Contemporary
Theatre, Film,
and Television

A Note About
Contemporary Theatre, Film, and Television
and
Who's Who in the Theatre

Contemporary Theatre, Film, and Television is a continuation of *Who's Who in the Theatre*, expanded to include film and television personalities. The editors believe this change in coverage of the series makes for a more representative and useful reference tool.

To provide continuity with *Who's Who in the Theatre (WWT)*, the cumulative index at the back of this volume interfiles references to *Contemporary Theatre, Film, and Television*, Volumes 1-5, with references to *Who's Who in the Theatre*, 1st-17th Editions, and *Who Was Who in the Theatre* (Gale Research Co., 1978).

ISSN 0749-064X

Contemporary Theatre, Film, and Television

A Biographical Guide Featuring Performers, Directors, Writers, Producers, Designers, Managers, Choreographers, Technicians, Composers, Executives, Dancers, and Critics in the United States and Great Britain

A Continuation of
Who's Who in the Theatre

Monica O'Donnell Hubbard
and **Owen O'Donnell,**
Editors

Sara J. Steen,
Associate Editor

Volume 5

Includes Cumulative Index Containing References to
Who's Who in the Theatre and *Who Was Who in the Theatre*

GALE RESEARCH COMPANY • BOOK TOWER • DETROIT, MICHIGAN 48226

STAFF

Monica O'Donnell Hubbard and Owen O'Donnell, *Editors*

Sara J. Steen, *Associate Editor*

Mel Cobb, James R. Kirkland, Jack Rosenberger, *Sketchwriters*
Sharon Gamboa, Vincent Henry, *Editorial Assistants*

Marilyn K. Basel, Christa Brelin, Diane L. Dupuis, Paul Gallagher, Anne Janette Johnson, James G. Lesniak,
Joanne M. Peters, Barbara J. Pruett, Bryan Ryan, Kenneth Shepherd, Thomas Wiloch, *Contributing Editors*

Linda S. Hubbard, *Senior Editor, Contemporary Theatre, Film, and Television*

Mary Beth Trimper, *Production Manager*
Darlene K. Maxey, *Production Associate*
Roger D. Hubbard, *Graphic Arts Coordinator*
Arthur Chartow, *Art Director*

Computerized photocomposition by
Roberts/Churcher

Printed in the United States

Contents

Preface

The worlds of theatre, film, and television hold an undeniable appeal, and the individuals whose careers are devoted to these fields are subjects of great interest. The people both behind the scenes and in front of the lights and cameras—writers, directors, producers, performers, and others—all have a significant impact on our lives, for they enlighten us as they entertain.

Contemporary Theatre, Film, and Television
Provides Broad Coverage in the
Entertainment Field

Contemporary Theatre, Film, and Television (CTFT) is a comprehensive biographical series designed to meet the need for information on theatre, film, and television personalities. Prior to the publication of *CTFT*, biographical sources covering entertainment figures were generally limited in scope; for more than seventy years *Who's Who in the Theatre (WWT)*, for example, provided reliable information on theatre people. But today few performers, directors, writers, producers, or technicians limit themselves to the stage. And there are also growing numbers of people who, though not active in the theatre, make significant contributions to other entertainment media. With its broad scope, encompassing not only stage notables but also film and/or television figures, *CTFT* is a more comprehensive and, the editors believe, more useful reference tool. Its clear entry format, allowing for the quick location of specific facts, combines with hundreds of photographs to further distinguish *CTFT* from other biographical sources on entertainment personalities.

Moreover, since *CTFT* is a series, new volumes can cover the steady influx of fresh talent into the entertainment media. The majority of the entries in each *CTFT* volume present information on people new to the series, but *CTFT* also includes updated versions of previously published *CTFT* sketches on especially active figures as well as complete revisions of *WWT* entries. The *CTFT* cumulative index makes all listings easily accessible.

Scope

CTFT is a biographical series covering not only performers, directors, writers, and producers but also designers, managers, choreographers, technicians, composers, executives, dancers, and critics from the United States and Great Britain. With nearly 700 entries in *CTFT* Volume 5, the series now provides biographies for more than 3,500 people involved in all aspects of the theatre, film, and television industries.

Primary emphasis is given to people who are currently active. *CTFT* includes major, established figures whose positions in entertainment history are assured, such as actor, singer, and producer Harry Belafonte; actress and film producer Goldie Hawn; playwright Jerome Lawrence; television executive William S. Paley; and theatrical producer Ellen Stewart. New and highly promising individuals who are beginning to make their mark are represented in *CTFT* as well—people such as actor and recording artist Ruben Blades; actress Kim Greist who has appeared in such films as *Brazil* and *Throw Momma from the Train;* award-winning playwright David Hwang; Elizabeth Pena, whose acting credits include the films *Down and Out in Beverly Hills* and *La Bamba* as well as a starring role in the television series *I Married Dora;* and writer, director, and actor Luis Valdez, who has gained renown for his plays *Actos* and *Zoot Suit* as well as for directing *La Bamba*.

CTFT also includes sketches on people no longer professionally active who have made significant contributions to their fields and whose work remains of interest today. This volume, for example, contains entries on actress and singer Vivian Blaine; actor Sterling Holloway; screenwriter Ring Lardner, Jr.; and producer, director, and screenwriter Joseph L. Mankiewicz. Selected sketches also record the achievements of recently deceased theatre, film, and television personalities. Among such notables with listings in this volume are Jean Anouilh, Michael Bennett, Jackie Gleason, Charles Ludlam, David Susskind, and Emlyn Williams.

With its broad coverage and detailed entries, *CTFT* is designed to assist a variety of users—a student preparing for a class, a teacher drawing up an assignment, a researcher seeking a specific fact, a librarian searching for the answer to a question, or a general reader looking for information about a favorite personality.

Compilation Methods

Every effort is made to secure information directly from biographees. The editors consult industry directories, biographical dictionaries, published interviews, feature stories, and film, television, and theatre reviews to identify people not previously covered in *CTFT*. Questionnaires are mailed to prospective listees or, when addresses are unavailable, to their agents, and sketches are compiled from the information they supply. The editors also select major figures included in *WWT* whose entries require updating and send them copies of their previously published entries for revision. *CTFT* sketches are then prepared from the new information submitted by these well-known personalities or their agents. Among the notable figures whose *WWT*, seventeenth edition, entries have been completely revised for this volume of *CTFT* are George Abbott, Gene Feist, Lucille Lortel, and Murray Schisgal. If people of special interest to *CTFT* users are deceased or fail to reply to requests for information, materials are gathered from reliable secondary sources. Sketches prepared solely through research are clearly marked with an asterisk (*) at the end of the entries.

Revised Entries

Each volume of *CTFT* is devoted primarily to people currently active in theatre, film, and television who are not already covered in the series or in *WWT*. However, to ensure *CTFT*'s timeliness and comprehensiveness, in addition to the updates of *WWT* sketches mentioned above, the editors also select *CTFT* listees from earlier volumes who have been active enough to require revision of their previous biographies. Such individuals will merit revised entries as often as there is substantial new information to provide. For example, the update of Gene Hackman's entry from *CTFT*, Volume 1, included in this volume adds eight titles to his list of screen acting credits; moreover, research has brought to light additional information about his early television and stage appearances, which has also been incorporated into his updated listing. Similarly, Volume 5 provides revised entries containing significant new information on Richard Benjamin, Richard Dreyfuss, Mark Hamill, and Dana Ivey, among others.

Format

CTFT entries, modeled after those in the Gale Research Company's highly regarded *Contemporary Authors* series, are written in a clear, readable style with few abbreviations and no limits set on length. So that a reader needing specific information can quickly focus on the pertinent portion of an entry, typical *CTFT* listings are clearly divided into the following sections:

Entry heading—Cites the form of the name by which the listee is best known followed by birth and death dates, when available.

Personal—Provides the biographee's full or original name if different from the entry heading, date and place of birth, family data, and information about the listee's education (including professional training), politics, religion, and military service.

Vocation—Highlights the individual's primary fields of activity in the entertainment industry.

Career—Presents a comprehensive listing of principal credits or engagements. The career section lists theatrical debuts (including Broadway and London debuts), principal stage appearances, and major tours; film debuts and principal films; television debuts and television appearances; and plays, films, and television shows directed and produced. Related career items, such as professorships and lecturing, are also included as well as non-entertainment career items.

Writings—Lists published and unpublished plays, screenplays, and scripts along with production information. Published books and articles, often with bibliographical data, are also listed.

Recordings—Cites album and single song releases with recording labels, when available.

Awards—Notes theatre, film, and television awards and nominations as well as writing awards, military and civic awards, and fellowships and honorary degrees received.

Member—Highlights professional, union, civic, and other association memberships, including official posts held.

Sidelights—Cites favorite roles, recreational activities, and hobbies. Frequently this section includes portions of agent-prepared biographies or personal statements from the listee. In-depth sidelights providing an overview of an individual's career achievements are compiled on selected personalities of special interest.

Addresses—Notes home, office, and agent addresses, when available. (In those instances where an individual prefers to withhold his or her home address from publication, the editors make every attempt to include at least one other address in the entry.)

Enlivening the text in many instances are large, clear photographs. Often the work of theatrical photographers, these pictures are supplied by the biographees to complement their sketches. This volume, for example, contains nearly 200 such portraits received from various individuals profiled in the following pages.

Brief Entries

CTFT users have indicated that having some information, however brief, on individuals not yet in the series would be preferable to waiting until full-length sketches can be prepared as outlined above under "Compilation Methods." Therefore, *CTFT* includes abbreviated listings on notables who presently do not have sketches in *CTFT*. These short profiles, identified by the heading "Brief Entry," highlight the person's career in capsule form.

Brief entries are not intended to replace sketches. Instead, they are designed to increase *CTFT*'s comprehensiveness and thus better serve *CTFT* users by providing pertinent and timely information about well-known people in the entertainment industry, many of whom will be the subjects of full sketches in forthcoming volumes.

This volume, for example, includes brief entries on such up-and-coming people as Alex Cox, Bronson Pinchot, Kiefer Sutherland, and Alfre Woodard.

Cumulative Index

To facilitate locating sketches on the thousands of notables profiled in *CTFT*, each volume contains a cumulative index to the entire series. As an added feature, this index also includes references to all seventeen editions of *WWT* and to the four-volume compilation *Who Was Who in the Theatre* (Gale, 1978). Thus by consulting only one source—the *CTFT* cumulative index—users have easy access to the tens of thousands of biographical sketches in *CTFT, WWT,* and *Who Was Who in the Theatre.*

Suggestions are Welcome

If readers would like to suggest people to be covered in future *CTFT* volumes, they are encouraged to send these names (along with addresses, if possible) to the editors. Other suggestions and comments are also most welcome and should be addressed to: The Editors, *Contemporary Theatre, Film, and Television,* 150 E. 50th Street, New York, NY 10022.

Forthcoming *CTFT* Entries

A Partial List of Theatre, Film, and Television Personalities
Who Will Appear in Forthcoming Volumes of *CTFT*

Allen, Debbie	Cassidy, Joanna	Forsyth, Bill	Keach, James
Anderson, Harry	Chomsky, Marvin	Franz, Elizabeth	Keller, Marthe
Anderson, Michael, Jr.	Clark, Oliver	French, Victor	Kennedy, Burt
Antonioni, Michelangelo	Cole, Toby	Friendly, Fred	Kirby, Bruno
Antony, Scott	Collins, Gary	Fuller, Penny	Klemperer, Werner
Archer, Anne	Collins, Pat	Gardner, Herb	Kopell, Bernie
Armstrong, Bess	Connors, Chuck	Gerard, Gil	Kozoll, Michael
Ashby, Hal	Copperfield, David	Gero, Frank	Kruschen, Jack
Astin, John	Correia, Don	Getty, Estelle	Kurosawa, Akira
Aston, John	Cosell, Howard	Gibson, Mel	Kurtz, Gary
Averback, Hy	Costa-Gavras, Constantin	Glass, Philip	Langdon, Sue Ane
Babcock, Barbara	Cox, Courteney	Gleason, Joanna	Laneuville, Eric
Babenco, Hector	Coyote, Peter	Gless, Sharon	Lazar, Irving Paul
Backus, Jim	Craven, Wes	Globus, Yorum	Leach, Wilford
Baer, Max, Jr.	Crisp, Quentin	Glover, Crispin	Lean, David
Baker, Joe Don	Cronenberg, David	Goldblum, Jeff	LeBeauf, Sabrina
Baker, Rick	Cronkite, Walter	Goldthwait, Bob	Lee, Spike
Bakshi, Ralph	Cross, Ben	Gossett, Louis, Jr.	Leno, Jay
Barkin, Ellen	Curry, Tim	Griffith, Melanie	Letterman, David
Barnes, Joanna	Curtis, Jamie-Lee	Grimes, Scott	Levinson, Barry
Barris, Chuck	Cwikowski, Bill	Gross, Michael	Lewis, Emmanuel
Bartel, Paul	Dahl, Roald	Hagerty, Julie	Link, Ron
Bartlett, Bonnie	Daltry, Roger	Hailey, Arthur	Link, William
Barty, Billy	Daly, Tyne	Hamlin, Harry	Lloyd, Norman
Beatty, Ned	D'Apollonia, James	Hamner, Earl, Jr.	Lunden, Joan
Belafonte-Harper, Shari	Davis, Clifton	Hannah, Daryl	MacCormick, Cara Duff
Beresford, Bruce	Derricks, Cleavant	Harper, Jessica	Mahoney, John
Bergen, Polly	DeSilva, Albert	Harrelson, Woody	Margolin, Stuart
Berman, Shelly	DeSilva, David	Hays, Robert	Martinez, A.
Bernhard, Sandra	De Vito, Danny	Hearn, George	Mason, Jackie
Bill, Tony	Dixon, Donna	Hogan, Paul	Matlin, Marlee
Blakely, Susan	Donahue, Phil	Holliday, Jennifer	McAnuff, Des
Bledsoe, Tempestt	Douglas, Mike	Hopkins, Telma	McArdle, Andrea
Bluth, Don	Downey, Robert	Horne, Lena	McCarthy, Andrew
Bochco, Steven	Duff, Howard	Hunt, Pamela	McGillin, Howard
Boorman, John	Dzundza, George	Hunter, Holly	McGovern, Maureen
Botsford, Sara	Edelman, Herb	Ingersoll, James	McHattie, Stephen
Branch, Gerard	Edwards, Anthony	Ireland, Jill	McKee, Lonette
Brandauer, Klaus Maria	Eichhorn, Lisa	Irwin, Bill	Melendez, Bill
Brickman, Marshall	Eilbacher, Lisa	Jason-Leigh, Jennifer	Miyori, Kim
Brillstein, Bernie	Elcar, Dana	Jennings, Peter	Montand, Yves
Brimley, Wilford	Ellerbee, Linda	Johnson, Don	Napier, Charles
Broccoli, Albert "Cubby"	Estabrook, Christine	Jones, Alan	Near, Holly
Brokaw, Tom	Esterhas, Joe	Jones, Chuck	Needham, Hal
Brooks, Albert	Evans, Robert	Jones, Henry	Neill, Sam
Brosnan, Pierce	Fabares, Shelly	Jones, Shirley	Nero, Franco
Brown, Blair	Falabella, John	Jordan, Richard	Newman, Laraine
Busch, Charles	Feldon, Barbara	Joseph, Robert	Nicholas, Denise
Buttons, Red	Ferrer, Mel	Jourdan, Louis	Nielsen, Brigitte
Byrne, David	Fingerhut, Arden	Kallis, Stanley	Nixon, Agnes
Cacaci, Joe	Flanagan, Kit	Kasem, Casey	Noiret, Philippe
Caine, Michael	Flanders, Ed	Kaufman, Philip	Norris, Chuck
Campanella, Joseph	Foreman, Richard	Kazurinsky, Tim	North, Sheree

O'Connor, Glynnis
O'Herlihy, Dan
Ohlmeyer, Don
Olkewicz, Walter
Olmos, Edward James
O'Neal, Ron
O'Neill, Dick
O'Neill, Jennifer
Orlando, Tony
O'Shea, Milo
Osmond, Cliff
Osmond, Marie
O'Toole, Annette
Paar, Jack
Parker, Ellen
Parker, Jameson
Parker, Sarah Jessica
Parks, Gordon
Pennebaker, D.A.
Perkins, Elizabeth
Perlman, Ron
Persky, Bill
Peters, Brock
Pickett, Cindy
Plunkett, Maryann
Pollan, Tracy
Post, Markie
Potts, Cliff
Prince
Prine, Andrew
Quade, John
Quibell, Kevin

Quintano, Gene
Rafelson, Bob
Railsback, Steve
Rashad, Phylicia
Reasoner, Harry
Reed, Alaina
Reed, Alyson
Reed, Jerry
Reed, Pamela
Reed, Robert
Rhoades, Barbara
Rich, Frank
Rich, Lee
Rifkin, Ron
Ritchie, Michael
Ritt, Martin
Rivera, Geraldo
Robbins, Matthew
Robinson, Charles
Roche, Eugene
Roeg, Nicholas
Rogers, Fred
Romero, George
Ross, Herbert
Rush, Richard
Russell, Nipsey
Ryan, Meg
Salkind, Alexander
Salt, Waldo
Sandy, Gary
Sargent, Joseph
Scarwid, Diana

Schell, Maria
Schoenfeld, Gerald
Schulberg, Budd
Scolari, Peter
Sellecca, Connie
Siegel, Don
Sikking, James B.
Sinatra, Frank
Singer, Abby
Singer, Marc
Skerritt, Tom
Sloan, Allan
Smith, Charles Martin
Smith, Dick
Smits, Jimmy
Soyinka, Wole
Spano, Vincent
Spiegel, Sam
Stacy, James
Stahl, Richard
Stark, Ray
Stevenson, McLean
Stevenson, Parker
Stiers, David Ogden
Stilwell, Diane
Stone, Dee Wallace
Storch, Larry
Susman, Todd
Sykes, Brenda
Talbott, Michael
Tambor, Jeffrey
Tarses, Jay

Taylor, Rod
Taylor-Young, Leigh
Thicke, Alan
Thinnes, Roy
Thomas, Dave
Thomas, Henry
Thomas, Philip Michael
Tierney, Lawrence
Tucker, Michael
Tyrrell, Susan
Uggams, Leslie
Uhry, Alfred
Uys, Jamie
Van Peebles, Mario
Venora, Diane
Voland, Herb
Vonnegut, Kurt, Jr.
Wagner, Jane
Waits, Tom
Walcott, Derek
Walters, Barbara
Ward, Rachel
Warfield, Marsha
Weaver, Lee
Weege, Reinhold
White, Jesse
Williams, Hal
Winfield, Paul
Yniguez, Richard
Zerbe, Anthony
Zimbalist, Stephanie

To ensure that *CTFT* meets users' needs for biographical information on entertainment figures of special interest, the editors welcome your suggestions for additional personalities to be included in the series.

Contemporary Theatre, Film, and Television

Contemporary Theatre, Film, and Television

* Indicates that a listing has been compiled from secondary sources believed to be reliable.

ABBOTT, George 1887-

PERSONAL: Full name, George Francis Abbott; born June 25, 1887, in Forestville, NY; son of George Burwell (a wholesale tailor) and May (a teacher; maiden name, McLaury) Abbott; married Ednah Levis, July 9, 1914 (died, 1930); married Mary Sinclair, March 27, 1946 (divorced, 1951); married Joy Valderrama (formerly a fashion consultant), November, 1983; children: (first marriage) Judith Ann. EDUCATION: University of Rochester, B.A., 1911; studied playwriting at Harvard University with G.P. Baker.

VOCATION: Director, producer, playwright, and actor.

CAREER: BROADWAY DEBUT—Babe Merrill, *The Misleading Lady,* Fulton Theatre, 1913. PRINCIPAL STAGE APPEARANCES— All in New York City, unless indicated: Second Yeoman, *The Yeoman of the Guard,* 48th Street Theatre, 1915; Henry Allen, *Daddies,* Belasco Theatre, 1918; Sylvester Cross, *The Broken Wing,* 48th Street Theatre, 1920; Texas, *Zander the Great,* Empire Theatre, 1923; Sverre Peterson, *The White Desert,* Princess Theatre, 1923; Sid Hunt, *Hell-Bent for Heaven,* Klaw Theatre, 1924; Steve Tuttle, *Lazy Bones,* Vanderbilt Theatre, 1924; Dynamite Jim, *Processional,* Garrick Theatre, 1925; Dirk Yancey, *A Holy Terror,* George M. Cohan Theatre, 1925; Frederick Williston, *Those We Love,* John Golden Theatre, 1930; title role, *John Brown,* Ethel Barrymore Theatre, 1934; Mr. Antrobus, *The Skin of Our Teeth,* Theatre Sarah Bernhardt, Paris, France, then American National Theatre Academy Playhouse, both 1955. Also appeared in *The Queen's Enemy,* 1916; *Cowboy Crazy,* 1926.

MAJOR TOURS—*Dulcy,* U.S. cities, early 1920s.

FIRST NEW YORK STAGE WORK—Assistant stage manager, *Three Wise Fools,* Criterion Theatre, 1918. PRINCIPAL STAGE WORK— All in New York City unless indicated: Director, *Love 'Em and Leave 'Em,* Harris Theatre, 1926; director, *Broadway,* Broadhurst Theatre, 1926; director, *Chicago,* Music Box Theatre, 1926; director, *Four Walls,* John Golden Theatre, 1927; director, *Spread Eagle,* Martin Beck Theatre, 1927; director, *Coquette,* Maxine Elliott's Theatre, 1927; director (with John Meehan), *Bless You Sister,* Forrest Theatre, 1927; director, *Ringside,* Broadhurst Theatre, 1928; director, *Gentlemen of the Press,* Henry Miller's Theatre, 1928; director, *Jarnegan,* Longacre Theatre, 1928; director, *Poppa,* Biltmore Theatre, 1928; director, *Those We Love,* John Golden Theatre, 1930; director, *Louder Please,* Masque Theatre, 1931; producer (with Philip Dunning) and director, *Lilly Turner,* Morosco Theatre, 1932; director, *The Great Magoo,* Selwyn Theatre, 1932; producer (with Dunning) and director, *Twentieth Century,* Broadhurst

Theatre, 1932; producer (with Dunning) and director, *Heat Lightning,* Booth Theatre, 1933; producer (with Dunning) and director, *The Drums Begin,* Shubert Theatre, 1933; producer and director, *John Brown,* Ethel Barrymore Theatre, 1934; producer (with Dunning) and director, *Kill That Story,* Booth Theatre, 1934; director, *Small Miracle,* John Golden Theatre, 1934; director, *Page Miss Glory,* Mansfield Theatre, 1934; director, *Ladies' Money,* Ethel Barrymore Theatre, 1934; director, *Three Men on a Horse,* Playhouse Theatre, 1935; producer and director, *Boy Meets Girl,* Cort Theatre, 1935; director, *Jumbo,* Hippodrome Theatre, 1935; producer and director, *Sweet River,* 51st Street Theatre, 1936; director, *Brother Rat,* Biltmore Theatre, 1936; director, *Room Service,* Cort Theatre, 1937; director, *Angel Island,* National Theatre, 1937; director, *Brown Sugar,* Biltmore Theatre, 1937; director, *All That Glitters,* Biltmore Theatre, 1938; director, *What a Life,* Biltmore Theatre, 1938; director, *The Boys from Syracuse,* Alvin Theatre, 1938; director, *The Primrose Path,* Biltmore Theatre, 1939; director, *Mrs. O'Brien Entertains,* Lyceum Theatre, 1939; director, *See My Lawyer,* Biltmore Theatre, 1939; director, *Ring Two,* Henry Miller's Theatre, 1939; director, *Too Many Girls,* Imperial Theatre, 1939.

Producer and director, *The Unconquered,* Biltmore Theatre, 1940; producer and director, *The White-Haired Boy,* Plymouth Theatre, Boston, 1940; producer and director, *Goodbye in the Night,* Biltmore Theatre, 1940; producer and director, *Pal Joey,* Ethel Barrymore Theatre, 1940; producer and director, *Best Foot Forward,* Ethel Barrymore Theatre, 1941; producer, *Jason,* Hudson Theatre, 1942; producer and director, *Beat the Band,* 46th Street Theatre, 1942; director, *Sweet Charity,* Mansfield Theatre, 1942; producer and director, *Kiss and Tell,* Biltmore Theatre, 1943; producer and director, *Get Away, Old Man,* Cort Theatre, 1943; producer and director, *A Highland Fling,* Plymouth Theatre, 1944; producer and director, *Snafu,* Hudson Theatre, 1944; director, *On the Town,* Adelphi Theatre, 1944; producer (with Richard Myers) and director, *Mr. Cooper's Left Hand,* Wilbur Theatre, Boston, MA, 1945; director, *Billion Dollar Baby,* Alvin Theatre, 1945; producer and director, *One Shoe Off,* Nixon Theatre, Pittsburgh, PA, then Shubert Theatre, New Haven, CT, 1946; producer (with Richard Oldrich) and director, *It Takes Two,* Biltmore Theatre, 1947; producer and director, *Barefoot Boy with Cheek,* Martin Beck Theatre, 1947; director, *High Button Shoes,* Century Theatre, 1947; producer and director, *Look, Ma, I'm Dancin,* Adelphi Theatre, 1948; director, *Where's Charley?,* St. James Theatre, 1948; producer and director, *Mrs. Gibbons' Boys,* Music Box Theatre, 1949.

All as director: *Call Me Madam,* Imperial Theatre, 1950; (also producer) *A Tree Grows in Brooklyn,* Alvin Theatre, 1951; *The Number,* Biltmore Theatre, 1951; (also producer with Jule Styne) *In Any Language,* Cort Theatre, 1952; *Wonderful Town,* Winter Garden Theatre, 1953; *Me and Juliet,* Majestic Theatre, 1953; (with Jerome Robbins) *The Pajama Game,* St. James Theatre, 1954; (also producer) *On Your Toes,* 46th Street Theatre, 1954; *Damn Yankees,* 46th Street Theatre, 1955, then Coliseum Theatre, London, 1957; *New Girl in Town,* 46th Street Theatre, 1957; *Drink to Me Only,* 54th Street Theatre, 1958; *Once Upon a Mattress,* Phoenix Theatre, then Alvin Theatre, both 1959; *Fiorello!,* Broadhurst Theatre, 1959; *Tenderloin,* 46th Street Theatre, 1960; *A Call on Kuprin,* Broadhurst Theatre, 1961; *Take Her, She's Mine,* Biltmore Theatre, 1961; *A Funny Thing Happened on the Way to the Forum,* Alvin Theatre, 1962, then Strand Theatre, London, 1963; *Never Too Late,* Playhouse Theatre, 1962; *Fade Out-Fade In,* Mark Hellinger Theatre, 1964, redirected and reopened at the Mark Hellinger Theatre, 1965; *Flora, the Red Menace,* Alvin Theatre, 1965; *Anya,* Ziegfeld Theatre, 1965; *The Well-Dressed Liar,* Royal Poinciana Playhouse, Palm Beach, FL, then Coconut Grove Playhouse, Coconut Grove, FL, both 1966; *Help Stamp Out Marriage,* Booth Theatre, 1966; *Agatha Sue, I Love You,* Henry Miller's Theatre, 1966; *How Now, Dow Jones,* Lunt-Fontanne Theatre, 1967; *The Education of H*Y*M*A*N K*A*P*L*A*N,* Alvin Theatre, 1968; *The Fig Leaves Are Falling,* Broadhurst Theatre, 1968; *Three Men on a Horse,* Lyceum Theatre, 1969.

All as director: *Norman, Is That You?,* Lyceum Theatre, 1970; *Not Now, Darling,* Brooks Atkinson Theatre, 1970; *The Pajama Game,* Lunt-Fontanne Theatre, 1973; *Life with Father,* Seattle Repertory Theatre, Seattle, WA, 1974; *Music Is,* St. James Theatre, 1976; *Winning Isn't Everything,* Hudson Guild Theatre, 1978; *On Your Toes,* Virginia Theatre, 1983; *Broadway,* Great Lakes Theatre Festival, Cleveland, OH, 1987. Also redirected plays including: *Beggar's Holiday,* Broadway Theatre, 1946; *Out of This World,* New Century Theatre, 1950; *Tickets, Please!,* Coronet Theatre, 1950; and *You Never Know,* 1947.

PRINCIPAL FILM WORK—Director, *The Bishop's Candlesticks,* Paramount, 1928; director, *Why Bring That Up?,* Paramount, 1929; director, *Manslaughter,* Paramount, 1930; director, *Secrets of a Secretary,* Paramount, 1931; *Stolen Heaven,* Paramount, 1931; director, *My Sin,* Paramount, 1931; director, *Too Many Girls,* RKO, 1940; director, *Kiss and Tell,* Columbia, 1945; producer and director (both with Stanley Donen), *The Pajama Game,* Warner Brothers, 1957; producer and director (both with Donen) *Damn Yankees,* Warner Brothers, 1958.

PRINCIPAL TELEVISION APPEARANCES—Series: Host (also director), *The U.S. Royal Showcase,* NBC, 1952. Specials: Mr. Antrobus, *The Skin of Our Teeth,* NBC, 1955.

NON-RELATED CAREER—Western Union messenger, telephone operator, steel plant worker, basketball coach, Sunday school teacher, ranch hand.

WRITINGS: PLAYS, PRODUCED—See above for production details unless indicated: *The Head of the Family,* Harvard Dramatic Club, Cambridge, MA, 1912; *Man in the Manhole,* Bijou Art Theatre, Boston, MA, 1912; (with James Gleason) *The Fall Guy,* Eltinge Theatre, New York City, 1925; (with Winchell Smith) *A Holy Terror;* 1926; (with John V.A. Weaver) *Love 'Em and Leave 'Em,* 1926; (with Philip Dunning) *Broadway,* 1926; (with Dana Burnet) *Four Walls,* 1927; (with Ann P. Bridgers) *Coquette,* 1927; (with Edward E. Paramore, Jr. and H. Daab) *Ringside,* 1928; (with S.K. Lauren) *Those We Love,* 1930; (with Dunning) *Lilly Turner,* 1932; (with Leon Abrams) *Heat Lightning,* 1933; *Ladies' Money,*

1934; (with John Cecil Holm) *Three Men on a Horse,* 1935; *The Ragged Edge,* Fulton Theatre, 1935; *Sweet River,* (with Richard Rogers and Lorenz Hart) *On Your Toes,* Imperial Theatre, 1936; *The Boys from Syracuse,* 1938; (with Holm) *Best Foot Forward,* 1941; (with George Marion, Jr.) *Beat the Band,* 1942; *Where's Charley?,* 1948; (with Betty Smith) *A Tree Grows in Brooklyn,* 1951; (with Richard Bissell) *The Pajama Game,* 1954; (with Douglas Wallop) *Damn Yankees,* 1955; *New Girl in Town,* 1957; (with Jerome Weidman) *Fiorello!,* 1959; (with Weidman) *Tenderloin,* 1960; (with Robert Russell) *Flora, the Red Menace,* 1965; (with Guy Bolton) *Anya,* 1965; *Music Is,* 1976.

SCREENPLAYS—Dialogue collaborator, *All Quiet on the Western Front,* Universal, 1930; (with Richard Bissell) *The Pajama Game,* Warner Brother, 1957; *Damn Yankees,* Warner Brothers, 1958.

AUTOBIOGRAPHY—*Mr. Abbott,* Random House, 1963.

FICTION—*Try-Out,* Playboy Press, 1979.

AWARDS: Boston Globe award, 1912, for *Man in the Manhole;* Best Director, Donaldson Award, 1946, for *Billion Dollar Baby;* Best Director, Donaldson Award, 1948, for *High Button Shoes;* Best Director, Donaldson Award, 1953, Best Musical Production, New York Drama Critics Circle Award, 1953, Best Musical, Antoinette Perry Award, 1953, all for *Wonderful Town;* Best Director, Donaldson Award, 1955, Best Author (Musical), Antoinette Perry Award, 1955, both for *The Pajama Game;* Best Author (Musical), Antoinette Perry Award, 1956, for *Damn Yankees;* Best Musical Production, New York Drama Critics Circle Award, 1960, Best Author (Musical), Antoinette Perry Award, 1960, Pulitzer Prize for Drama, 1960, all for *Fiorello!;* "Most over-all creative contribution to the season," Outer Critics Circle, 1962, Best Director (Musical), Antoinette Perry Award, 1963, both for *A Funny Thing Happened on the Way to the Forum;* Best Director (Dramatic), Antoinette Perry Award nomination, 1963, for *Never Too Late;* Award of Merit from the Society of Stage Directors and Choreographers, 1965; Best Dierctor (Musical), Antoinette Perry Award nomination, 1968, for *How Now, Dow Jones;* Theatre Hall of Fame and Museum, 1972; Antoinette Perry Award, 1976, for "Distinguished Career Achievement"; Lawrence Langer Award, 1976; Handel Medallion of the City of New York, 1976; Kennedy Center Honors Medal, 1983; Antoinette Perry Award, 1987. Honorary degrees: H.H.D. from University of Rochester, 1961, University of Miami, 1974.

MEMBER: Actors' Equity Association, Society of Stage Designers and Choreographers, Dramatists Guild, Academy of Motion Picture Arts and Sciences, Academy of Lighting Arts, American Federation of Television and Radio Artists, Writers Guild of America, Stage Designers Guild; Psi Upsilon; Coffee House Club, Dutch Treat Club, Indian Creek Country Club, Merriewold Club.

SIDELIGHTS: RECREATIONS—Golf. At the time of his one-hundredth birthday, George Abbott was writing a new musical titled *Irwin* and the book for a musical version of his 1926 play *Broadway,* according to *Playbill* (July, 1987).

ADDRESSES: HOME—Miami Beach, FL (winter). OFFICE—1270 Avenue of the Americas, New York, NY 10020.*

*   *   *

ABEL, Walter   1898-1987

PERSONAL: Born June 6, 1898, in St. Paul, MN; died in Essex, CT, March 26, 1987; son of Richard Michael and Christine (Becker)

Abel; married Marietta Bitter, September 24, 1926 (died, 1970); children: two sons. EDUCATION: Trained for the stage at the American Academy of Dramatic Art, 1917-1918.

VOCATION: Actor.

CAREER: BROADWAY DEBUT—Vincent Moretti, *Forbidden*, Manhattan Opera House, 1919. LONDON DEBUT—Michael Jeffery, *Coquette*, Apollo Theatre, 1929. PRINCIPAL STAGE APPEARANCES—All in New York City unless indicated: Acis, *Back to Methusela*, Garrick Theatre, 1922; Eugene Huckins, *A Square Peg*, Punch and Judy Theatre, 1923; Jacques, Lord, *As You Like It*, 44th Street Theatre, 1923; Sheriff, *Desire Under the Elms*, Greenwich Village Theatre, 1924; Sir Sampson Legend, *Love for Love*, Greenwich Village Theatre, 1925; Carl Behrend, *The Enemy*, Times Square Theatre, 1925; Hortensio, *The Taming of the Shrew*, Klaw Theatre, 1925; Dermot McDermot, *Hangman's House*, Forrest Theatre, 1926; John Roberts, *Seed of the Brute*, Little Theatre, 1926; Robert Mayo, *Beyond the Horizon*, Mansfield Theatre, 1926; Henry Bascom, *The House of Women*, Maxine Elliott's Theatre, 1927; Wayne Trenton, III, *Skidding*, Bijou Theatre, 1928; Elmer Gray, *First Mortgage*, Royale Theatre, 1929; Boris Trigorin, *The Seagull*, Comedy Theatre, 1929, then Waldorf Theatre, 1930.

Vaska, *At the Bottom*, Waldorf Theatre, 1930; George, *I Love an Actress*, Times Square Theatre, 1931; Orin Mannon, *Mourning Becomes Electra*, Alvin Theatre, 1932; Niko, *A Divine Drudge*, Jimmie Lee, *When Ladies Meet*, both Royale Theatre, 1933; Andre Roussel, *The Drums Begin*, Shubert Theatre, 1933; Morgan Chadwick, *Wife Insurance*, Ethel Barrymore Theatre, 1934; Dr. Linton, *Invitation to a Murder*, Masque Theatre, 1934; Jonathan Crale, *Merrily We Roll Along*, Music Box Theatre, 1934; Nathaniel McQuestion, *Wingless Victory*, Empire Theatre, 1936; John Shand, *What Every Woman Knows*, County Theatre, Suffern, NY, 1938; David Hudson, *The Birds Stopped Singing*, Princeton, NJ, 1939; Benjamin de Wolfe, *No Code to Guide Her*, Playhouse Theatre, 1939; Clement Waterlow, *The Mermaids Singing*, Empire Theatre, 1945; Charles Burnett, *Parlor Story*, Biltmore Theatre, 1947; Dr. Jay Stewart, *The Biggest Thief in Town*, Mansfield Theatre, 1949; Gavin Leon Andree, *The Wisteria Trees*, Martin Beck Theatre, 1950; Capt. Mike Dorgan, *The Long Watch*, Lyceum Theatre, 1952; narrator, *King David*, Philadelphia Orchestra, Carnegie Hall, 1952; title role, *Noah*, Parkland College, Seattle, WA, 1953; reader, *Under Milk Wood*, Kaufmann Auditorium, 1954; Jim Dougherty, *The Pleasure of His Company*, Longacre Theatre, 1958; Scrooge, *A Christmas Carol*, Fulton Theatre, 1959.

Nat Miller, *Take Me Along*, State Fair Theatre, Dallas, TX, 1962; Lew, *Night Life*, Brooks Atkinson Theatre, 1962; Malvolio, *Twelfth Night*, Fresno State College, Fresno, CA, 1963; Bill Hastings, *The Ninety-Day Mistress*, Biltmore Theatre, 1972; Antonio, *Saturday, Sunday, Monday*, Martin Beck Theatre, 1974; William Gower, *Trelawny of the Wells*, Vivian Beaumont Theatre, 1975. Appeared in *A Woman's Way*, *Harvest*, *Nocturne*, *Garside's Career*, all with the American Academy of Dramatic Art, 1918; *Affairs of State*, Papermill Playhouse, Millburn, NJ, 1965; *Maggie*, Goodspeed Opera House, East Haddam, CT, 1966; narrator, *Lincoln Portrait*, Philadelphia Orchestra; and in a number of summer theatre productions including *Romeo and Juliet*, *Our Town*, *The Skin of Our Teeth*, *Inherit the Wind*.

With the Provincetown Playhouse Company, Provincetown, MA, and New York City: student, *The Spook Sonata*, Colonel Howard, *Fashion*, Ted, *The Crime in the Whistler Room*, Olson, *S.S. Glencairn*, all 1924; Raul, *Beyond*, Armand Blondeau, *Michel Auclair*, both 1925; Olson, *S.S. Glencairn*, 1929.

MAJOR TOURS—Orin Mannon, *Mourning Becomes Electra*, U.S. cities, 1932; Cedric Trent, *West of Broadway*, U.S. cities, 1939; Claudius, *Hamlet*, Elsinore, Denmark, and West German cities, 1949; Argan (also director), *The Imaginary Invalid*, U.S. cities, 1964; Chief Justice Harry Griffin, *A Conflict of Interests*, U.S. cities, 1972; Mark Walters, *In Praise of Love*, U.S. cities, 1975; also *Come Out of the Kitchen*, U.S. cities, 1918; *Toby's Bow*, U.S. cities, *Friendly Enemies*, U.S. cities, both 1919.

FILM DEBUT—*Out of a Clear Sky*, Paramount, 1918. PRINCIPAL FILM APPEARANCES—*The North Wind's Malice*, Goldwyn, 1920; *Liliom*, Twentieth Century-Fox, 1930; *The Three Musketeers*, RKO, 1935; *The Lady Consents*, *Two in the Dark*, *The Witness Chair*, *Second Wife*, all RKO, 1936; *Fury*, *We Went to College*, both Metro-Goldwyn-Mayer (MGM), 1936; *Portia on Trial*, Republic, 1937; *Wise Girl*, RKO, 1937; *Green Light*, Warner Brothers, 1937; *Racket Busters*, Warner Brothers, 1938; *Men with Wings*, Paramount, 1938; *Arise, My Love*, Paramount, 1940; *Hold Back the Dawn*, Paramount, 1941; *Beyond the Blue Horizon*, *Wake Island*, *Star Spangled Rhythm*, *Holiday Inn*, all Paramount, 1942; *Follow the Boys*, Universal, 1943; *Mr. Skeffington*, Warner Brothers, 1944; *An American Romance*, MGM, 1944; *The Affairs of Susan*, Warner Brothers, 1945; *Kiss and Tell*, Columbia, 1945; *Duffy's Tavern*, Paramount, 1945; *The Kid from Brooklyn*, RKO, 1946; *13 Rue Madeleine*, Twentieth Century-Fox, 1946; *Dream Girl*, *That Lady in Ermine*, both Twentieth Century-Fox, 1948.

So This Is Love, *Island in the Sky* both Warner Brothers, 1953; *Night People*, Twentieth Century-Fox, 1954; *Indian Fighter*, United Artists, 1955; *The Steel Jungle*, Warner Brothers, 1956; *Bernardine*, Twentieth Century-Fox, 1957; *Raintree County*, MGM, 1957; *Zora* (also known as *Night of the Dark Full Moon*), Cannon, 1971; *Grace Quigley*, Cannon, 1983. Also appeared in *Miracle on Main Street*, 1939; *Michael Shayne, Private Eye*, and *Dance, Girl, Dance*, both 1940; *Skylark*, 1941; *So Proudly We Hail*, 1943; *The Fabulous Joe*, 1947; *Handle with Care*, 1958; *The Confession*, 1964 (unreleased); *Mirage*, 1965; *Silent Night, Bloody Night*, 1973; and in *Law of the Underworld*; *King of the Turf*; *Who Killed Auntie Maggie?*; *Glamour Boy*; *Fired Wife*.

PRINCIPAL TELEVISION APPEARANCES—Episodic: *East Side/West Side*, CBS, 1964. Specials: *Gaslight*, NBC, 1948; *The Enchanted*, NBC, 1961; *Eugene O'Neill: A Glory of Ghosts*, PBS, 1986; also *We've Come of Age*, 1973. Movies: *Man without a Country*, 1973.

MEMBER: Screen Actors Guild (vice-president), Episcopal Actors Guild (vice-president).*

OBITUARIES AND OTHER SOURCES: Variety, April 1, 1987.

*   *   *

ABRAHAMS, Doris Cole   1925-

PERSONAL: Born January 29, 1925, in New York City; daughter of Mark Harris and Florence May (Kleinman) Cole; married Gerald M. Abrahams, CBE. EDUCATION: Attended Goucher College and Ohio University; trained for the stage at the Leland Powers School of the Theatre.

VOCATION: Producer.

CAREER: FIRST NEW YORK STAGE WORK—Producer, *Blue Holiday*, Belasco Theatre, 1945. PRINCIPAL STAGE WORK—

Producer, *To Grandmother's House We Go,* Biltmore Theatre, New York City, 1981. Also producer for summer theatre company, Connecticut, 1946; *Enter a Free Man, Out of the Question,* both London, 1968; *Enemy,* London, 1969; *Child's Play,* London, 1971; *Equus,* New York City, 1974; *Travesties,* New York City, 1975; *Wild Oats,* London, 1977; *Once a Catholic,* London, 1977, then New York City, 1979.

RELATED CAREER—Theatrical agent; formerly an actress.

MEMBER: League of New York Theatres and Producers; Society of West End Theatre (London).

SIDELIGHTS: RECREATIONS—Boating, swimming, antique furniture collecting.

ADDRESSES: OFFICE—1501 Broadway, New York, NY 10036.*

*　　*　　*

ACKLAND, Joss　1928-

PERSONAL: Born February 29, 1928, in London, England; son of Sydney Norman and Ruth (Izod) Ackland; married Rosemary Kircaldy; children: seven (one son deceased). EDUCATION: Trained for the stage at the Central School of Speech and Drama.

VOCATION: Actor and director.

JOSS ACKLAND

CAREER: STAGE DEBUT—*The Hasty Heart,* Aldwych Theatre, London, 1945. PRINCIPAL STAGE APPEARANCES—All in London unless indicated: Gans, police constable, *The Rising Sun,* Arts Theatre, 1946; Simon, *Mary Rose,* Pitlochry Theatre, 1951; Father, *Life with Father,* Bottom, *A Midsummer Night's Dream,* both Oxford Playhouse Company, Oxford, U.K., 1957; Squeezum, *Lock Up Your Daughters,* Her Majesty's Theatre, 1962; Professor Gilbert Medlin, *The Professor,* Royal Court Theatre, 1965; title role, *Jorrocks,* New Theatre, 1966; Gus, *The Hotel in Amsterdam,* Royal Court Theatre, then New Theatre, later Duke of York's Theatre, all 1968; various roles, *Come As You Are,* New Theatre, then Strand Theatre, both 1970; Brassbound, *Captain Brassbound's Conversion,* Cambridge Theatre, 1971; Sam Brown, *Collaborators,* Duchess Theatre, 1973; Harold Mitchell, *A Streetcar Named Desire,* Piccadilly Theatre, 1974; Fredrik Egerman, *A Little Night Music,* Adelphi Theatre, 1975; Eustace Perrin State, *The Madras House,* Olivier Theatre, 1977; Juan Peron, *Evita,* Prince Edward Theatre, 1978; Gaev, *The Cherry Orchard,* Chichester Festival, Chichester, U.K., 1981; Falstaff, *Henry IV, Parts I and II,* Barbican Theatre, 1982; Mr. Darling/ Captain Hook, *Peter Pan,* Barbican Theatre, 1983, then Aldwych Theatre, 1985; Stewart, *Pack of Lies,* Lyric Theatre, 1984. Also appeared as Romain Gary, *Jean Seberg,* Olivier Theatre; had various minor roles during the 1947 Stratford-on-Avon season; played in numerous repertory companies throughout England during the late 1940s and early 1950s; performed in South Africa, 1955-57.

With the Old Vic Theatre Company, London: Sir Toby Belch, *Twelfth Night,* 1958; Caliban, *The Tempest,* Northumberland, *Richard II,* Falstaff, *The Merry Wives of Windsor,* all 1959; Archbishop of Rheims, *St. Joan,* Pistol, *Henry V,* both 1960; Aegisthus, *The Oresteia,* 1961.

At the Mermaid Theatre, London: Scrofulofsky, *The Bed Bug,* Bluntschli, *Arms and the Man,* Sotmore, *Lock Up Your Daughters,* all 1962; title role, *The Life of Galileo,* Kirilov, *The Possessed,* Long John Silver, Blind Pew, *Treasure Island,* all 1963; herdsman, *The Bacchae,* 1964.

PRINCIPAL STAGE WORK—Director, *The Plough and the Stars,* Mermaid Theatre, London, 1962.

MAJOR TOURS—Petruchio, *The Taming of the Shrew,* U.K. cities, 1977; Sir, *The Dresser,* U.K. cities, 1981; also with various repertory companies, U.K. cities, 1954; with the Old Vic Theatre Company, Soviet and U.S. cities, early 1960s.

FILM DEBUT—*Seven Days to Noon,* 1947. PRINCIPAL FILM APPEARANCES—Don Masino Croce, *The Sicilian,* Twentieth Century-Fox, 1987; Sir Jock Delves Broughton, *White Mischief,* 1987. Also appeared in *One of Our Dinosaurs Is Missing,* Buena Vista, 1975; *Royal Flash,* Twentieth Century-Fox, 1975; *Silver Bears,* Columbia, 1977; (voice) *Watership Down,* AVCO-Embassy, 1978; *Who Is Killing the Great Chefs of Europe?,* Warner Brothers, 1978; *Rough Cut,* Paramount, 1980; *Lady Jane,* Paramount, 1986; and in *Operation Daybreak,* 1975; *Saint Jack,* 1978; *The Apple,* 1980; *A Zed and Two Noughts,* 1985; *New World,* 1986.

PRINCIPAL TELEVISION APPEARANCES—Mini-Series: Sir Burton, *Queenie,* ABC, 1987; ''C,'' *Codename: Kyril,* 1987; *Tinker, Tailor, Soldier, Spy.* Movies: Moulton Barrett, *The Barretts of Wimpole Street,* 1985; C.S. Lewis, *Shadowland,* 1985; colonel, *The Colonel's Lady,* 1987; photographer, *When We Are Married,* 1987; also appeared in *The Lie; Constance Kent.*

RELATED CAREER—Associate director, Mermaid Theatre, London, 1962-64; broadcaster, disc jockey, scriptwriter.

NON-RELATED CAREER—Tea planter, Central Africa, 1954.

AWARDS: International Emmy, 1985, for *Shadowland.*

MEMBER: British Actors' Equity Association, Garrick Club.

SIDELIGHTS: RECREATIONS—Painting, writing.

Joss Ackland told *CTFT:* "After playing supporting parts in movies for many years, a big break came when Michael Cimino cast me as Don Masino Croce—the godfather in *The Sicilian*—a role for which I put on thirty-three pounds."

ADDRESSES: HOME—London. OFFICE—The Garrick Club, Garrick Street, London WC2, England.

* * *

AIELLO, Danny   1933-

PERSONAL: Born June 20, 1933, in New York, NY.

VOCATION: Actor.

CAREER: BROADWAY DEBUT—*Lampost Reunion,* 1975. PRINCIPAL STAGE APPEARANCES—Chester Grant, *Wheelbarrow Closers,* Bijou Theatre, New York City, 1976; Fran Geminiani, *Gemini,* Circle Repertory Theatre, New York City, 1977; Damie Ruffino, *Knockout,* Helen Hayes Theatre, New York City, 1979; Max Pollack, *The Floating Light Bulb,* Vivian Beaumont Theatre, New York City, 1981; Floyd, *A Destiny with Half Moon Street,* Coconut Grove Playhouse, Coconut Grove, FL, 1982; Phil, *Hurlyburly,* Ethel Barrymore Theatre, New York City, 1985; *The House of Blue Leaves,* Vivian Beaumont Theatre, New York City, 1986.

PRINCIPAL STAGE WORK—Fight coordinator, *Kid Purple,* Manhattan Punch Line Theatre, New York City, 1984.

PRINCIPAL FILM APPEARANCES—Danny La Gattuta, *The Front,* Columbia, 1976; Artie, *Blood Brothers,* Warner Brothers, 1979; Sal Carvello, *Hide in Plain Sight,* United Artists, 1980; Carmine, *Defiance,* American Internationl, 1980; Morgan, *Fort Apache, the Bronx,* Twentieth Century-Fox, 1981; Johnson, *Chu Chu and the Philly Flash,* Twentieth Century-Fox, 1981; first removal man, *Amityville II: The Possession,* Orion, 1982; Police Chief Aiello, *Once Upon a Time in America,* Warner Brothers, 1984; Mr. Brucker, *Old Enough,* Orion, 1984; Monk, *The Purple Rose of Cairo,* Orion, 1985; Carabello, *Key Exchange,* Twentieth Century-Fox, 1985; Vickers, *The Stuff,* 1985; Danny Garoni, *The Protector,* Warner Brothers, 1985; Captain Mike Gress, *Death Mask,* Art Theatre Guild, 1986; *Man on Fire,* Tri-Star, 1987; Rocco, *Radio Days,* Orion, 1987.

PRINCIPAL TELEVISION APPEARANCES—Pilots: Frank Ravelli, *Car Wash,* 1979. Movies: Carl, *The Last Tenant,* 1978; Bernie Serino, *Lovey: A Circle of Children, Part II,* 1978; Frank Caruso, *The Unforgivable Secret,* 1982; Martelli, *A Question of Honor,* 1982; Randy Powers, *Blood Feud,* 1983; Lt. Terrence McNichols,

Lady Blue, ABC, 1985; also appeared in *Daddy,* ABC, 1987; and *Family of Strangers.*

AWARDS: Theatre World Award, 1976, for *Lampost Reunion.*

ADDRESSES: AGENT—The Artists Agency, 10000 Santa Monica Boulevard, Suite 305, Los Angeles, CA 90067.*

* * *

AKALAITIS, JoAnne   1937-

PERSONAL: Born June 29, 1937, in Chicago, IL; daughter of Clement and Estelle (Mattis) Akalaitis; married Philip Glass (a composer; divorced). EDUCATION: University of Chicago, B.A., philosophy, 1960; trained for the stage at the Actors' Workshop.

VOCATION: Director, actress, and set designer.

CAREER: PRINCIPAL STAGE APPEARANCES—Colette, *Dressed Like an Egg,* Mabou Mines Theatre Group, Public Theatre, New York City, 1977; Mrs. Lammle, *Dark Ride,* Soho Repertory Theatre, New York City, 1981; also appeared in *The Red Horse Animation,* 1976, *Cascando,* 1976, *Southern Exposure,* 1979, all with Mabou Mines Theatre Group, Public Theatre.

PRINCIPAL STAGE WORK—Director: (Also set designer) *Dressed Like an Egg,* Mabou Mines Theatre Group, Public Theatre, 1977; (also set designer) *Dead End Kids,* Mabou Mines Theatre Group, Public Theatre, 1980; *Request Concert,* Interart Theatre, New York City, 1981; *Red and Blue,* Public Theatre, 1982; *Through the Leaves,* Mabou Mines Theatre Group, Interart Theatre, then Public Theatre, 1984; *Endgame,* American Repertory Theatre (ART), Cambridge, MA, 1984; *Tis Pity She's a Whore,* ART, 1988; also directed *The Balcony* for ART.

PRINCIPAL FILM WORK—Director: *Dead End Kids,* 1986; also directed *Other Children.*

AWARDS: Guggenheim Fellowship for Experimental Theatre, 1978; special Obie Award from the *Village Voice,* 1979, for *Southern Exposure;* also won two other Obie awards.

ADDRESSES: OFFICE—231 Second Avenue, New York, NY 10009.*

* * *

ALDERTON, John   1940-

PERSONAL: Born November 27, 1940, in Gainsborough, England; son of Gordon John and Ivy (Handley) Alderton; married Jill Browne (divorced); married Pauline Collins.

VOCATION: Actor.

CAREER: STAGE DEBUT—*Badger's Green,* Theatre Royal Repertory Company, York, U.K., 1961. LONDON DEBUT— Harold Crompton, *Spring and Port Wine,* Mermaid Theatre, then Apollo Theatre, 1965. PRINCIPAL STAGE APPEARANCES—Eric Hoyden, *Dutch Uncle,* Royal Shakespeare Company, Aldwych Theatre,

London, 1969; Jimmy Cooper, *The Night I Chased the Women with an Eel,* Comedy Theatre, London, 1969; Stanley, *Punch and Judy Stories,* Howff Theatre, London, 1973; Stanley, *Judies,* Comedy Theatre, 1974; Stanley, *The Birthday Party,* Shaw Theatre, London, 1975; four roles, *Confusions,* Apollo Theatre, London, 1976.

PRINCIPAL FILM APPEARANCES—First officer, *Cloepatra,* Twentieth Century-Fox, 1963; Nidge, *The Girl Getters,* American International, 1966; George, *Assignment K,* Columbia, 1968; Anthony Calvert, *Duffy,* Columbia, 1968; Bernard, *Hannibal Brooks,* United Artists, 1969; friend, *Zardoz,* Twentieth Century-Fox, 1974. Also appeared in *Please Sir,* Rank, 1971.

PRINCIPAL TELEVISION APPEARANCES—Series: *Please Sir; My Wife Next Door.*

MEMBER: Green Room Club, Lord's Taverners.

SIDELIGHTS: RECREATIONS—Golf, cricket.

ADDRESSES: AGENT—News Management, Ltd., 29 King's Road, London SW3, England.*

*   *   *

ALLEN, Nancy

PERSONAL: Born June 24, in New York, NY; married Brian De Palma, 1979 (divorced, 1983). EDUCATION: Attended the School for the Performing Arts.

VOCATION: Actress.

CAREER: FILM DEBUT—Nancy, *The Last Detail,* Columbia, 1973. PRINCIPAL FILM APPEARANCES—Chris Hargenson, *Carrie,* United Artists, 1976; Pam Mitchell, *I Wanna Hold Your Hand,* Universal, 1978; Kristina, *Home Movies,* United Artists, 1979; Donna, *1941,* Universal, 1979; Liz Blake, *Dressed to Kill,* Filmways, 1980; Sally, *Blow Out,* Filmways, 1981; Betty Walker, *Strange Invaders,* Orion, 1983; Carrie, *The Buddy System,* Twentieth Century-Fox, 1984; Lois, *Not for Publication,* Thorn-EMI, 1984; Allison, *The Philadelphia Experiment,* New World Pictures, 1984; Lewis, *Robo Cop,* Orion, 1987; Julian Grey, *Sweet Revenge,* Concorde, upcoming. Also appeared in *Forced Entry* (also known as *The Last Victim*), Century International, 1984; *Terror in the Aisles,* 1984.

PRINCIPAL TELEVISION APPEARANCES—Movies: Susan Neville, *The Gladiator,* 1986.

ADDRESSES: AGENT—c/o Toni Howard, William Morris Agency, 151 El Camino Drive, Beverly Hills, CA 90212.*

*   *   *

ALLEY, Kirstie

BRIEF ENTRY: In 1987 Kirstie Alley took on the prized— but challenging—assignment of replacing Shelley Long as the female lead on the popular NBC television series *Cheers.* As Rebecca Howe she is the new manager of the Boston bar in which the show is set, a role quite different from the one in which she made her professional debut. Audiences first saw her as Lt. Saavik, the pointy-eared Vulcan crew member in the 1982 film *Star Trek II: The Wrath of Khan.* Alley told Martin Burden of the *New York Post* (December 13, 1983) that for a time thereafter "Anything that was alien, I was offered. . . . But I knew that if I continued doing only that my career wouldn't last very long." Instead, Alley's subsequent roles included a CIA agent in the television series *Masquerade* and feminist Gloria Steinem in the 1984 television movie *A Bunny's Tale.* She also appeared in the feature films *Champions,* 1983, and *Runaway,* 1984, and in the mini-series *North and South, Book II,* 1986. The Kansas native has drawn attention with her husky voice and striking green eyes as well as with her acting skills.

*   *   *

ALMENDROS, Nestor   1930-

PERSONAL: Born October 30, 1930, in Barcelona, Spain; son of Herminio (a university professor) and Maria (a grammar school teacher; maiden name, Cuyas) Almendros. EDUCATION: Havana University, Ph.D, 1956; studied cinematography and film editing at City College of New York, 1956, and at the Centro Sperimentale de Cinematografia, 1957.

VOCATION: Cinematographer.

CAREER: PRINCIPAL FILM WORK—All as cinematographer unless indicated: *Cockfighter,* New World, 1974; *The Story of Adele H.,* New World, 1974; *Madame Rosa,* Atlantic, 1978; *Goin' South,*

NESTOR ALMENDROS

Days of Heaven, both Paramount, 1978; *Kramer vs. Kramer*, Columbia, 1979; *The Blue Lagoon*, Columbia, 1980; *Still of the Night*, Metro-Goldwyn-Mayer/United Artists, 1981; *Sophie's Choice*, Universal, 1982; *Places in the Heart*, Tri-Star, 1984; *Heartburn*, Paramount, 1986; (also director) *People at the Beach*, 1960; *Paris Vu Par . . .*, 1964; *La Collectionneuse*, 1966; *The Wild Racers*, 1967; *More*, 1968; *My Night at Maud's, The Wild Child*, both 1969; *Claire's Knee, Bed and Board*, both 1970; *The Valley, Obscured by the Clouds*, and *Two English Girls*, both 1971; *Chloe in the Afternoon, Poil de Carote*, both 1972; *L'Oiseau Rare, Femmes au Soleil, La Gueule Ouverte, The Gentleman Tramp*, all 1973; *General Idi Amin Dada, Mes Petites Amoureuses*, both 1974; *Maitresse, The Marquise of O.*, both 1975; *Des Journees Entieres Dans Les Arbres, Cambio de Sexo*, both 1976; *The Man Who Loved Women, Le Centre Georges Pompidou, The Green Room*, and *Koko, the Talking Gorilla*, all 1977; *Perceval, Love on the Run*, both 1978; *The Last Metro*, 1980; *Pauline at the Beach, Confidentially Yours*, both 1982; director (with Orlando Jimenez-Leal), *Improper Conduct*, 1984; *Nadine*, 1986; director (with Jorge Ulla), *Nobody Listened*, 1987. Also directed documentary films for ICAIC, Cuba, 1959-61.

NON-RELATED CAREER—Spanish teacher, Vassar College, 1957-59.

WRITINGS: NON-FICTION—*A Man with a Camera*, Farrar, Strauss & Giroux, 1980; *Improper Conduct*, 1984. Also contributed articles to *American Cinematographer* and *Film Comment*.

AWARDS: Best Photography Award, U.S. Association of Film Critics, 1969, for *The Wild Child;* Best Photography, Academy Award, 1979, U.S. Association of Film Critics Award, 1979, both for *Days of Heaven;* Best Photography Award, French Academy of Motion Picture Arts and Techniques, 1980, for *The Last Metro;* Cesar Award, 1982, New York Film Critics Award, 1982, both for *Sophie's Choice;* decorated Chevalier, Order of Arts and Letters, France.

MEMBER: American Society of Cinematographers, Academy of Motion Picture Arts and Sciences, International Alliance of Theatrical Stage Employees.

ADDRESSES: AGENT—c/o Ray Gosnell, Smith-Gosnell, P.O. Box 1166, Pacific Palisades, CA 90272.

*   *   *

ALPER, Jonathan L.   1950-

PERSONAL: Born September 14, 1950, in Washington, DC; son of Jerome M. and Janet (Levy) Alper. EDUCATION: Amherst College, B.A., 1971; trained for the stage at the Webber-Douglas Academy.

VOCATION: Director and actor.

CAREER: PRINCIPAL STAGE APPEARANCES—*The Madness of God*, Arena Stage, Washington, DC, 1974. *The Romance of Shakespeare*, Meadow Brook Theatre, Rochester, MI, 1979.

PRINCIPAL STAGE WORK—Director, all with Folger Theatre Group, Washington, DC: *The Comedy of Errors*, 1975; *All's Well That Ends Well, Black Elk Speaks, Much Ado about Nothing*, all 1976; (with Louis Scheeder) *Teeth and Smiles*, 1977; *Hamlet*,

1978. Also director, *Safe House*, Manhattan Theatre Club, New York City, 1978; director, *Rosencrantz and Guildenstern Are Dead*, Monmouth, ME, 1978; director, *The Romance of Shakespeare*, Meadow Brook Theatre, Rochester, MI, 1979; director, *Fishing*, Actors' Collective, New York City, 1979; director, *The Eccentricities of a Nightingale*, Bergen Stage, NJ, 1979; dramaturg, *Hunting Scenes from Lower Bavaria*, Manhattan Theatre Club, 1981; director, *Death of a Buick*, Manhattan Theatre Club, 1987.

MAJOR TOURS—Director, *The Romance of Shakespeare*, U.S. cities, 1979.

RELATED CAREER—Literary manager, Folger Theatre Group, Washington, DC, 1975-78; director and dramaturg, Sundance Playwrights Institute, Sundance, UT, 1982, then 1984-86; literary manager, Manhattan Theatre Club, 1980-84, then artistic associate, 1984—.

ADDRESSES: HOME—785 West End Avenue, New York, NY 10025. OFFICE—c/o Manhattan Theatre Club, 453 W. 16th Street, New York, NY 10011.

*   *   *

AMBROSE, David   1943-
(William Wales)

PERSONAL: Full name, David Edwin Ambrose; born February 21, 1943, in Chorley, England; son of Albert Edwin (an insurance salesman) and Annie Margery (Fairclough) Ambrose; married Laurence Huguette Hammerli (a sculptor), September 13, 1979. EDUCATION: Merton College, Oxford University, J.D., 1965.

VOCATION: Scriptwriter, playwright, and director.

CAREER: PRINCIPAL TELEVISION WORK—Director, *Comeback*, YTV, 1987.

WRITINGS: SCREENPLAYS—*The Pedestrian*, Cinerama, 1973; *The Fifth Musketeer* (also known as *Behind the Iron Mask*), Columbia, 1977; *The Final Countdown*, United Artists, 1980; *The Dangerous Summer*, McElroy and McElroy, 1982; (as William Wales) *Amityville 3D*, Orion, 1983; *D.A.R.Y.L.*, Paramount, 1985. Also *Battle for Rome*, 1968; *Passion Flower Hotel*, 1969; *Blackout*, 1985; *Taffin*, 1987.

TELEPLAYS—*Public Face*, ATV, 1969; *The Innocent Ceremony*, ATV, 1969; *The Undoing*, ATV, 1969; *The Professional*, YTV, 1972; *When the Music Stops*, YTV, 1972; *Reckoning Day*, YTV, 1973; *Love Me to Death*, YTV, 1974; *Goose with Pepper*, Anglia, 1975; *A Variety of Passion*, YTV, 1975; *Alternative 3*, Anglia, 1977; *Nanny's Boy*, BBC, 1977; *Disaster on the Coastliner*, ABC, 1979; *Survival 80*, cable, 1980; *Comeback*, YTV, 1987. TELEVISION SHOWS—*Colditz; Hadleigh; Justice; Public Eye; Orson Welles' Great Mysteries; Oil Strike North*.

PLAYS, PRODUCED—*Siege*, Cambridge Theatre, London, 1972. Also *Five to Six*, Oxford, U.K., 1963.

AWARDS: Best Screenplay, Sitges Film Festival Award, 1981, for *The Survivor* (produced as *Survival 80*).

MEMBER: Writers Guild of America-West, Writers Guild of Great Britian, Writers Guild of Australia, Dramatists Club (London).

ADDRESSES: HOME—London. AGENT—(New York) c/o Fred Milstein, William Morris Agency, 151 El Camino Drive, Beverly Hills, CA 90212. (London) Hatton & Baker, Ltd., 18 Jermyn Street, London SW1, England.

*   *   *

ANOUILH, Jean   1910-1987

PERSONAL: Surname is pronounced "Ahn-wee;" full name, Jean Marie Lucien Pierre Anouilh; born June 23, 1910, in Bordeaux, France; died of a heart attack at Vaudois University Hospital Center, Lausanne, Switzerland, October 3, 1987; son of Francois (a tailor) and Marie-Magdeleine (a musician; maiden name, Soulue) Anouilh; married Monelle Valentin (an actress; divorced); married Nicole Lancon, July 30, 1953; children: (first marriage) Catherine; (second marriage) Caroline, Nicolas, Marie-Colombe. EDUCATION: Received baccalaureate from College Chaptal; studied law at the Sorbonne, University of Paris, 1931-32. MILITARY: Served in France during the 1930's.

VOCATION: Playwright and director.

CAREER: PRINCIPAL STAGE WORK—Also see *WRITINGS* below; secretary to Louis Jouvet's theatrical company, Comedie des Champs-Elysees, Paris, France, 1931-32; general assistant to director Georges Pitoeff, Paris. PRINCIPAL FILM WORK—Director, *Le Voyageur sans bagage,* 1943, released in the United States as *Identity Unknown,* Republic Pictures, 1945; *Deux sous de violettes,* France, 1951.

RELATED CAREER—Free-lance writer of publicity scripts and comic gags for films; advertising copywriter for Publicite Damour, Paris, France, for two years.

WRITINGS: PLAYS—(With Jean Aurenche) *Humulus le muet,* published by Editions Francaises Nouvelles, c. 1929; *L'Hermine,* Theatre de l'Oeuvre, Paris, France, 1932, published in *Les Oeuvres libres,* No. 151, 1934, translation by Miriam John published as *The Ermine* in *Plays of the Year,* Vol. 13, Ungar, 1956; *Mandarine,* Theatre de l'Athenee, Paris, 1933; *Y'avait un prisonnier* (title means "There Was a Prisoner"), Theatre des Ambassadeurs, Paris, 1935, published in *La Petite illustration,* May 18, 1935; *Le Voyageur sans bagage,* Theatre des Mathurins, Paris, 1937, published in *La Petite illustration,* April 10, 1937, translation by John Whiting published as *Traveller without Luggage,* Methuen, 1959, produced at Arts Theatre, London, U.K., 1959, translation by Lucienne Hill produced at American National Theatre Academy (ANTA) Playhouse, New York City, 1964; *La Sauvage,* Theatre des Mathurins, 1938, published in *Les Oeuvres libres,* No. 201, 1938, translation by Lucienne Hill published as *Restless Heart,* Methuen, 1957, produced at St. James Theatre, London, 1957; *Le Bal des voleurs,* Theatre des Arts, Paris, 1938, Theatre des Quatre Saisons, New York City, 1938, published in *Les Oeuvres libres,* No. 209, 1938, and by Editions Francaises Nouvelles, 1945, translation by Lucienne Hill published as *Thieves' Carnival,* Methuen, 1952, and by Samuel French, Inc., 1952, produced at Cherry Lane Theatre, New York City, 1955.

Rendez-vous de Senlis, Theatre de l'Atelier, Paris, 1938, published by Editions de la Table Ronde, 1958, translation by Edwin O. Marsh published as *Dinner with the Family,* Methuen, 1958, produced at New Theatre, London, 1957, Gramercy Arts Theatre,

New York City, 1961; *Leocadia,* Theatre de l'Atelier, 1939, translation by Patricia Moyes published as *Time Remembered,* Methuen, 1955, and Coward, 1958, produced at Morosco Theatre, New York City, 1957; *Eurydice,* Theatre de l'Atelier, 1941, translation by Mel Ferrer produced at the Coronet Theatre, Los Angeles, CA, 1948, translation by Kitty Black published as *Point of Departure,* Samuel French, Inc., 1951, produced at Lyric Hammersmith Theatre, London, 1950, Mannhard't Theatre Foundation, New York City, 1967, also published as *Legend of Lovers,* Coward, 1952, produced at Plymouth Theatre, New York City, 1951.

Antigone, Theatre de l'Atelier, 1944, published by Editions de la Table Ronde, 1946, translation by Lewis Galantiere published under the same title, Random House, 1946, produced at the Cort Theatre, New York City, 1946; *Romeo et Jeannette,* Theatre de l'Atelier, 1946, adaptation by Donagh MacDonagh produced as *Fading Mansion,* Duchess Theatre, London, 1949, translation by Miriam John produced as *Jeannette,* Maidman Playhouse, New York City, 1960; *L'Invitation au chateau,* Theatre de l'Atelier, 1947, published by Editions de la Table Ronde, 1948, and by Cambridge University Press, 1962, translation by Christopher Fry published as *Ring Around the Moon,* Oxford University Press, 1950, produced at Martin Beck Theatre, New York City, 1950, adaptation by Clifford Bax published in London as *The Pleasure of Your Company; Ardele, ou La Marguerite,* Comedie des Champs-Elysees, Paris, 1948, adaptation by Cecil Robson produced as *Cry of the Peacock,* Mansfield Theatre, New York City, 1950, translation by Lucienne Hill published as *Ardele,* Methuen, 1951, produced at Cricket Theatre, New York City, 1958.

Episode de la vie d'un auteur, Comedie des Champs-Elysees, 1948, published in *Cahiers de la compagnie Madeleine Renaud—Jean-Louis Barrault,* Julliard, 1959, translation produced as *Episode in the Life of an Author,* Studio Arena, Buffalo, NY, 1969, later Off-Broadway; *Cecile, ou L'Ecole des peres,* Comedie des Champs-Elysees, 1949, published by Editions de la Table Ronde, 1954, translation by Luce Klein and Arthur Klein published as *Cecile, or the School for Fathers,* in *From the Modern Repertoire,* 3rd series, Indiana University Press, 1958; *La Repetition, ou L'Amour puni,* Theatre Marigny, Paris, 1950, and Ziegfeld Theatre, New York City, 1952, translation by Pamela Hansford Johnson and Kitty Black published as *The Rehearsal,* Coward, 1961, produced at Royale Theatre, New York City, 1963; *Colombe,* Theatre de l'Atelier, 1951, published by Livres de Poche, 1963, adaptation by Denis Cannan published under the same title, Coward, 1954, produced at the Longacre Theatre, New York City, 1954; *Monsieur Vincent,* Bayerisch Scheulbuch-Verlag, 1951; *La Valse des Toreadors,* published by Editions de la Table Ronde, 1952, translation by Lucienne Hill published as *The Waltz of the Toreadors,* Elek, 1956, and Coward, 1957, produced at Coronet Theatre, New York City, 1957; *L'Alouette* Theatre Montparnasse, Paris, 1953, published by Editions de la Table Ronde, 1953, Methuen, 1956, and Appleton, 1957, translation by Christopher Fry published as *The Lark,* Methuen, 1955, and Oxford University Press, 1956, translation by Lucienne Hill, originally titled "Joan" published as *The Lark,* Random House, 1956, adaptation by Lillian Hellman produced as *The Lark,* Longacre Theatre, New York City, 1955; *Medee,* Theatre de l'Atelier, 1953, published by Editions de la Table Ronde, 1953, translation by Lothian Small published as *Medea* in *Plays of the Year,* 1956, Vol. 15, Ungar, 1957.

Ornifle, ou Le Courant d'air, Comedie des Champs-Elysees, 1955, published by Editions de la Table Ronde, 1955, translation by Lucienne Hill published as *Ornifle: A Play,* Hill & Wang, 1970; *Pauvre Bitos, ou Le Diner de tetes,* Theatre Montparnasse, 1956, published by Editions de la Table Ronde, 1958, and by Harrap, 1958, translation by Lucienne Hill published as *Poor Bitos*, Coward, 1964, produced by Classic Stage Company, New York City, 1969; *Hurluberlu, ou Le Reactionnaire amoureux*, Comedie des Champs-Elysees, 1959, published by Editions de la Table Ronde, 1959, adaptation by Lucienne Hill published as *The Fighting Cock*, Coward, produced at ANTA Playhouse, New York City, 1959; *Madame De . . .*, translation by John Whiting, published by Samuel French, Inc., c. 1959, produced on the same bill with *Traveller without Luggage*, Arts Theatre, London, 1959; *Becket, ou L'Honneur de Dieu*, Theatre Montparnasse, 1959, published by Editions de la Table Ronde, 1959, translation by Lucienne Hill published as *Becket, or the Honor of God*, Coward, 1960, produced as *Becket*, St. James Theatre, New York City, 1960; (with Roland Laudenback), *La Petite Moliere*, Theatre Festival of Bordeaux, France, 1960, published in *L'Avant Scene*, December 15, 1959.

La Grotte, Theatre Montparnasse, 1961, published by Editions de la Table Ronde, 1961, translation by Lucienne Hill published as *The Cavern*, Hill & Wang, 1966, produced at Playhouse in the Park, Cincinnati, OH, 1967, and by Classic Stage Company, New York City, 1968; *La Songe du critique*, published by Lensing (Dortmund, Germany), 1963; *La Foire d' Empoigne*, produced in Paris, 1962, published by Editions de la Table Ronde, 1961; *L'Orchestre*, produced in Paris, 1962, published in *L'Avant Scene*, November 15, 1962, translation produced as *The Orchestra*, Studio Arena Buffalo, NY, 1969, and Off-Broadway; (translator) *Richard III*, Theatre Montparnasse, 1964; *Cher Antoine, ou l'Amour rate*, Comedie des Champs-Elysees, 1969, published by Editions de la Table Ronde, 1969, translation by Lucienne Hill, published as *Dear Antoine, or The Love That Failed*, by Hill & Wang, 1971, produced at Chichester Festival Theatre, Chichester, U.K., 1971, and Loeb Drama Center, Harvard University, 1973; *Le Boulanger, la boulangere et le petit mitron*, Comedie des Champs-Elysees, 1968, published by Editions de la Table Ronde, 1969, translation by Lucienne Hill produced as *The Baker, the Baker's Wife, and the Baker's Boy*, University Theatre, Newcastle, U.K., 1972.

Le Theatre, ou La Vie comme elle est (title means "Theatre, or Life as It Is"), Comedie des Champs-Elysees, 1970; *Ne reveillez pas Madame* (title means "Don't Wake Up Madame"), Comedie des Champs-Elysees, 1970, published by Editions de la Table Ronde, 1970; *Les Poissons rouges, ou Mon Pere, ce heros*, (title means "The Goldfish" or "The Red Fish"), Theatre de l'Oeuvre, 1970; *Tu etais si gentil quand tu etais petit*, (title means "You Were So Nice When You Were Little"), Theatre Antoine, Paris, 1972, published by Editions de la Table Ronde, 1972; *Le Directeur de l'Opera*, published by Editions de la Table Ronde, 1972. Also, *The Navel*, 1981.

COLLECTIONS—French-language; all published by Editions de la Table Ronde, unless indicated: *Pieces roses*, contains *Le Bal des voleurs*, *Le Rendez-vous de Senlis*, and *Leocadia*, Editions Balzac, 1942, second edition, adding *Humulus le muet*, Editions de la Table Ronde, 1958; *Pieces noires*, contains *L'Hermine*, *La Sauvage*, *Le Voyageur sans bagage*, and *Eurydice*, Editions Balzac, 1942; *Nouvelles pieces noires*, contains *Jezebel*, *Antigone*, *Romeo et Jeannette*, and *Medee*, 1946; *Pieces brillantes*, contains *L'Invitation au chateau*, *Colombe*, *La Repetition ou L'Amour puni*, and *Cecile, ou L'Ecole des peres*, 1951; *Pieces grincantes*, includes *Ardele, ou La Marguerite*, *La Valse des toreadors*, *Ornifle, ou Le Courant d'air*, and *Pauvre Bitos, ou Le Diner de tetes*, 1956; *Pieces costumees*, includes *L'Alouette*, *Becket, ou L'Honneur de Dieu*, and *La Foire d'Empoigne*, 1960; *Pieces grincantes*, contains *L'Hurluberlu, ou Le Reactionnaire amoureux*, *La Grotte*, *L'Orchestre*,

Le Boulanger, la Boulangere, et le petit mitron, and *Les Poissons rouges, our Mon Pere, ce heros*, 1970.

English-language: Collected plays in three volumes published by Hill & Wang; Vol. I published as *Five Plays*, contains *Antigone*, *Eurydice*, *The Ermine*, *The Rehearsal*, and *Romeo and Jeannette*, 1958, Vol. II published as *Five Plays*, containe *Restless Heart*, *Time Remembered*, *Ardele*, *Mademoiselle Colombe*, and *The Lark*, 1959, Vol. III published as *Seven Plays*, contains *Thieves' Carnival*, *Medea*, *Cecile, or the School for Fathers*, *Traveler without Luggage*, *The Orchestra*, *Episode in the Life of an Author*, and *Catch as Catch Can*, 1967; *The Collected Plays*, Methuen, Vol. I contains *The Ermine*, *Thieves' Carnival*, *Restless Heart*, *Traveller without Luggage*, and *Dinner with the Family*, 1966, Vol. II contains *Time Remembered*, *Point of Departure*, *Antigone*, *Romeo and Jeanette*, and *Medea*, 1967. Plays are widely represented in anthologies.

Other stage writings: (Editor and translator) *Trois Comedies: As You Like It, The Winter's Tale, Twelfth Night*, Editions de la Table Ronde, 1952; (with Pierre Imbourg and Andre Warnod) *Michel-Marie Poulain*, Braun, 1953; (with Nicole Anouilh) *L'Amant complaisant*, a translation of Graham Greene's *The Complaisant Lover*, Laffont, 1962; (adaptor) Roger Vitrac's *Victor*, in *L'Avant Scene*, November 15, 1962; (translator) *Il est important d'etre aime*, a translation of Oscar Wilde's *The Importance of Being Earnest*, in *L'Avant-Scene*, No. 101. Also co-author, with Leon Thoorens, *Le Dossier Moliere*, 1964; and translator and adaptator of *Desire Under the Elms*. Also wrote *Attile le magnifique*, 1930; *Le Petit bonheur*, 1935; *L'Incertain*, 1938.

SCREENPLAYS—(Author of dialogue, with Jean Aurenche) *Les Degourdis de la onzieme*, 1936; (dialogue, with Jean Aurenche) *Vous n' avez rien a declarer*, 1937; (dialogue, with Aurenche) *Les Otages*, 1939; (scenarist and author of dialogue, with Aurenche) *Le Voyageur sans bagage*, 1943, released in the United States as *Identity Unknown*, Republic Pictures, 1945; (adaptor and author of dialogue, with J. Duvivier and G. Morgan) *Anna Karenina*, 1947; (scenarist and author of dialogue, with J. Bernard-Luc), *Monsieur Vincent*, Lopert, 1949; (scenarist, adaptor, and author of dialogue, with Bernard-Luc) *Pattes Blanches*, 1948; (adaptor and author of dialogue) *Un Caprice de Caroline cherie*, 1950; (adaptor and author of dialogue, with Monelle Valentin) *Deux sous de violettes*, 1951; (adaptor, scenarist, and author of dialogue) *Le Rideau rouge (ce soir joue Macbeth)*, 1952; (adaptor and author of dialogue) *Le Chevalier de la nuit*, 1953; *The End of Belle*, released as *The Passion of Slow Fire*, Trans-Lux Distributing, 1962; *La Ronde*, 1964; *La Grain de beaute*, 1969; *Waterloo*, Paramount, 1971; *Time for Loving*, 1972; *A Room in Paris*.

Also author of *The Vicountess of Eristal Has Not Received Her Mechanical Carpet Sweeper* (autobiography), 1987; and of scenarios for the ballets *Les Demoiselles de la nuit* and *Le Loup*.

AWARDS: Grand Prix du Cinema Francais, 1949, for film *Monsieur Vincent;* Antoinette Perry Award and citation from the cultural division of the French Embassy, 1955, for *Thieves' Carnival;* New York Drama Critics' Circle Award for best foreign play of 1956-57, for *Waltz of the Toreadors;* First Prize for best play of the year from Syndicate of French Drama Critics, 1970, for *Cher Antoine* and *Les Poissons rouges;* Paris Critics Prize, 1971, for *Ne Reveillez pas Madame*.

SIDELIGHTS: Director Peter Brook, in the preface to *Ring Around the Moon*, said of Jean Anouilh: "[He] writes plays for performance rather than for paper. . . . His plays are recorded improvisations. . . . He is a poet, but not a poet of words: he is a poet of words-acted, of scenes-set, of players performing.''

Several of the playwright's works have been adapted by others for film and television performances. *Romeo and Jeannette* was adapted and produced as *Monsoon* (United Artists, 1953); *La Valse des toreadors* became *The Waltz of the Toreadors* (Continental Distributing, 1962); and the 1963 Paramount film *Becket* was based on Lucienne Hill's translation of *Becket, ou L'Honneur de Dieu.* Television productions include "The Lark," 1956-57, and "Time Remembered," based on Patricia Moyes's translation of *Leocadia,* 1961, both on *Hallmark Hall of Fame,* CBS; "Traveler without Luggage," on *NET Playhouse,* PBS, 1971; "Antigone," *Playhouse New York,* PBS, 1972; and *The Young Man and the Lion,* PBS, 1976.

OBITUARIES AND OTHER SOURCES: Leon Cabell Pronko, *The World of Jean Anouilh,* University of California Press, 1961; John Harvey, *Anouilh: A Study in Theatrics,* Yale University Press, 1964; A.M. della Fazia, *Jean Anouilh,* Twayne, 1969; K.W. Kelly, *Jean Anouilh: An Annotated Bibliography,* Scarecrow, 1973; *Contemporary Authors,* First Revision Series, Vol. 17-20, Gale, 1976; H.G. McIntyre, *The Theatre of Jean Anouilh,* Barnes and Nobel Imports, 1981; *Variety,* October 17, 1987.*

*   *   *

ANSTEY, Edgar   1907-1987

OBITUARY NOTICE—See *CTFT* index for sketch: Full name, Edgar Harold MacFarlane Anstey; born February 16, 1907, in Watford, England; died in London, September 26, 1987. Edgar Anstey was considered a pioneer of the documentary. At the start of his career in the early thirties, Anstey produced or directed such socially oriented films as *Housing Problems, Enough to Eat?,* and *On the Way to Work*—films lauded for both their realism and for their impressionistic style. In 1936 Anstey became director of productions for "March of Time," makers of theatrical newsreels, but left the position to create films for the Ministry of Information and Armed Services during World War II. After the war, Anstey briefly served as film critic for *The Spectator,* returning to filmmaking to serve as the head of the British Transportation Commission's film unit. Among the prizewinning films he created for the commission were *Journey into Spring, Between the Tides, Under Night Streets,* and *Terminus.* In 1966 Anstey's *Wild Wings* received an Academy Award for best non-fiction short subject. Among his numerous memberships and positions, Anstey served as chairman of the British Film Academy and was a senior fellow of the Royal College of Art.

OBITUARIES AND OTHER SOURCES: Variety, September 30, 1987.

*   *   *

ANTHONY, Michael   1920-

PERSONAL: Born Michael Chodzko, September 26, 1920, in St. Helier, Jersey, England; son of Alexander Victor (a mariner and journalist) and Letitia Caroline (Elrington) Chodzko; married Mary

MICHAEL ANTHONY

Stuart (an actress), November 15, 1948 (divorced); married Bernadette Milnes (an actress), June 20, 1973 (divorced); children: Frances Caroline, Lysette. POLITICS: "Conservative with a strong bias in preservation of Western culture." RELIGION: Roman Catholic. MILITARY: Royal Navy, 1939-45.

VOCATION: Actor, director, and writer.

CAREER: STAGE DEBUT—Christopher, *The Passing of the Third Floor Back,* Frank Forbes Robertson Company, tour of U.K. cities, 1933, for eighty-five performances. LONDON DEBUT—*Your Number's Up,* Gate Theatre, 1935, for fifty performances. PRINCIPAL STAGE APPEARANCES— Weekly repertory at Palladium Theatre, Edinburgh, Scotland, U.K., 1934-35; appeared in several revues, including *Gate Revue,* 1935-36, *Spread It Around,* 1936, *Floodlight Revue,* 1938, *Nine Sharp,* 1938-39, and *A la Carte,* 1946; played in repertory, Cambridge Arts Theatre, Cambridge, U.K., 1945; Prince Charming, *The Glass Slipper,* St. James Theatre, London; also appeared in *Peace in Our Time,* 1947, *King's Rhapsody,* 1948, and more recently in *The Sleeping Prince,* Royal Haymarket Theatre, *The Dresser,* Queen's Theatre, and as Mephistopheles in *Dr. Faustus,* Fortune Theatre, all London. Performed numerous roles at Chichester Festival Theatre, Chichester, U.K., 1981-83.

MAJOR TOURS—Sir, *The Dresser,* U.K. cities.

FILM DEBUT—Vicomte de Nanjac, *An Ideal Husband,* London Films, 1947. PRINCIPAL FILM APPEARANCES—Lieutenant James, *The Guards,* Rank, 1955; hotel manager, *To Paris with Love,* Rank,

1955; various roles, *Oh Rosalindha,* Rank, 1956; Le Cure Aumonier, *Wet Stuff,* Columbia, 1956; Kapt. Shultz, *Night Ambush* (also known as *Ill Met By Moonlight*), Rank, 1957; Captain Le Blanc, *I Accuse!,* Metro-Goldwyn-Mayer (MGM), 1958; hotel manager, *Indiscreet,* Rank, 1958; passenger on boat deck, *A Night to Remember,* Rank, 1958; Baron de Granville, *Becket,* Paramount, 1964; French porno director, *Darling,* Rank, 1965; French Ambassador, *Khartoum,* Rank/Columbia, 1966; Major Von Krauss, *The Dirty Dozen,* MGM, 1967; Pere Bellargue, *Mosquito Squadron,* Mirisch Films, 1969; Duc de Montmorency, *Mata-Hari,* Cannon, 1985. Also played Captain Jameson, *Moment Dangereuse,* Pathe; Mr. Smethson, *Une Nuit de Venise,* Pathe; and numerous roles in a series of British comedy films starring Norman Wisdom.

TELEVISION DEBUT—Dorothy Parker sketch, BBC, 1939. PRINCIPAL TELEVISION APPEARANCES—Episodic: Appeared on many British television series; also French detective, *Private Investigator,* BBC; "Antony and Cleopatra," "Timon of Athens," both *Jonathan Miller's Shakespearian Saga,* BBC. Mini-Series: Dr. Lacoste, *War and Remembrance,* ABC, upcoming. Specials: M. Dubois, *Svengali,* BBC; cobbler, *The Pickwick Papers,* BBC; Georges Clemenceau, *Lloyd George,* BBC; French foreign minister, *The Suez Affair,* BBC; Monsieur Dubois, *Trilby,* BBC.

RELATED CAREER—Actor and manager, Stage Arts Players and City Stage theatrical companies.

WRITINGS: FICTION—*Slip Road from Solombala; Bottom Right Hand Corner.*

MEMBER: British Actors' Equity Association; Naval Club (London).

ADDRESSES: HOME—Domaine des Emeraudes, 83420, La Croix Valmer, France. OFFICE—c/o Spotlight, 43 Cranbourne Sreet, London WC2 7AP, England.

*   *   *

ANTOON, A.J.   1944-

PERSONAL: Born December 7, 1944, in Lawrence, MA; son of Alfred J., Sr. and Josephine (Saba) Antoon. EDUCATION: Attended Boston College.

VOCATION: Director.

CAREER: FIRST STAGE WORK—Director, *Story Theatre from Chekhov and Tolstoy,* St. Clement's Church Theatre, New York City, 1971. FIRST LONDON STAGE WORK—Director, *Subject to Fits,* Palace Theatre, 1971. PRINCIPAL STAGE WORK—All as director unless indicated: *Subject to Fits,* Public Theatre, *The Tale of Cymbeline,* Delacorte Theatre, both New York City, 1971; *That Championship Season,* Public Theatre, then Booth Theatre, New York City, both 1972, later Garrick Theatre, London, 1974; *Much Ado about Nothing,* Delacorte Theatre, 1972; *The Good Doctor,* Eugene O'Neill Theatre, New York City, 1973; *The Dance of Death,* Vivian Beaumont Theatre, New York City, 1974; *Trelawny of the Wells,* Public Theatre, 1975; *Nasty Rumours and Final Remarks,* Old Prop Shop, New York City, 1979; *The Art of Dining,* Newman Theatre, New York City, 1979; *Derelict,* Studio Arena Theatre, Buffalo, NY, 1982; *The Rink,* Martin Beck Theatre, New York City, 1984; advisor, *My Life in Art,* New Directors Project, Perry Street Theatre, New York City, 1984; *South Pacific,* Dorothy

Chandler Pavilion, Los Angeles, CA, 1985; *Sherlock's Last Case,* Kennedy Center, Washington, DC, then Nederlander Theatre, New York City, both 1987.

PRINCIPAL TELEVISION WORK—Director, *Much Ado about Nothing,* 1972.

AWARDS: Best Director, Antoinette Perry Award, 1973, for *That Championship Season;* Best Director, Antoinette Perry Award nomination, 1973, for *Much Ado about Nothing.*

ADDRESSES: AGENT—c/o Richard Rosenthal, Esq., 424 Park Avenue, New York, NY 10022.*

*   *   *

APTED, Michael   1941-

PERSONAL: Born February 10, 1941, in London, England; son of Ronald William and Frances Amelia (Thomas) Apted; wife's name, Joan, married July 9, 1966; children: Paul, James. EDUCATION: Downing College, Cambridge University, B.A., 1961.

VOCATION: Director.

CAREER: PRINCIPAL FILM WORK—Director: *Triple Echo* (also known as *Soldier in Skirts*), Hemdale, 1973; *Stardust,* Goodtimes/Anglo, 1974; *The Squeeze,* Warner Brothers, 1976; *Agatha,* Casablanca/First Artists, 1978; *Coal Miner's Daughter,* Universal,

MICHAEL APTED

1980; *Continental Divide,* Universal, 1981; *Gorky Park,* Orion, 1983; *First Born,* Paramount, 1984; *Bring on the Night,* Goldwyn/A&M, 1985; *Critical Condition,* Paramount, 1986.

PRINCIPAL TELEVISION WORK—Director: *Another Sunday and Sweet F.A.,* Granada, 1972; *Kisses at Fifty,* BBC, 1974; *The Collection, "21",* both Granada, 1976; *Stronger Than the Sun,* BBC, 1977; *28 Up,* Granada, 1984. Also *P'Tang Yang Kipperband; Poor Girl; High Kampf; Highway Robbery.*

PRINCIPAL THEATRE WORK—Director, *Strawberry Fields,* National Theatre, London, 1978.

RELATED CAREER—Researcher, director, and producer for Granada television, London, during the 1960s.

AWARDS: TV Critics Best Play, 1972, for *Another Sunday and Sweet F.A.;* TV Critics Best Play, 1974, SFTA Best Director, 1974, both for *Kisses at Fifty;* International Emmy, 1976, for *The Collection;* International Emmy nomination, 1976, for *"21";* Directors Guild of America nomination, 1980, for *Coal Miner's Daughter;* British Academy Award, 1984, for *28 Up.*

MEMBER: Directors Guild of America.

ADDRESSES: AGENT—c/o Mike Marcus, Creative Artists Agency, 1888 Century Park E., Suite 1400, Los Angeles, CA, 90067.

*   *   *

MARK ARNOTT

ARNOTT, Mark   1950-

PERSONAL: Born June, 15, 1950, in Chicago, IL; son of George Peter (a psychologist) and Martha Adelade (a copy editor; maiden name, Wood) Arnott; married Jane Carr (an actress), May 30, 1987. EDUCATION: Dartmouth College, B.A., theatre, 1975; trained for the stage with Stella Adler and Michael Moriarty.

VOCATION: Actor.

CAREER: OFF-BROADWAY DEBUT—Quasimodo, *The Hunchback of Notre Dame,* Public Theatre, New York Shakespeare Festival, 1980. PRINCIPAL STAGE APPEARANCES—Quasimodo, *The Hunchback of Notre Dame,* American Theatre Festival, NH, 1980; Marlowe, *She Stoops to Conquer,* GeVa Theatre, Rochester, NY, 1982; Jerry, *Buddies,* Ensemble Studio Theatre, New York City, 1982; Spence, *Marmalade Skies,* Actors Outlet Theatre, New York City, 1983; *The Dining Room,* Astor Place Theatre, New York City, 1983; Colin, *The Knack,* Roundabout Theatre, New York City, 1984; Lenny, *The Homecoming,* Jewish Repertory Theatre, New York City, 1984; Leo Davis, *Room Service,* Eisenhower Theatre, Kennedy Center, Washington, DC, 1984; Peter, *The Common Pursuit,* Long Wharf Theatre, New Haven, CT, 1985; Jim O'Connor, *The Glass Menagerie,* Chatauqua, NY, 1985; Chirs Keller, *All My Sons,* Seattle Repertory Theatre, Seattle, WA, 1985; Mike Schwartz, *Arsenals,* Studio Arena Theatre, Buffalo, NY, 1986; also as Charlie, *What I Did Last Summer,* 1983; Michael Conklin, *House,* Ensemble Studio Theatre, New York City; David, *The Crashing of Moses Flying By,* Manhattan Punch Line Theatre, New York City; King of Navarre, *Love's Labour's Lost* and Valentine, *Two Gentlemen of Verona,* both with the Potters' Field Company, New York City; Renfield, *Count Dracula* and Edmund, *Long Day's Journey into Night,* both with the Nassau Repertory

Theatre, NY; Jack, *Charley's Aunt* and Puck, *A Midsummer Night's Dream,* both with the Eastern Slope Playhouse.

FILM DEBUT—Jeff, *The Return of the Secaucus Seven,* Salsipuedes Productions, 1978. PRINCIPAL FILM APPEARANCES—Kelly, *Tex,* Buena Vista, 1981; Brank, *Best Defense,* Paramount, 1983; Paul, *Chain Letters,* independent, 1985.

TELEVISION DEBUT—Jeff Sweetwater, *Leatherstocking Stories,* PBS, 1979. PRINCIPAL TELEVISION APPEARANCES—Episodic: *Hill Street Blues,* NBC, 1986; Mark, *Cheers,* NBC; *Kate & Allie,* CBS; *Hunter,* NBC; *Hard Copy,* CBS. Specials: Steve Lindquist, *Haunted,* PBS, 1984; *The Great Performance,* PBS.

RELATED CAREER—Formerly employed as a construction foreman for the Harlequin Dinner Theatre, Atlanta, GA, and Harlequin Dinner Theatre, Rockville, MD; worked extensively in technical theatre.

AWARDS: Marcus Heiman Fellowship Award, 1975, Dartmouth College.

MEMBER: Actors' Equity Association, Screen Actors Guild, American Federation of Television and Radio Artists.

SIDELIGHTS: FAVORITE ROLES—Chris Keller, *All My Sons,* Leo Davis, *Room Service,* Jim O'Connor, *The Glass Menagerie,* Peter, *The Common Pursuit,* Jeff, *The Return of the Secaucus Seven,* among others.

ADDRESSES: HOME—New York, NY. AGENT—c/o Susan

Smith, Smith, Freedman and Associates, 850 Seventh Avenue, New York, NY 10019.

*   *   *

ASKIN, Peter   1946-

PERSONAL: Born May 31, 1946; son of Alma (Durst) Askin; separated from wife; children: James; Sarah, Lida (stepchildren). EDUCATION: Received B.A., English literature, from Middlebury College; Ph.D., English literature, from Columbia University; trained for the stage with Wynn Handman and as a writer with Richard Brickner.

VOCATION: Director and writer.

CAREER: PRINCIPAL STAGE WORK—Director, *Down an Alley Filled with Cats*, Quaigh Theatre, New York City, 1986.

WRITINGS: SCREENPLAYS—*Smithereens*, New Line, 1983; *Season's Greetings*, Orion, 1987; *Selling Kate*, *Springfield Star*, both upcoming.

MEMBER: Writers Guild of America-East.

ADDRESSES: AGENT—Shore-Stille.

*   *   *

ASTAIRE, Fred   1899-1987

OBITUARY NOTICE—See index for *CTFT* sketch: Born Frederick Austerlitz, May 10, 1899, in Omaha, NE; died of pneumonia at Century City Hospital in Los Angeles, CA, June 22, 1987. Fred Astaire's style, grace, and flair won him high praise throughout his long career as a dancer, actor, choreographer, and singer. He started in vaudeville in a dance team with his sister, Adele, and their first Broadway appearance in the 1917 production *Over the Top* garnered rave reviews. They remained steady draws on Broadway and the London stage into the thirties with such hits as *The Passing Show of 1918*, *Lady Be Good*, 1924, *Funny Face*, 1929, and *The Band Wagon*, 1931. After his sister's retirement in 1932, Astaire continued on Broadway in Cole Porter's *Gay Divorce*, but it was to be his last appearance in a stage musical. Despite a screen test that was judged less than favorably, Astaire made his Hollywood debut in *Dancing Lady*, 1933. In his second film that year, *Flying Down to Rio*, he began his legendary partnership with Ginger Rogers. Although they did not receive top billing in the movie, their dance routines stole the spotlight and they went on to star in eight more features between 1934 and 1939, including *The Gay Divorcee*, 1934, *Top Hat*, 1935, and *The Story of Vernon and Irene Castle*, 1939. They reunited a decade later for *The Barkleys of Broadway*, but Astaire made a number of other films with such partners as Eleanor Powell, Rita Hayworth, Ann Miller, Judy Garland, Cyd Charisse, and Gene Kelly. He also choreographed and performed in several critically acclaimed television specials; *An Evening with Fred Astaire* in 1958 earned him an outstanding performance Emmy and won eight other Emmy awards. Among the many other major honors he received were a special Academy Award in 1949 "for raising the standards of all musicals" and lifetime achievement awards from the Kennedy Center for the Performing Arts in

1978 and the American Film Institute in 1981. His apparently effortless routines on film and stage were actually the product of hours of rigorous work. Such exacting perfectionism earned Astaire numerous accolades culminating in the *New York Times*'s description of him as "the ultimate dancer."

OBITUARIES AND OTHER SOURCES: New York Times, June 23, 1987; *Variety*, June, 1987.

*   *   *

ATKINS, Christopher   1961-

PERSONAL: Born February 21, 1961, in Rye, NY. EDUCATION: Attended Dennison University.

VOCATION: Actor.

CAREER: FILM DEBUT—Richard, *The Blue Lagoon*, Columbia, 1980. PRINCIPAL FILM APPEARANCES—Frederic, *The Pirate Movie*, Twentieth Century-Fox, 1982; Rick, *A Night in Heaven*, Twentieth Century-Fox, 1983.

PRINCIPAL TELEVISION APPEARANCES—Series: Peter Richards, *Dallas*, CBS, 1983-84. Movies: Isaac King, *Child Bride of Short Creek*, NBC, 1981; Allen Collier, *Secret Weapons*, 1985. Specials: *I Love Liberty*, ABC, 1982; *Night of 100 Stars*, ABC, 1982; *Celebrity Daredevils*, ABC, 1983; *Rock 'N' Roll Summer*, NBC, 1985; *The Tenth Annual Circus of the Stars*, CBS, 1985; *American Treasury*, CBS, 1985. Guest: *TV's Bloopers and Practical Jokes*, NBC, 1984.

PRINCIPAL STAGE APPEARANCES—*Night of 100 Stars*, Radio City Music Hall, New York City, 1982.

ADDRESSES: AGENT—c/o David Shapira and Associates, Inc., 15301 Ventura Boulevard, #345, Sherman Oaks, CA 91403. PUBLICIST—c/o Brad Turell, Rogers and Cowan, 10000 Santa Monica Boulevard, Los Angeles, CA 90067.*

*   *   *

AVALOS, Luis   1946-

PERSONAL: Surname is pronounced with accent on first "A"; born September 2, 1946, in Havana, Cuba; immigrated to the United States with his parents, 1946; son of Jose Antonio (a sugar refiner) and Estrella (a dressmaker; maiden name, De Leon) Avalos. EDUCATION: New York University, B.F.A., 1969.

VOCATION: Actor and writer.

CAREER: TELEVISION DEBUT—Roberto, *The Electric Company*, PBS, 1973-78. PRINCIPAL TELEVISION APPEARANCES—Episodic: Joe, *Barney Miller*, ABC, 1978; Primero, *The Incredible Hulk*, CBS, 1979; boxer, *The Jeffersons*, CBS, 1979; General Sandia, *Soap*, ABC, 1980; Melendez, *Fame*, NBC, 1981; Skippy, *Making a Living*, ABC, 1981; Hernandez, *Archie Bunker's Place*, CBS, 1982; Costa, *Mama's Family*, CBS, 1982; Detective Maldonado, *Second Family Tree*, CBS, 1982; Allan, *Jennifer Slept Here*, NBC, 1983; Detective Rubio, *Simon and Simon*, CBS, 1983;

LUIS AVALOS

Shiek Mamee, *Benson,* ABC, 1984; Louie, *You Again?,* NBC, 1986; also, *Kojak,* CBS. Series: Dr. Sanchez, *Highcliff Manor,* NBC, 1979; Jesse Rodriguez, *Condo,* ABC, 1983; Dr. Esquivel, *E.R.,* CBS, 1984; and on *I Had Three Wives,* CBS, 1986. Mini-Series: Juan, *Fresno,* CBS, 1986. Specials: Dr. Lyman, *George Burns Comedy Hour,* CBS, 1985. Pilots: Jesse Rodriguez, *Condo,* ABC, 1983; Detective Hernandez, *Boys in Blue,* CBS, 1983. Movies: Dr. Rojas, *The Long Journey Back,* ABC, 1979; cabbie, *The Fantastic World of D.C. Collins,* CBS, 1983.

BROADWAY DEBUT—King of Hearts, *Never Jam Today,* City Center Theatre, New York City, 1968. PRINCIPAL STAGE APPEARANCES—As a member of the ensemble, then resident actor, Lincoln Center Repertory Company, New York City, 1969-73: Abdullah, *Camino Real,* 1969; Jerry, *The Zoo Story;* also *The Good Woman of Setzuan, Kool Aid, The Architect and the Emperor of Assyria, Armedians, Payment as Pledged, Save Grand Central, Marco Polo, Beggar on Horseback, Antigone, A Streetcar Named Desire, Don Juan in Hell, Twelve Angry Men.* Appeared as Pepe, *El Grande de Coca-Cola,* Plaza Nine Theatre, New York City, 1975; Jacques de Boys, *As You Like It,* New York Shakespeare Festival, New York City, 1976.

FILM DEBUT—Chico, *Badge 373,* Paramount, 1970. PRINCIPAL FILM APPEARANCES—Ramon, *Hot Stuff,* Columbia, 1979; cabbie, *Stir Crazy,* Columbia, 1980; also appeared in *Sunday Lovers,* United Artists, 1981.

WRITINGS: SCREENPLAYS—Contributor, *Ghost Fever,* 1986; (with Julio Vera) *Diplomatic Ties,* Proctor & Gamble, 1987; *Cabaret Tijuana,* Cinestar, 1987; *Ay Caramba,* upcoming.

AWARDS: Best Actor in Theatre, Association of Hispanic Critics, 1974; Hispanic of the Year, *Caminos* magazine, 1984.

MEMBER: Actors' Equity Association, Screen Actors Guild, American Federation of Television and Radio Artists; National Foundation for the Arts (judge).

SIDELIGHTS: RECREATIONS—Swimming and tennis.

ADDRESSES: HOME—Hollywood Hills, CA. AGENT—Century Artists, Ltd., 9744 Wilshire Boulevard, Beverly Hills, CA 90212. PUBLICIST—Charisma Public Relations, 11500 W. Olympic Boulevard, Suite 400, Los Angeles, CA 90064.

*   *   *

AZENBERG, Emanuel   1934-

PERSONAL Born January 22, 1934, in Bronx, NY; son of Joshua Charles and Hannah (Kleiman) Azenberg; married Elinor Shanbaum; children: Lisa. EDUCATION: Attended New York University. MILITARY: U.S. Army.

VOCATION: Producer.

CAREER: PRINCIPAL STAGE WORK—Producer, all in New York City unless indicated: *Rendezvous at Senlis,* Gramercy Arts Theatre, 1961; *The Lion in Winter,* Ambassador Theatre, *Mark Twain Tonight,* Longacre Theatre, *The Investigation,* Ambassador Theatre, all 1966; *Something Different,* Cort Theatre, 1967; *The Sunshine Boys,* Broadhurst Theatre, 1972; *The Good Doctor,* Eugene O'Neill Theatre, 1973; *Scapino,* Brooklyn Academy of Music, Brooklyn, NY, then Circle in the Square, both 1974; *California Suite,* Eugene O'Neill Theatre, 1976; *Something's Afoot,* Lyceum Theatre, 1976, then Ambassador Theatre, 1977; *Chapter Two,* Imperial Theatre, 1977; *Ain't Misbehavin',* Longacre Theatre, 1978; *They're Playing Our Song,* Imperial Theatre, *Whose Life Is It, Anyway?,* Trafalgar Theatre, *Devour the Snow,* John Golden Theatre, *Last Licks,* Longacre Theatre, all 1979; *I Ought to Be in Pictures,* Eugene O'Neill Theatre, *Division Street,* Ambassador Theatre, *Children of a Lesser God,* Longacre Theatre, all 1980; *Fools,* Eugene O'Neill Theatre, *Einstein and the Polar Bear,* Cort Theatre, *Grownups,* Lyceum Theatre, *Duet for One,* Royale Theatre, all 1981; *Little Me,* Eugene O'Neill Theatre, *Master Harold. . .and the Boys,* Lyceum Theatre, both 1982; *Brighton Beach Memoirs,* Neil Simon Theatre, 1983; *Sunday in the Park with George,* Booth Theatre, *A Moon for the Misbegotten,* Cort Theatre, *Whoopi Goldberg,* Lyceum Theatre, *The Real Thing,* Plymouth Theatre, all 1984; *The Odd Couple,* Broadhurst Theatre, *Joe Egg,* Longacre Theatre, both 1985; *Biloxi Blues,* Neil Simon Theatre, 1985, then Fox Theatre, Atlanta, GA, 1986; *Long Day's Journey into Night, Broadway Bound,* both Broadhurst Theatre, 1986; *A Month of Sundays,* Ritz Theatre, 1987; *Barbara Cook: A Concert for the Theatre,* Ambassador Theatre, 1987. Also produced *Ain't Supposed to Die a Natural Death,* 1971; *God's Favorite,* 1974; *The Poison Tree,* Philadelphia, PA.

MAJOR TOURS—Producer: *They're Playing Our Song,* U.S. cities, 1979-81; *Whose Life Is It, Anyway?,* U.S. cities, 1980-81; *Children of a Lesser God,* U.S. cities, 1980-81.

RELATED CAREER: Lecturer, Duke University, New York University.

AWARDS: Best Musical, Antoinette Perry Award, 1978, New York Drama Critics Circle Award, 1978, Drama Desk Award, 1978, Outer Critics Circle Award, 1978, all for *Ain't Misbehavin';* Best Play, Antoinette Perry Award, 1980, for *Children of a Lesser God;* Best Play, Antoinette Perry Award, 1984, New York Drama Critics Circle Award, 1984, Drama Desk Award, 1984, all for *The Real Thing;* Best Musical, New York Drama Critics Circle Award, 1984, Drama Desk Award, 1984, Antoinette Perry Award nomination, 1984, all for *Sunday in the Park with George;* Best Play, New York Drama Critics Circle Award, 1984, for *Brighton Beach Memoirs;* Best Play, Antoinette Perry Award, 1985, for *Biloxi Blues;* Best Reproduction, Antoinette Perry Award, 1985, Outstanding Revival, Drama Desk Award, 1985, both for *Joe Egg;* Best Play, Antoinette Perry Award nomination, 1987, for *Broadway Bound.*

ADDRESSES: HOME—100 W. 57th Street, New York, NY 10019. OFFICE—Iron Mountain Productions, 165 W. 46th Street, New York, NY 10036.*

B

BABCOCK, Debra Lee   1956-

PERSONAL: Born July 3, 1956, in Seaford, NY; daughter of Ralph David (a businessman) and Paula Adele (a hospital geriatric activities director; maiden name, Schulleri) Babcock; married Stephen Paul Hamilton (an actor), September 8, 1984. EDUCATION: Attended the California College of Arts and Crafts; San Francisco Art Institute, B.F.A., 1978; studied acting with Madeleine Sherwood, Patrick Brafford, Michael Shurtleff, Terry Schreiber, and Leslie Ayvazion; trained in directing with Curt Dempster and Jack Garfein.

VOCATION: Actress, director, designer, and producer.

CAREER: STAGE DEBUT—With the Earth Thread Theatre, Fort Mason Foundation, San Francisco Art Institute, CA, 1978. PRINCIPAL STAGE APPEARANCES—Dancer and anger, *Laughing Souls-*

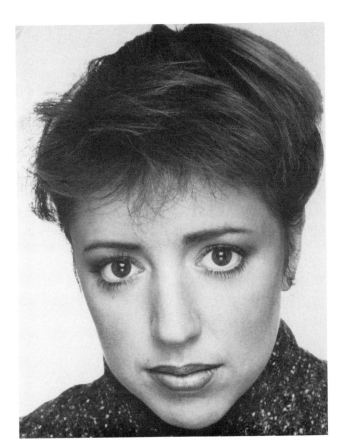

DEBRA LEE BABCOCK

Espiritus Sonriendas, 626 Performance Space, 1979; Mina, *Count Dracula,* 1980 and Elvira, *Blithe Spirit,* 1981, both Playhouse by the River, Mt. Bethel, PA; Rebecca, *Our Town,* Players' Club, New York City, 1982; Maria, *Cries and Whispers,* 3L Theatre, New York City, 1982; servant girl and nun, *Romeo and Juliet* and peasant and nurse, *The Caucasian Chalk Circle,* both with the Lion Theatre Ensemble at the Judith Anderson Theatre, New York City, 1982; Flute and Thisby, *A Midsummer Night's Dream,* Playhouse by the River, 1984; Mary, *Among the Fallen,* New Theatre, New York City, 1985; Carla, *Silver Bells,* Ensemble Studio Theatre Institute, New York City, 1985; Esther Miller, *The Miller's Tale,* Westbeth Theatre Center, New York City, 1986; the girl, *Hot L Baltimore* and Ann, *Balm in Gilead,* both at The Real Stage, New York City, 1986; Beverly, *Blind Hearts,* Ensemble Studio Theatre, New York City, 1986.

MAJOR TOURS—*Mr. Pim Passes By,* tour of shelters for the homeless, New York City, 1986.

PRINCIPAL STAGE WORK—Founding member, Earth Thread Theatre, 1978; scenic painter, *La Rondine,* University of Hartford, CT, 1979; scenic designer and painter: *The Infernal Machine,* Chameleon Theatrix, New York City, 1979; *Modigliani,* Cubiculo Theatre, New York City, 1983; director: *Of Mice and Men,* 1981 and *Cowboys II,* 1983, both Playhouse by the River, Mt. Bethel, PA; *A Christmas Carol,* Christ Church, Brooklyn, NY, 1984; *Thoughts on the Instant of Greeting a Friend on the Street* and *Cowboys II,* both 1984, *Goodnight Firefly Ravine* and *Small Corners,* both 1985, all at the Ensemble Studio Theatre, New York City.

PRINCIPAL FILM APPEARANCES—Woman of a Thousand Faces, *Blood and Dreams,* Castellon Inc. Films, 1978; assistant lawyer, *The Jury Film,* Playback Association.

TELEVISION DEBUT—*One Life to Live,* ABC, 1986.

NON-RELATED CAREER—Waitress, cook, and bartender, Great Performances Caterers, New York City, 1984-87; substitute teacher of art, English, and theatre, St. Ann's School, New York City, 1985-86; bookstore attendant, Museum of American Folk Art, New York City, 1984.

MEMBER: Actors' Equity Association, Screen Actors Guild, American Federation of Television and Radio Artists.

SIDELIGHTS: Debra Lee Babcock told *CTFT,* "I have travelled to the Hawaiian Islands, all over Canada, crossed the United States seven times, hiked in the Alps, and camped all over France. The most extraordinary trip has been my recent solo hike across the Grand Canyon to have my thirtieth birthday at the bottom."

ADDRESSES: HOME—26 W. 87th Street, Apartment 3A, New York, NY 10024.

*   *   *

BABE, Thomas   1941-

PERSONAL: Born March 13, 1941, in Buffalo, NY; son of Thomas James (in sales) and Ruth Ina (Lossie) Babe; married Susan Bramhall, April 1, 1967 (divorced, 1976); children: Charissa. EDUCATION: Harvard College, B.A. (summa cum laude), 1963; St. Catharine's College, Cambridge University, B.A., English, 1965; Yale University, J.D., 1972.

VOCATION: Writer and director.

CAREER: PRINCIPAL STAGE WORK—Also see *WRITINGS* below; director of nearly one hundred plays, many of which were performed at Playwrights Horizons, New York City.

WRITINGS: PLAYS—*The Pageant of Awkward Shadows,* Harvard College Theatre, Cambridge, MA, 1963; *Kid Champion,* Public Theatre, New York City, 1974; *Mojo Candy,* Yale Cabaret, New Haven, CT, 1975; *Rebel Women,* Public Theatre, 1976; *Billy Irish,* Manhattan Theatre Club, New York City, 1976; *A Prayer for My Daughter,* Public Theatre, then Royal Court Theatre, London, 1978; *Great Solo Town,* Yale Cabaret, 1977; *Fathers and Sons,* Public Theatre, 1978; *Taken in Marriage,* Public Theatre, 1979; *Salt Lake City Skyline,* Public Theatre, 1980; (with Twyla Tharp) *When We Were Very Young,* Winter Garden Theatre, New York City, 1980; *Buried Inside Extra,* Public Theatre, 1984; *Planet Fires,* GeVa Theatre, Rochester, NY, 1985, then Mark Taper Forum, Los Angeles, CA, 1986, later Stage Number One, Dallas, TX, 1987; *Carrying School Children,* Theatre for the New City, New York City, 1987; *Demon Wine,* Los Angeles Theatre Center, Los Angeles, CA, 1987. Also wrote *Daniel Boone,* 1979.

SCREENPLAYS—(With Michael Wadleigh) *The Sun Gods,* Warner Brothers, 1978; *The Vacancy,* Warner Brothers, 1979; *Kid Champion,* Music Fair, Inc., 1979.

RADIO PLAYS—"Hot Dogs and Soda Pop," *Ear Play,* National Public Radio (NPR), 1980; *The Volunteer Fireman,* NPR, 1981.

RELATED CAREER—Founder and co-director, Summer Players, Agassiz Theatre, Cambridge, MA, 1966-68; member of overview panel and playwriting fellowship panel of the National Endowment for the Arts.

AWARDS: Burns-Mantle Award, 1976, for *Rebel Women;* Burns-Mantle Award, 1978, for *A Prayer for My Daughter;* CBS Fellowship in Playwriting, 1976; Guggenheim Fellowship, 1977; Rockefeller Grant, 1978; also received a grant from the National Endowment for the Arts.

MEMBER: Writers Guild of America-East, Dramatists Guild of America; Phi Beta Kappa.

SIDELIGHTS: Thomas Babe told *CTFT:* "My work in the theatre began in the 1960s—about the time that the modern institutional theatre movement in America was finding itself. Though current fashion has shrunk somewhat the wider boundries I knew when I started, the theatre remains the place of maximum freedom in dramatic expression, representing as it does—in any given season and on a decentralized, nationwide basis—everything from theatricalized sit-coms to the liberating experiments of the Mabou Mines and Martha Clark. It is a financially terrorizing but creatively rewarding form to work in and serves as an important counterpoint to the equally exciting but different worlds of television and film.''

ADDRESSES: OFFICE—103 Hoyt Street, Darien, CT 06820. AGENT—c/o Robert Lantz, The Lantz Office, 888 Seventh Avenue, New York, NY 10106.

*   *   *

BACH, Catherine

PERSONAL: Grew up in South Dakota and Los Angeles, CA; married David Shaw (divorced).

VOCATION: Actress.

CAREER: PRINCIPAL TELEVISION APPEARANCES—Episodic: *Love Boat,* ABC, 1983; "Drive, She Said," *Trying Times,* PBS, 1987. Series: Daisy Duke, *The Dukes of Hazzard,* CBS, 1979-85; (cartoon) voice of Daisy Duke, *The Dukes,* CBS, 1983. Specials: *Battle of the Network Stars 6,* ABC, 1979; *Celebrity Challenge of the Sexes 4,* CBS, 1979; *Battle of the Network Stars 8,* ABC, 1980; *Celebrity Challenge of the Sexes 5,* CBS, 1980; *The Nashville Palace,* ABC, 1980; *The Magic of David Copperfield,* CBS, 1981; *Battle of the Network Stars 12,* ABC, 1982; *Circus of the Stars 6,* CBS, 1982; *Night of 100 Stars,* ABC, 1982; *Bob Hope's Merry Christmas Show,* NBC, 1983; *CBS All-American Thanksgiving Day Parade,* CBS, 1983 and 1984; *Blondes vs. Brunettes,* ABC, 1984; *George Burns' How to Live to Be 100,* NBC, 1984; *The 21st Annual Academy of Country Music Awards,* NBC, 1986; *Willie Nelson's Picnic,* syndicated, 1987. Movies: *Alice, Matt Helm,* ABC, 1975; Lara, *Strange New World,* ABC, 1975; Linda, *Murder in Peyton Place,* NBC, 1977; Trisha Parker, *White Water Rebels,* CBS, 1983.

PRINCIPAL FILM APPEARANCES—Natalie, *The Midnight Man,* Universal, 1974; Melody, *Thunderbolt and Lightfoot,* United Artists, 1974; Peggy Summers, *Hustle,* Paramount, 1975; Marcie, *Cannonball Run II,* Warner Brothers, 1984.

PRINCIPAL STAGE APPEARANCES—*Night of 100 Stars,* Radio City Music Hall, New York City, 1982; *Extremities,* Burt Reynolds' Jupiter Theatre, Jupiter, FL, 1985.

ADDRESSES: AGENT—c/o Rich Hersh, William Morris Agency, 151 El Camino Drive, Beverly Hills, CA 90212. PUBLICIST—c/o Alan Nierob, Rogers and Cowan, 10000 Santa Monica Boulevard, #400, Los Angeles, CA 90067.*

*   *   *

BACON, Kevin   1958-

PERSONAL: Born July 8, 1958, in Philadelphia, PA. EDUCATION: Trained for the stage as an apprentice at Circle in the Square Theatre School and at the Manning Street Actor's Theatre.

VOCATION: Actor.

CAREER: FILM DEBUT—Chip Diller, *National Lampoon's Animal House*, Universal, 1978. PRINCIPAL FILM APPEARANCES—Jack, *Friday the 13th*, Paramount, 1980; Don, *Only When I Laugh*, Columbia, 1981; Rickey, *Forty-Deuce*, Island, 1982; Timothy Fenwick, Jr., *Diner*, Metro-Goldwyn-Mayer/United Artists, 1982; Ren MacCormack, *Footloose*, Paramount, 1984; Jack Casey, *Quicksilver*, Columbia, 1985. Also appeared in *Starting Over*, Paramount, 1979; *Hero at Large*, United Artists, 1980; *Rites of Summer*, Columbia, 1987; *End of the Line*, Orion Classics, 1987.

OFF-BROADWAY DEBUT—Ronnie, *Getting Out*, Marymount Manhattan Theatre, 1978. BROADWAY DEBUT—Phil McCann, *Slab Boys*, Playhouse Theatre, 1983. PRINCIPAL STAGE APPEARANCES—Billy, *Album*, WPA Theatre, then Cherry Lane Theatre, both New York City, 1980; Ricky, *Forty-Deuce*, Perry Street Theatre, New York City, 1981; Michael, *Flux*, Second Stage, New York City, 1982; Frank Wozniak, *Poor Little Lambs*, Theatre at St. Peter's Church, New York City, 1982; Dennis, *Loot*, Manhattan Theatre Club, New York City, 1986. Also appeared as Murph, *Men without Dates*, New York City, 1985; and in *Mary Barnes*, Long Wharf Theatre, New Haven, CT, 1980; *Glad Tidyings*, New York City, then Actors Theatre of Louisville, Louisville, KY, 1979-80.

PRINCIPAL TELEVISION APPEARANCES—Episodic: Tim Werner, *The Guiding Light*, CBS; *Search for Tomorrow*, NBC. Movies: Teddy, *The Gift*, CBS, 1979; Dennis, *Enormous Changes at the Last Minute*, PBS 1982; also appeared in *The Demon Murder Case*, NBC, 1983. Specials: Ensign Pulver, *Mister Roberts*, NBC, 1984.

ADDRESSES: AGENT—c/o N. David, Triad Artists, 10100 Santa Monica Boulevard, Los Angeles, CA, 90067. PUBLICIST—c/o N. Koenisberg, D. Taylor, P/M/K Public Relations, Inc., 8436 W. Third Street, Los Angeles, CA 90048.*

*   *   *

BADEL, Sarah 1943-

PERSONAL: Born March 30, 1943, in London, England; daughter of Alan Firman and Yvonne (Owen) Badel.

VOCATION: Actress.

CAREER: STAGE DEBUT—*Hamlet*, Bristol Old Vic Company, tour of India, 1963. LONDON DEBUT—Bella Hedley, *Robert and Elizabeth*, Lyric Theatre, 1964. BROADWAY DEBUT—Helen, *The Right Honourable Gentleman*, Billy Rose Theatre, 1965. PRINCIPAL STAGE APPEARANCES—Miss Fanny, *The Clandestine Marriage*, Sophie, *The Fighting Cock*, Anya, *The Cherry Orchard*, all Chichester Festival, Chichester, U.K., 1966; Petronell Sweetland, *The Farmer's Wife*, Helene, *An Italian Straw Hat*, both Chichester Festival, 1967; Ellie Dunn, *Heartbreak House*, Chichester Festival, then Lyric Theatre, London, both 1967; Solveig, *Peer Gynt*, Raina Petkoff, *Arms and the Man*, both Chichester Festival, 1970; Vivie Warren, *Mrs. Warren's Profession*, National Theatre Company, London, 1970; Olivia, *Twelfth Night*, Juliet, *Romeo and Juliet*, both St. George's Playhouse, England, 1976.

PRINCIPAL TELEVISION APPEARANCES—Series: *The Pallisers*. Specials: *Cold Comfort Farm; King Lear*.

FILM DEBUT—*Every Home Should Have One*, 1970.

SIDELIGHTS: RECREATIONS—Gardening.

ADDRESSES: AGENT—c/o Plunket Greene, 91 Regent Street, London W1R 5RU, England.*

*   *   *

BAILEY, John 1942-

PERSONAL: Born August 10, 1942, in Missouri; married Carol Littleton (a film editor) March 11, 1972. EDUCATION: Attended University of Santa Clara, Loyola University, University of Southern California, and University of Vienna.

VOCATION: Cinematographer.

CAREER: PRINCIPAL FILM WORK—Cinematographer: *Premonition*, Transvue, 1972; *End of August*, Mica, 1974; *Legacy*, Kino International, 1976; *The Mafu Cage*, Clouds Productions, 1978; *Boulevard Nights*, Warner Brothers, 1979; *American Gigolo*, Paramount, 1980; *Ordinary People*, Paramount, 1980; *Honky Tonk Freeway*, Universal, 1981; *Continental Divide*, Universal, 1981; *Cat People*, Universal, 1982; *That Championship Season*, Cannon, 1982; *Without a Trace*, Twentieth Century-Fox, 1983; *The Big Chill*, Columbia, 1983; *Racing with the Moon*, Paramount, 1984; *The Pope of Greenwich Village*, Metro-Goldwyn-Mayer/United Artists, 1984; *Mishima: A Life in Four Chapters*, Warner Brothers, 1985; *Silverado*, Columbia, 1985; *Crossroads*, Columbia, 1986; *Brighton Beach Memoirs*, Universal, 1986; *Light of Day*, Tri-Star, 1987; *Swimming to Cambodia*, Cinecom, 1987; *Tough Guys Don't Dance*, Cannon, 1987.

PRINCIPAL TELEVISION WORK—Cinematographer: *Battered*, NBC, 1978; *City in Fear*, ABC, 1980.

RELATED CAREER—Lecturer, American Film Institute, 1982 and 1984.

AWARDS: Cannes Film Festival Award for Artistic Achievement, 1985, for *Mishima: A Life in Four Chapters*.

MEMBER: American Society of Cinematographers, Academy of Motion Picture Arts and Sciences.

ADDRESSES: AGENT—Bauer-Benedek, 9255 Sunset Boulevard, Suite 710, Los Angeles, CA, 90069.

*   *   *

BAIO, Scott 1961-

PERSONAL: Born in 1961, in Brooklyn, NY.

VOCATION: Actor.

CAREER: PRINCIPAL TELEVISION APPEARANCES—Episodic: *Operation: Runaway*, NBC, 1978; *Hotel*, ABC, 1983; *20/20*, ABC, 1983; *The Fall Guy*, ABC, 1985. Series: Anthony DeLuca, *Blansky's Beauties*, ABC, 1977; Frankie Vitola, *Who's Watching the Kids?,* NBC, 1978; Chachi Arcola, *Happy Days,* ABC, 1977-84; host, *We're Movin',* syndicated, 1981; Chachi Arcola, *Joanie Loves Chachi,* ABC, 1982-83; title role, *Charles in Charge,* CBS, 1984, then syndicated, 1986—; also hosted *Hollywood Teen* and *Shorts.* Pilots: Frankie Bates, *Legs,* ABC, 1978. Movies: Roger Ellis, *Senior Trip,* CBS, 1981; Pat the Pig, *Alice in Wonderland,* CBS, 1985; Brad, *The Truth about Alex,* HBO, 1987. Specials: *Magic with the Stars,* NBC, 1982; *Lily for President,* CBS, 1982; *CBS All-American Thanksgiving Day Parade,* CBS, 1984; *Dom De Luise and Friends Part 2,* ABC, 1984; *Night of 100 Stars II,* ABC, 1985; *Real Trivial Pursuit,* ABC, 1985; also appeared in *Battle of the Video Games,* 1983; "Run, Don't Walk," "Luke Was There," and "A House in the Woods," all *ABC Afterschool Specials,* ABC; "All the Kids Do It," "The Boy Who Drank Too Much," "Stoned," all *Schoolbreak Specials,* CBS; *Battle of the Network Stars,* ABC; *Celebrity Challenge of the Sexes,* CBS; *Circus of the Stars,* CBS. Guest: *The Mike Douglas Show; Dinah; Hollywood Squares; Us Against the World; Kids Are People Too; Joe Namath Special; Bay City Rollers Variety Hour.*

PRINCIPAL FILM APPEARANCES—Title role, *Bugsy Malone,* Paramount, 1976; Richie, *Skatetown, USA,* Columbia, 1979; Brad, *Foxes,* United Artists, 1980; Barney, *Zapped!,* AVCO-Embassy, 1982; Mario Cotone, *I Love N.Y.* Manhattan Films, 1987.

RELATED CAREER—Acted in and provided voice-over for television commercials.

ADDRESSES: AGENT—c/o Ruth Webb Enterprises, 7500 De Vista Drive, Los Angeles, CA 90046.*

*   *   *

BAIRD, Bil   1904-1987

PERSONAL: Full name, William Britton Baird; born August 15, 1904, in Grand Island, NE; died of pneumonia while suffering from bone cancer, March 18, 1987, in New York City; son of William Hull (a chemical engineer and playwright) and Louise (Hetzel) Baird; married Evelyn Schwartz, 1932 (divorced, 1934); married Cora Burlar, January 13, 1937 (died, December, 1967); married Patricia Courtleigh, June, 1969 (divorced, 1972); married Susanna Lloyd, December, 1974 (divorced, 1984); children: (second marriage) Peter Britton, Laura Jenne; (fourth marriage) Madeleine. EDUCATION: State University of Iowa, B.A., 1926; graduated from Chicago Academy of Fine Arts, 1927. MILITARY: U.S. Army Reserve, 1925.

VOCATION: Puppeteer, producer, writer, composer, and designer.

CAREER: PRINCIPAL STAGE APPEARANCES—Clyde, *Flahooley,* Broadhurst Theatre, New York City, 1951; also appeared in productions at the State University of Iowa, 1924-26. PRINCIPAL STAGE WORK—All as puppeteer: (Also director) *The A&P Show,* Chicago World's Fair, Chicago, IL, 1933; (also producer) *Bil Baird's Marionettes,* Chicago World's Fair, 1934; *Horse Eats Hat,* Maxine Elliott's Theatre, New York City, 1936; *Dr. Faustus,* Maxine Elliott's Theatre, 1937; *The Ziegfeld Follies,* Winter Garden Theatre, New York City, 1943; *Nellie Bly,* Adelphi Theatre, New York City, 1946; *Flahooley,* Broadhurst Theatre, New York City, 1951; (also producer) *Ali Baba and the Forty Thieves,* Phoenix Theatre, New York City, 1955; (also producer) *Davy Jones' Locker,* Morosco Theatre, New York City, 1959; (also

producer) *Man in the Moon,* Biltmore Theatre, New York City, 1961; *Chrysler Show Go Round,* New York World's Fair, Queens, NY, 1964; *Baker Street,* Broadway Theatre, New York City, 1965; (with the New York Philharmonic) *L'Histoire du Soldat,* Philharmonic Hall, New York City, 1969; *Once Upon a Dragon,* Busch Gardens, Williamsburg, VA, 1977; also *Pageant of Puppet Variety,* 1957; *Carnival of Animals, Suprise Box,* both with Tim Scherman's Little Orchestra.

Producer and puppeteer, all at the Bil Baird Theatre, New York City: *Davy Jones' Locker,* 1966; *People Is the Thing That the World Is Fullest Of, Winnie the Pooh,* both 1967; *The Wizard of Oz,* 1968; *The Whistling Wizard and the Sultan of Tuffet,* 1969; (also designer) *Holiday on Strings,* 1970; *Peter and the Wolf,* 1971; *The Magic Onion,* 1972; *Band Wagon, Pinocchio,* both 1973; (with Susanna Baird) *Alice in Wonderland,* 1975.

MAJOR TOURS—Puppeteer, *Ali Baba and the Forty Thieves,* Tony Sarg Marionettes, U.S. cities, 1927-28; choreographer, *Rip Van Winkle, Alice in Wonderland,* Tony Sarg Marionettes, U.S. cities, 1931-32; producer, puppeteer, *Davy Jones' Locker,* Bil and Cora Baird Marionettes, India, Nepal, and Afghanistan, 1962, then Soviet cities, 1963; also toured Inida and Turkey, 1970.

MAJOR CABARET WORK—With the Baird Marionettes: Le Reuban Bleu, New York City; Persian Room, New York City; French Casino Lounge.

PRINCIPAL TELEVISION WORK—All with the Baird Marionettes. Series: Producer, puppeteer, *Life with Snarky Parker,* CBS, 1949-50; producer, puppeteer, *The Whistling Wizard,* CBS, 1952-53; puppeteer, *The Morning Show,* CBS, 1954-55; puppeteer, *Babes in Toyland,* NBC, 1954-55. Specials: *Heidi,* NBC, 1955; *Art Carney Meets Peter and the Wolf,* ABC, 1958; *The Sorcerer's Apprentice,* ABC, 1959; *Winnie the Pooh,* 1960; *O'Halloran's Luck, Baird's Eye View,* both 1961; *Puppet Revue,* HBO (cable), 1979. Guest: *Galen Drake Show,* ABC, 1957; *Discovery '65,* ABC, 1965; *The Ed Sullivan Show,* CBS; *The Jack Paar Show,* NBC; *The Mike Douglas Show,* syndicated; *Wonderama,* WNEW, New York City; *Book Talk,* WNET, New York City; *New York Illustrated,* WNBC, New York City.

PRINCIPAL FILM WORK—Puppeteer, *The Sound of Music,* Twentieth Century-Fox, 1965; also puppeteer for U.S. government films.

RELATED CAREER—Founder, owner, manager, Bil Baird Theatre, New York City; also produced or performed as a puppeteer in over 400 television commericials.

NON-RELATED CAREER—Sign painter, steeplejack, jazz musician.

WRITINGS: See production details above. PUPPET SHOWS—Co-writer, *The A&P Show;* (story) *Davy Jones' Locker; The Magic Onion.* MUSIC—*The Whistling Wizard and the Sultan of Tuffet;* also songs for *Ali Baba and the Forty Thieves* (1955 production).

NON-FICTION—*The Art of the Puppet,* Macmillan, 1966; *Schnitzel, the Yodeling Goat,* Nelson, 1965; *Puppets and Population,* World Education, 1971.

AWARDS: Emmy Award, 1958, for *Art Carney Meets Peter and the Wolf;* Outer Circle Award, 1967, for the Bil Baird Theatre; Jennie Heiden Award, American Theatre Association, 1974, for excellence in children's theatre.

MEMBER; International Puppet Federation (director), National Academy of Television Arts and Sciences (governor, 1957-61); Sigma Chi, Omicron Delta Kappa; Lotos, Salmagundi.

OBITUARIES AND OTHER SOURCES: New York Times, March 20, 1987.*

*   *   *

BALDWIN, Alec   1958-

PERSONAL: Full name, Alexander Rae Baldwin III; born April 3, 1958 in Amityville, NY; son of Alexander Rae (a high school teacher) and Carol Newcomb (Martineau) Baldwin. EDUCATION: Attended George Washington University, 1976-79; New York University, 1979-80; trained for the stage at the Lee Strasberg Theatre Institute with Marcia Haufrecht and Geoffrey Horne; also studied with Mira Rostova. POLITICS: Democrat. RELIGION: Catholic.

VOCATION: Actor.

CAREER: STAGE DEBUT—Lysander, *A Midsummer Night's Dream,* Lee Strasberg Theatre Institute, New York City, 1980. BROADWAY DEBUT—Dennis, *Loot,* Music Box Theatre, 1986, for one hundred performances. PRINCIPAL STAGE APPEARANCES—Soldier, *Summertree,* Vandam Theatre, New York City, 1981; *The Wager,* New York City.

ALEC BALDWIN

FILM DEBUT—Davis McDonald, *She's Having a Baby,* Paramount, 1986. PRINCIPAL FILM APPEARANCES—*Forever Lulu,* Tri-Star, 1987; *Beetle Juice,* Warner Brothers, upcoming.

TELEVISION DEBUT—Billy Aldrich, *The Doctors,* NBC, 1980-82. PRINCIPAL TELEVISION APPEARANCES—Series: *Knot's Landing,* CBS, 1984-85. Movies: *Dress Grey,* NBC, 1986.

RELATED CAREER—Performs voice-over work for radio and television commercials.

AWARDS: Acting scholarship, New York University, Tisch School of the Arts, 1980; *Theatre World* Award, 1986, for Dennis in *Loot.*

MEMBER: Actors' Equity Association, Screen Actors Guild, American Federation of Television and Radio Artists.

SIDELIGHTS: Alec Baldwin told *CTFT* that his brother Billy is a model and brother Stephen is an actor.

ADDRESSES: HOME—New York City. OFFICE—c/o M. Lester, Jejenja Productions, Inc., Suite A, 328 S. Beverly Drive, Beverly Hills, CA 90212. AGENT—J. Michael Bloom Ltd., 9200 Sunset Blvd., Suite 202, Los Angeles, CA 90069.

*   *   *

BALL, William   1931-

PERSONAL: Born April 29, 1931, in Chicago, IL; son of Russell and Catherine (Gormaly) Ball. EDUCATION: Attended Fordham University, 1948-50; Carnegie Institute of Technology, B.A., acting and design, 1953, M.A., directing, 1955.

VOCATION: Director, producer, and actor.

CAREER: OFF-BROADWAY DEBUT—Acaste, *The Misanthrope,* Theatre East, 1956. PRINCIPAL STAGE APPEARANCES—Mark Anthony, *Julius Caesar,* Feste, *Twelfth Night,* Lorenzo, *The Merchant of Venice,* Ariel, *The Tempest,* Claudio, *Much Ado about Nothing,* all Oregon Shakespeare Festival, Ashland, OR, 1950-53; Richard, *Ah, Wilderness!,* Pittsburgh Playhouse, Pittsburgh, PA, 1952; Puck, *A Midsummer Night's Dream,* Devil, *L'Histoire du Soldat,* both Pittsburgh Symphony Orchestra, Pittsburgh, PA, 1954; Romeo, *Romeo and Juliet,* Trinculo, *The Tempest,* Old Gobbo, *The Merchant of Venice,* Puck, *A Midsummer Night's Dream,* Vincentio, *The Taming of the Shrew,* Montano, *Othello,* all Antioch Shakespeare Festival, Yellow Springs, OH, 1954; title role, *Hamlet,* San Diego Shakespeare Festival, San Diego, CA, 1955; Lion, *Androcles and the Lion,* Gonzalo, *The Tempest,* Witch, *Faust,* both Group 20 Players, Wellesley, MA, 1955-56; Rosencrantz, *Hamlet,* Theatre de Lys, New York City, 1957; Nicholas Devize, *The Lady's Not for Burning,* Carnegie Hall Playhouse, New York City, 1957; Mr. Horner, *The Country Wife,* Renata Theatre, New York City, 1957; Dubedat, *The Doctor's Dilemma,* Arena Stage, Washington, DC, 1957; Prince Hal, *Henry IV, Part II,* San Diego Shakespeare Festival, 1962.

FIRST NEW YORK STAGE WORK—Stage manager, *Back to Methuselah,* Ambassador Theatre, 1958. FIRST LONDON STAGE WORK—Director, *Six Characters in Search of an Author,* May Fair Theatre,

1963. PRINCIPAL STAGE WORK—Director: *As You Like It,* Antioch Shakespeare Festival, Yellow Springs, OH, 1954; *Twelfth Night, Antioch Shakespeare Festival, 1957; Ivanov,* Renata Theatre, New York City, 1958; *Once More with Feeling,* Alley Theatre, Houston, TX, 1958; *Henry IV, Part I, Julius Caesar,* both San Diego Shakespeare Festival, San Diego, CA, 1958; *The Devil's Disciple,* Actors Workshop Theatre, San Francisco, CA, 1958; *Six Characters in Search of an Author, Cosi Fan Tutti,* both New York City Opera, City Center Theatre, New York City, 1959; *A Month in the Country,* Arena Stage, Washington, DC, 1959; *The Inspector General,* New York City Opera, City Center Theatre, 1960; *The Tempest,* American Shakespeare Festival, Stratford, CT, 1960; *Under Milk Wood,* Circle in the Square, New York City, 1961; *Porgy and Bess,* New York City Opera, City Center Theatre, 1962; *Henry IV, Part II,* San Diego Shakespeare Festival, 1962; *Six Characters in Search of an Author,* Martinique Theatre, New York City, 1963; *Don Giovanni,* New York City Opera, City Center Theatre, 1963; *The Yeoman of the Guard,* Festival Theatre, Stratford, ON, Canada, 1964; *Natalia Petrovna,* New York City Opera, City Center Theatre, 1964; *Tartuffe,* Washington Square Theatre, New York City, 1965.

Producer and director for the American Conservatory Theatre (ACT): *Tartuffe, Tiny Alice, The Rose Tatoo, King Lear, Six Characters in Search of an Author, Antigone, Noah, The Servant of Two Masters, The Devil's Desciple, Death of a Salesman, Uncle Vanya,* all Pittsburgh Playhouse, Pittsburgh, PA, 1965-66; ACT resettled in San Francisco, CA, in 1967 where Ball has continued to produce and direct plays including: *Hamlet, Oedipus Rex, Twelfth Night, The Taming of the Shrew, Richard III, The Winter's Tale, Cyrano de Bergerac, Three Sisters, Rosencrantz and Guildenstern Are Dead, Equus,* and *Jumpers* among numerous others; also with ACT, directed *The Three Sisters, A Flea in Her Ear, Tiny Alice,* all American National Theatre Academy Playhouse, New York City, 1969, and *Hamlet,* Carnegie Hall, New York City, 1971.

MAJOR TOURS—Conrad, *Visit to a Small Planet,* U.S. cities, 1957; also assistant designer and actor in minor roles, Margaret Webster's Shakespeare Company, U.S. cities, 1948-50; general director of ACT tours of U.S. cities, 1966, Soviet cities, 1976, Soviet cities and Tokyo, Japan, 1978; and Hawaii, 1972-79.

PRINCIPAL TELEVISION WORK—Director: *Cyrano de Bergerac,* 1974; *The Taming of the Shrew,* 1976.

RELATED CAREER—Founder, general director, American Conservatory Theatre, 1966—; founder, American Conservatory Theatre School, 1971—.

AWARDS: Fulbright Scholarship, 1953; NBC/RCA Directors Fellowship, Carnegie Institute of Technology, 1955; Ford Foundation Grant, 1958; *Village Voice* Obie Award, 1959, Vernon Rice Award, 1959, both for *Ivanov;* Lola D'Annunzio Award, 1961, for *Under Milk Wood,* and 1963, for *Six Characters in Search of an Author;* Outer Circle Award, 1965, for *Tartuffe;* Antoinette Perry Award (presented to the American Conservatory Theatre), 1979, for "distinguished achievement in theatre." Honorary degrees: D.F.A., Carnegie-Mellon University, 1979.

MEMBER: Society of Stage Directors and Choreographers, Actors' Equity Association.

ADDRESSES: OFFICE—American Conservatory Theatre, 450 Geary Street, San Francisco, CA 94102.*

IAN BANNEN

BANNEN, Ian   1928-

PERSONAL: Born June 29, 1928, in Airdrie, Scotland; son of John James and Clare (Galloway) Bannen; married Marilyn Salisbury, 1978. EDUCATION: Attended Ratcliffe College.

VOCATION: Actor.

CAREER: FILM DEBUT—Bannister, *Battle Hell,* 1956. PRINCIPAL FILM APPEARANCES—Pvt. Horrock, *Private's Progress,* Charter, 1956; Vince, *Rotten to the Core,* Cinema V, 1956; Filippo Gozzi, *Miracle in Soho,* Rank, 1957; workman, *The Third Key,* Rank, 1957; Alan Crabtree, *Behind the Mask,* GW Films, 1958; Gabelle, *A Tale of Two Cities,* Rank, 1958; Colin Crane, *The French Mistress,* British Lion, 1960; Alan Andrews, *The Risk,* Kingsley International, 1961; Peter Howard, *She Didn't Say No!,* Warner Brothers, 1962; Kitson, *The World in My Pocket,* Corona, 1962; Paul, *Psyche 59,* Columbia, 1964; Fletcher, *Station Six—Sahara,* Allied Artists, 1964; Crow, *The Flight of the Phoenix,* Twentieth Century-Fox, 1965; Sgt. Charlie Harris, *The Hill,* Metro-Goldwyn-Mayer (MGM), 1965; Robert, *Mister Moses,* United Artists, 1965; James B. Elcott, *Penelope,* MGM, 1966; Alan, *The Sailor from Gibraltar,* Lopert, 1967; Ramble, *Lock Up Your Daughters,* Columbia, 1969; Pvt. Thornton, *Too Late the Hero* (also known as *Suicide Run*), Cinerama, 1970; Crawford, *The Deserter,* Paramount, 1971; Brian, *Fright* (also known as *Night Legs*), Allied Artists, 1971; Baxter, *The Offence* (also known as *Something Like the Truth*), United Artists, 1973; Slade, *The Mackintosh Man,* Warner Brothers, 1973; Christopher Lowe, *From*

Beyond the Grave (also known as *The Creatures* and *The Creatures from Beyond the Grave*), Warner Brothers, 1974; Antonio Braggi, *The Voyage*, Champion, 1974; Richard, *The Driver's Seat*, AVCO-Embassy, 1975; Norfolk, *Bite the Bullet*, Columbia, 1975; Baker, *Sweeney*, EMI, 1977; John Keller, *The Watcher in the Woods*, Buena Vista, 1980; Col. Buckner, *Counterfeit Commandos*, Aquarius, 1981; Godliman, *The Eye of the Needle*, United Artists, 1981; Josef Keller, *Night Crossing*, Buena Vista, 1982; senior police officer, *Gandhi*, Columbia, 1982; Iamskoy, *Gorky Park*, Orion, 1983. Also appeared in *Doomwatch*, Tigon, 1972; *Hope and Glory*, Columbia, 1987; and *Carlton-Browne of the F.O.*, 1958; *Darkness into Darkness*, 1977; *Prodigal*, 1984; *Lamb, Defense of the Realm, Attack on the Pope*, all 1985.

STAGE DEBUT—Emperor's son, *Armlet of Jade*, Gate Theatre, Dublin, Ireland, 1947. LONDON DEBUT— Captain Rickman, *Prisoners of War*, Irving Theatre, 1955. PRINCIPAL STAGE APPEARANCES—Customer, mayor, *Robinson*, Arts Theatre, Cambridge, U.K., 1954; Marco, *A View from the Bridge*, Comedy Theatre, London, 1956; title role, *The Waiting of Lester Abbs*, Royal Court Theatre, London, 1957; Hickey, *The Iceman Cometh*, Arts Theatre, then Winter Garden Theatre, both London, 1958; Jamie, *Long Day's Journey into Night*, Lyceum Theatre, Edinburgh, Scotland, U.K., later Globe Theatre, London, both 1958; Musgrave, *Sergeant Musgrave's Dance*, Royal Court Theatre, 1959; Julian Berniers, *Toys in the Attic*, Piccadilly Theatre, London, 1960; title role, *Hamlet*, Mercutio, *Romeo and Juliet*, Iago, *Othello*, all Memorial Theatre, Stratford-on-Avon, U.K., 1961; Orlando, *As You Like It*, Memorial Theatre, 1961, then Aldwych Theatre, London, 1962; Morris Pieterson, *The Blood Knot*, New Arts Theatre, London, 1963; Brutus, *Julius Caesar*, Royal Court Theatre, 1964; Brig Brown, *The Brass Hat*, Arnaud Theatre, Guildford, U.K., 1972; Judge Brack, *Hedda Gabler*, Duke of York's Theatre, London, then Edinburgh Festival, Edinburgh, Scotland, U.K., 1977; Jamie Tyrone, *A Moon for the Misbegotten*, American Repertory Theatre, Cambridge, MA, 1983, then Cort Theatre, New York City, 1984. Also appeared in *Translations*, National Theatre, London, 1981; as Cornelius Melody, *A Touch of the Poet*, Dublin, Ireland, then Venice, Italy, both 1962; Jamie Tyrone, *A Moon for the Misbegotten*, London, 1983. Performed with the Memorial Theatre Company, Stratford-on-Avon, U.K., 1951-55.

MAJOR TOURS—Dick Dudgeon, *The Devil's Disciple*, U.K. cities, 1965; with the Memorial Theatre Company, Australian and New Zealand cities, 1955.

PRINCIPAL TELEVISION APPEARANCES—Mini-Series: *Tinker, Tailor, Soldier, Spy*. Movies: Rev. St. John Rivers, *Jane Eyre*, NBC, 1970; Amos, *Jesus of Nazareth*, NBC. Specials: Macduff, *Macbeth*, NBC, 1960; Dr. Jack Richardson, *Johnny Belinda*, ABC, 1967; Adolph Hitler, "The Gathering Storm," *Hallmark Hall of Fame*, NBC, 1974; Frank Dean, *Terror from Within*, ABC, 1975; also appeared in *Death in Deep Water*, ABC, 1975.

NON-RELATED CAREER—Professional photographer.

AWARDS: Best Actor, Drama Critics Award, 1981, for *Translations*.

SIDELIGHTS: RECREATIONS—Swimming, riding.

ADDRESSES: AGENT—c/o Jean Diamond, London Management, 235-241 Regent Street, London W1, England.

BANNERMAN, Celia 1946-

PERSONAL: Born June 3, 1946, in Abingdon, England; daughter of Hugh and Hilda (Diamond) Bannerman; married Edward Klein. EDUCATION: Trained for the stage at the London Drama Center.

VOCATION: Actress and director.

CAREER: STAGE DEBUT—Juliet, *Romanoff and Juliet*, Leatherhead, U.K., 1965. LONDON DEBUT—Dolly, *You Never Can Tell*, Haymarket Theatre, 1966. PRINCIPAL STAGE APPEARANCES—All in London unless indicated: Lucy, *The Rivals*, Haymarket Theatre, 1966; Portia, *The Merchant of Venice*, Palace Theatre, Watford, U.K., 1967; Miranda, *The Tempest*, Citizens' Theatre, Glasgow, Scotland, U.K., 1968; Viola, *Twelfth Night*, Old Vic Theatre, Bristol, U.K., 1968; Silvia, *The Two Gentlemen of Verona*, Open Air Theatre, 1968; Cecily, *The Importance of Being Earnest*, Haymarket Theatre, 1968; Cynthia, *The Double Dealer*, Royal Court Theatre, 1969; Mrs. Adams, *Pirates*, Theatre Upstairs, 1970; *Come As You Are*, New Theatre, then Strand Theatre, 1970; Amy Spettigue, *Charley's Aunt*, 69 Theatre Company, 1971; Miranda, *The Tempest*, Open Air Theatre, 1972; Lady Katherine Gordon, *Perkin Warbeck*, Galy Gay's wife, *Man Is Man*, Lady Anne, *Richard III*, all Other Place Theatre, Stratford-on-Avon, U.K., 1975; Clea, *Black Comedy*, Shaw Theatre, 1976; Elizabeth, *The Circle*, Sorel, *Hay Fever*, both English Theatre, Vienna, Austria, 1977; Amanda, *Private Lives*, Birmingham Repertory Theatre, Birmingham, U.K., 1980.

PRINCIPAL STAGE WORK—Assistant director, *Lark Rise, The Passion, Strife, The Fruits of Enlightenment*, all National Theatre, London, 1978-79; director, *Lies in Plastic Smiles*, 1979.

MAJOR TOURS—Gloria, *You Never Can Tell*, U.K. cities, 1973.

PRINCIPAL TELEVISION APPEARANCES—*Pride and Prejudice; Vile Bodies*.

ADDRESSES: AGENT—International Creative Management, 22 Grafton Street, London W1, England.*

*   *   *

BARNES, Peter 1931-

PERSONAL: Born January 10, 1931, in London, England; son of Frederick and Martha (Miller) Barnes; married Charlotte Beck, 1960.

VOCATION: Writer and director.

CAREER: PRINCIPAL STAGE WORK—Co-director, *Lulu*, Nottingham Playhouse Theatre, Nottingham, U.K., 1970; director, *Frontiers of Farce*, Old Vic Theatre, London, 1976; co-director, *The Devil Is an Ass*, Edinburgh Festival, Edinburgh, Scotland, U.K., 1976, then National Theatre, London, 1977; director, *For All Those Who Get Despondent*, Theatre Upstairs, London, 1977; director, *Bartholomew Fair*, Round House Theatre, London, 1978; co-director, *Antonio*, Nottingham Playhouse Theatre, 1979.

RELATED CAREER—Critic, *Films and Filming*, London, 1954; story editor, Warwick Film Productions, Ltd., London, 1956.

WRITINGS: PLAYS—*The Time of the Barracudas*, Curran Theatre,

San Francisco, CA, 1963; *Sclerosis,* Traverse Theatre, Edinburgh, Scotland, U.K., then Aldwych Theatre, London, 1965; *The Ruling Class,* Nottingham Playhouse Theatre, Nottingham, U.K., 1968, then Piccadilly Theatre, London, 1969, later Kreeger Theatre, Washington, DC, 1971, published by Heinemann, 1969, then Grove Press, Inc., 1972; *Leonardo's Last Supper, Noonday Demons,* both Open Space Theatre, London, 1969, published in one volume by Heinemann, 1970; (adaptor) *The Alchemist,* Old Vic Theatre, London, 1970, revised version, Other Place Theatre, Stratford-on-Avon, U.K., then Aldwych Theatre, both 1977; (adaptor) *Lulu,* Nottingham Playhouse Theatre, then Royal Court Theatre, London, both 1970, published by Heinemann, 1971; (adaptor) *The Devil Is an Ass,* Nottingham Playhouse Theatre, 1973, revised version, Edinburgh Festival, Edinburgh, Scotland, U.K., 1976, then National Theatre, London, 1977; *The Bewitched,* Aldwych Theatre, 1974, published by Heinemann, 1974; *For All Those Who Get Despondent,* Theatre Upstairs, London, 1976; *The Frontiers of Farce,* Old Vic Theatre, 1976, published by Heinemann, 1977; *Laughter!,* Royal Court Theatre, 1978, published by Heinemann, 1978; (adaptor) *Bartholomew Fair,* Round House Theatre, London, 1978; (adaptor) *Antonio,* Nottingham Playhouse Theatre, 1979; (adaptor) *The Devil Himself,* Lyric Hammersmith Theatre, London, 1980; *Sommersaults,* Haymarket Theatre, Leicester, U.K., 1981. COLLECTIONS—*Collected Plays,* 1981.

SCREENPLAYS—*Violent Moment,* Anglo Amalgamated, 1958; *The White Trap, Breakout,* both Anglo Amalgamated, 1959; *The Professionals,* Anglo Amalgamated, 1961; *Off Beat,* British Lion, 1961; (with Frank Launder) *Ring of Spies* (also known as *Ring of Treason*), British Lion, 1965; (with Norman Panama and Larry Gelbart) *Not with My Wife, You Don't,* Warner Brothers, 1966; *The Ruling Class,* United Artists, 1972.

TELEPLAYS—*The Man with a Feather in His Hat,* ABC (Britain), 1960.

RADIO PLAYS—(Adaptor) *Eastward Ho!,* BBC, 1973; *My Ben Jonson,* BBC, 1973; (adaptor) *Lulu,* BBC, 1975; (adaptor) *Antonio,* BBC, 1977; (adaptor) *A Chaste Maid in Cheapside,* BBC, 1979; (adaptor) *Eulogy on Baldness,* BBC, 1980; (adaptor) *The Soldier's Fortune,* BBC, 1981; (adaptor) *The Atheist,* BBC, 1981; *Barnes' People,* BBC, 1981; (adaptor) *The Dutch Courtesan,* BBC, 1982.

AWARDS: John Whiting Playwrights Award, 1968, for *The Ruling Class; Evening Standard* Annual Drama Award, 1969, for "most promising playwright."

ADDRESSES: HOME—7 Archery Close, Connaught Street, London W2, England. AGENT—Margaret Ramsay, Ltd., 14-A Goodwin's Court, London WC2, England.*

*   *   *

BARON, Alec

PERSONAL: Born November 29; son of Hyman and Betsy Baron; married Judith Edelston, 1951; children: Michael, Helen, Olivia, Rebecca. MILITARY: Second Lothian and Border Horse, East Riding Yeomanry, 1940-45.

VOCATION: Director, playwright, producer, and theatre administrator.

CAREER: STAGE DEBUT—Director, *They Came to Leeds,* Civic

ALEC BARON

Theatre, Leeds, U.K., 1951. PRINCIPAL STAGE WORK—Director: *Asylum, Kafka: The Long Road Back,* both Edinburgh Festival, Edinburgh, Scotland, U.K., 1977; *Groucho at Large,* Edinburgh Festival, 1979; *Momma Golda,* Leeds Playhouse, Leeds, U.K., 1980; *Groucho at Large* (revised version), Citadel Theatre, Edmonton, SK, Canada, then New End Theatre, London, 1981; *Ethel and Julie,* Edinburgh Festival, 1982; *Groucho in Toto,* Edinburgh Festival, then Fortune Theatre, London, 1982. Also directed *Company Come,* 1980; *The Big Cats,* 1984.

MAJOR TOURS—Director: *Groucho at Large,* 1979; *Momma Golda,* 1980.

PRINCIPAL TELEVISION WORK—All as director. Series: *The Two Ronnies,* 1976-82; *Coronation Street,* 1979-81. Specials: *Company Come,* 1978; *Groucho in Toto,* 1982.

PRINCIPAL RADIO WORK—Director: *The Element of Doubt,* 1975; *The Trouble with Mother,* 1976; *Luxury Weekend, Company Come, The Colmar Killer,* all 1977; *The Merrion Case, A Case of Rare Vintage,* both 1982; *False Picture, Company Come,* both 1983; *The Big Cats,* 1984; *Rudi's First Case, Parkinson's War,* both 1985.

RELATED CAREER—Producer, Proscenium Players, 1948-69; administrator, Leeds Playhouse, Leeds, U.K., 1969-72; theatre correspondent for *Arts Yorkshire* and *Artscene,* 1973-87; lecturer on theatre studies.

WRITINGS: PLAYS, PRODUCED AND PUBLISHED—*Company Come,* produced in 1980, published by Samuel French, Inc.; *The Big Cats,* produced in 1984, published by Samuel French, Inc.;

Chimera, published by Samuel French, Inc.; *Absheid*, published in Holland.

ADDRESSES: HOME—19 Park View Crescent, Leeds LS8 2ES, England.

*   *   *

BARRY, B.H.   1940-

PERSONAL: Born Barry Halliday, February 19, 1940; son of Ronald (an architect) and Dorothy (Mansell) Halliday.

VOCATION: Fight choreographer, director, and actor.

CAREER: PRINCIPAL STAGE APPEARANCES—Bell boy, *Oh Dad, Poor Dad, Mama's Hung You in the Closet and I'm Feeling So Sad*, Piccadilly Theatre, London, 1962, for forty-eight performances.

FIRST NEW YORK WORK—Fight choreographer, *Hot Grog*, Marymount Manhattan Theatre, 1978. PRINCIPAL STAGE WORK—All as fight choreographer and stunt director unless indicated: *Hamlet*, Arena Stage, Washington, DC, 1978; *Cyrano de Bergerac*, Long Wharf Theatre, New Haven, CT, 1979, then Center Stage, Baltimore, MD, 1979, later Williamstown Theatre Festival, Williamstown, MA, then Santa Fe Stage Festival, Santa Fe, NM; *Holeville*, Brooklyn Academy of Music, Brooklyn, NY, 1979; *Othello*, New York Shakespeare Festival (NYSF), Delacorte Thea-

B.H. BARRY

tre, New York City, 1979; *Hamlet, Mary Stuart*, both Circle Repertory Company, New York City, 1979.

Macbeth, Vivian Beaumont Theatre, New York City, 1980; *Frankenstein*, Palace Theatre, New York City, then Toronto Arts Theatre, Toronto, ON, Canada, both 1981; *Hamlet*, Players State Theatre, Coconut Grove, FL, 1981; *Twelfth Night, As You Like It*, both Shakespeare and Company, Lenox, MA, 1981; *Henry V, Othello*, both American Shakespeare Theatre, Stratford, CT, 1981; *Romeo and Juliet, As You Like It*, both Dallas Shakespeare Festival, Dallas, TX, 1981; *After the Prize*, Marymount Manhattan Theatre, New York City, 1981; director, *Cyrano de Bergerac*, Alley Theatre, Houston, TX, 1981; *Henry IV, Part I*, NYSF, Delacorte Theatre, then American Shakespeare Theatre, 1982; *Hamlet*, NYSF, Public Theatre, New York City, 1982; *Mary Stuart*, Public Theatre, 1982; *Some Men Need Help*, 47th Street Theatre, New York City, 1982; *Geniuses*, Playwrights Horizons, Douglas Fairbanks Theatre, New York City, 1982; *Othello*, Winter Garden Theatre, New York City, 1982; *The Woods*, Second Stage, New York City, 1982; *Twelfth Night, Macbeth, The Comedy of Errors*, all Shakespeare and Company, 1982; *Extremities*, West Side Arts Theatre/Cheryl Crawford Theatre, New York City, 1982; *A View from the Bridge*, Ambassador Theatre, New York City, 1983; *Heartbreak House*, Circle in the Square, New York City, 1983; *Noises Off*, Brooks Atkinson Theatre, New York City, 1983; *Friends*, Manhattan Theatre Club, New York City, 1983; *Full Hook Up*, Circle Repertory Theatre, New York City, 1983; *Richard III*, NYSF, Delacorte Theatre, 1983; *Macbeth*, Ark Theatre Company, New York City, 1983; *Night Is Mother to the Day*, Yale Repertory Theatre, New Haven, CT, 1984; *A Midsummer Night's Dream, Romeo and Juliet*, both Shakespeare and Company, 1984; *Cinders, Fen, Found a Peanut* all Public Theatre, 1984; *Henry V, The Ballad of Soapy Smith*, both NYSF, Public Theatre, 1984; *Romance Language*, Playwrights Horizons, New York City, 1984; *Requiem for a Heavyweight*, Martin Beck Theatre, New York City, 1985; *The Boys of Winter*, Biltmore Theatre, New York City, 1985; *Big River*, Eugene O'Neill Theatre, New York City, 1985; *I'm Not Rappaport*, American Place Theatre, then Booth Theatre, both New York City, 1985; *Aunt Dan and Lemon, Rum and Coke*, both Public Theatre, 1986; *Little Footsteps*, Playwrights Horizons, 1986; *Sleight of Hand*, Cort Theatre, New York City, 1987.

All as fight choreographer and stunt director unless indicated: *King Lear*, Acting Company, New York City; *Troilus and Cressida*, Yale Repertory Theatre; *Mahagonny* (opera), Metropolitan Opera House, New York City; *Passione*, Playwrights Horizons; *Mary Stuart, Hamlet*, both Circle Repertory Company; *True West*, Public Theatre, *Mass Appeal*, Booth Theatre; *Romeo and Juliet*, Alley Theatre, then Long Wharf Theatre, later La Jolla Playhouse, La Jolla, CA; *Henry IV, Part I*, Public Theatre; *Three Musketeers*, Hartman Theatre, Stamford, CT; *As You Like It*, Arena Stage, *Macbeth*, Metropolitan Opera House; *Twelfth Night, Two Gentlemen of Verona*, both NYSF, Delacorte Theatre; *Porgy and Bess* (opera), Metropolitan Opera House; *Lucky Spot*, Manhattan Theatre Club; *Borges and Himself*, INTAR Theatre, New York City; *The Widow Clare*, Circle in the Square Downtown, New York City; *Roanoak*, American Playhouse, New York City; also, *Island of the Mighty, Titus Andronicus, Anthony and Cleopatra, Romeo and Juliet, Othello, As You Like It, Women Pirates, Too True to Be Good, Bewitched, The Taming of the Shrew, Julius Caesar*, all Royal Shakespeare Company, London; director, *Toad of Toad Hall*, Pittsburgh, PA; *Camelot*, New York City.

TELEVISION DEBUT—Billy Bunter, *Dixon of Dock Green*. PRINCIPAL TELEVISION APPEARANCES—Guest: *Mike Douglas Show*, syndicated; *Late Night with David Letterman*, NBC; *The Morning Show*, CBS.

PRINCIPAL TELEVISION WORK—All as fight choreographer. Specials: *Twelfth Night, Hamlet, Macbeth, Anthony and Cleopatra, Tales of Hoffman, The Legend of King Arthur*, all BBC.

PRINCIPAL FILM APPEARANCES—Prefect, *French Mistress*, 1960.

PRINCIPAL FILM WORK—Fight choreographer: *Crossed Swords*, Warner Brothers, 1978; *The Pirates of Penzance*, Universal, 1983; also *Macbeth*.

RELATED CAREER—Faculty member at Juilliard, New York University, and Circle in the Square Theatre School. Teacher, Shakespeare and Company (Lenox, MA), Southern Methodist University, Temple University, Yale School of Drama, Carnegie-Mellon University, Royal Academy of Dramatic Arts, Central School of Speech and Drama, London School of Music, Guildhall School of Music and Dramatic Arts, and the Corona Academy.

AWARDS: Drama Desk Award, 1982, for "consistent excellence."

MEMBER: Society of British Fight Directors (founding member), Stunt Man's Association, Actors' Equity Association.

ADDRESSES: AGENT—Jerold Couture, 551 Fifth Avenue, New York, NY 10176.

* * *

BARRY, Gene 1922-

PERSONAL: Born Eugene Klass, June 4, 1922, in New York, NY; son of Martin and Eva (Conn) Klass; married Betty Claire Kalb, October 22, 1944; children: Michael Lewis, Fredric James, Liza.

VOCATION: Actor.

CAREER: PRINCIPAL TELEVISION APPEARANCES—Episodic: "To Each His Own," *Lux Video Theatre*, CBS, 1950; *Fireside Theatre*, NBC; *Loretta Young Theatre*, NBC; *TV Reader's Digest*, ABC; *Hollywood Screen Test*, ABC; *Science Fiction Theatre*, syndicated; *Appointment with Adventure*, ABC; *The Clock*, ABC; *Ford Television Theatre*, NBC; *Honey West*, ABC; *Love Boat*, ABC; *Alfred Hitchcock Presents*. Series: Gene Talbot, *Our Miss Brooks*, CBS, 1955-56; title role, *Bat Masterson*, NBC, 1958-61; Amos Burke, *Burke's Law*, ABC, 1963-65, then *Amos Burke—Secret Agent*, ABC, 1965-66; Glenn Howard, *The Name of the Game*, NBC, 1968-71; Gene Bradley, *The Adventurer*, syndicated, 1972. Mini-Series: Carl Osborne, *Aspen* (also known as *The Innocent and the Damned*), NBC, 1977. Pilot: Sgt. Andy Pile, *War Correspondent*, CBS, 1959. Movies: Dr. Ray Flemming, *Prescription: Murder*, NBC, 1968; Michael London, *Istanbul Express*, NBC, 1968; Murray Jarvis, *Do You Take This Stranger?*, NBC, 1971; Rankin, *The Devil and Miss Sarah*, ABC, 1971; Harry Darew, *Ransom for Alice*, NBC, 1977; Gordon Harris, *A Cry for Love*, NBC, 1980; John Cockerill, *The Adventures of Nellie Bly*, NBC, 1981; Andrew Stovall, *The Girl, the Gold Watch, and Dynamite*, syndicated, 1981; also appeared in *Perry Mason: The Case of the Lost Love*, NBC, 1987. Specials: *Tiptoe through TV*, CBS, 1960; *Variety: The World of Show Biz*, CBS, 1960; *The 40th*

Annual Tony Awards, 1986; *The 38th Annual Emmy Awards*, 1986; *NBC's 60th Anniversary Celebration*, 1986.

PRINCIPAL FILM APPEARANCES—Dr. Addison, *Atomic City*, Paramount, 1952; Captain Beaton, *Girls of Pleasure Island*, Johnny Kisco, *Those Redheads from Seattle*, Dr. Clayton Forrester, *War of the Worlds*, all Paramount, 1953; Verne Williams, *Alaska Seas*, Raphael Moreno, *Red Garters*, both Paramount, 1954; Al Willis, *Naked Alibi*, Universal, 1954; Captain Laverne, *The Purple Mask*, Universal, 1955; Louis Hoyt, *Soldier of Fortune*, Twentieth Century-Fox, 1955; Ellis, *Back from Eternity*, RKO, 1956; Frank Duncan, *The Houston Story*, Columbia, 1956; Brock, *China Gate*, Twentieth Century-Fox, 1957; Wes Bonnell, *Forty Guns* (also known as *Woman with a Whip*), Twentieth Century-Fox, 1957; Jonathan Clark, *The 27th Day*, Columbia, 1957; Casey Reed, *Hong Kong Confidential*, Troy Barrett, *Thunder Road*, both United Artists, 1958; Simon Grant, *Maroc Seven*, Paramount, 1967; Donovan, *Subterfuge*, Commonwealth United Entertainment, 1969; Congressman Leo O'Brien, *Guyana: Cult of the Damned* (also known as *Guyana: Crime of the Century*), Universal, 1980. Also played a TV commentator in *The Second Coming of Suzanne*, 1974, for which Barry was executive producer.

PRINCIPAL STAGE APPEARANCES—Georges, *La Cage aux Folles*, Palace Theatre, New York City, 1983, then Pantages Theatre, Los Angeles, CA, 1985. Also appeared in *Rosalinda*, 44th Street Theatre, New York City, 1942; *Catherine Was Great*, Shubert Theatre, New York City, 1944; *Bless You All*, Mark Hellinger Theatre, New York City, 1950; *The Perfect Setup*, Cort Theatre, New York City, 1962; *Watergate: A Musical*, Alliance Theatre Company, Atlanta, GA, 1982; and in *Happy Is Larry*.

MEMBER: Actors' Equity Association, Screen Actors Guild (former first vice-president); Boy Scouts of America.

ADDRESSES: AGENT—International Creative Management, 40 W. 57th Street, New York, NY 10019.*

* * *

BARRY, Paul 1931-

PERSONAL: Born August 29, 1931, in Waterford, MI; son of Clement Stanley (an opera singer) and Doris (an actress; maiden name, Manier) Barry; married Ellen Frances Reiss (an actress), February 22, 1969; children: Kevin Michael, Timothy Brian, Shannon Elizabeth. EDUCATION: Received B.A. from Wayne State University; received M.A. from University of California, Los Angeles; studied for the theatre with Michael Chekhov and Peter Ballbusch.

VOCATION: Director, actor, and fencing choreographer.

CAREER: PRINCIPAL STAGE APPEARANCES—Mr. Keres, *Tiger, Tiger, Buring Bright*, Off-Broadway production. With the New York Shakespeare Festival, American Savoyards, and other companies played such roles as Quixote/Cervantes, *Man of La Mancha*, Littlechap, *Stop the World, I Want to Get Off*, Og, *Finian's Rainbow*, George, *Of Mice and Men*, Frank Elgin, *The Country Girl*, Shannon, *Night of the Iguana*, Berrenger, *Rhinoceros*, Bill Maitland, *Inadmissible Evidence*, Archie Rice, *The Entertainer*, and the title roles in *Hamlet, Richard III, Luther, Macbeth*, and *Cyrano de Bergerac*.

PAUL BARRY

MAJOR TOURS—*Macbeth* and *Spoon River Anthology*, Title I-III tours of New Jersey.

PRINCIPAL STAGE WORK—Director: *Richard III*, Asolo State Theatre, Sarasota, FL, 1978; *Transfiguration in Precinct 12*, Kennedy Center, Washington, DC, 1979. Also directed *Call a Spade a Shovel*, 81st Annual Triangle Show, Princeton University, Princeton, NJ; *The Rose Tattoo, The Tavern*, both New Orleans Repertory Theatre, New Orleans, LA; *Romeo and Juliet, West Side Story*, both Bucks County Playhouse, New Hope, PA; *Kismet*, Equity Library Theatre, New York; *Twelfth Night, The Rivals*, both with the Boston Herald-Traveler Repertory Company, Boston, MA.

Director, all with the New Jersey Shakespeare Festival, Madison, NJ, 1963-87: *The Taming of the Shrew, Richard III, Antony and Cleopatra, Luther, The Merry Wives of Windsor, The Devils, The Comedy of Errors, Marat/Sade, Much Ado about Nothing, Julius Caesar, Desire Under the Elms, Othello, A Midsummer Night's Dream, Hamlet, The Tempest, Rosencrantz and Guildenstern Are Dead, Troilus and Cressida, The Bourgeois Gentleman, Coriolanus, Summer and Smoke, As You Like It, Measure for Measure, Under Milk Wood, J.B., Steambath, Richard II, Henry IV--Parts I and II, Henry V, The Devil's Disciple, The Best Man, The Playboy of the Western World, Of Mice and Men, Cyrano de Bergerac, An Enemy of the People, The Glass Menagerie, Love's Labour's Lost, The Country Girl, King Lear, A Streetcar Named Desire, Travesties, Two for the Seesaw, Who's Afraid of Virginia Woolf?, Macbeth, Volpone, Romeo and Juliet, The Caretaker, A Christmas Carol, Cymbeline, Tartuffe, Da, That Championship Season, Sweet Bird of Youth, The Lady's Not for Burning, The Merchant of Venice, The*

School for Scandal, All the Way Home, The Sunshine Boys, The Crucible, Henry VIII, A Man for All Seasons.

Director, all with the Cape May Playhouse, Cape May, NJ: *Rashomon, The Hostage, South Pacific, Anna Christie, A Taste of Honey, My Fair Lady, The Rose Tattoo, The King and I, Incident at Vichy, How to Succeed in Business without Really Trying, Carnival, The Birthday Party, The Apple Tree, Beyond the Fringe.*

Director, all with the Keweenaw Playhouse, Calumet, MI: *The Rainmaker, Teahouse of the August Moon, The Diary of Anne Frank, Cat on a Hot Tin Roof, The Matchmaker, The Emperor Jones, Look Back in Anger, The Music Man, West Side Story, The Merry Widow, Paint Your Wagon.*

PRINCIPAL TELEVISION WORK—Both as director: "Cyrano de Bergerac," *Hallmark Hall of Fame*, NBC; *Hamlet*, WHDH, Boston.

RELATED CAREER—Fencing choreographer; teacher of acting, directing, movement, voice, and weaponry, New Jersey Shakespeare Festival, Madison, NJ, 1963—; director, guest artist, and/or lecturer: University of California, Riverside; Marymount College; State University of New York, New Paltz; Drew University; Rutgers University; Fairleigh-Dickinson College; University of Toledo; Pennsylvania State University.

WRITINGS: BOOKS—*The Care and Feeding of Dinosaurs: A Treatise on Acting.*

AWARDS: Holder of three New Jersey state titles, Amateur Fencers League of America, in sabre and epee.

ADDRESSES: HOME—34 Hillcrest Avenue, Morristown, NJ 07960. OFFICE—New Jersey Shakespeare Festival, Madison, NJ 07940.*

*   *   *

BARRYMORE, Drew   1975-

PERSONAL: Born February 22, 1975, in Los Angeles, CA; daughter of John, Jr. and Jaid Barrymore.

VOCATION: Actress.

CAREER: TELEVISION DEBUT—Commercial at age eleven months. PRINCIPAL TELEVISION APPEARANCES—Episodic: Passenger, *Amazing Stories*, NBC, 1985; Connie Sawyer, "Con Sawyer and Hucklemary Finn," *ABC Weekend Special*, ABC, 1985; host, "Hansel and Gretel," *Great Performances*, PBS, 1986. Movies: Leslie, *Bogie*, CBS, 1980; Heather Leany, *The Screaming Woman*, HBO, 1986; Jody Wykowski, *Conspiracy of Love*, CBS, 1987; also appeared as Lisa Piper, *Babes in Toyland*, 1986; and in *Suddenly Love*, 1978. Specials: *Night of 100 Stars II*, ABC, 1985; *Happy Birthday, Hollywood*, ABC, 1987; *Celebrating Gershwin*, PBS, upcoming; also appeared in *Screen Actors Guild 50th Anniversary Celebration Special*, 1984; *Disneyland's 30th Anniversary*, 1987.

FILM DEBUT—Margaret Jessup, *Altered States*, Warner Brothers, 1980. PRINCIPAL FILM APPEARANCES—Gertie, *E.T.: The Extra-Terrestrial*, Universal, 1982; Casey Brodsky, *Irreconcilable Differences*, Warner Brothers, 1984; Charlie McGee, *Firestarter*, Universal, 1984; also appeared in *Cat's Eye*, Metro-Goldwyn-Mayer/United Artists, 1985.

ADDRESSES: AGENT—William Morris Agency, 151 El Camino Drive, Beverly Hills, CA 90212.*

*   *   *

BARTLETT, D'Jamin   1948-

PERSONAL: Born May 21, 1948, in New York, NY; married William Bartlett. EDUCATION: Trained for the stage at the American Academy of Dramatic Arts.

VOCATION: Actress and singer.

CAREER: STAGE DEBUT—*Godspell*, Ford's Theatre, Washington, DC, 1971. BROADWAY DEBUT—Petra, *A Little Night Music*, Shubert Theatre, 1973. PRINCIPAL STAGE APPEARANCES—Liana, *The Glorious Age*, Theatre Four, New York City, 1974; Isabella, Sister Angelica, *Boccaccio*, Edison Theatre, New York City, 1975; *2 by 5*, Village Gate Theatre, New York City, 1976; title role, *Lulu*, Direct Theatre, New York City, 1977; Holly Beaumont, *Spotlight*, National Theatre, Washington DC, 1978; Sally Bowles, *Cabaret*, Pittsburgh Civic Light Opera, Pittsburgh, PA, 1979. Also appeared in *I Got a Song*, Studio Arena, Buffalo, NY, 1974; *Alec Wilder: Clues to a Life*, Vineyard Theatre, New York City, 1982; *Pal Joey*, Long Wharf Theatre, New Haven, CT, 1983.

MAJOR TOURS—Eliza Doolittle, *My Fair Lady*, U.S. cities, 1976; Fastrada, *Pippin*, U.S. cities, 1977.

PRINCIPAL CABARET APPEARANCES—Reno Sweeney, New York City; Chelsea Encore.

AWARDS: Theatre World Award, 1973, for *A Little Night Music*.

SIDELIGHTS: FAVORITE ROLES—Eliza Doolittle, Sally Bowles.

ADDRESSES: AGENT—Henderson-Hogan Agency, 200 W. 57th Street, New York, NY 10019.*

*   *   *

BASS, Alfie   1921-1987

PERSONAL: Full name, Alfred Bass; born April 8, 1921, in London, England; died of a heart attack in London, July 15, 1987; son of Jacob and Ada (Miller) Bass; married Bryl Margaret Bryson; children: one son, one daughter.

VOCATION: Actor.

CAREER: STAGE DEBUT—Izzie, *Plant in the Sun*, Unity Theatre, London, 1939. PRINCIPAL STAGE APPEARANCES—Title role, *Buster*, Arts Theatre, London, 1943; Cohen, *Mr. Bolfry*, Playhouse Theatre, London, 1943; Abel Drugger, *The Alchemist*, Liverpool Old Vic Company, Playhouse Theatre, Liverpool, U.K., 1945; Rooky, *Alice in Thunderland*, Unity Theatre, London, 1945; Morgan, *Those Were the Days*, Q Theatre, London, 1947; Tilly, *He Who Gets Slapped*, Duchess Theatre, London, 1947; Fred Bassett, *Headlights on A5*, Embassy Theatre, London, 1947; Og, *Finian's Rainbow*, Palace Theatre, London, 1947; Gurney, *King John*, Launcelot Gobbo, *The Merchant of Venice*, Second Gravedigger,

Hamlet, Grumio, *The Taming of the Shrew*, Autolycus, *The Winter's Tale*, all with the Stratford Memorial Theatre Company, Stratford-on-Avon, U.K., 1948; Benjamin Brownstein, *The Golden Door*, Philip Anagnos, *The Gentle People*, both Embassy Theatre, 1949; Augustus Colpoys, *Trelawny of the Wells*, Lyric Hammersmith Theatre, London, 1952; Jimmie Thomson, *Starched Aprons*, Embassy Theatre, 1953; Fender, *The Bespoke Overcoat*, Arts Theatre, 1953, then Embassy Theatre, 1954; Emmett, *The Silver Whistle*, Duchess Theatre, 1956; Tevye, *Fiddler on the Roof*, Her Majesty's Theatre, London, 1968; Eccles, *Caste*, Greenwich Theatre, London, 1972; *Cinderella* (pantomime), Palladium Theatre, London, 1973; *Jack and the Beanstalk* (pantomime), Palladium Theatre, 1974. Also appeared in *The World of Sholom Aleichem*, Embassy Theatre, 1955; *The Punch Revue*, Duke of York's Theatre, London, 1955.

PRINCIPAL FILM APPEARANCES—*Johnny Frenchman*, Ealing, 1945; *Holiday Camp*, Gainesborough, 1947; *The Hasty Heart*, Warner Brothers, 1949; *Pool of London*, Ealing, 1950; *The Lavender Hill Mob*, Ealing, 1951; *A Kid for Two Farthings*, Lopert, 1956; *Make Me an Offer*, Associated Artists, 1956; *The Angel Who Pawned Her Harp*, Associated Artists, 1956; *A Tale of Two Cities*, Rank, 1958; *The Millionairess*, Twentieth Century-Fox, 1961; *Help!*, United Artists, 1965; *A Funny Thing Happened on the Way to the Forum*, United Artists, 1966; *Alfie*, Paramount, 1966; *The Fearless Vampire Killers*, Metro-Goldwyn-Mayer (MGM), 1967; *Up the Junction*, Paramount, 1968; *The Fixer*, MGM, 1968; *A Challenge for Robin Hood*, Twentieth Century-Fox, 1969; *The Revenge of the Pink Panther*, United Artists, 1978; *Death on the Nile*, Paramount, 1978; *Moonraker*, United Artists, 1979; *Dick Turpin*, RKO, 1980 (unreleased). Also appeared in *The Monkey's Paw*, 1949; *The Galloping Major*, 1950; *Brandy for the Parson*, 1954; *Svengali*, 1955; *A Child in the House*, 1957; *The Night My Number Came Up*, 1959; *I Only Arsked*, 1959; *The Magnificent Seven Deadly Sins*, 1962; *It Always Rains on Sunday*, 1968; *The Bespoke Overcoat*, 1969; *High Rise Donkey*, 1978.

PRINCIPAL TELEVISION APPEARANCES—Series: *Bootsie and Snudge*; *Till Death Us Do Part*. Movies: *Danger UXB*; *Star Maidens*; *Our Mutual Friend*; *Robin Hood*; *The Army Game*; *You Are Being Served*.

MEMBER: British Actors' Equity Association, Screen Actors Guild.

OBITUARIES AND OTHER SOURCES: Variety, July 22, 1987.*

*   *   *

BATEMAN, Jason

PERSONAL: Son of Kent (an acting coach and theatrical manager) and Victoria (a flight attendant) Bateman.

VOCATION: Actor.

CAREER: PRINCIPAL TELEVISION APPEARANCES—Series: James Cooper, *Little House on the Prairie*, NBC, 1981-82; Derek Taylor, *Silver Spoons*, NBC, 1982-84; Matthew Burton, *It's Your Move*, NBC, 1984; David Hogan, *Valerie*, NBC, 1985-1987, then *Valerie's Family*, NBC, 1987—. Movies: Addison Cromwell, *The Fantastic World of D.C. Collins*, NBC, 1984; Steve Tilby, "The Thanksgiving Promise," *Disney Sunday Movie*, ABC, 1986; also appeared as Joseph Kennedy III, *Robert Kennedy and His Times*,

1985; Larry Nichols, *Can You Feel Me Dancing?*, 1986; Tony *The Bates Motel*, 1987. Specials: *Just a Little More Love*, NBC, 1984; *NBC Presents the American Film Institute Comedy Special*, NBC, 1987. Guest: *Body Language*.

PRINCIPAL FILM APPEARANCES—Todd Howard, *Teen Wolf, Too*, Atlantic, 1987.

PRINCIPAL STAGE APPEARANCES—*Journey to the Day*, Birmingham, AL.

ADDRESSES: AGENT—International Creative Management, 8899 Beverly Boulevard, Los Angeles, CA 90048. PUBLICIST—Michael Levine Public Relations Co., 8730 Sunset Boulevard, Los Angeles, CA 90069.*

*   *   *

BATEMAN, Justine 1966-

PERSONAL: Born in 1966; daughter of Kent (an acting coach and theatrical manager) and Victoria (a flight attendant) Bateman.

VOCATION: Actress.

CAREER: PRINCIPAL TELEVISION APPEARANCES—Episodic: "Mookie and Pookie," *Tales from the Darkside*, syndicated, 1984; *One to Grow On*, NBC, 1984; *It's Your Move*, NBC, 1984; *Glitter*, ABC, 1984. Series: Mallory Keaton, *Family Ties*, NBC, 1982—. Movies: Deborah Jahnke, *Right to Kill?*, ABC, 1985; Mallory Keaton, *Family Ties Vacation*, NBC, 1985; Karin Nichols, *Can You Feel Me Dancing?*, 1986. Specials: "First the Egg," *ABC Afterschool Special*, ABC, 1985; *Whatta Year . . . 1986*, ABC, 1986; *Fame, Fortune, and Romance*, ABC, 1986; *Disney's "Captain Eo" Grand Opening*, NBC, 1986; *The 39th Annual Emmy Awards*, Fox, 1987.

PRINCIPAL FILM APPEARANCES—*Sweet Little Rock & Roller*, upcoming.

PRINCIPAL STAGE APPEARANCES—*Journey to the Day*, Birmingham, AL.

ADDRESSES: AGENT—c/o Scott Schwartz, International Creative Management, 8899 Beverly Boulevard, Los Angeles, CA, 90048. PUBLICIST—c/o Justin Pierce, Michael Levine Public Relations Co., 8730 Sunset Boulevard, Los Angeles, CA 90069.*

*   *   *

BAUERSMITH, Paula 1909-1987

PERSONAL: Born July 26, 1909, in Oakmont, PA; died of cancer in New York City, August 6, 1987; daughter of William and Susan (Paul) Bauersmith; married B.M. Warren (deceased); children: Jennifer and one son. EDUCATION: Attended Carnegie Institute of Technology.

VOCATION: Actress.

CAREER: BROADWAY DEBUT—Carmen Bracegirdle, *Lean Har-*

vest, Forrest Theatre, 1931. PRINCIPAL STAGE APPEARANCES—Lora McDonald, *East of Broadway*, Belmont Theatre, New York City, 1932; First Sergeant, *Warrior's Husband*, Morosco Theatre, New York City, 1932; Mary Paterson, *The Anatomist*, Bijou Theatre, New York City, 1932; Jennie, *Three-Cornered Moon*, Cort Theatre, New York City, 1933; Miss Morehead, *All Good Americans*, Henry Miller's Theatre, New York City, 1933; Marge, *Mahogany Hall*, Bijou Theatre, 1934; Emma Martin, *Let Freedom Ring*, Broadhurst Theatre, New York City, 1935; Martha Webster, *Bury the Dead*, Ethel Barrymore Theatre, New York City, 1936; Jennie Walters, *Two Hundred Were Chosen*, 48th Street Theatre, New York City, 1936; Katya, *Winter Soldiers*, Studio Theatre, New York City, 1942; Augusta Stetson, *Battle for Heaven*, Educational Alliance Theatre, New York City, 1948; Dr. Johnson, *Twentieth Century*, American National Theatre Academy Playhouse, New York City, 1950; *Member of the Wedding, Tiger at the Gates, The Chalk Garden, The Solid Gold Cadillac*, all Ann Arbor Drama Festival, Ann Arbor, MI, 1956; Anna, *Thor with Angels*, Margaret, *A Box of Watercolors*, Anne, *Tobias and the Angel*, Bernoline, *The Marvellous History of Saint Bernard*, Miss Connolly, *The Potting Shed*, all Chapel Players, Broadway Congregational Church, New York City, 1957-58; maid, *The Lesson*, Phoenix Theatre, New York City, 1958; Mrs. Sweeney, *Sail Away*, Broadhurst Theatre, 1961; *Sweet of You to Say So*, Theatre de Lys, New York City, 1962. Also appeared in *It's Up to You*, 1943, and in summer theatre productions of *You Can't Take It with You, Anything Goes, The Other Devil, Separate Tables, The Mousetrap, Take Me Along, Write Me a Murder, Damn Yankees, Bells Are Ringing, Tunnel of Love*.

MAJOR TOURS—*Paths of Glory*, U.S. cities, 1947; *Tiger at the Gates*, U.S. cities, 1960. With the National Repertory Company: Aunt Julia, *Hedda Gabler*, Mrs. Hardcastle, *She Stoops to Conquer*, and *Liliom*, U.S. cities, 1964-65, then Luce, *Comedy of Errors*, various roles, *John Brown's Body*, U.S. cities, 1967-68.

PRINCIPAL TELEVISION APPEARANCES—Episodic: *Omnibus*, ABC; *The U.S. Steel Hour*, CBS; *East Side/West Side*, CBS; *Studio One*, CBS.

MEMBER: Actors' Equity Association, American Federation of Television and Radio Artists.

SIDELIGHTS: CTFT notes that Paula Bauersmith's favorite role was Jennie Walters in *Two Hundred Were Chosen* and that she enjoyed creating crossword puzzles for the *New York Times*. Bauersmith's daughter is the actress Jennifer Warren.

OBITUARIES AND OTHER SOURCES: Variety, September 16, 1987.*

*   *   *

BAXTER, Cash 1937-

PERSONAL: Born April 23, 1937, in San Benito, TX; son of Walter Hope (a seedsman) and Olga Juanita (Arnold) Baxter; married Betty Nan Carpenter (head of the Episcopal School, New York City) July 30, 1959; children: Stephen Barrington, Catherine Elaine. EDUCATION: Attended the University of Texas at Arlington, 1954-55; Southern Methodist University, B.A., speech, 1959; College of Communications and Fine Arts, Southern Illinois University, Carbondale, M.F.A., 1986. MILITARY: U.S. Air Force, motion picture officer, 1959-62.

CASH BAXTER

VOCATION: Director, producer, choreographer, and educator.

CAREER: PRINCIPAL STAGE WORK—Director, *Career,* Wiesbaden Little Theatre, Weisbaden, West Germany, 1961; director, *Anything Goes,* State University of New York, New Paltz, 1965; choreographer, *Of Thee I Sing,* Pennsylvania State University, Festival Theatre, 1968; producer, *Candida,* Longacre Theatre, New York City, 1970; producing director and executive vice-president, Windmill Dinner Theatre Chain, for twenty-two productions, 1970-71; director, *The Music Man,* State University of New York at Binghampton, 1971; producing director, Coachlight Dinner Theatre, CT, for forty-two productions, 1972-78, including *Zorba,* 1974, *An Evening with Who?,* 1975, and *Pippin,* 1978; executive producer, director, and owner, Parkway Casino Dinner Theatre, for six productions, 1973; director, *An Evening with Who?,* Town Hall Theatre, New York City, 1975; director, *Jaques Brel Is Alive and Well and Living in Paris,* Music Fairs, Inc., 1976; director, *A Noel Coward Tribute,* National Arts Club, New York City, 1977; *People and Other Aggravations,* National Arts Club, New York City, 1978; director, *Sunrise,* Candlewood Area Theatre, New Fairfield, CT, 1978; director, *A Funny Thing Happened on the Way to the Forum,* Equity Library Theatre, New York City, 1979.

Director, *The Sound of Music,* Nisei Theatre, Tokyo, Japan, 1982; director, *Starting Here, Starting Now* and *Arsenic and Old Lace,* both at the Meadow Brook Theatre, Rochester, MI, 1983; *Night Fishing in Beverly Hills,* Intar Theatre, New York City, 1984; *Mortally Fine,* Stage Arts Theatre, New York City, 1985; director, *The Sound of Music, Amadeus,* and *The Aztec Holiday Murders,* all at the Theaterfest, Santa Maria and Solvang, CA, 1985; *The Drunkard,* Asolo State Theatre, Sarasota, FL, 1985; at the McLeod Theatre, Southern Illinois University, Carbondale, IL, director: *Our Town,* 1986 and *Brighton Beach Memoirs* and *110 in the Shade,* both 1987.

MAJOR TOURS—Director, *The Sound of Music,* Chuchini Theatre, Nogoya, and Japanese cities, 1980.

PRINCIPAL FILM WORK—Director: *The Berlin Wall Affair,* also more than two hundred training and documentary films, Department of Defense and U.S. Air Force, 1959-62; *The Last Resort,* 1979.

PRINCIPAL TELEVISION WORK—Production supervisor and co-director, *This Is Ben Shahn,* WCBS, 1965; consulting director and director of European footage, *Beethoven, a Portrait,* BBC and PBS, 1985.

RELATED CAREER—Artist-in-residence, Pennsylvania State College, 1965-68; guest director and lecturer, Clark University, 1970; artist-in-residence and guest director, State University of New York, Binghampton, 1971; guest lecturer and master teacher, Southern Illinois University at Carbondale, 1984, head of acting and directing program, 1986-87; guest lecturer and guest director, Allan Hancock College, 1985; guest director, Stage/West, Springfield, MA; student Theatre Guild, Southern Illinois University (faculty advisor); Summer Playhouse '87, Southern Illinois University (selection committee); Department of Theatre (honors committee) Southern Illinois University.

AWARDS: Emmy Award nomination, 1965, for *This Is Ben Shahn;* Best Director, Chuchini Award, Japan, 1980, for *The Sound of Music.*

MEMBER: Society of Stage Directors and Choreographers, American Academy of Composers, Authors, and Publishers, Academy of Television Arts and Sciences.

ADDRESSES: HOME—504 Beadle Drive, Apt. C, Carbondale, IL, 62901; 316 W. 79th Street, New York, NY 10024.

*   *   *

BEALS, Jennifer   1963-

PERSONAL: Born in 1963, in Chicago, IL.

VOCATION: Actress.

CAREER: FILM DEBUT—Alex Owens, *Flashdance,* Paramount, 1983. PRINCIPAL FILM APPEARANCES—Eva, *The Bride,* Columbia, 1985; appearing in the upcoming films *Vampire Kiss,* Tri-Star; *Kid Gloves,* New Century/Vista Films; *Layover,* Sho Films; *Rider in the Dark,* Filmalpha Productions.

PRINCIPAL TELEVISION APPEARANCES—Movies: *The Picture of Dorian Grey.* Specials: Title role, "Cinderella," *Faerietale Theatre,* Showtime, 1985.

RELATED CAREER—Fashion model.

ADDRESSES: c/o Martha Luttrell, International Creative Management, 8899 Beverly Boulevard, Los Angeles, CA 90048.*

*   *   *

BELAFONTE, Harry   1927-

PERSONAL: Born March 1, 1927, in New York, NY; son of Harold George and Melvine (Love) Belafonte; married Marguerite Mazique (divorced); married Julie Robinson, March 8, 1957; children: Adrienne, Shari, David, Gina. EDUCATION: Trained for the stage at the Actors Studio, the New School for Social Research, and the American Negro Theatre. MILITARY: U.S. Navy, 1943-45.

VOCATION: Actor, singer, and producer.

CAREER: PRINCIPAL TELEVISION APPEARANCES—Episodic: *Stage '67*, ABC, 1967. Series: Regular, *Sugar Hill Times*, CBS, 1949. Movies: Eddie Robinson, *Grambling's White Tiger*, NBC, 1981. Specials: *Tonight with Belafonte*, CBS, 1959; *Belafonte, New York*, CBS, 1960; *The Dinah Shore Special*, NBC, 1965; *Petula*, NBC, 1968; *The Julie Andrews Special*, ABC, 1969; *An Evening with Julie Andrews and Harry Belafonte*, NBC, 1969; *A World of Love*, CBS, 1970; *Harry and Lena*, ABC, 1970; *The Diahann Carroll Show*, NBC, 1971; *The Rowan and Martin Special*, NBC, 1973; *Marlo Thomas and Friends in "Free to Be. . .You and Me,"* ABC, 1974; *Night of 100 Stars*, ABC, 1982; also appeared in *I Sing What I See*, German television special, 1980.

HARRY BELAFONTE

PRINCIPAL TELEVISION WORK—Producer: *A Time for Laughter*, ABC, 1967; *Harry and Lena*, ABC, 1970; also produced *The Strolling '20s*, 1965.

FILM DEBUT—School principal, *Bright Road*, Metro-Goldwyn-Mayer, 1953. PRINCIPAL FILM APPEARANCES—Joe, *Carmen Jones*, Twentieth Century-Fox, 1954; David Boyeur, *Island in the Sun*, Twentieth Century-Fox, 1957; Ralph Burton, *The World, the Flesh, and the Devil*, Metro-Goldwyn-Mayer, 1959; Johnny Ingram, *Odds Against Tomorrow*, United Artists, 1959; Alexander Levine, *The Angel Levine*, United Artists, 1970; Preacher, *Buck and the Preacher*, Columbia, 1972; Geechie Dan Beauford, *Uptown Saturday Night*, Warner Brothers, 1974. Also appeared in *First Look*, 1984.

PRINCIPAL FILM WORK—Producer, *Beat Street*, Orion, 1984.

STAGE DEBUT—*Juno and the Paycock*, American Negro Theatre. BROADWAY DEBUT—*John Murray Anderson's Almanac*, Imperial Theatre, 1953. PRINCIPAL STAGE APPEARANCES—*Three for Tonight*, Plymouth Theatre, New York City, 1955; *Night of 100 Stars*, Radio City Music Hall, New York City, 1982; *Parade of Stars Playing the Palace*, Palace Theatre, New York City, 1983.

PRINCIPAL STAGE WORK—Co-producer, *Asinamal!*, Jack Lawrence Theatre, New York City, 1987; producer, *To Be Young, Gifted, and Black*, 1969.

MAJOR TOURS—Recent tours as a concert singer have included: Cuban, Jamaican, and European cities, 1980; Australian, New Zealand, U.S., and European cities, 1981; Canadian cities, 1982; (with the Canadian Symphony Orchestra) U.S. and European cities, 1983; U.S. cities, 1985; U.S., Canadian, European, and Japanese cities, 1986.

PRINCIPAL CABARET APPEARANCES—Royal Roost Nightclub, New York City, 1950; Village Vanguard, New York City, 1950; Golden Nugget, Atlantic City, NJ, Las Vegas, NV, 1985 and 1986.

RELATED CAREER—President, Harry Belafonte Enterprises, Inc.

WRITINGS: SONGS—(With Millard Thomas) *Suzanne (Ev'ry Night When the Sun Goes Down)*, 1952; (with Irving Burgie) *Island in the Sun*, 1956; *Cocoanut Woman*, 1957; (with Alan Greene and Malvina Reynolds) *Turn Around*, 1958; also (with William Attaway and Norman Luboff) *Jump Down, Spin Around*.

RECORDINGS: SINGLES—*We Are the World*, 1985. VIDEO—*We Are the World*, 1985.

AWARDS: Best Supporting or Featured Actor in a Musical, Antoinette Perry Award, 1953, Theatre World Award, 1954, both for *John Murray Anderson's Almanac;* Outstanding Performance in a Variety or Musical Program or Series, Emmy Award, 1960, for *Tonight with Harry Belafonte;* Grammy Award, 1985, American Music Award, 1986, both for *We Are the World;* Award of Appreciation, American Music Center, 1986, for initiation of and work for "USA for Africa"; UNICEF goodwill ambassador, 1987—. Honorary degrees: Doctor of the Arts, New School for Social Research, 1968; Doctor of Humane Letters, Park College, 1968; Doctor of Music, Morehouse College, 1987; Doctor of Fine Arts, State University of New York, Purchase, 1987; Doctor of Humanities, Park College.

MEMBER: TransAfrica; Martin Luther King Center for Non-

Violent Social Change; New York State Martin Luther King, Jr. Commission (chairman, 1986—).

SIDELIGHTS: RECREATIONS—Photography.

ADDRESSES: OFFICE—Harry Belafonte Enterprises, P.O. Box 1700, Ansonia Station, New York, NY 10023. AGENT—c/o Richard Rosenberg, Triad Artists, Inc., 10100 Santa Monica Boulevard, Los Angeles, CA 90067.

*   *   *

BENCHLEY, Peter   1940-

PERSONAL: Full name, Peter Bradford Benchley; born May 8, 1940, in New York, NY; son of Nathaniel Goddard (an author) and Marjorie (Bradford) Benchley; married Wendy Wesson, September 19, 1964; children: Tracy, Clayton. EDUCATION: Harvard University, B.A. (cum laude), 1961. MILITARY: U.S. Marine Corps Reserve, 1962-63.

VOCATION: Novelist and screenwriter.

CAREER: Also see *WRITINGS* below. RELATED CAREER—Reporter, *Washington Post,* Washington, DC, 1963; associate editor, *Newsweek,* New York City, 1964-67; freelance writer and television correspondent, 1969—, with assignments including episodes of *American Sportsman,* ABC. NON-RELATED CAREER—Staff assistant to the President of the United States, 1967-69.

WRITINGS: Novels, unless indicated—*Time and a Ticket* (non-fiction), Houghton Mifflin, 1964; *Jonathan Visits the White House* (juvenile), McGraw-Hill, 1964; *Jaws* (also see below), Doubleday, 1974; *The Deep* (also see below), Doubleday, 1976; *The Island* (also see below), Doubleday, 1979; *The Girl of the Sea of Cortez,* Doubleday, 1982; *Q Clearance,* Random House, 1986.

Screenplays: All based on his novels of the same titles—(With Carl Gottlieb) *Jaws,* Universal, 1975; (co-author) *The Deep,* Columbia, 1977; *The Island,* Universal, 1980.

Contributor to periodicals, including *Holiday, New Yorker, Vogue, New York Times Magazine,* and *National Geographic.*

AWARDS: Golden Globe nomination, Writers Guild of America award, both 1975, for *Jaws;* Golden Eagle Award, 1975, for *American Sportsman* episode on sharks.

MEMBER: Coffee House.

ADDRESSES: AGENT—c/o Roberta Pryor, International Creative Management, 40 W. 57th Street, New York, NY 10019.*

*   *   *

BENJAMIN, Richard   1938-

PERSONAL: Born May 22, 1938, in New York, NY; married Paula Prentiss; children: Ross Thomas.

VOCATION: Actor and director.

RICHARD BENJAMIN

CAREER: PRINCIPAL FILM APPEARANCES—*Goodbye, Columbus,* Paramount, 1969; *Catch-22,* Paramount, 1970; *Diary of a Mad Housewife,* Universal, 1970; *The Marriage of a Young Stockbroker,* Twentieth Century-Fox, 1971; *The Steagle,* AVCO-Embassy, 1971; *Portnoy's Complaint,* Warner Brothers, 1972; *Westworld,* Metro-Goldwyn-Mayer, 1973; *The Last of Sheila,* Warner Brothers, 1973; *The Sunshine Boys,* United Artists, 1975; *House Calls,* Universal, 1978; *Love at First Bite,* American International, 1979; *Scavenger Hunt,* Twentieth Century-Fox, 1979; *The Last Married Couple in America,* Universal, 1980; *How to Beat the High Cost of Living,* Filmways, 1980; *The First Family,* Warner Brothers, 1980. PRINCIPAL FILM WORK— Director: *My Favorite Year,* Metro-Goldwyn-Mayer/United Artists, 1982; *Racing with the Moon,* Paramount, 1984; *City Heat,* Warner Brothers, 1984; *The Money Pit,* Universal, 1986; also *Little Nikita,* 1987.

PRINCIPAL STAGE APPEARANCES—*Star-Spangled Girl,* New York City, 1966; *The Little Black Book,* New York City, 1972; *The Norman Conquests,* New York City, 1976. Also appeared in *The Taming of the Shrew, As You Like It,* both Delacorte Theatre, New York City. PRINCIPAL STAGE WORK—Director, *Barefoot in the Park,* London, 1965; director, *Arf, The Great Airplane Snatch,* both Stage 73, New York City, 1969.

PRINCIPAL TELEVISION APPEARANCES—Series: Dick Hollister, *He and She,* CBS, 1967-68; title role, *Quark,* NBC, 1978. Specials: "Fame," *Hallmark Hall of Fame,* 1978.

ADDRESSES: AGENT—The Gersh Agency, 222 N. Canon Drive, Beverly Hills, CA 90210.

BENNETT, Michael   1943-1987

PERSONAL: Born Michael Bennett DeFiglia, April 8, 1943, in Buffalo, NY; died of AIDS-related lymphoma in Tucson, AZ, July 2, 1987; son of Salvatore Joseph (a factory worker) and Helen (a secretary; maiden name, Ternoff) DeFiglia; married Donna McKechnie (a dancer and actress), December, 1976 (divorced, 1977).

VOCATION: Choreographer, director, producer, and writer.

CAREER: STAGE DEBUT—Baby John, *West Side Story,* touring production, 1959. PRINCIPAL STAGE APPEARANCES— All as chorus performer, in New York City: *Subways Are for Sleeping,* St. James Theatre, 1961; *Here's Love,* Shubert Theatre, 1963; *Bajour,* Shubert Theatre, 1964.

FIRST NEW YORK STAGE WORK—Choreograper, *A Joyful Noise,* Mark Hellinger Theatre, 1966. PRINCIPAL STAGE WORK—All in New York City unless indicated: Choreographer, *Henry, Sweet Henry,* Palace Theatre, 1968; choreographer, *Promises, Promises,* Shubert Theatre, 1968; choreographer, *Coco,* Mark Hellinger Theatre, 1969; choreographer, *Company,* Alvin Theatre, 1970, then Her Majesty's Theatre, London, 1972; co-director (with Harold Prince), choreographer, *Follies,* Winter Garden Theatre, 1971; producer, director, *Twigs,* Broadhurst Theatre, 1971; director, choreographer, *Seesaw,* Uris Theatre, 1973; director, *God's Favorite,* Eugene O'Neill Theatre, 1974; director, co-choreographer (with Bob Avian), *A Chorus Line,* Newman Theatre, then Shubert Theatre, both 1975, later Drury Lane Theatre, London, 1976; producer, director, co-choreographer (with Bob Avian), *Ballroom,* Majestic Theatre, 1978; producer, director, co-choreographer (with Michael Peters), *Dreamgirls,* Imperial Theatre, 1981. Also contributed work to *By Jupiter,* Theatre Four, 1967; *How Now, Dow Jones,* Lunt-Fontanne Theatre, 1967; *Your Own Thing,* Orpheum Theatre, 1968.

MAJOR TOURS—Baby John, *West Side Story,* U.S. cities, 1959, then European cities, 1960.

PRINCIPAL TELEVISION WORK—All as choreographer and dancer. Episodic: *Hullabaloo,* NBC; *The Dean Martin Show,* NBC; *Hollywood Palace,* ABC; *The Ed Sullivan Show,* CBS.

PRINCIPAL FILM WORK—Choreographer, *What's So Bad About Feeling Good?,* Universal, 1968.

WRITINGS: PLAYS—See production details above: Reworked book for *Seesaw;* also credited with original conception of *A Chorus Line.*

AWARDS: Best Choreographer nomination, Antoinette Perry Award, 1967, for *A Joyful Noise;* Best Choreographer nomination, Antoinette Perry Award, 1968, for *Henry, Sweet Henry;* Best Choreographer nomination, Antoinette Perry Award, 1969, for *Promises, Promises;* Best Choreographer nomination, Antoinette Perry Award, 1970, for *Coco;* Best Choreographer nomination, Antoinette Perry Award, 1971, for *Company;* Best Director (with Harold Prince), Best Choreographer, both Antoinette Perry Award, 1972, for *Follies;* Best Director nomination, Best Choreographer, both Antoinette Perry Award, 1974, for *Seesaw;* Pulitzer Prize for Drama, 1975, Best Director, Antoinette Perry Award, Best Choreographer (with Bob Avian), Antoinette Perry Award, 1976, Theatre World Award, 1976, all for *A Chorus Line;* Best Musical nomination, Best Director nomination, Best Choreographer (with Bob Avian), all

Antoinette Perry Award, 1979, for *Ballroom;* Best Musical nomination, Best Director nomination, Best Choreographer (with Michael Peters), all Antoinette Perry Award, 1982, for *Dreamgirls;* also winner of three Drama Critics Circle awards, Outer Critics Circle Award, Boston Theatre Critics Award, Los Angeles Drama Critics Award, Astaire Award, Dance Educators of America Award, Harkness Award, and the NAACP Image Award.

OBITUARIES AND OTHER SOURCES: Variety, July 8, 1987.*

*   *   *

BERLINGER, Warren   1937-

PERSONAL: Born August 31, 1937, in Brooklyn, NY; son of Elias (a building contractor) and Frieda (Shapkin) Berlinger; married Betty Lou Keim, February 18, 1960; children: one son, one daughter. EDUCATION: Attended Columbia University.

VOCATION: Actor.

CAREER: PRINCIPAL FILM APPEARANCES—*Teenage Rebel,* Twentieth Century-Fox, 1956; *Three Brave Men,* Twentieth Century-Fox, 1957; *Blue Denim,* Twentieth Century-Fox, 1959; *Because They're Young,* Columbia, 1960; *The Wackiest Ship in the Army,* Columbia, 1960; *Platinum High School,* Metro-Goldwyn-Mayer (MGM), 1960; *All Hands on Deck,* Twentieth Century-Fox, 1961; *Billie,* United Artists, 1965; *Spinout,* MGM, 1966; *Thunder Alley,* American International, 1967; *Lepke,* Warner Brothers, 1974; *I Will . . . I Will . . . For Now,* Twentieth Century-Fox, 1976; *Harry and Walter Go to New York,* Columbia, 1976; *The Shaggy D.A.,* Buena Vista, 1976; *Cannonball Run,* Twentieth Century-Fox, 1981; *The World According to Garp,* Warner Brothers, 1982; *My African Adventure,* Cannon, 1987. Also appeared in *The Long Goodbye,* 1973; *Free Ride,* 1986; and in *The Four Deuces; The Magician of Dublin.*

PRINCIPAL TELEVISION APPEARANCES—Episodic: Over 1,000 appearances since 1951 including *The Alcoa Hour, Goodyear Television Playhouse, Bracken's World, Armstrong Circle Theatre, Matinee Theatre, London Palladium, Kilroy, Billie, The Most Wanted Woman, The Secret Storm,* and *The Other Woman.* Series: Larry Barnes, *Joey Bishop Show,* NBC, 1961-62; regular, *The Funny Side,* NBC, 1971-72; Walter Bradley, *A Touch of Grace,* ABC, 1973; Chief Engineer Dobritch, *Operation Petticoat,* ABC, 1978-79; Eddie, *Small and Frye,* CBS, 1983.

BROADWAY DEBUT—Various children's roles, *Annie Get Your Gun,* Imperial Theatre, 1946. LONDON DEBUT—J. Pierpont Finch, *How to Succeed in Business without Really Trying,* Shaftesbury Theatre, 1963. PRINCIPAL STAGE APPEARANCES—Bibi, *The Happy Time,* Plymouth Theatre, New York City, 1951; Dave Gibbs, *Bernadine,* Playhouse Theatre, New York City, 1952; Johnny Reynolds, *Take a Giant Step,* Lyceum Theatre, New York City, 1953; Okkie Walters, *Anniversary Waltz,* Broadhurst Theatre, New York City, 1954; Dick Hewitt, *A Roomful of Roses,* Playhouse Theatre, 1955; Ernie Lacey, *Blue Denim,* Playhouse Theatre, 1958; Buddy Baker, *Come Blow Your Horn,* Brooks Atkinson Theatre, New York City, 1961; title role, *Tom Jones,* Bucks County Playhouse, New Hope, PA, 1965; Richard Hallen, *Who's Happy Now?,* Mark Taper Forum, Los Angeles, CA, 1968; Eddie Bell, *A Broadway Musical,* Lunt-Fontanne Theatre, New York City, 1978. Also appeared in *The Other Foot,* East Hampton

Theatre, Andover, MA, 1955; *The Rubaiyat of Howard Klein,* Westbury Music Fair, Long Island, NY, 1967.

MAJOR TOURS—Bibi, *The Happy Time,* U.S. cities, 1951; Buddy Baker, *Come Blow Your Horn,* U.S. cities, 1962; Marvin, Mort, *California Suite,* U.S. cities, 1977.

AWARDS: Theatre World Award, 1958; Best Actor nomination, London Theatre Critics Award.

MEMBER: Academy of Motion Picture Arts and Sciences; National Academy of Television Arts and Sciences.

SIDELIGHTS: FAVORITE ROLES—J. Pierpont Finch, *How to Succeed in Business without Really Trying.* RECREATIONS—Theatre.

Warren Berlinger told *CTFT* that he served four years as honorary mayor and honorary sheriff of Chatsworth, CA.

ADDRESSES: OFFICE—15374 Dickens Street, Sherman Oaks, CA 91403. AGENT—Fred Amsel and Associates, 291 S. La Cienega Boulevard, Beverly Hills, CA 90214.

*　　*　　*

BERMAN, Ed   1941-

PERSONAL: Born March 8, 1941, in Lewiston, ME; son of Jack and Ida (Webber) Berman. EDUCATION: Harvard University, B.A., 1962; attended Exeter College, Oxford University, 1962-65, 1978-79.

VOCATION: Writer, director, producer, actor, and theatrical manager.

CAREER: PRINCIPAL STAGE APPEARANCES—Actor under such pseudonyms as Otto Premier Check, Professor R.L. Dogg, and Super Santa.

PRINCIPAL STAGE WORK—Producer, director, *Dirty Linen, New-Found-Land,* both Almost Free Theatre, then Arts Theatre, London, 1976, then John Golden Theatre, New York City, 1977; director, *Dogg's Hamlet/Cahoot's Macbeth,* British American Repertory Company, London, 1979.

RELATED CAREER—Artistic director: Ambiance Lunch-Hour Theatre Club, Almost Free Theatre, Professor Dogg's Troupe for Children, British American Repertory Company. Founder: Inter-Action Trust, 1968; Other Company, 1968; Community Arts Workshop (Chalk Farm), 1968; Labrys Trust, 1969; Inter-Action Advisory Service, 1970; Infilms, 1970; Inter-Action Housing Trust, Ltd., 1970; Inter-Action Imprint, 1972; City Farm One, 1972; Neighborhood Use of Building and Space (Community Design Center), 1974. Resident dramatist and director, International Theatre Club, Mercury Theatre, 1967.

WRITINGS: PLAYS, PRODUCED—All as ED.B.: *Freeze,* 1966; *Stamp, Super Santa,* both 1967; *Sagittarius, Virgo, The Nudist Campers Grow and Grow,* all 1968; *The Alien Singer,* 1978.

BOOKS—*Fun Art Bus* (coloring book for children), edited by Justin Wintle, Eyre Methuen, 1973, then Inprint, 1974; *Homosexual Acts: Five Short Plays from the Gay Season at the Almost Free Theatre,*

Inter-Action Imprint, 1975; also author of *Professor R.L. Dogg's Zoo's Who I and II,* 1975, and *The Creative Game,* 1979. Editor of *How to Do It Yourself, Community Newspapers, Community Bookshops, Basic Video and Community Work,* and *Converting a Bus.*

AWARDS: Member of Order of British Empire, 1979; Rhodes Scholar.

SIDELIGHTS: RECREATIONS—''Solitude, conversation, sensuality, music.''

ADDRESSES: OFFICE—Inter-Action Housing Co-operative, 75 Willes Road, London NW5, England.*

*　　*　　*

BERNSTEIN, Jay   1937-

PERSONAL: Surname is pronounced ''Bern-steen''; born June, 7, 1937; son of Jerome and Nathaline Bernstein.

VOCATION: Producer and manager.

CAREER: PRINCIPAL TELEVISION WORK—All as executive producer. Movies: *The Wild Wild West Revisited,* CBS, 1979; *More Wild Wild West,* CBS, 1980; *Mickey Spillane's Mike Hammer in ''Margin for Murder,''* CBS, 1981; *Mickey Spillane's Mike Hammer in ''Murder Me, Murder You,''* CBS, 1983; *Mickey Spillane's Mike Hammer in ''More Than Murder,''* CBS, 1984; *The Return of Mickey Spillane's Mike Hammer,* CBS, 1986. Series: *Bring 'Em Back Alive,* CBS, 1982-83; *Mickey Spillane's Mike Hammer,* CBS, 1984-87; *Houston Knights,* CBS, 1987—.

PRINCIPAL FILM WORK—Executive producer: *Sunburn, Paramount, 1979; Nothing Personal,* American International, 1980.

RELATED CAREER—Personal manager, Jay Bernstein Public Relations; clients have included Farrah Fawcett, Suzanne Somers, Kristy McNichol, William Shatner, Cicely Tyson, Mary Hart, Susan St. James, Susan Hayward, and William Holden.

MEMBER: Academy of Motion Picture Arts and Sciences, Academy of Television Arts and Sciences, Directors Guild of America, Hollywood Radio and Television Society.

ADDRESSES: OFFICE—Columbia Pictures, 4000 Warner Boulevard, Burbank, CA 91505.

*　　*　　*

BERRIDGE, Elizabeth   1962-

PERSONAL: Born May 2, 1962, in New Rochelle, NY; daughter of George B. (a lawyer) and Mary L. (a social worker; maiden name, Robinson) Berridge. EDUCATION: Trained for the stage at the Lee Strasberg Theatre Institute and the Warren Robertson Theatre Workshop.

VOCATION: Actress.

CAREER: STAGE DEBUT—Zivia, *The Vampires,* Astor Place Theatre, New York City, 1984. PRINCIPAL STAGE APPEARANCES—Subway girl, friend's wife, reporter, groupie, *The Incredibly Famous Willy Rivers,* WPA Theatre, New York City, 1985; Lashondra Phillips, *Outside Waco,* Hudson Guild Theatre, New York City, 1985; Angela, *The Ground Zero Club,* Playwrights Horizons, New York City, 1985; Suze, *Cruise Control,* WPA Theatre, 1986; Angie, *Wrestlers,* Hudson Guild Theatre, 1986; Jilly, *Sorrows and Sons,* Vineyard Theatre, New York City, 1986. Also appeared in *Harvey,* Elitch Theatre, CO, then Westport Country Playhouse, Westport, CT, 1985; *Never in My Lifetime,* Hartman Theatre, Stamford, CT, 1986; *Crackwalker,* Hudson Guild Theatre, 1987; *Tuesday's Child,* Williamstown Theatre Festival, Williamstown, MA, 1987.

FILM DEBUT—Amy, *Funhouse,* Universal, 1983. PRINCIPAL FILM APPEARANCES—Contanze Mozart, *Amadeus,* Orion, 1984; Melanie, *5 Corners,* Handmade Films, 1986.

TELEVISION DEBUT—Allison Linden, *Texas,* ABC. PRINCIPAL TELEVISION APPEARANCES—Episodic: *One of the Boys,* 1984. Movies: June, *Smooth Talk,* PBS, 1985.

AWARDS: Drama Desk Award nominations, 1986, for *Cruise Control* and *Wrestlers.*

MEMBER: Actors' Equity Association, Screen Actors Guild, American Federation of Television and Radio Artists.

ADDRESSES: AGENT—c/o Kevin Huvane, William Morris Agency, 1350 Avenue of the Americas, New York, NY 10019. MANAGER—Bill Treusch, 853 Seventh Avenue, New York, NY 10106.

*   *   *

BIGGS, Roxann
(Roxann Cabalero)

PERSONAL: Born September 11, in Los Angeles, CA. EDUCATION: Received B.A., theatre, from University of California, Berkeley; trained for the stage at the American Conservatory Theatre with Uta Hagen.

VOCATION: Actress and playwright.

CAREER: BROADWAY DEBUT—(As Roxann Cabalero) Diana Morales, *A Chorus Line,* Shubert Theatre, 1982. PRINCIPAL STAGE APPEARANCES—Cetta, *Daughters,* Philadelphia Drama Guild, Philadelphia, PA, 1984; Miranda, *The Tempest,* City Stage Company, New York City, 1985; George, *The Early Girl,* Circle Repertory Company, New York City, 1986; Teresa, *The Hostage,* Coconut Grove Playhouse, Coconut Grove, FL, 1987; Rosa, *The Rose Tattoo,* GeVa Theatre, Rochester, NY, 1987.

TELEVISION DEBUT—Adrienne Morrow, *Another World,* NBC, 1985. PRINCIPAL TELEVISION APPEARANCES—Episodic: *Ohara,* ABC, 1987. Mini-Series: Louisa, *The Fortunate Pilgrim,* NBC, 1987.

WRITINGS: PLAYS, PRODUCED—*Desire to Fall,* Circle Repertory Company workshop, 1986.

ROXANN BIGGS

ADDRESSES: AGENT—Bauman, Hiller, and Associates, 250 W. 57th Street, New York, NY 10019.

*   *   *

BIKEL, Theodore   1924-

PERSONAL: Born May 2, 1924, in Vienna, Austria; son of Josef and Miriam (Riegler) Bikel; married Ofra Ichilov (divorced); married Rita Weinberg, 1967; children: Robert Simon, Daniel Martin. EDUCATION: Attended University of London; trained for the stage at the Royal Academy of Dramatic Art.

VOCATION: Actor and singer.

CAREER: STAGE DEBUT—Village clerk, *Tevye the Milkman,* Habimah Theatre, Tel Aviv, Israel, 1943. LONDON DEBUT—*You Can't Take It with You,* 1948. BROADWAY DEBUT—Inspector Massoubre, *Tonight in Samarkand,* Morosco Theatre, 1955. PRINCIPAL STAGE APPEARANCES—Charley, *Charley's Aunt,* father, *The Insect Play,* both Chamber Theatre, Tel Aviv, Israel, 1945; Pablo Gonzalez, then Howard Mitchell, *A Streetcar Named Desire,* Aldwych Theatre, London, 1949; Colonel Ikonenko, *The Love of Four Colonels,* Wyndham Theatre, London, 1951; Jan, *Dear Charles,* New Theatre, London, 1954; Robert de Baudricourt, *The Lark,* Longacre Theatre, New York City, 1955; Dr. Jacobson, *The Rope Dancers,* Cort Theatre, New York City, 1957; Captain Georg von Trapp, *The Sound of Music,* Lunt-Fontanne Theatre, New York City, 1959; (concert reading) *Brecht on Brecht,* Theatre de

Lys, New York City, 1962; Samuel Cole, *Cafe Crown*, Martin Beck Theatre, New York City, 1964; Professor George Ritter, *Pousse-Cafe*, 46th Street Theatre, New York City, 1966; Tevye, *Fiddler on the Roof*, Caesar's Palace, Las Vegas, NV, 1967, then Honolulu, HI, 1969; Meyer Rothschild, *The Rothschilds*, Westbury Music Fair, Long Island, NY, 1972; Major, *The Inspector General*, Circle in the Square, New York City, 1978; Macheath, *Threepenny Opera*, Guthrie Theatre, Minneapolis, MN, 1984; Tevye, *Fiddler on the Roof*, St. Louis Municipal Opera, St. Louis, MO, 1984.

MAJOR TOURS—Harold Mitchell, *A Streetcar Named Desire*, U.K. cities, 1950; Tevye, *Fiddler on the Roof*, U.S. cities, 1969, 1971, 1979; *Jacques Brel Is Alive and Well and Living in Paris*, U.S. cities, 1972, 1974; Meyer Rothschild, *The Rothschilds*, U.S. cities, 1972; Paul Delville, *The Marriage Go Round*, U.S. cities, 1973; Al Lewis, *The Sunshine Boys*, U.S. cities, 1973; Michael, *I Do, I Do*, U.S. cities, 1974; Chekhov, *The Good Doctor*, U.S. cities, 1975; title role, *Zorba*, U.S. cities, 1976.

FILM DEBUT—First officer of the "Luisa," *The African Queen*, United Artists, 1951. PRINCIPAL FILM APPEARANCES—*Moulin Rouge, Melba* both United Artists, 1953; *Desperate Moment*, Universal, 1953; *Never Let Me Go*, Metro-Goldwyn-Mayer (MGM), 1953; *The Little Kidnappers*, United Artists, 1954; *Love Lottery*, Ealing, 1954; *Forbidden Cargo*, Fine Arts, 1956; *The Pride and the Passion*, United Artists, 1957; *The Enemy Below*, Twentieth Century-Fox, 1957; *The Vintage*, MGM, 1957; *Fraulein*, Twentieth Century-Fox, 1958; *I Want to Live, The Defiant Ones*, both United Artists, 1958; *Blue Angel, Woman Obsessed*, both Twentieth Century-Fox, 1959; *Angry Hills*, MGM, 1959; *A Dog of*

Flanders, Twentieth Century-Fox, 1960; *Chance Meeting*, Paramount, 1960; *My Fair Lady*, Warner Brothers, 1964; *Sands of the Kalahari*, Paramount, 1965; *The Desperate Ones*, David Films, 1966; *The Russians Are Coming, the Russians Are Coming*, United Artists, 1966; *Sweet November, My Side of the Mountain*, both Paramount, 1969; *Darker Than Amber*, National General, 1969; *The Little Ark*, National General, 1970; *200 Motels*, United Artists, 1971. Also appeared in *The Divided Heart*, 1954; *Prince Jack*, 1984; *Very Close Quarters*, 1986; and in *The Dark Tower*.

TELEVISION DEBUT—Episodic: *Star Tonight*, ABC, 1955; "Julius Caesar," *Studio One*, CBS, 1955; "The Bridge of San Luis Rey," *Dupont Show of the Month*, CBS, 1958; *Naked City*, ABC, 1961; *Twilight Zone*, CBS, 1962; *Dr. Kildare*, NBC, 1962; *Sam Benedict*, NBC, 1962; *East Side/West Side*, CBS, 1963; "Noon Wine," *Stage '67*, ABC, 1966; *Mission: Impossible*, CBS, 1968; *Ironside*, NBC, 1971; *Cannon*, CBS, 1972; also in "The Dybbuk," *Play of the Week; U.S. Steel Hour; Climax!; Trials of O'Brien; Gunsmoke; Playhouse 90; Hawaii Five-O; Alfred Hitchcock Presents; Wagon Train; Kraft Television Theatre; Producer's Showcase; Alcoa Hour; Danny Thomas Hour; Dick Powell Theatre; Bob Hope Presents the Chrysler Theatre; Combat; Mod Squad*. Series: *The Eternal Light*, NBC, 1958-60; *Look Up and Live*, CBS, 1958-60; *Directions '61*, ABC, 1961. Movies: *Killer by Night*, CBS, 1972. Specials: *The Cherry Orchard*, BBC, 1948; *Who Has Seen the Wind?*, ABC, 1965; *The Diary of Anne Frank*, ABC, 1967; "St. Joan," *Hallmark Hall of Fame*, NBC, 1967; also *Birthday of an Idea; Angry Harvest; There Shall Be No Night; The Hunted*.

PRINCIPAL TELEVISION WORK—Editor, *Directions '61*, ABC, 1961.

PRINCIPAL RADIO APPEARANCES—*At Home with Theodore Bikel*, 1957-62.

RELATED CAREER—Concert folksinger since 1955: Carnegie Recital Hall, 1956; toured New Zealand and Australia, 1963; has performed throughout the U.S., Canada, and Europe.

NON-RELATED CAREER—Photographer: Exhibition at Bank Street Gallery, New York City, 1961; contributor to *U.S. Camera* and *Popular Photography*.

WRITINGS: TELEVISION SHOWS—*The Eternal Light*, NBC, 1958-61. NON-FICTION—*Folksongs and Footnotes*, Meridian Books, 1961.

RECORDINGS: ALBUMS—All for Elektra Records unless indicated: *Israeli Folk Songs*, 1955; *An Actor's Holiday, Jewish Folk Songs, Folk Songs of Israel, Songs of a Russian Gypsy*, (with Cynthia Gooding) *A Young Man and a Maid: Love Songs of Many Lands*, all 1958; (with Geula Gill) *Folk Songs from Just About Everywhere, More Jewish Folk Songs, Bravo Bikel: Theodore Bikel's Town Hall Concerts*, all 1959; *Songs of Russia, Old and New*, 1960; *From Bondage to Freedom*, 1961; *A Harvest of Israeli Folk Songs, Poetry and Prophecy of the Old Testament, The Best of Bikel*, all 1962; *Theodore Bikel on Tour*, 1963; *A Folksinger's Choice*, 1964; *Yiddish Theatre and Folk Songs, Songs of the Earth*, both 1967; *Theodore Bikel Is Tevye*, 1968; *The Sound of Music* (original cast recording), Columbia, 1960; *The King and I*, Columbia, 1964; *A New Day*, Reprise, 1970; *Silent No More: Soviet Jewish Underground Songs*, Star American, Jewish Congress, 1972; *Theodore Bikel for the Young*, Ambassador, 1973.

THEODORE BIKEL

AWARDS: Antoinette Perry Award nomination, 1958, for *The Rope*

Dancers; Antoinette Perry Award nomination, 1960, for *The Sound of Music;* Academy Award nomination, 1961, for *The Defiant Ones;* "Citizen of the World and Friend of Humanity," Brandeis University Women's Committee, 1960; cited for distinguished philanthropic service, National Jewish Hospital, Denver, CO, 1960; Man of the Year, Mt. Sinai Hospital, 1960; award for "Distinguished Service in the Cause of Human Rights" from the Joint Defense Appeal of the American Jewish Committee and the Anti-Defamation League, 1961; Mar Mitzvah Award, Israel Bonds, 1961; New York Jewish War Veterans Public Service Award, 1961; Arts Chapter Citation, American Jewish Congress; 1964; Morim Award, Jewish Teacher's Association, 1964; Appreciation Award, Combined Jewish Philanthropies (Boston), 1965, for *Birthday of an Idea;* Israel Bonds (Detroit) Annual Award, 1966; Distinguished Achievment Award, Goodwill Industries of Philadelphia, 1966; Man of the Year, B'nai B'rith, 1967; Man of Conscience Award, American Jewish Congress (Southern California division), 1967; Keynoters Award, United Jewish Welfare Fund, 1968; Certificate of Honor, Hebrew University of Jerusalem, 1969; Bronze Medallion Award, Mizrachi Women's Organizations of America (West Coast), 1970; Certificate of Appreciation, National Press Club, 1972; Certificate of Honor, City and County of San Francisco, 1973; Jewish Heritage Award, Farband Labor Zionist Organization, 1973.

MEMBER: Actors' Equity Association (council member, 1961, vice-president, 1964-73, president, 1973-82, president emeritus, 1982—), Academy of Motion Picture Arts and Sciences, Screen Actors Guild, Academy of Television Arts and Sciences (board of governors, 1962- 65), American Federation of Television and Radio Artists, International Federation of Television Arts and Sciences, 1961-65; International Federation of Actors (vice-president, 1981—), American Federation of Musicians, National Council for the Arts, 1977; American Council for the Arts (board member), Jewish Music Council (board member), Ethnic Folk Arts Council (board member); American Jewish Congress (founder, vice-president, 1963-70, chairman of governing council, 1970-80, senior vice-president, 1980); delegate to Democratic National Convention, 1968.

SIDELIGHTS: FAVORITE ROLES—Zorba. RECREATIONS—Chess, photography.

ADDRESSES: AGENT—c/o Walter Kohner, Paul Kohner Agency, 9169 Sunset Boulevard, Beverly Hills, CA 90069.

*   *   *

BILLINGS, Josh   1947-

PERSONAL: Full name, Joshua L. Billings; born August 31, 1947, in Charleston, WV; son of Howard Lloyd and Effie Velma Billings (a nursery school director). EDUCATION: Received B.A., theatre, from Antioch College; trained for the stage at the Drama Studio, London.

VOCATION: Actor.

CAREER: STAGE DEBUT—*Paradise Mislaid,* Roundhouse Theatre, London, 1976, for sixteen performances. PRINCIPAL STAGE APPEARANCES—Andrew Wyke, *Sleuth,* King's Jester Theatre, Washington, DC, 1979; Droulliet, *Addis Ababa,* Kennedy Center, Washington, DC, 1980; Bob, *Split,* Circle Theatre, Los Angeles,

JOSH BILLINGS

CA, 1982. Also appeared as William, *As You Like It,* Folger Theatre, Washington, DC; Louis Post, *Splendid Rebels,* son, *White Horse/Black Horse,* Boyce, *Incidental Incidents,* Fulbert, *The Prodigal,* all New Playwrights Theatre, Washington, DC.

FILM DEBUT—Tom Moore, *The Image Maker,* Screenscope, 1984. PRINCIPAL FILM APPEARANCES—Caddy mechanic, *Tin Men,* Touchstone, 1986; Chyron operator, *Broadcast News,* Twentieth Century-Fox, upcoming; guard, *Young Lust,* Warner Brothers; also dubbed voices for the German documentary, *Viva Portugal.*

TELEVISION DEBUT—Walter Weisbrade, *Lime Street,* ABC, 1985. PRINCIPAL TELEVISION APPEARANCES—Series: Charlie Strickland, *Ossie and Ruby,* PBS, 1986. Specials: Christmas Future, *World Wrestling Federation,* USA (cable), 1986.

PRINCIPAL RADIO APPEARANCES—Series: *Just So Stories,* Children's Radio Workshop; *U.S. Surplus Soap,* Washington Ear for the Blind; also *Thinkabout,* Educational Film Center.

RELATED CAREER—Founder, producing director, and teacher, Poet and Peasant Theatre, Washington, DC, 1984—; board of directors, American Showcase Theatre, Alexandria, VA, 1987—; also appeared in numerous television and radio commercials and industrial films.

MEMBER: Actors' Equity Association, Screen Actors Guild, American Federation of Television and Radio Artists.

ADDRESSES: HOME—8500 16th Street, #219, Silver Spring, MD

20910. AGENT—Central Casting, 623 Pennsylvania Avenue, S.E., Washington, DC 20003.

*   *   *

BIRNEY, David

PERSONAL: Full name, David Edward Birney; born April 23, in Washington, DC; son of Edwin B. (a special agent for the Federal Bureau of Investigation) and Jeanne (McGee) Birney; married Joan Concannon, 1961 (divorced); married Meredith Baxter (an actress), April 10, 1974; children: Theodore, Eva, Kathleen Jeanne, Peter, Mollie. EDUCATION: Dartmouth College, A.B., 1961; University of California, Los Angeles, M.A., 1963. MILITARY: U.S. Army, 1963-65.

VOCATION: Actor and director.

CAREER: STAGE DEBUT—Simon, *Hay Fever,* Barter Theatre, Abingdon, VA, 1965. OFF-BROADWAY DEBUT—Antipholus of Syracuse, *The Comedy of Errors,* Delacorte Theatre, 1967. BROADWAY DEBUT—Antonio Salieri, *Amadeus,* Broadhurst Theatre, 1983. PRINCIPAL STAGE APPEARANCES— Streetsinger, *Threepenny Opera,* Damis, *Tartuffe,* narrator, *Pictures in the Hallway,* Cristoforov, *The Public Eye,* Tolar, *The Knack,* all Barter Theatre, Abingdon, VA, 1965; Algernon, *The Importance of Being Earnest,* Orsino, *Twelfth Night,* Tony, *You Can't Take It with You,* all Barter Theatre, 1966; Deschamps, *Poor Bitos,* Fedotik, *The Three Sisters,* Clov, *Endgame,* all Hartford Stage Company, Hartford, CT, 1966;

DAVID BIRNEY

chorus, *Under the Gaslight,* DiNolli, *Enrico IV,* Silvio, *Servant of Two Masters,* all Hartford Stage Company, 1967; Dauphin, *King John,* Chiron, *Titus Andronicus,* both Delacorte Theatre, New York City, 1967; chorus, Egg of Head, *MacBird,* Village Gate Theatre, New York City, 1967; Edmund, *Ceremony of Innocence,* American Place Theatre, New York City, 1968; young man, *Summertree,* Forum Theatre, New York City, 1968; Wilson, ''The Ruffian on the Stair,'' Kenny, ''The Erpingham Camp,'' *Crimes of Passion,* Astor Place Theatre, New York City, 1969, then University of Pennsylvania, Philadelphia, PA, 1969; Cleante, *The Miser,* Vivian Beaumont Theatre, New York City, 1969; Andocides, *The Long War,* Triangle Theatre, New York City, 1969.

Title role, *Hamlet,* University of Pennsylvania, 1970; Yang Sun, *The Good Woman of Setzuan,* Christy Mahan, *The Playboy of the Western World,* Mars and Haemon, *Antigone,* Jan and Hovstad, *An Enemy of the People,* all Vivian Beaumont Theatre, 1970; Adolphus Cusins, *Major Barbara,* Mark Taper Forum, Los Angeles, CA, 1971; Mercutio, *Romeo and Juliet,* Arena Stage, Buffalo, NY, 1972; Valentine, *You Never Can Tell,* Arlington Park Theatre, Chicago, IL, 1973; Romeo, *Romeo and Juliet,* American Shakespeare Festival, Stratford, CT, 1974; King Arthur, *Camelot,* St. Louis Municipal Opera, St. Louis, MO, 1975; Kentridge, *The Biko Inquest,* Mark Taper Forum, 1979; title role, *Richard III,* Hopkins Center, Dartmouth College, 1980; title role, *Hamlet,* Solvang Theatre Festival, Solvang, CA, 1985; David, *Benefactors,* Brooks Atkinson Theatre, New York City, 1986; Adam, *Diaries of Adam and Eve,* Hopkins Center, 1987. Also appeared in *Never Too Late,* Barter Theatre, 1965.

MAJOR TOURS—*Brecht and Strindberg,* Strolling Players Company, U.S. cities, 1967; Sky Masterson, *Guys and Dolls,* U.S. cities, 1973; Henry Higgins, *My Fair Lady,* U.S. cities, 1979; Matt Friedman, *Talley's Folly,* U.S. cities, 1981.

PRINCIPAL STAGE WORK—Director: *The Zoo Story,* Barter Theatre, Abingdon, VA, 1965; *Yanks 3, Detroit 0, Top of the Seventh,* American Shakespeare Festival, Stratford, CT, 1974; *A Life in the Theatre,* Matrix Theatre, Los Angeles, CA, 1980; *The Sorrow of Stephen,* Dartmouth Repertory Theatre, Dartmouth, NH, 1980; *Diaries of Adam and Eve,* Hopkins Center, Dartmouth College, Dartmouth, NH, 1987.

TELEVISION DEBUT—Mark Elliot, *Love Is a Many Splendored Thing,* CBS, 1968-69. PRINCIPAL TELEVISION APPEARANCES— Episodic: *Hawaii Five-O,* CBS; *Police Story,* NBC; *Cannon,* CBS, *The F.B.I.,* ABC. Series: Oliver Harrell, *A World Apart,* ABC, 1970-71; Bernie Steinberg, *Bridget Loves Bernie,* CBS, 1972-73; title role, *Serpico,* NBC, 1976-77; Ben Samuels, *St. Elsewhere,* NBC, 1982-83; Sam Dillon, *Glitter,* ABC, 1984. Mini-Series: John Quincy Adams, *The Adams Chronicles,* PBS, 1976; Bernard Lacey, *Seal Morning,* PBS, 1985; Lyon Burke, *Jacqueline Susann's The Valley of the Dolls,* 1985; Daniel, ''Daniel in the Lion's Den,'' *The Bible.* Movies: Lucas Cord, *Power's Play,* CBS, 1986; Carter Wells, *The Long Journey Home,* CBS, 1987; appeared as Willy Harvey, *Bronk,* 1975; Tony Gianetti, *High Midnight,* 1979; Jan, *Ohms,* 1980; Henry Hawksworth, *The Five of Me,* 1981; David, *The Master of the Game;* Paul Winkless, *High Rise;* Jonathan Ferrier, *Testimony of Two Men;* also in *Ghost Story; Murder or Mercy; Only with Married Men; The Champions—A Love Story; Mom, the Wolfman, and Me.* Specials: Brother Martin, ''Saint Joan,'' *Hallmark Hall of Fame,* NBC, 1967.

FILM DEBUT—Neil Bowman, *Caravan to Vaccares,* Rank, 1974. PRINCIPAL FILM APPEARANCES—John, *Trial by Combat,* Warner Brothers, 1976; Frank, *Somerville House,* 1980. Also appeared in *Oh God, Book II,* Warner Brothers, 1980; *Prettykill,* Lorimar, 1986; and in *Good Bye, See You Monday.*

RELATED CAREER—Visiting professor of Drama, Dartmouth College, 1980; board of overseers, Hopkins Center for the Arts, Dartmouth College, 1986-87.

RECORDINGS: The Miser, Caedmon, 1969; *An Enemy of the People,* Caedmon, 1971.

AWARDS: Barter Theatre Award, 1965; Theatre World Award, 1968, Clarence Derwent Award, 1968, both for *Summertree; Buffalo-Courier Express* Award, 1972, for *Romeo and Juliet;* Most Promising Newcomer, *Photoplay Magazine* Award, 1973, *Sixteen Magazine Award,* 1973, both for *Bridget Loves Bernie;* Best Director, *Los Angeles Weekly* Award, 1980, for *A Life in the Theatre.* Honorary degrees: Doctor of Humanities, Southern Utah State University, 1987.

MEMBER: Actors' Equity Association, Screen Actors Guild, American Federation of Television and Radio Artists, Academy of Motion Picture Arts and Sciences, National Endowment for the Arts, Players Club; Cystic Fibrosis Foundation, March of Dimes '85, American Diabetes Association (co-chairperson, 1986-87), American Lung Association; U.S. Ski Team.

SIDELIGHTS: RECREATIONS—Skiing, sailing, poetry, literature, music, running.

ADDRESSES: OFFICE—MAB Productions, Inc., c/o Zeiderman-Oberman Associates, 500 S. Sepulveda, Los Angeles, CA 90049. AGENT—David Shapiro and Associates, 5301 Ventura Boulevard, Suite 345, Sherman Oaks, CA 91403.

* * *

BISHOP, Carole
See BISHOP, Kelly

* * *

BISHOP, Kelly 1944-
(Carole Bishop)

PERSONAL: Born Carole Bishop, February 28, 1944, in Colorado Springs, CO; began using the name Kelly Bishop, 1975-76; daughter of Lawrence Boden and Jane Lenore (Wahtola) Bishop; married Peter Miller (divorced); married Lee Leonard. EDUCATION: Studied dance at the American Ballet Theatre School and the San Jose Ballet School.

VOCATION: Actress.

CAREER: STAGE DEBUT—(As Carole Bishop) corps de ballet, Radio City Music Hall, New York City, 1962. BROADWAY DEBUT—(As Carole Bishop) *Golden Rainbow,* Shubert Theatre, 1968. PRINCIPAL STAGE APPEARANCES— (As Carole Bishop) company nurse, *Promises, Promises,* Shubert Theatre, New York City, 1968; (as Carole Bishop) Sheila, *A Chorus Line,* Newman Theatre, then Shubert Theatre, both New York City, 1975; Mary, *Vanities,* Westside Theatre, Chicago, IL, 1977; Julie, *Piano Bar,* Chelsea Westside Theatre, New York City, 1978. Also appeared in *On the Town,* Imperial Theatre, New York City, 1971; *Rachael Lily Rosenblum,* Broadhurst Theatre, New York City, 1973; *Night of the*

Iguana, McCarter Theatre, Princeton, NJ, 1981, then Virginia Stage Company, Norfolk, VA, 1984; *Precious Sons,* Longacre Theatre, New York City, 1986; and as Anita, *West Side Story,* Chateau de Ville Theatre, 1974.

MAJOR TOURS—(As Carole Bishop) Helen McFudd, *Irene,* U.S. cities, 1974.

FILM DEBUT—*An Unmarried Woman,* Twentieth Century-Fox, 1978; PRINCIPAL FILM APPEARANCES—Marjorie Houseman, *Dirty Dancing,* Vestron, 1987; also *O'Hara's Wife,* 1982.

PRINCIPAL TELEVISION APPEARANCES—Episodic: *Hawaii Five-0,* CBS.

AWARDS: Best Featured Actress in a Musical, Antoinette Perry Award, 1976, for *A Chorus Line.*

SIDELIGHTS: FAVORITE ROLES—Sheila in *A Chorus Line.*

ADDRESSES: AGENT—c/o Lionel Larner, 850 Seventh Avenue, New York, NY 10019.*

* * *

BLADES, Ruben 1948-

PERSONAL: Born July 16, 1948, in Panama City, Republic of Panama; son of Ruben Dario (a detective) and Anoland Benita (an actress and singer; maiden name, Bellido de Luna); married Lisa A. Lebenzon (an actress), December 13, 1986. EDUCATION: University of Panama, law and political science, 1974; Harvard University, L.L.M., 1985; studied acting with George Loros. RELIGION: Roman Catholic.

VOCATION: Actor, composer, writer, and singer.

CAREER: FILM DEBUT—Andy Perez, *The Last Fight,* J. Masucci, 1982. PRINCIPAL FILM APPEARANCES—Rudy Yeloz, *Crossover Dreams,* Miramax, 1984; Louis Rodriguez, *Critical Condition,* Paramount, 1986; Bernabe Montoya, *The Milagro Beanfield War,* Universal, 1986; Carl Jimenez, *Fatal Beauty,* Warner Brothers, 1987; also appeared in *When the Mountains Tremble,* 1983; *Beat Street,* 1984.

PRINCIPAL TELEVISION APPEARANCES—*Sesame Street,* PBS, 1986.

RELATED CAREER—Singer, musician, and songwriter.

NON-RELATED CAREER—Attorney, Banco Nacional de Panama, 1972-74; legal advisor, Fania Records, Inc., 1975-78.

WRITINGS: SCREENPLAYS—(With L. Ichaso and M. Arce) *Crossover Dreams,* Miramax, 1983.

Also wrote songs contained on his albums as well as the score for the stage production, *The Balcony,* American Repertory Theatre, Cambridge, MA, 1986.

RECORDINGS: ALBUMS—All for Elektra/Asylum Records. *Buscando America,* 1984; *Escenas,* 1985; *Agua de Luna,* 1987.

AWARDS: Time magazine's "Top Ten Albums of the Year," 1984, for *Buscando America,* and 1985, for *Escenas;* New York Award, 1985, for *Buscando America,* and 1986, for *Escenas;* Best Latin Performance, Grammy Award, 1986, for *Escenas;* winner of three other Grammy Awards.

MEMBER: Screen Actors Guild; American Society of Composers, Authors, and Publishers; National Academy of Recording Arts and Sciences; American Federation of Television and Radio Artists; Colegio Nacional de Abogados (Panama); Harvard Law School Association.

SIDELIGHTS: RECREATIONS—Baseball, soccer, boxing, dominoes, collecting toy soldiers, old books, and reading.

Ruben Blades told *CTFT* that his motivation is to present "stories through music and film that will help people understand that our hopes are similar, regardless of country, race, sex, etc., and that the solution to our problems can and should be made by *all* of us." Blades has traveled throughout the United States, Central America, and Europe with his band "Seis del Solar," headlining concerts at the Hollywood Bowl, Carnegie Hall, and Madison Square Garden.

ADDRESSES: OFFICE—David Maldonado Management, 1674 Broadway, #703, New York, NY 10019. AGENT—c/o Paul Schwartman, International Creative Management, 8899 Beverly Hills Boulevard, Los Angeles, CA 90048.

RUBEN BLADES

BLAINE, Vivian   1921-

PERSONAL: Born Vivian S. Stapleton, November 21, 1921 (some sources say 1923 or 1924), in Newark, NJ; daughter of Lionel P. and Wilhelmina (Tepley) Stapleton; married Manuel George Frank (divorced); married Milton Rackmil (divorced); married Stuart Clark. EDUCATION: Trained for the stage at the American Academy of Dramatic Art.

VOCATION: Actress and singer.

CAREER: STAGE DEBUT—Variety acts, Mosque Theatre, Newark, NJ, then in New York City, 1939. LONDON DEBUT—Variety acts, Casino Theatre, 1947. PRINCIPAL STAGE APPEARANCES— Miss Adelaide, *Guys and Dolls,* 46th Street Theatre, New York City, 1950, then Coliseum Theatre, London, 1953; Celia Pope, *A Hatful of Rain,* Lyceum Theatre, New York City, 1956; Irene Lovelle, *Say, Darling,* American National Theatre Academy Playhouse, New York City, 1958; Rose, *Gypsy,* Shady Grove Music Fair, Washington, DC, 1962; Angela, *Enter Laughing,* Henry Miller's Theatre, New York City, 1963; Nell Henderson, *Mr. President,* Civic Arena, Pittsburgh, PA, 1964; Miss Adelaide, *Guys and Dolls,* City Center Theatre, New York City, 1966; Jo Anne, *Company,* Alvin Theatre, New York City, 1971, later Westbury Music Fair, Long Island, NY, 1973; Madame Hortense, *Zorba,* Broadway Theatre, New York City, 1983. Also appeared as Phyllis Rogers Stone, *Follies,* Westchester Country Playhouse, NY, 1973; and in *One Touch of Venus,* Dallas Starlight Theatre, 1948; *Light Up the Sky,* Lakeside Summer Theatre, Lake Hopatcong, NJ, 1949; *Panama Hattie,* Starlight Theatre, Dallas, TX, 1955; *The Best of Everybody,* Studebaker Theatre, Chicago, IL, 1975.

MAJOR TOURS—Celia Pope, *A Hatful of Rain,* U.S. cities, 1956; Miss Adelaide, *Guys and Dolls,* Nell Henderson, *Mr. President,* U.S. cities, both 1964; Edith Lambert, *Never Too Late,* U.S. cities, 1965; Stephanie, *Cactus Flower,* U.S. cities, 1967; Marion Hollander, *Don't Drink the Water,* U.S. cities, 1968; Madame Hortense, *Zorba,* U.S. cities, 1970; Phyllis Rogers Stone, *Follies,* U.S. cities, 1973; all female roles, *Twigs,* U.S. cities, 1973; Dolly Levi, *Hello Dolly!,* U.S. cities, 1974; Frances Black, *Light Up the Sky,* U.S. cities, 1975. Also *Bloomer Girl,* U.S. cities, 1949; and in *One Touch of Venus; Light Up the Sky; Born Yesterday; Gypsy; Rain; Cactus Flower; I Do, I Do; A Streetcar Named Desire.*

FILM DEBUT—*Through Different Eyes,* Twentieth Century-Fox, 1942. PRINCIPAL FILM APPEARANCES—*It Happened in Flatbush, Girl Trouble,* both Twentieth Century-Fox, 1942; *Jitterbugs, He Hired the Boss,* both Twentieth Century-Fox, 1943; *Something for the Boys, Greenwich Village,* both Twentieth Century-Fox, 1944; *Nob Hill, State Fair, Doll Face,* all Twentieth Century-Fox, 1945; *Three Little Girls in Blue, If I'm Lucky,* both Twentieth Century-Fox, 1946; *Skirts Ahoy,* Metro-Goldwyn-Mayer (MGM), 1952; *Guys and Dolls,* MGM, 1955; *Public Pigeon No. One,* Universal, 1957; *The Dark,* Film Ventures International, 1979; *Parasite,* Wizard Video, 1981. Also appeared in *Richard,* 1972; *I'm Going to Be Famous,* 1982.

PRINCIPAL TELEVISION APPEARANCES—Episodic: "Double Jeopardy," *Philco Television Playhouse,* ABC, 1953; "Heart of a Clown," *Elgin Hour,* ABC, 1954; *Center Stage,* ABC, 1954; "Pick the Winner," *Damon Runyon Theatre,* CBS, 1955; "The Awful Truth," *The Bob Hope Show,* NBC, 1956; "The Undesirable," *Lux Video Theatre,* NBC, 1957; *Route 66,* CBS; and *Ford Theatre.* Series: *Those Two,* NBC, 1951-52. Specials: "Dream Girl," *Hallmark Hall of Fame,* NBC, 1955; *Ray Bolger's Washing-*

ton Square Show, NBC, 1956. Guest: *The Jimmy Durante Show*, NBC, *The Milton Berle Show*, NBC; *The Jackie Gleason Show*, CBS.

PRINCIPAL RADIO APPEARANCES—*The Fitch Bandwagon.*

PRINCIPAL CABARET APPEARANCES—Cafe de la Paix, New York City, 1940; Glass Hat, New York City, 1941; Casino Theatre, London, 1947; Copacabana, New York City, 1948; Brothers and Sisters, New York City, 1975; Grand Finale, New York City, 1976.

RELATED CAREER—Performed in vaudeville at age three; band singer.

AWARDS: Musical Comedy Star of the Year, New York Theatre Goers Award, 1951, Best Female Supporting Performance in a Musical, Donaldson Award, 1951, both for *Guys and Dolls;* Best Dressed Woman, Fashion Academy Award, 1952.

MEMBER: Academy of Motion Picture Arts and Sciences, American Federation of Television and Radio Artists, Actors' Equity Association, Screen Actors Guild, American Guild of Variety Artists.

SIDELIGHTS: RECREATIONS—Golf, horseback riding, tennis.

CTFT learned that in 1967 Vivian Blaine played Miss Adelaide in a special performance of *Guys and Dolls* given at the White House at the request of President Johnson.

ADDRESSES: AGENT—Becker and London, 15 Columbus Circle, New York, NY 10019.*

*   *   *

BOLAM, James   1938-

PERSONAL: Born June 16, 1938, in Sunderland, England; son of Robert Alfred and Marion Alice (Drury) Bolam.

VOCATION: Actor.

CAREER: STAGE DEBUT—Michael, *The Kitchen,* Royal Court Theatre, 1959. BROADWAY DEBUT—Frank More, *How's the World Treating You?,* Music Box Theatre, 1966. PRINCIPAL STAGE APPEARANCES—Lord Mayor and Smith, *The Happy Haven,* Vakov, *Platonov,* both Royal Court Theatre, London, 1960; Michael, *The Kitchen,* Starveling, *A Midsummer Night's Dream,* both Royal Court Theatre, 1961; Tom, *The Knack,* Royal Court Theatre, 1962; Tom Midway, *Semi-Detached,* Saville Theatre, London, 1962; attendant, *Oedipus the King,* Mercury, *Four Thousand Brass Halfpennies,* both Mermaid Theatre, London, 1965; Private Meek, *Too True to Be Good,* Strand Theatre, then Garrick Theatre, both London, 1965; Evans, *Events While Guarding the Bofors Gun,* Hampstead Theatre Club, London, 1966; Frank, *White Lies,* Brindsley Miller, *Black Comedy,* both Lyric Theatre, London, 1968; Colin Shaw, *In Celebration,* Royal Court Theatre, 1969; Bamforth, *The Long and the Short and the Tall,* Belgrade Theatre, Coventry, U.K., 1971; Robespierre, *The Silence of Saint-Just,* Gardner Theatre, Brighton, U.K., 1971; Trevor Hollingshead, *Veterans,* Royal Court Theatre, 1972; title role, *Macbeth,* Young Vic Theatre, London, 1975; Dave, *Treats,* Royal Court Theatre, 1976; John Terry, *Who Killed "Agatha" Christie?,*

Ambassadors Theatre, London, 1978. Also appeared in *The Wakefield Mystery Cycle,* Mermaid Theatre, 1961; and *The Vicar of Soho,* Gardner Theatre, 1972.

MAJOR TOURS—Face, *The Alchemist,* Trepliov, *The Seagull,* both with the Cambridge Theatre Company, U.K. cities, 1970; title role, *Butley,* U.K. cities, 1973; Leonard, *Time and Time Again,* U.K. cities, 1974. Also in *Arms and the Man,* U.K. cities, 1980.

PRINCIPAL TELEVISION APPEARANCES—*The Beiderbecke Affair,* Yorkshire Television (YTV); *Room at the Bottom,* YTV; *Father Matthew's Daughter,* BBC; also *The Likely Lads; Only When I Laugh; When the Boat Comes In.*

PRINCIPAL FILM APPEARANCES—*A Kind of Loving,* Governor, 1962; *Half a Sixpence,* Paramount, 1968; *Otley,* Columbia, 1969.

SIDELIGHTS: RECREATIONS—Horses.

ADDRESSES: AGENT—c/o Barry Burnett, Suite 409, Prince's House, 119 Piccadilly, London W1, England.

*   *   *

BORIS, Robert M.   1945-

PERSONAL: Born October 12, 1945, in New York, NY; son of Sam (a manufacturer) and Leatrice (a bookkeeper; maiden name, More) Boris; married Joan Canning, December 20, 1978; children: Melissa Ann. EDUCATION: Studied drama for two years at Carnegie Mellon University. RELIGION: Jewish.

VOCATION: Director and writer.

CAREER: PRINCIPAL FILM WORK—Writer (see below); director: *Oxford Blues,* Metro-Goldwyn-Mayer/United Artists, 1984; *Steele Justice,* Atlantic Productions, 1987.

WRITINGS: SCREENPLAYS—*Electra-Glide in Blue,* United Aritsts, 1973; (with James Kirkwood) *Some Kind of Hero,* Paramount, 1982; (with Carl Gottlieb and Bruce Jay Friedman) *Dr. Detroit,* Universal, 1983; *Oxford Blues,* Metro-Goldwyn-Mayer/United Artists, 1984; *Steele Justice,* Atlantic Productions, 1987.

TELEPLAYS—*Birds of Prey,* CBS, 1973; *Blood Feud,* Operation Prime Time, 1983; (with David Kinghorn) *Deadly Encounter,* CBS, 1983; *Izzy and Moe,* NBC, 1985.

AWARDS: Writers Guild of America Award, 1984, for *Blood Feud.*

MEMBER: Writers Guild of America, Directors Guild of America, Producers Guild of America.

ADDRESSES: HOME—Los Angeles, CA. AGENT—c/o Rand Holston, Creative Artists Agency, 1888 Century Park East, Los Angeles, CA 90067.

*   *   *

BORREGO, Jesse

PERSONAL: Born in San Antonio, TX. EDUCATION: Attended College of the Incarnate Word; trained for the stage at California Institute of the Arts.

JESSE BORREGO

VOCATION: Actor.

CAREER: PRINCIPAL TELEVISION APPEARANCES—Series: Jesse Velasquez, *Fame,* syndicated, 1984—.

PRINCIPAL STAGE APPEARANCES—*Green Card,* Mark Taper Forum, Los Angeles, 1985.

ADDRESSES: PUBLICIST—Michael Levine Public Relations 9123 Sunset Boulevard, Los Angeles, CA 90069.

*   *   *

BOSTWICK, Barry   1945-

PERSONAL: Born February 24, 1945, in San Mateo, CA; son of Henry and Betty Bostwick. EDUCATION: Received B.F.A., acting, from U.S. International University; New York University, graduate work in theatre.

VOCATION: Actor.

CAREER: BROADWAY DEBUT—Title role, *Cock-A-Doodle Dandy,* Lyceum Theatre, 1969. PRINCIPAL STAGE APPEARANCES—Danny Zuko, *Grease,* Eden Theatre, New York City, 1972; Joey, *They Knew What They Wanted,* Marymount Manhattan Theatre, New York City, 1976; title role, *The Robber Bridegroom,* Mark Taper Forum, Los Angeles, CA, then Biltmore Theatre, New York City, 1976; George Nowack, *She Loves Me,* Town Hall, New York City, 1977. Also appeared in *Salvation,* Jan Hus Playhouse, New York City, 1969; *House of Leather, Colette,* both Ellen Stewart Theatre, New York City, 1970; *Soon,* Ritz Theatre, New York City, 1971; *The Screens,* Brooklyn Academy of Music, Brooklyn, New York, 1971; *L'Histoire du Soldat* (opera), State Theatre, New York City; and in *The Death of von Richthofen as Witnessed from Earth.*

MAJOR TOURS—Pirate King, *The Pirates of Penzance,* U.S. cities, 1981.

PRINCIPAL TELEVISION APPEARANCES—Series: Detective Tucker Pendleton, *Foul Play,* ABC, 1981; *Dads,* ABC, 1986. Mini-Series: Title role, *George Washington,* CBS; Paul McGill, *A Woman of Substance;* Spider Elliot, *Scruples,* CBS; title role, *Washington II: The Forging of a Nation,* CBS; Zachary Amberville, *I'll Take Manhattan,* CBS; *Deceptions,* NBC. Movies: *The Chadwick Family,* 1974; *The Quinns,* 1977; *Murder By Natural Causes,* 1979; *You Can't Take It with You; Once Upon a Family,* both 1980; *Moviola: The Silent Lovers,* 1980; *Red Flag,* 1981; *An Uncommon Love,* 1983; *Summer Girl,* 1983; *Betrayed by Innocence,* CBS, 1986. Specials: *Working,* PBS. Guest: *Saturday Night Live,* NBC.

PRINCIPAL FILM APPEARANCES—Brad Majors, *The Rocky Horror Picture Show,* Twentieth Century-Fox, 1975; also appeared in *Movie, Movie,* Warner Brothers, 1979; *Megaforce,* Twentieth Century-Fox, 1982.

RECORDINGS: The Robber Bridegroom (original cast album), Columbia.

BARRY BOSTWICK

AWARDS: Best Actor, Antoinette Perry Award nomination 1972, for *Grease;* Best Featured Actor in a Play, Antoinette Perry Award nomination, 1976, for *They Knew What They Wanted;* Best Actor in a Musical, Antoinette Perry Award, 1977, for *The Robber Bridegroom.*

MEMBER: Actors' Equity Association, Screen Actors Guild.

ADDRESSES: AGENT—William Morris Agency, 151 El Camino Boulevard, Beverly Hills, CA 90212. PUBLICIST—Gerald Siegel Public Relations, 1650 Broadway, New York, NY 10019.

* * *

BREGMAN, Martin 1926-

PERSONAL: Born May 18, 1926, in New York, NY; son of Leon and Ida (Granowski) Bregman; married Elizabeth Driscoll (divorced); married Cornelia Sharpe; children: Michael, Christopher, Marissa. EDUCATION: Attended Indiana University and New York University.

VOCATION: Producer.

CAREER: PRINCIPAL FILM WORK—Producer: *Serpico,* Paramount, 1974; *Dog Day Afternoon,* Warner Brothers, 1975; *The Next Man,* Allied Artists, 1976; *The Seduction of Joe Tynan,* Universal, 1979; *Simon,* Warner Brothers, 1980; *The Four Seasons,* Universal, 1981; *Venom,* Paramount, 1982; *Eddie Macon's Run,* Universal, 1983; *Scarface,* Universal, 1983; *Sweet Liberty,* Universal, 1986; *Real Men,* Metro-Goldwyn-Mayer/United Artists, upcoming.

PRINCIPAL TELEVISION WORK—All as producer. Series: *The Four Seasons,* CBS, 1984. Movies: *S*H*E,* 1980.

ADDRESSES: OFFICE—Martin Bregman Productions, Inc., 641 Lexington Avenue, New York, NY 10022. AGENT—William Morris Agency, 1350 Avenue of the Americas, New York, NY 10019.*

* * *

BREUER, Lee 1937-

PERSONAL: Born February 6, 1937, in Philadelphia, PA; son of Joseph B. (an architect) and Sara (a designer; maiden name, Leopold) Breuer; married Ruth Maleczech (an actress and director), July 27, 1978; children: Clove Galilee, Lute Ramblin'. EDUCATION: University of California, Los Angeles, B.A., 1958; also attended San Francisco State University.

VOCATION: Director and playwright.

CAREER: PRINCIPAL STAGE WORK—Director: *The House of Bernarda Alba,* San Francisco Actors' Workshop, San Francisco, CA, 1963; *The Messingkarf Dialogues,* Edinburgh Festival, Edinburgh, Scotland, U.K., 1968; *Lulu,* American Repertory Theatre, Cambridge, MA, 1980; *The Tempest,* New York Shakespeare Festival, Delacorte Theatre, New York City, 1981; *The Gospel at Colonus,* Brooklyn Academy of Music, Brooklyn, NY, then Grand Opera, Houston, TX, both 1983, later Arena Stage, Washington,

DC, 1984; also directed *Mother Courage,* Paris, France, 1967; *Play,* Paris, 1969, then New York City, 1970; (also choreographer) *The Saint and the Football Players,* American Dance Festival, 1976.

Director, all with Mabou Mines Theatre Group: *Red Horse Animation,* Guggenheim Museum, New York City, 1970, then La Mama Experimental Theatre Club, New York City, 1972; *B. Beaver Animation,* Whitney Museum of American Art, New York City, 1974, then Public Theatre, New York City, 1977; *Shaggy Dog Animation,* Public Theatre, 1978; *A Prelude to Death in Venice,* Public Theatre, 1980; *Hajj,* Public Theatre, 1982; also *Mabou Mines Presents Samuel Beckett,* 1975.

RELATED CAREER—Co-artistic director, Mabou Mines Theatre Group, 1970—; co-artistic director, Re.Cher.Chez., a studio for avant-garde performing arts; lecturer at Yale Drama School, 1978-80, Harvard Extension, 1981-82, New York University, 1981-82, and at various campuses of the University of California; panel member for National Endowment for the Arts.

WRITINGS: PLAYS—See additional production details above: (Adaptor) *The Best Ones,* Theatre for the New City, New York City, 1976, then Mark Taper Forum, Los Angeles, CA, 1979; *Red Horse Animation,* 1970; *B. Beaver Animation,* 1974; *Shaggy Dog Animation,* 1978; *A Prelude to Death in Venice,* 1980, published in *New Plays U.S.A.,* No. 1, 1982; *Sister Suzie Cinema,* Public Theatre, 1980; (with Ruth Maleczech, Craig Jones, and Julie Archer) *Hajj,* 1982, published by P.A.J. Press, 1983; (adaptor) *The Gospel at Colonus,* 1983. COLLECTIONS—*Animations,* includes *Red Horse Animation, B. Beaver Animation,* and *Shaggy Dog Animation,* P.A.J. Press, 1979.

AWARDS: Best Play, Obie Award from the *Village Voice,* 1978, for *Shaggy Dog Animation;* Playwrights' Award, Directors' Award, both Obies, 1980, for *A Prelude to Death in Venice;* Creative Arts Public Service Program Fellowship, 1980; Guggenheim Foundation Fellowship, 1980; National Endowment for the Arts Fellowship, 1980 and 1982; Rockefeller Foundation Fellowship, 1981.

MEMBER: Theatre Communications Group (board of directors, 1979-81), Inter-Art.

ADDRESSES: HOME—92 St. Mark's Place, No. 3, New York, NY 10009. OFFICE—c/o Performing Arts Services, 325 Spring Street, New York, NY 10013. AGENT—c/o Lynn Davis, Davis-Cohen Associates, 513-A Avenue of the Americas, New York, NY 10011.*

* * *

BROWNLOW, Kevin 1938-

PERSONAL: Born June 2, 1938, in Crowborough, England; son of Robert Thomas and Nina (Fortnum) Brownlow; married Virginia Keane, 1969; children: one daughter. EDUCATION: Attended University College School.

VOCATION: Film historian, writer, director, and film editor.

CAREER: PRINCIPAL FILM WORK—Director (with Andrew Mollo), *It Happened Here,* 1966; editor, *Charge of the Light Brigade,* 1967; director (with Mollo), *Winstanley,* 1975; oversaw restoration and served as editor for *Napoleon* (originally released in 1927), 1980.

PRINCIPAL TELEVISION WORK—Series: Director (with David Gill), *Hollywood,* Thames Television, 1980; director, *Unknown Chaplin,* 1983. Movies: Director (with Andrew Mollo), *Charm of Dynamite,* BBC.

RELATED CAREER—Film editor, World Wide Pictures, London, 1955-61, then joint director, 1964; film editor, Samaritan Films, London, 1961-65; film editor, Woodfall Films, London, 1965-68; also worked with Thames Television, 1980—.

WRITINGS: TELEPLAYS—*Hollywood,* Thames Television, 1980. NON-FICTION—*How It Happened Here,* Doubleday, 1968; *The Parade's Gone By . . .,* Knopf, 1968; *The War, the West, and the Wilderness,* Knopf, 1979; *Hollywood: The Pioneers,* Collins, 1980; *Napoleon: Abel Gance's Classic Film,* Knopf, 1983. Edited Karl Brown's *Adventures with D.W. Griffith,* Secker & Warburg, 1974.

AWARDS: Best Original Screenplay, Writers Guild Award, 1966, for *It Happened Here;* Best Editing, British Academy Award nomination, 1968, for *Charge of the Light Brigade;* Special Award, British Film Institute, for *Winstanley.*

MEMBER: British Film Institute (former member, board of governors).

ADDRESSES: AGENT—Harold Matson Co., Inc., 276 Fifth Avenue, New York, NY 10001.*

*   *   *

BRYAN, Dora   1924-

PERSONAL: Born Dora Broadbent, February 7, 1924, in Southport, England; daughter of Albert and Georgina (Hill) Broadbent; married William Lawton, 1954; children: two sons, one daughter (one son and daughter adopted). RELIGION: Christian.

VOCATION: Actress.

CAREER: PRINCIPAL STAGE APPEARANCES—Phyllis Mere, *Peace in Our Time,* Lyric Theatre, London, 1947; Eva, *Travellers Joy,* Criterion Theatre, London, 1948; Phyllis, *Accolade,* Aldwych Theatre, London, 1950; Janet Honeyman, *Simon and Laura,* Strand Theatre, London, 1954; Lily Bell, *The Water Gipsies,* Winter Garden Theatre, New York City, 1955; Julie Skidmore, *The Lovebirds,* Adelphi Theatre, London, 1957; Lorelei, *Gentlemen Prefer Blondes,* Prince's Theatre, London, 1962; title role, *Here's Dora,* Brighton Hippodrome, Brighton, U.K., 1964; Nurse Sweetie, *Too Good to Be True,* Edinburgh Festival, Edinburgh, Scotland, U.K., then Strand Theatre, both 1965; title role, *The Dora Bryan Show,* Royal Court Theatre, Liverpool, U.K., 1965; title role, *Hello Dolly!,* Drury Lane Theatre, London, 1966.

Dol Common, *The Alchemist,* Chichester Festival, Chichester, U.K., 1970; Alice GarthBander, *George and Margaret,* Arnaud Theatre, Guildford, U.K., 1973; Sheila, *Jack and the Beanstalk,* Palladium Theatre, London, 1973; Clarissa, *The Confederacy,* Chichester Festival, 1974; Mrs. Leverett, *Rookery Nook,* Her Majesty's Theatre, London, 1979; Mistress Quickly, *The Merry Wives of Windsor,* Regent's Park, London, 1984; Mrs. Pierce, *Pygmalion,* Plymouth Theatre, New York City, 1987. Also as Post Mistress General, *The Apple Cart,* Royal Haymarket Theatre, London; Mrs. Warren, *Mrs. Warren's Profession;* Mrs. Hardcastle, *She Stoops to Conquer;* and appeared in *The Lyric Revue,* Lyric-

DORA BRYAN

Hammersmith Theatre, then Globe Theatre, both London, 1951; *The Globe Revue,* Globe Theatre, 1952; *At the Lyric,* Lyric-Hammersmith Theater, 1953; *Going to Town,* St. Martin's Theatre, London, 1954; *Living for Pleasure,* Garrick Theatre, London, 1958; *Six of One,* Adelphi Theatre, London, 1963; *They Don't Grow on Trees,* Prince of Wales Theatre, London, 1968; *An Evening with Dora Bryan and Friends,* Palace Theatre, Westcliffe, U.K., 1973; *Charlie Girl,* Victoria Palace, London.

MAJOR TOURS—Sheila, *Relatively Speaking,* 1974.

PRINCIPAL CABARET APPEARANCES—Has performed in Canada, Hong Kong, and London.

FILM DEBUT—*The Fallen Idol,* 1949. PRINCIPAL FILM APPEARANCES—*A Taste of Honey,* 1961; *Two a Penny,* 1968.

PRINCIPAL TELEVISION APPEARANCES—*According to Dora,* 1968; *Both Ends Meet,* 1972; also *A to Z; Saturday Night at the London Palladium.*

AWARDS: Best Actress, British Academy Award, 1961, for *A Taste of Honey;* Best Actress, Variety Club of Great Britain, for *She Stoops to Conquer.*

SIDELIGHTS: RECREATIONS—Reading, quilting, and helping her husband and family run a hotel.

ADDRESSES: HOME—Clarges Hotel, 118 Marine Parade, Brighton, East Sussex BN2 1DD, England. AGENT—James Sharkey, 15 Golden Square, London W1R 3AG, England.

C

CABALERO, Roxann
 See BIGGS, Roxann

* * *

CADORETTE, Mary

PERSONAL: Born in East Hartford, CT; married Michael Eisen. EDUCATION: Received B.A., drama, from University of Connecticut.

VOCATION: Actress, singer, and dancer.

CAREER: PRINCIPAL STAGE APPEARANCES—Chorus and understudy, *42nd Street,* Winter Garden Theatre, then Majestic Theatre, both New York City, 1980; also appeared as Joan in a Florida dinner

MARY CADORETTE

theatre production of *Dames at Sea* and in a summer theatre production of *South Pacific.*

PRINCIPAL TELEVISION APPEARANCES—Series: Vicky Bradford, *Three's Company,* ABC, 1984. Episodic: *The Love Boat,* ABC.

PRINCIPAL FILM APPEARANCES—*Stewardess School,* Columbia, 1986.

NON-RELATED CAREER—Founder, owner, and chef of Gala Gatherings, a gourmet catering service in Los Angeles.

ADDRESSES: PUBLICIST—Michael Levine Public Relations, 8730 Sunset Boulevard, Los Angeles, CA 90069.

* * *

CAGE, Nicholas   1965-

PERSONAL: Born Nicholas Coppola, 1965, in Long Beach, CA. EDUCATION: Studied acting at the American Conservatory Theatre.

VOCATION: Actor.

CAREER: PRINCIPAL FILM APPEARANCES—Randy, *Valley Girl,* Atlantic, 1983; Smokey, *Rumble Fish,* Universal, 1983; Nicky, *Racing with the Moon,* Paramount, 1984; Al Columbato, *Birdy,* Tri-Star, 1984; Vincent Dwyer, *The Cotton Club,* Orion, 1984; Charlie, *Peggy Sue Got Married,* Tri-Star, 1986; H.I., *Raising Arizona,* Twentieth Century-Fox, 1986; also Ronnie, *Moonstruck,* Metro-Goldwyn-Mayer/United Artists, upcoming; *Vampire Kiss,* Tri-Star, upcoming; and appeared in *The Boy in Blue.*

SIDELIGHTS: CTFT learned Nicholas Cage changed his surname to avoid calling attention to the fact that he is the nephew of director Francis Ford Coppola.

ADDRESSES: AGENT—c/o Ed Limato, William Morris Agency, 151 El Camino Drive, Beverly Hills, CA, 90212.*

* * *

CAMERON, Kirk

BRIEF ENTRY: In September of 1986 Kirk Cameron reportedly was receiving four thousand letters a month from fans of his ABC television series *Growing Pains,* which was then beginning its second season. By March 28, 1987, *TV Guide* put the sixteen-year-old actor's fan mail count up to ten thousand letters a month and reported that he could no longer freely visit areas frequented by adolescent girls. According to his co-stars on the family comedy, Cameron nonetheless remained modest and continued to come to rehearsals with his lines fully memorized. He was already an experienced professional, having begun acting in commercials at age nine. Although his mother had expected her son's shyness to hamper his career, he found roles in episodes of various television series and on such made-for-television movies as *Goliath Awaits,* 1981. He also became a regular on the short-lived ABC series *Two Marriages.* At age fourteen Cameron landed the role of the wise-cracking, sometimes devious and smug Mike Seaver on *Growing Pains.* "In the hands of a lesser actor, the character might have been very unlikable," executive producer Steve Marshall told *TV Guide.* In fact, Cameron contrasts his own temperament with his character's, reporting that his gym teacher father and manager mother still expect him to share the chores in their Canoga Park, California home. The family, in turn, helps to handle his fan mail. In 1987 Cameron had his first starring film role in *Like Father, Like Son* with Dudley Moore. Although critics were unenthusiastic about the identity-switch comedy, they praised the young actor's comedic talents.

*   *   *

CANDY, John   1950-

PERSONAL: Full name, John Franklin Candy; born October 31, 1950, in Toronto, ON, Canada; son of Sidney James and Evangeline (Aker) Candy; married Rosemary Margaret Hobor, April 27, 1979; children: Jennifer Anne, Christopher Michael. EDUCATION: Attended Centennial Community College.

VOCATION: Actor, comedian, and writer.

CAREER: PRINCIPAL FILM APPEARANCES—*The Class of '44,* Warner Brothers, 1973; *1941,* Universal, 1979; *Lost and Found,* Columbia, 1979; *The Blues Brothers,* Universal, 1980; *Heavy Metal,* Columbia, 1981; *Stripes,* Columbia, 1981; *It Came from Hollywood,* Paramount, 1982; *Going Berserk,* Universal, 1983; *National Lampoon's Vacation,* Warner Brothers, 1983; *Brewster's Millions,* Universal, 1984; *Splash,* Buena Vista, 1984; *Sesame Street Presents: Follow That Bird,* Warner Brothers, 1985; *Summer Rental,* Paramount, 1985; *Volunteers,* Tri-Star, 1985; *Armed and Dangerous,* Columbia, 1986; *Three Amigos,* Orion, 1986; *Little Shop of Horrors,* Warner Brothers, 1986; *Planes, Trains, and Automobiles,* Paramount, 1987. Also appeared in *It Seemed Like a Good Idea at the Time,* 1975; *Tunnelvision,* 1976; *The Clown Murders,* 1976; *The Silent Partner,* 1978; *Double Negative,* 1980; *The Canadian Conspiracy,* 1986; and in *Find the Lady; Face Off; Tears Are Not Enough.*

PRINCIPAL TELEVISION APPEARANCES—Episodic: Albino Alien, "Cursed with Charisma," *Really Weird Tales,* 1987. Series: *Second City TV,* syndicated, 1977-79, then *SCTV Network 90,* NBC, 1981-83; *Big City Comedy,* syndicated. Movies: *Drums Over Malta.* Specials: *Comic Relief,* HBO, 1986; *Comic Relief 2,* HBO, 1987. Guest: *Saturday Night Live,* NBC.

PRINCIPAL STAGE APPEARANCES—Second City Comedy Troupe, Chicago, IL, 1972-74, then Toronto, ON, 1974-77; also appeared in a satirical revue, *Creeps.*

WRITINGS: TELEVISION SHOWS—*Second City TV; SCTV Network 90; Big City Comedy.* TELEPLAYS—*Drums Over Malta.*

AWARDS: Television and Radio Artists Award, 1978 and 1982; Outstanding Writing in a Variety Program, Emmy Award, 1983, for "The Energy Ball/Sweeps Week," *SCTV Network 90.*

MEMBER: Screen Actors Guild, Writers Guild of America, American Federation of Television and Radio Artists, Alliance of Canadian Cinema.

ADDRESSES: AGENT—c/o John Gaines, Agency for the Performing Arts, 9000 Sunset Boulevard, Suite 1200, Los Angeles, CA, 90069.*

*   *   *

CAPSHAW, Kate

PERSONAL: Born Kathy Sue Nail, in Fort Worth, TX; married John Capshaw (divorced); children: Jessica. EDUCATION: Attended the University of Missouri.

VOCATION: Actress.

CAREER: FILM DEBUT—Katherine, *A Little Sex,* Universal, 1982. PRINCIPAL FILM APPEARANCES—Willie Scott, *Indiana Jones and the Temple of Doom,* Paramount, 1984; Laura, *Best Defense,* Paramount, 1984; Jane Devries, *Dreamscape,* Twentieth Century-Fox, 1984; Emily Reubens, *Windy City,* Warner Brothers, 1984; Sydney Betterman, *Power,* Twentieth Century-Fox, 1986; Andie, *Spacecamp,* Twentieth Century-Fox, 1986; also in *Quite By Chance,* upcoming.

PRINCIPAL TELEVISION APPEARANCES—Series: *The Edge of Night,* ABC. Movies: Elaine Rogers, *Missing Children: A Mother's Story,* CBS, 1982; Susanna McKaskel, *The Quick and the Dead,* HBO, 1987; Annie Goodwin, *Her Secret Life,* ABC, 1987.

NON-RELATED CAREER—Formerly a school teacher.

MEMBER: Screen Actors Guild, American Federation of Television and Radio Artists.

ADDRESSES: AGENT—Creative Artists Agency, 1888 Century Park E., Los Angeles, CA, 90067. PUBLICIST—c/o John West, P/M/K Public Relations, Inc., 8436 W. Third Street, Los Angeles, CA 90048.*

*   *   *

CARA, Irene   1959-

PERSONAL: Born March 18, 1959, in Bronx, NY.

VOCATION: Actress and singer.

CAREER: FILM DEBUT—Angela, *Aaron Loves Angela,* Columbia, 1975. PRINCIPAL FILM APPEARANCES—Title role, *Sparkle,* Warner Brothers, 1976; Coco, *Fame,* Metro-Goldwyn-Mayer/United Artists, 1980; portrayed herself, *D.C. Cab,* Universal, 1983; Ginny

Lee, *City Heat,* Warner Brothers, 1984; Tracy Freeman, *A Certain Fury,* New World, 1985; Simone, *Busted Up,* Shapiro, 1986; also appeared as Jane Flores, *Killing 'em Softly,* 1985; and in *The Man in 5-A.*

BROADWAY DEBUT—*Maggie Flynn,* American National Theatre Academy Playhouse, 1968. PRINCIPAL STAGE APPEARANCES—*The Me Nobody Knows,* Orpheum Theatre, 1970; *Via Galactica,* Uris Theatre, New York City, 1972; *Got Tu Go Disco,* Minskoff Theatre, 1979; also appeared in *Ain't Misbehavin'.*

PRINCIPAL TELEVISION APPEARANCES—Series: *The Electric Company,* PBS, 1972. Mini-Series: Bertha Palmer, *Roots: The Next Generation,* ABC, 1979. Pilots: Irene Cannon, *Irene,* NBC, 1981. Movies: Alice Jefferson, *The Guyana Tragedy: The Story of Jim Jones,* CBS, 1980; Sissy Lovejoy, *Sister, Sister,* NBC, 1982; Myrlie Evers, *For Us, the Living,* PBS, 1983. Specials: *Bob Hope Goes to College,* NBC, 1983; *The 58th Annual Academy Awards Presentation,* ABC, 1986; also appeared in *Tribute to Martin Luther King, Jr.*

RECORDINGS: SINGLES—"Flashdance . . . What a Feeling;" "Fame;" "Out Here on My Own;" "Anyone Can See;" "The Dream;" "Breakdance."

AWARDS: Village Voice Obie Award for *The Me Nobody Knows;* Best Original Song, Academy Award, 1983, Grammy Award, 1983, both for "Flashdance . . . What a Feeling."

MEMBER: Actors' Equity Association, Screen Actors Guild.

ADDRESSES: HOME—104-60 Queens Boulevard, Forest Hills, NY 11375.*

*　　　*　　　*

CARR, Jane

PERSONAL: Born in England; daughter of Patrick (a steel erector) and Gwendoline Rose (a post office employee; maiden name, Clark) Carr; married Mark Arnott (an actor), May 30, 1987. EDUCATION: Attended the Arts Educational School, London; trained for the stage at the Corona Stage School, London.

VOCATION: Actress.

CAREER: STAGE DEBUT—Pippa, *The Spider's Web,* Sheffield Playhouse, U.K., 1964. LONDON DEBUT—Mary McGregor, *The Prime of Miss Jean Brodie,* Wyndham's Theatre, 1965. BROADWAY DEBUT—Fanny Squeers, Miss Snevelilli, and Peg Sliderskew, *The Life and Adventures of Nicholas Nickleby,* Broadhurst Theatre, 1986. PRINCIPAL STAGE APPEARANCES—*Once a Catholic, Mother's Day, What the Butler Saw, The Prime of Miss Jean Brodie, Lovers Dancing,* and *Friends of Dorothy,* all West End productions, London; with the Royal Shakespeare Company: *As You Like It, Look Out, Here Comes Trouble, Much Ado About Nothing, The Caucasian Chalk Circle, A Midsummer Night's Dream, The Twin Rivals, Money, Our Friends in the North, Poppy,* and *Peter Pan; The Merchant of Venice* and *The Way of the World,* both at the Chichester Festival, U.K.; *Spring Awakening* and *The Ticket of Leave Man,* both at the National Theatre, London.

FILM DEBUT—Mary McGregor, *The Prime of Miss Jean Brodie,*

JANE CARR

Twentieth Century-Fox, 1968. PRINCIPAL FILM APPEARANCES—*Something for Everyone,* National General, 1970; also appeared in *Lotte Von Ornstein.*

PRINCIPAL TELEVISION APPEARANCES—Series: Joan, *Upstairs, Downstairs,* BBC in U.K., P.B.S. in U.S. Teleplays: *The School Mistress, Love Among Artists, Daphne Laureola, The Higgler, Minder, Song of Songs, Singles Night, Starting Out,* and *What Mad Pursuit.*

RELATED CAREER—President, Interim Theatre for the Deaf, 1979-81.

AWARDS: Two Laurence Olivier Award nominations, for *Once a Catholic* and *A Midsummer Night's Dream;* co-winner, *Dramalogue* Award and L.A. Theatre Critics Award, both for *The Life and Adventures of Nicholas Nickelby.*

MEMBER: British Actors' Equity Association, British Academy of Film and Television Arts.

ADDRESSES: AGENT—Smith-Freedman & Associates, 121 N. San Vincente Blvd., Beverly Hills, CA 90211.

*　　　*　　　*

CARROLL, Vinnette

PERSONAL: Full name, Vinnette Justine Carroll; born in New York, NY; daughter of Edgar Edgerton (a dentist) and Florence (Morris) Carroll. EDUCATION: Long Island University, B.A.,

1944; Columbia University, graduate work, 1945-46; New York University, M.A., 1946; New School for Social Research, postgraduate work, 1948-50; trained for the stage with Erwin Piscator, Lee Strasberg, and Stella Adler.

VOCATION: Actress, director, writer, theatre administrator, and teacher.

CAREER: STAGE DEBUT—Addie, *The Little Foxes,* Southold Playhouse, Long Island, NY, 1948. LONDON DEBUT—Sophia Adams, *Moon on a Rainbow Shawl,* Royal Court Theatre, 1958. PRINCIPAL STAGE APPEARANCES—Bella, *Deep Are the Roots,* Southold Playhouse, Long Island, NY, 1949; woman, *A Streetcar Named Desire,* City Center Theatre, New York City, 1956; Catherine, *A Grass Harp,* Lakewood Summer Theatre, Lakewood, NJ, 1956; Amelie, *Small War on Murray Hill,* Ethel Barrymore Theatre, New York City, 1957; Tituba, *The Crucible,* Martinique Theatre, New York City, 1958; Dora, *Jolly's Progress,* Longacre Theatre, New York City, 1959; Dido, *The Octoroon,* Phoenix Theatre, New York City, 1961; Sophia Adams, *Moon on a Rainbow Shawl,* East 11th Street Theatre, New York City, 1962; narrator, *Black Nativity,* Criterion Theatre, London, then Festival of the Two Worlds, Spoleto, Italy, both 1962, later Piccadilly Theatre, London, 1963; narrator, *Your Arms Too Short to Box with God,* Festival of the Two Worlds, 1975; also appeared in *A Member of the Wedding,* 1960.

PRINCIPAL STAGE WORK—Director: *Dark of the Moon,* Equity Library Theatre, New York City, 1960; *Ondine,* Equity Library Theatre, 1961; *Black Nativity,* 41st Street Theatre, New York City, 1961; *The Disenchanted,* Equity Library Theatre, 1962; *Black*

© Linda Blase, 1985

VINNETTE CARROLL

Nativity, Criterion Theatre, London, 1962; *Trumpets of the Lord,* Astor Place Theatre, New York City, 1963; *Black Nativity,* Piccadilly Theatre, London, 1963, then Vaudeville Theatre, London, 1964; *The Prodigal Son,* Greenwich Mews Theatre, New York City, 1965; *But Never Jam Today,* City Center Theatre, New York City, 1969; *Bury the Dead, Croesus and the Witch,* both Urban Arts Corps Theatre, New York City, 1971; *Don't Bother Me, I Can't Cope,* Urban Arts Corps Theatre, 1971, then Playhouse Theatre, New York City, and Mark Taper Forum, Los Angeles, CA, both 1972; *Step Lively, Boy,* Urban Arts Corps Theatre, 1973; *The Flies, The Ups and Downs of Theophilus Maitland,* both Urban Arts Corps Theatre, 1974; *Power to Love, Old Judge Is Dead,* both Urban Arts Corps Theatre, 1975; *Your Arms Too Short to Box with God,* Festival of the Two Worlds, Spoleto, Italy, 1975, then Ford's Theatre, Washington, DC, and Lyceum Theatre, New York City, both 1976; *Play Mas, I'm Laughin' But I Ain't Tickled, But Never Jam Today,* all Urban Arts Corps Theatre, 1976; *Alice, The Gingham Dog,* both Urban Arts Corps Theatre, 1977; *When Hell Freezes Over, I'll Skate,* Black Theatre Festival, Lincoln Center, New York City, 1979; *But Never Jam Today,* Longacre Theatre, New York City, 1979; *Lost in the Stars,* San Francisco Opera, San Francisco, CA, 1980; *Your Arms Too Short to Box with God,* Ambassador Theatre, New York City, 1980, then Alvin Theatre, New York City, 1982; *Medea, Next Time I'll Rain Fire, The Green Bay Tree,* all with the Vinnette Carroll Repertory Company, New York City, 1986. Also directed *The Flies,* 1966; *Slow Dance on the Killing Ground,* 1968; *Desire Under the Elms,* 1974; *When Hell Freezes Over, I'll Skate,* 1984.

MAJOR TOURS—Ftatateeta, *Caesar and Cleopatra,* U.S. cities, 1950; one-woman variety show, U.S. and West Indian cities, 1952-57.

PRINCIPAL TELEVISION APPEARANCES—Episodic: Narrator, "Black Nativity," *Westinghouse Theatre,* CBS, 1962; appeared in "Jubilation," *Repertoire Workshop,* CBS, 1964. Specials: Bernice, *A Member of the Wedding,* Granada, 1960; Sojourner Truth, *We the Women,* CBS, 1974.

PRINCIPAL TELEVISION WORK—Director: "Black Nativity," *Westinghouse Theatre,* CBS, 1962; "Beyond the Blues," *Stage Two,* CBS, 1964; "Jubilation," *Repertoire Workshop,* CBS, 1964; *When Hell Freezes Over, I'll Skate,* 1979.

FILM DEBUT—Mother, *A Morning for Jimmy,* 1960. PRINCIPAL FILM APPEARANCES—Martha, *One Potato, Two Potato,* Cinema V, 1964; mother, *Up the Down Staircase,* Warner Brothers/Seven Arts, 1967; recruiting officer, *Alice's Restaurant,* United Artists, 1969.

RELATED CAREER—Director, Ghetto Arts Projects, New York State Council on the Arts; founder, artistic director, Urban Arts Corps Theatre, New York City; founder, director, Vinnette Carroll Repertory Company, New York City, 1986—; teacher of drama, School for the Performing Arts, New York City.

NON-RELATED CAREER—Clinical and industrial psychologist.

WRITINGS: PLAYS—See production details above. (Adaptor) *Trumpets of the Lord,* 1963; co-author, *The Ups and Downs of Theophilus Maitland,* 1974; co-author, *Your Arms Too Short to Box with God,* 1975; *Alice,* 1977; (adaptor) *When Hell Freezes Over, I'll Skate;* 1979. Creator of *But Never Jam Today,* 1969, revised 1976; *Don't Bother Me, I Can't Cope,* 1971; *Power to Love,* 1975; *I'm Laughing But I Ain't Tickled,* 1976.

AWARDS: Obie Award from the *Village Voice,* 1961, for *Moon on a Rainbow Shawl;* Emmy Award, 1964, for ''Beyond the Blues,'' *Stage Two;* Best Director, Outer Critics Circle Award, 1972, Los Angeles Drama Critics Circle Award, 1972, Antoinette Perry Award nomination, 1973, Harold Jackman Memorial Award, 1973, all for *Don't Bother Me, I Can't Cope;* also received Golden Circle Award, 1979; Black Filmmakers Hall of Fame Award, 1979; NAACP Image Award; Ford Foundation Grant for Directors.

MEMBER: Actors' Equity Association, Screen Actors Guild, American Federation of Television and Radio Artists.

SIDELIGHTS: RECREATIONS—Sports cars, horseback riding, building furniture.

ADDRESSES: OFFICE—Urban Arts Corps, 227 W. 17th Street, New York, NY 10011.

*   *   *

CARTER, Dixie   1939-

PERSONAL: Born May 25, 1939, in McLemoresville, TN; daughter of Halbert Leroy (a retail businessman and realtor) and Virginia (Hillsman) Carter; married Hal Holbrook (an actor), May 27, 1984; children: Ginna, Mary-Dixie. EDUCATION: Attended the University of Tennessee, Knoxville, Rhodes College, Memphis, and Memphis State University; studied music, piano, and voice with Robley Lawson, James Quillian, and Jerome Robertson. POLITICS: Republican. RELIGION: Methodist.

VOCATION: Actress and singer.

CAREER: STAGE DEBUT—Julie, *Carousel,* Front Street Theatre, Memphis, TN, 1961. OFF-BROADWAY DEBUT—Perdita, *A Winter's Tale,* with the New York Shakespeare Festival, 1963. LONDON DEBUT—Liz Conlon, *Buried Inside Extra,* Royal Court Theatre, 1983. PRINCIPAL STAGE APPEARANCES—Melba, *Pal Joey,* Circle in the Square Theatre, New York City, 1976; with the New York Shakespeare Festival, New York City: Belle Starr, *Jesse and the Bandit Queen,* 1976, Martha ''Calamity Jane'' Canary, *Fathers and Sons,* 1978, Dixie Avalon, *Taken in Marriage,* 1979; Hannah Mae Bindler, *A Coupla White Chicks Sitting Around Talking,* Astor Place Theatre, New York City, 1980; Liz Conlon, *Buried Inside Extra,* Martinson Hall, Public Theatre, New York City, 1983; appeared in *The King & I, Carousel,* and *The Merry Widow,* all at the Lincoln Center for the Performing Arts, New York City; also *Sextet.*

TELEVISION DEBUT—Brandy Henders, *The Edge of Night,* CBS. PRINCIPAL TELEVISION APPEARANCES—Series: April Baxter, *On Our Own,* CBS, 1977-78; Carlotta Beck, *Filthy Rich,* CBS, 1982-83; Julia Sugar Baker, *Designing Women,* CBS, 1986—. Movies: *OHMS,* 1980.

AWARDS: *Theatre World* Award, 1975-76, for *Jessie and the Bandit Queen,* 1978; Afternoon Television Award.

MEMBER: Actors' Equity Association, Screen Actors Guild, American Federation of Television and Radio Artists.

SIDELIGHTS: Dixie Carter told *CTFT* that she accompanied husband Hal Holbrook with their children on a world tour of his one-man show, *Mark Twain Tonight,* for the U.S. State Department.

ADDRESSES: OFFICE—c/o *Designing Women,* The Burbank Studios, 4000 Warner Blvd., Burbank, CA 91505.

*   *   *

CARTER, Lynda

PERSONAL: Full name Lynda Jean Carter, born July 24, in Phoenix, AZ; married Ron Samuels (divorced); married Robert A. Altman (a lawyer). EDUCATION: Attended Arizona State University; trained for the stage with Stella Adler and Charles Conrad.

VOCATION: Actress, singer, and dancer.

CAREER: PRINCIPAL TELEVISION APPEARANCES—Series: Diana Prince/Wonder Woman, *Wonder Woman,* ABC, 1976-77, then *The New Adventures of Wonder Woman,* CBS, 1977-79; Carole Stanwyck, *Partners in Crime,* NBC, 1984. Pilots: Diana Prince/Wonder Woman, *Wonder Woman,* ABC, 1975. Movies: Zelda, *A Matter of Wife . . . and Death,* NBC, 1976; Brooke Newman, *The Last Song,* CBS, 1980; Brianne O'Neil, *Hotline,* CBS, 1980; title role, *Rita Hayworth: The Love Goddess,* CBS, 1983; Patricia Traymore, *Stillwatch,* CBS, 1987; also appeared in *Born to Be Sold,* NBC, 1981. Specials: *The Olivia Newton-John Show,* ABC, 1976; *Battle of the Network Stars,* ABC, 1976; *A Special Olivia Newton-John,* ABC, 1976; *Circus of the Stars,*

LYNDA CARTER

CBS, 1977; *Lynda Carter's Special,* CBS, 1980; *Lynda Carter: Encore,* CBS, 1980; *Lynda Carter's Celebration,* CBS, 1981; *Lynda Carter: Street Lights,* CBS, 1982; *Happy Birthday, Bob!,* NBC, 1983; *Lynda Carter: Body and Soul,* CBS, 1984; *Bob Hope Buys NBC?,* NBC, 1985; *Night of 100 Stars II,* ABC, 1985; *Bob Hope with His Easter Bunnies and Other Friends,* NBC, 1987; *Happy Birthday, Hollywood,* ABC, 1987.

PRINCIPAL FILM APPEARANCES—Bobbie Jo James, *Bobbie Jo and the Outlaw,* American International, 1976.

PRINCIPAL CONCERT APPEARANCES—Palladium Theatre, London; Sporting Club, Monte Carlo, Monaco; Desert Inn Hotel, Las Vegas, NV; Hotel de la Reforma, Mexico City, Mexico. Also performed in Atlantic City, NJ, and Reno, NV.

NON-RELATED CAREER—Fashion director, Maybelline Cosmetics; member of rock group Garfin Gathering.

AWARDS: Miss World-USA, 1973; Hispanic Woman of the Year Award, 1983; Emmy Award nomination, 1985, for *Lynda Carter: Body and Soul;* Golden Eagle Award, 1986, for Consistent Performance in Television and Film; Ariel Award (Mexico) as International Entertainer of the Year.

MEMBER: American Ballet Theatre; American Cancer Society (national crusade chairperson, 1985-86), Exceptional Children's Foundation (honorary chairperson, 1987-88), United Service Organization (board of governors), National Committee on Arts for the Handicapped, Feed the Hungry, Committee for Creative Nonviolence.

SIDELIGHTS: From material supplied by Lynda Carter's publicist, *CTFT* learned that Carter became the first entertainer to associate herself with a major women's professional tennis tournament, "The Lynda Carter/Maybelline Tennis Challenge," held annually in Palm Springs, CA.

ADDRESSES: HOME—Washington, DC; Los Angeles, CA. OFFICE—Lynda Carter Productions, P.O. Box 5973, Sherman Oaks, CA 91413. AGENT—c/o Fred Westheimer, William Morris Agency, 151 El Camino Drive, Los Angeles, CA 90212. PUBLICIST—c/o Carla Schulman, Rogers and Cowan, 10000 Santa Monica Boulevard, Suite 400, Los Angeles, CA 90067.

*   *   *

CARTERET, Anna   1942-

PERSONAL: Born Anna Wilkinson, December 11, 1942, in Bangalore, India; daughter of Peter John and Patricia Carteret (Strahan) Wilkinson; married Christopher Morahan. EDUCATION: Trained for the stage at Arts Educational School.

VOCATION: Actress.

CAREER: STAGE DEBUT—Cloud, Jumping Bean, *Jack and the Beanstalk,* Palace Theatre, Watford, U.K., 1957. LONDON DEBUT—Wendy, *Peter Pan,* Scala Theatre, 1960. PRINCIPAL STAGE APPEARANCES—Honey, *Who's Afraid of Virginia Woolf?,* Titania, *A Midsummer Night's Dream,* Gloria Clandon, *You Never Can Tell,* Mariana, *Measure for Measure,* Polly Peachum, *The Beggar's Opera,* Cyprienne, *Let's Get a Divorce,* Constance, *She Stoops to*

Conquer, Anitra, green woman, *Peer Gynt,* all with the Bristol Old Vic Theatre Company, Bristol, U.K., 1964-66; Fiona Jones, *Big Bad Mouse,* Shaftesbury Theatre, London, 1966; Eliza, *Pygmalion,* Theatre Royal, Bristol, U.K., 1974; Fanny Wilton, *John Gabriel Borkman,* Lyttelton Theatre, London, 1976; Olivia, *Twelfth Night,* Greenwich Theatre, London, 1977; Portia, *The Merchant of Venice,* Isabella, *Measure for Measure,* Mistress Page, *The Merry Wives of Windsor,* all St. George's Theatre, London, 1977; Mrs. Cheveley, *An Ideal Husband,* Dona Elvira, *Don Juan,* both Greenwich Theatre, 1978; Ann Troubridge, *Daughters of Men,* Hampstead Theatre Club, London, 1979. Also appeared with repertory companies in Windsor, U.K. and Lincoln, U.K., 1962-63.

All with the National Theatre Company, performing at the Old Vic Theatre, London, unless indicated: Chorus, *Oedipus,* Elena, *The Advertisement,* both 1968; Norma, *Rites,* Nurse Sweet, *The National Health,* Jacquenetta, *Love's Labour's Lost,* Fusima, *Back to Methuselah,* Maria, *The Travails of Sancho Panza,* all 1969; Nerissa, *The Merchant of Venice,* 1970; Giacinta, *Scapino,* Young Vic Theatre, London, 1970; Roxane, *Cyrano,* Cambridge Theatre, London, 1970; Virgilia, *Coriolanus,* 1971; Lucille, *Danton's Death,* New Theatre, London, 1971; secretary, *Jumpers,* Queen Isabel, *Richard II,* Peggy Grant, *The Front Page,* maid, *School for Scandal,* all 1972; Anya, *The Cherry Orchard,* Olivia, *Twelfth Night,* Virginia, *Saturday, Sunday, Monday,* Susie Plaistow, *The Party,* all 1973; Fanny Wilton, *John Gabriel Borkman,* 1975; Denis Quilly, *Tribute to a Lady,* 1976; various roles, *Lark Rise,* Phoebe, *As You Like It,* Queen Elizabeth, *Richard III,* Adele Natter, *Undiscovered Country,* all 1979.

MAJOR TOURS—With the National Theatre Company: Anabella, *Tis Pity She's a Whore,* U.K. cities, 1972; gentlewoman, *Macbeth,* U.K. cities, 1973.

PRINCIPAL TELEVISION APPEARANCES—Series: *The Pallisers; The Glittering Prizes; Send in the Girls.*

PRINCIPAL FILM APPEARANCES—*The Plank; Dateline Diamonds.*

SIDELIGHTS: RECREATIONS—Gardening, walking, dancing.

ADDRESSES: AGENT—Fraser and Dunlop, 91 Regent Street, London W1, England.*

*   *   *

CASS, Ronald   1923-

PERSONAL: Born April 21, 1923, in Llanelli, Wales; son of Saul (a jeweler) and Rachel (a draper; maiden name, Palto) Cass; married Valerie Dorothy Carton (an actress and singer), June 30, 1955; children: Deborah Anne, Stephen Cecil, Nicola Jane. EDUCATION: Attended University College of Wales, 1941-42, 1946-48. RELIGION: Jewish. MILITARY: Royal Air Force.

VOCATION: Composer, musical director, and script editor.

CAREER: Also see *WRITINGS* below. PRINCIPAL STAGE WORK—Musical director: *Deja Revue, Move Along Sideways,* both 1975; *The Thoughts of Chairman Alf,* 1977. PRINCIPAL TELEVISION WORK—Episodic: Script editor, "Starbursts," *Entertainment Express,* Central Television. Series: Musical director, program associate, *Highway,* ITV, 1984—.

WRITINGS: REVUES—All as composer of score. *10:15 Revue,* Irving Theatre, London, 1951; *The Irving Revue,* Irving Theatre, 1952; (also book) *Jack and the Beanstalk,* Palladium Theatre, London, 1968; also provided score for *Just Lately, Intimacy at Eight,* both 1952; *High Spirits,* 1953; *Intimacy at 8:30,* 1954; *For Amusement Only,* 1956; *Harmony Close,* 1957; *For Adults Only,* 1958; *The Lord Chamberlain Regrets . . .,* 1961; *Enrico,* 1963; *Deja Revue,* 1975; *Blondes and Bombshells,* 1979. FILM SCORES— *Summer Holiday,* 1963; *Best House in London,* 1969; *The Virgin and the Gypsy,* 1970; also *The Young Ones; Go to Blazes; French Dressing; Wonderful Life.* TELEVISION SCORES—Series: *This Is Tom Jones.* Specials: *The Gentle Flame; Sing a Song of Sixpence; Easter in Rome.*

PLAYS, PRODUCED—Co-author, *Kingdom Coming,* 1972; *A Well-Ordered Affair,* 1976; *Blondes and Bombshells,* 1979. TELEPLAYS—(With Donald Ross) "Affair on Demand," *Love Boat,* ABC; (with Ron Moody) *The Other Side of London.*

NON-FICTION—*A Funny Thing Happened, or An Anthology of Pro's; The Highway Companion.* FICTION—*True Blue; Fringe Benefits.*

AWARDS: Best Musical Score for Film or Theatre, Ivor Novello Award, 1963, for *Summer Holiday;* received Burma Star from Royal Air Force.

SIDELIGHTS: RECREATIONS—Bridge, cricket.

ADDRESSES: HOME—27-A Elsworthy Road, London NW3,

RONALD CASS

England. OFFICE—15 Bloomsbury Square, London WC1, England. AGENT—c/o Nina Blatt, Coach House, One Larptent Avenue, London SW15, England.

*   *   *

CATES, Phoebe

BRIEF ENTRY: The lavish 1984 mini-series *Lace* made former model Phoebe Cates a recognizable star. The leading role of the long lost daughter grown to international sex symbol in the television adaptation of the bestselling novel was one Cates actively pursued despite being eight years younger than the character as written. Then twenty years old, she had already made one episode of a television series that was immediately cancelled—*Mr. and Mrs. Dracula*—and had roles in such films for the teenage market as *Paradise, Fast Times at Ridgemont High,* both 1982, and *Private School,* 1983. *Lace,* however, gave her the opportunity to work with such professionals as Angela Lansbury and was so successful that Cates reprised her role in *Lace 2,* 1985. She also became determined "to do serious theater," as she told the *New York Post* (June 28, 1984). Her resolve brought her back to her native New York, where she won a part in the New York Shakespeare Festival's 1984 production of the Russian play *The Nest of the Wood Grouse.* The same year she had a leading role in the hit movie *Gremlins.* Cates's original goal had been a career in dance; she won a scholarship to the School of American Ballet and was attending the Professional Children's School when a knee injury forced her to change her plans. She then became a model and did commercials, but she told *TV Guide* that modeling may not be good preparation for an acting career because it "puts such importance on mugging . . . making faces. And that's very different from acting" (February 25, 1984).

*   *   *

CHADBON, Tom   1946-

PERSONAL: Born February 27, 1946, in Luton, England; son of Thomas William (a banker) and Josie Yvonne (Cook) Chadbon; married Deborah Leathers, July 4, 1966 (divorced, 1970); married Jane Hennessy (a designer), July 20, 1977; children: Dominic, Nicholas, Amelia, Felicity. EDUCATION: Attended Victoria College; trained for the stage at the Webber-Douglas Academy and the Royal Academy of Dramatic Art.

VOCATION: Actor.

CAREER: STAGE DEBUT—Philosopher, *Galileo,* Phoenix Theatre, Leicester, U.K., 1967. LONDON DEBUT—Valentine, *Twelfth Night,* Royal Court Theatre, 1968. PRINCIPAL STAGE APPEARANCES—All in London unless indicated: Oliver, *The Houses by the Green,* Royal Court Theatre, 1968; Barry, *Saved,* Prince of Wales, *Early Morning,* Tommie White, *Inside-out,* all Royal Court Theatre, 1969; Laurie, *Cheek,* John Lennon, *No One Was Saved,* both Theatre Upstairs, 1970; Saturninus, *Titus Andronicus,* Round House Theatre, 1971; Said, *The Screens,* New Vic Theatre, Bristol, U.K., 1973; Stanley Kowalski, *A Streetcar Named Desire,* Playhouse Theatre, Liverpool, U.K., 1975; Gasparo, *The White Devil,* Old Vic Theatre, 1976; Alan Jeffcote, *Hindle Wakes,* Greenwich Theatre, 1978; Brian, *Middle-Age-Spread,* Lyric Theatre, 1979.

Photography by Beryl Vosburgh

Also Leontes, *A Winter's Tale,* Bristol Old Vic Theatre, Bristol, U.K.; Petie, *Moving House,* Farnham, U.K., 1977.

MAJOR TOURS—Brian, *Middle-Age-Spread,* U.K. cities, 1979-81.

TELEVISION DEBUT—*The Jazz Age,* BBC, 1968. PRINCIPAL TELEVISION APPEARANCES—Series: *The Expert.* Also over 100 episodic and series appearances including: *Hamlet; A Room with a View; The Liver Birds; The Creeper; Country Matters.*

FILM DEBUT—*Say Hello to Yesterday,* Cinerama, 1968. PRINCI-PAL FILM APPEARANCES—*Juggernaut,* United Artists, 1974; *Tess,* Columbia, 1981; *Dance with a Stranger,* Samuel Goldwyn, 1985. Also appeared in *The Beast Must Die; The Last of Linda Cleer; Sarnett Saga.*

AWARDS: Honors and Principals Medal, Royal Academy of Dramatic Art.

SIDELIGHTS: FAVORITE ROLES—Leontes, *A Winter's Tale.*

ADDRESSES: AGENT—c/o Michael Ladkin, 11 Garrick Street, London WC1, England.

*   *   *

CHAMBERLAIN, Richard   1935-

PERSONAL: Full name, George Richard Chamberlain; born March 31, 1935, in Los Angeles, CA; son of Charles (in sales) and Elsa Chamberlain. EDUCATION: Pomona College, B.A., art, 1956; studied voice at the Los Angeles Conservatory of Music; studied acting with Jeff Corey and in England. MILITARY: U.S. Army, 1956-58, served in Korea; became sergeant.

VOCATION: Actor, director, and producer.

CAREER: BROADWAY DEBUT—Jeff Claypool, *Breakfast at Tiffany's,* four performances (show closed in previews), 1966. PRINCIPAL STAGE APPEARANCES—Title role, *Hamlet,* Birmingham Repertory Theatre, Birmingham, U.K., 1969; title role, *Richard II,* Seattle Repertory Theatre, Seattle, WA, 1971, Ahmanson Theatre, Los Angeles, CA, 1972, then Eisenhower Theatre, Kennedy Center, Washington, DC, 1972; Thomas Mendip, *The Lady's Not for Burning,* Chichester Festival Theatre, Chichester, U.K., 1972; title role, *Cyrano de Bergerac,* Ahmanson Theatre, 1973; Reverend Shannon, *The Night of the Iguana,* Ahmanson Theatre, 1975, then Circle in the Square, New York City, 1976; Sergius, *Arms and the Man,* Williamstown Theatre Festival, Williamstown, MA, 1980; Wild Bill Hickock, *Fathers and Sons,* Public Theatre, New York Shakespeare Festival, then Other Stage, Los Angeles, 1981; Charles, *Blithe Spirit,* Neil Simon Theatre, New York City, 1987. Also appeared in *The Fantasticks,* Arlington Park, IL, 1973; in *Born Every Minute,* New York City; in stock productions of *Private Lives, The Philadelphia Story,* and *West Side Story;* as well as participating in *The Night of 100 Stars,* Radio City Music Hall, 1982.

PRINCIPAL STAGE WORK—Director, *The Shadow Box,* Williamstown Theatre Festival, 1978.

FILM DEBUT—*The Secret of Purple Reef,* Twentieth Century-Fox,

1960. PRINCIPAL FILM APPEARANCES—Sadistic husband, *Petulia,* Warner Brothers, 1968; Peter Ilyich Tchaikovsky, *The Music Lovers,* United Artists, 1971; Octavius, *Julius Caesar,* American International, 1971; Lord Byron, *Lady Caroline Lamb,* United Artists, 1972; Aramis, *The Three Musketeers,* Twentieth Century-Fox, 1974; son-in-law, *The Towering Inferno,* Twentieth Century-Fox, 1974; Aramis, *The Four Musketeers,* Twentieth Century-Fox, 1975; Prince Charming, *The Slipper and the Rose: The Story of Cinderella,* Universal, 1977; Dr. Hubbard, *The Swarm,* Warner Brothers, 1978; David Burton, *The Last Wave,* World Northal, 1979; Alan Quartermain, *King Solomon's Mines,* Cannon, 1985; Alan Quartermain, *Alan Quartermain and the Lost City of Gold,* Cannon, 1987. Also appeared in *A Thunder of Drums,* Metro-Goldwyn-Mayer (MGM), 1961; *Twilight of Honor,* MGM, 1963; *Joy in the Morning,* MGM, 1965; *The Madwoman of Chaillot,* Warner Brothers, 1969; and *Murder by Phone,* 1982.

PRINCIPAL TELEVISION APPEARANCES—Episodic: *Gunsmoke,* CBS; *Bourbon Street Beat,* ABC; *Thriller,* NBC; *Mr. Lucky,* CBS; *Alfred Hitchcock Presents,* CBS. Series: Dr. James Kildare, *Dr. Kildare,* NBC, 1961-66. Pilots: Title role, *Paradise Kid,* 1960. Mini-Series: Ralph Touchet, *Portrait of a Lady,* BBC, 1968; Alexander McKeag, *Centennial,* NBC, 1978; John Blackthorne, *Shogun,* NBC, 1980; Father Ralph de Bricassart, *The Thorn Birds,* ABC, 1983; Raoul Wallenberg, *Wallenberg,* NBC, 1985; John C. Fremont, *Dream West,* CBS, 1986. Movies: King Edward VIII, *The Woman I Love,* 1973; F. Scott Fitzgerald, *F. Scott Fitzgerald and "The Last of the Belles,"* 1974; Edmond Dantes, *The Count of Monte Cristo,* 1975; title role, *The Man in the Iron Mask,* 1978; Dr. Frederick Cook, *Cook and Perry: The Race to the Pole,* 1983. Specials: Title role, "Hamlet," *Hallmark Hall of Fame,* NBC, 1970; Thomas Mendip, *The Lady's Not for Burning,* PBS, 1974; Bobby, *Company,* PBS, 1979.

RELATED CAREER—Founder and executive producer, CHAM Enterprises, a production company operating on a non-exclusive agreement with Warner Brothers Television; founding member, Company of Angels, Los Angeles theatre company. Has released two record albums.

AWARDS: Favorite Male Performer, *TV Guide* Poll, 1963, three *Photoplay* Gold Medals and Hollywood Women's Press Club award, 1960s, for *Dr. Kildare,;* Best Actor, Golden Globe Award, 1980, Best Actor Award, *TV Times* London, 1980, Best Actor, Emmy Award nomination, 1980, all for *Shogun;* Best Actor, Golden Globe Award, People's Choice Award, Best Actor in a Dramatic Series or Mini-Series, *US Magazine* award, Emmy Award nomination, all 1983, for *The Thorn Birds;* Honorary degrees: doctorate from Pomona College.

MEMBER: Actors' Equity Association, Screen Actors Guild, American Federation of Television and Radio Artists.

SIDELIGHTS: Richard Chamberlain first achieved renown as the star of *Dr. Kildare* on network television, then went on to challenging stage and film roles before returning to the small screen as the acknowledged "king of prestige television" for his many acclaimed mini-series and dramatic specials. Those who have worked with Chamberlain commend his professionalism and the exacting attention he brings to his wide variety of roles. In a March 26, 1983 *TV Guide* article, producer David Victor commented that since his days as *Dr. Kildare,* Chamberlain has "never failed to be there for every scene, even if it was only to react to another actor, and he never stopped learning." Victor continued: "At one point, early on, a magazine critic called Richard 'a bland bottle of milk.' Now they call him the actor of the decade.''

Chamberlain first turned to acting while an undergraduate art major at Pomona College. ''I was extremely shy,'' he told *TV Guide* (March 16, 1963). ''In college I was a hermit. I sat in my little room and I painted pictures. . . . Then I discovered acting. The stage seemed like a place where you could be free. Free to express your emotions . . . free to move . . . free to shout. It seemed like a way to have fun without getting involved in life.''

After an army stint in Korea upon college graduation, Chamberlain returned to Los Angeles and to painting, but gradually he drifted back into the more social art of the stage play. Although he considered his acting skills to need improvement, he was able to secure small roles on such television shows as *Gunsmoke* and *Alfred Hitchcock Presents* and starred in the pilot for a series that did not go into production. In 1960 and 1961 he appeared in two films, *The Secret of the Purple Reef* and a western, *A Thunder of Drums;* neither was a box office hit.

Chamberlain was given the *Dr. Kildare* role almost by default, according to executive producer Norman Felton, but from its first episode on September 28, 1961, the show and Chamberlain were unqualified successes. In *TV Guide* Chamberlain attributed Kildare's appeal to ''neither mysterious nor heroic qualities, but rather the somewhat blank innocence of inexperience.'' Whatever his traits, the handsome physician-in-training was quite popular with women. Chamberlain received a then-unprecedented twelve thousand fan letters every week, and the show had an estimated eighty million viewers in thirty-one countries worldwide. It ran for five years—then Chamberlain decided he wanted to pursue more challenging work.

A December 26, 1983 *People* article observed that the actor ''shook off the pretty-boy stigma'' of Dr. Kildare by moving to England to study drama. His performance as Hamlet at the Birmingham Repertory Theatre received highly complimentary reviews; when he returned to the United States, it was as a serious stage actor with what *Time*'s T.E. Kalem characterized as ''a magnetic presence that holds an audience in thrall.'' The critic described Chamberlain's technique: ''His delivery is intelligent, inflectively exact, and he conducts his voice as if it were an orchestra of verse'' (April 26, 1971).

Television and popular films continued to lure Chamberlain, however. He unabashedly admitted in *TV Guide* that he appeared in such Hollywood extravaganzas as *The Towering Inferno* and *The Swarm* ''for money''—nearly a half-million dollars per film. He maintained his reputation as a marketable matinee idol when he played the swashbuckling Aramis in the comedy-adventure movies *The Three Musketeers* and *The Four Musketeers*. In 1978 a new career avenue opened for Chamberlain when he agreed to portray the Scottish trapper Alexander McKeag in the television mini-series production of James Michener's *Centennial*. Producers noted that Chamberlain still drew audiences to television, especially if he portrayed a romantic adventurer. After *Centennial*, he starred as John Blackthorne in the epic *Shogun*, another very popular miniseries, despite its unfamiliar subject and use of Japanese dialogue.

Chamberlain's made-for-television movies, such as *Cook and Peary: The Race to the Pole* and *The Count of Monte Cristo*, also combined interesting stories, top-line production techniques, and fine supporting casts, further enhancing the star's prestige. Although he suddenly had clout, according to *TV Guide*, he also found

himself laboring under ''a reputation as a cold, emotionless performer—a brilliant technical actor who could move across the stage with grace, who understood makeup and lighting, who had a resonant voice and eloquent gestures, but who lacked passion.''

That general opinion changed in 1983 when Chamberlain came to the television screen as Father Ralph de Bricassart in the twenty-one million dollar mini-series *The Thorn Birds*, based on Colleen McCullough's bestselling novel. The role of the handsome priest torn between his vows, his career ambitions, and his love for a beautiful woman was one ''that everyone . . . had said that Richard Chamberlain seemed destined to play,'' *TV Guide* remarked. More than 110 million viewers saw at least part of *The Thorn Birds*, making it the most popular mini-series of the 1980s thus far. Although the filming had its tense moments as its dedicated star argued for more creative control of his role, the immense attention the production received ultimately allayed his sense of frustration. ''I was very hyped up,'' Chamberlain told *People* when he heard about the ratings. ''I felt the energy of all those millions of people watching me on TV.'' Chamberlain received his third Emmy nomination for his work as Father Ralph, but he has yet to take home one of the awards. He told *People*, however, ''You can't be in this business for awards.''

A reclusive star, Chamberlain avoids the press and is zealous in his protection of his personal life. He shares his Los Angeles home with several cats and dogs, studying yoga and consciousness-expanding techniques with Dr. William Brugh Joy. The actor credits this holistic healer with showing him how to transcend his cool, withdrawn persona and let his emotions unfold. Chamberlain told *People* (September 22, 1980) that Brugh Joy's techniques have helped him come to a new and healthier position in his career. ''I have much more positive and creative directions,'' he said, ''a much better flow in my life. . . . I don't know what's around the next corner, and I'm fascinated to find out.''

ADDRESSES: AGENT—c/o Chasin-Park-Citron Agency, 9255 Sunset Boulevard, Los Angeles, CA 90069.*

                              *   *   *

CHELTON, Nick   1946-

PERSONAL: Born June 18, 1946, in London, England; son of Frederick Harold and Violet Maud (Ingram) Chelton. EDUCATION: Trained as a lighting designer with Theatre Projects, 1964-65.

VOCATION: Lighting designer.

CAREER: FIRST LONDON STAGE WORK—Lighting designer, *Hamlet*, Cambridge Theatre, 1971. PRINCIPAL STAGE WORK— Lighting designer: *Love's Labour's Lost, The Way of the World, Antony and Cleopatra,* and many others, all with the Royal Shakespeare Company. Has also lit numerous London productions at Sadler's Wells Theatre, Royal Court Theatre, Old Vic Theatre, Palladium Theatre, and for the English National Opera, Welsh National Opera, Scottish Opera, and Royal Opera.

RELATED CAREER—Lighting consultant, Kent Opera, Kent, U.K.

NON-RELATED CAREER—Electrician.

ADDRESSES: OFFICE—76 Rodwell Road, London SE22, England.*

CHONG, Tommy 1938-

PERSONAL: Born May 24, 1938, in Edmonton, AB, Canada; son of Stanley and Lorna Jean (Gilchrist) Chong.

VOCATION: Actor, writer, director, comedian, and musician.

CAREER: PRINCIPAL FILM APPEARANCES—Man Stoner, *Up in Smoke,* Paramount, 1978; Chong, *Cheech and Chong's Next Movie,* Universal, 1980; Chong, *Cheech and Chong's Nice Dreams,* Columbia, 1981; Chong, Prince Habib, *Things Are Tough All Over,* Columbia, 1982; Chong, *Still Smokin',* Paramount, 1983; El Nebuloso, *Yellowbeard,* Orion, 1983. Also appeared in *It Came From Hollywood,* Paramount, 1983; *The Corsican Brothers,* Orion, 1984; *After Hours,* Warner Brothers, 1985.

PRINCIPAL FILM WORK—See above for production details. Director: *Cheech and Chong's Next Movie; Cheech and Chong's Nice Dreams; Still Smokin'; The Corsican Brothers.*

RELATED CAREER—Member of the musical groups the Shades and Bobby Taylor and the Vancouvers; founder and performer, City Works, improvisational comedy troupe; with Richard "Cheech" Marin, member of comedy duo Cheech and Chong.

WRITINGS: SCREENPLAYS—See above for production details. All with Richard "Cheech" Marin: *Up in Smoke; Cheech and Chong's Next Movie; Cheech and Chong's Nice Dreams; Things Are Tough All Over; Still Smokin'; The Corsican Brothers.* SONGS— "Up in Smoke," 1978.

RECORDINGS: ALBUMS—*Sleeping Beauty; Los Cochimos.*

AWARDS: Best Comedy Album, Grammy Award, 1973, for *Los Cochimos.*

ADDRESSES: OFFICE—Monterey Peninsula Artists, P.O. Box 7308, Carmel, CA 93921.*

*   *   *

CHRISTIANSON, Catherine 1957-

PERSONAL: Born February 10, 1957, in Evanston, IL; daughter of Hilmar Bauman and Betty Marie (Hoelscher) Christianson. EDUCATION: Received B.A. from Vassar College; M.F.A. from Goodman School of Drama; trained for the stage with Uta Hagen at the Herbert Berghof Studios.

VOCATION: Actress.

CAREER: STAGE DEBUT—Ursula, *Much Ado about Nothing,* Center Stage, Baltimore, MD, 1981. OFF-BROADWAY DEBUT— Woman, *Romance,* Public Theatre 1984. BROADWAY DEBUT— Laurie, *I'm Not Rappaport,* Lyceum Theatre, 1986. PRINCIPAL STAGE APPEARANCES—Jule, *They Dance to the Sun,* Playhouse in the Park, Cincinnati, OH, 1984; Marie, *Come Back Little Sheba,* Delaware Theatre Company, Wilmington, DE, 1985. Appeared as wife, *The Animal Fair,* Ensemble Studio Theatre, New York City; Agnes, *Agnes of God,* Theatre Virginia, Richmond, VA; Bianca, *The Taming of the Shrew,* Walnut Street Theatre, Philadelphia, PA; Babe, *Crimes of the Heart,* Sheryl, *New Mexican Rainbow Fishing,* both Peterborough Players, Peterborough, NH; Laura, *The Glass*

CATHERINE CHRISTIANSON

Menagerie, Theatre Virginia, Hyde Park Festival Theatre, Hyde Park, NY.

MAJOR TOURS—Laurie, *I'm Not Rappaport,* U.S. cities, 1986.

PRINCIPAL FILM APPEARANCES—Mary, *Four Friends,* Filmways, 1981.

PRINCIPAL TELEVISION APPEARANCES—Series: Dr. Amy Stone, *All My Children,* ABC, 1986; Lula, *The Edge of Night.*

MEMBER: Actors' Equity Association, Screen Actors Guild, American Federation of Television and Radio Artists.

ADDRESSES: AGENT—c/o The Gage Group, 1650 Broadway, Suite 406, New York, NY 10019.

*   *   *

CILENTO, Diane 1933-

PERSONAL: Born October 5, 1933, in Brisbane, Australia; daughter of Sir Raphael West (a surgeon) and Phyllis (McGlew) Cilento; married Andrea Volpe, 1955 (divorced, 1962); married Sean Connery (an actor), 1962 (divorced, 1973); children: (first marriage) one daughter; (second marriage) Jason. EDUCATION: Trained for the stage at the American Academy of Dramatic Art and the Royal Academy of Dramatic Art.

VOCATION: Actress and writer.

CAREER: LONDON DEBUT—Louka, *Arms and the Man,* Arts Theatre, 1953. PRINCIPAL STAGE APPEARANCES—Juliet, *Romeo and Juliet,* Library Theatre, Manchester, U.K., 1953; Gina Hayworth, *One Fair Daughter,* Q Theatre, London, 1953; Diaphanta, *The Changeling,* Wyndham's Theatre, London, 1954; Dixie Evans, *The Big Knife,* Duke of York's Theatre, London, 1954; Helen, *Tiger at the Gates,* Apollo Theatre, London, then Plymouth Theatre, New York City, both 1955; title role, *Zuleika,* Manchester Opera House, Manchester, U.K., 1957; Mia, *Less Than Kind,* Arts Theatre, London, 1957; Carol Cutrere, *Orpheus Descending,* Royal Court Theatre, London, 1959; Ellie Dunn, *Heartbreak House,* Billy Rose Theatre, New York City, 1959; Marie-Paule, *The Good Soup,* Plymouth Theatre, 1960; Ersilia Drei, *Naked,* Oxford Playhouse, Oxford, U.K., 1960; title role, *Miss Julie,* Lyric Hammersmith Theatre, London, 1960; Dona Inez de Castro, *Queen After Death,* Oxford Playhouse, 1961; Leni, *Altona,* Royal Court Theatre, then Saville Theatre, both London, 1961; Anne Fox, *My Place,* Comedy Theatre, London, 1962; Eleonore, *Castle in Sweden,* Piccadilly Theatre, London, 1962; Ersilia Drei, *Naked,* Royal Court Theatre, 1963; Beatrice, *The Four Seasons,* Saville Theatre, 1965; Ludmila, *Marya,* Royal Court Theatre, 1967; Sarah, *I've Seen You Cut Lemons,* Fortune Theatre, London, 1969; Nastasya, *The Idiot,* Old Vic Theatre, London, 1970; Katherine Winter, *Collaborators,* Duchess Theatre, London, 1973; Rosaria, *The Artful Widow,* Greenwich Theatre, London, 1976; Laura, *The Father,* Open Space Theatre, London, 1979.

PRINCIPAL STAGE WORK—Director, Theatre Upstairs, *tuff,* London, 1977; director, *The Streets of London,* Stratford Theatre, London, 1980.

FILM DEBUT—*The Angel Who Pawned Her Harp.* PRINCIPAL FILM APPEARANCES—*The Admirable Crichton* (also known as *Paradise Lagoon*), Columbia, 1957; *The Truth About Women,* Continental, 1958; *Stop Me Before I Kill!,* Columbia, 1961; *I Thank a Fool,* Metro-Goldwyn-Mayer, 1962; *The Naked Edge,* United Artists, 1962; *Tom Jones,* Lopert, 1963; *Rattle of a Simple Man,* Continental, 1964; *The Agony and the Ecstasy,* Twentieth Century-Fox, 1965; *Hombre,* Twentieth Century-Fox, 1967; *Negatives,* Continental, 1968. Also appeared in *The Breaking Point,* 1964; *The Boy Who Had Everything,* 1984; *For the Term of His Natural Life,* 1985. and in *Passing Strangers; Passage Home; Woman for Joe; Jet Storm; The Full Treatment; Partners; Turning.*

PRINCIPAL TELEVISION APPEARANCES—Episodic: Sadie Thompson, *Rain,* ABC (Britain), 1960; Lina, "Festival of Pawns," *Espionage,* NBC, 1964; "Cut Yourself a Slice of Throat," *Blackmail,* ITV, 1965; Prince Boriarsi, *The Girl from U.N.C.L.E.,* NBC, 1967; *The Kiss of Blood,* BBC-2, 1968. Series: *La Bell France.* Specials: *The Small Servant,* NBC, 1955; Bianca, "Taming of the Shrew," *Hallmark Hall of Fame,* NBC, 1956; Geraldine, "Once Upon a Tractor," *UN Drama,* ABC, 1965. Also appeared in *Lysistrata; Court Martial; Rogues Gallery; Dial M for Murder.*

*WRITINGS:*BOOKS—*The Manipulator,* 1967; *Hybrid,* 1971.

AWARDS: Variety New York Drama Critics Poll, 1956, for *Tiger at the Gates;* Theatre World Award, 1956.

MEMBER: Actors' Equity Association, British Actors' Equity Association.

ADDRESSES: AGENT—Crouch Associates, 59 Frith Street, London W1, England.*

CLANCY, Deidre   1943-

PERSONAL: Born March 31, 1943, in London, England; adopted daughter of Julie M. Clancy; married Michael Steer. EDUCATION: Attended Birmingham College of Art.

VOCATION: Costume and set designer.

CAREER: FIRST STAGE WORK—Set designer, *Christmas Pantomime,* Theatre Royal, Lincoln, U.K., 1965. FIRST NEW YORK STAGE WORK—Costume designer, *Landscape and Silence,* Forum Theatre, 1970. PRINCIPAL STAGE WORK— Costume designer: *Cato Street,* Young Vic Theatre, London, 1971; (also set designer) *Hedda Gabler,* Stratford Festival of Canada, Stratford, ON, Canada, 1971; (also set designer) *Macbeth,* Stratford Festival of Canada, 1971; *Quetzalcoatl,* Round House Theatre, London, 1972; *Spring Awakening, Twelfth Night, Grand Manoeuvres,* all Old Vic Theatre, London, 1974; *The Playboy of the Western World,* Old Vic Theatre, 1975; *Watch It Come Down, Il Campiello,* both National Theatre, London, 1976; *Volpone, The Madras House, The Plough and the Stars,* all National Theatre, 1977; *Plenty, Strife,* both National Theatre, 1978; (also set designer) *Il Seraglio* (opera), Kent Opera, Kent, U.K., 1978; *Cosi Fan Tutte,* Metropolitan Opera House, New York City, 1980. Also costume designer for *June Evening,* Manchester, U.K., 1968; *Hamlet,* Nottingham, U.K., then London, both 1971; *Willie Rough,* Edinburgh, Scotland, U.K., 1972; *The Thrie Estates, The Bevellers,* both Edinburgh, U.K., 1974; (also set designer) *Trinity Tales,* Birmingham, U.K., 1975; *The Voysey Inheritance, How Mad Tulloch Was Taken Away,* both Edinburgh, U.K., 1975; *The White Devil, As You Like It,* both Nottingham, U.K., 1975; *Eugene Onegin* (opera), Scottish Opera, 1979.

Costume designer, all for the Royal Court Theatre, London: *The Daughter-in-Law,* (also set designer) *The Ruffian on the Stair,* (also set designer) *The Erpingham Camp,* all 1967; *A Collier's Friday Night, The Widowing of Mrs. Holyroyd,* both 1968; *Marya,* 1969; *Trixie and Baba,* (also set designer) *Early Morning,* (also set designer) *Uncle Vanya,* all 1970; *Sleeper's Den, Lear,* both 1971; *Crete,* (also set designer) *Sergeant Pepper,* (also set designer) *Hedda Gabler,* all 1971; (also set designer) *The Sea,* 1973; *Entertaining Mr. Sloane,* 1974.

PRINCIPAL FILM WORK—Costume designer: *The Virgin and the Gypsy,* Chevron, 1970; *The Girl from Petrovka,* Universal, 1974.

PRINCIPAL TELEVISION WORK—Costume designer for numerous series and plays.

SIDELIGHTS: RECREATIONS—Music.

ADDRESSES: AGENT—Simpson Fox Associates, 57 Fylmer Road, London SW6, England.*

*   *   *

CLARK, Mara   1930-

PERSONAL: Born Alice Maire Olds, March 29, 1930, in Middlefield, MA; daughter of George W. (a general store owner, town clerk, and town treasurer) and Grace H. (postal worker and librarian; maiden name, Cook) Olds; married Thomas J. Clark (in electronics sales), June 20, 1953; children: David, George. EDUCATION: Berkshire

MARA CLARK

Business College, 1948; Northern Essex Community College, A.B., arts, 1977; Salem State College, B.A., 1979; trained for the stage with Uta Hagen, and at the Randall Theatre School; studied voice with Alice Brady and Mady Christians.

VOCATION: Actress.

CAREER: STAGE DEBUT—Housekeeper, *Man of La Mancha,* Hampton Playhouse, Hampton, NH, 1966. PRINCIPAL STAGE APPEARANCES—Mother Fisher, *The Show Off,* Kate Keller, *All My Sons,* Madam Arcati, *Blithe Spirit,* Veta Louise, *Harvey,* all Lyric Stage, Boston, MA; Madam Xenia, *The Killing of Sister George,* Aunt Eller, *Oklahoma!,* both Theatre by the Sea, Portsmouth, NH; Mrs. Potter, *The Light in the Mill,* Theatre Express, Merrimack Repertory Theatre, Lowell, MA. Also appeared in *Mission Hill; The Autumn Garden; The Bat; Cabaret; Come Blow Your Horn; Don't Drink the Water; The Guardsman; Hedda Gabler; The Lion in Winter; The Music Man; See How They Run; Six Rms Riv Vu; The Shadow Box; The Sound of Music; Watch on the Rhine.*

MAJOR TOURS—One-woman shows throughout New England; also with the Chamber Repertory Theatre, 1960s and 1970s.

TELEVISION DEBUT—Village woman, *Summer Solstice,* ABC, 1980. PRINCIPAL TELEVISION APPEARANCES—Episodic: Bag lady, *Spencer for Hire,* ABC, 1986. Movies: Waitress, *Billy Galvin,* PBS, 1987; inspector, *Three Sovereigns for Sarah,* PBS; German grandmother, *I Love You, I Love You Not,* PBS. Also appeared in *Kennedy; A Question of Rape; Safety Net.* VIDEO—Games: Appeared as Madam Rose in *Clue* and *Clue II: Murder in Disguise,* both Parker Brothers, Inc.

FILM DEBUT—Widow Dee, *The Verdict,* Twentieth Century-Fox, 1982. PRINCIPAL FILM APPEARANCES—Animal officer, *The Parent Trap II,* Buena Vista, 1987.

RELATED CAREER—Producer, director, and teacher, YWCA children's theatre, Newburyport, MA, 1960-75; producer, director, and actor, Comedy Theatre Company.

MEMBER: Actors' Equity Association, American Federation of Television and Radio Artists, Screen Actors Guild, American Film Institute; Anna Saques Hospital Corporation (board of directors, 1968—), YWCA, Newburyport, MA (board of directors, 1961-69, president, 1968-69).

SIDELIGHTS: FAVORITE ROLES—Veta Louise in *Harvey,* Kate Keller in *All My Sons,* and Madam Arcati in *Blithe Spirit.*

ADDRESSES: HOME—4 Maple Terrace, Newbury, MA, 01951.

*   *   *

CLARKE, Richard   1930-

PERSONAL: Born January 31, 1930, in Durham, England; son of Robert William (a railroad worker) and Mary Eileen (Morrow) Clarke; EDUCATION: Received B.A. from Reading University.

VOCATION: Actor.

CAREER: PRINCIPAL STAGE APPEARANCES—Carr Gomm, con-

RICHARD CLARKE

ductor, *The Elephant Man,* Booth Theatre, New York City, 1979; Reverend Dodgson, Dean Liddell, *Looking-Glass,* Entermedia Theatre, New York City, 1982. Appeared in *Poor Richard,* Helen Hayes Theatre, New York City, 1964; *Cyrano de Bergerac, Tiger at the Gates, Saint Joan,* all Vivian Beaumont Theatre, New York City, 1968; *Conduct Unbecoming,* Ethel Barrymore Theatre, New York City, 1970; *Trelawny of the Wells,* Public Theatre, New York City, 1970; *The Trials of Oz,* Anderson Theatre, New York City, 1972; *Mrs. Warren's Profession,* Yale Repertory Theatre, New Haven, CT, 1981; *Over My Dead Body,* Hartman Theatre, Stamford, CT, 1984, *The Team,* Hartman Theatre, 1985; *Hay Fever,* Music Box Theatre, New York City, 1985; *Breaking the Code,* Neil Simon Theatre, New York City, 1987. Also *Design for Living, The Philanthropist, Much Ado about Nothing,* all Goodman Theatre, Chicago, IL; *No Time for Comedy,* McCarter Theatre, Princeton, NJ; *Love Letter on Blue Paper,* Syracuse Stage, Syracuse, NY.

PRINCIPAL FILM APPEARANCES—*A Night to Remember,* Rank, 1958; *Cleopatra,* Twentieth Century-Fox, 1963; *John and Mary,* Twentieth Century-Fox, 1969; *Midnight Cowboy,* United Artists, 1969; also appeared in *The Protector.*

PRINCIPAL TELEVISION APPEARANCES—Episodic: "Ghost Hunter," *Tales from the Darkside,* syndicated. Series: *The Edge of Night,* NBC; *As the World Turns,* CBS; *Search for Tomorrow,* CBS; *Another World,* NBC; *Ryan's Hope,* ABC; *The Guiding Light,* CBS. Movies: *The Elephant Man,* ABC. Specials: "Soldier in Love," *Hallmark Hall of Fame,* NBC; "The Chinese Prime Minister," *Hollywood Televison Theatre.*

MEMBER: Actors' Equity Association, Screen Actors Guild, American Federation of Television and Radio Artists.

ADDRESSES: AGENT—c/o Triad Artists, Inc., 888 Seventh Avenue, New York, NY 10106.

*   *   *

CLAYBURGH, Jill   1944-

PERSONAL: Born April 30, 1944 in New York, NY; daughter of Albert Henry (a manufacturing executive) and Julia (a former theatrical production secretary; maiden name, Door) Clayburgh; married David Rabe (a playwright), March, 1979; children: two. EDUCATION: Sarah Lawrence College, B.A., philosophy, 1966; trained for the stage with Uta Hagen and John Lehne.

VOCATION: Actress.

CAREER: FILM DEBUT—*The Wedding Party,* filmed 1963, released 1969. PRINCIPAL FILM APPEARANCES—Israeli soldier, *Portnoy's Complaint,* Warner Brothers, 1972; Carole Lombard, *Gable and Lombard,* Universal, 1976; Barbara Jane Bookman, *Semi-Tough,* United Artists, 1977; Erica Benton, *An Unmarried Woman,* Twentieth Century-Fox, 1978; Caterina, *Luna,* Twentieth Century-Fox, 1979; Marilyn, *Starting Over,* Paramount, 1979; mathematician, *It's My Turn,* Columbia, 1980; Judge Loomis, *First Monday in October,* Paramount, 1981; Barbara Gordon, *I'm Dancing as Fast as I Can,* Paramount, 1982; title role, *Hannah K.,* Universal, 1983; Diana Sullivan, *Shy People,* Cannon, 1987. Also appeared in *The Thief Who Came to Dinner,* Warner Brothers, 1972; *The Terminal Man,* Warner Brothers, 1974; *Silver Streak,*

Twentieth Century-Fox, 1976; and in *Where Are the Children?,* 1986.

OFF-BROADWAY DEBUT: *The Nest,* Mercury Theatre, 1970. BROADWAY DEBUT—Hannah Cohen, *The Rothschilds,* Lunt-Fontanne Theatre, 1970. PRINCIPAL STAGE APPEARANCES—Pippin's wife, *Pippin,* Imperial Theatre, New York City, 1972; Gilda, *Design for Living,* Circle in the Square, New York City, 1984. Also appeared as Desdemona in a 1971 Los Angeles production of *Othello* and in *Jumpers* at the Billy Rose Theatre, New York City, 1974. With Charles Street Repertory Company, Boston, MA, appeared in *America Hurrah, The Balcony, Love for Love,* and *Dutchman* in the late 1960s. Other roles include those in *It's Called the Sugarplum, Devil's Disciple,* and *In the Boom Boom Room.*

PRINCIPAL TELEVISION APPEARANCES—Series: Grace Bolton, *Search for Tomorrow,* CBS. Movies: Wanda, *Hustling,* 1975; *Griffin and Phoenix,* 1976. Guest: *Saturday Night Live,* NBC.

AWARDS: Emmy Award nomination, 1976, for *Hustling;* Best Actress, Cannes Film Festival Award, 1978, Best Actress, Academy Award nomination, 1979, and Best Film Actress, Golden Apple Award, all for *An Unmarried Woman;* Best Actress, Academy Award nomination, 1980, for *Starting Over.*

SIDELIGHTS: Critics have hailed Jill Clayburgh as one of Hollywood's most affecting embodiments of the 1980s woman. She has often portrayed vulnerable yet capable women who must juggle work, love, and parenthood while still searching for self-awareness. As Scot Haller noted in a March, 1982 *Saturday Review* profile: Clayburgh's films "grapple with social mores: divorce, the high anxieties of single life, the conflicts between careers and romance. . . . Her feisty women are the bruised but decorated heroes of the sexual revolution."

Two major dramatic films—*An Unmarried Woman,* for which she won the prestigious best actress award at the Cannes Film Festival, and *I'm Dancing as Fast as I Can*—established Clayburgh's credentials as a star. Both of these vehicles, as well as her comedies *Semi-Tough* and *Starting Over,* explore sensitive issues facing Americans in an era of failing marriages, drug dependency, and professional pressures. In an April 4, 1982 feature story in *Parade,* Anna Quindlen called Clayburgh "a kind of modern everywoman—smart, funny, accomplished, yet human and struggling with the demands of independence. At a time when women everywhere are learning about both the perquisites and the pitfalls of liberation, she has given life to its dilemmas onscreen."

Clayburgh claims to be apolitical, a performer who chooses her parts more for dramatic challenge than for social statement. However, her own career and personal life have reflected the issues her films depict. Raised in a privileged neighborhood in New York City, the strong-willed Clayburgh quarrelled with her parents and drove herself ambitiously from an early age. "I started going to a shrink in second grade," she told the *New York Times* (December 15, 1976). "I was very violent and self-destructive." In a September 7, 1978 *Rolling Stone* interview, she said: "I was very screwed up. . . . I didn't like the lives of the people I saw around me very much. I think I was always just searching for something I didn't have—it was frightening. Acting really gave me a chance to get out of that."

Clayburgh discovered theatre arts when her college roommate, a drama major, invited her to work in summer stock in Williamstown, Massachusetts. The atmosphere provided Clayburgh with a welcome release and she began to study acting with the same intensity that had previously seemed so self-destructive. By the time she graduated from college, her circle of friends included such other future notables as director Brian De Palma and actor Robert De Niro. After acting training with Uta Hagen in New York in 1966, Clayburgh joined the Charles Street Repertory Company in Boston. There she became romantically involved with another struggling young actor, Al Pacino.

They lived together in Boston and New York, with Clayburgh accepting many roles in order to finance the household. For a time she appeared as Grace Bolton on the soap opera *Search for Tomorrow* during the day and in Off-Broadway plays at night. Eventually she won roles on Broadway in *The Rothschilds* and *Pippin*, but was still regarded as "Al Pacino's girlfriend" in New York acting circles, according to Patricia Leigh Brown (*Rolling Stone*, September 7, 1978).

A turning point in Clayburgh's career came when she failed to win a role in the 1973 Lincoln Center production of David Rabe's *In the Boom Boom Room*. Clayburgh told Bernard Drew of *American Film* (April, 1979) that she was furious when Madeline Kahn got the part. "She had something of a Hollywood name," Clayburgh recalled, "and I thought if a Hollywood name is what they're so hot for in New York, well, then, California, here I come." She went west and garnered an Emmy nomination as best actress for the 1975 television movie *Hustling*, in which she gave a quirky edge to the part of a street prostitute. Then she starred in *Gable and Lombard*, a feature film that critics panned, although they praised her work. She next was asked to play the female lead in Gene Wilder's coast-to-coast train comedy *Silver Streak*. The film was a commercial success, and on the basis of its popularity Clayburgh was enlisted to appear in the offbeat Burt Reynolds comedy *Semi-Tough*. That too was a hit and she began to be approached for more serious roles.

In the 1978 film *An Unmarried Woman*, Clayburgh portrayed Erica Benton, a suddenly deserted spouse who must face life alone after more than fifteen years of marriage. *Saturday Review*'s Haller felt that in this work the actress "created a character of such timeliness and verisimilitude that Erica Benton immediately entered the cultural consciousness." Frank Rich was even more enthusiastic in his March 6, 1978 *Time* review: "Erica is a role this gifted actress had deserved for years, and now that she has it, she doesn't fool around. She swings gracefully from mood to mood—from hostile confrontations to hysterical shrink sessions to intimate and comic romantic interludes," he exclaimed, continuing, "She is vulnerable and tough, innocent and cynical, cool and sexy. Erica comes alive in a way film characters rarely do." Director Paul Mazursky told *American Film* that he was astonished with Clayburgh's performance; "Jill brought tons of things to the role I never put into it," he said. For her work Clayburgh received her first Oscar nomination as well as best actress honors at the Cannes Film Festival.

Clayburgh's roles subsequent to *An Unmarried Woman* spanned a wide range of characters and styles. She received her second Academy Award nomination for her part as a nursery school teacher in *Starting Over*. She played a mathematics professor in the romantic comedy *It's My Turn*, an opera diva in the dramatic art film *Luna*, and a Supreme Court justice in *First Moday in October*. A particularly demanding role was that of Barbara Gordon, a successful television producer whose addiction to Valium nearly destroyed her life, in the 1982 biographical feature *I'm Dancing as Fast as I Can*. Scot Haller wrote: "As played by Clayburgh, Barbara Gordon is . . . a self-made woman with self-inflicted wounds. . . . Swerving from utter confidence to utter fear in a split

second, Clayburgh captures Gordon's ambivalence about her business and love affairs.''

Clayburgh married playwright David Rabe in 1979 and gave birth to her first child in 1982. Since then she has had a lower profile in Hollywood, though she still reads numerous scripts for possible films. Back on September 30, 1979, she told the *New York Times*, "People think there's this wonderful garden of growing scripts," yet she found, ". . . There isn't much that's worth picking." Haller, however, predicted continuing success for her: "Depicting working women as facts of life instead of as pioneers, creating heroines who speak their minds instead of babbling polemic, presenting women motivated by personal feelings instead of by political ideology, Clayburgh's movies have given us a more sophisticated view than those of her colleagues. . . . Just when when you least expect it, the lady turns triumphant."

ADDRESSES: AGENT—Creative Artists Agency, 1888 Century Park E., Suite 1400, Los Angeles, CA 90067. PUBLICIST—c/o Press Relations, Universal Pictures, 445 Park Avenue, New York, NY 10022.*

*   *   *

CLAYTON, Jack   1921-

PERSONAL: Born March 1, 1921, in Brighton, England; married Christine Norden (divorced); married Katherine Kath (divorced). RELIGION: "Lapsed Catholic." MILITARY: Royal Air Force, 1939-46; became commanding officer in film unit.

VOCATION: Director, producer, and writer.

CAREER: PRINCIPAL FILM WORK—Director and co-cinematographer, *Naples Is a Battlefield*, Royal Air Force production, 1944; second unit director, *Bond Street*, 1948; production manager, *An Ideal Husband*, 1948; associate producer, *Queen of Spades*, 1949; associate producer, *Flesh and Blood*, 1949; associate producer, *Moulin Rouge*, 1952; associate producer, *Beat the Devil*, 1953; associate producer, *The Good Die Young*, 1954; associate producer, *I Am a Camera*, Distributors Corporation of America, 1955; producer and director, *The Bespoke Overcoat*, Romulus Films, 1956; producer, *Sailor Beware!* (also known as *Panic in the Parlor*), Distributors Corp. of America, 1956; producer, *Dry Rot*, 1956; producer, *Three Men in a Boat*, 1956; producer, *The Story of Esther Costello*, 1957; producer, *The Whole Truth*, Columbia, 1958; director, *Room at the Top*, Continental, 1959; producer and director, *The Innocents*, Twentieth Century-Fox, 1961; director, *The Pumpkin Eater*, Royal International, 1964; producer and director, *Our Mother's House*, Metro-Goldwyn-Mayer, 1967; director, *The Great Gatsby*, Paramount, 1974; director, *Something Wicked This Way Comes*, Buena Vista, 1983.

RELATED CAREER—Third assistant director, London Films, 1935; assistant director, then editor, London Films, 1936-40; former associate producer, Romulus Films.

WRITINGS: SCREENPLAYS—*Naples Is a Battlefield*, 1944.

AWARDS: Venice Festival Prize, 1956, for *The Bespoke Overcoat*; Best Director, British Academy Award and Academy Award nomination, 1959, for *Room at the Top*.

MEMBER: Directors Guild of America, Association of Cinematograph, Television, and Allied Technicians.

SIDELIGHTS: CTFT learned that before he entered a film-making career, Jack Clayton trained as a racing ice skater.

ADDRESSES: HOME—Heron's Flight, Highfield Park, Marlow, Buckinghamshire, England. AGENT—International Creative Management, 8899 Beverly Blvd., Los Angeles, CA 90048.

*   *   *

COE, Peter   1929-1987

OBITUARY NOTICE—See index for *CTFT* sketch: Born April 18, 1929, in London, England; died in an automobile accident, May 25, 1987. Director Peter Coe practiced his art throughout the world, having staged musicals, dramas, and operas in Europe, North America, Israel, India, and Australia. His first London success came in 1959 with the musical *Lock Up Your Daughters* and by 1961 he had three hits running simultaneously—*The Miracle Worker, The World of Suzie Wong,* and *Oliver!.* He also directed both the Australian and Broadway productions of *Oliver!* as well as its U.S. national tour and the 1983 London and 1984 Broadway revivals. Among Coe's many other directing achievements were the Broadway productions of *Golden Boy,* 1964, and *On a Clear Day You Can See Forever,* 1966, and the London productions of *Barnum,* 1981, and *Great Expectations,* 1984. His operatic credits included *The Love of Three Oranges, The Angel of Fire,* and *Ernani.* In 1981 Coe received an Antoinette Perry Award nomination as Best Director for *A Life,* and in 1982 he won the award for his revival of *Othello.*

OBITUARIES AND OTHER SOURCES: New York Times, June 3, 1987; *Variety,* May 27, 1987.

*   *   *

COHEN, Alexander H.   1920-

PERSONAL: Born July 24, 1920, in New York, NY; son of Alexander H., Sr. and Laura (Tarantous) Cohen; married Jocelyn Newmark, January 11, 1942 (divorced, February, 1956); married Hildy Parks (an actress, playwright, and producer), February 25, 1956; children: (first marriage) one daughter; (second marriage) two sons. EDUCATION: Attended New York University and Columbia University. MILITARY: U.S. Army, 1942-43.

VOCATION: Producer.

CAREER: FIRST BROADWAY STAGE WORK—Producer, *Ghost for Sale,* Daly's Theatre, 1941. PRINCIPAL STAGE WORK—Producer, all in New York City unless indicated: (With Shepard Straube) *Angel Street,* John Golden Theatre, 1941; (with Sam H. Grisman) *They Should Have Stood in Bed,* Mansfield Theatre, 1942; *Bright Lights of 1944,* Forrest Theatre, 1943; (with Joseph Kipness) *The Duke in Darkness,* Playhouse Theatre, 1944; (with James Russo and Michael Ellis) *Jenny Kissed Me,* Hudson Theatre, 1948; (with Robert L. Joseph) *King Lear,* National Theatre, 1950; (with Jule Styne and Harry Rigby) *Make a Wish,* Winter Garden Theatre, 1951; (with Michael Ellis and James Russo) *Courtin'*

Time, Royale Theatre, 1951; *Be Your Age,* 48th Street Theatre, 1953; (with Ralph Alswang) *The Magic and the Loss,* Booth Theatre, 1954; *The First Gentleman,* Belasco Theatre, 1957; *Love Me Little,* Helen Hayes Theatre, 1958; *At the Drop of a Hat,* John Golden Theatre, 1959.

An Evening with Mike Nichols and Elaine May, John Golden Theatre, 1960; *An Evening with Yves Montand,* John Golden Theatre, 1961; *Lena Horne's Nine O'Clock Revue,* Shubert Theatre, New Haven, CT, 1961; (also director) *Beyond the Fringe,* John Golden Theatre, 1962; *The School for Scandal,* Majestic Theatre, 1963; *An Evening with Maurice Chevalier,* Ziegfeld Theatre, 1963; *Lorenzo,* Plymouth Theatre, 1963; *Ages of Man,* Lyceum Theatre, 1963; *Karmon Israeli Dancers,* Royale Theatre, 1963; *Man and Boy,* Brooks Atkinson Theatre, 1963; *The Doctor's Dilemma,* Royal Haymarket Theatre, London, 1963; *Beyond the Fringe 1964,* John Golden Theatre, 1964; *The Roses Are Real,* Vaudeville Theatre, London, 1964; *Rugantino,* Mark Hellinger Theatre, 1964; *Hamlet,* Lunt-Fontanne Theatre, 1964; *Comedy in Music Opus 2,* John Golden Theatre, 1964; (also director) *Beyond the Fringe '65,* Ethel Barrymore Theatre, 1964; *Ivanov,* Yvonne Arnaud Theatre, then Phoenix Theatre, both London, 1965; *Baker Street,* Broadway Theatre, 1965; *Maurice Chevalier at 77,* Alvin Theatre, 1965; *Ken Murray's Hollywood,* John Golden Theatre, 1965; *The Devils,* Broadway Theatre, 1965; *You Never Can Tell, The Importance of Being Oscar, The Rivals,* all Royal Haymarket Theatre, London, 1966; *Ivanov,* Shubert Theatre, 1966; *A Time for Singing,* Broadway Theatre, 1966; *At the Drop of Another Hat,* Booth Theatre, 1966; *Halfway Up the Tree,* Brooks Atkinson Theatre, 1967; *The Merchant of Venice,* Royal Haymarket Theatre, London, 1967; *The Homecoming,* Music Box Theatre, 1967; *Black Comedy, White*

ALEXANDER H. COHEN

Lies, both Ethel Barrymore Theatre, 1967; *Little Murders,* Broadhurst Theatre, 1967; *The Unknown Soldier and His Wife,* Vivian Beaumont Theatre, then George Abbott Theatre, 1967; *Hellzapoppin' '67,* Garden of Stars, Montreal, PQ, Canada, 1967; *Marlene Dietrich,* Lunt-Fontanne Theatre, 1967, then Mark Hellinger Theatre, 1968; *Plaza Suite,* Lyric Theatre, 1969; *The Price,* Duke of York's Theatre, London, 1969; *We Who Are About To. . .,* Hampstead Theatre Club, London, restaged as *Mixed Doubles,* Comedy Theatre, London, both 1969; *His, Hers, Theirs,* Apollo Theatre, London, 1969; *Dear World,* Mark Hellinger Theatre, 1969.

(With Allan Davis) *Come As You Are,* New Theatre, then Strand Theatre, both London, 1970; (with Eddie Kulukundis) *The Happy Apple,* Apollo Theatre, London, 1970; (with Bill Freedman) *Who Killed Santa Claus?,* Piccadilly Theatre, London, 1970; *1776,* New Theatre, London, 1970; *Home,* Morosco Theatre, 1970; *Prettybelle,* Shubert Theatre, Boston, MA, 1971; (with Bernard Delfont) *Applause,* Her Majesty's Theatre, London, 1972; (with Rocky H. Aoki) *Fun City,* Morosco Theatre, 1972; (with Bernard Delfont) *6 Rms Riv Vu,* Helen Hayes Theatre, 1972; *Good Evening,* Plymouth Theatre, 1973; *Ulysses in Nighttown,* Winter Garden Theatre, 1974; (with Harvey Granat) *Words and Music,* John Golden Theatre, 1974; (with Bernard Delfont) *Who's Who in Hell,* Lunt-Fontanne Theatre, 1974; *We Interrupt This Program,* Ambassador Theatre, 1975; *Comedians,* Music Box Theatre, 1976; *Anna Christie,* Imperial Theatre, 1977; *I Remember Mama,* Majestic Theatre, 1979; (with Hildy Parks) *A Day in Hollywood/A Night in the Ukraine,* John Golden Theatre, 1980; (with Hildy Parks and Cynthia Wood) *84 Charing Cross Road,* Nederlander Theatre, 1982; *Beethoven's Tenth,* Ahmanson Theatre, Los Angeles, CA, 1983; *Parade of Stars Playing the Palace,* Palace Theatre, 1983; (with Hildy Parks) *Edmund Kean,* Brooks Atkinson Theatre, 1983; (with Hildy Parks) *La Tragedie de Carmen,* Vivian Beaumont Theatre, 1983; (with Hildy Parks) *Play Memory,* Longacre Theatre, 1983; (with Hildy Parks) *Accidental Death of an Anarchist,* Belasco Theatre, 1984; *Night of 100 Stars II,* Radio City Music Hall, 1985; (with Hildy Parks) *Bright Lights,* Mark Hellinger Theatre, 1987. Also produced *Season of Goodwill,* London, 1964; *Harvey,* London, 1975; *Overheard,* London, 1981; *Beethoven's Tenth,* London, 1983.

PRINCIPAL TELEVISION WORK—Producer: *A World of Love,* CBS, 1970; *Emmy Awards,* 1978; *Parade of Stars Playing the Palace,* 1983; *Emmy Awards,* 1985; *Emmy Awards,* 1986; *Happy Birthday Hollywood,* 1987; *CBS: On the Air (A Celebration of 50 Years),* CBS; *NBC 60th Anniversary Special,* NBC; *The Best of Everything; Steppin' Out with the Ladies;* has also produced the live broadcast of the Antoinette Perry (Tony) Awards annually since 1967. Executive producer: *Night of 100 Stars,* ABC, 1982; *Night of 100 Stars II,* ABC, 1985. PRINCIPAL TELEVISION APPEARANCES—Guest: *Musical Theatre,* CBS, 1964; *Hy Gardner Show,* 1965; *The Scene,* 1966.

RELATED CAREER: Founder of the Nine O'Clock Theatre.

AWARDS: Special Citation, Outer Circle Award, 1963, for "innovation befitting the development of the intimate revue in New York City through the production of the Nine O'Clock Theatre"; Sam S. Shubert Foundation Award, 1963, for "outstanding contribution to the legitimate theatre"; Outer Circle awards, 1967, for *Black Comedy, The Homecoming,* and for his contribution to the Antoinette Perry awards; Best Play, Antoinette Perry Award, 1967, for *The Homecoming;* Best Play, Antoinette Perry Award nomination, 1967, for *Black Comedy;* Best Play, Antoinette Perry Award

nomination, 1971, for *Home;* Emmy Award, 1971, for *The 1971 Tony Awards; Evening Standard* Award, 1972, for *Applause;* Theatre World Award, 1973, for his annual television production of the Antoinette Perry awards; Best Play, Antoinette Perry Award nomination, 1974, for *Ulysses in Nighttown;* Outstanding Program Achievement—Special Events, Emmy Award, 1980, for *The 34th Annual Tony Awards;* Outstanding Variety, Music, or Comedy Program, Emmy Award, 1982, for *Night of 100 Stars.*

MEMBER: Actors' Fund of America (vice-president; trustee), Players Club, Society of West End Theatre (London); City Athletic Club.

ADDRESSES: OFFICE—(New York) Shubert Theatre, 225 W. 44th Street, New York, NY 10036; (London) Eight Sloane Street, London SW1, England.

*   *   *

COLLIER, Patience   1910-1987

PERSONAL: Born Rene Ritcher, August 19, 1910, in London, England; died in London, July 13, 1987; daughter of Paul and Eva (Spitzel) Ritcher; married H.O.J. Collier (a biologist); children: one son, two daughters. EDUCATION: Trained for the stage at the Royal Academy of Dramatic Art, 1930-32.

VOCATION: Actress.

CAREER: STAGE DEBUT—Various roles, *Versailles,* Kingsway Theatre, London, 1932. BROADWAY DEBUT—Miss Gilchrist, *The Hostage,* Cort Theatre, 1960. PRINCIPAL STAGE APPEARANCES—Mrs. Blount, *Well, Gentlemen,* Cambridge Theatre, London, 1932; Italian peasant, *Josephine,* Haymarket Theatre, London, 1934; American wife, *Roulette,* Duke of York's Theatre, London, 1935; Madame Zaros, *The Velvet Moss,* Watergate Theatre, London, 1950; Charlotta, *The Cherry Orchard,* Lyric Hammersmith Theatre, London, 1954; Madame Parole, *My Three Angels,* Lyric Hammersmith Theatre, 1955; Maria, *The Power and the Glory,* Violet, *The Family Reunion,* both Phoenix Theatre, London, 1956; Anya Pavlikov, *Nude with Violin,* Globe Theatre, London, 1956; *Living for Pleasure,* Garrick Theatre, London, 1958; Putana, *Tis Pity She's a Whore,* Mermaid Theatre, London, 1961; Regan, *King Lear,* Theatre des Nations, Paris, France, 1963; Serena, *The Judge,* Cambridge Theatre, 1967; Bessie Berger, *Awake and Sing,* Hampstead Theatre Club, London, 1971; Sarah, *The Old Ones,* Royal Court Theatre, London, 1972; La Poncia, *The House of Bernarda Alba,* Greenwich Theatre, London, 1973; Anna, *A Month in the Country,* Chichester Festival, Chichester, U.K., 1974; Nurse Guiness, *Heartbreak House,* Old Vic Theatre, London, 1975; mother, *Brand,* Carlotta, *The Cherry Orchard,* both Olivier Theatre, London, 1978.

With the Royal Shakespeare Company, Memorial Theatre, Stratford-on-Avon, U.K. and Aldwych Theatre, London: Charlotta, *The Cherry Orchard,* 1961; Natella Abashwili, *The Caucasian Chalk Circle,* Queen, *Cymbeline,* Regan, *King Lear,* Aemilia, *The Comedy of Errors,* all 1962; Frau Lina Rose, *The Physicists,* Regan, *King Lear,* Mrs. Diana Traipes, *The Beggar's Opera,* all 1963; Duchess of York, *Richard II,* Mistress Quickly, *Henry IV, Parts I and II,* Alice, hostess, *Henry V,* all 1964; Lady Harriet Boscoe, *The Governor's Lady,* Alice, hostess, *Henry V,* Emma Takinainen, *Squire Puntila and His Servant Matti,* all 1965; Anna

Andreyevna, *The Government Inspector*, Eugenia, *Tango*, Frau Nomsen, *The Meteor*, Gratiana, *The Revenger's Tragedy*, all 1966; Edna, *A Delicate Balance*, Dame Purecraft, *Bartholomew Fair*, Mrs. Heegan, *The Silver Tassie*, duchess, *The Revenger's Tragedy*, all 1969-70; nurse, *All Over*, 1972; Mrs. Dudgeon, *The Devil's Disciple*, Avdotya, *Ivanov*, both 1976.

MAJOR TOURS—Swart Petry, *The Sea Shell*, U. K. cities, 1959.

PRINCIPAL FILM APPEARANCES—*House of Cards*, Universal, 1969; *Baby Love*, AVCO-Embassy, 1969; *Fiddler on the Roof*, United Artists, 1971; *Countess Dracula*, Twentieth Century-Fox, 1972; *The French Lieutenant's Woman*, United Artists, 1981. Also appeared in *Decline and Fall of a Bird Watcher*, 1969; *Every Home Should Have One* (also known as *Think Dirty*), 1970; *Endless Night*, 1971; *The National Health*, 1972; also *Perfect Friday*.

PRINCIPAL TELEVISION APPEARANCES—*Shoulder to Shoulder*; *Edward VII*; *Come Back Little Sheba*; *Who Paid the Ferry Man?*; *Love in a Cold Climate*.

RELATED CAREER—Associate artist, Royal Shakespeare Company.

AWARDS: Lady Tree's Elocution Award, Royal Academy of Dramatic Art, 1932.

MEMBER: British Actors' Equity Association, Screen Actors Guild.*

OBITUARIES AND OTHER SOURCES: *Variety*, July 22, 1987.

*   *   *

COLLINS, Barry 1941-

PERSONAL: Born September 21, 1941, in Halifax, England; wife's name, Anne. EDUCATION: Attended Queen's College, Oxford University.

VOCATION: Writer.

WRITINGS: PLAYS, PRODUCED—*And Was Jerusalem Builded Here?*, Leeds Playhouse, Leeds, U.K., 1972; *Beauty and the Beast*, Leeds Playhouse, 1973; *Judgment*, National Theatre, London, 1975, then 1977; *The Strongest Man in the World*, Nottingham Playhouse, Nottingham, U.K., 1978; *Toads*, Nottingham Playhouse, 1979. Also wrote *Judgment*.

TELEPLAYS—Series: *The Hills of Heaven*, 1978. Also wrote *The Lonely Man's Lover*, 1974; *The Witches of Pendle*, 1978; *Judgment*.

ADDRESSES: HOME—One Stafford Place, Halifax, West Yorkshire, England.*

*   *   *

COLLISON, David 1937-

PERSONAL: Full name, David John Collison; born August 5, 1937, in Ipswich, England; son of Douglas Roland and Molly (Hedgcock) Collison; married Annie Dodd (an actress).

VOCATION: Sound designer and consultant.

CAREER: FIRST STAGE WORK—Assistant stage manager, Arts Theatre Club, London, 1955. PRINCIPAL STAGE WORK— Sound designer and mixer for London stage productions of *Blitz!*, *Pickwick*, *A Funny Thing Happened on the Way to the Forum*, *Fiddler on the Roof*, *Cabaret*, *Company*, *Mame*, *Sweet Charity*, *Jesus Christ Superstar*, *A Little Night Music*, and many more. Has also designed sound for the Royal Shakespeare Company, the English Stage Company, and for theatres in Britain, Europe, Africa, and the Middle East.

RELATED CAREER—Managing director, Theatre Projects Sound, Ltd., 1963—; deputy managing director, Theatre Projects Services, Ltd., 1973—; director, Theatre Projects, Ltd., 1980—; lectures periodically at the London Academy of Music and Dramatic Art.

NON-RELATED CAREER—Formerly a trainee animal feed salesman.

WRITINGS: BOOKS—*Stage Sound*, 1976.

MEMBER: Society of Theatre Consultants, Association of British Theatre Technicians.

SIDELIGHTS: *CTFT* learned that David Collison was Britain's first independent theatre sound consultant. He has designed numerous pieces of unique sound equipment for the theatre.

ADDRESSES: HOME—Crowsnest, Rectory Lane, Kingston Bagpuize, Oxon, England. OFFICE—Theatre Projects, Ltd., 19 Long Acre, London WC2E 9LN, England.*

*   *   *

COLON, Miriam 1945-

PERSONAL: Born in 1945, in Ponce, Puerto Rico; married George P. Edgar, 1966. EDUCATION: Attended University of Puerto Rico; trained for the stage at the Erwin Piscator Dramatic Workshop and Technical Institute and with Lee Strasberg at the Actors Studio; also studied with Marcos Colon, Leopoldo Lavandero, and Ludwig Schajowicz.

VOCATION: Actress, director, and producer.

CAREER: BROADWAY DEBUT—Frederica, *In the Summer House*, Playhouse Theatre, 1953. PRINCIPAL STAGE APPEARANCES— All in New York City unless indicated: Esperanza, *The Innkeepers*, John Golden Theatre, 1956; Adelita Gomez, *Me, Candido!*, Greenwich Mews Theatre, 1965; Maria Esposito, Madonna, *Matty and the Moron and the Madonna*, Orpheum Theatre, 1965; Juanita, *The Ox Cart*, Greenwich Mews Theatre, 1966; then Puerto Rican Traveling Theatre, 1967; Dolores Gonzales, *The Wrong Way Light Bulb*, John Golden Theatre, 1967; Mirianne, *Winterset*, Puerto Rican Traveling Theatre, 1968; title role, *The Passion of Antigona Perez*, Cathedral Church, then New York City Parks, both 1972; Calpurnia, *Julius Caesar*, Public Theatre, 1979; Fifi, *Orinoco*, Lucy, *Simpson Street*, both Puerto Rican Traveling Theatre, 1985. Also appeared in *The Puppet Theatre of Don Cristobal*, *The Shoemaker's Prodigious Wife*, both Delacorte Mobile Theatre, 1964; *Fanlights*, Bilingual Foundation for the Arts, Los Angeles, CA, 1979; *The Eagle and the Serpent*, Puerto Rican Traveling Theatre.

PRINCIPAL STAGE WORK—Producer, *Crossroads,* New York City Parks, then Town Hall, 1969; producer, director, *The Golden Streets,* New York City Parks, 1970; producer, *Puerto Rican Short Stories,* New York City Parks, 1971.

Producer, all with the Puerto Rican Traveling Theatre: *El Malefico de la Mariposa,* 1970; *The Passion of Antigona Perez,* 1972; *Noo Yall, El Medico a Palos,* both 1973; *Scribbles, The Innocent, The Guest, At the End of the Street,* all 1974; *Arrabal's Ceremony for an Assassinated Black Man, The Two Executioners,* both 1975; *The Oxcart,* 1977; *The FM Safe,* 1978; *Orinoco,* (also director) *Simpson Street,* 1985; also *Winterset; La Farsa del Amor Compradito; Los Titeres de Cachiporra; Pipo Subway No Sabe Reir; Ceremonia por un Negro Asasinado; The Angels Are Exhausted;*

PRINCIPAL FILM APPEARANCES—*One-Eyed Jacks,* Paramount, 1961; *The Appaloosa,* Universal, 1966; *The Possession of Joel Delaney,* Paramount, 1972; also appeared in *Isabella Negra.*

PRINCIPAL TELEVISION APPEARANCES—Episodic: *Dick Van Dyke Show,* CBS; *Ben Casey,* ABC; *Dr. Kildare,* NBC; *Alfred Hitchcock Presents,* CBS; *Gunsmoke,* CBS; *Bonanza,* CBS.

RELATED CAREER—Founder, artistic director, Puerto Rican Traveling Theatre, New York City, 1966—.

ADDRESSES: OFFICE—Puerto Rican Traveling Theatre Company, Inc., 141 W. 94th Street, New York, NY 10025.*

*   *   *

COLUMBUS, Chris

BRIEF ENTRY: In his junior year at New York University, Chris Columbus received his first check as a screenwriter for a Hollywood movie. The exhilaration of the $50,000 payment disappeared, however, when he viewed the film—*Reckless,* 1984, starring Aidan Quinn as a troubled teenager and Daryl Hannah as his mainstream girlfriend—that resulted from a rewritten script. ''It came out as 'Last Tango in Weirton,' with a sex scene in the boiler room, of all places,'' he told Terri Minsky of the New York *Daily News* (June 30, 1985). By age twenty-six, however, Columbus wrote three screenplays that were produced by box office king Steven Spielberg. The first was *Gremlins,* which twenty-five directors and producers rejected before Spielberg purchased it and helped Columbus rewrite the script. They toned down some of the more macabre story elements and added more humor; the result was a phenomenal success. Their next project, *The Goonies,* 1985, featured a group of children in a treasure-hunting adventure story that was more popular with audiences than with critics, but *Young Sherlock Holmes,* released the same year, was highly praised on all fronts. His successful collaboration with Spielberg allowed Columbus to set up his own production company, 1492 Productions, and with the 1987 release of *Adventures in Babysitting* he added directing to his resume, a step he was determined to take. As a screenwriter, he felt, ''I only get to take it half-way. . . . Somebody else takes off with your baby,'' he told *Starlog* (May, 1985).

*   *   *

CONAWAY, Jeff   1950-

PERSONAL: Born October 5, 1950, in New York, NY; married Rona Newton-John; children: Emerson. EDUCATION: Attended North Carolina School of the Arts and New York University.

VOCATION: Actor.

CAREER: BROADWAY DEBUT—*All the Way Home,* Belasco Theatre, 1960. PRINCIPAL STAGE APPEARANCES—Danny Zuko, *Grease,* Royale Theatre, New York City, 1978; executive editor, *The News,* Helen Hayes Theatre, New York City, 1985; appeared as Billy, *Wanted,* Judson Poet's Theatre, New York City; and as a guest artist, Burt Reynolds Jupiter Theatre, Jupiter, FL, 1985-86.

MAJOR TOURS—*Critics Choice,* U.S. cities.

FILM DEBUT—*Jennifer on My Mind,* United Artists, 1971. PRINCIPAL FILM APPEARANCES—Kenicke, *Grease,* Paramount, 1978; also appeared in *The Eagle Has Landed,* Columbia, 1977; *Pete's Dragon,* Buena Vista, 1977; *I Never Promised You a Rose Garden,* New World, 1977; *Covergirl,* New World, 1984; and in *The Patriot,* 1986.

PRINCIPAL TELEVISION APPEARANCES—Episodic: *The Mary Tyler Moore Show,* CBS; *Happy Days,* ABC; *Movin' On,* NBC; *Barnaby Jones,* CBS; *Kojak,* CBS; *Berrenger's,* NBC. Series: Bobby Wheeler, *Taxi,* ABC, 1978-81. Movies: *Having Babies,* 1976; *Delta County, U.S.A.,* 1977; *Breaking Up Is Hard to Do,* 1979; *The Making of a Male Model,* 1983.

RELATED CAREER—Fashion model; formerly a singer and guitarist with a music group.

ADDRESSES: AGENT—c/o Jack Gilardi, International Creative Management, 8899 Beverly Boulevard, Los Angeles, CA 90040.*

*   *   *

CONRAD, William   1920-

PERSONAL: Born September 27, 1920, in Louisville, KY. EDUCATION: Attended Fullerton Junior College. MILITARY: U.S. Army Air Corps, 1943-45.

VOCATION: Actor, producer, director, and radio announcer.

CAREER: PRINCIPAL TELEVISION APPEARANCES—Series: Narrator, *The Bullwinkle Show,* NBC, 1961-62; narrator, *The Fugitive,* ABC, 1963-67; title role, *Cannon,* CBS, 1971-76; narrator, *The Wild, Wild World of Animals,* syndicated, 1973-78; narrator, *Tales of the Unexpected,* NBC, 1977; narrator, *Buck Rogers in the 25th Century,* 1979-80; title role, *Nero Wolfe,* NBC, 1981; J.L. McCabe, *Jake and the Fat Man,* CBS, 1987—. Movies: Title role, *The Return of Frank Cannon,* CBS, 1980; title role, *Turnover Smith,* 1980; narrator, *The Return of the King.* Also appeared in *The Brotherhood of the Bell,* 1970; *Conspiracy to Kill,* 1970; *Night Cries,* 1978; *The Rebels,* 1979; *Shocktrauma,* 1982; *In Like Flynn,* 1985.

PRINCIPAL TELEVISION WORK—Producer and director, *Klondike,* NBC, 1960-61; director, *77 Sunset Strip,* ABC, 1963-64; director, *General Electric True* (thirty-five episodes), CBS, 1962-63; producer, *Turnover Smith;* 1980.

FILM DEBUT—*The Killers,* Universal, 1946. PRINCIPAL FILM APPEARANCES—*Body and Soul,* United Artists, 1947; *Sorry, Wrong Number,* Paramount, 1948; *East Side, West Side,* 1949; *Cry Danger,* R.K.O., 1951; *The Naked Jungle,* 1954; narrator, *The*

Naked Sea, R.K.O., 1955; *The Conqueror*, R.K.O., 1956; —*30*—, Warner Brothers, 1959; *Moonshine County Express*, 1977.

PRINCIPAL FILM WORK—Director, *The Man from Galveston*, Warner Brothers, 1964; producer and director, *Two on a Guillotine*, Warner Brothers, 1965; producer and director, *Brainstorm*, Warner Brothers, 1965; producer, *An American Dream*, Warner Brothers, 1966; *A Covenant with Death*, Warner Brothers, 1967; *First to Fight*, Warner Brothers, 1967; *The Cool Ones*, Warner Brothers, 1967; producer, *Countdown*, Warner Brothers, 1968; producer, *Chubasco*, Warner Brothers, 1968; producer, *Assignment to Kill*, Warner Brothers, 1969.

PRINCIPAL RADIO WORK—Marshal Matt Dillon, *Gunsmoke*, 1949-60; announcer, KMPC, Los Angeles, CA.

ADDRESSES: AGENT—Creative Artists Agency, 1888 Century Park E., Suite 1400, Los Angeles, CA 90067.*

*   *   *

COPELAND, Stewart   1952-

PERSONAL: Born July 16, 1952, in Maclean, VA; son of Miles Axe, II (a Central Intelligence Agency operative) and Lorraine Elizabeth (an archeologist; maiden name, Adie) Copeland; married Sonja Kristina Shaw (an actress and singer), July 16, 1982; children: Sven, Patrick, Jordan, Scott.

STEWART COPELAND

VOCATION: Composer and director.

CAREER: PRINCIPAL FILM WORK—Director, *So What?*, CCCP, 1983.

NON-RELATED CAREER—Member of the music groups Curved Air and the Police.

WRITINGS: FILM SCORES—*Rumblefish*, Universal, 1983; *Bachelor Party*, Twentieth Century-Fox, 1983; *Out of Bounds*, Columbia, 1986; also *Texas Chainsaw Massacre 2*, 1986. TELEVISION SCORES—*The Equalizer*, CBS, 1986. STAGE SCORES—*Lear*, San Francisco Ballet, San Francisco, CA, 1985.

RECORDINGS: ALBUMS—*Music for the Equalizer and Other Cliffhangers*, upcoming. All with the Police, released on A&M Records: *Outlandos d'Amour*, 1978; *Regatta de Blanc*, 1979; *Zenyatta Mondatta*, 1980; *Ghost in the Machine*, 1981; *Synchronicity*, 1983. SINGLES—All with the Police, released on A&M Records unless indicated: *Fall Out*, Illegal Records, 1977; *Roxanne, Can't Stand Losing You, Message in a Bottle, Walking on the Moon*, all 1979; *So Lonely, Don't Stand So Close*, and *De Do Do Do, De Da Da Da*, all 1980; *Invisible Sun, Every Little Thing She Does Is Magic*, both 1981; *Spirits in the Material World*, 1982; *Every Breath You Take, Wrapped Around Your Finger, Synchronicity II*, all 1983; *King of Pain*, 1984. VIDEO—*The Rhythmatist*, A & M Video, 1985.

AWARDS: Winner of gold, platinum, and multiple platinum records and numerous other awards with the Police.

MEMBER: National Academy of Recording Arts and Sciences, Songwriters Guild (U.K.), Performing Right Society (U.K.), Musician's Union (U.K.).

ADDRESSES: OFFICE—c/o Derek Power, 633 N. La Brea, Los Angeles, CA 90036.

*   *   *

CORBETT, Gretchen   1947-

PERSONAL: Born August 13, 1947, in Portland, OR; daughter of Henry Ladd, Jr. and Katherine Minahen (Coney) Corbett; EDUCATION: Attended Carnegie Institute of Technology.

VOCATION: Actress.

CAREER: STAGE DEBUT—Desdemona, *Othello*, Oregon Shakespeare Festival, Ashland, OR. OFF-BROADWAY DEBUT—Louka, *Arms and the Man*, Sheridan Square Playhouse, 1967. BROADWAY DEBUT—Sonya, *After the Rain*, John Golden Theatre, 1967. PRINCIPAL STAGE APPEARANCES— Juliet, *Romeo and Juliet*, Amy, *Charley's Aunt*, Julia, *The Rivals*, all New Orleans Repertory Theatre, New Orleans, LA, 1967; title role, *Iphigenia in Aulis*, Circle in the Square, New York City, 1968; Jessie, *The Bench*, Gramercy Arts Theatre, New York City, 1968; Trina Stanley, *Forty Carats*, Morosco Theatre, New York City, 1968; wife, *The Unknown Soldier and His Wife*, Playhouse in the Park, Philadelphia, PA, 1969; Joan La Pucelle, *Henry VI, Part I*, New York Shakespeare Festival, Delacorte Theatre, New York City, 1970; title role, *Saint Joan*, American Theatre Company, Tulsa, OK, 1970; Joan, *The Survival of St. Joan*, Anderson Theatre, New York City, then Studio Arena, Buffalo, NY, 1971; Francoise, *The Justice Box*,

Theatre de Lys, New York City, 1971; Rosalind, *As You Like It,* New Jersey Shakespeare Festival, Madison, NJ, 1973; Hilda Wangel, *The Master Builder,* Long Wharf Theatre, New Haven, CT, 1973; Roxanne, *The Carome Brothers' Italian Food Products Corp.'s Annual Pasta Pageant,* Long Wharf Theatre, 1982; Eva, *The Traveler,* Center Theatre Group, Mark Taper Forum, Los Angeles, CA, 1987. Also appeared in *At the End of Long Island,* Mark Taper Forum, Los Angeles, CA, 1978; "Hopscotch," *The Queannapowitt Quartet,* Actors Theatre, Los Angeles, CA, 1983.

MAJOR TOURS—Ruth, *The Effect of Gamma Rays on Man-in-the-Moon Marigolds,* U.S. cities, 1972.

FILM DEBUT—*Out of It,* United Artists, 1969. PRINCIPAL FILM APPEARANCES—*Let's Scare Jessica to Death,* Paramount, 1971; *The Other Side of the Mountain—Part 2,* Universal, 1977. Also appeared in *Jaws of Satan,* 1979.

TELEVISION DEBUT—*N.Y.P.D.,* ABC, 1968. PRINCIPAL TELEVISION APPEARANCES—Episodic: *Ghost Story,* NBC; *Kojak,* CBS; *Ironside,* NBC; *Banacek,* NBC; *Gunsmoke,* CBS; *Colombo,* NBC. Movies: *North Beach and Rawhide,* CBS, 1985.

ADDRESSES: AGENT—c/o Richard H. Bauman, 1650 Broadway, New York, NY 10019.*

*   *   *

COSTNER, Kevin

BRIEF ENTRY: As the star of two of the biggest hits of the summer of 1987, Kevin Costner was widely hailed as Hollywood's new romantic leading man. He portrayed naval officer Tom Farrell, a man with secrets of his own who is caught in a Pentagon cover-up, in the political thriller *No Way Out.* The film provided him with steamy scenes of passion and sequences of action and suspense. Likewise, Costner alternated between tender family scenes and the stark violence of crime fighting in Brian De Palma's *The Untouchables.* Although audiences and critics alike acclaimed his work, this seeming overnight success actually followed years in which the thirty-two-year-old actor saw small parts in *Frances, Night Shift,* and *Table for Five* shrink even smaller in the movies' final cuts. His portrayal of the pivotal character Alex in the 1983 hit *The Big Chill* ended up as a cameo appearance as the corpse that is prepared for burial during the film's opening credits. Nevertheless, Costner regarded the experience of working with that project's writer-director, Lawrence Kasdan, as his "promised land," according to a September 7, 1987 profile in *Time,* because he found confirmation of his own feelings about what acting should be. Kasdan later cast him in the 1985 western *Silverado,* where reviewers felt he stole the show from co-stars Kevin Kline and Danny Glover with his humorous and sexy portrayal of the young cowboy Jake. Costner's other film credits include the nuclear holocaust drama *Testament* and *American Flyers,* a drama about two brothers in a marathon bicycle race. The actor takes a somewhat mystical approach to his craft; *Time* reported that Costner naps during shooting to help "keep the character alive in his dreams."

*   *   *

COURTENAY, Tom   1937-

PERSONAL: Born February 25, 1937, in Hull, England; son of Thomas Henry (a boat painter) and Anne Eliza (Quest) Courtenay;

married Cheryl Kennedy, November 12, 1973. EDUCATION: Attended University College, London; trained for the stage at the Royal Academy of Dramatic Art, 1960-61.

VOCATION: Actor.

CAREER: STAGE DEBUT—Konstantin Treplyef, *The Seagull,* Old Vic Theatre Company, Lyceum Theatre, Edinburgh, Scotland, U.K., 1960. LONDON DEBUT—Konstantin Treplyef, *The Seagull,* Old Vic Theatre, 1960. BROADWAY DEBUT—Simon, *Otherwise Engaged,* Plymouth Theatre, 1977. PRINCIPAL STAGE APPEARANCES—Poins, *Henry V, Part I,* Feste, *Twelfth Night,* both Old Vic Theatre, London, 1961; Billy Fisher, *Billy Liar,* Cambridge Theatre, London, 1961; Andri, *Andorra,* National Theatre Company, Old Vic Theatre, 1964; Trofimov, *The Cherry Orchard,* Malcolm, *Macbeth,* both Chichester Festival, Chichester, U.K., 1966; Lord Fancourt Babberly, *Charley's Aunt,* 69 Theatre Company, Manchester, U.K., 1966; Young Marlow, *She Stoops to Conquer,* Garrick Theatre, London, 1969; Lord Fancourt Babberly, *Charley's Aunt,* Apollo Theatre, London, 1971; Leonard, *Time and Time Again,* Comedy Theatre, London, 1972; Norman, *The Norman Conquests,* Greenwich Theatre, 1974, then Globe Theatre, London, 1975; John Clare, *The Fool,* Royal Court Theatre, London, 1975; Faulkland, *The Rivals,* Royal Exchange Theatre, Manchester, U.K., 1976; Raskolnikov, *Crime and Punishment,* Royal Exchange Theatre, 1978; Owen, *Clouds,* Duke of York's Theatre, London, 1978; Norman, *The Dresser,* Royal Exchange Theatre, then Queen's Theatre, London, both 1980, later Brooks Atkinson Theatre, New York City, 1981. Appeared as Captain Bluntschli, *Arms and the Man,* Manchester, U.K., 1973; and in *Playboy of the Western World,* Manchester, U.K., 1967; *Hamlet,* Garrick Theatre, 1969; *Peer Gynt,* University Theatre, Manchester, U.K., 1970; *The Prince of Homburg,* Royal Exchange Theatre, 1976; *Table Manners,* 1974; *The Misanthrope,* 1981; *Andy Capp,* 1983; *Jumpers,* 1984.

FILM DEBUT—Colin Smith, *The Loneliness of the Long Distance Runner,* Continental, 1963. PRINCIPAL FILM APPEARANCES—Billy Fisher, *Billy Liar,* Continental, 1963; title role, *Private Potter,* Metro-Goldwyn-Mayer (MGM), 1963; Pvt. Arthur Hamp, *King and Country,* Allied Artists, 1965; Pasha Strelnikoff, *Doctor Zhivago,* MGM, 1965; Lt. Grey, *King Rat,* Columbia, 1965; Robert Hemshaw, *Operation Crossbow,* MGM, 1965; navigator, *The Day the Fish Came Out,* International Classics, 1967; Cpl. Hartmann, *The Night of the Generals,* Columbia, 1967; Gatiss, *A Dandy in Aspic,* Columbia, 1968; title role, *Otley,* Columbia, 1969; Baxter, *Catch Me a Spy,* Rank, 1971; title role, *One Day in the Life of Ivan Denisovich,* Cinerama, 1971; Norman, *The Dresser,* Columbia, 1983. Also appeared in *Happy New Year.*

PRINCIPAL TELEVISION APPEARANCES—Series: Dobley, *The Lads.* Specials: *Ghosts,* 1967; title role, *Private Potter.* Movies: Father Tark Brian, *I Heard the Owl Call My Name,* CBS, 1973; *Jesus of Nazareth,* 1977.

AWARDS: Best Supporting Actor, Academy Award nomination, 1965, for *Doctor Zhivago;* Best Actor, French Academie du Cinema, 1967; Best Stage Actor, Variety Club of Great Britain, 1972, for *Time and Time Again;* Best Actor, Antoinette Perry Award nomination, 1977, for *Otherwise Engaged;* Best Actor, New York Drama Critics Circle Award, 1981, and New Standard Award, 1981, both for *The Dresser;* Best Actor, Academy Award nomination, 1984, for *The Dresser.*

SIDELIGHTS: RECREATIONS—Listening to music, playing golf.

ADDRESSES: AGENT—International Creative Management, 388
Oxford Street, London W1, England.*

*   *   *

COURTNEY, Richard   1927-

PERSONAL: Born June 4, 1927, in Newmarket, England; son of
Arthur John (a teacher) and Celia Annie Courtney; married Rosemary Gale (a writer and editor); children: Anne, John. EDUCA-
TION: University of Leeds, B.A., 1951, diploma in education,
1952. MILITARY: Royal Air Force, 1945-48.

VOCATION: Teacher, theatre scholar, writer, actor, and director.

CAREER: PRINCIPAL STAGE APPEARANCES—Various music
hall appearances in Northern England, 1951-54; also appeared with
the Arts Theatre, Leeds, the English Theatre Guild, and performed
in other repertory and amateur productions, all in England.

PRINCIPAL STAGE WORK—Director, Arts Theatre and Proscenium Players, both in Leeds.

PRINCIPAL TELEVISION APPEARANCES—With the Northern Repertory Company, BBC, 1954-64.

RELATED CAREER—Primary school teacher, Dalham, England,
1948; drama teacher, various high schools, Leeds, 1952-55;
founder, Four Valleys Youth Theatre, 1955; senior lecturer in
drama, Trent Park College, 1959-67, warden, Sir Phillip Sassoon
Hall, 1961-64; co-founder, Enfield Youth Theatre, 1961; associate
professor of theatre, University of Victoria, Canada, 1968-71; head
of Developmental Drama Summer School, 1970-72; professor of
drama, University of Calgary, Canada, 1971-74; lecturer, Gold-
smith's College, London, summers, 1973-74; professor of arts and
education, Ontario Institute for Studies in Education, Toronto, ON,
Canada, 1974—; member of faculty, University of Toronto,
1974—; visiting fellow, Melbourne State College, Victoria, Australia, 1979; visiting instructor, University of Western Ontario,
1980; lecturer at universities in England, U.S., Europe, and Asia.

WRITINGS: POEMS—*Wide Eyed Girl*, Stockwell, 1948. NON-
FICTION—(Editor) *College Drama Space*, Institute of Education,
University of London, 1964; *Teaching Drama*, Cassell, 1965; *The
School Play*, Cassell, 1966; *The Drama Studio*, Pitman, 1967;
*Play, Drama, and Thought: The Intellectual Background to Dra-
matic Education*, Cassell, 1968, second edition, Drama Book
Specialists, 1970, third edition, 1974; *Teaching and the Arts: Arts
Education in Australia, With Specific Reference to Drama Educa-
tion in Victoria*, Melbourne State College, 1979; (editor) *The Face
of the Future: The Report of the National Inquiry Into Arts and
Education in Canada*, Canadian Conference of the Arts, 1979; *The
Dramatic Curriculum*, Drama Book Specialists, 1980; (with Paul
Park) *Learning in the Arts*, Ministry of Education, Ontario, 1980;
(editor, with Gertrud Schattner) *Drama in Therapy* (two volumes:
Volume I, *Children*, Volume II, *Adults*), Drama Book Specialists,
1981; *History of British Drama*, Littlefield, Adams, 1982; *Re-
Play: Studies of Human Drama in Education*, Ontario Institute for
Studies in Education Press, 1982; *Outline History of British Dra-
ma*, Littlefield, 1982; *The Rarest Dream: "Play, Drama, and
Thought" Revisited*, 1984; (with Dr. Booth, J. Emerson, and N.
Kuzmich), *Teacher Education in the Arts*, 1986; *The Quest: Re-

search and Inquiry in Arts Education, University Press of America,
1987; *Dictionary of Developmental Drama*, C. C. Thomas, 1987.

Contributor: *Education and the Arts*, Australian National Universi-
ty, 1971; *Drama in Education*, Pitman, Volume I, 1973, Volume
II, 1974, Volume III, 1975; *Theatre for Young Audiences*, Longman,
1978; *Wholistic Dimensions in Healing*, Doubleday, 1978; *Fourth
Yearbook on Research in Arts and Aesthetic Education*, Central
Midwest Regional Educational Laboratory, 1981.

PERIODICALS—Contributor of more than one hundred articles,
stories, poems, and reviews to scholarly journals, popular magazines, and newspapers, including *Gryphon, Players, Connecticut
Review, Queen's Quarterly,* and *Orbit;* editor of monograph series
''Discussions in Developmental Drama,'' University of Calgary,
1971-74; contributing editor, *Curriculum Inquiry*, 1975-78.

AWARDS: Alberta Achievement Award, 1973, from the Government of Alberta, Canada; Canadian Silver Jubilee Medal, 1977,
from the Governor-General of Canada; Canadian Conference of the
Arts Fourtieth Anniversary Award, 1985; research awards: Design
Canada; Ontario Arts Council; Ontario Ministry of Education.

MEMBER: Canadian Child and Youth Drama Association (board of
directors, 1968-69, president, 1969-72), Canadian Conference of
the Arts (board of governors, 1970, executive committee, 1971,
vice-president, 1972, national president, 1973-76), American
Council of the Arts (board of directors, 1974-77), National Inquiry
Into Arts and Education in Canada (chairman, 1975), American
Theatre Association (Theatre Education Commission, 1979-81),
North Hertfordshire Youth Theatre (life patron), Task Force on Arts
and Education in Canada (chairman), Creative Education Founda-
tion, Educational Drama Association, Society for Teachers of
Speech and Drama, Folklore Society, Royal Society of Arts, British
Society of Drama Therapy, American Society for Aesthetics.

SIDELIGHTS: RECREATIONS—Creative writing and painting.

ADDRESSES: OFFICE—Ontario Institute for Studies in Education,
252 Bloor Street W., Toronto, Ontario M5S 1V6, Canada.

*   *   *

COX, Alex

BRIEF ENTRY: In 1984, just three years after leaving the film
school at the University of California, Los Angeles, Alex Cox
released his first commercial film, *Repo Man*. Critic Leonard
Maltin dubbed the quirky mixture of science fiction and punk
sensibility ''an instant cult movie'' and it proved a favorite on the
midnight film circuit. The young writer-director took another look
at the punk scene in *Sid and Nancy*, which quickly became
notorious for its bleak depiction of the drug-laden love affair
between rock performer Sid Vicious and his groupie girlfriend,
Nancy Spungen. Although reviews again were favorable, Cox
himself deemed making the film ''very harrowing,'' in a discussion
with Graham Fuller of the *Village Voice* (October 21, 1986). In
fact, his background stands in contrast to the subject matter of his
first two films. Cox grew up in Liverpool, England, and studied law
as an undergraduate at Oxford University, where he also directed
and acted in plays for the school's Drama Society. After graduation,
he went on to study film production at Bristol University and
received a Fulbright scholarship to attend UCLA. ''Education is not

a very hip thing to admit you've had in England,'' Cox has remarked. ''But if it hadn't been for education, I'd never be doing what I'm doing now.'' His third film, *Straight to Hell,* a humorous spaghetti western, did not achieve the critical or commercial success of its predecessors, and Cox once again shifted gears to make *Walker,* a historical drama based on the story of William Walker, an American who became the military dictator of Nicaragua in 1853.

*   *   *

CRICHTON, Michael   1942-
(Jeffery Hudson, John Lange, Michael Douglas—joint pseudonym)

PERSONAL: Surname is pronounced ''Cry-ton;'' full name, John Michael Crichton; born October 23, 1942, in Chicago, IL; son of John Henderson (a corporation president) and Zula (Miller) Crichton; married Joan Radam, January 1, 1965 (divorced, 1970); married Kathy St. Johns, 1978 (divorced, 1980). EDUCATION: Harvard University, A.B. (summa cum laude), 1964, M.D., 1969; Salk Institute for Biological Studies, La Jolla, CA, post-doctoral fellow, 1969-70.

VOCATION: Writer and director.

CAREER: PRINCIPAL FILM WORK—Director: *Westworld,* Metro-Goldwyn-Mayer, 1973; *Coma,* United Artists, 1978; *The Great Train Robbery,* United Artists, 1979; *Looker,* Warner Brothers, 1981; *Runaway,* Tri-Star, 1984.

PRINCIPAL TELEVISION WORK—Director, *Pursuit,* ABC, 1972.

WRITINGS: NON-FICTION—*Five Patients: The Hospital Explained,* Knopf, 1970; *Jasper Johns,* Abrams, 1977; *Electronic Life: How to Think about Computers,* Knopf, 1983.

FICTION—All published by Knopf unless indicated: *The Andromeda Strain,* 1969; (with Douglas Crichton under joint pseudonym Michael Douglas) *Dealing: Or, the Berkeley-to-Boston Forty-Brick Lost-Bag Blues,* 1971; *The Terminal Man,* 1972; (based on his screenplay of the same title) *Westworld* (also see below), Bantam, 1974; *The Great Train Robbery* (also see below), 1975; *Eaters of the Dead: The Manuscript of Ibn Fadlan Relating His Experiences with the Northmen in A.D. 922,* 1976; *Congo,* 1980; *Sphere,* 1987. All as John Lange and published by New American Library unless indicated: *Odds On,* 1966; *Scratch One,* 1967; (as Jeffery Hudson) *A Case of Need,* 1968; *Easy Go,* 1968, reissued as *The Last Tomb,* Bantam, 1974; *Zero Cool, The Venom Business,* both 1969; *Drug of Choice, Grave Descend,* both 1970; *Binary,* 1971.

SCREENPLAYS—*Westworld,* Metro-Goldwyn-Mayer, 1973; *Coma,* United Artists, 1977; (based on his novel of the same title) *The Great Train Robbery,* United Artists, 1978; *Looker,* Warner Brothers, 1981; *Runaway,* Tri-Star, 1984.

AWARDS: Edgar Award, Mystery Writers of America, 1968, for *A Case of Need;* Writer of the Year Award, Association of American Medical Writers, 1970, for *Five Patients: The Hospital Explained;* Edgar Award, 1979, for film, *The Great Train Robbery.*

MEMBER: Directors Guild of America, Authors Guild, Authors

League of America, P.E.N., Mystery Writers Guild of America-West; Aesculaepian Society, Phi Beta Kappa.

SIDELIGHTS: In addition to the films Michael Crichton has directed from his own writings, his novels *The Andromeda Strain* and *The Terminal Man* have also been made into films. In a 1983 interview in *Contemporary Authors,* New Revision Series, Vol. 13, Crichton talks about writing the same story for the two different media: ''When I wrote *The Terminal Man,* Warner Brothers bought it and then asked me to write the screenplay. I wrote a screenplay that was rather different, and they said, 'How could you do this? We thought the writer of the book would protect his project, and you have butchered it!' And I said, 'No, no, no, you don't understand: The book was the best book that I could write and the movie is the best movie. I've put into the movie all the scenes that I couldn't put into the book because they weren't really book scenes. I had a whole collection of scenes that I wanted to see in the movie, and here they are!' Well, they didn't understand that idea. They fired me. But books and movies are very different forms. And the extent to which they are different forms is something that you learn fully, I think, only with the experience of doing both.''

ADDRESSES: OFFICE—1750 14th Street, Suite C, Santa Monica, CA 90404. AGENT—c/o Lynn Nesbit, International Creative Management, 40 W. 57th Street, New York, NY 10025.*

*   *   *

CROSBY, Mary

PERSONAL: Full name, Mary Frances Crosby; daughter of Harry Lillis (''Bing'') (a singer and actor) and Kathryn (Grandstaff) Crosby; married Ebb Lottimer, November, 1978. EDUCATION: Attended University of Texas, Austin; studied acting at the American Conservatory Theatre.

VOCATION: Actress.

CAREER: PRINCIPAL TELEVISION APPEARANCES—Episodic: *The Fall Guy,* ABC, 1982, 1983, 1984; *Love Boat,* ABC, 1982, 1984; *The Finder of Lost Loves,* 1984; *Glitter,* ABC, 1984; *Hotel,* ABC, 1984, 1985; *The New Adventures of Beans Baxter,* Fox, 1987. Series: Suzi Cooper, *Brothers and Sisters,* NBC, 1979; Kristin Shepard, *Dallas,* CBS, 1979-1981. Mini-Series: Patricia North, *Pearl,* ABC, 1978; *Hollywood Wives,* NBC, 1985; *North and South, Book II,* ABC, 1986. Pilots: Natalie Kingsley, *Golden Gate,* ABC, 1981; Cynthia Hughes, *The Big Easy,* NBC, 1982; *Cover Up,* CBS, 1984. Movies: Lisa Harris, *With This Ring,* ABC, 1978; Eloise, *A Guide for the Married Woman,* ABC, 1978; Cathy Preston, *Midnight Lace,* NBC, 1981; Ellen Price, *Confessions of a Married Man,* ABC, 1983; Susan Campbell, *Final Jeopardy,* NBC, 1985; also appeared as Lucy Mallory, *Stage Coach,* 1986; and in *Johann Strauss: The King without a Crown,* upcoming. Specials: *Bing Crosby's Christmas Show,* NBC, 1970; *Bing Crosby and the Sounds of Christmas,* NBC, 1971; *Bing Crosby's Sun Valley Christmas Show,* NBC, 1973; *Bing Crosby's White Christmas,* CBS, 1976; *Bing! A 50th Anniversary Gala,* CBS, 1977; *Bing Crosby's Merrie Olde Christmas,* 1977; *Battle of the Network Stars,* ABC, 1979; *Twenty-First Annual Academy of Country Music Awards,* 1986.

PRINCIPAL FILM APPEARANCES—Princess Karina, *The Ice Pi-*

rates, Metro-Goldwyn-Mayer/United Artists, 1984; also appeared in *The Last Plane Out,* 1983; *Child's Play, 1984.*

ADDRESSES: AGENTS—c/o John Kimble, Triad Artists, 10100 Santa Monica Boulevard, Los Angeles, CA 90067; c/o International Creative Management, 40 W. 57th Street, New York, NY 10019. PUBLICIST—c/o Marilyn Heston, Michael Levine Public Relations, Inc., 8730 Sunset Boulevard, Los Angeles, CA 90069.*

*   *   *

CROW, Laura 1945-

PERSONAL: Born September 29, 1945, in Hanover, NH; daughter of James Franklin (a college professor) and Rebecca Ann (Crockett) Crow; children: Sarah Katherine Caine, Matthew Jordan Caine. EDUCATION: Boston University, B.F.A., 1967; University of Wisconsin, M.F.A., 1969; University of London, certificate of graduation, 1970; trained as a designer at the London College of Fashion, 1972.

VOCATION: Costume designer.

CAREER: FIRST LONDON STAGE WORK—Costume designer, *Electra,* Greenwich Theatre, 1971. FIRST NEW YORK STAGE WORK—Costume designer, *Warp,* Ambassador Theatre, 1973. PRINCIPAL STAGE WORK—Costume designer: *Hot l Baltimore,* Center Stage, Baltimore, MD, 1973; *Sweet Bird of Youth,* Kennedy Center, Washington, DC, 1975, then Harkness Theatre, New York City, 1976; *Angel City,* McCarter Theatre, Princeton, NJ, 1977; *A Streetcar Named Desire,* Arena Stage, Washington, DC, 1978; *The Water Engine, Mr. Happiness,* both Plymouth Theatre, New York City, 1978; *The Blood Knot, Of Mice and Men,* both Pittsburgh Public Theatre, Pittsburgh, PA, 1978; *Uncle Vanya,* Spreckles Theatre, San Diego, CA, 1979; *Fifth of July,* Apollo Theatre, New York City, 1980; *A Tale Told,* Mark Taper Forum, Los Angeles, CA, 1981; *The Great Grandson of Jedediah Kohler, Richard II,* both Entermedia Theatre, New York City, 1982; *Cloud 9,* Arena Stage, 1985; *Orchards,* Lucille Lortel Theatre, New York City, 1986; *Burn This,* Plymouth Theatre, 1987.

Costume designer, all with the Circle Repertory Company, New York City: *The Farm,* 1976; *Feedlot, Ulysses in Traction, Brontosaurus,* all 1977; *Fifth of July, Glorious Morning, In the Recovery Lounge,* all 1978; *Winter Signs, Mary Stuart, Hamlet,* all 1979; *A Tale Told,* 1981; *Full Hookup,* 1983; *Levitation, Love's Labour's Lost,* both 1984; *Who's Afraid of Virginia Woolf?, Talley and Son,* both 1985; *Burn This,* 1987.

Costume designer, all with the Seattle Repertory Theatre, Seattle, WA: *The Taming of the Shrew, An Enemy of the People, Born Yesterday, The Dance of Death, Tintypes,* all 1980-81; *Savages, Awake and Sing,* both 1982; *Girl Crazy, The Real Thing, End Game, The Merry Wives of Windsor,* all 1985-86.

PRINCIPAL TELEVISION WORK—All as costume designer. Movies: *The Lathe of Heaven,* PBS, 1978. Specials: *Charlie Smith and the Fritter Tree,* PBS, 1977; *Fifth of July,* Showtime, 1980.

RELATED CAREER—Resident designer, teacher of design and construction techniques, University of Wisconsin, 1968; resident designer, teacher of costume design, University of Illinois, Macomb, 1969; costume shop foreman, resident designer, Greenwich Thea-

tre, London, 1970-73; costume shop supervisor, head cutter, designer, Academy Festival Theatre, Chicago, IL, 1974-78 seasons; teacher of costume design, Brandeis University, 1987; associate professor of costume design, University of Massachusetts, Amherst, 1987.

NON-RELATED CAREER—Clothing designer, sample maker, Wells, Rich, Greene, New York City, 1976; clothing and fabric designer, ATEX/USA, Ashville, NC, 1978-79.

WRITINGS: BOOKS—Contributor, design section, *Introduction to the Theatre,* by Frank M. Whiting; photographs of work have appeared in *A Costumer's Handbook* and *A Costume Designer's Handbook,* both by Covey and Ingham and in *ITI—Design '70.*

AWARDS: Chicago Lyric Opera Design Contest Award, 1968, for *Salome;* Drama Desk Award, 1973, for *Warp;* Joseph Jefferson Award nomination, 1975, for *Sweet Bird of Youth;* Joseph Jefferson Award, 1976, for *Misalliance;* Joseph Jefferson Award nomination, 1977, for *Too True to Be Good;* Joseph Jefferson Award nomination, 1978, for *Twelfth Night;* Maharam Award nomination, 1980, for *Hamlet;* Villager awards, 1980, for *Hamlet* and *Mary Stuart;* Helen Hayes Award nomination, 1985, for *Cloud 9;* Fulbright scholarship, 1967.

MEMBER: United Scenic Artists.

ADDRESSES: HOME—401 25th Avenue E., Seattle, WA 98112. OFFICE—Circle Repertory Company, 161 Avenue of the Americas, New York, NY 10013.

*   *   *

CURRAN, Leigh 1943-

PERSONAL: Born Leigh Curran Griggs, December 5, 1943, in Santa Barbara, CA; daughter of John Van Benschoten (a teacher) and Barbara (Hansl) Griggs; married Edward Herrmann (an actor), September 9, 1978. EDUCATION: Graduated American Musical and Dramatic Academy, 1964.

VOCATION: Actress and writer.

CAREER: BROADWAY DEBUT—Singer, actress, *How Now, Dow Jones,* Lunt-Fontanne Theatre, 1968. PRINCIPAL STAGE APPEARANCES—Kate, *The Lunch Girls,* Long Wharf Theatre, New Haven, CT, 1977; Jessie, *'night, Mother,* Actors Theatre of Louisville, Louisville, KY, 1985; Yvette, *Stitchers and Starlight Talkers,* Yale Repertory Theatre, New Haven, CT, 1986.

FILM DEBUT—Manic depressive, *I Never Promised You a Rose Garden,* New World Pictures, 1977. PRINCIPAL FILM APPEARANCES—Ida Ram, *Reds,* Paramount, 1981.

TELEVISION DEBUT—Student, *Secret Storm,* CBS, 1966. PRINCIPAL TELEVISION APPEARANCES—Series: Delilah, *Adam's Rib,* ABC, 1974; Connie Nyquist, *St. Elsewhere,* NBC, 1985; Judge, *Another World,* NBC, 1986.

WRITINGS: PLAYS, PRODUCED AND PUBLISHED—*Lunch Girls,* Long Wharf Theatre, New Haven, CT, 1977, published by Samuel French, Inc., 1984; *Alterations,* Portland Stage Company, Portland, ME, 1982, then Whole Theatre Company, Montclair, NJ,

LEIGH CURRAN

1984, later WPA Theatre, New York City, 1987, published by Samuel French, Inc., 1987. TELEPLAYS—Episodic: *The Paper Chase,* CBS; *St. Elsewhere,* NBC.

MEMBER: Actors' Equity Association, Screen Actors Guild, American Federation of Television and Radio Artists, Writers Guild, Dramatists Guild.

ADDRESSES: AGENT—International Creative Management, 40 W. 57th Street, New York, NY 10019.

D

DALE, Grover 1935-

PERSONAL: Born Grover Robert Aitken, July 22, 1935, in Harrisburg, PA; son of Ronal Rittenhouse (a restauranteur) and Emma Bertha (Ammon) Aitken; married Anita Rose Morris (an actress). EDUCATION: Trained for the stage with Mary Tarcai, 1961-64; studied voice with David Craig, 1963-64.

VOCATION: Director, choreographer, and actor.

CAREER: STAGE DEBUT—Chorus, *Li'l Abner,* Pittsburgh, PA, 1953. BROADWAY DEBUT—Chorus, *Li'l Abner,* St. James Theatre, New York City, 1956. LONDON DEBUT—Barnaby Slade, *Sail Away,* Savoy Theatre, 1962. PRINCIPAL STAGE APPEARANCES— Chorus, *Call Me Madam,* Pittsburgh Civic Light Opera, Pittsburgh, PA, 1953; Snowboy, *West Side Story,* Winter Garden Theatre, New York City, 1960; Andrew, *Greenwillow,* Alvin Theatre, New York City, 1960; Barnaby Slade, *Sail Away,* Broadhurst Theatre, New York City, 1961; Mr. Mackintosh, *Too Much Johnson,* Phoenix Theatre, New York City, 1964; Pearce, *Half-a-Sixpence,* Broadhurst Theatre, New York City, 1965.

PRINCIPAL STAGE WORK—Assistant choreographer, *Ballets U.S.A.,* Alvin Theatre, New York City, 1958; choreographer, *Billy,* Billy Rose Theatre, New York City, 1969; director, *Pinkville,* Berkshire Theatre Festival, Stockbridge, MA, 1970; choreographer, *Steambath,* Truck and Warehouse Theatre, New York City, 1970; co-director, *Acrobats, Line,* both Theatre de Lys, New York City, 1971; director, choreographer, *Jump Crow,* Lenox Arts Center, New York City, 1972; choreographer, *Molly,* Alvin Theatre, 1973; choreographer, *Rachel Lily Rosenbloom and Don't You Ever Forget It,* Broadhurst Theatre, 1973; co-choreographer (with Michael Bennett), *Seesaw,* Uris Theatre, New York City, 1973; director, choreographer, *The Magic Show,* Cort Theatre, New York City, 1974; director, choreographer, *King of Schnorrers,* Harold Clurman Theatre, then Playhouse Theatre, both New York City, 1979; director, *One More Song, One More Dance,* Joyce Theatre, New York City, 1983.

MAJOR TOURS—Drum major, *The Amazing Adele,* U.S. cities, 1956; Snowboy, *West Side Story,* European cities, 1960-61.

PRINCIPAL FILM APPEARANCES—*The Unsinkable Molly Brown,* Metro-Goldwyn-Mayer, 1964; *Les Demoiselles de Rochefort,* Comacio, 1967; *Half-a-Sixpence,* Paramount, 1968; *The Landlord,* United Artists, 1970.

PRINCIPAL FILM WORK—Producer, director, *Douglas, James and Joe,* 1968.

PRINCIPAL TELEVISION APPEARANCES—All as a dancer. Series:

Jackie Gleason Show, CBS, 1954; *Martha Raye Show,* NBC, 1964; *The Gershwin Years,* CBS, 1960; *Look Up and Live,* CBS, 1965; *Perry Como Show,* NBC; *Milton Berle Show,* NBC; *Sid Caesar Show,* NBC; *Ed Sullivan Show,* CBS.

AWARDS: Best Choreography, Drama Desk Award, 1969, Antoinette Perry Award nomination, 1970, both for *Billy;* Best Choreographer (with Michael Bennett), Antoinette Perry Award, 1973, for *Seesaw.*

MEMBER: Actors' Equity Association, Screen Actors Guild, American Federation of Television and Radio Artists.

ADDRESSES: AGENT—c/o Eric Shepard, 40 W. 57th Street, New York, NY 10019.*

* * *

DAMON, Stuart 1937-

PERSONAL: Born Stuart Michael Zonis, February 5, 1937, in Brooklyn, NY; son of Marvin Leonard (a manufacturer) and Eva (Sherer) Zonis; married Deirdre Ann Ottewill (an actress, singer, and dancer) March 12, 1961; children: one daughter. EDUCATION: Brandeis University, B.A., psychology, 1958; trained for the stage with Charles Conrad and David Pressman at the Neighborhood Playhouse School of the Theatre, 1958, and with Uta Hagen, Frank Corsaro, and Maude Tweedy; studied dance with Luigi, ballet with Don Farnsworth.

VOCATION: Actor.

CAREER: STAGE DEBUT—Chorus, state trooper, *Plain and Fancy,* Lambertville Music Circus, Lambertville, NY, 1957. BROADWAY DEBUT—Chorus, *First Impressions,* Alvin Theatre, 1959. LONDON DEBUT—Jack Connor, *Charlie Girl,* Adelphi Theatre, 1965. PRINCIPAL STAGE APPEARANCES— Tony, *The Boy Friend,* Cape Playhouse, Dennis, MA, 1958; ghost, *The Enchanted,* Dominic, *Venus Observed,* George, *Twentieth Century,* gardener, *Monique,* Ambrose, *The Matchmaker,* all Theatre-by-the-Sea, Matunuck, RI, 1960; Frangipane, *Irma la Douce,* Plymouth Theatre, New York City, 1960, then as Nestor LeFripe in the same play, Riviera Hotel, Las Vegas, NV, 1961; Curt, *Entertain a Ghost,* Actors Playhouse, New York City, 1962; Antipholus of Syracuse, *The Boys from Syracuse,* Theatre Four, New York City, 1963; Conrad Birdie, *Bye Bye Birdie,* Melodyland Theatre, Berkeley, CA, 1963; Ed Farrish, *Y.M.2, Cool Off!,* Forrest Theatre, Philadelphia, PA, 1964; John Hardy, *Damn Yankees,* Packard Music Hall, Warren, OH, 1964; Sir Lancelot, *Camelot,* Paper Mill Playhouse, Milburn,

69

NJ, 1965; Eddie Yaeger, *Do I Hear a Waltz?*, 46th Street Theatre, New York City, 1965; title role, *Houdini: Man of Magic*, Piccadilly Theatre, London, 1966; title role, *Macbeth*, Marlowe Theatre, Canterbury, U.K., 1970; Eddie Payne, *Cadenza*, Thorndike Theatre, Leatherhead, U.K., 1973; Ben Silverman, *The Sunshine Boys*, Piccadilly Theatre, 1975. Also appeared in *From A to Z*, Plymouth Theatre, 1960, and as King Charles, *Nell*, Richmond, U.K., 1970.

MAJOR TOURS—Title role, *L'il Abner*, U.S. cities, 1959; John Shand, *Maggie*, U.S. cities, 1962; Joey, *The Most Happy Fella*, U.S. cities, 1962; Leadville Johnny Brown, *The Unsinkable Molly Brown*, U.S. cities, 1963.

TELEVISION DEBUT—*Look Up and Live*, CBS, 1960. PRINCIPAL TELEVISION APPEARANCES—Episodic: *Bell Telephone Hour*, NBC, 1960; *P.M. East*, WNEW, New York, 1961; *Naked City*, ABC, 1962; *Talent Scouts*, CBS, 1962; *A Really Good Jazz Piano*, 1964. Series: Craig Stirling, *The Champions*, NBC, 1968; Alan Quartermaine, *General Hospital*, ABC. Special: Prince, *Cinderella*, CBS, 1965. Guest: *Memory Lane*, independant, 1965-66; *Today Show*, NBC, 1965-66.

PRINCIPAL FILM APPEARANCES—*Young Doctors in Love*, Twentieth Century-Fox, 1982; *Star 80*, Warner Brothers, 1983.

AWARDS: Theatre World Award, 1963, for *The Boys from Syracuse*.

SIDELIGHTS: RECREATIONS—Riding, breeding, and training horses.

ADDRESSES: HOME—31 Shawfield Street, London SW3, England.*

*   *   *

D'ANGELO, Beverly

PERSONAL: Born in Columbus, OH; daughter of a bass player and his wife, a violinist.

VOCATION: Actress.

CAREER: FILM DEBUT—*The Sentinel*, Universal, 1977. PRINCIPAL FILM APPEARANCES—Stella, *Maid to Order*, New Century/Vista, 1987; Francine Glatt, *In the Mood*, Lorimar, 1987; also appeared in *Annie Hall*, United Artists, 1977; *Every Which Way But Loose*, Warner Brothers, 1978; *Hair*, United Artists, 1979; *Coal Miner's Daughter*, Universal, 1980; *Honky Tonk Freeway*, Universal, 1981; *Paternity* Paramount, 1981; *National Lampoon's Vacation*, Warner Brothers, 1983; *Finders Keepers*, Warner Brothers, 1984; *National Lampoon's European Vacation*, Warner Brothers, 1985; *Big Trouble*, Columbia, 1986; sequence four, "Rigoletto," *Aria*, RVP/Virgin Vision, 1987; also *First Love*, 1977.

NEW YORK DEBUT—Ophelia, *Rockabye Hamlet*. PRINCIPAL STAGE APPEARANCES—Marilyn, *Hey, Marilyn*, Charlottetown Festival Repertory Company; also appeared in an Off-Broadway production, *The Zinger*.

PRINCIPAL TELEVISION APPEARANCES—Movies: Stella Kowalski, *A Streetcar Named Desire*, ABC, 1984; Mary Hearn, *Hands of a Stranger*, CBS, 1987; also appeared in *Doubletake*, CBS, 1985.

RELATED CAREER: Cartoonist, Hanna-Barbera Studios, Hollywood, CA; formerly a singer with music group, Elephant.

ADDRESSES: MANAGER—Keith Addis and Associates, 8444 Wilshire Boulevard, Beverly Hills, CA 90211.*

*   *   *

DANIELS, Ron   1942-

PERSONAL: Born Ronald George Daniel, October 15, 1942, in Niteroi, Brazil; son of Percy and Nellie Daniel; married Anjula Harman. EDUCATION: Trained for the stage at Fundacao Brasileira de Teatro.

VOCATION: Director and actor.

CAREER: LONDON DEBUT—John Grass, *Indians*, Aldwych Theatre, 1968. PRINCIPAL STAGE APPEARANCES—Jimmy Porter, *Look Back in Anger*, Donal Davoren, *Shadow of a Gunman*, both Byre Theatre, St. Andrew's, Scotland, U.K., 1964; Orlando, *As You Like It*, Hotspur, *Henry IV, Part I*, Higgins, *Pygmalion*, title role, *Macbeth*, Brutus, *Julius Caesar*, Orgon, *Tartuffe*, Malvolio, *Twelfth Night*, all with the Victoria Theatre Repertory Company, Stoke-on-Trent, U.K., 1965-66; Benvolio, *Romeo and Juliet*, Richmond, U.K., 1967.

PRINCIPAL STAGE WORK—Director: *Electra*, *Pot O' Gold*, both Victoria Theatre, Stoke-on-Trent, U.K., 1966; *She Stoops to Conquer*, Victoria Theatre, 1967; *Who's Afraid of Virginia Woolf?*, *Sweeney Todd*, *Fighting Man*, *Hamlet*, *Major Barbara*, *The Recruiting Officer*, *Coriolanus*, *Drums in the Night*, all Victoria Theatre, 1969-71; *The Samaritan*, Victoria Theatre, then Shaw Theatre, London, 1971; *The Long, the Short and the Tall*, Shaw Theatre, 1971; *Bang*, Open Space Theatre, London, 1973; *The Children's Crusade*, National Youth Theatre, London, 1973; *Female Transport*, Half Moon Theatre, London, 1973; *The Motor Show*, Half Moon Theatre, 1974; *By Common Consent*, National Youth Theatre, 1974; *Afore Night Come*, Other Place Theatre, Stratford-on-Avon, U.K., 1974, then Long Wharf Theatre, New Haven, CT, 1975; *Ashes*, Young Vic Theatre, London, 1975; *Into the Mouth of Crabs*, National Theatre, London, 1975; *Made in Britain*, Oxford Playhouse, Oxford, U.K., 1976; *Bingo*, *Ivanov*, both Yale Repertory Theatre, New Haven, CT, 1976; *Destiny*, Other Place Theatre, 1976; *Tis Pity She's a Whore*, *The Lorenzaccio Story*, *The Sons of Light*, all Other Place Theatre, 1977; *Puntila and His Servant Matti*, Yale Repertory Theatre, 1977; *Man Is Man*, Yale Repertory Theatre, 1978; *The Women Pirates, Ann Bonney and Mary Read*, Aldwych Theatre, London, 1978; *Hyppolytus*, Other Place Theatre, 1978; *Pericles*, *The Suicide*, both Other Place Theatre, 1979; *Romeo and Juliet*, Guthrie Theatre, Minneapolis, MN, 1979, then Memorial Theatre, Stratford-on-Avon, U.K., 1980; *Timon of Athens*, *Hansel and Gretel*, both Other Place Theatre, 1980. Also directed *Serjeant Musgrave's Dance*, Bristol, U.K., 1975.

MAJOR TOURS—Marc Antony, *Julius Caesar*, U.K. cities, 1968.

RELATED CAREER—Founding member, Workshop Theatre, (Teatro Oficina) of Sao Paulo; assistant director, Victoria Theatre, Stoke-on-Trent, 1969-71; artistic director, then associate director, Other Place Theatre, Stratford-on-Avon, U.K., 1977—.

AWARDS: Obie Award, 1976, for *Bingo*; British Council Bursary to the British Drama League in Acting and Stagecraft.

ADDRESSES: OFFICE—Royal Shakespeare Theatre, Stratford-on-Avon, Warwickshire CV32 5XZ, England.*

*   *   *

DANNER, Blythe 1944-

PERSONAL: Full name, Blythe Katharine Danner; born in 1944, in Philadelphia, PA; daughter of Harry Earl (a bank executive) and Katharine Danner; married Bruce W. Paltrow (a writer and producer), December 14, 1969; children: Gwyneth Kate, Jake, Laura. EDUCATION: Bard College, B.A., drama, 1965.

VOCATION: Actress.

CAREER: OFF-BROADWAY DEBUT—Girl, *The Infantry,* 81st Street Theatre, 1966. PRINCIPAL STAGE APPEARANCES— Helena, *A Midsummer Night's Dream,* Irene, *The Three Sisters,* both Trinity Square Players, Providence, RI, 1967; Michele, *Mata Hari,* National Theatre, Washington, DC, 1967; girl, *Summertree,* Forum Theatre, New York City, 1968; Sister Martha, *Cyrano de Bergerac,* Vivian Beaumont Theatre, New York City, 1968; Violet Bean, *Up Eden,* Jan Hus Theatre, New York City, 1968; Connie Odum, *Someone's Comin' Hungry,* Pocket Theatre, New York City, 1969; Elsie, *The Miser,* Vivian Beaumont Theatre, 1969; Jill Tanner, *Butterflies Are Free,* Booth Theatre, New York City, 1969; title role, *Major Barbara,* Mark Taper Forum, Los Angeles, CA, 1971; Viola, *Twelfth Night,* Vivian Beaumont Theatre, 1972; Nina, *The Seagull,* Williamstown Theatre Festival, Williamstown, MA, 1974; Isabel, *Ring Around the Moon,* Williamstown Theatre Festival, 1975; Cynthia Karslake, *The New York Idea,* Brooklyn Academy of Music, Brooklyn, NY, 1977; Lisa, *Children of the Sun,* Williamstown Theatre Festival, 1979; Emma, *Betrayal,* Trafalgar Theatre, New York City, 1980; Tracy Lord, *The Philadelphia Story,* Vivian Beaumont Theatre, 1980; Elvira, *Blithe Spirit,* Morris Mechanic Theatre, Baltimore, MD, then Neil Simon Theatre, New York City, both 1987. Also appeared as Laura, *The Glass Menagerie,* 1965; and in *The Service of Joseph Axminster, The Way Out of the Way In,* and *The Knack,* all Theatre Company of Boston, Boston, MA, 1965-66.

FILM DEBUT—*To Kill a Clown,* Twentieth Century-Fox, 1972. PRINCIPAL FILM APPEARANCES—Martha Jefferson, *1776,* Columbia, 1972; *Lovin' Molly,* Columbia, 1974; *Hearts of the West,* United Artists, 1975; *Futureworld,* American International, 1976; *The Great Santini,* Warner Brothers, 1980; *Too Far To Go,* Zoetrope, 1982; *Man, Woman and Child,* Paramount, 1983; *Brighton Beach Memoirs,* Universal, 1986.

PRINCIPAL TELEVISION APPEARANCES—Episodic: *N.Y.P.D.,* ABC, 1968; *M*A*S*H,* CBS. Series: Amanda, *Adam's Rib,* ABC, 1973. Specials: Nina, *The Seagull,* PBS, 1975; Alma, *Eccentricities of a Nightingale,* PBS, 1976; Alice, *You Can't Take It with You,* PBS, 1979; also in *George M!,* 1970; *To Be Young, Gifted, and Black,* 1972. Movies: Zelda Fitzgerald, *F. Scott Fitzgerald and "The Last of the Belles,"* 1974; Eleanor Gehrig, *A Love Affair: The Eleanor and Lou Gehrig Story,* 1978; Joan Maple, *Too Far to Go,* 1979; also appeared in *Guilty Conscience,* CBS, 1985; *To Confuse an Angel,* 1970; *Doctor Cook's Garden,* 1971; and in *The Scarecrow.*

AWARDS: Theatre World Award, 1969, for *The Miser;* Antoinette Perry Award, 1971, for *Butterflies Are Free;* Antoinette Perry Award nomination, 1980, for *Betrayal;* Best Actress Award, Vevey

Film Festival, Switzerland, 1982. Honorary degrees—D.F.A., Bard College, 1981; L.H.D., Hobart-Smith College, 1981.

ADDRESSES: AGENT—Agency for the Performing Arts, Inc., 9000 Sunset Boulevard, Suite 315, Los Angeles, CA 90069.*

*   *   *

DANZA, Tony 1951-

PERSONAL: Born April 12, 1951, in Brooklyn, NY; married Tracy Robinson, June 28, 1986. EDUCATION: Received B.S., history, from the University of Dubuque.

VOCATION: Actor.

CAREER: PRINCIPAL TELEVISION APPEARANCES—Series: Tony Banta, *Taxi,* ABC, 1978-82, then NBC, 1982-83; Tony Micelli, *Who's the Boss?,* ABC, 1984—. Pilots: *Fast Lane Blues.* Movies: *Murder Can Hurt You,* 1981; *Singles Bars, Single Women,* ABC, 1984; *Doing Life,* NBC, 1986; *Wall of Tyranny,* NBC, 1987. Specials: *Night of 100 Stars II,* ABC, 1985.

PRINCIPAL FILM APPEARANCES—*Hollywood Knights,* Columbia, 1980; *Going Ape,* Paramount, 1981; *Cannonball Run,* Twentieth Century-Fox, 1983.

PRINCIPAL STAGE APPEARANCES—Participated in *Night of 100 Stars II,* Radio City Music Hall, New York City, 1985.

NON-RELATED CAREER—Boxer.

MEMBER: American Federation of Television and Radio Artists.

SIDELIGHTS: Tony Danza's prizefighting career began when he entered the New York Golden Gloves competition and made the lightweight semi-finals. Returning the next year as a middleweight, he advanced to the finals where a narrow decision cost him the title. Upon turning professional, Danza compiled a 12-3 record in the ring.

ADDRESSES: AGENT—c/o Frank Lieberman, FHL Company, 14319 Hartsook Street, Sherman Oaks, CA 91423.

*   *   *

Da SILVA, Howard 1909-1986

PERSONAL: Born Howard Silverblatt, May 4, 1909, in Cleveland, OH; died of lymphoma, February 16, 1986, in Ossining, NY; son of Benjamin (a dress cutter) and Bertha (Sen) Silverblatt; married Marjorie Nelson, 1950 (divorced, 1960); married Nancy Nutter (an actress), June 30, 1961; children: two sons, three daughters. EDUCATION: Attended Carnegie Institute of Technology.

VOCATION: Actor and director.

CAREER: OFF-BROADWAY DEBUT—*The Lower Depths,* Civic Repertory Theatre, 1929. PRINCIPAL STAGE APPEARANCES— Stationmaster, *The Cherry Orchard,* New Amsterdam Theatre, New York City, 1933; Astrov, *Uncle Vanya,* artist, *When We Dead*

Awaken, Don Victorio, *Fortunato,* all Brattle Hall Theatre, Cambridge, MA, 1933-34; (as Howard Solness) foreman, *Ten Million Ghosts,* St. James Theatre, New York City, 1936; Lewis, *Golden Boy,* Belasco Theatre, New York City, 1937; Larry Foreman, *The Cradle Will Rock,* Venice Theatre, then Windsor Theatre, both New York City, 1937; old man, *Casey Jones,* Fulton Theatre, New York City, 1938; Jack Armstrong, *Abe Lincoln in Illinois,* Plymouth Theatre, New York City, 1938; Speed, *Summer Night,* St. James Theatre, 1939; guide, *Two on an Island,* Broadhurst Theatre, New York City, 1940; Jud Fry, *Oklahoma!,* St. James Theatre, 1943; Friend Ed, *Burning Bright,* Broadhurst Theatre, 1950; Mendele, *The World of Sholom Aleichem,* Barbizon Plaza Theatre, New York City, 1953; Doc, *Mister Roberts,* Warwick Musical Theatre, Warwick, RI, then Oakdale Musical Theatre, Wallingford, CT, both 1954; fixer, Lt. Charles, *The Adding Machine,* Neel Fedoseitch Mamaev, *Diary of a Scoundrel,* both Phoenix Theatre, New York City, 1956; title role, *Volpone,* Rooftop Theatre, New York City, 1957; Prosecutor Horn, *Compulsion,* Ambassador Theatre, New York City, 1957; Ben Marino, *Fiorello!,* Broadhurst Theatre, 1959. Ottaker, *Romulus,* Music Box Theatre, New York City, 1962; Calchas, *La Belle,* Shubert Theatre, Philadelphia, PA, 1962; Max Hartman, *In the Counting House,* Biltmore Theatre, New York City, 1962; Paul Hirsch, *Dear Me, the Sky Is Falling,* Music Box Theatre, 1963; Claudius, *Hamlet,* New York Shakespeare Festival, Delacorte Theatre, New York City, 1964; Archbishop, *The Unknown Soldier and His Wife,* Vivian Beaumont Theatre, New York City, 1967; Benjamin Franklin, *1776,* 46th Street Theatre, New York City, 1969; title role, *Volpone,* Walnut Street Theatre, Philadelphia, PA, 1972.

With the Civic Repertory Theatre, New York City: Slave, *The Would-Be Gentleman,* apothecary, *Romeo and Juliet,* both 1929; Scaevola, *The Green Cockatoo,* orderly, *The Three Sisters,* Schumann, *Siegfried,* Cookson, Ostrich, *Peter Pan,* Hodges, *Alison's House,* second coastguardsman, *The Good Hope,* all 1930; guest, *Camille,* Mufti, *The Would-Be Gentleman,* Senator Lewis, *Inheritors,* stationmaster, *The Cherry Orchard,* all 1931; Wolf Biefeld, *Liliom,* Ferapont, *The Three Sisters,* countryman, *Cradle Song,* Dr. Samuel Johnson, *Dear Jane,* cook, White Knight, *Alice in Wonderland,* all 1932; Sepp Kriz, *Sailors of Cattaro,* 1934; Hansy McCulloh, *Black Pit,* 1935.

Also appeared in *Rain from Heaven, Between Two Worlds, The Master Builder,* all Cleveland Playhouse, Cleveland, OH, 1935; *Monday's Heroes, The Banker's Daughter,* both Actors Laboratory Theatre, Hollywood, CA, 1948-49; concert readings of Mark Twain, Sholom Aleichem, and Anton Chekhov, Actors Concert Theatre, 1951-52; *The Prodigious Snob, The Silver Tassle, The Caucasian Chalk Circle, The Cherry Orchard, The World of Sholom Aleichem, A Phoenix Too Frequent, The Gamblers,* all Crystal Lake Theatre, Crystal Lake, NY, 1955; *Anastasia, Tea and Sympathy, The Lesser Comores, The World of Sholom Aleichem,* all Bucks County Playhouse, New Hope, PA, 1956; *Nature's Way, Holiday for Lovers, The Little Foxes, Visit to a Small Planet, Three Men on a Horse,* all Valley Playhouse Theatre, Chagrin Falls, OH, 1958; *The Caucasian Chalk Circle,* Queensborough Community College, Queens, NY, 1975; *The Most Dangerous Man in America,* Coconut Grove Playhouse, Coconut Grove, FL, 1976.

PRINCIPAL STAGE WORK—All as director: *Waiting for Lefty, The Inheritors,* both People's Theatre, Cleveland, OH, 1935; *The Cradle Will Rock,* Mansfield Theatre, New York City, 1947; *Proud Accents,* Actors Laboratory Theatre, Hollywood, CA, 1949; concert readings of Mark Twain, Sholom Aleichem, and Anton Chekhov, Actors Concert Theatre, 1951-52; (also producer) *The World of*

Sholom Aleichem, Barbizon Plaza Theatre, New York City, 1953; *Sandhog,* Phoenix Theatre, New York City, 1954; (also producer) *The Prodigious Snob, The Silver Tassle, The Cherry Orchard, The Caucasian Chalk Circle, The World of Sholom Aleichem, A Phoenix Too Frequent, The Gamblers,* all Crystal Lake Theatre, Crystal Lake, NY, 1955; *The World of Sholom Aleichem, Anastasia, Tea and Sympathy, The Lesser Comores,* all Bucks County Playhouse, New Hope, PA, 1956; (also producer) *Tevya and His Daughters,* Carnegie Hall Playhouse, New York City, 1957; (also producer) *Nature's Way, Holiday for Lovers, The Little Foxes, Visit to a Small Planet, Three Men on a Horse,* all Valley Playhouse Theatre, Chagrin Falls, OH, 1958; *The Cradle Will Rock,* City Center Theatre, New York City, 1960; *Purlie Victorious,* Cort Theatre, New York City, 1961; *Fiorello!,* Paper Mill Playhouse, Milburn, NJ, 1962; *Cages,* York Playhouse, New York City, 1963; *The Advocate,* American National Theatre Academy Playhouse, 1963; *Thistle in My Bed,* Gramercy Arts Theatre, New York City, 1963; *The Cradle Will Rock,* Theatre Four, New York City, 1964; *My Sweet Charlie,* Longacre Theatre, New York City, 1966. Also directed productions at Stage Arts Laboratory, 1935.

MAJOR TOURS—Thorvald, *A Doll's House,* Brack, *Hedda Gabler,* Halvard Solness, *The Master Builder,* all with the Civic Repertory Theatre, U.S. cities, 1933-34; Benjamin Franklin, *1776,* U.S. cities, 1972 and 1973. Also appeared in and directed *The World of Sholom Aleichem,* U.S. cities, 1953.

FILM DEBUT—*Once in a Blue Moon* Paramount, 1936. PRINCIPAL FILM APPEARANCES—Jack Armstrong, *Abe Lincoln in Illinois,* RKO, 1940; Benjamin Franklin, *1776,* Columbia, 1972. Appeared in *I'm Still Alive,* RKO, 1941; *The Sea Wolf, Blues in the Night, Navy Blues, Bad Men of Missouri, Strange Alibi, Sergeant York, Nine Lives Are Not Enough, Wild Bill Hickock Rides Again, Steel Against the Sky,* all Warner Brothers, 1941; *Juke Girl, Bullet Scars, Big Shot* all Warner Brothers, 1942; *Keeper of the Flame, Reunion, Omaha Trail,* all Metro-Goldwyn-Mayer (MGM), 1942; *Tonight We Raid Calais,* Twentieth Century-Fox, 1942; *Duffy's Tavern, Blue Dahlia, The Lost Weekend,* all Paramount, 1945; *Two Years Before the Mast,* Paramount, 1946; *Blaze of Noon, Unconquered,* both Paramount, 1947; *They Live by Night,* RKO, 1948; *Border Incident,* MGM, 1949; *The Great Gatsby,* Paramount, 1949; *Three Husbands, The Underworld Story,* both United Artists, 1950; *Wyoming Mail,* Universal, 1950; *Tripoli,* Paramount, 1950; *Fourteen Hours,* Twentieth Century-Fox, 1951; *Slaughter Trail,* RKO, 1951; *M,* Columbia, 1951; *David and Lisa,* Continental, 1962; *The Outrage,* MGM, 1964; *Nevada Smith,* Paramount, 1966; *Mommie Dearest,* Paramount, 1981; *Garbo Talks,* United Artists, 1984. Also appeared in *Five Were Chosen,* 1942; *Hollywood on Trial; The Private Files of J. Edgar Hoover.*

PRINCIPAL TELEVISION APPEARANCES—Episodic: *Hollywood Premiere,* NBC, 1949; "My Heart's in the Highlands," *Silver Theatre,* NBC, 1950; *Blue Hotel,* CBC, 1961; *Man on Back,* CBC, 1962; *The Defenders,* CBS, 1963; *The Nurses,* CBS, 1963; *East Side/West Side,* CBS, 1963; narrator, "A Heritage of Freedom," *Look Up and Live,* CBS; also appeared on *The Outer Limits,* ABC; *Ben Casey,* ABC; *The Man from U.N.C.L.E.,* NBC; *The Loner,* CBS; *The Fugitive,* ABC. Series: Anthony Celese, *For the People,* CBS, 1965; title role, also co-directed) *The Walter Fortune Story,* NBC, 1950. Specials: *Verna: USO Girl,* PBS, 1978; Appeared as Claudius, *Hamlet,* CBS; Mr. Peachum, *The Beggar's Opera,* NET; Khrushchev, *The Missiles of October,* ABC, 1975; and in *Stop, Thief,* 1976; Guest: *Camera Three,* CBS.

PRINCIPAL RADIO APPEARANCES—Performed in the plays of

Arch Oboler and Norman Corwin, CBS, 1940. PRINCIPAL RADIO WORK—director, *Great Classics,* (Federal Theatre, WPA project), WHN, WEVD, 1936.

RELATED CAREER—Guest artist, Syracuse Repertory Theatre, Syracuse, NY, 1972-73; also teacher, Stage Arts Laboratory, 1935.

NON-RELATED CAREER—Steel worker.

WRITINGS: PLAYS, PRODUCED—(Co-author) *The Most Dangerous Man in America,* Coconut Grove Playhouse, Miami Beach, FL, 1976. Also (with Felix Coon) *The Zulu and the Zayda.*

AWARDS: Academy Award nomination, 1945, for *The Lost Weekend;* Academy Award nomination, 1946, for *Two Years Before the Mast;* British Academy of Motion Picture Arts and Sciences Award nomination, 1962, for *David and Lisa;* Outstanding Performance by a Supporting Actor in a Dramatic Special, Emmy Award, 1978, for *Verna: USO Girl.**

*   *   *

DAVIS, Brad   1949-

PERSONAL: Born November 6, 1949, in Florida.

VOCATION: Actor.

CAREER: PRINCIPAL STAGE APPEARANCES—Various theatres in Atlanta, GA; Carlton Pine, *The Elusive Angel,* Manhattan Marymount Theatre, New York City, 1977; title role, *Entertaining Mr. Sloane,* Cherry Lane Theatre, New York City, 1981; Gregor, *Metamorphosis,* Mark Taper Forum, Los Angeles, 1982; Ned Weeks, *The Normal Heart,* Public Theatre, New York Shakespeare Festival, New York City, 1985; *Crystal and Fox,* New York City production.

PRINCIPAL FILM APPEARANCES—*Midnight Express,* Columbia, 1978; *A Small Circle of Friends,* United Artists, 1980; *Chariots of Fire,* Warner Brothers, 1981; *Querelle,* Triumph Films, 1982; *Cold Steel* (also known as *Stiletto*), Cinetel Films, 1987; Eddie, *Heart,* New World Pictures, upcoming; *Out of Range,* Trans World Entertainment, upcoming; *The American Cousin,* Italian, upcoming.

PRINCIPAL TELEVISION APPEARANCES—Series: *How to Survive a Marriage,* for ten months. Mini-Series: Ol' George Johnson, *Roots,* ABC, 1977; *Chiefs,* CBS, 1983; *Robert Kennedy and His Times,* CBS, 1985. Movies: *Sybil,* 1976; *A Rumor of War,* 1980; Julian Salina, *Blood Ties,* Showtime, 1986; Tony Cimo, *Vengeance,* CBS, 1986; Dean McCurdy, *When the Time Comes,* ABC, 1987; also *The Greatest Man in the World; Walt Whitman.*

ADDRESSES AGENT—c/o Toni Howard, William Morris Agency, Inc., 151 El Camino Drive, Beverly Hills, CA 90212.*

*   *   *

DAVIS, Geena

BRIEF ENTRY: The 1986 remake of the science fiction movie *The Fly* marked a turning point in the career of actress Geena Davis. Having studied at Boston University's professional actors' training

program, she then performed with the Mount Washington Repertory Theatre Company in New Hampshire. When she came to New York City to further her career, however, the five-foot-ten-inch Davis found her first jobs in modeling instead of acting. After landing roles in television commercials, she made her screen debut as the scantily clad actress who shared a dressing room with Dustin Hoffman's character, Dorothy Michaels, in the 1982 hit film *Tootsie.* Dabney Coleman, who had a featured role in that movie, then suggested Davis for the role of the good-natured Wendy on his television series *Buffalo Bill.* In 1985 she appeared in the films *Fletch* and *Transylvania 6-5000,* a vampire spoof, as well as starring in her own comedy series, *Sara.* From there she took on the role of the reporter whose scientist boyfriend turns into a genetic mutation of human and housefly in *The Fly.* In the June, 1986 *Cable Guide* she described the film as ''a romantic tragedy'' as well as horror story and reported that with humorist Mel Brooks as producer and Jeff Goldblum, an actor with numerous comedy credits, in the title role, the filmmakers worried that audiences might expect *The Fly* to be a comedy. Its gruesome special effects quickly changed any such expectations and Davis's performance in the dramatic role received generally good notices. She teamed with Goldblum again in the upcoming science fiction comedy *Earth Girls Are Easy.*

*   *   *

DAWSON, Anna

VOCATION: Actress.

CAREER: PRINCIPAL STAGE APPEARANCES—Chorus, then title role, *Marigold,* Savoy Theatre, London, 1959; Carol Arden, *Wildest Dreams,* Vaudeville Theatre, London, 1961; Sally, *The Man in the Moon,* Palladium Theatre, London, 1963; Farina, *Stand by Your Bedouin,* Monica Johnson, *Uproar in the House,* Muriel Kitson, *Let Sleeping Wives Lie,* all with the Brian Rix Theatre of Laughter, Garrick Theatre, London, 1967; Hilaret, *Lock Up Your Daughters,* Mermaid Theatre, London, 1969; Mary Porter, *She's Done It Again,* Garrick Theatre, 1969; title role, *Irma La Douce,* Marlowe Theatre, Canterbury, U.K., 1972; Lady Arabella Harvey, *Stand and Deliver,* Edinburgh Festival, Edinburgh, Scotland, U.K., then Round House Theatre, London, both 1972; Madame Feydeau, Miss Trill, *The Feydeau Farce Festival of Nineteen Nine,* Greenwich Theatre, London, 1972; Marfa Zlotochienko, *R Loves J,* Chichester Festival Theatre, Chichester, U.K., 1973; Anne Finch, *The Sacking of Norman Banks,* Arnaud Theatre, Guildford, U.K., then (as *The Sack Race*) Ambassadors Theatre, London, 1974; Gloria, *Roger's Last Stand,* Duke of York's Theatre, London, 1975; Eva, *Absurd Person Singular,* Thorndike Theatre, Leatherhead, U.K., 1976; *Hats Off,* Arnaud Theatre, 1977; Jan, *Bedroom Farce,* Thorndike Theatre, London, 1979. Also appeared in *Jack and the Beanstalk,* Greenwich Theatre, London, 1971; *Move Over Mrs. Markham,* O'Keefe Centre Theatre, Toronto, ON, Canada, 1973; *Deja Revue,* New London Theatre, London, 1974.

MAJOR TOURS—Helga Philby, *A Bedful of Foreigners,* U.K. cities, 1974.

PRINCIPAL TELEVISION APPEARANCES—Episodic: *Dixon of Dock Green; The Benny Hill Show; Life Begins at Forty.*

ADDRESSES: AGENT—Barry Burnett, Ltd., Suite 409, Princes House, 190 Piccadilly, London W1, England.*

ROSEMARY De ANGELIS

De ANGELIS, Rosemary   1933-

PERSONAL: Born in April 26, 1933, in Brooklyn, NY; daughter of Francis and Antoinette (Donofrio) De Angelis; children: Laurel Ann Bridges. EDUCATION: The Fashion Institute of Technology and Design, A.A.S., textile design; studied with Herbert Berghof in New York City.

VOCATION: Actress.

CAREER: STAGE DEBUT—The Girl, *The Queen and the Rebels,* Bucks County Playhouse, PA. OFF-BROADWAY DEBUT—Mary of Nazareth, *Between Two Thieves,* Cherry Lane Theatre. PRINCIPAL STAGE APPEARANCES—Mother, *The Transformation of Benno Blimpie,* Astor Place Theatre, New York City, 1977; Vera Vasilyevna, *The Nest of the Woodgrouse,* Public Theatre, New York Shakespeare Festival (NYSF), New York City, 1985, then Eisenhower Theatre, Kennedy Center, Washington, DC, 1986; Mistress Overdone, *Measure for Measure,* Delacorte Theatre, NYSF, New York City, 1985; Catherine Reardon, *And Miss Reardon Drinks a Little,* Missouri Repertory Theatre, Kansas City, MO, 1987; also as Mrs. Lopez, *In the Summer House,* Little Fox Theatre, New York City; Kate, *Put Them All Together,* McCarter Theatre, Princeton, NJ; Marie, *High Time,* Milwaukee Repertory Theatre, WI; Mrs. Amber, *Monkey, Monkey,* Cincinnati Playhouse-in-the-Park, OH; *The Impossible Years,* Baltimore, MD; *Two for the Seesaw,* Atlanta, GA; *Luv,* Flint, MI; other Off-Broadway productions, New York City include: *The Ex-Patriot, Rocky Road, The Paradise Kid, Almost on a Runway,* and *Caravaggio.*

FILM DEBUT—*For Pete's Sake,* Columbia, 1974. PRINCIPAL

FILM APPEARANCES—*The Last Detail,* Columbia, 1974; *Just You and Me,* Columbia, 1979; *The Wanderers,* Warner Brothers, 1979; *Enormous Changes at the Last Minute,* A.B.C. Productions, 1983; Helen Flagella, *Nothing Lasts Forever,* Metro-Goldwyn-Mayer/United Artists, 1984.

TELEVISION DEBUT—Mrs. D'Amato, *The Doctors,* NBC, 1978. PRINCIPAL TELEVISION APPEARANCES—Series: Jean Blake, *Another World,* NBC, 1986. Episodic: Millie, *Baker's Dozen,* CBS, 1982; Mrs. Portman, *The Equalizer,* CBS, 1986. Teleplays: "Monkey, Monkey," *Theatre in America,* PBS; Praskovya, *The Death of Ivan Ilych,* NET; *The Living Room,* Aniforms. Movies: Nina, *Out of the Darkness,* 1985.

AWARDS: Outstanding Featured Actress, Drama Desk Award, 1977, for *The Transfiguration of Benno Blimpie.*

MEMBER: Actors' Equity Association, Screen Actors Guild, American Federation of Television and Radio Artists.

ADDRESSES: AGENT—Peggy Grant Associates, Inc., 1650 Broadway, Suite 711, New York, NY 10019.

*   *   *

De LIAGRE, Alfred   1904-1987

PERSONAL: Born October 6, 1904, in Passaic, NJ; died in New York City of lung cancer, March 5, 1987; son of Alfred, Sr. (a textile manufacturer) and Frida (Unger) De Liagre; married Mary Howard, July 25, 1945; children: one son, one daughter. EDUCATION: Graduated from Yale University, 1926.

VOCATION: Producer and director.

CAREER: FIRST STAGE WORK—Assistant stage manager, Woodstock Playhouse, Woodstock, NY, 1930. FIRST LONDON STAGE WORK—Producer, director, *Yes, My Darling Daughter,* St. James Theatre, 1937. PRINCIPAL STAGE WORK—All in New York City unless indicated: Stage manager, *Twelfth Night,* Maxine Elliott's Theatre, 1930; producer (with Richard Aldrich) and director, *Three Cornered Hat,* Cort Theatre, 1933; producer (with Aldrich) and director, *By Your Leave,* Morosco Theatre, 1934; producer (with Aldrich), *Pure in Heart,* Longacre Theatre, 1934; producer (with Aldrich) and director, *Petticoat Fever,* Ritz Theatre, 1935; producer (with Aldrich) and director, *Fresh Fields,* Empire Theatre, 1936; producer, director, *Yes, My Darling Daughter,* Playhouse Theatre, 1937; producer, director, *I Am My Youth,* Playhouse Theatre, 1938; producer, director, *Mr. and Mrs. North,* Belasco Theatre, 1941; producer, director, *The Walrus and the Carpenter,* Cort Theatre, 1941; producer, director, *Ask My Friend Sandy,* Biltmore Theatre, 1943; co-producer, director, *Hello Out There,* Lobero Theatre, Santa Barbara, CA, 1943; producer, *The Voice of the Turtle,* Morosco Theatre, 1943, then Piccadilly Theatre, London, 1947; producer, *The Mermaids Singing,* Empire Theatre, 1945; producer, *The Druid Circle,* Morosco Theatre, 1947; producer, director, *The Madwoman of Chaillot,* Belasco Theatre, 1948, then St. James Theatre, London, 1951.

Producer, director, *Second Threshold,* Morosco Theatre, 1951; director, *Amelia Goes to the Ball, The Lovely Galatea,* both Central City Opera, Central City, CO, 1951; producer (with John C. Wilson), *The Deep Blue Sea,* Morosco Theatre, 1952; producer (with Roger L. Stevens and Henry Sherek) and director, *Escapade,* 48th Street Theatre, 1953; producer (with the Phoenix Theatre), *The Golden Apple,* Alvin Theatre, 1954; producer, *Janus,* Plymouth Theatre, 1955, then Aldwych Theatre, London, 1957; producer, director, *Nature's Way,* Coronet Theatre, 1957; producer, *The Girls in 509,* Belasco Theatre, 1958; producer, *J.B.,* American National Theatre Academy (ANTA) Playhouse, 1958; producer (with Roger L. Stevens, in association with Laurence Olivier), *The Tumbler,* Helen Hayes Theatre, 1960; producer, *Kwamina,* 54th Street Theatre, 1961; producer (with Joseph E. Levine), *Photo Finish,* Brooks Atkinson Theatre, 1963; producer, *The Irregular Verb to Love,* Ethel Barrymore Theatre, 1963; director, *Janus,* Paper Mill Playhouse, Milburn, NJ, 1965; director, *Love in E Flat,* Paper Mill Playhouse, 1967; producer (with Martha Scott), *The Time of Your Life,* Eisenhower Theatre, Kennedy Center, Washington, DC, 1972; producer (with Stevens), *Deathtrap,* Music Box Theatre, 1978; producer (with Stevens), *On Your Toes,* St. James Theatre, 1983.

As producer for the American National Theatre Academy, presented numerous productions by regional companies at the ANTA Playhouse, New York City, including: *The Three Sisters, Tiny Alice, A Flea in Her Ear,* all American Conservatory Theatre, 1969; *Sganarelle, Songs from Milkwood,* both National Theatre of the Deaf, 1969; *Our Town,* Plumstead Playhouse, 1969; *Henry V,* American Shakespeare Festival production, 1969; *No Place to Be Somebody,* New York Shakespeare Festival production, 1969; *Watercolor, Criss-Crossing,* both Playwrights Unit of the Actors Studio, 1970; *Gloria and Esperanza,* La Mama Experimental Theatre Company, 1970; *Harvey,* Phoenix Theatre Company, 1970; *The Cherry Orchard,* John Fernald Company, 1970; *Wilson in the Promise Land,* Trinity Square Repertory Company, 1970.

PRINCIPAL FILM WORK—Director, *Springtime for Henry,* Twentieth Century-Fox, 1934; producer, *The Voice of the Turtle,* Warner Brothers, 1947.

RELATED CAREER—Board of directors, American National Theatre Academy; trustee, American Shakespeare Festival; Committee of Theatrical Producers.

NON-RELATED CAREER—Board of directors, National Book Committee, 1958; Yale University Council; formerly a journalist.

AWARDS: New York Drama Critics Circle Award, 1949, for *The Madwoman of Chaillot;* decorated Chevalier, French Legion of Honor, 1949, for *The Madwoman of Chaillot;* Best Musical, New York Drama Critics Circle Award, 1954, for *The Golden Apple;* Best Play, Antoinette Perry Award, 1958, for *J.B.*

MEMBER: Actors Fund of America; League of New York Theatres (board of directors, 1940-87), American Theatre Wing (board of directors, 1951-87); Century Association, River Club, Maidstone Club.

OBITUARIES AND OTHER SOURCES: Variety, March 11, 1987.*

*   *   *

DEMME, Jonathan 1944-

PERSONAL: Born in 1944, in Baldwin, NY; son of a publicist/magazine editor and his wife; married Evelyn Purcell (a director).

EDUCATION: Attended University of Miami. MILITARY: U.S. Air Force, 1966.

VOCATION: Director and screenwriter.

CAREER: PRINCIPAL FILM WORK—Also see *WRITINGS* below; music coordinator, *Sudden Terror,* National General, 1970; unit publicist, *Von Richthofen and Brown,* United Artists, 1971; producer, *Angels, Hard as They Come,* New World, 1971; producer and second unit director, *The Hot Box,* New World, 1972; director, *Caged Heat,* New World, 1974; director, *Crazy Mama,* New World, 1975; director, *Fighting Mad,* Twentieth Century-Fox, 1976; director, *Citizens Band* (also known as *Handle with Care*), Paramount, 1977; director, *Last Embrace,* United Artists, 1979; director, *Melvin and Howard,* Universal, 1980; co-director, *Swing Shift,* Warner Brothers, 1984; director, *Stop Making Sense,* Island Alive, 1984; director, *Swimming to Cambodia,* Cinecom, 1987. Early in his career, worked as a publicist for Embassy Films Corporation, New York City; and with Al Viola in London, promoting American investment in British films.

PRINCIPAL TELEVISION WORK—Director, ''Murder in Aspic,'' *Columbo,* NBC, 1977; director, ''Who Am I This Time,'' *American Playhouse,* PBS, 1982; director, ''Surviving a Family Tree,'' pilot for a comedy series, PBS, 1984, broadcast as ''A Family Tree,'' *Trying Times,* PBS, 1987. Also produced commercials for a U.S. company in Britain.

WRITINGS: SCREENPLAYS—See production details above. (With Joe Viola) *Angels, Hard as They Come,* 1971; (with Viola) *The Hot Box,* 1972; *Caged Heat,* 1974; *Fighting Mad,* 1976. Also wrote movie reviews for *Film Daily* and rock music reviews for *Fusion.*

AWARDS: Citizens Band and *Melvin and Howard* were selected for screening at the New York Film Festival.

SIDELIGHTS: Jonathan Demme broke into the film industry working for Roger Corman, a producer known for his low-budget, often violent ''B movies.'' Of the several screenplays he wrote for Corman's New World Pictures, Demme told *American Film* (January-February, 1984), ''Writing was a way to get to direct.''

ADDRESSES: OFFICE—c/o Lee Winkler, Global Business Management, 9000 Sunset Boulevard, Suite 1115, Beverly Hills, CA 90069. AGENT—c/o Arnold Stiefel, William Morris Agency, 151 El Camino Drive, Beverly Hills, CA 90212.*

*   *   *

DESMOND, Dan 1944-

PERSONAL: Born July 4, 1944; son of Halet Monroe and Louise Desmond. EDUCATION: University of Wisconsin, B.F.A., 1971; trained for the stage at the Yale School of Drama, 1973. MILITARY: U.S. Marine Corps, 1963-67.

VOCATION: Actor.

CAREER: PRINCIPAL STAGE APPEARANCES—Tilman, *On Mount Chimborazo,* Dodger Theatre, New York City, 1978; Rufio, *Caesar and Cleopatra,* Major, *The Cat and the Fiddle,* George, *Of Mice and Men,* Wallingford, *Get Rich Quick Wallingford,* Steven, *In Celebration,* Hastings, *Richard III,* Bill Cracker, *Happy End,* all

Cleveland Playhouse, Cleveland, OH, 1978-79; older son, *Table Settings*, Chelsea Theatre, New York City, 1979; Power, *Gossip*, PAF Playhouse, Long Island, NY, 1979; son, *Eve*, Loretto Hilton Theatre, St. Louis, MO, 1980; Theseus, *Oedipus at the Holy Place*, Indiana Repertory Theatre, Indianapolis, IN, 1981; Jack, *Angel Street*, Playmakers Repertory Theatre, Chapel Hill, NC, 1981; Paul, secretary, *Rip Van Winkle*, Yale Repertory Theatre, New Haven, CT, 1982; Bonnefoy, *The Imaginary Invalid*, Eugene, *Geniuses*, both Arena Stage, Washington, DC, 1982; senator, soldier, *Othello*, Winter Garden Theatre, New York City, 1982; Buck, *A Perfect Diamond*, Park Royale Theatre, New York City, 1984; Jim Bayliss, *All My Sons*, John Golden Theatre, New York City, 1987. Also Jack, *A Woman without Means*, Milwaukee Repertory Theatre, Milwaukee, WI; Fluellen, *Henry V*, Oregon Shakespeare Festival, Ashland, OR; Sam, *Wait Until Dark*, Cape Playhouse, Dennis, MA; title role, *Macbeth*, Theatre X, Milwaukee, WI; Smirov, *The Bear*, Spectrum Theatre, New York City; Henry Stubbs, *The Vienna Notes*, Playwrights Horizons Theatre, New York City; Herakles, *The Frogs*, Yale Repertory Theatre, New Haven, CT; Hildy, *The Front Page*, Indiana Repertory Theatre; Friar Lawrence, *Romeo and Juliet*, Weathervane Theatre. Also appeared in *Mornings at Seven*, Lyceum Theatre, New York City, 1980; *The Lady and the Clarinet*, Lucille Lortel Theatre, New York City, 1983.

PRINCIPAL TELEVISION APPEARANCES—Episodic: *Ryan's Hope*, ABC; *Search for Tomorrow*, CBS; *Another World*, NBC; *All My Children*, ABC. Movies: Mr. Walker, *No Big Deal*, HBO, 1983; photographer, *Kennedy*, 1983.

DAN DESMOND

MEMBER: Actors' Equity Association, Screen Actors Guild, American Federation of Television and Radio Artists.

ADDRESSES: AGENT—Abrams Artists and Associates, Ltd., 420 Madison Avenue, New York, NY 10017.

*   *   *

DEWELL, Michael   1931-

PERSONAL: Born March 21, 1931, in West Haven, CT; son of Mansfield Humphrey (an engineer) and Rolly (Dwy) Dewell; married Nina Foch, October 31, 1967. EDUCATION: Yale University, B.A., 1952; University of London, M.A., 1953; trained for the stage at the Royal Academy of Dramatic Art, 1954, and with Uta Hagen, 1954-56. MILITARY: U.S. Army, 1956-58.

VOCATION: Theatre executive, producer, and writer.

CAREER: PRINCIPAL STAGE WORK—Director, *The Heiress*, Carnegie Hall Theatre, New York City, 1954; assistant producer, stage manager, *Dragon's Mouth*, Cherry Lane Theatre, New York City, 1955; assistant producer, stage manager, *Dandy Dick*, Cherry Lane Theatre, 1956; *The Crucible, The Seagull*, both Belasco Theatre, New York City, 1964; *Tonight at 8:30, The Imaginary Invalid, A Touch of the Poet*, all American National Theatre Academy Playhouse, New York City, 1967; *John Brown's Body, She Stoops to Conquer, The Comedy of Errors;* all Ford's Theatre, Washington, DC, 1968; *As You Like It, Macbeth, The Comedy of Errors*, all Los Angeles Free Shakespeare Festival, Los Angeles, CA, 1963; *The Turn of the Screw* (opera), *Anatol*, both American Festival, Boston Arts Center, Boston, MA, 1974; translator, *Blood Wedding, The Shoemaker's Prodigious Wife*, both Theatre/Theatro, Los Angeles, CA, 1985.

Producer with the National Repertory Theatre: *Hedda Gabler, Liliom*, both 1963; *Ring Around the Moon, She Stoops to Conquer*, both 1965; *The Madwoman of Chaillot*, 1966; *The Rivals, The Trojan Women, A Touch of the Poet*, all 1966; *As You Like It*, 1973; *Macbeth, The Comedy of Errors*, both 1974; also *L'il Abner; Hotel Universe*, all with the National Repertory Theatre.

MAJOR TOURS—Performed in *Kiss and Tell*, U.S. cities, 1954. Producer: *Mary Stuart*, U.S. cities, 1959-60, then 1962; *Once Upon a Mattress*, U.S. cities, 1959-60; *Elizabeth the Queen*, U.S. cities, 1961; *Ring Around the Moon, The Crucible, The Seagull*, all U.S. cities, 1964.

PRINCIPAL TELEVISION WORK—Specials: Producer: "Mary Stuart," *Play of the Week*, WNTA, 1962; *Inaugural Night at Ford's*, 1968; *CBS All-Star Gala*. Also produced over 200 television programs for WRAMC-TV.

RELATED CAREER—Stage manager, Cherry Lane Theatre, 1954-56; entertainment director, U.S. Chemical Corps, 1956; assistant executive producer, writer, WRAMC-TV (Department of Defense), 1957-58; founder, National Phoenix Theater, New York City, 1958-60; board of directors, American National Theatre Academy, 1960-68; founder, American Festival, Boston Arts Center, Boston, MA, 1961; advisor, New York State Council on the Arts, Albany, NY, 1962-64; founder, producer, National Repertory Theatre, New York City, 1961-67, then Los Angeles,

1969—; founder, Los Angeles Free Shakespeare Festival, Los Angeles, CA, 1963; supervisor of restoration, U.S. Department of Interior, Ford's Theatre Foundation, Washington, DC, 1967; founder, Los Angeles Free Public Theatre, Los Angeles, CA, 1974; administrative director, president, Academy of Stage and Cinema Arts, Los Angeles, CA, 1975—; founder, National Play Award, 1976; project director, Humanities and Arts Computer Consortium, 1982.

WRITINGS: PLAYS—See production details above. Translator (with Carmen Zapata), *Blood Wedding, The Shoemaker's Prodigious Wife*, 1985. Also translated (with Zapata) *Yerma*, 1981; *House of Bernarda Alba*, 1982; *Child of the Moon* (opera), 1985. SCREENPLAY—*Ole Hollywood*, 1987. FICTION—Editor, *Hell and High Water* (short story anthology), 1956.

AWARDS: Special citations, Outer Critics Circle Award, 1960 and 1962, to the National Repertory Theatre, both for *Mary Stuart;* Drama-Logue Award, 1981, for translation of *Yerma.*

MEMBER: Academy of Stage and Cinema Arts; Company Theatre Foundation (trustee, 1968—), Foundation for Multi-Media and the Arts, Bilingual Foundation of the Arts (secretary, 1982-83, vice-president, 1982-85, trustee, 1977-85); El Hogar de los Ninos, Tijuana, Mexico (trustee, 1984—), El Pueblo Parks Association (trustee).

ADDRESSES: OFFICE—National Repertory Theatre, P.O. Box 1884, Beverly Hills, CA 90213.*

*   *   *

DEY, Susan   1952-

PERSONAL: Born Susan Smith, December 10, 1952, in Pekin, IL; daughter of Robert (a newspaper editor) and Gail (Dey) Smith; married Leonard Hirshan.

VOCATION: Actress.

CAREER: TELEVISION DEBUT—Laurie Partridge, *The Partridge Family*, ABC, 1970-74. PRINCIPAL TELEVISION APPEARANCES—Episodic: *Little Women*, NBC, 1979; *Barnaby Jones*, CBS; *Hawaii Five-O*, CBS; *The Streets of San Francisco*, ABC; *Switch*, CBS. Series: Jane, *Loves Me, Loves Me Not*, CBS, 1977; Celia Mallory Warren, *Emerald Point, N.A.S.*, CBS, 1983; Grace Van Owen, *L.A. Law*, NBC, 1986—. Movies: *Terror on the Beach*, 1973; *Cage without a Key*, 1975; *Mary Jane Harper Cried Last Night*, 1977; *The Comeback Kid*, 1980; *The Gift of Life*, 1982; *Sunset Limousine*, 1983.

PRINCIPAL FILM APPEARANCES—Diane, *The Trouble with Dick*, Frolix Productions, 1987. Also appeared in *Skyjacked*, Metro-Goldwyn-Mayer, 1972; *Looker*, Warner Brothers, 1981; *Echo Park*, Atlantic, 1986; *First Love*, 1977.

RELATED CAREER—As a model, appeared on the covers of *Seventeen, American Girl*, and *Simplicity* magazines.

ADDRESSES: AGENT—William Morris Agency, 151 El Camino Drive, Beverly Hills, CA 90212.*

DILLON, Matt   1964-

PERSONAL: Born February 18, 1964, in New Rochelle, NY.

CAREER: FILM DEBUT—*Over the Edge*, 1979. PRINCIPAL FILM APPEARANCES—Title role, *Tex*, Buena Vista, 1982; Dallas, *The Outsiders*, Warner Brothers, 1983. Appeared in *Little Darlings*, Paramount, 1980; *My Bodyguard*, Twentieth Century-Fox, 1980; *Rumble Fish*, Zoetrope, 1983; *The Flamingo Kid*, Twentieth Century-Fox, 1984; *Target*, Warner Brothers, 1985; *Native Son*, Cinecom, 1986; *The Big Town*, Columbia, 1987; also *Liar's Moon*, 1982; *The Rebel and the Lover*, 1985.

TELEVISION DEBUT—Episodic: Ralph, "The Great American Fourth of July . . . and Other Disasters," *American Playhouse*, PBS.

PRINCIPAL STAGE APPEARANCES—Participated in *Night of 100 Stars II*, Radio City Music Hall, New York City, 1985.

ADDRESSES: c/o Ed Limato, William Morris Agency, 151 El Camino Drive, Beverly Hills, CA 90212.*

*   *   *

DISHY, Bob

PERSONAL: Born in Brooklyn, NY; son of Nathan and Amy (Barazani) Dishy; married Judy Graubart. EDUCATION: Graduated from Syracuse University, 1955. MILITARY: U.S. Army, 1957-59.

VOCATION: Actor.

CAREER: BROADWAY DEBUT—Rocky, *Damn Yankees*, 46th Street Theatre, 1956. PRINCIPAL STAGE APPEARANCES— Charlie Paal, *There Is a Play Tonight*, Theatre Marquee, New York City, 1961; Theophile, *Can-Can*, City Center Theatre, NY, 1962; Harry Toukarian, *Flora, the Red Menace*, Alvin Theatre, New York City, 1965; Sapiens, *By Jupiter*, Theatre Four, New York City, 1965; inventor, *The Unknown Soldier and His Wife*, Vivian Beaumont Theatre, New York City, 1967; Sheldon "Bud" Nemerov, *Something Different*, Cort Theatre, New York City, 1967; Arthur Korman, *The Goodbye People*, Ethel Barrymore Theatre, New York City, 1968; Alex Krieger, *A Way of Life*, American National Theatre Academy Playhouse, New York City, 1969; Adam, *The Creation of the World and Other Business*, Shubert Theatre, New York City, 1972; Arnold Brody, *An American Millionaire*, Circle in the Square, New York City, 1974; Abner Truckle, *Sly Fox*, Broadhurst Theatre, New York City, 1976; Paul Miller, *Murder at the Howard Johnson's*, John Golden Theatre, New York City, 1979; Jake, *Grownups*, American Repertory Theatre, Cambridge, MA, then Lyceum Theatre, New York City, both 1981, later Mark Taper Forum, Los Angeles, CA, 1983; Mort, *What's Wrong with This Picture?*, Manhattan Theatre Club, New York City, 1985. Also appeared in *Chic*, Orpheum Theatre, New York City, 1959; *From A to Z*, Plymouth Theatre, New York City, 1960; *Dig We Must*, John Drew Theatre, East Hampton, NY, 1960; *Medium Rare, Put It in Writing*, both Happy Medium Theatre, Chicago, IL, 1962; *When the Owl Screams Revue*, Square East Theatre, New York City, 1963; *Open Season at Second City*, (also director) *The Wrecking Ball*, both Square East Theatre, New York City, 1964.

MAJOR TOURS—*Medium Rare*, U.S. cities, 1960-61.

PRINCIPAL FILM APPEARANCES—*The Tiger Makes Out,* Columbia, 1967; *Lovers and Other Strangers,* Cinerama, 1970; *The Big Bus,* Paramount, 1976; *Last Married Couple in America,* Universal, 1980; *The First Family,* Warner Brothers, 1980; *Author! Author!,* Twentieth Century-Fox, 1982; *Brighton Beach Memoirs,* Universal, 1986; *Critical Condition,* Paramount, 1986.

PRINCIPAL TELEVISION APPEARANCES—Episodic: *Columbo,* NBC. Series: *That Was the Week That Was,* NBC, 1964-65; (also director of individual skits) *Story Theatre,* syndicated.

RECORDINGS: *Flora, the Red Menace,* (original cast recording), RCA, 1965.

AWARDS: Best Featured Actor in a Play, Antoinette Perry Award nomination, 1977, for *Sly Fox;* Drama Desk Award; All-Army Entertainment Contest; Chancellor's Medal for Distinguished Achievement, Syracuse University.

ADDRESSES: HOME—20 E. 9th Street, New York, NY 10003.*

*   *   *

DONNER, Richard

PERSONAL: Born in New York, NY.

VOCATION: Director and producer.

CAREER: PRINCIPAL FILM WORK—Director: *X-15,* United Artists, 1961; *Salt and Pepper,* United Artists, 1968; *Twinky,* 1969; *The Omen,* Twentieth Century-Fox, 1976; *Superman,* Warner Brothers, 1978; *The Final Conflict,* Twentieth Century-Fox, 1981; *Inside Moves,* Associated Film Distributors, 1981; executive producer, *The Toy,* Columbia, 1982; producer and director, *Ladyhawke,* Warner Brothers, 1985; co-producer and director, *The Goonies,* Warner Brothers, 1985; producer and director, *Lethal Weapon,* Warner Brothers, 1987.

PRINCIPAL TELEVISION WORK—Director: Series—*Wanted: Dead or Alive,* CBS, 1959. Episodic—*Kojak,* CBS; *Bronk,* CBS. Teleplays: Co-director (with Martin Ritt), *Of Human Bondage;* director, *Portrait of a Teen-Age Alcoholic.*

PRINCIPAL STAGE APPEARANCES—Performed Off-Broadway prior to working in film and television.

RELATED CAREER—Director of commercials, industrial films, and documentaries.

ADDRESSES: MANAGER—Bresaluer, Jacobson & Rutman, 10802 Wilshire Blvd., Los Angeles, CA 90024.*

*   *   *

DONOVAN, Arlene

VOCATION: Producer and agent.

CAREER: FIRST FILM WORK—Assistant to director Robert Rosen, "Cocoa Beach" (uncompleted). PRINCIPAL FILM WORK—Pro-

ducer: *Still of the Night,* Metro-Goldwyn-Mayer/United Artists, 1982; *Places in the Heart,* Tri-Star, 1984; executive producer, *Nadine,* Tri-Star, 1987.

RELATED CAREER—Worked in publishing prior to entering motion picture industry; story editor, Columbia Pictures; literary head, motion picture department, International Creative Management, 1969-82; also worked on stage projects.

ADDRESSES: OFFICE—International Creative Management, 40 W. 57th Street, New York, NY 10019.*

*   *   *

DOUGLAS, Michael
See CRICHTON, Michael

*   *   *

DOWD, M'el

PERSONAL: Born February 2, in Chicago, IL; daughter of John J. and Catherine (an office manager; maiden name, O'Conner) Dowd; married Henri G. Eudes (a maitre d'hotel), July 1, 1962; children: one son. EDUCATION: Trained for the stage at the Goodman Theatre School.

VOCATION: Actress.

CAREER: BROADWAY DEBUT—Lady Macbeth, *Macbeth,* Jan Hus Theatre, 1955. PRINCIPAL STAGE APPEARANCES—All in New York City unless indicated: Titania, *A Midsummer Night's Dream,* Lady Capulet, *Romeo and Juliet,* both Jan Hus Theatre, 1956; Portia, *Julius Caesar,* Jan Hus Theatre, 1957; Lilith, *Back to Methuselah,* Ambassador Theatre, 1958; Katherine of Aragon, *Royal Gambit,* Sullivan Street Playhouse, 1959; Morgan Le Fey, *Camelot,* Majestic Theatre, 1960; Agrippina, *The Emperor,* Maidman Theatre, 1963; Anita Corcoran, *A Case of Libel,* Longacre Theatre, 1963; Mrs. Emilia Pattison, *The Right Honourable Gentleman,* Billy Rose Theatre, 1965; Elsa Schraeder, *The Sound of Music,* City Center Theatre, 967; woman, *The Unknown Soldier and His Wife,* Vivian Beaumont Theatre, 1967; Louise, *Everything in the Garden,* Plymouth Theatre, 1967; Hesione Hushabye, *Heartbreak House,* Arena Stage, Washington, DC, 1967; Mrs. Pelham, *The Right Honourable Gentleman,* Huntington Hartford Theatre, Los Angeles, CA, 1967; Andromache, *Tiger at the Gates,* Vivian Beaumont Theatre, 1968; Countess Aurelia, *Dear World,* Mark Hellinger Theatre, 1969; Great Aunt Amelia, *Mercy Street,* St. Clement's Church Theatre, 1969; Maude Bodley, *Not Now Darling,* Brooks Atkinson Theatre, 1970; Norma, *A Gun Play,* Cherry Lane Theatre, 1971; Amelia Newsome, *Ambassador,* Lunt-Fontanne Theatre, 1972; Mary Cassett, *Songs from the City Streets,* Manhattan Theatre Club, 1979; Frau Fahrenkopf, *The Night of the Iguana,* Morris Mechanic Theatre, Baltimore, MD, 1985. Also appeared in *Sweet Bird of Youth,* Martin Beck Theatre, 1959; *The Lady from Dubuque,* Morosco Theatre, 1980; *Mixed Couples,* Brooks Atkinson Theatre, 1980.

MAJOR TOURS—Lilith, *Back to Methuselah,* U.S. cities, 1958; Hattie, *Not Even in Spring,* U.S. cities, 1965.

FILM DEBUT—Miss O'Connor, *The Wrong Man*, Warner Brothers, 1957. PRINCIPAL FILM APPEARANCES—Mrs. Flint, *This Could Be the Night*, Metro-Goldwyn-Mayer (MGM), 1957; Rita, *Man on Fire*, MGM, 1957. Also appeared in *The 300 Year Weekend*, Cinerama, 1971.

PRINCIPAL TELEVISION APPEARANCES—Episodic: *Flipper*, NBC; *Education Exchange*, NBC. Series: Kate Farrow, *The Best of Everything*. Mini-series: *The Adams Chronicles*, 1975. Specials: *The Prince of Homburg; The Modern World of Shakespeare; The Trial Begins.*

NON-RELATED CAREER—Soda fountain attendant; switchboard operator.

MEMBER: Actors' Equity Association, Screen Actors Guild, American Federation of Television and Radio Artists.

SIDELIGHTS: FAVORITE ROLES—Lady Macbeth in *Macbeth*; Princess Kosmonopolis in *Sweet Bird of Youth*. RECREATIONS—Painting.

ADDRESSES: HOME—446 E. 86th Street, New York, NY 10028. OFFICE—Actors' Equity Association, 165 W. 46th Street, New York, NY 10036.*

*   *   *

DOWN, Lesley-Anne   1954-

PERSONAL: Born March 17, 1954, in London, England.

VOCATION: Actress.

CAREER: STAGE DEBUT—At age 14 in *All the Right Noises*. PRINCIPAL STAGE APPEARANCES—*Great Expectations, Hamlet.*

PRINICIPAL FILM APPEARANCES—Cecila, *Pope Joan*, 1972; *Scalawag*, Paramount, 1973; *Brannigan*, United Artists, 1975; Olga, *The Pink Panther Strikes Again*, United Artists, 1976; Anne Egerman, *A Little Night Music*, New World Pictures, 1977; *The Betsy*, Allied Artists, 1978; Miriam, *The Great Train Robbery*, United Artists, 1979; Margaret Sellinger, *Hanover Street*, Columbia, 1979; Gillian Bromley, *Rough Cut*, Paramount, 1980; Erica Baron, *Sphinx*, Warner Brothers, 1981; Dr. Flax, *Nomads*, Atlantic Releasing, 1986.

PRINCIPAL TELEVISION APPEARANCES—Mini-Series: Georgina Worsley, *Upstairs, Downstairs*, PBS, 1974; Chloe, *The Last Days of Pompeii*, ABC, 1984; Madeline Fabray, *North and South*, ABC, 1985; *North and South, Book II*, ABC, 1986. Movies: Phyllis Dixey, *Peek-a-Boo: The One and Only Phyllis Dixey*, 1979; Esmerelda, *The Hunchback of Notre Dame*, 1982; Bridget Conway, *Murder Is Easy*, 1982; Joan, *Arch of Triumph*, CBS, 1985. Teleplays: *Heartbreak House.*

RELATED CAREER—Began professional modeling at age ten for television commercials.

ADDRESSES: AGENT—c/o Lou Pitt, International Creative Management, 8899 Beverly Blvd., Los Angeles, CA 90048.*

DOWNS, Hugh   1921-

PERSONAL: Full name, Hugh Malcolm Downs; born February 14, 1921, in Akron, OH; son of Milton Howard and Edith (Hick) Downs; married Ruth Shaheen, February 20, 1944; children: Hugh Raymond, Deirdre Lynn. EDUCATION: Attended Bluffton College, 1938-39, Wayne State University, 1940-41, Columbia University, 1955-56.

VOCATION: Radio and televison broadcaster, actor, producer, and writer.

CAREER: PRINCIPAL TELEVISION WORK—Series: Announcer, *Kukla, Fran, and Ollie*, NBC, 1949; host, *Your Luncheon Date*, NBC, 1951; announcer, *The Home Show*, NBC, 1954; announcer, *Sid Caesar's Hour*, NBC, 1956-57; announcer, *The Jack Paar Show*, NBC, 1957-62; announcer, *The Tonight Show*, NBC, 1962; emcee, *Concentration*, NBC, 1961; host, *The Today Show*, NBC, 1962-72; host, *Not for Women Only*, 1972; host, *20/20*, ABC, 1978—; host, *Growing Old in America*, PBS, 1985; host, *Over Easy*, PBS. Pilots: Host, *Variety*, 1974. Movies: Portrayed himself, *Woman of the Year*, 1976. Specials: Moderator, *Broken Treaty at Battle Mountain: A Discussion*, 1975; reporter, *Liberty Weekend Preview*, 1986; *NBC's 60th Anniversary Celebration*, NBC, 1986; *Today at 35*, 1987. Guest: *Talent Scouts*, CBS, 1960; *Talent Search*, NBC, 1960.

PRINCIPAL FILM APPEARANCES—*Oh, God! Book II*, Warner Brothers, 1980. PRINCIPAL FILM WORK—Executive producer and narrator, *Nothing by Chance*, documentary, 1974.

PRINCIPAL RADIO WORK—Staff announcer and program director, WLOK, Lima, OH, 1939-40; staff announcer, WWJ, Detroit, MI, 1940-42; staff announcer, NBC, Chicago, IL, 1943-54; host, *Monitor*, NBC.

RELATED CAREER—Chairman, board of directors, Raylin Productions, Inc., 1960—; supervisor of science programming, NBC, for one year.

NON-RELATED CAREER—Science consultant to Westinghouse Laboratories and the Ford Foundation.

WRITINGS: NON-FICTION—(With Richard J. Roll) *Hugh Downs' Years Book*, Dell, 1982; *My Ten Thousand Hours on Television*, Putnam, 1986.

MEMBER: Actors' Equity Association, Screen Actors Guild, American Federation of Television and Radio Artists; National Space Institute (president), chairman for U.S. Committee of United Nations Children's Fund (UNICEF), Center for the Study of Democratic Institutions.

ADDRESSES: OFFICE—c/o *20/20*, American Broadcasting Corporation, 1330 Avenue of the Americas, New York, NY 10019.*

*   *   *

DREYFUSS, Richard   1947-

PERSONAL: Full name, Richard Stephan Dreyfuss; born October 29, 1947, in Brooklyn, NY; son of Norman (a lawyer and businessman) and Gerry Dreyfuss; married Jeramie Rain (also known as

RICHARD DREYFUSS

Susan Davis; an actress and writer), March 20, 1983; children: two. EDUCATION: Attended San Fernando Valley State College, 1965-67. MILITARY: Alternative service at Los Angeles County General Hospital, 1969-1971.

VOCATION: Actor and producer.

CAREER: PRINCIPAL FILM APPEARANCES—Curt Henderson, *American Graffiti*, Universal, 1973; Baby Face Nelson, *Dillinger*, American International, 1973; title role, *The Apprenticeship of Duddy Kravitz*, Universal, 1974; Matt Hooper, *Jaws*, Universal, 1975; Boy Wonder, *Inserts*, United Artists, 1976; Roy Neary, *Close Encounters of the Third Kind*, Columbia, 1977; Elliott Garfield, *The Goodbye Girl*, Warner Brothers, 1977; (also co-producer) Moses Wine, *The Big Fix*, Universal, 1979; Paul Dietrich, *The Competition*, Columbia, 1980; Ken Harrison, *Whose Life Is It, Anyway?*, Warner Brothers, 1981; Dave Whiteman, *Down and Out in Beverly Hills*, Touchstone, 1985; B.B., *Tin Men*, Touchstone, 1986; Aaron Levinsky, *Nuts*, Warner Brothers, 1987. Also appeared as Clavius, *The Second Coming of Suzanne*, 1974; narrator, *Stand by Me*, 1986; and in *The Graduate*, Embassy, 1967; *The Young Runaways*, Metro-Goldwyn-Mayer, 1968; *Hello Down There* (also known as *Sub-a-Dub-Dub*), Paramount, 1969; *The Buddy System*, Twentieth Century-Fox, 1984; *Stakeout*, Touchstone, 1987; *Moon Over Parador*, Universal, 1987.

STAGE DEBUT—*In Mama's House*, Gallery Theatre, Los Angeles, CA. BROADWAY DEBUT—Stanely, *But Seriously . . .*, Henry Miller's Theatre, 1969. OFF-BROADWAY DEBUT—Stephen, *Line*, Theatre de Lys, 1971. PRINCIPAL STAGE APPEARANCES—Adolphus Cusins, *Major Barbara*, Mark Taper Forum, Los Ange-

les, CA, 1972; Cassius, *Julius Caesar*, Brooklyn Academy of Music, Brooklyn, NY, 1978; Iago, *Othello*, Delacorte Theatre, New York City, then Alliance Theatre Company, Atlanta, GA, both 1979; Ken Harrison, *Whose Life Is It, Anyway?*, Williamstown Theatre Festival, Williamstown, MA, 1980; Joe, *A Day in the Death of Joe Egg*, Long Wharf Theatre, New Haven, CT, 1981; Lenny Keller, *Total Abandon*, Booth Theatre, New York City, 1983; Howard Bellman, *The Hands of Its Enemy*, Mark Taper Forum, 1984; Jean, *Miss Julie*, Napoleon, *A Man of Destiny*, both Chicago, IL, 1976; Harry, *The Time of Your Life*, Los Angeles, CA. Also appeared in *The Tenth Man*, Solari Ensemble, Los Angeles, CA, 1977; *Requiem for a Heavyweight*, Long Wharf Theatre, 1983; *Night of 100 Stars II*, Radio City Music Hall, New York City, 1985; *Journey to the Day, People Need People, Incident at Vichy*, and *Enemy, Enemy*, all Mark Taper Forum; *Aesop in Central Park*, Los Angeles, CA.

PRINCIPAL TELEVISION APPEARANCES—Episodic: *Love on a Rooftop*, ABC, 1966; *Judd for the Defense*, ABC, 1968; *The Big Valley*, ABC; *The Bold Ones*, NBC; *The Mod Squad*, ABC; *Room 222*, ABC; *The Young Lawyers*, ABC. Movies: *Victory at Entebbe*, 1976. Guest: *Saturday Night Live*, NBC.

AWARDS: Best Actor, Academy Award, 1977, Best Supporting Actor, Golden Globe, 1977, both for *The Goodbye Girl;* Los Angeles Drama Critics Award nominations for *The Time of Your Life* and *Aesop in Central Park*.

MEMBER: Screen Actors Guild, Actors' Equity Association, American Federation of Television and Radio Artists, Academy of Motion Picture Arts and Sciences; American Civil Liberties Union.

SIDELIGHTS: In the three decades he has worked as an actor, Richard Dreyfuss has brought life to a wide range of characters. Critics have praised the intelligence he evinces in parts as diverse as the thoughtful youth leaving for college in *American Graffiti*, the energetic unemployed actor in his Oscar-winning role in *The Goodbye Girl*, and the unscrupulous salesman in *Tin Men*, to mention only a few of his many film appearances. Dreyfuss's characters ''are real, accessible,'' wrote Jean Vallely in an October 10, 1978 *Esquire* profile. ''They show us courage. . . . They seem to be trying to live their lives honestly.''

If honesty and accessibility describe the actor's performances, they also characterized his recent well-publicized battle to overcome alcohol and drug addiction, which once threatened to destroy his career. Since successfully completing a drug rehabilitation program in 1983, Dreyfuss has achieved tranquility as an actor, a husband, and a father. He also increased his workload; having previously averaged one film every eighteen months, he completed five in a two-year period. Grateful for a second chance to work at his profession, ''I no longer feel so apart,'' he told *Parade* on March 23, 1986. ''I now feel like I belong [to the film community]. I'm not the crown prince. I never was the crown prince. But I'm a working stiff, which is what I always wanted to be. Ever since I was young.''

Dreyfuss's youth was unusual. The son of a lawyer who later became a restaurateur, he was born in Brooklyn and raised in Bayside, a neighborhood in Queens. When Dreyfuss was eight, his father returned home from work one day and said, ''Let's get out of here.'' As the actor remembered it in a January 15, 1978 *New York Times* feature, his family ''sold everything we owned and sailed to Europe, where we blew all our money in six months. We got back to New York with just enough money to buy an old 1950 Cadillac and drive to L.A., where we started all over again.'' A natural ham who competed for attention, Dreyfuss soon decided he wanted to perform. He told *Parade* that when he discussed his aspirations with his mother, she said, "Don't just talk about it. Do something about it." He continued: "I got up and walked down to the West Side Jewish Community Center and started acting that very afternoon." He has been a working actor, without the benefit of formal training, ever since that day.

By the time he finished high school in Beverly Hills, Dreyfuss had been acting professionally for more than five years. He spent a short time at San Fernando State College, dropped out, and was called to serve in the Vietnam War. He took conscientious objector status and worked as a file clerk in a Los Angeles hospital for two years. That obligation completed, he began performing in earnest, crossing the country to do stage work in New York and television appearances in Los Angeles. "I wanted to be a starving actor in New York," he noted in the *New York Times,* "but every time I went to New York I worked." He also took a variety of bit parts that he described in a July 31, 1975 *Rolling Stone* article as "father rapers, murderers, kidnappers, various psychopaths," for such shows as *The Mod Squad* and *The Young Lawyers.*

He was appearing in George Bernard Shaw's *Major Barbara* in Los Angeles when he was asked to play Curt Henderson in director George Lucas's *American Graffiti.* Dreyfuss has said that he accepted the part because he was recovering from a broken heart and wanted to get out of Los Angeles. He underestimated the impact the film would have. Costing $780,000 to make, *American Graffiti* earned in excess of fifty million dollars and boosted the careers of its many leads, including Dreyfuss.

Critics praised his work in *American Graffiti,* as well as his portrayals of a ruthless Jewish teenager in *The Apprenticeship of Duddy Kravitz* and as Baby Face Nelson in *Dillinger.* Audiences paid more attention to him in two Steven Spielberg blockbusters, *Jaws* and *Close Encounters of the Third Kind.* Although Dreyfuss gave creditable performances in both movies, he shocked the film community by making disparaging remarks about filming delays and about the superficiality of the characters he was playing. Rumors about his arrogant and self-indulgent temperament began to circulate, but these were quelled when *The Goodbye Girl* was relesed in 1977. In that Neil Simon comedy, Dreyfuss starred as Elliot Garfield, an energetic, romantic, would-be actor in Manhattan who not only launches his career, but finds the love of his life. "I liked my work, I liked me, I liked the people I was working with," Dreyfuss told the *New York Times* about that film. "I could do *The Goodbye Girl* as a 9-to-5 job for the rest of my life." His enjoyment was further rewarded by an Academy Award for best actor; he was thirty years old at the time. From that pinnacle, however, his life took a dramatic downturn.

In retrospect Dreyfuss recalled to *Esquire:* "I didn't anticipate the guilt and the fear of success. I didn't anticipate the down side of success at all. . . . I started to resist the position I was in by drinking a lot, doing drugs, eating too much, being childish, denigrating my talent." Under such strain, he pulled out of contractual obligations to appear in Bob Fosse's *All That Jazz;* then a string of his starring vehicles, *The Big Fix, The Competition,* and *Whose Life Is It, Anyway?,* were commercial failures. "Rock bottom was in 1982," he remembered in *Parade.* "I was in pain, real pain. I was completely out of control. I had also been blacking out regularly." When he flipped over in a convertible sportscar and was arrested in the hospital emergency room for cocaine possession, Dreyfuss realized his potential danger to others as well as to himself.

After his recovery, he put renewed emphasis on his work as an actor, not a star. Subsequent films, including *Down and Out in Bevery Hills, Stand by Me, Tin Men,* and *Stakeout* were critical and commercial successes, helping Dreyfuss to regain his stature in Hollywood. The actor who *Time* described on December 5, 1971 as generating "enough electricity to light up . . . Cleveland or Chicago" claimed in *Parade* that in the 1980s he has learned "the simple pleasure of behaving like a normal human being."

New York Times correspondent Michael Goodwin suggested that audiences respond to Dreyfuss because he mirrors "the characteristics of his generation. . . . Some of his characterizations have been more likable than others, but all of them are capable of drawing a line and holding it." Goodwin commended Dreyfuss for the sense of truthfulness and inner authenticity that he brings to his performances in both comedy and drama. All of his many and varied roles, the critic concluded, "reflect a facet of American character." Offstage Dreyfuss also reflects shared concerns with politics, the legacy of the Vietnam War, drug abuse, and the search for inner peace. Nevertheless, he remains constant to the ideal of his craft that he expressed to *U.S. News and World Report* (May 19, 1975)— "Actors express the common denominator of human experience."

ADDRESSES: AGENT—Richard Grant and Associates, 8500 Wilshire Boulevard, Suite 520, Beverly Hills, CA 90211.

*   *   *

DRURY, Alan   1949-

PERSONAL: Born May 22, 1949, in Hull, England; son of Harold (an insurance inspector) and Patricia (a teacher; maiden name, Tait) Drury. EDUCATION: Queens' College, Cambridge University, B.A., 1971.

VOCATION: Playwright and director.

CAREER: Also see *WRITINGS* below. PRINCIPAL STAGE WORK— Director: *Soap Opera,* York Theatre Royal, York, U.K., 1977; *The Training,* ICA Theatre, London, 1978.

RELATED CAREER—Resident dramatist: York Theatre Royal, York, U.K., 1976-78; Royal Court Theatre, London, 1979; drama critic, *Listener,* 1979-81.

NON-RELATED CAREER—Clerk, Department of Architecture, borough of Camden, London.

WRITINGS: PLAYS—*Shoreline,* (adaptor) *Godot Has Come,* both University Union, Edinburgh Festival, Edinburgh, Scotland, U.K., 1971; *Evening and Morning,* Pembroke College, Cambridge, U.K., 1971; *And How Are You This Bright and Early Morning?,* Tolcoons Theatre, Edinburgh Festival, 1972; (book and lyrics) *Silver,* Arts Theatre, London, 1972; *You Know Me,* Little Theatre, London, 1972; (adaptor) *The Ancient Mariner* (ballet scenario), Questor's Theatre, London, 1972; *Fall,* Little Theatre, 1973; (translator) *The Hills,* Kings Head Theatre, London, 1974, published by Fringescripts, 1973; *Glynis,* Oval House Theatre, London, 1974; *Asides,* Bush Theatre, London, 1974; *The Man Himself,* ICA Theatre, London, 1975; *The Railway Game, Antonio, Spotty Hilda,* all York Theatre Royal, York, U.K., 1975; (book and lyrics) *King David,* All Hallows by the Tower, London, 1975; *Sparrowfall,* Hampstead Theatre Club, London, 1976; *Black Dog,* University Theatre,

Saarbruecken, West Germany, 1976; *Sense of Loss*, Open Space Theatre, London, 1976; *Dick Turpin*, York Theatre Royal, 1976; (book and lyrics) *Up and Away*, York Theatre Royal, 1976; *Under the Skin*, Redgrave Theatre, Farnham, U.K., 1976; (adaptor) *Diary of a Madman*, (adaptor) *A Shorter Faustus*, both York Arts Centre, York, U.K., 1977; *Margaret Clitheroe*, York Theatre Royal, 1977; *A Change of Mind*, Lyttelton Theatre, London, 1977; *Soap Opera*, York Theatre Royal, 1977; *Simple Simon*, York Theatre Royal, 1978; (translator) *The Miser*, York Theatre Royal, 1978, published in *Moliere: Five Plays*, Methuen, 1982; *Looking Back*, Masonic Hall, Edinburgh Festival, 1978; *The Training*, ICA Theatre, 1978; *An Empty Desk*, Theatre Upstairs, London, 1979; *Mother Goose*, York Theatre Royal, 1980; (translator) *The Hypochondriac*, Olivier Theatre, London 1981, published in *Moliere: Five Plays*, Methuen, 1982. Also wrote *Other Views*, 1974; *Communion*, 1976; *An Honourable Man*, 1980.

RADIO PLAYS—*Mr. Jones*, BBC-Radio, 1979.

TELEPLAYS—*Winding Up*, ATV, 1981; *Keeping in Touch*, BBC, 1982.

MEMBER: Theatre Writers Union.

SIDELIGHTS: RECREATIONS—Conjuring, collecting old railway timetables.

ADDRESSES: AGENT—c/o John Rush, David Higham Associates, 5-8 Lower John Street, Golden Square, London W1, England.*

*   *   *

DUDLEY, William   1947-

PERSONAL: Born March 4, 1947, in London, England; son of William Stuart and Dorothy Irene Dudley. EDUCATION: Attended St. Martin's School of Art and Slade School of Art.

VOCATION: Designer.

CAREER: FIRST STAGE WORK—Designer, *Hamlet*, Nottingham Playhouse, Nottingham, U.K., 1970. PRINCIPAL STAGE WORK— All as designer: *Rooted, Magnificence, Sweet Talk, The Merry-Go-Round*, all Royal Court Theatre, London, 1973; *Anarchist Tyger, The Duchess of Malfi, Man Is Man, Cato Street, The Good-Natured Man*, all National Theatre, London, 1974; *Fish in the Sea, The Fool*, both Royal Court Theatre, 1975; *As You Like It*, Nottingham Playhouse, Nottingham, U.K., 1975, then Riverside Studios, London, 1976; *Small Change*, Royal Court Theatre, 1976; *Ivanov*, Aldwych Theatre, London, 1976; *The Cherry Orchard*, Riverside Studios, 1977; *That Good Between Us*, Warehouse Theatre, London, 1977; *Lavender Blue*, National Theatre, London, 1977; *Touched*, Old Vic Theatre, London, 1977; *The World Turned Upside Down, Has Washington Legs?*, both National Theatre, 1978; (also lighting designer) *Lark Rise* and *Lost Worlds*, both National Theatre, 1978; *Dispatches, Candleford*, both National Theatre, 1979; *Undiscovered Country*, Olivier Theatre, London, 1979; *Billy Budd* (opera), Metropolitan Opera House, New York City, 1978. Also designed *Live Like Pigs, I, Claudius*, and *The Baker, the Baker's Wife and the Baker's Boy*, all Newcastle, Scotland, U.K., 1972; *Ashes, The Corn Is Green*, both Watford, U.K., 1974; *Twelfth Night*, Stratford-on-Avon, U.K., 1974; *The Norman Conquests*, Berlin, 1976; *Harding's Luck*, 1974.

MEMBER: Society of British Theatre Designers.

SIDELIGHTS: RECREATIONS—Playing the concertina, browsing in bookshops, walking.

ADDRESSES: HOME—58 Earlswood Road, London SE10, England.*

*   *   *

Du KORE, Lawrence   1933-

PERSONAL: Born February 15, 1933, in Brooklyn, NY; son of Herman (a factory worker) and Leah (a secretary; maiden name, Herman) Du Kore. EDUCATION: University of Texas, Austin, B.A., English literature, 1954; studied drama with Harold Clurman at the Playwrights Unit of the Actors Studio; also studied at the Turtle Bay Music School.

VOCATION: Writer.

*WRITINGS:*PLAYS—*Virgin Territory*, Actors Studio, New York City; *The Emperor of My Baby's Heart*, New York City, 1984. SCREENPLAYS—*Greased Lightning*, Warner Brothers, 1977. TELEPLAYS—Episodic: "A Mistaken Charity," *American Playhouse*, PBS, 1987. Series: *One Life to Live*, ABC, 1979; *Search for Tomorrow*, NBC, 1984.

RELATED CAREER: Actor and film editor.

MEMBER: Writers Guild of America, Dramatists Guild; American Friends Service Committee (Quakers).

ADDRESSES: HOME—5008 Broadway, New York, NY 10034. AGENT—c/o Chris Tomasino, RLR Associates, Inc., Seven W. 51st Street, New York, NY 10019.

*   *   *

DURNING, Charles   1923-

PERSONAL: Born February 28, 1923, in Highland Falls, NY; first marriage ended in divorce, married Mary Ann Amelio, 1974; children: (first marriage) three. EDUCATION: Attended Columbia University and New York University. MILITARY: U.S. Army, World War II.

VOCATION: Actor.

CAREER: STAGE DEBUT—*The Andersonville Trial*, National touring company, 1960. LONDON DEBUT—Paul Rudd, *The Child Buyer*, Garrick Theatre, London England, 1964. PRINCIPAL STAGE APPEARANCES—With the New York Shakespeare Festival, New York City: Lucius, *Julius Caesar* and the porter and Seyton, *Macbeth*, both at the Heckscher Theatre, 1962; Stephano, *The Tempest* and first servant to Cornwall, *King Lear*, both at the Delacorte Theatre, 1962; the clown, *Antony and Cleopatra*, Corin, *As You Like It*, and the clown, *The Winter's Tale*, all at the Delacorte Theatre, 1963; Feste, *Twelfth Night*, Heckscher Theatre, 1963; a purser and a Cuban, *Too Much Johnson*, Phoenix Theatre, 1964; Pistol, *King Henry V* and Grumio, *The Taming of the Shrew*, both at the Delacorte Mobile Theatre, 1965; Lavatch, *All's Well That Ends Well*, Pompey, *Measure for Measure*, and the first murderer, *Richard III*, all at the Delacorte Theatre, 1966; Dromio of Ephesus, *The Comedy of Errors*, James Gurney, *King John*, and narrator, *Titus Andronicus*, all at the Delacorte Theatre, 1967; Daddy, *Huui, Huui*, Public Theatre, 1968; Rodion, *Invitation to a Beheading*, Public Theatre, 1969; Feste, *Twelfth Night*, Delacorte Theatre, 1969; Mayor of London, *Chronicles of King Henry VI, Part I* and Cade, *Chronicles of King Henry VI, Part II*, both at the Delacorte Theatre, 1970; the orderly, *The Happiness Cage*, Public Theatre, 1970; George Sikowski, *That Championship Season*, Public Theatre, then transferred to the Booth Theatre, 1972; first gravedigger, *Hamlet*, Delacorte Theatre, 1972.

Pincer, *Drat! The Cat!*, Martin Beck Theatre, New York City, 1965; Dean Stewart and Maurice, *Pousse-Cafe*, 46th Street Theatre, New York City, 1966; Point and the discussion leader, *The World of Gunther Grass*, Pocket Theatre, New York City, 1966; *A Man's a Man* and *The Entertainer*, both 1966, and *The Three Sisters*, 1967, all at the Pittsburgh Playhouse, PA; Louis Bonnard, *The Happy Time*, Ahmanson Theatre, Los Angeles, 1967, then Broadway Theatre, New York City, 1968; Ned Buntline, *Indians*, Brooks Atkinson Theatre, New York City, 1969; Douglas, *Lemon Sky*, Studio Arena Theatre, Buffalo, NY, then Playhouse Theatre, New York City, 1970; Harold, *In the Boom Boom Room* and Eugene Hartigan, *The Au Pair Man*, both at the Vivian Beaumont Theatre, Lincoln Center, New York City, 1973; *Knock, Knock*, New York City production, 1975; *On Golden Pond*, Mark Taper Forum, Los Angeles, 1980; Charley, *Death of a Salesman*, Broadhurst Theatre, New York City, 1985.

PRINCIPAL FILM APPEARANCES—Murphy, *Dealing*, Warner Brothers, 1972; private investigator, *Sisters*, American International, 1973; Lieutenant Snyder, *The Sting*, Universal, 1973; *The Front Page*, Universal, 1974; Detective Moretti, *Dog Day Afternoon*, Warner Brothers, 1975; Frank O'Brien, *Breakheart Pass*, 1975; Captain Pruss, *The Hindenburg*, Universal, 1975; United States President David T. Stevens, *Twilight's Last Gleaming*, Allied Artists, 1976; Rufus T. Crisp, *Harry and Walter Go to New York*, Columbia, 1976; "Spermwhale" Whalen, *The Choirboys*, Universal, 1977; Dr. McKeever, *The Fury*, Twentieth Century-Fox, 1978; Peter Stockman, *An Enemy of the People*, 1978; Michael Russell, *The Greek Tycoon*, Universal, 1978; John Clifford, *When a Stranger Calls*, Columbia, 1979; Arnold, *Die Laughing*, Warner Brothers, 1979; Michael Potter, *Starting Over*, Paramount, 1979; Doc Hopper, *The Muppet Movie*, Associated Film Distributors, 1979; Coach Johnson, *North Dallas Forty*, Paramount, 1979; Harold Remmens, *Tilt*, 1979.

Senator Samuel Chapman, *The Final Countdown*, United Artists, 1980; Frisco, *Sharky's Machine*, Warner Brothers, 1981; Jack Anderson, *True Confessions*, United Artists, 1981; Les, *Tootsie*, Columbia, 1982; Red Ball rider, *Deadhead Miles*, 1982; Governor, *The Best Little Whorehouse in Texas*, Universal, 1982; Charlie, *Two of a Kind*, Twentieth Century-Fox, 1983; Colonel Erhardt, *To Be or Not to Be*, Twentieth Century-Fox, 1983; Chucky, *Stick*, Universal, 1984; *Hadley's Rebellion*, ADI Marketing, 1984; Monsignor Burke, *Mass Appeal*, Universal, 1984; Ross, *The Man with One Red Shoe*, Twentieth Century-Fox, 1985; *Stand Alone*, New World Pictures, 1985; Father O'Reilly, *Where the River Runs Black*, Metro-Goldwyn-Mayer/United Artists, 1986; Deke Yablonski, *Tough Guys*, Universal, 1986; *Big Trouble*, Columbia, 1986; the warden, *Solarbabies*, 1986; *Happy New Year*, Columbia, 1987.

PRINCIPAL TELEVISION APPEARANCES—Series: Gil McGowen, *Another World*, NBC, 1964; Officer Frank Murphy, *The Cop and the Kid*, NBC, 1975-76; Big Ed Healey, *The Captains and the Kings*, NBC, 1976-77. Episodic: *High Chaparral*, NBC; *The Defenders*, CBS; *Madigan*, NBC; *All in the Family*, CBS. Pilots: D.A. Horn, *Rx for the Defense*, 1973; Phil Beckman, *Switch*, CBS, 1975; P. Oliver Pendergast, *P.O.P.*, 1984; Harry Deegan, *Side by Side*, 1984. Movies: Frank Devlin, *The Connection*, 1973; Al Green, *Queen of the Stardust Ballroom*, CBS, 1975; Stephen Douglas, *The Rivalry*, 1975; Budd Rogers, *The Trial of Chaplain Jensen*, 1975; Carl Gallitzin, *Special Olympics*, 1978; Bill Larson, *A Perfect Match*, 1980; Russel Oswald, *Attica*, 1980; Otis Hazelrig, *Dark Night of the Scarecrow*, 1981; Frank Powell, *The Best Little Girl in the World*, 1981; Jess Matthews, *Crisis at Central High*, 1981; Captain, *Mr. Roberts*, 1984; Charley, *Death of a Salesman*, CBS, 1985; Doffue, *The Legend of Sleepy Hollow*, 1986; also, *Dick and Tracy*, ABC.

Mini-Series: Paddy Lonigan, *Studs Lonigan*, NBC, 1979. Specials: *Working*, 1982; *The Best Little Special in Texas*, 1982; *The Screen Actors Guild 50th Anniversary Celebration*, 1984; *The Night of 100 Stars II*, 1985; *Dom DeLuise and Friends, Part III*, 1985; Oscar Poole, *Eye to Eye*, 1985; *The 40th Annual Tony Awards*, 1986; *The American Film Institute Salute to Billy Wilder*, 1986.

NON-RELATED CAREER—Worked as a boxer, cab driver, waiter, ironworker, construction worker, and an elevator operator.

AWARDS: Drama Desk Award and *Variety* Poll winner, both 1972, for *That Championship Season*.

MEMBER: Actors' Equity Association, Screen Actors Guild, American Federation of Television and Radio Artists; American Film Institute.

ADDRESSES: AGENT—Jack Fields and Associates, 9255 Sunset Blvd., Suite 1105, Los Angeles, CA 90069.*

                    *   *   *

DU SAUTOY, Carmen   1950-

PERSONAL: Born February 26, 1950, in London, England; daughter of Arthur John and Viola (Stocker) Du Sautoy; married Charles Savage (a director).

VOCATION: Actress.

CAREER: STAGE DEBUT—*The Lover*, University Theatre, Venice, Italy, 1968. PRINCIPAL STAGE APPEARANCES— Prossy, *Candida*, English Theatre, Vienna, Austria, 1974; Marie, *The Trial of Marie Stopes*, Miss Macdonald, *Cages*, both Bubble Theatre Company, London, 1975; Miss Leighton, *Once in a Lifetime*, Piccadilly Theatre, London, 1980; also appeared in numerous productions including *The Beggar's Opera*, *Twelfth Night*, *Under Milk Wood*, *The Lunatic*, *The Secret Sportsman*, *The Woman Next Door*, and *Puss in Boots* with the Nottingham Playhouse, Nottingham, U.K., Leeds Playhouse, Leeds, U.K., Oxford Playhouse, Oxford, U.K., Crewe Playhouse, Crewe, U.K., and with the Portable Theatre Company.

With the Royal Shakespeare Company: Courtesan, *The Comedy of*

Errors, Royal Shakespeare Theatre, Stratford-on-Avon, U.K., 1976, then Aldwych Theatre, London, and Newcastle, Scotland, U.K., 1977; Cassandra, *Troilus and Cressida,* Royal Shakespeare Theatre, then Aldwych Theatre, later Newcastle, all 1977; Hippolyta, faerie, *A Midsummer Night's Dream,* Royal Shakespeare Theatre, then Aldwych Theatre, both 1977; Mrs. Lynge, *Pillars of the Community,* Mrs. Fainall, *The Way of the World,* both Aldwych Theatre, 1978; Ceres, *The Tempest,* Royal Shakespeare Theatre, 1978; Lady Cummings, *Captain Swing,* Other Place Theatre, Stratford-on-Avon, 1978; Madeleine, *Piaf,* Other Place Theatre, 1978, then Aldwych Theatre, 1979, later Warehouse Theatre, London, 1979; Princess of France, *Love's Labour's Lost,* Other Place Theatre, then Aldwych Theatre, both 1979; Elena, *Children of the Sun,* Aldwych Theatre, 1979.

PRINCIPAL FILM APPEARANCES—*The Man with the Golden Gun,* United Artists, 1974. Also appeared in *Our Miss Fred.*

PRINCIPAL TELEVISION APPEARANCES—Mini-Series: Frances Lawrence, "The Citadel," *Masterpiece Theatre,* PBS, 1983; Julie Blane, "Lost Empire," *Masterpiece Theatre,* PBS, 1987.

SIDELIGHTS: FAVORITE ROLES—Mrs. Fainall in *The Way of the World;* Lucy Lockit in *The Beggar's Opera.* RECREATIONS—Science fiction, driving, jazz, skiing, tennis.

ADDRESSES: AGENT—c/o Duncan Heath, Studio One, 57 Redcliffe Road, London SW10, England.*

E

EASTON, Richard 1933-

PERSONAL: Full name, John Richard Easton, born March 22, 1933, in Montreal, PQ, Canada; son of Leonard Idell (a civil engineer) and Mary Louise (Withington) Easton. EDUCATION: Studied for the stage with the Children's Theatre, Montreal, 1948-49, with Eleanor Stuart in Montreal for one year, with Gwyneta Thurburn in London for three years, and at the Central School of Speech and Drama in London.

VOCATION: Actor and director.

CAREER: STAGE DEBUT—Wally, *Our Town,* Brae Manor Playhouse, Knowlton, Canada, June, 1947. OFF-BROADWAY DEBUT—Claudio, *Measure for Measure,* Luccentio, *The Taming of the Shrew,* and Delio, *The Dutchess of Malfi,* all at the Phoenix Theatre, 1957. LONDON DEBUT—Edward Kinnerton, *Both Ends*

RICHARD EASTON

Meet, Apollo Theatre, 1954. PRINCIPAL STAGE APPEARANCES—With the Montreal Repertory Theatre, 1949-50; Hortensio, *The Taming of the Shrew,* Ottawa, Canada, 1950; appeared with the Canadian Repertory Theatre, Ottawa, 1952-53; Sir Thomas Vaughan, *Richard III,* with the Shakespearean Festival Company, Stratford, ON, 1953; Edgar, *King Lear* and Claudio, *Much Ado About Nothing,* both with the Shakespeare Memorial Theatre Company at the Palace Theatre, London, 1955; appeared in *Anthony and Cleopatra, An Italian Straw Hat,* and *The Three Sisters,* all at the Crest Theatre, Toronto, Canada, 1956; Lord Scoop and Alexander Court, *Henry V* and Slender, *The Merry Wives of Windsor,* both with the Shakespearean Festival Company, Stratford, ON, and repeated roles in *Henry V* at the Edinburgh Festival, Scotland, 1956; Harcourt, *The Country Wife,* Adelphi Theatre, New York City, 1957; Cain, *Back to Methuselah,* Ambassador Theatre, New York City, 1958; Timothy, *Salad Days,* Barbizon Plaza Theatre, New York City, 1958; at the Shakespeare Festival, Stratford, CT: Roderigo, *Othello,* Claudio, *Much Ado About Nothing,* and Launcelot Gobbo, *The Merchant of Venice,* all 1957; Puck, *A Midsummer Night's Dream* and Osric and Florizel *The Winter's Tale,* both 1958; title role, *Romeo and Juliet,* Pistol, *The Merry Wives of Windsor,* the French Lord, *All's Well That Ends Well,* and repeated role of Puck, *A Midsummer Night's Dream,* all 1959; David, *Motel,* Wilbur Theatre, Boston, MA, 1960; with the Association of Producing Artists (APA) Repertory Company: Jack, *The Importance of Being Earnest,* Edgar, *King Lear,* title role, *Hamlet,* Amiens, *As You Like It,* Orsino, *Twelfth Night,* and Oberon, *A Midsummer Night's Dream,* all 1960.

Sir Harry Bumper and Joseph Surface, *The School for Scandal,* Haymarket Theatre, London, 1962 and later repeated the role at the Majestic Theatre, New York City, 1963; Nick, *Who's Afraid of Virginia Wolf?* Piccadilly Theatre, London, 1964; Barry, *Comfort Me With Apples,* Globe Theatre, London, 1965; Fagin, *Oliver!* Opera House, Manchester, U.K., 1965; Marlow, *She Stoops to Conquer,* the bishop, *The Balcony,* and the title role, *Richard III,* all at the Oxford Playhouse, U.K., 1967; with the APA, at the University of Michigan at Ann Arbor and at the Lyceum Theatre, New York City: A policeman, *Pantagleize* and King Berenger, *Exit the King,* both 1967-68; Trofimov, *The Cherry Orchard* (Lyceum Theatre only), 1968; Alceste, *The Misanthrope,* 1968; Claudius, *Hamlet,* 1968-69; Messenger, *Cock-A-Doodle Dandy* (Ann Arbor only), 1968-69; title role, *Macbeth* (Ann Arbor only), 1969; Brutus, *Julius Caesar,* Old Globe Theatre, San Diego, CA, 1969; James Bonham, *Murderous Angels,* Mark Taper Forum, Los Angeles, 1970.

Syd Sorokin, *The Pyjama Game,* Belgrade Theatre, Coventry, U.K., 1971; James Bonham, *Murderous Angels,* Playhouse Theatre, New York City, 1971; Walter Franz, *The Price,* Thorndike Theatre, Leatherhead, U.K., 1972; appeared in *Alexander and*

Friends and *Romans and Lovers,* both at the Arnaud Theatre, Guildford, U.K., 1972; Charles, *Blithe Spirit,* Haymarket Theatre, Leicester, U.K., 1975; Trigorin, *The Seagull,* Harrogate Theatre, London, 1975; title role, *Macbeth,* Marlowe Theatre, Canterbury, U.K., 1977; Dysart, *Equus,* Thorndike Theatre, Leatherhead, U.K., 1978; Aubrey Tanqueray, *The Second Mrs. Tanqueray,* Crucible Theatre, Sheffield, U.K., 1978; Theseus and Oberon, *A Midsummer Night's Dream* and Caliban, *The Tempest,* both at the Edinburgh Festival, 1978; Earnest Melton, *Canaries Sometimes Sing,* Arnaud Theatre, Guildford, U.K., 1979.

MAJOR TOURS—Edgar, *King Lear* and Claudio, *Much Ado About Nothing,* European and U.K. cities, 1955; title role, *Anatol,* Octavius Robinson, *Man and Superman,* and Constantine Trepleff, *The Seagull,* all at the City Hall Theatre, Hamilton, Bermuda, then at the Bucks County Playhouse, New Hope, PA, then the Theatre-by-the-Sea, Matanuck, RI, and at the John Drew Theatre, East Hampton, NY, 1960; Joseph Surface, *The School for Scandal,* U.S. cities, 1963; Fagin, *Oliver!,* U.K. cities, 1965; Marlow, *She Stoops to Conquer,* the bishop, *The Balcony,* and the title role, *Richard III,* U.K. cities, 1967; Berenger, *Exit the King,* a policeman, *Pantagleize,* Trofimov, *The Cherry Orchard,* and the title role, *Macbeth,* all with the APA Repertory Company, U.S. cities, 1967-69; Syd Sorokin, *The Pajama Game,* U.K. cities, 1971; *Caught on Hop,* U.K. cities, 1977; Aubrey Tanqueray, *The Second Mrs. Tanqueray,* U.K. cities, 1978; Earnest Melton, *Canaries Sometimes Sing,* U.K. cities, 1979.

PRINCIPAL THEATRE WORK—Director: *The Lady's Not For Burning,* 1961; *Julius Caesar,* Old Globe Theatre, San Diego, CA, 1969.

PRINCIPAL TELEVISION APPEARANCES—Series: *The Brothers,* BBC. Dramatic Specials: *As You Like It.* Also other appearances on television since 1952 in Canada, the US, and the U.K.

RELATED CAREER—Founding member, Association of Producing Artists, 1960.

AWARDS: Theatre World Award, 1958.

MEMBER: Actors' Equity Association.

SIDELIGHTS: FAVORITE ROLES—Nick, from *Who's Afraid of Virginia Woolf?,* Puck, from *A Midsummer Night's Dream,* and Hamlet. RECREATIONS—Singing German Lieder.

ADDRESSES: HOME—14 Earl's Terrace, London W8, England.*

*   *   *

EBB, Fred   1933-

PERSONAL: Born April 8, 1933, in New York, NY; son of Harry and Anna (Gritz) Ebb. EDUCATION: New York University, B.A., 1955; Columbia University, M.A., English literature, 1957.

VOCATION: Lyricist, writer, director, and producer.

CAREER: Also see *WRITINGS* below. PRINCIPAL STAGE WORK—Director, producer, *Liza in Concert at Carnegie Hall,* New York

City, 1979. PRINCIPAL TELEVISION WORK—*Liza with a "Z,"* NBC, 1972.

WRITINGS: LYRICS—(Also book) *Morning Sun,* Phoenix Theatre, New York City, 1963; *Flora, the Red Menace,* Alvin Theatre, New York City, 1965; *Cabaret,* Broadhurst Theatre, New York City, 1966; *The Happy Time,* Broadway Theatre, New York City, 1968; *Zorba,* Imperial Theatre, New York City, 1968; (also book with Norman L. Martin) *70, Girls, 70,* Broadhurst Theatre, 1971; (also book with Bob Fosse) *Chicago,* St. James Theatre, New York City, 1975; *The Act,* Martin Beck Theatre, 1978; *Woman of the Year,* Palace Theatre, New York City, 1981; lyrics, *The Rink,* Martin Beck Theatre, 1984.

Also contributed material to *From A to Z,* Plymouth Theatre, New York City, 1960; *Put It in Writing,* Theatre de Lys, New York City, 1963; *Two by Five,* Village Gate, New York City, 1976; *Joe Masiell, Not at the Palace,* Astor Place Theatre, New York City, 1977; *The Madwoman of Central Park West,* 22 Steps Theatre, New York City, 1979; *Parade of Stars Playing the Palace,* Palace Theatre, New York City, 1983; *Night of 100 Stars II,* Radio City Music Hall, New York City, 1985; *Diamonds,* Circle in the Square Downtown, New York City, 1985; adapted *By Jupiter,* Theatre Four, New York City, 1967; and wrote original material (with John Kander), *Liza,* Winter Garden Theatre, New York City, 1974.

FILM—Lyrics and contributed material: *Cabaret,* Allied Artists, 1972; *Funny Lady,* Columbia, 1975; *Lucky Lady,* Twentieth Century-Fox, 1975; *New York, New York,* United Artists, 1977; *French Postcards,* Paramount, 1979; also *A Matter of Time,* 1976.

TELEVISION—Series: *That Was the Week That Was,* NBC, 1963-64. Specials: Lyrics and contributed material: *Liza,* NBC, 1970; *Liza with a "Z",* NBC, 1972; *Three for the Girls,* CBS, 1973; *Gypsy in My Soul,* CBS, 1976; also *Ole Blue Eyes Is Back,* 1974; *Goldie and Liza Together, Baryshnikov on Broadway,* both 1980.

AWARDS: Best Composer and Lyricist (with John Kander), Antoinette Perry Award, League of New York Theatres and Producers Award, Drama Desk Award, all 1967, for *Cabaret;* Achievement Award, B'nai B'rith, 1967; Best Composer and Lyricist (with Kander), Antoinette Perry Award nomination, 1968, for *The Happy Time;* Outer Circle Award, 1968; Organization of Writers on Theatre Award, 1968 and 1969; Best Musical, Antoinette Perry Award nomination, 1969, for *Zorba;* George Foster Peabody Award, Grady School of Journalism, University of Georgia, 1972; Outstanding Single Program—Variety and Popular Music, Emmy Award, 1973, for *Liza with a "Z;"* NAACP Image Award, 1973; Christopher Award, Catholic Societies, 1976; Outstanding Special—Comedy-Variety or Music, Emmy Award, 1976, for *Gypsy in My Soul;* League of New York Theatres and Producers Award, 1981; Songwriters Hall of Fame, 1983. Honorary degrees: Emerson University, 1975.

MEMBER: Dramatists Guild; Actors' Equity Association; Academy of Television Arts and Sciences; American Society of Composers, Authors and Publishers; Academy of Motion Picture Arts and Sciences.

SIDELIGHTS: RECREATIONS—Collecting soundtrack albums for stage musicals.

ADDRESSES: AGENT—International Creative Management, 40 W. 57th Street, New York, NY 10019.*

EBERSOLE, Christine

PERSONAL: Born in Chicago, IL; married Peter Bergman (an actor; divorced). EDUCATION: Attended McMurray College; trained for the stage at the American Academy of Dramatic Arts.

VOCATION: Actress.

CAREER: BROADWAY DEBUT—Guinevere, *Camelot*, Palace Theatre, 1979. PRINCIPAL STAGE APPEARANCES—Dana, *Green Pond*, Chelsea Westside Theatre, New York City, 1978; Agnes, *On the Twentieth Century*, St. James Theatre, New York City, 1978; Ado Annie, *Oklahoma!*, Palace Theatre, New York City, then Kennedy Center, Washington, DC, both 1979; Natasha, *The Three Sisters*, Manhattan Theatre Club, New York City, 1982; Skye Bullene, *Geniuses*, Douglas Fairbanks Theatre, New York City, 1983; Gerta Granville, *Harrigan 'n Hart*, Longacre Theatre, New York City, 1985. Also appeared in *Gossip*, PAF Playhouse, Huntington Station, NY, 1978.

PRINCIPAL FILM APPEARANCES—Linda, *Tootsie*, Columbia, 1982; Katerina Cavalieri, *Amadeus*, Orion, 1984; Janie Pointer, *Thief of Hearts*, Paramount, 1984; also *Mac and Me*, New Star Entertainment, upcoming.

PRINCIPAL TELEVISION APPEARANCES—Episodic: Barbara Goodwin, *Valerie's Family*, NBC, 1986. Series: Katherine "Kit" Cavanaugh, *The Cavanaughs*, CBS, 1986; also cast member, *Saturday Night Live*, NBC. Movies: Lee Snyder, *Acceptable Risks*, ABC, 1986; also appeared as Miss Vashinski, *The Doll Maker*, 1984.

ADDRESSES: AGENT—c/o Toni Howard, William Morris Agency, 151 El Camino Drive, Beverly Hills, CA 90212.*

*   *   *

EBERT, Joyce   1933-

PERSONAL: Born Joyce Anne Womack, June 26, 1933, in Munhall, PA; daughter of John Leib (an engineer) and Bertha Louise (Friedel) Womack; married Michael Ebert (an actor; divorced); married Arvin Brown (a director) November 2, 1969. EDUCATION: Carnegie Institute of Technology, B.A., 1955; trained for the stage with Uta Hagen and at the Actors Studio with Lee Strasberg.

VOCATION: Actress.

CAREER: STAGE DEBUT—*White Sheep of the Family*, Pittsburgh Playhouse, Pittsburgh, PA, 1953. OFF-BROADWAY DEBUT—Julie, *Liliom*, Lenox Hill Playhouse, 1956. PRINCIPAL STAGE APPEARANCES—Portia, *The Merchant of Venice*, Ophelia, *Hamlet*, Bianca, *The Taming of the Shrew*, all Oregon Shakespeare Festival, Ashland, OR, 1953-54; Madge, *Picnic*, Mountain Playhouse, Jennerstown, PA, 1955; Alithea Pinchwife, *The Country Wife*, Renata Theatre, New York City, 1957; Emmanuelle, *Asmodee*, Flora, *Sign of Winter*, both Theatre 74, New York City, 1958; Maria, *The School for Scandal*, Clara Eynsford-Hill, *Pygmalion*, Jessica, *The Merchant of Venice*, all Group 20 Players, Wellesley, MA, 1958; Cordelia, *King Lear*, Players Theatre, New York City, 1959; Gertrude, *Fashion*, Royal Playhouse, New York City, 1959; Juliet, *Romeo and Juliet*, Princess of France, *Love's Labour's Lost*, Lady Mortimer, *Henry IV, Part I*, all San Diego Shakespeare

Festival, Old Globe Theatre, San Diego, CA, 1959; Camille, *No Trifling with Love*, St. Mark's Playhouse, New York City, 1959.

Margie, *The Iceman Cometh*, Isabella, *Ring Around the Moon*, both Arena Stage, Washington, DC, 1960; Miranda, *The Tempest*, American Shakespeare Festival, Stratford, CT, 1960; Annie, *Anatol*, McCarter Theatre, Princeton, NJ, 1960; Ophelia, *Hamlet*, Phoenix Theatre, New York City, 1961; Gwendolyn, *Becket*, Annie Sullivan, *The Miracle Worker*, Nina, *The Seagull*, Lady Larkin, *Once Upon a Mattress*, all Williamstown Theatre Festival, Williamstown, MA, 1962; Rosie Probert, Gossamer Beynon, Polly Garter, Mrs. Cherry Owen, Bessie Bighead, *Under Milk Wood*, Twelve O'Clock, *Pullman Car Hiawatha*, both Circle in the Square, New York City, 1962; Ann, *Man and Superman*, Elizabeth, *A Far Country*, Miss Fellows, *The Night of the Iguana*, Varya, *The Cherry Orchard*, Mrs. Booth, *Mr. Booth*, all Williamstown Theatre Festival, 1963; Pegeen Mike, *The Playboy of the Western World*, McCarter Theatre, 1963; stepdaughter, *Six Characters in Search of an Author*, Martinique Theatre, New York City, 1963; Andromache, *The Trojan Women*, Circle in the Square, 1963, then 1965; Mariane, *Tartuffe*, Washington Square Theatre, New York City, 1965; Vittoria Corombona, *The White Devil*, Circle in the Square, 1966; Sister Jeanne, *The Devils*, Mark Taper Forum, Los Angeles, CA, 1967; title role, *Saint Joan*, Williamstown Theatre Festival, 1967; wife, *Solitaire*, Barbara, *Double Solitaire*, both John Golden Theatre, New York City, 1971; matron, *The National Health*, Circle in the Square, 1974; Maggie, *The Shadow Box*, Morasco Theatre, New York City, 1977; Sara Muller, *Watch on the Rhine*, John Golden Theatre, 1980; Golda, *Requiem for a Heavyweight*, Martin Beck Theatre, New York City, 1985.

All at the Long Wharf Theatre, New Haven, CT: Laura Wingfield, *The Glass Menagerie*, 1967; Sheila, *A Day in the Death of Joe Egg*, 1970; Mrs. Hardcastle, *She Stoops to Conquer*, wife, *Solitaire*, Barbara, *Double Solitaire*, Blanche Dubois, *A Streetcar Named Desire*, all 1971; Gertrude, *Hamlet*, 1972; Mrs. Holyroyd, *The Widowing of Mrs. Holyroyd*, 1973; Madame Arkadina, *The Seagull*, matron, *The National Health*, both 1974; Ruth Ferrara, *You're Too Tall, but Come Back in Two Weeks*, Clara, *The Show-Off*, Maggie Wylie, *What Every Woman Knows*, all 1975; Bertha Dorset, *The House of Mirth*, Maisie Madigan, *Darlin' Juno*, both 1976; Maggie, *The Shadow Box*, 1977; Maria Lvovna, *Summerfolk*, 1979; Sara Muller, *Watch on the Rhine*, 1980; Maureen Johnson, *This Story of Yours*, 1981; Golda, *Requiem for a Heavyweight*, 1983. Also in *Misalliance, Mother Courage and Her Children, The Rehearsal, The Playboy of the Western World*, all 1967; *Room Service, A Doctor in Spite of Himself, Tiny Alice, The Lion in Winter, Epitaph for George Dillon*, all 1968; *America Hurrah, Under Milk Wood, Ghosts, Tango*, all 1969; *Country People, Black Comedy, Spoon River Anthology, The Skin of Our Teeth, Yegor Bulichov*, all 1970; *Heartbreak House, The Price*, both 1971; *The Way of the World, The Lady's Not For Burning*, "The Country Woman," *Troika: An Evening of Russian Comedy*, all 1972; *Juno and the Paycock, Forget-Me-Not-Lane, Dance of Death, Miss Julie*, all 1973; *The Autumn Garden*, 1977; *Hobson's Choice, Macbeth*, both 1978; *I Sent a Letter to My Love, Rosmersholm*, both 1979; *Solomon's Child, Close Ties*, both 1980; *Pal Joey, The Cherry Orchard*, both 1982; *The Hostage*, 1983; *Tobacco Road*, 1985.

TELEVISION DEBUT—*Frontiers of Faith*, NBC, 1956. PRINCIPAL TELEVISION APPEARANCES—Episodic: *The Big Valley*, ABC, 1967; *Kraft Television Theatre*, NBC; *Suspense*, CBS. Movies: Mrs. Holyroyd, *The Widowing of Mrs. Holyroyd*, PBS, 1974; *Forget-Me-Not-Lane*, 1975; *Ah! Wilderness*, 1976; *Blessings,*

1978; *James at 16,* 1978; *Close Ties,* 1983. Specials: "A Shropshire Lad," *Camera Three,* CBS, 1956; Mary, *A Dickens Chronicle,* CBS, 1963.

AWARDS: Atlas Award, San Diego Shakespeare Festival, 1959, for *Romeo and Juliet;* Clarence Derwent Award, 1964, Obie Award, from the *Village Voice,* 1964, both for *The Trojan Women; Variety* Award, 1970, for *Double Solitaire;* Drama Desk nomination, 1977, for *The Shadow Box.*

MEMBER: Actors' Equity Association, American Federation of Television and Radio Artists.

ADDRESSES: OFFICE—c/o Long Wharf Theatre, 222 Sargent Drive, New Haven, CT, 06511.*

*   *   *

eda-YOUNG, Barbara   1945-

PERSONAL: Born January 30, 1945, in Detroit, MI; daughter of Eddie and Ann Young.

VOCATION: Actress.

CAREER: STAGE DEBUT—Velma Sparrow, *Birdbath,* Theatre Genesis, New York City, 1965. OFF-BROADWAY DEBUT—*The Hawk,* Actors Playhouse, 1968. BROADWAY DEBUT—*Lovers and Other Strangers,* Brooks Atkinson Theatre, 1968. PRINCIPAL STAGE APPEARANCES—Babs, *The Time of Your Life,* Vivian Beaumont Theatre, New York City, 1969, Olympe, Eva, *Camino Real,* Honey, *Operation Sidewinder,* both Vivian Beaumont Theatre, 1970; girl, Doreen, *Kool Aid,* Forum Theatre, New York City, 1971; Stella Kowalski, *A Streetcar Named Desire,* St. James Theatre, New York City, 1973; Billie, *Born Yesterday,* Natasha, *The Three Sisters,* Carol, *Orpheus Descending,* all Williamstown Theatre Festival, Williamstown, MA, 1976; Carmel, *The Gathering,* Manhattan Theatre Club, New York City, 1977; Maggie, *After the Fall,* Williamstown Theatre Festival, 1977; Sylvia, *Two Brothers,* Liz, *The Philadelphia Story,* both Long Wharf Theatre, New Haven, CT, 1978; Claudette, *Drinks Before Dinner,* Public Theatre, New York City, 1978; Mrs. Forsythe, *Shout Across the River,* Marymount Manhattan Theatre, New York City, 1980; Velma Sparrow, *Birdbath,* Mirage, *Crossing the Crab Nebula,* both Harold Clurman Theatre, New York City, 1982; Margo Crosby, *Maiden Stakes,* St. Clement's Church Theatre, New York City, 1982; Martha Meier, *Mensch Meier,* Manhattan Theatre Club, New York City, 1984; Kate, *Goodbye Freddy,* INTAR Theatre, New York City, 1985; Pearl Rosen, *A Rosen By Any Other Name,* American Jewish Theatre, New York City, 1986. Also appeared in *Crimes of the Heart,* Center Stage, Baltimore, MD, 1980; *Grownups,* Lyceum Theatre, New York City, 1981; *The Two-Character Play,* Open Space Theatre New York City, 1982; *Angel Street,* Whole Theatre Company, Montclair, NJ, 1982; *Joe Egg,* Longacre Theatre, New York City, 1985; and in *The Terrorists; After Stardrive; Come Dog By Night; Glory in the Flower.*

PRINCIPAL FILM APPEARANCES—*Serpico,* Paramount, 1974.

PRINCIPAL TELEVISION APPEARANCES—*Another World,* NBC.

MEMBER: Actors' Equity Association, Screen Actors Guild, American Federation of Television and Radio Artists.

ADDRESSES: AGENT—c/o Coleman-Rosenberg, 667 Madison Avenue, New York, NY 10019.*

*   *   *

EDGLEY, Michael   1943-

PERSONAL: Full name, Michael Christopher Edgley; born December 17, 1943, in Perth, Australia; son of Eric (a theatre manager) and Edna (an actress and dancer; maiden name, Luscombe) Edgley; married Jennifer Gedge, 1972 (separated); children: Mark, Sasha, Capi, Gigi. EDUCATION: Attended Trinty College, Perth.

VOCATION: Producer and theatre manager.

CAREER: PRINCIPAL STAGE WORK—Producer of entertainment tours throughout Australia, the South Pacific, and Asia, including Great Moscow Circus, Bolshoi Ballet, Royal Winnipeg Ballet, Nederlands Dans Theatre, Kirov Ballet, Scottish Ballet, London Festival Ballet, Dance Theatre of Harlem, Georgian State Dance Company, Ballet Folklorico of Mexico, Moiseyev Company, Red Army Chorus, Disney on Parade, Chichester Festival Theatre Company, Vienna Boys Choir, and D'Oyly Carte Opera Company. Theatrical touring productions include: *Dracula, Annie, A Chorus Line,* and *Evita.* Performers produced include Nureyev, Fonteyn, Makarova and Baryshnikov, Shirley Bassey, Bette Davis, Shirley MacLaine, Rod McKuen, Marcel Marceau, Vincent Price, the Two Ronnies, and Liv Ullman.

RELATED CAREER— Office boy/accountant, later manager, then owner, His Majesty's Theatre, Perth, Australia.

AWARDS: Member of Order of British Empire for services to the performing arts, 1972; Citizen of Western Australia, 1975.

SIDELIGHTS: CTFT learned that Michael Edgley sponsored the first cultural exchange between Australia and the U.S.S.R. in 1973 and also produced the first attraction from mainland China to perform in Australia.

ADDRESSES: OFFICE—600 George Street, First Floor, Sydney, New South Wales 2000, Australia.

*   *   *

EGAN, Peter   1946-

PERSONAL: Born September 28, 1946, in London, England; son of Michael Thomas and Doris (Pilk) Egan; married Myra Frances (an actress), February 13, 1976; children: Rebecca. EDUCATION: Trained for the stage at the Royal Academy of Dramatic Art, 1964-66. RELIGION: Roman Catholic.

VOCATION: Actor and director.

CAREER: STAGE DEBUT—*Macbeth,* Chichester Festival Theatre, Chichester, U.K., 1966. LONDON DEBUT—Valentine, *Two Gentlemen of Verona,* Royal Shakespeare Company, Aldwych Theatre, 1970. PRINCIPAL STAGE APPEARANCES—Dandy, *The Italian Straw Hat,* Chichester Festival Theatre, Chichester, U.K., 1967; title role, *Hamlet,* Clare, *The Maids,* both Palace Court Theatre,

PETER EGAN

Bournemouth, U.K., 1967; Millais, *Ordeal By Marriage,* Arnaud Theatre, Guildford, U.K., 1967; Proteus, *Two Gentlemen of Verona,* Open Air Theatre, London, 1968; Romeo, *Romeo and Juliet,* Everyman Theatre, Cheltenham, U.K., 1969; Valentine, *Two Gentlemen of Verona,* Richmond, first murderer, *Richard III,* Osric, *Hamlet,* all Royal Shakespeare Company, Stratford-on-Avon, 1970; Jack Absolute, *The Rivals,* Apollodorus, *Caesar and Cleopatra,* Alexander, *Cher Antoine,* all Chichester Festival Theatre, 1971; Captain Stanhope, *Journey's End,* Mermaid Theatre, then Cambridge Theatre, both London, 1972; John Shand, *What Every Woman Knows,* Albery Theatre, London, 1974; Cheviot Hill, *Engaged,* National Theatre, London, 1975; Sergius, *Arms and the Man,* Oxford Playhouse, Oxford, U.K., 1976; Charles Rolls, *Rolls Hyphen Royce,* Shaftesbury Theatre, London, 1977; Valentine, *You Never Can Tell,* Lyric Hammersmith Theatre, London, 1979; Sergius, *Arms and the Man,* Lyric Hammersmith Theatre, 1981. Appeared as Henry Carr in *Travesties* and in *The Crucible,* both Sheffield, U.K., 1978.

MAJOR TOURS—Sergius, *Arms and the Man,* U.K. cities, 1976; *A Perfect Gentleman,* U.K. cities, 1977.

PRINCIPAL THEATRE WORK—Director, *Landmarks,* Lyric Studio, London, 1979; *A Midsummer Night's Dream,* Mills College, Oakland, CA, 1983.

FILM DEBUT—*One Brief Summer,* 1969. PRINCIPAL FILM APPEARANCES—*The Hireling,* Columbia, 1973; *Hennessey,* American International, 1975; *Chariots of Fire,* Warner Brothers, 1981. Also appeared in *Callan,* 1974.

PRINCIPAL TELEVISION APPEARANCES—Series: Title Role, *The Prince Regent,* BBC, 1978; also in *Ever Decreasing Circles,* 1984. Mini-Series: Earl of Southampton, *Elizabeth R,* PBS, 1971; Oscar Wilde, "Lillie," *Masterpiece Theatre,* PBS, 1978; Fothergill, "Reilly, Ace of Spies," *Mystery,* PBS, 1982; Henry Simcox, "Paradise Postponed," *Masterpiece Theatre,* PBS, 1985; Pym, *The Perfect Spy,* BBC, 1986; appeared in *A Woman of Substance,* syndicated, 1985; as Seth, *Cold Comfort Farm,* 1967; Hog, *Big Breadwinner Hog,* 1968; Millais, *The Love School,* 1974; and in *The Dark Side of the Sun; The Greeks.*

RELATED CAREER—Artistic director, Mill Theatre, Sonning, U.K.

AWARDS: London Theatre Critic's Award, 1972, for *Journey's End;* Best Actor, British Academy of Film and Television Arts, 1972, for *The Hireling;* Best Actor, *TV Times,* 1986, for *Paradise Postponed.*

MEMBER: British Actors' Equity Association, Screen Actors Guild, Garrick Club.

SIDELIGHTS: FAVORITE ROLES—Hamlet; Captain Stanhope in *Journey's End;* and "any good leading part." RECREATIONS—"Good wine and food, poker, snooker, swimming, travel."

ADDRESSES: HOME—Airdale Avenue, Chiswick, London, W4 England. AGENT—c/o James Sharkey Associate Ltd., Suite Three, 15 Golden Square, London, W11, England.

*   *   *

EIGSTI, Karl   1938-

PERSONAL: Second syllable of surname rhymes with "eye;" born September 19, 1938, in Goshen, IN; son of Orie Jacob (a scientist) and Agnes (a nutritionist; maiden name, Weaver) Eigsti; divorced from wife, 1984; children: Christina. EDUCATION: Attended Indiana University, 1956-59; American University, B.A., 1962; Bristol University, M.A., 1964; studied design at the School of Visual Arts, 1967-69. MILITARY: U.S. Army, 1959-62.

VOCATION: Designer.

*CAREER:*FIRST STAGE WORK—Set designer, *Billy Budd,* Arena Stage, Washington, DC, 1964. FIRST NEW YORK STAGE WORK—Set designer, *Bananas,* Forum Theatre, 1968. PRINICPAL STAGE WORK—Set designer, all in New York City unless indicated: *Boesman and Lena,* Circle in the Square, 1969; *Othello,* American Shakespeare Festival, American National Theatre Academy Playhouse, 1970; *Inquest,* Music Box Theatre, 1970; *The House of Blue Leaves,* Truck and Warehouse Theatre, 1971; lighting designer, *Grease,* Royale Theatre, 1972; (also lighting designer) *The Passion of Antigona Perez,* Cathedral of St. John the Divine, 1972; *The Karl Marx Play,* American Place Theatre, 1973; *Nourish the Beast,* Cherry Lane Theatre, 1973; *Baba Goya,* American Place Theatre, 1973; *Yentl, the Yeshiva Boy,* Brooklyn Academy of Music, Brooklyn, NY, 1974, then on Broadway, 1975; *Wings,* Lyceum Theatre, 1975; *Sweet Bird of Youth,* Harkness Theatre, 1975; *Jo Anne!,* Theatre of the Riverside Church, 1976; *On-the-Lock-In,* Public Theatre, 1977; (also costume designer) *Cold Storage,* Lyceum Theatre, 1977; *Once in a Lifetime,* Circle in the Square, 1978; *Eubie!,* Ambassador Theatre, 1978; *Annie Get Your Gun,* Jones

Beach, Long Island, New York, 1978; *The Diary of Anne Frank,* Theatre Four, 1978; *The Caretaker,* Long Wharf Theatre, New Haven, CT, 1979; *Losing Time,* Manhattan Theatre Club, 1979; *Murder at the Howard Johnson's,* John Golden Theatre, 1979; *Knockout,* Helen Hayes Theatre, 1979.

The Curse of the Starving Class, Arena Stage, Washington, DC, 1980; *The American Clock,* Biltmore Theatre, 1980; *Frimbo,* Grand Central Terminal, Tracks 39-42, 1980; (also costume designer) *Almost an Eagle,* Longacre Theatre, 1982; *Joseph and the Amazing Technicolor Dreamcoat,* Royale Theatre, 1982; *The World of Sholom Aleichem,* Rialto Theatre, 1982; *Richard II,* Circle Repertory Company, Entermedia Theatre, 1982; *Free and Clear,* Long Wharf Theatre, New Haven, CT, 1982; *Amen Corner,* Nederlander Theatre, 1983; *Julius Caesar,* Playhouse in the Park, Cincinnati, OH, 1984; *Joseph and the Amazing Technicolor Dreamcoat,* Paper Mill Playhouse, Milburn, NJ, 1984; *Alone Together,* Music Box Theatre, 1984; *Accidental Death of an Anarchist,* Belasco Theatre, 1984; *Downriver,* Musical Theatre Works, 1985; *Translations,* Alaska Repertory Theatre, Anchorage, AK, 1985; *Terra Nova,* Huntington Theatre Company, Boston, MA, 1985. Also designed *Dandelion Wine,* New York City, 1976; *Daddy,* New York City, 1977; *100% Alive,* Los Angeles, CA, 1979; and more than 40 productions at the Arena Stage, Washington, DC, as well as designs for the Actors Theatre of Louisville, Louisville, KY; the Milwaukee Repertory Theatre, Milwaukee, WI; the Los Angeles Theatre Centre, Los Angeles, CA; the South Coast Repertory Theatre, Costa Mesa, CA; and the Long Wharf Theatre, New Haven, CT.

MAJOR TOURS—Lighting designer: *Grease,* U.S. cities, 1971-80. Set designer: *Eubie!,* U.S. cities, 1979-80; *Albee Directs Albee,*

U.S. cities, then world tour, 1979; *One Mo' Time,* U.S. cities, 1981-82; *Joseph and the Amazing Technicolor Dreamcoat,* U.S. cities, 1981-83.

PRINCIPAL TELEVISION WORK—All as production designer. Episodic: "Guests of the Nation," *American Playhouse,* PBS, 1981; "The Shady Hill Kidnapping," *American Playhouse,* PBS, 1982; "File on Jill Hatch," *American Playhouse,* PBS, 1983; "Solomon Northrop's Odyssey," *American Playhouse,* PBS, 1984.

RELATED CAREER—Lecturer, New York University, School of the Arts, 1966-85; head of design, Brandeis University Theatre School, 1986—; visiting associate professor of drama, State University of New York, Purchase; board of directors, Theatre Communications Group, 1976-79.

AWARDS: Antoinette Perry Award nomination, 1969; Maharam Award, 1969, for outstanding set design; Dramalogue Award, 1986; also received Fulbright Fellowship, 1962.

MEMBER: United Scenic Artists (executive board, local 829, 1980-86), International Alliance of Theatrical Stage Employees and Moving Picture Machine Operators of the U.S. and Canada;

SIDELIGHTS: Karl Eigsti's work has been exhibited at the Museum of the City of New York, the New Jersey Arts and Cultural Center, the Milwaukee Art Museum, and in Prague, Czechoslovakia.

ADDRESSES: HOME—155 W. 15th Street, New York, NY 10011. OFFICE—One Union Square, Suite 801, New York, NY 10003.

*   *   *

KARL EIGSTI

EIKENBERRY, Jill   1947-

PERSONAL: Born January 21, 1947, in New Haven, CT; married Michael Tucker (an actor); children: one stepdaughter. EDUCATION: Attended the Yale School of Drama.

VOCATION: Actress.

CAREER: PRINCIPAL STAGE APPEARANCES—*Saints,* Broadway production, New York City, 1976; Kate Quin, *Uncommon Women and Others,* Marymount Manhattan Theatre, New York City, 1977; Marthe de Brancovis, *Watch on the Rhine,* Long Wharf Theatre, New Haven, CT, then John Golden Theatre, New York City, 1980; Victoria Woodhull, *Onward Victoria,* Martin Beck Theatre, New York City, 1980; *Holiday,* Long Wharf Theatre, New Haven, 1982; Amy, *Porch,* Lamb's Little Theatre, New York City, 1984; Zee, *Fine Line,* "Marathon '84," Ensemble Studio Theatre, New York City, 1984; Jinx, *Life under Water,* "Marathon '85," Ensemble Studio Theatre, New York City, 1985; also *All over Town,* Broadway production.

PRINCIPAL FILM APPEARANCES—Lynn, *Between the Lines,* Midwest Film Productions, 1977; Claire, *An Unmarried Woman,* Twentieth Century-Fox, 1977; Juilliard student, *Rich Kids,* United Artists, 1979; Mary, *Butch and Sundance: The Early Days,* Twentieth Century-Fox, 1979; Alisa Hacklin, *Hide in Plain Sight,* United Artists, 1980; Susan Johnson, *Arthur,* Warner Brothers, 1981; *Grace Quigley* (also known as *The Ultimate Solution of Grace Quigley*), Cannon, 1985; Elizabeth Stevens, *The Manhattan Project,* Twentieth Century-Fox, 1986.

PRINCIPAL TELEVISION APPEARANCES—Series: Ann Kelsey, *L.A. Law*, NBC, 1986—. Movies: Carole Eskanazi, *The Deadliest Season*, 1977; Emma Symms, *Orphan Train*, 1979; Anna, *Swan Song*, 1980; Matron, *Sessions*, NBC, 1983; Susan Lester, *Kane & Abel*, 1985. Teleplays: Kate, *Uncommon Women and Others*, 1978.

ADDRESSES: AGENT—S.T.E. Representation, Ltd., 211 S. Beverly Drive, Suite 201, Beverly Hills, CA 90212.*

*   *   *

ELGAR, Avril   1932-

PERSONAL: Born Avril Williams, April 1, 1932, in Halifax, England; daughter of Albert Elgar (in the British army) and Annie (Rose), Williams; married James Maxwell, 1952; children: two sons. EDUCATION: Trained for the stage at the Old Vic Theatre School.

VOCATION: Actress.

CAREER: LONDON DEBUT—Young Macduff, second witch, *Macbeth*, Royal Court Theatre, 1958. BROADWAY DEBUT—Norah, *Epitaph for George Dillon*, John Golden Theatre, 1958. PRINCIPAL STAGE APPEARANCES—Dodo, *The Sport of My Mad Mother*, Mrs. Ecto, *The Hole*, both Royal Court Theatre, London, 1958; Norah, *Epitaph for George Dillon*, Comedy Theatre, London, 1958; Lucille, *Danton's Death*, Lyric Hammersmith Theatre, London, 1959; Peony, *Farewell, Farewell, Eugene*, Garrick Theatre, London, 1959; night nurse, *The Death of Bessie Smith*, Grandma, *The American Dream*, both Royal Court Theatre, 1961; woman, *The Blood of the Bambergs*, Royal Court Theatre, 1962; Asta, *Little Eyolf*, 59 Theatre Company, Edinburgh Festival Theatre, Edinburgh, Scotland, U.K., 1963; Miss Sympathy, *Crawling Arnold*, Arts Theatre, London, 1965; various roles, *Shelley*, Lilian Fawcett, *The Cresta Run*, both Royal Court Theatre, 1965; Lady Kix, *A Chaste Maid in Cheapside*, Alice Maitland, *The Voysey Inheritance*, both Royal Court Theatre, 1966; Olga, *The Three Sisters*, Joyce, *The Ruffian on the Stair*, both Royal Court Theatre, 1967; Aase, *Peer Gynt*, 69 Theatre Company, University Theatre, Manchester, U.K., 1970; Sheila, *The Sandboy*, Greenwich Theatre, London, 1971; Miss Davitt, first nun, *A Pagan Place*, Royal Court Theatre, 1972; Agatha, *The Family Reunion*, 69 Theatre Company, 1972; Helen Mallock, *Half Life*, National Theatre, then Duke of York's Theatre, both London, 1978; Agatha, *The Family Reunion*, Round House Theatre, then Vaudeville Theatre, both London, 1979; Miss Moffatt, *The Corn Is Green*, Royal Exchange Theatre, Manchester, U.K., 1981; Hadezda Mandelstan, *Hope Against Hope*, Royal Exchange Theatre, 1983; Rosa, *Inner Voices*, Lyttelton Theatre, London, 1983; Queen, soothsayer, *Cymbeline*, Miss Havisham, *Great Expectations*, Lady Brocklehurst, *The Admirable Crichton*, all Royal Exchange Theatre, 1984-85; Aglae, *Court in the Act*, Royal Exchange Theatre, 1986, then Phoenix Theatre, London, 1987.

MAJOR TOURS—Young Macduff, second witch, *Macbeth*, U.K. cities, 1952; Rosa, *Inner Voices*, U.K. cities, 1983; Aglae, *Court in the Act*, U.K. cities, 1987.

TELEVISION DEBUT—*You Touched Me*, BBC, 1956. PRINCIPAL TELEVISION APPEARANCES—Episodic: ''Back for Christmas,'' *Tales of the Unexpected*, Anglia, 1980; ''The Moles,'' *Tales of the Unexpected*, Anglia, 1981. Series: *Looking for Mr. Wright*, BBC, 1980; also *Rosie; George and Mildred*. Movies: visa clerk, *Sakharov*, HBO, 1984; also in *13 for Dinner; Give Us This Day Arthur Daley's Bread*, both 1985. Also appeared in *Under the Skin*, BBC, 1981; *Winnie, The Citadel*, both BBC, 1982; *The Bank Manager's Wife*, Central, 1982; *Paying Guests*, BBC, 1985; *Children of Dynmouth*, *The Oldest Goose in the Business*, both BBC, 1986.

FILM DEBUT—Town hall office girl, *Room at the Top*, 1958. PRINCIPAL FILM APPEARANCES—Landlady, *Betrayal*, Twentieth Century-Fox, 1983; also in *Spring and Port Wine*, 1970.

MEMBER: British Actors' Equity Association.

SIDELIGHTS: RECREATIONS—Gardening and the ''Times'' crossword puzzle.

ADDRESSES: HOME—c/o John French, French's, 26-28 Binney Street, London, W1 England.

*   *   *

ELLIS, Leslie   1962-

PERSONAL: Born July 22, 1962, in Cambridge, MA; daughter of Allan B. (an educator) and Carole P. (an educator; maiden name, Mullen) Ellis. EDUCATION: Carnegie-Mellon University, B.F.A., acting, 1984.

LESLIE ELLIS

VOCATION: Actress and singer.

CAREER: STAGE DEBUT—Anne, *La Cage aux Folles,* tour of U.S. and Canadian cities, 1984-85. PRINCIPAL STAGE APPEAR-ANCES—*Broadway Applauds Lincoln Center,* New York City, 1986.

MAJOR TOURS—Grizabella, *Cats,* U.S. cities, 1986—.

MEMBER: Actors' Equity Association.

SIDELIGHTS: Leslie Ellis told CTFT: "I wanted to act after seeing Angela Lansbury in *Sweeney Todd.* I have toured the United States in two road shows and enjoy seeing the country as well as playing to the audiences." Ellis is currently learning sign language as she would like to work with handicapped children.

ADDRESSES: AGENT—c/o Peggy Hadley Enterprises, Ltd., 250 W. 57th Street, New York, NY 10019.

F

FABER, Ron 1933-

PERSONAL: Full name, Ronald Anthony Faber; born February 16, 1933, in Milwaukee, WI; son of Clarence Ernst and Ethel (Backus) Faber; married Elise Donahue (divorced); married Paula Ann Price. EDUCATION: Attended Marquette University.

VOCATION: Actor.

CAREER: STAGE DEBUT—Richard Talbot, *The Scarecrow,* Marquette Players Theatre, Milwaukee, WI, 1954. OFF-BROADWAY DEBUT—*An Enemy of the People,* Actors Playhouse, 1959. BROADWAY DEBUT—Creon, tutor, *Medea,* Circle in the Square, 1973. PRINCIPAL STAGE APPEARANCES—Promos, *And They Put Handcuffs on the Flowers,* patient, *Doctor Selavy's Magic Theatre,* both Mercer-O'Casey Theatre, New York City, 1972; Robert de Baudricourt, English soldier, *Saint Joan,* Williamstown Theatre Festival, Williamstown, MA, 1973; Nestor, Priam, *Troilus and Cressida,* Mitzi E. Newhouse Theatre, New York City, 1973; Captain, *Woyzeck,* Public Theatre, New York City, 1976; Edmund Scorn, *The Reason We Eat,* Dr. Einstein, *Arsenic and Old Lace,* both Hartman Theatre, Stamford, CT, 1976; Matti, *Puntila and His Chauffeur Matti,* Yale Repertory Theatre, New Haven, CT, 1977; Pierpont Mauler, *St. Joan of the Stockyards,* Encompass Theatre, New York City, 1978; Mr. Peachum, *The Beggar's Opera,* Guthrie Theatre, Minneapolis, MN, 1978; Blake, *First Monday in October,* Majestic Theatre, New York City, 1978; Carvalho, *Tunnel Fever,* American Place Theatre, New York City, 1979; Rosencrantz, *Hamlet,* Greenwich Mews Playhouse, New York City, 1979; John Garga, *In the Jungle of Cities,* Colonnades Theatre Lab, New York City, 1979; Pa Ubu, *Ubu Rex,* Ellis, *Curse of the Starving Class,* both Yale Repertory Theatre, 1979; Symmons, *Mary Stuart,* Public Theatre, 1981; Count Alphonse de Toulouse-Lautrec Monfa, Maurice Joyant, Vincent Van Gogh, puffy fellow, Oller, and Lauradour, *Times and Appetites of Toulouse-Lautrec,* American Place Theatre, 1985; Voltemand, fourth player, *Hamlet,* Public Theatre, 1986. Also appeared in *The Exception and the Rule,* Greenwich Mews Playhouse, 1965; *America Hurrah,* Pocket Theatre, New York City, 1966; *The Serpent—A Ceremony,* Public Theatre, then Washington Square Methodist Church, both New York City, 1970; *Terminal,* St. Clement's Church Theatre, then Washington Square Methodist Church, both New York City, 1970; *The Beauty Part,* American Place Theatre, 1974; *The Diary of Anne Frank,* Philadelphia Drama Guild, Philadelphia, PA, 1982; *The Day of the Picnic,* Yale Repertory Theatre, 1984; and in *Ubu Cocu, Opera, Scenes from Everyday Life, Three by Pirandello,* all New York City.

PRINCIPAL FILM APPEARANCES—*The Exorcist,* Warner Brothers, 1973. Also appeared in *The Private Files of J. Edgar Hoover,* 1980.

RELATED CAREER—Acting teacher, television floor director, lighting assistant.

NON-RELATED CAREER—Salesman, social worker, marionettist, factory worker, night porter.

AWARDS: Obie Award from the *Village Voice,* 1972, Drama Desk Award, 1972, both for *And They Put Handcuffs on the Flowers.*

ADDRESSES: HOME—155 Bank Street, New York, NY 10014.*

* * *

FAIRCHILD, Morgan 1950-

PERSONAL: Born Patsy McClenny, February 3, 1950, in Dallas, TX. EDUCATION: Attended Southern Methodist University.

VOCATION: Actress.

CAREER: TELEVISION DEBUT—Jennifer Phillips, *Search for Tomorrow,* CBS. PRINCIPAL TELEVISION APPEARANCES— Episodic: Susan Taylor, *Mork and Mindy,* ABC, 1978; Jenna Wade, *Dallas,* CBS, 1978; host, *Shape of Things,* NBC, 1982; appeared on *Switch,* CBS, 1977; *Big Shamus, Little Shamus,* CBS, 1979; *Magnum, P.I.,* CBS, 1982; *Simon and Simon,* CBS, 1982; also appeared on *Hotel,* ABC; *Barnaby Jones,* CBS; *Happy Days,* ABC; *Police Woman,* NBC; *Kojak,* CBS; *The Bob Newhart Show,* CBS; *A Man Called Sloane,* NBC. Series: Constance Weldon Carlyle, *Flamingo Road,* NBC, 1981-82; Racine, *Paper Dolls,* ABC, 1984; *Falcon Crest,* CBS, 1985. Mini-Series: Myrna Savitch, *79 Park Avenue,* NBC, 1977; Burdetta Halloran, *North and South,* ABC, 1985, then *North and South, Book II,* ABC, 1986. Pilots: Suzy, *Escapade,* CBS, 1979; Constance Weldon, *Flamingo Road,* NBC, 1980. Movies: Jennifer, *The Initiation of Sarah,* ABC, 1978; Dana Morgan, *Murder in Music City* (also known as *The Country Music Murders*), NBC, 1979; Kate Harper, Carla Wade, *Concrete Cowboys,* CBS, 1979; Lisa Eddington, *The Memory of Eva Ryker,* CBS, 1980; Dulcie Warren, *The Dream Merchants,* syndicated, 1980; Stella Walker, *The Girl, the Gold Watch, and Dynamite,* syndicated, 1981; Judy Wellman, *Honeyboy,* NBC, 1982; Lady Marian, *The Zany Adventures of Robin Hood,* ABC, 1984; Renee DeSalles, *Time Bomb,* NBC, 1984. Specials: *Bob Hope's Spring Fling of Comedy and Glamour,* NBC, 1981; *Women Who Rate a "10,"* NBC, 1981; *Bob Hope's Stars Over Texas,* NBC, 1982; *Magic with the Stars,* NBC, 1982; *Billy Crystal Comedy Hour,* NBC, 1982; *Whatever Became Of. . .?,* ABC, 1982; *Circus of the Stars,* CBS, 1982; *The Magic of David Copperfield,* CBS, 1983; *Battle of the Network Stars,* ABC, 1983; *Bob Hope Goes to College,* NBC,

1983; *Blondes vs. Brunettes,* ABC, 1984; *Love Boat Fall Preview Party,* ABC, 1984; *Our Planet Tonight,* NBC, 1987.

PRINCIPAL FILM APPEARANCES—Jamie, *The Seduction,* AVCO-Embassy, 1981; Catherine Van Buren, *Campus Man,* Paramount, 1987. Also appeared in *A Bullet for Pretty Boy,* American International 1970; *Pee-Wee's Big Adventure,* Warner Brothers, 1985; and *The Red Headed Stranger,* 1984.

OFF-BROADWAY DEBUT—Skye Bullene, *Geniuses,* Douglas Fairbanks Theatre, 1982. PRINCIPAL STAGE APPEARANCES— *Night of 100 Stars,* Radio City Music Hall, New York City, 1982; *Night of 100 Stars II,* Radio City Music Hall, 1985.

ADDRESSES: AGENT—Agency for the Performing Arts, 9000 Sunset Boulevard, Suite 1200, Los Angeles, CA 90069.*

* * *

FARQUHAR, Malcolm 1924-

PERSONAL: Born October 26, 1924, in Swansea, Wales; son of Allan and Florence Mary (Rees) Farquhar. EDUCATION: Attended Clevedon College.

VOCATION: Director and actor.

CAREER: LONDON DEBUT—Captain Absolute, *The Rivals,* St. James Theatre, 1948. PRINCIPAL STAGE APPEARANCES—With the Rapier Players, Bristol, U.K., and the Birmingham Repertory Company, Birmingham, U.K.

PRINCIPAL STAGE WORK—Director, all with the Everyman Theatre, Cheltenham, U.K.: *This Stratford Business, The Law and Order Gang,* both 1971; *As We Lie,* 1973; *The Daffodil Man,* 1974; *The Friendship of Mrs. Eckley,* 1975; *The Little Photographer,* 1978; *Time to Kill, Don't Look at Me,* both 1979. Also directed *A Woman of No Importance,* London, 1967; *A Boston Story,* London, 1968; *Highly Confidential,* London, 1969; *Lady Frederick, Winnie the Pooh,* both London, 1970; in South Africa, 1975-78; also at the Connaught Theatre, Worthing, U.K.; Alexandra Theatre, Birmingham, U.K.

RELATED CAREER—Artistic director, Everyman Theatre, Cheltenham, U.K., 1971-80.

SIDELIGHTS: RECREATIONS—Collecting old gramophone records, gardening.

ADDRESSES: HOME—Six Buckingham Road, Brighton BN1 3RA, England.*

* * *

FARRAH 1926-

PERSONAL: Full name, Abd' Elkader Farrah; born March 28, 1926, in Boghari, Algeria; son of Brahim and Fatima-Zohra (Missoumi) Farrah; married Simone Pieret (a painter).

VOCATION: Set designer.

CAREER: FIRST STAGE WORK—Set designer, *Samson et Dalila* (opera), Stadschouwberg, Amsterdam, Netherlands, 1953. PRINCIPAL STAGE WORK—Set designer: *The Burdies,* Edinburgh Festival, Edinburgh, Scotland, U.K., 1966; *Henry IV,* Pirandello Theatre, New York City, 1973; *Henry IV, Parts I and II, Henry V,* all Royal Shakespeare Theatre, Stratford-on-Avon, U.K., 1975, then Aldwych Theatre, London, 1976; *Henry V, Henry VI, Parts I, II, and III, Coriolanus,* all Royal Shakespeare Theatre, 1976; *Mardi Gras,* Prince of Wales Theatre, London, 1977, then Aldwych Theatre, 1978; *Carte Blanche,* Phoenix Theatre, London, 1976; *The Passion of Dracula,* Queen's Theatre, London, 1978. Also set designer for *The Cherry Orchard,* London, 1961; *The Tempest,* Stratford-on-Avon, U.K., 1963; *Puntila,* London, 1965; *The Three Sisters,* London, 1967; *Dr. Faustus,* Stratford-on-Avon, U.K., 1968; *Tiny Alice,* London, 1970; *Richard III,* Stratford-on-Avon, U.K., 1970; *Oh Calcutta!* London, 1970; *The Balcony,* London, 1971; *The Duchess of Malfi,* Stratford-on-Avon, U.K., 1971; *Murder in the Cathedral,* London, 1972; *Richard III,* Comedie Francaise, France, 1973; *Romeo and Juliet, The Taming of the Shrew,* both Stratford-on-Avon, U.K., 1973; *A Lesson in Blood and Roses,* London, 1973; *The Bewitched, The Can Opener,* both London, 1974.

RELATED CAREER—Teacher, theatrical design, National Theatre School, Strasbourg, France, 1955-62; National Theatre School of Canada, Montreal, PQ, Canada, 1968-1969; associate artist, Royal Shakespeare Company.

ADDRESSES: OFFICE—Royal Shakespeare Theatre, Stratford-on-Avon, Warwicks, England.*

* * *

FARRELL, Shea 1957-

PERSONAL: Born October 21, 1957, in Cornwall, NY; son of Edward Leo, Jr. (an attorney) and Mary Rose (Drummey) Farrell; married Ronda Pierson (an agent), August 3, 1982. EDUCATION: Lake Forest College, B.A., political science, psychology, 1980; trained for the stage with Howard Fine, Nina Foch, William Chow, Sonja Packer, and Stella Adler. RELIGION: Roman Catholic.

VOCATION: Actor, producer, and writer.

CAREER: TELEVISION DEBUT—Matt McCordless, *Capitol,* CBS, 1982. PRINCIPAL TELEVISION APPEARANCES—Episodic: *Murder, She Wrote,* CBS; *The Love Boat,* ABC; *Fantasy Island,* ABC; *Finder of Lost Loves,* ABC. Series: Mark Danning, *Hotel,* ABC, 1983-86; also *The Law and Harry McGraw,* CBS, 1987. PRINCIPAL TELEVISION WORK—Specials: Co-producer, *Streets of Shame,* ABC, 1986.

STAGE DEBUT—Brimsley Miller, *Black Comedy,* Tiffany's Attic Theatre, Kansas City, MO, 1986, for seventy-seven performances. PRINCIPAL STAGE APPEARANCES—Son, *Six Characters in Search of an Author,* Chicago, 1978; Tom, *The Glass Menagerie,* Chicago, 1980.

MAJOR TOURS—Producer, *The Pleasure of His Company,* U.S. cities; producer, *Bus Stop,* U.S. cities.

FILM DEBUT—*Ordinary People,* Paramount, 1980.

SHEA FARRELL

WRITINGS: DOCUMENTARIES—*Streets of Shame*, ABC, 1986.

AWARDS: American Film Institute Award nomination, 1986, for *Streets of Shame*.

MEMBER: Actors' Equity Association.

SIDELIGHTS: From material submitted by his office, *CTFT* learned that Shea Farrell gained firsthand insight into the plight of the homeless in the United States for his documentary *Streets of Shame* by living as a vagrant in Los Angeles, New York, Boston, and San Francisco.

ADDRESSES: OFFICE—Chatham Productions, Inc., 760 N. La Cienega Boulevard, Los Angeles, CA 90069. AGENT—c/o Doug Warner, Agency for the Performing Arts, 9000 Sunset Boulevard, Los Angeles, CA 90069.

*   *   *

FEIST, Gene   1930-

PERSONAL: Born January 16, 1930, in New York, NY; son of Henry (an automobile mechanic) and Hattie (a beautician; maiden name, Fishbein) Feist; married Kathe Schneider (professional name, Elizabeth Owens; an actress), February 10, 1957; children: Nicole, Gena. EDUCATION: Carnegie Mellon University, B.F.A., 1951; New York University, M.A., 1952; graduate work, Columbia University, Hunter College; trained for the stage with Lee Strasberg

at the American Theatre Wing and at the Actors Studio. MILITARY: U.S. Air Force.

VOCATION: Producer, director, and playwright.

CAREER: FIRST STAGE WORK—Director, *The Matchmaker*, New Theatre, Nashville, TN, 1958. FIRST NEW YORK STAGE WORK—Director, *Picnic on the Battlefield*, Cherry Lane Theatre, 1962. PRINCIPAL STAGE WORK—Producer and director: *Cat on a Hot Tin Roof*, *Separate Tables*, *Children of Darkness*, *The Crucible*, *Relative Strangers*, *The Boy Friend*, *A Clearing in the Woods*, all New Theatre, Nashville, TN, 1958-59; *Look Back in Anger*, *Does Poppy Live Here?*, *La Boheme*, *As You Like It*, *Orpheus Descending*, *Brigadoon*, *Fallen Angels*, *No Time for Sergeants*, *Stock and Trade*, and *Say, Darling*, all New Theatre, 1959-60. Also directed at numerous regionals theatres, 1963-65.

Producer and director, all Roundabout Theatre Company, Roundabout Theatre, New York City: *The Father*, *The Miser*, *Pelleas and Melisande*, *Pins and Needles*, all 1966-67; *Waiting for Lefty*, *The Bond*, *King Lear*, *The Importance of Being Earnest*, all 1968-69; *Journey's End*, *King Lear*, *Candida*, *Dance of Death*, *Trumpets and Drums*, *Jocasta and Oedipus*, *Lady from Maxim's*, all 1969-70; producer, *Macbeth*, 1970; *Hamlet*, 1970; producer, *Tug of War*, 1970; *Uncle Vanya*, *Charles Abbott and Son*, *She Stoops to Conquer*, *The Master Builder*, all 1971; producer, "Tales of Odessa" and "On the Harmfulness of Tobacco" as *An Evening of Russian Theatre*, 1971; *The Taming of the Shrew*, *Misalliance*, *John Whiting's Conditions of Agreement*, all 1972; *Right You Are If You Think You Are*, 1972; producer, *American Gothics*, *Anton Chekhov's Garden Party*, both 1972; *The Play's the Thing*, *Ghosts*, both 1973;

GENE FEIST

producer, *The Caretaker, Miss Julie, The Death of Lord Chatterly, The Father*, all 1973; *The Seagull, The Circle*, both 1974; producer, *The Burnt Flowerbed, Rosmersholm*, both 1974; producer, *All My Sons*, Roundabout Stage One Theatre, 1974.

Producer, all with the Roundabout Theatre Company, New York City: *The Rivals, James Joyce's Dublin, What Every Woman Knows, Summer and Smoke, Dear Mr. G.*, all Roundabout Stage One Theatre, 1975; *Clarence, The Cherry Orchard, The World of Sholom Aleichem, A Month in the Country, Love and Intrigue, The Merchant of Venice, The Philanderer, The Rehearsal*, all Roundabout Stage One Theatre, 1976; (also director) *John Gabriel Borkman*, Roundabout Stage One Theatre, 1977; (also director) *Endgame, Naked*, both Roundabout Stage Two Theatre, 1977; *Dear Liar, You Never Can Tell*, both Roundabout Stage One Theatre, 1977; (also director) *Othello, Pins and Needles*, both Roundabout Stage One Theatre, 1978; *The Promise, The Show-Off*, both Roundabout Stage Two Theatre, 1978; *Candida, Little Eyolf, Awake and Sing, Family Business, Diversions and Delights, A Month in the Country*, all Roundabout Stage One Theatre 1979; *Dark at the Top of the Stair*, Roundabout Stage Two Theatre, 1979.

Producer, all with the Roundabout Theatre Company, New York City: *Heartbreak House, Look Back in Anger, Here Are the Ladies, Don Juan in Hell, The Bloodknot, The Dance of Death, She Stoops to Conquer, The Winslow Boy*, all Roundabout Stage One Theatre, 1980; *A Taste of Honey*, Roundabout Stage Two Theatre, 1981; *Faces of Love, Hedda Gabler, Kurt Weill Cabaret, Inadmissible Evidence, Misalliance*, all Roundabout Stage One Theatre, 1981; *Martha Schlamme, Dear Liar, The Caretaker, The Fox, The Chalk Garden, Old Times*, all Roundabout Stage One Theatre, 1982; *The Twelve-Pound Look, The Browning Version*, both Roundabout Stage Two Theatre, 1982; (also director) *Playing with Fire, Miss Julie*, both Roundabout Stage Two Theatre, 1982; *The Learned Ladies*, Haft Theatre, 1982; *The Holly and the Ivy*, Susan Bloch Theatre, 1982; *The Entertainer, Duet for One, The Knack, The Master Builder*, all Roundabout Stage One Theatre, 1983; *Winners/ How He Lied to Her Husband, The Killing of Sister George*, both Susan Bloch Theatre, 1983; *Ah, Wilderness!*, Haft Theatre, 1983; *Old Times, Desire Under the Elms*, and *Come Back, Little Sheba*, all Roundabout Stage One Theatre, 1984; *On Approval*, Susan Bloch Theatre, 1984; *She Stoops to Conquer*, Triplex Theatre, 1984; *A Day in the Death of Joe Egg*, Haft Theatre, 1984; *The Playboy of the Western World, An Enemy of the People, Voice of the Turtle*, all New Roundabout Theatre, 1985; *Mrs. Warren's Profession, Room Service, The Master Class, A Raisin in the Sun*, all Christian C. Yeger Theatre, 1985-86; *A Man for All Seasons, The Miracle Worker, Rosencrantz and Guildenstern Are Dead*, all Christian C. Yeger Theatre, 1986-87.

MAJOR TOURS—Producer: *The Winslow Boy*, U.S. cities, 1980; *A Raisin in the Sun*, U.S. cities, 1985.

RELATED CAREER—General manager, Sharon Playhouse, Sharon, CT, 1957; founder, Fourth Street Theatre, New York City; founder, artistic director, Roundabout Theatre Company, New York City, 1965—; drama critic, *Chelsea Clinton News*, New York City.

NON-RELATED CAREER—Sociological researcher, Columbia University; social worker, New York City; teacher, secondary school and college.

WRITINGS: PLAYS—See production details above. (Adaptor) *Relative Strangers*, 1958; *Jocasta and Oedipus*, 1970; (adaptor) *Lady from Maxim's*, 1970; (adaptor) *Uncle Vanya*, 1971; (adaptor)

The Master Builder, 1971; (adaptor) *Ghosts*, 1973; (adaptor) *Naked*, 1978; *James Joyce's Dublin*, 1975. Also wrote *Wretched the Lionhearted, A Toy for the Clowns, Building Blocks*, and adapted works of Strindberg and Salacrou.

MEMBER: Society of Stage Directors and Choreographers, League of American Theaters and Producers, League of Resident Theatres; Players Club, New York State United Teachers.

SIDELIGHTS: RECREATIONS—Archeology, horticulture, collecting theatrical journals, biographies, and diaries.

ADDRESSES: OFFICE—Roundabout Theatre Company, 100 E. 17th Street, New York, NY 10003.

*				*				*

## FERRIS, Barbara			1943-

PERSONAL: Full name, Barbara Gillian Ferris; born 1943, in London, England; married John Quested (a producer), 1962.

VOCATION: Actress.

CAREER: LONDON DEBUT—Nellie, *Sparrows Can't Sing*, Stratford Theatre, 1960, then Wyndham's Theatre, 1961. BROADWAY DEBUT—Marion, *There's a Girl in My Soup*, Music Box Theatre, 1967. PRINCIPAL STAGE APPEARANCES—Cinderella, *The Merry Roosters' Panto*, Wyndham's Theatre, London, 1963; Jess, Prunella Flack, *A Kayf Up West*, first girl, *Carving a Statue*, both Stratford Theatre, London 1964; Pam, *Saved*, Royal Court Theatre, London, 1965; Moll, *A Chaste Maid in Cheapside*, Nancy, *The Knack*, girl, *Transcending*, all Royal Court Theatre, 1966; Marion, *There's a Girl in My Soup*, Globe Theatre, London, 1966; Ann, *Slag*, Royal Court Theatre, 1970; Jill Tanner, *Butterflies Are Free*, Apollo Theatre, London, 1970; Begonia Brown, *Geneva*, Mermaid Theatre, London, 1971; Mrs. Elvsted, *Hedda Gabler*, Royal Court Theatre, 1972; Marie-Louise Durham, *The Constant Wife*, Albery Theatre, London, 1973; Leslie, *Alphabetical Order*, Hampstead Theatre Club, then May Fair Theatre, both London, 1975; Mara, *Clouds*, Hampstead Theatre Club, 1976; Ethel Bartlett, *For Services Rendered*, Annie Parker, *When We Are Married*, both Lyttelton Theatre, London, 1979. Also appeared in *Honey, I'm Home*, Leatherhead, U.K., 1964.

PRINCIPAL FILM APPEARANCES—*Sparrows Can't Sing*, Janus, 1963; *Term of Trial*, Warner Brothers, 1963; *Children of the Damned*, Metro-Goldwyn-Mayer, 1964; *Having a Wild Weekend*, Warner Brothers, 1965; *The Girl Getters*, American International, 1966; *Interlude*, Columbia, 1968; *A Nice Girl Like Me*, AVCO-Embassy, 1969.

MEMBER: British Actors' Equity Association.

ADDRESSES: Crouch Associates, 59 Frith Street, London W1V 5TA, England.*

*				*				*

## FIELD, Jules			1919-

PERSONAL: Born Julius Blumenfeld, February 13, 1919, in New Castle, IN; son of Michael (a tailor) and Ida (Seeman) Blumenfeld;

married Muriel Joan Wolf (a businesswoman), September 10, 1961; children: Mark, Jimmy; Peggy (stepchild). POLITICS: Independent Democrat. RELIGION: Jewish. MILITARY: U.S. Navy, 1943-46.

VOCATION: Producer, theatre owner, and businessman.

CAREER: PRINCIPAL STAGE WORK—Producer, *Waltz of the Toreadors,* Jan Hus Theatre, New York City, 1959; producer, *John Gabriel Borkman,* Sullivan Street Playhouse, 1959; associate producer, *The Fantasticks,* Sullivan Street Playhouse, New York City, 1960—.

RELATED CAREER—Owner of the Sullivan Street Playhouse.

NON-RELATED CAREER—Riverdale Mental Health Association (board of directors and benefit chairman).

AWARDS: Honored guest at the Toledo, OH Sesquicentennial Celebration, 1986.

MEMBER: League of Off-Broadway Producers & Theatre Owners; Friars Club.

SIDELIGHTS: Jules Field is listed in the *Guiness Book of World Records* as the owner and associate producer of *The Fantasticks,* the world's longest-running musical. The musical opened on May 3, 1960, and is still playing in the same theatre.

ADDRESSES: HOME—679 W. 239th Street, Riverdale, NY 10463. OFFICE—181 Sullivan Street, New York, NY 10012.

JULES FIELD

FIELD, Ron

PERSONAL: Full name, Ronald Field; born in Queens, NY. EDUCATION: Graduated from the School for the Performing Arts, 1951.

VOCATION: Choreographer, director, and costume designer.

CAREER: STAGE DEBUT—*Lady in the Dark,* Alvin Theatre, New York City, 1941. PRINCIPAL STAGE APPEARANCES—*Seventeen,* Broadhurst Theatre, New York City, 1951; *Kismet,* Ziegfeld Theatre, New York City, 1953. FIRST BROADWAY STAGE WORK—Choreographer, *Anything Goes,* Orpheum Theatre, New York City, 1962. PRINCIPAL STAGE WORK—Choreographer, *Nowhere To Go But Up,* Winter Garden Theatre, New York City, 1962, then Municipal Opera, St. Louis, MO, 1963 and 1964; choreographer, *Cafe Crown,* Martin Beck Theatre, New York City, 1964; choreographer, *Show Boat,* State Theatre, New York City, 1966; choreographer, costume designer, *Cabaret,* Broadhurst Theatre, 1966, then Palace Theatre, London, 1968; choreographer, *Zorba,* Imperial Theatre, New York City, 1968; director, choreographer, *Applause,* Palace Theatre, New York City, 1969, then Her Majesty's Theatre, London, 1972; director, choreographer, *On the Town,* Imperial Theatre, 1971; choreographer, *Ashmedai* (opera), State Theatre, New York City, 1976; director, choreographer, *King of Hearts,* Minskoff Theatre, New York City, 1978; director, choreographer, *5-6-7-8 . . . Dance!,* Radio City Music Hall, New York City, 1983.

MAJOR TOURS—Marcel, Pepe, *The Boy Friend,* U.S. cities, 1955-57; also appeared in *Kismet,* U.S. cities, 1955. Choreographer, *Cabaret,* U.S. cities, 1967, then 1969; choreographer, *Zorba,* U.S. cities, 1969, then 1970; director, choreographer, *Applause,* U.S. and Canadian cities, 1971, then 1972; director, choreographer, *Mack and Mabel,* Florida cities, 1976; choreographer, *The American Dance Machine,* U.S. cities and Tokyo, Japan, 1978-79; production supervisor, *Peter Pan,* U.S. cities, 1981, then director, choreographer, U.S. cities, 1982-83; director, *South Pacific,* U.S. cities, 1987.

PRINCIPAL CABARET WORK—Choreographer of nightclub acts for Liza Minelli, Chita Rivera, Ann-Margret, Carol Lawrence, Gwen Verdon, and Shari Lewis; has also staged shows at the Latin Quarter, New York City, 1962; Casino du Liban, Beirut, Lebanon, 1967; Carillon Hotel, Miami Beach, FL; Casino de Paris, Paris, France.

PRINCIPAL TELEVISION APPEARANCES—As a dancer on more than 300 television shows during the 1950s. PRINCIPAL TELEVISION WORK—All as choreographer. Series: *Dean Martin Summer Show,* NBC, 1967; *Ed Sullivan Show,* CBS, 1967-68; *Hollywood Palace,* ABC. Specials: *Bell Telephone Jubilee,* NBC, 1976; *Pinocchio,* NBC, 1976; *America Salutes Richard Rodgers,* CBS, 1977; *The Sentry Collection Presents Ben Vereen—His Roots,* ABC, 1978; *Rodgers and Hart Revisited,* CBS; *Jerome Kern and the Princess,* CBS; also choreographed Angela Lansbury's "Thoroughly Modern Millie" number for the 1968 Academy Awards presentation and dances for Fred Astaire.

PRINCIPAL FILM WORK—Choreographer, *New York, New York,* United Artists, 1977.

RELATED CAREER—Performed with the Jack Cole Dancers.

AWARDS: Best Choreography, Antoinette Perry Award, 1967, for

Cabaret; Best Choreography, Antoinette Perry Award and Drama Desk Award, Best Director, Antoinette Perry Award and Drama Desk Award, all 1970, for *Applause;* Emmy Award, 1977, for *America Salutes Richard Rodgers;* Emmy Award, 1978, for *The Sentry Collection Presents Ben Vereen—His Roots.*

MEMBER: Society of Stage Directors and Choreographers.

ADDRESSES: OFFICE—Five W. 19th Street, New York, NY 10011.*

*   *   *

FIELDS, Freddie   1923-

PERSONAL: Born July 12, 1923, in Ferndale, NY; son of Jon Jacob (a journalist and showman) and Jeanette (a hotel operator) Fields; married Polly Bergen (an actress), February 13, 1957 (divorced, 1975); married Corinna Tsopei (an actress), July 12, 1981; children: Kathy, Peter, and P.K. MILITARY: U.S. Coast Guard.

VOCATION: Producer, motion picture executive, and agent.

CAREER: PRINCIPAL FILM WORK—Producer, *Lipstick,* Paramount, 1976; *Looking for Mr. Goodbar,* Paramount, 1977; *Citizen's Band* (also known as *Handle with Care*), Paramount, 1977; *American Gigolo,* Paramount, 1980; *Wholly Moses!,* Paramount, 1980; *Victory,* Paramount, 1981; *Fever Pitch,* Metro-Goldwyn-Mayer/United Artists (MGM/UA), 1985; *American Anthem,* MGM/UA, 1986; *Poltergeist II: The Other Side,* MGM/UA, 1986; *Crimes of the Heart,* MGM/UA, 1986.

RELATED CAREER—Vice-president, MCA-TV, MCA Canada, Ltd., and MCA Corporation, 1946-59; founder, president, and chief executive officer, Creative Management Associates, Ltd., (now known as International Creative Management, Inc.), 1960-75; independent consultant, International Creative Management, 1975—; president, chief operating officer, Metro-Goldwyn-Mayer Film Company; president, Metro-Goldwyn-Mayer/United Artists Film Division, 1981-83; president, Fields Organization, 1983—; president, Kam Entertainment, Ltd.; vice-president, F/B Productions, Inc.

MEMBER: Producers Guild of America; American Way, SHARE, Presidents' Club.

SIDELIGHTS: Freddie Fields has been the exclusive agent for Henry Fonda, Phil Silvers, Joanne Woodward, Peter Sellers, Barbra Streisand, Steve McQueen, Ali MacGraw, Woody Allen, Robert Redford, Ryan O'Neal, and Liza Minelli, among many other actors and actresses.

ADDRESSES: OFFICE—Fields Organization, Freddie Fields Productions, Inc., 152 N. Lapeer, Los Angeles, CA 90048.

*   *   *

FINLAY, Frank   1926-

PERSONAL: Born August 6, 1926, in Farnworth, England; son of Josiah and Margaret Finlay; married Doreen Joan Shepherd, 1954;

children: two sons, one daughter. EDUCATION: Trained for the stage with the Royal Academy of Dramatic Art.

VOCATION: Actor.

CAREER: PRINCIPAL STAGE APPEARANCES—Mr. Matthews, *Jessica,* Mr. Pinnock, *The Telescope,* Guilford Repertory Theatre Company, Guilford, U.K., 1957; gaoler, *The Queen and the Welshman,* Lyric Hammersmith Theatre, London, 1957; Peter Cauchon, *Saint Joan,* Belgrade Theatre, Conventry, U.K., 1958; Harry Kahn, *Chicken Soup with Barley,* Belgrade Theatre, then Royal Court Theatre, both London, 1958; Percy Elliott, *Epitaph for George Dillon,* John Golden Theatre, New York City, 1958; Eric Watts, *Sugar in the Morning,* Private Attercliffe, *Sergeant Musgrave's Dance,* both Royal Court Theatre, 1959; Harry Kahn, *Chicken Soup with Barley,* Stan Man, *Roots,* Libby Dobson, *I'm Talking about Jerusalem,* Mr. Crape Robinson, *The Happy Haven,* Ivan Triletski, *Platonov,* all Royal Court Theatre, 1960; Corporal Hill, *Chips with Everything,* Royal Court Theatre, then Vaudeville Theatre, London, 1962; Chaplain de Stogumber, *Saint Joan,* Alderman Butterthwaite, *The Workhouse Donkey,* both National Theatre, London, then Chichester Festival, Chichester, U.K., 1963; first gravedigger, *Hamlet,* Old Vic Theatre, London, 1963; Iago, *Othello,* Cocledemoy, *The Dutch Courtesan,* both National Theatre, then Chichester Festival, 1964; Giles Corey, *The Crucible,* Dogberry, *Much Ado about Nothing,* cook, *Mother Courage,* Iago, *Othello,* all National Theatre, 1965; Willie Mossop, *Hobson's Choice,* National Theatre, then Berlin and Moscow, 1965; Joxer Daly, *Juno and the Paycock,* Pavel Prokofyevich Dikoy, *The Storm,* National Theatre, 1966; Jesus, *Son of Man,* Phoenix Theatre, Leicester, U.K., then Round House Theatre, London, both 1969.

Bernard, *After Haggerty,* Aldwych Theatre, London, 1970, then Criterion Theatre, London, 1971; Sloman, *The Party,* Peppino, *Saturday, Sunday, Monday,* both National Theatre, then Old Vic Theatre, 1973, later Queen's Theatre, London, 1974; Freddy Malone, *Plunder,* Ben Prosse, *Watch It Come Down,* both Old Vic Theatre, 1976; Josef Frank, *Weapons of Happiness,* Lyttelton Theatre, London, 1976; Daniel Thorndike, *Tribute to a Lady,* Old Vic Theatre, 1976; Henry, *Kings and Clowns,* Phoenix Theatre, London, 1978; Domenico, *Filumena,* Lyric Theatre, London, then St. James Theatre, New York City, 1978; Salieri, *Amadeus,* National Theatre, 1982; Capt. Bligh, *Mutiny,* Piccadilly Theatre, London, 1985. Also appeared in *The Girl in Melanie Klein,* 1980; *The Cherry Orchard,* 1983.

PRINCIPAL FILM APPEARANCES—*The Loneliness of the Long Distance Runner,* Continental, 1963; *Agent 8 3/4,* Continental, 1963; *Doctor in the Wilderness,* Rank, 1963; *Private Potter,* Metro-Goldwyn-Mayer (MGM), 1963; *The Comedy Man,* British Lion, 1964; *Underworld Informers,* Continental, 1965; *A Study in Terror,* Columbia, 1966; *Othello,* Warner Brothers, 1966; *The Jokers,* United Artists, 1967; *The Shoes of the Fisherman,* MGM, 1968; *The Deadly Bees,* Paramount, 1967; *Robbery,* Embassy, 1967; *I'll Never Forget What's 'is Name,* Regional, 1968; *Cromwell,* Columbia, 1970; *The Molly Maguires,* Paramount, 1970; *Assault* (also known as *In the Devil's Garden* and *Tower of Terror*), Rank, 1971; *Gumshoe,* Columbia, 1972; *Shaft in Africa,* MGM, 1973; *The Three Musketeers,* Twentieth Century-Fox, 1974; *The Four Musketeers,* Twentieth Century-Fox, 1975; *The Wild Geese,* Allied Artists, 1978; *Murder by Decree,* AVCO-Embassy, 1979; *Enigma,* Embassy, 1983; *The Ploughman's Lunch,* Samuel Goldwyn, 1984; *1919,* British Film Institute, 1984; *Return of the Soldier,* European Classics, 1985. Appeared in *The Longest Day,* 1962;

Walk in the Sand, The Wild Affair, both 1966; *Inspector Clouseau,* 1968; *Twisted Nerve,* 1969; *Sitting Target,* 1972; *Neither the Sea nor the Sand,* 1974; also *A Life for Ruth; The Key; Hot Enough for June; The Sandwich Man; Victory for Danny Jones; Van Der Walk and the Girl; Van Der Walk and the Rich; Van Der Walk and the Dead; The Ring of Darkness.*

PRINCIPAL TELEVISION APPEARANCES—Episodic: *Tales of the Unexpected.* Mini-Series: Title role, *Casanova,* syndicated, 1981. Movies: Sancho Panza, *The Adventures of Don Quixote,* CBS, 1973; Abu Bakar, *The Thief of Baghdad,* NBC, 1978; Kravtsov, *Sakharov,* HBO, 1984; Marley's ghost, *A Christmas Carol,* CBS, 1984; Boris *Arch of Triumph,* CBS, 1985. Specials: *Julius Caesar; Les Miserables; This Happy Breed; The Lie; The Death of Adolf Hitler; Voltaire; The Merchant of Venice; Bouquet of Barbed Wire; 84 Charing Cross Road; Saturday, Sunday, Monday; Count Dracula; The Last Campaign; Napoleon in Betzi; Dear Brutus; Tales from One Thousand and One Nights; Aspects of Love.*

AWARDS: Best Actor, Clarence Derwent Award, 1962, for *Chips with Everything;* Best Actor, San Sebastian Award, 1966, for *Othello;* Society of Film and Television Arts Awards for *The Lie* and *The Adventures of Don Quixote;* Best Actor Award for *Bouquet of Barbed Wire.*

ADDRESSES: AGENT—Granstar Ltd., 50 Mount Street, London W 1, England.*

* * *

FINNEY, Albert   1936-

PERSONAL: Born May 9, 1936, in Salford, England; son of Albert, Sr. (a bookmaker) and Alice (Hobson) Finney; married Jane Wenham, 1957 (divorced, 1961); married Anouk Aimee (an actress), 1970 (divorced, 1975); children: (first marriage) Simon. EDUCATION: Trained for the stage at the Royal Academy of Dramatic Art.

VOCATION: Actor, producer, and director.

CAREER: STAGE DEBUT—Decius Brutus, *Julius Caesar,* Birmingham Repertory Company, Birmingham, U.K., 1956. LONDON DEBUT—Belzanor, *Caesar and Cleopatra,* Old Vic Theatre, 1956. BROADWAY DEBUT—Title role, *Luther,* St. James Theatre, 1963. PRINCIPAL STAGE APPEARANCES— Francis Archer, *The Beaux Strategem,* Face, *The Alchemist,* Malcolm, *The Lizard on the Rock,* all Birmingham Repertory Company, Birmingham, U.K., 1956-58; Soya Marshall, *The Party,* New Theatre, London, 1958; Edgar, *King Lear,* Cassio, *Othello,* Lysander, *A Midsummer Night's Dream,* all Memorial Theatre, Stratford-on-Avon, U.K., 1959; Ted, *The Lily-White Boys,* Royal Court Theatre, London, 1960; Billy Fisher, *Billy Liar,* Cambridge Theatre, London, 1960; title role, *Luther,* Paris International Festival, Theatre des Nations, Paris, France, then Holland Festival, later Royal Court Theatre, London, all 1961; Feste, *Twelfth Night,* Royal Court Theatre, 1962; title role, *Henry IV,* Glasgow Citizens Theatre, Glasgow, Scotland, U.K., 1963; Don Pedro, *Much Ado about Nothing,* Old Vic Theatre, London, 1965; John Armstrong, *Armstrong's Last Goodnight,* Jean, *Miss Julie,* Harold Gorringe, *Black Comedy,* all Chichester Festival, Chichester, U.K., 1966; Bri, *A Day in the Death of Joe Egg,* Brooks Atkinson Theatre, New York City, 1968; Mr. Elliot, *Alpha Beta,* Royal Court Theatre, then Apollo Theatre,

both London, 1972; Krapp, *Krapp's Last Tape,* O'Halloran, *Cromwell,* both Royal Court Theatre, 1973; Phil, *Chez Nous,* Globe Theatre, London, 1974; title role, *Hamlet,* National Theatre, London, then Old Vic Theatre, both 1975, later Lyttelton Theatre, London, 1976; title role, *Tamburlaine the Great,* Olivier Theatre, London, 1976; narrator, *Tribute to a Lady,* Old Vic Theatre, 1976; Mr. Horner, *The Country Wife,* Olivier Theatre, 1977; Lopakhin, *The Cherry Orchard,* title role, *Macbeth,* both Olivier Theatre, 1978; title role, *Uncle Vanya,* Gary Essendine, *Present Laughter,* both Royal Exchange Theatre, Birmingham, U.K., 1978; John Bean, *Has "Washington" Legs?,* Cottesloe Theatre, London, 1978. Also appeared in *Macbeth, Henry V,* both Birmingham Repertory Company, Birmingham, U.K., 1956-58; Musgrave, *Sergeant Musgrave's Dance,* 1984; *The Biko Inquest,* 1984; *Orphans,* 1986.

PRINCIPAL STAGE WORK—Director, *The Birthday Party, The School for Scandal,* both Glasgow Citizens Theatre, Glasgow, Scotland, 1963; director, *Armstrong's Last Goodnight,* Old Vic Theatre, London, 1965; producer, *A Day in the Death of Joe Egg,* Comedy Theatre, London, 1967; director, *The Freedom of the City,* Royal Court Theatre, London, 1973; *Loot,* Royal Court Theatre, 1975.

PRINCIPAL FILM APPEARANCES—Title role, *Tom Jones,* Lopert, 1963; Danny, *Night Must Fall,* Metro-Goldwyn-Mayer, 1964; title role, *Charlie Bubbles,* Universal, 1968; title role, *Scrooge,* National General, 1970; Mr. Elliot, *Alpha Beta,* Memorial, 1973; Hercule Poirot, *Murder on the Orient Express,* Paramount, 1974; Fouche, *The Duellists,* Paramount, 1978; Daddy Warbucks, *Annie,* Columbia, 1982; Sir, *The Dresser,* Columbia, 1983; Geoffrey Firmin, *Under the Volcano,* Universal, 1984. Appeared in *The Entertainer,* Continental, 1959; *Saturday Night and Sunday Morning,* Continental, 1960; *The Victors,* Columbia, 1963; *Two for the Road,* Twentieth Century-Fox, 1967; *Gumshoe,* Columbia, 1972; *The Adventures of Sherlock Holmes Smarter Brother,* Twentieth Century-Fox, 1975; *Wolfen,* Warner Brothers, 1981; *Shoot the Moon,* Metro-Goldwyn-Mayer/United Artists, 1982; *Orphans,* Lorimar, 1987; also *The Picasso Summer,* 1969; *Bleak Moment,* 1972; *Loophole,* 1980; *Looker,* 1981.

PRINCIPAL FILM WORK—Producer: *Gumshoe,* Columbia, 1963; (also director) *Charlie Bubbles,* Universal, 1968; *if . . .,* Paramount, 1969; *Bleak Moments,* British Film Institute, 1972; *O Lucky Man!,* Warner Brothers, 1973.

PRINCIPAL TELEVISION APPEARANCES—Movies: Title role, *Pope John Paul II,* CBS, 1984. Also appeared in *View Friendship and Marriage; The Claverdon Road Job; The Miser; Forget-Me-Not Lane.*

RELATED CAREER—Founder, Memorial Enterprises Ltd., 1965; associate artistic director, Royal Court Theatre, London, 1972-75.

RECORDINGS: ALBUMS—*Albert Finney's Album,* Motown Records, 1977; also *Scrooge* (original soundtrack), 1971.

AWARDS: Best Actor, British Academy Award, 1960, for *Saturday Night and Sunday Morning;* Best Actor, Academy Award nomination, 1963, for *Tom Jones;* Best Actor, Academy Award, 1974, for *Murder on the Orient Express;* Best Actor, Academy Award nomination, 1984, for *The Dresser.*

MEMBER: British Actors' Equity Association, Screen Actors Guild.

ADDRESSES: OFFICE—c/o Memorial Films, 74 Campden Hill Court, Campden Hill Road, London W8, England. AGENT—International Creative Management, 388-396 Oxford Street, London W1N 9HE, England.*

*   *   *

FITELSON, William H.   1905-

PERSONAL: Born January 21, 1905, in New York, NY. EDUCATION: Attended Columbia University and New York Law School.

VOCATION: Attorney.

CAREER: PRINCIPAL PROFESSIONAL AFFILIATIONS—Worked in story department and as counsel, Tiffany-Stahl Productions, 1929-32; U.S. counsel to British and foreign motion picture and theatrical producers; counsel to the Theatre Guild, New York City, and motion picture, theatre, publishing, newspaper, television, and radio industries; managing director of Theatre Guild television and radio divisions, including U.S. Steel Hour, ABC, CBS, 1953-63; non-legal consultant on communications projects, Allen & Company and Columbia Pictures Industries; partner, Fitelson, Lasky, Aslan & Couture law firm, specializing in communications, publishing, theatre, film, television, and radio.

RELATED CAREER—Librarian and tutor, New York Law School.

ADDRESSES: OFFICE—Fitelson, Lasky, Aslan & Couture, 551 Fifth Avenue, New York, NY 10176.*

*   *   *

FITZ, Paddy
See McGOOHAN, Patrick

*   *   *

FLANNERY, Peter   1951-

PERSONAL: Born October 12, 1951, in Jarrow, England; son of Andrew and Anne Flannery. EDUCATION: University of Manchester, B.A., 1973.

VOCATION: Playwright.

CAREER: Also see WRITINGS below.

RELATED CAREER—Actor, stage manager, singer, and director, 1974-76; resident dramatist, Royal Shakespeare Company, 1978-80.

WRITINGS: PLAYS—Heartbreak Hotel, Contact Theatre, Manchester, U.K., 1975, published by Woodhouse Books, 1979; Last Resort, Sidewalk Theatre, London, 1976; Are You with Me?, Nottingham Playhouse, Nottingham, U.K., 1977; Savage Amusement, Royal Shakespeare Company (RSC), Warehouse Theatre, London, 1978, published by Rex Collings, 1978; The Boy's Own Story, RAT Theatre, Manchester, U.K., 1978; (with Mick Ford)

The Adventures of Awful Knawful, RSC, Warehouse Theatre, 1978, published by Methuen, 1980; Jungle Music, Contact Theatre, Manchester, U.K., 1979; Our Friends in the North, Stratford-on-Avon, U.K., 1982.

TELEPLAYS—Joy Rise, Granada, 1980.

AWARDS: Best New Play, London Times, 1978, for Savage Amusement; Playwright Award, Thames Television, 1979; Writer's Bursary, Arts Council, 1980.

MEMBER: Theatre Writers Union.

SIDELIGHTS: RECREATIONS— Reading, walking, sports, music, "running away from dogs."

ADDRESSES: HOME—Ten Main Road, Langley, Cheshire, England. AGENT—c/o Harvey Unna and Stephen Durbridge, 14 Beaumont Mews, London W1N 4HE, England.*

*   *   *

FLEMING, Lucy   1947-

PERSONAL: Born May 15, 1947, in Nettlebed, England; daughter of Robert Peter Fleming and Celia Elizabeth Johnson (an actress).

VOCATION: Actress.

CAREER: STAGE DEBUT—Maggie, A Collier's Friday Night, Royal Court Theatre, London, 1965. PRINCIPAL STAGE APPEARANCES—Helen Shelley, Shelley, Royal Court Theatre, London, 1965; Gladys, The Performing Giant, Ethel Voysey, The Voysey Inheritance, both Royal Court Theatre, 1966; Sorel Bliss, Hay Fever, Duke of York's Theatre, London, 1968; Joanna Pilgrim, Out of the Question, St. Martin's Theatre, London, 1968; Lady Margaret, Edward the Second, Queen Isabel, Richard II, both Edinburgh Festival, Edinburgh, Scotland, U.K., 1969, then Mermaid Theatre, later Piccadilly Theatre, both London, 1970; Grazia, A Yard of Sun, Nottingham Playhouse, Nottingham, U.K., then Old Vic Theatre, London, both 1970; Ruth, Don't Start without Me, Garrick Theatre, London, 1971; Viola, Twelfth Night, Crucible Theatre, Sheffield, U.K., 1973; Olivia, Night Must Fall, Palace Theatre, Watford, U.K., 1980. Also appeared with repertory companies at University Theatre, Manchester, U.K., Arnaud Theatre, Guilford, U.K., and Welsh National Theatre, Cardiff, Wales, U.K.

MAJOR TOURS—Relatively Speaking, U.K. cities, 1974.

PRINCIPAL TELEVISION APPEARANCES—Series: The Survivors. Mini-Series: Molly Meahan, Smiley's People, syndicated, 1982.

ADDRESSES: AGENT—c/o Richard Stone, 18-20 York Buildings, London WC2, England.*

*   *   *

FLOWERS, Wayland   1939-

PERSONAL: Full name, Wayland Parrott Flowers, Jr.; born, November, 1939, in Dawson, GA; son of Wayland Parrott (a retailer)

WAYLAND FLOWERS

and Leila Elizabeth (Horsley) Flowers. EDUCATION: Attended Young Harris College and Rawlings College. MILITARY: U.S. Coast Guard.

VOCATION: Comedian, puppeteer, and writer.

CAREER: PRINCIPAL TELEVISION APPEARANCES—Series: *Keep On Truckin'*, ABC, 1975; regular, *The Andy Williams Show*, in syndication, 1976-77; *Hollywood Squares*, NBC, 1976-79; *Laugh-In*, NBC, 1979; *Solid Gold*, in syndication, 1980-84; *Madame's Place*, in syndication, 1982. Episodic: *The Paul Lynde Show*, ABC. Specials: *Madame Goes to Manhattan*, Showtime.

FILM DEBUT—*Norman, Is That You?*, Metro-Goldwyn-Mayer, 1976.

PRINCIPAL VIDEO APPEARANCES—*Madame Goes to Manhattan.*

OFF-BROADWAY DEBUT—*Kumquats*, Village Gate Theatre, 1970. PRINCIPAL CABARET APPEARANCES—*Madame Goes to Harlem*, Sahara Hotel, Las Vegas, NV, 1981; *One of a Kind*, Desert Inn, Las Vegas, 1982.

WRITINGS: BOOKS—*Madame*, Dodd-Mead, 1983.

TELEVISION—*Madame's Place*, in syndication, 1982.

AWARDS: Best Special Attraction, American Guild of Variety Artists (AGVA) Award, 1978.

ADDRESSES: OFFICE—Madame, Inc., 8033 Sunset Blvd., Suite

178, Los Angeles, CA 90046. MANAGER—Marlena Shell, 8033 Sunset Blvd., Los Angeles, CA 90046.

*   *   *

FOREMAN, John

PERSONAL: Born in Idaho Falls, ID.

VOCATION: Film producer.

CAREER: PRINCIPAL FILM WORK—Producer: *Winning*, Universal, 1969; *Butch Cassidy and the Sundance Kid*, Twentieth Century-Fox, 1969; *Puzzle of a Downfall Child*, Universal, 1970; *W.U.S.A.*, Paramount, 1970; *They Might Be Giants*, Universal, 1971; *Sometimes a Great Notion*, Universal, 1971; *The Life and Times of Judge Roy Bean*, National General, 1972; *The Effect of Gamma Rays on Man-in-the-Moon Marigolds*, Twentieth Century-Fox, 1973; *Pocket Money*, National General, 1973; *The Mackintosh Man*, Warner Brothers, 1973; *The Man Who Would Be King*, 1976; *Bobby Deerfield*, Columbia, 1977; *The Great Train Robbery*, United Artists, 1979; *Brainstorm*, Metro-Goldwyn-Mayer/United Artists (MGM/UA), 1983; *Eureka*, 1983; *The Ice Pirates*, MGM/UA, 1983; *Prizzi's Honor*, Twentieth Century-Fox, 1985.

RELATED CAREER—Co-founder, CMA Agency; co-founder, Newman-Foreman Company, 1968.

ADDRESSES: OFFICE—J.F. Productions, c/o TVI, 517 W. 35th Street, New York, NY 10001.*

*   *   *

FOSSE, Bob   1927-1987

OBITUARY NOTICE—See index for *CTFT* sketch: Full name, Robert Louis Fosse; born June 23, 1927, in Chicago, IL; died of a heart attack in Washington, DC, September 23, 1987. Bob Fosse was acknowledged by critics and audiences as one of the musical theatre's greatest choreographers and directors. After appearing as a dancer in such films as *Give a Girl a Break* and *Kiss Me, Kate*, both 1953, Fosse established himself as a top-flight choreographer with his first two Broadway efforts, *The Pajama Game*, 1954, and *Damn Yankees*, 1955. He brought an immediately recognizable, jazz influenced dance style of synchronized, undulating motions to some of Broadway's most successful and innovative shows such as *How to Succeed in Business without Really Trying*, 1960, *Chicago*, 1975, and *Dancin'*, 1977. Fosse was the recipient of nine Antoinette Perry Awards for his Broadway work, including one as Best Director for *Pippin*, 1972. His first film directing effort, *Cabaret*, 1973, was both a critical and box office success, garnering Fosse an Academy Award and establishing him as a creative force in Hollywood; other notable films he directed were *Lenny*, 1974, his semi-autobiographical *All That Jazz*, 1979, and his final film, *Star 80*, 1983. Fosse's sole directorial credit in television, the 1973 special *Liza with a ''Z''*, 1973, earned him an Emmy Award, thus making him the first person to win a top director's award in all three media.

OBITUARIES AND OTHER SOURCES: New York Times, September 24 and 25, 1987; *Variety*, September 24, 1987.

FOSTER, David   1929-

PERSONAL: Born November 25, 1929; son of George Israel (a salesman) and Anna Pauline (Feizenbaum) Foster; married Jackie Ann Pattiz, January 29, 1959; children: Gary Steven, Gregory Adam, Timothy George. EDUCATION: University of Southern California, B.A., business administration, also attended Georgetown University. MILITARY: U.S. Army, 1952-54.

VOCATION: Producer.

CAREER: PRINCIPAL FILM WORK—(With Mitchell Brower) Producer, *McCabe and Mrs. Miller,* Warner Brothers, 1971; producer, *The Getaway,* National General, 1972; executive producer, *The Nickel Ride,* Twentieth Century-Fox, 1975; co-producer, *The Drowning Pool,* Warner Brothers, 1975; producer, *First Love,* Paramount, 1977; co-producer, *Heroes,* Universal, 1977; producer, *The Legacy,* Universal, 1979; executive producer, *Tribute,* Twentieth Century-Fox, 1980; co-producer: *Caveman,* United Artists, 1981; *The Thing,* Universal, 1982; *Second Thoughts,* Universal, 1983; *Mass Appeal,* Universal, 1984; *The Mean Season,* Orion, 1984; *Short Circuit,* Tri-Star, 1986; *Running Scared,* Metro-Goldwyn-Mayer/United Artists, 1986.

MEMBER: Academy of Motion Picture Arts and Sciences; Georgetown University (board of trustees).

ADDRESSES: OFFICE—Turman-Foster Company, Laird Studios, 9336 W. Washington Blvd., Culver City, CA 90230.

*   *   *

FOX, Michael J.   1961-

PERSONAL: Born June 9, 1961, in Vancouver, BC, Canada; son of William (in the Canadian army) and Phyllis Fox.

CAREER: PRINCIPAL TELEVISION APPEARANCES—Episodic: *Trapper John, M.D.,* CBS, 1981; *Teachers Only,* NBC, 1982; *Love Boat,* ABC, 1983; *Night Court,* NBC, 1984; also *Lou Grant,* CBS. Series: Willy Joe Hall, *Palmerstown, U.S.A.,* CBS, 1980-81; Alex P. Keaton, *Family Ties,* NBC, 1983—; also *Leo and Me,* CBC. Movies: Ricky Miller, *Letters from Frank,* CBS, 1979; Jay Jay Manners, *High School U.S.A.,* NBC, 1983; Dennis Baxter, *Poison Ivy,* NBC, 1985; Alex Keaton, *Family Ties Vacation,* NBC, 1985. Specials: *Battle of the Network Stars,* ABC, 1984; *The Homemade Comedy Special,* NBC, 1984; *Time Travel: Fact, Fiction, and Fantasy,* syndicated, 1985; *David Letterman's Holiday Film Festival,* NBC, 1986; *Bruce Willis: The Return of Bruno,* HBO, 1987.

FILM DEBUT—Scott, *Midnight Madness,* Buena Vista, 1980. PRINCIPAL FILM APPEARANCES—Arthur, *Class of 1984,* United Film, 1982; Marty McFly, *Back to the Future,* Universal, 1985; *Teen Wolf,* Atlantic, 1985; Joe Rasnick, *Light of Day,* Tri-Star, 1987; Brantley Foster, *The Secret of My Success,* Universal, 1987. Also *Bright Lights, Big City,* upcoming.

PRINCIPAL STAGE APPEARANCES—*Night of 100 Stars II,* Radio City Music Hall, New York City, 1985.

AWARDS: Most Exciting Star, National Association of Theatre Owners, 1985; Outstanding Lead Actor in a Comedy Series, Emmy Award, 1986.

SIDELIGHTS: A familiar face to movie and television audiences alike, Michael J. Fox became one of the country's best known entertainers before reaching age twenty-five. His credits include *Family Ties,* for some time the second most popular series on television, and several top-grossing feature films, including *Back to the Future.* The five-foot-four Canadian native exudes a mixture of energy and vulnerability; most of his roles have stressed his youthful appearance and fair, small-town good looks. In an April, 1987 *Ladies' Home Journal* profile, Susan Granger suggested that Fox's appeal "cuts across the generations"—that to young girls he is a sex symbol, to men he is something of a kid brother, and to women of all ages he is simply adorable. "It's no wonder the actor gets twenty-one thousand fan letters a week," she asserted.

Fox is equally popular with producers and directors, both for his ability to wring profits out of somewhat marginal films and for what director Robert Zemeckis called his "incredible comic sensibility" in a February 9, 1987 *Maclean's* cover story. Both offstage and on, Fox has espoused such basic values as hard work, family togetherness, and a drug-free lifestyle; he has also expressed his obligation to fans. Accessible and humble despite his fame, Fox has, in Zemeckis's words, "that twinkle that all great movie stars need to have."

Fox is a veteran actor, having begun working as a professional at the age of fifteen. Although he discovered theatre in his high school drama class in Vancouver, he has admitted that having to move often due to his father's army career nurtured his flair for the dramatic from his earliest years. "I learned to adapt to new environments quickly," he told *Us* (July 29, 1985). "The attitude I took was, '. . . Right now I'm the New Short Kid, but in a couple of weeks I can be Funny Mike or Smart Mike.' " His parents and four siblings added their encouragement, too, even when Fox's acting duties on the Canadian situation comedy *Leo and Me* led him to drop out of high school. "When I came home and said I wanted to be an actor," Fox told Granger, "[my parents] weren't angry. There was a bit of concern that it was a difficult way to make a living and that I might get hurt, but there was never a feeling that I couldn't accomplish anything I wanted to accomplish."

His teachers were less charitable, however. One told him, "You're not going to be cute forever," he recalled in *Us.* But Fox had the marketable talent of playing younger than his age—at fifteen he was able to play a ten-year-old, and well into his twenties he made a plausible teenager. Arriving in Los Angeles soon after turning eighteen, he landed guest appearances on a number of television shows including *Trapper John, M.D.* and *Lou Grant,* and a recurring role on *Palmerstown, U.S.A.* He also starred in *Midnight Madness* for the Disney studio's Buena Vista division.

In 1981 Fox found himself deeply in debt, however, and offers of work simply stopped coming. Rather than return to Canada, he sold a sectional couch piece by piece, subsisted on macaroni and cheese, and used a phone booth on the street to call his agent. He had lost twenty pounds by the time he was asked to audition for *Family Ties* early in 1982. According to Brian D. Johnson in *Maclean's,* Fox "failed the first audition" for the family comedy, but the casting director won Fox a second chance with the new show's executive producer, Gary Goldberg, who then had trouble convincing NBC executives to accept the actor. According to Johnson, "The network's chief programmer, Brandon Tartikoff, told him 'The kid's good, but can you see his face on a lunch box?' " Nonetheless, most critics placed the overwhelming success of *Family Ties* squarely on Fox's shoulders. He has won an Emmy Award for his portrayal of arch-conservative Alex Keaton, oldest son of two ex-hippies who still espouse liberal ideals. In retrospect, Goldberg told *TV Guide* (April 14, 1984), that as a producer, he had failed to define the role of Alex, and thus was unprepared for Fox's imaginative treatment of the part. ''Michael defined [Alex] for me,'' Goldberg said, ''and now so much of the show revolves around him. Without Fox, we wouldn't be on the air.''

Rather than use his television experience merely as a steppingstone to films, Fox has attempted to schedule his movie appearances around the *Family Ties* production schedule. On at least one occasion—during shooting for *Back to the Future*—he worked on both simultaneously, logging sixteen-hour work days for three months in 1985. More typically, his films are shot in the *Family Ties* off-season. Fox's movie work is reaching beyond the limited, teen-comedy range. Although he portrays high school students in *Back to the Future* and *Teen Wolf*, he plays adults in both the rock film *Light of Day* and the comedy *The Secret of My Success*, and he has said he would consider any serious role, no matter how strongly it conflicts with his ''good guy'' image. He is also slated to direct and star in an upcoming Steven Spielberg production. Granger felt that directing ''could be the perfect vehicle for Michael to fall back on when he gets too old to play teenagers but remains too short to look the part of their parents.'' Meanwhile, Fox simply works as hard as he can on as many projects as possible. ''I don't want to sit around and enjoy all the temptations of success,'' he told Granger. ''I just like to . . . barrel through, keep my head down and work. The pace has been exhausting. . . . But the hard work has certainly kept me honest.''

Judging from the critical reaction to his work—especially his comedy—Fox may be unnecessarily anxious about the demise of his popularity. ''Fox is a prized talent,'' Johnson stated. ''Onscreen he displays agile timing and infallible charm. . . . As an actor, he has managed to work both sides of the generation gap—combining adolescent spirit with adult stability.'' He remains one of the most sought-after stars in Hollywood, a driven performer seeking new challenges, yet maintaining television contract commitments. ''I really have been lucky,'' he told the New York *Daily News* (July 20, 1986); ''I'm the sort of guy who falls through the ice in a river, and the water is only two feet deep.''

ADDRESSES: AGENT—Bauer/Benedeck, 9255 Sunset Boulevard, No. 710, Los Angeles, CA 90069.*

*   *   *

FRANCIS, Arlene   1908-

PERSONAL: Born Arlene Kazanjian, October 20, 1908, in Boston, MA; daughter of Aram and Leah (Davis) Kazanjian; married Martin Gabel(an actor), May 14, 1946 (died, May 22, 1986); children: Peter. EDUCATION: Attended Finch College; trained for the stage at the Theatre Guild School.

VOCATION: Actress.

CAREER: BROADWAY DEBUT—Anne, *One Good Year*, Fulton Theatre, 1936. PRINCIPAL STAGE APPEARANCES—All in New York City unless indicated: Princess Tamara, *The Women*, Ethel Barrymore Theatre, 1936; Sylvia Jordan, *Angel Island*, National Theatre, 1937; Elena, *All That Glitters*, Biltmore Theatre, 1938; Marion, *Danton's Death*, Mercury Theatre, 1938; Judy Morton, *Michael Drops In*, John Golden Theatre, 1938; Catherine Daly,

Young Couple Wanted, Maxine Elliott's Theatre, 1940; Miriam, *Journey to Jerusalem*, National Theatre, 1940; Doris, *The Walking Gentleman*, Belasco Theatre, 1942; Natalia Chodorov, *The Doughgirls*, Lyceum Theatre, 1942; Cora Overton, *The Overtons*, Booth Theatre, 1945; Jacqueline Carlier, *The French Touch*, Cort Theatre, 1945; Sheila Vane, *The Cup of Trembling*, Music Box Theatre, 1948; Madeleine Benoit-Benoit, *My Name Is Aquilon*, Carolyn Hopewell, *Metropole*, both Lyceum Theatre, 1949; Constance Warburton, *Late Love*, National Theatre, 1953; Dolly Fabian, *Once More, with Feeling*, National Theatre, 1958; Pamela Pew-Pickett, *Tchin-Tchin*, Ethel Barrymore Theatre, 1963; Pamela Piper, *Beekman Place*, Morosco Theatre, 1964; Evalyn, *Mrs. Dally*, Westport Country Playhouse, Westport, CT, then John Golden Theatre, both 1965; Carlotta Vance, *Dinner at Eight*, Alvin Theatre, 1966; Aunt Alicia, *Gigi*, Uris Theatre, 1974; Dona Ana, *Don Juan in Hell*, Roundabout Theatre, 1980. Also apppeared in *Horse Eats Hat*, Maxine Elliott's Theatre, 1936; *The Little Blue Light*, American National Theatre Academy Playhouse, 1951; *Don't Call Back*, Helen Hayes Theatre, 1975; *L'Empereur de Chine*, 1949; also *Pal Joey*.

MAJOR TOURS—Dolly Fabian, *Once More, with Feeling*, U.S. cities, 1958; Jane Kimball, *Kind Sir*, U.S. cities, 1963; Also *Old Acquaintance*, U.S. cities, 1967; *Who Killed Santa Claus?*, U.S. cities, 1972; *Call Me Back*, U.S. cities, 1974; *Sabrina Fair*, U.S. cities, 1975.

PRINCIPAL TELEVISION APPEARANCES—Episodic: ''Her Last Adventure,'' *Suspense*, CBS. Series: Emcee, *Blind Date*, ABC, then NBC, 1949-52; emcee, *By Popular Demand*, CBS, 1950; panelist, *Prize Performance*, CBS, 1950; panelist, *Answer Yes or No*, NBC, 1950; emcee, *Who's There?*, CBS, 1952; emcee, *Talent Patrol* (also known as *Soldier Parade*), ABC, 1953-55; emcee, *Comeback Story*, ABC, 1954; panelist, *What's My Line?* CBS, 1950-67; then syndicated, 1968-75; *Home*, NBC, 1954-57, *Arlene Francis Show*, NBC, 1957-58.

PRINCIPAL FILM APPEARANCES—*Stage Door Canteen*, United Artists, 1943; *All My Sons*, Universal, 1948; *One, Two, Three*, United Artists, 1961; *The Thrill of It All*, Universal, 1963.

PRINCIPAL RADIO APPEARANCES—*Arlene Francis Show*, WOR, New York; also *Emphasis; Monitor*.

WRITINGS: NON-FICTION—*That Certain Something*, 1960; *Arlene Francis—A Memoir*, 1978.

MEMBER: American Federation of Television and Radio Artists, Actors' Equity Association, Screen Actors Guild.

ADDRESSES: OFFICE—c/o Actors' Equity Association, 165 W. 46th Street, New York, NY 10036.*

*   *   *

FRANKEL, Gene   1923-

PERSONAL: Born December 23, 1923, in New York, NY; son of Barnet (a tailor) and Anna (a social worker; maiden name, Talerman) Frankel; married Pat Carter (an actress), May 1, 1963; children: Laura Ann, Ethan. EDUCATION: New York University, B.A., 1943; trained for the stage with Harold Clurman and Lee Strasberg at the Actors Studio. MILITARY: U.S. Army Air Force, 1941-44.

VOCATION: Director, producer, and actor.

CAREER: PRINCIPAL STAGE APPEARANCES—*A Man's Reach,* Provincetown Playhouse, New York City, 1946.

PRINCIPAL STAGE WORK—All as director unless indicated: *27 Wagons Full of Cotton,* Green Mansions Theatre, Warrenburg, NY, 1947; *They Shall Not Die, Nat Turner,* both People's Drama Theatre, New York City, 1950; *All My Sons, Stalag 17, My Heart's in the Highlands, The Country Girl, A Streetcar Named Desire,* all Resident Theatre, Kansas City, MO, 1951-53; (producer) *Volpone,* Rooftop Theatre, New York City, 1957; *Richard II,* McCarter Theatre, Princeton, NJ, 1958; (also producer) *An Enemy of the People,* Actors Playhouse, New York City, 1959; *Machinal,* Gate Theatre, New York City, 1960; *Once There Was a Russian,* Music Box Theatre, New York City, 1961; *The Blacks,* St. Marks Playhouse, New York City, 1961; *Brecht on Brecht,* Theatre de Lys, New York City, 1962; *The Firebugs,* Maidman Theatre, New York City, 1963; *Enrico IV,* Harper Theatre, Chicago, IL, 1964; *Oh, Dad, Poor Dad, Mama's Hung You in the Closet and I'm Feeling So Sad,* Atelje 212 Theatre, Belgrade, Yugoslavia, 1965; *Waiting for Godot,* Berkshire Theatre Festival, Stockbridge, MA, 1965; *A Cry of Players,* Berkshire Theatre Festival, 1966, then Vivian Beaumont Theatre, New York City, 1968; *Niggerlovers,* Orpheum Theatre, New York City, 1967; *Emperor Jones,* Royal Lyceum Theatre, Edinburgh, Scotland, U.K., 1968; *Dream Play,* Queens College, Queens, NY, 1968; *To Be Young, Gifted, and Black,* Cherry Lane Theatre, New York City, 1969; *Indians,* Arena Stage, Washington, DC, then Brooks Atkinson Theatre, both 1969; *The Engagement Baby,* Helen Hayes Theatre, New York City, 1970; *Pueblo,* Arena Stage, 1971; *A Gun Play,* Cherry Lane Theatre,

1971; *Lost in the Stars,* Imperial Theatre, New York City, 1972; *The Lincoln Mask,* Plymouth Theatre, New York City, 1972; *Othello,* Actors Studio, New York City, 1973; *The Night That Made America Famous,* Ethel Barrymore Theatre, New York City, 1975; *The Diary of Anne Frank,* Hartman Theatre, Stamford, CT, 1979; *Talk to me Like the Rain and Let Me Listen,* Lucille Lortel Theatre, 1986; *27 Wagons Full of Cotton,* Quaigh Theatre, New York City, 1986. Also directed *The Blacks,* Akademie der Kunst, Berlin, and Teatro la Fenice, Venice, Italy; *Salem Story,* New York City, 1946; *They Shall Not Die,* 1947; *Split Lip,* 1974; *The Mystery of Perricluse,* 1975; *The Countessa of Mulberry Street,* 1978; *White Pelicans,* 1986; and in numerous regional theatres, 1969-80.

MAJOR TOURS—Director: *The Blacks,* European cities, 1964; *Emperor Jones,* European cities, 1968; *Othello,* U.S. cities, 1973; *King Lear,* U.S. cities, 1982, then 1985.

PRINCIPAL TELEVISION WORK—All as director. Episodic: ''Volpone,'' *Play of the Week,* 1958. Specials: *To Be Young, Gifted, and Black,* PBS; *Moment of Fear,* NBC.

PRINCIPAL FILM APPEARANCES—Rocco, *G-Man,* Universal.

RELATED CAREER—Artistic director, Gene Frankel Theatre, New York City, 1963—, then executive director, 1973—; founding director, Berkshire Theatre Festival, Stockbridge, MA, 1965-66; cultural exchange director, U.S. State Department, Belgrade, Yugoslavia, 1968-69; visiting director, Arena Stage, Washington, DC, 1969-71; founder, executive director, producer, Media Center for the Performing Artist, 1974; professor: Boston University, 1968-69, Queens College, 1969-71, Columbia University, 1972-73; artist-in-residence, University of Wisconsin, New York University, American Theatre Wing.

WRITINGS: DOCUMENTARIES—*In Search of the Actor,* Cinefinance, upcoming.

AWARDS: Lola D'Annunzio Award for Outstanding Achievment, 1958; Best Director, Obie Award from the *Village Voice,* 1958, for *Volpone;* Best Director, Obie Award, Vernon Rice Award, both 1960, for *Machinal;* Burns Mantle Award, 1969, for *Indians;* Ford Foundation Fellowship to study European and Japanese theatre, 1960-62.

MEMBER: Society of Stage Choreographers and Directors, Actors' Equity Association, Screen Actors Guild.

SIDELIGHTS: RECREATIONS—Chess.

Gene Frankel told *CTFT:* ''My directing career began when I was hustling in a Brighton Beach pool emporium. Talking theatre and quoting Shakespeare, I zeroed in on this 'mark' who had been eyeing me keenly for the better part of the day. 'Wanna play?' 'No.' 'So what are you looking at?' He told me he was impressed by my spiel and he belonged to an actors' collective that had just lost its director. Would I be interested in replacing him? 'Pay?' 'No pay.' 'No thanks.' His response shook me. 'You'd better! Because if you don't you'll end up shooting your life away in a corner pocket.' I took the job.''

ADDRESSES: HOME—Four Washington Square Village, New York, NY 10012. OFFICE—Gene Frankel Theatre, 24 Bond Street, New York, NY 10012.

GENE FRANKEL

FRANKENHEIMER, John   1930-

PERSONAL: Born February 19, 1930, in New York, NY; son of Walter Martin and Helen Mary (Sheedy) Frankenheimer; married Carolyn Diane Miller, September 22, 1954 (divorced, 1961); married Evans Evans (an actress), 1964; children: (first marriage) Lisa Jean, Kristi. EDUCATION: Williams College, B.A., 1951, English. MILITARY: U.S. Air Force, Film Squadron, 1951-53.

VOCATION: Director, producer, and writer.

CAREER: PRINCIPAL FILM WORK—Director: *The Young Stranger*, Universal, 1957; *The Comedian*, 1958; *The Young Savages*, United Artists, 1961; also co-producer, *The Manchurian Candidate*, United Artists, 1962; *All Fall Down*, Metro-Goldwyn-Mayer (MGM), 1962; *Birdman of Alcatraz*, United Artists, 1962; *Seven Days in May*, Paramount, 1964; *The Train*, United Artists, 1965; *Grand Prix*, MGM, 1966; *Seconds*, Paramount, 1966; *The Fixer*, MGM, 1968; *The Extraordinary Seaman*, MGM, 1969; *The Gypsy Moths*, MGM, 1969; *I Walk the Line*, Columbia, 1970; *The Horsemen*, Columbia, 1971; *Impossible Object* (also known as *Story of a Love Story*,), French production, 1973; *The Iceman Cometh*, American Film Institute, 1973; *99 and 44/100% Dead* (U.K. title, *Call Harry Crown*), Twentieth Century-Fox, 1974; *French Connection II*, Twentieth Century-Fox, 1975; *Black Sunday*, Paramount, 1977; *Prophecy*, Paramount, 1979; *The Challenge*, Embassy, 1982; *The Holcroft Covenant*, Universal, 1985; *52 Pickup*, Canadian production, 1986.

PRINCIPAL TELEVISION WORK—Series: Assistant director, *The Garry Moore Show*, *Lamp Unto My Feet*, and *Person to Person*, all CBS, 1953-54; director, *Danger*, CBS, 1954-55; director, *Playhouse 90*, CBS, 1956-61. Episodic: Director—*You Are There*, *Climax*, *Studio One*, *DuPont Show of the Month*, and *Mama*, all CBS; *Ford Startime* and *Sunday Showcase*, both NBC. Dramatic Specials: *The Turn of the Screw*, 1959; *For Whom the Bell Tolls*; *The Browning Version*.

PRINCIPAL STAGE WORK—Director, *The Midnight Sun*, Broadway production, 1959.

RELATED CAREER—Actor between 1950-51; formed John Frankenheimer Productions, 1963.

WRITINGS: NON-FICTION—(With Gerald Pratley) *The Cinema of John Frankenheimer*, A.S. Barnes, 1969. ARTICLES—"7 Ways with *Seven Days in May*," *Films and Filming*, June, 1964; "Criticism as Creation," *Saturday Review*, December 26, 1964; "Filming *The Iceman Cometh*," *Action*, January-February, 1974.

AWARDS: Christopher Award, 1954; Best Film Direction of the Year, Grand Prize, Lacarno Film Festival, 1955; Best Direction of the Year, Critics Award, 1956 and 1959; Brotherhood Award, 1959; Acapulco Film Festival Award, 1962.

ADDRESSES: OFFICE—John Frankenheimer Productions, 2800 Olympic Blvd., Suite 201, Santa Monica, CA 90404. AGENT—c/o Jeff Berg, International Creative Management, 8899 Beverly Blvd., Los Angeles, CA 90048.*

*   *   *

FRASER, Alison   1955-

PERSONAL: Born July 8, 1955, in Natick, MA; daughter of Howard Melvin and Alyce Eleanor (Branagan) Fraser; married

Benjamin Rush Magee (a musician and actor), August 25, 1984. EDUCATION: Attended Carnegie Mellon University and the Boston Conservatory of Music; studied acting with Wynn Handman in New York City.

VOCATION: Actress.

CAREER: PRINCIPAL STAGE APPEARANCES—Ensemble, *The Dirtiest Show in Town 2*, Truck & Warehouse Theatre, New York City, 1975; Trina, *In Trousers*, Playwrights Horizons, New York City, 1978; Irina, *March of the Falsettos*, West Side Arts Theatre, New York City, 1981-82; Connie, Petula, and Brenda, *Beehive*, Village Gate, New York City, 1985-86; Helena Landless, *The Mystery of Edwin Drood*, New York Shakespeare Company production at the Imperial Theatre, New York City, 1986-87.

MEMBER: Actors' Equity Association, American Guild of Variety Artists, American Federation of Television and Radio Artists, Screen Actors Guild.

ADDRESSES: HOME—P.O. Box 250, Shawnee-on-Delaware, PA 18356. AGENT—Ambrosio/Mortimer, 165 W. 45th Street, New York, NY 10036.

*   *   *

FRASER, Bill   1908-1987

PERSONAL: Born June 5, 1908, in Perth, Scotland; died of emphysema in Hertfordshire, England, September 5, 1987; son of Alexander and Betty (Scott) Fraser; married Pamela Cundell (an actress). MILITARY: Royal Air Force, 1941-45.

VOCATION: Actor.

CAREER: STAGE DEBUT—Detective, *The Fourth Wall*, Playhouse Theatre, Broadstairs, U.K., 1931. LONDON DEBUT—*New Faces*, Comedy Theatre, 1940. PRINCIPAL STAGE APPEARANCES—John Mallory, *The Schoolmistress*, Saville Theatre, London, 1950; Palamede, *Albertine by Moonlight*, Westminster Theatre, London, 1956; Bullinger, *Schweyk in the Second World War*, Mermaid Theatre, London, 1963; Bert Mann, *The Subtopians*, New Arts Theatre, London, 1964; Mr. Sterling, *The Clandestine Marriage*, Pishchik, *The Cherry Orchard*, porter, *Macbeth*, all Chichester Festival, Chichester, U.K., 1966; Samuel Sweetland, *The Farmer's Wife*, Gibbet, *The Beaux Stratagem*, corporal, *An Italian Straw Hat*, all Chichester Festival, 1967; Boss Mangan, *Heartbreak House*, Chichester Festival, then Lyric Theatre, London, both 1967; Messerschmann, Lieutenant Barrow, *Ring Around the Moon*, Haymarket Theatre, London, 1968; Sir Toby Belch, *Twelfth Night*, Bishop Gardiner, *King Henry VIII*, both Royal Shakespeare Company (RSC), Memorial Theatre, Stratford-on-Avon, U.K., 1969; Sir George Crofts, *Mrs. Warren's Profession*, National Theatre Company (NTC), Old Vic Theatre, London, 1970; Obermuller, *The Captain of Kopenick*, Mr. Croaker, *The Good-Natured Man*, both NTC, Old Vic Theatre, 1971; King George, *Tyger*, NTC, New Theatre, London, 1971; John Tarleton, *Misalliance*, Mermaid Theatre, 1973; Sergeant Fender, *Something's Burning*, Mermaid Theatre, 1974; Morten Kiil, *An Enemy of the People*, Chichester Festival, 1975; Admiral Lord Radstock, *The Fool*, Royal Court Theatre, London, 1975; Sir Toby Belch, *Twelfth Night*, Chichester Festival, 1976; Lord Porteous, *The Circle*, Chichester Festival, 1976, then Haymarket Theatre, 1976. Also appeared as photographer, *When We Are Married,* London, 1986; and in *New Faces,* Apollo Theatre, London, 1941; *Between Ourselves,* Playhouse Theatre, Broadstairs, U.K., 1946; *Four, Five, Six,* Duke of York's Theatre, London, 1948; *Touch and Go,* Prince of Wales Theatre, London, 1950; *M. Perrichon's Travels,* Chichester Festival, 1976.

MAJOR TOURS—Inspector Goole, *An Inspector Calls,* U.K. cities, 1974; also appeared in *The Outsider,* U.K. cities, 1932; toured India with R.B. Salisbury's Company, 1931.

PRINCIPAL FILM APPEARANCES—*The Corn Is Green,* Warner Brothers, 1945; *Doctor at Large,* Universal, 1957; *The Americanization of Emily,* Metro-Goldwyn-Mayer (MGM), 1964; *Masquerade,* United Artists, 1965; *A Home of Your Own,* Cinema V, 1965; *That's Your Funeral,* Cinema V, 1965; *Captain Nemo and the Underwater City,* MGM, 1970. Appeared in *Meet Me Tonight* (also known as *Tonight at 8:30*), 1954; also *All the Way Up; Joey Boy.*

PRINCIPAL TELEVISON APPEARANCES—Series: Drill sergeant, *Bootsie and Snudge,* BBC; *Rumpole of the Bailey,* BBC, then PBS; also appeared in *Flesh and Blood; Comedians.* Movies: Squire, *The Corn Is Green,* CBS, 1979.

RELATED CAREER—Founder, Worthing Repertory Company, 1933-39.

AWARDS: Olivier Award from the Society of West End Theatre (London), 1986, for *When We Are Married.*

MEMBER: British Actors' Equity Association, Screen Actors Guild; Savage and Green Room Club.

OBITUARIES AND OTHER SOURCES: *Variety,* September 9, 1987.*

*   *   *

FRIEDKIN, William   1939-

PERSONAL: Born August 29, 1939, in Chicago, IL; married Jeanne Moreau (an actress), 1977 (divorced, 1979); married Lesley-Anne Down (an actress), 1982 (divorced, 1985); children: (second marriage) Jack.

VOCATION: Director, writer, and producer.

CAREER: PRINCIPAL FILM WORK—Director: *Good Times,* Columbia, 1967; *The Night They Raided Minsky's,* United Artists, 1968; *The Birthday Party,* Continental, 1968; *The Boys in the Band,* National General, 1970; *The French Connection,* Twentieth Century-Fox, 1971; *The Exorcist,* Warner Brothers, 1973; also producer, *Sorcerer,* Paramount and Universal, 1977; *The Brink's Job,* Universal, 1978; *Cruising,* United Artists, 1980; *Duet for One,* 1981; *Deal of the Century,* Warner Brothers, 1983; *To Live and Die in L.A.,* Metro-Goldwyn-Mayer/United Artists, 1985; *Sea Trial,* 1985; *Judgement Day,* 1986.

PRINCIPAL TELEVISION WORK—Between 1957 and 1967, directed documentaries for WGN, Chicago, including, *The People vs. Paul Crump,* 1962; director, *Putting It Together—The Making of ''The Broadway Album''* (Barbra Streisand), 1986.

RELATED CAREER—Began career working in the mailroom of WGN-TV, Chicago; formed partnership with Francis Ford Coppola and Peter Bogdanovich called the Directors Company, 1973-74.

WRITINGS: SCREENPLAYS—*Cruising,* United Artists, 1980; co-writer, *To Live and Die in L.A.,* Metro-Goldwyn-Mayer/United Artists, 1985.

ARTICLES—''Anatomy of a Chase,'' *Take One,* July/August, 1971; ''William Friedkin,'' *Dialogue on Film,* February/March, 1974; ''Mervyn LeRoy Talks with William Friedkin,'' *Action,* November/December, 1974.

AWARDS: Best Director, Academy Award, 1971, for *The French Connection;* Best Director, Academy Award nomination, 1973, for *The Exorcist.*

ADDRESSES: AGENT—c/o Tony Fantozzi, William Morris Agency, 151 El Camino Drive, Beverly Hills, CA 90212.*

G

GALLACHER, Tom 1934-

PERSONAL: Born February 16, 1934, in Alexandria, England; son of Edward and Rose (Connolly) Gallacher.

VOCATION: Playwright.

CAREER: Also see *WRITINGS* below.

RELATED CAREER—Writer-in-residence, Pitlochry Festival Theatre, Perthshire, U.K., 1975-78; writer-in-residence, Royal Lyceum Company, Edinburgh, Scotland, U.K., 1978—; Drama Committee, Scottish Arts Council, 1978—.

WRITINGS: PLAYS—*Personal Effects,* Pitlochry Festival Theatre, Perthshire, U.K., 1974; *A Laughing Matter,* St. Andrew's Theatre, Fife, Scotland, U.K., 1975; *Hallowe'en,* Dundee Theatre, Angus, Scotland, U.K., 1975; (adaptor) *A Presbyterian Wooing,* Pitlochry Festival Theatre, 1976; *Mr. Joyce Is Leaving Paris,* Stageworks, New York City, 1978. Also *Our Kindness to Five Persons,* Glasgow, Scotland, U.K., 1969; *Mr. Joyce Is Leaving Paris,* London, 1971, revised version produced in Dublin, Ireland, 1971, then London, 1972; *Revival!,* Dublin, 1972; *Schellenbrack,* London, 1973; *The Only Street,* Dublin, then London, both 1973; *The Sea Change,* Edinburgh, Scotland, U.K., 1976; (adaptor) *Cyrano de Bergerac,* 1977; (with Joan Knight) *The Evidence of Tiny Tim,* 1977; (with John Scrimger) *Wha's Like Us—Fortunately, Stage Door Canteen,* both 1978; (adaptor) *Deacon Brodie,* 1978; (adaptor) *An Enemy of the People,* 1979; *Jenny,* 1979.

TELEPLAYS—*The Trial of Thomas Muir,* 1977; *If the Face Fits,* 1978. RADIO PLAYS—*The Scar,* 1973.

ADDRESSES: AGENT—c/o Michael Imison, Dr. Jan van Loewen, Ltd., 81-83 Shaftesbury, London W1, England.*

*   *   *

GALLAGHER, Helen 1926-

PERSONAL: Born in 1926, in Brooklyn, New York; married Frank Wise, October 14, 1956. EDUCATION: Attended the American Ballet School.

VOCATION: Actress and singer.

CAREER: BROADWAY DEBUT—*The Seven Lively Arts,* Ziegfeld Theatre, 1947. LONDON DEBUT—*Touch and Go,* Prince of Wales Theatre, 1950. PRINCIPAL STAGE APPEARANCES—All in New York City unless indicated: Chorus, *Mr. Strauss Goes to Boston,* Century Theatre, 1945; flapper, *Billion Dollar Baby,* Alvin Theatre, 1945; chorus, *Brigadoon,* Ziegfeld Theatre, 1947; Nancy, *High Button Shoes,* Century Theatre, 1947; Poupette, *Make a Wish,* Winter Garden Theatre, 1951; Gladys Bumps, *Pal Joey,* Broadhurst Theatre, 1952; title role, *Hazel Flagg,* Mark Hellinger Theatre, 1953; Annie Oakley, *Annie Get Your Gun,* Oakdale Musical Theatre, Wallingford, CT, 1954; Miss Adelaide, *Guys and Dolls,* Sharon McLonergan, *Finian's Rainbow,* both City Center Theatre, 1955; Gladys, *The Pajama Game,* St. James Theatre, 1955; Meg Brockie, *Brigadoon,* City Center Theatre, 1957; Kitty O'Hara, *Portofino,* Adelphi Theatre, 1958; Ado Annie Carnes, *Oklahoma!,* City Center Theatre, then Municipal Opera, St. Louis, MO, both 1958; Miss Adelaide, *Guys and Dolls,* Municipal Opera, St. Louis, MO, 1958; small servant, *Pound in Your Pocket,* Palm Beach Playhouse, Palm Beach, FL, 1959; Gladys, *The Pajama Game,* St. Paul Civic Opera, St. Paul, MN, 1964; Lola, *Damn Yankees,* Municipal Opera, St. Louis, MO, 1964; Nickie, then Charity, *Sweet Charity,* Palace Theatre, 1966; Agnes Gooch, *Mame,* Winter Garden Theatre, 1968; Bessie Legg, *Cry for Us All,* Broadhurst Theatre, 1970; Lucille Early, *No, No, Nanette,* 46th Street Theatre, 1971; Roz Duncan, *Hothouse,* Brooklyn Academy of Music, Brooklyn, NY, 1974; Arsinoe, *The Misanthrope,* Public Theatre, 1977; title role, *Tallulah,* West Side Arts Center, 1983; Beth, *I Can't Keep Running in Place,* Westside Arts Theatre, 1981; Vic, *Red Rover Red Rover,* Park Royal Theatre, 1983. Also appeared in *Touch and Go,* Broadhurst Theatre, 1949; *The Pajama Game,* St. Paul Civic Opera, St. Paul, MN, 1964; *Tickles by Tucholsky,* Theater Four, 1976; *Sugar Babies,* Mark Hellinger Theatre, 1979; *Side by Side by Sondheim,* Paper Mill Playhouse, Milburn, NJ, 1985; also *The Gingerbread Lady,* Queens Festival, NY, 1977; and *A Broadway Musical.*

MAJOR TOURS—Nellie Forbush, *South Pacific,* U.S. cities, 1965; Nickie, *Sweet Charity,* U.S. and Canadian cities, 1967; Lucille Early, *No, No, Nanette,* U.S. cities, 1974; Cherie, *Bus Stop,* U.S. cities, 1956; *The Gershwin Years,* U.S. cities, 1973; also reconstructed dances for *The American Dance Machine,* U.S. cities, then Tokyo, Japan, 1977.

MAJOR CABARET APPEARANCES—Thunderbird, Las Vegas, NV, 1951; Mocambo, Hollywood, CA, 1951; Plaza Hotel, New York City, 1954; *Too Good for the Average Man* (revue), Camelot, New York City, 1960; Brothers and Sisters, Reno Sweeney, both New York City, 1974.

PRINCIPAL TELEVISION APPEARANCES—Episodic: *Manhattan Showcase,* CBS; *Colgate Comedy Hour,* NBC; *Ed Sullivan Show,* CBS; *Kraft Television Theatre,* NBC. Series: Maeve Ryan, *Ryan's Hope,* CBS. Specials: "Shangri-La," *Hallmark Hall of Fame,* NBC, 1960.

PRINCIPAL FILM APPEARANCES—*Strangers When We Meet,* Columbia, 1960.

AWARDS: Best Supporting Actress in a Musical, Antoinette Perry Award, 1952, for *Pal Joey;* Best Actress in a Musical, Antoinette Perry Award, 1971, for *No, No, Nanette.*

MEMBER: Actors' Equity Association, American Federation of Television and Radio Artists, American Guild of Variety Artists.

ADDRESSES: OFFICE—c/o Actors' Equity Association, 165 W. 46th Street, New York, NY 10036.*

*   *   *

GAMBON, Michael   1940-

PERSONAL: Born October 19, 1940, in Dublin, Ireland; son of Edward and Mary (Hoare) Gambon; married Anne Miller.

VOCATION: Actor.

CAREER: STAGE DEBUT—Second gentleman, *Othello,* Gaiety Theatre, Dublin, Ireland, 1962. PRINCIPAL STAGE APPEARANCES— Coster Pearmain, *The Recruiting Officer,* Diego, *The Royal Hunt of the Sun,* Herrick, *The Crucible,* Eilif, *Mother Courage,* Snap, *Love for Love,* Jerry Devine, *Juno and the Paycock,* all National Theatre Company, Old Vic Theatre, London, 1966; Flynn, *The Bofors Gun,* Palmer Anderson, *A Severed Head,* Patrick Cullen, *The*

MICHAEL GAMBON

Doctor's Dilemma, Cauchon, *Saint Joan,* button moulder, *Peer Gynt,* Escalus, *Romeo and Juliet,* title role, *Othello,* all Birmingham Repertory Theatre, Birmingham, U.K., 1967-68; title role, *Macbeth,* Forum Theatre, Billingham, U.K., 1968; Andrew, *In Celebration,* title role, *Coriolanus,* both Liverpool Playhouse, Liverpool, U.K., 1969; Wiebe, *The Plebeians Rehearse the Uprising,* Charles Lomax, *Major Barbara,* Surrey, *Henry VIII,* Hotspur, *When Thou Art King,* all Royal Shakespeare Company, Aldwych Theatre, London, 1970-71; Guy Holden, *The Brass Hat,* Arnaud Theatre, Guilford, U.K., 1972; Robin, *Not Drowning But Waving,* Greenwich Theatre, London, 1973; Tom, *The Norman Conquests,* Greenwich Theatre, 1974, then Globe Theatre, London, 1975; Gerry, *The Zoo Story,* Open Air Theatre, London, 1975; Simon, *Otherwise Engaged,* Queen's Theatre, London, 1976; Neil, *Just between Ourselves,* Queen's Theatre, 1977; Bertie, *Alice's Boys,* Savoy Theatre, London, 1978; Jerry, *Betrayal,* Henry, *Close of Play,* Buckingham, *Richard III,* Roderigo, *Othello,* all National Theatre, London, 1978-80; *A View from the Bridge,* National Theatre, 1987; Jack McCracken, *A Small Family Business,* Olivier Theatre, London, 1987.

MAJOR TOURS—Second gentleman, *Othello,* European cities, 1962.

PRINCIPAL FILM APPEARANCES—*Othello,* Warner Brothers, 1966; also appeared in *Nothing But the Night; The Beast Must Die.*

PRINCIPAL TELEVISION APPEARANCES—Episodic: *The Secret Agent,* BBC; *Tiptoe through the Tulips,* BBC. Specials: *The Seagull,* BBC.

NON-RELATED CAREER—Engineer.

MEMBER: British Actors' Equity Association, Screen Actors Guild.

SIDELIGHTS: RECREATIONS—Flying, guitar, "collecting heavy industrial machinery."

ADDRESSES: AGENT—Larry Dalzell Associates, Ltd., 126 Kennington Park Road, London SE11, England.

*   *   *

GARFEIN, Jack   1930-

PERSONAL: Full name, Jacob Garfein; born July 2, 1930, in Mukacevo, Czechoslovakia; son of Herman (in business) and Blanka (Spiegel) Garfein; married Carroll Baker (an actress), April 5, 1955 (divorced, 1969); children: Blanche Baker, Herschel Garfein. EDUCATION: Attended New School for Social Research, 1947-49; studied acting and directing at the American Theatre Wing, 1949-50, and with Erwin Piscator and Lee Strasberg. POLITICS: Democrat. RELIGION: Jewish.

VOCATION: Director, producer, writer, and actor.

CAREER: STAGE DEBUT—Moritz, *The Burning Bush,* Rooftop Theatre, New York City, 1948, for fifty performances. FIRST NEW YORK STAGE WORK—Director, *End As a Man,* Theatre de Lys, 1953. PRINCIPAL STAGE WORK— Director, *Girls of Summer,* Longacre Theatre, New York City, 1956; director, *The Sin of Pat Muldoon,* Cort Theatre, New York City, 1957; director, *Shadow of a Gunman,* Bijou Theatre, New York City, 1958; director, *Anna*

JACK GARFEIN

Christie, Huntington Hartford Theatre, Los Angeles, CA, 1965; director, *Don't Go Gentle,* Schonberg Hall, University of California, Los Angeles, 1967; director, *How Tall Is Toscanini?,* Schonberg Hall, 1968; producer, *The Price,* Festival of the Two Worlds, Spoleto, Italy, then Playhouse Theatre, New York City, 1979; producer, *The American Clock,* Festival of the Two Worlds, then Charleston, SC, both 1979, later Biltmore Theatre, New York City, 1980; producer (with Kilian C. Ganly), *All Strange Away,* Samuel Beckett Theatre, New York City, 1984; producer, *Avner the Eccentric,* Lamb's Theatre, New York City, then Samuel Beckett Theatre, 1984; producer, *Endgame,* Samuel Beckett Theatre, then Cherry Lane Theatre, New York City, 1984; producer (with Lucille Lortel), *Rockaby,* Samuel Beckett Theatre, 1984; director, "Ohio Impromptu," "Catastrophe," and "What Where" as *The Beckett Plays,* Edinburgh Festival, Edinburgh, Scotland, U.K., then (as producer also) Warehouse Theatre, London, 1984, later Jerusalem Festival, Jerusalem, Israel, 1985; director, *Master Harold . . . and the boys,* Renaud-Barrault Theatre, Paris, France, 1985; producer (with Carmella Ross and Ellen Oppenheim), *The Importance of Being Earnest,* Samuel Beckett Theatre, 1985. Also producer, *California Reich,* New York City, 1978; producer, *Flying Blind,* New York City, 1979; producer, *Paris Was Yesterday, These Men,* both New York City, 1980; director, *Arms and the Man,* Drury Lane Theatre, Chicago, IL; director, *The Sponsor,* Westwood Playhouse, Los Angeles, CA.

All as producer with the Harold Clurman Theatre, New York City: (also director) *The Lesson,* 1978; *The Two-Character Play,* 1980; *The Chekhov Sketchbook,* 1981; *With Love and Laughter, Chucky's Hunch, Birdbath, Crossing the Crab Nebula,* all 1982; *Hannah,* (with Lucille Lortel) *The Beckett Plays,* both 1983; *For No Good*

Reason, Childhood, (with Byron Lasky) *A Kurt Weill Cabaret,* (with Lortel) *An Evening with Ekkehard Schall,* (also director) *Rommel's Garden,* all 1985.

PRINCIPAL TELEVISION WORK—All as director. Episodic: *The Kate Smith Show,* NBC, 1952; *The Marriage,* NBC; *The Dwarf,* NBC. Documentaries: *Journey to Kenya; On Acting and Directing.*

PRINCIPAL FILM WORK—Director: *The Strange One,* Columbia, 1957; *Something Wild,* United Artists, 1961.

RELATED CAREER—Founder, director, Actors Studio West, Los Angeles, CA, 1967-71; artistic director, Harold Clurman Theatre, New York City, 1978—; founding member, Actors and Directors Lab, Los Angeles, CA and New York City; professor of cinema, University of Southern California, 1970-76; teacher, film directing, Berkeley Film Institute, Berkeley, CA, 1975-78; lecturer: Harvard University, University of California, Los Angeles, New York University, and Pacific Archives, San Francisco, CA.

WRITINGS: PLAYS—(Translator) *August, August, August.* SCREENPLAYS—Co-writer, *Something Wild,* United Artists, 1961; *The Farm.* TELEPLAYS—"A Man Dies," *The Web,* CBS, 1950. DOCUMENTARIES—*Journey to Kenya; On Acting and Directing.*

AWARDS: Best Director on Broadway, Show Business Award, 1954, for *End As a Man;* Cinematheque Francaise, tribute, 1984, for *The Strange One* and *Something Wild.*

MEMBER: Directors Guild of America; Player's Club; Holocaust Survivors of Slovakia (president).

ADDRESSES: HOME—61 W. 62nd Street, New York, NY 10023. OFFICE—412 W. 42nd Street, New York, NY 10036.

*   *   *

GEFFEN, David   1943-

PERSONAL: Born February 21, 1943, in Brooklyn, NY; son of Abraham and Batya (an owner of a corset business) Geffen. EDUCATION: Attended the University of Texas and Brooklyn College.

VOCATION: Producer and agent.

CAREER: PRINCIPAL STAGE WORK—Producer: *Dreamgirls,* Imperial Theatre, New York City, 1981-85; *Cats,* Winter Garden Theatre Theatre, New York City, 1982—; *Little Shop of Horrors,* Orpheum Theatre, New York City, 1982—; *Master Harold. . .and the Boys,* Lyceum Theatre, New York City, 1982; *Good,* Booth Theatre, New York City, 1982-83; *Social Security,* Barrymore Theatre, New York City, 1986-87.

PRINCIPAL FILM WORK—Executive producer, *Personal Best,* Warner Brothers, 1982; producer, *Risky Business,* Warner Brothers, 1983; producer, *Lost in America,* Warner Brothers, 1985; producer, *Little Shop of Horrors,* Warner Brothers, 1986; also producer, *Beastie,* upcoming.

PRINCIPAL TELEVISION APPEARANCES—Specials: *Putting It Together: The Making of "The Broadway Album,"* 1986.

PRINCIPAL RECORDING WORK—Producer of recordings by: Joni Mitchell; Crosby, Stills, and Nash; Neil Young; Jackson Browne; Linda Ronstadt; Queen; Carly Simon; Bob Dylan, and others.

RELATED CAREER—Mail room clerk, later talent agent, William Morris Agency, 1964-68; agent, Ashley Famous Agency, 1968; with Elliot Roberts, founder of Geffen-Roberts Management, 1968; founder and producer, Asylum Records, 1970; president, Elektra-Asylum Records, 1973-76; vice-chairman, Warner Brothers Pictures, 1975; founder and president, Geffen Records and David Geffen Company, 1980—. Also executive vice-president, Creative Management Associates; served on music faculty, Yale University.

NON-RELATED CAREER—Real estate investor.

SIDELIGHTS: David Geffen's unique entrepreneurial career spans the recording industry, the movies, and Broadway plays. By his mid-forties Geffen established himself as a bi-coastal mogul who earned rich profits by backing such varied projects as albums by Jackson Browne, the Broadway musical *Cats,* and the feature film *Risky Business.* In a July 21, 1985 *New York Times Magazine* feature, Don Shewey called Geffen a tastemaker with proven good judgment who "mediates between the interests of businessmen in making money and the interests of artists in doing good work."· A self-made man who earned a million dollars before he turned twenty-five, Geffen stepped away from the entertainment industry between 1976 and 1980 when he was told he had cancer. Since returning to the business, he has recouped his position as one of the most important individuals in its corporate structure. *New York Times* reporter John Duka wrote on October 3, 1982 that Geffen's recent triumphs "are proof that he is still capable of replicating the success he experienced when . . . he became the most sought after agent in the business. Proof, too, against those who forsook him during his retirement . . . that he has not lost his touch. And proof, finally, that he may not have been simply a pushy and loud upstart."

Geffen was born in Brooklyn, the second son in a struggling family who lived in a cramped, three-room apartment. His father was unemployed, but his mother strove ceaselessly to better the family's position. She created a company, Chic Corsetry by Geffen, that eventually moved from the family living room to its own storefront. "I was a terrible student," Geffen told the *New York Times.* "I learned by lessons by watching [my mother]. She taught me to tell the truth, to make sure that whatever I put out was good stuff. I believe that with every fiber of my body." While visiting his brother who was attending law school in Los Angeles, Geffen drove with a friend around the stars' homes in Beverly Hills. In a May 17, 1982 *New York* article, Geffen recalled: ". . . All I could think was how angry I was at my parents that they chose Brooklyn instead of Beverly Hills. I thought, 'Why . . . would anybody *not* want to live here. *Look* at this. This is fabulous! . . . I'm gonna live *here.*"

College did not seem to be the answer for Geffen. He flunked out of the University of Texas, then dropped out of Brooklyn College. He was dismissed from two entry-level jobs at CBS, and then he went to work in the mail room at the prestigious William Morris Agency. In order to advance at William Morris, Geffen fabricated the story that he had graduated from the University of California, Los Angeles. When he learned that the agency was trying to verify his claim, he haunted the mail room until he intercepted the college's answer, steamed it open, and forged a false response. "It was either give William Morris what they wanted or give up my dream," he told the *New York Times.* Even so, as a journeyman talent agent,

Geffen was almost fired for being "too aggressive." He had to plead for his job on at least one occasion.

In 1968 Geffen Geffen quit William Morris for the Ashley Famous Agency, where he "helped build its music department into the second largest in the business," according to Duka. After a term as executive vice president with Creative Management Associates, he joined with Elliot Roberts to form Geffen-Roberts, which quickly became one of the most profitable music management agencies in the country. Next he formed his own production company, Asylum Records, which found immediate success in 1971 with records from Joni Mitchell, Crosby, Stills, Nash & Young, America, and the Eagles. So formidable were Geffen's gains that Warner Communications quickly bought Asylum for seven million dollars, merged it with their own failing Elektra label, and gave Geffen direction of the new division. Once again, Geffen excelled. Out of forty Asylum-Elektra releases in 1973, thirty-eight were hits.

Warner Communications made Geffen vice-chairman of Warner Brothers Pictures in 1975. He oversaw production of *Oh! God* and a few less successful films, but he clashed with the bureaucracy of the movie business and alienated his associates with his forceful personality. Just as he was contemplating leaving the company, he was diagnosed as having cancer. He retired to await his expected death, but he did not stop making money. A series of lucrative real estate deals netted him an estimated $23 million between 1976 and 1980. Then it was determined that he did not have cancer after all. He decided to return to the entertainment industry—to prove a point. "By 1979 I was a forgotten guy," he told the *New York Times.* "I was called a flash in the pan. . . . The people I had thought were my friends and that I once had no trouble reaching by phone would not answer my calls." Of his comeback he went on to say, "I am driven." Geffen Records opened in 1980 with such top-name stars as Bob Dylan, Donna Summer, and Elton John in its ranks. *Dreamgirls* and *Cats,* two plays Geffen backed, opened to long and profitable runs on Broadway in 1981 and 1982 respectively. The film *Risky Business* earned in excess of $50 million. And once again, Geffen became the courted hero, making and receiving more than one hundred phone calls a day.

In the *New York Times,* Geffen has called himself "Billy the Kid, the fastest draw." He added: "It's not arrogance. It's the truth. I'm good at decidng what people like. I'm gifted at knowing what will be a success before it is a success." Where once his romances with singer Laura Nyro and with Cher, both clients, put him in the tabloids, Geffen has kept a lower profile since 1980. He spends some of his profits on fine art and works to keep in good physical condition. Although Geffen admits that he is happy only when the bottom line is securely in the black, he nonetheless told the *New York Times Magazine* that he loves his particular business. "The truth of the matter is I don't work to make a living," he claimed. "I work because I like this. If I had to pay somebody else for the opportunity to do this, I would."

ADDRESSES: OFFICE—Geffen Films, 9130 Sunset Boulevard, Los Angeles, CA 90069.*

* * *

GELBER, Jack   1932-

PERSONAL: Born April 12, 1932, in Chicago, IL; son of Harold (a sheet metal worker) and Molly (Singer) Gelber; married Carol

Westenberg, December 23, 1957; children: Jed, Amy. EDUCA-TION: University of Illinois, B.S., journalism, 1953.

VOCATION: Playwright, director, and writer.

CAREER: PRINCIPAL STAGE WORK—Director: *The Kitchen,* New Theatre, New York City, 1966; *The Cuban Thing,* Berkshire Theatre Festival, Stockbridge, MA, then Henry Miller's Theatre, New York City, both 1968; *Indians,* Royal Shakespeare Company, Aldwych Theatre, London, 1968; *Kool Aid,* Forum Theatre, New York City, 1971; *The Chickencoop Chinaman, The Kid,* both American Place Theatre, New York City, 1972; *Barbary Shore,* Public Theatre, New York City, 1974; *A Streetcar Named Desire,* Academy Festival Theatre, Lake Forest, IL, 1976; *Jack Gelber's New Play: Rehearsal,* American Place Theatre, 1976; *Eulogy for a Small Time Thief,* Ensemble Studio Theatre, New York City, 1977; *Seduced,* American Place Theatre, 1979.

RELATED CAREER—Writer-in-residence, City College of New York, 1965-66; adjunct professor of drama, Columbia University, 1967-72; professor of drama, Brooklyn College, 1972-80. Also playwright-in-residence, American Place Theatre, New York City.

NON-RELATED CAREER—Sheet metal worker; shipfitter's helper; mimeograph operator at the United Nations.

WRITINGS: PLAYS—*The Connection,* Living Theatre, New York City, 1959, published by Grove Press, 1960; *The Apple,* Living Theatre, 1961, published by Grove Press, 1961, later published in *Two Plays,* Viking, 1974; *Square in the Eye,* Theatre de Lys, New York City, 1965, published by Grove Press, 1966, later published in *Two Plays,* Viking, 1974; *The Cuban Thing,* Berkshire Theatre Festival, Stockbridge, MA, then Henry Miller's Theatre, New York City, both 1968, published by Grove Press, 1969; *Sleep,* American Place Theatre, New York City, 1972, published by Hill & Wang, 1972; (adaptor) *Barbary Shore,* New York Shakespeare Festival, Public Theatre, New York City, 1974; *Jack Gelber's New Play: Rehearsal,* American Place Theatre, 1976. FICTION—*On Ice,* Macmillan, 1964. SCREENPLAYS—*The Connection* (based on his play of the same name), 1962.

AWARDS: Vernon Rice Award, 1960, for Outstanding Contribu-tion to Off-Broadway; Obie Award from the *Village Voice,* Drama Desk Award, and *Variety's* New York Drama Critic's Poll Award, all 1960, for *The Connection;* Directing Award, Obie, 1972, for *The Kid;* Guggenheim Fellowship, 1963-64 and 1966-67, for creative writing for the theatre; Rockefeller Fellowship, 1972; National Endowment for the Arts Fellowship, 1974; CBS Fellow-ship, 1974-75.

MEMBER: Dramatists Guild, Writers Guild of America, Society of Stage Directors and Choreographers.

ADDRESSES: HOME—697 West End Avenue, New York, NY 10025. AGENT—Ronald S. Konecky, 1 Dag Hammarskjold Plaza, New York, NY 10017.*

*   *   *

GERROLL, Daniel   1951-

PERSONAL: Surname rhymes with "peril;" born October 16, 1951, in London, England; son of Harry (a clothing manufacturer)

DANIEL GERROLL

and Kathleen Cordelia (Norman) Gerroll. EDUCATION: Attended Nottingham University; trained for the stage at the Central School of Speech and Drama.

VOCATION: Actor, director, and writer.

CAREER: STAGE DEBUT—*A Public Mischief,* Southwold Summer Theatre, Southwold, U.K., 1974. PRINCIPAL STAGE APPEAR-ANCES—Bruno, *Marching Song,* Greenwich Theatre, New York City, 1974; Derek, *Once a Catholic,* Royal Court Theatre, London, 1977; friend, *A Respectable Wedding,* Open Space Theatre, Lon-don, 1978; Prince of Wales, *Love of a Good Man,* Royal Court Theatre, 1980; Phil McCann, *The Slab Boys,* Hudson Guild Thea-tre, New York City, 1980; Curly Delafield, *Knuckle,* Hudson Guild Theatre, 1981; Yolland, *Translations,* Manhattan Theatre Club, New York City, 1981; Mick, *The Caretaker,* Roundabout Theatre, New York City, 1982; John, *Scenes from La Vie de Boheme,* Manhattan Theatre Club, New York City, 1982; Mick, *Plenty,* Public Theatre, New York City, 1982, then Plymouth Theatre, New York City, 1983; Tom, *The Knack,* Roundabout Theatre, 1983; Oates, *Terra Nova,* American Place Theatre, New York City, 1984; John Faustus, *Doctor Faustus,* Susan Bloch Theatre, New York City, 1985; Clark Storey, *The Second Man,* Hudson Guild Theatre, 1986; Robert Greene, *Cheapside,* Roundabout Theatre, 1986. Also appeared in *Not Quite Jerusalem,* Long Wharf Theatre, New Haven, CT, 1984; "The Public Eye" and "Black Comedy" in *Light Comedies,* Hartman Theatre, Stamford, CT, 1985.

PRINCIPAL STAGE WORK—Director: *She Stoops to Conquer,* Roundabout Theatre, New York City, 1984; *On Approval,* Susan Bloch Theatre, New York City, 1984; *The Accrington Pals,* Hudson Guild Theatre, New York City, 1984; *A Backers' Audition,* Manhattan Theatre Club, New York City, 1985; *The Custom of the Country,* Second Stage Theatre, New York City, 1985.

MAJOR TOURS—*The Unexpected Guest,* U.K. cities, 1976; *Murder with Love,* U.K. cities, 1977.

FILM DEBUT—Rafe, *Sir Henry at Rawlinson End,* 1979. PRINCIPAL FILM APPEARANCES—Henry Stallard, *Chariots of Fire,* Warner Brothers, 1981; Brian, *84 Charing Cross Road,* Columbia, 1987.

TELEVISION DEBUT—*The Glums,* LWT, 1977. PRINCIPAL TELEVISION APPEARANCES—Walter Hartwright, *Woman in White,* 1981.

RELATED CAREER—Dialect coach.

WRITINGS: PLAYS—(Adaptor) *Doctor Faustus,* Susan Bloch Theatre, New York City, 1985.

Contributor, film criticism (under pseudonym) and feature articles for *Films in Review,* 1982—.

AWARDS: Theatre World Award, 1980, for *Translations;* Outer Critics Circle Award, 1981, for *Knuckle.*

MEMBER: Actors' Equity Association, Screen Actors Guild, American Federation of Television and Radio Artists.

ADDRESSES: AGENT—Lionel Larner, Ltd., 850 Seventh Avenue, New York, NY 19919.*

*   *   *

GERSTEN, Bernard   1923-

PERSONAL: Born January 30, 1923, in Newark, NJ; son of Jacob Israel (a garment worker) and Henrietta (Henig) Gersten; married Cora Cahan (a dancer), April 21, 1968. EDUCATION: Attended Rutgers University, 1940-42. MILITARY: U.S. Army Special Services.

VOCATION: Stage manager, actor, producer, and director.

CAREER: PRINCIPAL STAGE APPEARANCES—Jake, *Papa's All,* Hunterdon Hills Playhouse, Jutland, NJ, 1947. FIRST STAGE WORK—Technical director of Maurice Evans's U.S. Army Special Services Unit, Hawaii, two years. FIRST NEW YORK STAGE WORK—Assistant stage manager, *GI Hamlet,* International Theatre, 1945. FIRST LONDON STAGE WORK—Co-director, *Do Re Mi,* Prince of Wales Theatre, 1961. PRINCIPAL STAGE WORK—All as stage manager in New York City unless indicated: *Kathleen,* Mansfield Theatre, 1948; *Anna Christie,* City Center Theatre, 1950; *All You Need Is One Good Break,* Mansfield Theatre, 1950; producer, *Three O'Casey Plays,* Yugoslav Hall, 1951; *Tovarich,* City Center Theatre, 1952; general manager, lighting designer, *The World of Sholom Aleichem,* Barbizon Plaza Theatre, 1953; *Sand Hog,* Phoenix Theatre, 1954; *Guys and Dolls, South Pacific, Finian's Rainbow,* all City Center Theatre, 1955; *Mr. Wonderful,* Broadway Theatre, 1956; *Brigadoon,* City Center Theatre, 1957; *Edwin Booth,* 46th Street Theatre, 1958; *The Legend of Lizzie,* 54th Street Theatre, 1959; *Roman Candle,* Cort Theatre, 1960; *Laurette,*

Schubert Theatre, New Haven, CT, 1960; *Do Re Mi,* St. James Theatre, 1960, then director, Prince of Wales Theatre, London, 1961; executive stage manager, *Othello, The Merchant of Venice, Much Ado about Nothing,* all American Shakespeare Festival, Stratford, CT, 1957; executive stage manager, *Hamlet, A Midsummer Night's Dream, The Winter's Tale,* all American Shakespeare Festival, 1958; general stage manager, *L'Italiana in Algeria* (opera), Dallas Civic Opera, Dallas, TX, 1958; executive stage manager, *Romeo and Juliet, The Merry Wives of Windsor, All's Well That Ends Well, A Midsummer Night's Dream,* all American Shakespeare Festival, 1959.

All as associate producer, New York Shakespeare Festival (NYSF), New York City, unless indicated: *Henry V, Measure for Measure, The Taming of the Shrew,* all Central Park, 1960; director, *No for an Answer,* Circle in the Square, 1960; *Much Ado about Nothing, A Midsummer Night's Dream, Richard II,* all Wollman Memorial Skating Rink, 1961; *King Lear, The Tempest, The Merchant of Venice,* all Delacorte Theatre, 1962; *Antony and Cleopatra, As You Like It, The Winter's Tale,* all Delacorte Theatre, 1963; production stage manager, *Arturo Ui,* Lunt-Fontanne Theatre, 1963; *Othello,* Delacorte Theatre, then Martinique Theatre, 1964; *Hamlet, Electra, A Midsummer Night's Dream,* all Delacorte Theatre, 1964; *Coriolanus, Troilus and Cressida, Love's Labour's Lost,* all Delacorte Theatre, 1965; *All's Well That Ends Well, Measure for Measure, Richard III,* all Delacorte Theatre, 1966; co-director, *Potluck!,* Delacorte Mobile Theatre, 1966; co-director, *Lallapalooza,* Delacorte Mobile Theatre, 1967; *The Comedy of Errors, King John, Titus Andronicus,* all Delacorte Theatre, 1967; *Hair,* Public Theatre, 1967; *The Memorandum, Huui, Huui,* both Public Theatre, 1968; *Henry IV, Parts I and II, Romeo and Juliet,* all Delacorte Theatre, 1968; *Cities in Bezique, Invitation to a Beheading, No Place to Be Somebody, Sambo, The Owl Answers, A Beast's Story,* all Public Theatre, 1969; *Peer Gynt, Twelfth Night,* both Delacorte Theatre, 1969.

All as associate producer with NYSF in New York City unless indicated: "Henry VI, Parts I and II" and "Richard III" as *The Wars of the Roses,* Delacorte Theatre, 1970; *Mod Donna, Sambo, The Happiness Cage, Trelawny of the Wells, Jack MacGowran in the Works of Samuel Beckett,* all Public Theatre, 1970; *Subject to Fits, Slag, Here Are Ladies, Blood, Underground, The Basic Training of Pavlo Hummel, Dance wi' Me, Nigger Nightmare, Sticks and Bones, The Black Terror, The Wedding of Iphigenia, Iphigenia in Concert,* all Public Theatre, 1971; *Two Gentlemen of Verona, Timon of Athens, The Tale of Cymbeline,* all Delacorte Theatre, 1971; *Revenge of the Law, Harvey McLeod, Hallelujah, Black Visions, That Championship Season, Older People, The Hunter, The Corner, Wedding Band, The Children,* all Public Theatre, 1972; *Much Ado about Nothing,* Delacorte Theatre, then Winter Garden Theatre, 1972; *Hamlet, Ti-Jean and His Brothers,* both Delacorte Theatre, 1972; *Siamese Connections, The Orphan, Lotta,* all Public Theatre, 1973; *As You Like It, King Lear, Two Gentlemen of Verona,* all Delacorte Theatre, 1973; *Boom Boom Room, The Au Pair Man,* both Vivian Beaumont Theatre, 1973; *Troilus and Cressida,* Mitzi E. Newhouse Theatre, 1973; *More Than You Deserve, The Emperor of Late Night Radio, Short Eyes, Les Femmes Noires, Barbary Shore, The Killdeer,* all Public Theatre, 1974; *The Tempest, Macbeth,* both Mitzi E. Newhouse Theatre, 1974; *What the Wine Sellers Buy, The Dance of Death,* both Vivian Beaumont Theatre, 1974.

All as associate producer with NYSF in New York City unless indicated: *A Chorus Line,* Public Theatre, then Schubert Theatre, 1976; *Streamers,* Mitzi E. Newhouse Theatre, 1976; *For Colored*

Girls Who Consider Suicide When the Rainbow Is Enuf, Booth Theatre, 1976; *Agamemnon, The Cherry Orchard,* both Vivian Beaumont Theatre, 1977; *Miss Margarida's Way,* Public Theatre, then Ambassador Theatre, 1977; *Marco Polo Sings a Solo, Ashes, On-the Lock-In, Creditors/The Stronger, Landscape of the Boys, Mandrake, Where the Mississippi Meets the Amazon, A Photograph, The Dybbuk,* all Public Theatre, 1977; *The Water Engine/ Mr. Happiness, Runaways,* both Public Theatre, then Plymouth Theatre, 1978; *I'm Getting My Act Together and Taking It on the Road,* Public Theatre, then Circle in the Square, 1978; *A Prayer for My Daughter, Museum, Curse of the Starving Class, Sganarelle: An Evening of Moliere Farces, Spring Awakening,* all Public Theatre, 1978; *Catsplay,* Manhattan Theatre Club, 1978; *All's Well That Ends Well, The Taming of the Shrew,* both Delacorte Theatre, 1978; also, *Pericles, The Merry Wives of Windsor, Richard III, Mert and Phil, Where Do We Go from Here?, Sweet Talk, The Last Days of British Honduras, Boom Boom Room,* all 1974; *Kid Champion, Fishing, Time Trial, Black Picture Show, A Midsummer Night's Dream, A Doll's House, Taking of Miss Hanie, Little Black Sheep, Hamlet, Trelawny of the Wells, The Leaf People, Jesse and the Bandit Queen,* all 1975; *Henry V,* 1976; *Rich and Famous, Apple Pie, So Nice They Named It Twice, Rebel Women, The Threepenny Opera,* all 1977.

All in New York City: Independent co-producer, *Ballroom,* Palace Theatre, 1978; producer, *Bosoms and Neglect,* Longacre Theatre New York City, 1979; executive producer, *Porgy and Bess,* 5-6-7-8 . . . *Dance!,* both Radio City Music Hall, 1983; co-producer, *Play Memory,* Longacre Theatre, 1984; co-producer, *Accidental Death of an Anarchist,* Belasco Theatre, 1984; co-producer, *Night of 100 Stars II,* Radio City Music Hall, 1985; executive producer, *The Flying Karamazov Brothers,* Mitzi E. Newhouse Theatre, then Vivian Beaumont Theatre, 1986; "Terrors of Pleasure," "Sex and Death to the Age 14," "Swimming to Cambodia," three monologues billed as *Spalding Gray, Prairie du Chien/The Shawl,* both Mitzi E. Newhouse Theatre, 1986; *The House of Blue Leaves,* Vivian Beaumont Theatre, 1986.

MAJOR TOURS—Stage manager, *The Guardsman,* U.S. cities, 1950; *A Certain Joy,* U.S. cities, 1953; stage manager, *Much Ado about Nothing,* U.S. cities, 1987.

PRINCIPAL TELEVISION WORK—Episodic: Associate producer, *The Merchant of Venice,* CBS, 1962; associate producer, *Antony and Cleopatra,* CBS, 1963; associate producer, *Hamlet,* CBS, 1964; producer, *Sticks and Bones, Much Ado about Nothing, Wedding Band,* all PBS. Series: Production manager, *Showtime, USA,* ABC, 1951.

RELATED CAREER—Producer, Hunterdon Hills Playhouse, Jutland, NJ, 1947; technical director, Actors Laboratory, Hollywood, CA, 1948; production stage manager, New Stages, Inc., New York City, 1948-49; production supervisor, NBC, 1951; associate producer, New York Shakespeare Festival, 1960-78; vice-president, operations and development, Omni Zoetrope, 1979—; president, American Arts Alliance, 1979; president, Brentwood Television Productions, 1985.

AWARDS: Bronze Medallion of the City of New York, 1972.

MEMBER: Actors' Equity Association, American Guild of Musical Artists.

ADDRESSES: OFFICE—c/o Omni Zoetrope, 916 Kearny Street, San Francisco, CA 94133.*

GIBB, Lee
  See WATERHOUSE, Keith Spencer

* * *

GIBBS, Timothy   1967-

PERSONAL: Born April 17, 1967, in Burbank, CA; son of Raeford F. (an investment broker) and Paula (a designer; maiden name, Beck) Gibbs. EDUCATION: Attended University of California, Los Angeles; studied drama and improvisation with Peggy Feury and Terrance Hines at the Loft Studio; also studied with Kay Howell at the Stagecoach Theatre.

VOCATION: Actor.

CAREER: TELEVISION DEBUT—Binky, *The Jeffersons,* CBS, 1981. PRINCIPAL TELEVISION APPEARANCES—Series: Will Adams, *Father Murphy,* NBC, 1981-83; Michael Earp, *Rousters,* NBC, 1984-85; voice, *Get Along Gang* (cartoon), CBS, 1985-86. Mini-Series: John, *The Deliberate Stranger,* NBC, 1986. Movies: Artie Phillips, *Goldie and the Boxer Go to Hollywood,* NBC, 1982; *Huckleberry Finn,* NBC, 1984; *Dead Wrong,* CBS, 1985; *Family Honor,* ABC, 1986; *Contract for Life,* CBS, 1986. Guest: *The Morning Show,* CBS, 1985; *The Regis Philbin Show,* WABC, New York, 1986; "Showbiz," *CNN News,* CNN, 1986; *Good Morning New York,* 1986; *Good Morning L.A.,* 1986; *Mid-Morning L.A.,* 1986.

FILM DEBUT—Jeff Davis, *Just Between Friends,* Orion, 1986. PRINCIPAL FILM APPEARANCES—*The Kindred,* Film Enterprises, 1987; *AIDS in Teens* (documentary), MTM, 1987.

TIMOTHY GIBBS

PRINCIPAL STAGE APPEARANCES—George, *Alphabetical Order*, Stagecoach Theatre, Culver City, CA, 1985.

RELATED CAREER—Actor in television commercials; model; board of directors, Film Industry Council to Combat Drugs, 1986-87.

NON-RELATED CAREER—Chairor, Putter Productions, 1984-87; president, Spectrum Systems, 1986-87; chairman, Children's Liver Foundation.

AWARDS: Best Actor in a Television Series, Youth in Film Award, 1982 and 1983.

MEMBER: American Federation of Television and Radio Artists, Screen Actors Guild, Academy of Television Arts and Sciences.

SIDELIGHTS: RECREATIONS—Travel, sports cars, collecting watches, and "being an uncle to three nephews."

ADDRESSES: AGENT—c/o McCartt, Oreck, Barrett, 10390 Santa Monica Boulevard, Los Angeles, CA 90025.

*   *   *

GIBSON, Michael   1944-

PERSONAL: Born September 29, 1944, in Wilmington, DE; son of Alfred L. (a drug rehabilitation counselor) and Margaret A. Gibson; married Ellen Haight, April 16, 1984. EDUCATION: Graduated from Harvard College, 1966; attended Berklee College of Music, 1968.

VOCATION: Composer, orchestrator, and writer.

CAREER: FIRST NEW YORK STAGE WORK—Orchestrator, *Over Here*, Shubert Theatre, 1973. PRINCIPAL STAGE WORK—Orchestrator, all in New York City: *Peter Pan*, Lunt-Fontanne Theatre, 1979; *Manhattan Showboat*, Radio City Music Hall, *Onward Victoria*, Martin Beck Theatre, *Barnum*, St. James Theatre, all 1980; *Bravo!*, Entermedia Theatre, *Woman of the Year*, Palace Theatre, both 1981; *My One and Only*, St. James Theatre, 1983; *Gotta Getaway!*, Radio City Music Hall, *Ann Reinking . . . Music Moves Me*, Joyce Theatre, *The Rink*, Martin Beck Theatre, all 1984; *Night of 100 Stars II*, Radio City Music Hall, 1985; *Anything Goes*, Vivian Beaumont Theatre, *Roza*, Royale Theatre, *Cabaret*, Imperial Theatre, all 1987.

MAJOR TOURS—Orchestrator: *Dancin'*, U.S. and U.K. cities 1980; *Barnum*, U.S. cities, 1982; *My One and Only*, U.S. cities, 1985. Also orchestrated *Pippin*, U.S. cities.

PRINCIPAL CABARET WORK—Orchestrator for Joel Grey, Patti LuPone, Dorothy Loudon, Debbie Reynolds, Chita Rivera, and Liza Minelli.

PRINCIPAL FILM WORK—Orchestrator: *Roseland*, Cinema Shares, 1977; *Grease*, Paramount, 1978; *Grease 2*, Paramount, 1980; *Still of the Night*, Metro-Goldwyn-Mayer/United Artists, 1982; *Blue Skies Again*, Warner Brothers, 1983. Also orchestrated *Cold River*, 1981.

PRINCIPAL TELEVISION WORK—All as orchestrator. Specials: *A Tribute to Jule Styne*, PBS, 1987; *White House Concert*, PBS, 1987; also "Joel Grey and the Boston Pops," *Liberty Weekend Special*, 1986; *Ford's Theatre*, 1985, then 1986; *SRO: Liza in London*.

RELATED CAREER—Orchestrator for television commercials.

WRITINGS: FILM SCORES—*Roseland*, Cinema Shares, 1977; also *Cold River*, 1981; composed incidental music for *Grease*, Paramount, 1978. PROGRAM MUSIC—*Tribute to Alan Jay Lerner; Andrew Lloyd Webber Medley*.

RECORDINGS: All as orchestrator. ALBUMS—*Kathleen Battle Christmas Album; Grease* (original soundtrack); *The Rink* (original cast recording); *My One and Only*, (origninal cast recording); *Over Here!* (original cast recording).

AWARDS: Outstanding Orchestration, Drama Desk Award, 1983, for *My One and Only;* Clio Award for National Car Rental television commercials; platinum album for *Grease* (original soundtrack).

MEMBER: New York Arrangers and Orchestrators Committee (co-chairor).

ADDRESSES: HOME—200 W. 79th Street, New York, NY 10024. AGENT—c/o Michael Oubre, Schumer-Oubre Management, Inc., 1697 Broadway, New York, NY 10019.

*   *   *

GILBERT, Melissa   1964-

PERSONAL: Born May 8, 1964, in Los Angeles, CA; daughter of Paul (a comedian) and Barbara (a dancer and actress; maiden name, Crane) Gilbert. EDUCATION: Attended University of Southern California.

CAREER: PRINCIPAL TELEVISION APPEARANCES—Episodic: *The Hanna-Barbera Happy Hour*, NBC, 1978; "The Snow Queen," *Faerie Tale Theatre*, Showtime, 1985; also *Gunsmoke*, CBS; *Tenafly*, NBC; *The Love Boat*, ABC; *Emergency*, NBC. Series: Laura Ingalls Wilder, *Little House on the Prairie*, NBC, 1974-82, then *Little House: A New Beginning*, 1982-83. Movies: Laura Ingalls, *Little House on the Prairie*, NBC, 1974; Kelly Sullivan, *Christmas Miracle in Caufield, U.S.A.* (also known as *The Christmas Coal Mine Miracle*), NBC, 1977; Helen Keller *The Miracle Worker*, NBC, 1979; Anne Frank, *The Diary of Anne Frank*, NBC, 1980; Deanie Loomis, *Splendor in the Grass*, NBC, 1981; Laura Ingalls Wilder, *Little House: Look Back to Yesterday*, NBC, 1983; Jean Donovan, *Choices of the Heart*, NBC, 1983; Laura Ingalls Wilder, *Little House: Bless All the Dear Children*, NBC, 1984; Sara Calloway, *Family Secrets*, NBC, 1984; Laura Ingalls Wilder, *Little House: The Last Farewell*, NBC, 1984; Terry Granger, *Choices*, ABC, 1986; Leah Furman, *Penalty Phase*, CBS, 1986. Specials: *Battle of the Network Stars*, ABC, 1978, 1979, 1981, and 1982; *Celebrity Challenge of the Sexes*, CBS, 1980; *Circus Lions, Tigers, and Melissas Too*, NBC, 1977; *Dean Martin Celebrity Roast*, NBC, 1984; *Like Magic*, CBS, 1981.

FILM DEBUT—Clara, *Nutcracker Fantasy*, Sanrio, 1979. PRINCIPAL FILM APPEARANCES—*Sylvester*, Columbia, 1985.

PRINCIPAL STAGE APPEARANCES—*A Shayna Maidel*, Westside Arts Theatre, New York City, 1987; also Laura, *The Glass Menagerie*, Chautauqua, NY, 1985; and participated in *Night of 100 Stars*, Radio City Music Hall, New York City, 1982.

ADDRESSES: AGENT—International Creative Management, 8899 Beverly Boulevard, Los Angeles, CA 90048.*

DANA GILLESPIE

GILLESPIE, Dana 1949-

PERSONAL: Born Richenda Antoinette de Winterstein Gillespie, March 30, 1949, in London, England; daughter of Henry (a doctor) and Anne (Buxton) Gillespie. EDUCATION: Attended Arts Educational Trust.

VOCATION: Actress, singer, and songwriter.

CAREER: LONDON DEBUT—Bianca, *Catch My Soul,* Round House Theatre, 1970, then Prince of Wales Theatre, 1971. PRINCIPAL STAGE APPEARANCES—Mary Magdelene, *Jesus Christ Superstar,* Palace Theatre, London, 1973; Juno, *The Tempest,* National Theatre Company, Old Vic Theatre, London, 1974; Celandine, *Mardi Gras,* Prince of Wales Theatre, London, 1976; Acid Queen, *Tommy,* Queen's Theatre, London, 1979; title role, *Cora,* Edinburgh Festival, Edinburgh, Scotland, U.K., then Lyric Hammersmith Theatre, London, both 1983. Also appeared in *Liz,* Marlowe Theatre, Canterbury, U.K., 1968; *Playthings,* Vienna, Austria, then London, 1980; *Cinderella,* Eastbourne, U.K., 1980.

PRINCIPAL CABARET APPEARANCES—Reno Sweeney, New York City.

PRINCIPAL FILM APPEARANCES—*Mahler,* Mayfair Film Group, 1975; *The Lost Continent,* Twentieth Century-Fox, 1968; *People That Time Forgot,* American International, 1977; *Bad Timing: A Sensual Obsession,* World Northal, 1980; *Scrubbers,* Orion, 1982. Also appeared in *Sink or Swim,* 1976; *The Hound of the Baskervilles,* 1977; *Parker,* 1984.

TELEVISION DEBUT—*Ready, Steady, Go,* BBC, 1964. PRINCIPAL TELEVISION APPEARANCES—Episodic: *Little and Large,* BBC; *Hazell,* BBC. Also appeared in *Beat Room; Gadzooks; Seaside Special; Til Death Do Us Part; Mum's Boys.*

RELATED CAREER—Singer with the music groups the Cobras and the Mojo Blues Band.

WRITINGS: MUSICAL COMPOSITIONS—Contributed music, *Mahler,* Mayfair Film Group, 1975. Also has written numerous songs.

RECORDINGS: ALBUMS—*Foolish Seasons,* Decca, 1967; *Box of Surprises,* Decca, 1968; *Weren't Born a Man,* RCA, 1973; *Ain't Gonna Play No Second Fiddle,* RCA, 1974; *The Boogie Woogie Flu,* Bellaphon, 1981; *Blue Job,* Ace, 1982; *Solid Romance,* Bellaphon, 1984; *Below the Belt,* Ace, 1984; *It Belongs to Me,* Bellaphon, 1985; *Hot News,* Gig, 1987.

AWARDS: Number one single in Austria with ''Move Your Body Closer to Me.''

MEMBER: British Actors' Equity Association, Screen Actors Guild.

SIDELIGHTS: RECREATIONS—''Sports, especially riding and water sports.''

Dana Gillespie informed *CTFT* that she was the British water ski champion for four consecutive years.

ADDRESSES: AGENT—c/o Belinda Wright, Caroline Dawson Associates, 47 Courtfield Road, London SW7, England.

*   *   *

GILLIAM, Terry 1940-
(Jerry Gillian)

PERSONAL: Full name, Terry Vance Gilliam; born November 22, 1940, in Minneapolis, MN; immigrated to England, 1969; son of James Hall (a carpenter) and Beatrice (Vance) Gilliam; married Margaret Weston (a makeup artist), 1974; children: Amy Rainbow, Holly du Bois. EDUCATION: Occidental College, B.A., 1962.

VOCATION: Actor, writer, producer, director, animator, and illustrator.

CAREER: PRINCIPAL TELEVISION APPEARANCES—Series: *Monty Python's Flying Circus,* BBC, 1969-74, broadcast in the United States on PBS, 1974-82. Movies: *Pythons in Deutschland,* Bavaria Atelier, 1971.

PRINCIPAL TELEVISION WORK—Writer (see below). Series: Creator of animated film, *Do Not Adjust Your Set,* resident cartoonist, *We Have Ways of Making You Laugh,* and animator, *Marty,* all London, 1968; animator and director, *Monty Python's Flying Circus,* BBC, 1969-74, broadcast in the United States on PBS, 1974-82; creator of title sequence, *William,* CBS, 1972.

PRINCIPAL FILM APPEARANCES—*And Now for Something Completely Different,* Columbia, 1971; Patsy, a weird old man, and Keeper of the Bridge of Death, *Monty Python and the Holy Grail,* Cinema 5, 1975; *Pleasure at Her Majesty's,* 1976; *Jabberwocky,*

Cinema 5, 1977; a revolutionary, a masked commando, a prophet, a jailer, and Geoffrey, *Monty Python's Life of Brian,* Warner Brothers, 1979; *Monty Python Live at the Hollywood Bowl,* Columbia, 1982; *Monty Python's The Meaning of Life,* Universal, 1983; Dr. Imhaus, *Spies Like Us,* Warner Brothers, 1985.

PRINCIPAL FILM WORK—Writer (see below); co-director and animator of title sequence, *Cry of the Banshee,* American International, 1970; animator, *The Marty Feldman Comedy Machine,* 1971; director, *Jabberwocky,* Cinema 5, 1977; producer and director, *Time Bandits,* AVCO-Embassy, 1981; director, *Brazil,* Universal, 1985; director, *The Adventures of Baron Munchausen,* upcoming.

Animator for Monty Python feature films: *And Now for Something Completely Different,* Columbia, 1971; (also co-director) *Monty Python and the Holy Grail,* Cinema 5, 1975; (also set designer) *Monty Python's Life of Brian,* Warner Brothers, 1979; (also director) *Monty Python's The Meaning of Life,* Universal, 1983.

PRINCIPAL STAGE APPEARANCES—*Monty Python Live at the Hollywood Bowl,* Los Angeles, CA, 1970; *Monty Python Live!,* New York City, 1976.

MAJOR TOURS—As a member of the comedy troupe Monty Python, with Graham Chapman, John Cleese, Eric Idle, Terry Jones, and Michael Palin, performed in concert tours in U.S., U.K. and Canadian cities, 1970s.

RELATED CAREER—Associate editor, *Help!* (a satirical magazine), New York City, 1962-64; free-lance cartoonist, 1964-65; copywriter and art director, Carson Roberts Advertising Agency, Los Angeles, CA, 1966-67; free-lance illustrator for periodicals including Sunday editions of London *Times, Nova,* and *Queen,* 1967; artistic director of *Londoner Magazine,* 1967; animator of "The Great Gas Gala" campaign for British Gas Board, 1972.

WRITINGS: SCREENPLAYS—With Graham Chapman, John Cleese, Eric Idle, Terry Jones, and Michael Palin, except as noted: *And Now for Something Completely Different,* Columbia, 1971; *Monty Python and the Holy Grail,* Cinema 5, 1975; *Monty Python's Life of Brian,* Warner Brothers, 1979; (with Charles Alverson) *Jabberwocky,* Cinema 5, 1977; (with Palin) *Time Bandits,* AVCO-Embassy, 1981; *Monty Python Live at the Hollywood Bowl,* Columbia, 1982; *Monty Python's The Meaning of Life,* Universal, 1983; (with Tom Stoppard) *Brazil,* Universal, 1984; (with Charles McKeown) *The Adventures of Baron Munchausen,* upcoming.

TELEVISION—Series: *Do Not Adjust Your Set,* London, 1968; *We Have Ways of Making You Laugh,* London, 1968; (with Chapman, Cleese, Idle, Jones and Palin) *Monty Python's Flying Circus,* BBC, 1968-74. Movies: *Pythons in Deutschland,* Bavaria Atelier, 1971.

BOOKS—(Compiler with Harvey Kurtzman) *Harvey Kurtzman's Fun and Games* (text by Alverson), Fawcett, 1965; (with Joel Siegel) *The Cocktail People* (cartoons), Pisani Press, 1966; ((illustrator) Roger McGough, *Sporting Relations* (poems), Methuen, 1974; (with Lucinda Cowell) *Animations of Mortality* (cartoons), Methuen, 1978; (with Palin) *Time Bandits,* Hutchinson, 1981, also published as *Time Bandits: The Movie Script,* Doubleday, 1981.

Co-author of Monty Python books (with Chapman, Cleese, Idle, Jones, and Palin): *Monty Python's Big Red Book,* Methuen, 1972; (also illustrator, under pseudonym Jerry Gillian, with Peter Brookes) *The Brand New Monty Python Bok* (edited by Idle), Methuen, 1973,

later published as *The Brand New Monty Python Papperbok,* Methuen, 1974; *Monty Python and the Holy Grail (Book),* Methuen, 1977, also published as *Monty Python's Second Film: A First Draft,* Methuen, 1977; *Monty Python's Life of Brian (of Nazareth)* [and] *Montypyhonscrapbook,* Grosset, 1979; *The Complete Works of Shakespeare and Monty Python,* (contains *Monty Python's Big Red Book* and *The Brand New Monty Python Papperbok*), Methuen, 1981; *Monty Python's The Meaning of Life,* Methuen, 1983.

RECORDINGS: ALBUMS—(With Chapman, Cleese, Idle, Jones, and Palin) *The Worst of Monty Python's Flying Circus,* BBC Records, 1969; *Another Monty Python Record,* Charisma, 1970; *Monty Python's Previous Record,* Charisma, 1972; *Monty Python's Matching Tie and Handkerchief,* Charisma, 1973, Arista, 1975; *Monty Python Live at Drury Lane,* Charisma, 1974; *The Album of the Sound Track of the Trailer of the Film "Monty Python and the Holy Grail,"* Arista, 1975; *Monty Python Live at City Center,* Arista, 1976; *Monty Python's Instant Record Collection,* Charisma, 1977; *Monty Python's "Life of Brian,"* Warner Brothers, 1979; *Monty Python's Contractual Obligation Album,* Arista, 1980; *Monty Python's "The Meaning of Life,"* CBS Records, 1983. SINGLES—"Galaxy Song" and "Every Sperm Is Sacred."

AWARDS: Silver Rose Award from Montreux Festival for television series, *Monty Python's Flying Circus,* 1971; co-winner, Golden Palm Award, Cannes Film Festival, 1983, for *Monty Python's The Meaning of Life;* Best Screenplay, Academy Award nomination, 1985, for *Brazil.*

SIDELIGHTS: In a 1982 interview in *Contemporary Authors* (Volume 113, Gale Research Company), Terry Gilliam was asked where the name Monty Python originated: "We really wanted a name that meant nothing, that didn't relate to anything that anybody knew about. . . . [W]e were going on the air and I had to do some animated titles. The last name we had come upon was 'Monty Python's Flying Circus,' and that was the one we settled on."

ADDRESSES: HOME—London, England. OFFICE—14 Neal's Yard, London, WC2, England; Python Pictures, Ltd., 6 Cambridge Gate, London NW1, England.*

*   *   *

GILLIAN, Jerry
See GILLIAM, Terry

*   *   *

GINGOLD, Hermione   1897-1987

OBITUARY NOTICE—See index for *CTFT* sketch: Born Hermione Ferdinanda Gingold, December 9, 1897, in London, England; died at Lenox Hill Hospital, New York City, May 24, 1987. Although Hermione Gingold trained for the stage by acting classical roles in such renowned settings as the Old Vic, the Cambridge Festival Theatre, and London's West End, she was best known to audiences as a sharp-witted and skilled comedienne. The change in genre was due in part to her manager's decision to star her in the 1939 stage comedy *The Gate Revue.* Gingold continued to achieve success in revues, including the long-running *Sweet and Low,* which she performed for thousands of servicemen during World War II. In

1951 she made her U.S. debut starring in *It's About Time* at the Brattle Theatre in Cambridge, MA, and opened on Broadway to rave reviews in *John Murray Anderson's Almanac,* for which she received the Donaldson Award. After these triumphs on the stage, Gingold achieved film success in such Hollywood musicals as *Around the World in 80 Days,* 1956, and *The Music Man,* 1962. Her raspy-voiced duet of "I Remember It Well" with Maurice Chevalier was one of the most popular scenes in the 1958 film *Gigi.* Some of her other films included *Bell, Book, and Candle,* 1958, *Promise Her Anything,* 1966, and her final film, *Garbo Talks,* 1984. Gingold made frequent television appearances on such talk shows as those hosted by Jack Paar and Merv Griffin. Her sometimes ribald, tart-tongued responses to interviewers' questions made her an audience favorite.

OBITUARIES AND OTHER SOURCES: New York Times, May 25, 1987; *Variety,* May 27, 1987.

*   *   *

GIORDANO, Tony   1939-

PERSONAL: Full name, Anthony Giordano; born January 25, 1939, in Brooklyn, NY; son of Vincent and Evelyn Giordano. EDUCATION: Fairfield University, B.A., English literature, 1960; Catholic University, M.A., drama, 1962.

VOCATION: Director.

TONY GIORDANO

CAREER: PRINCIPAL STAGE WORK—Director: *The Chekhov Sketchbook,* Harold Clurman Theatre, New York City, 1980; *The Snow Orchid,* Circle Repertory Theatre, New York City, 1983; *The Day of the Picnic,* Yale Repertory Theatre, New Haven, CT, 1983; *The Further Adventures of Sally,* Pennsylvania Stage Company, Allentown, PA, 1984; *Daughters,* Philadelphia Drama Guild, Philadelphia, PA, 1984; *Glengarry Glen Ross,* Syracuse State Theatre, Syracuse, NY, 1985; *Sally's Gone, She Left Her Name,* Perry Street Theatre, New York City, 1985; *The Tavern,* Dallas Theatre Centre, Dallas, TX, then Trinity Square Repertory Company, Providence, RI, both 1985; *Noises Off, A Funny Thing Happened on the Way to the Forum, Quartermaine's Terms,* all Trinity Square Repertory Company, 1986; *Handy Dandy,* Pasadena Playhouse, CA, then Citadel Theatre, Edmonton, AL, Canada, 1987. Also directed *The Return of Herbert Bracewell, Long Day's Journey into Night,* both Citadel Theatre; *The Glass Menagerie, A View from the Bridge,* both Santa Fe Repertory Company, Santa Fe, NM; *Curse of the Starving Class, Hello and Goodbye,* both Yale Repertory Theatre, New Haven, CT; *On Borrowed Time,* Hartford Stage Company, Hartford, CT; *G.R. Point, Ladyhouse Blues,* both Association of Producing Artists, Phoenix Theatre, New York City.

PRINCIPAL TELEVISION WORK—Both as director. Series: *The Doctors,* NBC; *Another World,* NBC.

PRINCIPAL RADIO WORK—Director, *Earplay,* National Public Radio, 1978-79.

RELATED CAREER—Director, Eugene O'Neill Playwrights Conference, Waterford, CT, 1973-83; associate artistic director, Circle Repertory Company, New York City, 1980-81; adjunct professor, Yale School of Drama, 1982-83; founder, chairman of the board, Manhattan Plaza.

AWARDS: Best Director, Drama Desk Award nomination, for *G.R. Point;* Villager Award, for *The Snow Orchid;* awarded Italy's Grand Cross for cultural service to the U.S.; Catholic University Award for "a distinguished directing career;" National Endowment for the Arts grant.

MEMBER: Society of Stage Directors and Choreographers (executive vice president).

ADDRESSES: HOME—484 W. 43rd Street, New York, NY 10036.

*   *   *

GLASSCO, Bill   1935-

PERSONAL: Born August 30, 1935, in Quebec City, PQ, Canada; son of John Grant and Willa Glassco; divorced from wife, Jane. EDUCATION: Attended Princeton University, Oxford University, and University of Toronto; trained for the stage at New York University School of the Arts.

VOCATION: Director, producer, and writer.

CAREER: FIRST STAGE WORK—Director, *Creeps,* Factory Theatre Lab, Toronto, ON, Canada, 1971. PRINCIPAL STAGE WORK—Director: *Battering Ram, Leaving Home,* and *Forever-Yours, Marie-Lou,* all Tarragon Theatre, Toronto, ON, Canada, 1972; *Of the Fields, Lately,* both Tarragon Theatre, 1973; *You're Gonna Be*

Alright, Jamie Boy, Tarragon Theatre, 1974; *Hosanna,* Tarragon Theatre, then Bijou Theatre, New York City, both 1974; *One Crack Out, Bonjour, la, Bonjour,* both Tarragon Theatre, 1975; *Jitters,* Tarragon Theatre, 1979, then Walnut Street Theatre, Philadelphia, PA, 1981; *Damnee Manon, Sacree Sandra,* both Tarragon Theatre, 1979; *The Impromptu of Outremont,* Tarragon Theatre, 1980. Also directed *Le Temps d' Une Vie,* Tarragon Theatre, and productions at the Stratford Festival Theatre, Stratford, ON, Canada, the Vancouver Playhouse, Vancouver, BC, Canada, and at the Long Wharf Theatre, New Haven, CT.

RELATED CAREER—Founder, artistic director, Tarragon Theatre, Toronto, ON, Canada.

WRITINGS: PLAYS—See production details above unless indicated. Translator, all with John van Burek: *Forever-Yours, Marie-Lou,* 1972; *Hosanna,* 1974; *Bonjour, la, Bonjour,* 1975; *La Belles Soeurs,* North Light Repertory Theatre, Evanston, IL, 1982.

ADDRESSES: OFFICE—171 Robert Street, Toronto M5S 2K6, ON, Canada.*

*   *   *

GLEASON, Jackie   1916-1987

PERSONAL: Full name, Herbert John Gleason; born February 26, 1916, in Brooklyn, NY; son of Herb (an insurance auditor) and Mae (a subway change-booth attendant) Gleason; died June 24, 1987, of cancer, in Fort Lauderdale, FL; married Genevieve Halford, 1936 (divorced 1971); married Beverly McKittrick, July 4, 1971 (divorced 1974); married Marilyn Taylor; children: (first marrage) Geraldine, Linda.

VOCATION: Actor, comedian, composer, and conductor.

CAREER: PRINCIPAL TELEVISION APPEARANCES—Episodic: "No No Nanette," *Musical Comedy Time,* NBC, 1950; "The Laugh Maker," *Studio One,* CBS, 1953. Series: Chester A. Riley, *The Life of Riley,* NBC, 1949-50; emcee, *Cavalcade of Stars,* DuMont Television Network, 1950-52; host and creator of many characters including Reggie Van Gleason III, the Poor Soul, Joe the Bartender, Fenwick Babbit, Charley Bratten the Loudmouth, Ralph Kramden, *The Jackie Gleason Show,* CBS, 1952-55, 1957-59, 1966-70; Ralph Kramden, *The Honeymooners,* CBS, 1955-56; emcee, *You're in the Picture,* CBS, 1961. Movies: Isadore "Izzy" Einstein, *Izzy & Moe,* CBS, 1985; also appeared in *Mr. Halpern & Mr. Johnson,* HBO, 1983.

PRINCIPAL TELEVISION WORK—Producer, *Stage Show,* CBS, 1954-56.

PRINCIPAL FILM APPEARANCES—Tubby, *Navy Blues,* Warner Brothers, 1941; Hobart, *Larceny, Inc.,* Warner Brothers, 1942; Starchie, *All Through the Night,* Warner Brothers, 1942; Beck, *Orchestra Wives,* Twentieth Century-Fox, 1942; Dan's agent, *Springtime in the Rockies,* Twentieth Century-Fox, 1942; Hank, *Tramp, Tramp, Tramp,* Columbia, 1942; Aladdin, *The Desert Hawk,* Universal, 1950; Minnesota Fats, *The Hustler,* Twentieth Century-Fox, 1961; title role, *Gigot,* Twentieth Century-Fox, 1962; Maish Rennier, *Requiem for a Heavyweight,* Columbia, 1962; Jack "Papa" Griffith, *Papa's Delicate Condition,* Paramount, 1963; Maxwell Slaughter, *Soldier in the Rain,* Allied

Artists, 1963; Tony Banks, *Skidoo,* Paramount, 1968; Walter Hollander, *Don't Drink the Water,* AVCO-Embassy, 1969; Oliver Poe, *How to Commit Marriage,* Cinerama, 1969; Stanley Waltz, *How Do I Love Thee?,* Cinerama, 1970; John Cutler, *Mr. Billion,* Twentieth Century-Fox, 1977; Sheriff Buford T. Justice, *Smokey and the Bandit,* Universal, 1977; Sheriff Buford T. Justice, Reginald Van Justice, Gaylord Van Justice, *Smokey and the Bandit II,* Universal, 1980; U.S. Bates, *The Toy,* Columbia, 1982; Sheriff Buford T. Justice, *Smokey and the Bandit, Part III,* Universal, 1983; Gondorff, *The Sting II,* Universal, 1983. Also appeared in *Nothing in Common,* Tri-Star, 1986.

PRINCIPAL STAGE APPEARANCES—Uncle Sid, *Take Me Along,* Shubert Theatre, New York City, 1959-60. Also appeared in *Hellzapoppin',* 46th Street Theatre, New York City, 1938; *Keep Off the Grass,* Broadhurst Theatre, New York City, 1940; *Artists and Models,* Broadway Theatre, New York City, 1943; *Follow the Girls,* Century Theatre, New York City, 1944; *Along Fifth Avenue,* 1949; *Sly Fox,* 1978.

PRINCIPAL CABARET APPEARANCES—Stand-up comedian, Billy Rose's Diamond Horseshoe.

PRINCIPAL RADIO APPEARANCES—*Old Gold Radio Show,* NBC.

RELATED CAREER—Carnival barker and emcee.

WRITINGS: SCREENPLAYS—*Gigot,* Twentieth Century-Fox, 1962. TELEPLAYS—*The Million Dollar Incident.* TELEVISION SCORES—*Izzy and Moe,* CBS, 1985; also *The Million Dollar Incident;* composed and conducted movie and television theme songs, including "Melancholy Serenade," 1953, for *The Jackie Gleason Show,* and "The Honeymooners," for *The Honeymooners.*

RECORDINGS: With the Jackie Gleason Orchestra, recorded more than thirty-five albums, including *Lazy Lively Love, Lover's Rhapsody, Lonesome Echo, Tawny,* and *Oooo!.*

AWARDS: Best Comedian of the Year, *TV Guide,* 1952; Best Comedian, *Fame* poll, 1953; Best Comedy Show, *Fame* poll, 1954, for *The Jackie Gleason Show;* Best Actor, Antoinette Perry Award, for *Take Me Along,* 1959; Academy Award nomination, 1961, for *The Hustler;* elected to the Television Hall of Fame, 1985.

SIDELIGHTS: The six decades of Jackie Gleason's performing career included acclaimed appearances in nightclubs, on stage, and in films, but it was on television during the 1950's and 60's that he established himself as "the Great One." In the 1954-55 season, his hour-long series *The Jackie Gleason Show* achieved a 42.4 Nielsen rating, meaning that nearly half of the households in the country were tuning in to see the variety of amusing and endearing characters created by its star. Audienced particularly loved the "everyman" character of Ralph Kramden, a bus driver who lived in a tiny Brooklyn apartment with his wife, Alice (played by Audrey Meadows), and had numerous misadventures with his neighbor Ed Norton (Art Carney). The skits involving these characters proved so popular that a separate series, *The Honeymooners,* was created around them. The spinoff endured in syndication, winning new generations of fans—so much so that in 1984, nearly twenty years after the show originally aired, a convention of R.A.L.P.H. (the Royal Association for the Longevity and Preservation of the Honeymooners) drew over two thousand attendees and by 1987 the organization claimed over 12,000 members.

OBITUARIES AND OTHER SOURCES: Donna McCrohan, *The Honeymooners Companion,* Workman, 1978; *The New York Times,* June 25, 1987; *Variety,* July 1, 1987.*

*   *   *

GLEASON, John   1941-

PERSONAL: Born April 10, 1941, in Brooklyn, NY; son of John and Sue (Manzolillo) Gleason. EDUCATION: Attended Hunter College.

VOCATION: Lighting designer and writer.

CAREER: FIRST STAGE WORK—Lighting designer, *Tartuffe,* Repertory Theatre of Lincoln Center, New York City, 1965. PRINCIPAL STAGE WORK—Lighting designer, all in New York City unless indicated: *La Grosse Valise,* 54th Street Theatre, 1965; *Father Uxbridge Wants to Marry,* American Place Theatre, 1967; *Lovers and Other Strangers,* Brooks Atkinson Theatre, 1968; *The Great White Hope,* Alvin Theatre, 1968; *We Bombed in New Haven,* Ambassador Theatre, 1968; *A Midsummer Night's Dream,* Stratford Festival Theatre, Stratford, ON, Canada, 1968; *Cop Out/ Home Fires,* Cort Theatre, 1969; *Hamlet,* Lunt-Fontanne Theatre, 1969; *The Alchemist, Hamlet,* both Stratford Festival Theatre, 1969.

Lighting designer, all in New York City unless indicated: *Brightower,* John Golden Theatre, 1970; *Candida,* Longacre Theatre, 1970; *Othello,* American National Theatre Academy (ANTA) Playhouse, 1970; *Two by Two,* Imperial Theatre, 1970; *Songs from Milkwood,* National Theatre of the Deaf, ANTA Playhouse, 1970; *Hamlet, All's Well That Ends Well, Othello, The Devil's Disciple,* all American Shakespeare Festival, Stratford, CT, 1970; *Frank Merriwell,* Longacre Theatre, 1971; *The Tempest, The Merry Wives of Windsor, Mourning Becomes Electra,* all American Shakespeare Festival, 1971; *Love Suicide at the Schofield Barracks,* ANTA Playhouse, 1972; *Tough to Get Help,* Royale Theatre, 1972; *Small Craft Warnings,* Truck and Warehouse Theatre, 1972; *Veronica's Room,* Music Box Theatre, 1973; *A Streetcar Named Desire,* St. James Theatre, 1973; *The Pajama Game,* Lunt-Fontanne Theatre, 1973; *A Delicate Balance, A Streetcar Named Desire, A Raisin in the Sun, Kiss Me Kate, Old Times,* all Playhouse in the Park, Cincinnati, OH, 1973; *Lorelei,* Palace Theatre, 1974; *Over Here,* Shubert Theatre, 1974; *Perfect Pitch,* Eisenhower Theatre, Washington, DC, 1974; *Harvey, Travelers, Arsenic and Old Lace, Tartuffe,* and *Monkey, Monkey, Bottle of Beer,* all Playhouse in the Park, 1974; *Savages,* Mark Taper Forum, Los Angeles, CA, 1974; *Present Laughter, The Scarecrow, The Royal Family,* all Eisenhower Theatre, 1975; *Oh Coward!, Hot l Baltimore, That Championship Season,* all Playhouse in the Park, 1975; *Le Nozze Di Figaro* (opera), Manhattan School of Music, 1975; *The Four Temperaments, Le Sacre Du Printemps, The Life of the Bee, Dance for Six, Reflections in "D"* (ballets), all New Dance Group/Danscompany, 1975; *My Fair Lady,* Lunt-Fontanne Theatre, 1976; *Herzl,* Palace Theatre, 1976; *The Duchess of Malfi,* Mark Taper Forum, 1976; *Savages,* Hudson Guild Theatre, 1977; *Boris Godunov* (opera), Greater Miami Opera, Miami, FL, 1977; *Il Quattro Rusteghi,* Manhattan School of Music, 1977; *Macbeth* (opera), Dallas Civic Opera, Dallas, TX, 1977; *Angel,* Minskoff Theatre, 1978; *The Dodge Boys,* Hudson Guild Theatre, 1978; *Adriana Lecouvreur,* Greater Maimi Opera, 1978; *The Ballad of Baby Doe,* Dallas Civic Opera, 1978; *Getting Out,* Mark Taper Forum, 1978; *Crimes of the*

Heart, Center Stage, Baltimore, MD, 1979; *Manon Lescaut* (opera), Dallas Civic Opera, 1979.

Lighting designer, all in New York City unless indicated: *The Stitch in Time,* ANTA Playhouse, 1980; *The Philadelphia Story,* Vivian Beaumont Theater, 1980; *Really Rosie,* Chelsea Theatre Centre, then American Place Theatre, 1980; *The Lady and the Clarinet,* Mark Taper Forum, Los Angeles, CA, 1980; *Peter Grimes* (opera), Dallas Civic Opera, Dallas, TX, 1980; *The Survivor,* Morosco Theatre, 1981; *An Evening with Dave Allen,* Booth Theatre, 1981; *The Playboy of the Western World* (ballet), Irish Ballet, City Center Theatre, 1981; *Macbeth,* Vivian Beaumont Theatre, 1981; *Madame Butterfly* (opera), Dallas Civic Opera, 1981; *Black Angel,* Circle Repertory Theatre, 1982; *Number Our Days,* Mark Taper Forum, 1982; *Der Rosenkavalier* (opera), Dallas Civic Opera, 1982; *The Guys in the Truck,* New Apollo Theatre, 1983; *The Mikado,* New York City Opera, State Theatre, 1984, then 1985; *Enter a Free Man,* Perry Street Theatre, 1984; *Il Trittico,* Juilliard School of Music, 1984; *Don Giovanni* (opera), *La Nozze di Figaro* (opera), both Juilliard School of Music, 1986; *Werther* (opera), New York City Opera, State Theatre, 1986; *Albert Herring, Amelia al Ballo, Tamu Tamu, Jakob Lenz,* all Juilliard School of Music, 1987; *The Magic Flute* (opera), New York City Opera, State Theatre, 1987; *Beatrice and Benedict, A Midsummer Night's Dream,* both Juilliard School of Music, 1988. Also as lighting designer, all in New York City: *The Porcelain Year,* 1965; *The Woman,* 1973; *Who's Who in Hell, All Over Town,* both 1974; *Don't Call Back, Hello Dolly, Truckload,* all 1975; *Flowers,* 1975; *The Royal Family, Monty Python Live, An Evening with Diana Ross,* all 1976; *The Merry Widow* (ballet), Australian Ballet; *Let My People Come,* 1976; *Platinum, Halloween Bandit, Algonquin Sampler,* all 1978; *Sidewalkin' Bread and Circus,* 1980.

All as lighting designer with the Repertory Theatre of Lincoln Center, New York City: *The Alchemist,* Vivian Beaumont Theatre, 1966; *Saint Joan, Tiger at the Gates, Cyrano de Bergerac, King Lear, A Cry of Players,* all Vivian Beaumont Theatre, 1968; *Walking To Waldheim and Happiness, Summertree, Bananas, An Evening for Merlin Finch,* all Forum Theatre, 1968; *Inner Journey, The Year Boston Won the Pennant, The Increased Difficulty of Concentration, The Time of Your Life,* all Vivian Beaumont Theatre, 1969; *Camino Real, Operation Sidewinder, Beggar on Horseback, The Good Woman of Setzuan,* all Vivian Beaumont Theatre, 1970; *The Disintegration of James Cherry, Landscape and Silence, Amphitryon,* all Forum Theatre, 1970; *The Playboy of the Western World, An Enemy of the People, Antigone, Mary Stuart,* all Vivian Beaumont Theatre, 1971; *The Birthday Party, Pictures in the Hallway, Play Strindberg, People Are Living There,* all Forum Theatre, 1971; *Narrow Road to the Deep North, Twelfth Night, Enemies,* all Vivian Beaumont Theatre, 1972; *The Ride across Lake Constance, Duplex, Suggs in the City, Happy Days, Act without Words, Not I, Krapp's Last Tape,* all Forum Theatre, 1972; *The Plough and the Stars, A Streetcar Named Desire,* both Vivian Beaumont Theatre, 1973.

MAJOR TOURS—Lighting designer, *In the Matter of J. Robert Oppenheimer,* U.S. cities, 1969; also lighting designer for National Theatre of the Deaf tour of U.S. cities, 1968.

RELATED CAREER—Resident lighting designer: Eugene O'Neill Theatre Center, National Theatre of the Deaf, Repertory Theater of Lincoln Center, Cincinnati Playhouse in the Park, Dallas Civic Opera; assistant chairor of the design department and teacher, lighting design and cinematography courses, Tisch School of the Arts, New York University.

WRITINGS: SCREENPLAYS—*Over Due; Needing You; Final Cut.* NON-FICTION—Contributing editor, *Lighting Dimensions.*

AWARDS: Maharam Design Award, 1973; Los Angeles Drama Critics Circle Award, 1973, for *Savages.*

MEMBER: International Alliance of Theatrical Stage Employees and Motion Picture Camera Operators.

SIDELIGHTS: RECREATIONS—Painting, photography, reading, music.

ADDRESSES: HOME—170 W. 73rd Street, New York, NY 10023.

*   *   *

GLOVER, Danny   1947-

PERSONAL: Born in 1947, in Georgia (some sources say San Francisco, CA); son of postal workers; wife's name, Asake; children: Mandisa. EDUCATION: Graduated from San Francisco State College, economics; trained for the stage at American Conservatory Theatre's Black Actors' Workshop.

VOCATION: Actor.

CAREER: FILM DEBUT—*Escape from Alcatraz,* Paramount, 1979. PRINCIPAL FILM APPEARANCES—Morgan, *Chu Chu and the Philly Flash,* Twentieth Century-Fox, 1981; Loomis, *Iceman,* Universal, 1984; Moze, *Places in the Heart,* Tri-Star, 1984; Mal, *Silverado,* Columbia, 1985; James McFee, *Witness,* Paramount, 1985; Mister, *The Color Purple,* Warner Brothers, 1985; Roger Murtaugh, *Lethal Weapon,* Warner Brothers, 1987. Also *Out,* Cinegate, 1982; *Birdy,* Tri-Star, 1984; *Bat 21,* 1988.

OFF-BROADWAY DEBUT—Zachariah, *The Blood Knot,* Roundabout Theatre, 1980. BROADWAY DEBUT—Willie, *Master Harold . . . and the boys,* Lyceum Theatre, 1982. PRINCIPAL STAGE APPEARANCES—*The Island,* Eureka Theatre, San Francisco, CA; *Sizwe Banzi Is Dead, Macbeth,* both Actors Theatre, Los Angeles, CA; *Suicide in B Flat,* Magic Theatre, San Francisco; also, *Nevis Mountain Dew,* Los Angeles; *Jukebox,* Oakland, CA.

PRINCIPAL TELEVISION APPEARANCES—Episodic: *Hill Steet Blues,* NBC; *Lou Grant,* CBS; *Gimme a Break,* NBC; *Palmerstown, USA,* CBS; *B.J. and the Bear,* NBC; *Many Mansions,* PBS. Mini-Series: Marshall Peters, *Chiefs,* CBS, 1983. Movies: Gary, *The Face of Rage,* ABC, 1983; Nelson Mandela, *Mandela,* HBO, 1987.

NON-RELATED CAREER—Researcher, Mayor's office, San Francisco, CA, 1971-75; also worked for planning agency in Berkeley, CA.

AWARDS: Theatre World Award, 1982, for *Master Harold . . . and the boys.*

ADDRESSES: HOME—San Francisco, CA. AGENT—Writers and Artists Agency, 11726 San Vincente Boulevard, Suite 300, Los Angeles, CA 90049.*

GODFREY, Lynnie

PERSONAL: Full name, Caroline Godfrey; born September 11, in New York City; daughter of Fred and Maggie Mae (a caterer; maiden name, Wood) Godfrey; married Carl E. Lee (a financial analyst), June 10, 1979. EDUCATION: Received B.A., theatre, communications, and music, from Hunter College.

VOCATION: Actress, singer, and director.

CAREER: STAGE DEBUT—Vicky, *Juice Problem,* O'Neill Playwrights Conference, Waterford, CT. OFF-BROADWAY DEBUT—Belle, *Ragtime Blues,* AMAS Repertory Theatre. BROADWAY DEBUT—Member of company, *Eubie!,* Ambassador Theatre, 1978. PRINCIPAL STAGE APPEARANCES—Edna Walter, *Two Fish in the Sky,* Theatre at St. Peter's Church, New York City, 1982; Miss Bethesda, *Body Parts,* Ohio Theatre, New York City, 1983. Also Beverly, *Rock Festival,* Empire State Institute for the Performing Arts (ESIPA), Albany, NY; Alberta, *Take One Step,* Great Lakes Theatre Festival, Cleveland, OH; Jenny Diver, *The Threepenny Opera,* ESIPA; Lola, *Damn Yankees,* Hartford Stage Company, Hartford, CT; Azuri, *Desert Song,* Pittsburgh Civic Light Opera, Pittsburgh, PA; Elaine, *Nature and Purpose,* Direct Theatre, New York City. Appeared in *1,000 Years of Jazz,* Los Angeles Music Center, Los Angeles, CA; *If This Ain't It,* WPA Theatre, New York City; *Shuffle Along,* Theatre-Off-Park, New York City; *I Paid My Dues,* Astor Place Theatre, New York City; *A . . . My Name Is Alice,* American Place Theatre, New York City; *Knickerbocker Follies,* ESIPA; *Sweet Charity,* Starlight Theatre.

LYNNIE GODFREY

PRINCIPAL STAGE WORK—Director, *To Be Young, Gifted, and Black,* Theatre-Off-Park, New York City, 1981.

MAJOR TOURS—Woman #1, #2, #3, *Ain't Misbehavin'*, eastern U.S. cities; Josephine Baker, *Absurdities,* European cities.

PRINCIPAL TELEVISION APPEARANCES—Episodic: *One Life to Live,* ABC. Specials: *The Tony Awards,* CBS; *Eubie!,* Showtime; *Memories of Eubie,* PBS. Guest: *The Merv Griffin Show,* syndicated; *Good Morning America,* ABC; *The Joe Franklin Show,* WOR; *Midday Live,* WNEW, New York.

FILM DEBUT—Althea Cole, *Enemy Territory,* 1986.

RELATED CAREER—Performed at "Lyrics and Lyricists" series, Young Men's Hebrew Association, New York City, as well as in nightclubs, television commercials, and industrial films; National Advisory Council of the Empire State Institute for the Performing Arts.

MEMBER: Actors' Equity Association, Screen Actors Guild, American Federation of Television and Radio Artists.

SIDELIGHTS: RECREATIONS—Collects large-gauge toy trains.

ADDRESSES: AGENT—Peggy Grant Associates, Inc., 1650 Broadway, Suite 711, New York, NY 10019.

*   *   *

GOOCH, Steve   1945-

PERSONAL: Born July 22, 1945, in Surrey, England. EDUCATION: Trinty College, Cambridge University, B.A. (with honors), French and German, 1967; graduate work, St. Johns College, Cambridge University, 1967-68, then University of Birmingham, 1968-69.

VOCATION: Playwright and director.

CAREER: Also see *WRITINGS* below. PRINCIPAL STAGE WORK—Director, *Night Shift,* Theatre Venture, 1983; also directed plays by Writer's Workshop and West London Theatre Workshop students.

RELATED CAREER—Free-lance writer and stage director, 1969-72; assistant editor, *Plays and Players,* London, 1972-73; organized writing workshop, Half Moon Theatre, 1977; co-founder, editor, *Platform,* 1979. Resident playwright: Half Moon Theatre, London, 1973-74; Greenwich Theatre, London, 1974-75; Solent People's Theatre, 1982; Theatre Venture, 1986; Warehouse Theatre, Croyden, U.K., 1986. Teacher: Drama course, Essex University; playwriting courses, Royal Academy of Dramatic Art, Goldsmiths, City Lit, University of Kent, and Smith College.

WRITINGS: PLAYS—(Adaptor) *Great Expectations,* Liverpool Playhouse, Liverpool, U.K., 1970; (translator) *Man Is Man,* Royal Court Theatre, London, 1971; (translator) *Big Wolf,* Royal Court Theatre, 1972, published by Davis Poynter, 1972; (translator) *The Mother,* Half Moon Theatre, London, 1972, published by Eyre Methuen, 1978; (translator) *It's All for the Best,* Victoria Theatre, Stoke-on-Trent, U.K., 1972; *Will Wat: If Not, What Will,* Half Moon Theatre, 1972, published by Pluto Press, 1975; *Nick,* Northcott Theatre, Exeter, U.K., 1972; *Dick,* Half Moon Theatre, 1973;

Female Transport, Half Moon Theatre, 1973, then New York City, 1976, published by Pluto Press, 1975; (with Paul Thompson) *The Motor Show,* Dagenham, U.K., then Half Moon Theatre, 1974, published by Pluto Press, 1975; (translator) *Cock-Artist,* Almost Free Theatre, London, 1974, published in *Gambit 39-40,* John Calder, 1979; (with Frank McDermott) *Strike '26,* Popular Theatre, tour of U.K. cities, 1975; (with Thompson) *Made in Britain,* Oxford Playhouse, Oxford, U.K., 1976; *Our Land, Our Lives,* 7:84 Touring Theatre Company, U.K. cities, 1976; *Back Street Romeo,* Half Moon Theatre, 1977; (translator) *Rosie,* Half Moon Theatre, 1977; *The Women-Pirates Ann Bonney and Mary Read,* Royal Shakespeare Company, Aldwych Theatre, London, 1978, published by Pluto Press, 1978; *Floatsam,* published in *Gambit 39-40,* John Caler, 1979; *Landmark,* Essex University, Essex, U.K., 1980, published by Theatre Action Press, 1980; *Fast One,* produced and published by Solent People's Theatre, 1982; (adaptor) *Fuente Oeujuna,* Theatre Venture, Tom Allen Centre, London, 1982; *Taking Liberties,* Theatre Venture, 1984; *Good for You,* Phoenix Theatre, Leicester, U.K., 1985; *Mister Fun,* Metro Theatre Company, tour of U.K. cities, 1986; *Star Turns,* Warehouse Theatre, Croyden, U.K., 1987. Also wrote *How the Peace Was Lost, Passed On, What Brothers Are For, In the Club,* and translated *Home Work, Trumpets and Drums, Public Relations, Future Perfect.*

RADIO PLAYS—Translator: *The Kiosk,* 1970; *Delinquent,* 1978; *Santis,* 1980; *If It's What They Want,* 1984; *Bill of Health,* 1987.

TELEPLAYS—*The Women-Pirates Ann Bonney and Mary Read,* Thames, 1974.

NON-FICTION—(Translator) *Wolf Biermann: Poems and Ballads,* Pluto Press, 1977; (translator) *Wallraff: The Undesirable Journalist,* Pluto Press, 1978; *All Together Now,* Eyre Methuen, 1984.

AWARDS: Arts Council of Great Britain scholarship, 1973; Thames Television award, 1974, for *The Women-Pirates Ann Bonney and Mary Read.*

MEMBER: Theatre Writers Union.

ADDRESSES: AGENT—c/o Margaret Ramsay, Ltd., 14-A Goodwin's Court, London WC2N 4LL, England.

*   *   *

GORCEY, Elizabeth   1965-

PERSONAL: Full name, Elizabeth Ann Gorcey; born January 1, 1965, in Long Branch, NJ; daughter of Bernard (an electrical engineer) and Ruth Hilda (Marcus) Gorcey. EDUCATION: Attended the University of Arizona and Monmouth College; trained for the stage at the American Conservatory Theatre. RELIGION: Jewish.

VOCATION: Actress and producer.

CAREER: PRINCIPAL STAGE APPEARANCES—*Mango Tea,* Skylight Theatre, Los Angeles, CA, 1987; also appeared in *Carousel, Spoon River Anthology, Birdbath, Snow White and the Seven Dwarfs,* all Barn Theatre, Augusta, MI; and in *The Children's Hour; Seduced.* PRINCIPAL STAGE WORK—Producer, *Sleeping Beauty: Not the Fairytale, Mango Tea,* both Skylight Theatre, 1987.

ELIZABETH GORCEY

FILM DEBUT—June, *Kidco,* Twentieth Century-Fox, 1984. PRINCIPAL FILM APPEARANCES—Wendy Jo, *Footloose,* Paramount, 1984; Bonnie, *Grandview, USA,* Warner Brothers, 1984; Haley Dibble, *The Trouble with Dick,* Frolix Productions, 1987; also appeared in *Blizzard,* American Video Productions, 1987.

PRINCIPAL TELEVISION APPEARANCES—Episodic: *Max Headroom,* ABC, 1987; *The New Mike Hammer,* CBS; *Highway to Heaven,* NBC. Series: *3-2-1 Contact,* PBS, 1983. Movies: *Pecos Bill,* HBO.

RELATED CAREER—Mezzo-soprano, Metrolyric Opera Company.

NON-RELATED CAREER—Licensed real estate agent.

MEMBER: Actors' Equity Association, Screen Actors Guild, American Federation of Television and Radio Artists; American Film Institute; Smithsonian Associates; People Assisting the Homeless; Los Angeles World Affairs Council.

SIDELIGHTS: CTFT learned that while working on the PBS series *3-2-1 Contact,* Elizabeth Gorcey performed her own stunts including hang-gliding and aero-acrobatics.

ADDRESSES: AGENT—c/o Abrams Artists & Associates, Ltd., 9200 Sunset Boulevard, Los Angeles, CA 90069. PUBLICIST—c/o Michael Levine Public Relations Company, 967 N. La Cienega Boulevard, Los Angeles, CA 90069.

GORDY, Berry, Jr.   1929-

PERSONAL: Born 1929, in Detroit, MI; son of Berry Gordy (a plasterer) and his wife (an insurance agent); married; children: Berry IV, Hazel Joy, Terry James, Kerry A., Kennedy W., Stefan K. MILITARY: U.S. Army, 1953-53; served in Korea.

VOCATION: Record company executive, songwriter, film producer, and director.

CAREER: PRINCIPAL RECORDING WORK—Founder, Motown Industries, Inc. (founded as Hitsville, U.S.A., 1961); producer for such groups and singers as the Temptations, the Supremes, Marvin Gaye, Smokey Robinson, the Jackson Five, Stevie Wonder, and Diana Ross; expanded into music publishing, personal management, and film, television, and stage production.

PRINCIPAL FILM WORK—Producer, *Lady Sings the Blues,* Paramount, 1972; producer and director, *Mahogany,* Paramount, 1975; producer, *Bingo Long Traveling All-Stars and Motor Kings,* Universal, 1976; executive producer, *Almost Summer,* 1978; producer, *The Wiz,* Universal, 1978; executive producer, *The Last Dragon,* Tri-Star, 1985.

NON-RELATED CAREER—Professional featherweight boxer and auto assembly worker before entering the recording and producing industries.

WRITINGS: SINGLES—Co-writer: "Shop Around," "Lonely Teardrops," "Reet Peteet," "To Be Loved," "That's Why (I Love You So)," "I'll Be Satisfied," "You Got What It Takes," "Money (That's What I Want)," others.

AWARDS: Business Achievement Award, Interracial Council for Business Opportunity, 1967; Outstanding Contribution to the Music Industry, Second Annual American Music Award, 1975; named one of five Leading Entrepreneurs of the Nation, Babson College, 1978; Whitney M. Young, Jr. Award, Los Angeles Urban League, 1980; Gordon Grand Fellow, Yale University, 1985.

MEMBER: Directors Guild of America.

SIDELIGHTS: Berry Gordy, Jr. heads the largest black-owned business in the United States. His brainchild, Motown Industries, earns more than $100 million annually; it has long been a profitable trend-setter in the highly competitive recording industry. Nearly thirty years after he founded it, Gordy presides over the company in the same way he did when he started the operation in a run-down rowhouse in Detroit. Many of pop music's biggest stars—Smokey Robinson, Diana Ross, Stevie Wonder, Michael Jackson, and Lionel Richie—first came to fame for their recordings on the Motown label, and the music itself is praised for its exuberant appeal that cuts across racial lines. As Bill Barol noted in a *Newsweek* article of May 23, 1983, Motown "goes on and on. . . . It really *was* the Sound of Young America through much of the 1960s, instantly recognizable on a car radio or hi-fi: it was sweet but soulful, polished but nakedly emotional. And always, without fail, there was the beat." Of Motown's creator the reporter concluded, "Gordy's true genius was to recognize that, above all, young America—black and white—wanted to *dance.*"

America is still dancing to Motown music. The company has amassed more than 110 number one hits since its inception. This is even more astonishing when Motown's size is compared to industry giants such as Columbia or Atlantic Records. Gordy, however, has never been willing to rest on past achievements. Once a songwriter, then a determined entrepreneur, he has diversified his entertainment empire to include music publishing, talent scouting, and film and television production. In a September 1, 1967 *Fortune* profile, Stanley H. Brown suggested that with only the "most cursory" background in business, Gordy has "managed to fashion an organization whose premises, personnel, and relations with talent, tough unorthodox, have been effective and profitable."

Gordy was born and raised in Detroit. He told *Fortune* that he learned business techniques "through osmosis"—both his parents were self-employed, his father as a plasterer, his mother as an insurance salesperson. An unenthusiastic student, Gordy dropped out of high school in the eleventh grade, intending to pursue a boxing career. Betwee 1948 and 1951 he fought fifteen Golden Gloves bouts, winning twelve of them, but he was drafted and sent to Korea, where he served until 1953. After being discharged from the army, Gordy returned to Detroit and used his service pay and a loan from his father to open a record store, the Three-D Record Mart. The business failed in a short time, and Gordy was forced to seek work. He helped his father for a while, then took a job on the Ford Motor Company assembly line. He said that to keep from going crazy on his eight-hour shift, he would compose songs in his head, then write them down after hours. Decca Records bought two of these compositions, "Reet Peteet" and "Way Over There." Both achieved modest success, but Gordy discovered that his royalty payments were miniscule in comparison to what the record companies made on his work.

On the advice of another songwriter, William Robinson, Gordy decided to produce records under his own label, thereby keeping his rights to a far bigger share of the profits. He borrowed another sum from his father and formed Motown, though the company was first known as Hitsville, U.S.A. The first song published by Motown was "Shop Around," written and sung by William Robinson, who would soon be better known as Smokey Robinson. The record sold more than a million copies in 1960, and Motown was firmly established. Gordy kept the business in Detroit, renting a series of buildings on West Grand Boulevard, and he recruited talent from the choirs and schools in the neighborhood. The Supremes—Diana Ross, Florence Ballard, and Mary Wilson—came to Gordy right out of high school; they soon became his most recognized group. Gordy also worked with Marvin Gaye, the Four Tops, the Temptations, and the Jackson Five, to name only a few. He brought a high degree of perfectionism to what he called "the Motown sound," beat-laden rhythm-and-blues music marketed for teenagers of all races.

Motown was grossing $30 million by 1967 and analysts discerned several distinguishing characteristics to Gordy's operation. First, it was located in Detroit until 1970, and even after the move to Los Angeles, it was still situated in modest office buildings and studios. Second, Gordy hired his whole family, including his parents, brothers, sisters, and in-laws. Third, Gordy took immense personal interest in his performing artists; he founded a Motown subsidiary, International Talent Management, to teach his singers everything from proper table manners and personal grooming to investment strategies and how to pay taxes. A firm believer in quality at the expense of quantity, Gordy released as few as one or two singles a week—the industry average was five—but three out of four of his made the charts. According to Brown, Gordy's "somewhat isolated, tightly knit group . . . created an idiom close to the mainstream and yet with a distinctive family sound of its own."

In 1972 Gordy began a corollary career. He produced *Lady Sings the Blues,* a film about jazz singer Billie Holiday that starred Diana Ross. The movie was an immense success, both critically and commercially. Encouraged by the reception to that work, Gordy then directed and produced *Mahogany,* also with Ross in the lead. Critics panned the film, although it did well at theatres. An October 27, 1975 *Time* article suggested that the receipts alone made Gordy "the most powerful new director in the business." Gordy bowed out of directing, however, and has since remained content to act as producer. His most recent notable work was *The Wiz,* a sleeper hit that found bigger audiences after one of its players, Michael Jackson, became a music superstar. Gordy told *Newsweek* that he plans to continue producing films, but they are not his top priority. As Barol noted, even though Motown is "a diversified entertainment conglomerate," its name means "one thing only: music with 'the funky beat and the real good feeling.' "

Gordy has been described as autocratic, ostentatious, and sometimes even rude. Few would quarrel, however, with the quality and durability of his primary product, American popular music. As a successful black businessman, he is often both the recipient of prestigious awards and the object of careful case studies. One of his competitors, Atlantic Records chairman Ahmet Ertegun summed up Motown's and Gordy's success when he told *Newsweek,* "They make the records they know how to make, and they still make them better than anyone else."

ADDRESSES: HOME—Bel Air, CA. OFFICE—Motown Record Corporation, 6255 Sunset Boulevard, Los Angeles, CA 90028.*

*　　　*　　　*

GOTTLIEB, Morton　1921-

PERSONAL: Full name, Morton Edgar Gottlieb; born May 2, 1921, in Brooklyn, NY; son of Joseph William and Hilda (Newman) Gottlieb. EDUCATION: Yale University, B.A., 1941.

VOCATION: Producer, manager, actor, and press representative.

CAREER: STAGE DEBUT—Singer, *Go Home,* Brooklyn Academy of Music, Brooklyn, NY. PRINCIPAL STAGE APPEARANCES—*Liberty Jones,* Shubert Theatre, New Haven, CT.

PRINCIPAL STAGE WORK—All in New York City unless indicated: Press representative, *Pygmalion,* Ethel Barrymore Theatre, 1945; assistant business manager, *Dream Girl,* Coronet Theatre, 1945; assistant business manager, *Joan of Lorraine,* Alvin Theatre, 1946; company manager, *Eastward in Eden,* Royale Theatre, 1947; business manager, *Lamp at Midnight,* New Stages Theatre, 1947; business manager, *The Respectful Prostitute,* New Stages Theatre, then Cort Theatre, 1948; business manager, *To Tell You the Truth,* New Stages Theatre, 1948; general manager, *Edward, My Son,* Martin Beck Theatre, 1948; general manager, *An Enemy of the People,* Broadhurst Theatre, 1950: general manager, *Gigi,* Fulton Theatre, 1951; general manager, *Caesar and Cleopatra, Antony and Cleopatra,* both Ziegfeld Theatre, 1951; general manager, *Horses in Midstream,* Royale Theatre, 1953; company manager, *The Traveling Lady,* Playhouse Theatre, 1954; company manager, *Tea and Sympathy,* Ethel Barrymore Theatre, 1954; producer, *His and Hers,* 48th Street Theatre, 1954; company manager: *The Sleeping Prince,* Coronet Theatre, 1956; company manager, *The Rope Dancers,* Cort Theatre, 1957; company manager, *Gazebo,* Lyceum Theatre, 1958; company manager, *A Handful of Fire,*

Martin Beck Theatre, 1958; company manager, *Look After Lulu,* Henry Miller's Theatre, 1959; company manager, *Five Finger Exercise,* Music Box Theatre, 1959.

All in New York City unless indicated: Company manager, *Under the Yum Yum Tree,* Henry Miller's Theatre, 1960; company manager, *The Best Man,* Morosco Theatre, 1960; general manager, *Sail Away,* Broadhurst Theatre, 1961; general manager, *The Affair,* Henry Miller's Theatre, 1962; general manager, *The Hollow Crown,* Henry Miller's Theatre, 1963; producer, *Enter Laughing,* Henry Miller's Theatre, 1963; producer, *Chips with Everything,* Plymouth Theatre, 1963; producer, *The White House, P.S. I Love You,* both Henry Miller's Theatre, 1964; producer, *The Killing of Sister George,* Belasco Theatre, 1966; producer, *The Promise,* Henry Miller's Theatre, 1967; producer, *We Bombed in New Haven,* Ambassador Theatre, 1968; producer, *The Mundy Scheme,* Royale Theatre, 1969; producer, *Sleuth,* Music Box Theatre, 1970; producer, *Veronica's Room,* Music Box Theatre, 1973; producer, *Same Time Next Year,* Brooks Atkinson Theatre, 1975; producer, *Tribute,* Brooks Atkinson Theatre, 1978; producer, *Faith Healer,* Longacre Theatre, 1979; producer, *Romantic Comedy,* Ethel Barrymore Theatre, 1979; producer, *Special Occasions,* Music Box Theatre, 1982. Also produced *Waiting for Gillian,* London, 1954; *The Stronger Sex,* London, then pre-Broadway run, both 1954; *The Last Tycoon, The Facts of Life,* both pre-Broadway runs, 1954; *Lovers,* New York City, 1968; *Dancing in the End Zone,* New York City, 1985; *Cheri,* 1959.

MAJOR TOURS—General manager, *Edward My Son,* Australian cities, 1948; producer, *Arms and the Man,* U.S. cities, 1953; producer, *A Palm Tree in a Rose Garden, An Adventure, The Amazing Adele,* U.S. cities, all 1956; producer, *Duel of Angels,* U.S. cities, 1960; producer, *Tribute,* U.S. cities, 1980.

PRINCIPAL FILM WORK—Producer: *Sleuth,* Twentieth Century-Fox, 1972; *Same Time Next Year,* Universal, 1979; *Romantic Comedy,* Metro-Goldwyn-Mayer/United Artists, 1983.

RELATED CAREER—Assistant business manager and press representative, Theatre Inc., 1945; New York press representative, Old Vic Theatre Company, 1946; general manager, New Stages, New York City, 1946-48; general manager, press representative, Cape Playhouse, Dennis, MA, 1947-48; general manager, Gilbert Miller Productions, Henry Miller's Theatre, New York City, 1948-53; general manager, American Shakespeare Festival, Stratford, CT, 1956-57; general manager, Drama Festival, Cambridge, MA, 1959. Guest lecturer: Emerson College, Yale University, Columbia University, Northwestern University, Queens College, Harvard University, and Wesleyan University.

AWARDS: Best Play, Antoinette Perry Award, 1970, for *Sleuth.*

MEMBER: League of New York Theatres, Players Club; Yale Club.

ADDRESSES: HOME—Warren, CT 06754. OFFICE—26 W. Ninth Street, New York, NY 10011.*

*   *   *

GOULD, John 1940-

PERSONAL: Born July 1, 1940, in Newquay, England; son of Jack and Jeanette Rose (Paton) Gould. EDUCATION: Attended Clifton College and St. Edmund Hall, Oxford University.

VOCATION: Actor, director, composer, and pianist.

CAREER: STAGE DEBUT—*Hang Down Your Head and Die,* Comedy Theatre, London, 1964. PRINCIPAL STAGE APPEARANCES—All in London: *Four Degrees Over,* Mermaid Theatre, then Fortune Theatre, 1966; *Forty Years On,* Apollo Theatre, 1969. Also appeared in *Three to One On,* 1968; *Postscripts,* 1969; *Down Upper Street,* 1971; *Just the Ticket,* 1973; *Think of a Number,* 1975; *Bars of Gould,* 1977; *The Luck of the Bodkins,* 1978. Performed a one-man show, Jeanetta Cochrane Theatre, 1971, then May Fair Theatre, 1974.

PRINCIPAL STAGE WORK—Musical director, *Forty Years On,* Apollo Theatre, London, 1969.

PRINCIPAL RADIO APPEARANCES—*Bars of Gould,* 1977.

RELATED CAREER—Director: WSG Productions, Whirligig Children's Theatre.

NON-RELATED CAREER—Accountant.

WRITINGS: REVUES—See production details above. (Co-author) *Hang Down Your Head and Die,* 1964; *Four Degrees Over,* 1966; *Three to One On,* 1968; *Postscripts,* 1969; *Forty Years On,* 1969; *Down Upper Street,* 1971; *Just the Ticket,* 1973; *Think of a Number,* 1975; (co-adaptor) *The Luck of the Bodkins,* 1978. STAGE SCORES—*Sweet Fanny,* 1965; *A Present from the Corporation,* 1967; *Who Was That Lady,* 1970; *On the Boil,* 1972; *Betjemania,* 1976.

MEMBER: British Actors' Equity Association.

ADDRESSES: HOME—98 Nelson Road, London SW19, England.*

*   *   *

GRAINGER, Gawn 1937-

PERSONAL: Born October 12, 1937, in Glasgow, Scotland; son of Charles Neil and Elizabeth (Gall) Grainger; married Janet Key. EDUCATION: Trained for the stage at the Italia Conti School.

VOCATION: Actor and writer.

CAREER: STAGE DEBUT—Boy king, *King's Rhapsody,* Palace Theatre, London, 1950. BROADWAY DEBUT—Romeo, *Romeo and Juliet,* Bristol Old Vic Theatre Company, City Center Theatre, 1967. PRINCIPAL STAGE APPEARANCES—Title role, *Kean,* Christy Mahon, *The Playboy of the Western World,* Romeo, *Romeo and Juliet,* Laertes, *Hamlet,* Claudio, *Measure for Measure,* all Bristol Old Vic Theatre, Bristol, U.K., 1964-66; Jimmy, *There's a Girl in My Soup,* Music Box Theatre, New York City, 1967; Cyril Bishop, *The Giveaway,* Garrick Theatre, London, 1969; James Boswell, *The Douglas Cause,* Duke of York's Theatre, London, 1971; Oronte, *The Misanthrope,* St. James Theatre, New York City, 1975; Reverend Hale, *The Crucible,* Comedy Theatre, London, 1981. Also appeared in repertory at Dundee, Scotland, U.K., 1961, and at Ipswich, U.K., 1962-64.

With the National Theatre Company, London: McCue, *The Front Page,* Macduff, *Macbeth,* both Old Vic Theatre, 1972; Oronte, *The Misanthrope,* officer, *The Bacchae,* Roberto, *Saturday, Sunday,*

GAWN GRAINGER

Monday, Jeremy Haynes, *The Party*, all Old Vic Theatre, 1973; Stephen Lloyd, *Next of Kin*, Figaro, *The Marriage of Figaro*, both Old Vic Theatre, 1974; Osric, *Hamlet*, Old Vic Theatre, then Lyttelton Theatre, both 1976; *Tribute to a Lady*, Old Vic Theatre, 1976; Usumcasane, *Tamburlaine the Great*, Olivier Theatre, then National Theatre, both 1976; juggler, *Force of Habit*, National Theatre, 1976; Casca, *Julius Caesar*, soldier, *The Passion*, *To Those Born Later*, Corporal Stoddard, *The Plough and the Stars*, Mr. Dorilant, *The Country Wife*, all National Theatre, 1977; schoolmaster, *Brand*, Ajax, *The Woman*, Charles I, *The World Turned Upside Down*, Wesley, *Has "Washington" Legs?*, all National Theatre, 1978; Jack, Nick, *The Long Voyage Home*, George, General Heller, *Dispatches*, doctor, squire, landlord, rector, *Lark Rise*, Sir Timothy, *Candleford*, all National Theatre, 1979; Jimmy Tomorrow, *The Iceman Cometh*, National Theatre, 1980.

MAJOR TOURS—Romeo, *Romeo and Juliet*, Laertes, *Hamlet*, Claudio, *Measure for Measure*, all Bristol Old Vic Theatre Company, world tour, 1967; Oronte, *The Misanthrope*, National Theatre Company, U.S. cities, 1976; knight, *The Passion*, world tour, 1981.

PRINCIPAL TELEVISION APPEARANCES—Episodic: Henry, *Elizabeth Alone*, BBC, 1980; Hitler, *Private Schultz*, BBC, 1980; Pushkin, *The Marriage*, BBC, 1981; Ross, *Macbeth*, BBC, 1983; highwayman, *Beggar's Opera*, BBC, 1984; Dyson, *When We Are Married*, BBC, 1987; also appeared in *Tales of the Unexpected*, Thames, 1985; panelist, *What's My Line*, CBS. Series: Editor, *Mitch*, LWT; *Son of Man*, BBC.

PRINCIPAL FILM APPEARANCES—*Little Drummer Girl*, Warner Brothers, 1984; also appeared in *Mastermind*, 1976; *Blood Royal*; *Black Tower*.

WRITINGS: PLAYS—*Four to One*, BBC, 1976; *Vamp Till Ready*, 1978; *Lies in Plastic Smiles*, 1979; *Paradise Lost*, 1980. TELEPLAYS—*You Don't Have To Walk To Fly*, LWT; *To See Ourselves*, BBC; *Jack Solomon's Children*, Yorkshire Television; *Big Deal*, BBC; *Left Field*. NON-FICTION—Editor, *On Acting* by Laurence Olivier, published by Simon & Schuster.

MEMBER: British Actors' Equity Association, Screen Actors Guild.

SIDELIGHTS: FAVORITE ROLES—Figaro in *The Marriage of Figaro*; Serjeant Musgrave in *Sergeant Musgrave's Dance*. RECREATIONS—Pool, poker, tennis.

ADDRESSES: AGENT—c/o David White Associates, 31 Kings Road, London SW3, England.

*   *   *

GRAY, Dulcie   1919-

PERSONAL: Born Dulcie Bailey, November 20, 1919 in Kuala Lampur, Malaysia; daughter of Arnold Savage (a lawyer) and Kate Edith Clulow (Gray) Bailey; married Michael Denison (an actor), April 29, 1939. EDUCATION: Attended schools in Wallingford,

DULCIE GRAY

Workingham, and Swanage, U.K.; trained for the stage at the Webber-Douglas School of Dramatic Art.

VOCATION: Actress and writer.

CAREER: STAGE DEBUT—Sorel Bliss, *Hay Fever,* His Majesty's Theatre, Aberdeen, Scotland, May 8, 1939. LONDON DEBUT—Maria, *Twelfth Night,* Open Air Theatre, Hyde Park, July 16, 1942. PRINCIPAL STAGE APPEARANCES—With the HM Tennent Company in Edinburgh and Glasgow, Scotland, 1940; with the Harrogate Repertory Company, 1940-41; Hermia, *A Midsummer Night's Dream* and Bianca, *The Taming of the Shrew,* both at the Open Air Theatre, Hyde Park, London, 1942; Alexandra Giddens, *The Little Foxes,* Piccadilly Theatre, London, 1942; repeated role of Hermia, *A Midsummer Night's Dream,* Westminster Theatre, London, 1942; Rose Wilson, *Brighton Rock,* Garrick Theatre, London, 1943; Vivien, *Landslide,* Westminster Theatre, London, 1943; Greta, *The Lady from Edinburgh,* Playhouse Theatre, London, 1945; Ruth Wilkins, *Dear Ruth,* St. James's Theatre, London, 1946; Jean Ritchie, *The Wind Is Ninety,* Apollo Theatre, London, 1946; Nurse Ransom, *Rain on the Just,* Aldwych Theatre, London, 1948; Norah Fuller, *Queen Elizabeth Slept Here,* Strand Theatre, London, 1949.

Agnes, *The Four Poster,* Ambassador's Theatre, London, 1950; *See You Later Review,* Watergate Theatre, London, 1951; Nina, *The Dragon's Mouth,* Winter Garden Theatre, London, 1952; Robina Jevons, *Sweet Peril,* St. James's Theatre, London, 1952; Toni Oberon, *We Must Kill Toni,* Westminster Theatre, London, 1954; Mrs. Pooter, *The Diary of a Nobody,* Arts Theatre, London, 1954; White Queen, *Alice Through the Looking Glass,* Chelsea Palace Theatre, London, 1955; Marion Field, *Love Affair,* Lyric Theatre, Hammersmith, London, 1956; Sarah Banning, *Double Cross,* Duchess Theatre, London, 1958; title role, *Candida,* Oxford Playhouse, U.K., 1958; Duchess of Hampshire, *Let Them Eat Cake,* Cambridge Theatre, London, 1959.

Repeated title role, *Candida,* Bath Festival Theatre, U.K. and later at the Piccadilly Theatre, London, 1960; Mary, *The Bald Prima Donna* and the old woman, *The Chairs,* both at the Oxford Playhouse, 1961; Lady Utterword, *Heartbreak House,* Oxford Playhouse and later at the Wyndham's Theatre, London, 1961; Z, *A Village Wooing* and Lady Aline, *A Marriage Has Been Arranged,* both at the Hong Kong City Center Theatre, Hong Kong, 1962; appeared in *A Shakespeare Recital,* Berlin Drama Festival, Federal Republic of Germany, 1962; Katerina of Arragon, *Royal Gambit,* Ashcroft Theatre, Croydon, U.K., 1962; Caroline Abbott, *Where Angels Fear to Tread,* New Arts Theatre and later at the St. Martin's Theatre, London, 1963; Madame Arkadina, *The Seagull,* Birmingham Repertory Company, U.K., 1964; Lady Chiltern, *An Ideal Husband,* Strand Theatre, London, 1965; Maria Wislack, *On Approval* and Susan, *Happy Family,* both at the St. Martin's Theatre, London, 1966-67; Julia Pyrton, *Number Ten,* Strand Theatre, London, 1967; May, *Vacant Possession* and Yulya Glebova, *Confession at Night,* both at the Nottingham Playhouse, U.K., 1968; Celia Pilgrim, *Out of the Question,* St. Martin's Theatre, London, 1968.

Repeated role of Z, *A Village Wooing* and appeared as Mrs. Banger, *Press Cuttings,* both at the Fortune Theatre, London, 1970; Gina Ekdal, *The Wild Duck,* Criterion Theatre, London, 1970; Ellen Blake, *The Dragon Variation,* Royal Theatre, Windsor, U.K., 1972; *Through the Looking Glass,* Ashcroft Theatre, Croydon, 1972; Mabel Jackson, *At the End of the Day,* Savoy Theatre, London, 1973; Grace Bishop, *The Sack Race,* Ambassador's Thea-

tre, London, 1974; Olivia Cameron, *The Pay-Off,* Comedy Theatre, London, 1974; Miss Marple, *A Murder Is Announced,* Vaudeville Theatre, London, 1977; Delia, *Bedroom Farce,* Prince of Wales' Theatre, London, 1979.

Madame Ranyevskaia, *The Cherry Orchard,* Exeter Theatre, London, 1980; Evelyn, *The Kingfisher,* Royal Theatre, Windsor, 1980; Lady Ashbrook, *A Coat of Varnish,* Haymarket Theatre, London, 1982; Mrs. Cavell, *Cavell,* Chichester Festival Theatre, U.K., 1982; Lady Sneervell, *School for Scandal,* Haymarket Theatre, London, 1983; Madame Pernell, *Tartuffe,* Bromley Theatre, U.K., 1983; repeated role of Lady Sneervell and later appeared as Mrs. Candour, *School for Scandal,* Duke of York's Theatre, London, 1984; Miss Skillon, *See How They Run,* Royal Theatre, Windsor, 1986.

MAJOR TOURS—*Fools Rush In,* U.K. cities, 1946; Anna Lutcar, *The Distant Hill,* U.K. cities, 1953; Agnes, *The Four Poster,* South African cities, 1954-55; Lady Shotter, *South Sea Bubble,* South African and Australian cities, 1956-57; *Merely Players,* U.K. cities, 1964; Mrs. Heidelberg, *The Clandestine Marriage,* U.K. cities, 1971; *A Village Wooing,* U.K. cities, 1971; Ellen Creed, *Ladies in Retirement,* U.K. cities, 1976; Lady Twombley, *The Cabinet Minister,* U.K. cities, 1977; Evelyn, *The Kingfisher,* U.K. cities, 1980; Lady Boothroyd, *Lloyd George Knew My Father,* U.K. cities, 1980; Sheila, *Relatively Speaking,* Middle Eastern and Far Eastern cities, 1981; Carlotta Gray, *Song at Twilight,* U.K. cities, 1983; Mrs. Candour, *School for Scandal,* British Council Fiftieth Anniversary tour of European cities, 1984; Daphne Drimmond, *There Goes the Bride,* Middle Eastern and Far Eastern cities, 1985.

PRINCIPAL FILM APPEARANCES—*They Were Sisters,* 1945; *The Glass Mountain,* 1950; also appeared in *My Brother Jonathan* and *The Franchise Affair.*

PRINCIPAL TELEVISION APPEARANCES—Series: Kate Harvey, *Howard's Way,* 1985-87. Episodic: *Boyd, Q.C.,* 1957; *Rumpole of the Bailey,* 1983; *Cold Warrior,* 1984. Dramatic specials: *The Governess,* 1957; *The Importance of Being Earnest,* 1958; *Winter Cruise* and *The Letter,* both 1960; *Virtue,* 1962; *Beautiful Forever,* 1965; *Unexpectedly Vacant,* 1969; *This Is Your Life,* 1973; *The Voysey Inheritance,* 1978; *The Thirties,* 1983.

WRITINGS: PLAYS, PRODUCED AND PUBLISHED—*Love Affair,* published by Samuel French, 1957.

RADIO PLAYS—*Love a la Carte,* BBC.

FICTION—*Murder on the Stairs,* Arthur Barker, 1958; *Murder in Melbourne,* Arthur Barker, 1958; *Baby Face,* Arthur Barker, 1959; *Epitaph for a Dead Actor,* Arthur Barker, 1960; *Murder on a Saturday,* Arthur Barker, 1961; *Murder in Mind,* Macdonald & Company, 1963; *The Devil Wore Scarlet,* Macdonald & Company, 1964; *Quarter for a Star,* Macdonald & Company, 1964; *The Murder of Love,* Macdonald & Company, 1967; *Died in the Red,* Macdonald & Company, 1967; *Murder on Honeymoon,* Macdonald & Company, 1969; *For Richer, For Richer,* Macdonald & Company, 1970; *Deadly Lampshade,* Macdonald & Company, 1971; *Understudy to Murder,* Macdonald & Company, 1972; *Dead Give-Away,* Macdonald & Company, 1974; *Ride on a Tiger,* Macdonald & Company, 1975; *Stage Door Fright,* Macdonald & Company, 1977; *Death in Denims,* Macdonald & Company and Everest Books, 1977; *Dark Calypso,* Macdonald & Company, 1979; also the author of one book of short horror stories.

NON-FICTION—(With Michael Denison) *The Actor and His World*, Gollancz, 1964; *Butterflies on My Mind: On the Conservation of British Butterflies*, Angus and Robertson, 1978.

SHORT STORIES—*The Girl on the Bus* (short story anthology), Pan Books, 1966; also contributor to eleven anthologies of horror stories published by Pan Books.

PERIODICALS—*Sunday Express, Daily Sketch, Tatler, Evening Standard,* and the *Evening News.*

AWARDS: Created Companion of the British Empire, 1983; Queen's Silver Jubilee Medal, 1977; *London Times* Educational Supplement Senior Information Award, 1979, for *Butterflies on My Mind: On the Conservation of British Butterflies.*

MEMBER: British Actors' Equity Association, Crime Writers Association, Mystery Writers of America; Linnean Society of London (fellow); Royal Society of Arts (fellow).

SIDELIGHTS: FAVORITE ROLES—Rose Wilson, *Brighton Rock* and the Duchess of Hampshire, *Let Them Eat Cake.* RECREATIONS—Swimming and studying British butterflies.

ADDRESSES: AGENT—c/o Ronnie Waters, International Creative Management Ltd., 388 Oxford Street, London W1, England.

* * *

GREENE, Lorne   1915-1987

OBITUARY NOTICE—See index for *CTFT* sketch: Born February 12, 1915, in Ottawa, ON, Canada; died of pneumonia following abdominal surgery at St. John's Hospital Center in Santa Monica, CA, September 11, 1987. Actor Lorne Green attained fame for his portrayal of Ben Cartwright, the strong and caring head of the Ponderosa ranch on the television series *Bonanza,* 1959-73. With his deep voice and prominent stature, Greene not only embodied the prototypical man of the Old West, but represented a father figure with whom millions of viewers identified. Before his acting career, Greene was a top newscaster for the Canadian Broadcasting Corporation. At the height of his radio career he was often called "the Voice of Canada," hosting up to fifteen shows a week during World War II. He moved to New York City in the early fifies and appeared on the popular television show *Studio One* in 1953. That same year, Greene made his Broadway debut in *The Prescott Proposals* and subsequent Broadway credits included *Speaking of Murder,* 1956, and *Edwin Booth,* 1958. Between stage and television appearances, Greene landed roles in such films as *The Silver Chalice,* 1954, *Autumn Leaves,* 1956, and *Peyton Place,* 1957. Although Greene was best known for his *Bonanza* role, he also starred in other series, including *Battlestar Galactica,* 1978-80, and *Code Red,* 1981-82. In addition, he made numerous television movies and acted in the mini-series *The Moneychangers,* 1976, *Roots,* 1977, and *The Bastard,* 1978. At the time of his death, Greene was preparing to work on a television movie, *Bonanza—The Next Generation.*

OBITUARIES AND OTHER SOURCES: New York Times, September 12, 1987; *The Hollywood Reporter,* September 14, 1987; *Variety,* September 16, 1987.

GREIST, Kim

PERSONAL: Full name, Kimberley Bret Greist; born May 12, in Stamford, CT; daughter of E. Harold and Norma M. (Abtey) Greist. EDUCATION: Attended the New School for Social Research; trained for the stage with Freddie Kareman and Wynn Handman.

VOCATION: Actress.

CAREER: FILM DEBUT—Lauren Daniels, *C.H.U.D.*, New World Pictures, 1984. PRINCIPAL FILM APPEARANCES—Jill Leighton, *Brazil,* Universal/Twentieth Century-Fox, 1985; Molly Graham, *Manhunter,* DeLaurentis Films, 1986; Madeline Urie, *Punchline,* Columbia, 1987; Beth Ryan, *Throw Momma from the Train,* Orion, 1987.

PRINCIPAL STAGE APPEARANCES—Katya, *Second Prize: Two Months in Leningrad,* Perry Street Theatre, New York City, 1983; Viola, *Twelfth Night,* New York Shakespeare Festival, Delacorte Theatre, New York City, 1986.

TELEVISION DEBUT—*Miami Vice,* NBC, 1985. PRINCIPAL TELEVISION APPEARANCES—Episodic: Visiting alien, *Tales from the Darkside,* syndicated, 1986.

ADDRESSES: AGENT—Creative Artists Agency, 1888 Century Park E., Los Angeles, CA 90067. MANAGER—c/o Bill Treusch, 853 Seventh Avenue, New York, NY 10019.

KIM GREIST

ZACH GRENIER

GRENIER, Zach   1959-

PERSONAL: Born James Hampton Grenier, February 12, 1959, in Englewood, NJ; son of George Hampton (an electrical engineer) and Helen (a librarian; maiden name, Biadacweiwcz) Grenier; married Lynn Coutant Bailey (a creative consultant). EDUCATION: Attended the University of Michigan and Boston University, B.F.A.

VOCATION: Actor.

CAREER: STAGE DEBUT—Jacques, *As You Like It,* with the Boston Shakespeare Company, MA, 1978. OFF-BROADWAY DEBUT—Sid Greenberg, *Talk Radio,* Public Theatre, New York Shakespeare Festival, May 28, 1987. PRINCIPAL STAGE APPEAR-ANCES—Title role, *The Christopher Marlowe Show,* Boston, 1978; title role, *Baal,* Kozo Theatre, New York City, 1982; Monk, *Bhutan,* South Street Theatre, New York City, 1983; a general and a policeman, *The War on the Third Floor,* with the New Directors' Project at the Perry Street Theatre, New York City, 1984; Megs, *Strange Snow,* Philadelphia Theatre Company, PA, 1984; *Pantagleize,* with the Alaska Repertory Theatre in Anchorage and Fairbanks, 1985; *Der Inca Von Peru* and *Tomorrowland,* both at the Perform-ing Garage, New York City, 1985; Napoleon and Aitkin, *Citizen Tom Paine,* Williamstown Theatre Festival, MA, 1985, then at the Philadelphia Company, and at the Kennedy Center for the Perform-ing Arts, Washington, DC, 1987; Ali Hinkley, *Birth of the Poet,* Brooklyn Academy of Music, NY, 1986; Tanner, *Rum and Coke,* Coconut Grove Playhouse, FL, 1986; *The Cure,* Performing Ga-rage, New York City, 1986.

FILM DEBUT—Jesse Easterly, *Kid Brother,* Kinema Tokyo, 1986.

TELEVISION DEBUT—Officer Lacey, *One Life to Live,* ABC, 1983. PRINCIPAL TELEVISION APPEARANCES—Episodic: *The Equalizer,* CBS, 1986; *Miami Vice,* NBC, 1987.

MEMBER: Actors' Equity Association, Ensemble Studio Theatre.

ADDRESSES: HOME—571 10th Street, Brooklyn, NY 11215. AGENT—Bret Adams, 448 W. 44th Street, New York, NY 10036.

*   *   *

GROGG, Sam

PERSONAL: Son of Samuel Luther (a labor organizer) and Hazel Ellen (Bedwell) Grogg; married Susan Paulette Todoroff (an actress and choreographer), November 26, 1982; children: a son Keaton Harrison, a daughter Brady Ellen. EDUCATION: Western Illinois University, B.A., M.A., 1970; Bowling Green University, Ph.D., 1974.

VOCATION: Producer.

CAREER: PRINCIPAL FILM WORK—Executive producer, *The Trip to Bountiful,* Island Pictures, 1985; producer, *The Dirt Bike Kid,* Concorde-Cinema Group, 1985.

RELATED CAREER—Director of National Education, American

SAM GROGG

Film Institute, Washington, DC, 1974-80; executive director, USA Film Festival, Dallas, TX, 1981-84; president, Film Dallas, Inc., Dallas, 1984—.

ADDRESSES: OFFICE—Film Dallas, Inc., 2200 N. Lamar Street, Suite 103, Dallas, TX 75202.

*   *   *

GUERRA, Castulo   1945-

PERSONAL: Born August 24, 1945; son of Castulo (a politician and writer) and Maria (Sola) Guerra; married Christy Claire Risska (a production manager), December 15, 1972. EDUCATION: Attended Tucuman National University, Argentina; graduate work, Kansas University International Theatre Studies; trained for the stage at Tucuman Drama School.

VOCATION: Actor.

CAREER: OFF-BROADWAY DEBUT—Senator, *Coriolanus,* New York Shakespeare Festival (NYSF), Delacorte Theatre, 1979. PRINCIPAL STAGE APPEARANCES—Count Teck, *Watch on the Rhine,* Center Stage, Baltimore, MD, 1980; Doucet, *Animal Crackers,* Arena Stage, Washington, DC, 1982; ensemble, *Greencard,* Mark Taper Forum, Los Angeles, CA, 1986. Also appeared as officer, *Othello,* NYSF, Delacorte Theatre; Don John, *Much Ado about Nothing,* Center Stage; Stanzides, *Undiscovered Country,*

CASTULO GUERRA

Pugachev, musician, *The Suicide,* philosopher, *Galileo,* all Arena Stage; Dagomar, *Camaralenta,* Stages, Los Angeles, CA.

TELEVISION DEBUT—Sergeant Perez, *The Guiding Light,* CBS, 1980. PRINCIPAL TELEVISION APPEARANCES—Episodic: Don Luis, *Starman,* CBS; Rosario, *Houston Knights,* NBC; Segura, Carlos, *Riptide,* NBC; Ocean Jimmy, *Hunter,* NBC; Olvidado, *The Fall Guy,* ABC; Captain Fiero, *Falcon Crest,* CBS; Pavon, *The Shell Game,* ABC; Alexander Martien, *The A Team,* NBC; Fernando, *Remington Steele,* NBC. Movies: Enrique Vega, *Prisoner without a Name, Cell without a Number,* NBC, 1983; also appeared as Estabumante, *Desperate,* 1987.

FILM DEBUT—Gonzales the Angel, *Two of a Kind,* Twentieth Century-Fox, 1983. PRINCIPAL FILM APPEARANCES—Nestor, *Stick,* Universal, 1985; Orlando Santos, *Where the River Runs Black,* Metro-Goldwyn-Mayer/United Artists, 1986; Dr. Arantes, *Nuts,* Warner Brothers, 1987.

AWARDS: Fulbright Fellowship for theatre research in the United States, 1971; Ford Foundation Grant for experimental theatre research, New York, 1973.

MEMBER: Screen Actors Guild, American Federation of Television and Radio Artists, Actors' Equity Association.

ADDRESSES: HOME—4743 Frieda Drive, Los Angeles, CA 90065. AGENT—c/o STE Representation, Ltd., 211 S. Beverly Drive, Beverly Hills, CA 90212.

*   *   *

GUEST, Jean H.   1921-

PERSONAL: Born Genia P. Hindes, March 1, 1921, in New York, NY; daughter of Albert George (a doctor) and Frieda Muldavin (Sadvoronsky) Hindes; married Peter H. Guest (a British official to the United Nations), December 29, 1945; children: Christopher, Nicholas, Elissa. EDUCATION: Attended New York University, 1939-41, and the New School for Social Research; studied theatre at the Paul Mann Theatre Workshop and the New Theatre School.

VOCATION: Theatre and television executive.

CAREER: PRINCIPAL STAGE WORK—Party administrator, Playwrights Company, 1954-56; director, National Theatre Service Department, American National Theatre Academy, 1958-67; associate director, Theatre Communications Group, 1974—.

PRINCIPAL FILM WORK—Freelance script reader, United Artists Film Corporation, 1956-57; casting director, Frederick Brisson Productions, 1957-58.

PRINCIPAL TELEVISION WORK—Vice-president, casting, CBS, 1976-86.

RELATED CAREER—Vice-president, Wender & Associates, theatrical agents, 1968-74.

NON-RELATED CAREER—Worked for the Office of Scientific Research and Development, Cornell Medical School, during World War II.

MEMBER: Academy of Television Arts and Sciences; American Women in Film.

ADDRESSES: HOME—245 S. Spalding Drive, Beverly Hills, CA 90212.

*   *   *

GURNEY, Rachel

PERSONAL: Born March 5, in Eton, England; daughter of Samuel Gurney and Irene (Scharrer) Lubbock; married Denys Rhodes (divorced).

VOCATION: Actress.

CAREER: LONDON DEBUT—Lynne Hartley, *The Guinea Pig,* Criterion Theatre, 1946. OFF-BROADWAY DEBUT—Mrs. Clandon, *You Never Can Tell,* Roundabout Theatre, New York City, 1977. PRINCIPAL STAGE APPEARANCES—Lady Katherine, *The Sleeping Clergyman,* Criterion Theatre, London, 1947; Thea, *Black Chiffon,* Westminster Theatre, London, 1949; Mabel, *First Person Singular,* Mrs. Pless, *The Trap,* both Duke of York's Theatre, London, 1952; Alice, *The Voysey Inheritance,* Arts Theatre, London, 1952; Mrs. George Lamb, *Caro William,* Embassy Theatre, London, 1952; Valerie Carrington, *Carrington VC,* Westminster

Theatre, 1953; Avice Brunton, *The Bombshell,* Westminster Theatre, 1954; Oliva, *The Chalk Garden,* Haymarket Theatre, London, 1956; Hilary, *The Grass Is Greener,* St. Martin's Theatre, London, 1959; Lady Chiltern, *An Ideal Husband,* Piccadilly Theatre, London, 1966; Lady Chavender, *On the Rocks,* Dublin Festival, Dublin, Ireland, 1969; Freda Caplan, *Dangerous Corner,* Arnaud Theatre, Guildford, U.K., 1974; Mrs. Darling, *Peter Pan,* Palladium Theatre, London, 1975; Lady Chiltern, *An Ideal Husband,* O'Keefe Centre, Toronto, ON, Canada, 1976; Hesione Hushabye, *Heartbreak House,* McCarter Theatre, Princeton, NJ, 1979; Lady Britomart, *Major Barbara,* Circle in the Square, New York City, 1980; Her Ladyship, *The Dresser,* Brooks Atkinson Theatre, New York City, 1983; Sara, *Breaking the Code,* Neil Simon Theatre, New York City, 1987. Also appeared in *Rain on the Just,* Bristol Old Vic Theatre, Bristol, U.K., 1950; in a season of one-act plays by Bernard Shaw, Arts Theatre, 1951; and as Mrs. Prentice, *What the Butler Saw,* Academy Festival, Lake Forest, IL.

MAJOR TOURS—Lady Chavender, *On the Rocks,* U.K. cities, 1969; Freda Caplan, *Dangerous Corner,* U.K. cities, 1974; also toured India and Ceylon for the British Council in a program of Shakespeare's plays, 1958.

PRINCIPAL TELEVISION APPEARANCES—Series: Lady Marjorie Bellamy, *Upstairs, Downstairs,* PBS. Mini-Series: Grand Duchess Victoria, *Anastasia: The Mystery of Anna,* NBC, 1987.

ADDRESSES: AGENT—c/o London Management, 235 Regent Street, London W1, England.*

H

HACKMAN, Gene 1930-

PERSONAL: Born January 30, 1930, in San Bernardino, CA; son of Eugene Ezra Hackman; married Fay Maltese, 1956; children: Christopher, Elizabeth, Leslie.

VOCATION: Actor.

CAREER: PRINCIPAL FILM APPEARANCES—Cop, *Mad Dog Coll*, Columbia, 1961; Norman, *Lilith*, Columbia, 1964; Harmsworth, *A Covenant with Death*, Warner Brothers, 1966; John Whipple, *Hawaii*, United Artists, 1966; Tommy Del Gaddo, *Banning*, Universal, 1967; Sgt. Tweed, *First to Fight*, Warner Brothers, 1967; Buck Barrow, *Bonnie and Clyde*, Warner Brothers/Seven Arts, 1967; Lt. Walter Brill, *The Split*, Metro-Goldwyn-Mayer (MGM), 1968; Red Fletcher, *Riot!*, Paramount, 1969; Joe Browdy, *The Gypsy Moths*, MGM, 1969; Buzz Lloyd, *Marooned*, Columbia, 1969; Eugene Claire, *Downhill Racer*, Paramount, 1969; Gene Garrison, *I Never Sang for My Father*, Columbia, 1970; Dave Randolph, *Doctors' Wives*, Columbia, 1971; Popeye Doyle, *The French Connection*, Twentieth Century-Fox, 1971; Holland, *Cisco Pike*, Columbia, 1971; Rev. Frank Scott, *The Poseidon Adventure*, Twentieth Century-Fox, 1972; "Mary Ann," *Prime Cut*, National General, 1972; Max, *Scarecrow*, Warner Brothers, 1973; Harry Caul, *The Conversation*, Paramount, 1974; blind hermit, *Young Frankenstein*, Twentieth Century-Fox, 1974; Zandy Allen, *Zandy's Bride*, Warner Brothers, 1974; Popeye Doyle, *The French Connection II*, Twentieth Century-Fox, 1975; Sam Clayton, *Bite the Bullet*, Columbia, 1975; Harry Moseby, *Night Moves*, Warner Brothers, 1975; Kibby, *Lucky Lady*, Twentieth Century-Fox, 1975; Major General Sosabowski, *A Bridge Too Far*, United Artists, 1977; Brandt Ruger, *The Hunting Party*, United Artists, 1977; Roy Tucker, *The Domino Principle*, AVCO-Embassy, 1977; Major William Sherman Foster, *March or Die*, Columbia, 1977; Lex Lex Luthor, *Superman*, Warner Brothers, 1978; Lex Luthor, *Superman II*, Warner Brothers, 1980; George Dupler, *All Night Long*, Universal, 1981; Pete Van Wherry, *Reds*, Paramount, 1981; Jack McCann, *Eureka*, United Artists, 1983; Alex Grazier, *Under Fire*, Orion, 1983; Colonel Rhodes, *Uncommon Valor*, Paramount, 1983; Ned, *Misunderstood*, Metro-Goldwyn-Mayer/United Artists, 1984. Also appeared in *Two of a Kind*, Twentieth Century-Fox, 1983; *Target*, Warner Brothers, 1985; *Twice in a Lifetime*, Pan Canadian, 1985; *Power*, Lorimar, 1986; *Hoosiers*, Orion, 1986; also *Out by the Country Club*, 1967; *Kid Gloves*, 1988.

PRINCIPAL TELEVISION APPEARANCES—Episodic: "Little Tin God," *U.S. Steel Hour*, CBS, 1959; "Big Doc's Girl," *U.S. Steel Hour*, CBS, 1959; "Bride of the Fox," *U.S. Steel Hour*, CBS, 1960; *The Defenders*, CBS, 1961; "Brandenberg Gate," *U.S. Steel Hour*, CBS, 1961; "Far from the Shade Tree," *U.S. Steel Hour*, CBS, 1962; *The Defenders*, CBS, 1963; "Ride with Terror,"

Dupont Show of the Month, NBC, 1963; *Trials of O'Brien*, CBS, 1966; *Hawk*, ABC, 1966; *The F.B.I.*, ABC, 1967; *The Invaders*, ABC, 1967; *Iron Horse*, ABC, 1967; "My Father and My Mother," *CBS Playhouse*, CBS, 1968; *I Spy*, NBC, 1968; *Insight*, syndicated, 1971; also *Rowan and Martin's Laugh In*, NBC. Movies: Reverend Thomas Davis, *Shadow on the Land*, ABC, 1968. Specials: *Night of 100 Stars II*, ABC, 1985.

PRINCIPAL STAGE APPEARANCES—All in New York City: *Any Wednesday*, Music Box Theatre, 1964; *Poor Richard*, Helen Hayes Theatre, 1964; *Children from Their Games*, Morosco Theatre, 1963; *A Rainy Day in Newark*, Belasco Theatre, 1963; *The Natural Look*, Longacre Theatre, 1967; *Night of 100 Stars II*, Radio City Music Hall, 1985.

RELATED CAREER—Founder, Chelly, Ltd. (production company).

AWARDS: Best Supporting Actor, Academy Award nomination, 1968, for *Bonnie and Clyde;* Best Actor, Academy Award, National Association of Theatre Owners Star of the Year, Golden Globe Award, British Academy Award, New York Film Critics Award, all 1971, for *The French Connection;* British Academy Award, 1972, for *The Poseidon Adventure;* Cannes Film Festival Award, 1973, for *Scarecrow;* Best Actor, New York Film Critics Award nomination, 1975, for *The Conversation.*

MEMBER: Actors' Equity Association, Screen Actors Guild, American Federation of Television and Radio Artists, Academy of Motion Picture Arts and Sciences.

ADDRESSES: OFFICE—c/o Barry Haldeman, Haldeman & Peckerman, 9595 Wilshire Boulevard, Suite 700, Beverly Hills, CA 90212.*

*   *   *

HAILEY, Oliver 1932-

PERSONAL: Born July 7, 1932, in Pampa, TX; son of Oliver D., Sr. (a butcher) and Hallie May (Thomas) Hailey; married Elizabeth Ann Forsythe (a writer), June 25, 1960; children: Elizabeth Kendall, Melinda Brooke. EDUCATION: University of Texas at Austin, B.F.A., 1954; Yale University, M.F.A., 1962. POLITICS: Democrat. RELIGION: Protestant. MILITARY: U.S. Air Force.

VOCATION: Playwright.

CAREER: Also see *WRITINGS* below. RELATED CAREER—Feature writer, *Dallas Morning News*, 1957-59; story editor,

McMillan and Wife, NBC, 1972-74; creative consultant, *Mary Hartman, Mary Hartman,* syndicated; co-producer, *Another Day,* CBS; developer, *Love Sidney,* NBC.

WRITINGS: PLAYS—*Hey You, Light Man!,* University of Kansas, KS, 1961, then Mayfair Theatre, New York City, 1963, later New Theatre, Bromley, U.K., 1971, published by Dramatists Play Service, 1970; *Child's Play: A Comedy for Orphans,* Yale University, New Haven, CT, 1962; *Home by Hollywood,* Mitchell College, New London, CT, 1964; *Picture, Animal,* both Caffe Cino, New York City, 1965, both published in *Three Short Plays,* Dramatists Play Service, 1970; *First One Asleep, Whistle,* Belasco Theatre, New York City, 1966, published by S. Fischer Verlag, 1967; *Who's Happy Now?,* Mark Taper Forum, Los Angeles, CA, 1967, then Village South Theatre, New York City, 1969, published by Random House, 1969; *Crisscross,* Evergreen Theatre, Los Angeles, CA, 1970, published in *Three Short Plays,* Dramatists Play Service, 1970; *Orphan,* Evergreen Theatre, 1970; *Father's Day,* Los Angeles, CA, 1970, then John Golden Theatre, New York City, 1971, later Finborough Theatre, London, 1987, published by Dramatists Play Service, 1971; *Continental Divide,* Washington Theatre Club, Washington, DC, 1970, published by Dramatists Play Service, 1973; *For the Use of the Hall,* Trinity Square Theatre, Providence, RI, 1974, then Playwrights Horizon's, New York City, 1977, later Equity Library Theatre, New York City, 1983, published by Dramatists Play Service, 1976; *And Where She Stops Nobody Knows,* Mark Taper Forum, 1976; *Red Rover, Red Rover,* Cricket Theatre, Minneapolis, MN, 1977, then Park Royal Theatre, New York City, 1983, published by Dramatists Play Service, 1979; *Tryptych,* Mark Taper Forum, 1979; *I Can't Find It Anywhere,* Actors Theatre, Louisville, KY, 1979; *I Won't Dance,* Studio Arena Theatre, Buffalo, NY, 1980, then Helen Hayes Theatre, New York City, 1981, published by Samuel French, Inc., 1982; *About Time,* Back Alley Theatre, Los Angeles, CA, 1982, published by Dramatists Play Service, 1983; (adaptor) *The Father,* Philadelphia Drama Guild, Philadelphia, PA, 1984, published by Dramatists Play Service, 1984; *Round Trip,* Kalamazoo College, Kalamazoo, MI, 1984; *Inner/Inter Changes* (series of one act plays), American Theatre Arts, Los Angeles, CA, 1985; *Kith and Kin,* Dallas Theatre Center, Dallas, TX, 1986.

SCREENPLAYS—Co-writer, *Just You and Me Kid,* Columbia, 1979.

TELEPLAYS—Episodic: *Bracken's World* (three episodes), NBC; *McMillan and Wife* (nine episodes), NBC, 1972-74. Movies: *Sidney Shorr,* NBC, 1981; *Isabel's Choice,* CBS, 1981.

NON-FICTION—Contributor: *Three Plays from Yale School of Drama,* Dutton, 1964; *Collision Course,* Random House, 1968; *Showcase One, Plays from the Eugene O'Neill Foundation,* Grove Press, 1969; *New Theatre for Now,* Delta, 1971.

AWARDS: Phyllis S. Anderson Fellowship in Playwriting, 1961-62; Vernon Rice Award, 1963, for *Hey You, Light Man!;* Certificate of Merit, Los Angeles Drama Critics Circle, 1973, for *Father's Day;* Outstanding Writing in a Limited Series, Emmy Award nomination, Outstanding Comedy Written for Television, Writers Guild of America Award, both 1982, for *Sidney Shorr.*

MEMBER: Writers Guild of America.

ADDRESSES: HOME—11747 Canton Place, Studio City, CA 91604. AGENT—c/o Shirley Bernstein, Paramuse Artists Associates, 1414 Avenue of the Americas, New York, NY 10019.

HALES, Jonathan   1937-

PERSONAL: Born May 10, 1937, in London, England; son of James Alfred and Dorothy May (Broadbent) Hales; married Mary Jane Cherry (divorced); married Gillian Diamond; children: two sons. EDUCATION: Attended Christ's College, Cambridge University and University of Texas; trained for the stage with Ben Iden Payne.

VOCATION: Director, writer, and actor.

CAREER: PRINCIPAL STAGE WORK—Director: *The Knight of the Burning Pestle,* Marlowe Theatre, Canterbury, U.K., 1966; *Danton's Death, Galileo, The Three Musketeers,* all Phoenix Theatre, Leicester, U.K., 1967-68; *The Foursome,* Royal Court Theatre, then Fortune Theatre, both London, 1971; *The Lovers of Viorne,* Royal Court Theatre, 1971; *The Centaur,* Royal Court Theatre, 1972; *Brussels,* Royal Court Theatre, then Greenwich Theatre, London, 1972; *The Sea Anchor,* Royal Court Theatre, 1974; *Mrs. Grabowski's Academy,* Royal Court Theatre, 1975; *Judies,* Comedy Theatre, London, 1975; *The Entertainer,* Sherman Theatre, Cardiff, Wales, U.K., 1975; *Epitaph for George Dillon,* Young Vic Theatre, London, 1975; *Old Flames,* Bristol, U.K., 1975, then Arts Theatre, London, 1976; *The Sanctuary Lamp,* Abbey Theatre, Dublin, Ireland, 1976; *The Family Dance,* Criterion Theatre, London, 1976; *Mecca,* Open Space Theatre, London, 1977; *The Morning after Optimism,* Abbey Theatre, 1977; *Wild Oats,* Abbey Theatre, 1978.

RELATED CAREER—Director of productions, Phoenix Theatre, Leicester, U.K., 1967-68; formerly an actor appearing at the Oregon Shakespeare Festival, Ashland, OR, 1961, the Banff Festival, Banff, AB, Canada, 1963, and the Royal Shakespeare Company, Stratford-on-Avon, U.K.

WRITINGS: PLAYS—(Adaptor) *The Three Musketeers,* Phoenix Theatre, Leicester, U.K., 1968; *The Centaur,* Royal Court Theatre, London, 1972; *Brussels,* Royal Court Theatre, 1972; co-writer, *Alice's Boys,* Savoy Theatre, London, 1978. SCREENPLAYS—*The Mirror Crack'd,* American Film Distributors, 1980; *High Road to China,* Warner Brothers, 1983; *The Shipkiller.* TELEPLAYS—*The Comic, Places Where They Sing; Diane; The Chelsea Murders.*

AWARDS: Receipient of Open Scholarship and Fulbright Scholarship.

SIDELIGHTS: RECREATIONS—Reading, music, opera, and being with his two sons.

ADDRESSES: HOME—117 Canfield Gardens, London NW6, England.*

*   *   *

HALL, Adrian   1927-

PERSONAL: Born December 3, 1927, in Van, Texas; son of Lennie (a farmer) and Mattie (Murphee) Hall. EDUCATION: East Texas State Teachers College, B.S., 1948; received M.F.A. in 1950; trained for the stage with Margo Jones, Gilmore Brown, and Stella Holt. MILITARY: U.S. Army, 1951-53.

VOCATION: Director and writer.

CAREER: PRINCIPAL STAGE WORK—Director: *Another Part of*

© *Linda Blase, 1987*

ADRIAN HALL

the Forest, Lenox Hill Playhouse, New York City, 1956; *The Time of Your Life,* Lenox Hill Playhouse, 1957; *The Trip to Bountiful,* Theatre East, New York City, 1959; *Orpheus Descending,* Gramercy Arts Theatre, New York City, 1959; *The Mousetrap,* Maidman Playhouse, New York City, 1960; *Donogoo, Red Roses for Me,* both Greenwich Mews Theatre, New York City, 1961; *Riverwind,* Actors Playhouse, New York City, 1962; *The Milk Train Doesn't Stop Here Anymore,* Barter Theatre, Abingdon, VA, 1963; *The Hostage,* Fred Miller Theatre, Milwaukee, WI, 1964; *Mother Courage,* Milwaukee Repertory Theatre, Milwaukee, WI, 1966; *Peer Gynt,* Missouri Repertory Theatre, Kansas City, MO, 1975; *Enemy of the People,* Guthrie Theatre, Minneapolis, MN, 1977; *Buried Child,* Yale Repertory Theatre, New Haven, CT, 1979; *The Hothouse,* Playhouse Theatre, New York City, 1982; *Journey of the Fifth Horse,* American Repertory Theatre, Cambridge, MA, 1982. Directed summer theatre productions at the Playhouse Theatre and the Alley Theatre, both Houston, TX, 1953-54; at the Phoenicia Playhouse, Phoenicia, NY, 1957-60; and at the Civic Auditorium, Charlotte, NC, 1961. Also director for the Trinity Square Repertory Company, Providence, RI, and the Dallas Theatre Center, Dallas, TX.

MAJOR TOURS—Director, *Toys in the Attic,* U.S. cities, 1961; also directed various U.S. and world tours for the Trinity Square Repertory Company.

PRINCIPAL TELEVISION WORK—Episodic: Director, "Feasting with Panthers," *Theatre in America,* PBS, 1973; director, "Brother to Dragons," *Theatre in America,* PBS, 1975; director, "Life Among the Lowly," *Visions,* PBS, 1978. Series: Producer, *Theatre in America,* PBS; producer, *Visions,* PBS. Mini-Series: Producer

and director, *House of Mirth,* PBS, 1979. Specials: Producer and director, *Edith Wharton: A Biography,* PBS, 1980.

RELATED CAREER—Founder, artistic director, Trinity Square Repertory Company, Providence, RI, 1964—; board of directors, American National Theatre and Academy, 1969-72; consultant, Office of Planning and Analysis, National Endowment for the Humanities, 1977; Policy and Grants Panel member, National Endowment for the Arts, 1977-79; lecturer, University of Missouri, 1979; lecturer, Yale University, Graduate School of Drama, 1981; board of directors, Theatre Communications Group, 1981—; Overseer's Committee, Loeb Drama Center, Harvard University, 1981-82; Rhode Island Film Commission, 1982—; artistic director, Dallas Theatre Center, Dallas, TX, 1983—.

WRITINGS: PLAYS—All produced by the Trinity Square Repertory Company, Providence, RI, unless indicated. (With Timothy Taylor) *Son of Man and the Family,* 1970; (with Richard Cumming) *Feasting with Panthers,* 1973; (with Cumming) *Uncle Tom's Cabin: A History,* 1979; (adaptor) *In the Belly of the Beast,* Center Theatre Group, Mark Taper Forum, Los Angeles, CA, 1985.

TELEPLAYS—(Adaptor) "Brother to Dragons," *Theatre in America,* PBS, 1975; "Life Among the Lowly," *Visions,* PBS, 1978; (adaptor) *House of Mirth,* PBS, 1979.

AWARDS: Margo Jones Award, National Theatre Critics Association, 1969, for "continued professional productions of new American playwrights;" Shakespeare Festival Award, Old Globe Theatre, San Diego, CA, 1974, for "contributing to the classics;" Outstanding Creative Achievement Award, New England Theatre Conference, 1976; Elliot Norton Award, New England Theatre Conference, 1980, for "outstanding achievement in the theatre;" Antoinette Perry Award, 1981, for "outstanding contribution to the American theatre;" Rhode Island Theatre Arts Achievement Award, Community Theatres of Rhode Island, 1981; Rhode Island Governor's Award, 1982, for "bringing national and international acclaim to the state;" Person of the Year Award, National Theatre Conference, 1983, for "impact on the American Theatre as a thinker, leader, and practitioner of the highest order." Honorary degrees: Doctorate of Fine Arts (D.F.A.), Brown University, 1972; D.F.A., Rhode Island University, 1977; D.F.A., Roger Williams College, 1982; D.F.A., Bridgewater State College, 1985.

MEMBER: Actors' Equity Association, Writers Guild of America, Directors Guild of America.

ADDRESSES: OFFICE—Dallas Theatre Center, 3636 Turtle Creek Boulevard, Dallas, TX 75219.

*   *   *

HALLIWELL, David   1936-

PERSONAL: Born July 31, 1936, in Brighouse, England; son of Herbert and Ethel (Spencer) Halliwell. EDUCATION: Attended Huddersfield College of Art; trained for the stage at the Royal Academy of Dramatic Art.

VOCATION: Writer, actor, director, and producer.

CAREER: PRINCIPAL STAGE APPEARANCES—Vincentio, *The Taming of the Shew,* Seyton, *Macbeth,* both Nottingham Repertory

Theatre, Nottingham, U.K., 1962; Hortensio, *The Taming of the Shrew,* Leicester, U.K., 1962; Sydney Spooner, *Worms Eye View,* Colchester, U.K., 1962; General Madigan, *O'Flaherty, V.C.,* Jim Curry, *The Rainmaker,* both Stoke-on-Trent, U.K., 1962; Hero, *The Rehearsal,* Pozzo, *Waiting for Godot,* Common Man, *A Man for All Seasons,* all Stoke-on-Trent, 1963; Scrawdyke, *Little Malcolm and His Struggle against the Eunuchs,* London, 1965; Jackson McIver, *The Experiment,* London, 1967; policeman, *An Altercation,* London, 1973; Botard, *Rhinoceros,* London, 1974; Frankie, *Birdbath,* Bristol, U.K., 1975.

PRINCIPAL STAGE WORK—Director: *The Dumb Waiter, The Stronger, The Village Wooing,* and *Keep Out, Love in Progress,* all London, 1966; (with David Claderisi) *The Experiment,* London, then New York, both 1967; *A Day with My Sister,* Edinburgh, Scotland, U.K., 1971; *The Hundred Watt Bulb, I Am Real and So Are You, A Visit from the Family, Crewe Station at Two A.M.,* all London, 1972; *The Only Way Out,* London, 1973; *We Are What We Eat, The Knowall,* (with Gavin Eley) *The Quipu Anywhere Show,* all London, 1973; *The Last of the Feinsteins,* London, 1975; *Paint,* London, 1977; *Lovers,* Kingston, U.K., 1978; *Was It Her?, Meriel the Ghost Girl,* both London, 1982. Also director with the Quipu Group, London, 1966-76.

PRINCIPAL FILM APPEARANCES—Nightclub operator, *Mona Lisa,* Handmade Films, 1985; prison officer, *Defense of the Realm,* 1985.

PRINCIPAL RADIO APPEARANCES—Landlord, *Spongehenge,* BBC, 1982.

RELATED CAREER—Visiting fellow, Reading University, 1969-70; literary manager, 1976, then resident dramatist, Royal Court Theatre, London, 1976-77; resident dramatist, Hampstead Theatre Club, London, 1978-79.

WRITINGS: PLAYS—*Concerning Out and In,* 1958; *Little Malcolm and His Struggle against the Eunuchs,* London, 1965, then New York City (as *Hail Scrawdyke!*), 1966, published by Grove Press, 1967; *A Who's Who of Flapland,* London, 1967, published in *A Who's Who of Flapland and Other Plays,* Faber, 1971; (with David Calderisi) *The Experiment,* London, then New York City, 1967; *K.D. Dufford Hears K.D. Dufford Ask K.D. Dufford How K.D. Dufford'll Make K.D. Dufford,* London, 1969, published by Faber, 1970; *The Discussion,* Falmouth, U.K., 1969, published in *A Who's Who of Flapland and Other Plays,* Faber, 1971; *Muck from Three Angels,* Edinburgh, Scotland, U.K., then London, both 1971, published in *A Who's Who of Flapland and Other Plays,* 1971; *The Girl Who Didn't Like Answers, A Last Belch for the Great Auk, An Amour and a Feast,* all London, 1971; *Bleats from a Brighouse Pleasureground, Janitress Thrilled by Prehensile Penis, An Altercation,* all London, 1972; *The Freckled Bum, Minyip,* both London, 1974; *Progs, A Process of Elimination,* both London, 1975; *Prejudice,* Sheffield, U.K., 1978; *Persons in the Act of Mooting,* London, 1979; *The House,* London, 1979, published by Eyre Methuen, 1979; *A Rite Kwik Metal Tata,* Sheffield, U.K., then London, 1979; *Creatures of Another Kind,* London, 1981; *Meriel the Ghost Girl,* London, 1982, published in *The Mind Beyond,* Penguin, 1976; also wrote *Wychways along the Evenlode,* 1986; *A Tomato Who Grew into a Mushroom,* 1986.

PLAYS, UNPRODUCED—*Franklin and Wilkins; Demonstrations; The Cutteslowe Walls.*

TELEPLAYS—*A Plastic Mac in Winter,* 1963; *Cock, Hen, and*

Courting Pit, 1966; *Triptych of Bathroom Users,* 1972; *Blur and Blank via Checkheaton,* 1972; *Steps Back,* 1973; *Daft Mam Blues,* 1975; *Pigmented Patter (Crown Court* series), 1976; *Meriel the Ghost Girl,* 1976; *Tree Women of Jagden Crag,* 1978; *There's a Car Park in Witherton,* 1982; *Speculating about Orwell,* 1983; *Arrangements,* 1985; *Doctor Who* (two episodes), 1985.

SCREENPLAYS—*Little Malcolm and His Struggle against the Eunuchs,* 1973.

RADIO PLAYS—*A Who's Who of Flapland,* 1967; *Bleats from a Brighouse Pleasureground,* 1972; *Was It Her?,* 1980; *Spongehenge,* 1982; *Meriel the Ghost Girl,* 1983; *Grandad's Place,* 1984; *Shares of the Pudding,* 1985; *Do It Youself,* 1986; *Gifts,* 1987.

AWARDS: *London Evening Standard* award, 1967; John Whiting Award, 1977, for *Prejudice;* Silver Bear Award from the Berlin Film Festival, 1973, for *Little Malcolm and His Struggle against the Eunuchs.*

MEMBER: Fellow of the Royal Society of Literature.

SIDELIGHTS: RECREATIONS—''Animal parapsychology and indoor golf.''

ADDRESSES: HOME—Eight Crawborough Villas, Charlbury, Oxford OX7 3TS, England.

*   *   *

HAMILL, Mark   1951-

PERSONAL: Born September 25, 1951, in Oakland, CA; married Marilou York, 1978; children: Nathan Elias. EDUCATION: Attended Los Angeles City College.

VOCATION: Actor.

CAREER: FILM DEBUT—Luke Skywalker, *Star Wars,* Twentieth Century-Fox, 1977. PRINCIPAL FILM APPEARANCES—Kent Dantley, *Corvette Summer,* United Artists, 1978; Griff, *The Big Red One,* United Artists, 1980; Luke Skywalker, *The Empire Strikes Back,* Twentieth Century-Fox, 1980; cameo, *Britannia Hospital,* Universal, 1982; Luke Skywalker, *Return of the Jedi,* Twentieth Century-Fox, 1983. Also appeared in *The Night the Lights Went Out in Georgia,* AVCO-Embassy, 1981.

PRINCIPAL TELEVISION APPEARANCES—Episodic: David Bradford, *Eight Is Enough,* ABC, 1977; also appeared in *Headmaster,* CBS, 1970; *Manhunter,* CBS, 1974; *Medical Center,* CBS, 1976; *The Streets of San Francisco,* ABC, 1977; *One Day at a Time,* CBS; *The F.B.I.* ABC; *Owen Marshall, Counselor at Law,* ABC; *The Partridge Family,* ABC; *Room 222,* ABC. Series: Kent Murray, *General Hospital,* ABC, 1974; Doobie Wheeler, *The Texas Wheelers,* ABC, 1974-75. Pilots: Joe Celli, *Mallory: Circumstantial Evidence,* NBC, 1976. Movies: Paul Swenson, *Eric,* NBC, 1975; Ken Newkirk, *Sarah T.: Portrait of a Teenage Alcoholic,* NBC, 1975; Philip Donaldson, *Delancey Street: The Crisis Within,* NBC, 1975; Eugene Banks, *The City,* NBC, 1977. Specials: *Bob Hope Christmas Special,* NBC, 1977; *Night of 100 Stars II,* ABC, 1985.

BROADWAY DEBUT—John Merrick, *The Elephant Man,* Booth

Theatre, 1981. PRINCIPAL STAGE APPEARANCES—Wolfgang Amadeus Mozart, *Amadeus*, Broadhurst Theatre, New York City, 1983; Tony Hart, *Harrigan 'n Hart*, Goodspeed Opera House, East Haddam, CT, then Longacre Theatre, New York City, 1985; Gordon Miller, *Room Service*, Roundabout Theatre, New York City, 1986; *Night of 100 Stars II*, Radio City Music Hall, New York City, 1985; *The Nerd*, Helen Hayes Theatre, New York City, 1987.

MEMBER: Actors' Equity Association, Screen Actors Guild, American Federation of Television and Radio Artists.

ADDRESS: OFFICE—Lucas Films, P.O. Box 2009, San Rafael, CA 94912. AGENT—William Morris Agency, 1350 Avenue of the Americas, New York, NY 10019. *

*   *   *

HANDS, Terry   1941-

PERSONAL: Full name, Terence David Hands; born January 9, 1941, in Aldershot, England; son of Joseph Ronald and Luise Bertha (Kohler) Hands; married Josephine Barstow in 1964 (divorced); married Ludmila Mikael (divorced, 1980); children: Andrea-Marina. EDUCATION: Attended Birmingham University; trained for the stage at the Royal Academy of Dramatic Art, 1962-64.

VOCATION: Director and writer.

TERRY HANDS

CAREER: PRINCIPAL STAGE WORK—Director: *The Importance of Being Earnest, Look Back in Anger, Richard III, Fando and Lis*, all Everyman Theatre, Liverpool, U.K., 1964-66; *Richard III*, Comedie Francaise, Paris, France, then Avignon Festival, France, both 1972, later Aldwych Theatre, London, 1973; *Pericles*, Comedie Francaise, 1974; *Twelfth Night*, Comedie Francaise, 1976; *Otello* (opera), Paris, France, 1976; *Le Cid*, Comedie Francaise, 1977; *Murder in the Cathedral*, Comedie Francaise, 1978; *Troilus and Cressida*, Burgtheatre, Vienna, Austria, 1978; *As You Like It*, Burgtheatre, 1979; *Parsifal* (opera), Covent Garden, London, 1979.

Director, all with the Royal Shakespeare Company: *The Criminals*, Aldwych Theatre, London, 1967; *The Merry Wives of Windsor*, Royal Shakespeare Theatre, Stratford-on-Avon, U.K., then Aldwych Theatre, 1968; *The Latent Heterosexual*, Aldwych Theatre, 1968; *Pericles, The Merry Wives of Windsor, Women Beware Women*, all Stratford-on-Avon, U.K., 1969; *Bartholomew Fair*, Aldwych Theatre, 1969; *Richard III*, Royal Shakespeare Theatre, 1970; *The Merchant of Venice*, Royal Shakespeare Theatre, 1971; *Man of Mode, The Balcony*, both Aldwych Theatre, 1971; *The Merchant of Venice, Murder in the Cathedral*, both Aldwych Theatre, 1972; *Romeo and Juliet*, Royal Shakespeare Theatre, 1973; *Cries from Casement*, Other Place Theatre, Stratford-on-Avon, U.K., 1973; *Bewitched*, Aldwych Theatre, 1974; *Henry V*, Aldwych Theatre, then Brooklyn Academy of Music, Brooklyn, NY, both 1976; *Henry IV, Parts I and II, The Merry Wives of Windsor*, all Royal Shakespeare Theatre, then Aldwych Theatre, 1976; *Old World*, Aldwych Theatre, 1976; *Henry VI, Parts I, II, and III, Coriolanus*, all Royal Shakespeare Theatre, then Newcastle-on-Tyne, U.K., 1977, later Aldwych Theatre, 1978; *Henry V*, Royal Shakespeare Theatre, 1977, then Aldwych Theatre, 1978; *The Changeling*, Aldwych Theatre, 1978; *Children of the Sun*, Aldwych Theatre, 1979; *Twelfth Night*, Royal Shakespeare Theatre, 1979, then Aldwych Theatre, 1980; *As You Like It, Richard II, Richard III*, all Royal Shakespeare Theatre, 1980, then Aldwych Theatre, 1981; *Much Ado about Nothing*, Royal Shakespeare Theatre, 1982, then Barbican Theatre, London, 1983, later Gershwin Theatre, New York City, 1985; *Arden of Favorsham*, Other Place Theatre, 1982, then Barbican Theatre, 1983; *Poppy*, Barbican Theatre, 1982, then Adelphi Theatre, London, 1983; *Cyrano de Bergerac*, Barbican Theatre, 1983, then Gershwin Theatre, 1985; *Red Noses*, Barbican Theatre, 1985; *Othello*, Royal Shakespeare Theatre, then Barbican Theatre, both 1985; *The Winter's Tale*, Royal Shakespeare Theatre, 1986; *Scenes from a Marriage*, Barbican Theatre, 1986.

MAJOR TOURS—*The Proposal, The Second Shepherds' Play*, both Royal Shakespeare Company (RSC) Theatre-Go-Round, U.K. cities, 1966; *The Dumb Waiter, Pleasure and Repentance, Under Milk Wood*, all RSC Theatre-Go-Round, 1967; *The Merry Wives of Windsor*, RSC, Japanese cities, 1970; *The Merchant of Venice*, RSC, U.K. cities, 1972; *The Actor*, Australian cities, 1974; *Henry V*, RSC, U.K. and European cities, 1976; *Coriolanus*, RSC, European cities, 1979; *Much Ado about Nothing*, RSC, European and U.S. cities, 1984; *Cyrano de Bergerac*, RSC, U.S. cities, 1984.

RELATED CAREER— Founder, artistic director, Everyman Theatre, Liverpool, U.K., 1964-66; artistic director, RSC Theatre-Go-Round, 1966; associate director, Royal Shakespeare Company, 1967-77, then co-artistic director, 1978—; consultant and director, Comedie Francaise, 1975—.

WRITINGS: PLAYS—Translator (with Barbara Wright): *The Balcony*, 1971; *Pleasure and Repentance*, 1976.

RECORDINGS: Murder in the Cathedral, 1976.

AWARDS: Meilleur Spectacle de l'Annee (French critics award), 1972, for *Richard III,* 1976, for *Twelfth Night;* Chevalier des Ordes des Arts et des Lettres, 1975; *Plays and Players* Award, 1977, for *Henry VI;* Best Director, Society of West End Theatre Award, 1978, for *Henry V,* 1983, for *Cyrano de Bergerac;* Best Production, New York Drama League Award, 1985, for *Much Ado about Nothing* and *Cyrano de Bergerac.*

ADDRESSES: OFFICE—c/o Royal Shakespeare Company, Stratford-on-Avon, Warwicks CV37 6BB, England.

*   *   *

HANKS, Tom   1956-

PERSONAL: Born July 9, 1956, in Oakland, CA; married Samatha Lewes (an actress and producer), 1978 (divorced, 1987); children: two. EDUCATION: Attended California State University, Sacramento.

VOCATION: Actor.

CAREER: FILM DEBUT—*He Knows You're Alone,* United Artists, 1980. PRINCIPAL FILM APPEARANCES—Allan Bauer, *Splash,* Touchstone, 1984; Lawrence Bourne III, *Volunteers,* Columbia, 1985; also *Bachelor Party,* Twentieth Century-Fox, 1984; *The Man with One Red Shoe,* Twentieth Century-Fox, 1985; *The Money Pit,* Universal, 1986; *Nothing in Common,* Tri-Star, 1986; *Everytime We Say Goodbye,* 1986; *Love Is Ever Young.*

PRINCIPAL TELEVISION APPEARANCES—Episodic: Ned Donnelly, *Family Ties,* NBC, 1983, then 1984; also *Love Boat,* ABC, 1980; *Taxi,* ABC, 1982; *Happy Days,* ABC, 1982. Series: Kip Wilson/ Buffy Wilson, *Bosom Buddies,* ABC, 1980-82. Movies: *Mazes and Monsters,* CBS, 1982. Guest: *Saturday Night Live,* NBC, 1985; *The Tonight Show,* NBC; *Late Night with David Letterman,* NBC.

PRINCIPAL STAGE APPEARANCES—Performed with the Great Lakes Shakespeare Festival, Cleveland, OH, and the Riverside Shakespeare Company, New York City.

MEMBER: Actors' Equity Association, Screen Actors Guild, American Federation of Television and Radio Artists.

ADDRESSES: AGENT—c/o Mike Simpson, William Morris Agency, 151 El Camino Drive, Beverly Hills, CA 90212.*

*   *   *

HANNAFIN, Daniel   1933-

PERSONAL: Born February 8, 1933, in New York City; son of Daniel (a Wall Street order clerk) and Eleanor (Catterson) Hannafin; married Carol Ann Schmidt (a dancer), August 11, 1962; children: Matthew Brendan, Brian Patrick. EDUCATION: Attended the Juilliard School, 1954-56; studied voice with Milan Petrovic. RELIGION: Roman Catholic. MILITARY: U.S. Coast Guard, 1951-54.

VOCATION: Actor.

DANIEL HANNAFIN

CAREER: STAGE DEBUT—Chorus, *Detroit Melody Circus.* BROADWAY DEBUT—Cpl. Richard West, *South Pacific,* City Center Theatre, 1957. PRINCIPAL STAGE APPEARANCES—Jud Fry, *Oklahoma!,* City Center Theatre, 1963, then 1965; Red Regan, *The Animal Kingdom,* Hartman Theatre, Stamford, CT, 1978; Inspector Thomas, *The Unexpected Guest,* Hartman Theatre, 1980; Constable, *Fiddler on the Roof,* Paper Mill Playhouse, Milburn, NJ, 1983; Dunlap, *Inherit the Wind,* Paper Mill Playhouse, 1984; Lt. Shrank, *West Side Story,* Kennedy Center Opera House, Washington, DC, 1985. Also Pickering, *My Fair Lady;* Jigger, *Carousel;* Herbie, *Gypsy;* Sykes, *Oliver!;* Polyte, *Irma La Douce;* Big Julie, *Guys and Dolls;* Captain, *The Sound of Music;* Polpoch, *Marat/Sade;* Montano, *Othello;* and in *Baker Street, Wonderful Town, Brigadoon, The Tenth Man,* and *Flora, the Red Menace.*

MAJOR TOURS—Pedro, *Man of La Mancha,* U.S. cities, 1979; Lt. Shrank, *West Side Story,* U.S. cities, 1985-87.

FILM DEBUT—Lt. Cooper, *Shaft's Big Score,* Metro-Goldwyn-Mayer, 1972. PRINCIPAL FILM APPEARANCES—*The Taking of Pelham 1-2-3,* United Artists, 1974; *Harry and Tonto,* Twentieth Century-Fox, 1974; *Dog Day Afternoon,* Warner Brothers, 1975; *King Kong,* Paramount, 1976; *The Lonely Guy,* Universal, 1984.

TELEVISION DEBUT—*Kojak* CBS, 1977. PRINCIPAL TELEVISION APPEARANCES—Episodic: *The Andros Targets,* CBS, 1977; *Search for Tomorrow.* Movies: Menneker, *Contract on Cherry Street,* NBC, 1977; *Johnny, We Hardly Knew Ye,* 1977.

MEMBER: Actors' Equity Association, Screen Actors Guild, American Federation of Television and Radio Artists; Lamb's Club (board of directors).

ADDRESSES: HOME—117 Woodland Avenue, Ramsey, NJ 07446.

*   *   *

HARDIMAN, Terrence   1937-

PERSONAL: Born April 6, 1937, in London, England; son of Edward John and Rose (Breeden) Hardiman; married Rowena Cooper. EDUCATION: Attended Cambridge University.

VOCATION: Actor.

CAREER: STAGE DEBUT—*Dr. Faustus,* Old Vic Theatre, 1961. PRINCIPAL STAGE APPEARANCES—Roderigo, *Othello,* Boyet, *Love's Labour's Lost,* Dauphin, *Henry V,* all Bristol Old Vic Theatre, Bristol, U.K., 1962-65; Ambitioso, *The Revenger's Tragedy,* Royal Shakespeare Company (RSC), Stratford-on-Avon, U.K., 1966; Gremio, *The Taming of the Shrew,* Corin, *As You Like It,* both RSC, Stratford-on-Avon, U.K., 1967; Albany, *King Lear,* Mefistofilis, *Dr. Faustus,* Don John, *Much Ado about Nothing,* all RSC, Stratford-on-Avon, U.K., 1968; John Littlewit, *Bartholomew Fair,* RSC, Aldwych Theatre, London, 1969; Lucio, *Measure for Measure,* RSC, Stratford-on-Avon, U.K., 1970; Clarence, *Richard III,* RSC, Stratford-on-Avon, U.K., 1971; Starveling, *A Midsummer Night's Dream,* RSC, Stratford-on-Avon, U.K., 1971; Guppy, *Lying Figures,* Jeanneta Cochrane Theatre, London, 1972; Benedick, *Much Ado about Nothing,* Thorndike Theatre, Leatherhead, U.K., 1973; Bernard Link, *After Haggerty,* Thorndike Theatre, 1974; Mr. Horner, *The Country Wife,* Oxford Playhouse, Oxford, U.K., 1976; Hunt, *Scribes,* Greenwich Theatre, London, 1976; Mortensgaard, *Rosmersholm,* Haymarket Theatre, London, 1979; David Lister, *Daughters of Men,* Hampstead Theatre Club, London, 1979; *The Undisputed Monarch of the English Stage,* Old Vic Theatre, London, 1979.

PRINCIPAL FILM APPEARANCES—*Pope Joan,* 1972.

PRINCIPAL TELEVISION APPEARANCES—*Secret Army.*

RELATED CAREER—Lecturer and performer at universities in the United States as a member of the Actors in Residence project.

MEMBER: British Actors' Equity Association.

SIDELIGHTS: RECREATIONS—Writing, drawing, listening to music.

ADDRESSES: HOME—20 Elgin Mansions, Elgin Avenue, London W9 1JG, England.*

*   *   *

HARPER, Valerie   1940-

PERSONAL: Born August 22, 1940, in Suffern, NY; daughter of Howard and Iva (McConnell) Harper; married Richard Schaal (an actor and writer), 1964 (divorced, 1978). EDUCATION: Attended Hunter College and the New School of Social Research; studied acting with Mary Tarcai and John Cassavetes.

VALERIE HARPER

VOCATION: Actress.

CAREER: STAGE DEBUT—With the corps de ballet, Radio City Music Hall, New York City, 1956-57. PRINCIPAL STAGE APPEARANCES—*Li'l Abner,* St. James Theatre, New York City, 1958; *Take Me Along,* Shubert Theatre, New York City, 1959; *Wildcat,* Alvin Theatre, 1960; *Subways Are for Sleeping,* St. James Theatre, 1961; *Something Different,* Cort Theatre, New York City, 1968; *Story Theatre,* Ambassador Theatre, New York City, 1970-71; *Metamorphosis,* Ambassador Theatre, 1971; *Night of 100 Stars,* Radio City Music Hall, 1982; appeared with the Second City Repertory Company, Chicago, IL, 1964-69; with the Seattle Repertory Company, WA; and in summer stock theatres and nightclubs.

MAJOR TOURS—Dr. Martha Livingstone, *Agnes of God,* U.S. cities.

PRINCIPAL TELEVISION APPEARANCES—Series: Rhoda Morgenstern, *The Mary Tyler Moore Show,* CBS, 1970-74; Rhoda Morgenstern Gerard, *Rhoda,* CBS, 1974-78; *Valerie,* NBC, 1986-87. Pilots: Liz Farrell, *Farrell for the People,* NBC, 1982. Movies: Ann Menzente, *Thursday's Game,* ABC, 1974; Carol Turner, *Night Terror,* NBC, 1977; Maggie, *The Shadow Box,* ABC, 1980; Carol Hefferman, *Fun and Games,* ABC, 1980; Norma Danner, *The Day the Loving Stopped,* ABC, 1981; Laura, *Don't Go to Sleep,* ABC, 1982; Kate Bianchi, *An Invasion of Privacy,* CBS, 1983; Hannah Epstein, *The Execution,* NBC, 1985; *Strange Voices,* NBC, 1987; *Drop Out Mother,* CBS, upcoming. Specials: *I Love Liberty.*

PRINCIPAL FILM APPEARANCES—*Freebie and the Bean,* Warner

Brother, 1974; *Chapter Two,* Columbia, 1979; *The Last Married Couple in America,* Universal, 1980; *Blame It On Rio,* Twentieth Century-Fox, 1984.

AWARDS: Outstanding Performance by an Actress in a Supporting Role in Comedy, Emmy awards, 1971, 1972, and 1973, all for *The Mary Tyler Moore Show;* Outstanding Lead Actress in a Comedy Series, Emmy Award, 1975, for *Rhoda;* Golden Globe Award, Hollywood Foreign Press Association, 1975; Golden Apple Award, Hollywood Women's Press Club; Photoplay Gold Medal Award; Woman of the Year Award, Hasty Pudding Club, Harvard University.

MEMBER: American Federation of Television and Radio Artists; Hunger Project, LIFE (Love Is Feeding Everyone; founding member), End Hunger Network, Save the Children, Africare, Oxfam, Santa Monica Rape Treatment Center.

ADDRESSES: PUBLICIST—Michael Levine Public Relations Company, 8730 Sunset Boulevard, Los Angeles, CA 90069.

*   *   *

HARRIS, Cynthia

PERSONAL: Born August 9; daughter of Saul (a businessman) Harris and his wife. EDUCATION: Received B.A. from Smith College; studied acting with Lee Strasberg and George Morrison.

VOCATION: Actress and producer.

CYNTHIA HARRIS

CAREER: STAGE DEBUT—*The Premise,* Premise Theatre, New York City, 1961. BROADWAY DEBUT—*Natural Affection,* Booth Theatre, 1963. LONDON DEBUT—*America Hurrah,* Royal Court Theatre, 1968. PRINCIPAL STAGE APPEARANCES—*The Best Laid Plans,* Brooks Atkinson Theatre, New York City, 1966; *America Hurrah,* Pocket Theatre, New York City, 1966; *The Serpent—A Ceremony,* Public Theatre, then Washington Square Methodist Church, both New York City, 1970; *Company,* Alvin Theatre, New York City, 1970; *The White House Murder Case,* Circle in the Square, New York City, 1970; *Mystery Play,* Cherry Lane Theatre, New York City, 1973; *Bad Habits,* Astor Place Theatre, then Booth Theatre, both New York City, 1974; Ellen, Mrs. Saunders, *Cloud Nine,* Lucille Lortel Theatre, New York City, 1981; Charlotte Cushman, *Romance Language,* Plawrights Horizons, New York City, 1984. Also appeared in *Three by Saroyan,* Cherry Lane Theatre, New York City; *The Merry Wives of Windsor,* New York Shakespeare Festival, New York City; *Second Avenue Rag,* Association of Performing Artists, Phoenix Theatre, New York City; *The Shadow Box, Too Much Johnson,* both Mark Taper Forum, Los Angeles, CA; *Hold Me,* Westside Arts Theatre, New York City; *Make and Break,* Kennedy Center for the Performing Arts, Washington, DC; in *The Beauty Part, Any Wednesday,* and performed for three seasons at the Williamstown Theatre Festival, Williamstown, MA, and as a resident member of the Open Theatre, New York City, for eight years.

PRINCIPAL STAGE WORK—Co-producer, *Honky Tonk Nights,* workshop production, 1983.

FILM DEBUT—*Isadora* (also known as *The Loves of Isadora*), Universal, 1969. PRINCIPAL FILM APPEARANCES— *Been Down So Long It Looks Like Up to Me,* Paramount, 1971; *Up the Sandbox,* National General, 1972; *The Tempest,* Columbia, 1982; *Reuben, Reuben,* Twentieth Century-Fox, 1983; *Three Men and a Baby,* Touchstone, 1987. Also appeared in *I Could Never Have Sex with Any Man Who Has So Little Respect for My Husband,* 1973;

TELEVISION DEBUT—*The Bob Newhart Show,* CBS. PRINCIPAL TELEVISION APPEARANCES—Episodic: *Quincy, M.E.,* NBC; *Kojak,* CBS; *Nurse,* CBS; *Newhart,* CBS; *Three's Company,* ABC; *L.A. Law,* NBC; also *Everything's Relative.* Series: Maureen O'Connor, *Sirota's Court,* NBC, 1976; Paula Zuckerman, *Husbands, Wives & Lovers,* CBS, 1978. Mini-Series: Wallace Simpson, "Edward and Mrs. Simpson," *Masterpiece Theatre,* PBS, 1978. Movies: *The Princess and the Cabbie,* 1981; *Izzie and Moe,* 1985; also *A Special Friendship.*

AWARDS: Best Actress nomination, British Academy of Film and Television Arts, 1978, for *Edward and Mrs. Simpson;* Obie Award from the *Village Voice,* as a member of the Open Theatre ensemble.

MEMBER: Actors' Equity Association, Screen Actors Guild, American Federation of Television and Radio Artists.

ADDRESSES: HOME—New York, NY. AGENT—S.T.E. Representation, Ltd., 888 Seventh Avenue, New York, NY 10019.

*   *   *

HARRY, Jackee

BRIEF ENTRY: First name is pronounced "Jack-*kay.*" Jackee Harry is known to television audiences for the spice and laughs she has brought to NBC's family comedy series *227* since 1985. Playing the seductive upstairs neighbor Sandra Clark with a distinctive wardrobe, wiggle, and tendency toward double entendres has resulted in fan mail for the actress equalling that of the show's star, Marla Gibbs, and the producers have enlarged the part accordingly. Harry was playing another femme fatale, Lily Mason, on the soap opera *Another World* when she won the part of Sandra; for a while she commuted between the two shows' production facilities in Los Angeles and New York City, where she grew up. Her earlier New York credits included Broadway appearances in *Eubie!, The Wiz,* and *One Mo' Time,* small parts in Off-Broadway productions, and a successful cabaret act. Her first professional training, however, had been for an operatic career, a goal she gave up "because there's already one Leontyne Price," she told *TV Guide* (March 28, 1987). A graduate of Long Island University, Harry taught history at Brooklyn Technical High School for a short time before pursuing her entertainment career.

*   *   *

HARVEY, Peter 1933-

PERSONAL: Born January 2, 1933, in Quirigua, Guatemala; son of Francis William and Zena Erica (Henriquez) Harvey. EDUCATION: Attended Ridley College and University of Miami.

VOCATION: Set and costume designer.

CAREER: FIRST STAGE WORK—Set designer, *Pantomime for Lovers* (ballet), Dade County Auditorium, Miami, FL, 1954. PRINCIPAL STAGE WORK—All in New York City unless indicated: Set designer, *The Confederates,* Theatre Marquee, 1959; set designer, *Noontide,* Theatre Marquee, 1961; set designer, *The Thracian Horses,* Orpheum Theatre, 1961; set designer, *One Way Pendulum,* East 74th Street Theatre, 1961; set designer, *Plays for Bleecker Street,* Circle in the Square, 1962; set designer, *Put It in Writing,* Theatre de Lys, 1963; set and costume designer, *The Immoralist,* Bouwerie Lane Theatre, 1963; set and costume designer, *Baby Want a Kiss,* Little Theatre, 1964; set and costume designer, *All Women Are One,* Gate Theatre, 1965; set and costume designer, *The Sweet Enemy,* Actors Playhouse, 1965; costume designer, *All in Good Time,* Royale Theatre, 1965; set designer, *Good Day,* Cherry Lane Theatre, 1965; set and costume designer, *The Exhaustion of Our Son's Love,* Cherry Lane Theatre, 1965; set designer, *The Mad Show,* New Theatre, 1966; set and costume designer, *Hooray! It's a Glorious Day . . . And All That,* Theatre Four, 1966; set designer, *The Death of the Well Loved Boy,* St. Mark's Playhouse, 1967; set designer, *Walking to Waldheim, Happiness,* both Forum Theatre, 1967; set designer, *The Boys in the Band,* Theatre Four, 1968; set designer, *Red Cross, Muzeeka,* both Provincetown Playhouse, 1968; set designer, *Sweet Eros, Witness,* both Gramercy Arts Theatre, 1968; set designer, *Dames at Sea,* Bouwerie Lane Theatre, 1968; set designer, *The Boys in the Band,* Wyndham Theatre, London, 1969; set designer, *Dames at Sea,* Duchess Theatre, London, 1969.

Set and costume designer, *Watercolor, Criss-Crossing* both American National Theatre Academy (ANTA) Playhouse, 1970; set and costume designer, *Transfers,* Village South Theatre, 1970; set and costume designer, *Park,* John Golden Theatre, 1970; set designer, *Exchange,* Mercer-O'Casey Theatre, 1970; set designer, *One Night Stands of a Noisy Passenger,* Actors Playhouse, 1970; set designer, *The Nuns,* Cherry Lane Theatre, 1970; set and costume

designer, *The Survival of St. Joan,* Anderson Theatre, 1971; set designer, *Johnny Johnson,* Edison Theatre, 1971; set designer, *Welcome to Andromeda, Variety Obit,* both Cherry Lane Theatre, 1973; set and costume designer, *The Children's Mass,* Theatre de Lys, 1973; set designer, *Gloria and Esperanza,* ANTA Playhouse, 1973; set designer, *Sextet,* Bijou Theatre, 1974; set designer, *Kaboom!,* Bottom Line Theatre, 1974; set designer, *The Government Inspector,* Hartman Theatre, Stamford, CT, 1975; set designer, *Unsung Cole,* Circle Repertory Theatre, 1977; set and costume designer, *The Effect of Gamma Rays on Man-in-the-Moon Marigolds,* Biltmore Theatre, 1978; set designer, *Songs of Joy and Sorrow* (ballet), Colorado Ballet, Denver, CO, 1980; set designer, *Cyrano de Bergerac,* Santa Fe Festival, Santa Fe, NM, 1981; costume designer, *Firebird 2006* (ballet), Colorado Ballet, 1981; set designer, *Jane Avril,* Provincetown Playhouse, 1982; set designer, *a/k/a Tennessee,* South Street Theatre, 1982; set designer, *Rhinestone,* Richard Allen Center, 1982; set and costume designer, *Dames at Sea,* Asolo State Theatre, Sarasota, FL, 1984. Also in New York City unless indicated: set designer, *PS 193,* 1962; set and costume designer, *Noye's Fludde* (opera), 1964; set and costume designer, *Concerning Oracles* (ballet), 1966; set designer, *The Jewels* (ballet), 1967; set designer, a dramatized anthology of Puerto Rican short stories, 1971; set designer, *Black Picture Show,* 1975; set designer, *Straws in the Wind,* 1975; set and costume designer, *The Sorrows of Frederick the Great,* 1976; set designer, *A Midsummer Night's Dream* (ballet), Zurich, Switzerland, 1978; set designer, *The Nutcracker* (ballet), New Jersey Ballet, 1980; costume designer, *Who Cares?* (ballet), Zurich, Switzerland, 1980; set designer, *Capriccio for Piano and Orchestra* (ballet), Zurich, Switzerland, 1980; set designer, *Boris Godunov* (opera), 1986; set designer, *Foggy Day,* 1987.

PRINCIPAL TELEVISION WORK—Episodic: Set designer, four ballets, *Dance in America,* PBS.

RELATED CAREER—Teacher, scenic and costume design, scene painting, and history of costume design at the Pratt Institute, Brooklyn, NY, 1970-87.

AWARDS: Drama Critics Circle Award, Best Design, 1969; Graphics and Design Award, National Association of Educational Broadcasters, 1979.

MEMBER: United Scenic Artists, Local 829.

ADDRESSES: OFFICE—96 Perry Street, New York, NY 10014.

*   *   *

HAWN, Goldie 1945-

PERSONAL: Born November 21, 1945, in Washington, DC; daughter of Edward Rutledge (a musician) and Laura (Steinhoff) Hawn; married Gus Trinkonis in 1969 (divorced); married Bill Hudson in 1976 (divorced); children: Oliver Hudson, Kate Hudson, Wyatt Hawn-Russell. EDUCATION: Attended American University.

VOCATION: Actress and producer.

CAREER: FILM DEBUT—Toni Simmons, *Cactus Flower,* Columbia, 1969. PRINCIPAL FILM APPEARANCES—Marion, *There's a Girl in My Soup,* Columbia, 1970; Dawn Divine, *$ (Dollars),* Columbia, 1971; Jill Tanner, *Butterflies Are Free,* Columbia,

1972; Oktyabrina, *The Girl from Petrovka,* Universal, 1974; Lou Jean Poplin, *The Sugarland Express,* Univeral, 1974; Jill, *Shampoo,* Columbia, 1975; Amanda Quaid, *The Duchess and the Dirtwater Fox,* Twentieth Century-Fox, 1976; Gloria Mundy, *Foul Play,* Paramount, 1978; Judy Benjamin, *Private Benjamin,* Warner Brothers, 1980; Glenda, *Seems Like Old Times,* Columbia, 1980; Anita, *Lovers and Liars* (also known as *Travels with Anita* and *A Trip with Anita*), Pickman, 1981; Paula McCullen, *Best Friends,* Warner Brothers, 1982; Kay Walsh, *Swing Shift,* Warner Brothers, 1984; Sunny, *Protocol,* Warner Brothers, 1984; *Wildcats,* Warner Brothers, 1986; *Overboard,* Warner Brothers, 1987.

PRINCIPAL FILM WORK—Producer: *The Girl from Petrovka,* Universal, 1974; *Private Benjamin,* Warner Brothers, 1980; *Swing Shift,* Warner Brothers, 1984; *Wildcats,* Warner Brothers, 1986.

PRINCIPAL TELEVISION APPEARANCES—Series: Sandy Kramer, *Good Morning, World,* CBS, 1967-68; *Rowan and Martin's Laugh-In,* NBC, 1968-70. Specials: *Pure Goldie,* NBC, 1970; *Goldie Hawn Special,* CBS, 1978; *Goldie and Liza Together,* CBS, 1980; *Goldie and Kids: Listen to Me,* ABC, 1982; *George Burns's 100th Birthday Special,* NBC, 1982; also appeared as a dancer, *Andy Griffith Special.*

AWARDS: Best Supporting Actress, Academy Award, 1969, for *Cactus Flower.*

MEMBER: Actors' Equity Association, Screen Actors Guild, American Federation of Television and Radio Artists.

SIDELIGHTS: Once a dancer who was promoted because she couldn't read cue cards properly, Goldie Hawn is now considered one of the finest comic actresses in the entertainment industry. She is also a powerful and respected producer whose films, including *Private Benjamin, Protocol,* and *Wildcats,* have grossed more than $100 million since 1980. In a November, 1982 *Film Comment* feature, David Thomson described the source of Hawn's appeal: "She has very subtly shifted from Burbank airhead to the epitome of mature cuteness: wholesome, pretty, easily amused, responsive, warm, energetic, and, in her own words, 'an honest, decent, psychologically correct character. Solid.' " David Ansen also noted in his January 12, 1981 *Newsweek* profile that Hawn's "screen personality is a distillation of a long strain of funny-girl archetypes. . . . If Goldie . . . is the reigning comedienne of the moment, it may be because she safely appeals to both the conservative and the liberal currents in the culture—she can be rube and role model all at once." As a consequence of her wise choices of film roles, her business acumen, and her family-oriented lifestyle, Ansen stated, she has proven that "If Goldie Hawn is a dumb blonde, Henry Kissinger is a dopey brunet."

Hawn was raised in Takoma Park, Maryland, a suburb of Washington, DC. Her father was a professional musician who occasionally performed at White House functions and who enjoyed relating the antics of the very powerful to his family. "He'd come home with a funny, sarcastic look at things," she told *Newsweek.* "Maybe that's where I got my sense of satire." Hawn studied dancing and piano from the age of five and decided very early in life that she wanted to dance for a living. An interest in acting came later, when she was seventeen. In her first on-stage role she played Juliet in a summer stock production of *Romeo and Juliet* in Williamsburg, Virginia; she was moved, she told *Newsweek,* when "it started to rain and nobody left." Also at seventeen, Hawn opened her own dancing school and used the profits she earned from teaching ballet to study at American University. She stayed in college for less than two

years, eventually quitting to try her luck in New York. Her first dancing job there was in a chorus line for a 1964 World's Fair stage show. Then work became scarce and Hawn had to scrape to survive.

According to Rick Lyman in a February 17, 1985 *Philadelphia Inquirer* story, Hawn's early years as a performer "were filled with squalor and bohemian adventure; she danced at various go-go joints in Manhattan and North Jersey, gyrating in a cage to the disco din of that era." She was rejected at Broadway auditions and forced by financial circumstances to live in a dangerous neighborhood frequented by addicts and prostitutes. Finally she went to California with a group of friends, hoping for better luck there. She ended up in a Las Vegas chorus line. Hawn remembered those days in a New York *Daily News* interview of April 30, 1978: "I was up all night, sleeping all day, and I turned into a zombie. I saw myself one day on TV in a red wig, looking like somebody's pet monkey. That's when I quit. . . . I went back to L.A." She gave herself a nine-month deadline to "make it," promising her parents she would return to Maryland if she failed. She landed a spot as a dancer in an Andy Griffith special, and a William Morris agent decided to take her on as a client. Then she briefly played a small part on a CBS series entitled *Good Morning, World,* and thereby came to the attention of George Schlatter, a producer seeking talent for a new comedy-variety show called *Laugh-In.*

Originally Hawn was hired as a *Laugh-In* dancer who would perform while covered with body painted designs and comic slogans. As Lyman noted, however, her role soon burgeoned quite by accident. "Schlatter thought Hawn could introduce some of the guests," Lyman wrote, "but the first time she stepped in front of the camera, she began muffing her lines, giggling with what has now become her familiar style of uncomplicated merriment. Schlatter encouraged it, conspired with the other cast members to break her up on camera, tossed surprise buckets of water on her head from the wings. And she responded by peeling away her inhibitions and revealing, like a blossoming flower, a personality of such winning and natural innocence that the audience was captivated." In the space of a year Hawn became a major member of the *Laugh-In* ensemble, but her role—once spontaneous—became more and more difficult to maintain. "As the years went on it got harder," she told *Newsweek.* "I had to be consistently one character. There was no room for anything else." At the height of her popularity, Hawn left *Laugh-In* for other challenges, and the film industry welcomed her.

Hawn has appeared in more than fifteen major features since 1969. Her first movie role, as the young mistress of a dentist in *Cactus Flower,* won her an Academy Award as best supporting actress—an honor she viewed with ambivalence. Victory, she told *Newsweek,* had come too easily. "I wanted to win for working hard," she said. "That performance was just a drop in the bucket." Nevertheless, critics were impressed with the actress's ability to set aside the giggly stereotype for a characterization deemed both witty and sensitive. Her subsequent films continued to show a widening range; Lyman wrote: "She has played a criminal, a lawyer, several hippies, even a factory worker. Yet all of her characters do have the quality that Hawn refers to as 'moral fiber.' They are naive, maybe even innocent, but they are not stupid, and they are propelled by an unwavering sense of common-sensical decency." Hawn's most successful film to date is *Private Benjamin,* a comedy in which a wealthy young woman named Judy Benjamin joins the army. Ansen assessed the film's special achievement: "Judy Benjamin's transformation from spoiled Jewish princess to competent soldier to imperiled fiancee to rebellious feminist," Ansen declared, "is a kind of all-embracing collage of feminine comedic stereotypes, including a symbolic change from heiress to buck private. The contemporary twist is that she remains equally adorable as she changes from victim to avenger.''

Hawn's private life has not been without its challenges. She is twice divorced and is the mother of three young children, the youngest a son by her *Swing Shift* co-star, actor Kurt Russell. Busy as she is with her acting and producing duties, Hawn has expressed her determination to maintain a stable family life for her children. ''I will not have a neurotic Hollywood child on my hands,'' she told the *Daily News*. ''It might seem like an old-fashioned concept, but I think the family unit is something you can depend on even if everything else fails.'' A self-styled recluse who avoids industry parties, Hawn has also earned a reputation as a producer who cannot be bullied—and one who can apply pressure to achieve her own ends. ''You have to stand up for what you believe in,'' she told the *Philadelphia Inquirer*. ''Sometimes you know better what you are able to do than anyone else.''

Hawn brings this sort of confidence to her assessment of her own career. She is looking forward to more serious roles and is not overly concerned that age will diminish her marketability. As she told *Film Comment*, ''I think we must all be aware of—not burdened by— . . . our limitations, and that doesn't mean they're lasting. . . . Some of the worst mistakes are by actors who think they transcend all of it. So I think rather than being afraid of the 'industrial wisdom,' I'm being run by my own personal sense of wisdom. And that's the clock, that's the brain I listen to.'' With the transition from dizzy comic pin-up to consistent actress and businesswoman behind her, Hawn told the *New York Times* (July 23, 1978) that she got many fan letters saying, ''You're a woman now but you haven't let us down.'' That, she told the newspaper, ''was my dearest compliment.''

ADDRESSES: AGENT—c/o Ron Meyer, Creative Artists Agency, 1888 Century Park E., Los Angeles, CA 90067.

*   *   *

HAYDEN, Larry   1950-

PERSONAL: Born Larry Dill, October 8, 1950, in Union City, PA; son of Earl L. (an engineer) and Jaqueline Christina (a hotel and travel manager; maiden name, Gardei) Dill. EDUCATION: Trained as a dancer and choreographer at the National Ballet School of Canada, 1968-69; also trained with Bronislava Nijinska and Hans Brenaa at the Royal Danish Ballet and with Natalya Zolotova at the Bolshoi Ballet.

VOCATION: Dancer, choreographer, and teacher.

CAREER: STAGE DEBUT—Dancer, *Anne of Green Gables*, Royal Alexandra Theatre, Toronto, ON, Canada, 1969. PRINCIPAL STAGE APPEARANCES—Dancer, *Johnny Belinda*, Charlottetown Festival Theatre, Canada, 1969; principal dancer with the Alberta Ballet Company, Canada; soloist, *Carnaval, La Sylphide, Sleeping Beauty,* and *Graduation Ball,* all with the American Classical Ballet Company, Buffalo, NY, 1969-70; dancer with the Royal Winnipeg Ballet, Canada, 1970-75.

PRINCIPAL STAGE WORK—Choreographer, *Hijinks!,* Chelsea Theatre Center, New York City, 1980; director, *Libeslieder Waltzer,* Minnesota Orchestra Theatre, Minneapolis, 1981; choreogra-

pher: *The Abduction of Figaro*, Minnesota Opera Company, Minneapolis, 1984; *Camino Real*, Chautauqua Theatre Company, NY, 1985; *Casanova's Homecoming*, Minnesota Opera Company, 1985; with the Greater Miami Opera, FL: *Annie Get Your Gun, Carousel,* and *Salute to Broadway,* all 1985 and *A Sondheim Revue,* 1986; *As You Like It* and *Orchards,* both with The Acting Company, New York City, 1985-86; *Don Giovanni,* The Juilliard School, New York City, 1986; *Lucky Lucy* and *The Fortune Man,* both with The Writers Theatre, New York City, 1986; with the Music Theatre of Witchita, KS: *Man of La Mancha* and *Peter Pan,* both 1986 and *Girl Crazy* and *Brigadoon,* both 1987; *Rigoletto,* Greater Miami Opera, 1987.

Choreographer of original ballets: *The Pied Piper*, with the Alberta Ballet Company, Canada; also *Quest, Festive Airs, Moments Partita, Four Portraits, Collage, Forcefields, Divertimento, Mutations, Introduction, Beethoven Pas de Deux, Fete Brilliante, The Whims of Love, Easy Winners, The Passing Strange, Gloria, The Seasons, Holberg Suite, The Farewell, The Venetian Twins, Intermezzo, Pas Diamante,* and *Remembrance of Things to Come,* all for such companies as The Royal Winnepeg Ballet, Deutsch Opera Ballet, Banff Festival Ballet, American College in Paris, Minnesota Dance Theatre, Zenon Dance Company, Les Ballets Jazz de Montreal, and the Minnesota Jazz Dance Company.

PRINCIPAL TELEVISION WORK—Choreographer of dance specials, weekly variety shows, and ballet programs for CBC, Toronto, Montreal, and Winnipeg, Canada.

RELATED CAREER—Balletmaster and choreographer, Banff School of Fine Arts, 1972-82; teacher and choreographer, Royal Winnepeg

LARRY HAYDEN

Ballet, 1972-77; balletmaster and choreographer, Minnesota Dance Theatre, 1977-82; founder of ballet school, Minneapolis, 1981; teacher and choreographer, Juilliard School, New York City, 1986-87; also master teacher and choreographer, University of Calgary, University of Manitoba, University of Alberta, and University of Minnesota.

ADDRESSES: AGENT—Roseanne Kirk Associates, 161 W. 54th Street, New York, NY 10022.

*   *   *

HAYDEN, Sophie
(Sophie Schwab)

PERSONAL: Born Sophie Schwab, February 23, in Miami, FL; daughter of Leo J. (a construction worker) and Sophie M. (a waitress; maiden name, Ruba) Schwab; married David Rosen (a ceramacist), August 10, 1980. EDUCATION: Received B.F.A., theatre, from Northwestern University; studied for the stage with Robert Modica, Mira Rostova, and Harold Guskin.

VOCATION: Actress.

CAREER: PRINCIPAL STAGE APPEARANCES—(As Sophie Schwab) Deborah Da Costa, *King of Schnorrers,* Harold Clurman Theatre, then Playhouse Theatre, both New York City, 1979; (as Sophie Schwab) Mrs. Sherwood Stratton, *Barnum,* St. James Theatre, New York City, 1980; (as Sophie Schwab) Amalia, *She Loves Me,*

SOPHIE HAYDEN

Playwrights Horizons, New York City, 1981; (as Sophie Schwab) *The Passion of Dracula,* GeVa Theatre, Rochester, NY, 1981; (as Sophie Schwab) Adriana, *The Comedy of Errors,* Goodman Theatre, Chicago, IL, 1983; (as Sophie Schwab) Willa, *Jesse's Land,* American Jewish Theatre, New York City, 1984; (as Sophie Schwab) *The Three Moscowteers,* Goodman Theatre, 1984; Masha, *The Three Sisters,* Indiana Repertory Theatre, Indianapolis, IN, 1985; Annie, *Lies My Father Told Me,* Jewish Repertory Theatre, New York City, 1986; Adriana, *The Comedy of Errors,* Vivian Beaumont Theatre, New York City, 1987. Also appeared in *Working,* Union Square Theatre, New York City, 1980; and as Rebecca, *Rags,* pre-Broadway workshop, New York City.

TELEVISION DEBUT—Adriana, "The Comedy of Errors," *Live from Lincoln Center,* PBS, 1987.

MEMBER: Actors' Equity Association.*

ADDRESSES: HOME—New York, NY.

*   *   *

HEARD, John   1947-

PERSONAL: Born March 7, 1947, in Washington, DC; married Margot Kidder (an actress). EDUCATION: Clark University.

VOCATION: Actor.

CAREER: STAGE DEBUT—With the Organic Theatre. PRINCIPAL STAGE APPEARANCES—*Warp,* Chicago and New York City; also appeared in *Streamers;* Micah, *G.R. Point,* Marymount Manhattan Theatre, New York City, 1977; Adolf, "Creditors," part of the double bill, *Creditors/The Stronger,* New York Shakespeare Festival (NYSF), Newman/Public Theatre, New York City, 1977; Cassio, *Othello,* NYSF, Delacorte Theatre, New York City, 1979; Paul, *Split,* Second Stage, New York City, 1980; title role, "The Vagabond" and Savely, "The Witch," as part of the triple bill *The Chekov Sketchbook,* Harold Clurman Theatre, New York City, 1980; Henry Hirsch, *Total Abandon,* Perry Street Theatre, 1982, then at the Booth Theatre, New York City, 1983; Gentleman Caller, *The Glass Menagerie,* Eugene O'Neill Theatre, New York City, 1983-84.

PRINCIPAL FILM APPEARANCES—*Between the Lines,* Midwest, 1977; *On the Yard,* Midwest, 1979; *Head Over Heels* (also know as *Chilly Scenes of Winter),* United Artists, 1979; *Heartbeat,* Warner Brothers, 1980; *Cutter and Bone,* United Artists, 1981; *Cat People,* Universal, 1982; *Lies,* 1983; *Heaven Help Us,* Tri-Star, 1985; *The Trip to Bountiful,* Island, 1985; *After Hours,* Geffen, 1985.

PRINCIPAL TELEVISION APPEARANCES—Teleplays: *The Scarlet Letter; Tender Is the Night,* Showtime. Movies: David Manning, *Out on a Limb,* ABC, 1987.

AWARDS: Theatre World Award, 1976-77; Obie Award, 1980, for *Othello* and *Split.*

MEMBER: Actors' Equity Association, Screen Actors Guild.

ADDRESSES: AGENT—c/o Rick Nicita, Creative Artists Agency, 1888 Century Park East, Suite 1400, Los Angeles, CA 90067.*

NICKY HENSON

HENSON, Nicky   1945-

PERSONAL: Born May 12, 1945, in London, England; son of Leslie Lincoln and Harriet Martha (Collins) Henson; married Una Stubbs (divorced). EDUCATION: Trained for the stage at the Royal Academy of Dramatic Art.

VOCATION: Actor and composer.

CAREER: LONDON DEBUT—*All Square,* Vaudeville Theatre, 1963. PRINCIPAL STAGE APPEARANCES—Mordred, *Camelot,* Drury Lane Theatre, London, 1964; Ellis, *Passion Flower Hotel,* Prince of Wales Theatre, London, 1965; *London Laughs,* Palladium Theatre, London, 1966; soldier, *The Soldier's Tale,* Edinburgh Festival, Edinburgh, Scotland, U.K., 1967; Niko, *Climb the Greased Pole,* Mermaid Theatre, London, 1967; Squire, Nicholas, Damon, *Canterbury Tales,* Phoenix Theatre, London, 1968; Toad, *Toad of Toad Hall,* Strand Theatre, London, 1969; *The Ride Across Lake Constance,* Hampstead Theatre Club, then May Fair Theatre, both London, 1974; bus driver, *Mind Your Head,* Petruchio, *The Taming of the Shrew,* both Shaw Theatre, London, 1974; Laertes, *Hamlet,* Greenwich Theatre, London, 1974; Bottom, *A Midsummer Night's Dream,* Open Air Theatre, London, 1974; Buttons, *Cinderella,* Casino Theatre, London, 1974; Lorne, *Mardi Gras,* Prince of Wales Theatre, 1976; Leonardo da Vinci, *Later Leonardo,* Arnaud Theatre, Guilford, U.K., 1976; Lord Fancourt Babberley, *Charley's Aunt,* Young Vic Theatre, London, 1976; Captain Bluntschli, *Arms and the Man,* Thorndike Theatre, Leatherhead, U.K., then Hong Kong Festival, 1977; Henry Straker, *Man and Superman,* Malvern Festival, Malvern, U.K., then Savoy Theatre, London,

1977; title role, *Oedipus at the Crossroads,* King's Head Theatre, London, 1977; Gerald Popkiss, *Rookery Nook,* Birmingham Repertory Company, Birmingham, U.K., then Her Majesty's Theatre, London, 1979; Garn, *Noises Off,* Savoy Theatre, London, 1982; *The Relapse,* Lyric Theatre, London, 1983; *Sufficient Carbohydrates,* Hampstead Theatre Club, then Albery Theatre, London, 1983; *Mandragola,* National Theatre, London, 1984; Touchstone, *As You Like It,* Mr. Ford, *The Merry Wives of Windsor,* both with the Royal Shakespeare Company, 1985.

With the Young Vic Theatre Company, Young Vic Theatre, London, unless indicated: Ottavio, *The Cheats of Scapin,* 1970; soldier, *The Soldier's Tale,* 1970; Pozzo, *Waiting for Godot,* 1970; Grumio, *The Taming of the Shrew,* 1970; Herod, *The Wakefield Cycle,* 1970; messenger, *Oedipus,* 1970; Young Marlow, *She Stoops to Conquer,* 1971; Lucio, *Measure for Measure,* 1971; Mercutio, *Romeo and Juliet,* 1971; Solange, *The Maids,* 1972; Greeneyes, *Deathwatch,* 1972; Jack Sheppard, *Stand and Deliver,* Edinburgh Festival, then Round House Theatre, London, 1972; Jimmy Porter, *Look Back in Anger,* 1972; Rosencrantz, *Rosencrantz and Guildenstern Are Dead,* 1973.

With the National Theatre Company, Olivier Theatre, London: Yepihodov, *The Cherry Orchard,* 1979; Malcolm, *Macbeth,* 1979; Heros, *The Woman,* 1979; Mr. Brisk, *The Double Dealer,* 1979; Captain Ager, *A Fair Quarrel,* 1979; Constantin, *The Provoked Wife,* 1982; Treves, *The Elephant Man,* 1982; also appeared in *The Browning Version* and *Harlequinade,* 1980.

MAJOR TOURS—Bill, *Zoo, Zoo, Widdershins Zoo,* U.K. cities, 1969.

PRINCIPAL FILM APPEARANCES—*Witchfinder General,* 1965; *There's a Girl in My Soup,* Columbia, 1970; *The Bawdy Adventures of Tom Jones,* Universal, 1976. Also appeared in *Number 1 of the Secret Service.*

PRINCIPAL TELEVISION APPEARANCES—Series: *Prometheus,* BBC.

WRITINGS: THEATRICAL SCORES—*Oedipus,* Young Vic Theatre, London, 1970.

MEMBER: British Actors' Equity Association, Screen Actors Guild; Gerry's Club.

SIDELIGHTS: FAVORITE ROLES—Pozzo in *Waiting for Godot.* RECREATIONS—Songwriting, reading, motorcycling.

ADDRESSES: OFFICE—c/o Richard Stone, 18-20 York Buildings, London WC2, England.

*   *   *

HEPBURN, Katharine   1909-

PERSONAL: Full name, Katharine Houghton Hepburn; born November 9, 1909, in Hartford, CT; daughter of Dr. Thomas N. (a surgeon) and Katharine (a feminist; maiden name, Houghton) Hepburn; married Ludlow Ogden Smith, 1928 (divorced, 1934). EDUCATON: Hartford School for Girls; Bryn Mawr College, B.A., 1928.

VOCATION: Actress.

CAREER: FILM DEBUT—Sydney Fairfield, *A Bill of Divorcement,* RKO, 1932. PRINCIPAL FILM APPEARANCES— Cynthia, *Christopher Strong,* RKO, 1933; Eva Lovelace, *Morning Glory,* RKO, 1933; Jo, *Little Women,* RKO, 1934; Trigger Hicks, *Spitfire,* RKO, 1934; Lady Babbie, *The Little Minister,* RKO, 1934; title role, *Alice Adams,* RKO, 1935; title role, *Sylvia Scarlett,* RKO, 1935; Mary Stuart, *Mary of Scotland,* RKO, 1936; Pamela Thistlewaite, *A Woman Rebels,* RKO, 1936; Phoebe Throssel, *Quality Street,* RKO, 1937; Terry Randall, *Stage Door,* RKO, 1937; Susan Vance, *Bringing Up Baby,* RKO, 1938; Linda Seton, *Holiday,* Columbia, 1938; Tracy Lord, *The Philadelphia Story,* Metro-Goldwyn-Mayer (MGM), 1940; Tess Harding, *Woman of the Year,* MGM, 1942; Christine Forrest, *Keeper of the Flame,* MGM, 1942; cameo, *Stage Door Canteen,* United Artists, 1943; Jade, *Dragon Seed,* MGM, 1944; Jamie Rowan, *Without Love,* MGM, 1945; Ann Hamilton, *Undercurrent,* MGM, 1946; Lutie Cameron, *The Sea of Grass,* MGM, 1947; Clara Wieck Schumann, *Song of Love,* MGM, 1947; Mary Matthews, *State of the Union,* MGM, 1948; Amanda Bonner, *Adam's Rib,* MGM, 1949; Rose Sayer, *The African Queen,* Horizon Romulus, 1951; Pat Pemberton, *Pat and Mike,* MGM, 1952; cameo, *The Road to Bali,* Paramount, 1952; Jane Hudson, *Summertime,* United Artists, 1955; Lizzie Curry, *The Rainmaker,* Paramount, 1956; Vinka Kovelenko, *The Iron Petticoat,* MGM, 1956; Bunny Watson, *Desk Set,* Twentieth Century-Fox, 1957; Violet Venable, *Suddenly Last Summer,* Columbia, 1959; Mary Tyrone, *Long Day's Journey into Night,* Embassy, 1962; Christina Drayton, *Guess Who's Coming to Dinner,* Columbia, 1968; Queen Eleanor of Aquitaine, *The Lion in Winter,* AVCO-Embassy, 1968; Countess Aurelia, *The Madwoman of Chaillot,* Warner Brothers, 1969; Hecuba, *The Trojan Women,* Cinerama, 1971; Agnes, *A Delicate Balance,* American Film Institute, 1975; Eula Goodnight, *Rooster Cogburn,* Universal, 1975; Ethel Thayer, *On Golden Pond,* Universal, 1981; Miss Pudd, *Olly, Olly Oxenfree* (also known as *The Great Balloon Adventure*), Sanrio, 1983; title role, *Grace Quigley,* Cannon, 1984. Also appeared in *Break of Hearts,* RKO, 1935.

STAGE DEBUT—Lady-in-waiting, *The Czarina,* Baltimore, MD, 1928. BROADWAY DEBUT—Hostess, *Night Hostess,* Martin Beck Theatre, New York City, 1928. LONDON DEBUT—Lady, *The Millionairess,* New Theatre, 1952. PRINCIPAL STAGE APPEARANCES—Veronica Sims, *These Days,* Cort Theatre, New York City, 1928; understudy for the role of Linda Seton, *Holiday,* Plymouth Theatre, New York City, 1928; Katia, *A Month in the Country,* Guild Theatre, New York City, 1930; Judy Bottle, *Art and Mrs. Bottle,* Maxine Elliott's Theatre, New York City, 1930; Antiope, *The Warrior's Husband,* Morosco Theatre, New York City, 1932; Stella Surrege, *The Lake,* Martin Beck Theatre, New York City, 1933; Tracy Lord, *The Philadelphia Story,* Shubert Theatre, New York City, 1939; Jamie Rowan, *Without Love,* St. James Theatre, New York City, 1942; Rosalind, *As You Like It,* Cort Theatre, 1950; Lady, *The Millionairess,* Shubert Theatre, 1952; Portia, *The Merchant of Venice,* Beatrice, *Much Ado about Nothing,* American Shakespeare Festival, Stratford, CT, 1957; Viola, *Twelfth Night,* Cleopatra, *Antony and Cleopatra,* American Shakespeare Festival, 1960; Coco Chanel, *Coco,* Mark Hellinger Theatre, New York City, 1969; Mrs. Basil, *A Matter of Gravity,* Broadhurst Theatre, New York City, 1976; Margaret Mary Elderdice, *The West Side Waltz,* Ethel Barrymore Theatre, 1980. Also appeared in summer theatre productions, Ivoryton, CT, 1931.

MAJOR TOURS—Grazia, *Death Takes a Holiday,* U.S. cities, 1929; title role, *Jane Eyre,* U.S. cities, 1937; Rosalind, *As You Like*

It, 1950; Portia, *The Merchant of Venice,* Katherine, *The Taming of the Shrew,* Isabella, *Measure for Measure,* all with the Old Vic Theatre Company, Australian cities, 1955; Beatrice, *Much Ado about Nothing,* U.S. cities, 1958; Coco Chanel, *Coco,* U.S. cities, 1971; Mrs. Basil, *A Matter of Gravity,* U.S. cities, 1976; Mary Margaret Elderdice, *The West Side Waltz,* U.S. cities, 1980.

PRINCIPAL TELEVISION APPEARANCES—Movies: Amanda Wingfield, *The Glass Menagerie,* ABC, 1973; Jessica Medlicott, *Love among the Ruins,* ABC, 1975; Lilly Moffatt, *The Corn Is Green,* CBS, 1979; Margaret Delafield, *Mrs. Delafield Wants to Marry,* CBS, 1987. Specials: *The Selznick Years,* NBC, 1969; *A Tribute to Spencer Tracy,* PBS, 1986. Guest: *Dick Cavett Show,* ABC, 1973.

WRITINGS: NON-FICTION—*The Making of "The African Queen," or How I Went to Africa with Bogart, Bacall and Huston and Almost Lost My Mind,* Knopf, 1987.

AWARDS: Hollywood Reporter Gold Medal, 1933, Best Actress, Academy Award, 1934, both for *Morning Glory;* Best Actress, Venice Film Festival award, 1934, for *Little Women;* Best Actress, Academy Award nomination, 1936, for *Alice Adams;* Best Actress, New York Film Critics Award, 1940, Best Actress, Academy Award nomination, 1941, both for *The Philadelphia Story;* Best Actress, Academy Award nomination, 1943, for *Woman of the Year;* Best Actress, Academy Award nomination, 1952, for *The African Queen;* Best Actress, Academy Award nomination, 1956, for *Summertime;* Best Actress, Academy Award nomination, 1957, for *The Rainmaker;* Best Actress, Academy Award nomination, 1960, for *Suddenly Last Summer;* Best Actress, Cannes Film Festival award, 1962, Best Actress, Academy Award nomination, 1963, for *Long Day's Journey into Night,* 1962; Best Actress, Academy Award, Best Actress, British Academy Award, both 1968, for *Guess Who's Coming to Dinner;* Best Actress, Academy Award, Best Actress, British Academy Award, both 1969, for *The Lion in Winter;* Best Actress in a Musical, Antoinette Perry Award nomination, 1970, for *Coco;* Best Actress, Academy Award, 1982, for *On Golden Pond.*

MEMBER: Actors' Equity Association, Screen Actors Guild, American Federation of Television and Radio Artists.

SIDELIGHTS: Katharine Hepburn is one of the nation's most admired and beloved screen actresses, a Hollywood "legend" who has performed to high acclaim for more than sixty years. In their book *The MGM Stock Company: The Golden Era,* James Robert Parish and Ronald L. Bowers claimed that the feisty star's career "is unique in Hollywood history" because Hepburn is "the only actress who has been able to maintain her stellar position in today's realistic market." Indeed, Hepburn's four Academy Awards span five decades, from 1934 when she portrayed an aspiring starlet in *Morning Glory* to 1982 when she appeared as an aging woman trying to reconcile husband and daughter in *On Golden Pond.* In between she was nominated for Oscars for a long series of roles that uniformly stressed—in either comic or dramatic form—strength of character and firmness of resolve. "Katharine Hepburn has always played herself," Hubert Saal noted in a November 10, 1969 *Newsweek* feature. "It is her virtues, her beliefs, which are projected on the screen—through the indomitable missionary in *The African Queen* or in the great expectations of Jo in *Little Women.* She is versatile as a woman rather than adaptable as an actress. Her roles are reflections of what she is rather than what she can pretend to be." Saal summed up the typical Hepburn heroine: "The key to almost all her interpretations is a gallant mixture of individuality and femininity, the ambivalence of the tomboy, the straight-from-the-shoulder gruffness expressing the soft, womanly sentiment, the female meeting the male on his own ground, the Atalanta whose sexuality is in her challenge.'' Her spark, Parish and Bowers concluded, is ''in no way diminished'' by age. ''In her own eccentric fashion,'' they wrote, ''she is still the obstreperous showoff, but she has also become one of our finer actresses.''

A rather eccentric but genteel upbringing contributed to Hepburn's portrayals of cultured and semi-aristocratic screen personas. She was born in Hartford, Connecticut on November 9, 1909, to wealthy and politically active parents. Her father, a urologist, risked his career to bring the facts about venereal disease to a wider public, and her college-educated mother became a prominent spokesperson in the women's suffrage movement. Hepburn told the *Ladies' Home Journal* (August 1975): ''My first public appearance was carrying a flag in one of those [suffrage] parades and my first real, thrilling job was filling balloons with gas, then tying a string around them and making people buy them.'' Hepburn was an indifferent student, making sufficient grades to qualify for entrance into Bryn Mawr college, where she studied drama and just barely made passing grades. According to Romano V. Tozzi in a December, 1957 *Films in Review* profile, Shakespearean scholar Howard Furness picked Hepburn to play Pandora in a college pageant, and shortly thereafter she ''decided the stage could give the things her far from simple nature required.'' Against her parents' wishes, she journeyed to Baltimore to work in a stock company. She made her professional debut there in 1928 as a lady-in-waiting in *The Czarina*. By November of that same year she had a role on Broadway as a wealthy schoolgirl in *These Days*.

From 1929 until 1932 Hepburn had a series of theatrical roles on the East Coast, although on some occasions she was fired for clashing with directors and crews. Her brief marriage to socialite Ludlow Ogden Smith ended when it became apparent that she valued her career more than the relationship. In March of 1932 she was cast in the Broadway premier of a farce entitled *The Warrior's Husband*. Tozzi observed that in the play Hepburn ''was an athletic Amazon queen married to a handsome Greek, . . . whom she tried to keep in line by vigorous love-making.'' Although she was fired during rehearsals, she was re-hired and stole the show according to Tozzi. RKO Studios in Hollywood offered Hepburn a film contract based on her success in the play; she demanded fifteen hundred dollars per week in salary—she had been earning about eighty per week on stage—and, to her surprise, the studio agreed. She set out for Hollywood, determined to become a star.

''On July 4, 1932,'' Parish and Bowers exclaimed, ''a skinny, freckled, snooty typhoon Kate hit Hollywood. For eight years it kept hitting her back and almost knocked her out of the business.'' Tozzi also described the actress's early years in films: ''Hepburn arrived in Hollywood determined to put the movie industry in its place. She immediately set out to break all the rules and was as unpleasant and uncooperative as possible. She fought senselessly with practically everyone, from top producer to lowest technician. She was insulting and abusive to the press and gave out ridiculous, inane interviews in which she deliberately distorted the facts of her personal life. She allowed herself to be photographed without make-up in all her freckles, and, even worse, dressed hideously in mannish garb—sloppy slacks, sweaters, and men's trousers and suits.'' Hepburn was saved from dismissal at RKO by director George Cukor, who cast her in her first film, *A Bill of Divorcement*, even though he found her antics ''subcollegiate idiotic.'' The film—and Hepburn—were hits, and her long and tumultuous screen career was under way. In 1934 she won an Academy Award for *Morning Glory*, only her third film, and garnered a best actress

citation from the Venice Film Festival for her portrayal of Jo in *Little Women*. But success did not alter Hepburn's willful personality, and her next vehicles, the film *Spitfire* and the play *The Lake* were both flops. Nor did her luck improve substantially with such films as *Sylvia Scarlett* and *Quality Street;* even the comedies *Stage Door* and *Bringing Up Baby* did not make the first-run profits that were expected. In 1938 Hepburn was labelled ''box office poison'' by exhibitor Harry Brandt, and in an effort to salvage her career, she bought out of her RKO contract.

Hepburn's image was resurrected by two films of the early 1940s— *Holiday* and *The Philadelphia Story*. In the latter movie, according to Tozzi, she ''came of age as an actress. *The Philadelphia Story* was practically a flawless vehicle for her. Every line, every gesture, and every scene had been tailored to her particular talents.'' That success was closely followed in 1942 by *Woman of the Year,* the first of eight films that paired Hepburn with Spencer Tracy, to the benefit of both their careers. In films such as *Keeper of the Flame, Adam's Rib,* and *Pat and Mike,* Hepburn and Tracy ''may have seemed intractable opposites—the anchor and the sail—but a love of their craft and an eye for home truths brought them together and kept them there,'' in the words of a *Time* story of November 16, 1981. The two wre linked off-screen as well, although the actress remains reticent about their relationship.

Hepburn did not lack quality roles as she aged. The many notable films of her later life include *The African Queen, Long Day's Journey into Night, Guess Who's Coming to Dinner, A Lion in Winter,* and *On Golden Pond.* Richard Corliss noted in *Time* that roles in these movies gave the actress ''an opportunity to soar, and she played each lovely chance to the hilt. . . . Hepburn fashioned a career as distinctive as any in screen acting.'' Assessing her own talents, Hepburn told the *Ladies' Home Journal:* ''The only hold I've ever had on an audience that I felt was valid was that, in a curious way, from the time I was little, I understood instinctively the misgivings of the human race—the doubts, the fears and I could see through the bluffs. And when I played to an audience, I tried deliberately to present what I thought was elevating in the human being—which I think human beings automatically reach for.'' She added: ''People have told me how much this has meant to them.''

Although she has mellowed towards the press, Hepburn is still an intensely private person with little to say about her Hollywood acquaintances. Of her choice to remain single she told the *Ladies' Home Journal:* ''I remember making the decision. 'Well, I'll never marry and have children. I want to be a star, and I don't want to make my husband my victim. And I certainly don't want to make my children my victims.'' Hepburn's work has been her life, and she expresses no regrets. ''I chose to live as a man, and I'm very, very happy,'' she told the *Ladies' Home Journal.* ''I would not change any of the things I have done.'' Corliss in *Time,* concluding: ''In Hepburn's case art and life have blended to create an actress and woman of spectacular integrity. . . . Two dimensions couldn't hold her. The angular form, the tilted chin and cutting voice made her a secular Joan of Arc.''

ADDRESSES: HOME—Fenwick, CT and New York, NY.

*   *   *

HEPPLE, Peter   1927-

PERSONAL: Born January 2, 1927, in London, England; son of William (an executive) and Marjory (Mayes) Hepple; married

Josephine Barnett (a teacher), July 22, 1954; children: Clare Ruth, Julia Diane. MILITARY: British Army, Royal Corps of Engineers, 1945-48.

VOCATION: Editor, theatre critic, and publicist.

CAREER: See *WRITINGS* below.

RELATED CAREER—Theatre critic, *Where to Go in London,* 1966-77; drama critic and night life columnist, 1950—, *The Stage,* then editor, 1972—; secretary, Drama Section, Critics Circle, 1982—; secretary, Critics Circle, 1984—; director, British Section of the International Theatre Institute, 1985—; editor, *Television Today,* 1986. Also publicist for entertainers, clubs, and restaurants.

NON-RELATED CAREER—Editorial staff member, *Burkes Peerage and Burkes Landed Gentry* (reference book), 1948-51; editorial staff, Institute of Petroleum, 1952-62; editor, *Journal of the Institute of Petroleum* and *Institute of Petroleum Review,* 1965-72.

WRITINGS: PERIODICALS—Columnist: *Where to Go in London,* 1966-1971; *The Stage,* 1950—. Contributor: *Record Mirror, Show Pictorial, In Town Tonight, What's on in London, Plays and Players, Theatre World.*

SIDELIGHTS: RECREATIONS—Football, music of all types.

CTFT notes that Peter Hepple is considered to be an authority on London nightlife and entertainment and has been researching for a book on the subject.

PETER HEPPLE

ADDRESSES: HOME—12 Minchenden Crescent, Southgate, London N14 7EL, England. OFFICE—c/o *The Stage and Television Today,* 47 Bermondsey Street, London SE1, England.

*   *   *

HERRERA, Anthony   1944-

PERSONAL: Born January 19, 1944, in Biloxi, MS. EDUCATION: Received B.A., English and zoology, University of Mississippi; trained for the stage with Stella Adler.

VOCATION: Actor, director, and scriptwriter.

CAREER: PRINCIPAL TELEVISION APPEARANCES—Episodic: *The Rockford Files,* NBC; *The Incredible Hulk,* CBS; *The Blue Knight,* CBS; *Search for Tomorrow,* NBC; *Where the Heart Is,* ABC. Series: James Stenbeck, *As the World Turns,* CBS; Dane Hammond, *Loving,* ABC; *The Young and Restless,* CBS. Movies: Sergeant Smith, *Helter Skelter,* CBS, 1976; title role, *Mandrake the Magician,* NBC, 1979; Tru Sheridan, *The Night Rider,* ABC, 1979; also *It Must Be Love,* ABC.

PRINCIPAL TELEVISION WORK—Producer and director, *Mississippi Delta Blues* (documentary).

PRINCIPAL STAGE APPEARANCES—Malvolio, *Twelfth Night;* Trigorion, *The Seagull;* Petruchio, *The Taming of the Shrew;* Garcin, *No Exit;* Christian, *Cyrano de Bergerac;* Cleante, *Tartuffe;* First Knight, *Murder in the Cathedral;* Victor Belasco, *Barefoot in the Park;* Shep, *Bell, Book and Candle.*

PRINCIPAL FILM APPEARANCES—*The Nude Bomb,* Universal, 1980.

WRITINGS: TELEPLAYS—(Adaptor) "The Wide Net," *American Playhouse,* PBS, 1987.

AWARDS: Golden Eagle Award, for *Mississippi Delta Blues.*

MEMBER: American Federation of Television and Radio Artists, Screen Actors Guild, Actors' Equity Association.

ADDRESSES: OFFICE—360 E. 50th Street, New York, NY 10022. AGENT—c/o Herb Tobias & Associates, 1901 Avenue of the Stars, Los Angeles, CA 90069.

*   *   *

HICKMAN, Darryl   1933-

PERSONAL: Born July 28, 1933, in Hollywood, CA.

VOCATION: Actor and producer.

CAREER: FILM DEBUT—*Starmaker,* 1938. PRINCIPAL FILM APPEARANCES—*The Grapes of Wrath,* 1940; *Young People,* 1940; *Joe Smith, American,* Metro-Goldwyn-Mayer (MGM), 1941; *Men of Boys Town,* MGM, 1941; *Jackass Mail,* MGM, 1942; *Northwest Rangers,* MGM, 1942; *Keeper of the Flame,* MGM, 1942; *Assignment in Brittany,* MGM, 1943; *Song of Russia,* MGM, 1943; *The*

Human Comedy, MGM, 1943; *And Now Tomorrow*, 1944; *Salty O'Rourke*, 1945; *Captain Eddie*, 1945; *Kiss and Tell*, 1945; *Leave Her to Heaven*, 1945; *Boys' Ranch*, MGM, 1946; *Fighting Father Dunne*, 1948; *Any Number Can Play*, MGM, 1949; *The Happy Years*, MGM, 1950; *Submarine Command*, 1951; *Destination Gobi*, 1953; *Island in the Sky*, 1953; *Sea of Lost Ships*, 1953; *Prisoners of War*, MGM, 1954; *Southwest Passage*, 1954; *Tea and Sympathy*, MGM, 1956; *Network*, United Artists, 1977; *Looker*, Warner Brothers, 1981; *Sharky's Machine*, Warner Brothers, 1981.

PRINCIPAL TELEVISION APPEARANCES—Series: Davey Gillis, *The Many Loves of Dobie Gillis*, CBS, 1959-60; Ben Canfield, *The Americans*, NBC, 1961. Episodic: *Panic*, NBC, 1957.

PRINCIPAL TELEVISION WORK—Executive producer, daytime programming, CBS Television.

MEMBER: Screen Actors Guild, American Federation of Television and Radio Actors.

ADDRESSES: AGENT—Triad Artists, Inc., 10100 Santa Monica Blvd., 16th Fl., Los Angeles, CA 90067.*

*   *   *

HIGGINS, Colin   1941-

PERSONAL: Born July 28, 1941, in Noumea, New Caledonia; son of John Edward and Joy (Kelly) Higgins. EDUCATION: Stanford University, B.A., 1967; University of California, Los Angeles, M.A., 1969.

VOCATION: Playwright, scriptwriter, and director.

CAREER: PRINCIPAL FILM WORK—Director: *Foul Play*, Paramount, 1978; *Nine to Five*, Twentieth Century-Fox, 1980; *The Best Little Whorehouse in Texas*, Universal, 1982.

PRINCIPAL TELEVISION WORK—Co-producer, *Out on a Limb*, ABC, 1987.

RELATED CAREER—Playwright-in-residence, Theatre de National, Paris, France.

WRITINGS: SCREENPLAYS—*Harold and Maude*, Paramount, 1971; *Silver Streak*, Twentieth Century-Fox, 1976; *Foul Play*, Paramount, 1978; (with Patricia Resnick) *Nine to Five*, Twentieth Century-Fox, 1980; (with Larry L. King and Peter Masterson) *The Best Little Whorehouse in Texas*, Universal, 1982.

PLAYS—*Harold and Maude*, Martin Beck Theatre, New York City, 1980, published by Samuel French, Inc., 1981; (with Denis Cannan) *The Ik*, produced in 1974, French translation by Jean-Claude Carriere, published by Librairie Plon, Paris, France, 1986.

TELEPLAYS—(With Shirley MacLaine) *Out on a Limb*, ABC, 1987.

MEMBER: Writers Guild of America-West, Dramatists Guild.

ADDRESSES: AGENT—c/o Michael Ovitz, Creative Artists Agency, 1888 Century Park E., Los Angeles, CA 90067.

HILARY, Jennifer   1942-

PERSONAL: Full name, Jennifer Mary Hilary; born December 14, 1942, in Frimley, England; daughter of Richard Mounteney and Rosemary Lillian (Reynolds) Hilary. EDUCATION: Attended Elmhurst Ballet School; trained for the stage at the Royal Academy of Dramatic Art, 1961.

VOCATION: Actress.

CAREER: STAGE DEBUT—Nina, *The Seagull*, Liverpool Playhouse, Liverpool, U.K., 1961. LONDON DEBUT—Millie Theale, *Wings of a Dove*, Haymarket Theatre, 1964. BROADWAY DEBUT—Lucille, *The Rehearsal*, Royale Theatre, 1963. PRINCIPAL STAGE APPEARANCES—Isabel, *The Enchanted*, Lady Teazle, *School for Scandal*, Cilla Curtis, *Amateur Means Lover*, Cecily, *The Importance of Being Earnest*, all Liverpool Playhouse Company, Liverpool, U.K., 1961; Miranda, *The Tempest*, Lydia Languish, *The Rivals*, Lucille, *Duel of Angels*, Sarah Rigg, *Walker*, Alison, *Look Back in Anger*, Cheshire Cat, *Alice in Wonderland*, Cressida, *Troilus and Cressida*, all Birmingham Repertory Theatre Company, Birmingham, U.K., 1962; *A Scent of Flowers*, Duke of York's Theatre, London, 1964; Vera, *A Month in the Country*, Arnaud Theatre, Guildford, U.K., 1965; Sasha, *Ivanov*, Shubert Theatre, New York City, 1966; Virginia, *Relatively Speaking*, Duke of York's Theatre, 1967; Alison Ames, *Avanti!* (also known as *A Touch of Spring*), Booth Theatre, New York City, 1968; Milly, *Bodywork*, Phoenix Theatre, Leicester, U.K., 1972; Helen Saville, *The Vortex*, Greenwich Theatre, London, 1975; Gillian, *Dear Daddy*, Ambassadors Theatre, London, 1976; Lady Brute, *The*

JENNIFER HILARY

Provok'd Wife, Bristol Old Vic Theatre, Bristol, U.K., 1977; Adrienne, *Sisters,* Royal Exchange Theatre, Manchester, U.K., 1978. Also appeared in *Sufficient Carbohydrate,* Albery Theatre, London, 1984; *Festival of New Plays,* National Theatre, London, 1985.

MAJOR TOURS—Sasha, *Ivanov,* U.S. cities, 1966; Jennet Jourdemayne, *The Lady's Not for Burning,* U.K. cities, 1971; Alison Ames, *Avanti!* (also known as *A Touch of Spring*), South African cities, 1972. Also appeared in *Half Life,* U.K. and Canadian cities, 1978; *Some of My Best Friends Are Husbands,* U.K. cities, 1985.

PRINCIPAL FILM APPEARANCES—Peasant girl, *Becket,* Paramount, 1964; appeared in *The Heroes of Telemark,* Columbia, 1966; *The Idol,* Embassy, 1966; *Five Days One Summer,* Warner Brothers, 1982; also *One Brief Summer,* 1969; *North Sea Hijack,* 1979.

TELEVISION DEBUT—Girl, *The Tenpenny Scandal,* BBC, 1961. PRINCIPAL TELEVISION APPEARANCES—Mini-Series: *Winston Churchill: The Wilderness Years.* Movies: Lucy, *Alphabetical Order;* and in *The Woman in White; Exiles; Charades; Speed King; Sam; Miss A and Miss M; The Sun Also Rises.*

AWARDS: Bancroft Gold Medal, Tree Prize, both Royal Academy of Dramatic Art, 1961; Most Promising Newcomer from *Plays and Players,* 1964.

MEMBER: British Actors' Equity Association, Actors' Equity Association, Screen Actors Guild.

SIDELIGHTS: FAVORITE ROLES—Nina in *The Seagull,* Zoe in *A Scent of Flowers,* Lucy in *Alphabetical Order,* and Cressida in *Troilus and Cressida.*

ADDRESSES: AGENT—c/o Jean Diamond, London Management Ltd., 235-241 Regent Street, London W1, England.

*   *   *

Photography courtesy of Thames TV

BENNY HILL

1954; Variety Club's ITV Personality of the Year, 1969; comedy prize awarded by city of Montreux, 1984.

ADDRESSES: AGENT—Richard Stone, 18 York Buildings, Adelphi, London WC2N 6UU, England.

*   *   *

HILL, Benny   1925-

PERSONAL: Full name, Alfred Hawthorn Hill; born January 21, 1925, in Southampton, England; son of a chemist.

VOCATION: Actor and comedian.

CAREER: TELEVISION DEBUT—1952. PRINCIPAL TELEVISION APPEARANCES—Series: *The Benny Hill Show,* syndicated, U.K., 1969-82, U.S., 1979. Episodic: *The Service Show; Showcase.* Teleplays: *A Midsummer Night's Dream,* 1964. Specials: Has appeared in numerous specials.

FILM DEBUT—*Who Done It?,* 1955. PRINCIPAL FILM APPEARANCES—*Light Up the Sky,* 1960; *Those Magnificent Men in Their Flying Machines,* Twentieth Century-Fox, 1965; the toymaker, *Chitty Chitty Bang Bang,* United Artists, 1968; Professor Peach, *The Italian Job,* British production, 1969; also, *Tough It Light.*

NON-RELATED CAREER—Stockboy and milkman.

AWARDS: Personality of the Year, *Daily Mail* Television Award,

HILL, Debra

PERSONAL: Born in Haddonfield, NJ.

VOCATION: Producer, writer, and film executive.

CAREER: PRINCIPAL FILM WORK—Production assistant for documentaries, Adventure Films, in Africa and the Caribbean; script supervisor, assistant director, and second unit director for thirteen feature films; producer: *Halloween,* Universal, 1978; *The Fog,* AVCO-Embassy, 1980; *Escape from New York,* AVCO-Embassy, 1981; *Halloween II,* Universal, 1981; *Halloween III: Season of the Witch,* Universal, 1982; *The Dead Zone,* Paramount, 1983; *Head Office,* Paramount, 1985; *Clue,* Paramount, 1985; *Adventures in Baby Sitting,* Buena Vista, 1987.

WRITINGS: SCREENPLAYS—(With John Carpenter) *Halloween,* Universal, 1978.

ADDRESSES: OFFICE—Paramount Studios, 5555 Melrose Avenue, Los Angeles, CA 90038.*

HILL, Ken   1937-

PERSONAL: Full name, Kenneth Hill; born January 28, 1937, in Birmingham, England; son of Ernest (in sales) and Hilda Beryl (James) Hill.

VOCATION: Playwright, actor, director, and lyricist.

CAREER: STAGE DEBUT—*Forward—Up Your End,* Theatre Royal, Stratford, U.K., 1972. PRINCIPAL STAGE APPEARANCES—With the Theatre Workshop Company, U.K., 1972-73. PRINCIPAL STAGE WORK—Director: *Is Your Doctor Really Necessary?,* Theatre Workshop Company, U.K., 1973; *The Count of Monte Cristo, Land of the Dinosaurs, Dracula,* all Theatre Workshop Company, 1974; *Bloody Mary, Hancock,* both Theatre Workshop Company, 1975; *Turpin Time,* Theatre Workshop Company, 1976; *Joseph and the Amazing Technicolor Dreamcoat, The Mikado, Fiddler on the Roof,* all Musical Theatre Company, U.K., 1978-79; *The Phantom of the Opera,* Duke's Playhouse, Lancaster, U.K., 1976; *Curse of the Werewolf,* Contact Theatre, Manchester, U.K., 1976; *Mafeking,* Duke's Playhouse, 1977; *The Hunchback of Notre Dame,* National Theatre, London, 1977.

Director, all with the Newcastle Playhouse Theatre, Newcastle, U.K.: *The Mummy's Tomb, The Three Musketeers,* both 1978; *The Living Dead,* 1979; *Mrs. Tucker's Pageant,* 1981; *The Magic Sword,* 1982; *The Max Heiliger Account, Katie Mulholland,* both 1983; *Yellow Rain, The Lion the Witch and the Wardrobe,* both 1984; *The Gambling Man, Voyage of the Dawn Treader,* both 1985; *The Silver Chair,* 1986. Also *Tight at the Back, Sweeney Todd, A Little Shop of Horrors, Nightmare Rock, Hotel Dorado,* and *Andy Capp.*

PRINCIPAL TELEVISION APPEARANCES—Host, *ATV Today,* 1970.

PRINCIPAL TELEVISION WORK—Director, *All the Fun of the Fair,* 1979.

RELATED CAREER—Artistic director, Theatre Workshop Company, U.K., 1973-75; resident director, Newcastle Playhouse Theatre, Newcastle, U.K., 1983—.

NON-RELATED CAREER—Clerk, Education Department, Birmingham, U.K.; sldo basket weaver, insurance salesman, government officer, driver.

WRITINGS: PLAYS—*Night Season,* Alexander Theatre, Birmingham, U.K., 1963, published by Cambridge Press, 1963; *Forward—Up Your End,* Theatre Royal, Stratford, U.K., 1970; *Is Your Doctor Really Necessary?,* Theatre Workshop, U.K., 1973; *Gentlemen Prefer Anything,* (also lyrics) *Land of the Dinosaurs,* (adaptor) *The Count of Monte Cristo,* (adaptor) *Dracula,* all Theatre Workshop, 1974; (also lyrics) *Bloody Mary,* Theatre Workshop, 1975; (also lyrics) *The Phantom of the Opera,* Duke's Playhouse, Lancaster, U.K., 1976; (also lyrics) *Curse of the Werewolf,* Contact Theatre, Manchester, U.K., 1976, published by Samuel French, Inc., 1979; (also lyrics) *Mafeking,* Duke's Playhouse, 1977; (adaptor) *The Hunchback of Notre Dame,* National Theatre, London, 1977; (adaptor) *The Three Musketeers,* Newcastle Playhouse Theatre, Newcastle, U.K., 1978; (also lyrics) *The Mummy's Tomb,* Newcastle Playhouse Theatre, 1978, published by Samuel French, Inc., 1981; (also lyrics) *The Living Dead,* Newcastle Playhouse Theatre, 1979; (adaptor) *Dick Whittington,* Newcastle Playhouse Theatre, 1979; (adaptor) *Robin Hood,* Newcastle Playhouse Theatre, 1980; *Mrs. Tucker's Pageant,* (adaptor) *Sinbad the Sailor,* both

Newcastle Playhouse Theatre, 1981; (also lyrics) *The Magic Sword,* Newcastle Playhouse Theatre, 1982; *The Max Heiliger Account, Katie Mulholland,* both Newcastle Playhouse Theatre, 1983; *Yellow Rain,* Newcastle Playhouse Theatre, 1984; (adaptor) *The Lion, the Witch and the Wardrobe,* Newcastle Playhouse Theatre, 1984; *The Gambling Man, Voyage of the Dawn Treader,* both Newcastle Playhouse Theatre, 1985; *The Silver Chair,* Newcastle Playhouse Theatre, 1986.

TELEPLAYS—*The Second City,* BBC, 1964; *Wipets Three,* BBC, 1973; *All the Fun of the Fair,* BBC, 1979; also *Crossroads; Swizzlewick; The Newcomers; United; Castle Haven; Z Cars; Softly, Softly; Mickey Dunne; Adventures of Don Quick.*

RADIO PLAYS—*The Image,* Associated Rediffusion, 1964; *Wipets Three,* BBC, 1972.

MEMBER: British Actors' Equity Association, Writers Guild, Songwriters Guild.

SIDELIGHTS: RECREATIONS—Cricket, military history, science fiction.

ADDRESSES: OFFICE—17 Arlington Court, Arlington Road, Twickenham, Middlesex, England.

*   *   *

HILL, Walter   1942-

PERSONAL: Born January 10, 1942, in Long Beach, CA. EDUCATION: Attended Michigan State University.

VOCATION: Writer, director, and producer.

CAREER: PRINCIPAL FILM WORK—Writer (see below); also second assistant director, *The Thomas Crown Affair,* United Artists, 1968; assistant director, *Take the Money and Run,* Cinerama, 1969; director, *Hard Times,* Columbia, 1975; director, *The Driver,* Twentieth Century-Fox, 1978; co-producer, *Alien,* Twentieth Century-Fox, 1979; director, *The Warriors,* Paramount, 1980; director, *The Long Riders,* United Artists, 1980; director, *Southern Comfort,* Twentieth Century-Fox, 1981; director, *48 Hours,* Paramount, 1982; director, *Streets of Fire,* Universal, 1984; director, *Brewster's Millions,* Universal, 1985; director, *Crossroads,* Columbia, 1986; co-producer, *Aliens,* Twentieth Century-Fox, 1986; producer, *Blue City,* Paramount, 1986; director, *Extreme Prejudice,* Tri-Star, 1986; co-producer, *Aliens III,* Twentieth Century-Fox, upcoming; co-producer and director, *City Primevil,* United Artists, upcoming; director, *Dimitri,* Tri-Star, upcoming; executive producer, *Spanish Harlem,* Columbia, upcoming.

PRINCIPAL TELEVISION WORK—Series: Creator, *Dog and Cat,* ABC, 1977.

NON-RELATED CAREER—Formerly a construction worker and oil driller.

WRITINGS: SCREENPLAYS—*Hickey and Boggs,* United Artists, 1972; *The Getaway,* National General, 1972; *The Thief Who Came to Dinner,* Warner Brothers, 1973; *The Mackintosh Man,* Warner Brothers, 1973; (with Tracy Keenan Wynn and Lorenzo Semple) *The Drowning Pool,* Warner Brothers, 1975; (with Bruce Henstell and Bryan Gindoff) *Hard Times,* Columbia, 1975; *The Driver,*

Twentieth Century-Fox, 1978; (with David Shaber) *The Warriors,* Paramount, 1980; (with Michael Kane and David Giler) *Southern Comfort,* Twentieth Century-Fox, 1981; (with Larry Gross) *48 Hours,* Paramount, 1982; (with Gross) *Streets of Fire,* Universal, 1984; (with Lucas Heller) *Blue City,* Paramount, 1986; *Dimitri,* Tri-Star, upcoming.

ADDRESSES: AGENT—c/o Jim Wiatt, International Creative Management, 8899 Beverly Blvd., Los Angeles, CA 90048.*

*   *   *

HOFFMAN, Basil   1938-

PERSONAL: Full name, Basil Harry Hoffman; born, January 18, 1938, in Houston, TX; son of David (an antique dealer) and Beulah (Novoselsky) Hoffman. EDUCATION: Tulane University, B.B.A., 1960; trained for the stage at the American Academy of Dramatic Art, 1962, and with Clifford Jackson in New York City.

VOCATION: Actor.

CAREER: STAGE DEBUT—Mr. Paravicini, *The Mousetrap,* White Barn Theatre, Irwin, PA, 1963, for seven performances. PRINCI-PAL STAGE APPEARANCES—Professor, *South Pacific,* Jones Beach Theatre, NY, 1968.

FILM DEBUT—*Lady Liberty,* United Artists, 1972. PRINCIPAL FILM APPEARANCES—*At Long Last Love,* Twentieth Century-

BASIL HOFFMAN

Fox, 1975; *Lucky Lady,* Twentieth Century-Fox, 1975; *All the President's Men,* Warner Brothers, 1976; *Close Encounters of the Third Kind,* Columbia, 1977; *Comes a Horseman,* United Artists, 1978; *The Electric Horseman,* Columbia-Universal, 1979; *Ordinary People,* Paramount, 1980; *Night Shift,* Warner Brothers, 1982; *My Favorite Year,* Metro-Goldwyn-Mayer/United Artists, 1982; *All of Me,* Universal, 1984; *The Milagro Beanfield War,* Universal, 1987.

TELEVISION DEBUT—Walter Witherspoon, *One Life to Live,* ABC, 1973-74. PRINCIPAL TELEVISION APPEARANCES—Series: Principal Dingleman, *Square Pegs,* CBS, 1982-83; Ed Greenglass, *Hill Street Blues,* NBC, 1984-86. Mini-Series: Stanley Inchbeck, *The Moneychangers,* NBC, 1977.

MEMBER: Actors's Equity Association, Screen Actors Guild, American Federation of Television and Radio Artists, Academy of Motion Picture Arts and Sciences (Foreign Language Film Committee).

ADDRESSES: OFFICE—7060 Hollywood Blvd., Suite 206, Los Angeles, CA 90028. AGENT—c/o Michael Belson and Eric Klass, Belson and Klass, 211 S. Beverly Drive, Beverly Hills, CA 90212.

*   *   *

HOLLOWAY, Sterling   1904-

PERSONAL: Born January 14, 1904, in Cedartown, GA; son of Sterling Price (a cotton broker) and Rebecca de Haven (Boothby) Holloway; children: Richard Hargrove. EDUCATION: Attended Georgia Military Academy; trained for the stage at the American Academy of Dramatic Arts, 1921-23. MILITARY: U.S. Army, Special Services, 1941-45.

VOCATION: Actor.

*CAREER:*PRINCIPAL FILM APPEARANCES—*Casey at the Bat,* 1927; *Blonde Venus, Faithless, Rockabye,* all 1932; *Advice to the Lovelorn, Alice in Wonderland, Blondie Johnson, Dancing Lady, Elmer the Great, Fast Workers, Female, Gold Diggers of 1933, Hard to Handle, Hell Below, International House, Lawyer Man, Picture Snatcher, Professional Sweetheart, Wild Boys of the Road,* all 1933; *Back Page, Down to Their Last Yacht, Gift of Gab, The Merry Widow, Operator B, Strictly Dynamite, Tomorrow's Children, Wicked Woman,* all 1934; *Doubting Thomas, Girl o' My Dreams, I Live My Life, Life Begins at 40, Lottery Lover, Rendezvous, $1000 a Minute,* all 1935; *Career Woman, The Girl from Maxim's, Palm Springs,* all 1936; *Behind the Mike, Join the Marines, Maid of Salem, Varsity Show, When Love Is Young, The Woman I Love,* all 1937; *Dr. Rhythm, Of Human Hearts, Professor Beware, Spring Madness,* all 1938; *Nick Carter, Master Detective,* and *St. Louis Blues,* both 1939.

The Blue Bird, Hit Parade of 1941, Little Men, Remember the Night, Street of Memories, all 1940; *Cheers for Miss Bishop, Don't Get Personal, Dumbo, Look Who's Laughing, Meet John Doe, New Wine, Top Sergeant Mulligan,* all 1941; *Bambi, Iceland, The Lady Is Willing, Star Spangled Rhythm,* all 1942; *The Three Caballeros,* 1944; *A Walk in the Sun, Wildfire,* both 1945; *Death Valley, Make Mine Music, Sioux City Sue,* all 1946; *Robin of Texas, Saddle Pals, Trail to San Antone, Twilight on the Rio Grande,* all 1947; *The Beautiful Blonde from Bashful Bend,* 1949; *Her Wonderful Life,* 1950; *Alice in Wonderland,* 1951; *Kentucky Rifle,* 1956; *Shake,*

Rattle and Rock!, 1957; *The Adventures of Huckleberry Finn*, 1960; *Alakazam the Great!*, 1960; *It's a Mad, Mad, Mad, Mad World, My Six Loves*, both 1963; *Winnie the Pooh*, 1964; *The Jungle Book*, 1967; *Live a Little, Love a Little*, 1968; *The Aristocats*, 1970; *Won Ton Ton, the Dog Who Saved Hollywood, Super Seal*, both 1976; *Thunder and Lightening*, 1977.

PRINCIPAL STAGE APPEARANCES—Second phantom, *The Failures*, Garrick Theatre, New York City, 1923; Henry, *Fata Morgana*, New York City, 1924; Johnny Loring, *Get Me in the Movies*, Earl Carroll Theatre, New York City, 1928; barber, *The Grass Harp*, Martin Beck Theatre, New York City, 1952; Prologus, Pseudolus, *A Funny Thing Happened on the Way to the Forum*, Sacramento Music Circus, Sacramento, CA, 1965; Benjamin Kidd, *The Desert Song*, Sacramento Music Circus, 1966. Appeared in the revues *The Garrick Gaieties*, Garrick Theatre, 1925; *Shoe String Revue*, Lyric Theatre, Hoboken, NJ, 1929; *The Garrick Gaieties*, Garrick Theatre, 1930; *Hey Rookie*, U.S. Army Special Services, 1942; and in *The Seven Year Itch, Send Me No Flowers*, both Seattle, WA, 1960-61; *Song of Norway, The Wizard of Oz, Anything Goes*, all Sacramento Music Circus, 1959-63.

PRINCIPAL CABARET APPEARANCES—Ciro's, New York City, 1926.

PRINCIPAL TELEVISION APPEARANCES—Episodic: Pumpkinhead, *Shirley Temple's Storybook*, NBC, 1958; narrator, "Peter and the Wolf," *Walt Disney's Wonderful World of Color*, NBC, 1964; *Please Don't Eat the Daisies*, NBC, 1967. Series: Waldo Binney, *The Life of Riley*, CBS, 1953-58; Sorrowful Joe, *The Adventures of Rin Tin Tin*, ABC, 1954-61, then CBS, 1962-64; Buck Singleton, *The Baileys of Balboa*, CBS, 1964-65; voice of G.G., the Wizard, *Tony the Pony*, syndicated, 1979; voice of Amos, *Ben and Me*.

RELATED CAREER—Artist in residence, University of California, Irvine.

RECORDINGS: Narration and character voices for numerous children's story albums.

AWARDS: Best Children's Record, Grammy Award, 1975; Best Children's Record, Grammy Award nomination, 1976; Americana award from Cyprus College, 1978; Annie Award from the International Animated Film Society, 1985, for "distinguished contribution to the art of animation."

MEMBER: Actors' Equity Association, Screen Actors Guild, American Federation of Television and Radio Artists.

SIDELIGHTS: RECREATIONS—Collecting modern painting.

ADDRESSES: OFFICES—P.O. Box 38001, Los Angeles, CA 90038; c/o Brewen, 6355 Willoughby Avenue, Los Angeles, CA 90038. AGENT—c/o Kingsley Colton, 16661 Ventura Boulevard, Encino, CA 91436.

*   *   *

HOLT, Fritz   1940-1987

OBITUARY NOTICE: See index for *CTFT* sketch—Born George William Holt, III, October 9, 1940, in San Francisco, CA; died of complications due to pneumonia, July 14, 1987, in Montclair, NJ.

Fritz Holt began his career in 1965 as an assistant stage manager for the Mineola Playhouse in Long Island. In the same capacity he toured with the national production of *Cabaret* in 1967 and later served as production stage manager for *Company* and *Follies*, both on Broadway. In 1973, Holt co-produced (with Barry Brown) the successful London revival of *Gypsy* starring Angela Lansbury. He returned to Broadway where his stagings included *The Royal Family*, 1975, *The Madwoman of Central Park West*, 1979, *Perfectly Frank*, 1980, and he served as executive producer of *La Cage aux Folles*, 1983. Holt's last stage productions included *Best of the Best*, an all-star benefit at the Metropolitan Opera House for AIDS victims, and *Happy Birthday, Mr. Abbott!*, the Actors' Fund of America's celebration of George Abbott's one hundredth birthday.

OBITUARIES AND OTHER SOURCES: New York Times, July 15, 1987; *Variety,* July 15, 1987.

*   *   *

HONG, Wilson S.   1934-

PERSONAL: Born December 18, 1934, in Butte, MT. EDUCATION: Attended Montana State University and the Brooks Institute of Photography.

VOCATION: Cinematographer.

CAREER: PRINCIPAL FILM WORK—Cinematographer: *Velvet Vampire*, 1971; *Dear Dead Delilah*, 1972; *1776*, Columbia, 1972; *They Only Kill Their Masters*, Metro-Goldwyn-Mayer, 1972; *The Parallax View*, Paramount, 1974; *Drum*, United Artists, 1976; *White Buffalo*, 1977; *MacArthur*, Universal, 1977; *An Enemy of the People*, 1977; *Sergeant Pepper's Lonely Hearts Club Band*, Universal, 1978; *Winter Kills*, AVCO-Embassy, 1979; also *Bigfoot, Operation North Slope, No Substitute for Victory, The Hellcats, The Zodiac Killer, Mrs. McGrudy, The Day the Adults Died, Sundown in Watts, Don't Go West, Mulefeathers, Mission to Glory, The Unfinished, The Fearless Five.*

PRINCIPAL TELEVISION WORK—Cinematographer: Series—*Apple's Way*, CBS, 1974-75; *The Blue Knight*, CBS, 1975-76; *Young Maverick*, CBS, 1979-80. Episodic—*The Great Outdoors; The Jerry Show*. Pilots—*Gun Hawks, Keep It Up, Where Are They Now?, Moose, The Groovy Seven*. Specials—*Snowmobile Grand Prix, Indianapolis International Drag Races*, and *The Unser Story*, all ABC; also *Thank You America, Hunting and Fishing the North American Continent*, and *The Toy Game*. Movies—*A Dream for Christmas*, 1973.

RELATED CAREER—Free-lance photographer for worldwide magazine and newspaper syndication, 1965; photographic director, U.S. Forest Service Fire and Research Division, 1966; first cameraman for various documentaries, industrials, commercials, and sports specials, 1967.*

*   *   *

HOOKS, Robert   1937-

PERSONAL: Born April 18, 1937, in Washington, DC; son of Edward and Bertha (Ward) Hooks. EDUCATION: Attended Temple University.

VOCATION: Actor, director, and producer.

CAREER: STAGE DEBUT—George Murchison, *A Raisin in the Sun*, Wilbur Theatre, Boston, MA, 1960. BROADWAY DEBUT—Dewey Chipley, *Tiger, Tiger, Burning Bright*, Booth Theatre, 1962. PRINCIPAL STAGE APPERANCES—Dennis Thornton, *Ballad for Bimshire*, Mayfair Theatre, New York City, 1963; Deodatus Village, *The Blacks*, St. Marks Playhouse, New York City, 1963; stage assistant, *The Milk Train Doesn't Stop Here Anymore*, Brooks Atkinson Theatre, New York City, 1964; Clay, *The Dutchman*, Cherry Lane Theatre, New York City, 1964; title role, *Henry V*, Delacorte Mobile Theatre, New York Shakespeare Festival, New York City, 1965; Junie, *Happy Ending*, John, *Day oof Absence*, both St. Marks Playhouse, 1965; Razz, *Where's Daddy?*, Billy Rose Theatre, New York City, 1966; Clem, *Hallelujah, Baby!*, Martin Beck Theatre, New York City, 1967; Daoudu, *Kongi's Harvest*, Negro Ensemble Company (NEC), St. Marks Playhouse, 1968; Deodatus Village, *The Blacks*, DC Black Repertory Company, Eisenhower Theatre, Washington, DC, 1973; Captain Richard Davenport, *A Soldier's Play*, Mark Taper Forum, Los Angeles, CA, 1982. Also appeared in *Arturo Ui*, Lunt-Fontanne Theatre, New York City, 1963; *The Harangues*, NEC, St. Marks Playhouse, 1970.

FIRST LONDON STAGE WORK—Producer, *Song of the Lusitanian Bogey, God Is a (Guess What?)*, both with the Negro Ensemble Company, Aldwych Theatre, 1969. PRINCIPAL STAGE WORK—Co-producer with Gerald S. Krone, all with the Negro Ensemble Company, St. Marks Playhouse, New York City: *Song of the Lusitanian Bogey, Summer of the Seventeenth Doll, Kongi's Harvest, Daddy Goodness, God Is a (Guess What?)*, all 1968; *Ceremonies in Dark Old Men, An Evening of One Acts, Man Better Man, The Reckoning*, all 1969; *The Harangues, Ododo*, (also director) *Brotherhood*, (also director) *Day of Absence*, all 1970; *Perry's Mission, Rosalee Pritchett, The Dream on Monkey Mountain, Ride a Dark Horse, The Sty of the Blind Pig*, all 1971; *A Ballet Behind the Bridge, Frederick Douglass . . . through His Own Words, The River Niger*, all 1972-73; *The Great Macdaddy, Black Sunlight, Nowhere to Hide, Terraces, Heaven and Hell's Agreement, In the Deepest Part of Sleep*, all 1974; *The First Breeze of Summer, Liberty Call, Orrin, Sugar-Mouth Sam Don't Dance No More, The Moonlight Arms, The Dark Tower, Waiting for Mongo, Welcome to Black River*, all 1975; *Eden, Livin' Fat, The Brownsville Raid*, all 1976; *The Great Macdaddy, The Offering*, both 1977; *Black Body Blues, The Twilight Dinner, Nevis Mountian Dew, The Daughters of Mock*, all 1978; *Plays from South Africa, A Season to Unravel, Old Phantoms, Home, The Michigan*, all 1979. Also producer, *The River Niger*, Brooks Atkinson Theatre, New York City, 1973; directed, *The Blacks*, with the DC Black Repertory Company, Eisenhower Theatre, Washington, DC, 1973; producer, *The First Breeze of Summer*, Broadway production, 1975.

MAJOR TOURS—George Murchison, *A Raisin in the Sun*, U.S. cities, 1960-61; the boy, *A Taste of Honey*, U.S. cities, 1961-62.

PRINCIPAL TELEVISION APPEARANCES—Episodic: *Profiles in Courage*, NBC, 1965; *Mannix*, CBS, 1969; *The F.B.I.*, ABC, 1969; *Then Came Bronson*, ABC, 1969; *The Bold Ones*, NBC, 1970; *The Man and the City*, ABC, 1971; *Marcus Welby, M.D.*, ABC, 1974; *The Rookies*, ABC, 1973; *McMillan and Wife*, NBC, 1973; *The Streets of San Francisco*, ABC, 1974; *The F.B.I.*, ABC, 1974; *Police Story*, NBC, 1975; *Petrocelli*, NBC, 1975. Series: Jeff Ward, *NYPD*, ABC, 1967-69. Mini-Series: John Mays, *Backstairs at the White House*, NBC, 1979. Pilots: Stacey Robbins, *The Cliff Dwellers*, SBC, 1966; Larry Dean, *Two for the Money*,

ABC, 1972; Nate Simmons, *Down Home*, CBS, 1978. Movies: Lt. Edward Wallace, *Carter's Army*, ABC, 1970; Larry Storm, *Vanished*, NBC, 1971; Inspector Lou Van Alsdale, *The Cable Car Murder* (also known as *Cross Current*), CBS, 1971; Sergeant Connaught, *Trapped*, ABC, 1973; Nate Simmons, *Just an Old Sweet Song*, CBS, 1976; Commissioner Frank Wharton, *The Killer Who Wouldn't Die*, ABC, 1976; Major Stanley Norton, *The Courage and the Passion*, NBC, 1978; Captain Pete Rolf, *To Kill a Cop*, NBC, 1978; William Still, *A Woman Called Moses*, NBC, 1978; Paul Hendrix, *Hollow Image*, ABC, 1979; D.A. Roerich, *Madame X*, NBC, 1981; John Miller, *The Oklahoma City Dolls*, ABC, 1981; Ezzard Chops Jackson, *The Sophisticated Gents*, NBC, 1981; Harry Burton, *Sister, Sister*, NBC, 1982; Alton Reese, *The Execution*, NBC, 1985.

PRINCIPAL FILM APPEARANCES—*Hurry Sundown*, Paramount, 1967; *The Last of the Mobile-Hotshots*, Warner Brothers, 1970; *Trouble Man*, Twentieth Century-Fox, 1972; *Aaron Loves Angela*, Columbia, 1975; *Airport '77*, Universal, 1977; *Fast-Walking*, Lorimar, 1982; *Star Trek III: The Search for Spock*, Paramount, 1984.

RELATED CAREER— Co-founder, executive director, Negro Ensemble Company, New York City, 1968—; founder, DC Black Theatre, Washington, DC, 1973-77.

AWARDS: Theatre World Award, 1966.

MEMBER: Actor's Equity Association, American Federation of Television and Radio Artists, Screen Actors Guild.

ADDRESSES: OFFICE—c/o St. Marks Playhouse, 133 Second Avenue, New York, NY 10003.*

*   *   *

HOWES, Sally Ann

PERSONAL: Born July 20, in London, England; daughter of Robert (an actor) and Patricia (a singer; maiden name, Malone Clark) Howes; married Maxwell Coker (divorced); married Richard Adler (a composer), January 3, 1958 (divorced, 1966); married Andrew Maree; children: two sons. EDUCATION: Attended Queenswood College.

VOCATION: Actress and singer.

CAREER: STAGE DEBUT—*Caprice*, Alhambra Theatre, Glasgow, Scotland, U.K., 1951. LONDON DEBUT—*Fancy Free*, Prince of Wales' Theatre, 1951. BROADWAY DEBUT— Eliza, *My Fair Lady*, Mark Hellinger Theatre, 1957. PRINCIPAL STAGE APPEARANCES—Jan, *Bet Your Life*, Hippodrome Theatre, London, 1952; Jennifer Rumson, *Paint Your Wagon*, Her Majesty's Theatre, London, 1953; Margaret, *Romance in Candlelight*, Piccadilly Theatre, London, 1955; Karolka, *Summer Song*, Princes Theatre, London, 1956; Celia Pope, *A Hatful of Rain*, Pigalle Theatre, Liverpool, U.K., then Princes Theatre, both 1957; Eve, *Kwamina*, 54th Street Theatre, New York City, 1961; Fiona MacLaren, *Brigadoon*, City Center Theatre, New York City, 1962; Kit Sargent, *What Makes Sammy Run?*, 54th Street Theatre, 1964; Maria, *The Sound of Music*, Chandler Pavilion, Los Angeles, CA, 1972; Suzy Martin, *Lover*, St. Martin's Theatre, London, 1973; Anna, *The King and I*, Adelphi Theatre, Los Angeles, CA, 1974; Ann Whitefield, *Man* and *Superman*, Arnaud Theatre, Guildford, U.K., 1975; *Elizabeth Barrett*, *Robert and Elizabeth*, Arnaud Theatre, 1976; *Jenny Lind*, *Hans Anderson*, Palladium Theatre, London, 1977. Also appeared in the *Royal Variety Performance*, London, 1951; and as Robin Hood, *Babes in the Wood* (pantomime), Golder's Green Hippodrome, U.K., 1954.

MAJOR TOURS—Various variety shows, U.K. cities, 1951.

FILM DEBUT—*Thursday's Child*, 1943. PRINCIPAL FILM APPEARANCES—*Half-Way House*, 1945; *Dead of Night*, 1946; *Nicholas Nickleby*, 1947; *Anna Karenina*, *My Sister and I*, both 1948; *Fools Rush In*, *The History of Mr. Polly*, *Stop Press Girl*, all 1949; *Pink String and Sealing Wax*, 1950; *Honeymoon Deferred*, 1951; *The Admirable Crichton* (also known as *Paradise Lagoon*), 1957; *Chitty Chitty Bang Bang*, 1968; *Death Ship*, 1980.

PRINCIPAL TELEVISION APPEARANCES—Episodic: Beth, *Mission: Impossible*, CBS, 1969; also *Marcus Welby, M.D.*, ABC; *The Man from Shiloh*, ABC. Pilots: Prudence MacKenzie, *Prudence and the Chief*, ABC, 1970. Movies: Laura Frankland, *The Hound of the Baskervilles*, ABC, 1972; Sybil Townsend, *Female Artillery*, ABC, 1973. Specials: Della, *The Gift of the Magi*, CBS, 1958; title role, *Jane Eyre*, CBS, 1961; Fiona MacLaren, *Brigadoon*, ABC, 1966.

MEMBER: Actors' Equity Association, Screen Actors Guild, American Federation of Television and Radio Artists.

SIDELIGHTS: RECREATIONS—Reading, travel, decorating, cooking.

ADDRESSES: AGENTS—(Los Angeles) International Creative Management, 8899 Beverly Boulevard, Los Angeles, CA 90048; (London) c/o Fraser and Dunlop Ltd., 91 Regent Street, London W1R 8RU, England.*

*   *   *

HUDSON, Jeffery
See CRICHTON, Michael

*   *   *

HUGHES, John

VOCATION: Writer, director, and producer.

CAREER: PRINCIPAL FILM WORK—Writer and director: *Sixteen Candles*, Universal, 1984; *The Breakfast Club*, Universal, 1985; also producer, *Weird Science*, Universal, 1985; *Pretty in Pink*, Paramount, 1986; also co-producer, *Ferris Bueller's Day Off*, Paramount, 1986; writer and producer, *Some Kind of Wonderful*, Paramount, 1987.

RELATED CAREER—President, John Hughes Production Company, 1985—.

WRITINGS: SCREENPLAYS—(In addition to the credits above) *National Lampoon's Class Reunion*, Twentieth Century-Fox, 1982; *National Lampoon's Vacation*, Warner Brothers, 1983; (with

David Odell) *Nate and Hayes*, Paramount, 1983; *Mr. Mom*, Twentieth Century-Fox, 1983; *National Lampoon's European Vacation*, Warner Brothers, 1985.

PERIODICALS—Writer and editor, *National Lampoon*.

ADDRESSES: OFFICE—John Hughes Production Company, Paramount Pictures, 5555 Melrose Avenue, Los Angeles, CA 90038. AGENT—c/o Jack Rapke, Creative Artists Agency, 1888 Century Park East, Suite 1400, Los Angeles, CA 90067.*

*   *   *

HUNT, Charles W.   1943-

BRIEF ENTRY: Born July 17, 1943, in Jefferson, ME; son of Ernest Grayson (a mechanic) and Ida May (a teacher; maiden name Perry) Hunt. A graduate of Boston University, Hunt began painting scenery for the Boston Opera Company under the artistic direction of Sarah Caldwell during his college years. Following graduation in 1965, he went to work for Samuel French, Inc., a talent agency and publisher of plays, then moved to Hollywood where he worked for Paramount Pictures on such productions as *Rosemary's Baby*, *Skidoo*, *Darling Lilly*, *On A Clear Day You Can See Forever*, and *Paint Your Wagon*. On his return to New York City, he joined the Helen Harvey Agency, spending five years as a talent and casting agent. Currently a vice-president with the Oscard Agency, his clients include Janet Leigh, Dorothy Lyman, Rosalyn Drexler, and others.

ADDRESSES: HOME—593 Riverside Drive, New York, NY 10031. OFFICE—c/o The Oscard Agency, 19 W. 44th Street, New York, NY 10036.

*   *   *

HUNTER, Marian   1944-

PERSONAL: Full name, Marian Sears Hunter; born July 25, 1944, in New York, NY; daughter of B. Sears (an attorney) and Maryphyllis (a teacher; maiden name Barber) Hunter; divorced from husband; children: Larissa. EDUCATION: Attended the Juilliard School of Music; studied film production at the School of Visual Arts and at the New School for Social Research; studied dance with Martha Graham, Jose Limon, Merce Cunningham, and at the American Dance Festival.

VOCATION: Producer, director, and film editor.

CAREER: PRINCIPAL FILM WORK—Producer and director, *Roll Over*, 1974; producer and director, *Just Married for a While*, 1977; editor, *A Berger to Go*, 1979; editor, *Marathon Woman: Miki Gorman*, 1980; editor, *A Lady Named Baybie*, 1980; editor, *Home Sweet Homes*, 1982; producer and director, *Introducing Choreography and the Camera*, 1983; editor, *Joint Custody: A New Kind of Family*, 1984; producer and director, *The Big Apple Workout*, 1985; editor, *Kicking High: In the Golden Years*, 1986; editor, *The Rebuilding of Mascott Flats*, 1986. Also editor, *Hoopla, The New Yorker*, *Vladimir Horowitz: The Last Romantic*, *Hard Choices*.

RELATED CAREER—Founder, Herstory Films; teacher, videotape

workshops for dancers, Film Video Arts, Laban Institute, and Manhattanville College; Screening Committee member, New York Festival of Women's Films, Student Academy Awards; juror, American Film Festival; guest artist and lecturer: Museum of Modern Art, American Cultural Center, Chicago Art Institue, U.S. Military Academy, Florida International University, Indiana University, New School for Social Research, Brooklyn College, Manhattan Community College, Hunter College, Queens College, New York Community College, Intermedia Foundation, University of Massachusetts, Hampshire College.

NON-RELATED CAREER—Photographer.

AWARDS: Production award for editing from the National Council for Family Relations Film Festival, 1984, for *Joint Custody: A New Kind of Family;* selected by "Ms. Magazine," as one of "80 Women to Watch in the 1980's."

ADDRESSES: OFFICE—137 E. 13th Street, New York, NY 10003.

*   *   *

HURT, William   1950-

PERSONAL: Born March 20, 1950, in Washington, DC; married Mary Beth Hurt (an actress; divorced). EDUCATION: Attended Tufts University; trained for the stage at the Julliard School of Music and Drama.

VOCATION: Actor.

*CAREER:*OFF-BROADWAY DEBUT—Lord Scroop, Interpreter, John Bates, *Henry V,* New York Shakespeare Festival, Delacorte Theatre, 1977. BROADWAY DEBUT—Eddie, *Hurlyburly,* Ethel Barrymore Theatre, 1984. PRINCIPAL STAGE APPEARANCES— Jamie, *Long Day's Journey into Night,* Oregon Shakespeare Festival, Ashland, OR, 1975; Edward Howe, *My Life,* John Morrisey, *Ulysses in Traction,* both Circle Repertory Company (CRC), Circle Repertory Theatre, New York City, 1977; Alwa Schon, *Lulu,* Kenneth Talley, Jr., *Fifth of July,* both CRC, Circle Repertory Theatre, 1978; title role, *Hamlet,* Davison, *Mary Stuart,* both CRC, Circle Repertory Theatre, 1979; Lord Byron, *Childe Byron,* Melvin, *The Diviners,* both CRC, Circle Repertory Theatre, 1981; Ike McKee/Henry Jarvis, *The Great Grandson of Jedediah Kohler,* title role, *Richard II,* both CRC, Entermedia Theatre, New York City, 1982; Oberon, *A Midsummer Night's Dream,* New York Shakespeare Festival, Delacorte Theatre, New York City, 1982; Eddie, *Hurlyburly,* Goodman Theatre, Chicago, IL, 1984; Brother Dominic, *Joan of Arc at the Stake,* York Theatre Company, Church of the Heavenly Rest Theatre, New York City, 1985.

FILM DEBUT—Eddie Jessup, *Altered States,* Warner Brothers, 1980. PRINCIPAL FILM APPEARANCES—Ned Racine, *Body Heat,* Warner Brothers, 1981; Nick, *The Big Chill,* Columbia, 1983. Also appeared in *Eyewitness,* Twentieth Century-Fox, 1981; *Gorky Park,* Orion, 1983; *Kiss of the Spider Woman,* Island Alive Pictures, 1984; *Children of a Lesser God,* 1986.

PRINCIPAL TELEVISION APPEARANCES—Specials: Jay Follet, *All the Way Home,* NBC, 1981; *Verna: USO Girl,* PBS, 1980; *Best of Families.*

AWARDS: Theatre World Award, 1978; Academy Award, Best

Actor, Cannes Film Festival Award, Best Actor, both 1985, for *Kiss of the Spider Woman.*

MEMBER: Actors' Equity Association, Screen Actors Guild, American Federation of Television and Radio Artists.

ADDRESSES: AGENT—c/o Triad Artists, Inc., 1100 Santa Monica Boulevard, Los Angeles, CA 90067.*

*   *   *

HUSTON, John   1906-1987

OBITUARY NOTICE—See index for *CTFT* sketch: Born August 5, 1906, in Nevada, MO; died August 28, 1987, shortly after hospital treatment for pneumonia brought on by emphysema. Director, writer, and actor John Huston numbered several classics among the many films to his credit. He had already gained acclaim as a screenwriter for *Dr. Ehrlich's Magic Bullet, High Sierra, Sergeant York,* and other films when his 1941 directorial debut, *The Maltese Falcon,* earned both box office success and critical praise. One of the traits that most impressed viewers throughout Huston's career was his desire to present authentic detail in his films; this led him, for example, to be among the first directors to move a production away from the studio lot, as when he filmed much of *The Treasure of the Sierra Madre* in Mexico in 1948. His handling of actors was likwise lauded. In *The African Queen,* 1951, he successfully matched the disparate styles of Humphrey Bogart and Katharine Hepburn to create one of the most popular films of all time; moreover, he directed both his father, Walter Huston, and his daughter Anjelica Huston in Academy Award-winning performances. Huston's own acting abilities drew good notices as well; in addition to incidental appearances in a number of films, he had prominent roles in *The Cardinal* and *Chinatown,* earning a 1963 Academy Award nomination as best supporting actor for the former. This was one of fourteen nominations that he received in various categories from the Academy of Motion Picture Arts and Sciences over the years. Along with his other professional citations and honors, he was presented with the American Film Institute's Lifetime Achievement Award in 1983. Despite persistent health problems, Huston remained professionally active into his eighties. Although some of his later films, such as *Wise Blood* and *Under the Volcano,* drew support from the critics but not from the mass audience, the 1985 release of *Prizzi's Honor* saw him regain his hold on the box office. His last film, *The Dead,* based on a short story by James Joyce, was released in late 1987.

OBITUARIES AND OTHER SOURCES: Variety, September 2, 1987.

*   *   *

HWANG, David   1957-

PERSONAL: Full name, David Henry Hwang; born August 11, 1957, in Los Angeles, CA; married Ophelia Chong (an artist) September 21, 1985. EDUCATION: Stanford University, B.A., English, 1979.

VOCATION: Playwright.

CAREER: Also see *WRITINGS* below.

RELATED CAREER—Board of Directors, Theatre Communications Group, 1987—.

WRITINGS: PLAYS—*FOB*, O'Neill National Playwrights Conference, 1979, then New York Shakespeare Festival (NYSF), Public Theatre, 1980, also produced in Los Angeles, San Francisco, Seattle, Toronto, San Diego, Vancouver, Singapore, Hong Kong, and Honolulu; *The Dance and the Railroad*, Henry Street Settlement, New York City, then NYSF, Public Theatre, both 1981, also produced in Minneapolis, San Francisco, Seattle, and Amsterdam; *Family Devotions*, NYSF, Public Theatre, then San Francisco, both 1981; *Sound and Beauty*, NYSF, Public Theatre, 1983, also produced in San Francisco, Los Angeles, Minneapolis, and Portland, ME; *Rich Relations*, Second Stage, New York City, 1986.

PUBLICATIONS—*Broken Promises: Four Plays by David Henry Hwang*, Avon/Bard, 1983; *The Sound of a Voice*, Dramatists Play Service, 1984. Anthologies: *New Plays USA 1*, *Best Plays of 1981-82*, *Best Short Plays of 1983*, *Best Short Plays of 1985*.

WORKS IN PROGRESS—*M. Butterfly, House of Sleeping Beauties*, and an adaptation of H.G. Wells's *War of the Worlds*. Also working on screenplays for Warner Brothers and Columbia film studios.

AWARDS: Best Play, Obie Award from the *Village Voice*, 1981, for *The Dance and the Railroad;* Drama Desk Award nominations; CINE Golden Eagle Award; Drama-Logue awards; Guggenheim Fellowship; National Endowment for the Arts, Artistic Associate; New York State Council on the Arts Fellowship; Phi Beta Kappa.

Photography by Ophelia Hwang

DAVID HWANG

MEMBER: Dramatists Guild, Writers Guild of America, PEN.

ADDRESSES: AGENT—c/o William Craver, Writers and Artists Agency, 70 W. 36th Street, New York, NY 10018.

*   *   *

HYAMS, Peter   1943-

PERSONAL: Born July 26, 1943, in New York, NY. EDUCATION: Attended Hunter College and Syracuse University.

VOCATION: Writer, director, and producer.

CAREER: PRINCIPAL FILM WORK—Writer (see below); director, *Busting*, United Artists, 1974; director, *Our Time*, Warner Brothers, 1974; director, *Peeper*, Twentieth Century-Fox, 1975; director, *Telefon*, United Artists, 1977; director, *Capricorn One*, Warner Brothers, 1978; director, *Hanover Street*, Columbia, 1979; director, *Outland*, Warner Brothers, 1981; director, *Star Chamber*, Twentieth Century-Fox, 1983; producer and director, *2010*, Metro-Goldwyn-Mayer/United Artists (MGM/UA), 1984; executive producer and director, *Running Scared*, MGM/UA, 1986; executive producer, *The Monster Squad*, Tri-Star, 1987; executive producer, *Running Scared II*, MGM, upcoming.

PRINCIPAL TELEVISION WORK—Specials: Producer, Vietnam documentary, CBS, 1966. Movies: Writer (see below); director: *The Rolling Man*, ABC, 1972; *Goodnight, My Love*, ABC, 1972.

RELATED CAREER—Anchorman, CBS Television News, New York City; director of features, ABC Television.

WRITINGS: SCREENPLAYS—*T.R. Baskin*, 1971; *Busting*, United Artists, 1974; co-writer, *Telefon*, United Artists, 1977; *Capricorn One*, Warner Brothers, 1978; *Hanover Street*, Columbia, 1979; co-writer, *The Hunter*, Paramount, 1980; *Outland*, Warner Brothers, 1981; *Star Chamber*, Twentieth Century-Fox, 1983; *2010*, MGM/UA, 1984. Also writer for Paramount Pictures, 1970. TELEVISION—Movies: *The Rolling Man*, ABC, 1972; *Goodnight, My Love*, ABC, 1972.

ADDRESSES: AGENT—c/o Michael Ovitz, Creative Artists Agency, 1888 Century Park East, Los Angeles, CA 90067.*

*   *   *

HYDE-WHITE, Alex   1959-

PERSONAL: Full name, Alex Punch Hyde-White; born January 30, 1959, in London, England; son of Wilfred (an actor) and Ethel M. (a stage manager; maiden name, Korenman) Hyde-White; married Karen Y. Dotrice (an actress and writer), February 14, 1986. EDUCATION: Attended Georgetown University, 1975-76; studied at the Actors Centre and with Michael Shurtleff.

VOCATION: Actor, writer, and producer.

CAREER: STAGE DEBUT—Tom, *The Remarkable Mr. Pennypacker*, Los Angeles, CA, 1968. BROADWAY DEBUT— Maurice, *Kingdoms*, Cort Theatre, 1981. PRINCIPAL STAGE APPEARANCES—

ALEX HYDE-WHITE

Jack Merivale, Kenneth Tynan, *Vivien,* Melrose Theatre, Los Angeles, CA, 1987.

FILM DEBUT—*The Mani,* 1985. PRINCIPAL FILM APPEARANCES—Jim Ferguson, *Biggles,* New Century/Vista, 1986; also appeared in *Ishtar,* Columbia, 1987.

PRINCIPAL FILM WORK—Co-producer, *Some of These Days.*

TELEVISION DEBUT—*Quincy, M.E.,* NBC, 1978. PRINCIPAL TELEVISION APPEARANCES—Episodic: *Matlock,* NBC. Series: Dexter Sawyer, *Hill Street Blues,* NBC, 1984. Mini-Series: Blake, *The First Olympics,* NBC, 1984; *Worlds Beyond,* syndicated, 1986; Chris Pappas, *Echoes in the Darkness,* CBS, 1987.

WRITINGS: WORKS IN PROGRESS—Screenplays: "Dimensions."

MEMBER: Actors' Equity Association, Screen Actors Guild, American Federation of Television and Radio Artists.

SIDELIGHTS: RECREATIONS—Golf, skiing, softball.

ADDRESSES: AGENT—Artists Agency, 10000 Santa Monica Boulevard, Los Angeles, CA 90069.

I

IDLE, Eric 1943-

PERSONAL: Born March 29, 1943, in South Shields, Durham, England; son of Ernest (a Royal Air Force sergeant) and Norah (a health visitor; maiden name, Sanderson) Idle. EDUCATION: Attended Pembroke College, Cambridge, 1962-65.

VOCATION: Actor, writer, and editor.

CAREER: PRINCIPAL TELEVISION APPEARANCES—Series: *Monty Python's Flying Circus,* BBC, 1969-74, broadcast in the United States on PBS, 1974-82. Episodic: *The Legend of Sid Gottlieb,* Showtime, 1987; *Faerie Tale Theatre,* Showtime. Movies: *Pythons in Deutschland,* Bavaria Atelier, 1971.

PRINCIPAL TELEVISION WORK—Writer (see below); director, *Faerie Tale Theatre,* Showtime.

PRINCIPAL FILM APPEARANCES—*And Now for Something Completely Different,* Columbia, 1971; *Monty Python and the Holy Grail,* Cinema V, 1975; *Monty Python's Life of Brian,* Warner Brothers, 1979; *Monty Python Live at the Hollywood Bowl,* Columbia, 1982; *The Secret Policeman's Other Ball,* Amnesty International, 1982; *Monty Python's The Meaning of Life,* Universal, 1983; *National Lampoon's European Vacation,* Warner Brothers, 1985.

PRINCIPAL STAGE APPEARANCES—*Monty Python Live at the Hollywood Bowl,* Los Angeles, CA, 1970; *Monty Python Live!,* New York City, 1976.

MAJOR TOURS—As a member of the comedy troupe, Monty Python, with Graham Ghapman, John Cleese, Terry Gilliam, Terry Jones, and Michael Palin, performed in concert tours in U.S., U.K. and Canadian cities, 1970s.

WRITINGS: PLAYS, PRODUCED AND PUBLISHED—*Pass the Butler,* Globe Theatre, London, 1982, published by Methuen, 1982.

SCREENPLAYS—With Graham Chapman, John Cleese, Terry Gilliam, Terry Jones, and Michael Palin, except as noted: *And Now for Something Completely Different,* Columbia, 1972; *Monty Python and the Holy Grail,* Cinema 5, 1975; *Monty Python's Life of Brian,* Warner Brothers, 1979; *Monty Python Live at the Hollywood Bowl,* Columbia, 1982; *Monty Python's The Meaning of Life,* Universal, 1983; sole author: *National Lampoon's Vacation Down Under,* upcoming.

TELEVISION—Series: *The Frost Report,* London, 1965; *Do Not Adjust Your Set,* London, 1968; with Chapman, Cleese, Gilliam, Jones, and Palin, *Monty Python's Flying Circus,* BBC, 1969-74,

broadcast in the U.S. on PBS, 1974-82. Episodic: *Faerie Tale Theatre,* Showtime. Movies: *Pythons in Deutschland,* Bavaria Atelier, 1971.

BOOKS—Sole author: *Hello Sailor,* Weidenfeld and Nicholson, 1974; *The Rutland Dirty Weekend Book,* Eyre Methuen, 1976.

Co-author of Monty Python Books (with Champan, Cleese, Gilliam, Jones, and Palin) *Monty Python's Big Red Book* (also editor), Methuen, 1972; *The Brand New Monty Python Bok* (also editor; illustrated by Terry Gilliam under pseudonym Jerry Gillian, and Peter Brookes), Methuen, 1973, later published as *The Brand New Monty Python Papperbok,* Methuen, 1974; *Monty Python and the Holy Grail (Book),* Methuen, 1977, also published as *Monty Python's Second Film: A First Draft,* Methuen, 1977; *Monty Python's Life of Brian (of Nazareth)* (also editor) [and] *Montypythonscrapbook,* Grosset, 1979; *The Complete Works of Shakespeare and Monty Python* (contains *Monty Python's Big Red Book* and *The Brand New Monty Python Papperbok,* Methuen, 1981; *Monty Python's The Meaning of Life,* Methuen, 1983.

RECORDINGS: ALBUMS—(With Chapman, Cleese, Gilliam, Jones, and Palin) *Monty Python's Flying Circus,* BBC Records, 1969; *Another Monty Python Record,* Charisma, 1970; *Monty Python's Previous Record,* Charisma, 1972; *Monty Python's Matching Tie and Handkerchief,* Charisma, 1973, Arista, 1975; *Monty Python Live at Drury Lane,* Charisma, 1974; *The Album of the Soundtrack of the Trailer of the Film "Monty Python and the Holy Grail,"* Arista, 1975; *Monty Python Live at City Center,* Arista, 1976; *Monty Python's Instant Record Collection,* Charisma, 1977; *Monty Python's Life of Brian,* Warner Brothers, 1979; *Monty Python's Contractual Obligation Album,* Arista, 1980; *Monty Python's The Meaning of Life,* CBS Records, 1983; (with Neil Innes) *The Rutland Dirty Weekend Songbook,* BBC Records, 1975. SINGLES—"The Galaxy Song" and "Every Sperm Is Sacred."

AWARDS: Co-winner, Golden Palm Award, Cannes Film Festival, 1983, for *Monty Python's The Meaning of Life.*

ADDRESSES: OFFICE—Python Pictures, Ltd., 6 Cambridge Gate, London NW1, England.*

* * *

INGELS, Marty 1936-

PERSONAL: Born Martin Ingerman, March 9, 1936, in Brooklyn, NY; son of Jacob and Minnie (Crown) Ingerman; married Jean Marie Frassinelli, August 3, 1960 (divorced, 1969); married Shirley Jones (an actress and singer), 1977. MILITARY: U.S. Army, 1954-58.

VOCATION: Actor, comedian, theatrical agent, and executive.

CAREER: PRINCIPAL TELEVISION APPEARANCES—Series: Arch Fenster, *I'm Dickens, He's Fenster*, ABC, 1962-63; Norman Crump, *The Pruitts of South Hampton*, ABC, 1966-67. Episodic: *The Phil Silvers Show*, CBS; *The Bell Telephone Hour*, NBC; *Manhunt*, syndicated; *The Ann Southern Show*, CBS; *Peter Loves Mary*, NBC; *The Detectives*, ABC; *Hennessey*, CBS; *The Dick Van Dyke Show*, CBS; *Burke's Law*, ABC; *Hollywood Palace*, ABC. Guest: *The Steve Allen Show*, CBS; *The Jack Paar Show*, CBS; *The Joey Bishop Show*, CBS; *Playboy Penthouse*.

PRINCIPAL FILM APPEARANCES—*Ladies Man*, Paramount, 1961; *Armored Command*, Allied Artists, 1961; *The Horizontal Lieutenant*, Metro-Goldwyn-Mayer, 1962; *Wild and Wonderful*, 1964; *A Guide for the Married Man*, Twentieth Century-Fox, 1967; *If It's Tuesday, This Must Be Belgium*, United Artists, 1969.

PRINCIPAL CABARET APPEARANCES—*Sketchbook Revue*, Las Vegas, NV.

RELATED CAREER—Television and motion picture producer; founder, Ingels, Inc., 1975—; founder, Stoneypoint Productions, 1981—.

NON-RELATED CAREER—Active in various charities.

ADDRESSES: OFFICE—Ingles, Inc., 8322 Beverly Blvd., Hollywood, CA 90048.*

*   *   *

INGHAM, Barrie

PERSONAL: Born February 10, in Halifax, England; son of Harold Ellis Stead and Irene (Bolton) Ingham; married Tarne Phillips. MILITARY: Served with the Royal Artillery in the British army.

VOCATION: Actor.

CAREER: STAGE DEBUT—Llandudno, *Beggar My Neighbor*, Pier Pavillon, 1956. LONDON DEBUT—Fortinbras, *Hamlet*, Old Vic Theatre, 1957. BROADWAY DEBUT—Claudio, *Much Ado about Nothing*, Lunt-Fontanne Theatre, 1959. PRINCIPAL STAGE APPEARANCES—*Macbeth*, Old Vic Theatre, London, 1958; Lelie, *Sganarelle*, Damis, *Tartuffe*, Cecil Farringdon, *The Magistrate*, all Old Vic Theatre, 1959; Alan Howard, *Joie de Vivre*, Queen's Theatre, London, 1960; Henry Golightly, *The Happy Haven*, Royal Court Theatre, London, 1960; Percy French, *The Golden Years*, Gaiety Theatre, Dublin, Ireland, 1961; Young Fasion, *Virtue in Danger*, Mermaid Theatre, then Strand Theatre, both London, 1963; Nicholas Stavrogin, *The Possessed*, Dionysus, *The Bacchae*, both Mermaid Theatre, 1963; Jingle, *Pickwick*, Saville Theatre, London, 1964; Clancy Pettinger, *On the Level*, Saville Theatre, 1966; one-man show, *Love, Love, Love*, Mermaid Theatre, 1972; Herbie, *Gypsy*, Piccadilly Theatre, London, 1973; Ben, *Snap*, Vaudville Theatre, London, 1974; Tony Price, *Double Edge*, Vaudeville Theatre, 1975; Elyot Chase, *Private Lives*, Comedy Theatre, Melbourne, Australia, 1976; one-man show, *The Actor*, Neighborhood Playhouse, New York City, 1978; Uriah Heep,

Copperfield, American National Theatre Academy Playhouse, New York City, 1981; King Pellinore, *Camelot*, Winter Garden Theatre, New York City, 1981. Also appeared in *Julius Caesar*, *Mary Stuart*, both with the Old Vic Theatre Company, Edinburgh Festival, Edinburgh, Scotland, U.K., 1959; and in the revues *Pottering About*, Theatre Royal, London, 1961, and *England, Our England*, Prince's Theatre, London, 1962.

All with the Royal Shakespeare Company (RSC), Stratford-on-Avon, U.K., and London: Lalo, *Criminals*, 1967; Buffalo Bill, *Indians*, Lord Toppington, *The Relapse*, Brutus, *Julius Caesar*, 1968; Leontes, *The Winter's Tale*, Aguecheck, *Twelfth Night*, both 1969; Dazzle, *London Assurance*, 1970; Duke, *Measure for Measure*, 1974; also *Pleasure and Repentance*, RSC, Edinburgh, Scotland, U.K., 1970.

MAJOR TOURS—Richard Adam, *Strip the Willow*, U.K. cities, 1960; Leontes, *The Winter's Tale*, Japanese and Australian cities, 1969; one-man show, *Love, Love, Love*, Australian cities, 1971; one-man show, *The Actor*, Australian and South African cities, 1975, then U.S. cities, 1978-79.

PRINCIPAL STAGE WORK—Director, *Gypsy*, Her Majesty's Theatre, Melbourne, Australia, 1975.

PRINCIPAL FILM APPEARANCES—Robin, *A Challenge for Robin Hood*, Twentieth Century-Fox, 1969; St. Clair, *The Day of the Jackal*, Universal, 1973.

PRINCIPAL TELEVISION APPEARANCES—Series: *Hine*, *The Power Game*, *The Caesars*, *Beyond a Joke*, *The Victorians*, *Funny Man*.

RELATED CAREER—Associate artist, Royal Shakespeare Company, 1974; consultant to the International Theatre Arts Forum, 1976; visiting professor of drama, University of Texas, Austin, 1979; drama consultant, Baylor University, 1980.

AWARDS: Most Distinguished Actor, Australian Theatre award, 1975.

SIDELIGHTS: RECREATIONS—Songwriting, riding.

ADDRESSES: AGENTs—(New York) c/o Milton Goldman, International Creative Management, 40 W. 57th Street, New York, NY 10019; (London) c/o Dennis Sellinger, International Creative Management, 22 Grafton Street, London W1, England.*

*   *   *

IRELAND, Kenneth   1920-

PERSONAL: Born June 17, 1920, in Edinburgh, Scotland; son of Richard Morison and Erna (Herrmann) Ireland; married Moira Lamb. EDUCATION: Received Bachelor of Law from Edinburgh University; studied theatre at the Pasadena Playhouse, 1947. MILITARY: Served in the Royal Artillery, 1941-42, Intelligence Corps, 1942-46.

VOCATION: Festival director and secretary of Pitlochry Festival Theatre, United Kingdom.

CAREER: PRINCIPAL STAGE WORK—General manager, Park

Theatre, Glasow, Scotland, U.K., 1946-49; general manager, Pitlochry Festival Theatre, Pitlochry, U.K., 1951-53, then general manager and secretary, 1953-57, later director and secretary, 1957—.

MAJOR TOURS—Pitlochry Festival companies regularly tour the U.K.

RELATED CAREER—Secretary, Federation of Scottish Theatres, 1966-69, then chairor, 1974—; chairor, Association of British Theatre Technicians (Scotland), 1972—; has broadcast and lectured extensively in Scotland and abroad.

NON-RELATED CAREER—Chairman, Tourist Association of Scotland, 1967-69; vice-chairman, Scottish Tourist Consultative Committee, 1977—; founder fellow, Tourism Society (Scotland), 1978, chairman, 1979—.

AWARDS: Order of British Empire, 1966; William Thyne Award, 1970. Honary degrees: Doctor of the University, Stirling University, 1972.

SIDELIGHTS: RECREATIONS—Music, travel, going to the theatre and art galleries.

ADDRESSES: OFFICE—Knockendarroch House, Pitlochry, Perthshire PH16 5DR, Scotland.*

*   *   *

IVANEK, Zeljko   1957-

PERSONAL: Born August 15, 1957, in Ljubljana, Yugoslavia; immigrated to the United States, 1960. EDUCATION: Graduated from Yale University, 1978; trained for the stage at the London Academy of Music and Dramatic Arts.

VOCATION: Actor.

CAREER: BROADWAY DEBUT—Yankele, *The Survivor,* Morosco Theatre, 1981. PRINCIPAL STAGE APPEARANCES—Betty, Gerry, *Cloud 9,* Lucille Lortel Theatre, New York City, 1981; Stanley, *Brighton Beach Memoirs,* Center Theatre Group, Ahmanson Theatre, Los Angeles, CA, 1982, then Neil Simon Theatre, New York City, 1983; Hal, *Loot,* Music Box Theatre, New York City, 1986. Also appeared in *Hay Fever,* GeVa Theatre, Rochester, NY, 1980; *Master Harold . . . and the boys,* Yale Repertory Theatre, New Haven, CT, 1982; *A Map of the World,* New York Shakespeare Festival, Public Theatre, New York City, 1985; *The Cherry Orchard,* Majestic Theatre, Brooklyn Academy of Music, Brooklyn, NY, 1988; and *Hay Fever, Charley's Aunt, The Front Page,* all Williamstown Theatre Festival, Williamstown, MA.

PRINCIPAL FILM APPEARANCES—*Tex,* Buena Vista, 1982; *The Sender,* Paramount, 1982; *The Soldier,* Paramount, 1982; *Mass Appeal,* Universal, 1984.

PRINCIPAL TELEVISION APPEARANCES—Episodic: "All My Sons," *American Playhouse,* PBS, 1987. Movies: Bill Gorton, *The Sun Also Rises,* NBC, 1984; Vince Valaitis, *Echoes in the Darkness,* CBS, 1987.

AWARDS: Drama Desk Award, 1981, for *Cloud 9;* Antoinette

Perry Award nomination, 1983, for *Brighton Beach Memoirs;* Best Supporting Actor, Academy Award nomination, 1985, for *Mass Appeal.*

MEMBER: Actors' Equity Association, Screen Actors Guild, American Federation of Television and Radio Artists.

ADDRESSES: AGENT—Triad Artists, 10100 Santa Monica Boulevard, Los Angeles, CA 90067.

*   *   *

IVEY, Dana

PERSONAL: Born August 12, in Atlanta, GA; daughter of Hugh Daugherty (a physicist) and Mary Nell (an actress and teacher; maiden name, McKoin) Ivey. EDUCATION: Received A.B., theatre, from Rollins College; trained for the stage at the London Academy of Music and Dramatic Art for one year.

VOCATION: Actress and teacher.

CAREER: STAGE DEBUT—Seventh fairy and palace guard, *Sleeping Beauty,* Children's Civic Theatre, Atlanta, GA. BROADWAY DEBUT—Monica Reed, *Present Laughter,* Circle in the Square, 1982, for 176 performances. PRINCIPAL STAGE APPEARANCES—Hermia, *A Midsummer Night's Dream,* Sara, *Major Barbara,* Marian's mother, *The Music Man,* Mrs. Teale, *Roberta,* Madame Rosepettle, *Oh Dad, Poor Dad, Mama's Hung You in the Closet*

DANA IVEY

and I'm Feeling So Sad, wife, mother, *Ah! Wilderness,* wife, *The Seven Year Itch,* Mrs. Higgins, *My Fair Lady,* all Front Street Theatre, Memphis, TN, 1964-65; Mrs. Mullins, *Carousel,* Theatre of the Stars, Atlanta, GA, 1965; chorus, *Murder in the Cathedral,* Anna, *The Firebugs,* Sara Tansey, *The Playboy of the Western World,* all with the Canadian Players, Toronto, ON, Canada, 1965-66; Mrs. Sowerberry, *Oliver!,* Theatre of the Stars, 1966; Margaret, *Galileo,* Solange, *The Maids,* Kitty, *Charley's Aunt,* all Manitoba Theatre Centre, Winnipeg, MB, Canada, 1966; title role, *Antigone,* Lucy Brown, *The Threepenny Opera,* both Hartford Stage Company, Hartford, CT, 1968; Baroness, Clea, *White Liars/ Black Comedy,* Mia, *The Three Desks,* Amanda, *Private Lives,* pioneer woman, singer, *You Two Stay Here, the Rest Come with Me,* Gillian, *Bell, Book, and Candle,* Gwendolyn, *The Importance of Being Earnest,* Mrs. Gargary, *Great Expectations,* Fay, *Loot,* all Theatre Calgary, Calgary, AB, Canada, 1969-70.

Lill, *Revenge,* Ruth, *The Homecoming,* nurse, *The Death of Bessie Smith,* Miss Moscowitz, *The Eletronic Nigger,* Sonya, *Uncle Vanya,* Emilia, *Othello,* Mrs. Harford, *A Touch of the Poet,* all Centaur Theatre, Montreal, PQ, Canada, 1970-71; title role, *Electra,* Jean, *The Entertainer,* narrator, *At the Hawk's Well,* Queen, *Full Moon in March,* woman, *The Exception and the Rule,* Claire, *The Maids,* Isabelle, *Total Eclipse,* all Centaur Theatre, 1971-72; Gwendolyn Pidgeon, *The Odd Couple,* Theatre of the Stars, 1972; Helene, *En Pieces Detachees,* woman, *Thurber Carnival,* Stella, *A Streetcar Named Desire,* all Manitoba Theatre Centre, 1973; Shen-Te, *The Good Woman of Setzuan,* Theatre London, London, ON, Canada, 1973; Sara, *A Touch of the Poet,* St. Lawrence Center, National Arts Centre, Ottawa, ON, Canada, 1973; Sara, *Sunrise on Sara,* Festival Lennoxville, Lennoxville, PQ, Canada, 1973; Nurse, *Romeo and Juliet,* Sister Woman, *Cat on a Hot Tin Roof,* both Alliance Theatre, Atlanta, GA, 1974; Elizabeth Proctor, *The Crucible,* Alliance Theatre, 1975; Annie Sullivan, *The Miracle Worker,* Alliance Theatre, 1976; Mistress Quickly, *Henry IV, Part I,* Mary, *All the Way Home,* Lina, *Misalliance,* Mona, *Come Back to the Five and Dime, Jimmy Dean, Jimmy Dean,* title role, *Hedda Gabler,* all Alliance Theatre, 1977; Catherine, *Great Catherine,* Shaw Festival, Niagara-on-the-Lake, ON, Canada, 1977; Alma, *Eccentricities of a Nightingale,* Alaska Repertory Theatre, Anchorage, AK, 1978; Miss Casewell, *The Mousetrap,* Elaine, *The Last of the Red Hot Lovers,* both Newport Actors Company, Newport, RI, 1978; Mrs. Linde, *A Doll's House,* Manitoba Theatre Centre, 1978; Regina, *The Little Foxes,* Alliance Theatre, 1979; Claire, *The Taking Away of Little Willie,* Mark Taper Forum, Los Angeles, CA, 1979; Katherine, *The Taming of the Shrew,* Lady Capulet, *Romeo and Juliet,* California Shakespearean Festival, Visalia, CA, 1979; Miss Giddens, *The Innocents,* Vancouver Playhouse, Vancouver, BC, Canada, 1979; Elvira, *Blithe Spirit,* Vancouver Playhouse, 1979.

Julia, *The Philanderer,* Lucienne, *A Flea in Her Ear,* both Shaw Festival, 1980; gentlewoman, witch, *Macbeth,* Vivian Beaumont Theatre, New York City, 1980; Isabel, *A Call from the East,* Manhattan Theatre Club, New York City, 1981; madwoman, *The Hunchback of Notre Dame,* New York Shakespeare Festival, Public Theatre, 1981; Miss Prism, *The Importance of Being Earnest,* Ellie, *Bing and Walker,* both Peterborough Players, Peterborough, NH, 1981; Hilda, *Am I Blue?,* Renata, *Forbidden Copy,* Andrea, *Twinkle, Twinkle,* all Hartford Stage Company, 1981; Lizzie Borden, actress, *Blood Relations,* Centaur Theatre, 1981; Miss Tendesco, Vivien, Arc Theatre, New York City, 1982; Melanie Garth, *Quartermaine's Terms,* Long Wharf Theatre, New Haven, CT, 1982, then Playhouse 91, New York City, 1983; Nanny, Kate,

Principal, *Baby with the Bathwater,* Playwrights Horizons, New York City, 1983; Lady Ariadne Utterwod, *Heartbreak House,* Circle in the Square, New York City, 1983; Yvonne, Naomi, *Sunday in the Park with George,* Booth Theatre, New York City, 1984; Helen Kroger, *Pack of Lies,* Royale Theatre, New York City, 1984; Countess, *The Marriage of Figaro,* Circle in the Square, 1985; Daisy Werthan, *Driving Miss Daisy,* Playwrights Horizons, New York City, 1987. Also Jenny, *Everything in the Garden,* Druid Cellar Dinner Theatre, 1974; Pearl, Dot, *Patio/Porch,* Dallas, TX, 1978.

MAJOR TOURS—Chorus, *Murder in the Cathedral,* Anna, *The Firebugs,* Sara Tansey, *Playboy of the Western World,* all with the Canadian Players, Canadian cities, 1966; lady-in-waiting, *Twelfth Night,* Avdotya, *The Government Inspector,* both with the Stratford Shakespeare Festival Centennial tour, Canadian cities, 1967; Androgyne, *Volpone,* Viola, *Twelfth Night,* Juliet, *Romeo and Juliet,* all with the National Shakespeare Company, U.S. cities, 1967; Miss McCormack, Mimsey, *Plaza Suite,* U.S. cities, 1969; scenes from *The Taming of the Shrew,* Canadian schools, 1970.

TELEVISION DEBUT—Dr. Maria Thompson, *Search for Tomorrow,* CBS, 1978. PRINCIPAL TELEVISION APPEARANCES— Series: Eleanor Standard, *Easy Street,* NBC, 1986. Movies: *Little Gloria . . . Happy at Last,* NBC, 1982. Specials: Lady Utterwod, *Heartbreak House,* PBS/Showtime, 1984; Yvonne, Naomi, *Sunday in the Park with George,* PBS/Showtime, 1985.

FILM DEBUT—Mrs. Mueller, *Explorers,* Paramount, 1984. PRINCIPAL FILM APPEARANCES—Miss Millie, *The Color Purple,* Warner Brothers, 1985. Also appeared in *Heartburn,* Paramount, 1986.

RELATED CAREER—Director of Drama Tech, Georgia Institute of Technology, 1974-77; teacher: Circle in the Square Theatre School, National Theatre School of Canada, Academy Theatre School.

NON-RELATED CAREER—Disc jockey, interviewer, and classical music programmer, WGKA-AM, Atlanta, GA, 1974-76; teacher, Atlanta, GA, 1974-77.

AWARDS: Best Actress, Atlanta Circle of Drama Critics, 1977, for *Come Back to the Five and Dime, Jimmy Dean, Jimmy Dean;* Dramalogue Award, 1979, for *Romeo and Juliet;* Clarence Derwent Award, 1983; Drama Desk nominations, both 1983, for *Present Laughter* and *Quartermaine's Terms;* Obie Award from the *Village Voice,* 1983, for *Quartermaine's Terms;* Best Supporting Actress, Antoinette Perry Award nominations, both 1984, for *Heartbreak House* and *Sunday in the Park with George.*

MEMBER: Actors' Equity Association, American Federation of Television and Radio Artists, Screen Actors Guild, Canadian Actors' Equity Association, Association of Canadian Television and Radio Artists.

SIDELIGHTS: FAVORITE ROLES—Annie Sullivan in *The Miracle Worker.* RECREATIONS—Classical music, reading (historical fiction and mysteries).

Dana Ivey told *CTFT* that she supports animal rights groups and that her favorite places to visit are Scotland and Venice.

ADDRESSES: AGENT—c/o STE Representation, 888 Seventh Avenue, New York, NY 10019.

J

JACKSON, Gordon 1923-

PERSONAL: Full name, Gordon Cameron Jackson; born December 19, 1923, in Glasglow, Scotland; son of Thomas and Margaret (Fletcher) Jackson; married Rona Anderson, 1951; children: two sons.

VOCATION: Actor.

CAREER: STAGE DEBUT—Dudley, *George and Margaret,* MSU Theatre, Rutherglen, Scotland, U.K., 1943. LONDON STAGE DEBUT—Able Seaman McIntosh, *Seagulls Over Sorrento,* Apollo Theatre, 1951. BROADWAY DEBUT—Horatio, *Hamlet,* Lunt-Fontanne Theatre, 1969. PRINCIPAL STAGE APPEARANCES— Young Actor (Ismael), *Moby Dick,* Duke of York's Theatre, London, 1955; narrator, *The Soldier's Tale,* Sadler's Wells Thea-

tre, London, 1958; Banquo, *Macbeth,* Royal Court Theatre, London, 1966; narrator, *The Soldier's Tale,* Edinburgh Festival, Edinburgh, Scotland, U.K., 1967; Mr. Booker, *Wise Child,* Garrick Theatre, London, 1967; Baxter, *This Story of Yours,* Royal Court Theatre, 1968; Horatio, *Hamlet,* Round House Theatre, London, 1969; Alfred, *The Signalman's Apprentice,* Oxford Playhouse, Oxford, U.K., 1969; Tesman, *Hedda Gabler,* Stratford Theatre, Stratford, ON, Canada, 1970; Creon, *Oedipus,* narrator, *The Soldier's Tale,* both Young Vic Theatre, London, 1970; Interrogator, *The Lovers of Viorne,* Royal Court Theatre, 1971; Rodney, *Veterans,* Royal Court Theatre, 1972; Banquo, *Macbeth,* Aldwych Theatre, London, 1975; title role, *Noah,* Malvolio, *Twelfth Night,* both Chichester Festival, Chichester, U.K., 1976. Also appeared in *Death Trap,* 1981; *Cards on the Table,* 1982; *Mass Appeal,* 1983.

MAJOR TOURS—David, *What Every Woman Knows,* U.K. cities, 1973.

FILM DEBUT—*The Foreman Went to France,* 1941. PRINCIPAL FILM APPEARANCES—*Those Magnificent Men in Their Flying Machines,* Twentieth Century-Fox, 1956; *Tunes of Glory,* United Artists, 1960; *Greyfriars Bobby,* Buena Vista, 1961; *Mutiny on the Bounty,* Metro-Goldwyn-Mayer, 1962; *The Great Escape,* United Artists, 1963; *The Long Ships,* Columbia, 1964; *The Ipcress File,* Universal, 1965; *Cast a Giant Shadow,* United Artists, 1966; *The Fighting Prince of Donegal,* Buena Vista, 1966; *The Night of the Generals,* Columbia, 1967; *Triple Cross,* Warner Brothers-Seven Arts, 1967; *The Prime of Miss Jean Brodie,* Twentieth Century-Fox, 1969; *Run Wild, Run Free,* Columbia, 1969; *Hamlet,* Columbia, 1970; *Scrooge,* National General, 1970; *Kidnapped,* American International, 1971; *Russian Roulette,* AVCO-Embassy, 1975; *The Medusa Touch,* Warner Brothers, 1978. Also appeared in *Nine Men; San Demetrio; Millions Like Us; Pink String and Sealing Wax; Captive Heart; Against the Wind; Eureka Stockade; Whiskey Galore; Floodtide; Stop Press Girl; Bitter Strings; Happy Go Lovely; The Lady with the Lamp; Meet Mr. Lucifer; Malta Story; Castle in the Air; Quartermass Experiment; Pacific Destiny; The Baby and the Battleship; Sailor Beware; Seven Waves Away* (also known as *Abandon Ship*); *As Long As You're Happy; Hell Drivers; Rockets Galore; Bridal Path; Yesterday's Enemy; Blind Date; Cone of Silence; The Eliminator; Madame Sin; Golden Rendezvous; The Last Giraffe; The Shooting Party; The Masks of Death; Gunpowder; The Whistle Blower; Spectre.*

PRINCIPAL TELEVISION APPEARANCES—Episodic: *Hart to Hart,* ABC. Series: *Upstairs, Downstairs,* 1970-75; *The Professionals,* 1977-81. Mini-Series: *A Town Like Alice,* 1980; *Masks of Death,* 1984; also appeared in *Noble House.*

NON-RELATED CAREER—Draftsman.

GORDON JACKSON

161

AWARDS: Officer of Order of the British Empire; Royal Television Society Award, 1975, Emmy Award, 1976, both for *Upstairs, Downstairs;* Australian Logie Award, 1981, for *A Town Like Alice.*

SIDELIGHTS: RECREATIONS—Music, gardening.

ADDRESSES: HOME—London, England. AGENT—International Creative Management, 338 Oxford Street, London W1N 9HE, England.

*   *   *

JACOBS, Sally   1932-

PERSONAL: Born November 5, 1932, in London, England; daughter of Bernard Maxwell and Esther (Bart) Rich; married Alexander Jacobs (died, 1979). EDUCATION: Attended St. Martin's School of Art and Central School of Arts and Crafts, London, 1957-60.

VOCATION: Set designer, costume designer, and director.

CAREER: PRINCIPAL STAGE WORK—All as set designer unless indicated: *Wildest Dreams,* Colchester Repertory Theatre, Colchester, U.K., 1960; assistant set designer, *The Kitchen,* Royal Court Theatre, London, 1961; *Five Plus One,* Edinburgh Festival, Edinburgh, Scotland, U.K., 1961; *Twists, Women Beware Women, The Empire Builders,* all Arts Theatre, London, 1962; *The Day of the Prince,* Royal Court Theatre, 1963; *The Formation Dancers,* Globe Theatre, London, 1964; *Marat/Sade* Martin Beck Theatre, New York City, 1965; *The Golden Fleece, Muzeeka,* both Mark Taper Forum, Los Angeles, CA, 1968; *A Midsummer Night's Dream,* Billy Rose Theatre, New York City, 1971; *The Conference of the Birds,* Centre Centre, Paris, France, then Brooklyn Academy of Music, Brooklyn, NY, 1973; *Mahagonny Songplay, The Measures Taken, Brecht: Sacred and Profane,* all Mark Taper Forum, 1973; *Ajax,* Mark Taper Forum Laboratory, 1974; *Of Mice and Men* (opera), San Francisco Spring Opera, San Francisco, CA, 1974; *Savages,* Mark Taper Forum, 1974; *Il Trovatore* (opera), Houston Grand Opera, Houston, TX, 1974; director, *Oedipus at Colonus,* Mark Taper Forum Laboratory, 1975; *Cross Country, Where She Stops, Ashes, Three Sisters,* all Mark Taper Forum, 1976; *Much Ado about Nothing,* Los Angeles Shakespeare Festival, 1977; *Gethsemane Springs,* Mark Taper Forum, 1977; *Black Angel,* Mark Taper Forum, 1978; *Anthony and Cleopatra,* Aldwych Theatre, London, 1979; *Conference of Birds,* Centre Centre, 1979; *Ice,* Manhattan Theatre Club, New York City, 1979.

Endgame, Manhattan Theatre Club, then American Centre, Paris, France, 1980; *Selma,* Theatre for the New City, 1981; *Three Acts of Recognition,* New York Shakespeare Festival (NYSF), Public Theatre, 1981; *Antigone,* NYSF, Public Theatre, 1982; *Die Fledermaus* (opera), Paris Opera, Paris, France, 1982; *Black Angels,* Circle Repertory Theatre, New York City, 1982; *The Relapse,* Lyric Hammersmith Theatre, England, 1983; *Turandot* (opera), Los Angeles Olympic Arts Festival, Los Angeles, CA, then Royal Opera House, London, both 1984; *Otello* (opera), Royal Opera House, 1985; *Fidelio* (opera), Royal Opera House, 1986. Also set designer for Royal Shakespeare Company productions of *Theatre of Cruelty,* 1964; *The Screens,* 1964; *Marat/Sade,* 1964; *Love's Labour's Lost,* 1964; *Twelfth Night,* 1966; *Us,* 1966; *A Midsummer Night's Dream,* 1970; *Anthony and Cleopatra,* 1978.

MAJOR TOURS—Set designer: *A Midsummer Night's Dream,* U.S.

cities, 1970, then world tour, 1972; *Conference of the Birds,* European cities, 1979; *Turandot* (opera), Korean and Japanese cities, 1987. Also set designer for Peter Brook's International Centre for Theatre Research tour of West Africa, 1973.

PRINCIPAL FILM WORK—Costume designer, *Nothing But the Best,* Royal, 1964; costume designer, *Having a Wild Weekend,* Warner Brothers, 1965; set designer, *Marat/Sade,* United Artists, 1966.

PRINCIPAL TELEVISION WORK—Both as set designer. Specials: *The Ascent of Mount Fuji,* Hollywood Television Theatre, 1977; *Turnandot,* BBC, 1987.

RELATED CAREER—Production secretary, continuity girl for a number of British feature films, 1951-57; scenic painter, Colchester Repertory Theatre, Colchester, U.K., 1960; teacher of design classes: California Institute of the Arts, 1970-71; University of California, Los Angeles, 1977; Actors and Directors Laboratory, New York University, 1978-79; Theatre Arts Department of Stage Design, New York University, 1979-82; artist-in-residence, Theatre Arts Program, Rutgers University, 1980-82; senior lecturer, Central School of Art and Design, London, 1982—.

AWARDS: Best Scenic Design, Drama Desk Award, Antoinette Perry Award nomination, both 1970, for *A Midsummer Night's Dream;* Obie Award from the *Village Voice,* 1980, for *Endgame.*

ADDRESSES: HOME—Garden Flat, Five Primrose Gardens, London NW3 4UJ, England. OFFICE—A.C.T.A.C. Ltd., 16 Cadogan Lane, London SW1, England.

*   *   *

JAECKEL, Richard   1926-

PERSONAL: Full name, Richard Hanley Jaeckel; born October 10, 1926, in Long Beach, NY.

VOCATION: Actor.

CAREER: FILM DEBUT—Baby Marine, *Guadalcanal Diary,* 1943. PRINCIPAL FILM APPEARANCES—*Sands of Iwo Jima,* Republic, 1949; *Battleground,* Metro-Goldwyn-Mayer (MGM), 1949; *The Gunfighter,* 1950; *Sea Hornet,* 1951; *Hoodlum Empire,* 1952; *My Son John,* 1952; *Come Back, Little Sheba,* 1952; *Big Leaguer,* MGM, 1953; *Sea of Lost Ships,* 1953; *Shanghai Story,* 1954; *Violent Men,* Columbia, 1955; *Platinum High School,* MGM, 1960; *The Young and the Brave,* MGM, 1963; *Apache Ambush,* Columbia, 1965; *The Dirty Dozen,* MGM, 1967; *The Green Slime,* MGM, 1969; *Sometimes a Great Notion,* Universal, 1971; *Ulzana's Raid,* Universal, 1972; *Pat Garrett and Billy the Kid,* MGM, 1973; *The Outfit,* United Artists, 1974; *Chosen Survivors,* Columbia, 1974; *The Drowning Pool,* Warner Brothers, 1975; *Part II: Walking Tall,* American International, 1975; *Twilight's Last Gleaming,* Allied Artists, 1977; *All the Marbles,* United Artists, 1981; *Starman,* Columbia, 1984; also *Fragile Fox.*

PRINCIPAL TELEVISION APPEARANCES—Series: Tony Gentry, *Frontier Circus,* CBS, 1961-62; Lieutenant Pete McNeil, *Banyon,* NBC, 1972-73; Hank Myers, *Firehouse,* ABC, 1974; Klinger, *Salvage I,* ABC, 1979; Major Hawkins, *At Ease,* ABC, 1983; Lt. Martin Quirk, *Spencer: For Hire,* ABC, 1986-87. Episodic: *U.S.*

RICHARD JAECKEL

Steel Hour, ABC; *The Elgin TV Hour,* ABC; *Goodyear TV Playhouse,* NBC; *Kraft Television Theatre,* NBC, *Playhouse 90,* CBS; *Climax,* CBS; *Producers Showcase,* NBC; *Gunsmoke,* CBS; *Have Gun, Will Travel,* CBS; *Lou Grant,* CBS. Movies: *Firehouse,* 1972.

NON-RELATED CAREER—Delivery boy, Twentieth Century-Fox mailroom.

MEMBER: Screen Actors Guild, American Federation of Television and Radio Actors.

ADDRESSES: AGENT—David Shapira & Associates, Inc., 15301 Ventura Blvd., Suite 345, Sherman Oaks, CA 91403.

*   *   *

JAFFE, Herb

PERSONAL: Born in New York, NY. EDUCATION: Attended Brooklyn College and Columbia University.

VOCATION: Producer.

CAREER: PRINCIPAL FILM WORK—Producer: *The Wind and the Lion,* United Artists, 1975; *The Demon Seed,* United Artists, 1977; *Who'll Stop the Rain?,* United Artists, 1978; *Time After Time,* Warner Brothers, 1979; *Those Lips, Those Eyes,* United Artists, 1980; *Motel Hell,* 1980; *It's All in the Game,* 1982; co-producer,

The Lords of Discipline, Paramount, 1983; *Little Treasure,* Tri-Star, 1985; *Fright Night,* Columbia, 1985; *The Gate,* 1986; co-producer, *Tweeners* (also known as *Trading Hearts*), New Century, upcoming; co-executive producer, *Russkies,* New Century, upcoming; co-producer, *The Penitent,* New Century, upcoming; co-producer, *Pass the Ammunition* (also known as *Pass the Ammo*), New Century, upcoming; *Nightflyers,* New Century, upcoming; co-producer, *Maid to Order,* New Century, upcoming; *Federal Express,* Vista Films, upcoming; co-producer, *Dudes,* New Century, upcoming; *The Danger,* New Century, upcoming.

PRINCIPAL TELEVISION WORK—Co-producer, *The Desert Rose,* Vestron Video, upcoming.

RELATED CAREER—Free-lance press agent; talent agent, MCA, personal appearance division; sales executive, syndicated film division, MCA-TV, Ltd.; Eastern sales manager, Motion Pictures for Television, Inc.; vice-president and sales manager, Official Films, Inc.; president, Herb Jaffe Associates, 1957; president, TVO Productions, Inc.; vice-president of production, United Artists, 1965, then vice-president of West Coast operations, 1966, and vice-president of world wide productions, 1970; independent film producer, 1973—.

ADDRESSES: OFFICE—Vista Films Corporation, Laird Studios, 9336 W. Washington Blvd., Culver City, CA 90230.*

*   *   *

JAMES, Emrys   1930-

PERSONAL: Born September 1, 1930, in Machynlleth, Wales; son of James Harold and Elen (Roberts) James; married Sian Davis. EDUCATION: Attended University of Wales; trained for the stage at the Royal Academy of Dramatic Art.

VOCATION: Actor.

CAREER: STAGE DEBUT—Dudley, *The Young Elizabeth,* Liverpool Playhouse, Liverpool, U.K., 1954. PRINCIPAL STAGE APPEARANCES—Guildenstern, *Hamlet,* Claudio, *Measure for Measure,* both Royal Shakespeare Theatre, Stratford-on-Avon, U.K., 1956; Touchstone, *As You Like It,* narrator, *Under Milk Wood,* both Bristol Old Vic Theatre, Bristol, U.K., 1958; Private Evans, *The Long and the Short and the Tall,* New Theatre, London, 1959; Feste, *Twelfth Night,* Malcolm, *Macbeth,* Richmond, *Richard III,* all Old Vic Theatre, London, 1960-62; title role, *Hamlet,* Empire Theatre, Sunderland, U.K., 1963; juror nine, *Twelve Angry Men,* Lyric Theatre, London, 1964; title role, *Hamlet,* Ludlow Festival, Ludlow, U.K., 1965; Sir Hugh Evans, *The Merry Wives of Windsor,* Royal Shakespeare Company (RSC), Royal Shakespeare Theatre, then Aldwych Theatre, London, 1968; Sitting Bull, *Indians,* Worthy, *Relapse,* both RSC, Aldwych Theatre, 1968; Gower, *Pericles,* RSC, Royal Shakespeare Theatre, 1969.

Feste, *Twelfth Night,* Cranmer, *Henry VIII,* both RSC, Royal Shakespeare Theatre, 1969, then Aldwych Theatre, 1970; Boss, *The Plebeians Rehearse the Uprising,* RSC, Aldwych Theatre, 1970; Cardinal, *The Duchess of Malfi,* Shylock, *The Merchant of Venice,* Iago, *Othello,* RSC, Royal Shakespeare Theatre, 1971; Merlin, *The Island of the Mighty,* RSC, Aldwych Theatre, 1972; Mephistophilis, *Dr. Faustus,* RSC, Aldwych Theatre, 1974; title role, *King John,* RSC, Royal Shakespeare Theatre, then Aldwych

Theatre, both 1975; chorus, *Henry V,* title role, *Henry IV, Parts I and II,* Sir Hugh Evans, *The Merry Wives of Windsor,* all RSC, Royal Shakespeare Theatre, 1975, then Aldwych Theatre, 1976; Cauchon, *Saint Joan,* RSC, Old Vic Theatre, 1977; York, *Henry VI, Parts I, II, and III,* all RSC, Royal Shakespeare Theatre, 1977, then Aldwych Theatre, 1978; Jacques, *As You Like It,* RSC, Royal Shakespeare Theatre, 1977, then Aldwych Theatre, 1978; Edgar, *The Dance of Death,* RSC, Other Place Theatre, then Warehouse Theatre, London, 1978; De Flores, *The Changeling,* RSC, Aldwych Theatre, 1978.

PRINCIPAL FILM APPEARANCES—*Darling,* Embassy, 1965. Also appeared in *The Man in the Iron Mask; In Search of Eden.*

PRINCIPAL TELEVISION APPEARANCES—Mini-Series: "Testament of Youth," *Masterpiece Theatre,* PBS.

RELATED CAREER—Associate artist, Royal Shakespeare Company.

SIDELIGHTS: RECREATIONS—Cats, art, books, music.

ADDRESSES: AGENT—John Cadell Ltd., Two Southwood Lane, London N6, England.*

*   *   *

JAMES, Peter   1940-

PERSONAL: Born July 27, 1940, in Enfield, England; son of Arthur Leonard and Gladys (King) James. EDUCATION: Attended Birmingham University and Bristol University.

VOCATION: Director.

CAREER: FIRST STAGE WORK—Director, *The Caretaker,* Everyman Theatre, Liverpool, U.K., 1964. PRINCIPAL STAGE WORK—Director: *The Wakefield Mystery Plays, Little Malcolm, Happy Days, Endgame, Romeo and Juliet, Julius Caesar, The Dwarfs, The Shadow of the Gunman, The Painters, The Comedy of Errors,* all Young Vic Theatre, London, 1970-72; *Bakke's Night of Fame,* Shaw Theatre, London, 1972; *Oh, What a Lovely War!,* Crucible Theatre, Sheffield, U.K., 1972; *As You Like It,* Cameri Theatre, Tel Aviv, Israel, 1973; *Macbeth,* Shaw Theatre, 1973; *Tartuffe,* Edinburgh Festival, Edinburgh, Scotland, U.K., 1974; *Mind Your Head, The Importance of Being Ernest, The King,* all Shaw Theatre, 1974; *The Comedy of Errors* Cameri Theatre, 1974; *Landscape, A Slight Ache,* both Cameri Theatre, 1975; *Twelfth Night,* Sevriomennik, Moscow, USSR, 1975; *Equus, Three Sisters,* both Cameri Theatre, 1976; *Chicago,* Cambridge Theatre, London, 1979. Also directed over thirty productions for the Everyman Theatre, 1964-70; *Jumpers, Old Times,* Melbourne, Australia, 1973; *A Slight Ache,* Royal Shakespeare Company, 1973; *No Good Friday, Nongogo, Charley's Aunt, Waiting for Godot, Dracula, As You Like It, Cabaret, Travesties, The Second Mrs. Tanqueray, Much Ado about Nothing, Chicago,* all Crucible Theatre, Sheffield, U.K.

MAJOR TOURS—*Twelfth Night,* National Theatre Company, U.K. cities, 1972.

RELATED CAREER—Co-founder and associate director, Everyman Theatre, Liverpool, U.K., 1964-67, then artistic director, 1967-70; associate director, Young Vic Theatre, London, 1970-72;

artistic director, Shaw Theatre, London, 1974; artistic director, Crucible Theatre, Sheffield, U.K., 1974-80; member, Arts Council Drama Panel, 1968-75; member, Drama Board; president, New Theatre Committee, International Theatre Institute, 1974-77.

WRITINGS: MUSICALS—(Adaptor) *As You Like It,* Cameri Theatre, Tel Aviv, Israel, 1973; (adaptor) *The Comedy of Errors,* Cameri Theatre, 1975.

SIDELIGHTS: CTFT learned that Peter James was the first British director to stage a production in the USSR when he directed *Twelfth Night* in Moscow in 1975.

ADDRESSES: OFFICE—c/o Crucible Theatre, 55 Norfolk Street, Sheffield S1 1DA, England.*

*   *   *

JAMES, Polly   1941-

PERSONAL: Born Polly Devaney, July 9, 1941, in Blackborn, England; daughter of James Gerard and Alice (Howson) Devaney; married Clive Francis. EDUCATION: Attended Yorkshire College of Housecraft; trained for the stage at the Royal Academy of Dramatic Art.

VOCATION: Actress.

CAREER: LONDON DEBUT—Gladys, *A Cuckoo in the Nest,* Royal Court Theatre, 1964. BROADWAY DEBUT—Annie Pornick, *Half a Sixpence,* Broadhurst Theatre, 1965. PRINCIPAL STAGE APPEARANCES—Corrie, *Barefoot in the Park,* Piccadilly Theatre, London, 1966; Polly Peachum, *The Beggar's Opera,* Lika, *The Promise,* Northcott Theatre, Exeter, U.K., 1967-68; title role, *Anne of Green Gables,* New Theatre, London, 1969; Nerissa, *The Merchant of Venice,* Royal Shakespeare Company (RSC), Royal Shakespeare Theatre, Stratford-on-Avon, U.K., 1971; Margaret, *Much Ado about Nothing,* RSC, Royal Shakespeare Theatre, then Aldwych Theatre, London, both 1971; Katharine, *Henry V,* RSC, Theatre-Go-Round, Stratford-on-Avon, U.K., 1971; Queen Victoria, *I and Albert,* Piccadilly Theatre, 1972; Maggie, *Hobson's Choice,* Oxford Playhouse, Oxford, U.K., 1978; Effie, *Saratoga,* RSC, Aldwych Theatre, 1978; Babe, *Babes in the Woods,* Pavilion Theatre, Bournemouth, U.K., 1979; Princess Victoria, *Motherdear,* Birmingham Repertory Theatre, Birmingham, U.K., 1980. Also played various parts with the Arthur Brough Players, Lees Pavilion, Folkestone, United Kingdom, 1966; Celia Coplestone, *The Cocktail Party,* Manchester, U.K., 1975.

MAJOR TOURS—Cicely Courtneidge, *Once More with Music,* U.K. cities, 1976.

PRINCIPAL TELEVISION APPEARANCES—Series: *The Liver Birds,* 1968. Mini-Series: "Our Mutual Friend," *Masterpiece Theatre,* PBS. Movies: *A Divorce; Sweepstake's Game.*

AWARDS: Best Performance of 1969, *Variety* Critics' Award, for *Anne of Green Gables.*

SIDELIGHTS: RECREATIONS—Handicrafts, sewing.

ADDRESSES: AGENT—c/o James Sharkey, Fraser and Dunlop Ltd., 91 Regent Street, London W1R 8RU, England.*

JAMPOLIS, Neil Peter   1943-

PERSONAL: Born March 14, 1943, in New York, NY; son of Samuel and Beatrice (Swenken) Jampolis; married Jane Reisman (a lighting designer), July 24, 1971. EDUCATION: Art Institute of Chicago, B.F.A., 1966; University of Chicago, B.A., 1966; also attended University of Arizona.

VOCATION: Set, costume, and lighting designer.

CAREER: FIRST NEW YORK STAGE WORK—Set supervisor and lighting designer, *Borstal Boy,* Lyceum Theatre, 1969. PRINCIPAL STAGE WORK—Set designer, *The Barretts of Wimpole Street,* Goodman Memorial Theatre, Chicago, IL, 1965; set and lighting designer, *Uncle Vanya,* Theatre of the Living Arts, Philadelphia, PA, 1965; set designer, *Poor Bitos,* Hartford Stage Company, Hartford, CT, 1966; set and lighting designer, *Endgame, Act Without Words, The Three Sisters,* all Hartford Stage Company, 1966; set designer, *Under the Gaslight,* Hartford Stage Company, 1967; set designer, *The Balcony,* Center Stage, Baltimore, MD, 1967; lighting designer, *King Lear,* Morris Theatre, Morristown, NJ, 1967; lighting designer, *Not a Way of Life,* Sheridan Square Playhouse, New York City, 1967; lighting designer, *Tea Party, The Basement,* both Eastside Playhouse, New York City, 1968; *The People vs. Ranchman,* Fortune Theatre, New York City, 1968; *Little Murders,* Circle in the Square, New York City, 1969; set designer, *War Games,* Fortune Theatre, 1969; set and lighting designer, *In the Bar of a Tokyo Hotel,* Eastside Playhouse, 1969; lighting designer, *Arf, The Great Airplane Snatch,* both Stage 73, New York City, 1969; lighting designer, *Rondelay,* Hudson West Theatre, New York City, 1969.

All in New York City unless indicated: Lighting designer, *Show Me Where the Good Times Are,* Edison Theatre, 1970; lighting designer, *Les Blancs,* Longacre Theatre, 1970; set, lighting, and costume designer, *Acrobats, Line,* both Theatre de Lys, 1971; set, lighting, and costume designer, *One Flew over the Cuckoo's Nest,* Mercer-Hansberry Theatre, 1971; set and lighting designer, *To Live Another Summer, To Pass Another Winter,* Helen Hayes Theatre, 1971; lighting designer, *Wild and Wonderful,* Lyceum Theatre, 1971; *Wise Child,* Helen Hayes Theatre, 1972; English set supervisor, *Don't Bother Me, I Can't Cope,* Playhouse Theatre, 1972; lighting and costume designer, *Butley,* Morosco Theatre, 1972; lighting designer, *Let Me Hear You Smile,* Biltmore Theatre, 1973; lighting supervisor, *Warp I: My Battlefield, My Body,* Ambassador Theatre, 1973; lighting designer, set design supervisor, *The Emperor Enrico IV,* Ethel Barrymore Theatre, 1973; lighting designer, *Crown Matrimonial,* Helen Hayes Theatre, 1973; set supervisor, *The Wager,* Eastside Playhouse, 1974; set designer, *Anthony Newley/Henry Mancini,* Uris Theatre, 1974; set and lighting designer, *One Flew over the Cuckoo's Nest,* Huntington Hartford Theatre, Los Angeles, CA, 1974, then Arlington Park Theatre, IL, both 1974; lighting designer, *Sherlock Holmes,* Broadhurst Theatre, 1974; set designer, *Johnny Mathis and the Miracles,* Uris Theatre, 1974; set designer, *Raphael in Concert with the Voices of New York,* Imperial Theatre, 1974; set supervisor, *Brief Lives,* Booth Theatre, 1974.

All in New York City unless indicated: Set consultant, *A Gala Tribute to Joshua Logan,* Imperial Theatre, 1975; lighting designer, *The Innocents,* Morosco Theatre, 1976; set supervisor and lighting designer, *Otherwise Engaged,* Plymouth Theatre, 1977; set designer, *Comedy with Music,* Imperial Theatre, 1977; set designer, *The Brownsville Raid,* Theatre de Lys, 1977; lighting designer, *G.R. Point,* Center Stage, Baltimore, MD, 1978, then Playhouse Theatre, 1979; lighting designer, *Knockout,* Helen Hayes

Theatre, 1979; lighting designer, *Night and Day,* American National Theatre Academy Playhouse, 1979; lighting designer, *Night and Day,* Eisenhower Theatre, Washington, DC, 1979; lighting designer, *The American Clock,* Biltmore Theatre, 1980; lighting designer, *Harold and Maude,* Martin Beck Theatre, 1980; set and lighting designer, *Fishing,* Second Stage Theatre, 1981; set and costume designer, *The Life and Adventures of Nicholas Nickleby,* Plymouth Theatre, 1981; lighting designer, *El Bravo!,* Entermedia Theatre, 1981; set designer, *Vanities,* Virginia Stage Company, Norfolk, VA, 1983; set designer, *Great Days,* American Place Theatre, 1983; set designer, *Breakfast Conversations in Miami, What's a Nice Country Like You Still Doing in a State Like This?,* both American Place Theatre, 1984; lighting designer, *Julius Caesar,* Playhouse in the Park, Cincinnati, OH, 1984; set designer, *Rap Master Ronnie,* Village Gate Theatre, 1984; lighting designer, *Kipling,* Royale Theatre, 1984; lighting designer, *A Midsummer Night's Dream* (opera), Banff Festival, Banff, AB, Canada, 1984; lighting designer, *Translations,* Alaska Repertory Company, Anchorage, AL, 1985; lighting designer, *Down River,* Musical Theatre Works, 1985; lighting designer, *The Search for Signs of Intelligent Life in the Universe,* New York City, 1985; Also set, costume, and lighting designer, *Pieces of Eight,* Citadel Theatre; set and costume designer, *Journey to Rheims* (opera), Opera Theatre of St. Louis, St. Louis, MO; set, costume, and lighting designer, *Aida* (opera), Tulsa Opera, Tulsa, OK; set, costume, and lighting designer, *Eugene Onegin* (opera), 1986; also *Resurrection, Bolivar;* and more than eighty operas for Houston Grand Opera, Santa Fe Opera, St. Paul Opera, New York City Opera, Netherlands Opera, La Scala, Deutsche Oper, Berlin, Salzburg Festival, Vienna State Opera and OMAC, Caracas.

MAJOR TOURS—Lighting designer, *Butley,* U.S. cities, 1972.

RELATED CAREER—Designer, Playhouse in the Park, Cincinnati, OH, 1965-66; lighting designer, Arlington Park Theatre, IL, 1973-74; designer, Pilobolus Dance Theatre, 1976—; set and lighting designer, Playhouse in the Park, Pittsburgh, PA, 1979-80; lighting designer, Philadelphia Drama Guild, Philadelphia, PA, 1980-81. Faculty: Banff School of Fine Arts, Banff, AB, Canada, 1978-87; Music Theatre Program, Banff School of Fine Arts, 1982-85.

AWARDS: Best Lighting Design, Antoinette Perry Award, Drama Desk Award, both 1975, for *Sherlock Holmes;* Maharam Award for *One Flew over the Cuckoo's Nest;* Los Angeles Drama Critics Award nomination, Maharam Award nomination, both for *The Search for Signs of Intelligent Life in the Universe;* Maharam Award nomination for *Down River.*

MEMBER: United Scenic Artists, Local 829.

ADDRESSES: HOME—130 W. 57th Street, New York, NY 10019l. OFFICE—142 W. 44th Street, New York, NY 10036.

*   *   *

JARRE, Maurice   1924-

PERSONAL: Born 1924, in Lyon, France.

VOCATION: Composer and conductor.

CAREER: PRINCIPAL FILM WORK—Composer: *Crack in the Mirror,* Twentieth Century-Fox, 1960; *Sundays and Cybele,*

French, 1962; *The Longest Day,* Twentieth Century-Fox, 1962; *Lawrence of Arabia,* Columbia, 1962; *The Collector,* Columbia, 1965; *Is Paris Burning?,* Paramount, 1966; *Weekend at Dunkirk,* Twentieth Century-Fox, 1966; *Dr. Zhivago,* Metro-Goldwyn-Mayer (MGM), 1965; *The Night of the Generals,* Columbia, 1967; *The Professionals,* American International, 1961; *Grand Prix,* MGM, 1966; *Five Card Stud,* Paramount, 1968; *Isadora,* British, 1969.

The Damned, Warner Brothers, 1970; *Ash Wednesday,* Paramount, 1973; *The Life and Times of Judge Roy Bean,* National General, 1972; *The Mackintosh Man,* Warner Brothers, 1973; *The Effect of Gamma Rays on Man-in-the-Moon Marigolds,* Twentieth Century-Fox, 1973; *Island at the Top of the World,* Buena Vista, 1974; *Mandingo,* Paramount, 1975; *Posse,* 1975.

Winter Kills, AVCO-Embassy, 1980; *Taps,* Twentieth Century-Fox, 1981; *Firefox,* Warner Brothers, 1982; *Young Doctors in Love,* Twentieth Century-Fox, 1982; *The Year of Living Dangerously,* MGM/United Artists, 1983; *Dreamscape,* Twentieth Century-Fox, 1984; *A Passage to India,* Columbia, 1984; *Witness,* Paramount, 1985; *Mad Max, Beyond Thunderdome,* Warner Brothers, 1985; *The Mosquito Coast,* Warner Brothers, 1986; *Wildfire,* Vestron, upcoming; *Journal d' un Four* (*Diary of a Madman*), Amis du Cinema Populaire, upcoming; *Puccini,* upcoming; also *Hotel des Invalides, La Tete contre les Murs,* and *Eyes without a Face.*

PRINCIPAL STAGE WORK—Composer and conductor: Jean Louis Barrault's theatre company, Paris; Jean Vilar's national theatre company, Paris, 1951.

AWARDS: Best Original Score, Academy Awards, 1962, for *Lawrence of Arabia,* and 1965, for *Dr. Zhivago.*

ADDRESSES: AGENT—SACEM, 225 av Charles de Gaulle, 92521 Neuilly S/Sienne, France.*

*   *   *

JAYSTON, Michael   1936-

PERSONAL: Born Michael James, October 29, 1936, in Nottingham, England; son of Vincent and Myfanwy (Llewelyn) James; married Lynn Farleigh (divorced); married Heather Mary Sneddon (divorced); married Elizabeth Smithson. EDUCATION: Attended Nottingham University; trained for the stage at the Guildhall School of Music and Drama.

VOCATION: Actor.

CAREER: STAGE DEBUT—Corporal Green, *The Amorous Prawn,* Salisbury Playhouse, Salisbury, U.K., 1962. PRINCIPAL STAGE APPEARANCES—Various parts, *Beyond the Fringe,* Bristol Old Vic Theatre, Bristol, U.K., 1964; various parts and Exeter, *Henry V,* Royal Shakespeare Company, Aldwych Theatre, London, 1965; storyteller, *The Thwarting of Baron Bolligrew,* Aldwych Theatre, 1965; Laertes, *Hamlet,* Stratford Theatre, London, 1966; Lenny, *The Homecoming,* Music Box Theatre, New York City, 1967; Oswald, *Ghosts,* Bertram, *All's Well That Ends Well,* reader, *The Hollow Crown,* Custer, *Indians,* Young Fashion, *The Relapse,* all Aldwych Theatre, 1968; Henry II, *Becket,* Arnaud Theatre, Guildford, U.K., 1972; *Equus,* Charles Appleby, *Eden End,* Old Vic Theatre, London, 1974; Martin Dysart, *Equus,* Old Vic Theatre, 1974, then

Albery Theatre, London, 1976; Elyot Chase, *Private Lives,* Greenwich Theatre, then Duchess Theatre, both London, 1980. Also appeared in *The Sound of Music,* 1981; *Way of the World,* 1984.

MAJOR TOURS—Martin Dysart, *Equus,* U.K. cities, 1976.

PRINCIPAL FILM APPEARANCES—*A Midsummer Night's Dream,* Columbia, 1962; *Follow Me,* Cinerama, 1969; *Cromwell,* Columbia, 1970; *Nicholas and Alexandra,* Columbia, 1971; *The Nelson Affair,* Universal, 1972; *The Public Eye,* Universal, 1972; *The Homecoming,* AFT Distributing, 1973; *Tales That Witness Madness,* Paramount, 1973; *Craze,* Warner Brothers, 1973. Also appeared in *A Bequest to the Nation,* 1972; *The Internecine Project,* 1974; *Zulu Dawn.*

PRINCIPAL TELEVISION APPEARANCES—Mini-Series: *Quiller,* 1975; *Tinker, Tailor, Soldier, Spy,* 1979. Also appeared in *The Power Game; Beethoven; Jane Eyre; The Last Romantic; Gossip from the Forest; She Fell among Thieves; Power Game; Charles Dickens; Solo*—Wilfred Owen.

MEMBER: MMC, Lord's Taverners, Eccentrics, S.P.A.R.K.S.

SIDELIGHTS: RECREATIONS—Cricket, darts, riding, TV sports, gardening, gambling.

ADDRESSES: AGENT—c/o Leading Artists, 60 St. James Street, London SW1, England.*

*   *   *

JENS, Salome   1935-

PERSONAL: Born May 8, 1935, in Milwaukee, WI; daughter of Arnold John (a builder and farmer) and Salomea (Szujeuska) Jens; married Ralph Meeker (divorced); married Lee Leonard. EDUCATION: Attended the University of Wisconsin and Northwestern University; trained for the stage with Herbert Berghof, Stella Adler, Lee Strasberg, and at the Actors Studio; studied voice with John Mace; studied dance with Martha Graham.

VOCATION: Actress.

CAREER: BROADWAY DEBUT—Miss Ferguson, *Sixth Finger in a Five Finger Glove,* Longacre Theatre, 1956. PRINCIPAL STAGE APPEARANCES—Mary, *The Bald Soprano,* Roberta, *Jack,* both Sullivan Street Playhouse, New York City, 1958; Georgette, *The Disenchanted,* Coronet Theatre, New York City, 1958; title role, *Deirdre of the Sorrows,* Gate Theatre, New York City, 1959; girl, *The Balcony,* Circle in the Square, New York City, 1960; Martha Bernays Freud, *A Far Country,* Music Box Theatre, New York City, 1961; Lady Macbeth, *Macbeth,* Pittsburgh Playhouse, Pittsburgh, PA, 1962; Anna, *Night Life,* Brooks Atkinson Theatre, New York City, 1962; Abbie Putnam, *Desire Under the Elms,* Circle in the Square, 1963; Hermione, *The Winter's Tale,* Delacorte Theatre, New York City, 1963; Lizzie, *The Rainmaker,* Royal Poinciana Playhouse, Palm Beach, FL, 1963; Louise, *After the Fall,* Gilian Prosper, *But for Whom, Charlie,* both American National Theatre Academy (ANTA), Washington Square Theatre, New York City, 1964; Elmire, *Tartuffe,* ANTA, Washington Square Theatre, 1965; Elaine, *First One Asleep, Whistle,* Belasco Theatre, New York City, 1966; Amanda Prynne, *Private Lives,* Melodyland Theatre, Berkeley, CA, 1966; *Posterity for Sale,* American Place Theatre,

New York City, 1967; Nancy, *The Meeting,* Theatre de Lys, New York City, 1967; Makedah, *I'm Solomon,* Mark Hellinger Theatre, New York City, 1968; Josie Hogan, *A Moon for the Misbegotten,* Circle in the Square, 1968; Countess Sophia Delyanoff, *A Patriot for Me,* Imperial Theatre, New York City, 1969; Abigail, *John and Abigail,* Ford's Theatre, Washington, DC, 1971; title role, *Mary Stuart,* Vivian Beaumont Theatre, New York City, 1971; Cleopatra, *Anthony and Cleopatra,* American Shakespeare Festival, Stratford, CT, 1972; Julie Holliman, *A Break in the Skin,* Actors Studio, New York City, 1973; Queen Gertrude, *Hamlet,* Mark Taper Forum, Los Angeles, CA, 1974; Lorraine, *A Lie of the Mind,* Promenade Theatre, New York City, 1985. Also appeared in *U.S.A.,* Martinique Theatre, New York City, 1959, then Royal Poinciana Playhouse, 1961; *As You Like It, The Lady's Not for Burning,* both Toledo Festival, Toledo, OH, 1960; *The Skin of Our Teeth,* Olney Playhouse, MD, 1961; *Anna Christie,* Playhouse in the Park, Philadelphia, PA, 1962; *Crystal and Fox,* Mark Taper Forum, 1970; *The Ride across Lake Constance,* Forum Theatre, New York City, 1972; *One Flew over the Cuckoo's Nest,* Huntington Hartford Theatre, Los Angeles, CA, 1974; . . . *About Anne,* Interact Theatre, New York City, 1985; *A Short Happy Life,* Huntington Hartford Theatre; *Transformations, Lady of the House,* both Los Angeles; and *Shadows of Heroes; The Affairs of Anatol.*

MAJOR TOURS—*Will Success Spoil Rock Hunter?* U.S. cities, 1959; *The Owl and the Pussycat,* U.S. cities, 1966; *And Miss Reardon Drinks a Little,* U.S. cities, 1970; also *A Moon for the Misbegotten,* U.S. cities; *Tiny Alice,* U.S. cities; *Delicate Balance,* U.S. cities; *Private Lives,* U.S. cities; *Who's Afraid of Virginia Woolf?,* U.S. cities.

SALOME JENS

PRINCIPAL TELEVISION APPEARANCES: Episodic: *McMillan and Wife,* NBC; *Naked City,* ABC; *The Defenders,* CBS; *Gunsmoke,* CBS; *The Untouchables,* ABC; *Kraft Television Theatre,* NBC; *Stoney Burke,* ABC; *Medical Center,* CBS; *Kojak,* CBS; *The Blue Knight,* CBS; *Petrocelli,* NBC; *Hart to Hart,* ABC; *Trapper John, M.D.,* CBS; *Quincy, M.E.,* NBC; *Falcon Crest,* CBS; *Mary Hartman, Mary Hartman,* syndicated; *U.S. Steel Hour.* Mini-Series: Gert Kipfer, *From Here to Eternity,* NBC, 1979. Movies: Judge Kendis Winslow, *In the Glitter Palace,* NBC, 1977; Terri, *Sharon: Portrait of a Mistress,* NBC, 1977; Ilyena, *The Golden Moment: An Olympic Love Story,* NBC, 1980; Colleen Murphy, *A Matter of Life and Death,* CBS, 1981; Dr. Miller, *The Two Lives of Carol Letner,* CBS, 1981; Laura Pressburg, *Tomorrow's Child,* NBC, 1982; Nurse Ann Botts, *Uncommon Valor,* CBS, 1983; Alice Johnson, *A Killer in the Family,* ABC, 1983; Mady Christians, *Grace Kelly,* ABC, 1983; Dr. Becker, *Playing with Fire,* NBC, 1985. Also appeared in *Dial 911; Genesis; Hello from Bertha; The Purification; Barefoot in Athens.*

PRINCIPAL FILM APPEARANCES—Jenny Angel, *Angel Baby,* Allied Artists, 1961; also appeared in *Seconds,* Paramount, 1966; *Me, Natalie,* National General, 1969; *The Clan of the Cave Bear,* Warner Brothers, 1985; *Just Between Friends,* Orion, 1986; *The Fool Killer,* 1966; *Cold Sweat,* 1971; *Savages,* 1974; *Cloud Dancer,* 1980; *Harry's War,* 1981.

AWARDS: Clarence Derwent Award, 1980, for *The Balcony;* Straw Hat Award for *And Miss Reardon Drinks a Little;* Cliff Dwellers Award for *A Moon for the Misbegotten.*

MEMBER: Screen Actors Guild, Actors' Equity Association, American Federation of Television and Radio Artists.

ADDRESSES: AGENT—c/o Harris, Goldberg, 2121 Avenue of the Stars, Los Angeles, CA.

*　　　*　　　*

JOFFE, Roland　1945-

PERSONAL: Born November 17, 1945, in London, England. EDUCATION: Attended Carmel College and the University of Manchester, England.

VOCATION: Director and writer.

CAREER: PRINCIPAL STAGE WORK—Director, National Theatre of Great Britain, London, 1973.

PRINCIPAL FILM WORK—Director: *The Killing Fields,* Warner Brothers, 1984; *The Mission,* Warner Brothers, 1986.

PRINCIPAL TELEVISION WORK—Director: Documentaries— *Rope* and *Anne.* Teleplays—*The Spongers,* 1978; *No Mamma No,* 1980; also co-writer, *United Kingdom,* 1981; *Tis Pity She's a Whore,* 1982. Series—*The Stars Look Down.*

AWARDS: Prix Italia, 1978; Prix de la Presse, Prague, 1978; Premio San Fidele, 1985.

SIDELIGHTS: *CTFT* learned that Roland Joffe was the youngest director ever engaged at the National Theatre of Great Britain.

ADDRESSES: AGENT—Judy Daish Associates, 83 Eastbourne Mews, London W2 6CQ, England.*

*   *   *

JOHNS, Glynis   1923-

PERSONAL: Born October 5, 1923, in Pretoria, South Africa; daughter of Mervyn (an actor) and Alys Maude (a pianist; maiden name, Steele-Payne); married Anthony Forwood (divorced); married David Ramsey Foster, February 1, 1952 (divorced); married Cecil Peter L. Henderson, 1960 (divorced, 1961); married Elliot Arnold (a writer), October 4, 1964; children: one son.

VOCATION: Actress.

CAREER: LONDON DEBUT—Ursula, *Buckie's Bears*, Garrick Theatre, 1935. NEW YORK DEBUT—Title role, *Gertie*, Plymouth Theatre, New York City, 1952; PRINCIPAL STAGE APPEARANCES—Hortense, *St. Helena*, Old Vic Theatre, then Daly's Theatre, both London, 1936; Mary Tilford, *The Children's Hour*, Gate Theatre, London, 1936; elf, child, *The Melody That Got Lost*, Embassy Theatre, London, 1936; Sonia Kuman, *Judgment Day*, Embassy Theatre, then Strand Theatre, both London, 1937, later Phoenix Theatre, London, 1939; Cinderella, *A Kiss for Cinderella*, Phoenix Theatre, 1937, then 1939; Miranda, *Quiet Wedding*, Richmond Theatre, then Wyndham's Theatre, both London, 1938; Miranda Bute, *Quiet Week-End*, Wyndham's Theatre, 1941; title role, *Peter Pan*, Cambridge Theatre, London, 1943; Pam, *Fools Rush In*, Fortune Theatre, London, 1946; Mary Flemin, *The Way Things Go*, Phoenix Theatre, 1950; title role, *Major Barbara*, Martin Beck Theatre, New York City, 1956; Miss Mopply, *Too True to be Good*, 54th Street Theatre, New York City, 1963; Anne of Cleves, *The King's Mare*, Garrick Theatre, London, 1966; Desiree Armfeldt, *A Little Night Music*, Shubert Theatre, New York City, 1973; Madame Desmortes, *Ring Around the Moon*, Ahmanson Theatre, Los Angeles, CA, 1975; Leontine, *13 Rue de l'Amour*, Phoenix Theatre, 1976; Alma Rattenbury, *Cause Celebre*, Her Majesty's Theatre, London, 1977. Also appeared as Jennifer Wren, *Plaintiff in a Pretty Hat*, Coconut Grove, FL, 1958; and in *Come As You Are*, New Theatre, then Strand Theatre, both London, 1970; *Harold and Maude*, Canada, 1977; *The Boyfriend*, Toronto, ON, Canada, 1984.

MAJOR TOURS—Corinne, *I'll See You Again*, U.K. cities, 1944; Ann Stanley, *Forty Carats*, South African cities, 1971; title role, *The Marquise*, U.K., U.S., and Australian cities, 1971-72; also *Hay Fever*, U.K. cities, 1978.

FILM DEBUT—*South Riding*, United Artists, 1938. PRINCIPAL FILM APPEARANCES—*Prison without Bars*, United Artists, 1939; *The Fugitive*, Universal, 1940; *The Prime Minister*, Warner Brothers, 1940; *The Invaders* (also known as *49th Parallel*), Columbia, 1942; *Adventures of Tartu*, Metro-Goldwyn-Mayer (MGM), 1943; *Half-Way House*, AFE, 1945; *Vacation from Marriage*, MGM, 1945; *Frieda*, Universal, 1947; *An Ideal Husband*, Twentieth Century-Fox, 1948; *Miranda*, Eagle-Lion, 1949; *Lucky Mr. Prohack*, Pentagon, 1950; *The Great Manhunt*, Columbia, 1950; *Island Rescue*, RKO, 1950; *No Highway in the Sky*, Twentieth Century-Fox, 1951; *Encore*, Paramount, 1952; *The Promotor*, Universal, 1952; *The Sword and the Rose*, RKO, 1952; *Rob Roy*, RKO, 1952; *Personal Affair*, United Artists, 1954; *The Weak and the Wicked*, Allied Artists, 1954; *Mad about Men*, General Films,

1954; *Land of Fury*, Universal, 1955; *The Beachcomber*, United Artists, 1955; *All Mine to Give*, Universal, 1957; *The Court Jester*, Paramount, 1958; *Another Time, Another Place*, Paramount, 1958; *Shake Hands with the Devil*, United Artists, 1959; *The Sundowners*, Warner Brothers, 1960; *The Cabinet of Dr. Caligari*, Twentieth Century-Fox, 1962; *The Chapman Report*, Warner Brothers, 1962; *Papa's Delicate Condition*, Paramount, 1963; *Mary Poppins*, Buena Vista, 1965; *Dear Brigitte*, Twentieth Century-Fox, 1965; *Don't Just Stand There*, Universal, 1968; *Lock Up Your Daughters*, Columbia, 1969; *Vault of Horrors*, Cinerama, 1973. Also appeared in *Murder in the Family*, Twentieth Century-Fox; *Josephine and Men*, British Lion; *The Spider's Web*, Columbia; *Flesh and Blood*, 1949; *Loser Takes All*, 1950; *The Million Pound Note*, 1954; *Under Milk Wood*, 1973; and *Mr. Brigg's Family*; *This Man is Mine*; *Third Time*; *The Day They Gave Babies Away*.

PRINCIPAL TELEVISION APPEARANCES—Episodic: "Lily, the Queen of the Movies," *Studio One*, CBS, 1952; "Two for Tea," *Video Theatre*, CBS, 1953; "Party," *GE Theatre*, CBS, 1961; *Naked City*, ABC, 1961; "Windfall," *Dupont Show ot the Month*, NBC, 1963; "Safari," *The Dick Powell Show*, NBC, 1963; *Twelve O'Clock High*, ABC, 1964; *Burke's Law*, ABC, 1964; *Batman*, ABC, 1967; *Skag*, NBC, 1982; also *Dr. Kildare*, NBC; *Roaring Twenties*, ABC; *The Defenders*, CBS; *Danny Kaye Show*, CBS; *Noel Coward's Star Quality*. Series: Glynis Granville, *Glynis*, CBS, 1963-65. Pilots: Aunt Mary, *Spraggue*, ABC, 1984. Mini-Series: Lady Fitzpatrick Morgan, *Little Gloria . . . Happy at Last*, NBC, 1982. Also appeared in *Mrs. Amworth*; *All You Need Is Love*; *Across a Crowded Room*.

AWARDS: Academy Award nomination, 1960, for *The Sundowners*; Best Actress in a Musical, Antoinette Perry Award, 1973, for *A Little Night Music*.

MEMBER: Actors's Equity Association, Screen Actors Guild, American Federation of Television and Radio Artists.

ADDRESSES: AGENT—c/o International Creative Management Ltd., 22 Grafton Street, London W1, England.*

*   *   *

JOHNSON, Richard   1927-

PERSONAL: Born July 30, 1927, in Upminster, England; son of Keith Holcombe and Frances Louisa Olive (Tweed) Johnson; married Sheila Ann Sweet, 1957 (divorced); married Marilyn Kim Novak (an actress), 1965 (divorced); married Marie-Louise Nordlund, 1982; children: two sons, one daughter. EDUCATION: Trained for the stage at the Royal Academy of Dramatic Art. MILITARY: Royal Navy, 1945-48.

VOCATION: Actor, producer, and writer.

CAREER: STAGE DEBUT—*Hamlet*, Opera House, Manchester, U.K., 1944. BROADWAY DEBUT—Clive Root, *The Complaisant Lover*, Ethel Barrymore Theatre, New York City, 1961; PRINCIPAL STAGE APPEARANCES—Marius Tertius, *The First Victorian*, Embassy Theatre, London, 1950; Pierre, *The Madwoman of Chaillot*, St. James Theatre, London, 1951; Demetrius, *A Midsummer Night's Dream*, Open Air Theatre, London, 1951; George Phillips, *After My Fashion*, Ambassadors Theatre, London, 1952; Beauchamp, Earl of Warwick, *The Lark*, Lyric Hammersmith Theatre, London,

1955; Laertes, *Hamlet,* Moscow, U.S.S.R., then Phoenix Theatre, London, 1955; Jack Absolute, *The Rivals,* Saville Theatre, London, 1956; Lord Plynlimmon, *Plantiff in a Pretty Hat,* Duchess Theatre, then St. Martin's Theatre, both London, 1956; Orlando, *As You Like It,* Mark Antony, *Julius Caesar,* Leonatus, *Cymbeline,* Ferdinand, *The Tempest,* all Memorial Theatre, Stratford-on-Avon, U.K., 1957; Ferdinand, *The Tempest,* Drury Lane Theatre, London, 1957; Romeo, *Romeo and Juliet,* Sir Andrew Aguecheek, *Twelfth Night,* title role, *Pericles,* Don John, *Much Ado about Nothing,* all Memorial Theatre, 1958; Henry Lee, *The Wrong Side of the Park,* Cambridge Theatre, then St. Martin's Theatre, both London, 1960; Sir Andrew Aguecheek, *Twelfth Night,* Aldwych Theatre, London, 1960; Hans, Ondine, Urbain Grandier, *The Devils,* Aldwych Theatre, 1961; Mark Antony, *Julius Caesar,* Mark Antony, *Antony and Cleopatra,* both Stratford-on-Avon, U.K., 1972, then Aldwych Theatre, 1973; Thomas, *Thomas and the King,* Her Majesty's Theatre, 1975; Charles, *Blithe Spirit,* Lyttelton Theatre, London, 1976; Pontius Pilate, *The Passion,* Pinchwife, *The Country Wife,* both National Theatre, London, 1976; Nandor, *The Guardsman,* National Theatre, 1978. Also appeared in *Hamlet, Love for Love, The Circle, The Duchess of Malfi,* all Haymarket Theatre, London, 1944; *The Hollow Crown,* Aldwych Theatre, 1961; appeared in a season of old melodrama, Bedford Theatre, London, 1950; in repertory at the Perth Theatre, 1945 and 1948-49, and with the Bristol Old Vic Theatre Company, Bristol, U.K., 1953.

PRINCIPAL STAGE WORK—Producer, *Brief Lives,* Criterion Theatre, London, 1969; co-producer, *The Beloved.*

MAJOR TOURS—*The Paragon, The Happiest Days of Your Life* U.K. cities, both 1949; Romeo, *Romeo and Juliet,* Sir Andrew Aguecheek, *Twelfth Night,* both Soviet cities, 1958; also *The Hollow Crown,* European cities, 1963; *Death Trap,* U.K. cities, 1982.

FILM DEBUT—*Captain Horatio Hornblower,* 1950. PRINCIPAL FILM APPEARANCES—*Never So Few,* Metro-Goldwyn-Mayer (MGM), 1959; *The Haunting,* MGM, 1963; *The Pumpkin Eater,* Royal International, 1964; *Operation Crossbow,* MGM, 1965; *The Amorous Adventures of Moll Flanders,* Paramount, 1965; *Khartoum,* United Artists, 1966; *Deadlier than the Male,* Universal, 1967; *Danger Route,* United Artists, 1968; *A Twist of Sand,* United Artists, 1968; *Oedipus the King,* Universal, 1968; *The Deserter,* Paramount, 1971; *Hennessy,* American International, 1975; *Turtle Diary,* Samuel Goldwyn, 1986. Also appeared in *Julius Caesar,* American International; *80,000 Suspects; The Beloved; La Strega in Amore; The Rover; Trajan's Column; Lady Hamilton; Some Girls Do; Aces High; The Four Feathers.*

PRINCIPAL TELEVISION APPEARANCES—Specials: Claudius, *Hamlet;* Sir Charles Duke, *The Member for Chelsea;* also appeared in *Rembrandt; Antony and Cleopatra; Cymbeline; A Marriage; Murder in Your Mind.*

RELATED CAREER—Formed Pageant Entertainments Ltd., 1969; founder, chairman, chief executive officer, United British Artists, 1982—, then director, 1983—.

WRITINGS: PLAYS—*The Golden Age,* Lyceum Theatre, New York City, 1963. SCREENPLAYS—*Hennessy,* American International, 1975.

MEMBER: British Academy of Film and Television Arts (council member, 1976-78).

SIDELIGHTS: FAVORITE ROLES—Warwick in *The Lark.* RECREATIONS—Country pursuits, music, travel, gardening.

ADDRESSES: HOME—2 Stokenchurch Street, London SW6 3TR, England. AGENT—c/o Leading Artists, 60 St. James Street, London SW1, England.*

*   *   *

JONES, David   1934-

PERSONAL: Full name, David Hugh Jones; born February 19, 1934, in Poole, England; immigrated to the United States in 1979; son of John David and Gwendolen Agnes Langworthy (Ricketts) Jones; married Sheila Marion Essex Allen, October 20, 1964; children: Joseph Luke Allen, Jesse Gawain Allen. EDUCATION: Christ's College, Cambridge University, B.A. (first class honors), English, 1954, M.A., 1957. MILITARY: British Army, 1954-56.

VOCATION: Director and producer.

CAREER: FIRST LONDON STAGE WORK—Director, *Sweet Agonistes, Purgatory, Krapp's Last Tape,* all Mermaid Theatre, 1961. PRINCIPAL STAGE WORK—Director: *Saint's Day,* Stratford-on-Avon, U.K., 1965; *As You Like It,* Stratford-on-Avon, U.K., then London, 1967; *Diary of a Scoundrel,* Liverpool, U.K., 1968; *The Tempest,* Chichester, U.K., 1968; *As You Like It,* Los Angeles, CA, then Stratford-on-Avon, U.K., 1968; *The Marrying of Ann Leete, The Return of A.J. Raffles, Twelfth Night,* all Stratford, ON, Canada, 1975; *Summerfolk,* New York City, 1975; *Love's Labour's Lost,* New York City, then London, 1975; *All's Well That Ends Well,* Stratford, ON, Canada, 1977; also directed *The Empire Builders,* 1962; *The Governor's Lady* and (with Peter Brook) *The Investigation,* both 1965; *Belcher's Luck,* 1966; *The Silver Tassie,* 1969; *After Haggerty, The Plebians Rehearse the Uprising,* both 1970; *Enemies,* 1971; *The Lower Depths, The Island of the Mighty,* both 1972; *Love's Labour's Lost,* 1973; *Duck Song* and *Summerfolk,* both 1974; *The Zykovs, Ivanov,* both 1976; *Cymbeline, Baal,* both 1979.

Director, *A Midsummer Night's Dream,* Brooklyn Academy of Music, Brooklyn, NY, 1981; director, *Jungle of Cities,* Brooklyn Academy of Music, 1981; producer, *Particular Friendships,* Astor Place Theatre, New York City, 1981; director, *Rip Van Winkle, or "The Works,"* Yale Repertory Theatre, New Haven, CT, 1981-82; producer, *The Good Parts,* Astor Place Theatre, 1982.

PRINCIPAL FILM WORK—Director, *Betrayal,* Twentieth Century-Fox Classic, 1983.

PRINCIPAL TELEVISION WORK—Series: Producer, *Monitor* (arts magazine show), BBC, 1958-64; producer, *Play of the Month,* BBC, 1977-79; director, Shakespeare series, BBC, 1982-83; also introduced *The Present Stage,* 1965, and *Review* (arts magazine show), 1971-72. Introduced *The Case of Eliza Armstrong,* 1974; produced *Ice Age, The Beaux' Stratagem,* and *Langarishe Go Down.*

RELATED CAREER—Artistic controller, then associate director, Royal Shakespeare Company, London, 1964-75; artistic director, Royal Shakespeare Company at Aldwych Theatre, London, 1975-78; artistic director, Brooklyn Academy of Music Theatre Company, Brooklyn, NY, 1979-81; professor, Yale School of Drama, New Haven, CT, 1981.

AWARDS: Best Director, Obie Award from the *Village Voice,* 1976, for *Summerfolk;* Obie Award, 1980, for innovative programming at the Brooklyn Academy of Music.

SIDELIGHTS: RECREATIONS—Chess, reading modern poetry, and "escaping to the mountains and/or islands."

ADDRESSES: AGENT—Lantz Inc., 888 Seventh Avenue, New York, NY 10106.*

*   *   *

JONES, Paul   1942-

PERSONAL: Born Paul Pond, February 24, 1942, in Portsmouth, England; son of Norman Henry and Amelia Josephine (Hadfield) Pond; married Sheila MacLeod (a singer). EDUCATION: Attended Jesus College, Oxford University.

VOCATION: Actor.

CAREER: STAGE DEBUT—John Argue, *Muzeeka,* Open Space Theatre, 1969. LONDON DEBUT—Second Lieutenant Arthur Drake, *Conduct Unbecoming,* Queen's Theatre, 1969. NEW YORK DEBUT—Second Lieutenant Arthur Drake, *Conduct Unbecoming,* Ethel Barrymore Theatre, 1970. PRINCIPAL STAGE APPEARANCES—Noel Parker, *The Banana Box,* Hampstead Theatre Club, then Apollo Theatre, both London, 1973; title role, *Pippin,* Her Majesty's Theatre, London, 1973; Orestes, *You Were So Sweet When You Were Little,* Theatre at the New End, London, 1974; Edmund, *King Lear,* Trench, *Widower's Houses,* both Belgrade Theatre, Coventry, U.K., 1974; Christian, *Pilgrim,* Edinburgh Festival, Edinburgh, Scotland, U.K., then Round House Theatre, London, 1975; title role, *Hamlet,* Ludlow Festival, Ludlow, U.K., 1976; Cassio, *Othello,* Nottingham Playhouse, Nottingham, U.K., 1976; leading roles, *In Order of Appearance,* Chichester Festival, Chichester, U.K., 1977; Francis Drake, *Drake's Dream,* Shaftesbury Theatre, London, 1977; Joseph, *Joseph and the Amazing Technicolour Dreamcoat,* Westminster Theatre, London, 1978-79; Claudio, *Measure for Measure,* Riverside Theatre, London, 1979.

MAJOR TOURS—Romeo, *Romeo and Juliet,* with the Young Vic Theatre Company, U.K. cities, 1977.

PRINCIPAL FILM APPEARANCES—*Privilege,* Universal, 1967; *The Committee,* Commonwealth United Entertainment, 1969; also *Demons of the Mind.*

RELATED CAREER—Frequently sings and plays harmonica with "The Blues Band;" recordings include *Evita.*

SIDELIGHTS: RECREATIONS—Collecting blues records, Victorian and Edwardian theatre postcards, "avoiding musicals."

ADDRESSES: AGENT—c/o Michael Linnit, Globe Theatre, Shaftesbury Avenue, London W1, England.*

*   *   *

JOYCE, Stephen   1931-

PERSONAL: Born March 7, 1931, in New York, NY; son of Stephen and Ruth (Reilly) Joyce; married Billie J. Jones. EDUCATION: Attended Fordham University.

VOCATION: Actor.

CAREER: STAGE DEBUT—Sakini, *Teahouse of the August Moon,* Okinawa, 1953. NEW YORK DEBUT— Romeo, *Romeo and Juliet,* New York Shakespeare Festival, 1956. PRINCIPAL STAGE APPEARANCES—Michael Byrne, "The Tinker's Wedding," and Bartley, "Riders to the Sea," as part of a triple bill entitled *Three Plays by John Millington Synge,* Theatre East, New York City, 1957; Henry Appleton, *The Legend of Lizzie,* 54th Street Theatre, New York City, 1959; title role, *Coriolanus,* Edgar, *King Lear,* both American Shakespeare Festival, Stratford, CT, 1965; Leontes, *The Winter's Tale,* San Diego Shakespeare Festival, Old Globe Theatre, San Diego, CA, 1965; Biff, *Death of a Salesman,* title role, *Hamlet,* both Seattle Repertory Theatre, Seattle, WA, 1966; Archbishop of York, *Falstaff,* First Tempter, *Murder in the Cathedral,* Marcus Antonius, *Julius Caesar,* all American Shakespeare Festival, Stratford, 1966; Prince, *Those That Play the Clowns,* American National Theatre Academy (ANTA) Playhouse, New York City, 1966; Father Jerome Fogarty, "The Frying Pan," Tom Dorgan, "Eternal Triangle," and Denis Sullivan, "The Bridal Night," as a triple bill entitled *Three Hand Reel,* Renata Theatre, New York City, 1966; various roles, *The Hemingway Hero,* Shubert Theatre, New Haven, CT, 1967; Stephen Dedalus, *Stephen D,* East 74th Street Theatre, New York City, 1967; Brother Martin Ladvenu, *Saint Joan,* Vivian Beaumont Theatre, Lincoln Center, New York City, 1968; Actor, *The Exercise,* John Golden Theatre, New York City, 1968; *An Evening with James Agee,* Theatre de Lys, New York City, 1969; Ben Bran, "The Report," Coach, "Football," Old Local, "Fireworks for a Hot Fourth," as a triple bill entitled *Fireworks,* Village South Theatre, New York City, 1969.

Segismund, *Life Is a Dream,* Paul Holliman, *A Break in the Skin,* Larry Parks, *Are You Now or Have You Ever Been?,* all Yale Repertory Theatre, New Haven, CT, 1972; Charlie Now, *Da,* Olney Playhouse, Olney, MD, then Ivanhoe Theatre, Chicago, IL, 1973; Richard Halvey, *Summer,* Olney Playhouse, 1974; Father Rivard, *The Runner Stumbles,* Hartman Theatre, Stamford, CT, then Little Theatre, New York City, 1976; Mark Crawford, *Savages,* Hudson Guild Theatre, New York City, 1977; Hunt, *Scribes,* Phoenix Theatre, New York City, 1977; Captain Blakely, *The Caine Mutiny Court Martial,* Circle in the Square, New York City, 1983; Private John Brown, *Maneuvers,* South Street Theatre, New York City, 1985; Bartholmew Van Amburg, *Planet Fires,* Mark Taper Forum, Los Angeles, CA, 1985-86. Also appeared in *Happy End,* Yale Repertory Theatre, 1972; *The Glass Menagerie,* Olney Playhouse, 1975; *The Auction Tomorrow,* Hartman Theatre, 1978; *Angel Street,* Whole Theatre Company, Montclair, NJ, 1982; *The Father,* Philadelphia Drama Guild, Philadelphia, PA, 1984; and in *Devour the Snow, School for Wives,* and *Daisy.* Played Banco and Macol in *Macbeth,* Caliban, *The Tempest,* and appeared in Edward Bond's *Lear,* all 1973; Stanley Kowalski, *A Streetcar Named Desire;* Bri, *A Day in the Death of Joe Egg.*

PRINCIPAL STAGE WORK—Director, *The Tantalus,* Harold Clurman Theatre, New York City, 1981.

PRINCIPAL TELEVISION APPEARANCES—Episodic: *Matinee Theatre,* NBC; *Play of the Week,* NBC; *Omnibus,* CBS; *Ben Casey,* ABC; *Rawhide,* CBS.

AWARDS: Theatre World Award, 1967, *Stephen D.*

MEMBER: Actors' Equity Association, American Federation of Television and Radio Artists, Screen Actors Guild.

SIDELIGHTS: FAVORITE ROLES—Stanley Kowalski in *A Streetcar Named Desire*, Bri in *Joe Egg*. . . . RECREATIONS—Painting, physical exercise, horseback riding, farming.

ADDRESSES: HOME—145 Platt Lane, Milford, CT 06460.*

*   *   *

JULIAN, Pat   1947-

PERSONAL: Born Patrick Vellucci, Jr., July 5, 1947, in Jersey City, NJ. EDUCATION: St. Peter's College, B.A., 1972; Pacific

PAT JULIAN

Western University, M.A., 1987; trained for the stage at the American Academy of Dramatic Arts. MILITARY: U.S. Army, 1965-68.

VOCATION: Actor, director, and writer.

CAREER: STAGE DEBUT—Jeff, *Curious Savage,* tour, for fifty performances. PRINCIPAL STAGE APPEARANCES— *Arabesque,* Gramercy Arts Theatre, New York City, 1970; *Conduct Unbecoming,* Ethel Barrymore Theatre, New York City, 1978; Banjo, *The Man Who Came to Dinner;* Leo, *Chapter Two;* Eddie, *Born Yesterday;* Ben, *The Sunshine Boys;* Harvey, *Cactus Flower;* Kolenkov, *You Can't Take It with You;* Dolan, *Mr. Roberts;* Brad, *Opal;* Harry, *Barefoot in the Park;* El Gallo, *The Fantasticks;* Lt. Rooney, *Arsenic and Old Lace;* Dr. Mathews, *Harold and Maude;* Billy, *Forty Carats;* District Attorney, *The Night of January 16th;* Harry, *Guys and Dolls;* as well as roles in *South Pacific, Something Borrowed,* and *Mastercharge.*

PRINCIPAL STAGE WORK—Director: *Arabesque,* Gramercy Arts Theatre, New York City, 1970; *Botticelli,* La Mama Experimental Theatre Club, New York City; also directed *The Sunhine Boys, Relatively Speaking, South Pacific, Never Too Late, Tribute,* and *The Gin Game.*

PRINCIPAL TELEVISION APPEARANCES—Series: Paramedic, *The Doctors,* syndicated. Episodic: District attorney, *Kojak,* CBS; Lt. Marino, *Que Pasa, USA?,* syndicated; district attorney, *Miami Vice,* NBC. Movies: *Ellery Queen,* 1975.

PRINCIPAL TELEVISION WORK—All as director. Specials: *21 Days of America, Chanukah Story,* and *The Battle for the Ballot.*

FILM DEBUT—*Panic in Needle Park,* 1971. PRINCIPLE FILM APPEARANCES—*The Hospital,* 1971; *The Gang That Couldn't Shoot Straight,* 1971; *Mortadella* (also known as *Lady Liberty*), 1972.

WRITINGS: TELEVISION SCRIPTS—*21 Days of America, Chanukah Story,* and *The Battle for the Ballot.*

AWARDS: Gold Medal from New York Film and TV Festival, 1979; Freedoms Foundation Award, 1980; Silver Medal from Chicago Film and TV Festival, 1982.

MEMBER: Actors' Equity Association, Screen Actors Guild, American Federation of Television and Radio Artists, Society of Stage Directors and Choreographers, Writers Guild of America.

ADDRESSES: HOME—Paramus, NJ.

K

KALFIN, Robert 1933-

PERSONAL: Born April 22, 1933, in New York, NY; son of Alfred A. (a real estate broker) and Hilda (a kindergarten teacher; maiden name, Shulman) Kalfin. EDUCATION: Alfred University, B.F.A., 1954; Yale University, M.F.A., directing, 1957.

VOCATION: Director, producer, writer, and actor.

CAREER: FIRST NEW YORK STAGE WORK—Assistant stage manager, *Uncle Vanya,* Fourth Street Theatre, 1956. PRINCIPLE STAGE WORK—Co-producer and director, *The Golem,* St. Marks Playhouse, New York City, 1959; producer, *An Evening of European Theatre,* 41st Street Theatre, New York City, 1960; director, *The Good Soldier Schweik,* Actors Playhouse, New York City, 1961; director, *The Solid Gold Cadillac,* ART Repertory Theatre, Rockville, MD, 1962; director, *The Love of Four Colonels, Anniversary Waltz, Witness for the Prosecution, The Male Animal, The Little Hut, Night Must Fall, Private Lives,* all Tanglewood Barn Theatre, Clemmons, SC, 1964; director, *Five Days, One of Us Has Been Ignited, The Furthermost Finger of Fillmore,* all Chelsea Theatre Center, New York City, 1965-66; director, *The Rainmaker,* Manitoba Theatre Centre, Winnipeg, MB, Canada, 1966; director, *The Glass Menagerie,* Citadel Theatre, Edmonton, AB, Canada, 1966; director, *Puntila and His Hired Man,* Milwaukee Repertory Theatre, Milwaukee, WI, 1967; director, *Christophe, My Friend Weissmann Is Back!,* both Chelsea Theatre Center, 1968; director, *The Judas Applause,* Chelsea Theatre Center, 1969; director, *Things to Hear, Things to See—An Evening with Huckleberry Finn, The Universal Nigger,* both Chelsea Theatre Center, 1970; director, *Tarot,* Chelsea Theatre Center, 1970, then Circle in the Square, New York City, 1971; director, *Kaddish,* Chelsea Theatre Center, then Circle in the Square, both 1972; director, *Sunset,* Chelsea Theatre Center, 1972; director, *The Lady from the Sea,* New Repertory Company, Gotham Art Theatre, New York City, 1973; director, *Total Eclipse,* Chelsea Theatre Center, 1974; director, *Yentl, the Yeshiva Boy,* Chelsea Theatre Center, then (as *Yentl*) Eugene O'Neill Theatre, both 1975; director, *Polly,* Chelsea Theatre Center, 1975; *The Prince of Homburg,* Brooklyn Academy of Music, then Theatre Four, both 1976; *Happy End,* Brooklyn Academy of Music, then Martin Beck Theatre, both 1977; *Strider,* Chelsea Westside Theatre, then Helen Hayes Theatre, both 1979, later Cleveland Playhouse, Cleveland, OH, Seattle Repertory Theatre, Seattle, WA, both 1981, and in Israel.

Producer and director, *Hijinks!,* Cheryl Crawford Theatre, New York City, 1980-81; director, *The Upper Depths,* Wonderhorse Theatre, New York City, 1982; producer, *Shades of Brown* and *The Trial of Adam Clayton Powell, Jr.,* both New Federal Theatre, New York City, 1983; producer, *Shades of Brown The Big Holiday Broadcast, Amateurs, Paradise!, Sleuth,* producer and director, *The Seagull, Have, Amadeus,* all at Playhouse in the Park, Cincinnati, OH, 1984-85; director, *A Shayna Maidel: The Life of a Family,* Hartford Stage Company, Hartford, CT, Philadelphia Drama Guild, Philadelphia, PA, and National Jewish Theatre, Chicago, IL, all 1986; producer, *Song for a Saturday,* American Jewish Theatre, New York City, 1987. Also directed *Amadeus,* Citadel Theatre; *Lorca,* Lucille Lortel's White Barn Theatre; produced *Candide,* Chelsea Theatre Center, later on Broadway, both 1974, as well as over 100 other productions for the Chelsea Theatre Company.

MAJOR TOURS—Director, *The Skin of Our Teeth,* Chelsea Theatre Center, Scandinavian cities, 1968.

PRINCIPAL TELEVISION WORK—Director, "The Prince of Homburg," *Theatre in America,* PBS.

RELATED CAREER—Founder and artistic director, Chelsea Theatre Company, New York City, 1965—; artistic director, Playhouse in the Park, Cincinnati, OH, 1984-85; guest instructor, Yale School of Drama; instructor in the musical theatre program and graduate costume class, New York University.

WRITINGS: See production detail above. PLAYS—(Adaptor) *Golem,* 1959; (adaptor) *The Good Soldier Schweik,* 1961; (co-adaptor, with Leah Napolin) *Yentl,* 1975; (co-adaptor, with Steve Brown) *Strider,* 1979; (co-adapter) *Hijinks!,* 1980; all published by Samuel French, Inc.

AWARDS: Under Robert Kalfin's artistic direction, writers, directors, designers, and actors working at the Chelsea Theatre Center have received five Antoinette Perry Awards and nine nominations, as well as numerous Obie Awards, Drama Critics Circle Awards, Maharam Awards, and Margo Jones Awards.

MEMBER: Society of Stage Directors and Choreographers (executive board).

ADDRESSES: OFFICE—312 W. 20th Street, Apt. 2D, New York, NY 10011. AGENT—c/o Roseanne Kirk, 161 W. 54th Street, Suite 1204, New York, NY 10019.

*　　　*　　　*

KANDER, John 1927-

PERSONAL: Born March 18, 1927, in Kansas City, MO; son of Harold and Berenice (Aaron) Kander. EDUCATION: Oberlin College, B.A., 1951; Columbia University, M.A., 1954.

JOHN KANDER

VOCATION: Composer, director, conductor, and musician

CAREER: PRINCIPAL STAGE WORK—Also see *WRITINGS* below. Choral director and conductor, Warwick Musical Theatre, Warwick, RI, 1955-57; conductor, *Conversation Piece,* Barbizon-Plaza Theatre, New York City, 1957; arranged dance music for *Gypsy,* Broadway Theatre, New York City, 1959, and for *Irma la Douce,* Plymouth Theatre, 1960. Also pianist for *The Amazing Adele,* New York City, 1956, and for *An Evening with Bea Lillie,* Florida, 1956.

WRITINGS: MUSICAL SCORES—*Second Square* and *Opus Two,* Oberlin College, 1950; *Requiem for Georgie,* Oberlin College, 1951; *A Family Affair,* Billy Rose Theatre, New York City, 1962; *Never Too Late,* Playhouse Theatre, New York City, 1962; all Broadway productions with lyricist Fred Ebb: *Flora, the Red Menace,* Alvin Theatre, 1965, *Cabaret,* Broadhurst Theatre, 1966, *The Happy Time,* Broadway Theatre, 1968, *Zorba,* Imperial Theatre, 1968, *70 Girls 70,* Broadhurst Theatre, 1971, *Chicago,* St. James Theatre, 1979, *The Act,* Martin Beck Theatre, 1977, *Woman of the Year,* Palace Theatre, 1981, *The Rink,* Martin Beck Theatre, 1984.

SONGS—"Playing the Palace," *Parade of Stars Playing the Palace,* Palace Theatre, New York City, 1983; "A New Pair of Shoes," *Night of 100 Stars II,* Radio City Music Hall, New York City, 1985; contributor, *Diamonds,* Circle in the Square Theatre, New York City, 1985.

FILM SCORES—*Something for Everyone,* National General, 1970; (with Fred Ebb) *Cabaret,* Allied Artists, 1972; (with Ebb) *Funny*

Lady, Columbia, 1975; (with Ebb) *Lucky Lady,* Twentieth Century-Fox, 1975; (with Ebb) *New York, New York,* United Artists, 1977; *Kramer vs. Kramer,* Columbia, 1979; *Still of the Night,* Metro-Goldwyn-Mayer/United Artists, 1982; *Blue Skies Again,* Warner Brothers, 1983; *Places in the Heart,* Tri-Star, 1984; (with Ebb) *A Matter of Time,* 1976.

TELEVISION SCORES—*Liza with a Z,* NBC, 1972; *An Early Frost,* NBC, 1985.

AWARDS: All with Fred Ebb. Best Musical Score, Antoinette Perry Award, 1966, for *Cabaret;* Best Musical Score, Antoinette Perry Award nomination, 1968, for *The Happy Time;* Best Musical, Antoinette Perry Award nomination, 1969, for *Zorba;* Emmy Award, 1973, for *Liza with a Z;* Best Musical Score, Antoinette Perry Award, 1981, for *Woman of the Year.*

MEMBER: Dramatists Guild, National Institute of Musical Theatre, American Society of Composers, Authors, and Producers.

ADDRESSES: OFFICE—c/o Dramatists Guild, 234 W. 44th Street, New York, NY 10036.

*   *   *

KANTER, Marin   1960-

PERSONAL: Born February 20, 1960, in Cincinnati, OH; daughter of Joseph H. (a banker) and Nancy (a singer and songwriter; maiden

MARIN KANTER

name, Reed) Kanter. EDUCATION: Trained for the stage at Sarah Lawrence College with John Braswell and Wilford Leach.

VOCATION: Actress.

CAREER: FILM DEBUT—Tracey, *Ladies and Gentlemen, The Fabulous Stains,* Paramount, 1981. PRINCIPAL FILM APPEARANCES—Telena, *The Loveless,* Atlantic, 1982; Mac, *Endangered Species,* Metro-Goldwyn-Mayer/United Artists, 1982.

TELEVISION DEBUT—Janet Feldman, *Skokie,* CBS, 1981.

MEMBER: Screen Actors Guild.

ADDRESSES: HOME—6010 N. Bay Road, Miami Beach, FL 33140. AGENT—c/o Richard Schmenner, S.T.E. Representation, 888 Seventh Avenue, Suite 12, New York, NY 10106.

*   *   *

KAPLAN, Jonathan   1947-

PERSONAL: Born November 25, 1947, in Paris, France; son of Sol (a film composer) and Frances (an actress; maiden name, Heflin) Kaplan. EDUCATION: Attended the University of Chicago, 1965-67; New York University, B.F.A., film, 1970; graduate work, School of Film Making, Hollywood, CA, 1971-73; studied film production with Martin Scorsese and film editing with Carl Lerner and Dee Dee Allen.

Photography courtesy of Paramount

JONATHAN KAPLAN

VOCATION: Director and actor.

CAREER: PRINCIPAL STAGE APPEARANCES—*The Dark at the Top of the Stairs,* Music Box Theatre, New York City, 1957; also appeared in improvisational children's theatre, 1964.

PRINCIPAL STAGE WORK—Lighting designer, Filmore East Concert Hall, New York City, 1969-71.

PRINCIPAL FILM APPEARANCES—*Plaza Suite,* 1971.

PRINCIPAL FILM WORK—Director: *Stanley Stanley,* student film, 1970; *Night Call Nurses,* New World, 1972; *The Student Teachers,* New World, 1973; *The Slams,* Metro-Goldwyn-Mayer, 1973; *Truck Turner,* American International, 1974; *White Line Fever,* Columbia, 1974; *Mr. Billion,* Twentieth Century-Fox, 1976; *Over the Edge,* Orion-Warner Brothers, 1978; *Heart Like a Wheel,* Twentieth Century-Fox, 1983; *Project X,* Twentieth Century-Fox, 1987.

PRINCIPAL TELEVISION WORK—All as director. Movies: *The 11th Victim,* CBS, 1978; *The Hustler of Muscle Beach,* ABC, 1979; *The Gentleman Bandit,* CBS, 1980; *The Girls of the White Orchid,* NBC, 1983.

WRITINGS: FILMS—Co-writer, *White Line Fever,* Columbia, 1974.

AWARDS: First Prize, Schlitz National Student Film Festival, for *Stanley Stanley.*

ADDRESSES: HOME—760 N. La Cienega Boulevard, Los Angeles, CA 90069. OFFICE—Paramount Pictures, 5555 Melrose Avenue, Los Angeles, CA 90038. AGENT—c/o Michael Black, International Creative Management, Inc., 8899 Beverly Boulevard, Los Angeles, CA 90048.

*   *   *

KASDAN, Lawrence   1949-

PERSONAL: Born January 14, 1949, in Miami Beach, FL; son of Clarence Norman (a retail manager) and Sylvia (an employment counselor; maiden name, Landau) Kasdan; married Meg Goldman, November 28, 1971; children: Jacob, Jonathan. EDUCATION: University of Michigan, B.A., 1970, M.A., education, 1972.

VOCATION: Screenwriter, director, and producer.

CAREER: PRINCIPAL FILM WORK—Writer (see below); director, *Body Heat,* Warner Brothers, 1981; director and executive producer, *The Big Chill,* Columbia, 1983; director and producer, *Silverado,* Columbia, 1985.

RELATED CAREER—Advertising copywriter: W.B. Doner and Company, Detroit, MI, 1972-75 and Doyle, Dane, Bernbach Advertisers, Los Angeles, CA 1975-77; freelance screenwriter, 1977-80.

WRITINGS: SCREENPLAYS—(With Leigh Brackett) *The Empire Strikes Back,* Twentieth Century-Fox, 1980; (with George Lucas) *Raiders of the Lost Ark,* Paramount, 1981; *Body Heat,* Warner Brothers, 1981; *Continental Divide,* Universal, 1981; co-writer,

Return of the Jedi, Twentieth Century-Fox, 1983; (with Barbara Bendek) *The Big Chill,* Columbia, 1983; co-writer, *Silverado,* Columbia, 1985. SCREENPLAYS, UNPRODUCED—"The Bodyguard."

AWARDS: Writers Guild of America Award and Best Director nomination, Directors Guild of America Award, both 1983, for *The Big Chill;* recipient of Clio Awards for work in advertising.

MEMBER: Writers Guild of America West, Directors Guild of America West.

ADDRESSES: OFFICE—Kasdan Productions, 4117 Radford Avenue, Studio City, CA 91604.*

*   *   *

KAVNER, Julie   1951-

PERSONAL: Born September 7, 1951. EDUCATION: Graduated from San Diego State University.

VOCATION: Actress.

CAREER: PRINCIPAL TELEVISION APPEARANCES—Series: Brenda Morgenstern, *Rhoda,* CBS, 1974-78; *The Tracey Ullman Show,* Fox, 1987—. Movies: Margot Weiss Goldman, *Katherine,* ABC, 1975; Janet Michaels, *No Other Love,* CBS, 1979; Megan Brady, *Revenge of the Stepford Wives,* NBC, 1980. Specials: "The Girl Who Couldn't Lose," *ABC Afterschool Special* ABC, 1975.

PRINCIPAL FILM APPEARANCES—*Bad Medicine,* Twentieth Century-Fox, 1985; *Hannah and Her Sisters,* Orion, 1985. *Radio Days,* Orion, 1987; also *National Lampoon Goes to the Movies,* 1981.

PRINCIPAL STAGE APPEARANCES—Brooke Silver, *Particular Friendships,* Astor Place Theatre, New York City, 1981.

AWARDS: Outstanding Continuing Performance by a Supporting Actress in a Comedy Series, Emmy Award, 1978, for *Rhoda.*

ADDRESSES: OFFICE—Twentieth Century-Fox Television, 10201 W. Pico Boulevard, Los Angeles, CA 90035.*

*   *   *

KAY, Charles   1930-

PERSONAL: Born Charles Piff, August 31, 1930, in Coventry, England; son of Charles Beckingham and Frances (Petty) Piff. EDUCATION: Attended Birmingham University; trained for the stage at the Royal Academy of Dramatic Art, 1958.

VOCATION: Actor.

CAREER: STAGE DEBUT—Sadi, *Uncle Dunda,* Belgrade Theatre, Coventry, U.K., 1958. LONDON DEBUT—Jimmy Beales, *Roots,* Royal Court Theatre, 1959. PRINCIPAL STAGE APPEARANCES— Magpie, *The Naked Island,* Arts Theatre, London, 1960; Franciscus, *The Changeling,* Royal Court Theatre, London, 1961; Pope Leo, *Luther,* Royal Court Theatre, then Phoenix Theatre, London, both

1961; Sir Andrew Aguecheck, *Twelfth Night,* Royal Court Theatre, 1962; Eric Sawbridge, *The New Men,* Strand Theatre, London, 1962; Superintendent, General, *The Captain of Kopnick,* Sicinius Veletus, *Coriolanus,* Robespierre, *Danton's Death,* all New Theatre, London, 1971; Harold Twine, *Popkiss,* Arts Theatre, Cambridge, U.K., 1972; Fr. Vernon, *The Prodigal Daughter,* Mercury Theatre, Colchester, U.K., 1973; title role, *Tartuffe,* second messenger, *The Bacchae,* both with the Actors Company, Edinburgh Festival, Edinburgh, Scotland, U.K.; Shylock, *The Merchant of Venice,* Leeds Playhouse, Leeds, U.K., 1975; Dauphin, *St. Joan,* Old Vic Theatre, London, 1977; Cassius, *Julius Caesar,* Chichester Festival, Chichester, U.K., 1977; Sam, *The Homecoming,* Garrick Theatre, London, 1978; Doctor, *The Millionairess,* Haymarket Theatre, London, 1978; Daniel de Bosola, *The Duchess of Malfi,* Birmingham Repertory Theatre, Birmingham, U.K., 1979; appeared as James, *The Last Romantic,* Comte de Chagny, *The Phantom of the Opera,* Wimbledon, U.K., 1975; and as Lord Fancourt Babberly, *Charley's Aunt.*

All with the Royal Shakespeare Company, Stratford-on-Avon, U.K., and London: Octavius, *Julius Caesar,* Clarence, "Henry VI, Parts I and II" and "Richard III" as *The Wars of the Roses,* 1963; Archbishop of Canterbury, Dauphin, *Henry V,* 1964; Ferdinand of Navarre, *Love's Labour's Lost,* Lancelot Gobbo, *The Merchant of Venice,* Antipholus of Ephesus, *The Comedy of Errors,* Player Queen, Osric, *Hamlet,* all 1965; Dobchinsky, *The Government Inspector,* Jochen, *The Meteor,* Moloch, *The Thwarting of Baron Bolligrew,* 1966; Beau Clincher, *The Constant Couple,* 1967.

All with the National Theatre Company, National Theatre, London: Verges, *Much Ado about Nothing,* Celia, *As You Like It,* both 1967; Gaveston, *Edward II,* Sir Nathaniel, *Love's Labour's Lost,* both 1968; Hamlet, *Rosencrantz and Guildenstern Are Dead,* Loach, *The National Health,* both 1969; Arragon, *The Merchant of Venice,* Soloni, *The Three Sisters,* de Guiche, *Cyrano de Bergerac,* both 1970.

MAJOR TOURS—*The Hollow Crown,* Asian and Australian cities, 1976.

PRINCIPAL STAGE WORK—Director, *Tartuffe,* Wimbledon, U.K., 1975.

FILM DEBUT—*Bachelor of Hearts,* 1958. PRINCIPAL FILM APPEARANCES—*Nijinsky,* Paramount, 1980.

PRINCIPAL TELEVISION APPEARANCES—Specials: *The Duchess of Malfi,* BBC; *Fall of Eagles,* Thames; *Loyalties,* BBC.

MEMBER: British Actors' Equity Association, Screen Actors Guild.

SIDELIGHTS: FAVORITE ROLES—Lord Fancourt Babberly in *Charley's Aunt.* RECREATIONS—Reading, music, bridge.

ADDRESSES: HOME—18 Epple Road, London SW6, England.*

*   *   *

KEATING, Charles   1941-

PERSONAL: Born October 22, 1941, in London, England; son of Charles James and Margaret (Shevlin) Keating; immigrated to the

United States; married Mary Ellen Chobody. MILITARY: U.S. Army Special Services.

VOCATION Actor, director, and teacher.

CAREER: BROADWAY DEBUT—Pylades, *The House of Atreus,* Billy Rose Theatre, 1968. LONDON DEBUT—Consul Casimir, *The Marquis of Keith,* Royal Shakespeare Company, Aldwych Theatre, 1975. PRINCIPAL STAGE APPEARANCES— Valentine, *Love for Love,* Laertes, *Hamlet,* Eilif, *Mother Courage,* all Charles Playhouse, Boston, MA, 1967; Antony, *Julius Caesar,* Caliban, *The Tempest,* Hurst, *Sergeant Musgrave's Dance,* title role, *Baal,* Giri, *Arturo Ui,* Pylades, *The House of Atreus,* all at Guthrie Theatre, Minneapolis, MN, 1968-70; Ralph, *The Shoemaker's Holiday,* Crucible Theatre, Sheffield, U.K., 1972; Cromwell, *A Man for All Seasons,* Bankside Globe Playhouse, U.K., 1972; Rodd, *Richard II,* Oliver, *As You Like It,* lord, *The Taming of the Shrew,* Royal Shakespeare Company, Memorial Theatre, Stratford-on-Avon, U.K., 1973; King, *Escurial,* Other Place Theatre, Stratford-on-Avon, U.K., 1974; Ross, *Richard II,* Brooklyn Academy of Music, Brooklyn, NY, 1974; Cloten, *Cymbeline,* Memorial Theatre, 1974; Edmund, *King Lear,* Other Place Theatre, The Place, London, both 1974, then Brooklyn Academy of Music, 1975; Cloten, *Cymbeline,* Aldwych Theatre, 1975; Orsino, *Twelfth Night,* Ham, *Noah,* both Chichester Festival, Chichester, U.K., 1976; title role, *Macbeth,* Cleveland Playhouse, Cleveland, OH, 1977; Antony, *Julius Caesar,* American ambassador, *The Applecart,* Jerry, *The Zoo Story,* and appeared in *Murder in the Cathedral,* Chichester Festival, 1977; Ergun, *An Ounce of Prevention,* Hartley House, New York City, 1985; McLeavy, *Loot,* Manhattan Theatre Club, then Music Box Theatre, New York City, 1986. Also performed at the Cleveland Playhouse, Cleveland, OH, and the Provincetown Playhouse, Cape Cod, MA, 1959-60.

MAJOR TOURS—With the Guthrie Theatre, as a solo performer, *When I Was a Boy with Never a Crack in My Heart* and *What Is Past, Passing or to Come,* Midwest cities, 1968; with the Royal Shakespeare Company, *The Hollow Crown,* *Shall I Compare Thee,* and *Groupings,* U.S. universities, 1976.

PRINCIPAL STAGE WORK—All as director unless indicated: U.S. Army Special Services productions of Shakespeare's plays and of contemporary works, 1960-63; *The Madness of Lady Bright,* Guthrie Theatre, Minneapolis, MN, 1969; *Macbeth,* Crawford Livingston Theatre, St. Paul, MN, 1970; *The Scarecrow,* American College Theatre Festival, 1971; actor and director with the Crucible Theatre, Sheffield, U.K., 1972; co-director, *Murder in the Cathedral,* Chichester Cathedral, Chichester, U.K., 1976.

PRINCIPAL FILM APPEARANCES—*Charlie Muffin.*

PRINCIPAL TELEVISION APPEARANCES—Mini-Series: *Edward and Mrs. Simpson;* *Brideshead Revisited.* Specials: *Richard II;* *Dream of Living;* *The Professionals.*

PRINCIPAL CABARET WORK—One season at "The Moors," Cape Cod, MA, 1967.

MEMBER: Actors' Equity Association (U.S. and British), Screen Actors Guild, American Federation of Television and Radio Artists.

ADDRESSES: AGENT—c/o Dodo Watts Agency, 4 Broom Close, Teddington, Middlesex, England.*

KEITEL, Harvey 1941-

PERSONAL: Born 1941, in Brooklyn, NY. EDUCATION: Trained for the stage at the Actors Studio with Lee Strasberg and Frank Corsaro. MILITARY: U.S. Marine Corps.

VOCATION: Actor.

CAREER: FILM DEBUT—Lead, *Who's That Knocking at My Door?,* Brenner, 1968. PRINCIPAL FILM APPEARANCES—*Street Scenes,* 1973; *Mean Streets,* Warner Brothers, 1973; *Alice Doesn't Live Here Anymore,* Warner Brothers, 1975; Sport, *Taxi Driver,* Columbia, 1976; Coleman Buckmaster, *That's the Way of the World* (also known as *Shining Star*), United Artists, 1975; Speed, *Mother, Jugs, and Speed,* 1976; nephew, *Buffalo Bill and the Indians, or Sitting Bull's History Lesson,* United Artists, 1976; Ken Hood, *Welcome to L.A.,* Lion's Gate, 1977; *Fingers,* 1978; Gabriel Feraud, *The Duellists,* Paramount, 1978; Jerry Bartowski, *Blue Collar,* Universal, 1978; Henry, *Eagle's Wing,* 1978; Roddy, *La Mort en Direct,* 1979; Benson, *Saturn 3,* Associated Film, 1979.

Inspector Fredrich Netusil, *Bad Timing/A Sensual Obsession,* World Northal, 1980; Cat, *The Border,* Universal, 1981; Lieutenant Fred O'Connor, *Copkiller,* 1982; *Il Mondo Nuovo,* 1982; Mr. Legend, *Nemo,* 1983; fugitive, *Une Pierre dans la Bouche,* 1983; Rivas, *Exposed,* Metro-Goldwyn-Mayer/United Artists (MGM/UA), 1983; Ed Lasky, *Falling in Love,* Paramount, 1984; Clever, *El Caballero del Dragon* (*Knight of the Dragon,* also known as *Star Knight*), Cinetel Films, 1985; Frankie Acquasanta, *Un Complicato Intrigo di Donne, Vicoli, e Delitti* (*A Complex Plot about Women, Alleys, and Crimes*), Cannon, 1985; Mickey, *Off Beat,* Buena Vista, 1986; Bobby Dilea, *Wise Guys,* MGM/UA, 1986; Pontius Pilate, *L'Inchiesta* (*The Investigation*), Italian International, 1987.

PRINCIPAL TELEVISION APPEARANCES—Movies: *The Virginia Hill Story,* 1974; *Eagle's Way,* 1979; Solly Berliner, *The Men's Club,* Showtime, 1986; Pontius Pilate, *L'Inchiesta* (*The Investigation*), RAI-TV, Italy, 1987. Teleplays: *A Memory of Two Mondays.*

PRINCIPAL STAGE APPEARANCES—*Death of a Salesman,* Circle in the Square Theatre, New York City, 1975; *Hurlyburly,* Goodman Theatre, Chicago, 1983-84, then Promenade Theatre, New York City, 1984, transferring to the Ethel Barrymore Theatre, New York City, 1984-85.

MEMBER: Actors' Equity Association, Screen Actors Guild, American Federation of Television and Radio Artists.

ADDRESSES: AGENT—International Creative Management, 8899 Beverly Blvd., Los Angeles, CA 90048.*

*   *   *

KELLERMAN, Sally 1936-

PERSONAL: Full name, Sally Claire Kellerman; born June 2, 1936, in Long Beach, CA; daughter of John Helm and Edith Baine (Vaughn) Kellerman; married Richard Edelstein, December 19, 1970 (marriage ended); married Jonathan Krane, 1980; children: (first marriage) four step-daughters. EDUCATION: Attended Los Angeles City College; trained for the stage at the Actors Studio and with Jeff Corey.

VOCATION: Actress.

CAREER: PRINCIPAL FILM APPEARANCES—*The Boston Strangler,* Twentieth Century-Fox, 1968; *The April Fools,* National General, 1969; *M*A*S*H,* Twentieth Century-Fox, 1970; *Brewster McCloud,* Metro-Goldwyn-Mayer (MGM), 1970; *The Last of the Red Hot Lovers,* Paramount, 1972; *Slither,* MGM, 1973; *Reflection of Fear,* 1973; *Lost Horizon,* Columbia, 1973; *Rafferty and the Gold Dust Twins,* Warner Brothers, 1975; *The Big Bus,* Paramount, 1976; *Welcome to L.A.,* Lion's Gate, 1977; *A Little Romance,* Orion, 1979; *Foxes,* United Artists, 1980; *Loving Couples,* Twentieth Century-Fox, 1980; *Serial,* Paramount, 1980; *Head On,* Greentree Productions, 1980 (later retitled *Fatal Attraction* for U.S. release, 1985); *For Lovers Only,* 1982; *Dempsey,* 1983; *September Gun,* 1983; *Back to School,* Orion, 1986; *That's Life,* Columbia, 1986; Roxy Du Jour, *Meatballs III,* TMS Pictures, 1987; Edith Helm, *Someone to Love,* International Rainbow Pictures, 1987; Blanche, *Three for the Road,* New Century Vista, 1987.

PRINCIPAL TELEVISION APPEARANCES—Episodic: "Higher and Higher," *Premiere,* CBS, 1968; also *Chrysler Theatre,* NBC; *Mannix,* CBS; *It Takes a Thief,* ABC. Movies: *Verna: USO Girl,* 1978; *Elena,* NBC, 1985. Mini-Series: Lisa Bockweiss, *Centennial,* NBC, 1978-79.

PRINCIPAL STAGE APPEARANCES—Linda Seton, *Holiday,* with the Center Theatre Group at the Ahmanson Theatre, Los Angeles, 1980-81; also *Singular Man* and *Breakfast at Tiffany's,* both New York City productions.

MEMBER: Actors' Equity Association, Screen Actors Guild, American Federation of Television and Radio Artists.

AWARDS: Acadamy Award nomination, Golden Globe Award, 1970, for *M*A*S*H.*

ADDRESSES: AGENT—Creative Artists Agency, 1888 Century Park East, Suite 1400, Los Angeles, CA 90067. MANAGER—c/o Jonathan Krane, The Management Company (BEE), 1888 Century Park East, Suite 1616, Los Angeles, CA 90067.*

*   *   *

KENNEDY, Cheryl   1947-

PERSONAL: Born April 29, 1947, in Enfield, England; daughter of Richard Wilson and Margaret Rose (Hickson) Kennedy; married David Murphy (divorced); married Tom Courtenay (an actor). EDUCATION: Trained for the stage at the Corona Stage School.

VOCATION: Actress.

CAREER: STAGE DEBUT—Marilyn, *What a Crazy World,* Stratford Theatre, London, 1962. BROADWAY DEBUT—Eliza Doolittle, *My Fair Lady,* St. James Theatre, 1982. PRINCIPAL STAGE APPEARANCES—Victoria, *Half-a-Sixpence,* Cambridge Theatre, London, 1963. Agnes, *The Wayward Way,* Vaudeville Theatre, London, 1965; Winnie, *The Matchgirls,* Globe Theatre, London, 1966; Belinda, *Jorrocks,* New Theatre, London, 1967; Polly, *Queenie,* Polly Browne, *The Boy Friend,* both Comedy Theatre, London, 1967; Jo, *Little Women,* Arnaud Theatre, Guildford, U.K., 1970; Martha Jefferson, *1776,* New Theatre, 1970; Elizabeth Bennet, *First Impressions,* Birmingham Repertory Theatre, Birm-

ingham, U.K., 1971; Joan, *Time and Time Again,* Comedy Theatre, 1972; Miss Smith, *Springtime for Henry,* Oxford Festival, Oxford, U.K. 1974; Evelyn, *Absent Friends,* Garrick Theatre, London, 1975; Kay, *Time and the Conways,* Bristol Old Vic Theatre, Bristol, U.K., 1978; Alice Kinnian, *Flowers for Algernon,* Queen's Theatre, London, 1979; Katherine, *Love's Labour's Lost,* Berkeley Shakespeare Festival, Berkeley, CA, 1984.

FILM DEBUT—*Doctor in Clover,* 1965.

PRINCIPAL TELEVISION APPEARANCES—Movies: *The Sweeney; Couples; What Every Woman Knows; Schalcken; Rings on Their Fingers.*

MEMBER: British Actors' Equity Association, Screen Actors Guild.

SIDELIGHTS: RECREATIONS—Motor racing, swimming, stamp collecting.

ADDRESSES: AGENT—c/o Larry Dalzell Associates, 3 Goodwin's Court, St. Martin's Lane, London WC2, England.*

*   *   *

KENNEDY, Kathleen

PERSONAL: EDUCATION: Attended San Diego State University.

VOCATION: Producer.

CAREER: FIRST FILM WORK—Production assistant, *1941,* Universal, 1979. PRINCIPAL FILM WORK—Associate producer, *Raiders of the Lost Ark,* Paramount, 1981; associate producer, *Poltergeist,* Metro-Goldwyn-Mayer/United Artists, 1982; (with Steven Spielberg) co-producer, *E.T.: The Extra-Terrestrial,* Universal, 1982; associate producer, *Indiana Jones and the Temple of Doom,* Paramount, 1984; executive producer, *Gremlins,* Warner Brothers, 1984; executive producer, *Goonies,* Warner Brothers, 1985; executive producer, *Fandango,* Warner Brothers, 1985; executive producer, *Back to the Future,* Universal, 1985; (with Frank Marshall) co-producer, *The Money Pit,* Universal, 1986; producer, *Batteries Not Included,* upcoming.

PRINCIPAL TELEVISION WORK—Producer, *You're On.*

RELATED CAREER—Camera operator, video editor, floor director, and news production coordinator, KCST-TV, San Diego, CA.

ADDRESSES: OFFICE—c/o Universal Studios, 100 Universal City Plaza, Universal City, CA 91608.*

*   *   *

KENT, John B.   1939-

PERSONAL: Born September 5, 1939, in Jacksonville, FL. EDUCATION: Attended Yale University and the University of Florida Law School; New York University Law School, L.L.M., taxation, 1964.

VOCATION: Theatre executive and attorney.

CAREER: Director and officer, Kent Theatres, Inc., 1961—, president, 1967-70, then vice-president and general counsel, 1970—; partner, Kent, Watts, Durden, Kent, Nichols and Mickler (now Carlton, Fields and Kent), 1967—; vice-president, National Association of Theatre Owners, Florida, 1968-72, director, 1973—, President's Advisory Cabinet, 1979—; president and director, Kent Investments, Inc., 1977—.

MEMBER: American Bar Association, Florida Bar Association, American Judicature Society; Rotary Club of Jacksonville.

ADDRESSES: OFFICE—Carlton, Fields and Kent, 1400 Florida National Bank Tower, 225 Water Street, Jacksonville, FL 32202.*

*   *   *

KESTELMAN, Sara   1944-

PERSONAL: Born May 12, 1944, in London, England; daughter of Morris and Dorothy Kestelman; EDUCATION: Trained for the stage at the Central School of Speech and Drama.

VOCATION: Actress.

CAREER: STAGE DEBUT—Nymph, *The Tempest,* Open Air Theatre, London, 1960. LONDON DEBUT—Cassandra, *Troilus and Cressida,* Royal Shakespeare Company, Aldwych Theatre, 1969. BROADWAY DEBUT—Hippolyta/Titania, *A Midsummer Night's Dream,* Royal Shakespeare Company, Billy Rose Theatre, 1971. PRINCIPAL STAGE APPEARANCES— Abigail, *The Crucible,* Liverpool Playhouse, Liverpool, U.K., 1961; Cecily, *The Importance of Being Earnest,* Library Theatre, Manchester, U.K., 1961; Lechery, *Dr. Faustus,* Margaret, *Much Ado about Nothing,* Jessie Taite, *The Silver Tassie,* all Royal Shakespeare Company (RSC), Aldwych Theatre, London, 1969; Jane Shore, *Richard III,* RSC, Memorial Theatre, Stratford-on-Avon, U.K., 1970; Hippolyta/Tatania, *A Midsummer Night's Dream,* RSC, Memorial Theatre, then Aldwych Theatre, both 1970; Kleopatra, *Enemies,* RSC, Aldwych Theatre, 1971; Natasha, *Subject to Fits,* RSC, Other Place Theatre, Stratford-on-Avon, U.K., 1971; Messalina, *I Claudius,* Queen's Theatre, London, 1972; Lady Macbeth, *Macbeth,* Ruth, *The Homecoming,* both Birmingham Repertory Theatre, Birmingham, U.K., 1972; Yelena, *Uncle Vanya,* Bristol Old Vic Theatre, Bristol, U.K., 1973; Prudence, *Plunder,* Bristol Old Vic Theatre, 1973; Countess Werdenfels, *The Marquis of Keith,* Aldwych Theatre, 1974; Sally Bowles, *I Am a Camera,* Cambridge Theatre Company, Cambridge, U.K., 1976; Alexandra Kollontai, *State of Revolution,* Madame Petypon, *The Lady from Maxim's,* Susannah, *Bedroom Farce,* all National Theatre, London, 1977-78; Janet Achurch, *The Achurch Letters,* Greenwich Theatre, London, 1978; Lady Touchwood, *The Double Dealer,* Enid Underwood, *Strife,* both Olivier Theatre, London, 1978; lady with a monocle, *The Fruits of Enlightenment,* Mrs. Wahl, *Undiscovered Country,* Roslaind, *As You Like It,* all Olivier Theatre, 1979.

MAJOR TOURS—*The Hollow Crown, Pleasure and Repentance,* with the Royal Shakespeare Company, U.S. and Japanese cities, 1974-75.

FILM DEBUT—*Zardoz,* Twentieth Century-Fox, 1973. PRINCIPAL FILM APPEARANCES—*Liztomania,* Warner Brothers, 1975; *Break of Day,* 1978; *The Life of Nobel,* 1979.

PRINCIPAL TELEVISION APPEARANCES—Series: *Kean,* BBC; *The New Avengers,* BBC. Movies: *The Caucasian Chalk Circle,* BBC; *Under Western Eyes,* BBC. Specials: *Peer Gynt,* BBC.

MEMBER: British Actors' Equity Association, Screen Actors Guild.

SIDELIGHTS: FAVORITE ROLES—Prudence in *Plunder.* RECREATIONS—Singing, photography, indoor plants.

ADDRESSES: AGENT—c/o Saraband Associates, 59 Frith Street, London W1, England.*

*   *   *

KIMMINS, Kenneth   1941-

PERSONAL: Born September 4, 1941, in Brooklyn, NY; son of Edward F. (a distiller) and Charlotte (Duncan) Kimmins; divorced from wife. EDUCATION: Catholic University, B.A., drama. POLITICS: Democrat. RELIGION: Roman Catholic.

VOCATION: Actor, director, producer, and writer.

CAREER: PRINCIPAL TELEVISION APPEARANCES—Episodic: *Dynasty,* ABC; *Dallas,* CBS; *Hill Street Blues,* NBC; *Cheers,* NBC; *Newhart,* CBS; *Alice,* CBS; *Taxi,* ABC; *WKRP in Cincinnati,* CBS; *Our House,* NBC; *Brothers.* Series: *A Rock and a Hard Place,* NBC; *Mr. President,* Fox Television Network, 1987; *Leo and Liz in Beverly Hills,* CBS, 1987. Movies: *Andy, My Old Man,*

KENNETH KIMMINS

CBS, 1979; Dr. Lewis Halloran, *The Henderson Monster,* CBS, 1980; Joe Kimble, *I Was a Mail Order Bride,* CBS, 1982; Duward Sandifer, *Eleanor, First Lady of the World,* CBS, 1982; Bill, *My Body, My Child,* ABC, 1982; Fred Burns, *Your Place or Mine?,* CBS, 1983; Keith Mackerson, *Emergency Room,* syndicated, 1983; chief of surgery, *Why Me?,* ABC, 1984; network spokesman, *The Ratings Game,* Movie Channel, 1984; Dr. Barney Kay, *Blackout,* HBO, 1985; Fogerty, *If Tomorrow Comes,* CBS, 1986; Eugene Skerritt, *Something in Common,* CBS, 1986; Gary Cole, *A Fight for Jenny,* NBC, 1986; Principal, *Help Wanted: Kids,* ABC, 1986; also *All God's Children,* ABC, 1980. Mini-Series: Fuller, *Moviola: The Scarlett O'Hara War,* NBC, 1980; Broderick, *The Atlanta Child Murders,* CBS, 1985. Specials: "Rookie of the Year," *ABC Afterschool Special,* 1976.

STAGE DEBUT—Wally Myers, *The Male Animal,* Lakes Region Playhouse, Laconia, NH, 1960. BROADWAY DEBUT—*The Fig Leaves Are Falling,* Broadhurst Theatre, 1968. LONDON DEBUT—Harry, *Company,* Her Majesty's Theatre, 1971. PRINCIPAL STAGE APPEARANCES—*All My Sons,* Equity Library Theatre, New York City, 1968; *Adaptation/Next,* Greenwich Mews Theatre, New York City, 1969; *Company,* Alvin Theatre, New York City, 1970; *The Gingerbread Lady,* Plymouth Theatre, New York City, 1971; *Status Quo Vadis,* Brooks Atkinson Theatre, New York City, 1973; *The Magic Show,* Cort Theatre, New York City, 1974; *The Fantasticks,* Sullivan Street Playhouse, New York City; *Impressions on Love, Nasty Rumors and Final Remarks,* both Off-Broadway; *Twelve Angry Men* and *The Normal Heart,* both Los Angeles, CA.

PRINCIPAL STAGE WORK—Producer, *Just the Immediate Family,* Hudson Guild Theatre, New York City, 1978; director and co-producer, *Impressions on Love.*

MAJOR TOURS—Harvey Greenfield, *Cactus Flower,* U.S. cities, 1967-68.

FILM DEBUT—Role of associate producer, *Network,* United Artists, 1977. PRINCIPAL FILM APPEARANCES—*Thieves,* Paramount, 1977; *Annie Hall,* United Artists, 1977; *Shoot the Moon,* Metro-Goldwyn-Mayer/United Artists, 1982; *Invaders from Mars,* Cannon, 1986; *Some Kind of Wonderful,* Paramount, 1987; also, *I Was a Teenage Vampire,* 1987.

WRITINGS: PLAYS—*Impressions on Love,* produced in New York City.

MEMBER: Actors' Equity Association, Screen Actors Guild, American Federation of Television and Radio Artists.

SIDELIGHTS: Kenneth Kimmins told *CTFT* that he enjoys working with the Special Olympics.

ADDRESSES: HOME—357 N. Mansfield Avenue, Los Angeles, CA 90036. AGENT—c/o Gary Rado, International Creative Management, Inc., 40 W. 57th Street, New York, NY 10019.

*   *   *

KINNEY, Terry   1954-

PERSONAL: Born January 29, 1954, in Lincoln, IL; son of Kenneth C. (a tractor company supervisor) and Elizabeth L. (a telephone operator; maiden name, Eimer) Kinney; married Eliza-

TERRY KINNEY

beth Perkins (an actress), March 27, 1984. EDUCATION: Received B.S., theatre, Illinois State University.

VOCATION: Actor and director.

CAREER: STAGE DEBUT—Murphy, *The Indian Wants the Bronx,* Steppenwolf Theatre, Chicago, IL, 1976. PRINCIPAL STAGE APPEARANCES—Fick, *Balm in Gilead,* Steppenwolf Theatre, 1983; Treat, *Orphans,* Steppenwolf Theatre, 1984, and Westside Arts Theatre, New York City, 1985; also appeared in *The Glass Menagerie,* North Light Repertory Company, Evanston, IL, 1982. PRINCIPAL STAGE WORK—Director, *And a Nightingale Sang,* Mitzi Newhouse Theatre, New York City, 1981.

FILM DEBUT—Lew Ellis, *A Walk on the Moon,* Midwest, 1985. PRINCIPAL FILM APPEARANCES—Paul Deveneux, *No Mercy,* Tri-Star, 1986.

TELEVISION DEBUT—Mini-Series: Reverend Tom Bird, *Murder Ordained,* CBS, 1986. PRINCIPAL TELEVISION APPEARANCES—Episodic: Bill Pepin, *Miami Vice,* NBC, 1986.

RELATED CAREER—Founding member, Steppenwolf Theatre Company, Chicago, IL, 1976—.

AWARDS: Best Director, Joseph Jefferson Award, Drama Desk nomination, both 1981, for *And a Nightingale Sang.*

MEMBER: Actors' Equity Association, Screen Actors Guild, American Federation of Television and Radio Artists; Players Club.

ADDRESSES: AGENT—c/o Boaty Boatwright, William Morris Agency, 1350 Avenue of the Americas, New York, NY 10019.

KINSKI, Klaus 1928-

PERSONAL: Born Nicolaus Naksznski, 1928, in Poland; children: Nastassia. MILITARY: German Army, World War II.

VOCATION: Actor.

CAREER: PRINCIPAL FILM APPEARANCES—*Doctor Zhivago*, Metro-Goldwyn-Mayer, 1965; *For a Few Dollars More*, United Artists, 1967; *Aguirre: The Wrath of God* (West German), 1972; *Woyzeck* (West German), 1978; *Nosferatu, the Vampyre*, Twentieth Century-Fox, 1979; *Fitzcarraldo* (West German), 1982; *Love and Money*, Paramount, 1982; *The Soldier*, Embassy, 1982; *The Little Drummer Girl*, Warner Brothers, 1984; *Titan Find*, Trans World Entertainment, 1984; Boetius, *El Caballero del Dragon* (*The Knight of the Dragon*, also known as *Star Knight*), Cinetel Films, 1985; *Gor I*, Cannon, 1987; *Nosferatu in Venice* (also known as *Vampires in Venice*), Medusa, Italy, upcoming; Francisco Manoel da Silva, *Cobra Verde*, DeLaurentiis Entertainment Group, upcoming; *Revenge of the Stolen Stars* (also known as *Six Stars to Mindanao*), Dakota Entertainment, upcoming; *Crawlspace*, Empire, upcoming; also *Cold Blooded Beast, Pleasure Girls, The Bloody Hands of the Law*, and over 170 films in Europe.

PRINCIPAL STAGE APPEARANCES—Appeared in theatre productions in postwar Germany.

PRINCIPAL TELEVISION APPEARANCES—Episodic: "Love Sounds," *The Hitchhiker*, HBO, 1985. Movies: *Timestalkers*, CBS, 1987.

SIDELIGHTS: CTFT learned that Klaus Kinski was a prisoner of the British Forces during World War II.

ADDRESSES: AGENT—c/o Walter Kohner, Paul Kohner, Inc., 9169 Sunset Boulevard, Los Angeles, CA 90069.*

*   *   *

KIRKWOOD, James 1930-

PERSONAL: Born August 22, 1930, in Los Angeles, CA; son of James, Sr. (an actor and director) and Lila (an actress; maiden name, Lee) Kirkwood. EDUCATION: Attended New York University and University of California, Los Angeles; trained for the stage with Sanford Meisner. RELIGION: Roman Catholic. MILITARY: U.S. Coast Guard Reserve.

VOCATION: Actor and writer.

CAREER: STAGE DEBUT—Jean d'Arc, *Joan of Lorraine*, touring production, 1947. BROADWAY DEBUT—*Small Wonder*, Coronet Theatre, 1949. PRINCIPAL STAGE APPEARANCES—*Dance Me a Song*, Royale Theatre, New York City, 1950; *Junior Miss*, Lyceum Theatre, New York City; *Panama Hattie*, Dallas, TX; *Oh Men, Oh Women* and *The Tender Trap*, both Bucks County Playhouse, New Hope, PA.

MAJOR TOURS—*Wonderful Town, Call Me Madam, Welcome Darling, The Rainmaker, Oh Men, Oh Women, The Tender Trap*, and *Mary, Mary*, all U.S. cities; *Never Too Late*, South African cities.

PRINCIPAL CABARET APPEARANCES—(With Lee Goodman as a comedy-satire team) Bon Soir, The Blue Angel, and Number One Fifth Avenue, all New York City; Mocambo, Hollywood, CA; Embassy Club, London; Tic-Toc Club, Montreal, PQ, Canada; also appeared at Cafe Society and Le Ruban Bleu.

PRINCIPAL TELEVISION APPEARANCES—Episodic: *The Ed Sullivan Show*, CBS; *Alfred Hitchcock Presents*, CBS; *Kraft Theatre*, NBC. Series: Mickey Emerson, *Valiant Lady*, CBS; regular, *The Garry Moore Show*, CBS.

PRINCIPAL RADIO APPEARANCES—(With Lee Goodman) *Kirkwood-Goodman Show*, WOR, New York City; *Teenagers Unlimited*, Mutual Broadcasting Network; also *Henry Aldrich, Theatre Guild of the Air*.

WRITINGS: PLAYS—*There Must Be a Pony!*, touring production, 1962; *U.T.B.U. (Unhealthy to Be Unpleasant)*, Helen Hayes Theatre, New York City, 1965, published by Samuel French, Inc., 1966; *P.S. Your Cat Is Dead*, John Golden Theatre, New York City, 1975, published by Samuel French, Inc., 1976, then revised and produced Off-Broadway, 1978; (with Nicholas Dante) *A Chorus Line*, New York Shakespeare Festival, Newman Theatre, then Shubert Theatre, both New York City, 1975; *Surprise*, John Drew Theatre, Long Island, NY, 1981; *Legends*, Ahmanson Theatre, Los Angeles, CA, then Majestic Theatre, Dallas, TX, and subsequent tour, all 1986.

SCREENPLAYS—*Good Times/Bad Times*, United Artists, 1968; *Some Kind of Hero*, Paramount, 1982; *A Chorus Line*, Universal, 1985; also *Witch Story*, United Artists.

TELEPLAYS—*There Must Be a Pony!*, Columbia Pictures Television.

FICTION—*There Must Be a Pony!*, Little, 1960; *Good Times/Bad Times*, Simon & Schuster, 1968; *American Grotesque*, Simon & Schuster, 1970; *P.S. Your Cat Is Dead*, Stein & Day, 1972; *Some Kind of Hero*, Crowell, 1975; *Hit Me with a Rainbow*, Delacorte, 1980.

AWARDS: Best Musical, Tony Award, Drama Desk Award, Drama Critics Circle Award, Theatre World Award, and Pulitzer Prize in Drama, all 1976, for *A Chorus Line*.

MEMBER: Actors' Equity Association, American Federation of Television and Radio Artists, Screen Actors Guild, American Guild of Variety Artists, Dramatists Guild, Authors League.

SIDELIGHTS: *A Chorus Line* is the longest running play in the history of Broadway and is the only such production to run for more than 5,000 performances.

ADDRESSES: HOME—58 Oyster Shores Road, East Hampton, NY 11937. OFFICE—484 W. 44th Street, No. 45-R, New York, NY 10036. AGENT—(Novels) Jed Mattes, International Creative Management, 40 W. 57th Street, New York, NY 10019; (screenplays) Ron Mardigan, William Morris Agency, 151 El Camino Real, Beverly Hills, CA, 90069.*

*   *   *

KOENIG, Walter 1936-

PERSONAL: Born September 14, 1936, in Chicago, IL; son of Isadore (a businessman) and Sarah (Strauss) Koenig; married Judith

Levitt (a designer and actress), July 11, 1965; children: Joshua Andres, Danielle Beth. EDUCATION: Attended Grinnell College, 1954-56; University of California at Los Angeles, B.A., 1958; trained for the stage at the Neighborhood Playhouse School of the Arts, 1958-60. RELIGION: Jewish.

VOCATION: Actor, writer, and educator.

CAREER: TELEVISION DEBUT—*Day in Court,* ABC. PRINCIPAL TELEVISION APPEARANCES—Series: Ensign Pavel Chekov, *Star Trek,* NBC, 1967-69. Episodic: *Columbo,* NBC; *Medical Center,* CBS; *Ironside,* NBC; *Mannix,* CBS; *Alfred Hitchcock Presents,* NBC; *Mr. Novak,* NBC; *Ben Casey,* ABC; *The Untouchables,* ABC; *Combat,* ABC. Movies: *Goodbye Raggedy Ann,* 1971; *The Questor Tapes,* 1974.

PRINCIPAL FILM APPEARANCES—Pavel Chekov, *Star Trek: The Motion Picture,* Paramount, 1979; Pavel Chekov, *Star Trek II: The Wrath of Khan,* Paramount, 1982; Pavel Chekov, *Star Trek III: The Search for Spock,* Paramount, 1984; Pavel Chekov, *Star Trek IV: The Voyage Home,* Paramount, 1986; also *The Deadly Honeymoon.*

RELATED CAREER—Instructor: University of California at Los Angeles, 1972-78; California School of Professional Psychology, 1973; Sherwood Oaks Film College, 1978—.

WRITINGS: TELEVISION—Episodic: *Family,* ABC; *What Ever Happened to the Class of '65,* NBC; *The Powers of Matthew Star,* NBC; *The Incredible Hulk,* CBS; *Face to Face,* NBC. NONFICTION—*Chekov's Enterprise,* Pocket Books, 1980.

MEMBER: Screen Actors Guild, American Federation of Television and Radio Artists.

SIDELIGHTS: Walter Koenig told *Contemporary Authors* (Gale, volume 104), "If one can liken the happy experience of working as a regular in a prestigious television series—with its philosophical dignity, its aesthetic good taste, and its bountiful coffers—to an ideal, albeit, imaginary existence several fathoms deep in the fabled lost city of Atlantis, then, the cancellation of that program [*Star Trek*] has its concomitant parallel in the ruination of that aquamarine mecca, the violent ascension to a gray surface world and a miserable case of the bends. When the series ended, the phone stopped ringing. Faced with the prospect of life in a decompression chamber, I began to write. So far I've been able to keep the bad nitrogen bubbles away. I think I can write. I've decided to spend the next several years determining whether or not I can think accurately."

ADDRESSES: AGENT—Harry Gold & Associates, 12725 Ventura Blvd., Suite E, Studio City, CA 91604.*

* * *

KORNMAN, Cam 1949-

PERSONAL: Born June 12, 1949, in Madison, TN; daughter of Alec N. (in business) and Elsie (Brooks) Kornman. EDUCATION: Received B.S. from University of Wisconsin, Madison; trained in musical comedy with Rita Gardner; studied acting with Wynn Handeman and Sanford Meisner at the Goodman School of Theatre; studied voice with Mark Zeller. POLITICS: Democrat. RELIGION: Jewish.

VOCATION: Actress.

CAREER: PRINCIPAL STAGE APPEARANCES—Various roles, *Anna Karenina,* Actors Playhouse, New York City; Masha, *The Seagull,* Universalist Church Theatre, New York City; Jose, *The Grab Bag,* Astor Place Theatre, New York City; Lettuce, *And So to Bed,* Manhattan Theatre Club, New York City; Shelley, *Fishing,* Ariel, *The Tempest,* both Westbeth Theatre Centre, New York City; Deborah, *Rapes,* Cubiculo Theatre, New York City; Julia, *The Wood Demon,* Equity Library Theatre, New York City; Kaleria, *Summerfolk,* Spectrum Theatre, New York City; Nina Sue, *Separates,* WPA Theatre, New York City; Lois, *The Catch,* Playwrights Horizons, New York City; Boyet, *Change Favors,* 78th Street Theatre Lab, New York City; Kirstin, *Miss Julie,* TOMI Theatre, New York City; Miss Jepson, *Day for Surprises,* Quaig Theatre, New York City; Tessie, *The Miss Firecracker Contest,* Studio Arena Theatre, Buffalo, NY; Marie, *The Madwoman of Chaillot,* Goodman Theatre, Chicago, IL. Also Prossy, *Candida,* Green Ram Theatre; Alice, *You Can't Take It with You,* Lake Sunapee Playhouse.

PRINCIPAL TELEVISION APPEARANCES—Series: Geraldine, *The Secret Storm,* CBS. Specials: Ginny Dosh, *Where the Heart Is,* CBS.

PRINCIPAL FILM APPEARANCES—Miss Dixon, *Four Friends,* 1981.

MEMBER: Actors' Equity Association, Screen Actors Guild, American Federation of Television and Radio Artists.

SIDELIGHTS: FAVORITE ROLES—Masha in *The Seagull;* Miss

CAM KORNMAN

Jepson, *Day for Surprises*. RECREATIONS—Reading, folk dancing, swimming, hiking, bicycling.

ADDRESSES: HOME—161 W. 72nd Street, New York, NY 10023.

*   *   *

KOTTO, Yaphet 1944-

PERSONAL: Full name, Yaphet Fredrick Kotto; born November 15, 1944, in New York, NY; son of Yaphet Mangobell and Gladys Maria Kotto; married Antoinette Pettyjohn, January 29, 1975; children: Natascha, Fredrick, Robert, Sarada, Mirabai, Salina. POLITICS: Democrat.

VOCATION: Actor and producer.

CAREER: PRINCIPAL FILM APPEARANCES—*Nothing But a Man*, Cinema 5, 1965; *The Liberation of Lord Byron Jones*, Columbia, 1970; *Across 110th Street*, United Artists, 1972; *Live and Let Die*, United Artists, 1973; *Truck Turner*, American International, 1974; *Report to the Commissioner*, United Artists, 1975; *Shark's Treasure*, United Artists, 1975; *Friday Foster*, American International, 1975; *Drum*, United Artists, 1976; *Monkey Hustle*, 1977; *Alien*, Twentieth Century-Fox, 1978; *Blue Collar*, Universal, 1978; *Brubaker*, Twentieth Century-Fox, 1980; *Fighting Back*, Paramount, 1982; *Hey, Good Lookin'*, Warner Brothers, 1982; *Star Chamber*, Twentieth Century-Fox, 1983; *Warning Sign*, Twentieth Century-Fox, 1985; Harris, *Pretty Kill*, Spectra-Film, 1987; also appeared in *The Limit* and *Bone*.

PRINCIPAL FILM WORK—Producer, *The Limit*.

PRINCIPAL TELEVISION APPEARANCES—Series: Platoon Sgt. James "China" Bell, *For Love and Honor*, NBC, 1983. Movies: *Raid on Entebbe*, 1977; *Rage*, 1980; *Women of San Quentin*, 1983; *Badge of the Assassin*, CBS, 1985; *Harem*, ABC, 1986; *Desperado*, NBC, 1987.

PRINCIPAL STAGE APPEARANCES—Broadway: *The Great White Hope* and *The Zulu and the Zayda*. Off-Broadway: *The Blood Knot*, *Black Monday*, *In White America*, and *A Good Place to Raise a Boy*.

ADDRESSES: AGENT—The Artists Group, Ltd., 1930 Century Park West, Suite 303, Los Angeles, CA 90067.*

*   *   *

KRAMER, Larry 1935-

PERSONAL: Born 1935, in Bridgeport, CT. EDUCATION: Yale University, B.A., 1957.

VOCATION: Writer and producer.

CAREER: PRINCIPAL FILM WORK—Writer (see below); associate producer, *Here We Go Round the Mulberry Bush*, Lopert, 1968; producer, *Women in Love*, United Artists, 1970; director, *The Normal Heart*, Barwood Films, upcoming.

RELATED CAREER—Story editor, Columbia Pictures, New York City and London, 1960-65; assistant to David Picker and Herb Jaffe, United Artists, 1965.

WRITINGS: PLAYS, PRODUCED—*The Normal Heart*, Public Theatre, New York Shakespeare Festival, New York City, 1985. SCREENPLAYS—(Additional dialogue) *Here We Go Round the Mulberry Bush*, Lopert, 1968; *Women in Love*, United Artists, 1970; *A Sea Change*, 1972; *Lost Horizon*, Columbia, 1975; *The Normal Heart*, Barwood Films, upcoming.

ADDRESSES: AGENT—c/o Johnny Planco, William Morris Agency, Inc., 1350 Avenue of the Americas, New York, NY 10019.*

*   *   *

KRISTOFFERSON, Kris 1936-

PERSONAL: Born June 22, 1936, in Brownsville, TX; son of a U.S. Air Force major general; married Fran Beir, 1960 (divorced); married Rita Coolidge (a singer and composer), August 19, 1973 (divorced, 1979); married Lisa Meyers (an attorney), February 18, 1983; children: (first marriage) Tracy, Kris; (second marriage) Casey; (third marriage) two. EDUCATION: Pomona College, B.A., 1958; attended Oxford University. MILITARY: U.S. Army, 1960-65.

VOCATION: Actor, composer, and singer.

CAREER: FILM DEBUT—Drug dealer, *Cisco Pike*, Columbia, 1971. PRINCIPAL FILM APPEARANCES—Billy, *Pat Garrett and Billy the Kid*, Metro-Goldwyn-Mayer, 1973; Elmo, *Blume in Love*, Warner Brothers, 1973; Paco, *Bring Me the Head of Alfredo Garcia*, United Artists, 1974; David, *Alice Doesn't Live Here Anymore*, Warner Brothers, 1975; Averill, *Heaven's Gate*, United Artists, 1980; Hub Smith, *Rollover*, Warner Brothers, 1981; Blackie Buck, *Songwriter*, Tri-Star, 1984; Hawk, *Trouble in Mind*, Island Alive, 1986. Also appeared in *A Star Is Born*, Warner Brother, 1976; *Vigilante Force*, United Artists, 1976; *The Sailor Who Fell from Grace with the Sea*, AVCO-Embassy, 1976; *Semi-Tough*, United Artists, 1977; *Convoy*, United Artists, 1978; *Flashpoint*, Tri-Star, 1984.

PRINCIPAL FILM WORK—Singer (with Rita Coolidge) for the soundtrack of *The Last Movie*, Universal, 1971.

PRINCIPAL TELEVISION APPEARANCES—Movies: Abner Lait, *Freedom Road*, NBC, 1979; Ben Cole, *The Lost Honor of Kathryn Beck*, CBS, 1984; Jesse James, *The Last Days of Frank and Jesse James*, NBC, 1986; Curt Maddox, *Blood and Orchids*, CBS, 1986; Ringo, *Stagecoach*, 1986. Mini-Series: Devin Milford, *Amerika*, ABC, 1987. Guest: *Johnny Cash Show*, ABC; *Rollin' on the River*, syndicated; *The Tonight Show*, NBC; *Late Night with David Letterman*, NBC. Specials: *Welcome Home*, HBO, 1987.

PRINCIPAL STAGE APPEARANCES—Various concert tours and appearances including the Newport Folk Festival, Newport, RI, 1969; *Welcome Home*, Washington, DC, 1987. Also appeared in England as folk singer under the name Kris Carson.

VIDEO—*A Celebration*, DID Productions, 1981.

NON-RELATED CAREER—Formerly an English teacher at West Point; also a bartender and janitor.

WRITINGS: SONGS—"Vietnam Blues," Buckhorn Music Publishing Company, 1965; "For the Good Times," Buckhorn Music Publishing Company, 1968; (with Fred L. Foster) "Me and Bobby McGee," Combine Music Corporation, 1969; "Sunday Mornin' Comin' Down," Combine Music Corporation, 1969; "Help Me Make It through the Night," Combine Music Corporation, 1970; "Loving Her Was Easier (Than Anything I'll Ever Do Again)," Combine Music Corporation, 1970; (with Shel Silverstein) "Once More with Feeling," Combine Music Corporation, 1970; (with Silverstein) "The Taker," Evil Eye Music, Inc., 1970; "Please Don't Tell Me How the Story Ends," Combine Music Corporation, 1971; "I'd Rather Be Sorry," Buckhorn Music Publishing Company, 1971; "Why Me?," Resaca Music Publishing Company, 1972; also "Jody and the Kid," "When I Loved Her."

RECORDINGS: ALBUMS—*Kristofferson,* 1970; *The Silver-Tongued Devil and I,* 1971; *Border Lord,* 1974; *Jesus Was a Capricorn,* 1974; *Spooky Lady's Sideshow,* 1974; *Big Sur Festival,* 1978; *Songs of Kristofferson,* 1978; *Who's to Bless and Who's to Blame,* 1978; *Easter Island,* 1978; *Shake Hands with the Devil,* 1979; *Reposessed,* Mercury, 1987; also *To the Bone,* 1981; *Full Moon* and *Breakaway,* both with Rita Coolidge. SINGLES—"Loving Her Was Easier (Than Anything I'll Ever Do Again)," Monument, 1971; "From the Bottle to the Bottom," 1973, and "Lover Please," 1975, both with Rita Coolidge.

AWARDS: Song of the Year, Country Music Association Award, 1970, for "Sunday Mornin' Comin' Down"; Best Song, Grammy Award nominations, both 1971, for "Help Me Make It through the Night" and "Me and Bobby McGee"; Country Song of the Year, Grammy Award nominations, 1971, for "For the Good Times," and 1973, for "Why Me?"; Best Vocal Performance by a Duo (with Rita Coolidge), Grammy Awards, 1973, for "From the Bottle to the Bottom," and 1975, for "Lover Please"; Rhodes scholarship; honorary doctorate, Pomona College, 1974.

SIDELIGHTS: Kris Kristofferson is well known as a leading actor in productions as diverse as the films *A Star Is Born* and *Semi-Tough* or the television mini-series *Amerika,* but his talents as a songwriter have also won him consistent acclaim. In a December, 1976 *Esquire* profile, Tom Burke called the lanky Texas native "one of the most respected, and his work among the most performed, of contemporary songwriters." George T. Simon, author of *The Best of the Music Makers,* dubbed him "a balladeer of the dispossessed, the troubador of losing and losers," who has brought "a gentle intensity to his portraits of frustration, defeat, and lost romance." Kristofferson's songs have had a major influence on country music in particular; often melancholy and autobiographical, they challenge the "good old boy" image that was once central to that genre. *TV Guide*'s Neil Hickey numbered the writer among the leading members "of a new breed of Nashville songwriters who were more literary, more poetic, less insular in their approaches" (October 12, 1985). Indeed, Kristofferson can hardly be called "insular" in any respect. His wide travels, academic credentials—including a prestigious Rhodes scholarship for study at Oxford University—and his personal problems with marijuana and alcohol have provided him with insights that have fueled his writing and acting. The many years spent in the throes of addiction have also provided grist for the gossip mills, however, and given the modest performer an image of irresponsibility that he worked to change beginning in the 1980s.

Born in Brownsville, Texas, the eldest of three children, Kristofferson was in many respects a model son. In both high school and college he excelled in sports; he managed to become a Golden Gloves boxer while earning high grades. Upon graduating from Pomona College in Claremont, California, he won first- and third-place awards for stories he entered in the *Atlantic Monthly* collegiate short story contest, in addition to the Rhodes scholarship. Despite his many achievements, Kristofferson has expressed unhappiness with his early years. He was considered "square" in California because he liked the country music star Hank Williams and enjoyed playing guitar country style. At Oxford the other Rhodes scholars called him "Tex." He became disillusioned with both the academic world and with his fiction writing while in England, but found a brief stint as a folk singer under the name Kris Carson also unsatisfactory. Halfway through his degree program at Oxford, he quit school, returned to America, married, and joined the Army. For five years he seemed destined to follow in the footsteps of his major general father, as he moved through Ranger school, parachute jump school, and pilot training, eventually becoming an able helicopter pilot. In 1965, however, only weeks before he was to start a position as a literature instructor at West Point military academy, he decided to go to Nashville to try to sell some songs.

The following four years became for Kristofferson "a struggle just to stay alive and write," according to Paul Hemphill in a December 6, 1970 *New York Times Magazine* feature. All but disowned by his shocked parents, Kristofferson also became separated from his wife and two children as his fortunes waned. He took odd jobs tending bar and worked as night janitor at a Columbia Records studio; in his spare time he wrote songs and tried to meet the country stars who might sing them. Eventually singers Johnny Cash and Roger Miller responded to his talent and persistence. Miller was the first to record a Kristofferson song, the soulful "Me and Bobby McGee," which has since become a rock classic in the performance by the late Janis Joplin. Cash's version of Kristofferson's "Sunday Mornin' Comin' Down" had an even more profound effect on the songwriter's career. In 1970 it won the Song of the Year Award from the Country Music Association. Soon thereafter, Cash persuaded Kristofferson to perform his own songs, despite his stage fright and conviction that he did not deserve an audience. The songwriter began to give concerts and record albums. In 1973 he married singer Rita Coolidge, and he toured and performed with her to ever growing audiences of country, folk, and rock music fans.

At the same time, his acting career was progressing. As early as 1971 he appeared as a drug dealer in the movie *Cisco Pike*. Between 1973 and 1977 Kristofferson took roles in more than a half dozen fetures, including the acclaimed *Alice Doesn't Live Here Anymore* and Barbra Streisand's remake of *A Star Is Born*. Nevertheless, as Cheryl McCall noted in a 1981 *People* article, the actor-writer's "peculiar insecurity led to near panic in the face of adulation and stardom." Drinking and drug abuse had long been a part of Kristofferson's life, and as his fame increased, so did his chemical dependency. This in turn led to scandals, first with Sarah Miles, his co-star in *The Sailor Who Fell from Grace with the Sea* and in some explicit photographs that ran in *Playboy,* and then in widely publicized battles with Streisand during the filming of *A Star Is Born*. Discussing the latter movie in a 1976 *People* story, Robert Windeler wrote: "The part . . . called for a zonked out, self-destructing superstar, and Kristofferson seemed typecast." As he sat through a rough cut of the movie, however, the actor began to take stock of his performance; its very realism convinced him that alcohol was destroying his life and his second marriage. He dates the end of his drinking from September 21, 1976.

Kristofferson and Coolidge remained together until 1979; their only child, Casey, was born in 1977. When Coolidge sought a divorce in order to pursue a solo career, she gave major responsibility for their daughter to Kristofferson. He told *People* that the little girl pulled him "kicking and screaming into the '80's," but he had another moment of reckoning late in 1981. In November of that year, an *Esquire* featured emphasized his use of marijuana, which had become a substitute for alcohol. Embarrassed, he gave up the drug and discovered that sobriety gave him a new perspective on his work and himself. In his book *A Kiss Is Still a Kiss,* critic Roger Ebert quoted Kristofferson: "Getting high was supposed to be a method of opening the doors of perception for me, and what it was doing was shutting them. Rather than easing problems for me, it was aggravating them. . . . It took me thirty years to admit I had a problem." Kristofferson then quoted a line from one of his favorite poets, William Blake: "The road of excess leads to the palace of wisdom."

Since ending his chemical dependencies, Kristofferson has worked at a slower pace. He received critical acclaim for *Trouble in Mind,* a film about a love triangle, and he was cast as the heroic patriot Devin Milford in the 1987 television mini-series *Amerika.* As a songwriter he has also rebounded, cutting the well-received album *Repossessed* in 1987. With a new wife and two more children, the artist who once rebelled against his academic background now tries to reconcile the various segments of his life. An interest in liberal politics has made him a spokesperson for better understanding between citizens of the United States and the Soviet Union. He has also become a proponent of sobriety; he told *TV Guide* that he now looks at life "like an old alcoholic," who "is trying to take it one day at a time." Neil Hickey might have summed up the Kris Kristofferson of the late 1980s when he called the artist "a middle-aged gent who's dead serious about his fathering, husbanding, songwriting, acting, record-making, and concert-giving."

ADDRESSES: AGENT—International Creative Management, 8899 Beverly Boulevard, Los Angeles, CA 90048.*

*   *   *

KROEGER, Gary   1957-

PERSONAL: Born April 13, 1957; son of Glenn R. (an engineer) and Donna M. (a teacher; maiden name, Ward) Kroeger; married Leslie Peters (an executive secretary), July 28, 1984. EDUCATION: Received B.A., speech, Northwestern University; trained for the stage at the Art Institute of Chicago.

VOCATION: Actor and writer.

CAREER: STAGE DEBUT—Various roles, *The Brick and the Rose,* Northern University, high school auditorium, 1972, for two performances. PRINCIPAL STAGE APPEARANCES—Perchick, *Fiddler on the Roof,* Cahn Auditorium, Evanston, IL, 1978; Joe Smead, *Smead's Yuk Shack,* Northwestern University, Evanston, IL, 1979. Also appeared in *Thrills and Glory,* Practical Theatre, Evanston, IL, 1981; *50th Golden Anniversary,* Practical Theatre, Evanston, IL, 1982.

PRINCIPAL TELEVISION APPEARANCES—Series: Cast member, *Saturday Night Live,* NBC, 1982-85; Ben Smyth, *Spies,* CBS, 1986-87.

FILM DEBUT—Dan Glover, *A Kid with a Ray Gun,* Empire, 1987.

WRITINGS: SCREENPLAYS—(With Brad Hall, Paul Barrosse, and Julia Louis-Dreyfus) *The Space Commandoes,* Universal, upcoming.

SIDELIGHTS: Gary Kroeger told *CTFT:* "What motivated me? The Avon Lady laughed when I fell."

ADDRESSES: OFFICE—310 N. San Vicente, Los Angeles, CA 90048. AGENT—c/o Howard Klein, International Creative Management, 8899 Beverly Boulevard, Los Angeles, CA 90048.

*   *   *

KURALT, Charles   1934-

PERSONAL: Full name, Charles Bishop Kuralt; born September 10, 1934, in Wilmington, NC; son of Wallace Hamilton and Ina (Bishop) Kuralt; married second wife Suzanna Folsom Baird, June 1, 1962; children: (first marriage) Lisa Catherine Bowers, Susan Guthery Bowers. EDUCATION: University of North Carolina, B.A., 1955.

VOCATION: Television news correspondent and anchorman.

CAREER: PRINCIPAL TELEVISION WORK—With CBS Television network: Writer, *CBS News,* 1956, then news assignment writer, 1958; host, *Eyewitness,* 1960; news chief for Latin America, Rio de Janeiro, 1961, then for U.S. West Coast, 1963. Series: Anchorman, *Eyewitness to History,* 1960-61; narrator, *CBS News Adventure,* 1970; reporter, *Who's Who,* 1977; anchorman: *Sunday Morning,* 1979—; *On the Road with Charles Kuralt,* 1983; *The American Parade,* 1984. Episodic: Correspondent—*CBS Reports;* "On the

CHARLES KURALT

Road,'' *The CBS Evening News with Walter Cronkite* (segment later expanded to series).

PRINCIPAL RADIO WORK—Developer and anchorman, *Dateline America,* CBS Radio, 1972.

RELATED CAREER—Reporter and columnist, *Charlotte News,* NC, 1955-57.

WRITINGS: NON-FICTION—*To the Top of the World,* 1968; *Dateline America,* 1979; *On the Road with Charles Kuralt,* Putnam, 1985; *Southerners: Portrait of a People,* Oxmoor House, 1986; (with Loonis McGlohan) *North Carolina Is My Home,* East Woods, 1986.

AWARDS: Ernie Pyle Memorial Award, 1956; George Foster Peabody Broadcasting Awards, 1969, 1976, 1980; Outstanding Achievement within Regularly Scheduled News Program, Emmy Award, 1969, for ''On the Road,'' *The CBS Evening News with Walter Cronkite;* other Emmy Awards, 1978, 1981.

MEMBER: Players Club.

SIDELIGHTS: CTFT learned that as a high school student, Charles Kuralt won the American Legion Essay Contest, which included a trip to Washington, DC to meet President Harry Truman.

ADDRESSES: OFFICE—CBS News, 524 W. 57th Street, New York, NY 10019.*

* * *

KUREISHI, Hanif

BRIEF ENTRY: Anglo-Pakistani writer Hanif Kureishi (surname is pronounced ''koor-*ee*-shee'') captured the attention of American audiences with his first screenplay, *My Beautiful Laundrette.* Originally made for British television, the low-budget feature portraying the relationship of an unemployed English punk gang member and the son of middle class Pakistani immigrants was the sleeper hit of the art film circuit in 1986 and Kureishi received an Academy Award nomination for his screenplay. Its provocative treatment of homosexual romance, unemployment, and class and racial prejudices continued themes the author had earlier explored in such plays as *The Mother Country,* for which he won the Thames Television Playwright Award, and *Outskirts,* which was produced by the Royal Shakespeare Company in 1981.

Kureishi continued to spark controversy with his second film, whose title (*Sammy and Rosie Get Laid*) some newspapers refused to carry in full. Rejecting the image of England offered by such genteel costume dramas as *A Room with a View* or the television series *Brideshead Revisited,* the London University graduate told the *New York Times* (November 8, 1987), ''You want a movie to be wilder and dirtier and kind of rough and cheap—and defiant as well.'' In addition to plays and film scripts, Kureishi wrote four unpublished novels before he was twenty and more recently has had short stories printed in such magazines as *Harper's* in the United States and *Granta* in Britain; early in his career he wrote pornography under the pseudonym Antonia French. The author also has taken his politics to the streets, campaigning for Labour Party candidates in his native England.

* * *

KYLE, Barry 1947-

PERSONAL: Born March 25, 1947, in London, England; son of Albert Ernest and Edith Ivy (Gaskin) Kyle; married Chrissy Iddon. EDUCATION: Birmingham University, B.A., 1968, M.A., 1969.

VOCATION: Director.

CAREER: FIRST STAGE WORK—Director, *Saved,* Liverpool Playhouse, Liverpool, U.K., 1969. PRINCIPAL STAGE WORK—Director: *Oh What a Lovely War,* Liverpool Playhouse, Liverpool, U.K., 1970; *Prometheus Bound,* Liverpool Playhouse, 1971; *The Odd Couple,* Liverpool Playhouse, 1972; *The Merchant of Venice,* Cameri Theatre, Tel Aviv, Israel, 1980.

Director, all with the Royal Shakespeare Company, Stratford-on-Avon, U.K. and London: *Sylvia Plath: A Dramatic Portrait,* 1973; *Comrades, King John, Cymbeline,* all 1974; *Perkin Warbeck, Richard III, Cymbeline,* all 1975; *Dingo, Romeo and Juliet, Troilus and Cressida, King Lear,* all 1976; *That Good Between Us, Frozen Assets, Dingo,* all 1977; *Measure for Measure, The Churchill Play,* both 1978; *The Churchill Play, The White Guard, Sore Throats, Julius Caesar, Measure for Measure,* all 1979; *The Maid's Tragedy,* 1980.

SIDELIGHTS: RECREATIONS—Politics, sport, music, owls.

ADDRESSES: OFFICE—c/o Royal Shakespeare Company, Aldwych Theatre, London WC2, England.*

L

LAMAS, Lorenzo 1958-

PERSONAL: Born January 20, 1958, in Santa Monica, CA; son of Fernando (an actor) and and Arlene (an actress; maiden name, Dahl) Lamas; married Victoria Hilbert (a model), 1981 (divorced); married Michele Smith (a publicist), 1983 (divorced); children: Alvaro Joshua. EDUCATION: Trained as an actor at Tony Barr's Film Actors Workshop, Burbank Studios, CA; also attended Jim Russell School of Motor Racing, 1985. POLITICS: Democrat.

VOCATION: Actor and race car driver.

CAREER: PRINCIPAL TELEVISION APPEARANCES—Episodic: *The Love Boat,* ABC; *Switch,* CBS; *Sword of Justice,* NBC. Series: Rick, *California Fever,* CBS, 1979; Burt Carroll, *Secrets of Midland Heights,* CBS, 1980-81; Lance Cumson, *Falcon Crest,* CBS,

LORENZO LAMAS

1981—. Movies: Jaime, *Detour to Terror,* NBC, 1980. Specials: *Night of 100 Stars II,* 1985.

PRINCIPAL FILM APPEARANCES—*Grease,* Paramount, 1978; *Tilt,* 1978; *Take Down,* Buena Vista, 1979; *Body Rock,* New World, 1984.

PRINCIPAL STAGE APPEARANCES—*Night of 100 Stars II,* Radio City Music Hall, New York City, 1985.

NON-RELATED CAREER—Partner, LeConte Driving School, Willow Springs, CA, 1985—; race car driver, Phil Conte Racing, Paramount, CA.

AWARDS: Winner, Toyota Grand Prix, Long Beach, CA, 1985.

SIDELIGHTS: RECREATIONS—Surfing, skiing, golf, motorcyles, karate.

ADDRESSES: AGENT—Charter Management, 9000 Sunset Boulevard, Suite 1112, Los Angeles, CA 90069.

*　　*　　*

LAN, David 1952-

PERSONAL: Born June 1, 1952, in Cape Town, South Africa; son of Chaim Joseph and Lois (Carklin) Lan. EDUCATION: University of Cape Town, B.A., 1970; London School of Economics, B.Sc., 1976, Ph.D., 1983.

VOCATION: Playwright.

CAREER: Also see *WRITINGS* below.

NON-RELATED CAREER—Social anthropologist; research associate, University of Zimbabwe, 1980-82.

WRITINGS: PLAYS—*Painting a Wall,* Almost Free Theatre, London, 1974; *Bird Child,* Theatre Upstairs, London, 1974, published by Pluto Press, 1979; *Homage to Been Soup, Paradise,* both Theatre Upstairs, 1975; *The Winter Dancers,* Theatre Upstairs, 1977, then Mark Taper Forum, Los Angeles, CA, 1978, later Marymount Manhattan Theatre, New York City, 1979; *Not in Norwich,* Royal Court Young People's Theatre Scheme, London, 1977; *Red Earth,* Institute of Contemporary Arts, London, 1978; *Sergeant Ola and His Followers,* Royal Court Theatre, London, 1979, then Soho Repertory Company, New York City, 1987, published by Methuen, 1979; (with Caryl Churchill) *A Mouthful of*

Birds, Joint Stock Theatre Group, London, 1986, published by Methuen, 1986; *Flight,* Royal Shakespeare Company, Memorial Theatre, Stratford-on-Avon, U.K., 1986, published by Methuen, 1987.

TELEPLAYS—"The Sunday Judge," *Global Report,* BBC-2, 1985.

NON-FICTION—*Guns and Rain: Guerrillas and Spirit Mediums in Zimbabwe,* published by James Currey, London, University of California Press, Los Angeles, and Zimbabwe Publishing House, Harare, all 1985.

AWARDS: John Whiting Award, 1977, for *The Winter Dancers;* George Orwell Memorial Award, 1983.

ADDRESSES: AGENT—c/o Margaret Ramsay, Ltd., 14-A Goodwin's Court, St. Martin's Lane, London WC2, England.

*   *   *

LANDEN, Dinsdale   1932-

PERSONAL: Born September 4, 1932, in Margate, England; son of Edward James and Winifred Alice Landen; married Jennifer Daniel. EDUCATION: Trained for the stage at the Florence Moore Theatre Studio.

VOCATION: Actor.

CAREER: STAGE DEBUT—Bimbo, *Housemaster,* Dolphin Theatre, Brighton, U.K., 1948. PRINCIPAL STAGE APPEARANCES—Archie Gooch, *A Dead Secret,* Piccadilly Theatre, London, 1957; John Lester, *A Touch of the Sun,* Saville Theatre, London, 1958; Ben Birt, *My Friend Judas,* Arts Theatre, London, 1959; Launcelot Gobbo, *The Merchant of Venice,* Fabian, *Twelfth Night,* Biondello, *The Taming of the Shrew,* all Royal Shakespeare Company, Memorial Theatre, Stratford-on-Avon, U.K., 1960; title role, *Henry V,* Petruchio, *The Taming of the Shrew,* both Open Air Theatre, London, 1964; Jack, *Honeymoon,* Hampstead Theatre Club, London, 1967; Stanley, *Before You Go,* Hampstead Theatre Club, 1969; Francis, *Play on Love,* St. Martin's Theatre, London, 1970; Donald, *The Philanthropist,* Royal Court Theatre, then May Fair Theatre, both London, 1970; Captain Winkle, *The Owl on the Battlements,* Nottingham Playhouse Theatre, Nottingham, U.K., 1971; Dazzle, *London Assurance,* New Theatre, London, 1972; Michel Cagre, *Suzanna Andler,* Aldwych Theatre, London, 1973; Robert, *The Pleasure Principle,* Theatre Upstairs, London, 1973; John, *Alphabetical Order,* Hampstead Theatre Club, then May Fair Theatre, both 1975; D'Arcy Tuck, *Plunder,* National Theatre Company, Old Vic Theatre, then Lyttelton Theatre, both London, 1976; Mervyn, *Bodies,* Hampstead Theatre Club, 1978, then Ambassadors' Theatre, both London, 1979; Leonard Charteris, *The Philanderer,* National Theatre Company, Lyttelton Theatre, 1978.

MAJOR TOURS—Sir Andrew Aguecheek, *Twelfth Night,* Lieutenant Bannen, *No Man's Land,* Bluntschli, *Arms and the Man,* U.K. cities, all 1968; Edmund Cornhill, *Odd Girl Out,* U.K. cities, 1974; also toured Australia with the Old Vic Theatre Company, 1955.

PRINCIPAL FILM APPEARANCES—*The Valiant,* United Artists, 1962; also appeared in *Every Home Should Have One.*

PRINCIPAL TELEVISION APPEARANCES—Mini-Series: *The Glittering Prizes; Fathers and Families; Devenish; Pig in the Middle.*

MEMBER: Stage Golfing Society.

SIDELIGHTS: FAVORITE ROLES—Petruchio in *Taming of the Shrew;* Iago in *Othello.* RECREATIONS—Swimming, "thinking about boating."

ADDRESSES: AGENT—c/o International Creative Management, 388 Oxford Street, London W1, England.*

*   *   *

LANE, Diane   1963-

PERSONAL: Born January, 1963, in New York, NY.

VOCATION: Actress.

CAREER: FILM DEBUT—*A Little Romance,* Orion, 1979. PRINCIPAL FILM APPEARANCES—*Watcher in the Woods,* Buena Vista, 1980; *Touched By Love,* Columbia, 1980; *Cattle Annie and Little Britches,* Universal, 1981; *Six Pack,* Twentieth Century-Fox, 1982; *The Outsiders,* Warner Brothers, 1983; *Rumble Fish,* Universal, 1983; *The Cotton Club,* Orion, 1984; *Streets of Fire,* Universal, 1984; *Ladies and Gentlemen: The Fabulous Stains,* Films, Inc., 1985; *The Big Town,* Columbia, 1987. Also appeared in *National Lampoon Goes to the Movies,* 1981.

PRINCIPAL STAGE APPEARANCES—Jackie, *Runaways,* New York Shakespeare Festival, Public Theatre, then Plymouth Theatre, both New York City, 1978; Iphigenia, *Agamemnon,* Vivian Beaumont Theatre, New York City, 1977. Also appeared in *The Cherry Orchard,* Vivian Beaumont Theatre, 1977; *Medea, Electra, The Trojan Woman, The Good Woman of Setzuan, As You Like It,* all La Mama Experimental Theatre Club, New York City.

PRINCIPAL TELEVISION APPEARANCES—Movies: Jessie Jacobs, *Child Bride of Short Creek,* NBC, 1981; Sally Butterfield, *Miss All-America Beauty,* CBS, 1982; also appeared in *Summer,* PBS, 1981.

MEMBER: Actors' Equity Association, Screen Actors Guild, American Federation of Television and Radio Artists.

ADDRESSES: AGENT— International Creative Management, 8899 Beverly Boulevard, Los Angeles, CA 90048.*

*   *   *

LANG, Robert   1934-

PERSONAL: Born September 24, 1934, in Bristol, England; son of Richard Lionel and Lily Violet (Ballard) Lang; married Ann Bell (an actress). EDUCATION: Trained for the stage at the Bristol Old Vic Theatre School.

VOCATION: Actor and director.

CAREER: STAGE DEBUT—Doctor, *King Lear,* Bristol Old Vic Theatre, Bristol, U.K., 1956. PRINCIPAL STAGE APPEARANCES—

ROBERT LANG

Uncle Ernest, *Oh! My Papa*, Bristol Old Vic Theatre, Bristol, U.K., then Garrick Theatre, London, both 1957; Tony Lumpkin, *She Stoops to Conquer*, Bristol Old Vic Theatre, 1957; title role, *Platonov*, Nottingham Repertory Theatre, Nottingham, U.K., 1958; Polonius, *No Bed for Bacon*, Bristol Old Vic Theatre, 1959; Charles, *Blithe Spirit*, Archie Rice, *The Entertainer*, title role, *Richard III*, all Nottingham Repertory Theatre, 1959-61; Sergeant-Major Tommy Lodge, *Celebration*, Nottingham Repertory Theatre, then Duchess Theatre, London, both 1961; Theseus, *A Midsummer Night's Dream*, Royal Court Theatre, London, 1962; Louis of France, *Becket*, Royal Shakespeare Company (RSC), Aldwych Theatre, then Arts Theatre, both London, 1962; Petruchio, *The Chances*, Chichester Festival, Chichester, U.K., 1962; title role, *Becket*, Bristol Old Vic Theatre, 1962; Sergeant Lumber, *The Workhouse Donkey*, Chichester Festival, 1963; Cauchon, *Saint Joan*, Chichester Festival, then Edinburgh Festival, Edinburgh, Scotland, U.K., both 1963; John Colombo, *The Beheading*, Apollo Theatre, London, 1972. Also appeared in title role, *Othello*, Canterbury, U.K., 1961; in *The Lower Depths*, RSC, Aldwych Theatre, then Arts Theatre, both 1962; Roderigo, *Othello*, Scandal, *Love for Love*, both Moscow, U.S.S.R., then Berlin, East Germany, 1965; *Masquerade*, Young Vic Theatre, London; and with the Bristol Old Vic Theatre Company, 1956-58, and the Nottingham Repertory Company, 1958-60.

With the National Theatre Company, London: Cauchon, *Saint Joan*, first player, *Hamlet*, Yefim, *Uncle Vanya*, Captain Brazen, *The Recruiting Officer*, all 1963; Anyone, *Andorra*, Odysseus, *Philoctetes*, Roderigo, *Othello*, Martin Ruiz, *The Royal Hunt of the Sun*, Richard Greatham, *Hay Fever*, all 1964; Reverend Hale, *The*

Crucible, Scandal, *Love for Love*, both 1965; Etienne Plucheux, Chandebise, and Poche, *A Flea in Her Ear*, 1966; Kurt, *The Dance of Death*, 1967; Corvino, *Volpone*, Mortimer, *Edward II*, William Cardew, *Home and Beauty*, all 1968; General Havelock, *H*, Mirabell, *The Way of the World*, Franklyn Barnabas, *Back to Methuselah*, Ash, *The National Health*, all 1969; Shylock, *The Merchant of Venice*, 1970.

PRINCIPAL STAGE WORK—Director: *The Covent Garden Tragedy*, National Theatre Company, London, 1968; *Twelfth Night*, Open Air Theatre, London, 1973; *Fears and Miseries of the Third Reich, School for Scandal*, both Cambridge Theatre Company, Cambridge, U.K., 1974; *The Importance of Being Earnest*, Cambridge Theatre Company, 1975. Also directed *Home and Beauty*, Leatherhead, U.K., 1971; *Thark*, Exeter, U.K., 1975.

MAJOR TOURS—Tony Lumpkin, *She Stoops to Conquer*, U.K. cities, 1957; Roderigo, *Othello*, Chandebise, Poche, *A Flea in Her Ear*, Kurt, *The Dance of Death*, Canadian cities, all 1967; Sir Toby Belch, *Twelfth Night*, U.K. cities, 1972.

PRINCIPAL FILM WORK—Director: *Interlude*, Universal, 1957; *A Walk with Love and Death*, Twentieth Century-Fox, 1969; *Night Watch*, AVCO-Embassy, 1973; also directed *The First Great Train Robbery*.

PRINCIPAL TELEVISION WORK—All as director. Series: *1990*. Movies: *An Age of Kings; Mathilda's England; Donkey's Years; The Birthday Party; The Father; Lady Windemere's Fan; Antigone; Vanity Fair; On the Edge of Sand*, all BBC. Specials: *That Was the Week That Was*, BBC.

PRINCIPAL TELEVISION APPEARANCES—Mini-Series: Ambassador Grant, *Harem*, ABC, 1986. Movies: Beck, *And No One Could Save Her*, ABC, 1973; Albany, *King Lear*, Granada; *The Double Dealer*, Granada.

RELATED CAREER—Board of directors, New Shakespeare Company, 1972; artistic director, Cambridge Theatre Company, Cambridge, U.K., 1975-76.

SIDELIGHTS: FAVORITE ROLES—Scandal in *Love for Love;* also Platonov and Richard III. RECREATIONS— Pisciculture, photography.

ADDRESSES: AGENT—Julian Belfrange Associates, 60 St. James's Street, London SW1, England.

*   *   *

LANG, Stephen   1952-

PERSONAL: Born July 11, 1952, in New York, NY; son of Eugene M. (in business) and Theresa (Volmer) Lang; married Kristina Watson (a costume designer and teacher), June 1, 1980; children: Lucy Jane, Daniel. EDUCATION: Swarthmore College, B.A, 1975.

VOCATION: Actor.

CAREER: STAGE DEBUT—Brabantio, *Othello*, Hedgerow Theatre, Rose Valley, PA, 1969, for fifty performances. OFF-BROADWAY DEBUT—Prologue player, *Hamlet*, New York Shakespeare Festival, Delacorte Theatre, 1975. BROADWAY DEBUT—Duinois' page, *Saint Joan*, Circle in the Square, 1977. PRINCIPAL STAGE

APPEARANCES—First *Chronicle* reporter, *Johnny on a Spot,* young shepherd, *A Winter's Tale,* Matvey Gogin, *The Barbarians,* all Brooklyn Academy of Music, Brooklyn, NY, 1980; *Wild Oats, or The Strolling Gentlemen,* Folger Theatre Group, Washington, DC, 1980; *Rip Van Winkle, or The Works,* Yale Repertory Theatre, New Haven, CT, 1981; Vaslav Nijinsky, *The Clownmaker,* Wonderhorse Theatre, New York City, 1982; Ned Poins, Earl of Douglas, *Henry IV, Part I,* American Shakespeare Theatre, Stratford, CT, 1982; interrogator, *Hannah,* Harold Clurman Theatre, New York City, 1983; Happy, *Death of a Salesman,* Broadhurst Theatre, New York City, 1984; Rosencrantz, *Rosencrantz and Guildenstern Are Dead,* Roundabout Theatre, New York City, 1987. Also appeared in *Henry V, Shadow of a Gunman,* and *Ah, Men,* all New York City; performed with the Guthrie Theatre Company, Minneapolis, MN, 1978-80.

FILM DEBUT—Keith, *Twice in a Lifetime,* Yorkin Company, 1985. PRINCIPAL FILM APPEARANCES—Freddy Lounds, *Manhunter,* DEG, 1986; Tiger, *Band of the Hand,* Tri-Star, 1986; Joe Watts, *Project X,* Twentieth Century-Fox, 1987.

TELEVISION DEBUT—Janos, *We're Fighting Back,* CBS, 1980. PRINCIPAL TELEVISION APPEARANCES—Series: Prosecutor, *Crime Story,* NBC, 1986. Movies: Tim, *Stone Pillow,* CBS, 1985; Happy, *Death of a Salesman,* 1985.

AWARDS: Drama Desk Award nomination, 1984, for *Death of a Salesman.*

MEMBER: Actors' Equity Association, Screen Actors Guild; Players Club.

STEPHEN LANG

ADDRESSES: AGENT—c/o David Williams, International Creative Management, 40 W. 57th Street, New York, NY 10036.

*   *   *

LANGE, Hope   1933-

PERSONAL: Full name, Hope Elise Ross Lange; born November 28, 1933, in Redding Ridge, CT; daughter of John (a musician and arranger) and Minnette (an actress; maiden name, Buddecke) Lange; married Don Murray (an actor; divorced); married Alan S. Pakula, 1963 (a producer and director; divorced, 1971); married Charles Hollerith, Jr., 1986. EDUCATION: Attended Barmore Junior College and Reed College.

VOCATION: Actress and dancer.

CAREER: PRINCIPAL TELEVISION APPEARANCES—Episodic: *Kraft Television Playhouse,* NBC. Series: Assistant host, *Back That Fact,* ABC, 1953; dancer, *Jackie Gleason Show,* CBS, 1961; Carolyn Muir, *The Ghost and Mrs. Muir,* NBC, 1968-69, then ABC, 1969-70; Jenny Preston, *The New Dick Van Dyke Show,* CBS, 1971-74. Mini-Series: Deborah Kendrick, *Beulah Land,* MBC, 1980. Movies: Maggie Porter, *Crowhaven Farm,* ABC, 1970; Janet Salter, *That Certain Summer,* ABC, 1972; Karen Walsh, *The 500 Pound Jerk,* CBS, 1973; Elaine Wedell, *Fer de Lance,* CBS, 1974; Karen Chandler, *I Love You . . . Goodbye,* CBS, 1974; Pat Durant, *The Secret Night Caller,* NBC, 1975; Elaine Palmer, *The Love Boat II,* ABC, 1977; Roz Meyers, *Like Normal People,* ABC, 1979; Claudia, *The Day Christ Died,* CBS, 1980; Madelaine Calvert, *Pleasure Palace,* CBS, 1980; Mrs. Coles, *Private Lessons,* NBC, 1985.

PRINCIPAL FILM APPEARANCES—*Bus Stop,* Twentieth Century-Fox, 1956; *The True Story of Jesse James,* Twentieth Century-Fox, 1957; *Peyton Place,* Twentieth Century-Fox, 1957; *The Young Lions,* Twentieth Century-Fox, 1958; *The Best of Everything,* Twentieth Century-Fox, 1959; *A Pocketful of Miracles,* United Artists, 1961; *How the West Was Won,* Metro-Goldwyn-Mayer, 1962; *Love Is a Ball,* United Artists, 1963; *Jigsaw,* Beverly Pictures, 1965; *Death Wish,* Paramount, 1974; *I Am the Cheese,* Almi Films, 1983; *Nightmare on Elm Street 2,* New Line Cinema, 1985. Also appeared in *In Love and War,* 1958; *The Prodigal,* 1984.

BROADWAY DEBUT—*The Patriots,* National Theatre, 1943. PRINCIPAL STAGE APPEARANCES—Doris, *Same Time, Next Year,* Brooks Atkinson Theatre, New York City, 1978-79; Ellen, *The Supporting Cast,* Biltmore Theatre, New York City, 1981; also appeared in *The Hot Corner,* John Golden Theatre, New York City, 1956.

AWARDS: Outstanding Continued Performance by an Actress in a Leading Role in a Comedy Series, Emmy awards, 1968 and 1969, for *The Ghost and Mrs. Muir.*

MEMBER: Actors' Equity Association, Screen Actors Guild, American Federation of Television and Radio Artists.

ADDRESSES: AGENT—McCartt, Oreck, Barrett, 10390 Santa Monica Boulevard, Suite 310, Los Angeles, CA 90025.*

LANGE, John
  See CRICHTON, Michael

*   *   *

LARDNER, Ring, Jr.   1915-
  (Philip Rush)

PERSONAL: Full name, Ringgold Wilmer Lardner, Jr.; born August 19, 1915, in Chicago, IL; son of Ring W., Sr., (a writer and humorist) and Ellis (Abbott) Lardner; married Silvia Schulman, February 19, 1937 (divorced, 1945); married Frances Chaney (an actress), September 28, 1946; children: Peter, Ann, Katharine, Joseph, James. EDUCATION: Graduated from Phillips Andover Academy, 1932; attended Princeton University, 1932-34.

VOCATION: Writer and teacher.

CAREER: Also see *WRITINGS* below.

RELATED CAREER—Reporter, New York *Daily Mirror*, 1935; teacher of screenwriting, New York University Film School, 1984-85; advisor, Sundance Institute, Salt Lake City, UT, 1985—.

WRITINGS: SCREENPLAYS—(With Ian McLellan Hunter and Harvey Gates) *Meet Dr. Christian*, RKO, 1939; (with Hunter) *The Courageous Dr. Christian*, RKO, 1940; (with Michael Kanin) *Woman of the Year*, Metro-Goldwyn-Mayer (MGM), 1942; (with Kanin, Alexander Esway, and Robert Andrews) *The Cross of*

RING LARDNER, JR.

Lorraine, MGM, 1944; (with Leopold Atlas) *Tomorrow the World*, United Artists, 1944; (with Albert Maltz) *Cloak and Dagger*, Warner Brothers, 1946; (with Philip Dunne) *Forever Amber*, Twentieth Century-Fox, 1947; *The Forbidden Street*, Twentieth Century-Fox, 1949; *Four Days Leave*, Film Classics, 1950; (as Philip Rush; with Hunter and Pat Jackson) *Virgin Island*, 1959; (with Terry Southern) *The Cincinnati Kid*, MGM, 1965; *M*A*S*H*, Twentieth Century-Fox, 1970; *The Greatest*, Columbia, 1977.

TELEPLAYS—Series: *Sir Lancelot*, BBC; *The Adventures of Robin Hood*, BBC.

FICTION—*The Ecstasy of Owen Muir*, Cape, London, 1954, Cameron and Kahn, New York, 1954; *All for Love*, Watt, 1985. NON-FICTION—*The Lardners: My Family Remembered* (autobiography), Harper and Row, 1976.

AWARDS: (With Michael Kanin) Best Screenplay, Academy Award, 1942, for *Woman of the Year;* Best Screenplay, Academy Award, 1970, for *M*A*S*H.*

MEMBER: Authors Guild, Writers Guild of America, Academy of Motion Picture Arts and Sciences.

ADDRESSES: AGENT—Jim Preminger Agency, 1650 Westwood Boulevard, Los Angeles, CA 90024.

*   *   *

LAUGHLIN, Tom   1938-
  (Frank Cristina, Teresa Cristina, T.C. Frank, Donald Henderson, Lloyd E. James)

PERSONAL: Born 1938 (some sources say 1931 or 1933), in Minneapolis, MN; married Delores Taylor (an actress). EDUCATION: Attended University of Indiana.

VOCATION: Actor, producer, director, and writer.

CAREER: PRINCIPAL FILM APPEARANCES—*Tea and Sympathy*, Metro-Goldwyn-Mayer, 1956; *South Pacific*, Twentieth Century-Fox, 1958; *Gidget*, Columbia, 1959; Billy Jack, *Born Losers*, American International, 1967; title role, *Billy Jack*, Warner Brothers, 1971; title role, *The Trial of Billy Jack*, Taylor-Laughlin, 1974; *The Master Gunfighter*, Taylor-Laughlin, 1975; title role, *Billy Jack Goes to Washington*, Taylor-Laughlin, 1977; title role, *The Return of Billy Jack*, upcoming.

PRINCIPAL FILM WORK—Also see *WRITINGS* below. Director (as T.C. Frank), *Billy Jack*, Warner Brothers, 1971; producer and director, *The Trial of Billy Jack*, Taylor-Laughlin, 1974; producer and director, *Billy Jack Goes to Washington*, Taylor-Laughlin, 1977; also technical work as Donald Henderson and Lloyd E. James.

RELATED CAREER—Founder, Billy Jack Enterprises (production company).

NON-RELATED CAREER—Teacher and administrator, Montessori School, Santa Monica, CA.

WRITINGS: SCREENPLAYS—(As Frank and Teresa Cristina) *Billy Jack*, Warner Brothers, 1971; *The Trial of Billy Jack*, Taylor-

Laughlin, 1974; *Billy Jack Goes to Washington,* Taylor-Laughlin, 1977.

FICTION—*Billy Jack,* Avon, 1973.

ADDRESSES: OFFICE—753 N. Kings Road, Los Angeles, CA 90069.*

*   *   *

LAUTER, Ed   1940-

PERSONAL: Born October 30, 1940, in Long Beach, NY.

VOCATION: Actor.

CAREER: PRINCIPAL TELEVISION APPEARANCES—Movies: Dave McKay, *Class of '63,* ABC, 1973; Crees, *The Godchild,* ABC, 1974; Mr. Barlow, *The Migrants,* CBS, 1974; Bud Delaney, *Last Hours Before Morning,* NBC, 1975; Strickland, *Satan's Triangle,* ABC, 1975; Bender, *The Clone Master,* NBC, 1978; Rawley Porter, *Undercover with the KKK,* NBC, 1979; Sgt. Weed, *Love's Savage Fury,* ABC, 1979; Jerry Beloit, *The Jericho Mile,* ABC, 1979; Jim Jones, Sr., *Guyana Tragedy: The Story of Jim Jones,* CBS, 1980; Frank Morris, *Alcatraz: The Whole Shocking Story,* NBC, 1980; Gus Carpenter, *The Boy Who Drank Too Much,* CBS, 1980; Jack Claggert, *Rooster,* ABC, 1982; Judge Halloran, *In the Custody of Stranger,* ABC, 1982; Lydon Dean, *The Cartier Affair,* NBC, 1984; Carl, *The Seduction of Gina,* CBS, 1984; Mr. Grier, *The Three Wishes of Billy Grier,* ABC, 1984; Coach Gruniger, *The Thanksgiving Promise,* ABC, 1986; Jerry Tyler, *Yuri Nosenko, KGB,* HBO, 1986; B.C. Thompson, *Firefighter,* CBS, 1986; Sheriff LeRoy, *The Defiant Ones,* ABC, 1986; Lt. Col. Paul S. Hill, *The Last Days of Patton,* CBS, 1986.

PRINCIPAL FILM APPEARANCES—*The Last American Hero,* Twentieth Century-Fox, 1973; *Executive Action,* National General, 1973; *Lolly Madonna, XXX,* Metro-Goldwyn-Mayer, 1973; *The Longest Yard,* Paramount, 1974; *The French Connection II,* Twentieth Century-Fox, 1975; *Family Plot,* Universal, 1976; *King Kong,* Paramount, 1976; *Magic,* Twentieth Century-Fox, 1978; *Death Hunt,* Twentieth Century-Fox, 1981; *Cujo,* Warner Brothers, 1983; *Lassiter,* Warner Brothers, 1984; *Finders Keepers,* Warner Brothers, 1984; *Raw Deal,* De Laurentiis Entertainment, 1985; *Real Genius,* Tri-Star, 1985; *Death Wish III,* Cannon, 1985; *Youngblood,* Metro-Goldwyn-Mayer/United Artists, 1986; Skip, *Chief Zabu,* Howard Zucker Productions, upcoming. Also appeared in *Breakheart Pass,* 1976; *Timerider,* 1983.

MEMBER: Screen Actors Guild, American Federation of Television and Radio Artists.

ADDRESSES: AGENT—Camden Artists, 409 N. Camden Drive, Suite 200, Beverly Hills, CA 90210.*

*   *   *

LAWRENCE, Jerome   1915-

PERSONAL: Born Jerome Lawrence Schwartz, July 14, 1915, in Cleveland, Ohio; son of Samuel (a printer) and Sarah (a poet;

JEROME LAWRENCE

maiden name, Rogen) Schwartz. EDUCATION: Ohio State University, B.A., 1937; University of California, Los Angeles, graduate work, 1939-40. MILITARY: U.S. Army.

VOCATION: Playwright and director.

CAREER: Also see *WRITINGS* below. PRINCIPAL STAGE WORK—Director: *The Incomparable Max,* Barter Theatre, Abingdon, VA, 1969; *Mame,* Sacramento Music Circus, Sacramento, CA, 1969; (with Marty Bronson) *The Crocodile Smile,* State Theatre of North Carolina, Flat Rock, NC, 1970; *The Night Thoreau Spent in Jail,* Dublin Theatre Festival, Olympia Theatre, Dublin, Ireland, 1972; *Jabberwock,* Dallas Theatre Center, Dallas, TX, 1973; *Inherit the Wind,* Dallas Theatre Center, 1975; also directed summer theatre productions of *Androcles and the Lion, You Can't Take It with You, Anything Goes, H.M.S. Pinafore, The Pirates of Penzance, Room Service, Boy Meets Girl,* and *Green Pastures.*

RELATED CAREER—Reporter and telegraph editor, *Wilmington News Journal,* Wilmington, OH, 1937; editor, *New Lexington Daily News,* New Lexington, OH, 1937; continuity editor, KMPC (radio), Beverly Hills, CA, 1937-39; senior staff writer, Columbia Broadcasting System, New York City and Los Angeles, CA, 1939-41; professor, Banff School of the Arts, Banff, AB, Canada, 1952-53; president, Lawrence & Lee, Inc., New York City and Los Angeles, CA, 1955—; drama panel, U.S. State Department Cultural Exchange Program, 1963-71; master playwright, New York University, 1966-68; national vice-president, American National Theatre and Academy, 1968-69; visiting professor, Ohio State University, 1969; founder and trustee, American Playwrights

Theatre, Columbus, OH, also president, 1970-72; lecturer, American College Theatre Festival, 1970, 1971, and 1974; professor, Salzburg Seminar in American Studies, Salzburg, Austria, 1972; professor, Baylor University, Waco, TX, 1978; host (with Robert E. Lee) Chinese-American Writers Conference, University of California, Los Angeles, Los Angeles, CA, 1982; chairor, Filmex International's "Salute to Screenwriters," 1982; professor, University of Southern California, Los Angeles, CA, 1984; founder (with Lee), Armed Forces Radio Service; founder and judge (with Lee), Margo Jones Award; national advisory board member, William Inge Collection, Independence Community College, Independence, KS; chairor, National Repertory Theatre's annual playwriting award; advisory board member, Institute of Outdoor Drama, University of North Carolina; advisory board member, Performing Arts Theatre of the Handicapped; contributing editor, *Dramatics* (magazine); advisory council member, California Educational Theatre Association; advisory board member, Ohio State University School of Journalism; alumni advisor for academic affairs, Ohio State University. Member of the board of directors: National Repertory Theatre, American Conservatory Theatre, Eugene O'Neill Memorial Foundation, Board of Planning and Standards of the Living Theatre, U.S.D.A.N. Center for the Creative and Performing Arts, East-West Players, American National Theatre and Academy, Roy Harris Society, John F. Kennedy Memorial Library, California State University, alumni association of Ohio State University. Guest lecturer: University of California, Los Angeles, Yale University, Tufts University, Villanova University, University of Southern California, California State University, Boston University, Kent State University, Ohio State University, Southern Methodist University, Midwestern State University, American University, Squaw Valley Community of Writers, Eugene O'Neill Memorial Foundation, American Conservatory Theatre, Pasadena Playhouse, American Film Institute, and Gorki Writers School in Leningrad; also lectured in Japan, Thailand, Turkey, Greece, Romania, Poland, France, Spain, and England.

WRITINGS: PLAYS—All with Robert E. Lee, unless indicated: (book) *Look, Ma, I'm Dancin'!*, Adelphi Theatre, New York City, 1948; *The Laugh Maker*, Players Ring, Hollywood, CA, 1952, rewritten and restaged as *Turn on the Night*, Playhouse-in-the-Park, Philadelphia, PA, 1961, again rewritten and restaged as *The Crocodile Smile*, State Theatre of North Carolina, Flat Rock, NC, 1970; *Inherit the Wind*, Margo Jones's Dallas Theatre '5, Dallas, TX, then National Theatre, New York City, both 1955, published by Random House, 1955; (book and lyrics; also with James Hilton) *Shangri-La*, Winter Garden Theatre, New York City, 1956; *Auntie Mame*, Broadhurst Theatre, New York City, 1956, published by Vanguard Press, 1957; *The Gang's All Here*, Ambassador Theatre, New York City, 1959, published by World Publishing, 1960; *Only in America*, Cort Theatre, New York City, 1959, published by Samuel French, Inc., 1960; *A Call on Kuprin* (also known as *Checkmate*), Broadhurst Theatre, 1961, published by Samuel French, Inc., 1961; *Diamond Orchid*, Henry Miller's Theatre, New York City, 1965, rewritten and restaged as *Sparks Fly Upward*, McFarlin Auditorium, Dallas, TX, 1967, published by Dramatists Play Service, 1969; (sole author) *Live Spelled Backwards*, Beverly Hills Playhouse, Beverly Hills, CA, 1966, published by Dramatists Play Service, 1970; (book) *Mame*, Winter Garden Theatre, 1966, published by Random House, 1967; (book) *Dear World*, Mark Hellinger Theatre, New York City, 1969; *The Incomparable Max*, Royale Theatre, New York City, 1971, published by Hill & Wang, 1972; *The Night Thoreau Spent in Jail*, American Playwrights Theatre, Columbus, OH, 1971, published by Hill & Wang, 1970; *Jabberwock*, Dallas Theatre Center, Dallas, TX, 1973, published by Samuel French, Inc., 1974; *First Monday in October*, Majestic Theatre,

New York City, 1978, published by Samuel French, Inc., 1979. With Lee, unless indicated, also wrote: (Sole author) *Laugh, God!*, published in *Six Anti-Nazi One Act Plays*, Contemporary Play Publications, 1939; (with Budd Schulberg) *Tomorrow*, published in *Free World Theatre*, Random House, 1944; *Annie Laurie*, 1954; *Roaring Camp*, 1955; *The Familiar Stranger*, 1956; *Inside a Kid's Head; Top of the Mark; Paris, France; Eclipse; Some Say in Ice;* (book and lyrics) *Dilly; Houseboat in Kashmir; Short and Sweet; The Angels Weep;* (book and lyrics) *Actor;* (book and lyrics) *Barbara;* (also with Norman Cousins) *Whisper in the Mind*, and sole author of *Black Sunset, Make Believe*, and *Between Light and Darkness*.

TELEPLAYS—All with Robert E. Lee. Series: *Favorite Story*, syndicated, 1952-54; *The Unexpected* (also known as *Times Square Playhouse*) 1951. Specials: "Shangri-La," *Hallmark Hall of Fame*, NBC, 1960; "Inherit the Wind," *Hallmark Hall of Fame*, NBC, 1965; "The Unwilling Warrior," *Sandburg's Lincoln*, NBC, 1975; *Now Is the Time*, HBO, 1987; also wrote *West Point, Song of Norway*, and *Actor*.

SCREENPLAYS—(With Robert E. Lee) *First Monday in October*, Paramount, 1981.

RADIO SCRIPTS—Series: *Junior Theatre of the Air*, 1938; *Sunday Morning Maniacs*, 1938; *Let's Have a Party*, 1938-39; *Musical Portraits*, 1938-39; *Through the Years*, 1939; *I Was There*, 1939; *Under Western Skies*, 1939; *Nightcap Yarns* (also known as *One Man Theatre* and *Armchair Adventures*), 1939-40; *Stories from Life*, 1939-40; *Man about Hollywood*, 1940; *Hollywood Showcase*, 1940-41; (with Aleen Leslie) *A Date with Judy*, 1941-42; (with Robert E. Lee) *Columbia Workshop*, 1941-42; (with Howard Teichmann) *They Live Forever*, 1942; *Everything for the Boys*, 1944; (with Lee) *Screen Guild Theatre*, 1946; (with Lee) *Favorite Story*, 1946-49; (with Lee) *Frank Sinatra Show*, 1947; (with Lee) *Dinah Shore Program*, 1948; (with Lee) *Railroad Hour*, 1948-54; (with Lee) *Young Love*, 1949-50; (with Lee) *Halls of Ivy*, 1950-51; (with Lee) *Hallmark Playhouse*, 1950-51; (with Lee) *Charles Boyer Show*, 1951; also with Lee wrote numerous scripts for Armed Forces Radio Service programs. Specials: *To You, My Son*, 1934; (with Lee) *The Journey of Trygve Jones*, 1949; (with Lee) *The Birthday Story*, 1950.

Also sole author of the books *Oscar the Ostrich* (juvenile), Random House, 1940; *Off Mike* (non-fiction), Duell, Sloan & Pearce, 1944; *Actor: The Life and Times of Paul Muni* (biography), G.P. Putnam's Sons, 1974; and author with Robert E. Lee of numerous articles published in periodicals and anthologies.

RECORDINGS: ALBUMS—All written and directed with Robert E. Lee. *Rip Van Winkle*, Decca; *The Cask of Amontillado*, Decca; *A Tale of Two Cities*, Decca; *One God*, Kapp.

AWARDS: All with Robert E. Lee, unless indicated. New York Press Club Award, 1942; special citation from the Secretary of War, 1945; City College of New York award, 1948; *Radio-TV Life* awards, 1948, 1952; George Foster Peabody awards, 1949, 1952; *Radio-TV Mirror* awards, 1952-53; *Variety* Showmanship Award, 1954; Most Promising New Playwrights, *Variety* New York Drama Critics Poll award, and Best Play, Outer Circle Critics Award and Donaldson Award, all 1955, for *Inherit the Wind;* Bluebonnet Award from the Dallas *Times-Herald*, 1955; Ohioana Award, 1955; Ohio Press Club award, 1960; Playwrights of the Year, Baldwin-Wallace College Living Playwrights Festival, 1960; Best Foreign Play of the Year, London Critics Poll award, and Best

Foreign Play, British Drama Critics award, both 1960, for *Inherit the Wind;* Ben Franklin Award from the Poor Richard Club, 1966; Best Musical, Antoinette Perry Award nomination, 1966, for *Mame;* Moss Hart Memorial Award, 1967; (sole receipient) selected Man of the Year, Zeta Beta Tau fraternity, 1967; U.S. State Department medal, 1969; Pegasus Award from Ohioana Library, 1970; Centennial Award, Ohio State University, 1970; Ohio Governor's Award, 1973; Bar Association Award of Greater Cleveland, 1975; Lifetime Award, American Theatre Association, 1979, for "distinguished service to the theatre;" Directors' Award, National Thespian Association, 1980; Pacific Pioneer Broadcasting Award, 1981; Ohioana Library Career Medal, 1982; (sole receipient) Master of Arts Award, Rocky Mountain Writers Guild, 1982; (sole receipient) William Inge Award, 1983. Honorary degrees: Doctor of Humane Letters, Ohio State University, 1963; Doctor of Literature, Fairleigh Dickinson University, 1968; Doctor of Fine Arts, Villanova University, 1969; Doctor of Letters, College of Wooster, 1983.

MEMBER: Radio Writers Guild (founder, national president, 1954-55), Dramatists Guild (council member, 1969—), Authors League of America (council member, 1972—), Writers Guild of America-West (founder, trustee), American Society of Composers, Authors, and Publishers (ASCAP), American Guild of Authors and Composers, Academy of Motion Picture Arts and Sciences, National Academy of Television Arts and Sciences; Phi Beta Kappa, Sigma Delta Chi, Zeta Beta Tau; Players Club.

SIDELIGHTS: From materials supplied by Jerome Lawrence, *CTFT* learned that the Lawrence and Lee Theatre Research Institute, located on the campus of Ohio State University in Columbus, OH, is one of the major theatrical research centers in the world. Among its extensive collection covering the theatre history of the Western world from the Medieval period to the modern day are play texts, critical works, promptbooks, posters, playbills, original costume and scene designs, and biographies of actors, writers, producers, and directors.

ADDRESSES: OFFICE—21056 Las Flores Mesa Drive, Malibu, CA 90265.

*   *   *

LAYTON, Joe   1931-

PERSONAL: Born Joseph Lichtman, May 3, 1931, in Brooklyn, NY; son of Irving J. and Sally (Fischer) Lichtman; married Evelyn Russell (an actress), October 6, 1959; children: Jeb James. EDUCATION: Graduated from the School of Music and Art, 1948; studied ballet and Spanish dance with Joseph Levinoff, 1943-48. MILITARY: U.S. Army, 1952-54.

VOCATION: Choreographer and director.

CAREER: STAGE DEBUT—First performed in children's shows, Brooklyn, NY, 1937-41. BROADWAY DEBUT—Dancer, *Oklahoma!,* St. James Theatre, 1947. PRINCIPAL STAGE APPEARANCES—Dancer, *Gentlemen Prefer Blondes,* Ziegfeld Theatre, New York City, 1949; dancer, *Wonderful Town,* Winter Garden Theatre, New York City, 1953.

PRINCIPAL STAGE WORK—Assistant choreographer, *Kaleidoscope,* Provincetown Playhouse, New York City, 1957; choreogra-

pher, *The Princess and the Pea,* Tamiment Playhouse, Camp Tamiment, PA, 1958; choreographer, *On the Town,* Carnegie Hall Playhouse, New York City, 1959; choreographer, *Once upon a Mattress,* Phoenix Theatre, New York City, 1959, then Adelphi Theatre, London, 1960; choreographer, *The Sound of Music,* Lunt-Fontanne Theatre, New York City, 1959, then Palace Theatre, London, 1961; choreographer, *Greenwillow,* Alvin Theatre, New York City, 1960; choreographer and director, *South Pacific,* Arena Theatre, Toronto, ON, Canada, 1960; choreographer, *Tenderloin,* 46th Street Theatre, New York City, 1960; choreographer, *Sail Away,* Broadhurst Theatre, New York City, 1961, then Savoy Theatre, London, 1962; choreographer and director, *No Strings,* 54th Street Theatre, New York City, 1962; choreographer and director, *On the Town,* Prince of Wales Theatre, London, 1963; director, *The Girl Who Came to Supper,* Broadway Theatre, New York City, 1963; choreographer and director, *South Pacific,* O'Keefe Center, Toronto, ON, Canada, 1964; director, *Peterpat,* Longacre Theatre, New York City, 1965; choreographer and director, *Drat! The Cat!,* Martin Beck Theatre, New York City, 1965; choreographer and director, *Sherry,* Colonial Theatre, Boston, MA, then Alvin Theatre, 1967; director, *South Pacific,* State Theatre, New York City, 1967; choreographer and director, *George M!,* Palace Theatre, New York City, 1967; choreographer and director, *Dear World,* Mark Hellinger Theatre, New York City, 1969.

Director, *Scarlet,* Drury Lane Theatre, London, 1970; director, *Two by Two,* Imperial Theatre, New York City, 1970; choreographer, *Double Exposure,* Joffrey Ballet, State Theatre, New York City, 1972; choreographer, *The Grand Tour* (ballet), Royal Ballet, London, 1972; choreographer and director, *Platinum,* Mark Hellinger Theatre, 1978; director, *Barnum,* St. James Theatre, New York City, 1980; director, *Bring Back Birdie,* Martin Beck Theatre, 1981; choreographer and director, *Rock 'n' Roll! The First 5000 Years,* St. James Theatre, 1982; choreographer and director, *Woman of the Year,* Palace Theatre, New York City, 1980; director, *Harrigan 'n' Hart,* Longacre Theatre, New York City, 1985. Also director: *The Lost Colony,* Roanoke Island, NC, 1964; *Carol Channing and Her Ten Stout Hearted Men,* London, 1970; *Scarlet,* Tokyo, Japan, 1970; *Lorelei,* New York City, 1973; (also choreographer) *Bette Midler's "Clams on the Half Shell" Revue,* 1975. While serving in the U.S. Army choreographed and directed productions of *On the Town, Brigadoon, The Medium,* and *The Telephone,* and directed *The Moon Is Blue.*

MAJOR TOURS—Dancer, *High Button Shoes,* U.S. cities, 1949; dancer, *Miss Liberty,* U.S. cities, 1950; choreographer, *Once upon a Mattress,* U.S. cities, 1960; choreographer, *The Sound of Music,* U.S. cities, 1961 and 1962; *Gone with the Wind,* U.S. cities, 1973. Also directed world tours of Raquel Welch, Diana Ross, and the Carpenters, all 1976.

PRINCIPAL CABARET APPEARANCES—Dancer, Latin Quarter, New York City, 1950; singer, One Fifth Avenue, New York City, 1959. PRINCIPAL CABARET WORK—Director of Las Vegas nightclub acts for Connie Stevens, Diahann Carroll, and Dyan Cannon.

PRINCIPAL TELEVISION APPEARANCES—Dancer, *Cinderella,* CBS, 1956. PRINCIPAL TELEVISION WORK—Specials: Choreographer, *Mary Martin's Easter Show,* NBC, 1959; choreographer and director, *The Gershwin Years,* CBS, 1960; choreographer and director, *Once upon a Mattress,* CBS, 1964; choreographer and director, *My Name Is Barbra,* CBS, 1965; choreographer and director, *Color Me Barbra,* CBS, 1966; producer, *Jack Jones on the Move,* ABC, 1966; director, *On the Flip Side,* ABC, 1966; choreographer and director, *The Belle of 14th Street—Barbra*

Streisand, CBS, 1967; director, *Theater of the Deaf,* NBC, 1967; also directed, *Androcles and the Lion, Debbie Reynolds Special, Infancy,* all 1968; *The Littlest Angel,* 1969; *Raquel Welch: Las Vegas; Barbra Streisand and Other Musicial Instruments,* both 1974; *World Tour—The Carpenters; A Special Olivia Newton-John,* both 1976. Also director of specials for Cher, Melissa Manchester, Dolly Parton, and Carol Burnett.

PRINCIPAL FILM WORK—Choreographer, *Thoroughly Modern Millie,* Universal, 1967; choreographer, *Harry and Walter Go to New York,* Columbia, 1976; director, *Richard Pryor Live on the Sunset Strip,* Columbia, 1982; executive producer, *Annie,* Columbia, 1982.

RELATED CAREER—Dancer and choreographer, Ballet Ho de George Reich, Paris and Cannes, France, 1954-55; choreographer, Fashion Industrial Show, American Exhibition, Moscow, U.S.S.R., 1959.

WRITINGS: PLAYS—(Revisor) *The Lost Colony,* Roanoke Island, NC, 1964; *Bring Back Birdie,* Martin Beck Theatre, New York City, 1981. TELEPLAYS—Specials: *Color Me Barbra,* CBS, 1966; *The Belle of 14th Street—Barbra Streisand,* CBS, 1967.

AWARDS: Best Choreography, Antoinette Perry Award nomination, 1960, for *Greenwillow;* Best Choreography, Antoinette Perry Award, 1962, for *No Strings;* Best Choreography, Best Director, both Emmy Awards, 1965, for *My Name Is Barbra;* Best Choreography, Antoinette Perry Award, 1969, for *George M.!.*

MEMBER: Actors' Equity Association, American Federation of Television and Radio Artists, Society of Stage Directors and Choreographers.

SIDELIGHTS: RECREATIONS—Painting.

ADDRESSES: AGENT—c/o Roy Gerber Associates, 9200 Sunset Boulevard, Los Angeles, CA 90069.*

*   *   *

LEACH, Robin   1941-

PERSONAL: Born August 29, 1941, in Perivale, England; son of Douglas Thomas (a sales executive) and Violet Victoria (Phillips) Leach. EDUCATION: Trained as a journalist at the National Union of Journalists.

VOCATION: Producer, television host, and writer.

CAREER: TELEVISION DEBUT—Interviewer, Cable News Network, 1980. PRINCIPAL TELEVISION APPEARANCES— Correspondent, *Entertainment Tonight,* syndicated, 1980-83; host, *Lifestyles of the Rich and Famous,* syndicated, 1983—; host, *Runaway with the Rich and Famous,* syndicated, 1985—; host, *Fame Fortune and Romance,* ABC, 1986—.

PRINCIPAL TELEVISION WORK—All as executive producer; see production details above unless indicated. Series: *Lifestyles of the Rich and Famous; Runaway with the Rich and Famous; The Start of Something Big,* syndicated, 1984-86; *Fame Fortune and Romance.* Specials: *The Rich and Famous World's Best,* syndicated, 1987; also *Salute to the Superstars,* syndicated.

ROBIN LEACH

RELATED CAREER—Writer, show business journalist; executive producer, Leach Entertainment Features.

WRITINGS: NON-FICTION—*Lifestyles of the Rich and Famous,* Doubleday, 1986; also *Pyramid Books,* 1968; *The Year in Music,* 1969.

AWARDS: Best Informational Special, Emmy Award nomination, 1984, for *Lifestyles of the Rich and Famous.*

MEMBER: Screen Actors Guild, American Federation of Television and Radio Artists.

ADDRESSES: OFFICE—Telerep, 875 Third Avenue, New York, NY 10022. AGENT—William Morris Agency, 1350 Sixth Avenue, New York, NY 10019.

*   *   *

LEE, Eugene   1939-

PERSONAL: Born March 9, 1939; son of Eugene and Betty Lee; married Franne Newman (a designer). EDUCATION: Attended Carnegie Mellon University and Yale University.

VOCATION: Set, costume, and lighting designer.

CAREER: PRINCIPAL STAGE WORK—Set designer, *A Dream of*

Love, costume designer, *Belch,* both Theater of the Living Arts, Philadelphia, PA, 1966; set and lighting designer, *The Threepenny Opera, The Imaginary Invalid, H.M.S. Pinafore,* all Studio Arena Theatre, Buffalo, NY, 1967; set and lighting designer, *Enrico IV,* lighting designer, *A Delicate Balance,* both Studio Arena Theatre, 1968; set designer, *World War 2 1/2,* Martinique Theatre, New York City, 1969; production designer, *Slave Ship,* Brooklyn Academy of Music, Brooklyn, NY, 1969, then Theatre-in-the-Church, New York City, 1970; set designer, *The Recruiting Officer, Harry Noon and Night,* both Theatre of the Living Arts, 1969; set designer, *A Line of Least Existence,* Theatre of the Living Arts, 1970; set designer, *Wilson in the Promise Land,* American National Theatre Academy (ANTA) Playhouse, New York City, 1970; co-designer (with Franne Lee), *Alice in Wonderland,* Extension Theatre, New York City, 1970; co-designer (with Franne Lee), *Saved,* Brooklyn Academy of Music, then Cherry Lane Theatre, New York City, both 1970; co-designer (with Franne Lee), *Mother Courage,* Arena Stage, Washington, DC, 1970; set designer, *Son of Man and the Family,* set and lighting designer, *The Taming of the Shrew,* both Rhode Island School of Design Theatre, Providence, RI, 1970; lighting designer, *Love for Love,* set and lighting designer, *The Threepenny Opera,* both Rhode Island School of Design Theatre, 1971; co-designer (with Franne Lee and Roger Morgan), *Dude,* Broadway Theatre, New York City, 1972; co-designer (with Franne Lee), *Candide,* Brooklyn Academy of Music, 1973, then Broadway Theatre, 1974; set designer, *Gabrielle,* Studio Arena Theatre, 1974; set designer, *The Skin of Our Teeth,* Kennedy Center for the Performing Arts, Washington, DC, then Mark Hellinger Theatre, New York City, both 1975.

All as set designer unless indicated: *It's Me, Sylvia!,* Playhouse Theatre II, New York City, 1981; *Agnes of God,* Music Box Theatre, New York City, 1982; *Some Men Need Help,* 47th Street Theatre, New York City, 1982; *The Ballad of Soapy Smith,* New York Shakespeare Festival (NYSF), Public Theater, New York City, 1984; *The Normal Heart,* NYSF, Public Theater, 1985; *Misalliance, Amadeus, A Christmas Carol, Passion Play, The Three Sisters, You Can't Take It with You, Good,* all Dallas Theater Center, Dallas, TX, 1984-85; *The Skin of Our Teeth, A Christmas Carol, The Marriage of Bette and Boo, The Glass Menagerie, The Tavern, The Ups and Downs of Theophilus Maitland, A Folk Tale, Kith and Kin,* all Dallas Theater Center, 1985-86. Also *Some of My Best Friends,* 1977; *Gilda Radner Live from New York,* New York City, 1979; and *The Girl of the Golden West* (opera).

All with the Trinity Square Repertory Company, Trinity Square Theatre, Providence, RI. Set designer unless indicated: *The Threepenny Opera, The Importance of Being Earnest,* both 1967; *Year of the Locust, An Enemy of the People, Phaedra,* all 1968; *Macbeth, The Homecoming, Billy Budd, Old Glory, House of Breathe, Black/White, Wilson in the Promise Land,* all 1969; *The Skin of Our Teeth, Lovecraft's Follies,* (also lighting designer) *You Can't Take It with You,* all 1970; *Troilus and Cressida, Down by the River where Water Lilies Are Disfigured Every Day,* (also lighting designer) *The Good and Bad Times of Cady Francis McCullum and Friends,* all 1971; *Old Times,* 1972; *The Royal Hunt of the Sun, Feasting with Panthers, Brother to Dragons, Ghost Dance,* scenery and environment designer, *Aimee,* all 1973; *Well Hung,* scenery and environment designer, *A Man for All Seasons,* both 1974; (also lighting designer) *Peer Gynt, Tom Jones, Seven Keys to Baldpate,* all 1975; *El Grande de Coca-Cola, An Almost Perfect Person, Deathtrap, Arsenic and Old Lace, Betrayal, On Golden Pond, A Christmas Carol, The Iceman Cometh, Inherit the Wind, How I Got That Story, Whose Life Is It, Anyway?, The Whales of August,* all 1980-81; (also lighting designer) *Tintypes, The Crucifer of Blood,*

13 Rue de L'Amour, The Dresser, Translations, A Christmas Carol, The Front Page, The Tempest, Pygmalion, The Web, Letters from Prison, all 1982-83; *Beyond Therapy, What the Butler Saw, Terra Nova, Passion Play, Tartuffe, A Christmas Carol, Misalliance, And a Nightingale Sang, The Country Wife, Master Harold . . . and the boys, Present Laughter,* all 1984-85; *The Marriage of Bette and Boo, Cat on a Hot Tin Roof, The Beauty Part, A Christmas Carol, The Crucible, The Tavern, Life and Limb, Pasta, The Country Girl, Baby, Not by Bed Alone,* all 1985-86.

MAJOR TOURS—Set designer, *Sweeney Todd,* U.S. cities, 1980, then U.S. and Canadian cities, 1982.

PRINCIPAL FILM WORK—Set designer: *One Trick Pony,* Warner Brothers, 1980; *Easy Money,* Orion, 1982; also (with Franne Lee) *Mr. Mike's Mondo Video,* 1979; *Hammett,* 1982.

PRINCIPAL TELEVISION WORK—Series: Set designer, *Saturday Night Live,* NBC.

RELATED CAREER—Designer, Trinity Square Repertory Company, Providence, RI, 1968—.

AWARDS: All with Franne Lee. Most Promising New Designer, Drama Desk Award, 1970-71, for *Alice in Wonderland;* Best Set Design, Antoinette Perry Award, Drama Desk Award, Maharam Foundation Award, all 1973-74, for *Candide.*

ADDRESSES: OFFICE—31 Union Square W., New York, NY 10003.*

*   *   *

LEE, Fran   1910-

PERSONAL: Born Frances Laderman, September 28, 1910, in New York, NY; daughter of Max (a garment worker) and Anna (a seamstress; maiden name, Siegelbaum) Laderman; married Samuel Weiss (an attorney), November 27, 1929; children: Barry L. and Gene Lee. EDUCATION: Attended New York Teachers Training. POLITICS: Liberal.

VOCATION: Actress, consumer advocate, and journalist.

CAREER: PRINCIPAL TELEVISION APPEARANCES—Episodic: Fourth century woman, "Teias the King," *Actors Studio,* ABC; countess, *Car 54, Where Are You?,* NBC; secretary, *The Defenders,* CBS; supervisor, *The Nurses,* CBS; also appeared on *Studio One,* CBS; *Lux Video Theatre,* CBS; *Treasury Men in Action,* ABC; *Lights Out,* NBC; *The Play's the Thing,* CBS; *Buck Rogers,* ABC; *Big Town,* NBC; *The Clock,* ABC; *We the People,* NBC; *Edge of Night; Guiding Light; Secret Storm.* Series: Chinese godmother, *Major Dell Conway of the Flying Tigers,* DuMont, 1951; appeared regularly as "Mrs. Fixit" and "Tidy Dee Lady," *Don Ameche/Frances Langford Show,* ABC, 1951; consumer reporter, *Great American Homemaker,* USA, 1984; *Good Morning, New York,* WABC, New York City; also on her own consumer affairs show, WPIX, New York City. Specials: *Granny Franny's Winter of Happiness,* KYW, 1982. Guest: *People Are Talking,* WPIX, 1979; *A.M. Indiana,* 1979; *Midday,* WNEW, New York; *Maury Povich,* KYW QUBE; *Tonight Show,* NBC; *Steve Allen Show,* CBS; *Tomorrow Show,* NBC; *Joe Franklin Show,* WOR, New York; *Mike Douglas Show; Missing Links; Betty Furness*

FRAN LEE

Show; Virginia Graham Show; Sonny Fox Show; David Susskind Show; David Frost Show; Stanley Siegel Show; Regis Philbin Show; Sally Jessy Raphael.

BROADWAY DEBUT—*Medea,* Royale Theatre, 1947. PRINCIPAL STAGE APPEARANCES—Mama Lucasta, *Anna Lucasta,* Old Towne Theatre, Smithtown, NY, 1950; landlady of the house, old lady of the levee, *Show Boat,* Rye Music Theatre, Rye, NY, 1958; Martha, *Simon's Wife,* Blackfriar's Guild Theatre, New York City, 1958. Also appeared in *A Season in Hell,* Cherry Lane Theatre, New York City, 1950; peasant woman, *Embezzled Heaven;* mother, *The Drunkard;* and in *Across the Blue.*

FILM DEBUT—*Miracle on 34th Street,* Twentieth Century-Fox, 1947. PRINCIPAL FILM APPEARANCES—*Splendor in the Grass,* Warner Brothers, 1961; *Funny Girl,* Columbia, 1968; *Madigan,* Universal, 1968; *The Producers,* Embassy, 1968. Also appeared in *Kiss of Death,* 1947; *A Face in the Crowd,* 1957; *Something Wild,* 1961; and cameo roles in over five hundred movies.

RELATED CAREER—Consumer advocate, 1939—; consumer affairs editor, WNEW-TV, New York City, 1969; founder, Children Before Dogs (a consumer education organization).

WRITINGS: NON-FICTION—*Fran Lee's Intimate Fix-It Book,* Hawthorne.

AWARDS: New York Television Academy Board of Governors Award nomination, 1986; Special Merit Award, New York Consumer Assembly, 1986; New York County Medical Society Award for Service to Public Health.

MEMBER: Screen Actors Guild, Actors' Equity Association, American Federation of Television and Radio Artists; American Society of Topical Medicine and Hygiene; Hadassah.

ADDRESSES: OFFICE—Children Before Dogs, 565 West End Avenue, New York, NY 10024.

*   *   *

LEE, Franne   1941-

PERSONAL: Born December 30, 1941; daughter of Martin and Ann (Elton) Newman; married Eugene Lee (a designer). EDUCATION: Received M.F.A. from the University of Wisconsin.

VOCATION: Costume and set designer.

CAREER: PRINCIPAL STAGE WORK—Costume designer, *Harry Noon and Night,* Theatre of the Living Arts, Philadelphia, PA, 1969; costume designer, *A Line of Least Existence,* Theatre of the Living Arts, 1970; co-designer (with Eugene Lee), *Alice in Wonderland,* Extension Theatre, New York City, 1970; co-designer (with Eugene Lee), *Saved,* Brooklyn Academy of Music, Brooklyn, NY, then Cherry Lane Theatre, New York City, both 1970; co-designer (with Eugene Lee), *Mother Courage,* Arena Stage, Washington, DC, 1970; costume designer, *The Good and Bad Times of Cady Francis McCullum and Friends,* Trinity Square Repertory Company, Trinity Square Theatre, Providence, RI, 1971; co-designer (with Eugene Lee and Roger Morgan), *Dude,* Broadway Theatre, New York City, 1972; costume designer, *The Tooth of Crime,* Performing Garage, New York City, 1973; co-designer (with Eugene Lee), *Candide,* Brooklyn Academy of Music, 1973, then Broadway Theatre, 1974; costume designer, *Love for Love,* Helen Hayes Theatre, New York City, 1974; costume designer, *Gabrielle,* Studio Arena Theatre, Buffalo, NY, 1974; costume designer, *The Skin of Our Teeth,* Kennedy Center for the Performing Arts, Washington, DC, then Mark Hellinger Theatre, New York City, both 1975; costume designer, *The Moony Shapiro Songbook,* Morosco Theatre, New York City, 1981; costume designer, *Rock 'n' Roll! The First 5000 Years,* St. James Theatre, New York City, 1982; costume designer, *Three Acts of Recognition,* Public Theater, New York City, 1982; set designer, *The Disappearance of the Jews, Gorilla, Hot Line,* all Goodman Theatre, Chicago, IL, 1983; costume designer, *Wild Life,* Vandam Theatre, New York City, 1983; costume designer, *Streetheat,* Studio 54, New York City, 1985.

MAJOR TOURS—Costume designer, *Sweeney Todd,* U.S. cities, 1980.

PRINCIPAL FILM WORK—Set and costume designer, *Gilda Live,* Warner Brothers, 1980; costume designer, *One Trick Pony,* Warner Brothers, 1980; costume designer, *Baby, It's You,* Paramount, 1982. Also set designer (with Eugene Lee), *Mr. Mike's Mondo Video,* 1979; set designer, *Dead Ringer,* 1982.

AWARDS: (With Eugene Lee) Most Promising New Designer, Drama Desk Award, 1970-71, for *Alice in Wonderland;* (with Eugene Lee) Best Set Design, Maharam Foundation Award, Antoinette Perry Award, Drama Desk Award, all 1973-74, for *Candide;* Best Costume Design, Maharam Foundation Award, Antoinette

Perry Award, Drama Desk Award, and *Best Plays* citation, all 1973-74, for *Candide*.

ADDRESSES: OFFICE—31 Union Square W., New York, NY 10003.*

*   *   *

LENZ, Kay   1953-

PERSONAL: Born March 4, 1953, in Los Angeles, CA; daughter of Ted and Kay Lenz; married David Cassidy (an actor and singer), April 3, 1977 (divorced).

VOCATION: Actress.

CAREER: PRINCIPAL TELEVISION APPEARANCES—Episodic: *Jigsaw John*, NBC; *Love Story*, NBC; *Gunsmoke*, CBS; *Medical Center*, CBS; *Kodiak*, ABC; *McCloud*, NBC; *Nakia*, ABC; *Cannon*, CBS; *Petrocelli*, NBC. Mini-Series: Kate Jordache, *Rich Man, Poor Man, Books I and II*, ABC, 1976-77. Movies: Audree Prewitt, *The Weekend Nun*, ABC, 1972; Lisa Schilling, *Lisa, Bright and Dark*, NBC, 1973; Ruth Hailey, *A Summer without Boys*, ABC, 1973; Vicky Simmons, *Unwed Father*, ABC, 1974; Sue Crandall, *The Underground Man*, NBC, 1974; Shirley, *The FBI Story: The FBI Versus Alvin Karpus, Public Enemy Number One*, CBS, 1974; Sherry Williams, *Journey from Darkness*, NBC, 1975; Sarah, *The Initiation of Sarah*, ABC, 1978; Sarah Burns, *The Seeding of Sarah Burns*, CBS, 1979; Carol Bain, *Sanctuary of Fear*, NBC, 1979; Barbara Chilcoate, *Escape*, CBS, 1980; Jenny O'Rourke, *The Hustler of Muscle Beach*, ABC, 1980; Carrie Madison, *Prisoners of the Lost Universe*, Showtime, 1983.

PRINCIPAL FILM APPEARANCES—*American Graffiti*, Universal, 1973; *Breezy*, Universal, 1973; *White Line Fever*, Columbia, 1975; *The Great Scout and Cathouse Thursday*, American International, 1976; *The Passage*, United Artists, 1979; *Fast-Walking*, Lorimar, 1982; *House*, New World, 1986; *Death Wish IV*, Cannon, upcoming; *Stripped to Kill* (also known as: *Deception* and *Murder at the Burlesque*), New Horizon, upcoming. Also appeared in *Moving Violation*, 1976.

AWARDS: Golden Apple Award nomination, 1973; Hollywood Foreign Press Award nomination, 1973; Emmy Award, 1974-75; Emmy Award nomination, 1975-76.

MEMBER: Screen Actors Guild, American Federation of Television and Radio Artists.

ADDRESSES: AGENT—Gage Group, Inc., 9229 Sunset Boulevard, Suite 306, Los Angeles, CA 90069.*

*   *   *

LEONARD, Robert Sean   1969-

PERSONAL: Born February 28, 1969, in Washington Township, NJ; son of Robert Howard (a musician) and Joyce P. (a nurse; maiden name, Peterson) Leonard. EDUCATION: Attended Fordham University; trained for the stage with Marty Winkler; studied voice with Margaret Leary.

VOCATION: Actor.

CAREER: STAGE DEBUT—Artful Dodger, *Oliver!*, New Players Summerstock Theatre, NJ, for eighteen performances. OFF-BROADWAY DEBUT—Christopher, *The Beach House*, Circle Repertory Theatre, 1985. PRINCIPAL STAGE APPEARANCES—Chris Decker, *Sally's Gone, She Left Her Name*, Perry Street Theatre, New York City, 1985; Eugene, *Brighton Beach Memoirs*, 48th Street Theatre, New York City, 1986; Christopher Morcom, *Breaking the Code*, Neil Simon Theatre, New York City, 1987. Also Jack, *Into the Woods* (workshop production), New York City; appeared in *Coming of Age in Soho*, New York Shakespeare Festival, Public Theatre, New York City.

MAJOR TOURS—Eugene, *Brighton Beach Memoirs*, U.S. cities, 1986; Eugene, *Biloxi Blues*, U.S. cities, 1987.

FILM DEBUT—Max, *The Manhattan Project*, Twentieth Century-Fox, 1985. PRINCIPAL FILM APPEARANCES—Jeremy, *I Was a Teenage Vampire*, Kings Road Productions, 1986.

TELEVISION DEBUT—Pilot: Garret, *The Robert Klein Show*, 1986. PRINCIPAL TELEVISION APPEARANCES—Movies: Larry, *My Two Loves*, ABC, 1986; Rusty, *Bluffing It*, ABC, 1987.

MEMBER: Actors' Equity Association, Screen Actors Guild, American Federation of Television and Radio Artists.

ADDRESSES: AGENT—Peggy Hadley Enterprises, Ltd., 250 W. 57th Street, New York, NY 10107.

ROBERT SEAN LEONARD

LEONE, Sergio   1929-

PERSONAL: Born January 3, 1929, in Rome, Italy; married wife Carla, 1960; children: Raffaella, Francesca, Andrea. EDUCATION: Attended law school in Rome.

VOCATION: Director, actor, and screenwriter.

CAREER: PRINCIPAL FILM APPEARANCES—*The Bicycle Thief,* 1947.

PRINCIPAL FILM WORK—Assistant director, *Helen of Troy,* Warner Brothers, 1956; assistant director, *The Nun's Story,* Warner Brothers, 1959; assistant director, *Ben-Hur,* Metro-Goldwyn-Mayer (MGM), 1959; co-director, *The Last Days of Pompeii,* United Artists, 1959; director, *The Colossus of Rhodes,* MGM, 1961; second unit director, *Sodom and Gomorrah,* Twentieth Century-Fox, 1962; director, *A Fistful of Dollars,* United Artists, 1967; director, *For a Few Dollars More,* United Artists, 1967; director, *The Good, the Bad and the Ugly,* United Artists, 1967; director, *Once Upon a Time in the West,* Paramount, 1969; director, *Duck, You Sucker!,* United Artists, 1972; director, *Un genio due compari e un pollo,* 1975; producer, *Il gatto,* 1978; director, *Once Upon a Time in America,* Warner Brothers, 1984; director, *Nine Hundred Days,* Cinecom International, upcoming.

RELATED CAREER—Assistant to Italian filmmakers and American directors, 1947-56; president, Rafran Cinematografica.

WRITINGS: SCREENPLAYS—Co-writer: *Sign of the Gladiator,* American International, 1958; *The Last Days of Pompeii,* United Artists, 1959; *The Colossus of Rhodes,* MGM, 1961; *A Fistful of Dollars,* United Artists, 1967; *For a Few Dollars More,* United Artists, *The Good, the Bad, and the Ugly,* United Artists, 1967; *Once Upon a Time in the West,* Paramount, 1969; *Duck, You Sucker!,* United Artists, 1972; *Once Upon a Time in America,* Warner Brothers, 1984. Also credited with story idea for *My Name Is Nobody,* Universal, 1973.

ADDRESSES: OFFICE—c/o Ministry of Tourism, Via Della Ferra Tella, Rome, Italy.*

*   *   *

LESLIE, Joan   1925-

PERSONAL: Born Joan Brodell, January 26, 1925, in Detroit, MI; daughter of John and Agnes Brodell.

VOCATION: Actress and model.

CAREER: PRINCIPAL FILM APPEARANCES—Velma, *High Sierra,* Warner Brothers, 1941; Mary, *Yankee Doodle Dandy,* Warner Brothers, 1942; Joan, *The Sky's the Limit,* RKO, 1943; Eileen Dibble, *This Is the Army,* Warner Brothers, 1943; Sally, *Where Do We Go from Here?,* Twentieth Century-Fox, 1945. Also appeared in *The Wagons Roll at Night,* Warner Brothers, 1941; *Thank Your Lucky Stars,* Warner Brothers, 1943; *Rhapsody in Blue,* Warner Brothers, 1945; *The Skipper Surprised His Wife,* Metro-Goldwyn-Mayer, 1950; *The Revolt of Mamie Stover,* Twentieth Century-Fox, 1956; and *Hollywood Canteen,* 1944; *Too Young to Know,* 1945; *Cinderella Jones,* 1946; *Repeat Performance,* 1947; *Northwest Stampede,* 1948; *Born to Be Bad,* 1950; *Man in the Saddle,*

JOAN LESLIE

1951; *Toughest Man in Arizona, Hellgate,* both 1952; *The Woman They Almost Lynched,* 1953; *Flight Nurse, Jubilee Trail, Hell's Outpost,* all 1954.

PRINCIPAL TELEVISION APPEARANCES—Episodic: *Police Story,* NBC, 1973; also *Ford Theatre,* CBS; *General Electric Theatre,* CBS; *Queen for a Day.* Pilots: Sandy Hannah, *Charley Hannah,* ABC, 1986. Movies: Mary Keegan, *The Keegans,* CBS, 1976.

RELATED CAREER—Model; actress, television commercials.

NON-RELATED CAREER—Board of directors: Damon Runyon Foundation; St. Anne's Hospital.

AWARDS: Star of Tomorrow, 1946.

MEMBER: Screen Actors Guild, American Federation of Television and Radio Artists.

ADDRESSES: AGENT—c/o Chris Shiffrin, Shiffrin Artists, Inc., 7466 Beverly Boulevard, Suite 205, Los Angeles, CA 90036.

*   *   *

LEVENTON, Annabel   1942-

PERSONAL: Born April 20, 1942; daughter of Gerald and Avril (Wright) Leventon; married John Adams. EDUCATION: Attended St. Anne's College, Oxford University; trained for the stage at the

London Academy of Music and Dramatic Art and at La Mama Experimental Theatre Club, New York City.

VOCATION: Actress, singer, and director.

CAREER: STAGE DEBUT—Vera Alexandrovna, *A Month in the Country,* Oxford Playhouse, Oxford, U.K., 1962. PRINCIPAL STAGE APPEARANCES—Sheila, *Hair,* Shaftesbury Theatre, London, then Porte St. Martin, Paris, France, both 1969; Helena, *A Midsummer Night's Dream,* Open Air Theatre, London, 1970; Jocasta, *Oedipus,* Bianca, *The Taming of the Shrew,* Mary, *The Wakefield Navity,* all Young Vic Theatre, London, 1970; Celia, *The Philanthropist,* May Fair Theatre, London, 1971; Lucienne, *A Flea in Her Ear,* Lika, *The Promise,* both Bristol Old Vic Theatre, Bristol, U.K., 1976; Daisy Bell, *Spokesong,* King's Head Theatre, London, 1976, then Vaudeville Theatre, London, 1977; Daphne Kershaw, *Daughters of Men,* Hampstead Theatre Club, London, 1979; Beatrice, *Much Ado about Nothing,* Open Air Theatre, 1980. Also appeared in Bournemouth, U.K.; with the Traverse Theatre, Edinburgh, Scotland, U.K.; and with La Mama Experimental Theatre Club, New York City.

PRINCIPAL STAGE WORK—Director, *Morecambe,* Edinburgh Festival, Edinburgh, Scotland, U.K., then Hampstead Theatre Club, London, 1975; director, *Flux,* London, then New York City, both 1976; assistant director, *Elvis,* 1977.

PRINCIPAL FILM APPEARANCES—*Every Home Should Have One,* 1969; *La Mur de l'Atlantique,* 1971.

PRINCIPAL TELEVISION APPEARANCES—Episodic: *The New Avengers,* CBS, 1978; also appeared in *Penmarric.*

SIDELIGHTS: FAVORITE ROLES—Cherie in *Bus Stop;* Lika in *The Promise.*

ADDRESSES: AGENT—Susan Angel Associates, Ten Greek Street, London W1, England.*

*   *   *

DAVID E. LeVINE

OFFICE—c/o Dramatists Guild, 234 W. 44th Street, New York, NY 10036.

*   *   *

LeVINE, David E.   1933-

PERSONAL: Born June 22, 1933, in New York, NY; son of Harry Louis (an art director) and Esther H. (Hartman) LeVine; married Stephanie D. Reichman, September 18, 1956 (divorced, 1971); married Barbara Ann Grande (a model), March 1, 1974. EDUCATION: Harvard College, B.A., 1955; Columbia University, L.L.B., 1960. MILITARY: U.S. Naval Reserve, 1955-57.

VOCATION: Theatre executive and lawyer.

CAREER: PRINCIPAL STAGE WORK—Assistant treasurer, Dramatists Guild Fund, New York City, 1968—; assistant treasurer, Authors League Fund, New York City, 1968—; board of directors, International Theatre Institute, New York City, 1974—; trustee, Eugene O'Neill Theatre, Waterford, CT; administrative vice-president, Foundation of the Dramatists Guild, New York City, 1980—.

MEMBER: Harvard Club.

ADDRESSES: HOME—315 E. 68th Street, New York, NY 10021.

LEVINE, Joseph E.   1905-

PERSONAL: Full name, Joseph Edward Levine; born September 9, 1905, in Boston, MA; died July 31, 1987, in Greenwich, CT; married Rosalie Harrison (a singer with Rudy Vallee's orchestra), 1939; children: one son, one daughter.

VOCATION: Producer.

CAREER: FIRST FILM WORK—Producer (with Maxwell Finn), *Gaslight Follies,* Embassy, 1955. PRINCIPAL FILM WORK—Producer: *Godzilla: King of the Monsters,* Embassy, 1956; *Attila,* Embassy, 1958; *Hercules,* Warner Brothers, 1959; *Jack the Ripper,* Paramount, 1960; *Hercules Unchained,* Warner Brothers, 1960; *Two Women,* Embassy, 1961; *Bimbo the Great,* Warner Brothers, 1961; *The Fabulous World of Jules Verne,* Warner Brothers, 1961; *The Wonders of Aladdin,* Metro-Goldwyn-Mayer (MGM), 1961; *Morgan the Pirate,* MGM, 1961; *The Thief of Baghdad,* MGM, 1961; *Boy's Night Out,* MGM, 1961; *Sodom and Gomorrah,* Twentieth Century-Fox, 1961; *The Sky Above, the Mud Below,* Embassy, 1961; *Divorce, Italian Style,* Embassy, 1962; *Salvatore Guiliano,* Embassy, 1962; *Boccaccio '70,* Embassy,

1962; *Long Day's Journey into Night*, Embassy, 1962; *What a Curve Up!* (also known as *No Place Like Homicide!*), Embassy, 1962; *Conjugal Bed*, Embassy, 1963; *8 1/2*, Embassy, 1963; *The Easy Life*, Embassy, 1963; *Landru* (also known as *Bluebeard*), Embassy, 1963; *Contempt*, Embassy, 1963; *Fury at Smuggler's Bay*, Embassy, 1963; *A Face in the Rain*, Embassy, 1963; *Yesterday, Today and Tomorrow*, Embassy, 1964; *Marriage, Italian Style*, Embassy, 1964; *The Carpetbaggers*, Paramount, 1964; *The Empty Canvas*, Embassy, 1964; *Zulu*, Embassy, 1964; *Santa Claus Conquers the Martians*, Embassy, 1964; *Where Love Has Gone*, Paramount, 1964.

Casanova '70, Embassy, 1965; *Darling*, Embassy, 1965; *Harlow*, Embassy, 1965; *The Tenth Victim*, Embassy, 1965; *Dingaka*, Embassy, 1965; *Sands of the Kalahari*, Embassy, 1965; *The Second Best Secret Agent in the Whole Wide World* (also known as *Licensed to Kill*), Embassy, 1965; *Git!*, Embassy, 1965; *The Idol*, Embassy, 1966; *Romeo and Juliet*, Embassy, 1966; *The Spy with a Cold Nose*, Embassy, 1966; *The Oscar*, Embassy, 1966; *A Man Called Adam*, Embassy, 1966; *Nevada Smith*, Paramount, 1966; *Woman Times Seven*, Embassy, 1967; *The Graduate*, Embassy, 1967; *Robbery*, Embassy, 1967; *The Caper of the Golden Bulls*, Embassy, 1967; *The Producers*, AVCO-Embassy, 1968; *The Lion in Winter*, AVCO-Embassy, 1968; *A Nice Girl Like Me*, AVCO-Embassy, 1968; *Generation*, AVCO-Embassy, 1969; *Stiletto*, AVCO-Embassy, 1969; *Don't Drink the Water*, AVCO-Embassy, 1969; *The Adventurers*, Paramount, 1970; *The Man Who Had Power over Women*, AVCO-Embassy, 1970; *Sunflower*, AVCO-Embassy, 1970; *The People Next Door*, AVCO-Embassy, 1970; *C.C. and Company*, AVCO-Embassy, 1970; *Macho Callahan*, AVCO-Embassy, 1970; *Promise at Dawn*, AVCO-Embassy, 1970; *Soldier Blue*, AVCO-Embassy, 1970; *Carnal Knowledge*, AVCO-Embassy, 1971; *Thumb Tripping*, AVCO-Embassy, 1972; *The Ruling Class*, AVCO-Embassy, 1972; *Day of the Dolphin*, AVCO-Embasssy, 1973; *A Touch of Class*, AVCO-Embassy, 1963; *A Bridge Too Far*, United Artists, 1977; *Magic*, Twentieth Century-Fox, 1978; *Tatoo*, Twentieth Century-Fox, 1981. Also produced *Arruza*, 1972; *They Call Me Trinity*, 1972; *Paper Tiger*, 1974; *Night Porter*, 1974; *Only One New York*, Embassy; *The Hellfire Club*, Embassy; *Baby Love; A House Is Not a Home; Strangers in the City;* and *Light Fantastic*.

PRINCIPAL STAGE WORK—Producer, *Kelly*, Broadhurst Theatre, New York City, 1965.

RELATED CAREER—Owner, motion picture theatres; president, AVCO-Embassy Pictures; president, Joseph E. Levine Presents, 1974—.

NON-RELATED CAREER—Garment factory worker, restaurant manager.

AWARDS: Showman of the Year Award, 1960; Producer of the Year Award from the Allied States Association of Motion Picture Exhibitions, 1962; Master Showman of the World Award, 1963; Cecil B. DeMille Award from the Hollywood Foreign Press, 1964; Conference of Personal Managers-East Award, 1965, for "Outstanding Contributions to the World of Entertainment;" also Pioneer of the Year Award, Variety Club of New York. Honorary degrees: L.H.D., Emerson College, 1968.

OBITUARIES AND OTHER SOURCES: Variety, August 5, 1987.

LEVINSON, Richard   1934-1987

PERSONAL: Full name, Richard Leighton Levinson; born August 7, 1934, in Philadelphia, PA; died of a heart attack, March 12, 1987, in Los Angeles, CA; son of William (in business) and Georgia (Harbert) Levinson; married Rosanna Huffman (an actress), April 12, 1969; children: Christine. EDUCATION: University of Pennsylvania, B.S., economics, 1956. MILITARY: U.S. Army, 1957-58.

VOCATION: Writer and producer.

CAREER: PRINCIPAL TELEVISION WORK—Also see *WRITINGS* below; all with William Link. Series: Creator, *Mannix*, CBS, 1967-75; creator of "The Lawyers" segments of *The Bold Ones*, NBC, 1969-73; creator, *The Psychiatrist*, NBC, 1971; creator and producer, *Tenafly*, NBC, 1971; creator and producer, *Columbo*, NBC, 1971-76; developer and producer, *Ellery Queen*, NBC, 1975-76; creator (also with Peter S. Fischer), *Murder, She Wrote*, CBS, 1984-87. Pilots: Executive producer, *Tenafly*, NBC, 1973; producer, *Ellery Queen: Too Many Suspects*, NBC, 1975; executive producer, *Charlie Cobb: Nice Night for a Hanging*, NBC, 1977. Movies: Producer, *My Sweet Charlie*, NBC, 1970; producer, *Two on a Bench*, ABC, 1971; producer, *That Certain Summer*, ABC, 1972; producer, *The Judge and Jake Wyler*, NBC, 1972; executive producer, *Savage*, NBC, 1973; executive producer, *Partners in Crime*, NBC, 1973; producer, *The Gun*, ABC, 1974; executive producer, *The Execution of Private Slovik*, NBC, 1974; executive producer, *A Cry for Help*, ABC, 1975; producer, *The Storyteller*, NBC, 1977; executive producer, *Murder by Natural Causes*, CBS, 1979; executive producer (also with David Susskind), *Crisis at Central High*, CBS, 1981; executive producer, *Rehearsal for Murder*, CBS, 1982; executive producer, *Take Your Best Shot*, CBS, 1982; executive producer, *Prototype*, CBS, 1983; executive producer (also with Stanley Chase), *The Guardian*, HBO, 1984; executive producer, *Guilty Conscience*, CBS, 1985; executive producer, *Murder in Space*, Showtime, 1985; executive producer, *Vanishing Act*, CBS, 1986.

RELATED CAREER—Writer and producer, Universal Studios, Universal City, CA, 1966-77; co-president, Richard Levinson/William Link Productions, Los Angeles, CA, 1978-87.

WRITINGS: All with William Link. Series: Contributor of more than one hundred scripts for various series, beginning with "Chain of Command" for *Desilu Playhouse*, 1959, and including *General Motors Presents*, *Dr. Kildare*, *The Fugitive*, and *Alfred Hitchcock Hour*.

TELEPLAYS—Movies (see additional production details above): *Prescription: Murder*, NBC, 1968; *Istanbul Express*, NBC, 1968; *The Whole World Is Watching*, NBC, 1969; *My Sweet Charlie*, NBC, 1970; (also with Stanford Whitmore) *McCloud: Who Killed Miss U.S.A.?*, NBC, 1970; *Sam Hill: Who Killed the Mysterious Mr. Foster?*, NBC, 1971; *Two on a Bench*, ABC, 1971; (also with David Shaw) *The Judge and Jake Wyler*, NBC, 1972; *That Certain Summer*, ABC, 1972; *Savage*, NBC, 1973; *Tenafly*, NBC, 1973; *The Execution of Private Slovik*, NBC, 1974; *The Gun*, ABC, 1974; *Ellery Queen: Too Many Suspects*, NBC, 1975; *The Storyteller*, NBC, 1977; *Murder by Natural Causes*, CBS, 1979; *Crisis at Central High*, CBS, 1981; *Rehearsal for Murder*, CBS, 1982; *Take Your Best Shot*, CBS, 1982; *Prototype*, CBS, 1983; *The Guardian*, HBO, 1984; *Guilty Conscience*, CBS, 1985; *Vanishing Act*, CBS, 1986.

Also with William Link: *Prescription: Murder* (three-act play), Samuel French, Inc., 1963; *Fineman* (novel), Laddin Press, 1972; *Stay Tuned: An Inside Look at the Making of Prime-Time Television*, St. Martin's, 1981; book for *Merlin* (two-act musical play), produced on Broadway at Mark Hellinger Theatre, 1983; *The Playhouse* (novel), Berkeley, 1984; and more than thirty short stories for such periodicals as *Playboy*.

AWARDS: All with William Link. Emmy Award, Image Award from the National Association for the Advancement of Colored People (NAACP), both 1970, for *My Sweet Charlie;* Emmy Award, Golden Globe Award, both 1972, for *Columbo;* Golden Globe Award, Writers Guild of America Award, Silver Nymph Award from the Monte Carlo Film Festival, all 1973, for *That Certain Summer;* George Foster Peabody Award, 1974, for *The Execution of Private Slovik;* Christopher Award, 1981, for *Crisis at Central High;* Antoinette Perry Award nomination, 1983, for *Merlin;* also won four Edgar awards from the Mystery Writers of America.

MEMBER: Academy of Television Arts and Sciences, Caucus for Writers, Producers, and Directors (member of steering committee), Writers Guild of America, Actors Studio West (chairperson of playwrights committee).

SIDELIGHTS: Richard Levinson's long collaboration with William Link yielded some of television's most popular mystery series, including *Columbo*, starring Peter Falk, and *Murder, She Wrote*, starring Angela Lansbury. The team also earned numerous awards for such issue-oriented television movies as *My Sweet Charlie*, concerning an interracial friendship, and *That Certain Summer*, about homosexuality. Levinson's *New York Times* obituary quoted him about the duo's philosophy: "What we try to do is the highest quality popular entertainment we can do, with an occasional thought sticking through."

OBITUARIES AND OTHER SOURCES: Richard Levinson and William Link, *Stay Tuned: An Inside Look at the Making of Prime-Time Television*, St. Martin's, 1981; *American Film*, December, 1983; *Contemporary Authors*, New Revision Series, Vol. 13, Gale, 1984; *New York Times*, March 13, 1987; *Variety*, March 18, 1987.*

*   *   *

LEWIS, Jerry   1926-

PERSONAL: Born Joseph Levitch, March 16, 1926, in Newark, NJ; son of Danny (a master of ceremonies) and Mona (an entertainer) Levitch; married Patti Palmer (a singer), 1944 (divorced); married Sandra Pitnick, 1983; children: (first marriage) Gary, Ronnie (adopted), Scott, Christopher, Anthony, Joseph.

VOCATION: Actor, comedian, producer, writer, and director.

CAREER: PRINCIPAL FILM APPEARANCES—Seymour, *My Friend Irma*, Paramount, 1949; Seymour, *My Friend Irma Goes West*, Paramount, 1950; Soldier Korwin, *At War with the Army*, Paramount, 1950; Junior Jackson, *That's My Boy*, Paramount, 1950; Melvin Jones, *Sailor Beware*, Paramount, 1951; Ted Rogers, *The Stooge*, Paramount, 1952; Hap Smith, *Jumpin' Jacks*, Paramount, 1952; Harvey Miller, *The Caddy*, Paramount, 1953; Myron Mertz, *Scared Stiff*, Paramount, 1953; Virgil Yokum, *Money from Home*, Paramount, 1953; Homer Flagg, *Living It Up*, Paramount, 1954; Jerry Hotchkiss, *Three Ring Circus*, Paramount, 1954; Wilbur

Hoolick, *You're Never Too Young*, Paramount, 1955; Eugene Fullstack, *Artists and Models*, Paramount, 1955; Wade Kingsley, Jr., *Pardners*, Paramount, 1956; Malcolm Smith, *Hollywood or Bust*, Paramount, 1956; Sydney Pythias, *The Delicate Delinquent*, Paramount, 1957; Meredith T. Bixley, *The Sad Sack*, Paramount, 1957; Clayton Poole, *Rockabye Baby*, Paramount, 1958; Gilbert Wooley, *The Geisha Boy*, Paramount, 1958; John Paul Steckley III, *Don't Give Up the Ship*, Paramount, 1959; Frank, *Li'l Abner*, Paramount, 1959.

Kreton, *Visit to a Small Planet*, Paramount, 1960; title role, *The Bellboy*, Paramount, 1960; Fella, *Cinderfella*, Paramount, 1960; Herbert H. Heebert and Mrs. Heebert, *The Ladies Man*, Paramount, 1961; Morty S. Tachman, *The Errand Boy*, Paramount, 1961; Lester March, *It's Only Money*, Paramount, 1962; man who ran over Culpepper's hat, *It's a Mad, Mad, Mad, Mad World*, United Artists, 1963; Raymond Phiffier, *Who's Minding the Store?*, 1963; Julius F. Kelp and Buddy Love, *The Nutty Professor*, Paramount, 1963; Stanley Belt, *The Patsy*, Paramount, 1964; Jerome Littlefield, *Disorderly Orderly*, Paramount, 1964; Willard Woodward, Uncle James Peyton, Uncle Eddie Peyton, et al., *The Family Jewels*, Paramount, 1965; Robert Reed, *Boeing, Boeing*, Paramount, 1965; Christopher Prise, Warren, et al., *Three on a Couch*, Columbia, 1966; Peter Matamore, *Way, Way Out*, Twentieth Century-Fox, 1966; Gerald Clamson and Sid Valentine, *The Big Mouth*, Columbia, 1967; George Lester, *Don't Raise the Bridge, Lower the River*, 1968; Peter Ingersoll, alias Dobbs, *Hook, Line and Sinker*, Columbia, 1969.

Brendan Byers III and Kesselring, *Which Way to the Front?*, Warner Brothers, 1970; unemployed circus clown, *Hardly Working*, Twentieth Century-Fox, 1981; Jerry Langford, *The King of Comedy*, Twentieth Century-Fox, 1983; Paul, *Slapstick (Of Another Kind)*, International Film Marketing, 1984; also, "Smorgasbord" (also known as "Cracking Up"; unreleased), 1983; *To Catch a Cop*, French release, 1984; and "The Day the Clown Cried" (unreleased).

PRINCIPAL FILM WORK—Director of comedy shorts: *Fairfax Avenue; A Spot in the Shade; Watch on the Lime; Come Back Little Shicksa; Son of Lifeboat; The Re-Inforcer; Son of Spellbound; Melvin's Revenge; I Should Have Stood in Bedlam; The Whistler*.

Producer, *The Delicate Delinquent*, Paramount, 1957; producer, director, and screenwriter, *The Bellboy*, Paramount, 1960; producer, director, and screenwriter, *The Ladies Man*, Paramount, 1961; director and screenwriter, *The Errand Boy*, Paramount, 1961; director and screenwriter, *The Nutty Professor*, Paramount, 1963; director and screenwriter, *The Patsy*, Paramount, 1964; producer, director, and screenwriter, *The Family Jewels*, Paramount, 1965; producer and director, *Three on a Couch*, Paramount, 1966; producer, director, and screenwriter, *The Big Mouth*, Columbia, 1967; director, *One More Time*, United Artists, 1970; producer and director, *Which Way to the Front?*, Warner Brothers, 1970; director and screenwriter, *Hardly Working*, Twentieth Century-Fox, 1981; director and screenwriter, "Smorgasbord" (also known as "Cracking Up"), 1983.

PRINCIPAL TELEVISION APPEARANCES—Guest: *Startime*, Du-Mont; *Ed Sullivan Show*, CBS. Specials: Master of ceremonies, annual Labor Day Muscular Dystrophy Telethon, 1966—. Movies: Bernie Abrams, *Fight for Life;* also, *The Jazz Singer*.

RELATED CAREER—Comedian at Catskill Mountain resorts; partner with singer and straight-man Dean Martin in comedy team of

Martin and Lewis, performing in nightclubs and films, 1946-56; professor of cinema, University of Southern California; president of production companies including Jerry Lewis Productions, Jerry Lewis Films, Inc., P.J. Productions, Inc., and Patti Enterprises; chairman of National Muscular Dystrophy Association of America.

WRITINGS: SCREENPLAYS—See PRINCIPAL FILM WORK. BOOKS— *The Total Film-Maker,* Random House, 1971; (with Herb Gluck) *Jerry Lewis in Person* (autobiography), Atheneum, 1982.

AWARDS: Most Promising Male Star, *Motion Picture Daily* Award, 1950; Top Ten Money Making Stars, *Herald-Fame* Award, 1951, 1952 (number one), 1953, 1954, 1957; Best Comedy Team, *Motion Picture Daily* Radio Poll Award, 1951, 1952, 1953, 1956; Best Picture, from French critics, for *The Nutty Professor,* 1964, and twice named best director by them; nominated for Nobel Peace Prize, 1978; named Commander of the Order of Arts and Letters and Commander of Legion of Honor by French government, both 1984.

MEMBER: Screen Producers Guild, Screen Directors Guild, Screenwriters Guild.

SIDELIGHTS: A slapstick comedian of international renown, Jerry Lewis has also earned the respect of his fellow Americans for his longstanding commitment to fundraising for muscular dystrophy research and the adulation of French critics for what they regard as his brilliant social satire. Throughout the 1950s until the mid-sixties, his highly visual comic style, relying on pratfalls, goofy faces, and other tricks reminiscent of burlesque theatre, made him a top-drawing Hollywood star, first in a team with singer-straight man Dean Martin and then on his own. Almost a decade before such comedians as Mel Brooks and Woody Allen wrote and directed their own films, Lewis had responsibility for many of his movies, from scripting and directing to editing the final cut. Audiences' changing tastes and his own problems with drug addiction led to his having no films released for a decade after 1970, however, and in 1982 he suffered a near fatal heart attack that necessitated open heart surgery. "I'm a very lucky man," he told *Parade* (April 22, 1984). "It's because I almost died that saved my life. It changed me." In the 1980s he returned to making movies, including a highly regarded dramatic performance in Martin Scorsese's *The King of Comedy,* and enjoyed renewed acclaim at home and abroad.

Lewis's climb to international stardom started in Newark, New Jersey, where he was born in 1926. Both his parents were entertainers, principally on the summer "Borscht Belt" at resorts in the Catskill Mountains. As a child he often traveled with his parents, occasionally singing a song or dancing a small part in their show. He told *Parade* that his early exposure to applause and audience appreciation made him feel more alive onstage than elsewhere. "I don't want to be one of the 200 drummers in the parade," he said. I knew that as a kid. . . . I wanted to *lead* the parade. I wanted the baton!" Growing up in Newark, Lewis found his family's poverty personally humiliating. He determined to make a name for himself as a performer, and at the age of fifteen he quit high school, worked up a comedy act, and took it on the road to burlesque palaces on the East Coast. Dotson Rader in *Parade* noted that at first Lewis was "promptly booed off the stage" for pantomiming the words to popular songs as they were played on a phonograph offstage. By 1942, however, he had honed his act and was working regularly in the Catskills. In 1946 he teamed up with another struggling young performer, Dean Martin.

By the time they had been together eight months, Martin and Lewis

were earning $5000 a week at the most exclusive night clubs. From clubs and theatres, they graduated to films in 1949. *The Great Movie Comedians* described the pair's typical routine: "Dean Martin was the nominal straight man, carrying the romantic interest, singing an occasional tune, and providing a character contrast to Jerry Lewis. Lewis was the lovable fool, often trod upon, faced with troubles both comic and serious, a juvenile cutup who played off Martin's sober stoicism. From the outset it was clear that Jerry Lewis was the comedy star of this comedy team." From 1951 to 1956, through sixteen films, they were consistently ranked among the ten biggest Hollywood stars. Critics found their humor indecent, tasteless, and lunatic, but audiences thronged to their pictures in the United States and abroad. At the height of their popularity in 1956, the team broke up. There were rumors of name-calling and intense incompatibility; the two men have never reconciled.

Rader noted that when Martin and Lewis disbanded, critics speculated that Lewis "couldn't survive on his own." From *The Delicate Delinquent* on, however, not only did Lewis survive, he prospered—at least until the late 1960s, when age began to alter the boyish contours of his face. His films were generally loosely structured farces that gave ample display to Lewis's "frantic misfit" persona. Most American critics still either ignored or disparaged his work for its boisterous vulgarity, especially when he also directed, wrote, or produced his films. *Sight and Sound* commentator John Russell Taylor was an exception, writing in the spring of 1965 that Lewis's development had been "spectacular." The critic continued: "The addition of directing, producing and writing to his repertoire of cinematic activities is the most striking evidence of this, but it is really only symptomatic of a much longer, slower and harder-won development of Jerry Lewis as a performer and inventor on film." He assessed that Lewis had become "a stunningly varied and inventive performer . . . a performer perfectly able to regulate his own effects, apply his own disciplines and get better results under his own direction than under anyone else's."

It was in France, however, that Lewis's films consistently met with greater critical appreciation. Intellectuals there saw his work as a satirical statement about America so subtle that Americans couldn't grasp its meaning. Luc Moullet told the February 20, 1966 *New York Times Magazine:* "We began to understand several years ago that [Lewis] was more than a clown, that actually his comical way was very conscious and elaborate, and that in his movies he played too much of the idiot to be idiotic to that degree. The answer was that he had to be, actually, very intelligent." More than one French critic suggested that Lewis was the last practitioner of the American comic tradition popularized by silent film stars Charlie Chaplin and Buster Keaton; they found his use of the film medium inspired by a cinematic awareness rather than an intellectual preoccupation with meaning. Lewis remained in such high regard in France that in 1984 he received two of that country's highest honors, when he was named commander of both the Order of Arts and Letters and of the Legion of Honor.

In the United States his film making opportunities were limited throughout the 1970s and he concentrated primarily on stage performances and on his annual Labor Day telethon to raise funds for muscular dystrophy. His 1981 film *Hardly Working* did well at the box office, but ill health intervened in his return to that medium. In December of 1982 Lewis suffered a heart attack and required bypass surgery. His recuperation under the care of his second wife included emotional self-analysis during which Lewis rid himself of the addictions to Percodan, a pain-killer, and cigarettes that he had suffered for years. He was able to assess his life crises, including the break-up of his thirty-six-year first marriage. Some have attributed the effectiveness of his portrayal of a lonely victim of fame in *The King of Comedy* to this newfound self-awareness; Lewis offered *Parade* his own views on performing. "I don't need other people's pain to make comedy," he said. "I just call on my own. I need only to call upon my sorrow to create laughter. Sorrow and laughter are so close, hand-in-glove." He added that his one outstanding aspiration is to see muscular dystrophy, a disease that "is like all the evil in the world," eradicated from the globe.

ADDRESSES: OFFICE—Plaza Vegas, Suite One, 3305 W. Spring Mountain Road, Las Vegas, NV 89102; Jerry Lewis Films, Inc., 1888 Century Park E., Suite 830, Los Angeles, CA 90067. AGENT— William Morris Agency, 151 El Camino Drive, Beverly Hills, CA 90212.*

*   *   *

LEWIS, Marcia   1938-

PERSONAL: Born August 18, 1938, in Melrose, MA. EDUCATION: Attended the University of Cincinnati.

VOCATION: Actress.

CAREER: PRINCIPAL STAGE APPEARANCES—Miss Hannigan, *Annie,* Alvin Theatre, then Uris Theatre, both New York City, 1981; Miss Hannigan, *Annie,* Papermill Playhouse, Milburn, NJ, 1983; various roles, *Romance Language,* Playwrights Horizons, New York City, 1984; Kitty Katz, *Miami,* Playwrights Horizons,

MARCIA LEWIS

1986; Rachel Halpern, *Rags,* Mark Hellinger Theatre, New York City, 1986; Madame Katz, *Roza,* Royale Theater, New York City, 1987. Also Ernestine Money, *Hello, Dolly!,* St. James Theatre, New York City; Lorene, *The Time of Your Life,* Vivian Beaumont Theatre, New York City; appeared as Sister Mary Hubert, *Nunsense;* Golde, *Fiddler on the Roof;* Jan, *Woman of the Year;* Mrs. Schinn, *The Music Man;* Aunt Eller, *Oklahoma;* Rose, *Gypsy;* and Off-Broadway in *The Impudent Wolf, Who's Who Baby, God Bless Coney,* and *Let Yourself Go.*

PRINCIPAL CABARET APPEARANCES—Freddy's, New York City; The Gardenia, Los Angeles, CA; Studio One, Los Angeles, CA; Upstairs-at-the-Downstairs, New York City; Mayfair Music Hall, Los Angeles, CA; Harrah's, Reno, NV.

PRINCIPAL TELEVISION APPEARANCES—Episodic: *All My Children,* ABC; *Ryan's Hope,* ABC; *The Bionic Woman,* ABC; *Bob Newhart Show,* CBS; *Happy Days,* ABC; *One Life to Live; Out of the Blue; Working Stiffs; Pinky; Don Rickles Show; Rowan and Martin Reports; Sesame Street.* Mini-Series: *Rich Man, Poor Man.* Series: Mitzie Logan, *Who's Watching the Kids?,* NBC, 1978; Irma Coolidge, *The Good Time Girls,* ABC, 1980. Movies: Mrs. Gilmore, *The Great Ice Rip-Off,* ABC, 1974; Mrs. Barrett, *The Night They Took Miss Beautiful,* NBC, 1977; Gloria, *When She Was Bad . . .,* ABC, 1979; also appeared in *Legs,* NBC; *How to Survive a Happy Divorce,* ABC; *Bobby and Sarah,* NBC.

PRINCIPAL FILM APPEARANCES—*The Ice Pirates,* Metro-Goldwyn-Mayer/United Artists, 1984; also *Curtain Call; Night Warning.*

RELATED CAREER—Singer.

ADDRESSES: HOME—250 W. 74th Street, Apt. B, New York, NY 10023. AGENT—Gage Group, 1650 Broadway, New York, NY 10019; 9229 Sunset Boulevard, Suite 306, Los Angeles, CA 90069.

*   *   *

LIBERATORE, Lou   1959-

PERSONAL: Born August 4, 1959, in Jersey City, NJ; son of Ernest Raymond (a stock broker) and Madeline Theresa (a bookkeeper; maiden name, Collaro) Liberatore. EDUCATION: Received B.A., theatre, from Fordham University; trained for the stage with William Esper.

VOCATION: Actor.

CAREER: STAGE DEBUT—Singer, *Godspell,* John Harms Theatre, Englewood, NJ, 1977, for six performances. OFF-BROADWAY DEBUT—Nub, *Threads,* Circle Repertory Company, 1981, for two performances. BROADWAY DEBUT— Various roles, *As Is,* Lyceum Theatre, 1985. PRINCIPAL STAGE APPEARANCES—Servant, *Richard II,* Johnny Two Dance, *The Great Grandson of Jedediah Kohler,* both Entermedia Theatre, New York City, 1982; M.P., second hooded man, *Black Angel,* Circle Repertory Company (CRC),Circle Repertory Theatre, New York City, 1983; various roles, *As Is,* CRC, Circle Repertory Theatre, 1985; Larry, *Burn This,* Mark Taper Forum, Los Angeles, CA, then Plymouth Theatre, New York City, both 1987. Also appeared in *Thymus Vulgaris.*

TELEVISION DEBUT—Russian cadet, *Combat High,* NBC, 1986.

LOU LIBERATORE

PRINCIPAL TELEVISION APPEARANCES—Marty Bacon, *If It's Tuesday, It Still Must Be Belgium,* NBC, 1987.

MEMBER: Actors' Equity Association; Amnesty International.

ADDRESSES: OFFICE—c/o Circle Repertory Company, 161 Avenue of the Americas, New York, NY 10013. AGENT—c/o Paul Martino, International Creative Management, 40 W. 57th Street, New York, NY 10019.

*   *   *

LINDSAY, Robert

BRIEF ENTRY: Robert Lindsay starred in the first big hit of the 1986-87 Broadway season, the revival of the 1937 British musical *Me and My Girl.* His portrayal of the Cockney Bill Snibson earned him comparisons to Charlie Chaplin for his comedic talents and to Gene Kelly for his singing and dancing; according to the August 24, 1986 *New York Times,* many of the quarter-million dollars' worth of tickets sold the day after the show opened on Broadway were bought "on the strength of Mr. Lindsay's notices." During the show's earlier London run, the English actor won the 1985 Laurence Olivier Award; in New York he took the 1987 Antoinette Perry Award and the Drama Desk Award as best actor in a musical as well. Although *Me and My Girl* was his American debut, Lindsay was known to British audiences before he opened on the West End. A graduate of the Royal Academy of Dramatic Art, he had toured England in a modern dress production of *Hamlet* with

Manchester's Royal Exchange Theatre Company, with whom he also did *The Cherry Orchard, The Lower Depths,* and *The Beaux' Stratagem.* His previous musical credits included *Godspell* and *The Three Musketeers,* though he may have been more widely recognized for his television role as Wolfie on *Citizen Smith* and work on the BBC series *Give Us a Break.* He played opposite Laurence Olivier in the Emmy Award-winning production of *King Lear* and had parts in other televised productions of Shakespeare. Lindsay returned to England in 1987 where he was scheduled to start filming *Loser Takes All,* a romantic comedy based on a Graham Greene story.

*   *   *

LINK, Peter   1944-

PERSONAL: Born June 19, 1944, in St. Louis, MO; son of Lyman and Virginia (Anderson) Link; married Marta Heflin. EDUCATION: Attended Principia College and the University of Virginia.

VOCATION: Composer and director.

CAREER: FIRST STAGE WORK—Director, *Salvation,* Village Gate Theatre, New York City, 1969. PRINCIPAL STAGE WORK—Director, *Island,* Virginia Stage Company, Norfolk, VA, 1983; director, *Waitin' in the Wings,* Triplex Theatre, New York City, 1986. Also produced *Milwaukee,* 1978.

WRITINGS: PLAYS—(Co-author) *Island,* Portland Stage Company, Portland, ME, 1980-81. MUSICALS—Music and lyrics, *Salvation,* Village Gate Theatre, New York City, 1969; music and lyrics, *Island,* Portland Stage Company, Portland, ME, 1981, then Virginia Stage Company, Norfolk, VA, 1983-84; music, *King of Hearts,* 1978. Composed indicental music for *Earl of Ruston, The Wedding of Iphigenia, Iphigenia in Concert,* all 1971; *Older People, The Hunter, Much Ado about Nothing, Lysistrata,* all 1972; *The Orphan, The Good Doctor,* both 1973; *Ulysses in Nighttown,* 1974; *Trelawny of the Wells, The Comedy of Errors,* both 1975; *The Nightly Gents,* 1978. FILM SCORES—*Nightmare,* 1974. TELEVISION SCORES—*Much Ado about Nothing,* 1972; *Vegetable Soup,* 1974.

SIDELIGHTS: RECREATIONS—Photography.

ADDRESSES: OFFICE—285 Central Park W., New York, NY 10024.*

*   *   *

LINN-BAKER, Mark

PERSONAL: Born in New York, NY.

VOCATION: Actor, director, and playwright.

CAREER: PRINCIPAL STAGE APPEARANCES—William Evans, *The Death of von Richthofen as Witnessed from Earth,* New York Shakespeare Festival (NYSF), Public Theatre, 1982; Mark, *Doonesbury,* Biltmore Theatre, New York City, 1983; Delmount Williams, *The Miss Firecracker Contest,* Manhattan Theatre Club, then Cheryl Crawford Theatre, both New York City, 1984. Also appeared in *Alice in Concert,* Public Theater, New York City, 1980; *Randy Newman's Maybe I'm Doing It Wrong,* Production Company Theatre, New York City, 1981, then Astor Place Theatre, New York City, 1982; *The Laundry Hour,* Public Theatre, 1981; *Waiting for Godot,* American Repertory Theatre, Cambridge, MA, 1982.

PRINCIPAL STAGE WORK—Director: *Baby with the Bath Water,* American Repertory Theatre Company, Pudding Theatre, Cambridge, MA, 1982; *Savage in Limbo,* Double Image Theatre, New York City, 1985; *L.A. Freewheeling,* Hartley House Theater, New York City, 1986.

PRINCIPAL FILM APPEARANCES—*Manhattan,* United Artists, 1979; *My Favorite Year,* Metro-Goldwyn-Mayer/United Artists, 1982; also appeared in *The End of August,* 1981.

PRINCIPAL TELEVISION APPEARANCES—Series: Host, *The Comedy Zone,* CBS, 1985; Larry, *Perfect Strangers,* ABC, 1986—.

MEMBER: Artists in Action.

ADDRESSES: AGENT—c/o John Kimble or Judy Schoen, Triad Artists, 10100 Santa Monica Boulevard, 16th Floor, Los Angeles, CA 90067. PUBLICIST—c/o Neil Koenigsberg or Susan Culley, PMK Public Relations, Inc., 8436 W. Third Street, No. 650, Los Angeles, CA 90048.*

*   *   *

LIPMAN, Maureen   1946-

PERSONAL: Born May 10, 1946, in Hull, England; daughter of Maurice and Zelma Lipman; married Jack Rosenthal (a playwright). EDUCATION: Trained for the stage at the London Academy of Music and Dramatic Art.

VOCATION: Actress.

CAREER: STAGE DEBUT—Nancy, *The Knack,* Watford, U.K., 1967. PRINCIPAL STAGE APPEARANCES—Lucy, *Dracula,* Zanche, *The White Devil,* both Stables Theatre Company, Manchester, U.K., 1968-70; Eleanor Rigby, *No One Was Saved,* Theatre Upstairs, London, 1970; second randy woman, *Tyger,* National Theatre Company, New Theatre, London, 1971; Miss Richland, *The Good-Natured Man,* National Theatre Company, National Theatre, London, 1971; hospital visitor, *The National Health,* maid, *The School for Scandal,* Molly Malloy, *The Front Page,* third witch, *Macbeth,* all National Theatre Company, Old Vic Theatre, London, 1972; maid, *A Long Day's Journey into Night,* 1973; Celia, *As You Like It,* Royal Shakespeare Theatre, Stratford-on-Avon, U.K., 1973; Proserpine Garnett, *Candida,* Albery Theatre, London, 1977; Janis, *The Ball Game,* Open Space Theatre, London, 1978; Maggie, *Outside Edge,* Hampstead Theatre Club, then Queen's Theatre, both London, 1979.

FILM DEBUT—*Up the Junction,* Paramount, 1968. PRINCIPAL FILM APPEARANCES—*The Knowledge; Dangerous Davies; St. Trinian's.*

PRINCIPAL TELEVISION APPEARANCES—Series: *Agony; Dissident.* Movies: Sheila Craven, *Smiley's People,* syndicated, 1982.

SIDELIGHTS: FAVORITE ROLES—Molly Malloy in *The Front Page;* Maggie in *Outside Edge.*

ADDRESSES: AGENT—c/o Sara Randall, 348A Upper Street, London N1, England.*

*   *   *

LITTLE, Rich   1938-

PERSONAL: Full name, Richard Caruthers Little; born November 26, 1938, in Ottawa, ON, Canada; son of Lawrence Peniston (a doctor) and Elizabeth Maud (Wilson) Little; married Jeanne E. Worden, October 16, 1971; children: Bria Christianne. EDUCATION: Lisgar Collegiate, B.A., 1957.

VOCATION: Actor, comedian, and impressionist.

CAREER: TELEVISION DEBUT—Guest, *Judy Garland Show,* CBS, 1964. PRINCIPAL TELEVISION APPEARANCES—Episodic: Guest host, *Operation Entertainment,* ABC, 1968; *Love American Style,* ABC. Series: Stan Parker, *Love on a Rooftop,* ABC, 1966-71; regular, *The John Davidson Show,* ABC, 1969; regular, *ABC Comedy Hour,* ABC, 1972; regular, *The Julie Andrews Hour,* ABC, 1972-73; host, *The Rich Little Show,* NBC, 1975-1976; host, *You Asked for It,* syndicated, 1981-83; also *Wait till Your Father Gets Home* (animated), syndicated. Guest: *On Broadway Tonight,* CBS, 1965; *Barbara McNair Show,* syndicated, 1969;

RICH LITTLE

The David Frost Show, syndicated. Specials: *Rich Little's Christmas Carol; Rich Little's Washington Follies; The Christmas Raccoons; Rich Little and Friends in New Orleans.*

PRINCIPAL FILM APPEARANCES—Mr. X, *Happy Hour,* Movie Store, 1987; also appeared in *Dirty Tricks,* AVCO-Embassy, 1981.

PRINCIPAL CABARET APPEARANCES—As an impressionist and comedian, has appeared in nightclubs and cabarets throughout the world.

RECORINGS: ALBUMS—*My Fellow Comedians; The First Family Rides Again.*

AWARDS: Entertainer of the Year Award, 1974; Maple Leaf Distinguished Arts and Letters Award, 1983; Comedy Star of the Year, American Guild of Variety Artists Award; two-time winner, Best Guest on a Television Talk Show, Cleveland Amory Award.

SIDELIGHTS: From material submitted by Rich Little's publicist, *CTFT* learned that the children's nursery at the Ottawa Civic Hospital was named the "Rich Little Special Care Nursery" in 1983.

ADDRESSES: OFFICE—9200 Sunset Boulevard, Suite 607, Los Angeles, CA 90069. AGENT—c/o Frank Rio, 10100 Santa Monica Boulevard, Suite 1600, Los Angeles, CA 90067. PUBLICIST—c/o David Baiz, Baker Winokur Public Relations, Inc., 9348 Civic Center Drive, Beverly Hills, CA, 90210.

*   *   *

LOCKE, Sondra   1947-

PERSONAL: Born May 28, 1947, in Shelbyville, TN; daughter of Alfred Taylor and Pauline (Bayne) Locke; married Gordon Leigh Anderson, September 25, 1967 (divorced). EDUCATION: Attended Middle Tennessee State University.

VOCATION: Actress and director.

CAREER: FILM DEBUT—*The Heart Is a Lonely Hunter,* Warner Brothers-Seven Arts, 1968. PRINCIPAL FILM APPEARANCES— *Run Shadow Run,* 1969; *Willard,* Cinerama, 1970; *Second Coming of Suzanne,* Michael Barry, 1972; *The Daughter* (also known as *A Reflection of Fear*), 1973; *Death Game,* First American Films, 1973; *The Outlaw Josie Wales,* Warner Brothers, 1976; *Wishbone Cutter,* 1976; *The Gauntlet,* Warner Brothers, 1977; *Every Which Way But Loose,* Warner Brothers, 1978; *Bronco Billy,* Warner Brothers, 1980; *Any Which Way You Can,* Warner Brothers, 1980; *Sudden Impact: Dirty Harry IV,* Warner Brothers, 1983; *Ratboy,* 1985.

PRINCIPAL FILM WORK—Director, *Ratboy,* 1985.

PRINCIPAL TELEVISION APPEARANCES—Movies: Jessie Dunne, *Friendships, Secrets and Lies,* NBC, 1979; title role, *Rosie: The Rosemary Clooney Story,* CBS, 1982.

AWARDS: Academy Award nomination, 1968, for *The Heart Is a Lonely Hunter.*

ADDRESSES: AGENT—William Morris Agency, 151 El Camino Drive, Beverly Hills, CA 90212.*

*   *   *

LOLLOBRIGIDA, Gina   1927-

PERSONAL: Born July 4, 1927, in Subiaco, Italy; daughter of Giovanni and Giuseppina Mercuri; married Milko Skofic, 1949; children: one son. EDUCATION: Attended Liceo Artistico.

VOCATION: Actress, model, and photojournalist.

CAREER: FILM DEBUT—*Love of a Clown.* PRINCIPAL FILM APPEARANCES—*Aquila Nera,* 1946; *Il Delitto di Giovanni Episcopo,* 1947; *Campane a Martello,* 1949; *Achtung, Banditti!,* 1951; *Fanfan la Tulipe* (*Fanfan the Tulip*), 1951; *Altri Tempi,* 1951; *Les Belles de Nuit* (*Night Beauties*), 1952; *The Wayward Wife,* 1952; *Pane, Amore e Fantasia* (*Bread, Love, and Dreams*), 1953; *Le Grand Jeu,* 1953; *Pane, Amore e Gelosia* (*Bread, Love, and Jealousy*), 1954; *La Bella di Roma,* 1954; *La Romana* (*Woman of Rome*), 1954; *Beat the Devil,* 1954; *La Donna piu Bella del Mondo* (*The Most Beautiful Woman in the World*), 1955; *Trapeze,* United Artists, 1956; *The Hunchback of Notre Dame,* Allied Artists, 1957; *Anna di Brooklyn,* 1958; *La Loi,* 1958; *Solomon and Sheba,* United Artists, 1959; *Never So Few,* Metro-Goldwyn-Mayer (MGM), 1959; *Where the Hot Wind Blows,* MGM, 1960; *Go Naked in the World,* MGM, 1961; *Come September,* Universal, 1961; *Venus*

GINA LOLLOBRIGIDA

Imperiale, 1961; *Mare Matto*, 1962; *Woman of Straw*, United Artists, 1964; *Strange Bedfellows*, Universal, 1965; *Le Bambole*, 1964; *Les Sultans*, 1965; *Hotel Paradiso*, MGM, 1966; *Cervantes*, 1967; *La Morte la Fatto L'Uovo*, 1967; *Un Bellissimo Novembre (That Splendid November)*, 1968; *Buona Sera, Mrs. Campbell*, United Artists, 1969; *Bad Man's River*, 1971; *King, Queen, Knave*, AVCO-Embassy, 1972.

PRINCIPAL TELEVISION APPEARANCES—Series: Francesca Gioberti, *Falcon Crest*, CBS, 1984—. Movies: Princess Alexandra, *Deceptions*, NBC, 1985. Specials: *Love Boat Christmas*, ABC, 1986.

PRINCIPAL STAGE APPEARANCES—*Night of 100 Stars*, Radio City Music Hall, New York City, 1982.

RELATED CAREER—Photojournalist and model.

WRITINGS: BOOKS—*Italia Mia* (photography), 1974; *Il Segreto Delle Rose*, 1984; also, *The Philippines, Manila*.

ADDRESSES: AGENT—c/o Richard Heckenkamp, Film Artists Associates, 470 S. San Vicente Boulevard, Suite 104, Los Angeles, CA 90048.

*   *   *

LONG, Shelley   1949-

PERSONAL: Born August 23, 1949, in Fort Wayne, IN; married Bruce Tyson; children: Juliana. EDUCATION: Attended Northwestern University.

VOCATION: Actress, producer, director, and writer.

CAREER: FILM DEBUT—*A Small Circle of Friends*, United Artists, 1980. PRINCIPAL FILM APPEARANCES—*Caveman*, United Artists, 1981; *Nightshift*, Warner Brothers, 1982; *Losin' It*, Embassy, 1983; *Irreconcilable Differences*, Warner Brothers, 1984; *The Money Pit*, Universal, 1986; *Outrageous Fortune*, Touchstone, 1986; *Hello Again*, Touchstone, 1987.

PRINCIPAL TELEVISION APPEARANCES—Series: Co-host, *Sorting It Out*, Chicago, IL; Diane Chambers, *Cheers*, NBC, 1982-87.

PRINCIPAL TELEVISION WORK—Associate producer, *Sorting It Out*.

PRINCIPAL STAGE APPEARANCES—With the Second City Troupe, Chicago, IL.

RELATED CAREER—Former television model and spokesperson; writer, director, and producer of industrial and educational films.

AWARDS: Recipient of three local Emmy Awards, for *Sorting It Out;* Outstanding Leading Actress in a Comedy Series, Emmy Award, 1983, for *Cheers;* also two Golden Globe Awards for *Cheers*.

ADDRESSES: AGENT—William Morris Agency, 151 El Camino Drive, Beverly Hills, CA 90212. MANAGER—Mickelson-Littman Management, 329 N. Weatherly Drive, Suite 205, Beverly Hills, CA 90211.*

LORTEL, Lucille   1905-

PERSONAL: Born Lucille Mayo, December 16, 1905, in New York, NY; daughter of Harry (a garment industry executive) and Anna Mayo; married Louis Schweitzer (a chemical engineer and manufacturer), March 23, 1931 (died, September 19, 1971). EDUCATION: Attended Adelphi College; trained for the stage at the American Academy of Dramatic Arts and with Arnold Korf and Max Reinhardt.

VOCATION: Producer and actress.

CAREER: PRINCIPAL STAGE APPEARANCES—Handmaiden, then Iras, *Caesar and Cleopatra*, Guild Theatre, New York City, 1925; Inez, *The Dove*, Empire Theatre, New York City, 1925; Clara Rathbone, *One Man's Woman*, 48th Street Theatre, New York City, 1926; Elsa, *The Virgin Man*, Princess Theatre, New York City, 1927; French maid, *The Man Who Reclaimed His Head*, Broadhurst Theatre, New York City, 1932. Also appeared in *Two by Two*, Selwyn Theatre, New York City, 1925; *The Man Who Laughed Last*, Palace Theatre, New York City, 1927; and in summer theatre productions in Albany, NY, and Lewiston, ME, both 1924.

MAJOR TOURS—Poppy, *The Shanghai Gesture*, U.S. cities, 1927; also toured in summer theatre and vaudeville, and with the Merkle Harder Repertory Company, 1924.

PRINCIPAL STAGE WORK—Producer, all with the White Barn Theatre, Westport, CT: *The Painted Wagon*, 1947; *Red Roses for Me, Jim Dandy, Alive and Kicking*, all 1948; *Don Perlimplin and Belisa in the Garden, The Stranger* (opera), both 1949; *Murder in the Cathedral*, 1950; *Loaves and Fishes*, 1951; *Brewsie and Willie, The Lottery*, both 1952; *Geoffrey Holder and His Company of Dancers*, 1953; *Juno and the Paycock*, 1954; *Three Players of a Summer Game, Pere Goriot*, both 1955; *Dona Rosita, Ghosts, I Knock at the Door*, all 1956; *Baty's Dulcinea, The Chairs, Saint's Day*, all 1957; *Irene Innocente, Talk to Me Like the Rain, Triple Cross, Song of Songs, Blood Wedding*, all 1958; *Shakespeare in Harlem*, 1959; *Mishima's Noh Plays, Fam and Yam, Embers*, all 1960; *The Typists, The Deceased and the Grand Vizir*, both 1961; *Brecht on Brecht, The World of Kurt Weill in Song*, both 1963; *The Blood Knot, The After Dinner Opera Company*, both 1964; *The Long Valley, The Dream Watcher*, both 1965.

Producer, all with Theatre de Lys, New York City: *The Threepenny Opera*, 1955; *Hamlet*, 1955; *The Mark Anthony Dance Theatre, Curtains Up*, both 1958; *Two Philoctetes, Sweet Confession, Electra, Harlequinade*, and *I Rise in Flames, Cried the Phoenix*, all 1959; *Figure in the Night, The Moon Shines on Kylenamoe, The Lunatic View*, all 1962; *The Crown, The Ring and the Roses, Put It in Writing*, all 1963; *Pictures in the Hallway, I Knock at the Door*, both 1964; *Square in the Eye*, and *The Old Glory: Benito Cereno, Theatre Songs*, all 1965; *Serjeant Musgrave's Dance, The Israel Mime Theatre, The Seven Ages of Bernard Shaw, The Deadly Art*, and *Come Slowly, Eden*, all 1966; *The Viewing, Conditioned Reflex, Willie Doesn't Live Here Anymore, A Funny Kind of Evening with David Kossof, The Deer Park, Postcards, The Club Bedroom, Limb of Snow, The Meeting*, all 1967; *Our Man in Madras, On Vacation, A Madrigal of Shakespeare, Mr. and Mrs. Lyman, Hello and Goodbye, Cuba Si, The Guns of Carrar*, all 1968; *The Projection Room, Neighbors, An Evening with James Agee, A Round with Ring*, and *Oh, Pioneers*, all 1969; *Dream of a Blacklisted Actor, Cruising Speed 600 MPH, Mrs. Snow*, all 1970; *Heritage, A Biography in Song*, and *Sally, George, and Martha*, all

1971; *Madame de Sade, Wilde!*, both 1972; *Love Gotta Come by Saturday Night, Orrin, Three on Broadway, The Interview, The Epic of Buster Friend*, all 1973; *Scott and Zelda, Fire and Ice, The Prodigal Sister, Drums at Yale*, all 1974; *Medal of Honor Rag*, 1976; *Buried Child*, 1978; *Getting Out*, 1979.

Producer, all at the Lucille Lortel Theatre (formerly Theatre de Lys): *The Lady and the Clarinet*, 1983; *Woza Albert!, Isn't It Romantic?*, both 1984; *Not about Heroes*, 1985; *Gertrude Stein and a Companion, Elisabeth Welch: Time to Start Living*, both 1986.

Producer, all in New York City: *A Sleep of Prisoners*, St. James Church, 1951; *The River Line*, Carnegie Hall Playhouse, 1957; *I Knock at the Door*, Belasco Theatre, 1957; *Cock-a-Doodle Dandy*, Carnegie Hall Playhouse, 1958; *The Balcony*, Circle in the Square, 1960; *Happy As Larry*, Martinique Theatre, 1961; *The Blood Knot*, Cricket Theatre, 1964; *A Streetcar Named Desire*, Vivian Beaumont Theatre, then St. James Theatre, 1973; *Glasshouse*, Theatre at St. Peter's Church, 1981; *Marvelous Gray*, Lion Theatre, 1982; *Angels Fall*, Longacre Theatre, 1983; "Ohio Impromptu," "Catastrophe," "What Where," as *Samuel Beckett Plays*, all Harold Clurman Theatre, 1983-84; *Isn't It Romantic?*, Playwrights Horizons Theatre, 1983; *Rockaby*, Samuel Beckett Theatre, 1984; *As Is*, Lyceum Theatre, 1985; *Blood Knot*, John Golden Theatre, 1985; *An Evening with Ekkehard Schall*, Harold Clurman Theatre, 1985.

PRINCIPAL FILM APPEARANCES—*The Man Who Laughed Last*, Warner Brothers, 1930; also appeared in a series of short films for Warner Brothers.

RADIO DEBUT—*Advice to the Lovelorn* WHN, New York City, 1935. PRINCIPAL RADIO APPEARANCES—*Great Women of History*, WHN.

RELATED CAREER—Founder and artistic director, White Barn Theatre, Westport, CT, 1947—; owner, operator, and producer, Theatre de Lys (later Lucille Lortel Theatre), New York City, 1955—; co-founder, American Shakespeare Festival Theatre and Academy, 1955; founder and artistic director, Matinee Theatre Series for the Greater New York Chapter of the American National Theatre and Academy (ANTA), 1956-76; member of the national and New York boards of directors, ANTA; member of the advisory committee, Institute for Advanced Study of Theatre Arts (IASTA), 1959—; trustee, National Repertory Theatre, 1961—; member of the citizen's advisory council, Office of Cultural Affairs for the City of New York, 1963—; member of the board of directors, Lincoln Center for the Performing Arts, 1971—.

AWARDS: Best Play, Obie Award from the *Village Voice*, 1956, for *The Threepenny Opera*; special citation, Obie Award, 1958, for "fostering and furthering the spirit of theatrical experiment;" Greater New York Chapter of ANTA awards, both 1959, for "outstanding achievement as artistic director of the ANTA Matinee Series," and for "unselfish devotion to the art of theatre;" Whistler Society Award, 1959, for "outstanding merit in the field of theatre;" Best Play, Obie Award, 1960, for *The Balcony;* National ANTA Award, 1962, for "pioneering work fostering new playwrights, directors, and actors;" Margo Jones Award 1962, for "significant contribution to the dramatic art with hitherto unproduced plays;" Lee Strasberg Lifetime Achievement Award, 1985; Kennedy Center Lifetime Achievement Award, 1987. Honorary degrees: University of Bridgeport, 1985; Fairfield University, 1987.

MEMBER: New Dramatists Committee (advisory council, 1959—);

Pickwick Club (London; honorary member), Ziegfeld Club, Woman Pays Club.

SIDELIGHTS: Lucille Lortel, the "Queen of Off-Broadway," is a pioneering theatre producer and proprietor whose singular commitment to innovative drama is perhaps unparalleled in the history of the American stage. For more than forty years the diminutive and self-effacing Lortel has been producing shows by heretofore unknown playwrights, including Tennessee Williams, Athol Fugard, Eugene Ionesco, Federico Garcia Lorca, Edward Albee, William Inge, and Paul Zindel. Having founded two thriving experimental theatres, the White Barn Theatre in Westport, Connecticut, and Theatre de Lys (now Lucille Lortel Theatre) in New York City, Lortel continues to spend "the overwhelming share of her time helping artistic anarchists," according to Ward Morehouse in the June 18, 1985 *Christian Science Monitor*. Lortel, who was the first recipient of the annual Lee Strasberg Lifetime Achievement Award and who has also been honored with a prestigious Kennedy Center Lifetime Achievement Award, explained her theatrical philosophy thus: "I want something to think about when I leave the theatre. With comedy, you sometimes forget it as soon as you see it. So that's why I put on plays of a more serious nature." Her more than three hundred productions of such plays have garnered numerous awards and launched the careers of such varied show business talents as movie directors Peter Bogdanovich and Sidney Lumet and performers Eva Marie Saint, Vincent Gardenia, Sada Thompson, and George Peppard. In a June, 1980 *Fifty Plus* interview, Lortel noted: "If you love the theatre, you must be innovative. You must try new ideas and new faces. That's the only way the theatre can develop. . . . You must take a chance."

Lortel was born in New York City, the daughter of a garment industry executive. From an early age the theatre captivated her, so much so that by 1920 she was attending acting classes at the American Academy of Dramatic Arts. She then continued her education in Germany, where she worked with Arnold Korf and producer-director Max Reinhardt. Her stage debut occurred in 1924, with a stock company in Albany, New York, and within a year she was appearing on Broadway in a variety of minor parts. Gradually she began to receive larger roles on Broadway and in national touring companies—Clara Rathbone in the comedy *One Man's Woman*, Elsa in the comedy *The Virgin Man*, and Poppy in *The Shanghai Gesture*. Her acting career was cut short in 1931 by her marriage to Louis Schweitzer, a wealthy manufacturer of cigarette paper. At Schweitzer's insistence, Lortel retired from the stage, though for a few years she continued to work in short films and provided a voice for radio dramas.

Lortel told the *New York Times* of August 5, 1979 that the endless round of cocktail parties and the routine of married life caused her to become increasingly restless and dissatisfied as the years wore on. In the summer of 1947, while her husband was away on a business trip, she was approached by actor Canada Lee and playwright Philip Huston about the possibility of staging a new play for a private audience. Thrilled by the opportunity, Lortel volunteered the barn on her Connecticut estate, empty of horses because of a scarcity of oats. Huston's *The Painted Wagon* premiered there on a hastily built platform and the White Barn Theatre was born. At first Lortel was producer, decorator, and publicist for the tiny experimental theatre. As she told the *New York Times* (September 30, 1980): "I began without any idea or purpose. I was staging dramatic readings for anybody who wanted to give me a script. All I knew was that I wanted to do new plays." By 1951 the White Barn Theatre was a successful nonprofit foundation; Lortel acted as president of the organization, a post she still holds. Actress Mildred Dunnock recalled in a 1981 *Avenue* profile of Lortel that the White Barn "was a wonderful opportunity, a place to try out new things, with great freedom to live and work. And yet, as progressive as it was, no actor who ever worked there ever felt he was taking a chance with his career because he knew no production would be shoddy."

Even Louis Schweitzer became drawn in by his wife's enthusiasm for the finest avant-garde theatrical works. In 1955 he bought the Theatre de Lys for Lortel so that she would have a New York base to continue her experimentations. That theatre quickly became a pacesetter for Off-Broadway productions and a valuable precursor to the Off-Off Broadway movement. Lortel's first production at Theatre de Lys, *The Threepenny Opera,* was an unprecedented success that ran for seven years through 2,611 performances. Although Lortel appreciated the play's popularity, she felt it somewhat thwarted her purpose, namely, to stage numerous and varied artistic dramas. So in 1956 she inaugurated a Tuesday matinee series supported by the American National Theatre and Academy (ANTA). Once again she personally chose all the productions, giving emphasis to new and foreign playwrights, inviting dance troupes, and offering actors an opportunity to give readings from works of their own choosing. Helen Hayes, Dame Sybil Thorndike, and Richard Burton were among the many performers who read during these matinees. The series ran until 1975 and served as a debut forum for plays by Fugard, Williams, Albee, and Inge.

Now called the Lucille Lortel Theatre, the former Theatre de Lys is among the most prestigious of Off-Broadway venues. Under both names it has played host to numerous notable modern plays, from the comedic *Isn't It Romantic* to Sam Shepard's caustic Pulitzer Prize-winning drama *Buried Child.* As a widow well into her eighties, Lortel continued to nurture her consuming passion with unabated vigor. "I think I've gotten as much a kick out of producing plays as I did acting," she told the *Christian Science Monitor,* "because I got just as nervous. But I don't have to look pretty when I'm backstage as a producer. So I can be nervous and look the way I look!" Although she sometimes claims that she may one day retire, Lortel continues to encourage new talent and to discover tomorrow's seminal dramatists. All of her time and much of her wealth goes into the support of nonprofit theatres because, as she commented in the *New York Times,* "I've got a one-track mind and it's theater, theater, theater. I have no time for anything else."

ADDRESSES: OFFICE—Lucille Lortel Theatre, 12 Christopher Street, New York, NY 10014.*

*　　*　　*

LUDLAM, Charles   1943-1987

PERSONAL: Born April 12, 1943, in Floral Park, NY; died of AIDS-related pneumonia in New York City, May 28, 1987; son of Joseph William and Marjorie (Braun) Ludlam. EDUCATION: Hofstra University, B.A., dramatic literature, 1965.

VOCATION: Actor, playwright, director, producer, and designer.

CAREER: OFF-OFF BROADWAY DEBUT—Peeping Tom, *The Life of Lady Godiva,* Seventeenth Street Studio, 1967. LONDON DEBUT—Title role, *Bluebeard,* Open Space Theatre, 1971. PRINCIPAL STAGE APPEARANCES—All with the Ridiculous Theatrical Company (see production details below): Svengali, Norma Desmond, *Big Hotel;* Cosroe, Zabina, *When Queens Collide;* the Fool, *The*

Grand Tarot; Saint Obnoxious, *Turds in Hell;* title role, *Bluebeard;* An Te Hai, *Eunuchs of the Forbidden City;* Paw Hatfield, *Corn;* title role, *Camille;* Buck Armstrong, *Hot Ice;* Carleton Stone, Jr., *Stage Blood; Professor Bedlam's Educational Punch and Judy Show* (puppet show); title role, *Caprice;* featured role, *The Adventures of Karagoz;* Hagen, *Der Ring Gott Farblonjet;* Charles, *The Ventriloquist's Wife;* Botchup, *Utopia, Incorporated;* Anti-Galaxie Nebula (puppet show); Ebenezer Scrooge, *A Christmas Carol;* Leonard Silver, *Reverse Psychology;* Bram Taylor, *Love's Tangled Web;* Phil Landers, *Secret Lives of the Sexists;* Count Benito Neroni, *Exquisite Torture;* Mr. Foufas, *Le Bourgeois Avant-Garde;* Maria Magdelena Galas, *Galas;* various roles, *The Mystery of Irma Vep;* title role, *Salammabo;* Chester Nurdiger, *The Artificial Jungle.* Also appeared in later Off-Off Broadway revivals of these productions and in the title role in the American Ibsen Theatre's production of *Hedda Gabler,* Pittsburgh, PA, 1984.

PRINCIPAL STAGE WORK—Producer and director for the Ridiculous Theatrical Company: *Big Hotel,* Gate Theatre, New York City, 1967; *When Queens Collide* (also known as *Conquest of the Universe*), Gate Theatre, 1967, restaged as *Conquest of the Universe, or When Queens Collide,* One Sheridan Square, New York City, 1979; *The Grand Tarot,* Millenium Film Workshop, New York City, 1969; *Turds in Hell,* Gate Theatre, then Masque Theatre, New York City, 1969; *Bluebeard,* La Mama Experimental Theatre Club, then the Trocadero at Christopher's End, later the Performing Garage, all New York City, 1970; *Eunuchs of the Forbidden City,* European tour, 1971, then Theatre for the New City, later the Performing Garage, both New York City, 1972; *Corn,* Thirteenth Street Theatre, New York City, 1972; *Camille,* Thirteenth Street Theatre, 1973; *Hot Ice,* Tamanous Playhouse, Vancouver, BC, Canada, 1973; *Professor Bedlam's Educational Punch and Judy Show* (puppet show), Evergreen Theatre, New York City, 1975; *Stage Blood,* Evergreen Theatre, 1975, restaged at the Truck and Warehouse Theatre, New York City, 1977; *The Adventures of Karagoz,* Festival Mondial de Theatre, Nancy, France, 1976; *Caprice,* Provincetown Playhouse, then Performing Garage, both New York City, 1976; (also designer) *Der Ring Gott Farblonjet,* Truck and Warehouse Theatre, 1977; *The Ventriloquist's Wife, Anti-Galaxie Nebula* (puppet show), and *Utopia, Incorporated,* all One Sheridan Square, 1978; *The Enchanted Pig, The Elephant Woman, A Christmas Carol,* all One Sheridan Square, 1979; (also designer) *Reverse Psychology,* One Sheridan Square, 1980; *Love's Tangled Web,* One Sheridan Square, 1981; *Secret Lives of the Sexists, Exquisite Torture,* both One Sheridan Square, 1982; (also designer) *Le Bourgeois Avant-Garde, Galas,* both One Sheridan Square, 1983; (also designer) *The Mystery of Irma Vep,* One Sheridan Square, 1984; *Salammbo,* One Sheridan Square, 1985; *The Artificial Jungle,* One Sheridan Square, 1986. Dates are for original productions; in early years of the Ridiculous Theatrical Company, plays were done in repertory, later in individual runs.

MAJOR TOURS—Produced, directed, and acted in Ridiculous Theatrical Company tours of European cities, 1971 and 1973, U.S. cities, 1978, and West Coast, 1980.

PRINCIPAL FILM APPEARANCES—*The Big Easy,* Columbia, 1987; also appeared in *Forever, Lulu,* 1987; *Imposters; The Sorrows of Dolores; Museum of Wax; She Must Be Seeing Things.* PRINCIPAL FILM WORK—Producer and director: *The Sorrows of Dolores; Museum of Wax.*

PRINCIPAL TELEVISION APPEARANCES—Episodic: *Oh Madeline,* ABC, 1984; *Miami Vice,* NBC, 1985; *Tales from the Darkside,* syndicated, 1986.

RELATED CAREER—Directed Santa Fe Opera Company productions of *The English Cat,* 1985, and *Die Fledermaus,* 1986. Lecturer at University of Massachusetts, 1972, University of Connecticut, 1974-75, American University, 1976, New York University, 1977 and 1979-80, Yale University, 1977; adjunct associate professor, Yale University, 1982-83.

WRITINGS: PLAYS—See production details above unless indicated. *Big Hotel,* 1967; *When Queens Collide* (also known as *Conquest of the Universe*), 1967; *The Grand Tarot,* 1969; (with Bill Vehr) *Turds in Hell,* 1969, published in *Drama Review,* edited by Erika Munk, New York University, 1969; *Bluebeard,* 1970, published in *Best Plays of Off Broadway, 1970,* edited by Michael Smith, Bobbs-Merrill, 1970, in *The Off-Off Broadway Book,* edited by Albert Poland and Bruce Mailman, Bobbs-Merrill, 1972, and by Samuel French, Inc., 1987; *Eunuchs of the Forbidden City,* 1971, published in *Scripts,* edited by Erika Munk and Bill Coco, New York Shakespeare Festival, 1972; *Corn,* 1972; (adaptor) *Camille,* 1973, published by Samuel French, Inc., 1987; *Hot Ice,* 1973, published in *Drama Review,* edited by Michael Kirby, New York University, 1974; *Professor Bedlam's Educational Punch and Judy Show* (puppet show), 1975; *Stage Blood,* 1975, published in *Theatre of the Ridiculous,* edited by Bonnie Marranca and Gautum Dasgupta, Performing Arts Journal Publications, 1979, and by Samuel French, Inc., 1987; *The Adventures of Karagoz,* 1976; (adaptor) *Jack and the Beanstalk,* Brooklyn Academy of Music, Brooklyn, NY, 1976; *Caprice,* 1976; *Der Ring Gott Farblonjet,* 1977; *The Ventriloquist's Wife,* 1978; *Utopia, Incorporated,* 1978; (with Bill Vehr and Everett Quinton) *Anti-Galaxie Nebula* (puppet show), 1978; *The Enchanted Pig,* 1979; *The Elephant Woman,* 1979; (adaptor) *A Christmas Carol,* 1979; *Reverse Psychology,* 1980; *Love's Tangled Web,* 1981; *Secret Lives of the Sexists,* 1982; *Exquisite Torture,* 1982; *Le Bourgeois Avant-Garde,* 1983; *Galas,* 1983; *The Mystery of Irma Vep,* 1984, published by Samuel French, Inc., 1987; (adaptor) *Salammbo,* 1985; *The Artificial Jungle,* 1986, published by Samuel French, Inc., 1987.

SCREENPLAYS—*The Sorrows of Dolores; Museum of Wax.*

ESSAYS—"The Totalitarian Theatre of Energy" in *Drama Review,* edited by Erika Munk, New York University, 1970; "The Seven Levels of the Theatre" in *Performance,* edited by Erika Munk and Bill Coco, New York Shakespeare Festival, 1972; "Ridiculous Theatre: Scourge of Human Folly" in *Drama Review,* edited by Michael Kirby, New York University, 1975.

Also author of libretto for operas *The Production of Mysteries,* performed by City Symphony, Bennington, VT, 1980, then Brooklyn Philharmonic Orchestra, Brooklyn, NY, 1985, and *Die Fledermaus,* performed by Santa Fe Opera, Santa Fe, NM, 1986; wrote scenario for Paul Taylor Dance Company production *Aphrodisiamania,* Brooklyn Academy of Music, Brooklyn, NY, 1977, and subsequent tour.

AWARDS: Obie Award from the *Village Voice,* 1969, for "Distinguished Achievement in the Off-Broadway Theatre;" Second Prize, BITEF (International Avant-Garde Theatre Festival, Belgrade, Yugoslavia), 1971, for *Bluebeard;* Guggenheim Fellowship in Playwriting, 1971; Outstanding Performance, Obie, 1973, for *Corn* and *Camille;* Outstanding Performance, Obie, 1975, for *Professor Bedlam's Educational Punch and Judy Show;* New York State Council on the Arts commission, 1975; Rockefeller Brothers Fund Grant in Playwriting, 1976; Outstanding Design, Obie, 1977, for *Der Ring Gott Farblonjet;* Ford Foundation New American Plays

commission, 1977; Association of Comedy Artists Award, 1978, for Excellence and Originality in Comedy; National Endowment for the Arts Fellowship in Playwriting, 1981, and 1984; Drama Desk Special Award, 1982, for "Outstanding Achievement in the Theatre;" Excellence in Design, Maharam Foundation Award, 1985, for *The Mystery of Irma Vep;* Outstanding Performance, Obie, Drama Desk Award, both 1985, for *The Mystery of Irma Vep;* Rosamund Gilder Award, 1986, for "Distinguished Achievement in the Theatre;" Obie, 1987, for "Distinguished Achievement in the Off-Broadway Theatre."

SIDELIGHTS: At the time of his death, the *New York Times* called Charles Ludlam "one of the most prolific and flamboyant artists in the theatre of the avant-garde." His obituary went on to compare the highly regarded impressario to the theatrical entrepreneurs of the nineteenth century for his actions as playwright, director, producer, and star of the Ridiculous Theatrical Company.

OBITUARIES AND OTHER SOURCES: New York Times, April 7, 1972, December 28, 1977, December 5, 1978, April 24, 1979, May 29, 1987.

*   *   *

LUEDTKE, Kurt   1939-

PERSONAL: Surname is pronounced "Lud-key"; full name, Kurt Mamre Luedtke; born September 28, 1939, in Grand Rapids, MI; son of Herman Ernst (a lumber broker) and Virginia (Victory) Luedtke; married Eleanor Kruglinski (a symphony vice-president), May 1, 1965. EDUCATION: Brown University, B.A., 1961.

VOCATION: Writer.

CAREER: Also see *WRITINGS* below.

RELATED CAREER—Reporter, *Grand Rapids Press,* Grand Rapids, MI, 1961-62; reporter, *Miami Herald,* Miami, FL, 1963-65; reporter, 1965-66, assistant city editor, 1966-67, photography director, 1967-69, assistant managing editor, 1969-70, assistant executive editor, 1970-73, executive editor, 1973-78, all with the Detroit *Free Press,* Detroit, MI.

WRITINGS: SCREENPLAYS—*Absence of Malice,* Columbia, 1981; *Out of Africa,* Universal, 1985; *Walls,* upcoming.

AWARDS: Professional Journalism Fellow, Stanford University, 1973; Best Original Screenplay, Academy Award nomination, 1982, for *Absence of Malice;* Best Screenplay Adaptation, Academy Award, 1985, for *Out of Africa.*

MEMBER: OFFICE—600 W. Brown Street, Birmingham, MI 48009. AGENT—c/o George Diskant, 1033 Gayley Avenue, Suite 202, Los Angeles, CA 90024.

*   *   *

LuPONE, Patti   1949-

PERSONAL: Born April 21, 1949, in Northport, NY; daughter of Orlando Joseph and Angela Louise (Patti) LuPone. EDUCATION: Received B.F.A. from the Juilliard School of Music and Drama.

VOCATION: Actress and singer.

CAREER: STAGE DEBUT—Title role, *Iphigenia,* Young Vic Theatre, London, 1970. BROADWAY DEBUT—Irina, *The Three Sisters,* Lucy Lockit, *The Beggar's Opera,* Lizzie, *Next Time I'll Sing to You,* all with the Acting Company, Billy Rose Theatre, 1973. PRINCIPAL STAGE APPEARANCES— Lady Teazle, *The School for Scandal,* Kathleen, *The Hostage,* Natasha, *The Lower Depths,* all with the Acting Company, Good Shepherd Faith Church, New York City, 1972; Rosamund, *The Robber Bridegroom,* Prince Edward, *Edward II,* Kitty Duval, *The Time of Your Life,* all with the Acting Company, Harkness Theatre, New York City, 1975; Genevieve, *The Baker's Wife,* Kennedy Center for the Performing Arts, Washington, DC, 1976; Ruth, *The Woods,* St. Nicholas Theatre Company, Chicago, IL, 1977; Rita, Lily La Pon, *The Water Engine,* Plymouth Theatre, New York City, 1978; call girl, *Working,* 46th Street Theatre, New York City, 1978; Monagh, *Catchpenny Twist,* Hartford Stage Company, Hartford, CT, 1979; title role, *Evita,* Broadway Theatre, New York City, 1979; Rosalind, *As You Like It,* Guthrie Theatre, Minneapolis, MN, 1981; Ruth, *The Woods,* Second Stage Theatre, New York City, 1981; Edmond's wife, *Edmond,* Provincetown Playhouse, New York City, 1983; Cleo, *America Kicks Up Its Heels,* Playwrights Horizons Mainstage Theatre, New York City, 1983; Nancy, *Oliver!,* Mark Hellinger Theatre, New York City, 1984; Reporter, *Accidental Death of an Anarchist,* Belasco Theatre, New York City, 1984; Fantine, *Les Miserables,* Royal Shakespeare Company, Barbican Theatre Center, London, then Broadway Theatre, both 1987; Reno Sweeney, *Anything Goes,* Vivian Beaumont Theatre, New York City, 1987. Also appeared as Moll, *The Cradle Will Rock,* with the Acting Company, New York City, 1982; and in *Stars of Broadway,* Colonie Coliseum, Albany, NY, 1983. Also *Women Beware Women, Scapin, Stage Directions,* all New York City.

MAJOR TOURS—Title role, *Evita,* U.S. cities, 1979.

PRINCIPAL FILM APPEARANCES—*King of the Gypsies,* Paramount, 1978; *1941,* Universal, 1979; *Fighting Back,* Paramount, 1982; *Cat's Eye,* Metro-Goldwyn-Mayer/United Artists, 1985.

PRINCIPAL TELEVISION APPEARANCES—Episodic: Kitty, "The Time of Your Life," *American Playhouse,* PBS; also appeared in "The Cradle Will Rock," *American Playhouse,* PBS. Movies: Lady Bird Johnson, *LBJ: The Early Years,* NBC, 1987.

AWARDS: Best Actress in a Musical, Antoinette Perry Award, 1980, for *Evita.*

MEMBER: Actors' Equity Association, Screen Actors Guild, American Federation of Television and Radio Artists.

ADDRESSES: AGENT—Triad Artists, Inc., 10100 Santa Monica Boulevard, Los Angeles, CA 90067.*

*   *   *

LYNCH, David   1947-

PERSONAL: Born 1947, in Montana. EDUCATION: Attended Pennsylvania Academy of Fine Arts.

VOCATION: Director and writer.

CAREER: PRINCIPAL FILM WORK—Also see *WRITINGS* below. Director: *The Grandmother* (16mm), independent, 1970; *Eraserhead,* American Film Institute, 1978; *The Elephant Man,* Paramount, 1980; *Dune,* Universal, 1984; *Blue Velvet,* De Laurentiis Entertainment Group, 1986.

WRITINGS: SCREENPLAYS—*Eraserhead,* American Film Institute, 1978; co-writer, *The Elephant Man,* Paramount, 1980; *Dune,* Universal, 1984; *Blue Velvet,* Twentieth Century-Fox, 1987.

AWARDS: Best Director, Los Angeles Film Critics Award, National Society of Film Critics Award Academy Award nomination, all 1986, for *Blue Velvet;* American Film Institute Grant.

ADDRESSES: AGENT—c/o Rick Nicita, Creative Artists Agency, 1888 Century Park E., Suite 1400, Los Angeles, CA 90067.*

*   *   *

LYNCH, Richard   1936-

PERSONAL: Born April 29, 1936.

VOCATION: Actor.

CAREER: PRINCIPAL TELEVISION APPEARANCES—Movies: Zane, *Starsky and Hutch,* ABC, 1975; Shirley, *Dog and Cat,* ABC, 1977; Mr. Rimmin, *Good Against Evil,* ABC, 1977; Curt Blair, *Roger and Harry: The Mitera Target,* ABC, 1977; Anton Voytek, *Vampire,* 1979; Sam Shockley, *Alcatraz: The Whole Shocking Story,* NBC, 1980; Johnny O'Brien, *Sizzle,* ABC, 1981; William Devine, *White Water Rebels,* CBS, 1983; Professor Gustav Norden, *The Last Ninja,* ABC, 1983.

FILM DEBUT—*Scarecrow,* Warner Brothers, 1973. PRINCIPAL FILM APPEARANCES—*The Premonition,* AVCO-Embassy, 1976; *Delta Fox,* 1977; *Steel,* 1980; *The Formula,* United Artists, 1980; *Little Nikita,* Columbia, upcoming; also *Savage Dawn* and *Cut and Run.*

BROADWAY DEBUT—*The Devils.* PRINCIPAL STAGE APPEARANCES—Sergeant Brisbey, *The Basic Training of Pavlo Hummel,* Longacre Theatre, New York City, 1977; also *The Balcony* and *The Lion in Winter,* both New York City.

ADDRESSES: AGENT—c/o Mike Greenfield, Charter Management, 9000 Sunset Boulevard, Suite 1112, Los Angeles, CA 90069.*

*   *   *

LYNLEY, Carol   1942-

PERSONAL: Born Carol Ann Jones, February 13, 1942, in New York, NY; daughter of Cyril and Frances (Felch) Jones; children: Jill Veronica.

VOCATION: Actress.

CAREER: PRINCIPAL FILM APPEARANCES—*Light in the Forest,* Buena Vista, 1958; *Holiday for Lovers,* 1959; *Blue Denim,* Twentieth Century-Fox, 1959; *The Last Sunset*, 1961; *Return to Peyton Place*, Twentieth Century-Fox, 1961; *The Cardinal*, 1963; *Under the Yum Yum Tree*, Columbia, 1963; *The Pleasure Seekers*, 1964; *Harlow*, 1965; *Bunny Lake Is Missing*, Columbia, 1965; *The Shuttered Room*, Warner Brothers, 1968; *Danger Route*, United Artists, 1968; *The Maltese Bippy*, Metro-Goldwyn-Mayer, 1969; *Norwood*, Paramount, 1970; *The Poseiden Adventure*, Twentieth Century-Fox, 1972; *Cotter*, 1972; *The Shape of Things to Come*, 1979; *The Cat and the Canary*, Grenadier Films, Ltd., 1982; *Vigilante*, Artists Releasing Corporation, 1983; *Dark Tower*, Spectrafilm, upcoming.

PRINCIPAL TELEVISION APPEARANCES—Episodic: *Goodyear Playhouse*, NBC, 1956; *Alfred Hitchcock Presents*, CBS, 1957; *DuPont Show of the Month*, NBC, 1957; *General Electric Theatre*, CBS, 1958, 1959; *Pursuit*, CBS, 1958; *Shirley Temple Story Book*, ABC, 1958; *Laf Hit*, 1962; *Alcoa Premiere*, ABC, 1962; *The Virginian*, NBC, 1962; *Dick Powell Theatre*, CBS, 1963; *Bob Hope Chrysler Theatre*, NBC, 1965-66; *Run for Your Life*, NBC, 1966; *The Man from U.N.C.L.E.*, NBC, 1967; *The Invaders*, ABC, 1967; *Journey to the Unknown*, ABC, 1968; *Big Valley*, ABC, 1968; *It Takes a Thief*, ABC, 1969; *The Bold Ones*, NBC, 1970; *Mannix*, CBS, 1971; *Night Gallery*, NBC, 1972; *Quincy, M.E.* NBC, 1976; *Police Woman*, NBC, 1976. Pilots: Sylvia Cartwright, *The Immortal*, ABC, 1969; Liz Hollander, *Fantasy Island*, ABC, 1977. Movies: Abagail Turner, *Shadow on the Land*, ABC, 1968; Jo Hudson, *The Smugglers*, NBC, 1968; Sister Meredith, *Weekend of Terror*, ABC, 1970; Kathy Cooper, *The Cable Car Murder* (also known as *Cross Current*), CBS, 1971; Gail Foster, *The Night Stalker*, ABC, 1971; Irene Turner, *The Elevator*, ABC, 1974; Cathy Webster, *Death Stalk*, NBC, 1974; Abbie Adams, *Flood!*, NBC, 1976; Sally Magee, *Having Babies II*, ABC, 1977; Dr. Alice Alcott, *Cops and Robin*, NBC, 1978; Dr. Clair McCauley, *The Beasts Are on the Streets*, NBC, 1978.

AWARDS: Theatre World Award, 1956-57.

ADDRESSES: AGENT—c/o Paul Kohner, 9169 Sunset Boulevard, Los Angeles, CA 90069.*

*   *   *

LYNN, Jonathan   1943-

PERSONAL: Born April 3, 1943, in Bath, England; son of Robin (a physician) and Ruth Helen (a sculptor; maiden name, Eban) Lynn; married Rita Eleanora Merkelis (a psychotherapist), August 1, 1967. EDUCATION: Pembroke College, Cambridge University, M.A., 1964; trained for the stage with Mira Rostova.

VOCATION: Director, writer, and actor.

CAREER: NEW YORK DEBUT—*Cambridge Circus on Broadway*, with the Footlights Company, Plymouth Theatre, 1954. LONDON DEBUT—Bob Lacey, *Green Julia*, Traverse Theatre Company, New Arts Theatre, 1965. PRINCIPAL STAGE APPEARANCES—Motel the tailor, *Fiddler on the Roof*, Her Majesty's Theatre, London, 1967; Angus, Bill, *Blue Comedy*, Open Space Theatre, London, 1968; Hitler, *A Comedy of the Changing Years*, Theatre Upstairs, London, 1969; Gerald Forbes, *When We Are Married*, Strand Theatre, London, 1970.

PRINCIPAL STAGE WORK—Director: *Four Degrees Over*, Northcott

JONATHAN LYNN

Theatre, Exeter, U.K., 1970; *The Glass Menagerie, The Gingerbread Man*, both Cambridge Theatre Company, Cambridge, U.K., 1977; *The Unvarnished Truth*, Cambridge Theatre Company, then Phoenix Theatre, London, both 1978; *The Matchmaker*, Cambridge Theatre Company, then Her Majesty's Theatre, London, both 1978; *Songbook*, Cambridge Theatre Company, then Globe Theatre, London, both 1979; *Anna Christie*, Royal Shakespeare Company, Stratford-on-Avon, U.K., 1979, then London, 1980; *The Moony Shapiro Songbook*, Morosco Theatre, New York City, 1981; *Jacobowsky and the Colonel, The Magistrate, Three Men on a Horse*, all National Theatre Company, 1986-87. Also directed John Gould's one-man show, 1970; *The Plotters of Cabbage Patch Corner*, 1971.

PRINCIPAL FILM APPEARANCES—*Suspicion*, upcoming.

PRINCIPAL FILM WORK—Director, *Clue*, Paramount, 1985.

PRINCIPAL TELEVISION APPEARANCES—Specials: *Barmitzvah Boy; The Knowledge*.

RELATED CAREER—Artistic director, Cambridge Theatre Company, 1977-81.

WRITINGS: PLAYS—*Pig of the Month*. SCREENPLAYS—*Clue*, Paramount, 1985; *The Internecine Project*; also training films for Video Arts. TELEPLAYS—Series: (With George Layton) *My Brother's Keeper*, Granada, 1974-75; (with Antony Jay) *Yes, Minister*, BBC, 1980-81; (with Jay) *Yes, Prime Minister*, BBC; also *Doctor in Charge, Doctor at Sea, My Name Is Harry Worth*, all London Weekend Television; and co-author of more than sixty television scripts. FICTION—*A Proper Man,* Heinemann, 1976; (with Jay) *Yes, Minister: The Diaries of the Right Honourable James Hacker, Volume 1,* BBC Publications, 1981; *The Complete "Yes, Minister,"* Salem House, 1987; also *The Diaries of a Cabinet Minister: 3 Volumes.*

AWARDS: Best Musical, Society of West End Theatre Award, *Evening Standard* Award, both 1979, for *Songbook;* Ivor Novello Award, 1979; Best Television Comedy, British Academy of Film and Television Arts, Broadcasting Press Guild, both for *Yes, Minister.*

ADDRESSES: HOME—29 Etheldene Avenue, London N10, England.

*   *   *

LYONS, Stuart   1928-

PERSONAL: Born in 1928, in Manchester, England. EDUCATION: Attended Manchester University.

VOCATION: Producer and casting director.

CAREER: PRINCIPAL FILM WORK—Casting director, Associated British Films, 1956-60; freelance casting director, 1960-63; casting director, Twentieth Century-Fox, 1963-67; during this entire period, casted more than thirty films, including *Those Magnificent Men in Their Flying Machines,* Twentieth Century-Fox, 1956; *Cleopatra,* Twentieth Century-Fox, 1963; *The Long Ships,* Columbia, 1964; *Guns at Batasi,* Twentieth Century-Fox, 1964; *High Wind in Jamaica,* Twentieth Century-Fox, 1965; *Rapture,* International Classics, 1965; *The Blue Max,* Twentieth Century-Fox, 1966. Director, Twentieth Century-Fox Productions, Ltd., 1967, then managing director, 1968-71; head of production, Hemdale Group, 1972-73; independent producer, 1973—, including *The Slipper and the Rose,* Universal, 1977; *Meetings with Remarkable Men; Danses Sacrees.* Production consultant, *Eleni,* Warner Brothers, 1985; executive producer, *Turnaround,* Cinema Group, upcoming.

RELATED CAREER—Assistant director, BBC, 1955-56.*

M

MacBRIDGE, Aeneas
See MACKAY, Fulton

*   *   *

MacDEVITT, Brian 1956-

PERSONAL: Born October 6, 1956; son of William Gerard (a teacher) and Julie (a nurse; maiden name, Powers) MacDevitt. EDUCATION: Received B.F.A. from the State University of New York, Purchase; studied lighting design with Bill Mintzer.

VOCATION: Lighting designer.

CAREER: FIRST STAGE WORK—Lighting designer, *Oh, Coward!*, Woodstock Playhouse, Woodstock, NY, 1979. FIRST NEW YORK STAGE WORK—Lighting designer, *A Girl's Guide to Chaos*, American Place Theatre, 1986. PRINCIPAL STAGE WORK—Lighting designer: *Show Boat, Naughty Marietta, Candide, Sayonara,* all Paper Mill Playhouse, Milburn, NJ; *The Price,* Philadelphia Drama Guild, Philadelphia, PA; *The Bar Mitzvah Boy, Song for a Saturday,* both American Jewish Theatre, New York City.

MAJOR TOURS—Lighting designer: *Seven Brides for Seven Brothers, Gigi,* U.S. cities, both 1984; *Oliver!,* U.S. cities, 1985; *Brigadoon,* U.S. cities, 1986; *Can-Can,* U.S. cities, 1988.

RELATED CAREER—Guest instructor, design department, State University of New York, Purchase, 1986-87.

MEMBER: United Scenic Artists.

ADDRESSES: HOME—761 Union Street, Brooklyn, NY 11204.

*   *   *

MacGRAW, Ali 1939-

PERSONAL: Born April 1, 1939, in Pound Ridge, NY; parents, commercial artists; married Robin Hoen (a banker; divorced); married Bob Evans (a producer), October, 1970 (divorced); married Steve McQueen (an actor), 1973 (divorced, 1977); children: (second marriage) Joshua. EDUCATION: Graduated from Wellesley College, 1960.

VOCATION: Actress and model.

CAREER: FILM DEBUT—*A Lovely Way to Die,* Universal, 1968. PRINCIPAL FILM APPEARANCES—*Goodbye, Columbus,* Paramount, 1969; *Love Story,* Paramount, 1970; *The Getaway,* National General, 1972; *Convoy,* United Artists, 1978; *Players,* Paramount, 1979; *Just Tell Me What You Want,* Warner Brothers, 1980.

PRINCIPAL TELEVISION APPEARANCES—Episodic: *Dynasty,* ABC, 1985. Mini-Series: Natalie Jastrow, *The Winds of War,* ABC, 1983. Movies: Rose Arrow, *China Rose,* CBS, 1983.

RELATED CAREER—Model, *Mademoiselle* magazine; assistant to Diana Vreeland; assistant to fashion photograper Mel Sokolsky; actress, television commercials; editorial assistant, *Harper's Bazaar* magazine.

AWARDS: Best Actress, Academy Award nomination, 1970, for *Love Story.*

ADDRESSES: AGENT—International Creative Management, 8899 Beverly Boulevard, Los Angeles, CA 90048.*

*   *   *

MACKAY, Fulton 1922-1987
(Aeneas MacBridge)

PERSONAL: Born Fulton McKay, August 12, 1922, in Paisley, Scotland; died June 6, 1987, in London, England; son of William and Agnes (McDermid) McKay; married Sheila Manahan. EDUCATION: Trained for the stage at the Royal Academy of Dramatic Art. MILITARY: Royal Air Force, 1941-1945.

VOCATION: Actor, director, and writer.

CAREER: STAGE DEBUT—*Angel,* tour of U.K. cities, 1947. LONDON DEBUT—*Angel,* Strand Theatre, 1947. PRINCIPAL STAGE APPEARANCES—King Humanitie, *The Thrie Estates,* Assembly Hall, Edinburgh Festival, Edinburgh, Scotland, U.K., 1950; Oscar, *Naked Island,* Arts Theatre, London, 1960; Kleshch, *The Lower Depths,* Arts Theatre, 1962; preacher, Solveig's father, *Peer Gynt,* Salerio, *The Merchant of Venice,* Dapper, *The Alchemist,* all Old Vic Theatre, London, 1962-63; Mr. Miller, *Justice Is a Woman,* Vaudeville Theatre, London, 1966; Reardon, *In Celebration,* Royal Court Theatre, London, 1969; Solveig's father, Bergriffenfeldt, button moulder, *Peer Gynt,* 69 Theatre Company, University Theatre, Manchester, U.K., 1970; Dr. Wangel, *The Lady from the Sea,* Greenwich Theatre, London, 1971; Duke of Hamilton, Andrew Stuart, *The Douglas Cause,* Duke of York's Theatre, London, 1971; Hughie, *Willie Rough,* Lyceum Theatre, Edinburgh, Scotland, U.K., then Shaw Theatre, London, both 1972; John the Commonweal, *The Thrie Estates,* Edinburgh Festival, 1973; Davies, *The Caretaker,* Shaw Theatre, 1976; Bill Ford, *Old Movies,* National Theatre, London, 1977; St. Peter, blind man, *The Passion,* National Theatre, 1978; McNab, *Balmoral,* Arnaud Theatre, Guildford, U.K., 1978; Jardine, *The Hang of the Gaol,* Royal Shakespeare Company (RSC), Warehouse Theatre, London,

1978; Chris Christopherson, *Anna Christie,* RSC, Other Place Theatre, Stratford-on-Avon, U.K., 1979. Also appeared as Squeers, *The Life and Adventures of Nicholas Nickleby,* RSC, London, 1980; in *The Man with a Flower in His Mouth,* Edinburgh Festival, 1973; and in repertory at the Citizens Theatre, Glasgow, Scotland, U.K., 1949-51 and 1953-58.

PRINCIPAL STAGE WORK—Director, *The Wild Duck,* Scottish Actors Company, Edinburgh Festival, Edinburgh, Scotland, U.K., 1969.

PRINCIPAL FILM APPEARANCES—*Gumshoe,* Columbia, 1972; *Local Hero,* Warner Brothers, 1983; voice characterization, *Dreamchild,* Universal, 1985; *Water,* Atlantic, 1986; also appeared in *Defence of the Realm,* 1985.

PRINCIPAL TELEVISION APPEARANCES—Series: Prison guard, *Porridge,* BBC; *Special Branch,* BBC; *The Foundation,* BBC. Movies: *To Catch a King,* HBO, 1984; also appeared in *A Sense of Freedom; Slip-Up; The Holy City.*

RELATED CAREER—Founder, actor, and director, Scottish Actors Company.

WRITINGS: TELEPLAYS—(As Aeneas MacBridge) *Diamond's Progress; The Girl with Flowers in Her Hair; Dalhousie's Luck.*

MEMBER: British Actors' Equity Association, Screen Actors Guild.

OBITUARIES AND OTHER SOURCES: Variety, June 10, 1987.*

*   *   *

JOHN MacKAY

MacKAY, John   1924-

PERSONAL: Surname is pronounced ''Mac-Eye;'' born John MacKay Elliott, September 23, 1924, in Los Angeles, CA; son of Robert Peel (a banker) and Corennah (DePue) Elliott; married Mary Foskett (an actress), January 31, 1983. EDUCATION: Fordham University, B.A., 1972; City College of New York, M.A., 1975, Ph.D., theatre, 1977; trained for the stage with Stella Adler. POLITICS: Democrat. MILITARY: U.S. Naval Reserve, 1942-46.

VOCATION: Actor, director, teacher, and writer.

CAREER: BROADWAY DEBUT—Justin, *The Lovers,* Martin Beck Theatre, 1956. PRINCIPAL STAGE APPEARANCES—Old Mahon, *The Playboy of the Western World,* Irish Players, Tara Theatre, New York City, 1958; title role, *Henry VIII,* Stratford Shakespeare Festival, Stratford, ON, Canada, 1961; John Hersey, *Gift of Time,* Ethel Barrymore Theatre, New York City, 1962; Inspector O'Sullivan, *The Borstal Boy,* Lyceum Theatre, New York City, 1970; chorus, *Oedipus* cycle, Classic Stage Company, New York City, 1980-81; Domenico Soriano, *Filumena,* St. Lawrence Theatre Centre, Toronto, ON, Canada, 1981; King Agamemnon, *Hecuba,* Directors Collective, New York City, 1982; title role, *Macbeth,* Britain Salutes New York Festival, New York City, 1983; Thor, *Mornings at Seven,* Walnut Street Theatre, Philadelphia, PA, 1984; mayor, *The Front Page,* Indiana Repertory Theatre, Indianapolis, IN, 1985; Gardner Church, *Painting Churches,* Seattle Repertory Theatre, Seattle, WA, 1986; Yens, *Vikings,* Pittsburgh Public Theatre, Pittsburgh, PA, 1987; Junius Brutus, *Coriolanus,* McCarter Theatre, Princeton, NJ, 1987. Also appeared as Claudius, *Hamlet,*

New York City, 1959; and in *Under the Yum Yum Tree,* Henry Miller's Theatre, New York City, 1960; *A Man for All Seasons,* American National Theatre Academy Playhouse, New York City, 1961; *The Subject Was Roses,* John Cleary Theatre, New Brunswick, NJ, 1979; *You Never Can Tell,* Circle in the Square, New York City, 1986; with the Guthrie Theatre Group, Minneapolis, MN, 1961, 1964, 1965; and with the Inner City Repertory Company, Los Angeles, CA, 1966-69.

MAJOR TOURS—Title role, *Mister Roberts,* U.S. cities, 1953; Bruce, *Peccadillo,* U.S. cities, 1985.

PRINCIPAL FILM APPEARANCES—Lieutenant Guard, *The Court Martial of Billy Mitchell,* Warner Brothers, 1957; *The Dead One,* New Orleans Mardi Gras Productions, 1958; *Secret Life of an American Wife,* Metro-Goldwyn-Mayer, 1966; *The Next Man,* Allied Artists, 1976. Also appeared in *Cuban Rebel Girls,* 1960.

PRINCIPAL FILM WORK—Assistant director, *Captain Horatio Hornblower,* Warner Brothers, 1948.

TELEVISION DEBUT—''The Peacock,'' *Studio One,* CBS, 1955. PRINCIPAL TELEVISION APPEARANCES—Episodic: *The Andros Targets,* CBS, 1976; also *Philco TV Playhouse,* NBC; *Goodyear TV Playhouse,* NBC. Series: Bowie Kuhn, *Ball Four,* CBS, 1972; Ambassador Eden, *The Edge of Night,* NBC, 1983; *Texas,* 1983; *One Life to Live,* ABC, 1986; *As the World Turns,* CBS. Movies: *Billion and Connection,* PBS, 1977. Specials: Gascon, ''Cyrano de Bergerac,'' *Hallmark Hall of Fame,* 1965.

RELATED CAREER—Teacher, Fordham University, New York

City, 1975-76; teacher, John Jay College, 1976-77; producer, Hunter Playwrights, Hunter College, New York City, 1978; executive producer, City University of New York Alumni Educational Television.

NON-RELATED CAREER—General manager, Hunter Mountain Ski Bowl, Hunter, NY, 1960-61.

WRITINGS: PLAYS—*The Castle of Perseverance,* City University of New York, New York City, 1977.

MEMBER: Actors' Equity Association, Screen Actors Guild, American Federation of Television and Radio Artists; Ph.D. Alumni Association, City University of New York (director, 1980-85).

SIDELIGHTS: John MacKay told *CTFT:* ''Performing in the theatre keeps me honest as an actor and helps keep me honest as a human being. I find the craft of acting complex and always interesting even on its most pedestrian levels. Comedy and farce fascinate me with their techniques of mathematical precision and the warmth of the resulting laughter . . . and then once in a while the opportunity comes to do a classic in a favorable situation—Shakespeare, Moliere, Beckett, O'Casey—and the full extent of your good fortune opens up for you, like music. I consider myself very fortunate to be able to work at what I love.''

ADDRESSES: HOME—361 E. 50th Street, Apartment 2H, New York, NY 10022. AGENT—(Television) Cunningham, Escott & Dipene, 118 E. 25th Street, New York, NY 10010. (Theatre) Michael Hartig Agency, 114 E. 28th Street, New York, NY 10016.

*   *   *

MADDEN, Ciaran   1945-

PERSONAL: Born December 27, 1945; daughter of James George (a doctor) and Maria Elizabeth (Dawson) Madden. EDUCATION: Trained for the stage at the Royal Academy of Dramatic Art.

VOCATION: Actress.

CAREER: STAGE DEBUT—Shirley Hughes, *The Man Most Likely To . . .,* Alexandria Theatre, Birmingham, U.K. PRINCIPAL STAGE APPEARANCES—Constance Neville, *She Stoops to Conquer,* 69 Theatre Company, Manchester, U.K., then Garrick Theatre, London, 1969; Heloise, *Abelard and Heloise,* Wyndam's Theatre, London, 1970; Angela, *The Director of the Opera,* Chichester Festival, Chichester, U.K., 1973; Isabella, *Measure for Measure,* Arnaud Theatre, Guildford, U.K., 1973; Elizabeth, *The Circle,* Arnaud Theatre, 1974, then in Hong Kong, 1975; Miss Forsythe, *Death of a Salesman,* Arnaud Theatre, 1975; Isabella, *Measure for Measure,* Open Space Theatre, London, 1975; title role, *Saint Joan,* Thorndike Theatre, Leatherhead, U.K., 1979; Vittoria, *Country Life,* Hammersmith Lyric Theatre, London, 1980. Also Blanche, *Widower's Houses,* Wimbledon, U.K., 1976.

PRINCIPAL TELEVISION APPEARANCES—Movies: Claire Strickland, *A Married Man,* syndicated, 1984. Specials: *Sense and Sensibility; Hamlet; Jennie; Gawaine and the Green Knight.*

SIDELIGHTS: RECREATIONS—Playing piano, drawing, eating.

ADDRESSES: HOME—Glebe House, Tollesbury, Essex, England.*

MADIGAN, Amy

VOCATION: Actress.

CAREER: PRINCIPAL FILM APPEARANCES—*Love Child,* Warner Brothers, 1982; *Streets of Fire,* Universal, 1984; *Places in the Heart,* Tri-Star, 1984; *Alamo Bay,* Tri-Star, 1985; *Twice in a Lifetime,* Bud Yorkin Productions, 1985; *Nowhere to Hide,* New Century, 1987.

PRINCIPAL TELEVISION APPEARANCES—Pilot: Billy Jean Bailey, *Travis McGee,* ABC, 1983. Movies: Marilyn, *Crazy Times,* ABC, 1981; Molly Slavin, *The Ambush Murders,* CBS, 1982; Chloe Brill, *Victims,* NBC, 1982; Alison Ransom, *The Day After,* ABC, 1983; also appeared in *The Laundromat.*

ADDRESSES: MANAGER—c/o Alan Somers Management, 8335 Sunset Boulevard, Los Angeles, CA 90069.

*   *   *

MALKOVICH, John   1953-

PERSONAL: Born December 9, 1953, in Christopher, IL; married Glenne Headley (an actress), August 2, 1982. EDUCATION: Attended Eastern Illinois State University.

VOCATION: Actor, director, and sound designer.

CAREER: OFF-BROADWAY DEBUT—Lee, *True West,* Cherry Lane Theatre, 1982. PRINCIPAL STAGE APPEARANCES—*Curse of the Starving Class,* Goodman Theatre, Chicago, 1978-79; Biff, *Death of a Salesman,* Broadhurst Theatre, New York City, 1984; Captain Bluntschli, *Arms and the Man,* Circle in the Square, New York City, 1985; *Burn This,* Plymouth Theatre, New York City, 1987.

PRINCIPAL STAGE WORK—Director: *The Rear Column,* North Light Repertory Theatre, Evanston, IL, 1981-82; *Arms and the Man,* Circle in the Square, New York City, 1985; also sound designer, *Balm in Gilead,* with the Steppenwolf Theatre Company and the Circle Repertory Company, Minetta Lane Theatre, New York City, 1984-85; *The Caretaker,* Steppenwolf Theatre Company, Chicago, 1985; *Coyote Ugly,* produced in Chicago and at the Kennedy Center, Washington, DC, 1986.

FILM DEBUT—*The Killing Fields,* Warner Brothers, 1984. PRINCIPAL FILM APPEARANCES—*Places in the Heart,* Tri-Star, 1984; *Eleni,* Warner Brothers, 1985; Jeff Peters/Ulysses, *Making Mr. Right,* Orion, 1987; *Empire of the Sun,* Warner Brothers, 1987; Tom, *The Glass Menagerie,* Cineplex Odeon, 1987.

PRINCIPAL TELEVISION APPEARANCES—Movies: Gary, *Word of Honor,* CBS, 1981; Biff, *Death of a Salesman,* CBS, 1985; also appeared in *American Dream,* ABC, 1981.

RELATED CAREER—Co-founder and member, Steppenwolf Theatre Ensemble, Chicago.

AWARDS: Obie Award from the *Village Voice,* Clarence Derwent Award, Theatre World Award, all 1982, for *True West;* Best Supporting Actor, Academy Award nominations, both 1984, for *The Killing Fields* and *Places in the Heart;* Best Direction, Drama

Desk Award, 1985, for *Balm in Gilead;* Outstanding Supporting Actor, Emmy Award, 1986, for *Death of a Salesman.*

MEMBER: Actors' Equity Association, Screen Actors Guild.

ADDRESSES: MANAGER—Phyllis Carlyle Management, 4000 Warner Boulevard, Producers Building 7, Room 205, Burbank, CA 91522.*

*   *   *

MALONE, Dorothy   1925-

PERSONAL: Born Dorothy Maloney, January 30, 1925, in Chicago, IL. EDUCATION: Attended Southern Methodist University.

VOCATION: Actress.

CAREER: FILM DEBUT—*Falcon and the Co-Eds,* 1943. PRINCIPAL FILM APPEARANCES—*One Mysterious Night,* 1944; *Show Business,* 1944; *Hollywood Canteen,* 1945; *The Big Sleep,* Warner Brothers, 1946; *Night and Day,* Warner Brothers, 1946; *To the Victor,* 1948; *Two Guys from Texas,* 1948; *One Sunday Afternoon,* 1949; *Colorado Territory,* 1949; *South of St. Louis,* 1949; *The Nevadan,* 1950; *Mrs. O'Malley and Mr. Malone,* Metro-Goldwyn-Mayer (MGM), 1950; *Pushover,* 1954; *Private Hell 36,* Filmmakers, 1954; *Young at Heart,* Warner Brothers, 1955; *Battle Cry,* Warner Brothers, 1955; *Five Guns West,* American Releasing Corporation, 1955; *Pillars of the Sky,* Universal, 1956; *Tension at Table Rock,* Universal, 1956; *Written on the Wind,* Universal, 1956; *Man of a Thousand Faces,* Universal, 1957; *Tip on a Dead Jockey,* MGM, 1957; *The Tarnished Angels,* Universal, 1958; Diana Barrymore, *Too Much, Too Soon,* Warner Brothers, 1958; *Warlock,* Twentieth Century-Fox, 1959; *The Last Voyage,* MGM, 1959; *The Last Sunset,* Universal, 1961; *Beach Party,* American International, 1963; *Gli Insaziablili,* 1969; *Abduction,* 1975; *The November Plan,* 1976; *Golden Rendezvous,* Film Trust, 1977; *Winter Kills,* AVCO-Embassy, 1979; *Rest in Pieces* (also known as *A Thousand Ways to Die*), Overseas Filmgroup, upcoming.

PRINCIPAL TELEVISION APPEARANCES—Episodic: "To Each His Own," *Lux Video Theatre,* ABC, 1954; *Dick Powell Theatre,* CBS; *Dr. Kildare,* NBC; *The Bob Hope Show,* NBC; *The Jack Benny Show,* CBS; *The Untouchables,* ABC; *The Greatest Show on Earth,* ABC. Series: *Fireside Theatre,* NBC, 1954-55; Constance MacKenzie, *Peyton Place,* ABC, 1964-68. Mini-Series: Irene Goodwin, *Rich Man, Poor Man,* ABC, 1976. Movies: Elaine Hagen, *The Pigeon,* ABC, 1969; Constance MacKenzie, *Murder in Peyton Place,* NBC, 1977; Maggie, *Little Ladies of the Night,* ABC, 1977; Myrtle Cutler, *Katie: Portrait of a Centerfold,* NBC, 1978; Molly Denniver, *Condominium,* syndicated, 1980; Dr. Sullivan, *He's Not Your Son,* CBS, 1984; Constance Mackenzie Carson, *Peyton Place: The Next Generation,* NBC, 1985.

AWARDS: Best Supporting Actress, Academy Award, 1956, for *Written on the Wind.*

MEMBER: Screen Actors Guild, American Federation of Television and Radio Artists.

ADDRESSES: AGENT—Ann Waugh Talent Agency, 4731 Laurel Canyon Boulevard, Suite 5, North Hollywood, CA 91607.*

MANGANO, Silvana   1930-

PERSONAL: Born 1930, in Rome, Italy; married Dino de Laurentiis (a film producer), July 17, 1949; children: Veronica, Rafaella, Federico, Francesca. EDUCATION: Attended the Dance Academy of Jia Ruskaja.

VOCATION: Actress.

CAREER: FILM DEBUT—*Il Delitto di Giovanni Episcopo,* 1947. PRINCIPAL FILM APPEARANCES—*L'Elisior d'Amore,* 1948; *Bitter Rice,* 1949; *Black Magic,* 1949; *Il Brigante Musolino,* 1950; *Anna,* 1951; *Mambo,* 1954; *Gold of Naples,* 1954; Penelope, *Ulysses,* 1955; *Uomini e Lupi,* 1956; *Tempest,* 1957; *The Sea Wall,* 1958; *Five Branded Women,* Paramount, 1960; *La Grande Guerra,* 1960; *Crimen,* 1960; *Una Vita Difficlie,* 1961; *Il Giudizio Universale,* 1961; *Barabbas,* Columbia, 1962; *Il Processo di Verona,* 1962; *La Mia Signora,* 1964; *Il Disco Volante,* 1965; *Le Streghe,* 1966; *Oedipus Rex,* Universal, 1968; *Medea,* 1969; *Death in Venice,* Warner Brothers, 1971; *The Decameron,* United Artists, 1971; *Ludwig,* Metro-Goldwyn-Mayer, 1973; *Conversation Piece,* 1975; *Dune,* Universal, 1984; *The Ship Ulysses and a Wife,* SACIS, upcoming.

RELATED CAREER—Model.

ADDRESSES: OFFICE—DeLaurentiis Entertainment Group, 8670 Wilshire Boulevard, Beverly Hills, CA 90211.*

*   *   *

MANKIEWICZ, Joseph L.   1909-

PERSONAL: Full name, Joseph Leo Mankiewicz; born February 11, 1909, in Wilkes-Barre, PA; son of Frank (a teacher) and Johanna (Blumenau) Mankiewicz; married Elizabeth Young, 1934 (divorced, 1937); married Rosa Stradner, 1939 (died, 1958); married Rosemary Matthews, 1962; children: (first marriage) Eric; (second marriage) Christopher, Thomas; (third marriage) Alexandra. EDUCATION: Columbia University, B.A., 1928.

VOCATION: Screenwriter, director, and producer.

CAREER: PRINCIPAL FILM WORK—Producer: *Three Godfathers,* Metro-Goldwyn-Mayer (MGM), 1936; *Fury,* MGM, 1936; *The Gorgeous Hussy,* MGM, 1936; *Love on the Run,* MGM, 1936; *The Bride Wore Red,* MGM, 1937; *Double Wedding,* MGM, 1937; *Mannequin,* MGM, 1937; *Three Comrades,* MGM, 1938; *The Shining Hour,* MGM, 1938; *A Christmas Carol,* MGM, 1938; *The Adventures of Huckleberry Finn,* MGM, 1939; *Strange Cargo,* MGM, 1940; *The Philadelphia Story,* MGM, 1940; *The Wild Man of Borneo,* MGM, 1941; *The Feminine Touch,* MGM, 1941; *Woman of the Year,* MGM, 1942; *Reunion in France,* MGM, 1942.

Director: *The Late George Apley,* Twentieth Century-Fox, 1946; *The Ghost and Mrs. Muir,* Twentieth Century-Fox, 1947; *Five Fingers,* 1952; *Julius Caesar,* MGM, 1953; *Guys and Dolls,* Samuel Goldwyn/MGM, 1955; *Suddenly, Last Summer,* Columbia, 1959; *There Was a Crooked Man,* Warner Brothers, 1970; *Sleuth,* Twentieth Century-Fox, 1972.

PRINCIPAL STAGE WORK—Director, *La Boheme* (opera), Metropolitan Opera House, New York City, 1952.

PRINCIPAL TELEVISION WORK—Specials: Director, *Carol for Another Christmas*, 1964.

RELATED CAREER—Foreign correspondent for the *Chicago Tribune*, Berlin, Germany, 1928; subtitle translator, Universum-Film Aktien-Gesellschaft, Berlin, Germany, 1928; founding member and secretary, Screen Writers Guild, 1933; formed own production company, Figaro Inc., 1952-61.

WRITINGS: SILENT FILMS—Titles for Paramount-Famous-Lasky: *The Dummy, Close Harmony, The Man I Love, The Studio Murder Mystery, Thunderbolt, River of Romance, The Mysterious Dr. Fu Manchu, The Saturday Night Kid, Fast Company, The Virginian,* all 1929.

SCREENPLAYS—(With Howard Estabrook) *Slightly Scarlet,* Paramount-Famous-Lasky, 1930; (adaptation and dialogue) *The Social Lion,* Paramount, 1930; (dialogue) *Only Saps Work,* Paramount, 1930; (dialogue) *The Gang Buster,* Paramount, 1931; (dialogue) *Finn and Hattie,* Paramount, 1931; (with Keene Thompson and Vincent Lawrence) *June Moon,* Paramount, 1931; (with Norman Z. McLeod and Don Marquis) *Skippy,* Paramount, 1931; (with McLeod and Edward Paramore, Jr.) *Newly Rich* (also known as *Forbidden Adventure*), Paramount, 1931; (with McLeod and Sam Mintz) *Sooky,* Paramount, 1931; *This Reckless Age,* Paramount, 1932; (with Agnes Brand Leahy and Grover Jones) *Sky Bride,* Paramount, 1932; (with Henry Myers) *Million Dollar Legs,* Paramount, 1932; co-writer, *If I Had a Million,* Paramount, 1932; (with Myers) *Diplomaniacs,* RKO, 1933; (with John B. Clymer) *Emergency Call,* RKO, 1933; *Too Much Harmony,* Paramount, 1933; (with William Cameron Menzies) *Alice in Wonderland,* Paramount, 1933; (with Oliver H.P. Garrett) *Manhattan Melodrama,* MGM, 1934; (dialogue) *Our Daily Bread,* United Artists, 1934; *Forsaking All Others,* MGM, 1934; *I Live My Life,* MGM, 1935.

(With Nunnally Johnson) *Keys to the Kingdom,* Twentieth Century-Fox, 1945; *Dragonwyck,* Twentieth Century-Fox, 1946; (with Howard Dimsdale) *Somewhere in the Night,* Twentieth Century-Fox, 1946; *A Letter to Three Wives,* Twentieth Century-Fox, 1949; *All About Eve,* Twentieth Century-Fox, 1950; (with Lesser Samuels) *No Way Out,* Twentieth Century-Fox, 1950; *People Will Talk,* Twentieth Century-Fox, 1951; *Julius Caesar,* MGM, 1953; *The Barefoot Contessa,* United Artists, 1954; *Guys and Dolls,* MGM, 1955; *The Quiet American,* United Artists, 1958; (with Sidney Buchman and Ranald MacDougal) *Cleopatra,* Twentieth Century-Fox, 1963; *The Honey Pot,* United Artists, 1967.

Contributor: *Paramount on Parade,* 1930; *Sap from Syracuse,* 1930; *Dude Ranch,* 1931; *Touchdown,* 1931; *Three Godfathers,* MGM, 1936; *Fury,* MGM, 1936; *The Gorgeous Hussy,* MGM, 1936; *Love on the Run,* MGM, 1936; *The Bride Wore Red,* MGM, 1937; *Double Wedding,* MGM, 1937; *Mannequin,* MGM, 1937; *Three Comrades,* MGM, 1938; *The Shopworn Angel,* MGM, 1938; *The Shining Hour,* MGM, 1938; *A Christmas Carol,* MGM, 1938; *The Adventures of Huckleberry Finn,* MGM, 1939; *Strange Cargo,* MGM, 1940; *The Philadelphia Story,* MGM, 1940; *The Wild Man of Borneo,* MGM, 1941; *The Feminine Touch,* MGM, 1941; *Woman of the Year,* MGM, 1942; *Cairo,* MGM, 1942; *Reunion in France,* MGM, 1942; *The Late George Apley,* Twentieth Century-Fox, 1946; *The Ghost and Mrs. Muir,* Twentieth Century-Fox, 1947; *Escape,* 1948; *House of Strangers,* 1949; *Five Fingers,* 1952; *Suddenly, Last Summer,* Columbia, 1959; *There Was a Crooked Man,* Warner Brothers, 1970; *Sleuth,* Twentieth Century-Fox, 1972.

FICTION—*All About Eve: A Screenplay,* Random House, 1951; (with Gary Carey) *More About All About Eve: A Colloquy,* Random House, 1972.

AWARDS: Best Screenplay, Academy Award nomination, 1931, for *Skippy;* Best Screenplay and Best Director, Academy awards, Screen Directors Guild Award, and Screen Writers Guild Award, all 1949, for *A Letter to Three Wives;* Best Screenplay and Best Director, Academy awards, Best Screenplay and Best Director, British Academy awards, Best Screenplay and Best Director, New York Critics awards, Screen Directors Guild Award, and Screen Writers Guild Award, all 1950, for *All About Eve;* Order of Merit from the Italian Republic, for contributions to the arts, 1965; Erasmus Award from the City of Rotterdam, 1984; D.W. Griffith Award from the Directors Guild of America, 1986, for lifetime achievement in film.

MEMBER: Academy of Motion Picture Arts and Sciences, Screen Directors Guild of America (president, 1950); Yale University (associate fellow, 1979—), Bedford Golf and Tennis Club.

ADDRESSES: HOME—R.F.D. 2, Box 110, Bedford, NY 10506.*

* * *

MANKIEWICZ, Tom 1942-

PERSONAL: Full name, Thomas Mankiewicz; born June 1, 1942, in Los Angeles, CA; son of Joseph L. (a film writer, producer, and director) and Rosa (Stradner) Mankiewicz.

VOCATION: Writer, director, and producer.

CAREER: PRINCIPAL TELEVISION WORK—Series: Writer (see below) director, *Hart to Hart,* 1979-84.

PRINCIPAL FILM WORK—Writer (see below); director, *Dragnet,* Universal, 1987; executive producer, *Hot Pursuit,* Paramount, 1987.

WRITINGS: SCREENPLAYS—*The Sweet Ride,* Twentieth Century-Fox, 1968; *Diamonds Are Forever,* United Artists, 1971; *Live and Let Die,* United Artists, 1973; *The Man with the Golden Gun,* United Artists, 1974; *Mother, Jugs and Speed,* 1976; (with Robert Kate and George Cosmatos) *The Cassandra Crossing,* AVCO-Embassy, 1977; *The Eagle Has Landed,* Columbia, 1977; *Ladyhawke,* Warner Brothers, 1985; co-writer, *Dragnet,* Universal, 1987.

TELEPLAYS—Series: *Hart to Hart,* ABC.

ADDRESSES: AGENT—Creative Artists Agency, 1888 Century Park E., Suite 1400, Los Angeles, CA 90067.*

* * *

MANN, Abby 1927-

PERSONAL: Born Abraham Goodman, December 1, 1927, in Philadelphia, PA; son of Ben Goodman (a jeweler); married Harriet Carr (divorced). EDUCATION: Attended Temple University and New York University. MILITARY: U.S. Army.

VOCATION: Writer, producer, and director.

CAREER: PRINCIPAL FILM WORK—Executive producer, *The Schmid Case,* National General, 1969; executive producer, *After the Fall,* Paramount, 1969.

PRINCIPAL TELEVISION WORK—Series: Creator, *Kojak* (adapted from the movie *The Marcus-Nelson Murders,* see below), CBS, 1973; executive producer, *Medical Story,* NBC, 1975-76. Mini-Series: Executive producer and director, *King,* NBC, 1978. Pilots: Executive producer, *Medical Story,* NBC, 1975; executive producer, *Skag,* NBC, 1980. Movies: Executive producer, *The Marcus-Nelson Murders,* CBS, 1973; executive producer, *This Man Stands Alone,* NBC, 1979; executive producer, *The Atlanta Child Murders,* CBS, 1985.

WRITINGS: SCREENPLAYS—*Judgment at Nuremburg,* United Artists, 1961, published by Cassell, 1961; *A Child Is Waiting,* United Artists, 1963, published by Popular Library, 1963; *The Condemned of Altona,* Twentieth Century-Fox, 1963; *Ship of Fools,* Columbia, 1965, published by Pressbook, 1965; *Andersonville,* Columbia, 1966; *The Detective,* Twentieth Century-Fox, 1968; *After the Fall,* Paramount, 1969; *The Back Room,* Universal, 1969; *The Schmid Case,* National General, 1969; (with Ernest Tidyman) *Report to the Commissioner,* United Artists, 1975; *The Children of Sanchez,* Lone Star International, 1978; *War and Love,* Cannon, 1985; also *What Are We Going to Do Without Skipper?,* National General; *Light in August.*

PUBLISHED SCREENPLAYS—*Judgment at Nuremberg,* Cassell, 1961; *A Child Is Waiting,* Popular Library, 1963; *Ship of Fools,* Pressbook, 1965.

TELEVISION—Teleplays: "A Child Is Waiting," *Studio One,* CBS, 1957; "Judgment at Nuremberg," *Playhouse 90,* CBS, 1959; also wrote for *Alcoa Theatre,* NBC; *Goodyear TV Playhouse,* NBC. Pilots: *Medical Story,* NBC, 1975; *Skag,* NBC, 1980. Movies: *The Marcus-Nelson Murders,* CBS, 1973; *King,* NBC, 1978; *The Atlanta Child Murders,* CBS, 1985.

PLAYS, PRODUCED—While attending college, all student productions: *Just Around the Corner* (musical); *Freud Has a Word for It* (musical); (with Herbert Cobey) *The Happiest Days* and *Sweet Lorraine; Exodus.*

FICTION—*Judgment at Nuremburg,* New American Library, 1961; *Medical Story,* Signet, 1975; *Tuesdays and Thursdays,* Doubleday, 1978; *Massacre at Wounded Knee,* Zebra, 1979.

AWARDS: Best Screenplay, Academy Award and Writers Guild Award nomination, both 1961, for *Judgment at Nuremburg;* Best Screenplay, Academy Award nomination and Writers Guild Award nomination, both 1965, for *Ship of Fools;* co-winner, New York Film Critics Award, 1965, for *Ship of Fools;* Outstanding Writing Achievement in Drama, Original Teleplay, Emmy Award, 1973, for *The Marcus-Nelson Murders;* nominated for over twenty awards for television films, including for *King* and *Skag;* honorary doctorate, Columbia University.

MEMBER: Writers Guild of America.

ADDRESSES: HOME—Beverly Hills, CA. OFFICE—c/o Columbia Pictures Corporation, 711 Fifth Avenue, New York, NY 10022.*

MANN, Michael

PERSONAL: Born in Chicago, IL. EDUCATION: Attended the University of Wisconsin and the London Film School.

VOCATION: Producer, director, and writer.

CAREER: PRINCIPAL FILM WORK—Writer (see below); director, *Jaunpuri* (short film), 1971; director, *Eighteen Days Down the Line* (documentary), 1972; executive producer and director, *Thief,* United Artists, 1981; director, *The Keep,* Paramount, 1983; executive producer, *Band of the Hand,* Tri-Star, 1986.

PRINCIPAL TELEVISION WORK—Series: Executive producer, *Miami Vice,* NBC, 1985—; executive producer, *Crime Story,* NBC, 1986—. Movies: Director, *The Jericho Mile,* 1979.

RELATED CAREER—Director, documentaries and commercials, England, 1965-72.

WRITINGS: SCREENPLAYS—*Thief,* United Artists, 1981; *The Keep,* Paramount, 1983.

TELEVISION—Episodic: *Starsky and Hutch,* ABC; *Police Story,* NBC; *Vega$,* ABC. Movies: *The Jericho Mile,* 1979.

AWARDS: Juris prize, Cannes Film Festival, 1971, for *Jaunpuri;* Outstanding Writing in a Limited Series or Special, Emmy Award, 1979, for *The Jericho Mile;* Best Director Award, Directors Guild of America, 1980, for *The Jericho Mile.*

MEMBER: Directors Guild of America.

ADDRESSES: AGENT—c/o Jeff Berg, International Creative Management, 8899 Beverly Blvd., Los Angeles, CA 90048.*

*   *   *

MARCUS, Louis   1936-

PERSONAL: Born 1936, in Cork, Ireland. EDUCATION: National University of Ireland, B.A., 1959.

VOCATION: Producer, director, and writer.

CAREER: PRINCIPAL FILM WORK—Producer and director of over thirty documentary films, including: *Fleadh Cheoil, Horse Laughs, Woes of Golf, Children at Work, Conquest of Light.*

RELATED CAREER—Founder, Louis Marcus Documentary Film Production, Dublin and Louis Marcus Films Ltd., London.

WRITINGS: BOOKS—*The Irish Film Industry,* 1968.

MEMBER: Academy of Motion Picture Arts and Sciences, Abbey Theatre (board); Cultural Relations Commission of the Department of Foreign Affairs.

ADDRESSES: OFFICE—c/o Abbey Theatre, Dublin, Ireland.*

MARGOLIN, Janet   1943-

PERSONAL: Born 1943, in New York, NY; married Ted Wass (an actor), 1979; children: Julian. EDUCATION: Attended the High School for the Performing Arts.

VOCATION: Actress.

CAREER: PRINCIPAL STAGE APPEARANCES—*Daughter of Silence,* Broadway production.

FILM DEBUT—Lisa, *David and Lisa,* Continental, 1963. PRINCIPAL FILM APPEARANCES—*The Greatest Story Ever Told,* United Artists, 1965; *Bus Riley's Back in Town,* Universal, 1965; *Morituri,* Twentieth Century-Fox, 1965; *Nevada Smith,* Paramount, 1966; *Enter Laughing,* Columbia, 1967; *Take the Money and Run,* Cinerama, 1969; *Annie Hall,* United Artists, 1977; *Last Embrace,* United Artists, 1979. Also appeared in *Buona Sera, Mrs. Campbell,* 1968.

PRINCIPAL TELEVISION APPEARANCES—Series: Betty Anderson Roerick, *Peyton Place,* 1964-69; Miriam Small, *Lanigan's Rabbi,* NBC, 1977. Pilots: Miriam Small, *Lanigan's Rabbi,* NBC, 1976. Movies: Karen Miller, *The Last Child,* ABC, 1971; Carol Rutledge, *Family Flight,* ABC, 1972; Krissie Kincaid, *Pray for the Wildcats,* ABC, 1974; Harper-Smythe, *Planet Earth,* ABC, 1974; Betty Anderson Roerick, *Murder in Peyton Place,* NBC, 1977; Carol, *Sharon: Portrait of a Mistress,* NBC, 1977; Rose, *The Triangle Factory Fire Scandal,* NBC, 1979; Judith Longdon, *The Plutonium Incident,* CBS, 1980.

AWARDS: Theatre World Award, 1962; Best Actress, San Francisco Film Festival Award, 1962.

ADDRESSES: AGENT—The Gersh Agency, 222 N. Canon Drive, Suite 202, Beverly Hills, CA 90210.

*   *   *

MAROWITZ, Charles   1934-

PERSONAL: Born January 26, 1934, in New York, NY; son of Julius (a butler) and Tillie (Rosencrantz) Marowitz; married Julia Crosthwait (marriage ended); married Jane Windsor (an actress), February, 1982.

VOCATION: Director and playwright.

CAREER: FIRST NEW YORK STAGE WORK—Director, *Doctor Faustus,* Labor Temple Theatre, 1948. FIRST LONDON STAGE WORK—Director, *Marriage,* Unity Theatre, 1958. PRINCIPAL STAGE WORK—All as director: *Trigon,* New Arts Theatre, London, 1964; (with Peter Brook) *Theatre of Cruelty* season, Royal Shakespeare Company (RSC), London Academy of Musica and Dramatic Art Theatre, London, 1964; *The Bellow Plays,* Fortune Theatre, London, 1966; *Loot,* Criterion Theatre, London, 1966; *Fanghorn,* Fortune Theatre, 1967; *Fortune and Men's Eyes,* Comedy Theatre, London, 1968; *Section Nine,* Aldwych Theatre, London, 1973; *Macbett,* Globe Playhouse, London, 1973; *Laughter!,* Royal Court Theatre, London, 1978; *Artaud at Rodez,* Actors Theatre, Los Angeles, CA, 1983; *Enemy of the People,* Actors Theatre, 1984; *The Petrified Forest,* Los Angeles Theatre Center, Los Angeles, CA, 1985; also directed *Sclerosis,* RSC, Aldwych

CHARLES MAROWITZ

Theatre, *Introducing Dominic Behan,* New Arts Theatre; *The Screens,* Donmar Theatre, London; *Crawling Arnold,* New Arts Theatre; (with Brook) *King Lear,* RSC, Aldwych Theatre; *Hedda,* Round House Theatre, London; *The Shrew,* Ensemble Studio Theatre, Los Angeles, CA; *The Inspector General,* Bing Theatre, Los Angeles, CA; *Hamlet,* Great Lakes Shakespeare Festival, Cleveland, OH; *The White Crow, Hamlet, The Fair Penitent, The Importance of Being Earnest,* all Los Angeles Theatre Centre, Los Angeles, CA.

Director, all Open Space Theatre, London: *Blue Comedy, Muzeeka, The Fun War,* all 1969; *Chicago Conspiracy, Palach,* both 1970; *Sweet Eros, Next,* both 1971; *The Four Little Girls, Sam Sam, The Tooth of Crime, The Old Man's Comforts,* all 1972; *Woyzeck, The Houseboy, And They Put Handcuffs on the Flowers,* all 1973; *Sherlock's Last Case,* 1974; *Artaud at Rodez,* 1975; *Anatol, Hanratty in Hell,* both 1976; *Boo Hoo,* 1978; *The Father,* 1979; *Ubu Roi,* 1980; also *Measure for Measure, Marowitz Hamlet, The Merchant of Venice, The Shrew, A Macbeth, Leonardo's Last Supper, The Snob, The Investigation, Jump, Cave Dwellers, An Othello, And Noonday Demons, The Typists, The Tiger, Hot Buttered Roll.*

RELATED CAREER—Founder, artistic director, Open Space Theatre, London, 1968-81; associate director, Los Angeles Theatre Centre, Los Angeles, CA, 1982—; artistic director, Santa Monica Stage Company, Santa Monica, CA; theatre critic.

WRITINGS: PLAYS—See production details above, unless indicated. *Palach,* 1970; (adaptor) *Woyzeck,* 1973; (translator) *And They Put Handcuffs on the Flowers,* 1973; *Sherlock's Last Case,* 1974, later produced at the Nederlander Theatre, New York City, 1987; *Artaud at Rodez,* 1975, published by Calder & Boyars; (adaptor) *The Father,* 1979; *The Removal,* Actors Theatre, Los Angeles, CA, 1983; (adaptor) *Enemy of the People,* 1984; (adaptor) *Hedda,* published by Aschehough and Company; (adaptor) *An Othello,* published by Penguin; (adaptor) *Measure for Measure,* published by Hansom; (adaptor) *The Shrew,* published by Marion Boyars; also wrote *Disciples; Clever Dick; Tea with Lady Bracknell.*

COLLECTIONS—*Potboilers,* published by Marion Boyars; *Sex Wars,* published by Marion Boyars; *The Marowitz Shakespeare,* published by Marion Boyars; *Open Space Plays,* published by Penguin; *Marowitz Hamlet and Doctor Faustus,* published by Penguin; *Confessions of a Counterfeit Critic,* published by Eyre-Methuen.

NON-FICTION—(Editor) *Theatre at Work,* published by Eyre-Methuen; (editor) *The Encore Reader,* published by Eyre-Methuen; *The Critic As Artist,* published by S. Fischer Verlag; *Stanislavsky: The Method,* published by Citadel Press; *The Method As Means,* published by Barrie & Rockliffe; *Prospero's Staff,* published by Indiana University Press.

Also has written for periodicals including the *Village Voice, Drama Review, New Statesman, Los Angeles Times, New York Times, Plays and Players, American Theatre,* and *The Observer.*

AWARDS: Louis B. Mayer Playwriting Award; Order of the Purple Sash.

MEMBER: Dramatists Guild, Screenwriters Guild.

ADDRESSES: HOME—3058 Sequit Drive, Malibu, CA 90265. AGENT—c/o Gary Salt, Paul Kohner Agency, 9169 Sunset Boulevard, Los Angeles, CA 90069.

*　　*　　*

MARSHALL, Alan Peter   1938-

PERSONAL: Born August 12, 1938, in London, England; married Carol Christina; children: Lorraine, Jamie.

VOCATION: Film and television producer.

CAREER: PRINCIPAL FILM WORK—Producer: *Bugsy Malone,* Paramount, 1976; *Midnight Express,* Columbia, 1978; *Fame,* United Artists, 1980; *Shoot the Moon,* Metro-Goldwyn-Mayer/United Artists (MGM/UA), 1982; *Pink Floyd: The Wall,* MGM/UA, 1982; *Another Country,* Orion Classics, 1983; *Birdy,* Tri-Star, 1984; *Angel Heart,* Tri-Star, 1986.

PRINCIPAL TELEVISION WORK—All as producer: Movies: *No Hard Feelings,* BBC; *Our Cissy, Footsteps,* both EMI.

RELATED CAREER—Founder, Alan Parker Film Company, 1970; film editor.

AWARDS: All with Alan Parker. Best Artistic Contribution, Cannes Film Festival Award, 1984, for *Another Country;* Grand Prix Special du Jury Award, Cannes Film Festival, 1985, for *Birdy;* Michael Balcon Award, British Academy, for Outstanding Contribution to Cinema, 1985; ten Academy Award nominations; four

ALAN PETER MARSHALL

Academy Awards; seven Golden Globe Awards; ten British Academy Awards.

MEMBER: British Film and Television Producers Association (executive committee); British Academy of Film and Television Arts (executive committee); Association of Independent Producers; Independent Programme Producers Association.

ADDRESSES: HOME—Surrey, England. AGENT—c/o Judy Scottfox, William Morris Agency, 151 El Camino Drive, Beverly Hills, CA 90212.

*　　*　　*

MARTIN, Christopher   1942-

PERSONAL: Full name, John Christopher Martin; born December 7, 1942, in New York City; son of Ian (an actor and writer) and Inge (an actress; maiden name, Adams) Martin. EDUCATION: New York University, B.S., M.A., 1967.

VOCATION: Actor, director, producer, and designer.

CAREER: PRINCIPAL STAGE APPEARANCES—John Tanner, Don Juan, *Man and Superman,* Astrov, *Uncle Vanya,* Creon, *Antigone,* Thomas Mendip, *The Lady's Not for Burning,* Max, *The Homecoming,* Ben Jonson, *Bingo,* title role, *Hamlet,* title role, *Richard II,* Musgrave, *Serjeant Musgrave's Dance,* all with the Classic Stage Company, New York City.

PRINCIPAL STAGE WORK—All with the Classic Stage Company, New York City. Producer, director, and/or designer: *Moby Dick, Woyzeck, Rashomon, The Hound of the Baskervilles, Tartuffe, Hedda Gabler, Rosemersholm, The Marquis of Keith, Don Juan, Oedipus Rex, Oedipus at Colonus, Antigone, Gilles de Rais, Leonce and Lena,* all 1980-81; *Faust, Parts I and II, Ghost Sonata, Wild Oats, Balloon, Danton's Death,* all 1982-83; *Big and Little/ Scenes, Hamlet, Baal, Dance of Death,* all 1984; and over sixty other productions since 1967; also directed or co-directed *Twelfth Night, Timon of Athens, Wild Oats, Our Town, Cat on a Hot Tin Roof, Fifth of July,* all New Jersey Shakespeare Festival, Madison, NJ; and directed plays while at New York University, including *The Caretaker,* 1963.

RELATED CAREER—Founder, artistic director, Classic Stage Company, 1967—; founding president, Off-Off Broadway Alliance, 1972-75; teacher, New York University and Fordham University.

WRITINGS: PLAYS—(Translator) *Civil Wars,* American Repertory Theatre, Cambridge, MA, 1984; also adapted plays for the Classic Stage Company.

SIDELIGHTS: FAVORITE ROLES—Max in *The Homecoming;* Ben Jonson in *Bingo;* Falstaff.

ADDRESSES: OFFICE—564 Hudson Street, New York, NY 10014.*

*   *   *

MARTIN, Quinn   1922-1987

PERSONAL: Born Martin Cohen, Jr., May 22, 1922, in New York, NY; died of a heart attack, September 5, 1987, in Rancho Santa Fe, CA; son of Martin Cohen, Sr. (a film editor and producer); married wife, Marianne, March 28, 1961; children: Jill, Cliff, Michael. EDUCATION: University of California, Berkeley, B.A., 1949. MILITARY: U.S. Army Air Corps, 1940-45.

VOCATION: Producer and writer.

CAREER: PRINICPAL TELEVISION WORK—All as executive producer unless indicated. Series: Producer and principal writer, *Jane Wyman Show,* NBC, 1957; producer, *Westinghouse Desilu Playhouse,* CBS, 1958-59; *The Untouchables,* ABC, 1959-63; *The Fugitive,* ABC, 1963-67; *Twelve O'Clock High,* ABC, 1964-67; *The F.B.I.,* ABC, 1965-74; *The Invaders,* ABC, 1967-68; *Cannon,* CBS, 1971-76; *The Streets of San Francisco,* ABC, 1972-77; *Barnaby Jones,* CBS, 1973-80; *Manhunter,* CBS, 1974-75; *Bert D'Angelo, Superstar,* ABC, 1976; *Most Wanted,* ABC, 1976-77; *Tales of the Unexpected,* NBC, 1977. Pilots: *Incident in San Francisco,* ABC, 1971; *Cannon,* CBS, 1971; *Travis Logan, D.A.,* CBS, 1971; *Streets of San Francisco,* ABC, 1972; *Manhunter,* CBS, 1974; *Crossfire,* NBC, 1975; *Most Wanted,* ABC, 1976; *Law of the Land* (also known as *The Deputies*), NBC, 1976; *The Hunted Lady,* NBC, 1977; *Code Name: Diamond Head,* NBC, 1977; *The City,* NBC, 1977. Movies: *House on Green Apple Road,* ABC, 1970; *The Face of Fear,* CBS, 1971; *Murder or Mercy,* ABC, 1974; *The F.B.I. Story: The F.B.I. Versus Alvin Karpis, Public Enemy Number One,* CBS, 1974; *Panic on the 5:22,* ABC, 1974; *The Abduction of Saint Anne* (also known as *They've Kidnapped Anne Benedict*), ABC, 1975; *Attack on Terror: The F.B.I. Versus the Ku Klux Klan,* CBS, 1975; *A Home of Our Own,* CBS, 1975;

Brink's: The Great Robbery, CBS, 1976; *Standing Tall,* NBC, 1978.

PRINCIPAL FILM WORK—Producer, *The Mephisto Waltz,* Twentieth Century-Fox, 1971.

RELATED CAREER—Head of post production, Universal Studios, 1950-54; president and chief executive officer, QM Productions, 1960-79; president, Quinn Martin Communications Group, 1982-87; board chairor, chief executive officer, Quinn Martin Films; consultant, Taft Broadcasting; adjunct professor of drama, University of California, San Diego; president, La Jolla Playhouse, La Jolla, CA.

NON-RELATED CAREER—President, Del Mar Fair Board.

SIDELIGHTS: CTFT notes that Quinn Martin, as head of QM Productions, was responsible for more than two thousand hours of television programming among the sixteen series and twenty movies he produced. After selling his television production company to Taft Broadcasting in 1979, Martin endowed a chair of drama at the University of California, San Diego.

OBITUARIES AND OTHER SOURCES: New York Times, September 7, 1987; *Variety,* September 9, 1987.*

*   *   *

MARTIN, Steve   1945-

PERSONAL: Born in 1945, in Waco, TX; son of Glenn and Mary (Lee) Martin; married Victoria Tennant (an actress), 1986. EDUCATION: Attended Long Beach State College (now California State University, Long Beach) and the University of California, Los Angeles.

VOCATION: Comedian, actor, writer, and producer.

CAREER: PRINCIPAL FILM APPEARANCES— Navin, *The Jerk,* Universal, 1979; Arthur, *Pennies from Heaven,* United Artists, 1981; Rigby Reardon, *Dead Men Don't Wear Plaid,* Universal, 1982; Dr. Michael Hfuhruhurr, *The Man with Two Brains,* Warner Brothers, 1983; title role, *The Lonely Guy,* Universal, 1984; Roger Cobb, *All of Me,* Universal, 1984; Orin Scrivello, D.D.S., *Little Shop of Horrors,* Geffen Company/Warner Brothers, 1986; Lucky Day, *Three Amigos,* Orion, 1986; C.D. Bales, *Roxanne,* Columbia, 1987; Neal Page, *Planes, Trains, and Automobiles,* Paramount, 1987. Also appeared in the short *The Absent Minded Waiter,* Paramount, 1977; and in *Sergeant Pepper's Lonely Hearts Club Band,* 1978; *The Kids Are Alright,* 1979; and *The Muppet Movie,* 1979.

PRINCIPAL FILM WORK—Also see *WRITINGS* below; executive producer, *Three Amigos,* Orion, 1986.

PRINCIPAL TELEVISION APPEARANCES—Series: Regular, *Andy Willams Presents Ray Stevens,* NBC, 1970; *The Ken Berry "Wow" Show,* ABC, 1972; *The Sonny and Cher Comedy Hour,* CBS, 1972-73; *The Smothers Brothers Comedy Hour,* CBS, 1975; *The Johnny Cash Show,* CBS, 1976. Episodic: Host, *The Tonight Show,* NBC, for over fifty appearances; host, *Saturday Night Live,* NBC; guest, *The Muppet Show,* syndicated; guest, *The Carol Burnett Show,* CBS; guest, *Cher,* CBS; *The Steve Allen Comedy Hour,* NBC.

Specials: *Steve Martin: A Wild and Crazy Guy,* NBC, 1978; *Comedy Is Not Pretty,* NBC, 1980, *Steve Martin's Best Show Ever,* NBC, 1981.

PRINCIPAL TELEVISION WORK—Also see *WRITINGS* below; executive producer, *Domestic Life,* CBS, 1984.

RELATED CAREER—Partner in Aspen Film Society (an independent production company) and 40 Share Productions (a television production company).

WRITINGS: SCREENPLAYS—*The Absent-Minded Waiter,* Paramount, 1977; (with Carl Gottlieb and Michael Elias) *The Jerk,* Universal, 1979; (with Carl Reiner and George Gipe) *Dead Men Don't Wear Plaid,* Universal, 1982; *Easy Money,* Orion, 1983; co-writer, *The Man with Two Brains,* Warner Brothers, 1983; (with Carl Reiner) *All of Me,* Universal, 1984; (with Lorne Michaels and Randy Newman) *Three Amigos,* Orion, 1986; *Roxanne,* Columbia, 1987.

TELEVISION—Series: *The Smothers Brothers Comedy Hour,* CBS; *The Sonny and Cher Comedy Hour,* CBS; also comedy writer for Pat Paulsen, Ray Stevens, Dick Van Dyke, John Denver, and Glen Campbell.

BOOKS—*Cruel Shoes* (humorous sketches), Press of the Pegacycle Lady, 1977, revised and enlarged edition, Putnam, 1979.

RECORDINGS: COMEDY ALBUMS—*Let's Get Small,* 1977; *A Wild and Crazy Guy,* 1978; *Comedy Is Not Pretty,* 1979; *The Steve Martin Brothers,* 1982, all Warner Brothers. SINGLES—"King Tut," 1978.

AWARDS: Co-winner, Outstanding Writing Achievement in Comedy, Variety, or Music Series, Emmy Award, 1969, for *The Smothers Brothers Comedy Hour;* Best Writing in a Comedy, Variety, or Music Special, Emmy Award nomination, 1975, for *Van Dyke and Company;* Georgie Award, American Guild of Variety Artists, 1977 and 1978; Best Comedy Album, Grammy Award, 1977, for *Let's Get Small,* 1978, for *A Wild and Crazy Guy;* Academy Award nomination, 1978, for *The Absent- Minded Waiter;* Best Actor, National Society of Film Critics Award and New York Film Critics Circle Award, both 1984, for *All of Me.*

MEMBER: Screen Actors Guild, American Guild of Variety Artists, American Federation of Television and Radio Artists.

SIDELIGHTS: Over the course of two decades, Steve Martin has "evolved from a coolly absurdist stand-up comic to a fully formed, amazingly nimble comic actor," noted Janet Maslin in a June 19, 1987 *New York Times* article. Martin became the hottest comic of the seventies by perfecting the persona of a "wild and crazy guy" who parodied the very idea of doing comedy. A frequent host of the *Tonight Show* and *Saturday Night Live,* he successfully parlayed his routines into numerous television appearances, two Grammy Award-winning albums, *Let's Get Small* and *A Wild and Crazy Guy,* as well as a best-selling book of comic sketches, *Cruel Shoes,* before bringing his comedic talents to the screen in *The Jerk*—the third biggest hit of 1980. Since then he has devoted himself to filmmaking as a writer and actor. Though his films have met with uneven success, he earned the 1984 award as best actor from both the New York Film Critics Circle and the National Society of Film Critics for *All of Me,* and his 1987 hit *Roxanne* led *Time* in its August 24, 1987 cover story to proclaim him "America's most charming and resourceful comic actor."

Born in Waco, Texas in 1945, Martin grew up in southern California just two miles from Disneyland, where he first learned to perform magic and balloon tricks, tell jokes, and play the banjo. As a child he studied and later performed with Wally Boag, a former vaudeville comic whose act was showcased at Disneyland's Golden Horseshoe Revue. After eight years at the Magic Kingdom, Martin left for nearby Knott's Berry Farm to act in melodrama at the Birdcage Theatre and to perform his own fifteen-minute routines of comedy, magic, and banjo music. While working at the Birdcage, Martin met a young woman who convinced him that knowledge was the most important thing in life. Persuaded to go to college, he entered Long Beach State and majored in philosophy.

Despite earning excellent grades and at one point considering a career teaching philosophy, Martin lost interest in the subject after a while. "As I studied the history of philosophy, the quest for ultimate truth became less important to me, and by the time I got to Wittgenstein it seemed pointless," he told *Time.* "Then I realized that in the arts you don't have to discover meaning, you create it. There are no rules, no true and false, no right and wrong. Anyway, these were the musings of a 21-year-old kid." In 1967 Martin transferred to the University of California, Los Angeles, changed his major to theatre and television writing, and began performing at night in the local clubs. When he caught the attention of Mason Williams, the head writer for *The Smothers Brothers Comedy Hour* on CBS, and was offered a chance to earn $500 a week as a staff writer, Martin decided his college days were over. Although CBS cancelled the controversial program in 1968, the following year Martin and the show's other ten writers received an Emmy Award for their work. The Emmy not only increased Martin's renown, it also tripled his salary as a writer. He subsequently earned $1500 a week writing material for such entertainers as Glen Campbell, John Denver, Pat Paulsen, Ray Stevens, and Sonny and Cher.

In spite of the financial reward, writing for other performers left Martin unfulfilled. When he was twenty-five, he launched his own career as a stand-up comedian performing in small clubs and appearing at rock concerts as the opening act for groups like the Nitty Gritty Dirt Band. But the first few years were dismal ones, since the drugged, impatient audiences at rock concerts had little interest in comedy. Even the audiences in Las Vegas, where Martin opened for Ann Margret and other headliners, were often unreceptive. "He made balloon animals and did the magic, and it just seemed weird to be trying that stuff," recalled Carl Gottlieb in an April 3, 1978 *Newsweek* profile of Martin.

Between his first appearance on the *Tonight Show* in 1973 and the dawning of success in 1975, Martin literally cleaned up his act. He got rid of the turquoise jewelry, the conch belt, the long hair, and the beard he had acquired while trying to create an image that would succeed with the rock crowd, and began wearing a white, custom-tailored, three-piece suit. Stardom, however, remained elusive. Still occasionally bombing, he was $17,000 dollars in debt and seriously considering quitting show business, but he made two additional changes that proved to be significant. First, he vowed never again to open for anyone, but rather to build his own audience. Second, he revised his whole approach to comedy, opting for an absurdist, nonsensical brand of humor that contrasted sharply with his clean-cut, business-like image. The change in approach led him to develop a persona—a stage personality or attitude holding all the jokes and tricks together—that parodied the very idea of doing comedy. Pauline Kael described Martin's act in the June 27, 1983 *New Yorker:* "Onstage, he puts across the idea that he's going to do some cornball routine, and then when he does it it has quotation marks around it, and that's what makes it hilarious. He does the routine straight, yet he's totally facetious."

By the end of 1975 Martin was selling out such prestigious clubs as the San Francisco Boarding House and was appearing with regularity on programs like the *Merv Griffin Show, Dinah!, Dick Cavett Show,* and *Hollywood Squares.* His national breakthrough came in 1976, when he was featured on a Home Box Office (HBO) special taped at the Troubadour in Los Angeles, and when he first guest-hosted *Saturday Night Live,* where he and Dan Ackroyd created the now-famous Czechoslovakian playboys, the Festrunk brothers. In October and November of 1977 the self-proclaimed "wild and crazy guy" went on a fifty-city tour across the country, grossing over one million dollars and performing for 500,000 fans at college campuses and auditoriums, where some of the audiences were as large as 20,000. Greeting him with ovations normally reserved for rock superstars, fans imitated features of Martin's act by sporting novelty-store arrows on their heads, screaming "Well, EXCUUUUSE MEEE!!!" and requesting balloon animals in the shape of "a venereal disease" or "the Sistine Chapel."

Martin's success carried over into other areas as well, making him the hottest comic of the seventies. His two Grammy Award-winning albums had combined sales of six million copies, and a gag disco tune called "King Tut" sold more than 1.5 million in 1978. The next year he published a revised edition of his book, *Cruel Shoes,* and it topped the bestseller list. While at the height of his popularity, Martin gave up his stage work to concentrate on films. "I quit because it was over for me emotionally," he explained in a conversation with *U.S. News and World Report* (June 17, 1985). "You just can't maintain that kind of momentum. . . . Besides, there is a critical cycle [of discover, acceptance, rejection, and rediscovery]."

Martin incorporated much of his stage act into the 1980 film *The Jerk,* a $74 million box-office bonanza that he wrote with Carl Gottlieb and Michael Elias. Though he had previously written and starred in *The Absent-Minded Waiter*—a 1977 Paramount short that was nominated for an Academy Award—*The Jerk* was his first feature-length film. In the September-October, 1984 issue of *Film Comment,* Jack Barth accounted for the movie's success: "It was the first chance to hear the Wild and Crazy Guy swear, and the first chance to pay to see him up close, since his concert venues by that time were too large for his own good. The film was stuffed with sight gags. . . . The sheer density of the humor combined with the truth-in-advertising title put this one over the top."

"Since 'The Jerk,' Martin's movie career has been pretty slumpy," observed Tom Shales in the June 19, 1987 *Washington Post,* though Barth detected "moments of mirth worth the price of admission" in all his films. One of his pictures was a departure from his comedic roles—Martin played the lead in *Pennies from Heaven,* a downbeat musical drama about small people with oversize dreams. "It was a breath of fresh air I needed in my life," the actor told David Ansen and Janet Huck of *Newsweek* (June 22, 1987), but he also conceded that the box-office flop was "the worst career move of my life." Martin co-wrote his next film, *Dead Men Don't Wear Plaid,* which Vincent Canby described in the May 21, 1982 *New York Times* as "a technically and artistically risky, impertinent adventure that integrates clips from approximately two dozen old movies into the action of Rigby Reardon's lastest caper." The film included "plenty of vintage Steve Martin," according to Barth, but was another disappointment in drawing power.

Though some of his more recent films have been highly praised, Martin's cinematic standouts since *The Jerk* have been *All of Me* and *Roxanne.* "With *All of Me* in 1984, he proved that he could locate the soul of a character while surrounding it with spectacular physical comedy," wrote Richard Corliss in the August 24, 1987 *Time* cover story. *Los Angeles Times* arts editor Charles Champlin described Martin's award-winning performance in a December 27, 1984 review of the movie: "Martin's portrayal of a klutzy young lawyer who becomes semi-inhabited by a dead but irascible lady [played by Lily Tomlin] was one of his most skillful works. . . . He also invested the character with likability as well as foolishness, and even . . . preserved the sensitivity that made 'Pennies from Heaven' such an engrossing try as a film."

Martin's most critically acclaimed screen performance was the 1987 hit *Roxanne,* an adaptation of Edmond Rostand's play *Cyrano de Bergerac* that Martin spent nearly three years and twenty-five drafts writing. "Critics have adored the writing," said Shales, "but have also likened Martin's comedic agility onscreen to Charlie Chaplin's. There have been reference to things like 'comic genius' bursting forth." Calling *Roxanne* "a charmer" that "honors Rostand while skimming off the fat and the play's creepier masochistic undertones," Ansen claimed that the protagonist, C.D. Bales "is Martin's most fully rounded character. Always brilliant at standing outside himself, mocking silliness while creating it, here [Martin] does his high-wire act without the protective net of irony and shows he can be both funny *and* real. . . . This is the culmination of a long quest to exorcise his stage persona as a wild and crazy guy."

ADDRESSES: HOME—Aspen, CO. OFFICE—P.O. Box 929, Beverly Hills, CA 90213. AGENT—c/o Marty Klein, Agency for the Performing Arts, 9000 Sunset Boulevard, Suite 1200, Los Angeles, CA 90069. PUBLICIST—c/o Paul Bloch, Rogers and Cowan, 10000 Santa Monica Boulevard, Los Angeles, CA 90067.*

*   *   *

MARVIN, Lee   1924-1987

OBITUARY NOTICE—See index for *CTFT* sketch: Born February 19, 1924, in New York City; died of a heart attack, August 29, 1987, at Tucson Medical Center, Tucson, AZ. With nearly sixty films to his credit, actor Lee Marvin was well known for his tough guy roles in such movies as *Bad Day at Black Rock, Violent Saturday, The Man Who Shot Liberty Valance, The Killers,* and *The Dirty Dozen.* Nevertheless, it was for a dual role in the comedic western *Cat Ballou* that he won the 1965 Academy Award for best actor. Prior to his Hollywood success, Marvin had acted in a number of Off-Broadway productions and made his Broadway debut in *Billy Budd* in 1951. His career also included over two hundred television appearances, notably the starring role as Lieutenant Frank Ballinger on the NBC series *M Squad* from 1957 to 1960. Marvin's personal life also drew public attention when a support suit brought against him by his former live-in lover, Michele Triola Marvin, made headlines in 1979 and introduced the term "palimony" for such cases. Marvin's last feature film, *The Delta Force,* was released in 1986.

OBITUARIES AND OTHER SOURCES: Variety, September 2, 1987.

*   *   *

MASON, Brewster   1922-1987

PERSONAL: Born August 30, 1922, in Kidsgrove, England; died after a fall while playing the title role in *Richard II,* August 14,

1987; son of Jesse and Constance May (Kemp) Mason; married Lorna Whittaker (divorced); married Kate Meredith; children: (first marriage) one daughter. EDUCATION: Trained for the stage at the Royal Academy of Dramatic Art. MILITARY: Royal Navy.

VOCATION: Actor, director, and lecturer.

CAREER: STAGE DEBUT—Dick Dudgeon, *The Devil's Disciple*, Finsbury Park Open Air Theatre, 1947. LONDON DEBUT—Flight Sergeant John Nabb, *An English Summer*, Lyric Hammersmith Theatre, 1948. BROADWAY DEBUT—Sir Lewis Eliot, *The Affair*, Henry Miller's Theatre, September, 1962. PRINCIPAL STAGE APPEARANCES—Caesar French, *The King of Friday's Men*, Lyric Hammersmith Theatre, London, 1949; Polixenes, *The Winter's Tale*, Phoenix Theatre, London, 1951; Borachio, *Much Ado about Nothing*, Phoenix Theatre, 1952; Earl of Northumberland, *Richard II*, Lyric Hammersmith Theatre, 1952; Sir Wilful Witwoud, *The Way of the World*, Bedemar, *Venice Preserves*, both Lyric Hammersmith Theatre, 1953; Earl of Northumberland, *Richard II*, Rhodes Centenary, Bulawayo, Rhodesia (now Zimbabwe), 1953; Dr. Farley, *A Day by the Sea*, Haymarket Theatre, London, 1954; Mr. Badger, *Toad of Toad Hall*, Prince's Theatre, London, 1954; David Bowman, *Flowering Cherry*, Haymarket Theatre, 1957; Victor Hodges, QC, *Look on Tempests*, Comedy Theatre, London, 1960; General Allenby, *Ross*, Haymarket Theatre, 1960. Also member of the Brighton Repertory Company, Brighton, U.K., 1948-49.

All with the Royal Shakespeare Company: Kent, *King Lear*, Aldwych Theatre, London, 1963; Earl of Warwick, *The Wars of the Roses*, Memorial Theatre, Stratford-on-Avon, U.K., 1963, then Aldwych Theatre, 1964; Goldberg, *The Birthday Party*, Aldwych Theatre, 1964; Antonio, *The Merchant of Venice*, Boyet, *Love's Labour's Lost*, Alcibiades, *Timon of Athens*, Claudius, ghost, *Hamlet*, all Memorial Theatre, 1965; judge, *The Government Inspector*, Claudius, ghost, *Hamlet*, Sir Toby Belch, *Twelfth Night*, Menenius, *Coriolanus*, Lafeu, *All's Well That Ends Well*, Banquo, *Macbeth*, all Memorial Theatre, 1967, then Aldwych Theatre, 1968; Falstaff, *The Merry Wives of Windsor*, Sir Tunbelly Clumsy, *The Relapse*, both Memorial Theatre, then Aldwych Theatre, 1968; title role, *Julius Caesar*, Memorial Theatre, 1968; Duke of Florence, *Women Beware*, Wolsey, *Henry VIII*, Falstaff, *The Merry Wives of Windsor*, all Memorial Theatre, 1969; Andrew Undershaft, *Major Barbara*, Wolsey, *Henry VIII*, both Memorial Theatre, then Aldwych Theatre, 1970; *Othello*, Memorial Theatre, 1971, then Aldwych Theatre, 1972; Falstaff, *Henry IV, Parts I and II*, *The Merry Wives of Windsor*, all Memorial Theatre, then Aldwych Theatre, 1976; Earl of Warwick, *The Wars of the Roses*, Memorial Theatre, 1984.

MAJOR TOURS—Menenius, *Coriolanus*, Lafeu, *All's Well That End's Well*, Royal Shakespeare Company (RSC), Finland and Soviet cities, 1967; title role, *Othello*, RSC, Japan cities, 1972.

PRINCIPAL STAGE WORK—Directed three plays at the Monomoy Theatre, Cape Cod, MA, 1976-79.

PRINCIPAL FILM APPEARANCES—*The Dam Busters*, Warner Brothers, 1955; *Private Potter*, Metro-Goldwyn-Mayer, 1963.

PRINCIPAL TELEVISION APPEARANCES—*The Pallisers*, BBC; *Edward VIII*, BBC.

RELATED CAREER—Lecturer on drama, University of California,

Irvine; drama instructor, Guildhall School of Music and Drama, London.

AWARDS: Bancroft Gold Medal, Royal Academy of Dramatic Art; elected a Fellow of the Guildhall School of Music and Drama.

MEMBER: British Actors' Equity Association, Screen Actors Guild; Garrick Club, Players Club, New York City; Stage Golfing Club; Naval Club.

OBITUARIES AND OTHER SOURCES: Variety, September, 2, 1987.*

*   *   *

MASTROIANNI, Marcello   1924-

PERSONAL: Born September 28, 1924, in Fontana Liri, Italy; married Flora Carabella (an actress); children: two daughters. EDUCATION: Attended the University of Rome.

VOCATION: Actor.

CAREER: STAGE DEBUT—*Angelica*, Rome, Italy, 1948. PRINCIPAL STAGE APPEARANCES—*Death of a Salesman*, *A Streetcar Named Desire*, *Ciao Rudy;* title role, *Henry IV*, Paris, 1983; others.

FILM DEBUT—*I Miserabili*, Italian, 1947. PRINCIPAL FILM APPEARANCES—*Domenica d'Agosto*, 1950; *Parigi e Sempre Parigi*, 1951; *Le Ragazze di Piazza di Spagna*, 1952; *Tempi Nostri*, 1954; *Peccato che Sia una Canaglia*, 1954; *Cornache di Poveri Amanti*, 1954; *Giorni d'Amore*, 1954; *Il Bigamo*, 1956; *Padre e Figli*, 1957; *White Nights*, CISA-Vides-Intermondia, 1957; *La Loi*, 1958; *I Soliti Ignoti*, 1958; *Racconti d'Estate*, 1958; *La Dolce Vita*, Rlama-Pathe, 1960; *Il Bell'Antonio*, Del Duca-Arco, 1960; *Adua e le Compagne*, 1960; *La Notte*, Nepi-Sofited-Silver, 1961; *The Assassin*, Titanus-Vides, 1961; *A Very Private Affair*, Metro-Goldwyn-Mayer, 1961; *Divorce, Italian Style*, Lux-Vides-Galatea, 1961; *Vie Privee*, 1962; *Family Chronicle*, Titanus, 1962; Guido, *8 1/2*, Cineriz, 1963; *Yesterday, Today and Tomorrow*, Champion, 1963; *Marriage, Italian Style*, 1963; *Fantasmi a Roma*, 1964; *Casanova 70*, 1965; *The Organizer*, Lux-Vides, 1965; *The 10th Victim*, AVCO-Embassy, 1965; *Shout Louder, I Don't Understand*, 1966; *The Stranger*, De Laurentiis, 1967; *The Man with the Balloons*, 1968; *Diamonds for Breakfast*, 1968; *A Place for Lovers*, 1969; *Sunflower*, 1969.

Drama of Jealousy, 1970; *Leo the Last*, United Artists, 1970; *La Moglie del Prete*, 1971; *What?* 1972; *Mordi e Fuggi*, 1972; *Blow-Out*, Mara-Films, 1973; *Rappresaglia*, 1973; *The Slightly Pregnant Man*, S. J. International, 1973; *Allonsanfan*, 1974; *The Priest's Wife*, 1975; *Gangster Doll*, 1976; *A Special Day*, Cinema V, 1977; *Bye-Bye Monkey*, 1978; *Cosi Come Sei*, 1978; *Revenge*, 1979; *City of Women*, 1979; *Wifemistress*, Quartet Films, 1979; *It Only Happens to Others*, 1979; *Blood Feud*, ITC Entertainment, 1981; *The New World*, 1981; *Henry IV*, 1985; *Saturday, Sunday, Monday*, 1985; *Storia di Piera*, Macaroni, 1986; *Ginger and Fred*, 1986; Mandrake, *Intervista*, Al Josha Productions, 1987; Romano, *Dark Eyes*, UGC, 1987.

RELATED CAREER—Formed independent film production company, Master Films, 1966.

NON-RELATED CAREER—Formerly a draftsman in Rome, 1940-43.

AWARDS: Best Actor, Cannes Film Festival, 1970, for *Drama of Jealousy;* 1986, for *Dark Eyes.*

ADDRESSES: OFFICE—c/o Avv. Cav Via Maria Adelaide 8, Rome, Italy. AGENT—The William Morris Agency, 151 El Camino Drive, Beverly Hills, CA 90212.*

*   *   *

MAY, Elaine   1932-

PERSONAL: Born April 21, 1932, in Philadelphia, PA; daughter of Jack Berlin; married Marvin May (divorced); married Sheldon Harnick (divorced); children: (first marriage) Jeannie Berlin. EDUCATION: Trained for the stage with Maria Ouspenskaya.

VOCATION: Actress, film director, comedienne, and screenwriter.

CAREER: BROADWAY DEBUT—*An Evening with Mike Nichols and Elaine May,* John Golden Theatre, 1960; PRINCIPAL STAGE APPEARANCES—Shirley, *The Office,* Henry Miller's Theatre, New York City, 1966; Martha, *Who's Afraid of Virginia Woolf?,* Long Wharf Theatre, New Haven, CT, 1980. Also appeared with the Playwright's Theatre in a student performance of *Miss Julie,* University of Chicago, Chicago, IL.

PRINCIPAL STAGE WORK—Technical assistant, *Bruno and Sidney,* New Stages Theatre, New York City, 1949; director, *The Third Ear,* Premise Theatre, New York City, 1964; director, *Adaptation, Next,* both Greenwich Mews Playhouse, Mew York City, 1969; director, *The Goodbye People,* Berkshire Theater Festival, Stockbridge, MA, 1971; director, *The Disappearance of the Jews, Gorilla, Hotline,* all Goodman Theatre, Chicago, IL, 1983.

MAJOR TOURS—*Adaptation, Next,* U.S. cities, both 1969.

PRINCIPAL CABARET APPEARANCES—Performed with Mike Nichols and others at The Compass, Chicago, IL, 1954-57; with Mike Nichols, appeared at the Village Vanguard, the Blue Angel, and many other nightclubs.

PRINCIPAL FILM APPEARANCES—*Luv,* Columbia, 1967; *A New Leaf,* Paramount, 1971; *California Suite,* Columbia, 1978; also appeared in *Enter Laughing,* 1970.

PRINCIPAL FILM WORK—Director: *A New Leaf,* Paramount, 1971; *The Heartbreak Kid,* Twentieth Century-Fox, 1973; *Mikey and Nicky,* Paramount, 1977; *Ishtar,* Columbia, 1987.

TELEVISION DEBUT—*The Jack Parr Show,* 1957. PRINCIPAL TELEVISION APPEARANCES—Episodic: *Omnibus,* NBC, 1958; *Laugh Line,* NBC, 1959; *Laugh-In,* NBC; *Dinah Shore Show,* NBC; *Perry Como Show,* NBC; also appeared in *The Fabulous Fifties.*

PRINCIPAL RADIO APPEARANCES—Appeared weekly on *Nightline,* NBC; also numerous other appearances.

WRITINGS: PLAYS—*A Matter of Position,* Walnut Street Theatre,

Philadelphia, PA, 1962; *Not Enough Rope,* Maidman Theatre, New York City, 1962; *Adaptation,* Greenwich Mews Playhouse, New York City, 1969; *Hot Line,* Goodmnan Theatre, Chicago, IL, 1983; *Better Part of Valour,* 1983. SCREENPLAYS—*A New Leaf,* Paramount, 1971; *Such Good Friends,* Paramount, 1971; *Mikey and Nicky,* Paramount, 1977; co-author, *Heaven Can Wait,* Paramount, 1978; (also co-writer of songs) *Ishtar,* Columbia, 1987.

RECORDINGS: ALBUMS—*Improvisations to Music,* Mercury; *An Evening with Mike Nichols and Elaine May,* Mercury; *Mike Nichols and Elaine May Examine Doctors,* Mercury.

AWARDS: Most Promising New Playwright, Drama Desk Award, Best Director, Outer Circle Award, both 1969, for *Adaptation.*

ADDRESSES: OFFICE—c/o Directors Guild of America, 110 W. 57th Street, New York, NY 10019.*

*   *   *

McCAMBRIDGE, Mercedes   1918-

PERSONAL: Born Charlotte Mercedes McCambridge, March 17, 1918, in Joliet, IL; daughter of John Patrick and Marie (Mahaffry) McCambridge; married William Fifield, 1939 (divorced, 1946); married Fletcher Markle, February 19, 1950 (divorced, 1962); children: (first marriage) John. EDUCATION: Mundelein College, A.B., 1937.

VOCATION: Actress and writer.

CAREER: BROADWAY DEBUT—Mary Lorimer, *A Place of Our Own,* Royale Theatre, April 2, 1945. PRINCIPAL STAGE APPEAR-ANCES—Betty Lord, *Woman Bites Dog,* Belasco Theatre, New York City, 1946; Frances Morritt, *The Young and Fair,* Fulton Theatre, New York City, 1948; replacement, *Who's Afraid of Virginia Woolf?,* Billy Rose Theatre, New York City, 1962 and 1964; *Cages,* York Theatre, New York City and in Montreal, Canada, 1963; Regina Giddens, *The Little Foxes,* Ann Arbor Drama Festival, MI, 1963; Annie Sullivan, *The Miracle Worker,* Moorestown Theatre, NJ, 1966; Nettie Cleary, *The Subject Was Roses* and Amanda, *The Glass Menagerie,* both at the Mineola Theatre, NY, 1966; Lucy Lake, *The Love Suicide at Schofield Barracks,* American National Theatre and Academy (ANTA), New York City, 1972; title role, *Medea,* Hartke Theatre, Catholic University, Washington, DC, 1973; also appeared in *Hope for the Best* and *'Night, Mother.*

MAJOR TOURS—Mary, *Twilight Bar,* pre-Broadway tour, Ford's Theatre, Baltimore, MD, Walnut Street Theatre, Philadelphia, PA, 1946; Mother Miriam Ruth, *Agnes of God,* National tour, Curran Theatre, San Francisco, 1983, Fox Theatre, San Diego, CA, 1984; *'Night, Mother,* National tour, 1984.

FILM DEBUT—Wife, *All the King's Men,* Columbia, 1949. PRIN-CIPAL FILM APPEARANCES—*Inside Straight,* Metro-Goldwyn-Mayer (MGM), 1951; *The Scarf,* United Artists, 1951; *Lightning Strikes Twice,* Warner Brothers, 1951; *Johnny Guitar,* Republic, 1954; *Giant,* Warner Brothers, 1956; *A Farewell to Arms,* Twentieth Century-Fox, 1957; *Suddenly, Last Summer,* Columbia, 1959; *Cimarron,* MGM, 1960; *Angel Baby,* Allied, 1961; *Run Home, Slow,* Joshua, 1964; *Last Generation,* 1965; *Jigsaw,* 1969; *99 Women,* Commonwealth, 1971; voice of the possessed girl, *The*

Exorcist, Warner Brothers, 1973; *Thieves,* 1977; *The Concorde—Airport '79,* 1979.

PRINCIPAL TELEVISION APPEARANCES—Episodic: *Tele-Theatre,* NBC, 1950; *Video Theatre,* CBS, 1950, 1952; *Ford Theatre,* NBC, 1952; *Studio One,* CBS, 1953, 1956; *Wire Service,* ABC, 1956; *The Loretta Young Show,* NBC, 1956; *Wagon Train,* NBC, 1957; *Jane Wyman Theatre,* NBC, 1958; *Rawhide,* CBS, 1959, 1960; *Bonanza,* NBC, 1962, 1970; *Dr. Kildare,* NBC, 1964; *The Nurses,* CBS, 1964; *The Defenders,* CBS, 1964; *Lost in Space,* CBS, 1966; *Stage 67,* ABC, 1966; *Bewitched,* ABC, 1968; *Medical Center,* CBS, 1970; *The Name of the Game,* NBC, 1971; *Gunsmoke,* CBS, 1971. Movies: *Killer by Night,* CBS, 1972; *Two for the Money,* ABC, 1972.

PRINCIPAL RADIO APPEARANCES—Series: Ruth, *Big Sister,* CBS, 1936; title role, *Nora Drake;* supplied all female voices, *I Love a Mystery.* Episodic: *Ford Theatre, CBS Radio Mystery Theatre,* others.

WRITINGS: NON-FICTION—Autobiography, *The Two of Us,* 1960; *The Quality of Mercy,* Berkley, 1982.

AWARDS: Best Supporting Actress, Academy Award, Associated Press Poll Award, *Look* Award, *Photoplay* Award, and the Foreign Correspondents Award, all 1949, for *All the King's Men;* Best Supporting Actress, Academy Award nomination, 1956, for *Giant;* Best Supporting Actress, Antoinette Perry Award nomination, 1972, for *The Love Suicide at Schofield Barracks;* special citation from United Jewish Welfare; two awards from the "City of Hope"; awarded with a certificate for volunteer work for the National Council on Alcoholism, presented by Mrs. Richard M. Nixon, 1971; Gold Key Award, Kansas City, MO, 1972; seven honorary doctorate degrees.

MEMBER: Actors' Equity Association, Screen Actors Guild, American Federation of Television and Radio Artists, Motion Picture Academy of Arts and Sciences.

ADDRESSES: AGENT—Michael Hartig Agency, 114 E. 28th Street, New York, NY 10016; Contemporary Artists, 132 Lasky Drive, Beverly Hills, CA 90212.*

*　　*　　*

McCLURE, Doug   1935-

PERSONAL: Born May 11, 1935, in Glendale, CA. EDUCATION: Attended the University of California at Los Angeles.

VOCATION: Actor.

CAREER: PRINCIPAL FILM APPEARANCES—*Because They're Young,* Columbia, 1960; *The Unforgiven,* United Artists, 1960; *Shenandoah,* Universal, 1965; *Beau Geste,* Universal, 1966; *The King's Pirate,* Universal, 1967; *Nobody's Perfect,* Universal, 1968; *The Land That Time Forgot,* American International, 1975; *At the Earth's Core,* American International, 1976; *Warlords of Atlantis,* British, 1978; *Humanoids from the Deep,* New World, 1980; *Cannonball Run II,* Warner Brothers, 1984.

PRINCIPAL TELEVISION APPEARANCES—Series: Frank "Flip" Flippen, *The Overland Trail,* NBC, 1960; Trampas, *The Virginian,*

NBC, 1962-71. Movies: *The Longest Hundred Miles,* 1967; *Terror in the Sky,* 1971; *The Birdmen,* 1971; *The Death of Me Yet,* 1971; *Playmates,* 1972; *The Judge and Jake Wyler,* 1972; *Shirts-Skins,* 1973; *Death Race,* 1973; *Satan's Triangle,* 1974; *SST—Death Flight,* 1977; *Wild and Woolly,* 1978; *The Rebels,* 1979. Mini-Series: Jemmy Brent, *Roots,* ABC, 1977-78.

PRINCIPAL STAGE APPEARANCES—Charles Browning, *The Roast,* Winter Garden Theatre, New York City, 1980.

MEMBER: Screen Actors Guild, American Federation of Television and Radio Artists.

ADDRESSES: AGENT—c/o Dan Pietragallo, William Morris Agency, Inc., 151 El Camino Drive, Beverly Hills, CA 90212.*

*　　*　　*

McCOOK, John

PERSONAL: Second marriage to Laurette Spang (an actress); children: Seth (first marriage), Jake, Becky.

VOCATION: Actor.

CAREER: PRINCIPAL TELEVISION APPEARANCES—Episodic: *Murder, She Wrote,* CBS; *Three's Company,* ABC; *Alice,* ABC; *Too Close for Comfort,* ABC; *Moonlighting,* ABC; *Amazing Stories,* NBC. Series: Lance Prentiss, *The Young and the Restless,*

JOHN McCOOK

1975-80; Eric Forrester, *The Bold and the Beautiful,* CBS, 1987; *Codename: Foxfire.* Mini-Series: Interrogator, *Robert Kennedy and His Times,* CBS, 1985. Movies: Captain Shafer, *O'Hara, United States Treasury: Operation Cobra,* CBS, 1971; Pepi Virgil, *Tourist,* syndicated, 1980; Dr. Kenner, *Beverly Hills Cowgirl Blues,* CBS, 1985.

PRINCIPAL STAGE APPEARANCES—All in summer theatre: Captain Hook, *Peter Pan;* Billy Bigelow, *Carousel;* Adam, *Seven Brides for Seven Brothers;* Pirate King, *The Pirates of Penzance.*

RELATED CAREER—Pianist and composer.

SIDELIGHTS: RECREATIONS—Golf, scuba diving, fishing, backpacking.

ADDRESSES: PUBLICIST—c/o Monique Moss, Michael Levine Public Relations Company, 8730 Sunset Boulevard, Los Angeles, CA 90069.

*   *   *

McDOUGALL, Gordon 1941-

PERSONAL: Born May 4, 1941, in Inverness, Scotland; son of Donald James and Sheila (McDonald) McDougall; married Lynda Britten; children: Abigail and Jack. EDUCATION: Kings College, B.A., English, 1963.

GORDON McDOUGALL

VOCATION: Director and producer.

CAREER: PRINCIPAL STAGE WORK—All as director: *The Restoration of Arnold Middleton,* Traverse Theatre, Edinburgh, Scotland, U.K., 1966; *The Daughter-in-Law,* Traverse Theatre, 1967; *Mourning Becomes Electra,* Traverse Theatre, then Arts Theatre, London, both 1967, later Baalbek Festival, Baalbek, Lebanon, and Edinburgh Festival, Edinburgh, Scotland, U.K., both 1968; *Aberfan, Would You Look at Them Smashing All the Lovely Windows,* Traverse Theatre, 1968; *Tom Paine, Romeo and Juliet,* both Stables Theatre, Manchester, U.K., 1969; *Occupations,* Stables Theatre, 1970; *Serjeant Musgrave's Dance,* Stables Theatre, 1971; *The Changeling,* Gardener Arts Centre, Brighton, U.K., 1971: *The Vicar of Soho, The Dark River,* both Gardener Arts Centre, 1972; *Twelfth Night,* Gardener Arts Centre, 1972, then Globe Playhouse, Bankside, U.K., 1973; *Henry IV, Part I,* and *King Lear,* both Citadel Theatre, Edmonton, AB, Canada, 1983; *Richard III,* Three Rivers Shakespeare Festival, Pittsburgh, PA, 1987. Also directed *The Country Wife,* Prospect Theatre, 1973; *Every Good Boy Deserves Favor, The Soldier's Tale, An English Soldier's Tale,* all Oxford Music Theatre, Oxford, U.K., 1977-82; *The Country Holiday, Peter Pan, Mephisto, Clay, Women Beware Women, The Master Class, The Tempest, Trafford Tanzi, Traveller in the Dark,* all Citadel Theatre, 1984-87; *The Master Class,* Centaur Theatre, Montreal, PQ, Canada; *Mephisto,* Round House Theatre, London; *All's Well That Ends Well,* Hong Kong Arts Centre.

Director, all with the Oxford Playhouse, Oxford, U.K., 1974-84: *The Government Inspector, As You Like It, Happy End, Uncle Vanya, Fitting Ladies, For Heaven's Sake Don't Walk around with Nothing On, The Country Wife, The Tempest, Dog Days, The Norman Conquests, The Threepenny Opera, Brand, The Magicalympical Games, What the Butler Saw, All's Well That Ends Well, Heartbreak Hotel, The Country Holiday, King Lear, Touch and Go, Much Ado about Nothing, Peer Gynt, Mephisto, The Philadelphia Story, The White Devil, Macbeth, Women Beware Women, The Oedipus Plays, Clay, The Dance of Death.*

MAJOR TOURS—Director: *Heartbreak Hotel,* Latin American cities; *Touch and Go,* Hong Kong and Latin America cities; *Every Good Boy Deserves Favour,* U.K. cites.

PRINCIPAL TELEVISION WORK—Series: Director, *World in Action,* Granda TV, 1963-66; producer, *Crown Court,* a Granada TV, 1973-74. Also served as assistant director, director, and producer of plays, educational films, and documentaries, Granada TV, 1963-71.

RELATED CAREER—Artistic director, Traverse Theatre, Edinburgh, U.K., 1966-68; founder and artistic director, Stables Theatre, Manchester, U.K., 1969; secretary, North West Arts Association Committee on Theatre in Manchester, 1971; artist in residence, University of York, 1971; North West Arts Association Advisory Panel member, 1971; founder and artistic director, Oxford Playhouse Company, Oxford, U.K., 1974-84; founder and artistic director, Oxford Music Theatre, Oxford, U.K., 1977-82; artistic director, Oxford International Festival, 1980-84; artistic director, Citadel Theatre, Edmonton, AB, Canada, 1984-87; artistic director, Gardener Arts Centre, Brighton, U.K. Also professor of drama: University of Edinburgh, 1966-68; University of Waterloo, 1973-74; Oxford University, 1974-78; University of California, Davis, 1982-83; University of Alberta, 1985; University of Pittsburgh, 1987-88.

WRITINGS: NON-FICTION—*The Theatrical Metaphor,* 1971.

MEMBER: British Actors' Equity Association (secretary, subcommittee on theatre directors, 1971), Association of Cinematographers and Television Technicians, Directors Guild of Great Britain.

SIDELIGHTS: RECREATIONS—Music, squash, travel.

ADDRESSES: HOME—27 Gloucester Place, London W1, England. AGENT—c/o Patricia MacNaughton, MLR Limited, 200 Fulham Road, London SW10 9PN, England.

*　　*　　*

McDOWELL, Malcolm 1943-

PERSONAL: Born June 13, 1943, in Leeds, England; married Mary Steenburgen (an actress), 1980; children: two.

VOCATION: Actor.

CAREER: PRINCIPAL STAGE APPEARANCES—With the Royal Shakespeare Company, Stratford, England, 1965-66; Jimmy Porter, *Look Back in Anger*, Roundabout Theatre, Stage Two, New York City, 1980; Andrew Shaw, *In Celebration*, with the Manhattan Theatre Club at the New York City Center, 1984.

FILM DEBUT—*Poor Cow*, 1967. PRINCIPAL FILM APPEARANCES—*If. . .*, Paramount, 1969; *Figures in a Landscape*, National General, 1971; *The Raging Moon*, 1971; *A Clockwork Orange*, Warner Brothers, 1971; *O Lucky Man*, Warner Brothers, 1973; *Royal Flash*, Twentieth Century-Fox, 1975; *Aces High*, 1976; *Voyage of the Damned*, AVCO-Embassy, 1977; *Caligula*, 1977; *The Passage*, United Artists, 1978; H.G. Wells, *Time after Time*, Warner Brothers, 1979; *Cat People*, Universal, 1982; narrator, *The Compleat Beatles*, Metro-Goldwyn-Mayer/United Artists, 1982; *Blue Thunder*, Columbia, 1983; *Cross Creek*, Universal, 1983; *Get Crazy*, Embassy, 1983; *Britannia Hospital*, United Artists Classics, 1984.

PRINCIPAL TELEVISION APPEARANCES—Series: Dixon of the Dock, Z Cars, BBC. Episodic: "Little Red Riding Hood," *Faerie Tale Theatre*, Showtime, 1983. Movies: *Arthur the King*, BBC and CBS, 1985; *Gulag*, HBO, 1985. Mini-Series: Christopher Quinn, *Monte Carlo*, CBS, 1986.

ADDRESSES: AGENT—International Creative Management, 8899 Beverly Blvd., Los Angeles, CA 90048 and 22 Grafton Street, London W1, England.*

*　　*　　*

McENERY, Peter 1940-

PERSONAL: Born February 21, 1940, in Walsall, England; son of Charles and Mary Ada (Brinson) McEnery. EDUCATION: Trained for the stage with Iris Warren.

VOCATION: Actor.

CAREER: STAGE DEBUT—Stanley Chadwick, *Bed, Board and Romance*, Palace Pier Theatre, Brighton, U.K., 1956. LONDON DEBUT—Tom, *Flowering Cherry*, Haymarket Theatre, 1958.

PRINCIPAL STAGE APPEARANCES—Eugene Gant, *Look Homeward, Angel*, Pembroke Theatre, Croydon, U.K., 1960; Eugene Grant, *Look Homeward, Angel*, Phoenix Theatre, London, 1962; Johnny Hobnails, *Afore Night Come*, New Arts Theatre, London, 1962; Rudge, *Next Time I'll Sing to You*, Criterion Theatre, London, 1963; Konstantin, *The Seagull*, Queen's Theatre, London, 1964; Johnny Hobnails, *Afore Night Come*, Aldwych Theatre, London, 1964; Ithamore, *The Jew of Malta*, title role, *Hamlet*, Hamlet, *Rosencrantz and Guildenstern Are Dead*, both Phoenix Theatre, Leicester, U.K., 1970; Mike, *Disabled*, Hampstead Theatre Club, London, 1971; Guildenstern, *Rosencrantz and Guildenstern Are Dead*, Nottingham Playhouse, Nottingham, U.K., 1971; Donal Davoren, *The Shadow of the Gunman*, Cassius, *Julius Caesar*, Young Vic Theatre, London, 1972; Henry Winter, *Collaborators*, Duchess Theatre, London, 1973; Colin, *Ashes*, Open Space Theatre, London, 1974; Trigorin, *The Seagull*, Lyric Theatre, London, 1975.

With the Royal Shakespeare Company, Stratford-on-Avon, U.K., and London: Laertes, *Hamlet*, Clarence, *Richard III*, Silvius, *As You Like It*, Tybalt, *Romeo and Juliet*, all 1961; Philip of France, *Curtmantle*, Patroclus, *Troilus and Cressida*, De Laubardemont, *The Devils*, all 1962; Bassanio, *The Merchant of Venice*, 1965; Duke of Suffolk, *Henry VI, Parts I and II*, Orlando, *As You Like It*, Lorenzo, *The Lorenzaccio Story*, Yescanalo, *Sons of Light*, Albie Sachs, *The Jail Diary of Albie Sachs*, all 1977-78; title role, *Pericles*, Jerry Hyland, *Once in a Lifetime*, both 1979-80. Also appeared in *Romeo and Juliet*, St. George's Theatre, London, 1976.

PRINCIPAL STAGE WORK—Director, *Richard III*, Nottingham Playhouse, Nottingham, U.K., 1971.

MAJOR TOURS—Clive Harrington, *Five Finger Exercise*, U.K. cities, 1960.

PRINCIPAL FILM APPEARANCES—*Tunes of Glory*, United Artists, 1960; *Negatives*, Continental, 1968; *Entertaining Mr. Sloane*, Continental, 1970; *La Curee; The Cat and the Canary*, Grenadier, 1979.

PRINCIPAL TELEVISION APPEARANCES—Specials: *Candida; Progress to the Park; Clayhanger*.

SIDELIGHTS: FAVORITE ROLES—Albie Sachs in *The Jail Diary of Albie Sachs*. RECREATIONS—Skiing, squash, military history.

ADDRESSES: AGENT—Fraser and Dunlop, Ltd., 91 Regent Street, London W1R SRU, England.*

*　　*　　*

McGAVIN, Darren 1922-

PERSONAL: Born May 7, 1922, in Spokane, WA; son of Reid Delano Richardson and Grace (Bogart) McGavin; married Melanie York (an actress), March 20, 1944 (divorced); married Katherine Browne (an actress), December 31, 1969; children: York, Megan, Bridget, Bogart. EDUCATION: Attended the University of the Pacific; trained for the stage at the Neighborhood Playhouse and at the Actors Studio.

VOCATION: Actor, director, and producer.

DARREN McGAVIN

CAREER: STAGE DEBUT—*Lady Windermere's Fan,* college production, 1941. PRINCIPAL STAGE APPEARANCES—Judge Advocate, *Liliom,* Actors Lab, Hollywood, CA, 1945; walk-on, *The Old Lady Says No!,* Mansfield Theatre, New York City, 1948; Joe, *Cock-a-Doodle-Doo,* Lenox Hill Playhouse, New York City, 1949; Happy, *Death of a Salesman,* Morosco Theatre, New York City, 1949; Heracles, *The Thracian Horses,* Brandeis University, 1951; Alfred, *My Three Angels,* Morosco Theatre, New York City, 1953; Bill Starbuck, *The Rainmaker,* Cort Theatre, New York City, 1954; King, *The King and I,* St. Louis Municipal Opera, MO, 1955; Hal Carter, *Picnic,* Playhouse-in-the-Park, Philadelphia, PA, 1955; Matt Burke, *Anna Christie* (staged reading), Phoenix Theatre, New York City, 1955; David McGregor, *The Innkeepers,* John Golden Theatre, New York City, 1956; Chrysagon de la Crux, *The Lovers,* Martin Beck Theatre, New York City, 1956; Dick Pepper, *The Tunnel of Love,* Royale Theatre, New York City, 1957; the wreck, *Wonderful Town,* U.S. Pavilion, Brussels World's Fair, Belgium, 1958; First Lieutenant Stanley Poole, *Blood Sweat, and Stanley Poole,* Morosco Theatre, New York City, 1961; Joe Kelly, *The Happiest Man Alive,* Westport Country Playhouse, CT, 1962; King, *The King and I,* New York State Theatre, New York City, 1964; title role, *Destry Rides Again,* Meadowbrook Dinner Theatre, Ceder Grove, NJ, 1964; Charlie Bickle, *Here Lies Jeremy Troy,* Lakewood Theatre, Skowhegan, ME, 1965; *Fairy Tale,* Royal Alexandra Theatre, Toronto, ON, Canada, 1966; Larry Renault, *Dinner at Eight,* Alvin Theatre, New York City, 1966; title role, *Captain Brassbound's Conversion,* Ahmanson Theatre, Los Angeles, 1968; Vern, *California Dog Fight,* Manhattan Theatre Club at the New York City Center, 1985.

MAJOR TOURS—*The Late Christopher Bean,* U.S.O. Tour, 1946;

Happy, *Death of a Salesman,* national tour, 1949-51; Professor Harold Hill, *The Music Man,* summer tour, 1962; Murray Burns, *A Thousand Clowns,* summer tour, 1964; Harry Roat, Jr., *Wait Until Dark,* winter tour, FL, 1967.

PRINCIPAL STAGE WORK—Co-Producer, *Dark Legend,* President Theatre, New York City, 1952; director, *With Respect for Joey,* for the Theatre Guild, New York City, 1957; director, *The Happiest Man Alive,* Westport Country Playhouse, CT, 1962; director, *A Thousand Clowns,* summer tour, 1964; director, *Fairy Tale,* Royal Alexandra Theatre, Toronto, 1966.

FILM DEBUT—*A Song to Remember,* Columbia, 1945. PRINCIPAL FILM APPEARANCES—*Kiss and Tell,* Columbia, 1945; *She Wouldn't Say Yes,* Columbia, 1945; *Counter-Attack,* Columbia, 1945; *Fear,* Monogram, 1946; *Queen for a Day,* United Artists, 1951; *Summertime,* United Artists, 1955; *The Court Martial of Billy Mitchell,* Warner Brothers, 1955; *The Man with the Golden Arm,* United Artists, 1956; *The Delicate Delinquent,* Paramount, 1957; *Beau James,* Paramount, 1957; *The Case Against Brooklyn,* Columbia, 1958; *Bullet for a Bad Man,* Universal, 1964; *The Great Sioux Massacre,* Columbia, 1965; *Ride the High Wind,* Emerson, 1966; *Mission: Mars,* Associated Artists, 1968; *Mrs. Polifax—Spy,* United Artists, 1971; *The Petty Story,* Rowland-Lasko, 1972; *B Must Die,* 1973; *No Deposit, No Return,* 1975; *Airport '77,* Universal, 1977; *Hot Lead and Cold Feet,* Walt Disney, 1978; *Zero to Sixty,* Katherine Browne, 1980; *Hanger 18,* Sun Classic, 1980; *Firebird 2015 A.D.,* 1981; *A Christmas Story,* Metro-Goldwyn-Mayer/United Artists, 1984; *The Natural,* Tri-Star, 1984; *Turk 182!,* Twentieth Century-Fox, 1985; Craig Duncan, *From the Hip,* De Laurentis, 1987.

PRINCIPAL FILM WORK—Producer and director, *Happy Mother's Day—Love, George,* Cinema V, 1973.

PRINCIPAL TELEVISION APPEARANCES—Series: Casey, *Crime Photographer,* CBS, 1951-52; Mike Hammer, *Mickey Spillane's Mike Hammer,* in syndication, 1957-59; Grey Holden, *Riverboat,* NBC, 1959-61; David Ross, *The Outsider,* NBC, 1968-69; Carl Kolchak, *Kolchak: The Night Stalker,* ABC, 1974-75. Episodic: "Sunset Boulevard," *Robert Montgomery Presents,* NBC, 1956; *Bob Hope Chrysler Theatre,* NBC, 1963-64; *Games People Play,* NBC, others. Pilots: *Banyon,* NBC, 1971; *The Rookies,* ABC, 1972; Carl Kolchak, *The Night Stalker,* ABC, 1972; Carl Kolchak, *The Night Strangler,* ABC, 1973. Movies: *The Challenge,* 1970; *Tribes,* 1970; *Something Evil,* 1972; *Law and Order,* 1976; *Brinks,* 1976; *The Baron and the Kid,* CBS, 1984; Dr. Gerrit Koets, *My Wicked, Wicked Ways,* CBS, 1985.

PRINCIPAL TELEVISION WORK—All as director. Episodic: "Cousin Casey" and "Sally's Old Beau," both for *Buckskin,* NBC, 1959; "Diamonds Ahead," *Riverboat,* NBC, 1960; "Queen of Spades," *Death Valley Days,* syndicated, 1960.

RELATED CAREER—Chief executive, Taurean Films (S.A.), Tympanum Corporation.

MEMBER: Actors' Equity Association, American Federation of Television and Radio Artists, Screen Actors Guild, Directors Guild of America, Writers Guild of America.

ADDRESSES: OFFICE—8643 Holloway Plaza, Los Angeles, CA 90069. AGENT—c/o B. Gale and D. Pietragallo, William Morris Agency, 151 El Camino Drive, Beverly Hills, CA 90212.

McGOOHAN, Patrick   1928-
(Paddy Fitz, Archibald Schwartz, Joseph Serf)

PERSONAL: Full name, Patrick Joseph McGoohan; born March 19, 1928, in Astoria, NY; family returned to Ireland in 1928; came to United States in early 1970s; son of Thomas and Rose McGoohan; married Joan Drummond (an actress), May 19, 1951; children: Catherine, Anne, Frances. EDUCATION: Attended Ratcliffe College; trained for the stage with Geoffrey Ost at the Sheffield Repertory Company.

VOCATION: Actor, director, producer, and writer.

CAREER: PRINCIPAL TELEVISION APPEARANCES—Episodic: "The Hanging of Alfred Wadham," *Rendezvous,* 1957; "The New People" and "Paper Dolls," *Journey into Darkness,* 1968; "By Dawn's Early Light," *Columbo,* NBC, 1974; "Identity Crisis," *Columbo,* NBC, 1975; "Witness for the Defense," *Murder, She Wrote,* CBS, 1987; also *You Are There,* CBS; *The Vice,* BBC. Series: John Drake, *Danger Man,* ITC, 1960-61, broadcast in the U.S. by CBS, 1961; John Drake, *Danger Man* (retitled *Secret Agent* for U.S. television), ITC, 1964-66, CBS, 1965-66; Number Six, *The Prisoner,* ITC, 1967, CBS, 1968-69; Sid Rafferty, M.D., *Rafferty,* CBS, 1977. Mini-Series: *The Makepeace Story,* BBC, 1956. Movies: John Drake, *Koroshi,* 1966; Nicholas Fouquet, *The Man in the Iron Mask,* 1979; John Connor, *The Hard Way,* 1980; chief magistrate, *Three Sovereigns for Sarah,* PBS, 1985; Joss Merlin, *Jamaica Inn,* 1985; also *Of Pure Blood,* CBS, 1986. Teleplays: *Disturbance,* BBC, 1957; *The Third Miracle,* BBC, 1957; *Rest in Violence,* BBC, 1958; *This Day in Fear,* BBC, 1958; Jack "Pat" Smurch, *The Greatest Man in the World,* BBC, 1958;

PATRICK McGOOHAN

title role, *Brand,* BBC, 1959; Charlie Castle, *The Big Knife,* BBC, 1959; *The Iron Harp,* BBC, 1959; *Terminus Number One,* BBC, 1959; prosecutor, *Shadow of a Pale Horse,* BBC, 1959; *Dead Secret,* BBC, 1961; interrogator, *The Prisoner,* BBC, 1962.

PRINCIPAL TELEVISION WORK—Executive producer and director (under such pseudonyms as Paddy Fitz, Archibald Schwartz, and Joseph Serf, in addition to his own name), *The Prisoner,* ITC, 1967, CBS, 1968-69; director, "Identity Crisis," *Columbo,* NBC, 1975; director, "Last Salute to the Commodore," *Columbo,* NBC, 1976; director, "The Wild Child," *Rafferty,* CBS, 1977.

FILM DEBUT—*The Dam Busters,* 1954. PRINCIPAL FILM AP-PEARANCES—Red, *Hell Drivers,* Rank, 1958; Jess, *The Gypsy and the Gentleman,* Rank, 1958; Andrew Miller, *Nor the Moon by Night* (also known as *Elephant Gun*), Rank, 1958; Dr. James Brown, *Life for Ruth* (also known as *Walk in the Shadow*), Continental, 1962; Andrew McDhui, *The Three Lives of Thomasina,* Buena Vista, 1963; title role, *Dr. Syn, Alias the Scarecrow,* Buena Vista, 1963; Thomas Crimmin, *The Quare Fellow,* Ajay, 1966; David Jones, *Ice Station Zebra,* Metro-Goldwyn-Mayer (MGM), 1969; Frank Long, *The Moonshine War,* MGM, 1970; James Stuart, *Mary Queen of Scots,* Universal, 1971; Roger Devereau, *Silver Streak,* Twentieth Century-Fox, 1976; Col. Mike McCauley, *Brass Target,* United Artists, 1979; warden, *Escape from Alcatraz,* Paramount, 1979; Dr. Paul Ruth, *Scanners,* AVCO-Embassy, 1981; Dr. Eric Kiviat, *Baby: Secret of the Lost Legend,* Buena Vista, 1985. Also appeared as Sir Oswald, *The Dark Avenger* (also known as *The Warrior*), 1955; Simon Breck, *High Tide at Noon,* 1957; Johnny Cousin, *All Night Long,* 1961; Erik Berger, *Two Living, One Dead,* 1961; John Kingsley, *Kings and Desperate Men,* 1977; Fred Welles, *Trespasses* (also known as *Finding Katie*), 1983; and in *Passage Home,* 1955; *I Am a Camera,* Distributors Corporation of America, 1955; *Zarak,* Columbia, 1956; *The Genius* (also known as *Un Genio, Due Compari e Un Pollo*), 1975.

PRINCIPAL FILM WORK—Director, *Catch My Soul,* Cinerama, 1974.

LONDON DEBUT—Rev. William Weightman, *The Brontes,* St. James Theatre, 1948. PRINCIPAL STAGE APPEARANCES—Roy Mawson, *Spring Model,* Leonard White, *Time on Their Hands,* both Q Theatre, London, 1954; Howard Phillips, *Serious Charge,* Garrick Theatre, London, 1955; Starbuck, *Moby Dick,* Duke of York's Theatre, London, 1955; Leonard White, *Ring for Catty,* Lyric Theatre, London, 1956; St. Just, *Danton's Death,* title role, *Brand,* both Lyric Theatre, London, 1959; Stewart, *Pack of Lies,* Royale Theatre, New York City, 1985. Also performed in many other plays, including as Petruchio in *The Taming of the Shrew,* in other Shakespearean plays, in *The Rivals,* and in works by Shaw, Chekhov, and Coward, all with the Sheffield Repertory Company, Sheffield, U.K., 1948-52; also performed with the Midland Theatre Company, Coventry, U.K., and the Bristol Old Vic Theatre Company, Bristol, U.K., 1952-54;

PRINCIPAL STAGE WORK—Stage manager, Sheffield Repertory Company, Sheffield, U.K.

NON-RELATED CAREER—Steel mill hand, bank employee, and manager of a chicken farm.

WRITINGS: TELEVISION—(Under such pseudonyms as Paddy Fitz, Archibald Schwartz, and Joseph Serf, in addition to his own name) *The Prisoner,* ITC, 1967, CBS, 1968-69; *Rafferty,* CBS, 1977. Also writes poetry.

AWARDS: London Drama Critics' Award, 1959, for *Brand;* Best Television Actor of the Year, 1959, for *The Greatest Man in the World;* Outstanding Performance by a Supporting Actor in a Dramatic Series, Emmy Award, 1975, for "By Dawn's Early Light," *Columbo.*

SIDELIGHTS: For some forty years, actor, producer, director, and scriptwriter Patrick McGoohan has found success in the entertainment industry. He is a versatile actor whose credits range from a 1959 London stage production of Ibsen's *Brand* that is still recognized as the definitive presentation to starring roles in the popular television series *Secret Agent* and *The Prisoner* in the 1960s. Describing himself simply as a working actor, he has played both heroes and villains, but in a 1987 *Classic Images* series Barbara Pruett characterized his work as "a lifetime playing roles of men in isolation, apart from the mainstream of society; loners who, for better or worse, rejected the rules and lived their own way."

Patrick Joseph McGoohan was born March 19, 1928, in the Astoria district of Queens, New York. His parents had immigrated to the United States from Ireland, but decided to return to their homeland a few months after he was born. They settled on a farm in County Leitrim, but the impoverished life there set them to move to Sheffield, England, seven or eight years later. His warm family life was interrupted when he was evacuated to the countryside during World War II and by the time he was sixteen, he was on his own, working at a series of jobs and acting in as many as five amateur theatrical companies around the city.

In 1948 McGoohan took a job as stage manager with the Sheffield Repertory Theatre and shortly thereafter made his professional acting debut replacing an ailing player. He quickly became one of the leading actors at in the company, where he remained until 1952. He has estimated that, including his amateur work, he appeared in over two hundred plays by the time he left Sheffield. McGoohan described this period of his life to Pruett: "When one is going through that many plays, like I did at Sheffield, that's the healthiest form of acting. . . . Do one play and immediately start rehearsing another one so that one feeds the other. The one you are rehearsing during the day stimulates the acting juices and carries over to one's performance in the evening. They add to each other."

McGoohan followed his work at Sheffield with a season at the Midland Theatre, Coventry, and two seasons at the Bristol Old Vic before moving to London. By 1954 he was appearing on television and in 1955 he had a small role in the film *Passage Home.* The same year, he had two successful plays on London's West End—*Serious Charge* and *Moby Dick.* Of his work in the later play, critic Kenneth Tynan remarked in the *Observer;* "Patrick McGoohan as Starbuck, the mate who dares to oppose Ahab's will, is Melville's long, earnest man to the life, whittled out of immemorial teak. His is the best performance of the evening." A filmed version of the production was lost when its backers seized it because of the director's debts.

Much of the actor's other early film work was as a contract player for Rank Films. The limited range of roles he received—he was cast as the heavy in most of the movies—made this an unhappy experience for him. His objections on this score contributed to his early reputation in the industry as a rebel, as did his outspokenness on other matters and his insistence on keeping his family and private life out of the studio's publicity stories.

In April of 1959 McGoohan achieved his greatest success to date in the title role of a widely acclaimed production of the Ibsen play *Brand.* Concerning his portrayl of a pastor dedicated to living with uncompromising commitment to his values, regardless of the personal cost, McGoohan told Pruett: "All the plays I did, all the training, really came together in that one. The play was bigger than me. I found it to be bigger than Lear. It's such an extraordinatry piece of work, the crying out to be 'all or nothing.' " He repeated the role in a live broadcast of the same production by the British Broadcasting Corporation several months later. His starring role as the first man on the moon in a television production of James Thurber's short story "The Greatest Man in the World"earlier in the season also earned him notice. Together these two dissimilar roles won him awards as England's top stage actor and best television actor within the same year.

In 1960 Lew Grade, head of ITC Entertainment, sought McGoohan out to play the lead role of John Drake in a television series called *Danger Man.* By now the actor had three young daughters and he accepted the role for the financial security it would give his family. Although the series ended production a year later, it established a theme and direction for what would in 1964 become a highly successful revival, the show known in the United States as *Secret Agent.* John Drake was not a James Bond style secret agent (a role McGoohan turned down, despite being the first actor to whom it was offered); in fact, the star's own ideas of morality and individuality strongly influenced the character's development. The actor told Pruett: "[Drake] was an agent who never carried a gun, never shot anyone. He used his wits instead. And he didn't go to bed with a different girl each night." McGoohand's rationale: "I felt that television was a guest in one's home and should behave that way. I'd rather that young children saw a hero than an antihero. That's what I tried to go for." He stipulated that the scripts include no romantic involvements and none did. By the time the series ended, McGoohan was contributing to the writing as well as directing several episodes. At that point, he was England's most popular and highly paid television star.

He soon tired of playing John Drake, however, and approached Grade with an idea for a new limited-episode series to be called *The Prisoner.* With Grade's backing, he became the creator and moving force behind a controversial project that many consider to be among the best series ever on television. McGoohan acted as producer and star, and frequently as director and writer, for the seventeen-episode saga. *The Prisoner* tells of a man who resigns from a top secret job, is kidnapped, and awakes to find himself held in "the Village," where residents have numbers instead of names and are controlled by a mysterious Number One. His captors attempt to find out why Number Six, McGoohan's character, resigned; he, meanwhile, repeatedly attempts escape. Number Six's most familar line—"I will not be pushed, filed, stamped, indexed, briefed, debriefed, or numbered. My life is my own"—was penned by the star, who elaborated: "People are the prisoners of our society. The series is a comment about life. The general theme of the man in isolation against authority and bureaucracy, the idea of being a rebel against suppression and stupid rules has been with me since I was able to start thinking of anything at all."

The show was an allegory and highly political, but was so written that no specific political element could clearly be identified as the captor. The final episode, revealing Number Six's jailer as himself, enraged many viewers. Critics in Britain and the United States called the series futuristic and made comparisons to the writings of George Orwell and Franz Kafka. The production quality and acting received considerable praise, but some reviewers found the show too philosophical and difficult for the average viewer to understand. Twenty years after it first aired, it is established as a small screen classic.

Once *The Prisoner* was completed, McGoohan moved his family to Switzerland. He spent much of the next two years relaxing and helping a friend with the production of several African documentaries. He made a few films and in the early 1970s decided to move to the United States, settling his family first in Santa Fe, New Mexico, and later in Pacific Palisades, California. In America he found opportunities to act, direct, and write, including work on three episodes of Peter Falk's popular television series, *Columbo;* for "By Dawn's Early Light" he won a 1975 Emmy as best supporting actor. His movies included the popular theatrical releases *Silver Streak* (1976) and *Escape from Alcatraz* (1979), as well as the television movie *Man in the Iron Mask*. He also made a short-lived television series, *Rafferty*, but did not enjoy the experience.

More films followed in the 1980s, but in 1985 he returned to the stage. He made his Broadway debut as Stewart in *Pack of Lies,* which was considered one of the season's successes. In taking on new projects, McGoohan has said he looks for roles as men who are different or for scripts with appealing themes. In the July, 1985 *Video Magazine,* Tom Soter noted that the themes of personal identity, trust, and imagination continually recur in McGoohan's work. As Pruett observed, "The public role may, after all, be the clearest insight into the . . . private man."

ADDRESSES: HOME—Pacific Palisades, CA. AGENT—Jack Fields & Associates, 9255 Sunset Boulevard, Suite 1105, Los Angeles, CA 90069.*

*   *   *

McHALE, Rosemary   1944-

PERSONAL: Born February 17, 1944; daughter of John William and Muriel Agnes (Evans) McHale; married Trevor Bowen. EDUCATION: Trained for the stage at Central School and Drama Centre.

VOCATION: Actress.

CAREER: LONDON DEBUT—Nellie Lambert, *A Collier's Friday Night,* Royal Court Theatre, 1965. PRINCIPAL STAGE APPEARANCES—Louka, *Arms and the Man,* Everyman Theatre, Liverpool, U.K., 1965; Maureen, *The Restoration of Arnold Middleton,* Traverse Theatre, Edinburgh, Scotland, U.K., 1966; Minnie, *The Daughter-in-Law,* Traverse Theatre, 1977; Helena, *The Ha-Ha,* Julia, *The Rivals,* Bianca, *Othello,* all Lyceum Theatre, Edinburgh, Scotland, U.K., 1967-68; Helena, *The Ha-Ha,* Hampstead Theatre Club, London, 1968; Joanne, *Slag,* Hampstead Theatre Club, 1970; Fontanelle, *Bond's Lear,* Royal Court Theatre, London, 1971; Virgilia, *Coriolanus,* Luciana, *The Comedy of Errors,* Charmian, *Antony and Cleopatra,* all Royal Shakespeare Company (RSC), Memorial Theatre, Stratford-on-Avon, 1972; Charmian, *Antony and Cleopatra,* RSC, Aldwych Theatre, London, 1973; Mme. Voiture, *A Lesson in Blood and Roses,* Place Theatre, London, 1973; Queen Ana, *The Bewitched,* Aldwych Theatre, 1974; Abel, *Comrades,* Laria, *The Beast,* Place Theatre, 1974; Jule, *Objections to Sex and Violence,* Royal Court Theatre, 1975; Mrs. Elvsted, *Hedda Gabler,* Duke of York's Theatre, London, 1977; Eliza, *Pygmalion,* Ellida, *The Lady from the Sea,* Birmingham Repertory Theatre, Birmingham, U.K., 1977; Myra Bruhl,

Deathtrap, Garrick Theatre, London, 1978. Appeared in repertory with the Everyman Theatre Company, Liverpool, U.K., 1965-66; also appeared in *Cries from Casement,* Place Theatre, 1973.

MAJOR TOURS—Masha, *The Seagull,* Cambridge Theatre Company, U.K. cities, 1970.

PRINCIPAL TELEVISION APPEARANCES—*The Brontes; The Way of the World; When the Actors Come; Just Between Ourselves; Memories.*

RELATED CAREER—Council member, Drama Centre, London.

AWARDS: Clarence Derwent awards, both 1970, for *Slag* and *The Seagull.*

SIDELIGHTS: RECREATIONS—Birds, bridge, sewing.

ADDRESSES: AGENT—Patrick Freeman Management, Four Cromwell Grove, London W6, England.*

*   *   *

McLERIE, Allyn Ann   1926-

PERSONAL: Born December 1, 1926, in Grand'Mere, PQ, Canada; daughter of Allan Gordon (an aviator) and Vera Alma MacTaggart (Stewart) McLerie; married Adolph Green (a playwright and lyricist), March 21, 1947 (divorced, 1953); married George Gaynes (an actor), December 20, 1953; children: Iya, Matthew. EDUCATION: Studied ballet with Martha Graham, Agnes DeMille, and Hanya Holm; trained for the stage with Tamara Daykarhanova and with Lee Strasberg at the Actors Studio.

VOCATION: Actress, singer, and dancer.

CAREER: BROADWAY DEBUT—Dancer, *One Touch of Venus,* Imperial Theatre, 1943. PRINCIPAL STAGE APPEARANCES—Second ballet girl, doll girl, then Ivy Smith, *On the Town,* Adelphi Theatre, New York City, 1945; Eustasia, *Bonanza Bound!,* Shubert Theatre, Philadelphia, PA, 1947; Susan, *Finian's Rainbow,* 46th Street Theatre, New York City, 1948; Amy Spettigue, *Where's Charley?,* St. James Theatre, New York City, 1948; Monique DuPont, *Miss Liberty,* Imperial Theatre, 1949; Amy Spettigue, *Where's Charley?,* Broadway Theatre, New York City, 1951; Myrtle, *To Dorothy, a Son,* Garrick Theatre, London, 1951; Lady India, *Ring Around the Moon,* Hyde Park Playhouse, Hyde Park, NY, 1955; WAC Corporal Jean Evans, *Time Limit!,* Booth Theatre, New York City, 1956; Gwynne, *Bells Are Ringing,* Coliseum Theatre, London, 1957; Lola, *Damn Yankees,* Ninotchka, *Silk Stockings,* Gladys, *The Pajama Game,* all Sacramento Music Circus, Sacramento, CA, 1957; Anita, *West Side Story,* Winter Garden Theatre, New York City, 1960; Ensign Nellie Forbush, *South Pacific,* City Center Theatre, New York City, 1961; Claudine, *Can-Can,* Garden Court Dinner Theatre, San Francisco, CA, 1962; various roles, *The Beast in Me,* Plymouth Theatre, New York City, 1963; Ellie, *Show Boat,* State Theater, New York City, 1966; Tlimpattia, *Dynamite Tonight,* Martinique Theatre, New York City, 1967; Elmire, *Tartuffe,* Clytemnestra, *The Flies,* both Inner City Repertory, Los Angeles, CA, 1967; Irma, *Irma La Douce,* Anita, *West Side Story,* both Sacramento Music Circus, 1967; Lenore, *LA under Siege,* Mark Taper Forum, Los Angeles, CA, 1970; Alma Stone, *The Mind with the Dirty Man,* Mark Taper

Forum, 1973; Judith Fellowes, *The Night of the Iguana*, Ahmanson Theatre, Los Angeles, CA, 1975; Calpurnia, *Julius Caesar*, Matrix Theatre, Los Angeles, CA, 1979. Also played in a scene from *Floradora* at a benefit for the American National Theatre and Academy, Ziegfeld Theatre, New York City, 1950; appeared in *You Never Can Tell*, La Jolla Playhouse, La Jolla, CA, 1952; *King of Hearts*, Fall River, MA, 1955; *Our Town*, Long Beach Theatre, Long Beach, CA, 1978; *Dancing in the Dark*, Manhattan Theatre Club, New York City, 1979.

MAJOR TOURS—Dancer, *Rodeo and Fancy*, with the Ballet Theatre, European cities, 1950; Anita, *West Side Story*, U.S. cities, 1963; Eliza Doolittle, *My Fair Lady*, U.S. cities, 1964.

PRINCIPAL CABARET APPEARANCES—Appeared as part of a dance team with John Butler throughout the U.S., 1947-48.

PRINCIPAL FILM APPEARANCES—*Words and Music*, Metro-Goldwyn-Mayer, 1948; *Where's Charley?*, Elstree, 1951; *Battle Cry*, Warner Brothers, 1955; *Calamity Jane*, Warner Brothers, 1953; *Phantom of the Rue Morgue*, Warner Brothers, 1954; *The Reivers*, National General, 1969; *They Shoot Horses, Don't They?*, Warner Brothers, 1969; *Monte Walsh*, National General, 1970; *The Cowboys*, Warner Brothers, 1972; *Jeremiah Johnson*, Warner Brothers, 1972; *The Magnificent Seven Ride*, Universal, 1972; *The Way We Were*, Columbia, 1973; *Cinderella Liberty*, Twentieth Century-Fox, 1974; *All The President's Men*, Warner Brothers, 1976.

PRINCIPAL TELEVISION APPEARANCES—Episodic: *The Delphi Bureau*, ABC; *The Walton*, CBS; *Cannon*, CBS; *The F.B.I.*, ABC; *Love Story*, NBC; *Ghost Story*, NBC; *Bonanza*, NBC; *My World and Welcome to It*, NBC; *Nichols*, NBC; *We'll Get By*, CBS; *Kodiak*, ABC; *Lou Grant*, CBS; *Young Dr. Kildare*, syndicated. Series: Janet Reubner, *Tony Randall Show*, ABC, 1976-77, then CBS, 1977-78; mother, *The Days and Nights of Molly Dodd*, NBC, 1987—. Mini-Series: Edna Davis, *Beulah Land*, NBC, 1980; Mrs. Smith, *The Thorn Birds*, ABC, 1983. Movies: Miss Martin, *A Tree Grows in Brooklyn*, NBC, 1974; Emma Lasko, *Born Innocent*, NBC, 1974; Jean, *Someone I Touched*, ABC, 1975; Alice Whitmore, *Death Scream*, ABC, 1975; Mrs. Pasko, *The Entertainer*, NBC, 1976; Polly Baker, *A Shining Season*, CBS, 1979; Dora, *And Baby Makes Six*, NBC, 1979; Shirley, *Fantasies*, ABC, 1982; Aunt Polly, *Rascals and Robbers: The Secret Adventures of Tom Sawyer and Huck Finn*, CBS, 1982; Aunt Emily, *Two Kinds of Love*, CBS, 1983; Audrey Williams, *Living Proof: The Hank Williams, Jr. Story*, NBC, 1983.

AWARDS: Theatre World Award, 1948, for *Where's Charley?*.

MEMBER: Screen Actors Guild, Academy of Motion Picture Arts and Sciences, Actors' Equity Association.

ADDRESSES: OFFICE—c/o Actors' Equity Association, 6430 Sunset Boulevard, Los Angeles, CA 90028.*

*   *   *

MEEK, Barbara

PERSONAL: Born February 26, in Detroit, MI; daughter of Harold Talmadge (a bus driver) and Juanita (a beautician; maiden name Coleman) Meek; married Martin Molson (an actor and director)

BARBARA MEEK

February, 1968 (died, 1980); children: Leslie Matuko. EDUCATION: Wayne State University, B.A., 1965.

VOCATION: Actress.

CAREER: PRINCIPAL STAGE APPEARANCES—Singer, *Wilson in the Promise Land*, American National Theatre Academy Playhouse, New York City, 1970; Mrs. Bruchinski (understudy), *Division Street*, Ambassador Theatre, New York City, 1980. Also Mrs. Sorby, *The Wild Duck*, Dallas Theatre Center, Dallas, TX; Hallelujah Lil, *Happy End*, Cleveland Playhouse, Cleveland, OH; judge, *Nuts*, Jewel, *The Best Little Whorehouse in Texas*, both Hampton Playhouse, Hampton, NH.

With the Trinity Square Repertory Company, Providence, RI, 1968—: Jenny, *The Threepenny Opera;* Katherine, *The Taming of the Shrew;* Lena, *Boseman and Lena;* Hester Saloman, *Equus;* Maggie, *The Shadow Box;* Miss Fancy, *Sly Fox;* Cleopatra Mahimovna, *The Suicide;* Madge, *The Dresser;* Grace, *Bus Stop;* Agnes, *Passion Play;* Dorine, *Tartuffe;* Melanie Garth, *Quartermaine's Terms;* Claire Zachanassian, *The Visit.*

MAJOR TOURS—*A Funny Thing Happened on the Way to the Forum*, U.S.O. Pacific tour, 1967.

PRINCIPAL TELEVISION APPEARANCES—Episodic: "House of Mirth," *Theatre in America*, PBS; "Brother to Dragons," *Theatre in America*, PBS. Series: Mrs. Canby, *Archie Bunker's Place*, CBS, 1980-82; Rose, *Melba*, CBS, 1986. Movies: Evelyn Parnell, *See How She Runs*, CBS, 1979; Roxanne, *Jimmy B. and Andre*, CBS, 1979; Mrs. Sawyer, *Parole*, CBS, 1982; also *Life among the Lowly*, PBS.

AWARDS: Achievement Award in theatre, Wayne State University, 1982.

MEMBER: Actors' Equity Association, American Federation of Television and Radio Artists, Screen Actors Guild.

ADDRESSES: AGENT—Gersh Agency, Inc., 130 W. 42nd Street, New York, NY 10036.

* * *

MERCOURI, Melina   1925-

PERSONAL: Born Maria Amalia Mercouri, October 18, 1925, in Athens, Greece; daughter of a member of the Greek Parliament; married Jules Dassin (a director and producer), 1957.

VOCATION: Actress, singer, writer, and politician.

CAREER: PRINCIPAL STAGE APPEARANCES—*Stella,* 1954; *Ilya, Darling,* Broadway production, 1967; *Lysistrata,* Broadway production, title role, *The Medea,* Mount Lycabettos, Greece, 1972; Clytaemnestra, *The Oresteia,* 1980; *Mourning Becomes Electra,* Athens, Greece; also appeared in *Sweet Bird of Youth,* 1979; *La Nuit de Samaracande, Les Compagnons de la Marjolaine, Il Etait une Gare, A Streetcar Named Desire, Helen or the Joy of Living, The Queen of Clubs,* and *The Seven Year Itch.*

PRINCIPAL FILM APPEARANCES—*Stella,* United Artists, 1955; *He Who Must Die,* United Artists, 1956; *Where the Hot Wind Blows* (also known as *The Law*), French, 1958; *The Gypsy and the Gentleman,* Rank, 1959; *Never on Sunday,* United Artists, 1959; *Phaedra,* United Artists, 1961; *The Victors,* Columbia, 1963; *Light of Day,* 1963; *Les pianos mecaniques,* 1964; *Topkapi,* United Artists, 1964; *A Man Could Get Killed,* 1966; *10:30 p.m. Summer,* United Artists, 1966; *Gaily, Gaily,* United Artists, 1969; *Promise at Dawn,* AVCO-Embassy, 1971; *Earthquake,* Universal, 1974; *Once Is Not Enough,* Paramount, 1975; *Nasty Habits,* Brut, 1976; *Maya and Brenda,* 1977; *A Dream of Passion,* Dassin Productions, 1978.

NON-RELATED CAREER—Member of Greek Parliament, for the Port of Piraeus, 1977—; Minister of Culture and Sciences for the Greek Government, 1981-85; Minister of Culture, Youth and Sports, 1985—.

WRITINGS: NON-FICTION—Autobiography, *I Was Born Greek,* 1971.

AWARDS: Best Actress, Cannes Film Festival Award and Academy Award nomination, both 1960, for *Never on Sunday;* Tregene Prize, 1984.

SIDELIGHTS: Melina Mercouri is fluent in French, German and English.

ADDRESSES: OFFICE—c/o Ministry of Culture, Youth and Sports, Odos Aristidou 14, Athens, Greece.*

* * *

METRANO, Art   1937-

PERSONAL: Born September 22, 1937, in Brooklyn, NY; son of Aron Harry and Rebecca (Russo) Metrano; married Rebecca Chute; children: Howard, Roxanne Elena, Harry, Zoe Bella. EDUCATION: Attended College of the Pacific, 1957-59; studied acting with John Cassavetes, Stella Adler and Harold Clurman.

VOCATION: Actor, comedian, and playwright.

CAREER: STAGE DEBUT—*Stage Door.* BROADWAY DEBUT—*Desire Under the Elms.* LONDON DEBUT—*Light Up the Sky,* Globe Theatre, June, 1987. PRINCIPAL STAGE APPEARANCES—*Awake & Sing,* Rapport Theatre, 1974; *Death and Life of Jesse James,* Mark Taper Forum, Los Angeles, CA, 1979; *Fatty,* Tiffany Theatre, Los Angeles, CA, 1985.

FILM DEBUT—*They Shoot Horses Don't They,* Warner Brothers, 1969. PRINCIPAL FILM APPEARANCES—*They Only Kill Their Masters,* Metro-Goldwyn-Mayer, 1972; *The All-American Boy,* Warner Brothers, 1973; *Matilda,* American International, 1978; *The Choirboys,* Universal, 1977; *How to Beat the High Cost of Living,* Filmways, 1980; *Going Ape,* Paramount, 1981; *History of the World—Part 1,* Twentieth Century-Fox, 1981; *Breathless,* Orion, 1983; *Teachers,* Metro-Goldwyn-Mayer/United Artists, 1984; *Police Academy 2: Their First Assignment,* Warner Brothers, 1985; *Police Academy 3: Back in Training,* Warner Brothers, 1986. Also *Seven,* 1979; *Cheaper to Keep Her,* 1980; *Maibu Express,* 1985.

TELEVISION DEBUT—*The Outcast,* CBS. PRINCIPAL TELEVISION APPEARANCES—Episodic: *Benson,* ABC; *All in the Family,* CBS. Series: Regular performer, *The Tim Conway Comedy Hour,* 1970; Nick Marr, *The Chicago Teddy Bears,* CBS, 1971; Benjy, *Movin' On,* NBC, 1974-76; Tom, *Loves Me, Loves Me Not,* CBS,

ART METRANO

1977; Uncle Rico, *Joanie Loves Chachi*, ABC, 1982-83. Mini-Series: Meurice Cartwright, "The Storm," *Centennial*, NBC, 1979. Movies: Joe, *In Name Only*, ABC, 1969; Barker, *Then Came Bronson*, ABC, 1969; Julius Merano, *Brink's: The Great Bank Robbery*, CBS, 1976; also appeared in *A Cry for Love*, NBC, 1980. Guest: *Mike Douglas Show*, syndicated; *Merv Griffin Show*, syndicated.

WRITINGS: PLAYS—*The Chicken and the Cheerleader*, 1981; *AMAM*, 1984; *Sultans of Style*, 1985; *Army Brats*, 1986.

MEMBER: Actors' Equity Association, Screen Actors Guild, American Federation of Television and Radio Artists; End Hunger Network; Crippled Children's Society.

ADDRESSES: OFFICE—9229 Sunset Boulevard, No. 520, Los Angeles, CA 90069. AGENT—Rodney Sheldon Management, 4000 Warner Boulevard, Producers 6 Suite 3, Burbank, CA 90105.

*   *   *

MIFUNE, Toshiro   1920-

PERSONAL: Born April 1, 1920, in Tsingtao, China; son of Japanese doctors serving in China; married Takeshi Shiro, 1950; children: two sons, one daughter. EDUCATION: Attended Japanese schools. MILITARY: Served in the Japanese Army for five years.

VOCATION: Actor and producer.

CAREER: FILM DEBUT—*Shin Baka Jidai*, (*These Foolish Times*), 1947. PRINCIPAL FILM APPEARANCES—*Snow Trail*, 1947; *Drunken Angel*, 1948; *The Stray Dog*, 1948; *Eagle of the Pacific*, 1949; *Rashomon*, Daiei, 1950; *The Seven Samurai*, Toho, 1954; *I Live in Fear*, 1954; *The Last Gunfight*, 1955; *I Bombed Pearl Harbor*, 1955; *The Legend of Miyamoto*, 1955; *The Lower Depths*, Toho, 1957; *Throne of Blood*, Toho, 1957; *The Rickshawman*, 1958; *The Hidden Fortress*, Toho, 1958; *The Three Treasures*, 1959; *The Storm of the Pacific*, 1959; *Yojimbo*, Toho, 1961; *Animus Trujano*, 1961; *Kiska*, 1962; *Sanjuro*, Toho, 1962; *High and Low*, Toho, 1963; *Judo Sag*, 1963; *The Lost World of Sinbad*, 1964; *Rebellion*, Mifune, 1964; *Life of Oharu*, 1965; *Red Beard*, Toho, 1965; *Grand Prix*, Metro-Goldwyn-Mayer (MGM), 1966; *Hell in the Pacific*, 1967; *Admiral Yamamoto*, 1968; *Furinkazan*, 1969; *Red Sun*, National General, 1972; *Paper Tiger*, 1974; *The Battle of Midway*, 1975; *Winter Kills*, AVCO-Embassy, 1979; *1941*, Universal, 1979; Shogun, *The Bushido Blade*, 1979; *The Equals*, 1981; *The Challenge*, Embassy, 1982; *Inchon*, Metro-Goldwyn-Mayer/United Artists, 1982.

PRINCIPAL TELEVISION APPEARANCES—Mini-Series: *Shogun*, 1981.

RELATED CAREER—Head of film production company, Mifune Productions Co., Ltd.

SIDELIGHTS: RECREATIONS—Hunting, yachting, flying, and horseback riding.

ADDRESSES: OFFICE—Mifune Productions Company, Ltd., 9-30-7, Seijyo, Setagayaku, Tokyo, Japan.*

MILES, Vera   1930-

PERSONAL: Born August 23, 1930, in Boise City, OK; daughter of Thomas and Burnice (Wyrick) Ralston; married Gordon Scott (divorced); married Keith Larson (divorced); children: Debra, Kelley, Michael, Erik.

VOCATION: Actress.

CAREER: FILM DEBUT—*For Men Only* 1952. PRINCIPAL FILM APPEARANCES—*The Rose Bowl Story*, 1953; *Backstreet*, 1953; *Charge at Feather River*, 1954; *Pride of the Blue Grass*, 1955; *Wichita*, Allied Artists, 1955; *The Searchers*, 1956; *23 Paces to Baker Street*, Twentieth Century-Fox, 1956; *Autumn Leaves*, 1956; *The Wrong Man*, Warner Brothers, 1957; *Beau James*, Paramount, 1957; *Web of Evidence*, Allied Artists, 1959; *The FBI Story*, Warner Brothers, 1959; *A Touch of Larceny*, 1959; *Beyond This Place*, 1959; *Five Branded Women*, Paramount, 1960; *Psycho*, Paramount, 1960; *The Lawbreakers*, Metro-Goldwyn-Mayer (MGM), 1961; *The Man Who Shot Liberty Valance*, Paramount, 1962; *The Hanged Man*, 1962; *The Spirit Is Willing*, 1964; *One of Our Spies Is Missing*, MGM, 1966; *The Gentle Giant*, Paramount, 1967; *Sergeant Ryker*, Universal, 1968; *Kona Coast*, Warner Brothers, 1968; *It Take All Kinds*, 1968; *Hellfighters*, Universal, 1969; *Mission Batangos*, 1971; *The Wild Country*, Buena Vista, 1971; *Baffled!*, 1972; *One Little Indian*, Buena Vista, 1973; *Castaway Cowboy*, 1974; *Run for the Roses*, 1978; *Brainwaves*, 1982; *Psycho II*, Universal, 1983.

PRINCIPAL TELEVISION APPEARANCES—Episodic: *Climax*, CBS; *Pepsi Cola Playhouse*, CBS; *Twilight Theatre*, ABC; *Ford Theatre*, NBC. Movies: *Runaway!*, 1973; *The Underground Man*, 1974; *The Strange and Deadly Occurence*, 1974; *Judge Horton and the Scottsboro Boys*, 1976; *McNaughton's Daughter*, 1976; *State Fair*, 1976; *Smash-Up on Interstate 5*, 1976; *Our Family Business*, 1981; *Rona Jaffe's Mazes and Monsters*, 1982; *Travis McGee*, 1983; *Helen Keller—The Miracle Continues*, 1984.

MEMBER: Actors' Equity Association, Screen Actors Guild, American Federation of Television and Radio Artists.

ADDRESSES: AGENT—Craig Agency, 8485 Melrose Plaza, Suite E, Los Angeles, CA 90069; Abrams Artists, 9200 Sunset Boulevard, Los Angeles, CA 90069.*

*   *   *

MILLER, Jonathan   1934-

PERSONAL: Full name, Jonathan Wolfe Miller; born July 21, 1934, in London, England; son of Emanuel (a psychiatrist) and Betty Bergson (a writer; maiden name, Spiro) Miller; married Helen Rachel Collet (a physician), July 27, 1956; children: Thomas, William, Kate. EDUCATION: St. John's College, Cambridge University, B.Ch., M.B., 1959; graduated from University College School of Medicine, London University.

VOCATION: Actor, director, producer, writer, editor, and physician.

CAREER: LONDON DEBUT—*Out of the Blue*, Cambridge Footlights Club, Phoenix Theatre, London, 1954. BROADWAY DEBUT—*Beyond the Fringe*, John Golden Theatre, 1962. PRINCIPAL STAGE APPEARANCES—*Between the Lines*, Scala Theatre, London, 1955; *Out of the Blue*, Lyceum Theatre, Edinburgh, Scotland, U.K., 1960; *Beyond the Fringe*, Fortune Theatre, London, 1961.

PRINCIPAL STAGE WORK—Director: *Under Plain Cover*, Royal Court Theatre, London, 1962; *The Old Glory*, American Place Theatre, New York City, 1964; *Benito Cereno*, Theatre de Lys, New York City, 1965, then Mermaid Theatre, London, 1967; *Come Live with Me*, Yale Repertory Theatre, New Haven, CT, 1966; *Prometheus Bound*, Yale Repertory Theatre, 1967; *The School for Scandal*, Nottingham Playhouse Theatre, Nottingham, U.K., 1968; *King Lear*, Nottingham Playhouse Theatre, then Old Vic Theatre, London, both 1969; *The Merchant of Venice*, National Theatre Company, Old Vic Theatre, 1970; *The Tempest*, National Theatre Company, Mermaid Theatre, 1970; *Hamlet*, National Theatre Company, Cambridge Arts Theatre, Cambridge, U.K., 1970; *Prometheus Bound*, Mermaid Theatre, 1971; *Richard II*, Ahmanson Theatre, Los Angeles, CA, 1971; *Julius Caesar*, New Theatre, London, 1972; *The Taming of the Shrew*, Chichester Festival Theatre, Chichester, U.K., 1972; *The School for Scandal*, National Theatre Company, 1972; *Measure for Measure*, National Theatre Company, 1973; *The Malcontent*, Nottingham Playhouse Theatre, 1973; *The Seagull*, Chichester Festival Theatre, 1973; *The Marriage of Figaro*, *The Freeway*, both Old Vic Theatre, 1974; *The School for Scandal*, American Repertory Theatre, Cambridge, MA, 1982; *Hamlet*, Warehouse Theatre, London, 1982; *Long Day's Journey into Night*, Broadhurst Theatre, New York City, 1986; also *The Seagull*, 1968; *Danton's Death, Hamlet*, both 1971; *The Devil Is an Ass*, 1973.

Director, Greenwich Theatre Company, London: *Ghosts, The Seagull, Hamlet*, 1974; *The Importance of Being Earnest, All's Well That Ends Well, Measure for Measure*, all 1975; *The Three Sisters*, 1976; *She Would If She Could*, 1979.

Director of operas: *Arden Must Die*, Sadler's Wells Theatre, London, 1974; *Cosi fan Tutte*, Kent Opera Company, Congress Theatre, Eastbourne, U.K., 1974; *Rigoletto*, Kent Opera Company, 1975; *The Cunning Little Vixen*, Glyndebourne Theatre, Sussex, U.K., 1975, 1977; *Orfeo*, Kent Opera Company, 1976; *Eugene Onegin*, Kent Opera Company, 1977; *The Marriage of Figaro*, English National Opera, London, 1978; *La Traviata*, Kent Opera Company, 1979; *The Turn of the Screw*, English National Opera, 1979; *Arabella*, English National Opera, 1980; *Falstaff*, Kent Opera Company, 1980, 1981; *Cosi fan Tutte*, Opera Theatre of St. Louis, St. Louis, MO, 1982; *Fidelio*, Kent Opera Company, 1982, 1983; *The Magic Flute*, Glasgow Opera House, Glasgow, Scotland, U.K., 1983; *Rigoletto*, New York City, 1984; *Don Giovanni*, English National Opera, 1985; *Mikado*, English National Opera, 1986; also *The Flying Dutchman*, Frankfurt Opera, Frankfurt, West Germany.

PRINCIPAL TELEVISION APPEARANCES—Episodic: *A Trip to the Moon*, CBS, 1964; *Intimations*, BBC, 1965; *Review*, BBC, 1974; also *Books for Our Times*, 1964. Series: Host, *The Body in Question*, BBC, 1978, then PBS, 1980; host, *States of Mind*, BBC, 1983. Specials: *Beyond the Fringe*, BBC-2, 1964. Guest: *Jack Paar Show*, NBC, 1962; *Review*, BBC, 1974; *Late Night with David Letterman*, NBC, 1987; also appeared on *Tempo*, 1961; *Tonight Show*, NBC; *David Susskind Show*, syndicated.

PRINCIPAL TELEVISION WORK—Director, *What's Going On Here?*, Metromedia, 1963; producer and director: *Plato's Dialogues*, BBC, 1966, then NET, 1971; *Alice in Wonderland*, BBC, 1966; *From Chekhov with Love*, BBC, 1972; *Whistle and I'll Come to You*, BBC; *The Body in Question*, BBC, 1978, then PBS, 1979.

Also executive producer, *Jonathan Miller's Shakespearian Saga*, BBC, 1979-81; editor, *Monitor*, BBC, 1964-65.

FILM DEBUT—Kirby Groomkirby, *One Way Pendulum*, Paramount, 1964.

PRINCIPAL FILM WORK—Director, *Take a Girl Like You*, Columbia, 1970.

PRINCIPAL RADIO WORK—Director: *Saturday Night on the Light, Monday Night at Home*, both BBC-Radio.

RELATED CAREER—Associate director, National Theatre, London, 1973-75; associate director, Greenwich Theatre, London, 1975—; associate director, English National Opera; visiting professor of drama at Westfield College, London; drama teacher, Yale University.

NON-RELATED CAREER—Physician; researcher in neuropsychology at Sussex University; resident fellow in history of medicine, University College of Medicine, London University.

WRITINGS: PLAYS—(With Peter Cook, Alan Bennett, and Dudley Moore) *Beyond the Fringe*, published by Samuel French, Inc., 1963.

BOOKS—*Harvey and the Circulation of the Blood*, Grossman, 1968; *McLuhan* (biography), Fontana, 1971, published in the U.S. as *Marshall McLuhan*, Viking, 1971; editor, *Freud: The Man, His World, His Influence*, Little, Brown, 1972; *The Body in Question*, Random House, 1979; (with Borin Van Loon) *Darwin for Beginners*, Random House, 1982; *States of Mind: Conversations with Psychological Investigators*, Pantheon, 1983; *The Human Body* (illustrated by David Pelham), Viking, 1983; *The Facts of Life* (illustrated by David Pelham), Viking, 1984.

TELEPLAYS—"The Anne Hutchinson Story," *Profiles in Courage*, NBC, 1965; *Alice in Wonderland*, BBC, 1966; *The Body in Question*, BBC, 1978, then PBS, 1980.

PERIODICALS—Film and television critic, *The New Yorker*, 1963; contributor of articles and reviews to *New York Herald Tribune, Partisan Review, Commentary, Spectator*, and *New Statesman*.

AWARDS: Best Revue or Musical, *London Evening Standard Award*, 1961, special citation, New York Drama Critics Circle, 1962, special Antoinette Perry Award, 1963, all for *Beyond the Fringe;* Director of the Year, Society of West End Theatres, 1976; Silver Medal, Royal Television Society, 1981. Honorary degrees: D.Litt., University of Leicester; honorary fellow, St. John's College, Cambridge University, 1982.

MEMBER: British Actors' Equity Association, Arts Council of Great Britain, 1975-76; British Medical Association.

SIDELIGHTS: Englishman Jonathan Miller "is as near to a Renaissance man as contemporary Britain can decently boast," according to Benedict Nightingale in the September 5, 1982 *New York Times.* "Imagine him stomping the streets en route from directing 'Macbeth' or 'Rigoletto' to examining a cancer patient in Charing Cross Hospital, making mental notes for a lecture on the influence of Dostoevsky on Freud as he goes, and you won't have an unduly exaggerated picture of his cross-disciplinary enthusiasms." A certified physician, Miller has made contributions to his scientific field, but his renown as a writer, a director of theatre, television, and opera productions, a comedian, and as the host of an important public television series is greater. In Britain Miller's achievements are considered almost legendary, from his ground-breaking comedy revue, *Beyond the Fringe,* to his inspired resuscitation of the British Broadcasting Corporation's series *The Shakespeare Plays.* Erudite and controversial, Miller continues to live a dual life, alternating his interests in physiology and psychology with the demands of directing classical opera and drama. His career, noted a January 9, 1983 *Observer* profile, "would have exhausted and satisfied a dozen lesser humans"; the writer continued, "The cultural landscape of the past two decades would have been much poorer without him."

Nothing in Miller's youth seemed to promise him a place in the international limelight. By his own admission he was a bookish youngster, interested in science, psychology, and philosophy. He attended Cambridge University, where he studied the natural sciences in preparation for a career as a pathologist. Miller told the *New York Times* (May 29, 1983): "My stumbling into the theater and staying there was a series of accidents. I left medicine reluctantly and have never been able to repress a deep sorrow for abandoning the career I originally chose." Indeed, Miller's entry into show business only came about during a two-week holiday from his internship at London's University College Hospital in 1959. With three friends—Allan Bennett, Peer Cook, and Dudley Moore—he authored and staged a satiric revue for the annual Edinburgh Festival. That show, *Beyond the Fringe,* was an unexpected success, and it changed the direction of Miller's career overnight. "One after another, people made me irresistible propositions," he told the *New York Times.* "In England, I was offered a John Osborne play nobody else would direct. In America, Robert Lowell called me up and asked me to direct 'The Old Glory.' I didn't have any experience directing. I didn't even know what 'blocking' meant, but I could tell an interesting play when I read one, so of course I said yes." Miller never shelved his interest in medicine, he simply made room in his life for artistic pursuits as well. *The Observer*'s contributor suggested that the range of his interests "almost forbids [his] concentrating on any one of them," but Miller has nevertheless won enormous respect for his work both on stage and in television.

As a director Miller has concentrated primarily on classical drama and opera. He explained in an August 1, 1982 *New York Times* profile that "one of the privileges of doing works from the past is to be able to break bread with the dead." Whatever his directorial task of the moment, from guiding Sir Laurence Olivier through a portrayal of Shylock in Shakespeare's *The Merchant of Venice* to bringing authenticity to a staging of Mozart's *Cosi fan Tutte* with the Opera Theatre of St. Louis, Miller brings strong opinions but gentle techniques to bear. In his June 3, 1984 *New York Times* piece, Mel Gussow wrote: "Because of his iconoclastic interpretations of classics, [Miller] has acquired detractors as well as admirers on both sides of the Atlantic. For him, each production represents a leap of his faith in his own intuitive judgement, reached after considerable contemplation as well as research. . . . Even when criticized for his divergence from tradition, he insists that he is faithful to the spirit of the source—as he sees it." Linda Blandford addressed Miller's methods in her *New York Times* profile: "Miller's directing style is to play the distinguished and dedicated doctor at the bedside of a favored patient. His unspoken message is : 'Together, we shall make you well.' He listens intently, reacts passionately—his approval fills the room. He is carefully sensitive, waiting for natural breaks . . . to have his say, meticulously handing out compliments, concealing suggestions in his enthusiatic responses as if he and the [cast] were back . . . at Cambridge

experiencing together the joy of learning." The *Observer* contributor declared that both actors and singers "relish the relaxed playground atmosphere he creates in rehearsal. He sets them free with the tumultuous force of his comic invention."

Although he began his show business career acting in a comic revue, Miller rarely steps before the camera anymore. He did, however, host *The Body in Question,* a medical/philosophical exploration of human anatomy that critics consider one of the finest works ever aired on public television. In a September, 1980 *Saturday Review* article, Miller explained his reasons for doing the series: "Talking to friends, I began to realize that the thing they tended to know least about was that part of the world nearest to them, the one that moves with them wherever they go." Miller's series explored anatomy and physiology by using analogies to technology and by demonstrating physical experiments. It remains, in *Saturday Review* correspondent Timothy Mason's words, "a work of memorable insight, a distinctly personal vision of the tortuous and exquisite mechanisms of human biology." For a short time after the series aired in the early 1980s, Miller announced plans to retire from directing for full-time medical work. But interesting projects have continued to pull him away from scientific research, despite his contention that such achievements have more lasting value than anything produced for the stage. Miller once told the *New York Times:* "A great performance of a great play hangs suspended in the air like an iridescent soap bubble. It shimmers for a moment with meaning and beauty and then disappears forever. The art of the director is the art of the ephemeral. But while it lasts it is an epiphany." He further assessed: "What makes the theatre special is not making 'art' but making friends with the people who make the art. There's a special and irreplaceable bond that grows up between directors, designers, technicians and actors. . . . We players know that the theater—like life itself—is a doomed enterprise. Putting on a show is like being on a mad, ship-wrecked vessel with the engine gone. You keep it all afloat for a while and then it disappears into the night."

Miller has for many years disassociated himself from the publicly funded British theatrical troupes, partly because he deplores the lax standards of quality under which much modern theatre operates and partly because of his feud with the powerful Sir Peter Hall, director of Britain's National Theatre. In the moments between his far-flung projects, he lives quietly in the Camden Town district of London with his wife, a practicing physician. A director, lecturer, educator, and author, Miller has an "artistic productivity [that] seems to continue with unabated enthusiasm and eclecticism," according to Mel Gussow. Taking his international celebrity in stride, Miller claimed in the *New York Times* that fame, for all its imagined importance, is "merely an arithmetical arrangement by which you are known by more people than you know."

ADDRESSES: HOME—63 Gloucester Crescent, London, NW1, England.*

*   *   *

MILLIAN, Andra

PERSONAL: Surname rhymes with "Dillon"; born May 7, in Bucharest, Romania; daughter of Paul L. and Babette (Stevenson) Millian. EDUCATION: California Institute of the Arts, B.F.A., 1981; also attended the University of Texas at Austin and the Parsons School of Design; trained for the stage with Robert Lewis,

ANDRA MILLIAN

Robert Benedetti, and Steven Kent; studied Shakespearian technique with Robert Lloyd and Kate Fitzmaurice; studied voice with Grace de la Cruz.

VOCATION: Actress and writer.

CAREER: TELEVISION DEBUT—Amy, "Having It All," *ABC Movie of the Week,* 1982. PRINCIPAL TELEVISION APPEARANCES—Series: Laura, *The Paper Chase,* Showtime, 1983-86. Episodic: Wendy, *Tucker's Witch,* CBS; Babette, *Casablanca,* NBC, 1983; Janey, *Jessie,* ABC; Sabrina, *Murder, She Wrote,* CBS, 1986.

FILM DEBUT—Stacey Lancaster, *Stacey's Knights* (also known as *Stacey and Her Gangbusters*), 1983.

STAGE DEBUT—Dierdre, *Bosoms and Neglect,* Odyssey Theatre Ensemble, Los Angeles, 1986; leading role, *Glass Houses,* Cal Arts Theatre Ensemble, Los Angeles; *The Human Voice* (one-woman show), Figtree Theatre, Hollywood, CA; with the Cal Arts Repertory Company: Kathy, *Lovers and Other Strangers;* Cassandra, *The Trojan Women;* Sonja, *Uncle Vanya;* the bride, *Blood Wedding.*

WRITINGS: TRANSLATIONS—*The Human Voice,* by Jean Cocteau.

AWARDS: Best Actress in a Dramatic Series, ACE Award nomination, 1985, for *The Paper Chase.*

SIDELIGHTS: Andra Millian told *CTFT* that she is an excellent swimmer and a certified scuba diver.

ADDRESSES: AGENT—Contemporary Artists, 132 Lasky Drive,

Beverly Hills, CA 90211 and the Monty Silver Agency, 200 W. 57th Street, New York, NY 10019. MANAGER—Marcelli-Heller Management, 8235 Santa Monica Boulevard, Suite 302, Los Angeles, CA 90046.

*   *   *

MILWARD, Kristin

PERSONAL: Full name Kristin Corbet-Milward; daughter of Roger (a naval officer) and Erna (Von Tangen) Corbet-Milward. EDUCATON: Received B.A. (with honors) from University of East Anglia; trained for the stage at the Royal Academy of Dramatic Art, 1971-74.

VOCATION: Actress.

CAREER: PRINCIPAL STAGE APPEARANCES—Sarah, *The Sheffield Flood,* Crucible Theatre, Sheffield, U.K.; Beatrice, *A View from a Bridge,* Library Theatre, Manchester, U.K.; Portia, *The Merchant of Venice,* Phoenix Theatre, Leicester, U.K.; Ruth, *The Constant Wife,* Arts Theatre, Cambridge, U.K.; Tatyana, *Vanity,* Tron Theatre, Glasgow, Scotland, U.K., then Young Vic Theatre, London; *The Triumph of Death,* Birmingham Repertory Theatre, Birmingham, U.K.; stepdaughter, *Six Characters in Search of an Author,* Edinburgh Festival, Edinburgh, Scotland, U.K.; Diomedes, *Troilus and Cressida,* Roundhouse Theatre, London; Mary, *Strip*

KRISTIN MILWARD

Show, Elephant Theatre, London; *Plunder*, National Theatre, London; *Plenty*, National Theatre, Philippine, *Devour the Snow*, Bush Theatre, London; Arkadina, *The Seagull*, Rostrum Theatre, London; Volargisn, *Les Liasons Dangereuse*, Royal Shakespeare Company, Stratford-on-Avon, U.K., then London, later Music Box Theatre, New York City, 1987. Also Bronya, *Nijinski;* Maja, *When We Dead Awaken;* Gertrude, *Hamlet;* and in *Romeo and Juliet; Rosencrantz and Guildenstern Are Dead; Dracula.*

PRINCIPAL TELEVISION APPEARANCES—Specials: Marie, *To the Lighthouse*, BBC; Nellie Bonser, *Poppyland*, BBC.

PRINCIPAL FILM APPEARANCES—Marietta, *City of the Dead*, American Independent; Craven, *Scene of the Crime*, upcoming.

ADDRESSES: HOME—London. OFFICE—c/o Spotlight, 42 Cranbourn Street, London W4, England.

* * *

MIMIEUX, Yvette 1944-

PERSONAL: Born January 8, 1944, in Los Angeles, CA.

VOCATION: Actress.

CAREER: PRINCIPAL STAGE APPEARANCES—*I Am a Camera*, 1963; *The Owl and the Pussycat*, 1966; *Night of 100 Stars II*, Radio City Music Hall, New York City, 1985.

PRINCIPAL CONCERT APPEARANCES—*Persephone*, with the Oakland Orchestra, CA, 1965, the New York Philharmonic Orchestra at Lincoln Center, New York City, the Los Angeles Philharmonic Orchestra at the Hollywood Bowl, the Houston Symphony Orchestra, and with the London Royal Philharmonic.

FILM DEBUT—*The Time Machine*, Metro-Goldwyn-Mayer (MGM), 1960. PRINCIPAL FILM APPEARANCES—*Where the Boys Are*, MGM, 1960; *The Four Horsemen of the Apocalypse*, MGM, 1962; *Light in the Piazza*, MGM, 1962; *The Wonderful World of the Brothers Grimm*, MGM, 1962; *Diamond Head*, Columbia, 1963; *Toys in the Attic*, United Artists, 1963; *Joy in the Morning*, MGM, 1965; *The Reward*, Twentieth Century-Fox, 1965; *Monkeys, Go Home!*, Buena Vista, 1967; *Dark of the Sun*, MGM, 1968; *Caper of the Golden Bulls*, Embassy, 1968; *Picasso Summer*, 1969; *Three in the Attic*, 1970; *Skyjacked*, MGM, 1972; *The Neptune Factor*, Twentieth Century-Fox, 1973; *Jackson County Jail*, MGM, 1975; *The Black Hole*, Buena Vista, 1979.

PRINCIPAL TELEVISION APPEARANCES—Series: Vanessa Smith, *The Most Deadly Game*, ABC, 1970-71. Episodic: *Berrengers*, NBC, 1985; *Lime Street*, ABC, 1985. Movies: *Tyger, Tyger*, 1964; *Death Takes a Holiday* 1971; *Black Noon* 1971; *Obsessive Love*, 1973. *The Fifth Missile*, NBC, 1986. Specials: *Night of 100 Stars II*, 1985.

MEMBER: Actors' Equity Association, Screen Actors Guild, American Federation of Television and Radio Artists.

ADDRESSES: AGENT—c/o Mark Teitelbaum, William Morris Agency, Inc., 151 El Camino Drive, Beverly Hills, CA 90212.*

MR. T 1952-

PERSONAL: Born Lawrence Tureaud, May 21, 1952, in Chicago, IL. EDUCATION: Attended college in Texas.

VOCATION: Actor and professional bodyguard.

CAREER: FILM DEBUT—Mr. T, *Rocky III*, Metro-Goldwyn-Mayer/United Artists, 1983. PRINCIPAL FILM APPEARANCES—*D.C. Cab*, Universal, 1983.

PRINCIPAL TELEVISION APPEARANCES—Series: Sergeant Bosco "B.A." Barcus, *The A-Team*, NBC, 1983—. Episodic: *Games People Play*, NBC, 1980. Movies: *The Toughest Man in the World*, 1984. Guest: *Thicke of the Night*, syndicated.

ADDRESSES: AGENT—c/o Peter Young, Triad, 10100 Santa Monica Blvd., 16th Floor, Los Angeles, CA 90067.*

* * *

MITCHELL, Cameron 1918-

PERSONAL: Born November 4, 1918, in Dallastown, PA. EDUCATION: Trained for the stage at the Theatre School in New York City and with the New York Theatre Guild, 1938-40. MILITARY: U.S. Army Air Force, 1942-44.

VOCATION: Actor.

CAREER: PRINCIPAL FILM APPEARANCES—*They Were Expendable*, Metro-Goldwyn-Mayer (MGM), 1945; *Mighty McGurk*, MGM, 1946; *High Barbaree*, MGM, 1947; *Cass Timberlane*, MGM, 1947; *Leather Gloves*, MGM, 1948; *Homecoming*, MGM, 1948; *The Sellout*, MGM, 1951; *Death of a Salesman*, MGM, 1951; *Flight to Mars*, Monogram, 1951; *Man in the Saddle*, 1951; *Japanese War Bride*, 1952; *Outcasts of Poker Flat*, 1952; *Okinawa*, 1952; *Les Miserables*, 1952; *Pony Soldiers*, 1952; *Powder River*, 1953; *Man on a Tightrope*, 1953; *How to Marry a Millionaire*, Twentieth Century-Fox, 1953; *Hell and High Water*, 1954; *Gorilla at Large*, 1954; *Garden of Evil*, 1954; *Desiree*, 1954; *Strange Lady in Town*, Warner Brothers, 1955; *Love Me or Leave Me*, MGM, 1955; *House of Bamboo*, Twentieth Century-Fox, 1955; *Tall Men*, Twentieth Century-Fox, 1955; *View from Pompey's Head*, Twentieth Century-Fox, 1955; *Carousel*, Twentieth Century-Fox, 1956; *Monkey on My Back*, United Artists, 1957; *Face of Fire*, Allied Artists, 1959; *Inside the Mafia*, 1959; *The Unstoppable Man*, 1959.

The Last of the Vikings, Medallions, 1960; *Three Came to Kill*, United Artists, 1960; *Blood and Black Lace*, Allied Artists, 1965; *Ride in the Whirlwind*, 1965; *Hombre*, Twentieth Century-Fox, 1967; *Island of the Doomed* (also known as *Man-Eater of Hydra*), 1967; *Nightmare in Wax*, Crown International, 1969; *Buck and the Preacher*, Columbia, 1972; *Slaughter*, American International, 1972; *The Midnight Man*, Universal, 1974; *The Klansman*, Paramount, 1974; *Viva Knieval!*, Warner Brothers, 1977; *The Swarm*, Warner Brothers, 1978; *Night Train to Terror*, Visto International, 1985; *Low Blow*, Crown International, 1986; Police Captain Carter, *The Messenger*, Snizzlefritz, 1987.

PRINCIPAL TELEVISION APPEARANCES—Series: Buck Cannon, *High Chaparral*, NBC, 1967-71; Jeremiah Worth, *Swiss Family*

Robinson, ABC, 1975-76. Episodic: "Return to Vienna," *Campbell Soundstage,* NBC, 1952; "The Last Night of August," *Pursuit,* CBS, 1959; "Meeting at Apalachian," *Westinghouse Desilu Playhouse,* CBS, 1960. Movies: *The Andersonville Trial.*

PRINCIPAL STAGE APPEARANCES—*Death of a Salesman,* Morosco Theatre, New York City, 1949; Mitch, *The November People,* Billy Rose Theatre, New York City, 1978; also appeared in *The Taming of the Shrew.*

PRINCIPAL RADIO WORK—Announcer and sportscaster before joining military.

AWARDS: Theatre World Award, 1948-49; Star of Tomorrow Award, 1954.

ADDRESSES: AGENT—Contemporary Artists, 132 Lasky Drive, Beverly Hills, CA 90212.*

*　　*　　*

MONASH, Paul

PERSONAL: Born in New York, NY. EDUCATION: Attended the University of Wisconsin and Columbia University. MILITARY: U.S. Army Signal Corps and Merchant Marine.

VOCATION: Producer and writer.

CAREER: FIRST FILM WORK—Executive producer, *Butch Cassidy and the Sundance Kid,* Twentieth Century-Fox, 1969. PRINCIPAL FILM WORK—Producer, *Slaughterhouse-Five,* Universal, 1972; producer, *The Friends of Eddie Coyle,* Paramount, 1973; producer, *The Front Page,* Universal, 1974; producer, *Carrie,* United Artists, 1976.

PRINCIPAL TELEVISION WORK—Executive producer, *Peyton Place,* ABC, 1964-69.

NON-RELATED CAREER—Newspaper reporter; high school teacher; civilian employee of the U.S. government in Europe.

WRITINGS: SCREENPLAYS—*The Friends of Eddie Coyle,* Paramount, 1973. TELEVISION—Movies: *All Quiet on the Western Front,* CBS, 1979. Pilots: *The Untouchables,* ABC, 1959; *Cain's Hundred,* NBC, 1961; *Peyton Place,* ABC. Mini-Series: *Salem's Lot,* CBS, 1979. Teleplays: "The Lonely Wizard," *Schlitz Playhouse of Stars,* CBS, 1957; also episodes for *Playhouse 90, Studio One,* and *Climax,* all CBS; *Theatre Guild of the Air.*

BOOKS—*How Brave We Live; The Ambassadors.*

AWARDS: Best Teleplay Writing, Emmy Award, 1958, for "The Lonely Wizard," *Schlitz Playhouse of Stars.*

MEMBER: Writers Guild, West.

SIDELIGHTS: RECREATIONS—Islamic history, anthropology, and primitive art.

ADDRESSES: OFFICE—c/o Writers Guild, West, 8955 Beverly Boulevard, Los Angeles, CA 90048.*

ROBERTO MONTICELLO

MONTICELLO, Roberto   1954-

PERSONAL: Born June 7, 1954, in Cuba; son of Marcello (a trapeze flyer) and Maria (a flamenco dancer) Monticello. POLITICS: "Human Rights Activist." RELIGION: "Humanitarian."

VOCATION: Director and writer.

CAREER: PRINCIPAL STAGE WORK—Director: *Break Loose,* Victoria Theatre, London, 1975; *Double Image,* Greene Street Theatre, Key West, FL, 1977; *Mind Games,* Impossible Ragtime Theatre, New York City, 1977; *A Tale of Two Cities,* Berlin Opera House, Berlin, West Germany, 1978; *Act Scared,* Greene Street Theatre, 1978; *The Changeling,* American Academy of Dramatic Art, Ansonia Hotel, New York City, 1979; *The Merry Go-Round,* Vandam Theatre, New York City, 1979; *Mind Games—Part 2,* Edinburgh Festival, Edinburgh, Scotland, U.K., 1979; *Changes,* Greene Street Theatre, 1980; *Consumer Society,* Empire Theatre, Albany, NY, 1981; *Angle Of Repose,* Empire Theatre, then Douglas Way Theatre, London, both 1982; *The Levels of Carmine,* Las Palmas de Santa Fe, Santa Fe, NM, 1982; *Lying and Other Misdomenors,* Vandam Theatre, 1984; *Extremes,* Transformation Theatre, New York City, 1985. Also directed five plays for the Drama Ensemble, New York City, 1977-81; *Camilian,* New York City, 1980; *Lover of Dreams,* New York City, 1981; *Flowers at Sea,* Madrid, Spain, 1983; a benefit for Ethiopian famine relief, Theatre Space Cabaret, New York City, 1984; *Blood Wedding,* Spoleto Theatre Festival, Spoleto, Italy; and at the following theatres: Salzburg Music Festival, Salzburg, Austria; American Center, Paris, France; Shelter West Company, New York City; St. Xavier Church, New York City; Ice and Fire Theatre, New York

City; Playwrights Preview Productions, New York City; 18th Street Playhouse, New York City; Three Muses Theatre, Ansonia Hotel, New York City; Phoenix Theatre Company, Marymount Manhattan College, New York City; Hartley House, New York City; Island Civic Theatre, Honolulu, Hawaii; Waterfront Players, Key West, FL; Mickery Theatre, Amsterdam, Holland.

MAJOR TOURS—Director: *Mother Courage,* Italian cities, 1977; *Splendor and Death of Joaquin Murieta,* U.S. cities, 1979. Also directed touring productions by the Players Company, European cities.

PRINCIPAL FILM WORK—Director: *The Rhythm of Violence, Games,* both 1979; *The Awakening,* 1981; *The Serpent's Head, Loving Persuasions,* both 1982; *Pebble Beach,* 1983; *To Whom It May Concern, Passions,* both 1984; *Ramblin' Gal,* 1986.

PRINCIPAL TELEVISON WORK—All as director. Episodic: *Miami Vice,* NBC, 1985-86. Movies: *The Cookie Crumbles,* ABC, 1982; *The Talent,* NBC, 1985; also *Pandering to the Masses* in West Germany, 1983, and *Whisper of Doubt* in England.

RELATED CAREER—Actor and stuntman for films in Europe, 1960-75; head of school programs, Drama Ensemble, Inc., 1981-83. Also creative writing and/or drama teacher: Universidad Central de Barcelona, 1976-77; American Academy of Dramatic Arts, West Pasadena, CA, 1977-78; University of California, San Diego, 1978; Association of Hispanic Artists, 1979-80; East Harlem Rehabilitation Center, 1980-82; New York School of the Arts, 1983; Arts for the Handicapped, 1984.

NON-RELATED CAREER—Trapeze flyer, Parrici Circus Europe, 1957-67; trapeze flyer, Ringling Brothers & Barnum and Bailey Circus, 1968-72.

WRITINGS: PLAYS—See production details above unless indicated: *Break Loose,* 1975; *Double Image,* 1977; *Mind Games,* 1977; (adaptor) *A Tale of Two Cities,* 1978; *Act Scared,* 1978; *Merry Go-Round,* 1979; (adaptor) *Splendor and Death of Joaquin Murieta,* 1979; *Changes,* 1980; *Of Heros, Bandits and Myths,* International Arts Relations Theatre, New York City, 1980; *The Consumer Society,* 1981; *The Truth about Lies* (staged reading), Ensemble Studio Theatre, New York City, 1981; *Angle Of Repose,* 1982; *Flowers at Sea,* 1983; *Lying and Other Misdomenors,* 1984; *Survivors,* Off-Center Theatre, New York City, 1984; *Will* (staged reading), Staten Island Shakespeare Company, Staten Island, NY, 1987; *The Big Bad Wolf,* American Theatre of Actors, New York City, 1987.

SCREENPLAYS—*The Rhythm of Violence, Games,* both 1979; *The Awakening,* 1981; *To Whom It May Concern, Passions,* both 1984.

TELEPLAYS—Episodic: *Miami Vice,* NBC, 1985-86. Also *Pandering to the Masses,* West German television, 1983; *Run Wild,* NBC, 1984.

FICTION—*Amazing Tales,* Humboldt, 1981; *Heat,* Humbolt, 1982. POETRY—*One from the Heart,* Aragon Press, 1983.

AWARDS: Performing Arts Award and Grant, from Philanthropists International, Switzerland, 1978-82, for "sustained excellence through the years;" Edinburgh Theatre Festival awards, 1979, for *Mind Games-Part 2,* 1983, for *Midnight Mother,* and 1985, for *Passion Play;* Creative Arts Public Services of New York Grant, 1978; Most Promising Playwright from New York Curtain Call,

1979; Best Director awards from *The Villager,* 1980, for *Camilian* and 1981, for *Lover of Dreams; Soho Weekly News* directing award, 1980, for *The Truth about Lies;* Playwriting Grant from the Edward Albee Foundation, 1980-1982; Best Director, U.S. Virgin Islands Film Festival awards, 1981, for *Games,* and 1982, for *Loving Persuasions;* Special Honorary Mention, Spoleto Theatre Festival, Spoleto, Italy, 1982, for *Grand Passion;* Best Director Award, from *Arriba* magazine, Madrid, Spain, 1983, for *Flowers at Sea;* Icaro Award, 1983, for Dramatic Excellence; Ford Foundation Latin Playwright Grant, 1983; INTAR-Lab Playwriting Grant, 1983; Best Documentary, Berlin Film Festival, 1984, for *Pebble Beach;* Unitas Literary Award, First Prize, 1985, for *Obsession* (short story); Honorable Mention, International Theatre Festival, Nancy, France, 1985, for *Series of Plays on Tour.*

MEMBER: Dramatists Guild, National Writers Union, Poets and Writers, Inc., Authors League of America, P.E.N., Directors Guild of America, Association of Residence Theatres.

ADDRESSES: OFFICE—c/o R.M. Productions, P.O. Box 372, Village Station, New York, NY 10014.

*   *   *

MOORE, Roger   1927-

PERSONAL: Born October 14, 1927, in London, England; son of George (a London policeman) and Lily (Pope) Moore; married Doorn van Steyn (divorced, 1953); married Dorothy Squires (divorced); married Luisa Mattioli (an actress), April 11, 1968; children: Deborah, Geoffrey, Christian. EDUCATION: Attended the Art School, London; trained for the stage at the Royal Academy of Dramatic Arts, 1944-45. MILITARY: British Army, 1945-48.

VOCATION: Actor and writer.

CAREER: PRINCIPAL FILM APPEARANCES—*The Last Time I Saw Paris,* Metro-Goldwyn-Mayer (MGM), 1954; *Interrupted Melody,* MGM, 1955; *King's Thief,* MGM, 1955; *Diane,* MGM, 1956; *The Miracle,* Warner Brothers, 1959; *Gold of the Seven Saints,* Warner Brothers, 1961; *Crossplot,* 1969; *The Man Who Haunted Himself,* Associated, 1970; *Live and Let Die,* United Artists, 1973; *The Man with the Golden Gun,* United Artists, 1974; *That Lucky Touch,* 1975; *Save Us from Our Friends,* 1975; *Street People,* American International, 1976; *Sherlock Holmes in New York,* 1976; *Shout at the Devil,* American International, 1976; *Gold,* Allied Artists, 1977; *The Spy Who Loved Me,* United Artists, 1977; *The Wild Geese,* Allied Artists, 1978; *Escape to Athena,* Associated, 1979; *Moonraker,* United Artists, 1979; *Esther, Ruth, and Jennifer,* 1979.

Ffolkes, Universal, 1980; *The Sea Wolves,* Paramount, 1981; *Sunday Lovers,* United Artists, 1981; *For Your Eyes Only,* United Artists, 1981; *The Cannonball Run,* Twentieth Century-Fox, 1981; *Octopussy,* Metro-Goldwyn-Mayer/United Artists (MGM/UA), 1983; *The Naked Face,* Cannon, 1984; *A View to a Kill,* MGM/UA, 1984; also, *Rachel Cade, No Man's Land, Rape of the Sabines.*

PRINCIPAL TELEVISION APPEARANCES—Series: *Ivanhoe,* 1957-58; Silky Harris, *The Alaskans,* ABC, 1959-60; Cousin Beauregard Maverick, *Maverick,* ABC, 1960-61; Simon Templar, *The Saint,*

NBC, 1967-69; Lord Brett Sinclair, *The Persuaders,* ABC, 1971-72. Episodic: *The Muppet Show,* syndicated, 1981.

PRINCIPAL STAGE APPEARANCES—*A Pin to See the Peepshow,* Playhouse Theatre, New York City, 1953; *Night of 100 Stars,* Radio City Music Hall, New York City, 1982; also appeared in *Mr. Roberts, I Capture the Castle,* and *Little Hut.*

WRITINGS: BOOKS—*James Bond Diary,* 1973.

MEMBER: St. James's Club, Garrick Club.

ADDRESSES: AGENT—London Management, 235-241 Regent Street, London W1, England; c/o Tom Chasin, The Gersh Agency, 222 N. Canon Drive, Suite 202, Beverly Hills, CA 90210. PUBLICIST—Guttman and Pam, 8500 Wilshire Boulevard, Suite 801, Beverly Hills, CA 90211.

*   *   *

MORALES, Esai

BRIEF ENTRY: Esai Morales has protested against being typecast as a Hispanic; "I'm as American as anybody else. I was born in Brooklyn," he told the *New York Times* (July 4, 1986). Nevertheless, the actor, whose heritage is Puerto Rican, has thus far achieved attention in Latin ethnic roles. He played a street tough engaged in a jailhouse vendetta against Sean Penn in the 1983 film *Bad Boys,* a Mexican-American cancer victim in *Rainy Day Friends* (1986), and Bob Morales, half-brother to rock star Ritchie Valens in the 1987 hit *La Bamba.* He called the latter part "the most rounded role I've ever done" and critics and audiences responded favorably to his work in the film. Morales's youthful determination to become an actor drove him to complete New York's prestigious High School for the Performing Arts even after he became a ward of the state and voluntarily entered a home for wayward boys at age fifteen. In addition to his movie work, his television credits include the 1986 NBC mini-series *On Wings of Eagles* with Burt Lancaster.

*   *   *

MORGAN, Gareth   1940-

PERSONAL: Born February 15, 1940, in Carmarthen, Wales; son of Gwyn Hughes and Lily May (Williams) Morgan; married Patricia England. EDUCATION: Trained for the stage at the Rose Bruford College of Drama.

VOCATION: Director.

CAREER: FIRST STAGE WORK—Director, *The Miracles,* Southwark Cathedral, Lonodn, 1963. PRINCIPAL STAGE WORK—Director: *Room for Company, Waiting for Godot, Men-at-Arms,* all Royal Shakespeare Company (RSC), 1968; *When Thou Art King, The Merry Month of May, The Trial and Execution of Charles I, Two Gentlemen of Verona,* all RSC, 1969; *Dr. Faustus, When Thou Art King,* both RSC, 1970; *Macbeth,* Dramski Teatar, Skopje, Yugoslavia, 1969; *Prisoners of War, Slip Road Wedding,* both Tyneside Theatre Company, Newcastle-on-Tyne, U.K., 1971; *Play Strindberg,* Tyneside Theatre Company, then Hampstead Theatre Club, London, both 1972; *The Baker, the Baker's Wife, and the*

Baker's Boy, Tyneside Theatre Company, 1972; *The Faery Queen, Peer Gynt, A Worthy Guest,* all Tyneside Theatre Company, 1973; *Cyrano de Bergerac, Rock Natvity,* both Tyneside Theatre Company, 1974. Also assistant director, *Puntila,* 1965; director, *The Comedy of Errors,* New Zealand, 1966; director, *Small Change and Shifts,* Theatre Yr Yuslon, 1977; director, *Much Ado about Nothng,* Nottingham, U.K., 1977; director, *Relatively Speaking,* Coventry, U.K., 1978; director, *Ashes,* Bristol, U.K., 1978; director, *St. Joan,* Birmingham, U.K., 1979; also directed productions for drama schools including the London Academy of Music and Dramatic Art.

PRINCIPAL TELEVISION WORK—Series: Director, *Northern View.*

RELATED CAREER—Director of productions, Welsh Theatre Company, 1966-68; artistic director, Royal Shakespeare Company's Theatre-Go-Round, 1968-70; artistic director, 1971, then theatre director, 1972-77, Tyneside Theatre Company, Newcastle-on-Tyne, U.K.; actor with the Royal Shakespeare Company and the BBC Repertory Company; Young People's Theatre Committee, Arts Council, 1974-80; governor, Rose Bruford College of Drama.

ADDRESSES: OFFICE—63 Church Road, Gosforth, Newcastle-on-Tyne, England.*

*   *   *

MORGENSTERN, Susan   1954-

PERSONAL: Born May 13, 1954, in Glens Falls, NY; daughter of John Jesse (a psychologist) and Kathleen Amy (an executive administrator; maiden name, Harris) Morgenstern; married Gerard Gerald Prendergast, Jr. (a restaurant consultant), September 24, 1983. EDUCATION: University of California, Santa Cruz, B.A., 1975; trained for the stage with Suzanne Shepherd, John Hellweg, Audrey Stanley, Larry Hecht, Kristin Linklater, Tina Packer, Dennis Krausnick, Merry Conway, Tom Lehrer, John Kroner, and Roland Wyatt.

VOCATION: Actor, director, and music director.

CAREER: STAGE DEBUT—Child, *Teahouse of the August Moon,* Glens Falls Community Theatre, NY, 1961, six performances. OFF-BROADWAY DEBUT—Winnie, *Female Transport,* Cubiculo Theatre, 1979, for fifteen performances. PRINCIPAL STAGE APPEARANCES—Hope, *Dracula: A Musical Nightmare,* Rosalie, *Carnival,* both Staircase Theatre, Santa Cruz, CA, 1975; Tessie Tura, *Gypsy,* Staircase Theatre, 1976; Fraulein Schneider, *Cabaret,* Catherine, *Arms and the Man,* Mrs. Anderson, *A Little Night Music,* Rosemary, *Picnic,* all Summer Repertory Theatre, Santa Rosa, CA, 1977; Nurse Ratched, *One Flew over the Cuckoo's Nest,* Jill Tanner, *Butterflies Are Free,* both Staircase Theatre, 1977; Yente, *Fiddler on the Roof,* Lady Bracknell, *The Importance of Being Earnest,* Bloody Mary, *South Pacific,* all Summer Repertory Theatre, 1978; Toinette, *The Imaginary Invalid,* Lina, *Misalliance,* both Staircase Theatre, 1978; Amy, *Wings,* Holly Kaplan, *Uncommon Women and Others,* Mrs. Varec, *The Water Engine,* June, *The Killing of Sister George,* all Palisades Theatre, St. Petersburg, FL, 1981; June, *The Killing of Sister George,* Westside Arts Theatre, New York City, 1981; Gertrude Blum, *The Sea Horse,* Performing Arts Showcase, New York University, New York City, 1982; Duchess of Trent, *Ball,* Greene Street Cafe, New York City, 1984; Viornia Popeilska, *The Sylvanian Shakespearean Sircus,* Raft

SUSAN MORGENSTERN

Theatre, New York City, 1987. Also Mrs. Mopply, *Too True to Be Good*, Ten-Ten Players, New York City; Mistress Quickly, *The Merry Wives of Windsor*, Studio T, New York City; Myrna, *Pontifex*, Berkeley Stage Company, Berkeley, CA.

PRINCIPAL FILM APPEARANCES—Pinball player, *Tilt*, 1978.

PRINCIPAL TELEVISION APPEARANCES—Tourist, *The Entertainer*, NBC, 1976.

RELATED CAREER—Teacher: University of California at Santa Cruz, 1975-78; Stagedoor Manor, Lock Sheldrake, NY, 1985; Brearley School, New York City, 1986.

ADDRESSES: HOME—344 E. 85th Street, New York, NY 10028.

*   *   *

MORLEY, Christopher

VOCATION: Set designer.

CAREER: PRINCIPAL STAGE WORK—All as set designer: *As You Like It*, Open Air Theatre, London, 1973; *Sticks and Bones*, New End Theatre, *The Achurch Letters*, Greenwich Theatre, *Molly*, Comedy Theatre, all London, 1978; *Mary Barnes*, Royal Court Theatre, London, 1979; *The Merchant, The Beggar's Opera, St. Joan*, all Birmingham Repertory Theatre, Birmingham, U.K., 1978-79. Also designed *Edward II*, Leicester, U.K., then London, both 1964; *Their Very Own and Golden City, Three Men for*

Colverton, Macbeth, all 1966; *The Sunshine Boys*, 1975; *Liza of Lambeth*, 1976; and numerous operas.

All as set designer with the Royal Shakespeare Company, Stratford-on-Avon, U.K., and London: *The Revenger's Tragedy*, 1966; *The Taming of the Shrew, The Relapse*, both 1967; *King Lear, Much Ado about Nothing*, both 1968; *The Winter's Tale, Twelfth Night*, both 1969; *Hamlet, King John, The Tempest*, all 1970; *Twelfth Night*, 1971; *Coriolanus, Julius Caesar, Antony and Cleopatra, Titus Andronicus*, all 1972; *The Merchant of Venice*, 1978, *Measure for Measure, Cymbeline, The White Guard*, all 1979; *The Maid's Tragedy*, 1980.

RELATED CAREER—Founder, Christopher Morley Associates, 1974; associate artist, Royal Shakespeare Company.

ADDRESSES: OFFICE—c/o Royal Shakespeare Theatre, Stratford-on-Avon, England.*

*   *   *

MORTON, Arthur   1908-

PERSONAL: Born August 8, 1908, in Duluth, MN. EDUCATION: Attended University of Minnesota, 1929.

VOCATION: Composer and arranger.

CAREER: PRINCIPAL FILM WORK—Arranger: *Laura*, Metro-Goldwyn-Mayer (MGM), 1944; *The Jolson Story*, MGM, 1946; *No Sad Songs for Me*, 1950; *Born Yesterday*, 1950; *From Here to Eternity*, MGM, 1953; *Salome*, 1953; *Phifft*, 1954; *The Long Gray Line*, Columbia, 1955; *The Man from Laramie*, Columbia, 1955; *My Sister Eileen*, Columbia, 1955; *Queen Bee*, Columbia, 1955; *Picnic*, Columbia, 1956; *Jubal*, Columbia, 1956; *Autumn Leaves*, Columbia, 1956; *Johnny Concho*, United Artists, 1956; *The Harder They Fall*, 1956; *3:10 to Yuma*, Columbia, 1957; *Full of Life*, Columbia, 1957; *The Garment Jungle*, Columbia, 1957; *They Came to Cordura*, Columbia, 1959.

Strangers When We Meet, Columbia, 1960; *That Touch of Mink*, Universal, 1962; *Critic's Choice*, Warner Brothers, 1963; *Diamond Head*, Columbia, 1963; *Toys in the Attic*, United Artists, 1963; *The Man from the Diner's Club*, Columbia, 1963; *What a Way to Go*, Twentieth Century-Fox, 1964; *The New Interns*, Columbia, 1964; *Rio Conchos*, Twentieth Century-Fox, 1964; *Von Ryan's Express*, Twentieth Century-Fox, 1965; *Sabateur: Code Name Morituri*, Twentieth Century-Fox, 1965; *In Harm's Way*, Paramount, 1965; *Dear Briggitte*, Twentieth Century-Fox, 1965; *The Flim-Flam Man*, Twentieth Century-Fox, 1967; *The Traveling Executioner*, MGM, 1967; *Our Man Flint*, Twentieth Century-Fox, 1968; *Planet of the Apes*, Twentieth Century-Fox, 1968; *Justine*, Twentieth Century-Fox, 1969.

The Ballad of Cable Hogue, Warner Brothers, 1970; *Patton*, Twentieth Century-Fox, 1970; *Tora! Tora! Tora!*, Twentieth Century-Fox, 1970; *The Mephisto Waltz*, Twentieth Century-Fox, 1971; *Escape from the Planet of the Apes*, Twentieth Century-Fox, 1971; *Cold Turkey*, United Artists, 1971; *The Wild Rovers*, MGM, 1971; *The Other*, Twentieth Century-Fox, 1972; *Ace Eli*, Twentieth Century-Fox, 1973; *One Little Indian*, Buena Vista, 1973; *The Don Is Dead*, Universal, 1973; *Papillion*, Allied Artists, 1973; *Chinatown*, Paramount, 1974; *Breakout*, 1975; *The Wind and the*

Lion, United Artists, 1975; *Logan's Run,* United Artists, 1976; *The Omen,* Twentieth Century-Fox, 1976; *Islands in the Stream,* Paramount, 1977; *The Passover Plot,* Paramount, 1977; *Twilight's Last Gleaming,* Allied Artists, 1977; *Damnation Alley,* Twentieth Century-Fox, 1977; *MacArthur,* Universal, 1977; *Capricorn One,* Warner Brothers, 1978; *Coma,* United Artists, 1978; *The Swarm,* Warner Brothers, 1978; *Damien: The Omen II,* Twentieth Century-Fox, 1978; *Magic,* Twentieth Century-Fox, 1978; *Superman,* Warner Brothers, 1978; *The Boys from Brazil,* Twentieth Century-Fox, 1979; *Alien,* Twentieth Century-Fox, 1979; *Players,* Paramount, 1979; *Meteor,* American International, 1979; *Star Trek,* Paramount, 1979.

The Final Conflict, Twentieth Century-Fox, 1981; *Outland,* Warner Brothers, 1981; *Raggedy Man,* Universal, 1981; *Night Crossing,* Buena Vista, 1982; *Poltergeist,* Metro-Goldwyn-Mayer/United Artists (MGM/UA), 1982; *The Secret of NIMH,* MGM/UA, 1982; *First Blood,* Orion, 1982; *Inchon,* MGM/UA, 1983; *Psycho II,* Universal, 1983; *Twilight Zone,* Warner Brothers, 1983; *Under Fire,* Orion, 1983; *The Lonely Guy,* Universal, 1984; *Gremlins,* Warner Brothers, 1984; *Supergirl,* Tri-Star, 1984; *The Explorers,* Paramount, 1985; *King Solomon's Mines,* Cannon, 1985; *Poltergeist II,* MGM/UA, 1986; also, *Night Life of the Gods, Princess O'Hara, Fit for a King, Smokey, Masoda,* and *Link.*

PRINCIPAL TELEVISION WORK—Composer and arranger: Series—*Black Saddle,* NBC; *Laramie,* ABC; *Bus Stop,* ABC; *Follow the Sun,* ABC; *My Three Sons,* ABC; *Peyton Place,* ABC; *Medical Center,* CBS; *Daniel Boone,* NBC; *Lancer,* CBS; *The Waltons,* CBS; *Apple's Way,* CBS; *Medical Story,* NBC. Specials—*National Geographic.* Movies—*Say Goodbye, Maggie Cole,* 1972; also, *How to Stay Alive, Hooray for Hollywood.*

RELATED CAREER—Composer for film companies including Universal, RKO, United Artists, and with Columbia since 1948.

WRITINGS: COMPOSITIONS—*Riding on Air,* 1937; *Turnabout,* 1946; *Walking Hills,* 1949; *The Nevadan,* 1950; *Father Is a Bachelor,* 1951; *Never Trust a Gambler,* 1951; *Harlem Globetrotters,* 1953; *The Big Heat,* 1955; *Pushover,* 1954; *He Laughed Last,* Columbia, 1956; *Rogues of Sherwood Forest,* 1958.

MEMBER: American Society of Composers, Authors, and Publishers.

ADDRESSES: AGENT—c/o American Society of Composers, Authors, and Publishers, One Lincoln Plaza, New York, NY 10023.*

*   *   *

MOSES, Gilbert, III   1942-

PERSONAL: Born August 20, 1942, in Cleveland, Ohio; son of Gilbert, Jr., and Bertha Mae (Jones) Moses. EDUCATION: Attended Oberlin College, the Sorbonne, and New York University.

VOCATION: Director.

CAREER: FIRST STAGE WORK—Director, *Roots,* Free Southern Theatre, New Orleans, LA, 1964. FIRST NEW YORK STAGE WORK—Director, *Slaveship,* Chelsea Theatre Center, Brooklyn Academy of Music, Brooklyn, NY, 1969. PRINCIPAL STAGE WORK—Director: *Bloodknot,* American Conservatory Theatre,

San Francisco, CA, 1970; *Mother Courage, No Place to Be Somebody,* both Arena Stage, Washington, DC, 1971; *Ain't Supposed to Die a Natural Death,* Ethel Barrymore Theatre, New York City, 1971; *The Duplex,* Forum Theatre, New York City, 1972; *Rigoletto,* San Francisco Opera House, San Francisco, CA, 1972; *Don't Let It Go to Your Head,* Henry Street Playhouse, New York City, 1972; *Louis,* Henry Street Playhouse, 1981. Also directed *Every Night When the Sun Goes Down,* New York City, 1975; *1600 Pennsylvania Avenue,* New York City, 1976; *The Taking of Miss Janie,* New York City, 1977; and with the Capital Repertory Company, Albany, NY.

PRINCIPAL FILM WORK—Director: *Willie Dynamite,* Universal, 1973; *The Fish That Saved Pittsburgh,* United Artists, 1979.

FIRST TELEVISION WORK—Episodic: *Roots* (two episodes), 1977. Movies: *The Greatest Thing That Almost Happened,* 1977.

RELATED CAREER—Co-founder, artistic director, Free Southern Theatre, 1963—, board of directors, 1966—.

NON-RELATED CAREER—Staff member, *Free Press,* Jackson, Mississippi, 1963-64, then editor, 1964; copy boy, *New York Post,* 1964; guitarist, composer, Nick Gravenitis Group, 1967, then The Street Choir, 1968.

WRITINGS: FILM SCORES—*Willie Dynamite,* Universal, 1973.

AWARDS: Obie Award from the *Village Voice,* 1970, for *Slaveship;* Drama Desk Award, 1973, for *Ain't Supposed to Die a Natural Death;* Obie Award, New York Drama Critics Award, Outer Circle Award, all 1977, for *The Taking of Miss Janie;* Emmy Award nomination, Humanitas Award, both 1977, for *Roots.*

ADDRESSES: AGENT—Irv Schechter Agency, 9300 Wilshire Boulevard, Suite 410, Beverly Hills, CA 90212.*

*   *   *

MUDD, Roger   1928-

PERSONAL: Born February 9, 1928, in Washington, DC; son of Kostka and Irma Iris (Harrison) Mudd; married Emma Jeanne Spears, October 28, 1957; children: Daniel H., Maria M., Jonathan, Matthew M. EDUCATION: Washington and Lee University, A.B., 1950; University of North Carolina, M.A., 1953. MILITARY: U.S. Army, 1945-47.

VOCATION: Television news reporter and anchorman.

CAREER: PRINCIPAL TELEVISION WORK—Reporter, WTOP, Washington, DC, 1956-61; news correspondent, *CBS Evening News with Walter Cronkite,* 1961-80; anchorman, *The CBS Saturday News,* CBS, 1966-71; narrator of episodes, *CBS Reports,* including "The Selling of the Pentagon," CBS, 1971; chief Washington correspondent, *NBC Television News,* 1980—; co-anchorman, *NBC Television News,* 1982-83; co-host, *Meet the Press,* NBC, 1980-85; host, *American Almanac,* NBC, 1985-86.

PRINCIPAL RADIO WORK—News director, WRNL, Richmond, VA, 1953-56; reporter, WTOP, Washington, DC, 1956-61.

RELATED CAREER—Teacher, Darlington School, Rome, GA,

ROGER MUDD

1951-52; reporter, *News Leader,* Richmond, 1953; Fund for Investigative Journalism (board of directors); PEN-Faulkner, Robert F. Kennedy Journalism Awards Committee, 1971-78.

NON-RELATED CAREER—Randolph-Macon Women's College, (board of trustees, 1971-78), Blue Ridge School (board of directors, 1978-84), Citizens Scholarship Foundation (board of directors).

AWARDS: Co-winner, Outstanding Achievement within Regularly Scheduled News Programs, Emmy Awards, 1973, for "Coverage of the Shooting of Governor Wallace," 1974, for "The Agnew Resignation," both *CBS Evening News with Walter Cronkite;* co-winner, Outstanding Documentary Program Achievements (Current Events), Emmy Award, 1974, for *CBS News Special Report: The Senate and the Watergate Affair.*

MEMBER: Radio-Television Correspondents Association (chairman of executive committee, 1969-70).

ADDRESSES: OFFICE—c/o NBC Television News, 4001 Nebraska Avenue, Washington, DC 20016.*

MURDOCH, Rupert 1931-

PERSONAL: Full name, Keith Rupert Murdoch; born March 11, 1931, in Melbourne, Victoria, Australia; came to the U.S. in 1974, naturalized in 1985; son of Sir Keith (a journalist and newspaper owner) and Dame Elisabeth (a welfare activist) Murdoch; married second wife, Anna Maria Tory, 1967; children: (first marriage) Prudence; (second marriage) Elisabeth, James, Lachlan. EDUCATION: Attended Oxford University, M.A., 1953.

VOCATION: Publisher and executive.

CAREER: Owner and publisher, *The Adelaide News,* Australia, 1952—; owner and publisher: Newspapers—*The New York Post, The Village Voice,* New York City; *The San Antonio Express, San Antonio News,* TX; *The Boston Herald,* MA; *The Chicago Sun-Times,* IL; *The Times of London, The Sunday Times, The Times Literary Supplement, The Times Educational Supplement, The Times Higher Education Supplement,* all London; *The Australian, The Daily Telegraph, The Sunday Telegraph, The Daily Mirror, The Sunday Sun, The News and Sunday Mail, The Sunday Times,* all Australia. Magazines—*New York Magazine, TV Week, New Idea, The Star, Antique Collector's Guide, The Trader, Licensed Bookmaker.*

PRINCIPAL TELEVISION WORK—Owner: Channel 10, Sydney, Channel 10, Melbourne, both Australia; News Group Productions, Skyband, and Fox Television Network, all U.S.; Satellite Television PLC, and part-owner, London Weekend Television, both U.K.

PRINCIPAL FILM WORK—Co-owner and chairman, Twentieth Century-Fox Film Corporation.

RELATED CAREER—Vice-President, *Times* Newspaper Holdings, 1981—; director, Reuters Holdings PLC, 1984; co-owner, Cruden Investments; chief executive officer and former managing director, News International Group, Ltd. and associated companies, Australia; chairman, News America Publishing, Inc. and City Post Publishing Corporation; owner, Bemrose Publishing Company, Bay Books, and Townsend Hook Paper Company; director, United Technologies, U.S.

NON-RELATED CAREER—Chief executive officer, Ansett Transport Industries, U.K.; owner, Santos Energy Company and Convoys Transport Company; director, New York State Lotto.

AWARDS: First Class, Commander of the White Rose Award, 1985.

SIDELIGHTS: RECREATIONS—Swimming, playing tennis, and skiing.

ADDRESSES: OFFICE—*New York Post,* 210 South Street, New York, NY 10002.*

N

NAPIER, John 1944-

PERSONAL: Born March 1, 1944, in London, England; son of James Edward Thomas and Florence (Godbold) Napier; married Andreane Neofitou (marriage ended); married Donna King (an actress); children: Julian, Elise, James. EDUCATION: Attended Hornsey College of Art; trained as a designer at the Central School of Arts and Crafts.

VOCATION: Designer.

CAREER: FIRST STAGE WORK—Set designer, *A Penny for a Song,* Phoenix Theatre, Leicester, U.K., 1967. FIRST LONDON WORK—Set designer, *Fortune and Men's Eyes,* Comedy Theatre, 1968. FIRST BROADWAY WORK—Set and costume designer, *Equus,* Plymouth Theatre, 1974. PRINCIPAL STAGE WORK—Co-designer for the Memorial Theatre, Stratford-Upon-Avon, U.K., 1976; set designer: Phoenix Theatre, Leicester, 1967-68; in London—*The Ruling Class, The Fun War, Muzeeka,* and *La Turista,* all 1969; *George Frederick,* Ballet Rambert, 1969; *Cancer* and *Isabel's a Jezabel,* both 1970; *Mister, The Foursome, The Lovers of Viorne,* and *Lear,* all 1971; *Jump, Sam Sam,* and *Big Wolf,* all 1972; *Equus* and *The Party,* both at the National Theatre, 1973; *The Devils,* English National Opera, 1973; *Knuckle,* 1974; *Kings and Clowns* and *The Traveling Music Show,* both 1978; *George Friedric,* Ballet Rambert, 1974; *The Devils of Loudon,* Sadler's Wells, 1974; for the Royal Shakespeare Company: *King John, Richard II, Cymbeline, Macbeth,* and *Richard III,* all 1974; *Hedda Gabler,* Aldwych Theatre, 1975; *Much Ado About Nothing, The Comedy of Errors,* and *King Lear,* all 1976; *Macbeth, A Midsummer Night's Dream,* and *As You Like It,* all 1977; *The Merry Wives of Windsor* and *Twelfth Night,* both 1979; *The Three Sisters,* Other Place Theatre and *Once In A Lifetime,* Aldwych Theatre, both 1979; *The Greeks* and *The Life and Adventures of Nicholas Nickleby,* both at the Aldwych Theatre, 1980.

Set and costume designer: *The Life and Adventures of Nicholas Nickleby,* Plymouth Theatre, New York City, 1981; *Cats,* London and at the Winter Garden Theatre, New York City, 1982; *Starlight Express,* Apollo Victoria Theatre, London, 1984 and at the Gershwin Theatre, New York City, 1987; *Les Miserables,* Barbican Theatre and at the Palace Theatre, London, 1985 and at the Broadway Theatre, New York City, 1987; *Time,* Dominion Theatre, London, 1986; also *Peter Pan, Fair Maid of the West,* and *Mother Courage,* all for the Royal Shakespeare Company.

Operas: For the Royal Opera House, London—*Lohengrin,* 1974 and 1978; *King Lear,* 1977; *Idomeneo,* Glyndebourne Opera House, U.K.; *Macbeth.*

PRINCIPAL FILM WORK—Costume designer, *Hedda,* Brut Productions, 1976.

PRINCIPAL TELEVISION WORK—Designer, *Macbeth* and *The Comedy of Errors,* both independent television.

AWARDS: Society of West End Theatres (SWET) Awards: 1977, for *King Lear,* 1978, for *Lohengrin;* Best Set and Costume Design, Antoinette Perry Award, 1981, for *The Life and Adventures of Nicholas Nickleby;* Best Set and Costume Design, Antoinette Perry Award, 1982, for *Cats.*

MEMBER: British Society of Theatre Designers (founding member), Royal Shakespeare Company (associate member).

SIDELIGHTS: RECREATIONS—Photography and football.

ADDRESSES: AGENT—ML Representation, 194 Old Brompton Road, London SW5 0AS, England.

JOHN NAPIER

NAUGHTON, James 1945-

PERSONAL: Born December 6, 1945, in Middletown, CT; son of Joseph (a teacher) and Rosemary (a teacher; maiden name, Walsh) Naughton; married Pamela Parsons; children: Gregory, Keira. EDUCATION: Brown University, A.B., 1967; Yale University, M.F.A., drama, 1970.

VOCATION: Actor.

CAREER: STAGE DEBUT—Narcissus, *Olympian Games,* Yale Repertory Company, John Drew Theatre, East Hampton, NY, 1970. BROADWAY DEBUT—Wally, *I Love My Wife,* Ethel Barrymore Theatre, 1977. PRINCIPAL STAGE APPEARANCES— Edmund, *Long Day's Journey into Night,* Promenade Theatre, New York City, 1971; doctor, *Whose Life Is It, Anyway?,* Royale Theatre, New York City, 1980; Nick, *Who's Afraid of Virginia Woolf?,* Long Wharf Theatre, New Haven, CT, 1980; Jim, *The Glass Menagerie,* Long Wharf Theatre, 1986; also appeared in *Free and Clear,* Long Wharf Theatre, 1982.

TELEVISION DEBUT—Ben, *Look Homeward, Angel,* CBS, 1972. PRINCIPAL TELEVISION APPEARANCES—Series: Steve Faraday, *Faraday and Company,* NBC, 1973-74; Pete Burke, *Planet of the Apes,* CBS, 1974; Harry Barnes, *Making the Grade,* CBS, 1982; Dr. Michael "Cutter" Royce, *Trauma Center,* ABC, 1983. Movies: Captain John Haines, *F. Scott Fitzgerald and "The Last of the Belles,"* ABC, 1974; Dr. Baxter, *The Last 36 Hours of Dr. Durant,* ABC, 1975; James O'Donnell, *The Bunker,* CBS, 1981; Dr. Dan Berenson, *My Body, My Child,* ABC, 1982; Andy Driscoll, *Parole,* CBS, 1982; Richard Wylie, *The Last of the Great Survivors,* CBS, 1984; Jack Parrish, *Between Darkness and the Dawn,* ABC, 1985; Andy Colleran, *Sin of Innocence,* CBS, 1986.

FILM DEBUT—Kevin Brooks, *The Paper Chase,* Twentieth Century-Fox, 1972. PRINCIPAL FILM APPEARANCES—Jim, *The Glass Menagerie,* Cineplex Odeon, 1987; also *Second Wind,* 1975; *A Stranger Is Watching,* 1981; *Cat's Eye,* Metro-Goldwyn-Mayer/ United Artists, 1984.

AWARDS: Theatre World Award, Drama Desk Award, New York Critics Circle Award, all 1971, for *Long Day's Journey into Night.*

MEMBER: Actors' Equity Association, Screen Actors Guild, American Federation of Television and Radio Artists.

ADDRESSES: AGENT—STE Representation, 888 Seventh Avenue, New York, NY 10106.*

*   *   *

NEILSON, Perlita 1933-

PERSONAL: Born Margaret Sowden, June 11, 1933, in Bradford, England; daughter of Wilson and Isabella (Gibson) Sowden; married Bruce Sharman (divorced).

VOCATION: Actress.

CAREER: LONDON DEBUT—Minnie, *Annie Get Your Gun,* Coliseum Theatre, 1947. NEW YORK DEBUT—Alexandra Carmichael, *Lace on Her Petticoat,* Booth Theatre, 1951. PRINCIPAL STAGE APPEARANCES—Lisa, *Peter Pan,* Scala Theatre, London, 1948;

Anukta, *The Power of Darkness,* Lyric Theatre, London, 1949; Alexandra Carmichael, *Lace on Her Petticoat,* Ambassadors' Theatre, London, 1950; Lucy, *The Enchanted,* Arts Theatre, London, 1954; Meg, *The Sun Room,* Arts Theatre, 1954; Sophia Truelove, *The Road to Ruin,* Dido, *The Marching Song,* Hero, *Much Ado about Nothing,* Nerissa, *The Merchant of Venice,* Mary Warren, *The Crucible,* Perdita, Mamilius, *The Winter's Tale,* all Bristol Old Vic Theatre Company, Bristol, U.K., 1954-55; Nina, *The Seagull,* Saville Theatre, London, 1956; title role, *The Diary of Anne Frank,* Phoenix Theatre, London, 1956; Cecily Cardew, *The Importance of Being Earnest,* Dublin Festival, Dublin, Ireland, 1957; Patty O'Neil, *The Moon Is Blue,* Nottingham Repertory Theatre, Nottingham, U.K., 1958; Pernette, *The Green Years,* Oxford Playhouse, Oxford, U.K., 1959; Felicity, *Will You Walk a Little Faster?,* Duke of York's Theatre, London, 1960; girl, *The Pleasure Garden,* Pembroke Theatre, Croydon, U.K., 1960; Ellie Dunn, *Heartbreak House,* Oxford Playhouse, then Wyndham's Theatre, London, 1961; Natasha, *War and Peace,* New Theatre, Cardiff, Wales, U.K., 1963; Miss Chiltern, *An Ideal Husband,* Strand Theatre, London, 1965; Edith, *Getting Married,* Strand Theatre, 1967; Fenny, *Dear Octopus,* Haymarket Theatre, London, 1967; Queen Victoria, *My Dearest Angel,* Arnaud Theatre, Guildford, U.K., 1968; Portia, *The Merchant of Venice,* Open Air Theatre, London, 1969; Kate, *She Stoops to Conquer,* Reardon Smith Theatre, Cardiff, Wales, U.K., 1970; title role, *Mary Rose,* Casson Theatre, Cardiff, Wales, U.K., 1970, then Arnaud Theatre, 1971; Judy, *Flowering Cherry,* Arnaud Theatre, 1973; Celia, *As You Like It,* Open Air Theatre, 1973; Freda, *Dangerous Corner,* Theatre Royal, York, U.K., 1974; Duchess of York, *Crown Matrimonial,* Thorndike Theatre, Leatherhead, U.K., 1974; performed in repertory at Theatre Royal, York, U.K., 1972, then 1975; with the Brighton Youth Concert, introduced and narrated Queen's Jubilee Concert, 1977.

MAJOR TOURS—Lesley Paul, *Matilda Shouted Fire,* U.K. cities, 1958; Ellie Dunn, *Heartbreak House,* Prossy, *Candida,* both with the Birmingham Repertory Company, European cities, 1965; Judy, *Flowering Cherry,* U.K. cities, 1973.

PRINCIPAL TELEVISION APPEARANCES—Specials: *The Boy David; Fall of Eagles.*

PRINCIPAL FILM APPEARANCES—*She Didn't Say No.*

SIDELIGHTS: RECREATIONS—Gardening, reading.

ADDRESSES: AGENT—c/o John Hunter, Film Rights, 113-117 Wardour Street, London W1V 4EH, England.*

*   *   *

NELSON, Barry 1925-

PERSONAL: Born Robert Nielson, in 1925, in Oakland, CA; son of Trygve and Betsy (Christophsen) Nielson; married Teresa Celi (divorced). EDUCATION: Received B.A. from the University of California, Berkeley. MILITARY: U.S. Army Air Force.

VOCATION: Actor.

CAREER: BROADWAY DEBUT—Bobby Grills, *Winged Victory,* 44th Street Theatre, 1943. PRINCIPAL STAGE APPEARANCES— Peter Sloan, *Light Up the Sky,* Royale Theatre, New York City,

1948; Gus Hammer, *The Rat Race*, Ethel Barrymore Theatre, New York City, 1949; Donald Gresham, *The Moon Is Blue*, Henry Miller's Theatre, New York City, 1951; Don Emerson, *Wake Up Darling*, Ethel Barrymore Theatre, 1956; Will Stockdale, *No Time for Sergeants*, Her Majesty's Theatre, London, 1956; Bob McKellaway, *Mary, Mary*, Helen Hayes Theatre, New York City, 1961; Nat Bentley, *Nobody Loves an Albatross*, Lyceum Theatre, New York City, 1964; Julian, *The Cactus Flower*, Royale Theatre, 1965; Richard, *Everything in the Garden*, Plymouth Theatre, New York City, 1967; Joe Grady, *The Only Game in Town*, Broadhurst Theatre, New York City, 1968; Harry Stone, *The Fig Leaves Are Falling*, Broadhurst Theatre, 1969; Walter Whitney, *The Engagement Baby*, Helen Hayes Theatre, 1970; Detective McLeod, *Detective Story*, Shubert Theatre, Philadelphia, PA, 1973; Charlie, *Seascape*, Shubert Theatre, New York City, then Shubert Theatre, Los Angeles, CA, both 1975; Reg, *The Norman Conquests*, Morosco Theatre, New York City, 1975; Dan Connors, *The Act*, Majestic Theatre, New York City, 1977; Julian Marsh, *42nd Street*, Majestic Theatre, 1981; Owen Turner, *Light Up the Sky*, Ahmanson Theatre, Los Angeles, CA, 1987; also appeared in *Suite in Two Keys*, Paper Mill Playhouse, Milburn, NJ, 1982.

PRINCIPAL STAGE WORK—Director, *The Only Game in Town*, Broadhurst Theatre, New York City, 1968.

MAJOR TOURS—Joe Bannon, *Heartsong*, U.S. cities, 1947; Sam Nash, Jesse Kiplinger, Roy Hubley, *Plaza Suite*, U.S. cities, 1971; Julian Marsh, *42nd Street*, U.S. cities, 1983; also *Conflict of Interest*, U.S. cities, 1972; *Lovers and Other Strangers*, U.S. cities, 1974.

PRINCIPAL FILM APPEARANCES—*A Guy Named Joe*, Metro-Goldwyn-Mayer, 1943; *Winged Victory*, Twentieth Century-Fox, 1944; *The Man with My Face*, United Artists, 1951; *The First Traveling Saleslady*, RKO, 1956; *Mary, Mary*, Warner Brothers, 1963; *Cactus Flower*, Columbia, 1969; *Airport*, Universal, 1970; *Pete 'n' Tillie*, Universal, 1973; *The Shining*, Warner Brothers, 1980.

PRINCIPAL TELEVISION APPEARANCES—Episodic: James Bond, "Casino Royale," *Climax*, CBS; "Drive a Desert Road," *Lux Playhouse*, CBS; *Starlight Theatre*, CBS. Series: Bart Adams, *The Hunter*, CBS, 1952; George Cooper, *My Favorite Husband*, 1953-57. Mini-Series: Bob Bailey, *Washington: Behind Closed Doors*, ABC, 1977. Movies: Hal Carter, *The Borgia Stick*, NBC, 1967; Alex Swain, *Seven in Darkness*, ABC, 1969; Lieutenant Frank Bryant, *Climb an Angry Mountain*, NBC, 1972.

AWARDS: Best Actor in a Musical, Antoinette Perry Award nomination, 1978, for *The Act*.

SIDELIGHTS: RECREATIONS—Reading, listening to music, traveling.

ADDRESSES: AGENT—William Morris Agency, 1350 Avenue of the Americas, New York, NY 10019.*

*   *   *

NELSON, David   1936-

PERSONAL: Born October 24, 1936, in New York City; son of Ozzie (an actor and bandleader) and Harriet (an actress and singer;

maiden name, Hilliard) Nelson; married. EDUCATION: Attended the University of Southern California.

VOCATION: Actor and director.

CAREER: PRINCIPAL TELEVISION APPEARANCES—As himself, *The Adventures of Ozzie and Harriet*, ABC, 1952-66.

PRINCIPAL TELEVISION WORK—Series: Director, *OK Crackerby*, ABC, 1965-66. Specials: Director, *Easy to Be Free*.

PRINCIPAL FILM APPEARANCES—*The Remarkable Mr. Pennypacker*, Twentieth Century-Fox, 1950; *Here Come the Nelsons*, 1952; *Peyton Place*, Twentieth Century-Fox, 1957; *Day of the Outlaw*, United Artists, 1959; *30*, Warner Brothers, 1959; *The Big Show*, Twentieth Century-Fox, 1961; *No Drums, No Bugles*, Cinerama, 1971; also *The Wheel* and *The Sinners*.

MEMBER: Directors Guild of America.

ADDRESSES: OFFICE—c/o Directors Guild of America, 7950 Sunset Blvd., Los Angeles, CA 90046.*

*   *   *

NELSON, Willie   1933-

PERSONAL: Born April 30, 1933, in Abbott, TX; married third wife, Connie, 1972; children: Paula Carlene, Amy, Lana, Susie, Billy. MILITARY: U.S. Air Force.

Photography by Randee St. Nicholas

WILLIE NELSON

VOCATION: Songwriter, singer, and actor.

CAREER: FILM DEBUT—*The Electric Horseman,* Columbia, 1979. PRINCIPAL FILM APPEARANCES—*Honeysuckle Rose,* Warner Brothers, 1980; *Thief,* United Artists, 1981; title role, *Barbarosa,* Universal, 1982; Doc Jenkins, *Songwriter,* Tri-Star, 1984; *Red Headed Stranger,* Alive Film, 1987.

PRINCIPAL TELEVISION APPEARANCES—Series: Announcer and host of various country music shows. Movies: *The Last Days of Frank and Jesse James,* NBC, 1986; *Stagecoach,* 1986. Specials: *Don Johnson's Heartbeat,* HBO, 1987.

PRINCIPAL CONCERT APPEARANCES—Grand Ole Opry, Nashville; Universal Amphitheatre, Los Angeles; Farm Aid I, 1985, Farm Aid II, 1986, Farm Aid III, 1987; numerous concerts and tours with his band, "Willie Nelson and Family," U.S. and international cities.

RELATED CAREER—Bass player with Ray Price Band.

NON-RELATED CAREER—Formerly a salesman.

WRITINGS: SONGS—"Crazy" (recorded by Patsy Cline), Decca, 1961; "Hello Fool" (recorded by Ralph Emory), Liberty, 1961; "Hello Walls" (recorded by Faron Young), Capitol, 1961; (with Faron Young) "Three Days" (recorded by Faron Young), Capitol, 1961; "Touch Me," Liberty, 1961; "Funny" (also known as "Funny How Time Slips Away"; recorded by Joe Hinton), Back Peat, 1964; "Healing Hands of Time," RCA Victor, 1964; "I'm Still Not Over You" (recorded by Ray Price), Decca, 1967; (with Waylon Jennings) "Good Hearted Woman" (recorded by Jennings), RCA, 1972; "On the Road Again," Columbia, 1980; "Angel Flying Too Close to the Ground," Columbia, 1981; "Opportunity to Cry" (recorded with Waylon Jennings in *Poncho and Lefty*), Epic, 1983; "Forgiving You Was Easy," Columbia, 1985; (with Merle Haggard and Freddy Powers) "A Place to Fall Apart" (recorded by Merle Haggard), Epic, 1985.

FILM SCORES—"On the Road Again," introduced in *Honeysuckle Rose,* Warner Brothers, 1980; *Red Headed Stranger,* Alive Film, 1987.

TELEVISION—Movies: Co-composer of musical score, *Stagecoach,* 1986.

RECORDINGS: ALBUMS—*One for the Road,* 1963; *Here's Willie Nelson,* 1963; *Shotgun Willie,* 1973; *Country Willie,* 1973; *Red Headed Stranger,* 1975; *The Troublemaker,* 1976; *Willie Nelson and His Friends,* 1976; *Willie Before His Time,* 1978; *Wanted: The Outlaws,* 1978; *The Willie Way,* 1978; *The Best of Willie Nelson,* 1978; *Stardust,* 1978; *Family Bible,* 1980; *Tougher Than Leather,* 1983; *City of New Orleans,* 1984; *Me and Paul* (with Johnny Cash, Kris Kristofferson and Waylon Jennings), Columbia, 1985; *The Highwayman,* Columbia, 1985; *The Promise Land,* 1986; *Partners,* 1986; *Island in the Sea,* 1987,

SONGS—Many original songs including: "Blue Eyes Crying in the Rain," Columbia, 1975; (with Waylon Jennings) "Mamas Don't Let Your Babies Grow Up to Be Cowboys," RCA, 1978; "Always on My Mind," Columbia, 1982; (with Julio Inglesias) "For All the Girls," 1984; (with Jennnings, Kristofferson, and Cash) "The Highwayman," Columbia, 1985; also "City of New Orleans";

"As Time Goes By"; "She's Gone"; "Pretend I Never Happened," others.

AWARDS: Best Single, Country Music Award, 1972, for "Good Hearted Woman"; Grammy Award nomination, 1975, for "Blue Eyes Crying in the Rain"; Top Album, Artists Award, *Billboard* magazine, 1976; Grammy Awards, 1978, for "Georgia on My Mind" and "Mamas Don't Let Your Babies Grow Up to Be Cowboys"; Best Album, Country Music Association Award, 1978 for *Wanted: The Outlaws;* Best Album, Grammy Award, 1984, for *City of New Orleans;* Best Vocal Duo, Country Music Association Award (with Julio Iglesias), 1984; Country Song of the Year, Grammy Award, 1985, for *The Highwayman.*

ADDRESSES: AGENT—c/o Jim Wiatt, International Creative Management, 8899 Beverly Blvd., Los Angeles, CA 90048. MANAGER—c/o Mark Rothbaum, P.O. Box 2689, Danbury, CT 06813.

*　　*　　*

NESMITH, Michael   1942-

PERSONAL: Born December 30, 1942, in Houston, TX; son of Warren and Bette Nesmith; first wife's name, Phyliss (marriage ended); second wife's name, Kathryn; children: Christian, Jonathan, Jessica. RELIGION: Christian Scientist. MILITARY: U.S. Air Force.

VOCATION: Musician, singer, producer, actor, and writer.

CAREER: PRINCIPAL TELEVISION APPEARANCES—Series: Mike, *The Monkees,* NBC, 1966-68. PRINCIPAL TELEVISION WORK—All as producer. Series: *Television Parts,* NBC, 1985. Pilots: *Poplips.*

PRINCIPAL FILM WORK—Executive producer: *Timerider,* Jensen Farley, 1983; *Repo Man,* Universal, 1984.

PRINCIPAL VIDEO WORK—Producer, *Elephant Parts.*

NON-RELATED CAREER—Gihon Foundation (trustee), McMurray Foundation (trustee).

WRITINGS: TELEPLAYS—Co-writer, *Poplips.*

SONGS—"The Girl I Knew Somewhere" (recorded with The Monkees), Colgems, 1967; "Tapioca Tundra" (recorded with The Monkees), Colgems, 1968; "Joanne," RCA, 1970; "Silver Moon," RCA, 1970; "Some of Shelly's Blues" (recorded by the Nitty Gritty Dirt Band), Liberty, 1971; others.

RECORDINGS: SINGLES—With The Monkees: "Last Train to Clarksville," Colgems, 1966; "I'm a Believer," Colgems, 1966; "Words," Colgems, 1967; others.

AWARDS: Video Grammy Award, for *Elephant Parts.*

ADDRESSES: MANAGER—Kragen & Company, 1112 N. Shelbourne Drive, Los Angeles, CA 90069.*

NETTLETON, John 1929-

PERSONAL: Born February 5, 1929, in London, England; son of Alfred and Dorothy (Pratt) Nettleton; married Deirdre Doone. EDUCATION: Attended St. Dunstan's College; trained for the stage at the Royal Academy of Dramatic Art.

VOCATION: Actor.

CAREER: LONDON DEBUT—*Snow White and the Seven Dwarfs,* St. James Theatre, 1951. PRINCIPAL STAGE APPEARANCES— Peasant, *The Burnt Flower Bed,* Arts Theatre, London, 1955; husband, *The Good Woman of Setzuan,* Royal Court Theatre, London, 1956; Lord Mulligan, *Camino Real,* Phoenix Theatre, London, 1957; Harry, *All Kinds of Men,* Arts Theatre, 1957; doctor, *Shadow of Heroes,* Piccadilly Theatre, London, 1958; Albert, *Rollo,* Strand Theatre, London, 1959; Mr. McBryde, *A Passage to India,* Comedy Theatre, London, 1960; Subtle, *The Alchemist,* Cambridge Theatre Company, Cambridge, U.K., 1970; headmaster, *A Voyage 'round My Father,* Greenwich Theatre, London, 1970; Dr. Kroll, *Rosmersholm,* Greenwich Theatre, 1973; Sicinius Velutus, *Coriolanus,* Aldwych Theatre, 1973; Agydus, *Tamburlaine the Great, Part I,* Sigismund, *Tamburlaine the Great, Part II,* both Olivier Theatre, London, 1976; Polonius, *Hamlet,* Old Vic Theatre, London, 1977; Serapion, *All for Love,* Lepidus, *Antony and Cleopatra,* both Old Vic Theatre, 1977; Lord Summerhays, *Misalliance,* Windsor Theatre, London, 1978; Fenwick, *Then and Now,* Hampstead Theatre Club, London, 1979; Roy Jenkins, *Anyone for Denis?,* Whitehall Theatre, London, 1981; also performed in repertory at Nottingham, U.K., 1955.

JOHN NETTLETON

All with the Royal Shakespeare Company: Mannoury, *The Devils,* Agamemnon, *Troilus and Cressida,* Gilbert Foliot, *Curtmantle,* all Aldwych Theatre, London, 1962; Bubnov, *The Lower Depths,* Arts Theatre, 1962; Snug, *A Midsummer Night's Dream,* Archbishop Orsenigo, *The Representative,* both Aldwych Theatre, 1963; Taffy, *Afore Night Come,* General Lonsegur, *Victor,* Barnadine, *The Jew of Malta,* Sir Hugh Evans, *The Merry Wives of Windsor,* and appeared in *The Hollow Crown,* all Aldwych Theatre, 1964; Fluellen, Archbishop of Canterbury, *Henry V,* Aldwych Theatre, 1965.

MAJOR TOURS—Aguecheek, *Twelfth Night,* Morocco, Duke, *The Merchant of Venice,* Elizabethan Theatre Company, U.K. cities, 1954; Oliver, *Me Times Me,* U.K. cities, 1972; Jaques, *As You Like It,* National Theatre Company, North American cities, 1974; Jim, *When the Wind Blows,* U.K. cities, 1984-85; also played small parts with the Royal Shakespeare Company's tour of New Zealand and Australian cities, 1953, and appeared in *The Hollow Crown,* Royal Shakespeare Company, U.K. and U.S. cities, 1964.

PRINCIPAL FILM APPEARANCES—*A Man for All Seasons,* Columbia, 1966; *Black Beauty,* Paramount, 1971; also *And Soon the Darkness.*

PRINCIPAL TELEVISION APPEARANCES—Series: *Yes, Prime Minister.* Movies: *A Perfect Spy.* Specials: *The Country Wife; Henry VII; The Tempest; East of Ipswich.*

SIDELIGHTS: FAVORITE ROLES—Jaques in *As You Like It;* Polonius in *Hamlet.* RECREATIONS—Listening to music, making bread.

ADDRESSES: OFFICE—24 The Avenue, St. Margaret's, Twickenham, Middlesex, England.

*   *   *

NEUBERGER, Jan 1953-

PERSONAL: Born January 21, 1953, in Amityville, NY; daughter of Frederick O. (a travel agent) and Jean Rose (Potts) Neuberger; married Randall Easterbrook, May 29, 1978 (divorced, 1986). EDUCATION: Attended American College, Paris, 1986; trained for the stage at the New York City Theatre Workshop with Gordon Duffi. POLITICS: Independent.

VOCATION: Actress.

CAREER: BROADWAY DEBUT—Hollywood Blonde, *Gypsy,* Winter Garden Theatre, 1974, for twenty-eight performances. PRINCIPAL STAGE APPEARANCES—Chuck Karel, *Chase a Rainbow,* Theatre Four, New York City, 1980; Joan, *Dames at Sea,* Syracuse Stage, Syracuse, NY, 1981; Bonnie, *Anything Goes,* Master Theatre, New York City, 1981; title role, *Peter Pan,* Playhouse in the Park, Cincinnati, OH, 1982; company member, *Forbidden Broadway,* Palsson's Supper Club, New York City, 1984, then 1985; also Sally Bowles, *Cabaret,* Virginia Museum Theatre, Richmond, VA; *Starting Here, Starting Now,* Walnut Street Theatre, Philadelphia, PA; and appeared in Off-Broadway productions of *Silk Stockings* and *A Little Madness.*

PRINCIPAL STAGE WORK—Choreographer, *Forbidden Broad-*

JAN NEUBERGER

way, Palsson's Supper Club, New York City, 1985; director, *Forbidden Broadway,* Washington, DC.

MAJOR TOURS—Minnie Fay, *Hello Dolly!,* U.S. cities, 1982.

ADDRESSES: AGENT—c/o Jim Wilhelm, Barry Douglas Talent, 1650 Broadway, New York, NY 10036.

*   *   *

NEWLEY, Anthony 1931-

PERSONAL: Full name, Anthony George Newley, born September 24, 1931, in London, England; son of George Anthony (a shipping clerk) and Frances Grace (Gardiner) Newley; married Anne E. Lynn (an actress), August 30, 1956 (divorced, 1963); married Joan Collins (an actress), May 27, 1963 (divorced, 1971); children: Tara Cynara, Alexander Anthony. EDUCATION: Trained for the stage with Dewsbury Repertory Company and Italia Conti. RELIGION: Jewish.

VOCATION: Actor, director, playwright, composer, lyricist, and singer.

CAREER: FILM DEBUT—Dusty Bates, *The Adventures of Dusty Bates,* Elstree, 1946. PRINCIPAL FILM APPEARANCES— Johnnie, *Little Ballerina,* Nettleford, 1947; Dick Bultitude, *Vice Versa,* Denham, 1948; Artful Dodger, *Oliver Twist,* Metro-Goldwyn-Mayer (MGM), 1948; Dudley, *Vote for Huggett,* Islington, 1949; Jimmy Knowles, *Don't Ever Leave Me,* Shepherds Bush, 1949;

Charley Ritchie, *A Boy, a Girl, and a Bike,* Shepherds Bush, 1949; Arab street urchin, *Golden Salamander,* Pinewood, 1950; dispensary assistant, *Madeleine,* Pinewood, 1950; wireless operator, *Highly Dangerous,* Ealing, 1950; Bob Twigg, *Those People Next Door,* Film Studios, 1952; Percy, *Top of the Form,* Pinwood, 1953; Bob, *The Weak and the Wicked,* Elstree, 1954; Tommy, *Up to His Neck,* Pinewood, 1954; Sparrow, *Blue Peter,* Beaconsfield, 1955; X-2 engineer, *Above Us the Waves,* Republic, 1956; marine clerk, *Cockleshell Heroes,* Columbia, 1956; Pedro, *Port Afrique,* MGM, 1956; Gaskin, *Last Man to Hang,* Columbia, 1956; Pvt. Spider Web, *X the Unknown,* Warner Brothers, 1956; *Battle of the River Plate,* Pinewood, 1956; Milbrau, *The Good Companions,* Elstree, 1957; Miguel, *Fire Down Below,* MGM, 1957; Edward, *How to Murder a Rich Uncle,* Columbia, 1958; Roger Endicott, *High Flight,* Columbia, 1958; Noakes, *No Time to Die,* Elstree, 1958; Ernest, *The Man Inside,* Columbia, 1958; Stokes, *The Bandit of Zhobe,* Columbia, 1959; Freddy, *The Lady Is a Square,* 1959; Jeep Jackson, *Idle on Parade,* Shepperton, 1959; Johnnie, *The Heart of a Man,* Pinewood, 1959; Hooky, *Killers of Kilimanjaro,* Columbia, 1960; Bert, *Jazz Boat,* Columbia, 1960; Dr. Newcombe, *In the Nick,* Borham Wood, 1960; Dicky, *Let's Get Married,* Elstree, 1960; Sammy, *The Small World of Sammy Lee,* Seven Arts, 1963; Matthew Mugg, *Doctor Doolittle,* Twentieth Century-Fox, 1967; Charlie Blake, *Sweet November,* Warner Brothers-Seven Arts, 1968; Heironymus Merkin, *Can Heironymus Merkin Ever Forget Mercy Humppe and Find True Happiness?,* Regional, 1969. Also Miles Minor, *The Guinea Pig,* 1948; *Task Force,* 1958; *Play It Cool,* Allied Artists, 1961; *Mr. Quilp,* AVCO-Embassy, 1975; *Old Dracula,* American International, 1975; *A Good Idea at the Time,* 1976; *Sammy Stops the World,* 1978.

PRINCIPAL FILM WORK—Producer and director, *Can Heironymus Merkin Ever Forget Mercy Humppe and Find True Happiness?,* Regional, 1969; director, *Summertree,* Columbia, 1971.

STAGE DEBUT—Gwynn, *The Wind of Heaven,* Colchester Repertory Theatre, Colchester, U.K., 1946. LONDON DEBUT—*Cranks,* New Watergate Theatre, 1956. BROADWAY DEBUT—*Cranks,* Bijou Theatre, 1956. PRINCIPAL STAGE APPEARANCES—Littlechap, *Stop the World, I Want to Get Off,* Queen's Theatre, London, 1961, then Shubert Theatre, New York City, 1962, later Ambassador Theatre, New York City, 1963; Cocky, *The Roar of the Greasepaint, the Smell of the Crowd,* Royal Theatre, Nottingham, U.K., 1964, then Shubert Theatre, New York City, 1965; Bubba, *The Good Old Bad Old Days,* Prince of Wales Theatre, London, 1972; title role, *Chaplin,* Dorothy Chandler Pavillion, Los Angeles, CA, 1983; also appeared in *Royalty Follies,* Royalty Theatre, London, 1974; *The World's Not Entirely to Blame; It's a Funny Old World We Live In;* and in concert with Henry Mancini at the Uris Theatre, New York City, 1974.

PRINCIPAL STAGE WORK—All as director; see production details above. *Cranks Revue; Stop the World, I Want to Get Off; The Roar of the Greasepaint, the Smell of the Crowd; The Good Old Bad Old Days; Chaplin.*

MAJOR TOURS—Peter Howard, *Lady of the House,* U.K. cities, 1953.

PRINCIPAL CABARET APPEARANCES—Caesar's Palace, Las Vegas, NV, 1969; Empire Room, Waldorf-Astoria, New York City, 1969; Harrah's Casino, Lake Tahoe, NV, 1970; (with Buddy Hackett) Fisher Theatre, Detroit, MI, 1971; (with Henry Mancini) Uris Theatre, New York City, 1974; (with Burt Bacharach) Westbury Music Fair, New York, 1976; and numerous other appearances.

PRINCIPAL TELEVISION APPEARANCES—Series: *Sammy,* 1958; *The Strange World of Gurney Glade,* 1960-61; *The Anthony Newley Show,* 1972. Movies: Wilson Mahoney, *Malibu,* ABC, 1983; Mad Hatter, *Alice in Wonderland,* CBS, 1985; Tommy T., *Blade in Hong Kong,* CBS, 1985; Victor Coles, *Outrage!,* CBS, 1986; Peacock, *Stagecoach,* CBS, 1986. Specials: *Lucky in London,* 1966; *Burt Bacharach!,* 1972; also *Sunday Night at the Palladium; Saturday Spectaculars.* Guest: *Vic Oliver show; Alfred Marks Show; Shirley Bassey Show; Music Shop; Tom Jones Show; Merv Griffin Show; Tonight Show, Hollywood Squares; Johnny Darling Show.* Also appeared on *Picture Parade; Focus on Youth; The Wharf Road Mob.*

NON-RELATED CAREER—Office boy in an insurance company, 1945.

WRITINGS: SONGS—"Tribute," 1963. With Leslie Bricusse: "Gonna Build a Mountain," "Lumbered," "Once in a Lifetime," "Someone Nice Like You," "This Dream," "Typically English," "What Kind of Fool Am I?," all 1961; "The Beautiful Land," "Feeling Good," "Goldfinger," "The Joker," "Look at That Face," "My First Love Song," "Sweet Beginning," "Who Can I Turn To (When Nobody Needs Me)?," "A Wonderful Day Like Today," all 1964; "The Candy Man," 1970.

PLAYS—See poduction details above. All with Leslie Bricusse unless indicated: *Stop the World, I Want to Get Off,* 1961; *The Roar of the Greasepaint, the Smell of the Crowd,* 1964; *The Good Old Bad Old Days,* 1972; (with John Taylor) *Royalty Follies,* 1974; (with Stanley Ralph Ross) *Chaplin,* 1983.

FILM SCORES—*Mr. Quilp,* AVCO-Embassy, 1975; *Willie Wonka and the Chocolate Factory,* Paramount, 1971.

SCREENPLAYS—*Can Heironymus Merkin Ever Forget Mercy Humppe and Find True Happiness?,* Regional, 1969.

AWARDS: Song of the Year, Grammy Award, Ivor Novello Award, Broadcast Music Inc. Award, all 1962, for "What Kind of Fool Am I?;" Best Original Screenplay, British Writers Guild Award, 1969, for *Can Heironymus Merkin Ever Forget Mercy Humppe and Find True Happiness?;* Las Vegas Male Musical Star of the Year award, 1972; also received gold records for "Goldfinger," "The Candy Man," and "What Kind of Fool Am I?."

MEMBER: British Actors' Equity Association, Actors' Equity Association, American Federation of Television and Radio Artists.

ADDRESSES: OFFICE—c/o Taralex Corporation, Suite 1101, 9255 Sunset Boulevard, Los Angeles, CA 90069.*

*   *   *

NEWMAN, David   1937-

PERSONAL: Born February 4, 1937, in New York, NY; son of Herman (a clothing manufacturer) and Rose (a bookkeeper; maiden name Spatz) Newman; married Leslie Harris England (a writer), June 2, 1958; children: Nathan, Catherine. EDUCATION: University of Michigan, B.A., 1958, M.A., 1959.

VOCATION: Writer and editor.

CAREER: PRINCIPAL FILM WORK—Writer (see below).

RELATED CAREER—Editor, *Esquire* magazine, 1960-64, contributing editor, 1964—.

WRITINGS: PLAYS, PRODUCED—*It's a Bird, It's a Plane, It's Superman,* Alvin Theatre, New York City, 1966; contributor, *Oh! Calcutta,* Eden Theatre, New York City, 1969, transferring to the Belasco Theatre, New York City, 1971, then to the Edison Theatre, New York City, 1976—.

SCREENPLAYS—(With Robert Benton) *Bonnie and Clyde,* Warner Brothers, 1967; (with Benton) *Hubba, Hubba,* 1968; (with Benton) *There Was a Crooked Man,* Warner Brothers, 1969; (with Benton and Buck Henry) *What's Up, Doc?,* Warner Brothers, 1971; (with Benton) *Bad Company,* Paramount, 1972; (with Benton, Mario Puzo, and Leslie Newman) *Superman,* Warner Brothers, 1978; (with Benton) *Stab,* 1981; (with Leslie Newman) *Superman II,* Warner Brothers, 1981; (with Frank Gilroy) *Jinxed,* Metro-Goldwyn-Mayer/United Artists (MGM/UA), 1982; (with Benton) *Still of the Night,* MGM/UA, 1982; (with Leslie Newman) *Superman III,* Warner Brothers, 1983; *Santa Claus: The Movie,* Tri-Star, 1985.

BOOKS—(With Robert Benton) *Extremism: A Non Book,* Viking, 1964.

PERIODICALS—(With Robert Benton) Co-author of column, "Man Talk," *Mademoiselle* magazine, 1964-74.

AWARDS: Avery Hopwood Fiction Award, University of Michigan, 1957, for short stories; Avery Hopwood Drama Award, University of Michigan, 1958, for three plays; Best Screenplay, Academy Award nomination, Best Drama, Writers Guild of America Award, Best Screenplay, New York Film Critics Award, and Best Screenplay, National Film Critics Award, all 1967, for *Bonnie and Clyde;* Best Comedy, Writers Guild of America Award, 1972, for *What's Up, Doc?*

ADDRESSES: AGENT—c/o Sam Cohn, International Creative Management, 40 W. 57th Street, New York, NY 10019. OFFICE—250 W. 57th Street, Room 1430, New York, NY 10019.*

*   *   *

NEWMAN, Edwin   1919-

PERSONAL: Full name, Edwin Harold Newman; born January 25, 1919, in New York, NY; son of Myron (a credit manager) and Rose (Parker) Newman; married Rigel Grell, August 14, 1944; children: Nancy Livia. EDUCATION: University of Wisconsin, B.A., 1940, Louisiana State University, graduate study, 1940-41. MILITARY: U.S. Navy, 1942-45.

VOCATION: Television news commentator, reporter, and writer.

CAREER: PRINCIPAL TELEVISION APPEARANCES—With NBC: Series—Host and reporter, *Edwin Newman Reporting,* 1960; anchorman, *This Is NBC News,* 1961—; news reporter and substitute host, *Today,* 1961—; moderator, *The Nation's Future,* 1961; *JFK Reports,* 1962; alternate moderator, *Meet the Press,* 1965—; host, *Speaking Freely,* WNBC-TV (New York City affiliate), 1967-76; host, *What's Happening to America?,* 1968; host, *Comment,* 1971-72; *Sports Journal,* 1980—. Episodic—Commentator, New York City, 1961-83; narrator, *Actuality Specials,* NBC, 1962; drama critic, WNBC-TV, New York City, 1965-71; critic-at-large, New York City, 1967-83. Specials—Moderator of the first Ford-Carter Television Debate, 1976; narrator: *Japan: East Is West,* 1961; *Orient Express,* 1964; *Who Shall Live?,* 1965; *Pensions: The Broken Promise,* 1972; *Violence in America,* 1977; *I Want It All Now,* 1978; *Spying for Uncle Sam,* 1978; *Oil and American Power,* 1979; *The Billionaire Hunts,* 1981; *Kids, Drugs, and Alcohol,* 1983; others. Guest: Host, *Saturday Night Live,* NBC.

PRINCIPAL TELEVISION WORK—With *NBC News:* Reporter, London bureau, 1952-56; bureau chief: London, 1956-57, Rome, 1957-58, Paris, 1958-61.

RELATED CAREER—Dictation writer, International News Service, Washington, DC, 1941; reporter, United Press, Washingtion, DC, 1941-42 and 1945-46; Washington, DC, bureau reporter, *PM,* New York City, 1946; reporter, Tufty News Bureau, Washington, DC, 1946-47; writer for evening news with Eric Sevareid, *CBS News,* Washington, DC, 1947-49; free-lance journalist and broadcaster in London, 1949-52.

NON-RELATED CAREER—Worked for the European Recovery Program, 1951-52.

WRITINGS: FICTION—*Sunday Punch* (novel), Houghton, 1979.

NON-FICTION—(Contributor) *Memo to JFK,* Putnam, 1961; (contributor) *The Best of Emphasis* (anthology), Newman Press, 1962; *Strictly Speaking: Will America Be the Death of English?* (also see below), Bobbs-Merrill, 1974; *A Civil Tongue* (also see below), Bobbs-Merrill, 1976; *Edwin Newman on Language: Strictly Speaking and A Civil Tongue,* Warner Paperback, 1980.

PERIODICALS—Contributor of articles to British and American periodicals, including *Harper's, Atlantic Monthly, Esquire, Punch, Progressive,* and *Listener.*

AWARDS: Overseas Press Club Award, 1961, for foreign news; Emmy Awards: 1966, 1967, 1970, 1972, 1973, 1974, and 1982, all for dramatic criticism and writing, and 1983, for *Kids, Drugs, and Alcohol;* Peabody Award, 1966; Boston Press Club Award, 1966; University of Wisconsin School of Journalism Award, 1967; San Francisco State University Award, 1970; Chevalier Legion of Honor, France, 1972; University of Missouri School of Journalism Award, 1975; also recipient of Headliners Award.

MEMBER: Association of Radio and Television News Analysts (president, 1966), American Federation of Television and Radio Artists.

SIDELIGHTS: By the time Edwin Newman retired from regular appearances on NBC television, his reporting career had spanned thirty-five countries and seven U.S. national political conventions.

ADDRESSES: HOME—New York, NY. OFFICE—NBC, 30 Rockefeller Plaza, New York, NY 10020.*

*   *   *

NEWTON-JOHN, Olivia   1948-

PERSONAL: Born September 26, 1948, in Cambridge, England; daughter of Brin (a Welsh university don) and Irene (Born) Newton-John; married Matt Lattanzi, 1984; children: Chloe.

VOCATION: Singer and actress.

CAREER: PRINCIPAL FILM APPEARANCES—*Grease,* Paramount, 1978; *Xanadu,* Universal, 1980; *Two of a Kind,* Twentieth Century-Fox, 1983.

PRINCIPAL TELEVISION APPEARANCES—Series: *It's Cliff Richard,* BBC.

PRINCIPAL CONCERT APPEARANCES—Numerous appearances, including at the Metropolitan Opera House, New York City.

NON-RELATED CAREER—Co-owner, *Koala Blue Boutique,* West Hollywood, CA.

RECORDINGS: SONGS—''Let Me Be There,'' MCA, 1974; ''If You Love Me (Let Me Know),'' MCA, 1974; ''I Honestly Love You,'' MCA, 1974; ''Have You Never Been Mellow,'' MCA, 1975; ''Come on Over,'' MCA, 1976; ''Don't Stop Believin','' MCA, 1976; ''Hopelessly Devoted to You,'' RSO, 1978; (with John Travolta) ''You're the One That I Want,'' RSO, 1978; (with the Electric Light Orchestra) ''Xanadu,'' MCA, 1980; ''Physical,'' MCA, 1981; ''Heart Attack,'' 1982; ''Soul Kiss,'' MCA, 1985; others.

ALBUMS—*Clearly Love, Come on Over, Don't Stop Believing, Have You Never Been Mellow, If You Love Me (Let Me Know), Let Me Be There, Making a Good Thing Better, Physical, Totally Hot, Soul Kiss.*

VIDEOS—*Let's Get Physical,* 1981; *Heart Attack,* 1982.

AWARDS: Created an Officer of the Order of the British Empire; Best British Girl Singer Award, 1971; Best Country Vocalist, Academy of Country Music Award, 1973, for ''Let Me Be There''; Country Music Association Awards, U.K., 1974 and 1975; Song of the Year, Grammy Award, 1974, for ''I Honestly Love You''; American Guild of Variety Artists Award, 1974; *Billboard* magazine Awards, 1974 and 1975; People's Choice Awards, 1974, 1976, and 1979; *Record World* Awards: 1974, 1975, 1976, and 1978; *Cashbox* Award, National Association of Retail Merchandisers, 1974-75; American Music Awards, 1974, 1975, and 1976; National Juke Box Award, 1980.

SIDELIGHTS: RECREATIONS—Horseback riding, song writing, cycling, astrology, conservation, and animals.

ADDRESSES: MANAGER—c/o Roger Davis Management, 3575 Cahuenga Blvd. West, Suite 580, Los Angeles, CA 90068.*

*   *   *

NORMINGTON, John   1937-

PERSONAL: Born January 28, 1937, in Dukinfield, England; son of John and Annie (Taylor) Normington. EDUCATION: Trained as an opera singer at the Northern School of Music.

VOCATION: Actor and director.

CAREER: STAGE DEBUT—Hopcroft Minor, *The Happiest Days of Your Life,* Oldham Repertory Theatre, Oldham, U.K., 1950. LONDON DEBUT—Jerry Lassiter, *Infanticide in the House of Fred*

Ginger, Arts Theatre, 1962. BROADWAY DEBUT—Sam, *The Homecoming,* Music Box Theatre, 1967. PRINCIPAL STAGE APPEARANCES—Gunner, *Misalliance,* Criterion Theatre, London, 1963; Feste, *Twelfth Night,* Commander, *The Houses by the Green,* both Royal Court Theatre, London, 1968; Harry, *On Such a Night,* Arnaud Theatre, Guildford, U.K., 1969; Adam Hepple, *Revenge,* Royal Court Theatre, 1969; Kenilworth, *The Happy Apple,* Apollo Theatre, London, 1970; Old Man, *History of a Poor Old Man,* Soho Poly Theatre, London, 1970; David, *Me Times Me,* Phoenix Theatre, Leicester, U.K., 1972; Father Vernon, *The Prodigal Daughter,* Theatre Royal, Brighton, U.K., 1974; George, *Taking Stock,* Royal Court Theatre, 1974; Muller, *Underground,* Forum Theatre, Billingham, U.K., 1974; Jaques, *As You Like It,* Nottingham Playhouse Theatre, then Edinburgh Festival, Edinburgh, Scotland, U.K., 1975; Parson, Napoleon, *The Fool,* Royal Court Theatre, 1975; Sainsbury, *Donkey's Years,* Theatre Royal, Bath, U.K., 1976; Jaques, *As You Like It,* Riverside Studio Theatre, London, 1976; Martin Jones, *German Skerries,* Bush Theatre, London, 1977; Dzershinsky, *State of Revolution,* National Theatre, London, 1977; W.H. Auden, *Letter to Lord Byron,* National Theatre, 1977; Etienne, *The Lady from Maxim's,* Lyttleton Theatre, London, 1977; Thomas, *Rooting,* Traverse Theatre, Edinburgh, Scotland, U.K., 1978; Jimmy, *Comings and Goings,* Hampstead Theatre Club, 1978; Touchstone, *As You Like It,* Olivier Theatre, London, 1979; Clarence, *Richard III,* Emperor Joseph II, *Amadeus,* both National Theatre, 1979. Also appeared in *Protest,* Lyttelton Theatre, 1980.

With the Royal Shakespeare Company, Stratford-on-Avon, U.K., and London: Mortimer, Simpcox, Young Clifford, *The Wars of the Roses,* 1963; Bardolph, *Henry IV, Parts I and II,* both 1964; Dean, Puntila, Sam, *The Homecoming,* Antipholus, *The Comedy of Errors,* Oblong Fitz Oblong, *The Thwarting of Baron Bolligrew,* all 1965; Glendower, Shallow, *Henry IV,* Osric, Player Queen, *Hamlet,* both 1966.

PRINCIPAL STAGE WORK—Director: *Rip,* Soho Theatre, London, 1973; *Hay Fever,* Summer Theatre, Southwold, U.K., 1973.

FILM DEBUT—*Inadmissible Evidence,* Paramount, 1968. PRINCIPAL FILM APPEARANCES—*Rollerball,* United Artists, 1975; *The Thirty-Nine Steps,* 1978.

PRINCIPAL TELEVISION APPEARANCES—Series: *Her Majesty's Pleasure.* Specials: *Will Shakespeare; The Chester Mystery Plays; John Vassall, Spy.*

SIDELIGHTS: FAVORITE ROLES—Feste in *Twelfth Night;* Martin Jones in *German Skerries.* RECREATIONS—Opera, travel (especially to the Greek islands).

ADDRESSES: HOME—66 Redcliffe Gardens, London SW10, England.*

*   *   *

NUREYEV, Rudolf   1938-

PERSONAL: Full name, Rudolf Hametovich Nureyev; born March 17, 1938, in Tartar, Ufa, Union of Soviet Socialist Republics (U.S.S.R.); defected to France, May, 1961; naturalized Austrian citizen in 1982. EDUCATION: Trained for the ballet at the Ufa and Leningrad Choreographic Schools.

VOCATION: Dancer, choreographer, ballet company executive, actor, and writer.

CAREER: STAGE DEBUT—Soloist with the Kirov Ballet, Leningrad, U.S.S.R., 1958. LONDON DEBUT—Solo dancer, *Giselle,* Royal Ballet, 1962. PRINCIPAL STAGE APPEARANCES—Solo dancer, Kirov Ballet, Leningrad, 1958-61; dancer, Grand Ballet du Marquis de Cuevas, Paris, 1961; dancer, Royal Ballet, London, 1962; Chicago Opera Ballet, IL, 1962; also danced in over eighty ballets, including nineteeth century classics and contemporary roles, performing in both classical and modern style; has appeared with twenty-five ballet companies, including: the American Ballet Theatre, the Australian Ballet, the Colon Theatre Ballet, the Deutsche Opera Ballet, Berlin, the Dutch National Ballet, the National Ballet of Canada, the Paris Opera Ballet, and the Royal Danish Ballet.

PRINCIPAL STAGE WORK—Choreographer: *La Bayadere,* 1963; *Raymonda,* 1964, revised, 1983; *Swan Lake,* 1964; *Tancredi,* 1966; *Sleeping Beauty,* 1966; *The Nutcracker,* 1967, revised, 1983; *Don Quixote,* 1970; *Romeo and Juliet,* 1977; *Manfred,* 1979; *The Tempest,* 1982; *The Nutcracker,* 1983; *Washington Square,* 1985.

TELEVISION DEBUT—Dancer, *Bell Telephone Hour,* NBC, 1962. PRINCIPAL TELEVISION APPEARANCES—Specials: *Julie Andrews Invitation to the Dance with Rudolf Nureyev.*

PRINCIPAL FILM APPEARANCES—*An Evening with the Royal Ballet,* 1963; *Romeo and Juliet,* Embassy, 1966; *The Bible,* Twentieth Century-Fox, 1966; *The Dancer,* 1970; *I Am a Dancer,* Thorn-EMI, 1972; *Don Quixote,* 1972; *Valentino,* 1977; *Exposed,* Metro-Goldwyn-Mayer/United Artists, 1983.

RELATED CAREER—Artistic director, Paris Opera Ballet, France, 1983—.

WRITINGS: BOOKS—*Nureyev: An Autobiography.*

ADDRESSES: OFFICE—Paris Opera Ballet, 8 Rue Scribe, Paris, F-75009, France.*

*   *   *

NYE, Carrie

PERSONAL Born in Mississippi; married Dick Cavett (a television personality). EDUCATION: Attended Stephens College and Yale University.

VOCATION: Actress.

CAREER: BROADWAY DEBUT—Inez, *A Second String,* Eugene O'Neill Theatre, 1960. PRINCIPAL STAGE APPEARANCES— Title role, *Ondine,* Equity Library Theatre, New York City, 1961; Tiffany Richards, *Mary, Mary,* Helen Hayes Theatre, New York City, 1962; Celia, *As You Like It,* Lady Macduff, *Macbeth,* Cressida, *Troilus and Cresida,* all American Shakespeare Festival, Stratford, CT, 1961; Regina Engstrand, *Ghosts,* Fourth Street Theatre, New York City, 1961; Cecily Cardew, *The Importance of Being Earnest,* Madison Avenue Playhouse, New York City, 1963; Regan, *King Lear,* Adriana, *The Comedy of Errors,* Cleopatra, *Caesar and Cleopatra,* all American Shakespeare Festival, 1963; Cassandra, *The Trojan Women,* Circle in the Square, New York City, 1963; Helen Walsingham, *Half a Sixpence,* Broadhurst Theatre, New York City, 1965; Ursula Bailey, *A Very Rich Woman,* Belasco Theatre, New York City, 1965; Vittoria Corombona, *The White Devil,* Circle in the Square, 1965; Lady Macbeth, *Macbeth,* American Shakespeare Festival, 1967; Margaret Ross-Hughes, *Home Fires,* Cort Theatre, New York City, 1969; Elinor of Aquitaine, *The Lion in Winter,* Studio Arena Theatre, Buffalo, NY, 1969; Thelma, *After Magritte,* Cynthia, *The Real Inspector Hound,* both Theatre Four, New York City, 1972; Blanche du Boise, *A Streetcar Named Desire,* Playhouse in the Park, Cincinnati, OH, 1973; Gilda, *Design for Living,* Goodman Theatre, Chicago, IL, 1976; Anna Petrovna, *Platonov,* Williamstown Theatre Festival, Williamstown, MA, 1977; Regina Giddens, *The Little Foxes,* Stage West, Springfield, MA, 1977; *No Time for Comedy,* McCarter Theatre, Princeton, NJ, 1979; Yelena, *Children of the Sun,* Williamstown Theatre Festival, 1979; Lorraine Sheldon, *The Man Who Came to Dinner,* Circle in the Square, 1980; *a/k/a Tennessee,* South Street Theatre, New York City, 1982; Lucy Ransdell, *The Wisteria Trees,* York Theatre Company, New York City, 1982; Angela Langtry, *Paducah,* American Place Theatre, New York City, 1985; *The Madwoman of Chaillot,* Mirror Theatre Company, Theatre of St. Peter's Church, New York City, 1986.

PRINCIPAL TELEVISION APPEARANCES—Mini-Series: Tallulah Bankhead, *Moviola: The Scarlett O'Hara War,* NBC, 1980. Movies: Diana Proctor, *Divorce His/Divorce Hers,* ABC, 1973; Nancy Baker, *The Users,* NBC, 1978.

ADDRESSES: OFFICE—c/o Actors' Equity Association, 165 W. 46th Street, New York, NY 10036.*

*   *   *

NYKVIST, Sven   1922-

PERSONAL: Full name, Sven Vilhelm Nykvist; born December 3, 1922, in Moheda, Sweden; son of Gustaf Nathanael and Gerda Emilia (Nilson) Nykvist; children: Carl-Gustaf. EDUCATION: Attended Stockholm Photographic School.

VOCATION: Cinematographer, director, and writer.

CAREER: PRINCIPAL FILM WORK—Cinematographer: *Sawdust and Tinsel,* Janus, 1953; *Karin Mansdotter,* 1954; *The Virgin Spring,* 1960; *Winter Light,* Janus, 1962; *The Silence,* Janus, 1964; *Loving Couples,* Prominent, 1966; *Persona,* Lopert, 1967; *Hour of the Wolf,* Lopert, 1968; *One Day in the Life of Ivan Denisovich,* Cinerama, 1971; *Cries and Whispers,* New World, 1973; *The Dove,* Paramount, 1974; *Black Moon,* Twentieth Century-Fox, 1975; *The Magic Flute,* Surrogate Releasing, 1975; *Monismania 1995,* 1975; *Scenes from a Marriage,* Cinema V, 1976; *Face to Face,* Paramount, 1976; *The Tenant,* Paramount, 1976; *The Serpent's Egg,* Paramount, 1978; *Pretty Baby,* Paramount, 1978; *One and One,* 1978; *King of the Gypsies,* Paramount, 1978; *Starting Over,* Paramount, 1979; *Autumn Sonata,* New World, 1979; *Hurricane,* Paramount, 1979; *Willie and Phil,* Twentieth Century-Fox, 1980; *The Postman Always Rings Twice,* Paramount, 1981; *Cannery Row,* Metro-Goldwyn-Mayer/United Artists (MGM/UA), 1982; *Star 80,* Warner Brothers, 1983; *Swann in Love,* Orion, 1983; *The Tragedy of Carmen,* Orion, 1983; also director, *The Man on the Island,* 1983; *Fanny and Alexander,* Embassy, 1983; *After the Rehearsal,* Triumph, 1984; *Agnes of God,* Columbia, 1985; *Dream Lover,* MGM/UA, 1985; *The Sacrifice,* 1986.

PRINCIPAL TELEVISION WORK—Movies: Cinematographer, *Nobody's Child,* CBS, 1986.

RELATED CAREER—Assistant cameraman, Stockholm, 1941-44; co-owner, Josephson-Nykvist Film Productions.

WRITINGS: BOOKS—*Resan Till Lambarene.*

AWARDS: Best Cinematography, Academy Awards, 1973, for *Cries and Whispers* and 1983, for *Fanny and Alexander;* French Academy Award (Caesar); Swedish Academy Award.

MEMBER: American Society of Cinematographers, Swedish Film Academy, Svenska Teaterforbundet.

ADDRESSES: OFFICE—Dove Films, 625 N. Michigan Avenue, Fifth Floor, Chicago, IL 60611. AGENT—Milton Forman, 10390 Wilshire Blvd., Los Angeles, CA 90024.*

O

O'BRIEN, Maureen   1943-

PERSONAL: Born June 29, 1943, in Liverpool, England; daughter of Leo and Eileen (Connolly) O'Brien; married Michael B. Moulds. EDUCATION: Trained for the stage at the Central School of Speech and Drama.

VOCATION: Actress and playwright.

CAREER: STAGE DEBUT—Lady Mortimer, *Henry IV, Part I,* Everyman Theatre, Liverpool, U.K., 1964. PRINCIPAL STAGE APPEARANCES—Beauty, *Beauty and the Beast,* Hampstead Theatre Club, London, 1965; Celia, *Volpone,* Garrick Theatre, London, 1967; Sibley Sweetland, *The Farmer's Wife,* Dorinda, *The Beaux' Stratagem,* both Chichester Festival, Chichester, U.K., 1967; Miranda, *The Tempest,* Gladys, *The Skin of Our Teeth,* both Chichester Festival, 1968; Isabelle, *Ring Around the Moon,* Haymarket Theatre, London, 1968; Portia, *The Merchant of Venice,* Imogen, *Cymbeline,* both Shakespeare Festival, Stratford, ON, Canada, 1970; Rana, *Arms and the Man,* Theatre Royal, Windsor, U.K., 1972; Emilia, *The Director of the Opera,* Chichester Festival, 1973; Nina, *The Seagull,* Chichester Festival, 1973, then Greenwich Theatre, London, 1974; girl, *Rape,* Basement Theatre, London, 1974; Molly, *The Iron Harp,* ICA Theatre, London, 1974; Vivie, *Mrs. Warren's Profession,* Crucible Theatre, Sheffield, U.K., 1975; young witch, *Woodpainting,* Young Vic Theatre, London, 1975; Rosalind, *As You Like It,* Crucible Theatre, 1976; Evelyn Daly, *Waters of the Moon,* Chichester Festival, 1977; Leontine, *13 Rue de l'Amour,* Ann, *Treats,* both Belgrade Theatre, Coventry, U.K., 1977; Beth, *Confession Fever,* King's Head Theatre, London, 1977; stepdaughter, *Six Characters in Search of an Author,* Belgrade Theatre, 1978; Levidulcia, *The Atheist's Tragedy,* Belgrade Theatre, 1979.

TELEVISION DEBUT—*Doctor Who,* 1965. PRINCIPAL TELEVISION APPEARANCES—Movies: *The Lost Boys; The Serpent Son.*

WRITINGS: PLAYS—*The Great Gobstopper Show,* 1977.

SIDELIGHTS: FAVORITE ROLES—Imogen in *Cymbeline;* Rosalind in *As You Like It.*

ADDRESSES: AGENT—William Morris Agency, 149 Wardour Street, London W1, England.*

*   *   *

O'DONNELL, Mary Eileen   1948-

PERSONAL: Born May 2, 1948; daughter of Harry Joseph (a wine and spirit merchant) and Mary Louise (a teacher and librarian; maiden name, Kane) O'Donnell. EDUCATION: Received B.A. from the State University of New York, Albany; trained for the stage at the Guildhall School of Music and Drama. POLITICS: Democrat. RELIGION: ''Roman Catholic/Unitarian.''

PERSONAL: Actress.

CAREER: OFF-BROADWAY DEBUT—Head of the control commission, *The Measures Taken,* New York Shakespeare Festival, Public Theatre, 1974, for thirty performances. PRINCIPAL STAGE APPEARANCES—Mistress Quickly, *Henry IV, Parts I and II,* Duchess of York, *Richard II,* Emer, *Cuchulain,* Nerissa, *Merchant of Venice,* La Meffraye, *Gilles De Rais,* Ismene, *Oedipus at Colonus,* Ismene, *Antigone,* Margaret, *Woyzeck,* governess, *Leonice and Lena,* all with the City Stage Company (CSC), New York City, 1980-81; Voice, *The Girl Who Ate Chicken Bones,* Soho Repertory Theatre, New York City, 1982; Madame Helvetius, *Balloon,* Amelia, *Wild Oats,* Mathurine, *Don Juan,* Amelia, *Ghost Sonata,*

MARY EILEEN O'DONNELL

259

Duchess of Vanholt, *Dr. Faustus,* all CSC, 1982-83; Marthe, witch, *Faust, Parts I and II,* morphine addict, *Big and Little,* Gertrude, *Hamlet,* all CSC, 1983-84; Sonya, *Uncle Vanya,* June, *The Killing of Sister George,* nymph of the grotto, *Love in the Country,* widow, *Mandrake,* all CSC, 1984; Mrs. Cratchit, *A Christmas Carol,* Pennsylvania Stage Company, Allentown, PA, 1984. Also appeared as Catherine, *Arms and the Man,* Helen Hobart, *Once in a Lifetime,* Dorina, *Tartuffe,* all Guildhall Theatre, London; Pele, *The Shining House,* Theatre of the Open Eye, New York City; appeared with Soho Repertory Theatre, 1977-84.

MAJOR TOURS—Singer, *The Chorus Angelorum of Pan America,* world tour, 1987.

TELEVISION DEBUT—Sister Margaret, *Search for Tomorrow,* CBS, 1978. PRINCIPAL TELEVISION APPEARANCES—Episodic: *Search for Tomorrow,* CBS; *Nurse,* CBS; *Seize the Day,* PBS.

RELATED CAREER—Associate, Guildhall School of Music and Drama.

AWARDS: Gold Medal Award, Guildhall School of Music and Drama, London, 1974; Outstanding Actress, *The Villager* Award, 1983, for *Balloon.*

MEMBER: Actors' Equity Association, Screen Actors Guild, American Federation of Television and Radio Artists, Society of British Fight Directors.

ADDRESSES: HOME—New York, NY. AGENT—Fifi Oscard Associates, 19 W. 44th Street, New York, NY 10036.

*   *   *

O'DONOVAN, Desmond   1933-

PERSONAL: Born February 2, 1933, in Burbage, England; son of Charles and Mary (Allen) O'Donovan. EDUCATION: Attended Stonyhurst College and Oxford University.

VOCATION: Director.

CAREER: FIRST STAGE WORK—Director, *The Tiger and the Horse,* Playhouse Theatre, Salisbury, U.K., 1961. FIRST LONDON STAGE WORK—Director, *A Cheap Bunch of Nice Flowers,* Arts Theatre, 1962. PRINCIPAL STAGE WORK— Director: *The Royal Hunt of the Sun,* Chichester Festival, Chichester, U.K., then Old Vic Theatre, London, both 1964; *Trelawny of the Wells,* Chichester Festival, then Old Vic Theatre, both 1965; *The Clandestine Marriage,* Chichester Festival, 1966; *Hamlet, The Tempest,* both St. John's Theatre, London, 1970. Also directed *Spring Awakening,* London, 1963; *The Sleepers' Den, Spring Awakening, Easter,* all London, 1965; *The Knack, Three Men for Colverton, The Lion and the Jewel,* all London, 1966; *The Duchess of Malfi,* New York City, 1966; *Chikamatzu Suicides, A View to the Common,* both London, 1967.

SIDELIGHTS: RECREATIONS—Talking.

ADDRESSES: HOME—29 Wandsworth Common, North Side, London SW18, England.*

O'HEARN, Robert   1921-

PERSONAL: Full name, Robert Raymond O'Hearn; born July 19, 1921, in Elkhart, IN; son of Robert Raymond, Sr. and Ella May (Stoldt) O'Hearn. EDUCATION: Indiana Univeristy, B.F.A., 1943; further studies at Art Students League, 1943-45.

VOCATION: Scenic designer.

CAREER: FIRST STAGE WORK—Scenic designer, *Shadow and Substance,* Brattle Theatre, Cambridge, MA, 1948; set designer at Brattle Theatre, 1948-52. FIRST NEW YORK STAGE WORK—Scenic designer, *The Relapse,* 1951. PRINCIPAL STAGE WORK—Assistant designer: *Kismet,* 1953, *Pajama Game,* 1955, *My Fair Lady,* 1956, *West Side Story,* 1958, all on Broadway. Scenic designer: *Love's Labour's Lost,* New York City, 1953; *Othello,* New York Shakespeare Festival, 1955; *The Apple Cart, Child of Fortune,* both New York City, 1956; *Troilus and Cressida,* Stratford, CT, 1961; *Kiss Me, Kate,* Los Angeles Civic Light Opera, 1964, then City Center Theatre, New York City, 1965; *La Sylphide,* American Ballet Theatre, New York City, 1964, then Italian Symphony, 1971; *Adam Cochrane,* New York City, 1964; *Porgy and Bess,* Vienna Volksoper, Austria, 1965, then Bregenzer Festspiele, Austria, 1971; *Otello,* Boston Opera, then Hamburg State Opera, West Germany, both 1967; *The Nutcracker,* San Francisco Ballet, 1967, then Los Angeles Ballet, 1979; *La Traviata,* Santa Fe Opera, 1968; *Rosalinda,* Los Angeles Civic Light Opera, 1968; *Tallis Fantasia,* New York City Ballet, 1969.

The Enchanted, Kennedy Center for the Performing Arts, Washington, DC, 1973; *The Mind with the Dirty Man,* Los Angeles, 1973; *Coppelia,* Ballet West, Salt Lake City, UT, 1974, then Pacific Northwest Ballet, Seattle, WA, 1978; *Carmen,* Strasbourg, France, 1974; *Swan Lake,* Strasbourg, France, 1975; *Die Meistersinger,* Karlsruhe, West Germany, 1975, then Chicago Lyric Opera, 1977; *Boris Godunov,* Strasbourg, France, 1976; *Girl of the Golden West,* Houston Opera, then Vienna Staatsoper, Austria, both 1976, later New York City Opera, 1977; *Der Rosenkavelier,* Karlsruhe, West Germany, 1976, then Canadian Opera Company, Toronto, ON, 1978; *Don Quixote,* Ballet West, Salt Lake City, UT, 1977; *Andrea Chenier,* New York City Opera, 1978; *The Taming of the Shrew,* Pennsylvania State University, College Park, PA, 1980; *West Side Story,* Bregenzer Festspiele, Austria, 1981, then Michigan Opera Theatre, Detroit, MI, 1985; *Pique Dame,* San Francisco Opera, 1982.

Production designer, all with the Metropolitan Opera Company, New York City: *L'Elisir d'Amore,* 1960; *Die Meistersinger,* 1962; *Aida,* 1963. Stage designer, all with the Metropolitan Opera Company: *Samson and Delila,* 1964; *Pique Dame,* 1965; *La Ventana, Die Frau Ohne Schatten,* both 1966; *Hansel and Gretel,* 1967; *Der Rosenkavelier,* 1969; *Parsifal,* 1970; *The Marriage of Figaro,* 1975; *Porgy and Bess,* 1985; also designed *Boris Godunov,* 1970, unproduced.

Stage designer, all with the Central City Opera House, Central City, CO: *Falstaff, The Marriage of Figaro, Gianni Schicci,* all 1972; *The Barber of Seville,* 1973; *A Midsummer Night's Dream,* 1974; *Scipio Africanus,* 1975.

Stage designer, all with the Miami Opera, Miami, FL: *The Pearl Fishers,* 1974; *Don Pasquale,* 1976; *Adriana Lecouvreur, La Boheme,* both 1978; *Die Fledermaus,* 1980; *Tosca,* 1981; *La Traviata,* 1982; *Lucia di Lammermoor,* 1984; *L'Italiana in Algeri,* 1985; also *Annie Get Your Gun, Carousel.*

Stage designer, all with Opera Colorado, Denver, CO: *Aida, Don Giovanni,* both 1986; *Samson and Delila, Manon Lescaut,* both 1987.

PRINCIPAL FILM WORK—Designer, *A Clerical Error,* 1955.

RELATED CAREER—Stage design teacher, Studio and Forum of Stage Design, New York City, 1968—.

MEMBER: United Scenic Artists; Costume Institute at the Metropolitan Museum of Art (visitors committee).

ADDRESSES: HOME—New York City.

*   *   *

O'NEIL, Colette

PERSONAL: Born Colette McCrossan, in Glasgow, Scotland; daughter of Neil and Mary (Ellis) McCrossan; married Michael Ellis.

VOCATION: Actress.

CAREER: STAGE DEBUT—Monica, *Mr. Kettle and Mrs. Moon,* Palace Court Theatre, Bournemouth, U.K., 1956. LONDON DEBUT—Anne Gascoyne, *Gay Landscape,* Royal Court Theatre, 1958. PRINCIPAL STAGE APPEARANCES—Mrs. Keegan, *Progress to the Park,* Stratford Theatre, London, 1960; May Becket, *Celebration,* Duchess Theatre, London, 1961; title role, *Hedda Gabler,* Pitlochry Theatre Festival, Pitlochry, U.K., 1963; Lady Bona, *Edward IV,* Duchess of Gloucester, *Henry VI,* both Royal Shakespeare Company, Stratford-on-Avon, U.K., 1964; Lady Percy, Doll Tearsheet, *Henry IV, Parts I and II,* both Mermaid Theatre, London, 1970; Anne Butley, *Butley,* Criterion Theatre, London, 1971; Josie, *A Pagan Place,* Royal Court Theatre, London, 1972; Lady Macbeth, *Macbeth,* Welsh National Theatre, Wales, U.K., 1975; Dora Strang, *Equus,* National Theatre Company, Albery Theatre, London, 1977; Constance, *The Autumn Garden,* Watford Palace Theatre, Watford, U.K., 1979; title role, *Candida,* Perth Festival, Perth, U.K., 1979; Marianne, *Close of Play,* National Theatre Company, Dublin, Ireland, 1979.

PRINCIPAL FILM APPEARANCES—*A Smashing Bird I Used to Know* (also known as *School for Unclaimed Girls*), 1969; also appeared in *Frankenstein Must Be Destroyed.*

PRINCIPAL TELEVISION APPEARANCES—*Blue Skies from Now On; Between the Covers; The Standard; The Spoils of War.*

ADDRESSES: AGENT—c/o Joy Jameson, Ltd., 7 W. Eaton Place Mews, London SW1, England.*

*   *   *

O'NEILL, Edward   1946-

PERSONAL: Born April 12, 1946, in Youngstown, OH; son of Edward Phillip (a truck driver) and Ruth Ann (a social worker; maiden name, Quinlan) O'Neill; married Cathy Rusoff (an actress) February 30, 1986. EDUCATION: Attended Ohio State University and Youngstown State University.

EDWARD O'NEILL

VOCATION: Actor.

CAREER: BROADWAY DEBUT—Paddy Klonski, *Knockout,* Helen Hayes Theatre, 1979, for one hundred fifty performances. PRINCIPAL STAGE APPEARANCES—Ferrovius, *Androcles and the Lion,* Hartford Stage Company, Hartford, CT, 1986; also appeared in *Lakeboat,* Long Wharf Theatre, New Haven, CT, 1983; *Elm Circle,* Playwright's Horizons, New York City, 1984; *Of Mice and Men,* Hartford Stage Company, 1984.

TELEVISION DEBUT—Pilot: Title role, *Popeye Doyle,* NBC, 1986. PRINCIPAL TELEVISION APPEARANCES—Episodic: ''Peter Gray Story,'' *Miami Vice,* NBC; ''Right to Die,'' *Spencer for Hire,* ABC. Series: Al Bundy, *Married . . . with Children,* Fox, 1987. Pilots: Ed, *The Day the Women Got Even,* NBC, 1980; Jay Brennan, *Farrell for the People,* NBC, 1982; Danny Buckner, *Braker,* ABC, 1985. Movies: Mack Shore, *When Your Lover Leaves,* NBC, 1983; Whitey Gray, *A Winner Never Quits,* ABC, 1986.

FILM DEBUT—Lieutenant Schreiber, *Cruising,* United Artists, 1980. PRINCIPAL FILM APPEARANCES—Terry, *Dogs of War,* Orion, 1981.

MEMBER: Actors' Equity Association, Screen Actors Guild, American Federation of Television and Radio Artists.

SIDELIGHTS: RECREATIONS—Handball, history, literature.

ADDRESSES: HOME—Pacific Palisades, CA. AGENT— International Creative Management, 8899 Beverly Boulevard, Los Angeles, CA 90048.

*   *   *

O'NEILL, Sheila   1930-

PERSONAL: Born May 5, 1930, in London, England; daughter of Reuen and Marie (Long) O'Neill; married Don Lawson. EDUCATION: Attended the Arts Education Trust; trained as a dancer with Madeleine Sharpe.

VOCATION: Actress, dancer, and choreographer.

CAREER: LONDON DEBUT—Chorus, *Song of Norway,* Palace Theatre, 1949. PRINCIPAL STAGE APPEARANCES—Dancer, *Brigadoon,* Her Majesty's Theatre, London, 1949; Yvonne Sorel, *Paint Your Wagon,* Her Majesty's Theatre, 1953; Fritzie, then title role, *Sweet Charity,* Prince of Wales Theatre, London, 1967; Sheila, *Applause,* Her Majesty's Theatre, 1972; Princess of Ababu, *Kismet,* Shaftesbury Theatre, London, 1978. Also appeared in *Jokers Wild,* Victoria Palace Theatre, London, 1954; *Kismet,* Prince's Theatre, London, 1957; *One over the Eight,* Duke of York's Theatre, London, 1961; *Six of One,* Adelphi Theatre, London, 1963; *Chaganog,* Vaudeville Theatre, London, 1964, then St. Martin's Theatre, London, 1965.

PRINCIPAL STAGE WORK—Choreographer: *Kiss Me Kate,* Coliseum Theatre, then Sadler's Wells Theatre, both London, 1970; *The Beggar's Opera,* Chichester Festival, Chichester, U.K., 1972;

SHEILA O'NEILL

South Pacific, Prince of Wales Theatre, London, 1988; also *Kismet,* Canada, 1985; *The King and I,* 1973; *Dad's Army,* 1975; *The Importance,* 1984; *The Comeback,* 1986; and productions at Coventry, Cambridge, Greenwich and Edinburgh, Scotland.

MAJOR TOURS—Choreographer, *The Pajama Game,* U.K. cities, 1974.

PRINCIPAL FILM APPEARANCES—*Half a Sixpence,* Paramount, 1968; also appeared in *Summer Holiday,* 1963.

PRINCIPAL TELEVISION WORK—Has appeared on over one hundred programs and served choreographer on many British shows.

SIDELIGHTS: FAVORITE ROLES—Charity in *Sweet Charity.* RECREATIONS—Listening to jazz.

ADDRESSES: MANAGER—Stella Richards Management, 42 Hazlebury Road, London SW6 2ND, England.

*   *   *

ORNBO, Robert   1931-

PERSONAL: Born September 13, 1931, in Hessle, England; son of Karl Gerhardt (a shipbroker) and Gwendoline Ciceley (Fenner) Ornbo; married Rose Harris (a production assistant), August 10, 1974; children: George Alexander, Sam Fenner. EDUCATION: Received B.S., economics, from Hull University.

VOCATION: Lighting designer.

CAREER: FIRST LONDON STAGE WORK—Lighting designer, *Urfaust,* 1959. FIRST NEW YORK STAGE WORK—Lighting designer, *Company,* Alvin Theatre, 1970. PRINCIPAL STAGE WORK—Lighting designer, all in London unless indicated: *England, Our England,* Princess Theatre, 1962; *Period of Adjustment,* Royal Court Theatre, 1962; *Escape from Eden,* Lyric Hammersmith Theatre, 1962; *Love of Three Oranges,* Sadler's Wells Theatre, 1963; *A Funny Thing Happened on the Way to the Forum,* Strand Theatre, 1963; *Creation Du Monde* (opera), Royal Opera House, 1963; *Scent of Flowers,* Duke of York's Theatre, 1964; *Julius Caesar,* Royal Court Theatre, 1964; *Wings of a Dove,* Haymarket Theatre, 1964; *Ride a Cock Horse,* Piccadilly Theatre, 1965; *Trelawny of the Wells,* National Theatre Company, Old Vic Theatre, 1965; *Spring Awakening,* Royal Court Theatre, 1965; *The Anniversary,* Duke of York's Theatre, 1966; *There's a Girl in My Soup,* Globe Theatre, 1966; *Macbeth,* Royal Court Theatre, 1966; *Relapse,* Royal Shakespeare Company (RSC), Aldwych Theatre, 1967; *Flip Side,* Apollo Theatre, 1967; *Tartuffe,* National Theatre Company, Old Vic Theatre, 1967; *Midsummer Marriage,* Royal Opera House, 1968; *As You Like It,* National Theatre Company, Old Vic Theatre, 1968; *40 Years On,* Apollo Theatre, 1968; *Pelleas and Melisande* (opera), Royal Opera House, 1969; *Back to Methuselah,* National Theatre Company, Old Vic Theatre, 1969; *The Ruling Class,* Piccadilly Theatre, 1969.

Lighting designer, all in London unless indicated: *The Merchant of Venice,* National Theatre Company, Old Vic Theatre, 1970; *Turco in Italia,* Glyndebourne Theatre, 1970; *Voyage 'round My Father,* Haymarket Theatre, 1971; *Anastasia,* Royal Opera House, 1971; *Oedipus Now,* Hampstead Theatre Club, 1972; *I and Albert,* Piccadilly Theatre, 1972; *Il Travatore* (opera), Orange, France,

ROBERT ORNBO

1972; *Tannhauser* (opera), Sydney Opera House, Sydney, Australia, 1973; *Hello Revue,* Cadono du Liban, Beirut, Lebanon, 1973; *Ring Cycle,* Coliseum Theatre, 1973; *Travesties,* RSC, Aldwych Theatre, 1974; *Say Goodnight to Grandma,* Birmingham Repertory Company, Birmingham, U.K., 1974; *Male of the Species,* Piccadilly Theatre, 1974; *The Gay Lord Quex,* RSC, Aldwych Theatre, 1975; *Dad's Army,* Shaftesbury Theatre, 1975; *Otello* (opera), Orange, France, 1975; *Military Tattoo,* Wolf Trap Festival, Washington, DC, 1976; *Midsummer Marriage,* Welsh National Opera, Cardiff, Wales, U.K., 1976; *Wild Oats,* RSC, Aldwych Theatre, 1976; *Cavaliera Rusticana* (opera), *Pagliacci* (opera), both Theatre de la Monnaie, Brussels, Belgium, 1977; *Spinechiller,* Duke of York's Theatre, 1977; *Country Matters,* 69 Theatre Company, Manchester, U.K., 1977; *Salome* (opera), L'Opera, Lyons, France, 1978; *Two Ronnies,* Palladium Theatre, 1978; *Brand,* National Theatre, Oslo, Norway, 1978; *Turandot* (opera), Orange, France, 1979; *Leyline,* London Contemporary Dance Company, 1979; *The Misanthrope,* Frefolksbuhne, Berlin, West Germany, 1979.

Lighting designer, all in London unless indicated: *Poppea* (opera), Welsh National Opera, 1980; *Half Life,* The Hague, Netherlands, 1980; *A Midsummer Night's Dream,* Ataturk Theatre, Istanbul, Turkey, 1980; *Bent,* Theatre de la Poche, Brussels, Belgium, 1981; *Der Rosenkavalier* (opera), Theatre Royal de la Monnaie, Brussels, Belgium, 1981; *Tattoo,* Edinburgh Castle, Edinburgh, Scotland, U.K., 1981; *A Midsummer Night's Dream,* Opera North, Leeds, U.K., 1982; *The King and I,* Stadsteater, Malmo, Sweden, 1982; *Royal Tournament,* Earls Court Theatre, 1982; *Heart of the Nation,* Horseguards Parade Grounds, 1983; *Pack of Lies,* Lyric Theatre, 1983; *Hard Shoulder,* Aldwych Theatre, 1983; *Top People,* Am-

bassadors Theatre, 1984; *Mr. Gillie,* Scottish Theatre Company, Edinburgh, Scotland, U.K., 1984; *Peter Pan,* Theatre Clywd, Edinburgh, Scotland, U.K., 1984; *Concert for the Queen Mother,* Albert Hall, London, 1985; *Hair,* Theatre Clywd, 1985; *Grand Military Concert,* Waldbuhne, Berlin, Germany, 1985; *Royal Tournament,* Earls Court Theatre, 1985; *Military Tatoo,* Edinburgh Castle, 1985; *The Heart of the Nation,* Horseguards Parade Grounds, 1985; *I'm Not Rappaport,* Apollo Theatre, 1986; *Berlin Tatoo,* Deutschland Halle, Berlin, West Germany, 1986; *Jane Eyre,* Chichester Festival, Chichester, U.K., 1986; *Magic Flute* (opera), Kent Opera, Kent, U.K., 1987; *The Seagull,* Norske Teater, Oslo, Norway, 1987; *My Fair Lady,* Malmo Stadsteater, Malmo, Sweden, 1987.

RELATED CAREER—Lecturer: Dramatic Institute, Stockholm, Sweden; National Theatre School, Oslo, Norway; National Theatre School, Helsinki, Finland; British Theatre Association, London; drama panel, Eastern Arts Association; assessment panel, British Arts Council.

AWARDS: Freedom Award, from the city of Orange, France, 1976.

MEMBER: British Association of Lighting Designers (chairor, 1986—), British Actors' Equity Association, United Scenic Artists of America.

ADDRESSES: HOME—4 Worlington Road, Milenhall, Suffolk 1P28 7DY, England. OFFICE—Theatre Projects, 14 Langley Street, London WC2H 9J6, England. AGENT—c/o Kenneth Cleveland, 34 Roland Gardens, London SW7 3PL, England.

*   *   *

OSBORNE, John   1929-

PERSONAL: Full name, John James Osborne; born December 12, 1929, in London, England; son of Thomas Godfrey (a commercial artist) and Nellie Beatrice (a barmaid; maiden name, Grove) Osborne; married Pamela Elizabeth Lane (an actress), 1951 (divorced, 1957); married Mary Ure (an actress), November 8, 1957 (divorced, 1963); married Penelope Gilliatt (a drama critic and novelist), May 24, 1963 (divorced 1967); married Jill Bennett (an actress), April 1968 (divorced); married Helen Dawson, 1978; children: Nolan Kate (third marriage).

VOCATION: Playwright and actor.

CAREER: STAGE DEBUT—Mr. Burrells, *No Room at the Inn,* Empire Theatre, Sheffield, U.K., 1948. LONDON DEBUT— Antonio, *Don Juan,* English Stage Company, Royal Court Theatre, London, 1956. PRINCIPAL STAGE APPEARANCES— Lionel, *The Death of Satan,* English Stage Company, Royal Court Theatre, London, 1956; Dr. Scavenger, custodian, aunt, *Cards of Indentity,* Lin To, *The Good Woman of Setzuan,* both English Stage Company, Royal Court Theatre, 1956; commissionnaire, *The Apollo de Bellac,* Donald Blake, *The Making of Moo,* both English Stage Company, Royal Court Theatre, 1957; Claude Hickett, *A Cuckoo in the Nest,* English Stage Company, Royal Court Theatre, 1964; also appeared in repertory at Leicester, Camberwich, Kidderminster, Derby, and Bridgewater.

PRINCIPAL STAGE WORK—Director, *Meals on Wheels,* Royal Court Theatre, London, 1965.

MAJOR TOURS—*No Room at the Inn,* U.K. cities, 1948.

PRINCIPAL FILM APPEARANCES—*First Love,* UMC Pictures, 1970; also appeared in *Flash Gordon,* 1980.

PRINCIPAL TELEVISION APPEARANCES—*The Parachute; First Night of Pygmalion.*

RELATED CAREER—Manager of a seaside resort theatrical company; founder, director, Woodfall Films, 1958—; director, Oscar Lewenstein Plays, Ltd., London, 1960—; writer, *Gas World, Miller,* both trade journals; tutor to juvenile actors; assistant stage manager.

WRITINGS: PLAYS—*The Devil Inside Him,* Huddersfield, U.K., 1950; (with Anthony Creighton) *Personal Enemy,* Harrogate, U.K., 1955; *Look Back in Anger,* London, 1956, then New York City, 1957, published by Criterion, 1957; *The Entertainer,* London, 1957, then New York City, 1958, published by Faber, 1957, and Criterion, 1958; (with Anthony Creighton) *Epitaph for George Dillon,* Oxford, U.K., 1957, then London, later New York City, both 1958, published by Criterion, 1958; *The World of Paul Slickey,* London, 1959, published by Faber, 1959, and Criterion, 1961; *A Subject of Scandal and Concern,* Nottingham, U.K., 1962, then New York City, 1965, published by Faber, 1961; *Luther,* London, 1961, then New York City, 1963, published by Dramatic Publishing, 1961; *Plays for England: The Blood of the Bambergs, Under Plain Cover,* both London, 1963, then New York City, 1965, published by Faber, 1963, and Criterion, 1964; *Inadmissible Evidence,* London, 1964, then New York City, 1965, published by Grove Press, 1965; *A Bond Honoured,* London, 1966, published by Faber, 1966; *A Patriot for Me,* London, 1965, then New York City, 1969, published by Faber, 1966, and Random House, 1970; *Time Present, The Hotel in Amsterdam,* both London, 1968, published by Faber, 1968; *West of Suez,* London, 1971, published by Faber, 1971; (adaptor) *Hedda Gabler,* London, 1972, published by Faber, 1972; *A Sense of Disenchantment,* London, 1972, published by Faber, 1973; *The End of Me Old Cigar,* London, 1975, published by Faber, 1975.

SCREENPLAYS—*Tom Jones,* Lopert, 1963, published as *Tom Jones: A Film Script,* by Faber, 1964, and Grove Press, 1965; *Look Back in Anger,* Warner Brothers, 1959; *The Entertainer,* Continental, 1960; *Inadmissible Evidence,* Paramount, 1968.

TELEPLAYS—*Billy Bunter,* 1952; *Robin Hood,* 1953; *A Matter of Scandal and Concern,* 1960; *The Right Prospectus,* 1970, published as *The Right Prospects: A Play for Television,* by Faber, 1970; *Very Like a Whale,* 1970, published by Faber, 1971; *The Hotel in Amsterdam,* 1971; *The Gifts of Friendship,* 1972, published by Faber, 1972; *Ms., or Jill and Jack,* 1974; *Almost a Vision,* 1976; *You're Not Watching Me, Mummy,* 1978; *Try a Little Tenderness,* 1978.

AWARDS: *Evening Standard* Award, 1956; New York Drama Critics Circle Award, 1958, for *Look Back in Anger;* Antoinette Perry Award, 1963, for *Luther;* Best Screenplay, Academy Award, 1963, for *Tom Jones; Evening Standard* Award, 1965, for *A Patriot for Me; Evening Standard* Award, 1968, for *The Hotel in Amsterdam;* honorary doctorate, Royal College of Art, London, 1970.

MEMBER: Writers' Guild of Great Britain, Royal Society of Arts, Saville Club, Garrick Club.

ADDRESSES: OFFICE—Woodfall Films, 27 Curson Street, Lon-

don W1, England. AGENT—c/o Margery Vosper, Ltd., Suite 8, 26 Charing Cross Road, London WC2H 0DG, England.*

*   *   *

OSTERHAGE, Jeffrey   1953-

PERSONAL: Born March, 12, 1953, in Columbus, IN; son of Bruce Henry (a sales manager) and Ruth Anna (Thomas) Osterhage; children: Parker Lee Buehler. EDUCATION: Western Michigan University, B.B.A., 1976.

VOCATION: Actor.

CAREER: TELEVISION DEBUT—Christopher Sumner, *True Grit—A Further Adventure,* ABC, 1978. PRINCIPAL TELEVISION APPEARANCES—Episodic: *Murder, She Wrote,* CBS; *Scarecrow and Mrs. King,* CBS; *Riptide,* NBC; *T.J. Hooker,* ABC; *Knight Rider,* NBC; *This Is the Life,* ABC. Pilots: John Golden, *The Legend of the Golden Gun,* NBC, 1979. Mini-Series: Tyrel Sackett, *Louis L'Amour's The Sacketts,* NBC, 1979; Jesse Traven, *Louis L'Amour's The Shadow Riders,* CBS, 1982. Also appeared in *The Texas Ranger.*

FILM DEBUT—*Sky Bandits,* Galaxy International, 1986. PRINCIPAL FILM APPEARANCES—*South of Reno; Buckeye; Dark before Dawn.*

MEMBER: Screen Actors Guild, American Federation of Television and Radio Artists.

JEFFREY OSTERHAGE

ADDRESSES: HOME—210 N. Cordova, Apartment D, Burbank, CA 91505. AGENT—The Artists Group, 1930 Century Park W., Los Angeles, CA 90067. PUBLICIST—Cassidy/Watson Public Relations, 1717 N. Vine, Hollywood, CA 90028.

*   *   *

OVERMYER, Eric   1951-

PERSONAL: Born September 25, 1951, in Boulder, CO; married Melissa Cooper, April 2, 1978 (divorced, 1987). EDUCATION: Reed College, B.A., 1976; also attended City University of New York; trained for the stage at the Asolo Conservatory Program, 1977. RELIGION: Buddhist.

VOCATION: Writer.

CAREER: Also see *WRITINGS* below.

RELATED CAREER—Literary Manager, Playwrights Horizons, New York City, 1981-85; television story editor, *Cheek to Cheek,* 1986-87. Also resident writer: Squaw Valley Writer's Conference for Poetry; Fine Arts Work Center for Poetry, Provincetown, MA; River Arts Repertory, Woodstock, NY.

WRITINGS: PLAYS—*Native Speech,* produced at the Actors Theatre, Los Angeles, CA, 1983-84, published by Broadway Play Publishing, and in *Wordplays 3,* Performing Artist Journal Publications; *On the Verge,* produced at Baltimore Center Stage, Baltimore, MD, 1987, published by Broadway Play Publishing; *In a Pig's Valise,* produced at Baltimore Center Stage. Also wrote *Hawker,* published in *Plays from New Dramatists,* Broadway Play Publishing; and *In Perpetuity throughout the Universe,* 1987.

SCREENPLAYS—(With Jim McConnell) *Nematodes!,* upcoming.

TELEPLAYS—Series: *St. Elsewhere,* NBC, 1985-86.

PERIODICALS, POETRY—*The Paris Review, Shankpainter.*

AWARDS: Le Comte Du Nouy Award for Playwriting, 1986; New York Foundation for the Arts Fellowship, 1986; McKnight Fellowship.

MEMBER: Writers Guild-East, Dramatists Guild.

ADDRESSES: HOME—c/o Cooper, 118 W. 27th Street, New York, NY 10001. AGENT—c/o George Lane, William Morris Agency, 1350 Avenue of the Americas, New York, NY 10019.

*   *   *

OWENS, Rochelle   1936-

PERSONAL: Born Rochelle Bass, April 2, 1936, in Brooklyn, NY; daughter of Maxwell and Molly (Adler) Bass; married George D. Economou (a university professor), June 17, 1962. EDUCATION: Trained for the stage at the Herbert Berghof Studios and the New School for Social Research. POLITICS: ''Variable.'' RELIGION: Jewish.

ROCHELLE OWENS

VOCATION: Playwright.

CAREER: Also see *WRITINGS* below.

RELATED CAREER—Playwrights Unit of the Actors Studio; New Dramatists Committee, New York Theatre Strategy.

WRITINGS: PLAYS—*The String Game,* Judson Poet's Theatre, New York City, 1965, published by Methuen, 1969; *Futz,* Tyrone Guthrie Workshop Theatre, Minneapolis, MN, 1965, then Cafe La Mama Theatre, New York City, 1966, published by Hawk's Well Press, 1962, and Methuen, 1969; *Istanbul,* Judson Poet's Theatre, 1968, then Actors Playhouse, New York City, 1971, published by Hawk's Well Press, 1968; *Homo,* Cafe La Mama Theatre, 1966, later Ambiance Theater, London, 1966, published by Hawk's Well Press, 1968; *Beclch,* Theatre for the Living Arts, Philadelphia, PA, then Gate Theatre, New York City, 1968, published by Hawk's Well Press, 1968; *Futz and What Came After,* produced in New York City, 1968, published by Random House, 1968; *The Karl Marx Play,* American Place Theatre, New York City, 1973, published by Dutton, 1974; *He Wants Shih,* produced in New York City, 1971, published by Dutton, 1974; *Emma Instigated Me,* produced in New York City, 1976, published in *Performance Arts Journal,* 1976; *The Widow and Me Colonel,* produced in New York City, 1977, published in *Best Short Plays, 1977,* by Crown, 1977; *Who Do You Want, Piere Vidal?,* Theatre for the New City, New York City, 1982; *Chucky's Hunch,* Harold Clurman Theatre, New York City, 1982.

SCREENPLAYS—*Futz,* Commonwealth United, 1969.

POETRY—*Not Be Essence That Cannot Be,* Trobar, 1961; *Salt and Core,* Black Sparrow Press, 1968; *I Am the Babe of Joseph Stalin's Daughter: Poems, 1961-71,* Kulchur Press, 1972; *Poems from Joe's Garage,* Wittenborn, 1973; *The Joe Eighty-Two Creation Poems,* Black Sparrow Press, 1974; *The Joe Chronicles II,* Black Sparrow Press, 1977; also *Shemuel,* 1979; *French Light,* 1984; *Constructs, Anthropoligists at a Dinner Party,* both 1985. Anthologies: *Four Young Lady Poets,* Totem-Corinth Press, 1962; *A Controversy of Poets,* Doubleday, 1965; *Technicians of the Sacred,* Doubleday, 1969; *Inside Outer Space,* Anchor Books, 1970.

RADIO PLAYS—*Sweet Potatoes,* 1977.

AWARDS: Obie Award from the *Village Voice,* 1968, for *Futz;* Rockefeller Office for Advanced Drama Research, 1965; Ford Grant, 1965; Creative Artists Public Service Award, 1966; Yale University Drama School award, 1968; Guggenheim Fellowship, 1971; National Endowment for the Arts Grant, 1974; Rockefeller Grant, 1975. Also received New York Drama Critics Circle Award.

MEMBER: Dramatists Guild, American Society of Composers, Authors, and Publishers, PEN.

ADDRESSES: HOME—606 W. 116th Street, No. 34, New York, NY 10027. AGENT—(New York) Elisabeth Marton, 96 Fifth Avenue, New York, NY 10011; (London) c/o Michael Imison, Dr. Jan Van Loewen, Ltd., 81-83 Shaftesbury Avenue, London W1V 8BX, England.

P

PAGE, Geraldine 1924-1987

OBITUARY NOTICE—See index for *CTFT* sketch: Full name Geraldine Sue Page; born November 22, 1924, in Kirksville, MO; died of a heart attack in New York City, June 13, 1987. Geraldine Page was widely acknowledged to be one of America's most gifted performers. Playwright Tennesee Williams, whose troubled heroines she often portrayed on stage and screen, described her as "the most disciplined and dedicated of actresses." In fact it was as the female lead in the 1952 Off-Broadway production of his *Summer and Smoke* that Page first won critical notice, after earlier appearances in summer stock and bit parts in New York shows. In 1953 she made her Broadway debut in *Midsummer* and, although the play received mixed reviews, Page's performance was cited with a Donaldson Award, a New York Critics Circle Award, and a Drama Desk Award. Page also received her first Academy Award nomination that year, as best supporting actress in *Hondo*. Her next film, *Summer and Smoke*, 1961, saw her recreate her Off-Broadway role and she was again nominated for an Academy Award, but it was not until her eighth nomination, for *The Trip to Bountiful*, 1985, that she finally won. In addition, Page received Emmy awards for her television work in *A Christmas Memory*, 1966, and *A Thanksgiving Visitor*, 1968, and continued to create memorable stage portrayals throughout her career in such plays as *Sweet Bird of Youth*, 1959, *Black Comedy* and *White Lies*, both 1967, *Absurd Person Singular*, 1974, *Agnes of God*, 1982, and *Blithe Spirit*, in which she was appearing at the time of her death. A great proponent of Off-Broadway and regional theatre, throughout her career Geraldine Page appeared with a number of repertory companies around the country.

OBITUARIES AND OTHER SOURCES: New York Times, June 15, 1987; *Variety,* June 17, 1987.

*   *   *

PAGETT, Nicola 1945-

PERSONAL: Born Nicola Scott, June 15, 1945, in Cairo, Egypt; daughter of Herbert Wyndham Fitzgerald and Barbara Joan (Black) Scott; married Graham Swannell. EDUCATION: Trained for the stage at the Royal Academy of Dramatic Art.

VOCATION: Actress.

CAREER: STAGE DEBUT—Title role, *Cornelia,* Connaught Theatre, Worthing, U.K., 1964. LONDON DEBUT—Nora Lambert, *A Boston Story,* Duchess Theatre, 1968. PRINCIPAL STAGE APPEAR-ANCES—Hermia, *A Midsummer Night's Dream,* Open Air Theatre, London, 1967; Blanche, *Widowers' Houses,* Nottingham Playhouse Theatre, Nottingham, U.K., 1969, then Royal Court Theatre, London, 1970; Celimene, *The Misanthrope,* Nottingham Playhouse Theatre, 1970; Elizabeth, *A Voyage 'round My Father,* Haymarket Theatre, London, 1971; *The Ride across Lake Constance,* Hampstead Theatre Club, London, 1973; Regina Engstrand, *Ghosts,* Masha, *The Seagull,* Ophelia, *Hamlet,* all Greenwich Theatre, London, 1974; Suzanne, *The Marriage of Figaro,* National Theatre Company, Old Vic Theatre, London, 1974; Justine, *A Family and a Fortune,* Apollo Theatre, London, 1975; Bella Manningham, *Gaslight,* Criterion Theatre, London, 1976; Stella, *Yahoo,* Queen's Theatre, London, 1976; Kate, *Old Times,* Henry Fonda Theatre, Los Angeles, CA, 1985. Also appeared with the Citizen's Repertory Theatre, Glasgow, Scotland, U.K.

MAJOR TOURS—Carmela, *La Contessa,* U.K. cities, 1965.

NICOLA PAGETT

PRINCIPAL FILM APPEARANCES—*There's a Girl in My Soup*, Columbia, 1970; *Oliver's Story*, Paramount, 1978; *Privates on Parade*, Orion, 1984; also appeared in *Anne of the Thousand Days*, 1970; *Operation Daybreak*, 1976.

PRINCIPAL TELEVISION APPEARANCES—Series: Elizabeth Bellamy, *Upstairs Downstairs*, PBS. Mini-Series: Adele Fairley, *A Woman of Substance*, syndicated, 1984; title role, "Anna Karenina," *Masterpiece Theatre*, PBS. Movies: Elizabeth Fanschawe, *Frankenstein: The True Story*, NBC, 1973. Also appeared in *The Sweeney; Aren't We All; Love Story*.

SIDELIGHTS: FAVORITE ROLES—Celimene in *The Misanthrope*. RECREATIONS—Gardening, cats, cooking.

ADDRESSES: AGENT—c/o James Sheikey, 15 Golden Square, London W1, England.

*   *   *

PALANCE, Jack   1920-

PERSONAL: Born Vladimir Palanuik (some sources say Walter Palanuik; also other versions) February 18, 1920, in Lattimer, PA. EDUCATION: Attended the University of North Carolina and Stanford University. MILITARY: U.S. Army Air Corps.

VOCATION: Actor.

CAREER: PRINCIPAL FILM APPEARANCES—*Panic in the Streets*, Twentieth Century-Fox, 1950; *The Halls of Montezuma*, 1950; *Sudden Fear*, RKO, 1952; *Second Chance*, RKO, 1953; *Flight to Tangiers*, 1953; Stark Wilson, *Shane*, Paramount, 1953; Jack the Ripper, *Man in the Attic*, 1953; *Sign of the Pagan*, Universal, 1954; *Silver Chalice*, Warner Brothers, 1955; *Kiss of Fire*, Universal, 1955; *The Big Knife*, United Artists, 1955; *I Died a Thousand Times*, Warner Brothers, 1955; *The Lonely Man*, Paramount, 1957; *The House of Numbers*, Metro-Goldwyn-Mayer (MGM), 1957; *Attack!*, United Artists, 1958; *Ten Seconds to Hell*, United Artists, 1959; *The Mongols*, 1961; *Warriors Five*, 1962; *Barabbas*, Columbia, 1962; *Contempt*, Embassy, 1963; *Once a Thief*, MGM, 1965; *The Professionals*, Columbia, 1966; *The Spy in the Green Hat*, MGM, 1966; *The Torture Garden*, 1967; *Kill a Dragon*, United Artists, 1967; *Justine: Le Disavventure della Virtu*, 1968; *They Came to Rob Las Vegas*, Warner Brothers/Seven Arts, 1969; *The Desperados*, Columbia, 1969; Castro, *Che!*, Twentieth Century-Fox, 1969; *Legion of the Damned*, 1969; *The McMasters*, Chevron, 1970; *Monte Walsh*, National General, 1970; *The Mercenary*, United Artists, 1970; *The Horsemen*, Columbia, 1971; *Chato's Land*, United Artists, 1972; *Te Deum*, 1973; *Oklahoma Crude*, Columbia, 1973; *Craze*, Warner Brothers, 1974; *The Four Deuces*, Thorn EMI, 1975; *The Diamond Mercenaries*, 1980; *Hawk the Slayer*, 1981; also *A Bullet for Rommel*.

PRINCIPAL TELEVISION APPEARANCES—Series: Johnny Slate, *The Greatest Show on Earth*, ABC, 1963-64; Lieutenant Alex Bronkov, *Bronk*, CBS, 1975-76; host, *Ripley's Believe It or Not*, NBC, 1982—. Episodic: "Last Chance," *The Web*, CBS, 1953; "Requiem for a Heavyweight," *Playhouse 90*, CBS, 1956; *Motorola TV Theatre*, ABC. Pilots: Lieutenant Alex Bronkov, *Bronk*, CBS, 1975. Movies: *Dr. Jekyll and Mr. Hyde*, 1972; *Dracula*, 1973; also *Welcome to Blood City*.

BROADWAY DEBUT—*Panic in the Streets*, 1950. PRINCIPAL STAGE APPEARANCES—*Night of 100 Stars II*, Radio City Music Hall, New York City, 1985; also appeared in *The Big Two, Temporary Island, The Vigil, A Streetcar Named Desire*, and *Darkness at Head*.

PRINCIPAL RADIO WORK—Writer, prior to acting career.

NON-RELATED CAREER—Former professional boxer.

AWARDS: *Theatre World* Award, 1950-51; Best Supporting Actor, Academy Award nomination, 1952, for *Sudden Fear;* Best Supporting Actor, Academy Award nomination, 1953, for *Shane;* Best Single Performance by an Actor, Emmy Award, 1957, for "Requiem for a Heavyweight," *Playhouse 90*.

SIDELIGHTS: CTFT learned that Jack Palance's renowned taut facial expressions are the result of extensive plastic surgery following severe burns during World War II.

ADDRESSES: OFFICE—P.O. Box 1933, Beverly Hills, CA 90213. AGENT—c/o Jim Shimier, David Shapira & Associates, Inc., 15301 Century Blvd., Suite 345, Sherman Oaks, CA 91403.*

*   *   *

PALEY, William S.   1901-

PERSONAL: Full name, William Samuel Paley; born September 28, 1901, in Chicago, IL; son of Samuel (an owner of a cigar

WILLIAM S. PALEY

business) and Goldie (Drell) Paley; married Dorothy Hart Hearst, May 11, 1932 (marriage ended); married Barbara Cushing Mortimer, July 28, 1947 (died, 1978); children: (first marriage) Jeffrey, Hillary; (second marriage) William Cushing, Kate Cushing; (stepchildren) Stanley Mortimer III, Amanda Ross. EDUCATION: Attended the University of Chicago, 1918-1919; University of Pennsylvania, B.S., 1922. MILITARY: U.S. Army, 1944-45.

VOCATION: Broadcasting and newspaper executive.

CAREER: President, Columbia Broadcasting System (CBS, Inc.; originally United Independent Broadcasters, a radio network, later also a television network), New York City, 1928-46, chairman of the board, 1946-83, consultant, 1983-86, chairman of the board, 1986—.

RELATED CAREER—Co-chairman, International *Herald Tribune,* Paris, France; founder and chairman of the board, Museum of Broadcasting, New York City, 1976.

NON-RELATED CAREER—Production director, Congress Cigar Company, Philadelphia, PA, 1922-28, vice-president, 1923-28, and secretary, 1925-28; director and partner, Whitcom Investment Company, 1983—. Also active in many civic and philanthropic organizations, including: Museum of Modern Art (trustee, 1937-68, president, 1968-72, chairman, 1972—); North Shore University Hospital (trustee, 1949-73, co-chairman, board of trustees 1954-73); Committee for White House Conference on Education, 1954-56; President's Materials Policy Committee (chairman, 1951-52); Resources for the Future (executive committee, 1952-69, chairman, 1966-69, honorary board of directors, 1969); Columbia University (life trustee, 1950-73, trustee emeritus, 1973—); Bedford-Stuyvesant D and S Corporation (founding member; also director, 1967-72); New York City Task Force on Urban Design (chairman, 1968-71); Committee on Critical Choices for America, 1973-77; Committee for Cultural Affairs, New York City, 1975-78; Federation of Jewish Philanthropies of New York (life trustee); president and director, William S. Paley Foundation and the Greenpark Foundation, Inc.

WRITINGS: As It Happened: A Memoir (autobiography), Doubleday, 1979.

AWARDS: Keynote Award, National Association of Broadcasters; George Foster Peabody Award, 1958 and 1961; Broadcast Pioneer Award; Concert Artists Guild Award, 1965; First Annual Governor's Award, Academy of Television Arts and Sciences (Emmy Award), 1978; Robert Eunson Distinguished Service Award, Association of Press Broadcasting; Gold Achievement Medal of the Poor Richard Club; Skowhegan Gertrude Vanderbilt Whitney Award; Gold Medal Award, National Planning Association; Medallion of Honor Award, City of New York; First Amendment Freedoms Award, Anti-Defamation League of B'nai B'rith; Legion of Merit; Medal of Merit; officer, Legion of Honor, France; Croix de Guerre with Palm, France; Commander of the Order of St. John of Jerusalem; Order of Merit, Italy.

Honorary L.L.D. degrees from Adelphi University, 1957, Bates College, 1963, University of Pennsylvania, 1968, Columbia University, 1975, Brown University, 1975, Pratt Institute, 1977, Dartmouth College, 1979; and L.H.D., Ithaca College, 1978.

MEMBER: River Club, Century Association, Metropolitan Club (Washington, DC), Turf and Field Club, National Golf Club, Links Golf Club, Deepdale Golf Club, Meadowbrook Club, Economic Club (New York City), Lyford Cay Club, Bucks Club.

SIDELIGHTS: Despite his advancing age, William S. Paley remains a primary helmsman of the Columbia Broadcasting System (CBS), the company he founded and ran for more than fifty years. Paley is arguably the single most important creator of network television as viewers know it today; under his guidance, CBS was the premier network throughout the first twenty years of television's reign as an entertainment medium. In an *Atlantic* profile of January, 1975, David Halberstam contended that Paley "was, in the savage, predatory world of network broadcasting, the best. . . . He achieved a power over American taste and wrought an effect on American culture and sociology that had never been envisioned before." Paley is more than an arbiter of national tastes, however—he is also an enormously successful businessman whose company's after-tax profits have exceeded $100 million every year since 1974. According to Harry F. Waters's March 5, 1979 *Newsweek* piece, Paley "purchased a floundering little New York-based radio network and, over the next half century, transformed it into a $3 billion-a-year communications colossus. He may have been handed the financial means, but Paley also brought to his ends a relentless competitive drive, a high roller's daring and an instinct for divining America's mass-cultural appetite." Waters concluded, "Paley [created] standards for broadcast journalism and entertainment that uplifted the entire face of television."

Most accounts of Paley's life suggest that he grew up in Philadelphia. Actually he was born and raised in Chicago and moved east with his family when he was in college. The son of a highly successful cigar marker, he was accustomed to wealth; some observers have claimed he indulges too much in good food, fine automobiles, and stylish clothing. Paley was an indifferent student, but he graduated from the Wharton School of Finance in 1922 and entered the family business as production chief. Within three years he had been promoted to advertising manager, vice-president, and secretary of the company. Paley was among the first businessmen to detect the potential of radio as an advertising medium. Radio commercials for "La Palina" cigars boosted sales of his product as early as 1924. In gratitude, Paley's father gave him slightly less than a half million dollars to buy the failing United Independent Broadcasters network that was based in New York City. In 1928 the twenty-six-year-old Paley was elected president of the company, which he renamed the Columbia Broadcasting System. In a *New York Times* magazine interview with Tony Schwartz, Paley remembered the confidence with which he attacked his new challenge: "At a very early age, I took it for granted that I would be rich and successful, so I was prepared for it and I was not the least bit embarrassed by it. I just thought that if I put my mind to something I'd accomplish it. I wasn't going to have to worry, because I was going to be my father's heir anyway. If the gamble with CBS hadn't worked out, my father had a very successful cigar business in Philadelphia that I could have gone back to."

Needless to say, Paley never returned to the cigar business. Establishing offices at 485 Madison Avenue, he and his associates began to innovate "in a major and entirely new field, one unbound by tradition, unhampered by bureaucracy," according to Robert Metz (*New York,* July 21, 1975). Metz added that under Paley's guidance, "CBS, the upstart network, became a contender." The company's growth was unimpeded by the Great Depression; Halberstam reported that gross earnings went from $1.4 million in 1928 to $28.7 million by 1937 and the number of affiliated stations increased sevenfold. This steady rise in revenues and influence continued into the war years, as American listeners tuned in for the frontline broadcasts of CBS journalist Edward R. Murrow. Paley stepped away from CBS during World War II in order to serve in Europe as a top radio propagandist under General Eisenhower. He returned to the network in 1946, determined to make it number one in the nation.

Paley's method of achieving his goal revolutionized radio and set the precedent for the nascent television industry: he put his network into the programming field. Until then, most radio shows were produced by advertising agencies or outside packagers for a specific product line being sold during commercial breaks. Paley hired a team to create and produce shows right at CBS, then sold commercial time during those shows to a variety of advertisers. The idea was controversial, but eventually the advertisers came to appreciate that CBS was bearing the costs of developing programs and they found other uses for their money. To cement his dominance over the entertainment field, Paley raided other networks and bought away their talent—most notably Jack Benny, Red Skelton, Amos 'n' Andy, and Burns and Allen. By the time television was ready for commercial broadcast, Paley had the most popular stars in the nation working for him and their transition to the visual medium was accomplished with ease. As CBS burst into the lead as a network, Paley began to concentrate more and more on programming. A few of his corporate acquisitions, including Hytron, a television manufacturer, and Holt, Rinehart and Winston publishers, were financial drains that eroded his confidence in his business acumen.

As he aged and CBS grew too large for any one person to participate knowledgeably in all its facets, Paley began to leave daily business operations to others while he poured his efforts into generating good Nielsen ratings, a measure of the network's audience size. In that realm he was both comfortable and extremely successful. The CBS program roster has included such standards as the *Ed Sullivan Show, Playhouse 90, Sixty Minutes, All in the Family, The Beverly Hillbillies,* and *M*A*S*H.* But Paley did not spend his time on the hits; he told Tony Schwartz, "I'd rather watch the [shows] that aren't working to figure out why." The network's program directors could expect frequent calls from the chairman on so fine a detail as why an actor wore a hat in a given scene. Mike Dann, a former programming chief, remembered that Paley was receptive to discussing problems. "You could call him at home at 11:30 at night and he'd always talk to you," Dann said.

This close involvement has brought Paley criticism as well as praise. Always a controversial figure in his field, Paley's reluctance to relinquish his corporate power keeps him one. In 1987, at the age of eighty-five, he was once again elected chairman of CBS after engineering the ouster of a fifth chief executive officer and heir apparent. Paley protests that his role in the company these days is that of an advisor, someone who "kibbitzes" and forces executives to look carefully at all decisions. But with his 1987 reinstatement, Paley became again the person who makes the final programming choices in an era that has seen CBS lose some of its ratings share. A widower, Paley claims to relish the opportunity to continue his pioneering career, possibly into his nineties. "I thought about death more when I was younger than I do now," he told Schwartz. As Waters noted in *Newsweek:* "William Paley could have gone into his father's business and, conceivably, someone else could have invented CBS. The cigar industry probably would not be drastically different from what it is today. But it is impossible to imagine anyone other than Paley exerting a greater influence over what the wired nation has seen and heard—or one whose exercise of that power has been, by and large, so salutary."

ADDRESSES: OFFICE—CBS, 51 W. 52nd Street, New York, NY 10019.*

*   *   *

PALIN, Michael   1943-

PERSONAL: Born May 5, 1943, in Sheffield, Yorkshire, England. EDUCATION: Attended Oxford University.

VOCATION: Actor, writer, and producer.

CAREER: PRINCIPAL TELEVISION APPEARANCES—Series: *Do Not Adjust Your Set,* London, 1968; *Monty Python's Flying Circus,* BBC, 1969-74, broadcast in the United States on PBS, 1974-82; *Ripping Yarns,* 1976-77. Episodic: *The Marty Feldman Comedy Machine,* ABC, 1972; *Saturday Night Live,* NBC. Movies: *Pythons in Deutschland,* Bavaria Atelier, 1971; also *How to Irritate People* and *Secrets.*

PRINCIPAL TELEVISION WORK—Writer (see below).

PRINCIPAL FILM APPEARANCES—*And Now for Something Completely Different,* Columbia, 1972; *Monty Python and the Holy Grail,* Cinema V, 1975; *Jabberwocky,* Cinema V, 1977; *Monty Python's Life of Brian,* Warner Brothers, 1979; *Time Bandits,* AVCO-Embassy, 1981; *Monty Python Live at the Hollywood Bowl,* Columbia, 1982; *The Secret Policeman's Other Ball,* Amnesty International, 1982; *The Missionary,* Columbia, 1982; *Monty Python's The Meaning of Life,* Universal, 1983; *Brazil,* Universal, 1985; *A Private Function,* Island Alive, 1985.

PRINCIPAL FILM WORK—Writer (see below); also producer, *The Missionary,* Columbia, 1982.

PRINCIPAL STAGE APPEARANCES—*Monty Python Live at the Hollywood Bowl,* Los Angeles, 1970; *Monty Python Live!,* New York City, 1976.

MAJOR TOURS—With Monty Python, various concert tours, U.S., U.K., and Canadian cities, 1970s.

WRITINGS: SCREENPLAYS—(With Graham Chapman, John Cleese, Terry Gilliam, Terry Jones, and Eric Idle:) *And Now for Something Completely Different,* Columbia, 1972; *Monty Python and the Holy Grail,* Cinema V, 1975; *Monty Python's Life of Brian,* Warner Brothers, 1979; *Monty Python Live at the Hollywood Bowl,* Columbia, 1982; *Monty Python's The Meaning of Life,* Universal, 1983; (with Gilliam) *Time Bandits,* AVCO-Embassy, 1981; *The Missionary,* Columbia, 1982.

TELEVISION—Series: *The Frost Report,* London, 1965; (with Chapman, Cleese, Jones, and Idle) *Do Not Adjust Your Set,* BBC, 1968; (with Chapman, Cleese, Gilliam, Jones, and Idle) *Monty Python's Flying Circus,* BBC, 1969-74, broadcast in the United States on PBS, 1974-82; (with Jones) *Ripping Yarns,* PBS, 1979. Movies: (With Chapman, Cleese, Gilliam, Jones, and Idle) *Pythons in Deutschland,* Bavaria Atelier, 1971.

BOOKS—(With Chapman, Cleese, Gilliam, Jones, and Idle:) *Monty Python's Big Red Book,* Methuen, 1972; (with Chapman, Cleese, Jerry Gillian [pseudonym of Gilliam], Jones, and Idle) *The Brand New Monty Python Bok,* Methuen, 1973, later published as

The Brand New Monty Python Paperbok, Methuen, 1974; *Monty Python and the Holy Grail,* Methuen, 1977, also published as *Monty Python's Second Film: A First Draft,* Methuen, 1977; *Monty Python's Life of Brian (of Nazareth)* [and] *Montyphythonscrapbook,* Grosset, 1977; *The Complete Works of Shakespeare and Monty Python* (contains *Monty Python's Big Red Book* and *The Brand New Monty Python Paperbok*), Methuen, 1981; *Monty Python's The Meaning of Life,* Methuen, 1983.

(With Jones:) *Bert Fegg's Nasty Book for Boys and Girls,* Methuen, 1974, also published as *Dr. Fegg's Nasty Book of Knowledge,* Berkley; *Ripping Yarns* (stories adapted from the television series [also see above]; contains "Tomkinson's Schooldays," "Across the Andes by Frog," "Murder at Moorstones Manor," "The Testing of Eric Olthwaite," "Escape from Stalag Luft 112B," and "The Curse of the Claw"), Metheun, 1978, Pantheon, 1979; *More Ripping Yarns* (from the television series; contains "Whinfrey's Last Case," "Golden Gordon," and "Roger of the Raj") Methuen, 1980, Pantheon, 1981; *Dr. Fegg's Encyclopedia of All World Knowledge,* Bedrick Books, 1985; (with Gilliam) *Time Bandits: The Movie Script,* Doubleday, 1981.

The Mirrorstone: A Ghost Story with Holograms (children's), Knopf, 1986.

RECORDINGS: ALBUMS—(With Chapman, Cleese, Gilliam, Jones, and Idle) *Monty Python's Flying Circus,* BBC Records, 1969; *Another Monty Python Record,* Charisma, 1970; *Monty Python's Previous Record,* Charisma, 1972; *Monty Python's Matching Tie and Handkerchief,* Charisma, 1973, Arista, 1975; *Monty Python Live at Drury Lane,* Charisma, 1974; *The Album of the Soundtrack of the Trailer of the Film "Monty Python and the Holy Grail,"* Arista, 1975; *Monty Python Live at City Center,* Arista, 1976; *Monty Python's Instant Record Collection,* Charisma, 1977; *Monty Python's Life of Brian,* Warner Brothers, 1979; *Monty Python's Contractual Obligation Album,* Arista, 1980; *Monty Python's The Meaning of Life,* CBS Records, 1983.

AWARDS: Best Comedy Show, Press Critics of Great Britain Award, 1977, for *Ripping Yarns;* co-winner, Golden Palm Award, Cannes Film Festival, 1983, for *Monty Python's The Meaning of Life.*

ADDRESSES: OFFICE—Handmade Films, 26 Cadogan Square, London, SW1, England.*

*   *   *

PANTOLIANO, Joe   1951-

PERSONAL: Born in 1951, in Hoboken, NJ.

VOCATION: Actor.

CAREER: PRINCIPAL STAGE APPEARANCES—Tommy MacMillan, *Brothers,* South Coast Repertory Theatre, Costa Mesa, CA, 1982; Phillip, *Orphans,* Matrix Theatre, Los Angeles, CA, 1983; also appeared in *One Flew over the Cuckoo's Nest,* South Coast Repertory Theatre; *Italian American Reconciliation,* Gnu Theatre; and Off-Broadway in *The Death Star* and *Visions of Kerouac.*

PRINCIPAL FILM APPEARANCES—Pimp, *Risky Business,* Warner Brothers, 1983; Bob Keene, *La Bamba,* Columbia 1987; Frank, *Empire of the Sun,* Warner Brothers, 1987; also appeared in *The Godfather, Part II,* Paramount, 1974; *The Idol Maker,* United

JOE PANTOLIANO

Artists, 1980; *Monsignor,* Twentieth Century-Fox, 1982; *Eddie and the Cruisers,* AVCO-Embassy, 1983; *The Mean Season,* Orion, 1985; *Goonies,* Warner Brothers, 1985; *Running Scared,* Metro-Goldwyn-Mayer/United Artists, 1986; *The In Crowd, The Squeeze, Scenes from the Goldmine,* all 1987; and as Sy Swertlow, *Amazon Women from Outer Space,* 1987.

PRINCIPAL TELEVISION APPEARANCES—Episodic: *Amazing Stories,* NBC; *Hart to Hart,* ABC; *Hill Street Blues,* NBC; *Simon & Simon,* CBS. Pilots: *LA Law,* NBC, 1987; also appeared in *McNamara's Band; Free Country.* Mini-Series: Angelo Maggio, *From Here to Eternity,* NBC, 1979; Roy Cohen, *Robert Kennedy and His Times,* CBS, 1985. Movies: Ralphie, *More Than Friends,* ABC, 1978; Ray Neal, *Alcatraz: The Whole Shocking Story,* NBC, 1980; Lieutenant Amico, *Destination: America,* ABC, 1987. Specials: *Mr. Roberts,* NBC, 1984.

AWARDS: Drama Critics Circle nomination, 1983, for *Orphans.*

ADDRESSES: AGENT—Sumski, Green & Company, 8380 Melrose Avenue, Suite 200, Los Angeles, CA 90069.

*   *   *

PARE, Michael   1959-

PERSONAL: Born 1959, in Brooklyn, NY.

VOCATION: Actor and singer.

CAREER: FILM DEBUT—*Eddie and the Cruisers,* Embassy, 1983. PRINCIPAL FILM APPEARANCES—*The Philadelphia Experiment,* New World, 1984; *Streets of Fire,* Universal, 1984; Scott Youngblood, *Instant Justice,* Warner Brothers, 1987 (filmed in 1985).

PRINCIPAL TELEVISION APPEARANCES—Series: Tony Villicana, *The Greatest American Hero,* ABC, 1981-83; Sgt. LaFiamma, *Houston Knights,* CBS, 1987. Movies: Sgt. LaFiamma, *Houston Knights,* CBS, 1987.

ADDRESSES: PUBLICIST—Slade, Grant, Hartman & Hartman, 9145 Sunset Blvd., Suite 218, Los Angeles, CA 90069.*

*   *   *

PARKER, Alan   1944-

PERSONAL: Full name, Alan William Parker; born February 14, 1944, in London, England; son of William Leslie and Elsie Ellen Parker; married Annie Inglis, July 30, 1966; children: Lucy Kate, Alexander James, Jake William, Nathan Charles.

VOCATION: Director, writer, and film company executive.

CAREER: PRINCIPAL FILM WORK—Director: *Our Cissy,* 1973; *Footsteps,* 1973; *No Hard Feelings,* 1976; *Bugsy Malone,* Paramount, 1976; *Midnight Express,* Columbia, 1978; *Fame,* United Artists, 1980; *Shoot the Moon,* Metro-Goldwyn-Mayer/United Artists (MGM/UA), 1982; *Pink Floyd: The Wall,* MGM/UA, 1982; *Birdy,* Tri-Star, 1984; *Angel Heart,* Tri-Star, 1987.

ALAN PARKER

PRINCIPAL TELEVISION WORK—Movies: Director, *The Evacuees,* 1976.

RELATED CAREER—Advertising copywriter, 1966-69; director of television commercials, 1969-75; owner, Alan Parker Film Company, Buckinghamshire, England, 1970—.

WRITINGS: SCREENPLAYS—*Melody,* Levitt-Pickman, 1971; *No Hard Feelings,* 1972; *Our Cissy,* 1973; *Footsteps,* 1973; *Bugsy Malone,* Paramount, 1976; *Angel Heart,* Tri-Star, 1987.

FICTION—*Bugsy Malone,* 1975; *Puddles in the Lane,* 1977; *Hares in the Gate* (cartoons), 1983.

AWARDS: Best Screenplay, British Academy Award, 1976, for *Bugsy Malone;* British Academy Award, International Emmy Award, Press Guild U.K. Award, all 1976, for *The Evacuees;* Best Director, Academy Award nomination, Best Director, British Academy Award, both 1978, for *Midnight Express;* Grand Prix Special du Jury, Cannes Film Festival, 1985, for *Birdy;* Michael Balcon Award for Outstanding Contributions to British Film.

MEMBER: British Academy of Film and Television (member of council), Directors Guild of Great Britain (vice-chairor), Directors Guild of America, British Screen Advisory Council.

SIDELIGHTS: RECREATIONS—Cartooning.

ADDRESSES: AGENT—c/o Judy Scott-Fox, William Morris Agency, Inc., 151 El Camino Drive, Beverly Hills, CA 90212.

*   *   *

PARKER, Eleanor   1922-

PERSONAL: Born June 26, 1922, in Cedarville, OH.

VOCATION: Actress.

CAREER: FILM DEBUT—*They Died with Their Boots On,* Warner Brothers, 1941. PRINCIPAL FILM APPEARANCES—*Buses Roar,* 1942; *Mission to Moscow,* 1943; *Between Two Worlds,* 1944; *The Very Thought of You,* 1944; *Crime by Night,* 1944; *The Last Ride,* 1944; *Pride of the Marines,* 1945; *Never Say Goodbye,* 1946; Mildred, *Of Human Bondage,* Metro-Goldwyn-Mayer (MGM), 1946; *Escape Me Never,* 1947; *The Voice of the Turtle,* MGM, 1947; *Woman in White,* 1948; *Chain Lightning,* 1950; *Caged,* Warner Brothers, 1950; *Three Secrets,* 1950; *Valentino,* 1951; *Millionaire for Christy,* 1951; *Detective Story,* Paramount, 1951; *Scaramouche,* MGM, 1952; *Above and Beyond,* 1952; *Escape from Fort Bravo,* MGM, 1953; *The Naked Jungle,* 1954; *Valley of the Kings,* MGM, 1954; *Many Rivers to Cross,* MGM, 1955; *Interrupted Melody,* MGM, 1955; *The Man with the Golden Arm,* United Artists, 1956; *King and Four Queens,* United Artists, 1956; *Lizzie,* MGM, 1957; *The Seventh Sin,* MGM, 1957; *A Hole in the Head,* 1959; *Home from the Hill,* MGM, 1960; *Return to Peyton Place,* Twentieth Century-Fox, 1961; *Madison Avenue,* Twentieth Century-Fox, 1962; *The Sound of Music,* Twentieth Century-Fox, 1965; *The Oscar,* Embassy, 1966; *An American Dream,* Warner Brothers, 1966; *Warning Shot,* Paramount, 1967; *Il Tigre,* 1967; *How to Steal the World,* MGM, 1968; *The Eye of the Cat,* Universal, 1969; *Sunburn,* Paramount, 1979.

PRINCIPAL TELEVISION APPEARANCES—Series: Sylvia Caldwell, *Bracken's World*, NBC, 1969-70.

PRINCIPAL STAGE APPEARANCES—Appeared with the Cleveland Play Group, OH, and in summer stock at Martha's Vineyard, MA, and at the Pasadena Playhouse, CA.

AWARDS: Best Actress, Academy Award nominations, 1950, for *Caged*, 1951, for *Detective Story*, 1955, for *Interrupted Melody*.

MEMBER: Screen Actors Guild, American Federation of Television and Radio Artists.

ADDRESSES: AGENT—Smith-Freedman & Associates, 123 N. San Vicente Blvd., Beverly Hills, CA 90211; Contemporary Artists, 132 Lasky Drive, Beverly Hills, CA 90212.*

*   *   *

PARKS, Bert   1914-

PERSONAL: Born December 30, 1914, in Atlanta, GA; son of Aaron and Hattie (Spiegel) Jacobsen; married Annette Liebman, June 8, 1943; children: Jeffrey, Joel, Annette. EDUCATION: Attended Marist College, Atlanta, 1926-32. MILITARY: U.S. Army, 1942-45.

VOCATION: Emcee and announcer.

CAREER: PRINCIPAL TELEVISION APPEARANCES—Series: Emcee, *Party Line*, NBC, 1947; host, *Break the Bank*, ABC, NBC, and CBS, 1948-57; emcee, *Stop the Music*, ABC, 1949-56; emcee, *The Big Payoff* (daytime version), NBC, 1951; emcee, *Balance Your Budget*, CBS, 1952-53; emcee, *Double or Nothing*, NBC, 1953; emcee, *Two in Love*, CBS, 1954; emcee, *Giant Step*, CBS, 1956-57; emcee, *Hold That Note*, NBC, 1957; moderator, *Masquerade Party*, CBS and NBC, 1958-60; emcee, *Yours for a Song*, ABC, 1961-62; host, *Circus*, syndicated, 1971-73; host, *Strike It Rich*, CBS, 1973. Specials: Emcee, *The Miss America Beauty Pageant*, 1954-79.

PRINCIPAL RADIO WORK—Emcee: *Break the Bank; Stop the Music; Double or Nothing;* also announcer with a station in Atlanta and for Eddie Cantor; emcee for Xavier Cugat, New York City network station.

PRINCIPAL STAGE APPEARANCES—*Night of 100 Stars II*, Radio City Music Hall, New York City, 1985.

AWARDS: City of Hope Award, 1948; TV Forecast Award, 1950; Poor Richard Award, 1957; March of Dimes Man of the Year Award, 1963; Bronze Star Medal.

ADDRESSES: AGENT—c/o Dean Parker, Abrams-Rubaloff, 9012 Beverly Blvd., Los Angeles, CA 90048.*

*   *   *

PARKS, Hildy   1926-

PERSONAL: Full name, Hildy de Forrest Parks; born March 12, 1926, in Washington, DC; daughter of Steve McNeil (a high school

principal) and Cleo Lenore (a concert singer; maiden name, Scanland) Parks; married Sidney Morse (a talent representative), March, 1946 (divorced, 1949); married Jackie Cooper (an actor; divorced, 1951); married Alexander Cohen (a producer), February 24, 1956; children: (third marriage) Gerry, Christopher. EDUCATION: Mary Washington College, B.A., 1945; also attended the University of Virginia.

VOCATION: Actress, producer, and writer.

CAREER: STAGE DEBUT—Curley's wife, *Of Mice and Men*, Dramatic Workshop, New School for Social Research, New York City, 1945. BROADWAY DEBUT—Shari, *Bathsheba*, Ethel Barrymore Theatre, 1947. LONDON DEBUT—Lieutenant Ann Gerard, *Mister Roberts*, Coliseum Theatre, 1950. PRINCIPAL STAGE APPEARANCES—Girl, *Summer and Smoke*, Music Box Theatre, New York City, 1948; Joadie, *Magnolia Alley*, Mansfield Theatre, New York City, 1949; Alice, *To Dorothy, a Son*, John Golden Theatre, New York City, 1951; Gwendolyn Holly, *Be Your Age*, 48th Street Theatre, New York City, 1953; Alice Pepper, *The Tunnel of Love*, Royale Theatre, New York City, 1957. Also appeared in *The Time of Your Life*, Brussels World's Fair, Brussels, Belgium, 1958.

PRINCIPAL STAGE WORK—All as production associate unless indicated: *Baker Street, The Devils*, both Broadway Theatre, New York City, 1965; *Ivanov*, Shubert Theatre, New York City, 1966; *A Time for Singing*, Broadway Theatre, 1966; *Black Comedy, White Lies*, both Ethel Barrymore Theatre, New York City, 1967; *Little Murders*, Broadhurst Theatre, New York City, 1967; associate producer, *The Unknown Soldier and His Wife*, Vivian Beaumont Theatre, New York City, 1967; associate producer, *Dear World*, Mark Hellinger Theatre, New York City, 1969; *Home*, Morosco Theatre, New York City, 1970; *Prettybelle*, Shubert Theatre, Boston, MA, 1971; *Fun City*, Morosco Theatre, 1972; *6 Rms Riv Vu*, Helen Hayes Theatre, New York City, 1972; *Ulysses in Nighttown*, Winter Garden Theatre, New York City, 1974; *Who's Who in Hell*, Lunt-Fontanne Theatre, New York City, 1974; *We Interrupt This Program*, Ambassador Theatre, New York City, 1975; co-producer (with Alexander Cohen), *A Day in Hollywood/ A Night in the Ukraine*, John Golden Theatre, New York City, 1980; co-producer (with Cohen and Cynthia Wood), *84 Charing Cross Road*, Nederlander Theatre, New York City, 1982; co-producer (with Cohen), *Edmund Kean*, Brooks Atkinson Theatre, New York City, 1983; co-producer (with Cohen), *La Tragedie de Carmen*, Vivian Beaumont Theatre, 1983; co-producer (with Cohen), *Play Memory*, Longacre Theatre, New York City, 1983; co-producer (with Cohen), *Accidental Death of an Anarchist*, Belasco Theatre, New York City, 1984; co-producer (with Cohen), *Bright Lights*, Mark Hellinger Theatre, 1987. Also produced *The Unknown Soldier and His Wife*, London, 1973.

PRINCIPAL TELEVISION APPEARANCES—Episodic: *Studio One*, CBS; *Armstrong Circle Theatre*, NBC; *Philco Television Playhouse*, NBC; *Kraft Television Theatre*, NBC; *Danger*, CBS; *Suspense*, CBS; *The Web*, CBS. Series: Panelist, *Down You Go*, NBC, 1956; panelist, *To Tell the Truth*, CBS, 1956-57; also appeared in *Love of Life*, for five years.

PRINCIPAL TELEVISION WORK—Producer: *Antoinette Perry Award Show*, CBS, 1977-86; *Night of 100 Stars*, ABC, 1982; *Night of 100 Stars II*, ABC, 1985.

PRINCIPAL FILM APPEARANCES—*The Night Holds Terror*, Columbia, 1955; *Fail Safe*, Columbia, 1964; *The Group*, United Artists, 1966.

WRITINGS: TELEPLAYS—Specials: *Antoinette Perry Award Show,* CBS, 1967-86; *Emmy Awards,* 1978; *Night of 100 Stars,* ABC, 1982; *Parade of Stars Playing the Palace,* 1983; *Night of 100 Stars II,* ABC, 1985; *Emmy Awards,* 1985; *Emmy Awards,* 1986; *Happy Birthday Hollywood,* 1987; *CBS: On the Air (A Celebration of 50 Years),* CBS; *NBC 60th Anniversary Special,* NBC; *Ace Awards; William Shakespeare for Kids.*

AWARDS: (With Roy A. Somylo) Outstanding Program Achievement, Special Events, Emmy Award, 1980, for *The 34th Annual Tony Awards;* (with Somylo and Alexander Cohen) Outstanding Variety, Music, or Comedy Program, Emmy Award, 1982, for *Night of 100 Stars..*

MEMBER: Actors' Equity Association, Screen Actors Guild, American Federation of Television and Radio Artists, Writers Guild, Dramatists Guild; Manhattan Community Board #5, New York City Advisory Board for City Harvest.

ADDRESSES: OFFICE—225 W. 44th Street, New York, NY 10036.

*   *   *

PARRY, Chris   1952-

PERSONAL: Born May 23, 1952, in Manchester, England; son of Sydney (a journalist) and Kathleen (Pomfret) Parry; married Vivien Eadie; children: Richard Michael.

VOCATION: Lighting designer.

CAREER: PRINCIPAL STAGE WORK—Lighting designer: *Les Liaisons Dangereuses,* Royal Shakespeare Company (RSC), Stratford-on-Avon, U.K., then Barbican Theatre, London, later Music Box Theatre, New York City, all 1987; *Macbeth,* RSC, Barbican Theatre; *Flight* RSC, Stratford-on-Avon, U.K., then Barbican Theatre; *The Daughter-in-Law,* Birmingham Repertory Company, Birmingham, U.K.; *from the House of the Dead* (opera), Welsh National Opera, Cardiff, Wales, U.K.; *Il Pygmalioni* (opera), *L'occasione fa il Ladro* (opera), *Don Quixote in Sierra Morena* (opera), all Buxton Opera Festival, Buxton, U.K.; *Nicholas Nickleby,* RSC, Newcastle, U.K., then Manchester, U.K, later Los Angeles, CA; *Henry V, Twelfth Night, Henry VIII, Hamlet, Measure for Measure, Richard II,* all RSC, Newcastle, U.K., then London; *Carmen* (opera), Birmingham, U.K; *Dr. Jekyll and Mr. Hyde, Clouds, All My Sons, Pygmalion, Breezeblock Park, Blood Brothers, Funny Peculiar, Cinderella, Rookery Nook, The Oily Levantine, Relatively Speaking, Sisterly Feelings, Night and Day, Habeas Corpus, A Midsummer Night's Dream,* all Derby, U.K., then Nottingham, U.K.; *Rigoletto* (opera), New Opera Company.

MAJOR TOURS—Lighting designer: *Private Lives, Blithe Spirit, It Ain't Half Hot Mum,* all U.K. cities.

RELATED CAREER—Deputy Head of stage lighting, Royal Shakespeare Company.

AWARDS: Best Lighting Design, Antoinette Perry Award nomination, Most Outstanding Lighting, Drama Desk Award, both 1987, for *Les Liaisons Dangereuses.*

MEMBER: Association of Lighting Designers, Association of British Theatre Technicians.

ADDRESSES; AGENT—c/o Richard Haight, Performing Arts, One Hinde Street, London WC2, England.

*   *   *

PARTON, Dolly   1946-

PERSONAL: Full name, Dolly Rebecca Parton; born January 19, 1946, in Locust Ridge, TN; daughter of Robert Lee (a farmer) and Avie Lee (Owens) Parton; married Carl Dean, May 30, 1966.

VOCATION: Singer, composer, and actress.

CAREER: FILM DEBUT—*Nine to Five,* Twentieth Century-Fox, 1980. PRINCIPAL FILM APPEARANCES—*The Best Little Whorehouse in Texas,* Universal, 1982; *Rhinestone,* Twentieth Century-Fox, 1984.

PRINCIPAL TELEVISION APPEARANCES—Series: Hostess, *Dolly,* syndicated, 1976; *The Dolly Show,* ABC, 1987—. Specials: *Kenny and Dolly: A Christmas to Remember,* 1984. Guest: *Pop! Goes the Country,* syndicated; *The Barbara Mandrell and the Mandrell Sisters Show,* NBC; *Captain Kangaroo,* CBS; *The Porter Wagoner Show; The Cass Walker Program; The Bill Anderson Show; The Wilbur Brothers Show.*

PRINCIPAL VIDEO APPEARANCES—*Captain Kangaroo and His Friends,* Encyclopedia Britannica Educational, 1985.

PRINCIPAL RADIO WORK—*The Grand Ole Opry,* WSM, Nashville; *The Cass Walker Program,* Knoxville, TN.

PRINCIPAL CONCERT APPEARANCES—Numerous appearances, including at the Grand Ole Opry, Nashville; the Felt Forum, New York City, 1974; also Los Angeles, Oahu, HI, and others.

RELATED CAREER—Co-founder, Owepar Music Publishing Company, Nashville.

NON-RELATED CAREER—Owner, The Blue Indigo Club, Oahu, HI.

WRITINGS: SONGS—(With Bill Owens) "Put It Off Until Tomorrow," Combine Music, 1965; (with Dorothy Jo Hope) "Daddy Was an Old Time Preacher Man," RCA, 1970; "Joshua," RCA, 1970; "Coat of Many Colors," RCA, 1971; "I Will Always Love You," RCA, 1974; "Jolene," RCA, 1974; "To Daddy," Velvet Apple Music, 1976; "Two Doors Down," RCA, 1978; "Nine to Five," RCA, 1981; "Appalachian Memories," RCA, 1983; "Tennessee Homesick Blues," RCA, 1984; others.

RECORDINGS: ALBUMS—*Just Between You and Me,* 1968; *Here You Come Again,* 1977; *Burlap and Satin,* RCA, 1983; *Real Love,* RCA, 1986; *Just the Way I Am,* 1986; *Portrait,* 1986; also *Heartbreaker, Great Balls of Fire, The Best of Dolly Parton, Dolly Parton's Greatest Hits,* and (with Kenny Rogers) *Once Upon a Christmas.*

AWARDS: (With Porter Wagoner) Vocal Group of the Year Award, 1968; (with Porter Wagoner) Vocal Duo of the Year Award, All Country Music Association, 1970, 1971; Grammy Award nomination, 1974, for "I Will Always Love You"; Female Vocalist of the Year, 1975, 1976; Country Star of the Year, Sullivan Productions,

1977; Entertainer of the Year Award, Country Music Association, 1978; Female Vocalist of the Year, Grammy Award, 1978; Nashville Metronome Award, 1979; Best Song, Academy Award nomination, 1980, for *Nine to Five;* People's Choice Award, 1980; Female Vocalist of the Year, Academy of Country Music, 1980; Best Country Song and Song of the Year nomination, Grammy Awards, both 1981, for "Nine to Five"; Grammy Award nomination, 1983, for *Burlap and Satin;* American Music Award, 1984; Grammy Award nominatin, 1984, for "Tennessee Homesick Blues"; Dolly Parton Day Proclaimed, Sevier County, TN, October 7, 1967, Los Angeles, September 20, 1979.

ADDRESSES: AGENT—c/o Rick Nicita, Creative Artists Agency, 1888 Century Park E., Suite 1400, Los Angeles, CA 90067. MANAGER—Gallin, Morey, & Addis, 8730 Sunset Boulevard Penthouse West, Los Angeles, CA 90069. PUBLICIST—c/o Mac Newberry, Solters/Roskin/Friedman, 5455 Wilshire Boulevard, Suite 2200, Los Angeles, CA 90036.

*   *   *

PATRICK, Q.
See WHEELER, Hugh

*   *   *

PAULEY, Jane   1950-

PERSONAL: Full name, Margaret Jane Pauley; born October 31, 1950, in Indianapolis, IN; married Garry Trudeau (a cartoonist), 1980; children: Rachel and Ross (twins), Thomas. EDUCATION: Indiana University, B.A., political science, 1971.

VOCATION: Television journalist and host.

CAREER: PRINCIPAL TELEVISION APPEARANCES—Reporter, WISH-TV, Indianapolis, IN, 1972-75; co-anchor, *WMAQ News,* WMAQ-TV, Chicago, IL, 1975-76; co-host, *The Today Show,* NBC, 1976—; reporter, *NBC Nightly News,* 1980-82; co-anchor, *Early Today,* NBC, 1982-83; anchor for occasional *NBC White Paper* documentaries, including "Women, Work, and Babies: Can America Cope?," 1985, and "Divorce Is Changing America," 1986.

PRINCIPAL TELEVISION WORK—Writer, *NBC Nightly News,* 1980-82.

NON-RELATED CAREER—Worked in state politics in Indianapolis.

AWARDS: Honorary doctorate, DePauw University, 1978.

SIDELIGHTS: Jane Pauley's rise from local television reporter to replacement for Barbara Walters on network television's longest running morning news program, *The Today Show,* was rapid, but her acceptance among media critics was slower in coming. In 1972, with no experience in journalism or television, she landed a job as a reporter at the Indianapolis station WISH-TV. "Three years later," noted Joanmarie Kalter in *TV Guide* (August 18, 1984), "she became Chicago's first woman co-anchor of the nightly news." Pauley's exposure there brought her to the attention of the NBC team that was searching for a replacement for the departing

Walters; she was selected from a list of 250 candidates. At that time, related Jane Hall in the December 5, 1983 *People,* "Pauley was derided as a triumph of corn-fed style over experience-bred substance."

Tom Brokaw, Pauley's first co-anchor on *Today,* characterized her early years with the show in Sherryl Connelly's July 20, 1986 article in the New York *Daily News:* "She obviously did not have a lot of experience in interviews. . . . And she did not have a lot of experience in the world." But now, after more than a decade with *Today,* Pauley holds the distinction of having appeared on a morning news show longer than anyone else. "I've gained a reservoir of experience," she told Hall in an interview in *People* (October 27, 1986), "and I'm proud of my credibility." *Washington Post* television critic Tom Shales told Kalter, "[Pauley has] improved a lot over the years. . . . In those hours of the morning, we don't need interviewers who pummel people. I think she treads the line nicely between being rude and being easy."

In her tenure, Pauley has covered political conventions, the British royal weddings of Prince Charles and Lady Diana Spencer and Prince Andrew and Sarah Ferguson, as well as the funeral of Princess Grace of Monaco. She has gone on the road with the *Today* team, across the nation and to a number of foreign countries. Even her personal life has added a dimension to her role on the show. She has a two-career marriage to *Doonesbury* cartoonist Garry Trudeau, has worked through two on-air pregnancies, and now leads the life of a working mother. Her identification with issues confronting contemporary women made her the natural choice to anchor two *NBC White Paper* documentaries, "Women, Work, and Babies: Can America Cope?," broadcast in 1985, and "Divorce Is Changing America," which aired in 1986.

Since 1982 Pauley's partner on *Today* has been Bryant Gumbel; although they have slightly different roles and different approaches to the news, "They go together like bagels and cream cheese," wrote James Kelley in the June 24, 1985 *Time.* "Pauley displays a more empathetic style, laced with a self-deprecating wit," assessed Kelley, "that works best when she is discussing topics of high emotion." In a New York *Daily News* article published June 3, 1986, Kay Gardella maintained that Pauley's "ladylike presence, in contrast to Bryant Gumbel's more aggressive, take charge style, is one of the reasons 'Today' is leading the daytime pack." Her rapid rise and inexperience behind her, Pauley now speaks confidently of her place in television news. "Jane Pauley was a talk show hostess," she told Melba Tolliver in the November 8-10, 1985 issue of *USA Weekend.* "But I seem now to have outlived that. Now I am the grande dame of morning television and a journalist."

ADDRESSES: OFFICE—*Today Show,* NBC Television, 30 Rockefeller Plaza, New York, NY 10020.*

*   *   *

PAXTON, Bill   1955-

PERSONAL: Born May 17, 1955, in Fort Worth, TX; son of John Lane (a business executive) and Mary Lou (Gray) Paxton; married Louise Newbury. EDUCATION: Attended New York University; trained for the stage with Stella Adler and with Vincent Chase.

VOCATION: Actor, producer, director, and screenwriter.

BILL PAXTON

CAREER: FILM DEBUT—*Mortuary,* Hickmar Productions, 1981. PRINCIPAL FILM APPEARANCES—*Stripes,* Columbia, 1981; *The Lords of Discipline,* Paramount, 1982; *Streets of Fire,* Universal, 1983; *Impulse,* Twentieth Century-Fox, 1983; *Weird Science,* Universal, 1984; *Terminator,* Orion, 1984; *Commando,* Twentieth Century-Fox, 1985; *Aliens,* Twentieth Century-Fox, 1985. Also appeared in *Near Dark,* 1986; *Pass the Ammo,* 1987.

PRINCIPAL FILM WORK—Director, *Fish Heads* (theatrical short), 1982; producer, *Scoop* (theatrical short), 1983.

PRINCIPAL TELEVISION APPEARANCES—Episodic: *Miami Vice,* NBC, 1986. Series: *The Hitch Hiker,* HBO, 1986. Mini-Series: Billy Jo Bobb, *Fresno,* CBS, 1986. Movies: Eddie Fox, *Deadly Lessons,* ABC, 1983; Campbell, *The Atlanta Child Murders,* CBS, 1985; Bob Maracek, *An Early Frost,* NBC, 1985.

WRITINGS: SCREENPLAYS—Co-author, *Scoop* (theatrical short), 1983.

AWARDS: Special Award, Melbourne Film Festival, 1982, for *Fish Heads;* Honorable Mention, U.S.A. Film Festival, 1983, for *Scoop;* Best Supporting Actor, Saturn Award, Academy of Science Fiction, Fantasy, and Horror Films, 1986, for *Aliens.*

MEMBER: Screen Actors Guild.

ADDRESSES: AGENT—c/o Hildy Gottlieb, International Creative Management, 8899 Beverly Boulevard, Los Angeles, CA 90048.

PUBLICIST—c/o Carla Schalman, Rogers and Cowan, 10000 Santa Monica Boulevard, Los Angeles, CA 90067.

* * *

PAYTON-WRIGHT, Pamela 1941-

PERSONAL: Born November 1, 1941, in Pittsburgh, PA; daughter of Gordon Edgar and Eleanor Ruth (McKinley) Payton-Wright; married David Arthur Butler; children: Oliver Dickon Hedley. EDUCATION: Birmingham Southern College, B.A., 1963; trained for the stage at the Royal Academy of Dramatic Art, 1963-65. RELIGION: Episcopalian.

VOCATION: Actress.

CAREER: BROADWAY DEBUT—Amy, *The Show-Off,* Lyceum Theatre, 1967. PRINCIPAL STAGE APPEARANCES—Juliette, *Exit the King,* Anya, *The Cherry Orchard,* both with the Phoenix Repertory Company, New York City, 1968; Constance Fry, *Jimmy Shine,* Brooks Atkinson Theatre, New York City, 1968; Tillie, *The Effect of Gamma Rays on Man-in-the-Moon Marigolds,* Mercer-O'Casey Theatre, New York City, 1970; Abigail Williams, *The Crucible,* Vivian Beaumont Theatre, New York City, 1972; Lavinia Mannon, *Mourning Becomes Electra,* Joseph E. Levine Theatre, New York City, 1972; Aimee Semple McPherson, *Aimee,* Trinity Square Repertory Company, Providence, RI, 1973; Millie, *All Over Town,* Booth Theatre, New York City, 1974; Belle, *Jesse and the Bandit Queen,* Other Stage Theatre, New York City, 1975; Laura, *The Glass Menagerie,* Circle in the Square, New York City, 1975; Juliet, *Romeo and Juliet,* Circle in the Square, 1977; Clare, *The Lunch Girls,* Long Wharf Theatre, New Haven, CT, 1977; Kaleria, *Summerfolk,* Long Wharf Theatre, 1979; Masha, *The Sea Gull,* Public Theatre, New York City, 1980; title role, *Hamlet,* Public Theatre, 1982; *Hedda Gabler,* Hartman Theatre, Stamford, CT, 1982; Dona Elvire, *Don Juan,* Delacorte Theatre, New York City, 1982; *The Misanthrope,* Hartford Stage Company, Hartford, CT, 1983; Eleanor, *Passion Play,* Hartford Stage Company, 1985; Mary, *On the Verge, or The Geography of Yearning,* Hartford Stage Company, 1986; *Little Eyolf,* Yale Repertory Theatre, New Haven, CT, 1986. Also appeared with the Trinity Square Repertory Theatre, 1969-70; and the Long Wharf Theatre Company, New Haven, CT, 1973-74.

MAJOR TOURS—Anya, *The Cherry Orchard,* U.S. cities, 1968.

PRINCIPAL FILM APPEARANCES—*Going in Style,* Warner Brothers, 1979; *Resurrection,* Universal, 1980; also appeared in *Corky,* 1972; *The Dark End of the Street,* 1981; *My Little Girl,* 1986.

PRINCIPAL TELEVISION APPEARANCES—Episodic: "Look Homeward, Angel," *Playhouse 90,* 1972. Mini-series: Louisa Catherine Adams, *The Adams Chronicles,* PBS, 1975.

AWARDS: Drama Desk Award, 1972, for *Mourning Becomes Electra;* Clarence Derwent Award, Obie Award from the *Village Voice,* both 1976, for *The Effect of Gamma Rays on Man-in-the-Moon Marigolds;* Obie Award, 1976, for *Jessie and the Bandit Queen.*

MEMBER: Actors' Equity Associaton, Screen Actors Guild, American Federation of Television and Radio Artists.

ADDRESSES: OFFICE—c/o Actors' Equity Association, 165 W. 46th Street, New York, NY 10019.*

*   *   *

PEACOCK, Trevor   1931-

PERSONAL: Born May 19, 1931, in London, England; son of Victor Edward and Alexandria Peacock; married Iris Jones (divorced); married Tilly Tremayne (an actress).

VOCATION: Actor, lyricist, and writer.

CAREER: BROADWAY DEBUT—Sidney Prime, *Sherlock Homes,* Broadhurst Theatre, 1974. PRINCIPAL STAGE APPEARANCES—Grumio, *The Taming of the Shrew,* Open Air Theatre, London, 1964; Jimmy Beales, *Roots,* Royal Court Theatre, London, 1967; Estragon, *Waiting for Godot,* 69 Theatre Company, Manchester, U.K., 1967; Horatio, *Hamlet,* 69 Theatre Company, Manchester, U.K., 1968, then Edinburgh Festival, Edinburgh, Scotland, U.K., 1968; Tony Lumpkin, *She Stoops to Conquer,* 69 Theatre Company, Manchester, U.K., then Garrick Theatre, London, 1969; title role, *Erb,* Strand Theatre, London, 1970; Bottom, *A Midsummer Night's Dream,* Open Air Theatre, 1970; Sergeant Charles Fairchild, *Man Is Man,* Royal Court Theatre, London, 1971; title role, *Titus Andronicus,* Round House Theatre, London, 1971; title role, *The Novelist,* Hampstead Theatre Club, London, 1971; Petruchio, *The Taming of the Shrew,* Young Vic Theatre, London, 1971; Nathan Detroit, *Guys and Dolls,* University Theatre, Manchester, U.K., 1972; Clov, *Endgame,* Manchester Theatre, Manchester, U.K., then Shaw Theatre, 1973; Sidney Prime, *Sherlock Holmes,* Royal Shakespeare Company (RSC), Aldwych Theatre, London, 1974; Friar Mauro Tenda, Diego Lopez Duro, *The Bewitched,* Aldwych Theatre, 1974; Bishop of Ely, Fluellen, *Henry V,* Poins, *Henry IV, Parts I and II,* Sir Hugh Evans, *The Merry Wives of Windsor,* all RSC, Memorial Theatre, Stratford-on-Avon, U.K., 1975, then Aldwych Theatre, 1976; Bob Acres, *The Rivals,* Colonel Kottwitz, *The Prince of Homberg,* title role, *Zack,* Police Sergeant, *What the Butler Saw,* all Royal Exchange Theatre, Manchester, U.K., 1976; Mark Twain, *White Suit Blue,* Old Vic Theatre, London, 1977, then Nottingham, U.K., later Edinburgh, Scotland, U.K., 1978; Tom Price, *A Family,* Haymarket Theatre, London, 1978; Aramis, *The Three Musketeers,* Royal Exchange Theatre, 1979. Also appeared with the Old Vic Theatre Company, London, 1962-64; and as Sir John Brute, *The Provok'd Wife,* Watford Palace Theatre, 1973.

MAJOR TOURS—Sergeant Kite, *The Recruiting Officer,* Cambridge Theatre Company, U.K. cities, 1970.

PRINCIPAL TELEVISION APPEARANCES—Specials: *The Old Curiosity Shop; Twelfth Night; Born and Bred.*

WRITINGS: PLAYS—(Lyricist) *Passion Flower Hotel,* 1965; (lyricist) *Saturday Night and Sunday Morning,* 1966; *Cinderella,* 1978; also *Collapse of Stout Party.*

SIDELIGHTS: FAVORITE ROLES—Estragon in *Waiting for Godot;* Tony Lumpkin in *She Stoops to Conquer.* RECREATIONS—Cricket, soccer.

ADDRESSES: AGENT—c/o Peter Crouch, 59 Frith Street, London W1V 5TA, England.*

PELUCE, Meeno   1970-

PERSONAL: Born February 26, 1970, in Amsterdam, Netherlands; son of Floyd N. (a certified public accountant) and Sondra N. (a personal manager) Peluce.

VOCATION: Actor.

CAREER: TELEVISION DEBUT—*Starsky and Hutch,* ABC. PRINCIPAL TELEVISION APPEARANCES—Series: Tanner Boyle, *The Bad News Bears,* 1979-80; Daniel Best, *Best of the West,* ABC, 1981-82; Jeffrey Jones, *Voyagers,* NBC, 1982-83. Movies: Ian Whitney, *Night Cries,* ABC, 1978; Billy, *The Ghost of Flight 401,* NBC, 1978; young Muhammed, *Harold Robbins' "The Pirate,"* CBS, 1978; Josh Roman, *Fast Friends,* NBC, 1979; Big Ace, *Scout's Honor,* NBC, 1980; Andrei Gorney, *World War III,* NBC, 1982; Joshua Miller, *The Million Dollar Infield,* CBS, 1982.

FILM DEBUT—Son, *The Amityville Horror,* American International, 1979.

AWARDS: Youth in Film Award; Academy of Science Fiction Award.

MEMBER: Screen Actors Guild, American Federation of Television and Radio Artists; Youth in Film.

SIDELIGHTS: RECREATIONS—Guitar.

ADDRESSES: AGENT—Herb Tannen and Associates, 6640 Sunset Boulevard, Suite 203, Hollywood, CA 90028.

MEENO PELUCE

ELIZABETH PENA

PENA, Elizabeth

PERSONAL: Born September 23, in Elizabeth New Jersey; daughter of Mario (an actor, writer, and director) and Estella Marguerita (a producer; maiden name, Toirac) Pena. EDUCATION: Graduated from the School of the Performing Arts; studied acting with Curt Dempster at the Ensemble Studio Theatre and with Endre Hules at La Mama Experimental Theatre Club.

VOCATION: Actress.

CAREER: PRINCIPAL STAGE APPEARANCES—All in New York City: Jesse, *Dog Lady,* International Arts Relations Theatre, 1984; Jane, *Becoming Garcia,* Louis Abron Arts for Living Center, 1984; also Maria, *Bring on the Night,* Sutton Theatre; Cynthia, *Shattered Image,* American Theatre of Actors; Teresa, *La Morena,* Henry Street Playhouse; Juliet, *Romeo and Juliet,* Gramercy Arts Theatre; Beba, *Night of the Assassins,* La Mama Experimental Theatre Club; barmaid, *Act One and Only,* Public Theatre; Teresa, *Italian-American Reconciliation,* GNU Theatre; appeared in *Cinderella,* Off-Broadway production.

PRINCIPAL FILM APPEARANCES—Aurelita, *El Super,* New Yorker Films, 1979; *Times Square,* Associated Film Distributors, 1980; Rita, *They All Laughed,* 1981; Liz, *Crossover Dreams,* Crossover Films Ltd., 1984; Carmen, *Down and Out in Beverly Hills,* Buena Vista, 1985; Rosie, *La Bamba,* Columbia, 1986; Marisa, *Batteries Not Included,* 1987; Consuelo, *Vibes,* 1988; *Fat Chance.*

PRINCIPAL TELEVISION APPEARANCES—Episodic: *Saturday Night Live,* NBC; *Feeling Good,* PBS. Series: *Tough Cookies,* CBS, 1986; Dora, *I Married Dora,* ABC, 1987; also *As The World Turns.*

MEMBER: Actors' Equity Association, Screen Actors Guild, American Federation of Television and Radio Artists.

ADDRESSES: AGENT—c/o David Eidenberg, S.T.E. Representation, 211 Beverly Drive, Suite 201, Beverly Hills, CA 90212.

*　　*　　*

PEREZ, Lazaro   1945-

PERSONAL: Born December 17, 1945, in Havana, Cuba; son of Emilio (a shoe shiner) and Josefina (Gazquez) Perez; married Dianne Reutter, 1970 (divorced, 1978). RELIGION: Roman Catholic.

VOCATION: Actor.

CAREER: STAGE DEBUT—*In the Jungle of Cities,* Theatre Company of Boston, Boston, MA, 1964. BROADWAY DEBUT—*Does a Tiger Wear a Necktie?,* Belasco Theatre, 1969. PRINCIPAL STAGE APPEARANCES—Tito, *G.R. Point,* Playhouse Theatre, New York City, 1978; Juan Riber, *Animals,* Princess Theatre, New York City, 1981; Double, *The Man and the Fly,* with the Puerto Rican Traveling Theatre, New York City, 1982; Carlo, *Balm in Gilead,* with the Circle Repertory Company, Steppenwolf Theatre, Chicago, IL, then Minetta Lane Theatre, New York City, 1984-85. Also appeared in *The Architect and the Emperor of Assyria,* La Mama Experimental Theatre Club, New York City, 1976; *The Life of Galileo,* Pittsburgh Public Theatre, Pittsburgh, PA, 1981; *The Good Woman of Setzuan, Dirty Hands, Marat/Sade, Picnic on the*

Photography by Carol Rosegg

LAZARO PEREZ

Battlefield, all with the Theatre Company of Boston, Boston, MA; *A Streetcar Named Desire, Room Service,* both Pittsburgh Public Theatre, Pittsburgh, PA; *Pericles,* Hartford Stage Company, Hartford, CT; *Cabal of Hypocrites, Alive, Twelve Angry Men, And They Put Handcuffs on the Flowers, The Wonderful Years, Romeo and Juliet,* all Off-Broadway productions.

MAJOR TOURS—*The Architect and Emperor of Assyria,* European cities, 1977; Double, *THe Man and the Fly,* Spanish cities, 1983.

TELEVISION DEBUT—*The Name of the Game,* NBC, 1969. PRINCIPAL TELEVISION APPEARANCES—Episodic: *Baretta,* ABC; *Joe Forrester,* NBC; *The Streets of San Francisco,* ABC; *Ironside,* NBC; *Sarge,* NBC; *The Partridge Family,* ABC; *Feeling Good,* ABC; *The Equalizer,* CBS; *Miami Vice,* NBC; *One Life To Live,* ABC; *All My Children,* ABC; *The Guiding Light,* CBS. Movies: *Jax, A Short Walk to Daylight,* ABC, 1972. Specials: *Liberty,* PBS.

FILM DEBUT—*Fortune and Men's Eyes,* Metro-Goldwyn-Mayer, 1970. PRINCIPAL FILM APPEARANCES—*Gumball Rally,* Warner Brothers, 1977; *Desperately Seeking Susan,* Orion, 1985; also *Nightflowers.*

AWARDS: Best Actor, ACE Award from the Association of New York Critics, 1984, for *Balm in Gilead.*

MEMBER: Actors' Equity Association, Screen Actors Guild, American Federation of Television and Radio Artists.

ADDRESSES: AGENT—c/o Shelia Robinson, International Creative Management, 40 W. 57th Street, New York, NY 10019.

*   *   *

JILL PERRYMAN

PERRYMAN, Jill   1933-

PERSONAL: Born May 30, 1933, in Melbourne, Australia; daughter of William Thomas (a singer) and Dorothy Eileen (a singer; maiden name, Duval) Perryman; married Kevan Johnston (a dancer and choreographer), September 14, 1959; children: Tod Andrew, Trudy Jane. RELIGION: Christian Scientist.

VOCATION: Actress.

CAREER: STAGE DEBUT—*White Horse Inn,* King's Theatre, Melbourne, Australia, 1935. PRINCIPAL STAGE APPEARANCES—Chorus, *Call Me Madam,* Her Majesty's Theatre, Melbourne, 1953; chorus, *South Pacific,* Mormon's wife, *Paint Your Wagon,* both Her Majesty's Theatre, 1954; chorus, *Can Can,* Her Majesty's Theatre, 1955; Mabel, *The Pajama Game,* Her Majesty's Theatre, 1957; Rosalie, *Carnival,* Her Majesty's Theatre, 1962; Mrs. Molloy, *Hello Dolly!,* Her Majesty's Theatre, 1965; Fanny Brice, *Funny Girl,* Her Majesty's Theatre, 1966; Agnes, *I Do, I Do,* Her Majesty's Theatre, 1969; *When We Are Married,* Phillip Theatre, Sydney, Australia, 1970; various roles, *The Two of Us,* St. Martin's Theatre, Melbourne, 1971; Lucille, *No, No, Nanette,* Her Majesty's Theatre, 1972; Countess Malcolm, *A Little Night Music,* Her Majesty's Theatre, Sydney, 1973; various roles, *Leading Lady,* Music Loft Theatre, Sydney, 1976, then St. Martin's Theatre, 1977; *Side by Side by Sondheim,* Theatre Royal, Sydney, 1977; Miss Hannigan, *Annie,* Her Majesty's Theatre, Sydney, 1979; Anna I, *Seven Deadly Sins,* W.A. Ballet Company, Perth, Australia, 1987. Also appeared in the following revues, Phillip Theatre:

Bats, 1958; *Birthday Show, Hey Diddle Diddle, The Phillip Revue,* all 1959; *Yes Please, At It Again,* both 1960; *Do You Mind,* 1961. Appeared as narrator and singer with the Sydney Dance Company, South Australia, 1981; Dame Lollipop, *Puff, the Magic Dragon,* Queensland, Australia, 1982; Molly, *Gulls,* Sydney, 1986.

MAJOR TOURS—Dotty Ottley, *Noises Off,* Australian cities, 1983; Jess, *'night Mother,* Australian cities, 1984; Blanche, *Brighton Beach Memoirs,* Australian cities, 1985.

PRINCIPAL TELEVISION APPEARANCES—Episodic: *Bellbird; Dynasty; Perryman on Parade.* Series: Wife, *Palace of Dreams,* ABC (Australia), 1979-80; sister, *Flight into Hell,* ABC (Australia), 1985. Specials: *Africa: The Dispossessed,* 1981.

FILM DEBUT—Mother, *Maybe This Time,* Cherrywood, 1980. PRINCIPAL FILM APPEARANCES—Miss Dodge, *Windrider,* Barron Films, 1985.

AWARDS: Member of the Order of the British Empire, 1979; Best Actress, Erik Award, 1966, for *Funny Girl;* Best Actress, Erik Award, 1972, for *No, No, Nanette;* Best Variety Entertainer, Television Society of Australia Award, 1973, for *Perryman on Parade;* Best Supporting Actress, Australian Film Award, 1980, for *Maybe This Time;* Best Single Performance by an Actress, Penguin Award, Television Society of Australia, 1980, for *Palace of Dreams;* Gold Citation Award, United Nations, 1981, for *Africa: The Dispossessed.*

SIDELIGHTS: FAVORITE ROLES—Fanny Brice in *Funny Girl;*

Agnes in *I Do, I Do;* Countess Malcolm in *A Little Night Music.* RECREATIONS—Listening to classical music, reading.

ADDRESSES: HOME—Four Hillside Crescent, Gooseberry Hill 6076, Western Australia. AGENT—c/o Shanahan Management, 129 Bourke Street, Woolomoloo 2011, New South Wales, Australia.

*   *   *

PETERSON, Lenka   1925-

PERSONAL: Born Lenke Isacson, October 16, 1925, in Omaha, NE; daughter of Sven (a physician) and Lenke (a lab technician; maiden name, Leinweber) Isacson; married Daniel P. O'Connor (a film producer), May 8, 1948; children: Kevin, Brian, Darren, Glynnis, Sean. EDUCATION: Attended University of Iowa, 1943-45, and Northwestern University, 1945; trained for the stage at the Actors Studio with Lee Strasberg and Elia Kazan and with Robert Lewis, Sanford Meisner, Etienne DeCreux, Anna Sokol, and Mimi Kellerman.

VOCATION: Actress and director.

CAREER: STAGE DEBUT—Doll Susan, *Raggedy Ann and Andy,* Omaha Community Playhouse, NE, 1937. BROADWAY DEBUT— *Years Ago,* Mansfield Theatre, 1947. PRINCIPAL STAGE APPEARANCES—Orphie, *Bathsheba,* Ethel Barrymore Theatre, New York City, 1947; Ella, *Sundown Beach,* Belasco Theatre, New York

LENKA PETERSON

City, 1948; Jenny Nelson, *Harvest of Years,* Hudson Theatre, New York City, 1948; Selma Keeney, *The Young and Fair,* Fulton Theatre, New York City, 1948; Maude Riordan, *The Grass Harp,* Martin Beck Theatre, New York City, 1952; Kitty, *The Time of Your Life,* City Center Theatre, New York City, 1955; Binnie Brookman, *Girls of Summer,* Longacre Theatre, New York City, 1956; Laura, *Look Homeward, Angel,* Ethel Barrymore Theatre, 1957; Mary Follett, *All the Way Home,* Belasco Theatre, 1960; various roles, *Brecht on Brecht,* Theatre de Lys, New York City, 1962; Mary Mercer, *Leaving Home,* Theatre of the Riverside Church, New York City, 1974; Mrs. Hardcastle, *She Stoops to Conquer,* Studio Arena Theatre, Buffalo, NY, 1982; Kate, *All My Sons,* Philadelphia Drama Guild, Philadelphia, PA, 1982; Sarah, *Quilters,* Jack Lawrence Theatre, New York City, 1984.

Mrs. Krekelberg, *El Bravo,* Entermedia Theatre, New York City; Ada Dahl, *Levitation,* Circle Repertory Theatre, New York City; Polly, *Cliffhanger,* Lambs Theatre, New York City; Charlotte, *Little Footsteps,* Playwrights Horizons, New York City; Lucy Potter, *The Bone Ring,* Theatre of the Open Eye, New York City; Sally, *Threads,* Paul Green Theatre, Chapel Hill, NC; Mrs. Light, *Dynamo,* Syracuse Stage, Syracuse, NY; Madame Parnell, *Tartuffe,* Hartman Theatre, Stamford, CT; Aunt Martha, *Arsenic and Old Lace,* Hartman Theatre; title role, *Candida,* Long Wharf Theatre, New Haven, CT; Henny, *Bosoms and Neglect,* Charles Playhouse, Boston, MA; Mrs. Stilson, *Wings,* Met Theatre, Los Angeles, CA; Henny, *Bosoms and Neglect,* Aunt Abby, *Arsenic and Old Lace,* Ethel, *On Golden Pond,* all Trinity Square Theatre, Providence, RI; Bessie, *Madonna of the Power Room,* Portland Stage Comapny, Portland, ME; Dorothea, *Eleemosynary,* Philadelphia Festival Theatre, Philadelphia, PA; Linda, *Death of a Salesman,* Actors Theatre, Louisville, KY; Eleanor, *A Lion in Winter,* Westchester Theatre, NY; Selma, *The Young and the Fair,* New York City; Maude, *The Grass Harp,* New York City; Rose Kirk, *Nuts,* New York City; and portrayed various roles, Eugene O'Neill Playwrights Conference, Waterford, CT.

MAJOR TOURS—*Kiss and Tell,* USO Pacific tour, 1945-46.

TELEVISION DEBUT—*Hollywood Screen Test.* PRINCIPAL TELEVISION APPEARANCES—Episodic: *I, Bonino,* NBC; *Philco Television Playhouse,* NBC; *Actors Studio Playhouse,* ABC; *Westinghouse Theatre,* CBS; *U.S. Steel Hour,* CBS; *Armstrong Circle Theatre,* CBS; *Ed Sullivan Show,* CBS; *The Defenders,* CBS; *General Hospital,* ABC; *Route 66,* CBS; *Robert Montgomery Presents,* NBC; *Suspense,* CBS; *Look Up and Live,* CBS; *Lamp Unto My Feet,* CBS; *Danger,* CBS; *The Web,* CBS; *Inner Sanctum,* CBS; *My True Story,* NBC; *Love, Sidney,* NBC; *Kojak,* CBS; *Quincy, M.E.,* NBC; *All My Chldren,* ABC; *Lucas Tanner,* NBC; *Playhouse 90,* CBS; *Kraft Theatre,* NBC; *Pulitzer Prize Playhouse,* ABC; *Hill Street Blues,* NBC; *Love of Life,* CBS; *Another World,* NBC; *Guiding Light,* CBS; *Ryan's Hope,* ABC; *One Life to Live,* ABC. Series: *Young Doctor Malone,* NBC, 1959-61; *Search for Tomorrow,* CBS. Movies: *Seizure; Visions; Code of Vengeance; Someone I Touched; Pennsylvania Dutch; Pals.*

FILM DEBUT—Ann, *Answer for Ann,* 1948. PRINCIPAL FILM APPEARANCES—Ellie, *Take Care of My Little Girl,* Twentieth Century-Fox, 1950; Mrs. Griffin, *Black Like Me,* United Artists, 1964; Granny Mundy, *Dragnet,* Universal, 1987; also *Panic in the Streets,* Twentieth Century-Fox, 1950; *Lifeguard,* Paramount, 1976; Mary Jo Patterson, *The Phoenix City Story;* Mother, *Homer.*

RADIO DEBUT—WOW, Omaha, NB, 1941. PRINCIPAL RADIO APPEARANCES—*Road of Life,* CBS; *My True Story,* ABC; *Grand*

Central Station, CBS; *The Romance of Helen Trent,* CBS; *Henry Aldrich,* NBC.

NON-RELATED CAREER—NBC Guide, 1945.

AWARDS: Best Actress, Dorothy Maguire Award, Omaha Community Playhouse, 1942; Antoinette Perry Award nomination, Helen Hayes Award nomination, both 1985, for *Quilters.*

MEMBER: Actors' Equity Association, Screen Actors Guild, American Federation of Television and Radio Artists; New Rochelle Council of the Arts.

SIDELIGHTS: RECREATIONS— Reading, playing the piano, swimming, driving.

ADDRESSES: AGENT—Smith-Freedman Associates, 850 Seventh Avenue, New York, NY 10019.

*   *   *

PETERSON, Roger   1928-

PERSONAL: Born March 8, 1928, in Minnesota; son of Adler E. (a pharmacist) and Ella Julia (a teacher; maiden name, Eklund) Peterson; divorced from wife. EDUCATION: Received B.A., business administration, from University of Minnesota; also attended Gustavus Adolphus College; trained for the stage with Bobby Lewis, Tamara Daykarhanova, Joseph Anthony, and Madelyn

ROGER PETERSON

Burns; also studied at the Actors Studio and the American National Theatre and Academy. MILITARY: U.S. Navy.

VOCATION: Actor and producer.

CAREER: TELEVISION DEBUT—Captain of the Space Pilots, *Choose Up Sides,* NBC, 1953. PRINCIPAL TELEVISION APPEARANCES—Episodic: *Playhouse 90,* CBS; *Studio One,* CBS; *Robert Montgomery Presents,* NBC; *General Hospital,* ABC; *As the World Turns,* CBS; *The Equalizer,* CBS; *Search for Tomorrow; One Life to Live; The Guiding Light.* Movies: *Women at West Point,* 1979; *Rage of Angels II.*

PRINCIPAL TELEVISION WORK—Associate producer for Goodson-Todman Productions: *I've Got a Secret,* CBS, 1954-67; *Snap Judgement,* syndicated, 1967-69; *To Tell the Truth,* syndicated, 1969-78. Production manager for all West Coast-based Goodson-Todman Productions game shows, including: *Family Feud, The Price Is Right, Tattletales, Child's Play, Match Game, Password Plus, Card Sharks,* all syndicated, 1979-84.

PRINCIPAL FILM APPEARANCES—*Fourteen Hours,* Twentieth Century-Fox, 1951; *Sabrina,* Paramount, 1954; *Firepower,* Associated Film Distributors, 1979; *Kramer vs. Kramer,* Columbia, 1979; *Hello Again,* Touchstone, 1987.

PRINCIPAL STAGE APPEARANCES—*The Insect Comedy,* City Center Theatre, New York City, 1948; *Joy to the World,* Plymouth Theatre, New York City, 1948; also appeared in summer theatre productions of *The Glass Menagerie, Hedda Gabbler, The Seagull,* and numerous summer theatre productions at the Green Mountain Playhouse, Middlebury, VT, the Old Log Playhouse, Minneapolis, MN, and the Suffern Playhouse, Suffern, NY.

RELATED CAREER—Radio announcer; model; actor and voice for radio and television commercials.

MEMBER: Actors' Equity Association, Screen Actors Guild, National Academy of Television Arts and Sciences, American Federation of Television and Radio Artists.

ADDRESSES: OFFICE—225 E. 74th Street, Apt. 5-P, New York, NY 10021.

*   *   *

PHILLIPS, Michelle   1944-

PERSONAL: Born June 4, 1944, in Long Beach, CA; daughter of Gardner Burnett (a merchant marine) and Joyce Leon (an accountant; maiden name, Poole) Gilliam; married John Phillips (a musician), December 31, 1962 (divorced, 1970); children: Gilliam Chynna Phillips, Austin Devereux Hines. POLITICS: Democrat. RELIGION: "Druid."

VOCATION: Actress, singer, writer, and composer.

CAREER: PRINCIPAL TELEVISION APPEARANCES—Episodic: *Knots Landing,* CBS; *Fantasy Island,* ABC. Mini-Series: Gloria Osborne, *Aspen* (also known as *The Innocent and the Damned*),

MICHELLE PHILLIPS

NBC, 1979; Jennie Barber, *The French Atlantic Affair*, ABC, 1979. Movies: Maggie, *The California Kid*, ABC, 1974; Joyce Kreski, *Death Squad*, ABC, 1974; Marina Brent, *The Users*, ABC, 1978; Meredith Tyne, *Moonlight*, CBS, 1982; Chris Jameson, *Mickey Spillane's Mike Hammer in "Murder Me, Murder You,"* CBS, 1983; Katie Jordan, *Secrets of a Married Man*, NBC, 1984; Claire Noble, *The Covenant*, NBC, 1985; Jennifer Clayton, *Stark: Mirror Image*, CBS, 1986.

FILM DEBUT—*Dillinger*, American International, 1973. PRINCI-PAL FILM APPEARANCES—*Valentino*, United Artists, 1977; *Bloodline*, Paramount, 1979; *The Man with Bogart's Face*, 1980; *Savage Harvest*, Twentieth Century-Fox, 1981; also *American Anthem*, 1986.

RELATED CAREER—Member of The Mamas and the Papas, singing group, 1965-68.

WRITINGS: AUTOBIOGRAPHIES—*Californa Dreamin': The Sto-ry of The Mamas and the Papas*, Warner Books, 1986.

AWARDS: Received a Grammy Award, 1966, and four gold albums as a member of The Mamas and the Papas.

MEMBER: American Federation of Television and Radio Artists, Screen Actors Guild.

ADDRESSES: OFFICE—P.O. Box 396, Releda, CA 91335. AGENT—International Creative Management, 8899 Beverly Boulevard, Los Angeles, CA 90048.

PHILLIPS, Robin   1942-

PERSONAL: Born February 28, 1942, in Haslemere, England; son of James William and Ellen Anne (Barfoot) Phillips. EDUCATION: Trained for the stage at the Bristol Old Vic Theatre School with Duncan Ross.

VOCATION: Director and actor.

CAREER: STAGE DEBUT—Mr. Pubb, *The Critic*, Bristol Old Vic Theatre Company, Theatre Royal, Bristol, U.K., 1959. PRINCIPAL STAGE APPEARANCES—Romeo, *Romeo and Juliet*, Konstantin, *The Seagull*, Geoffrey, *A Taste of Honey*, all Bristol Old Vic Theatre Company, Theatre Royal, Bristol, U.K., 1959-60; Eric MacClure, *South*, Lyric Hammersmith Theatre, London, 1961; Curio, *The Chances*, Prophilus, *The Broken Heart*, both Chichester Festival, Chichester, U.K., 1962; son, *Six Characters in Search of an Author*, May Fair Theatre, London, 1963; Louis Dubedat, *The Doctor's Dilemma*, Chichester Festival, 1972; also appeared with the Oxford Playhouse Company, 1964.

PRINCIPAL STAGE WORK—All as director unless indicated: As-sistant director, *Timon of Athens, Hamlet*, both Royal Shakespeare Company (RSC), Stratford-on-Avon, U.K., 1965; *The Ballad of the False Barman*, Hampstead Theatre Club, London, 1966; *The Seagull*, Thorndike Theatre, Leatherhead, U.K., 1969; *Tiny Alice*, RSC, Aldwych Theatre, London, 1970; *Sing a Rude Song*, Green-wich Theatre, then Garrick Theatre, both London, 1970; *Abelard and Heloise*, Wyndham's Theatre, London, 1970; *Two Gentlemen of Verona*, RSC, Memorial Theatre, Stratford-on-Avon, U.K., then Aldwych Theatre, 1970; *Abelard and Heloise*, Brooks Atkinson Theatre, New York City, 1970; *Dear Antoine*, Chichester Festival, Chichester, U.K., 1971; *The Beggars Opera, The Lady's Not for Burning*, both Chichester Festival, 1972; *The Three Sisters, The House of Bernarda Alba, Rosmersholm, Catsplay, Zorba, Not Drowning But Waving*, all Company Theatre, Greenwich, U.K., 1973. Also directed *Dear Antoine*, London, 1971; *Caesar and Cleopatra*, London, 1971; *Miss Julie*, London, 1971; *Notes on a Love Affair*, London, 1972; *The Guardsman*, Los Angeles, CA, 1976; *Long Day's Journey into Night*, London, 1977.

Director, all with the Stratford Shakespeare Festival, Stratford, ON, Canada: *The Comedy of Errors, Two Gentlemen of Verona, Measure for Measure, Trumpets and Drums, The Importance of Being Earnest*, all 1975; *Antony and Cleopatra, A Midsummer Night's Dream, The Way of the World, Hamlet, The Tempest, Measure for Measure, The Importance of Being Earnest*, all 1976; *A Midsummer Night's Dream, The Guardsman, Richard III, As You Like It, Hay Fever*, all 1977; *Macbeth, The Winter's Tale, Uncle Vanya, Private Lives, Judgement, The Devils*, all 1978; *Love's Labour's Lost, The Importance of Being Earnest, King Lear*, all 1979; *The Beggar's Opera, Virginia, Much Ado about Nothing, Foxfire, The Seagull, Long Day's Journey into Night*, all 1980.

MAJOR TOURS—Co-director, *The Comedy of Errors, Two Gentle-men of Verona*, U.S. cities, both 1975.

PRINCIPAL FILM APPEARANCES—*Decline and Fall*, Twentieth Century-Fox, 1969.

PRINCIPAL TELEVISION APPEARANCES—Movies: Title role, *Da-vid Copperfield*, NBC, 1970. Specials: *The Seagull*.

RELATED CAREER—Associate director, Bristol Old Vic Theatre, 1959-60; associate director, Northcott Theatre, 1967-68; artistic director, Company Theatre, Greenwich, U.K., 1973; artistic director, Stratford Shakespeare Festival, Stratford, ON, Canada, 1974—.

SIDELIGHTS: RECREATIONS—Painting.

ADDRESSES: OFFICE—Stratford Shakespeare Festival, Box 520, Stratford, ON, Canada.*

*   *   *

PIAZZA, Ben   1934-

PERSONAL: Born July 30, 1934, in Little Rock, AR; son of Charles and Elfreida (Spillman) Piazza; married Dolores Dorn-Heft. EDUCATION: Attended Princeton University; trained for the stage at the Actors Studio.

VOCATION: Actor and writer.

CAREER: STAGE DEBUT—Venetian Senator, *Othello*, Theatre Intime, Princeton, NJ, 1952. BROADWAY DEBUT—George Willard, *Winesburg, Ohio*, National Theatre, 1958. PRINCIPAL STAGE APPEARANCES—Alvin, *Kataki*, Ambassador Theatre, New York City, 1959; Paul, *A Second String*, Eugene O'Neill Theatre, New York City, 1960; young man, *The American Dream*, York Playhouse, then Cherry Lane Theatre, both New York City, 1961; Clov, *Endgame*, Green Eyes, *Deathwatch*, young man, *The American Dream*, Jerry, *The Zoo Story*, all Cherry Lane Repertory Theatre, New York City, 1962; Leopold, *The Fun Couple*, Lyceum Theatre, New York City, 1962; Nick, *Who's Afraid of Virginia Woolf?*, Billy Rose Theatre, New York City, 1963; *One in a Row*, Playhouse Theatre, Paramus, NJ, 1964; *The Zoo Story*, Cherry Lane Theatre, New York City, 1965; Alfredo, *The Song of the Grasshopper*, American National Theatre Academy Playhouse, New York City, 1967; *You Know I Can't Hear You When the Water's Running*, Coconut Grove Playhouse, Coconut Grove, FL, 1968; intern, *The Death of Bessie Smith*, Jerry, *The Zoo Story*, Billy Rose Theatre, New York City, 1968; Stanley Kowalski, *A Streetcar Named Desire*, New Orleans Repertory Theatre, New Orleans, LA, 1970; Buck, *Bus Stop*, Ivanhoe Theatre, Chicago, IL, 1970; Mark Crawford, *Savages*, Mark Taper Forum, Los Angeles, CA, 1974.

MAJOR TOURS—Isherwood, *I Am a Camera*, Jerry, *The Zoo Story*, Chance Wayne, *Sweet Bird of Youth*, South American cities, both 1961; Isherwood, *I Am a Camera*, South American cities, 1962.

FILM DEBUT—*Dangerous Age*. PRINCIPAL FILM APPEARANCES—*The Hanging Tree*, Warner Brothers, 1959; *Tell Me That You Love Me Junie Moon*, Paramount, 1970; *The Outside Man*, United Artists, 1973; also *No Exit*.

PRINCIPAL TELEVISION APPEARANCES—Episodic: *Ben Casey*, ABC; *The Defenders*, CBS; *Naked City*, ABC; *Kraft Theatre*, NBC.

WRITINGS: PLAYS—*Lime Green* and *Khaki Blue*, both Provincetown Playhouse, New York City, 1969. NOVELS—*The Exact and Very Strange Truth*, 1964.

AWARDS: Theatre World Award, 1959.

ADDRESSES: OFFICE—300 E. 59th Street, New York, NY 10022.*

PINCHOT, Bronson

BRIEF ENTRY: Full name, Bronson Alcott Pinchot; named after the nineteenth-century transcendentalist teacher and writer Amos Bronson Alcott. In the 1984 hit film *Beverly Hills Cop*, Bronson Pinchot managed to steal a scene from star Eddie Murphy, even though he had only about twenty lines of dialogue. The indeterminate accent the actor used as the art gallery employee Serge made a great impression on audiences and Pinchot told *TV Guide* (September 27, 1986) that the role was a turning point in his career. Having studied theatre at Yale University, the southern California native started out as a stage actor in New York. He broke into the movies with supporting roles in *Risky Business*, 1983, and *The Flamingo Kid*, 1984. He was already committed to the NBC series *Sara* when *Beverly Hills Cop* was released, but that show's early demise freed him to accept a co-starring role on *Perfect Strangers*. Pinchot was the producers' first choice for the character of Balki, the immigrant shepherd whose innocent misunderstanding of American ways causes constant complications for his roommate-cousin, Larry. Although they felt Pinchot would do any kind of accent, they asked him to stay close to what he had developed as Serge. He did so, and the show, which began as a mid-season replacement in the 1985-86 season, has been renewed twice to date. In his spare time, Pinchot collects antique painted Scandinavian furniture.

*   *   *

PLEASANCE, Angela

PERSONAL: Born in Chapeltown, England; daughter of Donald (an actor) and Miriam (Raymond) Pleasance; married Michael Cadman (divorced). EDUCATION: Trained for the stage at the Royal Academy of Dramatic Art.

VOCATION: Actress.

CAREER: STAGE DEBUT—Titania, *A Midsummer Night's Dream*, Birmingham Repertory Theatre, Birmingham, U.K., 1964. PRINCIPAL STAGE APPEARANCES—Josephine, *The Ha-Ha*, Lyceum Theatre, Edinburgh, Scotland, U.K., 1967, then Hampstead Theatre Club, London, 1968; Irina, *The Three Sisters*, Lyceum Theatre, 1968; Juliet, *Romeo and Juliet*, Ludlow Festival Theatre, Ludlow, U.K., 1969; Miranda, *The Tempest*, Mermaid Theatre, London, 1970; title role, *Saint Joan*, Mermaid Theatre, 1970; Moliser, *The Plough and the Stars*, Nottingham Playhouse Theatre, Nottingham, U.K., 1973; Electra, *You Were So Sweet When You Were Little*, Theatre at New End, London, 1974; Jean Rice, *The Entertainer*, Greenwich Theatre, London, 1974; *The Journey*, Round House Theatre, London, 1976; *The Bitter Tears of Petra von Kant*, Theatre at New End, 1976; Juliet, *Romeo and Juliet*, Shaw Theatre, London, 1976; Water Sprite, *Better Days, Better Knights*, King's Head Theatre, London, 1976; girl, *The Square*, Theatre at New End, 1979; Miss Cutts, *The Hothouse*, Hampstead Theatre Club, 1980.

MAJOR TOURS—*The Hollow Crown*, U.K. cities, 1967.

PRINCIPAL FILM APPEARANCES—*Here We Go Round the Mulberry Bush*, 1967; *Hitler: The Last Ten Days*, 1973.

PRINCIPAL TELEVISION APPEARANCES—Mini-Series: *The Six Wives of Henry VIII*. Movies: Peace girl, *Destiny of a Spy*, NBC, 1969; Fantine, *Les Miserables*, CBS, 1978; Ghost of Christmas

Past, *A Christmas Carol*, CBS, 1984; interpreter, *Gulag*, HBO, 1985; madwoman, *Anastasia: The Mystery of Anna*, NBC, 1986; also *Marching Song; Breath; Murder at the Wedding.*

ADDRESSES: AGENT—c/o Joyce Edwards, Eight Theed Street, London SE1, England.*

*   *   *

POLIAKOFF, Stephen   1952-

PERSONAL: Born in 1952 in London, England.

VOCATION: Playwright.

CAREER: Also see *WRITINGS* below.

RELATED CAREER—Writer-in-residence, British National Theatre, London, 1976-80.

WRITINGS: PLAYS—*Bambi Ramm*, Abbey Community Centre, London, 1970; *The Summer Party*, Crucible Theatre, Sheffield, U.K., 1980; *Hitting Town*, South Street Theatre, New York City, 1979, published by Methuen, 1976, then Samuel French, Inc., 1977; *City Sugar*, Comedy Theatre, London, 1976, then Marymount Manhattan Theatre, New York City, 1978, published by Methuen, 1976, then Samuel French, Inc., 1977; *Strawberry Fields*, Young Vic Theatre, London, 1976, then Manhattan Theatre Club, New York City, 1978, published by Methuen, 1977; *Shout across the River*, Warehouse Theatre, London, 1978, then Marymount Manhattan Theatre, 1980, published by Methuen, 1979; *American Days*, ICA Theatre, London, 1979, then Manhattan Theatre Club, 1980, published by Methuen, 1980. Also wrote *Granny*, produced in London, 1969; *A Day with My Sister*, produced in Edinburgh, Scotland, U.K., 1971; *Pretty Boy*, produced in London, 1972; *Theatre Outside, Berlin Days, The Carnation Gang*, all produced in London, 1973; *Clever Soldiers*, produced in London, 1974; *Heroes, Join the Dance*, both produced in New York City, 1975.

SCREENPLAYS—*Bloody Kids.*

AWARDS: Evening Standard Award, 1976.

ADDRESSES: AGENT—Margaret Ramsay, Ltd., 14-A Goodwin's Court, London WC2N 4LL, England.*

*   *   *

POWELL, Robert   1944-

PERSONAL: Born June 1, 1944, in Salford, England; son of John Wilson and Kathleen (Davis) Powell; married Barbara Lord. EDUCATION: Attended Manchester University.

VOCATION: Actor.

CAREER: LONDON DEBUT—Various roles, *Ubu Roi*, Royal Court Theatre, 1966. PRINCIPAL STAGE APPEARANCES—Title role, *Hamlet*, Leeds Playhouse, Leeds, U.K., 1971; Lyngstrand, *The Lady from the Sea*, Greenwich Theatre, London, 1971; Jean Misson, *Pirates*, Theatre Upstairs, London, 1971; Scythrop Glowery, *Nightmare Abbey*, Arnaud Theatre, Guildford, U.K., 1972; Oberon, *The*

ROBERT POWELL

Fairy Queen, University Theatre, Newcastle, U.K., 1973; Branwell Bronte, *Glasstown*, Westminster Theatre, London, 1973; Tristan Tzara, *Travesties*, Royal Shakespeare Company, Aldwych Theatre, then Albery Theatre, both London, 1975. Also appeared in *Terra Nova*, Watford Theatre, 1982; *Private Dick*, Westminster Theatre, 1982.

PRINCIPAL FILM APPEARANCES—*Mahler*, Mayfair, 1975; *Tommy*, Columbia, 1975; *Jigsaw Man*, United Film Distributors, 1984. Also appeared in *Lumiere*, 1976; *Beyond Good and Evil*, 1977; *The Thirty-Nine Steps*, 1978; *The Harlequin*, 1980; *Jane Austen in Manhattan*, 1980; *The Survivor*, 1981; *Imperative*, 1982; *Secrets of the Phantom Caverns*, 1983.

PRINCIPAL TELEVISION APPEARANCES—Series: *Hannay*. Mini-Barrymore Theatre, 1957. PRINCIPAL STAGE APPEARANCES—*Nazareth*, NBC, 1977; Jack Durrance, *The Four Feathers*, NBC, 1978; Phoebus, *The Hunchback of Notre Dame*, CBS, 1982; Also appeared in *Doomwatch; Jude the Obscure; Looking for Clancy; Frankenstein; Pygmalion.*

ADDRESSES: AGENT—International Creative Management, 388-396 Oxford Street, London W1N 9HE, England.

*   *   *

PRESSMAN, Lawrence   1939-

PERSONAL: Born July 10, 1939, in Cynthiana, KY. EDUCATION: Attended Kentucky Northwestern University.

VOCATION: Actor.

CAREER: PRINCIPAL FILM APPEARANCES—*Shaft*, Metro-Goldwyn-Mayer, 1971; *Making It*, Twentieth Century-Fox, 1971; *The Hellstrom Chronicle*, Cinema V, 1971; *The Crazy World of Julius Vrooder*, Twentieth Century-Fox, 1974; *The Man in the Glass Booth*, American Film Theatre, 1975; *Walk Proud*, Universal, 1979; *Nine to Five*, Twentieth Century-Fox, 1980; *Some Kind of Hero*, Paramount, 1982; Cathcart, *The Hanoi Hilton*, Cannon Group, 1987.

PRINCIPAL TELEVISION APPEARANCES—Series: Michael Mulligan, *Mulligan's Stew*, NBC, 1977; Alan Thackery, *Ladies' Man*, CBS, 1980-81. Episodic: *Cannon*, CBS; *The Snoop Sisters*, NBC. Pilots: *The Marcus-Nelson Murders* (pilot for *Kojak* series), CBS, 1973. Mini-Series: Bill Denton, *Rich Man, Poor Man*, ABC, 1976-77. Movies: *Winter Kill*, 1974; *The First 36 Hours of Dr. Durant*, 1975; *The Man from Atlantis*, 1977; *The Trial of Lee Harvey Oswald*, 1977; *The Gathering*, 1977; *Like Mom, Like Me*, 1978; *The Gathering, Part II*, 1979; *Diary of a Perfect Murder*, NBC, 1986; *The Deliberate Stranger*, NBC, 1986; *A Fighting Choice*, ABC, 1986; also *Blind Ambition*.

PRINCIPAL STAGE APPEARANCES—*Bodies*, South Coast Repertory Theatre, Costa Mesa, CA, 1981-82; Arkady Sergeich Islaev, *A Month in the Country*, with the Center Theatre Group at the Mark Taper Forum, Los Angeles, 1982-83; also appeared in *The Man in the Glass Booth* and *Play It Again Sam*, both Broadway productions.

AWARDS: Theatre World Award, 1963-64.

MEMBER: Actors' Equity Association, Screen Actors Guild, American Federation of Television and Radio Artists.

*ADDRESSES:*OFFICE—15033 Encanto Drive, Sherman Oaks, CA 91403. AGENT—S.T.E. Representation, Ltd., 211 S. Beverly Drive, Suite 201, Beverly Hills, CA 90212.*

*   *   *

PRESTON, Robert   1918-1987

OBITUARY NOTICE—See index for *CTFT* sketch: Born Robert Preston Meservey, June 8, 1918, in Newton Highlands, MA; died of lung cancer, March 21, 1987, in Santa Barbara, CA. Although best known for his portrayal of the fast-talking con artist Professor Harold Hill in *The Music Man*, Robert Preston was an accomplished actor for more than fifty years on stage, screen, and television. Beginning his career with the Pasadena Community Theatre where he appeared in more than forty productions in two years, Preston was then signed as a contract player at Paramount, starring in a number of low-budget films. Making his Broadway debut in 1951 in *Twentieth Century*, Preston continued on Broadway in *The Male Animal*, 1952, *The Tender Trap*, 1952, and other plays, but it was his performance in *The Music Man*, 1957, that won him rave notices, an Antoinette Perry Award, and lasting fame. After this success he appeared in *Ben Franklin in Paris*, 1964, *I Do! I Do!*, 1966 (for which he won a second Antoinette Perry Award), in a national tour of *Mack and Mabel*, 1974, and in *Sly Fox*, 1977. Preston recreated the role of Harold Hill for the hit film version of *The Music Man*, 1962, and later won enthusiastic reviews for his work in *S.O.B.*, 1981, and an Academy Award nomination as best supporting actor for *Victor/Victoria*, 1982. Preston acted in a

number of television anthology series and appeared in such made-for-television movies as *Rehearsal for Murder*, 1982, *Finnigan, Begin Again*, 1985, and his final role, *Outrage!*.

OBITUARIES AND OTHER SOURCES: New York Times, March 23, 1987.

*   *   *

PRINCIPAL, Victoria   1945-

PERSONAL: Born January 3, 1945, in Fukuoka, Japan; daughter of Victor (a U.S. Air Force officer) and Ree (Veal) Principal; married Christopher Skinner (an actor; divorced); married Harry Glassman (a plastic surgeon), 1985. EDUCATION: Attended Miami-Dade Community College; trained for the stage with Max Croft, Al Sacks, and Estelle Harman.

VOCATION: Actress, writer, model, and talent agent.

CAREER: PRINCIPAL TELEVISION APPEARANCES—Series: Pamela Barnes Ewing, *Dallas*, CBS, 1978-87. Episodic: *Love, American Style*, ABC. Pilots: *Fantasy Island*, ABC, 1977. Movies: *Last Hours Before Morning*, 1975; *The Night They Stole Miss Beautiful*, 1977; *Pleasure Palace*, 1980; *Not Just Another Affair*, 1982; also appeared in *Sixty Years of Seduction* and *Delaney*.

FILM DEBUT—*The Life and Times of Judge Roy Bean*, National General, 1972. PRINCIPAL FILM APPEARANCES—*The Naked Ape*, Universal, 1973; *Earthquake*, Universal, 1974; *I Will, I Will. . .for Now*, Twentieth Century-Fox, 1976; *Vigilante Force*, United Artists, 1976; *Greatest Heroes of the Bible*, Sunn Classic Pictures, 1979.

PRINCIPAL STAGE APPEARANCES—*Night of 100 Stars*, Radio City Music Hall, New York City, 1982.

RELATED CAREER—Fashion model; talent agent, 1975-78; television commercial actress.

WRITINGS: NON-FICTION—Self-Improvement: *The Body Principal: The Exercise Program for Life*, Simon & Shuster, 1983, reprinted in 1985; *The Beauty Principal: The Beauty Program for Life*, Simon & Shuster, 1984.

MEMBER: Screen Actors Guild, American Federation of Television and Radio Artists.

ADDRESSES: OFFICE—9755 Oak Pass Road, Beverly Hills, CA 90210. AGENT—Triad Artists, 10100 Santa Monica Blvd., 16th Floor, Los Angeles, CA 90067.*

*   *   *

PRYOR, Nicholas   1935-

PERSONAL: Born Nicholas David Probst, January 28, 1935, in Baltimore, MD; son of J. Stanley (a pharmaceutical manufacturer) and Dorothy (Driskill) Probst; married Joan Epstein (an actress), December 21, 1958 (divorced, 1968); married Melinda Plank (an actress and dancer), February 27, 1968 (divorced); married third

NICHOLAS PRYOR

wife, Pamela; children: (third marriage) Stacey. EDUCATION: Yale University, B.A., drama, 1956.

VOCATION: Actor.

CAREER: STAGE DEBUT—Peter, *Light Up the Sky*, Drummond Players, Baltimore, MD, 1951. BROADWAY DEBUT—(As Nicholas Probst) Captain Dupont, *Small War on Murray Hill*, Ethel Barrymore Theatre, 1957. PRINCIPAL STAGE APPEARANCES—Trock, *Winterset*, Haimon, *Antigone*, John, *John Loves Mary*, Loevborg, *Hedda Gabler*, all Drummond Players, Baltimore, MD, 1951; Lord Chancellor, *Iolanthe*, Arthur Kindred, *Detective Story*, Randy Curtis, *Lady in the Dark*, singer, *My Heart's in the Highlands*, Cromwell, *Henry VIII*, Gremio, *The Taming of the Shrew*, Owen, *Jenny Kissed Me*, all Camden Hills Theatre, Camden, ME, 1952; Launcelot Gobbo, *The Merchant of Venice*, Hortensio, *The Taming of the Shrew*, Suffolk, *Henry IV, Part I*, all Oregon Shakespeare Festival, Ashland, OR, 1953; Paul Verrall, *Born Yesterday*, Ernest, *The Importance of Being Earnest*, Turk, *Come Back, Little Sheba*, Arthur, *Detective Story*, Don, *The Moon Is Blue*, Simon, *Hay Fever*, all Star Theatre, Minneapolis, MN, 1954; John, *The Old Maid*, Drew Theatre, East Hampton, NY, 1957; Roger Parson, *The Egghead*, Ethel Barrymore Theatre, New York City, 1957; Bill, *Love Me Little*, Helen Hayes Theatre, New York City, 1958; Bezano, *He Who Gets Slapped*, Falmouth Playhouse, Falmouth, MA, 1958; Jimmie Keefe, *Howie*, 46th Street Theatre, New York City, 1958; Buzz, *The Highest Tree*, Longacre Theatre, New York City, 1959.

Fredricks, *Craig's Wife*, Tappan Zee Playhouse, Nyack, NY, 1960; Schuyler Grogan, *Invitation to a March*, Ogunquit Playhouse,

Ogunquit, ME, 1961; Ed Hughes, *The Advocate*, Bucks County Playhouse, New Hope, PA, 1962; James Keller, *The Miracle Worker*, Bucks County Playhouse, 1962; Romeo, *Romeo and Juliet*, Casino Park Playhouse, Holyoke, MA, 1963; young man, *Moments of Love*, Westport County Playhouse, Westport, CT, 1963; Barney, *A Party for Divorce*, Provincetown Playhouse, New York City, 1966; Tiger, *The Rehearsal*, Theatre of Living Arts, Philadelphia, PA, 1968; James Daley, *That Championship Season*, Booth Theatre, New York City, 1974; Gordon, *Thieves*, Broadhurst Theatre, New York City, 1974. Also appeared in *The Father* and *Peg o' My Heart*, with the Drummond Players, 1951; *Coriolanus*, Oregon Shakespeare Festival, 1953; and as an understudy in *Who's Afraid of Virginia Woolf?*, Billy Rose Theatre, New York City, 1964.

MAJOR TOURS—Alan, *The Boys in the Band*, U.S. cities, 1969-70.

TELEVISION DEBUT—Tom, *Star for Tonight*, NBC, 1955. PRINCIPAL TELEVISION APPEARANCES—Episodic: *Kraft Television Theatre*, NBC, 1955; *U.S. Steel Hour*, CBS, 1958; *Omnibus*, ABC, 1958; *Hallmark Hall of Fame*, NBC, 1959; *The Dupont Show of the Month*, NBC, 1960; *Ford Startime*, NBC, 1960; *Alfred Hitchcock Presents*, NBC, 1961; *Murder, She Wrote*, CBS; *Falcon Crest*, CBS; *Hill Street Blues*, NBC; *St. Elsewhere*, NBC. Series: Ernie, *Young Dr. Malone*, NBC, 1959; Rex Stern, *The Brighter Day*, CBS, 1960-61; Johnny Ellis, *The Secret Storm*, CBS, 1963; Tom Baxter, *Another World*, NBC, 1964; Ken Cora, *The Nurses*, ABC, 1965-67; Paul Bradley, *Love Is a Many Splendored Thing*, CBS, 1968; Lincoln Tyler III, *All My Children*, ABC, 1971-72; Joel Gantry, *The Edge of Night*, CBS, 1973; Jack Felspar, *The Bronx Zoo*, NBC, 1986. Mini-Series: Hank Ferris, *Washington: Behind Closed Doors*, ABC, 1977. Movies: Art Beresford, *Fear on Trial*, CBS, 1975; James T. O'Neil, *Force Five*, CBS, 1975; Mack, *Widow*, NBC, 1976; Manners, *The Life and Assassination of the Kingfish*, NBC, 1977; man in sports car, *Night Terror*, NBC, 1977; Jeff Kramer, *Having Babies II*, ABC, 1977; Will Gilmore, *Rainbow*, NBC, 1978; Dick Owens, *Reunion*, CBS, 1980; Dave Gildea, *The Plutonium Incident*, CBS, 1980; Larry Wax, *Marriage Is Alive and Well*, NBC, 1980; Ryan, *The Last Song*, CBS, 1980; Jacob, *Gideon's Trumpet*, CBS, 1980; Ed Lissik, *The $5.20 an Hour Dream*, CBS, 1980; Ralph Dortlund, *Desparate Voyage*, CBS, 1980; Elwin Potter, *A Few Days in Weasel Creek*, CBS, 1981; James Grew, *John Steinbeck's "East of Eden,"* ABC, 1981; Dr. Judd, *Splendor in the Grass*, NBC, 1981; Greg Baker, Sr., *The Kid from Nowhere*, NBC, 1982; John Cye Cheasty, *Blood Feud*, syndicated, 1983; Dr. Thompson, *Amazons*, ABC, 1984; Mitchell McKay, *Second Sight: A Love Story*, CBS, 1984; Larry Walker, *Into Thin Air*, CBS, 1985; Freddie Dayton, *Agatha Christie's "Murder in Three Acts,"* CBS, 1986. Guest: *Tonight Show*, NBC, 1987.

PRINCIPAL FILM APPEARANCES— *Smile*, United Artists, 1975; *Damien: Omen II*, Twentieth Century-Fox, 1978; *Risky Business*, Warner Brothers, 1983.

NON-RELATED CAREER—Cabinet maker.

AWARDS: National scholarship from the Oregon Shakespeare Festival, 1953; RCA-NBC Scholarship for Acting, Yale University, School of Drama, 1955-56.

MEMBER: Actors' Equity Association, American Federation of Television and Radio Artists, Screen Actors Guild, Writers Guild of America-East.

SIDELIGHTS: CTFT learned that Nicholas Pryor is also an inventor who has recently developed and patented an accessory that improves the usefulness and storage capacity of household closets.

ADDRESSES: AGENT—c/o Ronald Muchnick and Yvette Schumer, Suite 1102, 1697 Broadway, New York, NY 10019. PUBLICIST—c/o Michael Levine Public Relations Company, 8730 Sunset Boulevard, Los Angeles, CA 90069.

*   *   *

PURL, Linda

PERSONAL: Born in Greenwich CT; daughter of Raymond and Marcie Purl. EDUCATION: Attended Finch College; trained for the stage with Marguerite Beale, 1970-71, at the Lee Strasberg Institute, 1972-74, and with Milton Katselas, 1978—.

VOCATION: Actress and singer.

CAREER: TELEVISION DEBUT—Host, NHK-TV (National Educational Network), Tokyo, Japan, 1962. PRINCIPAL TELEVISION APPEARANCES—Episodic: *The Waltons,* CBS, 1974; *Lucas Tanner,* NBC, 1974; *Sons and Daughters,* CBS, 1974; *Hawaii Five-O,* CBS, 1975; *Medical Center,* CBS, 1975; *Serpico,* ABC, 1976; *Murder, She Wrote,* CBS, 1985; *Alfred Hitchcock Presents,* NBC, 1985. Series: Doreen Post, *The Secret Storm,* CBS, 1973; Betsy Bullock, *Beacon Hill,* CBS, 1975; Ashley Pfister, *Happy Days,* ABC, 1982; *Weekends,* ABC, 1983; Charlene, *Matlock,* NBC, 1986. Mini-Series: Mavis Eaton, *Testimony of Two Men,* syndicated, 1977. Movies: Laurie Mathews, *Bad Ronald,* ABC, 1974; Molly Beaton, *Young Pioneers,* ABC, 1976; Deborah Randal, *Pioneer Trail,* NBC, 1976; Laura Gorman, *Having Babies,* ABC, 1976; Alice Roosevelt, *Eleanor and Franklin,* ABC, 1976; Molly Beaton, *Young Pioneers Christmas,* ABC, 1976; Anne Macarino, *Black Market Baby,* ABC, 1977; Hailey Atkins, *Little Ladies of the Night,* ABC, 1977; Nydia, *The Last Days of Pompeii,* ABC, 1978; Jennifer Scott, *Women at West Point,* CBS, 1979; Virginia Rae Hensler, *Like Normal People,* ABC, 1979; Sharon Muir, *A Last Cry for Help,* ABC, 1979; Emaline Nevada "Vada" Holtz, *The Flame Is Love,* NBC, 1979; Brenda Farrell, *The Night the City Screamed,* ABC, 1980; title role, *The Adventures of Nellie Bly,* NBC, 1981; Deirdre O'Manion, *The Manions of America,* ABC, 1981; Annie Gilson, *Money on the Side,* ABC, 1982; Sarah, *Midas Valley,* ABC, 1985; Arlene Robbins, *Outrage!,* CBS, 1986; Eve Harper, *Pleasures,* ABC, 1986; Shellane Victor, *Dark Mansions,* ABC, 1986. Guest: *Merv Griffin Show.*

STAGE DEBUT—Title role, *A Day in the Death of Joe Egg,* Tokyo International Players, Tokyo, Japan, 1966. PRINCIPAL STAGE APPEARANCES—Helen Keller, *The Miracle Worker,* Tokyo International Players, Tokyo, Japan, 1967; Isobel, *Hallelujah,* CBS Workshop, Los Angeles, CA, 1973; *Fourth Floor Walk Up,* CAST Theatre, Los Angeles, CA, 1977; *Spoon River Anthology,* Theatre 40, Los Angeles, CA, 1980; Portia, *The Merchant of Venice,* Globe Theatre, Los Angeles, 1981; Nora, *A Doll's House,* Allied International Productions, 1982; Ellen, *The Man Who Could See through Time,* South Coast Repertory Theatre, Costa Mesa, CA, 1982; Prudence, *Beyond Therapy,* Los Angeles Public Theatre, Los Angeles, CA, 1984; Daisy, *On a Clear Day You Can See Forever,* San Bernardino Civic Light Opera, San Bernardino, CA, 1984; Juliet, *Romeo and Juliet,* Starlight Theatre, Los Angeles, CA, 1985; Annie, *The Real Thing,* Mark Taper Forum, Los Angeles,

CA, 1986; Thea, *Hedda Gabler,* Mark Taper Forum, 1986. Also appeared in *The Relapse,* International Players, Tokyo, 1967; *The King and I,* Japan, 1968; *Oliver,* Imperial Theatre, Tokyo, Japan, 1968; and as Sandy, *Grease,* Sacramento, CA, 1980; Betty, *Snacks,* Los Angeles, CA, 1984.

PRINCIPAL CABARET APPEARANCES—Gardenia, Los Angeles, CA, 1986; Roosevelt's Cinegrill, Los Angeles, CA, 1986.

FILM DEBUT—*The Travelers.* PRINCIPAL FILM APPEARANCES—*Jory,* AVCO-Embassy, 1972; *Crazy Mama,* New World, 1975; *W.C. Fields and Me,* Universal, 1976; *Visiting Hours,* Twentieth Century-Fox, 1980; also *Leo and Loree,* 1979; *High Country,* 1979;

RECORDINGS: ALBUMS—Spoken Word: *Teaching English,* Columbia, 1967. *If We Could Turn Back Time* (original soundtrack to the film *Leo and Loree*), 1979.

AWARDS: Best Song, Best Performance, Tokyo Music Festival, 1974; Best Actress, Robby Award, 1981, for *The Merchant of Venice;* Best Actress, Drama-Logue awards, 1982, for *The Man Who Could See through Time,* 1984, for *Beyond Therapy,* 1985, for *Romeo and Juliet,* 1986, for *The Real Thing.*

MEMBER: Actors' Equity Association, Screen Actors Guild, American Federation of Television and Radio Artists.

SIDELIGHTS: RECREATIONS—Painting, swimming, horseback riding.

ADDRESSES: OFFICE—337 S. Bedford Drive, Beverly Hills, CA 90212. AGENT—International Creative Management, 8899 Beverly Boulevard, Los Angeles, CA 90069.

*   *   *

PURNELL, Louise   1942-

PERSONAL: Born May 29, 1942, in Purley, England; daughter of Douglas Southey and Jeanne Marie (de Guingand) Purnell; married Andrew Robertson (an actor). EDUCATION: Attended Coloma Convent; trained for the ballet at the Royal Ballet School and for the stage at Italia Conti Stage School.

VOCATION: Actress.

CAREER: STAGE DEBUT—*Puss in Boots,* New Theatre, Oxford, U.K., 1959. LONDON DEBUT—Lady Mabelle, *Once Upon a Mattress,* Adelphi Theatre, 1960. PRINCIPAL STAGE APPEARANCES—Sophie, *Fiorello!,* Piccadilly Theatre, London, 1962; Cecily Cardew, *The Importance of Being Earnest,* Shaw Theatre, London, 1974; Mrs. Dangerfield, *The Ginger Man,* Shaw Theatre, 1976; Julie Price, *The Ghost Train,* Old Vic Theatre, London, 1976; Rosaline, *Love's Labour's Lost,* Princess Katherine, *Henry V,* Open Air Theatre, London, 1977; Olivia, *Twelfth Night,* Anna Petrovna, *Ivanov,* both with the Prospect Theatre Company, Old Vic Theatre, 1978.

With the National Theatre Company, all at the Old Vic Theatre, London, unless indicated: Sorel Bliss, *Hay Fever,* 1964; Abigail, *The Crucible,* Rose, *Trelawny of the Wells,* both 1965; Carol Melkett, *Black Comedy,* 1966; Irina, *The Three Sisters,* Mariane,

Tartuffe, both 1967; Manto, *Seneca's Oedipus,* Elena, *The Advertisement,* Princess of France, *Love's Labour's Lost,* all 1968; Eve, Zoo, Cleopatra, *Back to Methuselah,* 1969; Aglaya, *The Idiot,* 1970; Susan Mountford, *A Woman Killed with Kindness,* Lady, *Danton's Death,* all 1971; Lady Byron, *Byron: The Naked Peacock,* Juliet, *Romeo and Juliet,* both Young Vic Theatre, London, 1971; Lady Teazle, *The School for Scandal,* Lady Macduff, *Macbeth,* 1972; Dunyasha, *The Cherry Orchard,* Guilianella, *Saturday, Sunday, Monday,* both 1973.

MAJOR TOURS—Viola, *Twelfth Night,* with the National Theatre Company, U.K. cities, 1973.

PRINCIPAL FILM APPEARANCES—*The Three Sisters,* American Film Theatre, 1974.

PRINCIPAL TELEVISION APPEARANCES—Specials: *The Bear; Clayhanger; Cork and Bottle.*

SIDELIGHTS: RECREATIONS—Music, travel.

ADDRESSES: AGENT—c/o Peter Crouch, 60-66 Wardour Street, London W1, England.*

Q

QUAYLE, Anthony 1913-

PERSONAL: Full name, John Anthony Quayle; born September 7, 1913, in Ainsdale, England; son of Arthur and Esther (Overton) Quayle; married Hermione Hannen (divorced); married Dorothy Hyson, 1947; children: one son, two daughters. EDUCATION: Royal Academy of Dramatic Art. MILITARY: British Army, Royal Artillery, 1939-45.

VOCATION: Actor, director, and writer.

CAREER: STAGE DEBUT—Richard Coeur de Lion, Will Scarlett, *Robin Hood,* Q Theatre, London, 1931. BROADWAY DEBUT—Mr. Harcourt, *The Country Wife,* Henry Miller's Theatre, 1936. PRINCIPAL STAGE APPEARANCES—Hector, *Troilus and Cressida,* Cambridge Festival Theatre, Cambridge, U.K., 1931; Ferdinand, *Love's Labour's Lost,* Westminster Theatre, London, 1932; Aumerle, *Richard of Bordeaux,* New Theatre, London, 1932; Bennie Edelman, *Magnolia Street,* Adelphi Theatre, London, 1934; Matt Burke, *Anna Christie,* Imperial Institute, then Embassy Theatre, both London, 1934; Guildenstern, *Hamlet,* New Theatre, 1934; Captain Courtine, *The Soldier's Fortune,* Ambassadors' Theatre, London, 1935; St. Denis, *St. Helena,* Old Vic Theatre, London, 1936; Mr. Wickham, *Pride and Prejudice,* St. James Theatre, London, 1936; Laertes, *Hamlet,* Elsinore Castle, Denmark, 1937; Horatio, *Hamlet,* Westminster Theatre, 1937; Duke of Surrey, *Richard II,* Queen's Theatre, London, 1937; Beppo, *The Silent Knight,* St. James Theatre, 1937; Earl of Essex, *Elizabeth, La Femme sans Homme,* Gate Theatre, then Haymarket Theatre, both London, 1938; Jack Absolute, *The Rivals,* Criterion Theatre, London, 1945; Enobarbus, *Antony and Cleopatra,* Piccadilly Theatre, London, 1946; Iago, *Othello,* Piccadilly Theatre, 1947; Claudius, *Hamlet,* Iago, *Othello,* Petruchio, *The Taming of the Shrew,* all with the Royal Shakespeare Company (RSC), Memorial Theatre, Stratford-on-Avon, U.K., 1948.

Falstaff, *Henry IV, Parts I and II,* RSC, Memorial Theatre, 1951; title role, *Othello,* Bottom, *A Midsummer Night's Dream,* Pandarus, *Troilus and Cressida,* all RSC, Memorial Theatre, 1954; Falstaff, *The Merry Wives of Windsor,* Aaron, *Titus Andronicus,* both RSC, Memorial Theatre, 1955; title role, *Tamburlaine the Great,* Winter Garden Theatre, New York City, 1956; Eddie, *A View from the Bridge,* Comedy Theatre, London, 1956; Aaron, *Titus Andronicus,* Paris Theatre Festival, Paris, France, 1957; Moses, *The Firstborn,* Habimah Theatre, Tel Aviv, Israel, 1958; then Coronet Theatre, New York City, 1958; James, *Long Day's Journey into Night,* Edinburgh Festival, Edinburgh, Scotland, U.K., then New Theatre, both 1959; Cesareo Grimaldi, *Chin-Chin,* Wyndham's Theatre, London, 1960; Nachtigall, *Power of Persuasion,* Garrick Theatre, London, 1963; Sir Charles Duke, *The Right Honourable Gentleman,* Her Majesty's Theatre, London, 1964; Leduc, *Incident*

at Vichy, Phoenix Theatre, London, 1966; title role, *Galileo,* Vivian Beaumont Theatre, New York City, 1967; General Fitzbuttress, *Halfway up the Tree,* Brooks Atkinson Theatre, New York City, 1967; Andrew Wyke, *Sleuth,* St. Martin's Theatre, London, then Music Box Theatre, New York City, both 1970; Rodion Nikolayevich, *The Old World,* RSC, Aldwych Theatre, London, 1976, then 48th Street Theatre, New York City, 1978; Hilary, *The Old Country,* Queen's Theatre, 1978; Sir Anthony Absolute, *The Rivals,* title role, *King Lear,* both with the Old Vic Theatre Company, National Theatre, London, 1978. Also performed with the Old Vic Theatre Company, 1932, at the Empire Theatre, Chiswick, U.K., in a season of Shakespeare's plays, 1933; appeared as Demetrius, *A Midsummer Night's Dream,* Cassio, *Othello,* Ferdinand, *Trelawny of the Wells,* Laertes, *Hamlet,* John Tanner, *Man and Superman,* Captain Absolute, *The Rivals,* all 1938; and in *Look After Lulu,* Edinburgh Festival, then New Theatre, both 1959.

PRINCIPAL STAGE WORK—Director: *Crime and Punishment,* New Theatre, London, 1946; *The Relapse,* Lyric Hammersmith Theatre, London, 1948; *Harvey,* Prince of Wales Theatre, London, 1949; *Who Is Sylvia?,* Criterion Theatre, London, 1950; *Cycle of Histories,* Royal Shakespeare Company (RSC), Memorial Theatre, Stratford-on-Avon, U.K., 1951; *Othello,* RSC, Memorial Theatre, 1954; *Measure for Measure,* Memorial Theatre, 1956; *The Firstborn,* Habimah Theatre, Tel Aviv, Israel, then Coronet Theatre, New York City, both 1958; *Power of Persuasion,* Garrick Theatre, London, 1963; *Lady Windermere's Fan,* Phoenix Theatre, London, 1966; *The Idiot,* with the Old Vic Theatre Company, National Theatre, London, 1970; *Harvey,* Prince of Wales Theatre, 1975; *The Rivals,* with the Old Vic Theatre Company, National Theatre, 1978; *The Clandestine Marriage,* Compass Theatre, 1984.

MAJOR TOURS—Title role, *Henry V,* with the Old Vic Theatre Company, European and Egyptian cities, 1939; title role, *Macbeth,* title role, *Henry VIII,* both with the Royal Shakespeare Company (RSC), Australian and New Zealand cities, 1949-1950; director, *As You Like It, Othello,* and *Henry IV, Part I,* all RSC, Australian and New Zealand cities, 1953; Aaron, *Titus Andronicus,* European cities, 1957; Rodion Nikolayevich, *Do You Turn Somersaults?* (retitled from *The Old World*), RSC, U.S. cities, 1977-78. Also appeared in *Heartbreak House,* U.K. cities, 1980; *The Devil's Disciple, The Skin Game,* U.K. cities, both 1981; *Hobson's Choice, Rules of the Game,* and (also director) *A Coat of Varnish,* U.K. cities, all 1982.

FILM DEBUT—*Saraband for Dead Lovers.* PRINCIPAL FILM APPEARANCES—*Hamlet,* Universal, 1948; *Oh, Rosalinda,* Powell and Pressburger, 1955; *No Time for Tears,* ABPC, 1956; *Pursuit of the Graf Spee,* Rank, 1957; *The Wrong Man,* Warner Brothers, 1957; *Woman in a Dressing Gown,* Warner Brothers, 1957; *Ice Cold in Alex,* (also known as *Desert Attack*), ABPC, 1957; *Serious*

Charge, Alva, 1958; *Tarzan's Greatest Adventure,* Paramount, 1959; *The Challenge* (also known as *It Takes a Thief*), Alexandra, 1960; *The Man Who Wouldn't Talk,* Showcorporation, 1960; *The Guns of Navarone,* Columbia, 1961; *H.M.S. Defiant,* Paramount, 1961; *Lawrence of Arabia,* Columbia, 1962; *The Fall of the Roman Empire,* Paramount, 1964; *East of Sudan,* Columbia, 1964; *Operation Crossbow,* Metro-Goldwyn-Mayer (MGM), 1965; *Fog,* Columbia, 1965; *A Study in Terror,* Columbia, 1966; *MacKenna's Gold,* Columbia, 1969; *Before Winter Comes,* Columbia, 1969; *Anne of the Thousand Days,* Universal, 1970; *Bequest to the Nation* (also known as *The Nelson Affair*), Universal, 1972; *Everything You Always Wanted to Know about Sex,* United Artists, 1972; *The Tamarind Seed,* AVCO-Embassy, 1974; *The Eagle Has Landed,* Columbia, 1977; *Murder by Decree,* AVCO-Embassy, 1979. Also appeared in *Holocaust 2000,* 1977; *The Chosen,* 1978; *After the Ball Is Over,* 1985.

PRINCIPAL TELEVISION APPEARANCES—Mini-Series: Aaron, *Moses, the Lawgiver,* CBS, 1975. Movies: Colonel Maledin, *Destiny of a Spy,* NBC, 1969; Bassett Cosgrove, *Jarrett,* NBC, 1973; Tom Bannister, *QB VII,* ABC, 1974; Jaggers, *Great Expectations,* NBC, 1974; King Saul, *The Story of David,* ABC, 1976; General Zvi Zemir, *21 Hours at Munich,* ABC, 1976; Quintus, *Last Days of Pompeii,* ABC, 1978; Rubrius Gallus, *Masada,* ABC, 1981; Inspector Hubbard, *Dial M for Murder,* NBC, 1981; Lord Montgomery, *The Manions of America,* ABC, 1981; Dr. Geneste, *Lace,* ABC, 1984; Abdullah, *The Key to Rebecca,* syndicated, 1985. Specials: *Benjamin Franklin,* 1974; *Ice Age,* 1978; *Henry IV, Parts I and II,* BBC, 1979; *Beethoven,* 1983; *The Last Bottle in the World,* 1985; *Testament of John,* 1984; *Quoth the Raven,* 1985; *Oedipus at Colonnus,* 1986; also appeared in *Strange Report.*

PRINCIPAL TELEVISION WORK—Producer, *The Idiot,* BBC, 1970; director, *Caesar and Cleopatra,* NBC, 1979.

RELATED CAREER— Director, Royal Shakespeare Company, Stratford-on-Avon, U.K., 1948-56; guest director and lecturer, University of Tennessee, 1975.

WRITINGS: BOOKS—*Eight Hours from England,* 1945; *On Such a Night,* 1947.

AWARDS: Commander of the British Empire, 1952; Emmy Award, 1974, for *QB VII.*

MEMBER: British Actors' Equity Association, Screen Actors Guild, American Federation of Television and Radio Artists; Garrick Club.

ADDRESSES: AGENT—International Creative Management, Ltd., 22 Grafton Street, London W1, England.*

*　　　*　　　*

QUENTIN, Patrick
See WHEELER, Hugh

*　　　*　　　*

QUILLEY, Denis   1927-

PERSONAL: Born December 26, 1927, in London, England; son of Clifford Charles and Ada Winifred (Stanley) Quilley; married Stella Chapman.

VOCATION: Actor.

CAREER: STAGE DEBUT—Lyngstrand, *The Lady from the Sea,* Birmingham Repertory Theatre Company, Birmingham, U.K., 1945. LONDON DEBUT—Richard, *The Lady's Not for Burning,* Globe Theatre, 1950. BROADWAY DEBUT—Nestor-le-Fripe, *Irma La Douce,* Plymouth Theatre, 1961. PRINCIPAL STAGE APPEARANCES—Leading Seaman Kendall, *Red Dragon,* Phoenix Theatre, London, 1950; Richard Shelton, *Black Arrow,* Gratiano, *The Merchant of Venice,* both Old Vic Theatre, London, 1950-51; Mathias, *Point of Departure,* Duke of York's Theatre, London, 1951; *Airs on a Shoestring,* Royal Court Theatre, London, 1953; Geoffrey Morris, *Wild Thyme,* Duke of York's Theatre, 1955; Laurie, *A Girl Called Jo,* Piccadilly Theatre, London, 1955; Tom Wilson, *Grab Me a Gondola,* Lyric Hammersmith Theatre, London, 1957; Brassbound, *Captain Brassbound's Conversion,* Orlando, *As You Like It,* both Bristol Old Vic Theatre, Bristol, U.K., 1958; title role, *Candide,* Saville Theatre, London, 1959.

Mike Polaski, *Bachelor Flat,* Piccadilly Theatre, London, 1960; Mark Raven, *Wildest Dreams,* Everyman Theatre, Cheltenham, U.K., 1960; Nestor-le-Fripe, *Irma La Douce,* Lyric Theatre, London, 1961; Benedick, *Much Ado about Nothing,* Open Air Theatre, London, 1963; Antipholus of Ephesus, *The Boys from Syracuse,* Drury Lane Theatre, London, 1963; Charles Condamine, *High Spirits,* Savoy Theatre, London, 1964; Archie Rice, *The Entertainer,* title role, *Macbeth,* both Nottingham Playhouse Theatre, Nottingham, U.K., 1969; Krogstad, *A Doll's House,* Gardner Center, Sussex University, Sussex, U.K., 1970; Alec Hurley, *Sing a Rude Song,* Greenwich Theatre then Garrick Theatre, both London, 1970; Aufidius, *Coriolanus,* Scofield, *Tyger,* Jamie, *Long Day's Journey into Night,* all National Theatre, London, 1971; Bolingbroke, *Richard II,* Crabtree, *The School for Scandal,* Hildy Johnson, *The Front Page,* Banquo, *Macbeth,* all National Theatre, 1972; title role, *Macbeth,* Lopakhin, *The Cherry Orchard,* Luigi Ianiello, *Saturday, Sunday, Monday,* Andrew Ford, *The Party,* all National Theatre, 1974; Caliban, *The Tempest,* National Theatre, 1975; John Tanner, *Man and Superman,* Arnaud Theatre, Guilford, U.K., 1975; Claudius, *Hamlet,* Old Vic Theatre, then Lyttelton Theatre, London, 1975; Hector, *Troilus and Cressida,* Young Vic Theatre, London, 1976; Bajazeth, Callapine, *Tamburlaine the Great,* Olivier Theatre, London, 1976; Captain Terri Dennis, *Privates on Parade,* Aldwych Theatre, London, 1977, then Piccadilly Theatre, 1978; Reverand James Morell, *Candida,* Albery Theatre, London, 1977; Sidney Bruhl, *Deathtrap,* Garrick Theatre, London, 1978; title role, *Sweeney Todd,* Drury Lane Theatre, 1980. Also appeared with the Birmingham Repertory Theatre Company, Birmingham, U.K., 1945; Nottingham Repertory Theatre Company, Nottingham, U.K., 1952.

MAJOR TOURS—Fabian, *Twelfth Night,* Old Vic Theatre Company, Italian cities, 1950; Nestor-le-Fripe, *Irma La Douce,* U.S. cities, 1962; Robert Browning, *Robert and Elizabeth,* Australian cities, 1966.

PRINCIPAL FILM APPEARANCES—*Anne of the Thousand Days,* Universal, 1970; *Murder on the Orient Express,* Paramount, 1974; also *Life at the Top,* 1965.

PRINCIPAL TELEVISION APPEARANCES—Series: *Clayhanger,* BBC. Specials: *The Father, Henry IV, Murder in the Cathedral,* all BBC.

MEMBER: British Actors' Equity Association, Screen Actors Guild.

SIDELIGHTS: FAVORITE ROLES—Jamie in *Long Day's Journey into Night;* Hildy Johnson in *The Front Page.* RECREATIONS—Flute, cello.

ADDRESSES: AGENT—NEMS Management, 29-31 King's Road, London SW3, England.*

*　　*　　*

QUINLAN, Kathleen   1954-

PERSONAL: Born in 1954 in Pasadena, CA.

VOCATION: Actress.

CAREER: PRINCIPAL TELEVISION APPEARANCES—Pilots: Joyce Howell, *Lucas Tanner,* NBC, 1974; Cass Donner, *She's in the Army Now,* ABC, 1981. Movies: Melissa, *Can Ellen Be Saved?,* ABC, 1974; Deborah Anders, *Where Have All the People Gone?,* NBC, 1974; Michelle, *The Missing Are Deadly,* ABC, 1975; Edith Evans, *The Turning Point of Jim Malloy,* NBC, 1975; Anne Benedict, *The Abduction of Saint Anne* (also known as *They've Kidnapped Anne Benedict*), ABC, 1975; Karen Brodwick, *Little Ladies of the Night,* ABC, 1977; Rose Michaels, *When She Says No,* ABC, 1984; Chris Graham, *Blackout,* HBO, 1985; Lois Lee, *Children of the Night,* CBS, 1985.

FILM DEBUT—*One Is a Lonely Number,* 1972. PRINCIPAL FILM APPEARANCES—*American Graffiti,* Universal, 1973; *Lifeguard,* Paramount, 1976; *Airport '77,* Universal, 1977; *I Never Promised You a Rose Garden,* New World, 1977; *The Promise,* Universal, 1979; *The Runner Stumbles,* Twentieth Century-Fox, 1979; *Sunday Lovers,* United Aritists, 1981; *Hanky Panky,* Columbia, 1982; *Independance Day,* Warner Brothers, 1982; *Twilight Zone: The Movie,* Warner Brothers, 1983; *Warning Sign,* Twentieth Century-Fox, 1985; Jane, *Wild Thing,* Atlantic, 1987.

PRINCIPAL STAGE APPEARANCES—Annie, *Taken in Marriage,* New York Shakespeare Festival, Public Theatre, New York City, 1979; *Accent on Youth,* Long Wharf Theatre, New Haven, CT, 1983.

AWARDS: Theatre World Award, 1979, for *Taken in Marriage.*

MEMBER: Actors' Equity Association, Screen Actors Guild.

ADDRESSES: AGENT—c/o Steve Dontanville, International Creative Management, 8899 Beverly Boulevard, Los Angeles, CA 90048.*

R

RAFFIN, Deborah 1953-

PERSONAL: Born March 13, 1953, in Los Angeles, CA; married Michael Viner (a producer and manager). EDUCATION: Attended Valley College.

VOCATION: Actress and model.

CAREER: FILM DEBUT—*40 Carats,* Columbia, 1973. PRINCIPAL FILM APPEARANCES—*The Dove,* Paramount, 1974; *Once Is Not Enough,* Paramount, 1975; *God Told Me To,* 1976; *The Sentinel,* Universal, 1977; *Touched by Love,* Columbia, 1980; *Dance of the Dwarfs,* 1983; *Death Wish III,* Filmways, 1985.

PRINCIPAL TELEVISION APPEARANCES—Movies: *Nightmare in Badham County,* ABC, 1976; *Haywire,* 1980; *Running Out,* 1983; *Lace II,* ABC, 1985; also *The Last Convertible* and *Dinner Date.*

PRINCIPAL STAGE APPEARANCES—Ophelia, *Hamlet,* with the National Theatre of Great Britain, London.

RELATED CAREER—Former fashion model.

AWARDS: Emmy Award nomination, 1977, for *Nightmare in Badham County.*

MEMBER: Screen Actors Guild.

ADDRESSES: HOME—Beverly Hills, CA and Vermont. AGENT—David Shapira & Associates, 15301 Ventura Blvd., Suite 345, Sherman Oaks, CA 91403. MANAGER—Michael Viner, 2630 Eden Place, Beverly Hills, CA 90210.*

*   *   *

RAIN, Douglas

PERSONAL: Born in Winnipeg, MB, Canada. EDUCATION: Studied theatre at the Banff School of Fine Arts and the Old Vic Theatre School.

VOCATION: Actor and director.

CAREER: BROADWAY DEBUT—Bajazeth, Almeda, *Tamburlaine the Great,* Winter Garden Theatre, 1956. PRINCIPAL STAGE APPEARANCES—Henry Higgins, *Pygmalion,* Crest Theatre, Toronto, ON, Canada, 1957; Christopher Mahon, *The Playboy of the Western World,* Gottlieb Biedermann, *The Firebugs,* both Central

Library Theatre, Toronto, ON, Canada, 1965; Father William Rolfe, *Hadrian VII,* Mermaid Theatre, London, 1965; Giovanni Mocenigo, *The Heretic,* Duke of York's Theatre, London, 1970; Claudius, *Hamlet,* Thorndike Theatre, Leatherhead, U.K., 1970; Fourteenth Earl of Gurney, *The Ruling Class,* Arena Stage, Washington, DC, 1971; Cecil, *Vivat! Vivat! Regina!,* Broadhurst Theatre, New York City, 1972; Tesman, *Hedda Gabler,* Andrew Wyke, *Sleuth,* both Manitoba Theatre Center, Winnipeg, MB, Canada, 1972. Also appeared in *The Golden Age* (concert reading), Lyceum Theatre, New York City, 1963; *Mother Courage,* Manitoba Theatre Center, 1964; *The Ottawa Man,* Festival Lennoxville, 1972.

With the Stratford Festival Theatre Company, Stratford, ON, Canada: Marquis of Dorset, Tyrrel, Richard (understudy), *Richard III,* 1953; Claudio, *Measure for Measure,* Biondello, *The Taming of the Shrew,* messenger, *Oedipus the King,* all 1954; Decius Brutus, Titinius, *Julius Caesar,* 1955; Michael Williams, *Henry V,* Simple, *The Merry Wives of Windsor,* both 1956; first player, *Hamlet,* Malvolio, *Twelfth Night,* both 1957; Tony Lumpkin, *She Stoops to Conquer,* Prince Hal, *Henry IV, Part I,* clown, *The Winter's Tale,* all 1958; Iago, *Othello,* Silvius, *As You Like It,* both 1959; title role, *King John,* Tybalt, *Romeo and Juliet,* both 1960; Wolsey, *Henry VIII,* Boyet, *Love's Labour's Lost,* Grandad, *The Canvas Barricade,* all 1961; Ragueneau, *Cyrano de Bergerac,* 1962; Ulysses, *Troilus and Cressida,* Dromio of Syracuse, *The Comedy of Errors,* Apemantus, *Timon of Athens,* all 1963; Monsieur Jourdain, *Le Bourgeois Gentilhomme,* Edgar, *King Lear,* Pinchwife, *The Country Wife,* all 1964; Prince Henry, *Henry IV, Parts I and II,* 1965; title role, *Henry V,* Sir Toby Belch, *Twelfth Night,* both 1966; Orgon, *Tartuffe,* D'Artagnan, *The Three Musketeers,* both 1968; Mosca, *Volpone,* 1971; Iago, *Othello,* 1973; Bastard, *King John,* Lysimachus, *Pericles,* both 1974; Judge Danforth, *The Crucible,* 1975; Angelo, *Measure for Measure,* 1976; Jean, *Miss Julie,* 1977; de la Rochepozay, Prince Conde, *The Devils,* Monologue, *From an Abandoned Work,* both 1978; title role, *Henry IV, Parts I and II,* Gloucester, *King Lear,* both 1979; Weller, *The Gin Game,* John Aubrey, *Brief Lives,* and appeared in *Henry V,* all 1980.

PRINCIPAL STAGE WORK—Director: *Rosencrantz and Guildenstern Are Dead,* Manitoba Theatre Center, Winnipeg, MB, Canada, 1973.

MAJOR TOURS—All with the Stratford Festival Theatre Company: Speed, *Two Gentlemen of Verona,* Huish, *The Broken Jug,* Canadian cities, both 1957; Holofernes, *Love's Labour's Lost,* Monsieur Jourdain, *Le Bourgeois Gentilhomme,* Apemantus, *Timon of Athens,* U.K. cities, all 1964; also *Two Programs of Shakespearean Comedy,* Canadian and U.S. universities, 1962.

PRINCIPAL TELEVISION APPEARANCES—Title role, *Henry VI;*

also *The Crucible; Hedda Gabler; The Circle; Talking to a Stranger,* all for Canadian television.

RELATED CAREER—Associate director, Avon Stage, Stratford Theatre Festival, Stratford, ON, Canada, 1974; head of the English section, National Theatre School, Montreal, PQ, Canada.

MEMBER: Canadian Actors' Equity Association.

ADDRESSES: AGENT—c/o Elspeth Cochrane Agency, One The Pavement, London SW4, England.*

*   *   *

RAITT, John   1917-

PERSONAL: Born January 19, 1917, in Santa Ana, CA; son of Archie John and Stella Eulalie (Walton) Raitt; married Marjorie Geraldine Haydock (marriage ended); married Kathy Landry. EDUCATION: Studied voice with Richard Cummings.

VOCATION: Actor and singer.

CAREER: BROADWAY DEBUT—Billy Bigelow, *Carousel,* Majestic Theatre, 1945. PRINCIPAL STAGE APPEARANCES— Chorus, *H.M.S. Pinafore,* Los Angeles Civic Light Opera Company, Curran Theatre, San Francisco, CA, 1940; Figaro, Count Almaviva, *The Barber of Seville* (opera), Escamillo, *Carmen* (opera), all Pasadena Civic Auditorium, Pasadena, CA, 1941; Curly, *Oklahoma,* Erlanger

JOHN RAITT

Theatre, Chicago, IL, 1944; Pedro, *Magdalena,* Ziegfeld Theatre, New York City, 1948; Robert, *New Moon,* Creek Theatre, Los Angeles, CA, 1949; Jamie McRuin, *Three Wishes for Jamie,* Mark Hellinger Theatre, New York City, 1952; duke, *Carnival in Flanders,* Century Theatre, New York City, 1953; Sid Sorokin, *The Pajama Game,* St. James Theatre, New York City, 1954, then Stadium Theatre, Pittsburgh, Pittsburgh, PA, 1957, later St. Paul Civic Opera, St. Paul, MN, 1964; Billy Bigelow, *Carousel,* Curran Theatre, San Francisco, CA, 1963, then State Theatre, New York City, 1965, later Music Theatre, Houston, TX, 1967; Shade Motley, *A Joyful Noise,* Mark Hellinger Theatre, 1966; title role, *Zorba,* Westbury Music Fair, Long Island, NY, 1970; Billy Bigelow, *Carousel,* Royal Alexandra Theatre, Toronto, ON, Canada, 1972. Also appeared as Frank Butler, *Annie Get Your Gun,* San Francisco then Los Angeles, CA, 1957; in *A Musical Jubilee,* St. James Theatre, 1975.

MAJOR TOURS—Destry, *Destry Rides Again,* Billy Bigelow, *Carousel,* Curley, *Oklahoma,* U.S. cities, all 1960; Sid Sorokin, *The Pajama Game,* Curley, *Oklahoma,* Billy Bigelow, *Carousel,* U.S. cities, all 1961; Curly, *Oklahoma,* U.S. cities, 1964; Sid Sorokin, *The Pajama Game,* Billy Bigelow, *Carousel,* U.S. cities, both 1965; Dr. Mark Buckner, *On a Clear Day You Can See Forever,* U.S. cities, 1967-68; Hajj, *Kismet,* U.S. cities, 1971; Edward Rutledge, *1776,* U.S. cities, 1973; Charlie Anderson, *Shenandoah,* U.S. cities, 1976; Don Quixote, *Man of La Mancha,* U.S. cities, 1978.

PRINCIPAL FILM APPEARANCES—*The Pajama Game,* Metro-Goldwyn-Mayer, 1957; also appeared in *Flight Command,* 1940: *Ziegfeld Girl,* 1941.

PRINCIPAL TELEVISION APPEARANCES—Series: Host, *The Chevy Show,* CBS, 1958-59. Specials: Frank, *Annie Get Your Gun,* 1960. Guest: *The Bell Telephone Hour.*

AWARDS: Best Performance in a Musical Production, Drama Critic's Award, Donaldson Award, both 1945, for *Carousel.*

MEMBER: Actors' Equity Association, Screen Actors Guild, American Federation of Television and Radio Artists.

SIDELIGHTS: RECREATIONS—Golf; water skiing.

ADDRESSES: OFFICE—c/o James Fitzgerald Enterprises Inc., 1061 Ravoli Drive, Pacific Palisades, CA, 90272.*

*   *   *

RAMBO, Dack

PERSONAL: Born Norman J. Rambo, November 13, in Delano, CA; son of Lester and Beatrice Rambo. EDUCATION: Studied acting with Lee Strasberg and Vincent Chase.

VOCATION: Actor.

CAREER: PRINCIPAL TELEVISION APPEARANCES—Episodic: *Hotel,* ABC; *The Love Boat,* ABC; *Fantasy Island,* ABC; *Charlie's Angels,* ABC; *Wonder Woman,* CBS; *House Calls,* CBS; *The Mississippi,* CBS; *Murder, She Wrote,* CBS. Series: Dack Massey, *The New Loretta Young Show,* CBS, 1962-63; Jeff Sonnett, *The Guns of Will Sonnett,* ABC, 1967-69; Cyrus Pike, *Dirty Sally,* CBS, 1974; Jack Cole, *The Sword of Justice,* NBC, 1978-79; Wesley Harper, *Paper Dolls,* ABC, 1984; Jack Ewing, *Dallas,* CBS, 1985-87; also appeared in *All My Children,* ABC; *Never Too*

DACK RAMBO

Young. Pilots: Ronnie Browning, *Waikiki,* ABC, 1980; Pat Connell, *No Man's Land,* 1984; Wesley Harper, *Paper Dolls,* ABC, 1982. Movies: Riley Briggs, *River of Gold,* ABC, 1971; Doug Reynolds, *Hit Lady,* ABC, 1974; Andy Stuart, *Good Against Evil,* ABC, 1977.

PRINCIPAL FILM APPEARANCES—*Nightmare Honeymoon,* Metro-Goldwyn-Mayer, 1972; *Shades of Love,* Lorimar, 1987; also appeared in *Rich and Famous,* 1981; and *Wild Flowers.*

RELATED CAREER—Founder, Dack Rambo Productions.

MEMBER: National Academy of Television Arts and Sciences; Mothers Against Drunk Drivers (M.A.D.D.).

SIDELIGHTS: RECREATIONS—Horseback riding, raquetball, tennis, jogging.

ADDRESSES: AGENT—c/o Gary Rado, International Creative Management, 8899 Beverly Boulevard, Los Angeles, CA 90048. MANAGER—Sterling/Winters Company, 1901 Avenue of the Stars, Los Angeles, CA 90067.

*   *   *

RANSLEY, Peter   1931-

PERSONAL: Born October 12, 1931, in Leeds, England; son of Arthur (a manager) and Hilda (Taylor) Ransley; married Hazel Rew, June 1955 (divorced, 1970); married Cynthia Harris (a social worker), December 14, 1974. EDUCATION: Attended London University, 1950-52.

VOCATION: Playwright, editor, and manager.

CAREER: Also see WRITINGS below.

RELATED CAREER—Contributor to the periodicals, *Plays and Players* and *Listener.*

NON-RELATED CAREER—Editor of business publications and development manager for a publishing company, 1959-70; chairman, Blenheim Project, 1974—.

WRITINGS: PLAYS—*Disabled,* Hampstead Theatre Club, London, 1971, then Stables Theatre Club, Manchester, U.K.; *Ellen,* Hampstead Theatre Club, 1971; *The Thompson Report,* produced in London, 1972; *Runaway,* Royal Court Theatre, London, 1974. TELEPLAYS—*Dear Mr. Welfare,* BBC, 1970; *Black Olives,* BBC, 1971; *Night Duty,* BBC, 1972; *Blinkers,* London Weekend Television, 1973; *A Fair Day's Work,* BBC, 1973; *Kate the Good Neighbour,* BBC, 1980; *Minor Complications,* BBC, 1981; *House on the Hill,* BBC; *Bread or Blood,* BBC; *The Story of Ruth,* BBC; *Shall I Be Mother?,* BBC; *Tales of the Unexpected,* Anglia Television; *Inside Story,* Anglia Television; *The Price,* RTE. SCREENPLAYS—*Geronimo,* Zenith Productions; *A Matter of Honor,* Amblin/Universal.

AWARDS: Gold Medal, Commonwealth Film and Television Festival, 1980, for *Kate the Good Neighbour;* Best Single Play, Royal Television Society Award, 1981, for *Minor Complications.*

MEMBER: Theatre Writers Group.

ADDRESSES: HOME—33 Dordrecht Road, London W2 3EW, England. AGENT—c/o The Artists Agency, 10000 Santa Monica Boulevard, No. 305, Los Angeles, CA 90067.

*   *   *

RAPF, Matthew   1920-

PERSONAL: Born October 22, 1920, in New York, NY; son of Harry Rapf (a producer). EDUCATION: Dartmouth College, B.A., 1942. MILITARY: U.S. Navy.

VOCATION: Producer and writer.

CAREER: PRINCIPAL TELEVISION WORK—Producer: Series—*The Web,* CBS, 1950-54; *The Loretta Young Show,* NBC, 1953-61; *Frontier,* NBC, 1955-56; *Ben Casey,* ABC, 1961-66; *Slattery's People,* CBS, 1964-65; *Iron Horse,* ABC, 1967-68; *Young Lawyers,* ABC, 1970-71; *Kojak,* CBS, 1973-78; *Switch,* CBS, 1975-78; *Doctor's Hospital,* NBC, 1975-76; *The Gangster Chronicles,* NBC, 1981; *Eischied,* NBC, 1979-83. Pilots—*The Marcus-Nelson Murders* (pilot for *Kojak* series), CBS, 1973. Movies—*Hardcase,* 1971; *Terror in the Sky,* 1971; *Oklahoma City Dolls,* 1981; also *The Great Gildersleeve, Jefferson Drum, The Man From Blackhawk, Two Faces West,* and *Shadow in the Land.*

PRINCIPAL FILM WORK—Writer (see below); co-producer, *The Adventures of Gallant Bess,* 1948; co-producer, *The Unknown Man,* Metro-Goldwyn-Mayer (MGM), 1951; producer: *Desperate*

MATTHEW RAPF

Search, MGM, 1952; *Big Leaguer,* MGM, 1953; *Half a Hero,* MGM, 1953.

WRITINGS: SCREENPLAYS—*The Adventures of Gallant Bess,* 1948; story, *The Sellout.*

MEMBER: Writers Guild of America.

ADDRESSES: HOME—120 Malibu Colony Road, Malibu, CA 90265. OFFICE—Writers Guild West, 8955 Beverly Blvd., Los Angeles, CA 90048.

*   *   *

RAPHAEL, Gerrianne   1939-

PERSONAL: Born February 23, 1939, in New York, NY; daughter of Sidney (a concert pianist) and Evelyn Raphael; children: Kathleen, Kristen, Deirdre. EDUCATION: Attended the Professional Childrens School, the New School for Social Research, and Columbia University; trained for the stage with Paul Mann at Paul Mann's Actor's Workshop, and with Sanford Meisner at the Neighborhood Playhouse.

VOCATION: Actress.

CAREER: PRINCIPAL STAGE APPEARANCES—Polly, Jenny, *The Threepenny Opera,* Theatre De Lys, New York City, 1954; Aldonza,

Man of La Mancha, American National Theatre Academy, Washington Square Theatre, New York City, 1965, then Vivian Beaumont Theatre, New York City, 1972; Amelia, *Catch My Soul,* Ahmanson Theatre, Los Angeles, CA, 1969; Vera, *King of Hearts,* Minskoff Theatre, New York City, 1978; Angela, *The Butler Did It,* Players Theatre, New York City, 1981; Joanna Wheeler, *The Ninth Step,* Riverwest Theatre, New York City, 1984. Also appeared in *Goodbye My Fancy,* Morosco Theatre, New York City, 1950; *Seventh Heaven,* Virginia Theatre, New York City, 1954; *Li'l Abner,* St. James Theatre, New York City, 1959; *Saratoga,* Winter Garden Theatre, New York City, 1960; *Milk and Honey,* Martin Beck Theatre, New York City, 1962; *Hallelujah Baby,* Martin Beck Theatre, 1968; *Solitaire,* John Golden Theatre, New York City, 1971; title role, *The Prime of Miss Jean Brodie,* Manhattan Theatre Club, New York City; Cecily, *Ernest in Love,* Gramercy Arts Theatre, New York City; Maizie, *The Boy Friend,* Cherry Lane Theatre, New York City; *Stauf* (opera), Cubiculo Theatre, New York City; *Noah* (opera), Pratt Institute, Brooklyn, NY; *The Conjurer* (opera), New York Shakespeare Festival, Public Theatre, New York City; *A Guest in the House,* New York City, 1972; *Violet,* New York City, 1974.

MAJOR TOURS—Maria, *West Side Story* and in *Gypsy,* U.S. cities, both 1964; Aldonza, *Man of La Mancha,* U.S. cities, 1975.

PRINCIPAL TELEVISION APPEARANCES—Episodic: *As the World Turns,* CBS; also appeared in *The First Hundred Years; From These Roots; One Man's Family.* Series: Elinor, *The Aldrich Family,* NBC, 1954; voices of Pumyra and Chilla, *Thundercats* (animated), syndicated.

GERRIANNE RAPHAEL

RELATED CAREER—Provides voice-over for television commercials.

NON-RELATED CAREER—Clothing designer.

MEMBER: Actors' Equity Association, American Federation of Television and Radio Artists.

SIDELIGHTS: CTFT learned that one of Gerianne Raphael's clothing designs is among the permanent collection of the Metropolitan Museum of Art.

ADDRESSES: AGENT—Don Buchwald and Associates, 10 E. 44th Street, New York, NY 10017.

*   *   *

RATHER, Dan   1931-

PERSONAL: Full name, Daniel Irvin Rather; born October 31, 1931, in Wharton, TX; son of Irvin (an oil pipeliner) and Byrl (a waitress; maiden name, Page) Rather; married Jeannine Grace Goebel (a painter); children: Dawn Robin, Daniel Martin. EDUCATION: Sam Houston State Teachers College (now Sam Houston State University), B.A., journalism, 1953; attended University of Houston Law School, 1957-59, and South Texas School of Law, 1959. POLITICS: Independent. RELIGION: Protestant.

VOCATION: Television news anchorman, reporter, and writer.

DAN RATHER

CAREER: PRINCIPAL TELEVISION WORK—News and public affairs director, KHOU-TV (CBS affiliate), Houston, TX, 1960-61; with CBS News (network), New York City, 1961—, as reporter in Dallas and New Orleans, 1961-63, White House correspondent, 1964, chief of London bureau, 1965-66, correspondent in Vietnam, 1966, White House correspondent, 1966-74, anchorman and correspondent, *CBS Reports,* 1974-75, co-editor and co-anchorman, *60 Minutes,* 1975-81, managing editor and anchorman, *CBS Evening News with Dan Rather,* 1981—; other duties for CBS News include team coverage of national political conventions, 1964—, anchorman on Midwest desk for national election coverage, 1972-80, reporter and co-editor, *Who's Who,* 1977, anchorman, *Campaign '84,* 1984, and anchorman for various special programs.

PRINCIPAL RADIO WORK—News writer, reporter, and sportscaster, KSAM, Huntsville, TX, 1950-54; news writer, reporter, and news director, KTRH (CBS affiliate), Houston, 1954-1959; anchorman, *Dan Rather Reporting,* CBS Radio Network, 1977—.

RELATED CAREER—Reporter, Associated Press, 1951-52, and United Press International, 1953, both in Huntsville, TX; journalism teacher, Sam Houston State Teachers College (now Sam Houston State University), 1953-54; part-time writer and reporter, *Huntsville Item* and *Houston Chronicle,* mid-1950s.

WRITINGS: NON-FICTION—(With Gary Paul Gates) *The Palace Guard,* Harper & Row, 1974; (with Mickey Herskowitz) *The Camera Never Blinks: Adventures of a TV Journalist* (autobiography), Morrow, 1977.

AWARDS: Co-winner, Outstanding Achievement within Regularly Scheduled News Programs, Emmy Awards, 1973, for "Coverage of the Shooting of Governor Wallace," and for "The Watergate Affair," and 1974, for "The Agnew Resignation," all *CBS Evening News with Walter Cronkite;* co-winner, Outstanding Documentary Program Achievements (Current Events), Emmy Award, 1974, for *CBS News Special Report: The Senate and the Watergate Affair;* Distinguished Achievement for Broadcasting Award, University of Southern California Journalism Alumni Association; Bob Considine Award, 1983.

SIDELIGHTS: Widely regarded as an outstanding television journalist, Dan Rather has been anchorman and managing editor of the *CBS Evening News* since March 9, 1981. His estimated three-million-dollar-a-year salary makes him one of television's highest paid newsmen, but he has drawn criticism as well as accolades in facing the challenge to maintain his network's foremost position among broadcast news operations.

Rather, the son of an oil pipeliner and a waitress, grew up in Houston, Texas, during the 1940s. The first member of his family to attend college, he graduated from Sam Houston State Teachers College in 1953 with a bachelor's degree in journalism. He began his professional career contributing stories to the national wire services and to Texas newspapers. In 1954 he joined the staff of the CBS radio affiliate in Houston, but made the move to the network's television affiliate, KHOU-TV, in 1960. Rather's big break came in 1961, when, as a KHOU-TV reporter, for three days he withstood the onslaught of Hurricane Carla to file reports for the network news operation in New York City. The network hired him as a correspondent shortly thereafter, and his reputation as a tough, indefatigable reporter began to build as he moved through assignments ranging from the civil rights struggle in the South, President

John F. Kennedy's assassination, and the Vietnam War, to the White House years of Lyndon Johnson and Richard Nixon.

That image crystallized during the closing years of the Nixon administration, when he was, by his own admission, "the reporter the White House hates." His aggressive style set the stage for a memorable exchange during a March 19, 1974 news conference. Then-President Nixon responded to the audience's applause and jeers when Rather stood up to query him by asking the newsman, "Are you running for something?" Rather shot back, "No sir, Mr. President, are you?" Shortly after Nixon resigned and Gearld Ford took office, Rather was transferred from the White House beat. His time in Washington had, however, encompassed the Watergate era, and in *The Palace Guard*—a 1974 book he wrote with fellow CBS staffer Gary Paul Gates—Rather chronicled the political machinations that culminated in the Watergate scandal. When he arrived in New York, he not only took on the role of anchorman-correspondent for the documentary-style *CBS Reports*, but also acted as anchor for the network's Saturday and Sunday evening newscasts.

During his two years with *CBS Reports*, Rather wrote and narrated numerous documentaries, including several highly acclaimed ones on the assassinations of John F. Kennedy, Robert Kennedy, and Martin Luther King, Jr. In 1976 Rather joined the anchor team of Mike Wallace and Morley Safer on *60 Minutes*. Described by Rather in his 1977 autobiography, *The Camera Never Blinks,* as a show that "falls between the banzai charge of daily journalism and the thoughtful, reflective, one-hour-to-do-it of 'CBS Reports,'" *60 Minutes* further enhanced the veteran correspondent's reputation and gave him additional stature, making him a serious candidate to succeed Walter Cronkite, who was approaching retirement as the head of the network's on-air news hierarchy.

Nevertheless, despite the departure of many members of the news staff to rival networks ABC and NBC during the late 1970s, CBS approached Rather about signing a long-term contract without any mention of replacing Cronkite. Rather then began to contact the other networks about a possible anchor spot, thus touching off what *Newsweek* referred to in its February 25, 1980 issue as "the hottest bidding war in the history of broadcast journalism." After six weeks of intensive negotiations, Rather made the decision to stay with CBS. "The attraction of ABC and NBC was getting a fresh start under conditions I never dreamed were possible," Rather remarked at the time of the announcement, according to *Newsweek.* "But I want to be the best there is in my time, and CBS is still the leader. And the symbolism of that anchor chair is so heavy."

Taking over Cronkite's anchor role was a momentous occasion for Rather, who described himself as "humbled and astounded" at the thought of inheriting the most coveted post in the CBS news operation. It was also a momentous occasion for the network. "By choosing Rather," a writer for *Time* observed in the February 25, 1980 issue, "CBS is gambling that the time has come for an electrifying anchorman rather than an avuncular one, a younger, more dynamic personality to replace an old familiar face." Rather refused to be intimidated by comparisons to his revered predecessor and quickly took command of *CBS Evening News.* Unlike Cronkite, who remained aloof from his staff, Rather worked closely with his, effecting several changes in the program's look, style, and story selection. He encouraged correspondents to file stories that ran longer than the usual minute-and-a-half whenever the content justified the extra time. He helped edit copy and screen tapes. At first, however, CBS dropped from the top of the ratings for evening news shows and Rather's performance was widely scrutinized.

Rather and his news staff persisted with a bold change in format. In the past, the evening news featured straightforward wire-service reports—mostly headlines from Congressional hearings told with pictures. With the guidance of CBS News president Van Gordon Sauter, the Rather team shifted emphasis from such reports to stories for television, built around people and their emotions. Stories were told not through correspondents standing against static backgrounds and reciting dry facts gleaned mostly from official government sources, but by people affected by them, no matter where in the country they happened to live. The result was more dramatic and stirring material, better suited to Rather's personality. Feeling more at ease, he became more effective, and the show's ratings climbed back up.

By the sixth year into the job, Rather dispelled any initial doubts about his capacity as anchorman. His "unique strength," according to *New York* contributor Tony Schwartz (February 3, 1986), is "the ingenuousness and passion with which he has played the role of himself." Schwartz described the shaping of that role in his profile of Rather: "He grew up deeply influenced by simple, homespun values—good manners, the importance of hard work, loyalty to the boss, love of country, and humility. These qualities are amplified by Rather's exceptional intensity. He is not simply loyal; he is loyal to a fault. He is considerate and gentlemanly not only to colleagues and to underlings but to his worst enemies as well." Schwartz further assessed: "The same is true of his approach to his job. Journalism is not just his profession; it is a higher calling, missionary work. He is not merely competitive; he is driven to win. He does not simply work hard; he works relentlessly."

Rather's career certainly demonstrates his drive to improve himself. From the start he went after assignments he recognized as part of a top correspondent's portfolio. He sought out such veteran journalists as Eric Sevareid for advice and followed it. He worked his way through Montaigne's essays and other serious books. He listened to recordings of Edward R. Murrow's voice, trying to learn from his cadence and rhythms. Even after taking over the *CBS Evening News,* Rather prepped to anchor his first space shot by reading several briefing books and encyclopedia articles on space as well as Tom Wolfe's bestseller *The Right Stuff* and by watching videotapes of Cronkite covering previous space launches.

According to Schwartz, Rather does not need to sell himself as an intellectual or sophisticate. Instead, comfortable that he has done his homework, he can "nurture the down-home persona that comes naturally to him—speech laced with Texas homilies, heart worn on the sleeve, a simple, blunt style of writing, a direct manner as a reporter." By way of illustration, the reporter recalled Rather's behavior at the press briefing for Soviet premier Mikhail Gorbachev during the October, 1985, Paris summit conference. Rather sat in the front row and asked "the first hard, confrontational question: Why not let all the Jews who seek to emigrate do so, and how many political prisoners are there in the Soviet Union?" Critics accused Rather of "grandstanding" or of "asking a question he knew would not be answered." The reality, averred Schwartz, is that "for better or for worse, Rather was simply 'being himself.'"

Rather has learned to accept his celebrity status, but he is still uncomfortable about its possible interference with his professional responsibilities. "The good journalist does *not* become a part of the story he covers," he declared in his autobiography. "A newsman does not make news. The idea of the reporter as *pop media star* is offensive to me. . . . That way is simply not compatible with the vision Ed Murrow had of the scholar-correspondent, a vision still good enough for me." Rather also refused to express undue concern about the highly publicized three-way ratings battle among the television evening news shows. ''I think we're doing the best broadcast today, and we're going to keep on doing the best reporting,'' he told *People*'s Jane Hall (August 10, 1987). ''That's what lasts in this business. The rest is seashells and smoke.''

ADDRESSES: OFFICE—CBS News, 524 W. 57th Street, New York, NY 10019.*

* * *

RAY, James 1932-

PERSONAL: Born January 1, 1932, in Calgra, OK; son of Sherman Gentry and Ora Catherine (Mitchell) Ray. EDUCATION: Attended Oklahoma A & M University; trained for the stage with Uta Hagen, 1957-60, and with Fanny Bradshaw, 1958-61.

VOCATION: Actor.

CAREER: STAGE DEBUT—Friar John, *Romeo and Juliet,* Margo Jones Theatre, Dallas TX, 1949. BROADWAY DEBUT— Witch boy, *Dark of the Moon,* Circle in the Square, 1950. LONDON DEBUT—Adolf, *The Creditors,* Mermaid Theatre, 1962. PRINCIPAL STAGE APPEARANCES—Vernon, *Summer and Smoke,* Circle in the Square, New York City, 1952; Lyman, *Compulsion,* Ambassador Theatre, New York City, 1957; title role, *Henry V,* New York Shakespeare Festival (NYSF), New York City, 1960; Katz, *The Wall,* Billy Rose Theatre, New York City, 1960; Malcolm, *Macbeth,* Diomedes, *Troilus and Cressida,* Oliver, *As You Like It,* all American Shakespeare Festival, Stratford, CT, 1961; title role, *Henry IV, Part I,* Mowbray, *Richard II,* both American Shakespeare Festival, 1962; James, *The Collection,* Cherry Lane Theatre, New York City, 1962; Edgar, *King Lear,* title role, *Henry V,* Apollodorus, *Caesar and Cleopatra,* all American Shakespeare Festival, 1963; Brinnin, *Dylan,* Plymouth Theatre, New York City, 1964; Mephistophilis, *The Tragical Historie of Doctor Faustus,* Phoenix Theatre, New York City, 1964; Ferdinand, *Love's Labour's Lost,* NYSF, Delacorte Theatre, New York City, 1965; title role, *Henry IV, Parts I and II,* NYSF, Delacorte Theatre, 1968; Stott, *The Basement,* Eastside Playhouse, New York City, 1968; William Cherry, *The Disintegration of James Cherry,* Mercury, *Amphitryon,* both Forum Theatre, New York City, 1970; Lord Capulet, *Sensations,* Theatre Four, New York City, 1970; son, *All Over,* Martin Beck Theatre, New York City, 1971; Chris, *This Way to the Rose Garden,* Alliance Theatre, Atlanta, GA, 1972; Cleante, *Tartuffe,* Walnut Street Theatre, Philadelphia, PA, 1972; Deeley, *Old Times,* Playhouse in the Park, Cincinnati, OH, 1973; George, *Who's Afraid of Virginia Woolf?,* Playhouse in the Park, 1974; Colin, *Ashes,* Mark Taper Forum, Los Angeles, CA, 1976; Dysart, *Equus,* Seattle Repertory Theatre, Seattle, WA, 1977; Congressman Gary, *Raw Youth,* Playwrights Horizons, New York City, 1986.

MAJOR TOURS—Roustabout, *J.B.,* U.S. cities, 1959; Dr. Rank, *A Doll's House,* Canadian and U.S. cities, 1971.

PRINCIPAL TELEVISION APPEARANCES—Mini-Series: Arnold Beecham, *Arthur Hailey's ''Wheels'',* NBC, 1978; Reese Claremont, *The Winds of War,* ABC, 1983; Mr. Stanhope, *If Tomorrow Comes,* CBS, 1986. Movies: First senator, *Little Ladies of the Night,* ABC, 1977; attorney, *Crisis in Midair,* CBS, 1979; Tom Adams, *Moviola: The Scarlett O'Hara War,* NBC, 1980; Donald Curdy, *The Seduction of Miss Leona,* CBS, 1980; Mr. Bain, *Lois*

Gibbs and the Love Canal, CBS, 1982; Irv, *Not in Front of the Children,* CBS, 1982; Norbert Ashley, *The Rules of Marriage,* CBS, 1982; *The Day the Bubble Burst,* NBC, 1982.

PRINCIPAL FILM APPEARANCES—*The People That Time Forgot,* American International, 1977; *Straight Time,* Warner Brothers, 1977; *Mass Appeal,* Universal, 1984; also appeared in *Charlie Chan and the Curse of the Dragon Queen,* 1980.

MEMBER: Actors' Equity Association, Screen Actors Guild, American Federation of Television and Radio Artists.

ADDRESSES: AGENT—c/o Arcara, Bauman and Hiller, 9220 Sunset Boulevard, Los Angeles, CA, 90069.*

* * *

REDDY, Helen 1942-

PERSONAL: Born October 25, 1942, in Melbourne, Australia; daughter of Max (a producer, actor, and writer) and Stella (an actress; maiden name, Lamond) Reddy; married first husband, Jeff Wald (an agent), November 1, 1966 (divorced); married third husband, Milton Ruth (a drummer); children: (first marriage) Traci, Jordan.

VOCATION: Singer, songwriter, and actress.

CAREER: PRINCIPAL TELEVISION APPEARANCES—Series: Host,

HELEN REDDY

Helen Reddy Sings, Australian, 1960; host, *The Helen Reddy Show,* NBC, 1973; host, *The Midnight Special,* NBC, 1975-76. Guest: *David Frost Show,* NBC; *Flip Wilson Show,* NBC; *Mike Douglas Show,* syndicated; *Tonight Show,* NBC; *Mac Davis Show,* NBC; guest host, *Merv Griffin Show,* syndicated; *Sesame Street,* PBS; *The Muppet Show,* syndicated.

FILM DEBUT—*Airport '75,* Universal, 1975. PRINCIPAL FILM APPEARANCES—*Pete's Dragon,* Buena Vista, 1977.

PRINCIPAL STAGE APPEARANCES—Reno Sweeny, *Anything Goes,* Sacramento Music Circus, Sacramento, CA, 1986, then Long Beach Civic Light Opera, Long Beach, CA, 1987; also appeared as Mrs. Sally Adams, *Call Me Madam.*

RELATED CAREER—As a singer, has appeared at Carnegie Hall, New York City, Royal Albert Hall and the Palladium in London, and at the Opera House in Sydney, Australia.

NON-RELATED CAREER—Commissioner, California Department of Parks and Recreation.

WRITINGS: SONGS—(With Ray Burton) "I Am Woman," 1971.

RECORDINGS: ALBUMS—*Love Song for Jeffrey, Free & Easy, No Way to Treat a Lady, Music Music, I Am Woman, Long Hard Climb, Imagination, Lust for Life, Helen Reddy's Greatest Hits,* others. SINGLES—"I Don't Know How to Love Him," Capitol, 1971; "Crazy Love," Capitol, 1971; "I Am Woman," Capitol, 1972; "Peaceful," Capitol, 1973; "Ruby," Capitol, 1973; "Delta Dawn," Capitol, 1973; "Leave Me Alone," Capitol, 1973; "Keep on Singing," Capitol, 1974; "You and Me Against the World," Capitol, 1974; "You're My World," Capitol, 1977; also "Angel Baby" and others.

AWARDS: Nine gold albums, three platinum albums, four gold singles; Best Singer of the Year, Grammy Award, 1973, for "I Am Woman;" Most Played Artist, Music Operators of America Award, 1974; American Music Award, 1974; Image Award from the NAACP, 1974; Woman of the Year, *Los Angeles Times,* 1975; Number One Female Vocalist, *Record World, Cash Box* and *Billboard,* 1975, 1976; B'nai B'rith Humanitarian Award, 1975; Maggie Award, People Helping People, 1976.

MEMBER: National Women's Political Caucus, National Organization for Women (NOW), Women's Center, Alliance for Women in Prison.

ADDRESSES: PUBLICIST—c/o Dale Olson, Dale C. Olson & Associates, 292 S. La Cienega Boulevard, Suite 315, Beverly Hills, CA 90211-3305.

*   *   *

REDGRAVE, Corin   1939-

PERSONAL: Born July 16, 1939, in London, England; son of Sir Michael Redgrave (an actor) and Rachel Kempson (an actress); married Deirdre Hamilton-Hill. EDUCATION: Attended Westminster College and King's College, Cambridge University.

VOCATION: Actor and director.

CAREER: STAGE DEBUT—Lysander, *A Midsummer Night's Dream,* English Stage Company, Royal Court Theatre, London, 1962. BROADWAY DEBUT—Pilot officer, *Chips with Everything,* Plymouth Theatre, 1963. PRINCIPAL STAGE APPEARANCES—Sebastian, *Twelfth Night,* English Stage Company, Royal Court Theatre, London, 1962; pilot officer, *Chips with Everything,* English Stage Company, Royal Court Theatre, then Vaudeville Theatre, London, both 1962; Mr. Bodley, *The Right Honourable Gentleman,* Her Majesty's Theatre, London, 1964; Mr. Cecil Graham, *Lady Windermere's Fan,* Phoenix Theatre, London, 1966; Abelard, *Abelard and Heloise,* Wyndham's Theatre, London, 1971; Antipholus of Ephesus, *The Comedy of Errors,* Royal Shakespeare Company (RSC), Memorial Theatre, Stratford-on-Avon, U.K., 1972; Octavius Caesar, *Julius Caesar* and in *Antony and Cleopatra,* both RSC, Memorial Theatre, 1972, then Aldwych Theatre, 1973; Norman, *The Norman Conquests,* Forum Theatre, Wythenshaw, U.K., 1976.

PRINCIPAL STAGE WORK—Director, *The Scarecrow,* English Stage Company, Royal Court Theatre, London, 1961.

PRINCIPAL FILM APPEARANCES—*A Man for All Seasons,* Columbia, 1966; *The Deadly Affair,* Columbia, 1967; *The Charge of the Light Brigade,* United Artists, 1968; *Oh! What a Lovely War,* Paramount, 1969; *The Magus,* Twentieth Century-Fox, 1969; *When Eight Bells Toll,* Cinerama, 1971; *Serail,* Paramount, 1980; *Excalibur,* Warner Brothers, 1981. Also appeared in *Between Wars,* 1968; *Eureka,* 1982.

PRINCIPAL TELEVISION APPEARANCES—Movies: Steerforth, *David Copperfield,* NBC, 1970; also appeared in *Hassan* and *The Governor,* both for New Zealand television, 1977.

MEMBER: Actors' Equity Association, Screen Actors Guild.

SIDELIGHTS: RECREATIONS—Music.

ADDRESSES: AGENT—c/o Sandra Marsh, 50 Glebe Road, London SW13, England.*

*   *   *

REDMAN, Joyce   1918-

PERSONAL: Born in 1918, in County Mayo, Ireland; married Charles Wynne Roberts. EDUCATION: Trained for the stage at the Academy of Dramatic Arts.

VOCATION: Actress.

CAREER: STAGE DEBUT—First Tiger Lilly, *Alice through the Looking Glass,* Playhouse Theatre, London, 1935. BROADWAY DEBUT—Doll Tearsheet, *Henry IV, Part II,* Century Theatre, 1946. PRINCIPAL STAGE APPEARANCES— Mrs. Cricket, *The Insect Play,* Little Theatre, London, 1936, then Playhouse Theatre, London, 1938; title role, *Lady Precious Stream,* Little Theatre, 1936; Katherine Carew, *The King's Pirate,* St. Martin's Theatre, London, 1937; Suzanne, *Thou Shalt Not . . .,* Playhouse Theatre, 1938; Hsiang Fei, *The Fragrant Concubine,* Little Theatre, 1938; Hung Niang, *The Western Chamber,* Torch Theatre, London,

1938; Alice, *Alice in Wonderland*, Queen's Theatre, London, 1938; Emanuelle, *Asmodee*, Gate Theatre, London, 1939; title role, *Lady Precious Stream*, Kingsway Theatre, London, 1939; Essie, *The Devil's Disciple*, Piccadilly Theatre, London, 1940; Maria, *Twelfth Night*, Arts Theatre, London, 1942; Rose, *Lottie Dundass*, Wimbledon Theatre, London, 1942; Roberta, *The House of Jeffreys*, Orpheum Theatre, London, 1942; Wendy, *Peter Pan*, Winter Garden Theatre, U.K., 1942; Brigid, *Shadow and Substance*, Duke of York's Theatre, London, 1943; title role, *Claudia*, St. Martin's Theatre, 1943; Solveig, *Peer Gynt*, Louka, *Arms and the Man*, Lady Anne, *Richard III*, Sonya, *Uncle Vanya*, all Old Vic Company, New Theatre, London, 1944; Doll Tearsheet, *Henry IV, Part II*, Jocasta's attendant, *Oedipus Rex*, confidante, *The Critic*, all Old Vic Company, New Theatre, 1945-46; Cordelia, *King Lear*, Dol Common, *The Alchemist*, both Old Vic Company, New Theatre, 1946-47; Valentine North, *Angel*, Strand Theatre, London, 1947; Abigail Sarclet, *Duet for Two Hands*, Booth Theatre, New York City, 1947; Jessica, *Crime and Passionnel*, Lyric Hammersmith Theatre, then Garrick Theatre, both London, 1948; Anne Boleyn, *Anne of the Thousand Days*, Shubert Theatre, New York City, 1948.

Gay Butterworth, *Count Your Blessings*, Wyndham's Theatre, 1951; title role, *Colombe*, New Theatre, 1951; Irene Elliott, *Affairs of State*, Cambridge Theatre, London, 1952; Helena, *Alls Well That Ends Well*, Mistress Ford, *The Merry Wives of Windsor*, both Shakespeare Memorial Theatre, Stratford-on-Avon, U.K., 1955; Fay Edwards, *The Long Echo*, St. James Theatre, London, 1956; Frances Brough, *The Party*, New Theatre, 1958; Hippolyte, *The Rape of the Belt*, Martin Beck Theatre, New York City, 1960; Hedda Rankin, *The Irregular Verb to Love*, Criterion Theatre, London, 1961; Therese, *Power of Persuasion*, Garrick Theatre, 1963; Laura, *The Father*, Piccadilly Theatre, 1964; Emilia, *Othello*, Crispinella, *The Dutch Courtesan*, both National Theatre Company, Old Vic Theatre, London, then Chichester Festival, Chichester, U.K., both 1964; Elizabeth Proctor, *The Crucible*, Mrs. Frail, *Love for Love*, both National Theatre Company, Old Vic Theatre, 1965; Juno Boyle, *Juno and the Paycock*, Mrs. Frail, *Love for Love*, both National Theatre Company, Old Vic Theatre, then Queen's Theatre, London, both 1966; Vivian Fairleigh, *The Lionel Touch*, three roles, *Plaza Suite*, both Lyric Theatre, London, 1969; Estelle, *Dear Antoine*, Chichester Festival, 1971; mistress, *The Fruits of Enlightenment*, Mrs. Von Aigner, *Undiscovered Country*, both Olivier Theatre, London, 1979. Also appeared as Laura, *Drawing Room*, Streatham Hill, U.K. 1939; Titania, *A Midsummer Night's Dream*, Old Vic Company, London, 1957.

MAJOR TOURS—Laura, *Drawing Room*, U.K. cities, 1939; title role, *Claudia*, U.K. cities, 1943; appeared with the Old Vic Company at the Comedie Francaise, Paris, France, 1945; Emilia, *Othello*, Mrs. Frail, *Love for Love*, both with the National Theatre Company, Moscow, U.S.S.R., and Berlin, East Germany, 1965.

PRINCIPAL FILM APPEARANCES—*Tom Jones*, Lopert, 1963; *Prudence and the Pill*, Twentieth Century-Fox, 1968; *Othello*, Warner Brothers, 1966.

PRINCIPAL TELEVISION APPEARANCES—Magliorie, *Les Miserables*, CBS, 1978.

MEMBER: British Actors' Equity Association, Screen Actors Guild.

ADDRESSES: AGENT—International Creative Management, 22 Grafton Street, London W1, England.*

PAT REEDY

REEDY, Pat   1940-

PERSONAL: Full name, Patricia M. Reedy; born May 1, 1940, in Mount Vernon, NY; daughter of William V. and Gertrude E. (a business executive; maiden name, Mongarell) Reedy. EDUCATION: Attended the Berkerly School of Business and the City University of New York; trained for the stage with Michael Shurtleff, Julie Bovasso, Bob Gorman, Charles Regan, Hubert Whitfield, Judy Murray, and David Cohen.

VOCATION: Actress, singer, director, stage manager, designer, and playwright.

CAREER: STAGE DEBUT—Fran, *Promises, Promises*, Tidewater Dinner Theatre, Norfolk, VA, 1973. PRINCIPAL STAGE APPEARANCES—Anita, *Black Mountain*, Lincoln Center Library, New York City, 1974; Wonder Woman, *Paranoia Pretty*, Theatre for the New City, New York City, 1974; Maggie, *It's Only Temporary*, Gate Theatre, New York City, 1976; Delores, *Sisters and Brothers*, Women's Interart Theatre, New York City, 1978; Irma, *Bagging It*, American Theatre of Actors, New York City, 1981.

PRINCIPAL STAGE WORK—Director, *A Bundle for Brunch*, American Theatre of Actors, New York City, 1979; director, *Trapped in the Basement*, American Theatre of Actors, 1983; stage manager, light and sound designer, *Legend of the Sword*, American Theatre of Actors Outdoor Theatre, New York City, 1982.

PRINCIPAL CABARET APPEARANCES—As a singer, performed at the Red Door Inn and U.S. military bases.

PRINCIPAL TELEVISION APPEARANCES—Episodic: *Another*

World, NBC, 1978. Movies: *Stage Struck,* CBS, 1978. Guest: *The Dick Lamb Show,* 1973; *Blankedy Blanks,* ABC, 1977; *Hotline,* 1979; *Joe Franklin Show,* WOR-New York, 1979; *Go for It,* 1983.

PRINCIPAL RADIO WORK—Director, *Ebbanflo Duo,* KBCS-FM.

WRITINGS: PLAYS—*It's Only Temporary,* Gate Theatre, New York City, 1976; *A Bundle for Brunch,* American Theatre of Actors, New York City, 1980; *The Stop Over, A Step Beyond, Bagging It,* all American Theatre of Actors, 1981.

MEMBER: American Federation of Television and Radio Artists, Actors' Equity Association, Screen Actors Guild, Dramatists Guild; Smithsonian Institute.

ADDRESSES: HOME—125 Argyll Avenue, New Rochelle, NY; AGENT—c/o Bertha Klausner, 71 Park Avenue, New York, NY 10016.

*   *   *

REID, Kate   1930-

PERSONAL: Full name, Daphne Kate Reid; born November 4, 1930, in London, England; daughter of Walter C. (a soldier) and Helen Isabel (Moore) Reid; married Austin Willis, July 13, 1953 (divorced, 1962); children: Reid, Robin. EDUCATION: Attended Havergal College, the University of Toronto, and the Toronto Conservatory of Music; trained for the stage with Uta Hagen at the Herbert Berghof Studio.

VOCATION: Actress.

CAREER: STAGE DEBUT—Daphne, *Damask Cheek,* Hart House, University of Toronto, Toronto, ON, Canada. LONDON DEBUT—Lizzie, *The Rainmaker,* St. Martin's Theatre, 1956. BROADWAY DEBUT—Martha, *Who's Afraid of Virginia Woolf?,* 1962. PRINCIPAL STAGE APPEARANCES—*Years Ago,* Straw Hat Players, Gravenhurst, ON, Canada, 1948; Catherine Ashland, *The Stepmother,* St. Martin's Theatre, London, 1958; Caitlin Thomas, *Dylan,* Plymouth Theatre, New York City, 1964; Martha, *Who's Afraid of Virginia Woolf?,* Manitoba Theatre Centre, Winnipeg, MB, Canada, 1965; Celeste, "The Mutilated," Moyla, "The Gnadiges Fraulein," on a bill as *Slapstick Tragedy,* Longacre Theatre, New York City, 1966; medical officer, *The Adventures of Private Turvey,* mayor's wife, *The Ottawa Man,* both Confederation Memorial Centre, Charlottetown, PE, Canada, 1966; writer's wife, *What Do You Really Know about Your Husband?,* Shubert Theatre, New Haven, CT, 1967; Lady Kitty, *The Circle,* Shaw Festival, Court House Theatre, Niagra-on-the-Lake, ON, Canada, 1967; Esther Franz, *The Price,* Morosco Theatre, New York City, 1968, then Duke of York's Theatre, London, 1969; Juno Boyle, *Juno and the Paycock,* Walnut Street Theatre, Philadelphia, PA, 1973; Lily, *The Freedom of the City,* Eisenhower Theatre, Washington, DC, then Alvin Theatre, New York City, both 1974; nurse, *Romeo and Juliet,* American Shakespeare Festival, Stratford, CT, 1974; Big Mama, *Cat on a Hot Tin Roof,* American Shakespeare Festival, then American National Theatre Academy Playhouse, New York City, both 1974; Rummy Mitchens, *Major Barbara,* Shaw Festival, 1978; Gwyneth Price, *I Sent a Letter to My Love,* Long Wharf Theatre, New Haven, CT, 1978; Henny, *Bosoms and Neglect,* Longacre Theatre, 1979; Ida Bolton, *Mornings at Seven,* Lyceum Theatre, New York City, 1981; Linda Loman, *Death of a*

Salesman, Broadhurst Theatre, New York City, 1984. Also appeared in *Leaving Home,* Vancouver, BC, Canada, 1973; *Mrs. Warren's Profession, The Apple Cart,* both Shaw Festival, 1976; *The Corn Is Green,* Alley Theatre, Houston, TX, 1977.

With the Stratford Shakespeare Festival, Stratford, ON, Canada: Celia, *As You Like It,* Emilia, *Othello,* both 1959; nurse, *Romeo and Juliet,* Helena, *A Midsummer Night's Dream,* both 1960; Katherine, *Henry VIII,* Jacquenetta, *Love's Labour's Lost,* Elly Cassidy, *The Canvas Barricade,* all 1961; Lady Macbeth, *Macbeth,* Katharine, *The Taming of the Shrew,* both 1962; Cassandra, *Troilus and Cressida,* Adriana, *The Comedy of Errors,* Lisa, Sister Marthe, *Cyrano de Bergerac,* all 1963; Portia, *Julius Caesar,* Madame Ranevskaya, *The Cherry Orchard,* both 1965; Gertrude, *Hamlet,* Masha, *The Three Sisters,* Esther, *The Friends,* 1970; Henny, *Bosoms and Neglect,* 1980.

MAJOR TOURS—Lizzie, *The Rainmaker,* U.K. cities, 1956; appeared in *Two Programs of Shakespearean Comedy,* Canadian and U.S. universities, 1962.

PRINCIPAL TELEVISION APPEARANCES—Episodic: "An Enemy of the People," *NET Playhouse,* NET, 1966; "Enemies," *NET Playhouse,* NET, 1974. Series: Marion Jaworski, *Gavilan,* NBC, 1982-83; Aunt Lil Trotter, *Dallas,* CBS, 1983-86. Pilots: Julia Dayton, *Hawkins on Murder,* CBS, 1973. Movies: Maggie Knowlton, *She Cried Murder,* CBS, 1973; Lieutenant Shirley Ridgeway, *Death among Friends,* NBC, 1975; Hilda, *Loose Change,* NBC, 1978; Madame Blomart, *The Blood of Others,* HBO, 1984; Linda Loman, *Death of a Salesman,* CBS, 1985; Molly Gottchalk, *Christmas Eve,* NBC, 1986; also appeared in *Friendly Persuasion,* 1972; *Happy Birthday to Me,* 1981; and *Nellie McClung, Crossbar,* and *Robbers, Rooftops and Witches.* Specials: Queen Victoria, "The Invincible Mr. Disraeli," *Hallmark Hall of Fame,* NBC, 1963; Mary Todd Lincoln, "Abe Lincoln in Illinois," *Hallmark Hall of Fame,* NBC, 1964; also in "The Holy Terror," *Hallmark Hall of Fame,* NBC, 1965; "Neither Are We Enemies," *Hallmark Hall of Fame,* NBC, 1970.

PRINCIPAL FILM APPEARANCES—*One Plus One,* Selected, 1961; *This Property Is Condemned,* Paramount, 1966; *Pigeons* (also known as *The Sidelong Glances of a Pigeon Kicker*), Metro-Goldwyn-Mayer, 1970; *The Andromeda Strain,* Universal, 1971; *A Delicate Balance,* American Film Theatre, 1973; *The Rainbow Boys,* Mutual, 1973; *Shoot,* AVCO-Embassy, 1976; *Equus,* Warner Brothers, 1977; *High Point,* New World Pictures, 1979; *Atlantic City,* Paramount, 1981; *Monkey Grip,* Cinecom International, 1983; *Heaven Help Us,* Tri-Star, 1984; *Fire with Fire,* Paramount, 1986. Also appeared in *Plague,* 1978; *Double Negative,* 1980; *Death Ship,* 1980; *The Blood of Others,* 1984; *No Sad Songs,* 1985.

AWARDS: Best Actress, Antionette Perry Award nomination, 1964, for *Dylan;* Best Actress, Antoinette Perry Award nomination, 1966, for *Slapstick Tragedy;* Outstanding Single Performance by an Actress in a Leading Role, Emmy Award nomination, 1963, for "The Invincible Mr. Disraeli," *Hallmark Hall of Fame;* Outstanding Single Performance by an Actress in a Leading Role, Emmy Award nomination, 1964, for "Abe Lincoln in Illinois," *Hallmark Hall of Fame;* Office of the Order of Canada, 1976. Honorary degrees: Ph.D., York University.

MEMBER: Actors' Equity Association, American Federation of Television and Radio Artists, Association of Canadian Television and Radio Artists.

REINER

ADDRESSES: OFFICE—14 Binsearth Road, Toronto, ON, Canada. AGENT—c/o Contemporary-Korman Artists, Ltd., 132 Lasky Drive, Beverly Hills, CA 90212.*

*   *   *

REINER, Carl   1922-

PERSONAL: Born March 20, 1922, in New York, NY; son of Irving and Bessie (Mathias) Reiner; married Estelle Lebost, December 24, 1943; children: Robert, Sylvia A., Lucas. EDUCATION: Attended the School of Foreign Service, Georgetown University, 1943. MILITARY: U.S. Army, 1942-46.

VOCATION: Actor, writer, director, and producer.

CAREER: PRINCIPAL STAGE APPEARANCES—Broadway productions: *Call Me Mister*, 1947-48; *Inside U.S.A.*, 1948-49; *Alive and Kicking*, 1949.

PRINCIPAL STAGE WORK—Director: *The Roast*, Winter Garden Theatre, New York City, 1980; *Something Different*, South Street Theatre, New York City, 1983.

MAJOR TOURS—With Major Maurice Evans' Special Services Unit, South Pacific tour for the armed services, World War II; *Call Me Mister*, national tour, 1947.

PRINCIPAL FILM APPEARANCES—*Happy Anniversary*, United Artists, 1959; *The Gazebo*, Metro-Goldwyn-Mayer, 1960; *Gidget Goes Hawaiian*, Columbia, 1961; *It's a Mad, Mad, Mad, Mad, World*, 1963; *The Russians Are Coming, The Russians Are Coming*, United Artists, 1966; *The End*, United Artists, 1978; *Dead Men Don't Wear Plaid*, Universal, 1982.

PRINCIPAL FILM WORK—Writer (see below); producer and director, *Enter Laughing*, Columbia, 1967; co-producer, *The Comic*, Columbia, 1969; director, *Where's Poppa?*, United Artists, 1970; executive producer (with Mel Brooks) and director, *Oh God!*, Warner Brothers, 1977. Director: *The One and Only*, Paramount, 1978; *The Jerk*, Universal, 1979; *The Man with Two Brains*, Warner Brothers, 1983; *All of Me*, Universal, 1984; *The Lonely Guy*, Universal, 1984; *Summer Rental*, Paramount, 1985.

PRINCIPAL TELEVISION APPEARANCES—Series: Regular, *Your Show of Shows*, NBC, 1950-54; George Hansen, *Caesar's Hour*, NBC, 1954-57; regular, *Sid Caesar Invites You*, ABC, 1958; emcee, *Keep Talking*, CBS, 1958-59; Alan Brady, *The Dick Van Dyke Show*, CBS, 1961-66; *The Dinah Shore Show*, NBC, 1963; Mr. Angel, *Good Heavens*, ABC, 1976. Specials: *The Sid Caesar, Imogene Coca, Carl Reiner, Howard Morris Special*, NBC, 1967; *A Carol Burnett Special: Carol, Carl, Whoopi & Robin*, ABC, 1987.

PRINCIPAL TELEVISION WORK—Writer (see below); producer: *The Dick Van Dyke Show*, CBS, 1961-66; *The New Dick Van Dyke Show*, CBS, 1973; *Heaven Help Us*, 1976.

WRITINGS: PLAYS, PRODUCED—*Something Different*, South Street Theatre, New York City, 1983, published by Samuel French, 1967; *Enter Laughing*, Mercer Street Theatre, New York City, 1983, then with the American Jewish Theatre at the 92nd Street YMHA, New York City, 1984-85.

SCREENPLAYS—*The Thrill of It All*, Universal, 1963; co-screenwriter, *Enter Laughing*, Columbia, 1967; co-screenwriter, *The Comic*, Columbia, 1969; *Generation*, AVCO-Embassy, 1969; co-screenwriter, *The Man with Two Brains*, Warner Brothers, 1983; co-screenwriter, *All of Me*, Universal, 1984.

TELEVISION—Series: *Your Show of Shows*, NBC, 1950-54; *Sid Caesar Invites You*, ABC, 1958; *The Dick Van Dyke Show*, CBS, 1961-66. Specials: *The Sid Caesar, Imogene Coca, Carl Reiner, Howard Morris Special*, NBC, 1967.

FICTION—*Enter Laughing* (autobiographical novel), Simon & Shuster, 1958.

RECORDINGS—*Carl Reiner and Mel Brooks, The 2000 Year Old Man; The 2001 Year Old Man; The 2013 Year Old Man*.

AWARDS: Emmy Awards: Best Supporting Actor in a Comedy Series, 1957, for *Caesar's Hour*, 1958, for *Sid Caesar Invites You;* Outstanding Writing Achievement in Comedy, 1962, 1963, and 1964, and Outstanding Program Achievement in Entertainment (as producer), 1965, all for *The Dick Van Dyke Show;* (co-winner) for Outstanding Writing Achievement in a Variety, 1967, for *The Sid Caesar, Imogene Coca, Carl Reiner, Howard Morris Special.*

MEMBER: Actors' Equity Association, Screen Actors Guild, American Federation of Television and Radio Artists, Writers Guild, Dramatists Guild, Directors Guild.

ADDRESSES: OFFICE—714 N. Rodeo Drive, Beverly Hills, CA 90210. AGENT—c/o Paula Wagner, Creative Artists Agency, 1888 Century Park East, Suite 1400, Los Angeles, CA 90067.*

*   *   *

REINER, Rob   1945-

PERSONAL: Full name, Robert Reiner; born March 6, 1945, in New York, NY; son of Carl (an actor, writer, director, and producer) and Estelle (Lebost) Reiner; married Penny Marshall (an actress and director), 1971 (divorced). EDUCATION: Attended the University of California at Los Angeles.

VOCATION: Actor, writer, and director.

CAREER: PRINCIPAL STAGE APPEARANCES—Danny, *The Roast*, Winter Garden Theatre, New York City, 1980; also appeared with various regional theatre companies and improvisational troupes.

PRINCIPAL FILM APPEARANCES—*This Is Spinal Tap*, Embassy, 1984.

PRINCIPAL FILM WORK—Writer (see below); director: *This Is Spinal Tap*, Embassy, 1984; *The Sure Thing*, Embassy, 1985; *Stand by Me*, Columbia, 1986.

PRINCIPAL TELEVISION APPEARANCES—Series: Mike Sitivic, *All in the Family*, CBS, 1971-78; Joseph Bresner, *Free Country*, ABC, 1978. Movies: *Thursday's Game*, 1974; *More Than Friends*, 1978; *Million Dollar Infield*, 1982. Specials: *The Billy Crystal Comedy Special*, Home Box Office, 1986. Guest: *People*, CBS, 1978; *The Billy Crystal Comedy Hour*, NBC, 1982.

PRINCIPAL TELEVISION WORK—Writer (see below); co-producer, *Free Country*, ABC, 1978.

WRITINGS: SCREENPLAYS—Co-writer, *Enter Laughing*, Columbia, 1967; *Halls of Anger*, United Artists, 1970; *Where's Poppa?*, United Artists, 1970; *Summertree*, Columbia, 1971; *Fire Sale*, 1977; *How Come Nobody's on Our Side*, 1977.

TELEVISION—Creator and co-writer (with Phil Mishkin), *The Super*, ABC, 1972; co-writer, *Free Country*, ABC, 1978.

AWARDS: Best Supporting Actor in a Comedy, Emmy Award, 1974, for *All in the Family;* Outstanding Continuing Performance by a Supporting Actor in a Comedy Series, Emmy Award, 1978, for *All in the Family;* Best Director, Directors Guild nomination, 1986, for *Stand by Me*.

MEMBER: Actors' Equity Association, Screen Actors Guild, American Federation of Television and Radio Artists, Directors Guild.

ADDRESSES: OFFICE—6400 Sunset Blvd., Los Angeles, CA 90069. AGENT—Creative Artists Agency, 1888 Century Park East, Los Angeles, CA 90067.*

*   *   *

REINHOLD, Judge

PERSONAL: Born in Wilmington, DE. EDUCATION: Attended Mary Washington College and the North Carolina School of the Arts.

VOCATION: Actor.

CAREER: FILM DEBUT—*Running Scared*, EMI Films, 1979. PRINCIPAL FILM APPEARANCES—*Stripes*, Columbia, 1981; *Thursday the Twelfth*, 1982; *Fast Times at Ridgemont High*, Universal, 1982; *Gremlins*, Warner Brothers, 1984; *Beverly Hills Cop*, Paramount, 1984; *Roadhouse*, 1985; *Ruthless People*, Buena Vista, 1986; *Head Office*, Tri-Star, 1986; *Off Beat*, Buena Vista, 1986; *Beverly Hills Cop II*, Paramount, 1987; Glenn, *Pandemonium*, Metro-Goldwyn-Mayer/United Artists, 1988.

PRINCIPAL TELEVISION APPEARANCES—Episodic: *Wonder Woman*, CBS; *Magnum P.I.*, CBS. Movies: *The Survival of Dana*, 1979; also *Brothers and Sisters*, *A Step Too Slow*, *The Wilmar Eight*, and *Booker*.

MEMBER: Screen Actors Guild, American Federation of Television and Radio Artists.

ADDRESSES: AGENT—c/o Todd Smith, Creative Artists Agency, 1888 Century Park E., Suite 1400, Los Angeles, CA 90067. PUBLICIST—c/o N. Koenigsberg and G. Freeman, P/M/K, 8436 W. Third Street, Suite 650, Los Angeles, CA 90048.

*   *   *

REISER, Paul

PERSONAL: Born in New York, NY. EDUCATION: Graduated from the State University of New York, Binghamton, with a major in music, 1977.

VOCATION: Actor and comedian.

CAREER: PRINCIPAL CABARET APPEARANCES—As a standup comedian: Catch a Rising Star, the Comic Strip, and the Improv, all New York City, 1979—; also appeared at other clubs nationally.

FILM DEBUT—Modell, *Diner*, MGM/UA, 1982. PRINCIPAL FILM APPEARANCES—Burke, *Aliens* (also known as *Alien II*), Twentieth Century-Fox, 1986; Jerry Friedman, *Beverly Hills Cop, II*, Paramount, 1987; also *Summer Jobs*, upcoming.

PRINCIPAL TELEVISION APPEARANCES—Series: *The Investigator*, Home Box Office (HBO); *My Two Dads*, NBC, 1987—; also *The Comedy Zone*. Specials: *Paul Reiser: Out on a Whim*, HBO, 1987. Pilots: *Diner*, CBS; *Just Married*, ABC. Movies: *Sunset Limousine*, 1983. Guest: *The Tonight Show*, NBC; *Late Night with David Letterman*, NBC.

ADDRESSES: AGENT—c/o Michael Menchel, Creative Artists Agency, Inc., 1888 Century Park E., Suite 1400, Los Angeles, CA 90067.*

*   *   *

REISMAN, Jane

PERSONAL: Married Neil Peter Jampolis (a set, lighting, and costume designer), July 24, 1971. EDUCATION: Attended Vassar College; studied at the Bayreuth Festival Master Classes, 1963, and at the Polakov Studio and the Forum of Stage Design, 1967-69.

VOCATION: Lighting designer.

CAREER: PRINCIPAL STAGE WORK—Lighting designer: *Shadow of Heroes*, York Playhouse, New York City, 1961; *Come Out Carol, Metamorphosis*, both 41st Street Playhouse, New York City, 1962; *A Man's a Man*, Masque Theatre, New York City, 1962; *Amorous Flea*, East 78th Street Playhouse, New York City, 1964; *Saint Joan*, American Conservatory Theatre, San Francisco, CA, 1970; *Inner City*, Ethel Barrymore Theatre, New York City, 1971; *Madame Butterfly, A Village Romeo and Juliet, La Boheme, Die Walkure, The Crucible*, (operas) all St. Paul Opera, St. Paul, MN, 1972-73; *He Who Gets Slapped*, Greer Garson Theatre, Santa Fe, NM, 1974; *Warp*, Ambassador Theatre, New York City, 1974; *Il Tabarro, Gianni Schicci, Il Ritorno D'Ulisse In Patria*, (operas) all Opera Society of Washington, DC, Kennedy Center, Washington, DC, 1974; *La Traviata, The Barber of Seville, Rigoletto, Lucia di Lammermoor, Madame Butterfly*, (operas) all New Orleans Opera, New Orleans, LA, 1975-77; *The Ballad of Baby Doe* (opera), Tulsa Opera, Tulsa, OK, 1976; *Little Me, West Side Story*, both Music Hall Theatre, Houston, TX, 1976; *Me Jack, You Jill*, John Golden Theatre, New York City, 1976; *Oliver!*, Playhouse in the Park, Cincinnati, OH, 1976; *The Taming of the Shrew*, Alliance Theatre, Atlanta, GA, 1978; *Summer and Smoke, Faust, The Mikado, The Marriage of Figaro*, (operas) all Lake George Opera Company, Lake George, NY, 1978; *Macbeth* (opera), Memphis Opera, Memphis, TN, 1978; *I Puritani* (opera), Tulsa Opera, 1978; *Tales of Hoffman, Don Giovanni, La Traviata, Don Pasquale*, (operas) all Mobile Opera, Mobile, AL, 1978-81; *La Traviata* (opera), Tulsa Opera, 1979; *Angel Street, Long Day's Journey into Night, Look Back in Anger*, and *Oh, Coward!*, all Cohoes Music Hall, Cohoes, NY, 1979; *Erismena* (opera), New Opera Theatre, Brooklyn Academy of Music, Brooklyn, NY, 1979; (with Neil

Peter Jampolis), *G.R. Point,* Playhouse Theatre, New York City, 1979.

Lighting designer: *South Pacific,* Music Hall Theatre, 1980; *Dracula,* Manitoba Theatre Centre, Winnipeg, MB, Canada, 1980; *Die Fledermaus* (opera), Tulsa Opera, 1980; *La Boheme, Daughter of the Regiment, Andrea Chenier,* (operas) all Tulsa Opera, 1981; *Enrico IV,* Theatre Plus, St. Lawrence Centre, Toronto, ON, Canada, 1981; *Of Mice and Men,* Philadelphia Drama Guild, Philadelphia, PA, 1981; *Die Kluge, Suor Angelica,* (operas) both Manhattan School of Music, New York City, 1981; *Barber of Seville* (opera), Tulsa Opera, 1982; *The Three Sisters, The Music Man,* both Banff Festival, Banff, AB, Canada, 1982; *Madame Butterfly* (opera), Tulsa Opera, 1983; *Women of Fortune,* St. Clement's Church Theatre, New York City, 1983; *Black Elk Speaks,* American Indian Theatre Company, Tulsa Performing Arts Centre, Tulsa, OK, 1984; *Findings* (ballet), Banff School of the Arts, Banff, AB, Canada, 1984; *Pirates of Penzance,* Tulsa Opera, 1984; *Breakfast Conversations in Miami, The Women's Project,* both American Place Theatre, New York City, 1984; *A Midsummer Night's Dream,* Walnut Street Theatre Company, Philadelphia, PA, 1984; *The Fantasticks,* Central Opera Theatre, Beijing, China, 1987. Also lighting designer for *Saint Joan of the Stockyards,* Philadelphia, PA, 1971; *Children of Darkness* (ballet), Pennsylvania Ballet, 1973; *A Ring of Time* (ballet), Nederlands Dans Theatre, 1974; concert series, Uris Theatre, New York City, 1974; *Cat on a Hot Tin Roof,* Chicago, IL, 1975; *Telecast,* New York City, 1979; *Adriana Lecouvreur, Il Trovatore, Lucia Di Lammermoor, Tosca, Marina, La Traviata,* (operas) all Caracas, Venezuela, 1980-81; Summer Dance Festival, Banff School of the Arts, Banff, AB, Canada, 1983; *Findings* (ballet), Les Grands Ballets Canadiens, 1984; Rome Opera Ballet, 1987.

RELATED CAREER—Resident lighting designer, Pittsburgh Playhouse, Pittsburgh, PA, 1966-67; guest lecturer and lighting designer for dance, Bennington College, 1968-69; visiting professor of lighting design, Emerson College, 1981-83; also guest observer, Royal Opera House, London, and with the Royal Shakespeare Company, Aldwych Theatre, London.

AWARDS: Institute of International Education grant, 1963.

MEMBER: United Scenic Artists, Local 829.

ADDRESSES: OFFICE—130 W. 57th Street, New York, NY 10019.

*   *   *

REISS, Alvin H.   1930-

PERSONAL: Born June 15, 1930, in Brooklyn, NY; son of Samuel (a manufacturer) and Anne (Elowsky) Reiss; married Ellen Komoroff (a travel agent), August 26, 1956; children: Steven, Robert, Michael. EDUCATION: University of Wisconsin, B.A., 1952, M.A., 1953. MILITARY: U.S. Army, 1953-55.

VOCATION: Writer, publisher, arts administrator, teacher, and producer.

CAREER: Assistant producer, Gordon Pollack Productions, New York City, 1955-56; executive director, Related Arts Counsellors, New York City, 1962—; editor, publisher, *Arts Management*

ALVIN H. REISS

(magazine), New York City, 1962—; editor, newsletter for the New York State Council on the Arts, 1963-66; business and arts columnist, *Cultural Affairs* (magazine), New York City, 1967-70; program director, Albert Dorne Memorial Foundation, 1968-71; director, Arts and Business Technical Assistance Program, 1972-73; communications director, American Council for Arts in Education, 1972-74; director, Management of Arts (graduate program), Aldelphi University, 1978-85.

PRINCIPAL RADIO APPEARANCES—Co-host, *World of Dance,* WNYC, New York City, 1965-68; host and moderator, *Monthly Arts Forum,* WNYC, 1968-79.

RELATED CAREER—Visiting professor, Philadelphia College of the Arts, Philadelphia, PA, 1986-87; board member, National Guild of Community Schools of the Arts; international advisory council, Symphony for United Nations; board member, Organization of Independent Artists; board member, Periwinkle Productions; advisory council, arts administration program, University of Toronto, Scarborough, ON, Canada; advisory board member, West Side Arts Coalition; past vice-president, Arts & Business Council.

WRITINGS: NON-FICTION—*The Arts Management Handbook,* Law-Arts, 1970, revised edition, 1974; *Culture & Company,* Twayne Publishers, 1972; *The Arts Management Reader,* Marcel Dekker, Inc., 1979; *Cash In! Funding and Promoting the Arts,* Theatre Communications Group, 1986. Also contributor of articles to the *New York Times, Esquire, American Way, Coronet, Family Health, Art News, Mainliner,* and *Cue.*

AWARDS: Outstanding Achievement Award, 1986, from the International Society of Performing Arts Administrators.

MEMBER: American Society of Journalists and Authors (past executive vice-president), Music Critics Association.

SIDELIGHTS: CTFT notes the following highlights of Alvin Reiss' career: Co-founder, editor, and publisher of the first national periodical for cultural administrators, *Arts Management;* organized the nation's first college course in arts management at The New School, 1963; author of the first Resolution on the Arts passed by the U.S. Conference of Mayors and National League of Cities, 1974; organized the first business/arts seminars for business oriented groups, and directed the first extended college seminar series on business and the arts; initiated the Visiting Arts Consultant Program for the State University of New York, 1973-75; developed and directed one of the first arts management graduate programs.

ADDRESSES: HOME—110 Riverside Drive, New York, NY 10024. OFFICE—c/o Arts Management, 408 W. 57th Street, New York, NY 10019.

*   *   *

REISS, Stuart   1921-

PERSONAL: Born July 15, 1921, in Chicago, IL. MILITARY: U.S. Army Air Corps, 1942-45.

VOCATION: Set decorator.

STUART REISS

CAREER: FIRST FILM WORK—Property man with Twentieth Century-Fox, 1939-42. PRINCIPAL FILM WORK—Set decorator, with Twentieth Century-Fox: *Titanic,* 1953; *How to Marry a Millionaire,* 1953; *Hell and High Water,* 1954; *There's No Business Like Show Business,* 1954; *Soldier of Fortune,* 1955; *The Seven Year Itch,* 1955; *The Man in the Grey Flannel Suit,* 1956; *Teenage Rebel,* 1956; *The Diary of Anne Frank,* 1959; *What a Way to Go,* 1964; *Doctor Doolittle,* 1967; *Fantastic Voyage,* 1967.

Oh God!, Warner Brothers, 1977; *The Swarm,* Warner Brothers, 1978; *Beyond the Poseidon Adventure,* Warner Brothers, 1979; *Carbon Copy,* Embassy, 1981; *All the Marbles,* United Artists, 1981; *The Man Who Loved Women,* Columbia, 1983; *Micki and Maude,* Columbia, 1984; *A Fine Mess,* Columbia, 1986.

AWARDS: Best Set Decoration, Academy Awards, 1959, for *The Diary of Anne Frank* and 1966, for *Fantastic Voyage;* Best Set Decoration, Academy Award nominations, 1953, for *The Titanic,* 1956, for *Teenage Rebel,* 1964, for *What a Way to Go,* and 1967, for *Doctor Dolittle.*

MEMBER: International Association of Technical Stage Employees (IATSE), Academy of Motion Picture Arts and Sciences.

ADDRESSES: HOME—4337 Reyes Drive, Tarzana, CA 91356. OFFICE—c/o IATSE, P.O. Box 5304, North Hollywood, CA 91616.

*   *   *

REISZ, Karel   1926-

PERSONAL: Born July 21, 1926, in Ostrava, Czechoslovakia; emmigrated to England in 1939; son of Dr. Josef and Frederika Reisz; married Julia Coppard (divorced); married Betsy Blair, 1963; children: three sons. EDUCATION: Attended Emmanuel College. MILITARY: R.A.F., Czechoslovakian section, 1944-46.

VOCATION: Director, producer, and writer.

CAREER: PRINCIPAL FILM WORK—Director (with Tony Richardson), *Momma Don't Allow,* 1956; co-producer, *Every Day Except Christmas,* 1957; producer, *We Are the Lambeth Boys,* 1959; director, *Saturday Night and Sunday Morning,* 1960; producer, *This Sporting Life,* 1963; co-producer and director, *Night Must Fall,* Metro-Goldwyn-Mayer, 1964; director, *Morgan: A Suitable Case for Treatment* (also known as *Morgan!*), British Lion, 1966; director, *Isadora* (also known as *The Loves of Isadora*), 1968; director, *The Gambler,* Paramount, 1974; director, *Who'll Stop the Rain?,* United Artists, 1978; co-producer and director, *The French Lieutenant's Woman,* United Artists, 1981; director, *Sweet Dreams,* Tri-Star, 1985.

RELATED CAREER—Film critic, *Sequence* and *Sight and Sound* magazines, London, 1950-52; program director, National Film Theatre, London, 1952-55; Officer of Commercials, film division, Ford Motor Company, 1956-57.

NON-RELATED CAREER—Teacher at a London grammer school, 1947-49.

WRITINGS: NON-FICTION—(With Gavin Miller) *The Technique of Film Editing,* 1953, reprinted by Focal Press, 1968. ARTICLES—

(With Marie Seton and L. McLeod) "Unfair to Eisenstein," *Sight and Sound,* London, June 1951; "Interview with John Huston," *Sight and Sound,* January-March 1952; "Stroheim in London," *Sight and Sound,* April-June, 1954; "Experiment at Brussels," *Sight and Sound,* 1958; "From 'Free Cinema' to Feature Film: Interview," *London Times,* 1960; "Karel Reisz and Experimenters: An Exchange of Correspondence," *Films and Filming,* London, December, 1961; "Desert Island Films," *Films and Filming,* August, 1963; "How to Get Into Films—By the People Who Got In Themselves," *Films and Filming,* July, 1963.

SIDELIGHTS: RECREATIONS—Gardening.

ADDRESSES: HOME—11 Chalcot Gardens Off England's Lane, London NW3, England. OFFICE—Film Contracts, Two Lower James Street, London, W1, England. AGENT—William Morris Agency, 151 El Camino Drive, Beverly Hills, CA 90212.*

*   *   *

RESNAIS, Alain 1922-

PERSONAL: Born June 3, 1922, in Vannes, France; son of Pierre and Jeanne (Gachet) Resnais; married Florence Malraux, October 7, 1969. EDUCATION: Attended the Institut des Hautes Etudes Cinematographiques, Paris, 1943-45; studied acting with Rene Simon. MILITARY: Served with the occupation army in Germany and Austria as a member of the travelling theatrical company "Les Arlequins."

VOCATION: Film director, writer, cinematographer, and editor.

CAREER: FIRST FILM WORK—Lighting cameraman, *Le Sommeil d'Albertine,* 1945. PRINCIPAL FILM WORK—Director, *Ouvert pour cause d'inventaire,* 1946; director, film shorts about artists: *Visite a Lucien Coutaud, Visite a Felix Labisse, Visite a Hans Hartung, Visite a Cesar Domela, Visite a Oscar Dominguez, Portrait d'Henri Goetz, La Bague,* and *Journee naturell,* all 1947; director, cinematographer, and editor, *L'Alcool tue,* 1947; editor, *Paris 1900,* 1947; director, cinematographer, and editor, *Les jardins de Paris,* 1948; director, cinematographer, and editor, *Chateaux de France,* 1948; director and editor, *Van Gogh,* 1948; co-director, *Malfray,* 1948; co-director (with Robert Hessens) and co-editor, *Guernica,* 1950; director and editor, *Gauguin,* 1950; editor, *Saint-Tropez, devior de vacances,* 1952; co-director (with Chris Marker) and co-editor, *Les Statues meurent aussi (The Statues Also Die),* 1953; director, *Nuit et brouillard (Night and Fog),* 1955; editor, *La Pointe courte,* 1956; director and editor, *Toute la memoire du monde,* 1956; co-director, *Le Mystere de l'Atelier Quinze,* 1957; editor, *L'Oeil du maitre,* 1957; editor, *Broadway by Light,* 1957; director and editor, *Le Chant de Styrene,* 1958; editor, *Paris a l'automne,* 1958; director, *Hiroshima, mon amour,* 1959; director, *L'Annee derniere a Marienbad (Last Year at Marienbad),* 1961; director, *Muriel, ou le temps d'un retour,* 1963; director, *La Guerre est finie (The War Is Over),* 1966; co-director (with Jean Luc-Godard), *Loin du Viet-Nam (Far from Vietnam),* 1967; director, *Je t'aime, je t'aime,* 1968; director, *Stavisky,* 1974; director, *Providence,* 1977; director, *Mon Oncle d'Amerique,* 1980; director, *La Vie est un roman,* 1983; director, *L'amour a mort,* 1984.

RELATED CAREER—Film editor, with the Institut des Hautes Etudes Cinematographiques, Paris, 1947-58.

WRITINGS: SCREENPLAYS—*Chateaux de France,* 1948; co-writer, *Les Statues meurent aussi (The Statues Also Die),* 1953; co-writer, *Je t'aime, je t'aime,* 1968.

AWARDS: Special Prize, Cannes Film Festival, 1980, for *Mon Oncle d'Amerique.*

ADDRESSES: HOME—70 rue des Plantes, 75014 Paris, France. OFFICE—Artmedia, 10 avenue George V, 75008 Paris, France.*

*   *   *

RICHARD, Cliff 1940-

PERSONAL: Born Harry Roger Webb, October 14, 1940, in India; son of Roger and Dorothy Webb.

VOCATION: Actor, singer, and writer.

CAREER: PRINCIPAL STAGE APPEARANCES—Title role, *Aladdin,* Palladium Theatre, London, U.K., 1964-65; *Five Finger Exercise,* 1970; *The Potting Shed,* 1971; also in other repertory and variety productions, U.K.

FILM DEBUT—*Serious Charge,* Paramount, 1959. PRINCIPAL FILM APPEARANCES—All British productions: *Expresso Bongo,* 1960; *The Young Ones,* 1961; *Summer Holiday,* 1962; *Wonderful Life,* 1964; *Finders Keepers,* 1966; *Two a Penny,* 1968; *His Land,* 1972; *Take Me High,* 1973.

PRINCIPAL TELEVISION APPEARANCES—Series: *The Cliff Richard Show,* BBC and ITV, U.K. Episodic: (With The Drifters) *Oh, Boy,* BBC, 1958, ABC, 1959; *Sunday Night at the London Palladium,* BBC; also represented the United Kingdom in two Eurovision Song Contests.

WRITINGS: SONGS—(With Bruce Welch) "Bachelor Boy," 1962, recorded with The Shadows, Epic, 1962; others.

BOOKS—*Questions,* 1970; *The Way I See It,* 1972; *The Way I See It Now,* 1975; *Which One's Cliff?,* 1977; *Happy Christmas from Cliff,* 1980; *You, Me, and Jesus,* 1983; *Mine to Share,* 1984; *Jesus, Me, and You,* 1985.

RECORDINGS: "Living Doll," Paramount, 1959; *Lucky Lips,* Epic, 1963; *Devil Woman,* Rocket, 1976; *We Don't Talk Anymore,* EMI America, 1979; also, "Move It," 1958; *The Young Ones,* 1961; and "Congratulations," "Power to All Our Friends," "Daddy's Home," and others.

AWARDS: Awarded the Order of the British Empire; Voted Top British Singer, 1960-71; voted Top Box Office Star of Great Britain, 1962-63 and 1963-64; ten Gold Discs, for selling over one million recordings and thirty Silver Discs, for selling over two hundred and fifty thousand recordings.

SIDELIGHTS: RECREATIONS—Swimming and tennis.

ADDRESSES: MANAGER—Gormley Management, P.O. Box 46C, Esher, Surrey, KT10 9AF, England.*

RICHARDS, Angela   1944-

PERSONAL: Born December 18, 1944. EDUCATION: Trained for the stage at the Royal Academy of Dramatic Art.

VOCATION: Actress and songwriter.

CAREER: LONDON DEBUT—Henrietta, *Robert and Elizabeth*, Lyric Theatre, 1964. PRINCIPAL STAGE APPEARANCES— Kathie, *On the Level*, Saville Theatre, London, 1966; Millie Jackson, *Annie*, Westminster Theatre, London, 1967; Jenny Diver, *The Beggar's Opera*, Prospect Theatre Company, Apollo Theatre, London, 1968; Sally, *Love on the Dole*, Nottingham Playhouse Theatre, Nottingham, U.K., 1970; Titania, *A Midsummer Night's Dream*, Countess Sophia, *A Patriot for Me*, both Bristol Old Vic Theatre, Bristol, U.K., 1971; Angela, *A Close Shave*, Eurydice, *Antigone*, both Nottingham Playhouse Theatre, 1971; Fanny, *Ride a Cock-horse*, Hampstead Theatre Club, London, 1972; Lucy Lockit, *The Beggar's Opera*, Minnie Tinwell, *The Doctor's Dilemma*, Chichester Festival, Chichester, U.K., 1972; Eve Harrington, *Applause*, Her Majesty's Theatre, London, 1972; widow, *Zorba*, Greenwich Theatre, London, 1973; *Cole*, Mermaid Theatre, London, 1974; Celia, *As You Like It*, Lieutenant Lillian Holliday, *Happy End*, Oxford Playhouse, Oxford, U.K., then Lyric Theatre, London, both 1975; title role, *Liza of Lambeth*, Shaftesbury Theatre, London, 1976.

MAJOR TOURS—Catherine Winslow, *The Winslow Boy*, U.K. cities, 1980.

PRINCIPAL TELEVISION APPEARANCES—Series: *Secret Army*, BBC. Specials: *Women—Which Way Now?*, BBC; *King of the Castle*, BBC.

WRITINGS: Songs for the BBC television series, *Secret Army*.

MEMBER: Brtish Actors' Equity Association.

ADDRESSES: AGENT—c/o Bryan Drew, 81 Shaftesbury Avenue, London W1, England.*

*   *   *

RIDDLE, Nelson   1921-1985

PERSONAL: Born June 1, 1921, in Hackensack, NJ; died of heart and kidney failure in Los Angeles, CA, October 6, 1985.

VOCATION: Composer, conductor, and actor.

CAREER: PRINCIPAL FILM APPEARANCES—*Fugitive Girls*, 1979.

PRINCIPAL FILM WORK—Composer: *Johnny Concho*, 1956; *A Kiss Before Dying*, 1956; *St. Louis Blues*, 1958; *L'il Abner*, Paramount, 1959; *Ocean's Eleven*, Warner Brothers, 1960; *Can-Can*, Twentieth Century-Fox, 1960; *Lolita*, Metro-Goldwyn-Mayer, 1962; *What a Way to Go!*, 1964; *Robin and the Seven Hoods*, Warner Brothers, 1964; *Marriage on the Rocks*, Warner Brothers, 1965; *El Dorado*, Paramount, 1967; *Paint Your Wagon*, Paramount, 1969; *The Great Gatsby*, Paramount, 1974; *Guyana: Cult of the Damned*, 1980.

PRINCIPAL TELEVISION WORK—Composer and conductor: Se-

ries—*The Nat "King" Cole Show*, NBC, 1956-57; *The Frank Sinatra Show*, ABC, 1957-58; *The Smothers Brothers Comedy Hour*, CBS, 1967-69; *The Smothers Brothers Show*, CBS, 1968; *The Leslie Uggams Show*, CBS, 1969; *The Tim Conway Comedy Hour*, CBS, 1970; *CBS Newcomers*, CBS, 1971; *The Julie Andrews Hour*, ABC, 1972-73; *The Helen Reddy Show*, NBC, 1973. Specials—*The Carpenters: Music, Music, Music.*

RELATED CAREER—Guest conductor, Hollywood Bowl, CA, 1954-60; music director, Reprise Records, 1963-85.

WRITINGS: COMPOSITIONS AND RECORDINGS—(In addition to the above) Theme music: *The Untouchables*, ABC, 1959-63; *Route 66*, CBS, 1960-64; "Johnny Concho's Theme" (also known as "Wait for Me"), 1956; "Lolita Ya-Ya," from *Lolita*, Metro-Goldwyn-Mayer, 1962, recorded by The Ventures on Dolton records; "Louisa's Theme," from *What a Way to Go!*, 1964; "New 'Naked City' Theme," ABC, 1962-63, recorded on Capitol records.

AWARDS: Hit theme song, number thirty on *Billboard's* top sixty, 1962, *Route 66;* Best Musical Score, Academy Award, 1974, for *The Great Gatsby.*

MEMBER: American Society of Composers, Authors, and Publishers, Broadcast Music, Inc.*

*   *   *

RIFKIN, Bud   1942-

PERSONAL: Full name, Harmon Rifkin; born April 1, 1942, in Springfield, MA. EDUCATION: Clark University, A.B., 1964; Boston College, Graduate School of Business Administration, M.B.A., 1967.

VOCATION: Entertainment executive.

CAREER: PRINCIPAL FILM WORK—Film and equipment purchasing agent for Rifkin Theatre chain; financial manager, Rifkin Theatre chain; co-founder, Cinema Centers Corporations and Theatre Management Services, 1972—, currently president in charge of theatre development and general operations.

MEMBER: National Association of Theatre Owners (executive committee); National Association of Theatre Owners (co-chairman, technical advancement committee); Theatre Owners of New England (past program chairman, vice-president, and chairman).

ADDRESSES: OFFICE—Cinema Center Corp., 39 Church Street, Boston MA 02116.*

*   *   *

RINEHART, Elaine   1952-

PERSONAL: Born August 16, 1952, in San Antonio, TX; daughter of James Howell (in the U.S. Marine Corps) and Evolyn Majoria (a speech therapist; maiden name, Dyer) Rinehart. EDUCATION: Received B.F.A., drama, from the North Carolina School of the Arts; attended the Rose Bruford Academy of Speech and Drama;

trained for the stage with Mira Rostova, Lee Strasberg, and with Jerzy Grotowski in Poland; studied voice with Tom Rexdale; ballet with Larry Stevens and Evee Lynn; and jazz with David Harris. RELIGION: Protestant.

VOCATION: Actress.

CAREER: STAGE DEBUT—Celimene, *The Misanthrope,* North Carolina School of the Arts, NC, 1974. PRINCIPAL STAGE APPEARANCES—Dawn, *The Best Little Whorehouse in Texas,* Actors Studio, New York City, 1978; Monica, *Dumping Ground,* Ensemble Studio Theatre, New York City, 1982; Simone, *Bedful of Foreigners,* Royal Poinciana Playhouse, Palm Beach, FL, 1981; Aurore, *Joan of Lorraine,* Mirror Repertory Theatre, New York City, 1983; Rita, *Educating Rita,* Lake George Dinner Theatre, Lake George, NY, 1984; Carla, Pearl, *Roots,* Jewish Repertory Theatre, New York City, 1986; Philomena, *Sister Mary Ignatius Explains It All for You,* Dock Street Theatre, Charleston, SC, 1987. Also appeared as Caroline, *Go Back for Murder,* St. Michael's Playhouse, VT, 1984; Ceil, *American Beef,* Gloucester Stage Company, MA, 1987; Miranda, *The Tempest,* Lost Colony Outdoor Drama Theatre, Manteo, VA; Ana, *Tropicana,* Cissy, *Internal Combustion,* both Musical Theatre Works, New York City; courtesan, *Comedy of Errors,* Ensemble Studio Theatre; Roxanne, *From Behind the Moon,* Theatre for the New City, New York City; Marya, *Chopin in Space,* American Place Theatre, New York City; Mary Dalton, *Native Son,* American Folk Theatre, New York City; Melinda, *Fairweather Friends,* Playwrights Horizons, New York City; Bridgett, *Tenderloin,* Equity Library Theatre, New York City; Nancy, *Angel Street,* Theatre at the Inn, NJ; Sherri, *Griev-*

ELAINE RINEHART

ances, Mirror Repertory Theatre; Mary, *The Wonder Years,* New Arts Theatre, New York City; Gwendolyn, *The Importance of Being Earnest,* Unified Field Production; Hermia, *A Midsummer Night's Dream,* Trumpet in the Land Outdoor Drama Theatre; and appeared in *Improv Comedy Corps,* Manhattan Punch Line, New York City.

MAJOR TOURS—Barbara Smith, *Run for Your Wife,* U.S. cities, 1985; Sally, *Pack of Lies,* U.S. cities, 1985.

PRINCIPAL CABARET APPEARANCES—As a stand-up comedienne, *Live Skro Acts on Stage,* New York City nightclubs.

PRINCIPAL FILM APPEARANCES—College girl, *The Bell Jar,* AVCO-Embassy, 1979; punk rocker, *Fame,* United Artists, 1980; stand in, *A Chorus Line,* Columbia, 1985. Also appeared as nurse, *Seizure,* 1974.

PRINCIPAL TELEVISION APPEARANCES—Series: Dixie, *The Edge of Night,* CBS. Mini-Series: *Kane & Abel,* CBS, 1985. Movies: *Sentimental Journey,* CBS, 1984; *Izzy & Moe,* CBS, 1985.

MEMBER: Actors' Equity Association, Screen Actors Guild, American Federation of Television and Radio Artists.

ADDRESSES: HOME—400 W. 43rd Street, New York, NY 10036. AGENT—c/o Steve Unger, Gage Group, 1650 Broadway, New York, NY 10019.

*   *   *

RITCHIE, June

PERSONAL: Married Marcus Turnbull. EDUCATION: Trained for the stage at the Royal Academy of Dramatic Art.

VOCATION: Actress.

CAREER: LONDON DEBUT—Miss Mopply, *Too True to Be Good,* Strand Theatre, 1965. PRINCIPAL STAGE APPEARANCES— Doreen, *Saturday Night and Sunday Morning,* Prince of Wales Theatre, London, 1966; Shirley, *The Anniversary,* Duke of York's Theatre, London, 1966; Becky Sharp, *Vanity Fair,* Arnaud Theatre, Guildford, U.K., 1971; Emily, *His Monkey Wife,* Hampstead Theatre Club, London, 1971; Scarlett O'Hara, *Gone with the Wind,* Drury Lane Theatre, London, 1972; Lady Macbeth, *Macbeth,* Dotty, *Jumpers,* Ruth, *The Homecoming,* all Gardner Center Theatre, Brighton, U.K., 1974; Natasha, *The Three Sisters,* Arnaud Theatre, then Cambridge Theatre, London, both 1976; Mrs. Kopecka, *Schweyk in the Second World War,* Bristol Old Vic Theatre, Bristol, U.K., 1977; countess, *A Patriot for Me,* Center Theatre Group, Ahmanson Theatre, Los Angeles, CA, 1985. Also appeared in *Tonight We Improvise,* Chichester Festival, Chichester, U.K., 1974.

MAJOR TOURS—Becky Sharp, *Vanity Fair,* U.K. cities, 1971; Beverly, *The Shadow Box,* U.K. cities, 1979.

FILM DEBUT—*A Kind of Loving,* Governor, 1962. PRINCIPAL FILM APPEARANCES—*Live Now, Pay Later; This is My Street.*

MEMBER: British Actors' Equity Association, Screen Actors Guild.

ADDRESSES: AGENT—c/o Fraser and Dunlop, 91 Regent Street, London W1, England.*

ROBB, R.D. 1972-

PERSONAL: Born March 31, 1972, in Philadelphia, PA.

VOCATION: Actor.

CAREER: BROADWAY DEBUT—Little Charlie, *Charlie and Algernon* 1980. PRINCIPAL STAGE APPEARANCES—Leonard Bernstein, *A Broadway Baby,* Goodspeed Opera House, East Haddam, CT, 1984; title role, *Oliver!,* Mark Hellinger Theatre, New York City, 1984; Gavroche, *Les Miserables,* Broadway Theatre, New York City, then Eisenhower Theatre, Washington, DC, both 1987; Lester, *House in the Woods,* Musical Theatre Works, New York City. Also appeared as Jimmy, *Calling All Kids,* Los Angeles.

MAJOR TOURS—Tiny Tim, *A Christmas Carol,* U.S. cities.

FILM DEBUT—Schwartz, *A Christmas Story,* Metro-Goldwyn-Mayer/United Artists, 1985.

PRINCIPAL TELEVISION APPEARANCES—Episodic: *Highway to Heaven,* NBC. Specials: Arliss, "Little Arliss," *ABC Afterschool Specials,* ABC; Martin, "Out of Time," *Young People's Special,* NBC.

MEMBER: Actors' Equity Association, Screen Actors Guild, American Federation of Television and Radio Artists.

ADDRESSES: MANAGER—c/o Talent Works, Philadelphia, PA.

* * *

ROBBINS, Carrie Fishbein 1943-

PERSONAL: Born February 7, 1943, in Baltimore, MD; daughter of Sidney W. and Betty A. (Berman) Fishbein; married Richard D. Robbins (a doctor). EDUCATION: Attended Pennsylvania State University; received M.F.A. from Yale School of Drama.

VOCATION: Costume and scenic designer.

CAREER: FIRST STAGE WORK—Scenic designer, *Bells Are Ringing,* Schwab Auditorium, University Park, PA, 1962. FIRST NEW YORK STAGE WORK—Costume designer, *Leda Had a Little.Swan,* Cort Theatre, 1968. PRINCIPAL STAGE WORK—Costume designer, all in New York City unless indicated: *Inner Journey, The Year Boston Won the Pennant,* both Forum Theatre, 1969; *The Time of Your Life,* Vivian Beaumont Theatre, 1969; *The Good Woman of Setzuan,* Vivian Beaumont Theatre, 1970; *Look to the Lilies,* Lunt-Fontanne Theatre, 1970; *An Enemy of the People,* Vivian Beaumont Theatre, 1971; *Narrow Road to the Deep North, The Crucible,* both Vivian Beaumont Theatre, 1972; *Grease,* Eden Theatre, then Royale Theatre, both 1972; *The Hostage,* Good Shepherd-Faith Church, 1972; *Sunset; The Beggar's Opera,* both Chelsea Theatre Center, 1972; *The Secret Affairs of Mildred Wild,* Ambassador Theatre, 1972; *Let Me Hear You Smile,* Biltmore Theatre, 1973; *The Plough and the Stars,* Vivian Beaumont Theatre, 1973; *Molly,* Alvin Theatre, 1973; *The Iceman Cometh,* Circle in the Square, 1973; *The Beggar's Opera,* Billy Rose Theatre, 1973; *Over Here,* Shubert Theatre, 1974; *Yentl, the Yeshiva Boy,* Chelsea Theatre Center, 1974; *Polly,* Chelsea Theatre Center, 1975; *The Boss,* Chelsea Theatre Center, 1976; *The Creditors, The Stronger,* both Public Theatre, 1977; *Happy End,* Martin Beck Theatre, 1977;

CARRIE FISHBEIN ROBBINS

Old Man Joseph and His Family, Chelsea Westside Theatre, 1978; *Fearless Frank,* Princess Theatre, 1980; (also designed puppets) *Frankenstein,* Palace Theatre, 1981; *El Bravo,* Entermedia Theatre, 1981; *The First,* Martin Beck Theatre, 1981; *Agnes of God,* Music Box Theatre, 1983; (also designed special effects) *The Boys of Winter,* Biltmore Theatre, 1985; *The Octette Bridge Club,* Music Box Theatre, 1985; *Twelfth Night,* Alaska Repertory Theatre, Anchorage, AL, 1986. Also costume designer, *Merry Wives of Windsor,* New York Shakespeare Festival (NYSF), 1974; *Rebel Women,* NYSF, 1976; *The Misanthrope,* NYSF, 1977; with Center Stage, Baltimore, MD; Studio Arena Theatre, Buffalo, NY; Inner City Repertory Theatre, Mark Taper Forum, both Los Angeles, CA; Guthrie Theatre, Minneapolis, MN; Long Wharf Theatre, New Haven CT; McCarter Theatre, Princeton, NJ; American Conservatory Theatre, San Francisco, CA; Seattle Repertory Theatre, Seattle, WA; Kennedy Center, Washington, DC; Williamstown Theatre Festival, Williamstown, MA; designed operas at the Boston Opera Company and the Hamburg State Opera.

PRINCIPAL TELEVISION WORK—All as costume designer. Specials: *The Seagull; In Fashion; The Beggar's Opera.*

RELATED CAREER—Faculty member, theatre design department, New York University; visiting lecturer in advanced costume design, University of Illinois, 1977-78.

AWARDS: Drama Desk Award, 1972, for *Grease;* Drama Desk Award, 1973, for *The Beggar's Opera.*

MEMBER: International Association of Stage Employees and Motion Picture Camera Operators; Phi Beta Kappa Society.

ADDRESES: HOME—22 E. 36th Street, New York, NY, 10016.*

ROBERTSON, Dale 1923-

PERSONAL: Born Dayle Robertson, July 14, 1923, in Oklahoma City, OK. EDUCATION: Attended Oklahoma Military College. MILITARY: U.S. Army, 1942-45.

VOCATION: Actor and producer.

CAREER: FILM DEBUT—Jesse James, *Fighting Man of the Plains*, 1949. PRINCIPAL FILM APPEARANCES—*Caribou Trail*, 1950; *Two Flags West*, 1950; *Call Me Mister*, 1951; *Take Care of My Little Girl*, 1951; *Golden Girl*, 1951; *Lydia Bailey*, 1952; *Return of the Texan*, 1952; *The Outcasts of Poker Flat*, 1952; *O. Henry's Full House*, 1952; *The Farmer Takes a Wife*, 1953; *Gambler from Natchez*, 1954; *Sitting Bull*, 1954; *Son of Sinbad*, 1954; *Day of Fury*, 1956; *Dakota Incident*, 1956; *Hell Canyon Outlaws*, Republic, 1957; *View from the Terrace*, 1960; *Fast and Sexy*, Columbia, 1960; *Law of the Lawless*, 1964; *Blood on the Arrow*, Allied Artists, 1964; *The Walking Major*, 1964; *Coast of Skeletons*, 1964; *The One-Eyed Soldiers*, 1966.

PRINCIPAL TELEVISION APPEARANCES—Episodic: "A Tale of Wells Fargo," *Schlitz Playhouse of Stars*, CBS, 1956; *Undercurrent*, CBS; guest host, *The Hollywood Palace*, ABC. Series: Jim Hardie, *Tales of Wells Fargo*, NBC, 1957-62; Ben Calhoun, *The Iron Horse*, ABC, 1966-68; host, *Death Valley Days* (also known as *Frontier Adventure*), syndicated, 1968-72; Walter Lankershim, *Dynasty*, ABC, 1981; title role, *J.J. Starbuck*, NBC, 1987—. Pilots: Ben Calhoun, *Scalplock*, ABC, 1966. Movies: Title role, *Melvin Purvis: G-Man*, ABC, 1974; Melvin Purvis, *The Kansas City Massacre*, ABC, 1975; Judge Isaac Parker, *The Last Ride of the Dalton Gang*, NBC, 1979.

PRINCIPAL TELEVISION WORK—Producer, *Star of Tomorrow*, 1951.

NON-RELATED CAREER—Former professional prizefighter.

MEMBER: Screen Actors Guild, American Federation of Television and Radio Artists.

ADDRESSES: HOME—Box 226, Yukon, OK 73099.*

*   *   *

RODD, Marcia 1940-

PERSONAL: Born July 8, 1940, in Lyons, KS; daughter of Charles C. and Rosetta (Thran) Rodd; married Dale W. Hagen, 1963. EDUCATION: Northwestern University, B.A., 1963; trained for the stage with Alvina Krause.

VOCATION: Actress, singer, and director.

CAREER: OFF-BROADWAY DEBUT—*Oh Say Can You See!*, Provincetown Playhouse, 1962. LONDON DEBUT—Olivia, *Your Own Thing*, Comedy Theatre, 1969. PRINCIPAL STAGE APPEARANCES—Various roles, *Oh! What a Lovely War*, Broadhurst Theatre, New York City, 1964; various roles, *Cambridge Circus*, Square East, New York City, 1964; various roles, *The Mad Show*, New Theatre, New York City, 1966; Lotte, *Chu Chem*, New Locust Theatre, Philadelphia, PA, 1966; Bea, *Love in E-Flat*, Brooks Atkinson Theatre, New York City, 1967; Viola, *Love and Let Love*,

Sheridan Square Playhouse, New York City, 1968; Olivia, *Your Own Thing*, Huntington Hartford Theatre, Los Angeles, CA, 1968; Bobbi Michele, *Last of the Red Hot Lovers*, Eugene O'Neill Theatre, New York City, 1970; Maud, *Shelter*, John Golden Theatre, New York City, 1973; Mistress Page, *The Merry Wives of Windsor*, New York Shakespeare Festival, Delacorte Theatre, New York City, 1974; voice of Mrs. Blustone, *Pinocchio* (puppet show), Bil Baird Puppet Theatre, New York City, 1974; May Daniels, *Once in a Lifetime*, Mark Taper Forum, Los Angeles, CA, 1975; K.C. Wofford, *And If That Mockingbird Don't Sing*, Circle Theatre, Los Angeles, CA, 1977; *The Goodbye People*, Center Stage, Baltimore, MD, 1977.

MAJOR TOURS—Dorothy, *Gentlemen Prefer Blondes*, U.S. cities, 1966; Daisy Gamble, *On a Clear Day You Can See Forever*, U.S. cities, 1967; Aldonza, *Man of La Mancha*, U.S. cities, 1971.

PRINCIPAL STAGE WORK—Director: *After We Eat the Apple*, Cubiculo Theatre, New York City, 1972; *Blithe Spirit*, Center Stage, Baltimore, MD, 1978.

PRINCIPAL TELEVISION APPEARANCES—Episodic: *All in the Family*, CBS; *The Dumplings*, ABC; *The Dick Van Dyke Show*, CBS; *My Friend Tony*, ABC; *CBS Repertory Theatre*, CBS; *Wednesday Revue*, NET. Movies: Eve, *How to Break Up a Happy Divorce*, NBC, 1976; Lily, *Between the Darkness and the Dawn*, NBC, 1985. Guest: *Tonight Show*, NBC; *Ed Sullivan Show*, NBC; *David Frost Show*, CBS.

PRINCIPAL FILM APPEARANCES—Patsy Newquist, *Little Murders*, Twentieth Century-Fox, 1972; Dayle, *T.R. Baskin*, Paramount, 1972.

MEMBER: Actors' Equity Association, Screen Actors Guild, American Federation of Television and Radio Artists.

SIDELIGHTS: RECREATIONS—Tennis, carpentry, painting, needle-point, crossword puzzles, reading mysteries, playing cards.

ADDRESSES: AGENT—c/o STE Representation, 888 Seventh Avenue, New York, NY 10019.*

*   *   *

ROLIN, Judi 1946-

PERSONAL: Full name, Judith Marie Rolin; born November 6, 1946, in Chicago, IL; daughter of Kenneth Carl (a designing engineer) and Marcy Marie (Neson) Rolin; married Edward B. Self (a physician), December 18, 1971 (divorced, February 1, 1982); married Joseph P. Skirpek (an attorney), September 6, 1985; children: Anton William, Edward Badwin III, Rachel Marie. EDUCATION: Studied jazz with Ron Demarco and Kim Fitzner; guitar with Murray Phillips; voice with Peggy Fowler.

VOCATION: Actress, singer, and dancer.

CAREER: PRINCIPAL STAGE APPEARANCES— Fiona, *Brigadoon*, Mei Ling, *Flower Drum Song*, Lisle, *The Sound of Music*, Louisa, *The Fantasticks*, Dorothy, *The Wizard of Oz*, Sharon, *Finian's Rainbow*, all summer theatre productions, 1964; Dorothy, *The Wizard of Oz*, Mei Ling, *Aladdin's Golden Lamp*, Melisande, *Sleeping Beauty*, all with the Prince Street Players, New York City,

JUDI ROLIN

1965; Trina, *Forty Carats,* Morosco Theatre, New York City, 1970; lead singer, *Rodgers and Hart,* Broadway production, 1975.

PRINCIPAL CABARET APPEARANCES—The Duplex, New York City, 1986; Jason's Park Royal, 1987.

PRINCIPAL TELEVISION APPEARANCES—Episodic: Little Joe's girlfriend, "Shining in Spain," *Bonanza,* NBC, 1966; *Dean Martin Show,* NBC, 1965-1966; *Hullabaloo,* NBC, 1966; *Bell Telephone Hour,* NBC, 1966. Series: Regular, *Dean Martin Summer Show,* NBC, 1966; Minnie's niece, *Minnie Pearl Show,* 1968; Didi Claybourn, *The Secret Storm,* CBS, 1970; Nancy Ryan, *As the World Turns,* CBS, 1971. Specials: Title role, *Alice through the Looking Glass,* 1966. Guest: *Steve Lawrence Hour,* CBS, 1965; *Tonight Show,* NBC, 1965-1966; *Mike Douglas Show,* syndicated, 1966; *Ed Nelson Show,* 1968.

PRINCIPAL FILM APPEARANCES—Maeve, *A Change in the Wind,* 1971.

AWARDS: Best Actress, Emmy Award nomination, 1966, for *Alice through the Looking Glass.*

MEMBER: Actors' Equity Association, Screen Actors Guild, American Federation of Television and Radio Artists, American Guild of Variety Artists.

SIDELIGHTS: RECREATIONS—Breeding Paso Fino horses.

ADDRESSES: OFFICE—235 W. 56th Street, New York, NY 10019. AGENT—Michael Thomas Agency, Inc., 305 Madison Avenue, Suite 4419, New York, NY 10017.

ROLLINS, Jack

VOCATION: Film producer.

CAREER: PRINCIPAL FILM WORK—Producer, with Charles H. Joffe: *Take the Money and Run,* Cinerama, 1969; *Bananas,* United Artists, 1971; *Everything You Always Wanted to Know About Sex but Were Afraid to Ask,* United Artists, 1972; *Sleeper,* United Artists, 1973; *Love and Death,* United Artists, 1975; *The Front,* Columbia, 1976; *Annie Hall,* United Artists, 1977; *Interiors,* United Artists, 1978; *Manhattan,* United Artists, 1979; *Stardust Memories,* United Artists, 1980; *A Midsummer Night's Sex Comedy,* Warner Brothers, 1982; *Zelig,* Warner Brothers, 1983; *Broadway Danny Rose,* Orion, 1984; *The Purple Rose of Cairo,* Orion, 1985; *Hannah and Her Sisters,* Orion, 1986; *Radio Days,* Orion, 1987.

PRINCIPAL TELEVISION WORK—Producer: *The Dick Cavett Show,* CBS; *The David Letterman Show,* NBC.

ADDRESSES: OFFICE—Rollins-Joffe-Morra-Brezner Productions, 130 W. 57th Street, New York, NY 10019; Rollins-Joffe-Morra-Brezner Productions, c/o Paramount Studios, 5555 Melrose Avenue, Los Angeles, CA 90038.*

*   *   *

ROLSTON, Mark   1956-

PERSONAL: Born December 7, 1956, in Baltimore, MD; son of Thomas George (a computer programmer) and Evelyn Beverly (Sturm) Rolston; married Sally Anne Hughes (an actress), May 9, 1981; children: Adam, Timothy, Thomas. EDUCATION: Attended Frostburg State College, 1975-77; University of London, 1977-78; trained for the stage with John Blatchlem, Christopher Fettes, and Yat Malmgrem at the Drama Centre, London.

VOCATION: Actor.

CAREER: STAGE DEBUT—Sergeant, *Are You Now or Have You Ever Been?,* Bush Theatre, London, 1976, for sixty performances. PRINCIPAL STAGE APPEARANCES—Jean, *Miss Julie,* Edinburgh Theatre Festival, Edinburgh, Scotland, U.K., 1976; Jeep, *Action,* Fringe Festival, London, 1981; Bo Decker, *Bus Stop,* Mill Theatre, Sonning, U.K., 1984.

MAJOR TOURS—Title role, *Richard II,* National Shakespeare Company, U.S. cities, 1981.

FILM DEBUT—Drake, *Aliens,* Twentieth Century-Fox, 1985. PRINCIPAL FILM APPEARANCES—Jake Conner, *Survival Quest,* Universal, 1986; Dave, *Weeds,* DeLaurentiis Entertaiment Group, 1987.

TELEVISION DEBUT—Cop, *Sledgehammer,* ABC, 1987. PRINCIPAL TELEVISION APPEARANCES—Episodic: Renaldo Sykes, *Wiseguy,* CBS, 1987; Jeremiah Ennis, "Burn Baby, Burn," *Tour of Duty,* CBS, 1987. Mini-Series: Attendant, *Master of the Game,* CBS, 1984.

MEMBER: British Actors' Equity, Actors' Equity Association, Screen Actors Guild, American Federation of Television and Radio Artists; North American Artists (board member, 1986-87).

MARK ROLSTON

ADDRESSES: AGENT—c/o Pearl Wexler, Paul Kohner Agency, 9169 W. Sunset Boulevard, Los Angeles, CA 90069; c/o Michael Ladkin, 11 Garrick Street, London WC 2, England.

*   *   *

ROMAN, Arlene   1959-

PERSONAL: Born Arlene Ramos, March 21, 1959, in Bronx, NY; daughter of Modesto (a police officer) and Ada Mina (Hernandez) Ramos; married Peter Campbell Dawns, July 21, 1984 (separated). EDUCATION: Graduated from the School for the Performing Arts, New York City; attended New York University; trained for the stage with Herbert Berghof at the Herbert Berghof Studios, and with Curt Dempster at the Ensemble Studio Theatre. POLITICS: Democrat. RELIGION: "Higher Power."

VOCATION: Actress.

CAREER: STAGE DEBUT—Estelita, *Love Is Not for Sale,* La Mama Experimental Theatre Club, New York City, 1979. PRINCIPAL STAGE APPEARANCES—Martivio, *The House of Bernada Alba,* Spanish Repertory Company, Gramercy Arts Theatre, New York City, 1980; I-Love-Lucy, *La Chefa,* New Federal Theatre, Henry Street Settlement, New York City, 1984; Gabriele von Kant, *The Bitter Tears of Petra von Kant,* Puerto Rican Traveling Theatre, New York City, 1986; Gueria, *Birthrites,* American Folk Theatre, New York City, 1987.

ARLENE ROMAN

MAJOR TOURS—Lady-in-Orange, *For Colored Girls Who Have Considered Suicide When the Rainbow Is Enuf,* U.S. cities.

FILM DEBUT—Arlene, *Crossover Dreams,* Crossover Films, 1982.

TELEVISION DEBUT—*Reflections on Our Past,* 1978. PRINCIPAL TELEVISION APPEARANCES—Episodic: Inez Quinnes, "Golden Boy," *Oye Willie,* PBS, 1981.

RELATED CAREER—Improvisation teacher at children's workshops.

AWARDS: Obie Award from the *Village Voice,* 1980, for *The House of Bernarda Alba.*

SIDELIGHTS: RECREATIONS—Dancing, arts and crafts, studing Impressionist art.

ADDRESSES: AGENT—c/o Wendy Curiel, Oppenhiem & Christie, 13 E. 37th Street, New York, NY 10016.

*   *   *

ROMAN, Ruth   1924-

PERSONAL: Born December 23, 1924, in Boston, MA. EDUCATION: Attended Bishop Lee Dramatic School.

VOCATION: Actress.

CAREER: PRINCIPAL STAGE APPEARANCES—With the New England Repertory Company and Elizabeth Peabody Players.

FILM DEBUT—*Queen of the Jungle*, Universal. PRINCIPAL FILM APPEARANCES—*The House of Seven Gables*, 1940; *Good Sam*, 1948; *Belle Starr's Daughter*, 1948; *Whip Son*, 1948; *The Window*, RKO, 1949; *Champion*, United Artists, 1949; *Beyond the Forest*, 1949; *Always Leave Them Laughing*, 1949; *Colt .45*, 1950; *Barricade*, 1950; *Three Secrets*, 1950; *Dallas*, 1950; *Strangers on a Train*, Warner Brothers, 1951; *Tomorrow Is Another Day*, 1951; *Starlift*, 1951; *Invitation*, 1952; *Mara Maru*, 1952; *Young Man With Ideas*, Metro-Goldwyn-Mayer, 1952; *Blowing Wild*, 1953; *Shanghai Story*, 1954; *The Far Country*, 1955; *Tanganyika*, 1954; *Down Three Dark Streets*, 1954; *Joe Macbeth*, 1955; *The Bottom of the Bottle*, 1956; *Great Day in the Morning*, 1956; *Rebel in Town*, 1956; *Bitter Victory*, 1958; *Look in Any Window*, 1961; *Miracle of the Cowards*, 1962; *Love Has Many Faces*, 1965; *The Day of the Animals*, 1976; *Echoes*, Herbeval, 1983.

PRINCIPAL TELEVISION APPEARANCES—Series: Minnie Littlejohn, *The Long, Hot Summer*, ABC, 1965-66. Episodic: *Naked City*, ABC; *Route 66*, CBS; *The Defenders*, CBS; *Dr. Kildare*, NBC; *Producers Showcase*, NBC; *Eleventh Hour*, NBC; *Breaking Point*, ABC. Movies: *Go Ask Alice*, 1972.

MEMBER: Actors' Equity Association, Screen Actors Guild, American Federation of Television and Radio Artists.

ADDRESSES: HOME—1225 Cliff Drive, Laguna Beach, CA 92651.*

*   *   *

ROONEY, Andy   1920-

PERSONAL: Full name, Andrew Aitken Rooney; born January 14, 1920, in Albany, NY; son of Walter S. and Elinor (Reynolds), Rooney; married Marguerite Howard, April 21, 1942; children: Ellen, Martha, Emily, Brian. EDUCATION: Attended Colgate University, 1941. MILITARY: U.S. Army, 1941-45.

VOCATION: Writer, columnist, essayist, and producer.

CAREER: PRINCIPAL TELEVISION APPEARANCES—Documentaries: "Black History: Lost, Stolen, or Strayed," *CBS News Hour*, 1968; *An Essay on War*, PBS; also *In Praise of New York City, Mr. Rooney Goes to Dinner, Mr. Rooney Goes to Washington*, and *Mr. Rooney Goes to Work*; essayist, *60 Minutes*, CBS, 1979—.

PRINCIPAL TELEVISION WORK—Director, "Black History: Lost, Stolen, or Strayed," *CBS News Hour*, 1968; producer and director: *An Essay on War, In Praise of New York City, Mr. Rooney Goes to Dinner, Mr. Rooney Goes to Washington*, and *Mr. Rooney Goes to Work*.

RELATED CAREER—Journalist, *Stars & Stripes*, 1941-45; newspaper columninst, Tribune Corporation Syndicate, 1979—.

WRITINGS: NON-FICTION—(With O.C. Hutton) *Air Gunner*, 1944; *The Story of the Stars and Stripes*, 1946; *Conquerors' Peace*, 1947; *The Fortunes of War*, 1962; *A Few Minutes with Andy Rooney*, Atheneum, 1981; *And More by Andy Rooney*, Atheneum, 1982; *Pieces of My Mind*, Atheneum, 1984; *Word for Word*, Putnam, 1986.

TELEVISION—Series: Writer for Arthur Godfrey, Garry Moore,

Sam Levenson, and Victor Borge; essayist, *60 Minutes*, CBS, 1979—. Documentaries: "Black History: Lost, Stolen, or Strayed," *CBS News Hour*, 1968; *An Essay on War*, PBS; *In Praise of New York City, Mr. Rooney Goes to Dinner, Mr. Rooney Goes to Washington*, and *Mr. Rooney Goes to Work*.

AWARDS: Best Written Television Documentary, Writers Guild of America Awards, 1966, 1968, 1971, 1975, 1976; Outstanding News Documentary, Individual Achievement, Emmy Award, 1969, for "Black History: Lost, Stolen, or Strayed," *CBS News Hour;* Air Medal, Bronze Star, 1945.

MEMBER: Writers Guild of America, American Federation of Television and Radio Actors.

ADDRESSES: OFFICE—CBS, 51 W. 52nd Street, New York, NY 10019.*

*   *   *

RORKE, Hayden   1910-1987

OBITUARY NOTICE: Born October 23, 1910, in Brooklyn, NY; died of cancer, August 19, 1987, in Toluca Lake, CA. Best remembered as Dr. Alfred Bellows in the television comedy *I Dream of Jeannie*, Hayden Rorke's extensive acting credits also included more than fifty films and seventy Broadway productions. After studying acting at the American Academy of Dramatic Arts, he appeared in such shows as *Three Men on a Horse*, 1935, *The Philadelphia Story*, 1939; *Dream Girl*, 1945, *A Moon for the Misbegotten*, 1957, and in numerous summer theatre productions throughout the U.S. and Canada. Rorke made his movie debut in *This Is the Army*, 1943, and subsequent films included *Father's Little Dividend*, 1951, *An American in Paris*, 1951, *Pocketful of Miracles*, 1961, *The Thrill of It All*, 1963, and *The Unsinkable Molly Brown*, 1964. In addition to his continuing role in *I Dream of Jeannie*, he also was a regular on the television series *Mr. Adams and Eve*, 1957-58, and *No Time for Sergeants*, 1964-65, as well as guest appearances on *I Love Lucy, Dr. Kildare, Bonanza, Perry Mason, Cannon*, and *Barnaby Jones*. In 1985 Rorke made his last television appearance, reprising the role of Dr. Bellows in the reunion movie, *I Dream of Jeannie . . . 15 Years Later*.

OBITUARIES AND OTHER SOURCES: Variety, August 26, 1987.

*   *   *

ROSS, Diana   1944-

PERSONAL: Born Diane Ross, March 26, 1944, in Detroit, MI; daughter of Fred and Ernestine Ross; married Robert Ellis Silberstein, January, 1971 (divorced, 1976); married Arne Naess, October 23, 1985; children: (first marriage) Rhonda, Tracee, Chudney; (second marriage) one son, two stepchildren. EDUCATION: Graduated from public high school, Detroit, MI.

VOCATION: Singer and actress.

CAREER: FILM DEBUT—Billie Holiday, *Lady Sings the Blues*, Paramount, 1972. PRINCIPAL FILM APPEARANCES— Title role, *Mahogany*, 1975; Dorothy, *The Wiz*, Universal, 1978.

PRINCIPAL TELEVISION APPEARANCES—Specials: *An Evening with Diana Ross*, NBC, 1977; also, *Diana*, 1971.

PRINCIPAL STAGE APPEARANCES—*An Evening with Diana Ross*, Palace Theatre, New York City, 1976.

RELATED CAREER—President of Diana Ross Enterprises, Inc., with divisions including Anaid Film Productions, Inc.; Diana Ross Foundation; RTC Management Corporation; Chondee, Inc.; Rosstown, Inc.; Rossville, Inc.

RECORDINGS: ALBUMS—Those with the Supremes (Ross, Florence Ballard, and Mary Wilson; in 1967 Cindy Birdsong replaced Ballard and the group was billed as Diana Ross and the Supremes) include: *Meet the Supremes; At the Copa; Bit of Liverpool; Country Western and Pop; Supremes A-Go-Go; Greatest Hits, Vols. 1-3*, all Motown, 1964-70; also represented on such compilation albums as *Motown Legends* and *Detroit Girl Groups*. Top-ten singles for the Supremes include: "Where Did Our Love Go," "Baby Love," and "Come See about Me," all 1964; "Stop! In the Name of Love," "Back in My Arms Again," and "I Hear a Symphony," all 1965; "My World Is Empty without You," "Love Is Like an Itching in My Heart," "You Can't Hurry Love," and "You Keep Me Hanging On," all 1966; "Love Is Here and Now You're Gone," "The Happening," "Reflections," and "In and Out of Love," all 1967; "Love Child," 1968; "I'm Livin' in Shame" and "Someday We'll Be Together," both 1969.

Solo albums include: *Baby It's Me, Touch Me in the Morning, Lady Sings the Blues, Live at Caesar's Palace*, and *The Boss*, all Motown; *Eaten Alive, Ross, Swept Away, Why Do Fools Fall in Love*, and *Red Hot Rhythm and Blues*, all RCA. Top-ten singles as a solo artist include: "Ain't No Mountain High Enough," 1970; "Touch Me in the Morning," 1973; "Theme from Mahogany (Do You Know Where You're Going To)," 1975; "Love Hangover," 1976; "Upside Down," "I'm Coming Out," and "It's My Turn," all 1980; "Why Do Fools Fall in Love," 1981; "Mirror, Mirror" and "Muscles," both 1982; "Missing You," 1985; "Chain Reaction," 1986. Also represented on numerous Motown compilation albums

AWARDS: Vice-President Hubert H. Humphrey Citation Award for work with Youth Opportunity Program; Mrs. Martin Luther King and Reverend Abernathy Citation Award; named Female Entertainer of the Century, *Billboard* magazine; named World's Outstanding Singer, *Cashbox* and *Record World;* Female Entertainer of the Year, Grammy Award, 1970; National Association for the Advancement of Colored People (NAACP) Award, 1970; Entertainer of the Year, *Cue* Magazine Award, 1972; Golden Apple Award, 1972; Gold Medal Award, *Photoplay*, 1972; Best Actress, Academy Award nomination and Golden Globe Award, both 1972, for *Lady Sings the Blues;* Best Actress, Cesar Award (French), 1975, for *Mahogany;* Antoinette Perry Award, 1977, for *An Evening with Diana Ross*.

SIDELIGHTS: "It is not just the music that makes her a star," a prescient critic assessed of a Diana Ross performance in the August 5, 1970 *Variety*. At that time Ross had already established herself as the lead singer for the Supremes, the nonpareil female group of the 1960s, but her talent, personal style, and ambition were then carrying her to a successful solo career and she would soon make noteworthy appearances in films and on television. Under the management of Motown, the record company that had launched the Supremes, Ross was a millionaire while still in her teens, but in 1981 she became "a walking corporation" according to Susan L.

Taylor (*Essence,* December, 1985), "controlling her own management, film and music production, and music publishing." She was also, in Taylor's words, "an international megastar."

Ross's position, wrote Taylor, was "earned the old fashioned way: through hard work and determination." Diane, as she is still known to friends and family, was living in a Detroit housing project when a singer for the the Primes (a local group that later became the Temptations) asked Ross's parents to let their daughter sing with a "sister group" called the Primettes. With her parents' support, Ross began taking classes in cosmetology and performing at dances and talent shows. After two Primettes left the group to be married, the remaining members—Mary Wilson, Forence Ballard, and Diana, as she began to call herself—developed the look and the sound that prompted singer-songwriter Smokey Robinson to arrange for them to audition for Motown founder Berry Gordy. Although Gordy was impressed, he did not offer the girls a recording contract until they had finished school. Dubbed the Supremes by Gordy, the trio became Motown's favored act when their tenth single rose to the top of the charts.

The hit, "Where Did Our Love Go?," was their first single to make industry news. Arranged by Eddie Holland, Lamont Dozier, and Brian Holland (the team Gordy hired to write for the trio), the song "would launch the Supremes as the only Americans to seriously contend with the Beatles for the top chart spot,"wrote Gerri Hirshey in the May, 1984 *Esquire*. As described in *Time* (August 17, 1970), Mary and Florence "purred" the background "while Diana did the lead in a voice that was equal parts coyness, sexiness, nicotene, and velvet." For the first time, a large white audience was finding black pop-harmony with a gospel flavor accessible and irresistible. Diana Ross's role in this phenomenally successful crossover also involved being a glamorous illustration "of the idea that black is beautiful," explained Geoffrey Cannon in the May 1, 1972 *Guardian*. "Dressed and made up extravagantly to look like a cat-goddess, Diana Ross exploited her wide-mouthed, small-nosed beauty to its limit," he added. The Supremes had six consecutive gold records in 1964, seven in 1967, and a dozen bestselling albums by 1969 when Ross was ready to start her solo career.

That new phase also included film appearances, where Ross revealed both her acting talents and her flair for fashion design. While preparing for her debut as Billie Holiday in *Lady Sings the Blues*, Ross, who had studied fashion illustration in high school, where she also was voted best-dressed, rejected the costumes that had been made for her and replaced them with her own designs. The film's producer, Berry Gordy, told *New York Times* contributor Aljean Harmetz that the extra money it cost him for the new wardrobe was well spent. Years before, Hirshey related, Ross had designed an appealing look for the Primettes even before they had developed a characteristic sound. Ross brought more than a "look" to the challenging role in *Lady*, however. Harmetz observed that Ross "did not in any way try to make pretty the drug dazed Billie." Perhaps recalling scenes that show the incarcerated jazz singer suffering heroin withdrawal, Gordy told Harmetz that viewers were "surprised Diana would allow herself to look so *real*." Ross's acting ability, unexpected by some critics, was recognized in the awards her performance garnered. In addition to a Golden Globe, she was nominated for an Academy Award as best actress and named *Cue* magazine's entertainer of the year.

Ross again proved herself adept at acting and couture with a non-singing role in her second film. For *Mahogany*, the story of a fashion madel who is put through harrowing paces by an ambitious photographer, she again wore her own designs. The star also won the respect of colleagues by suffering some of her character's perils herself, diving into frigid waters for retakes on location in Rome, a feat noted in the February 24, 1975 *Time*. Her performance brought her a Cesar, the French equivalent of Hollywood's Oscar.

In the early 1970s Ross devoted time to her three daughters by then-husband Robert Silberstein, a rock promoter; this limited her availability for concerts, as Derek Jewell noted in the London *Sunday Times*. His September 23, 1983 review of the singer's Albert Hall appearance credits the show's success to Ross's eagerness to perform for a live audience and to a "new artistry" born of experience. In addition to her "sweet, husky, big yet intimately curled-up voice as well as a skinny frame which sudden small curves make beautiful," Jewell perceived vocal excellence "and a commanding presence able to make even the Albert Hall seem small."

Cue magazine's Daphne Davis reported in the September 29, 1978 issue that Ross's eagerness to perform for the camera piqued again when she heard that the Broadway hit *The Wiz*, a musical version of *The Wizard of Oz* with a black cast, was to be filmed as one of the first projects at New York City's revitalized Astoria Studios. Taking the lead as Dorothy, Ross co-starred with Michael Jackson, who had been her protege since his early years as a child star with the Jackson Five. Together they sang and romped the yellow brick road from Harlem to the World Trade Center, the film's urban analogues of Kansas and the Emerald City. As with so much else in her career to this point, this role was secured for Ross by Motown manager and friend, Berry Gordy.

When Ross left Motown in 1981, she was independent of Gordy's supervision for the first time in twenty years. In his place Ross installed RTC Management, her own company, which is named after daughters Rhonda, Tracee, and Chudney. RTC is just one part of Diana Ross Enterprises, which also includes Anaid Films, the Diana Ross Foundation, and a music publishing company. As her own manager, Ross has actively pursued projects ranging from the production of a free concert in New York's Central Park to seeking financing for a film about American expatriate entertainer Josephine Baker.

The joys of self-determination have sometimes, as in the case of the free concert, been dampened by the problems that can beset large-scale ventures. A thunderstorm interrupted that show and injuries resulted as the crowd rushed to leave the park during the downpour, reported Frank J. Prial in the *New York Times*. His July 23, 1983 article noted that some who attended the rescheduled concert were assaulted by roving gangs. In the end, the concert, which was taped both nights for broadcast to raise money for a city playground, instead cost the city and the show's producer more than 1.5 million dollars in damages. The press made much of the fact that Mayor Edward I. Koch had not received the promised percentage of profits from the broadcast of the concert some time afterward. According to Hirshey, Ross accused reporters of pressuring her to do what she had intended from the beginning, and she paid some $250,000 of her own money to compensate for what the concert failed to net, since the cost of taping the show on two nights exceeded what it earned when broadcast.

Ross has had other confrontations with the press, notably over the Broadway hit *Dreamgirls*, which depicts the rise of a black "girl group" very similar to the Supremes in some respects. "*Dreamgirls* came out, and they started writing that I was angry. It wasn't that," the former Supreme told Taylor, who went on to report the snger's

judgment that the show may be inaccurate since its makers had solicited neither her input nor her endorsement.

The superstar enjoys good relations with Motown if not with the press. After describing her close friendship with Berry Gordy and Suzanne de Passe, the president of Motown Productions, Ross told Taylor, "Going out on my own has made me really value how good Motown was to me. It's made me see that they did a whole lot that I'm doing for myself now. But it's so much better to control your own life." Later in the interview, Ross added that Gordy, whom Davis identified as the star's "permanent mentor and father figure," is pleased with her independence.

Ross has had much to enjoy for herself. She has made number one records in recent years both as a soloist and in duets with Lionel Richie and Julio Iglesias. She set a box office record at Radio City Music Hall with proceeds in excess of 1.7 million dollars. As Taylor related, she has also participated in projects that reach beyond "Diana Ross—the image," such as the "We Are the World" video and record that raised sixty million dollars for famine relief. She has continued the concerts around the world that give her stardom an international dimension. On a more personal level, the birth of a son to Ross and her second husband, Norwegian shipping magnate Arne Naess, realized the determination she expressed when her first marriage ended—"I want to marry again, and, more important, have a boy. I'll keep trying until I die."

Diana Ross told *CTFT*: "Most performers are real insecure. No, I'm not secure. I should be. Being insecure is not necessary, but it makes you better. I'll never be satisfied. I like to win, and I always set my goals for myself."

ADDRESSES: AGENT—c/o Shelly Berger, 6255 Sunset Boulevard, Los Angeles, CA 90028.

*   *   *

ROURKE, Mickey   1956-

PERSONAL: Full name, Philip Andre Rourke, Jr.; born in 1956, in Schenectady, NY; married Debra Feuer (a dancer and actress), 1980. EDUCATION: Studied acting with Sandra Seacat.

VOCATION: Actor.

CAREER: PRINCIPAL FILM APPEARANCES—*1941*, Universal, 1979; *Heaven's Gate*, United Artists, 1980; *Fade to Black*, 1980; arsonists, *Body Heat*, Warner Brothers, 1981; Boogie, *Diner*, Metro-Goldwyn-Mayer/United Artists (MGM/UA), 1982; Motorcycle Boy, *Rumblefish*, Universal, 1983; Charlie Moran, *The Pope of Greenwich Village*, MGM/UA, 1984; *9 1/2 Weeks*, 1985; *Eureka*, MGM/UA, 1985; *Year of the Dragon*, MGM/UA, 1985; Harry Angel, *Angel Heart*, Tri-Star, 1987; Henry Chiansky, *Barfly*, Cannon, 1987.

PRINCIPAL TELEVISION APPEARANCES—Movies: Joseph Cybulkowski, *Act of Love*, NBC, 1980; Tony Pate, *City in Fear*, ABC, 1980; John Rideout, *Rape and Marriage: The Rideout Case*, CBS, 1980.

MEMBER: Screen Actors Guild.

ADDRESSES: AGENT—Progressive Artists Agency, 400 S. Beverly Drive, Suite 216, Beverly Hills, CA 90212.*

PAMELA ROUSSEL

ROUSSEL, Pamela

PERSONAL: Born January 17, in Fort Sill, OK; daughter of Wallace Clifton, Jr. (in the U.S. Army) and Margaret MacGregor (an artist and actress; maiden name, Bailey) Magathan; married Coco Roussel (a drummer and composer), May 1, 1976. EDUCATION: Received B.A., dramatic art, from George Washington University; also attended the University of Kansas and the University of Bordeaux, France; trained for the stage with Sanford Meisner; studied voice with Margaret Riddleberger.

VOCATION: Actress and singer.

CAREER: STAGE DEBUT—Botticelli's Springtime, *Cactus Flower,* Hayloft Dinner Theatre, Manassas, VA, 1984, for fifty-nine performances. PRINCIPAL STAGE APPEARANCES—*The Seven Year Itch,* Hayloft Dinner Theatre, Manassas, VA, 1986; Marilyn Monroe, ensemble, *Mrs. Foggybottom and Friends,* New Playwrights Theatre, Washington, DC, 1986.

TELEVISION DEBUT—Singer, *Double Image,* BBC, 1986. PRINCIPAL TELEVISION APPEARANCES—Movies: Singer, *Yuri Nosenko, KGB,* HBO, 1986; Karol Levitt, *The Arch Campbell Show,* 1986.

AWARDS: Paul Parady Memorial Award from George Washington University, 1981, for outstanding contributions to the University Theatre.

MEMBER: Actor' Equity Association, Screen Actors Guild, American Federation of Television and Radio Artists.

ADDRESSES: HOME—Hollywood, CA.

ROWLANDS, Gena   1936-

PERSONAL: Full name, Gena Catherine Rowlands; born June 19, 1936, in Cambria, WI; daughter of Edwin Merwin (a banker) and Mary Allen (a painter; maiden name, Neal) Rowlands; married John Cassavetes (an actor and director), March 19, 1954; children: Nicholas, Alexandra, Zoe. EDUCATION: Attended the University of Wisconsin, 1952-53; trained for the stage at the American Academy of Dramatic Art, 1953.

VOCATION: Actress.

CAREER: BROADWAY DEBUT—Elaine, *The Seven Year Itch,* 1954. PRINCIPAL STAGE APPEARANCES—Mistress of Ceremonies, *All About Love,* Versailles Night Club Theatre, New York City, 1951; performed at the Provincetown Playhouse and other Off-Broadway theatres in New York City and in stock companies, 1951-53; Elaine, *The Seven Year Itch,* Cass Theatre, Detroit, MI, 1953; the girl, *Middle of the Night,* American National Theatre Academy (ANTA) Theatre, New York City, 1956.

MAJOR TOURS—Elaine, *The Seven Year Itch,* National, 1951-53.

PRINCIPAL FILM APPEARANCES—*The High Cost of Loving,* Metro-Goldwyn-Mayer, 1958; *Lonely Are the Brave,* Universal, 1962; *The Spiral Road,* Universal, 1962; *A Child Is Waiting,* United Artists, 1962; *Tony Rome,* Twentieth Century-Fox, 1967; *Faces,* Continental, 1968; *Machine Gun McCain,* Columbia, 1970; Minnie, *Minnie and Moskowitz,* Universal, 1971; Mabel Longhetti, *A Woman Under the Influence,* Faces International, 1974; *Two Minute Warning,* Universal, 1976; *Opening Night,* 1978; *The Brinks Job,* Universal, 1978; *One Summer Night,* 1979; title role, *Gloria,* Columbia, 1980; *Tempest,* Columbia, 1982; *Love Streams,* Cannon, 1983; Jeanette Rasnick, *Light of Day,* Tri-Star, 1987.

PRINCIPAL TELEVISION APPEARANCES—Series: Teddy Carella, *87th Precinct,* NBC, 1961-62; Adrienne Van Leyden, *Peyton Place,* ABC, 1967.

Episodic: *Actors on Acting,* PBS, 1984; also *Philco Playhouse,* NBC; *Armstrong Circle Theatre,* NBC; *Studio One,* CBS; *Goodyear Playhouse,* NBC; *Robert Montgomery Presents,* NBC; *Appointment with Adventure,* CBS; *General Electric Theatre,* CBS; *Staccato,* NBC; *Danger,* CBS; *Suspense,* CBS; *Martin Kane,* NBC; *U.S. Steel Hour,* CBS; *Riverboat,* NBC; *Adventures in Paradise,* ABC; *Markham,* CBS; *The Tab Hunter Show,* NBC; *The Islanders,* ABC; *Target: The Corrupters,* ABC; *Dick Powell Theatre,* NBC; *77 Sunset Strip,* ABC; *The Lloyd Bridges Show,* NBC; *Alfred Hitchcock Presents,* CBS; *Bob Hope Chrysler Theatre,* NBC; *Dr. Kildare,* NBC; *Bonanza,* NBC; *The Virginian,* NBC; *Kraft Mystery Theatre,* NBC; *Run for Your Life,* NBC; *The Long, Hot Summer,* ABC; *Road West,* NBC; *The Girl from U.N.C.L.E.,* NBC; *Breaking Point,* ABC; *Burke's Law,* ABC; *Medical Center,* CBS; *Garrison's Gorillas,* ABC; *Ghost Story,* NBC. Movies: *A Question of Love,* 1978; *Strangers: The Story of a Mother and Daughter,* CBS, 1979; *Thursday's Child,* CBS, 1983; *An Early Frost,* NBC, 1985; title role, *The Betty Ford Story,* ABC, 1987.

AWARDS: Best Actress, Academy Award nomination, New York Film Critics Award nomination, both 1975, for *A Woman Under the Influence;* Best Actress, Academy Award nomination, 1980, for *Gloria.*

MEMBER: Actors' Equity Association, Screen Actors Guild, American Federation of Television and Radio Artists, American Guild of Variety Artists.

ADDRESSES: AGENT—c/o Lou Pitt, International Creative Management, 8899 Beverly Blvd., Los Angeles, CA 90048.*

*   *   *

RUDD, Paul   1940-

PERSONAL: Full name, Paul Ryan Rudd; born May 15, 1940, in Boston, MA; son of Frank Stanley and Katherine Frances (Ryan) Rudd; married Joan Mannion, September 5, 1965 (divorced November, 1983); married Martha Bannerman. EDUCATION: Fairfield University, A.B., 1962; also attended Fordham University.

VOCATION: Actor and director.

CAREER: STAGE DEBUT—*Henry IV, Part I,* New York Shakespeare Festival, Delacorte Theatre, New York City, 1968. PRINCIPAL STAGE APPEARANCES—Messenger, *Henry IV, Part II,* herald, *King Lear,* both Repertory Theatre of Lincoln Center, Vivian Beaumont Theatre, New York City, 1968; Copley, *The Changing Room,* Long Wharf Theatre, New Haven, CT, 1972, then Morosco Theatre, New York City, 1973; Caimi, *A Pagan Place,* Long Wharf Theatre, 1974; Ken, *The National Health,* Long Wharf Theatre, then Circle in the Square, New York City, both 1974; Skip Hampton, *The Last Meeting of the Knights of the White Magnolia,* Arena Stage, Washington, DC, 1975; Arthur Miller, *Ah, Wilderness!,* Jim, *The Glass Menagerie,* both Circle in the Square, 1975; Billy Willson, *Streamers,* Mitzi E. Newhouse Theatre, New York City, 1976; Romeo, *Romeo and Juliet,* Circle in the Square, 1977; title role, *Henry V,* New York Shakespeare Festival, Delacorte Theatre, 1976; Oliver, *Da,* Hudson Guild Theatre, New York City, 1978; Aubrey Piper, *The Show-Off,* Roundabout Stage II Theatre, New York City, 1978; Scooper, *Bosoms and Neglect,* Longacre Theatre, New York City, 1979; Jack, *The Lady and the Clarinet,* Lucille Lortel Theatre, New York City, 1983; Adolphus Cusins, *Major Barbara,* Christy, *All in Favour, Said No!,* both South Coast Repertory Theatre, Costa Mesa, CA, 1983; Robert, *Stage Struck,* Old Globe Theatre, San Diego, CA, 1985; *Alcestis,* American Repertory Theatre, Cambridge, MA, 1986. Also Charly Gordon, *Flowers for Algernon,* Canada, 1979; *A Cry of Players,* Vivian Beaumont Theatre, 1968; *In the Matter of J. Robert Oppenheimer,* Vivian Beaumont Theatre, 1969; *Loose Ends,* South Coast Repertory Theatre, 1981; *A Midsummer Night's Dream, An Evening with Merlin Finch,* and *Elagabalus,* all Off-Broadway productions, New York City; and appeared at the Goodman Theatre, Chicago, IL; Hartford Stage Company, Hartford, CT; American Shakespeare Festival, Stratford, CT; and the San Diego Shakespeare Festival, San Diego, CA.

FIRST STAGE WORK—Director, *Coming Attractions,* 1982. PRINCIPAL STAGE WORK—Director, *Men's Singles,* 1983-84.

MAJOR TOURS—*The Boys in the Band,* U.S. cities, 1971.

TELEVISION DEBUT—Brian Mallory, *Beacon Hill,* CBS, 1975. PRINCIPAL TELEVISION APPEARANCES—Episodic: *Hart to Hart,* ABC, 1982; *Quincy, M.E.,* NBC, 1983. Series: Earl Trent, *Knots Landing,* CBS, 1980-81. Mini-Series: Leon Kendrick, *Beulah Land,* NBC, 1980; Lane Lyman, *Family Reunion,* NBC, 1981. Movies: John F. Kennedy, *Johnny, We Hardly Knew Ye,* NBC,

1977; Dennis, *End of Summer,* PBS, 1977; Yankee, *A Connecticut Yankee in King Arthur's Court,* BBC/PBS, 1978; Gary Aronson, *The Last Song,* CBS, 1980; Reverend Lawrence Perkins, *Kung Fu: The Movie,* CBS, 1986.

FILM DEBUT—Loren Hardeman, Jr., *The Betsy,* Allied Artists, 1978.

NON-RELATED CAREER—Advertising executive.

AWARDS: Outer Critics Circle Award, 1975-76; Man of the Year Award, Fairfield University, 1977.

MEMBER: Actors' Equity Association, Screen Actors Guild, American Federation of Television and Radio Artists.

ADDRESSES: OFFICE—145 W. 55th Street, New York, NY 10019.*

*   *   *

RUDOLPH, Alan   1948-

PERSONAL: Born 1948, in Los Angeles, CA; son of Oscar Rudolph (a television director). EDUCATION: Studied in the Assistant Directors Training Program of the Directors Guild.

VOCATION: Director and writer.

CAREER: PRINCIPAL FILM WORK—Writer (see below); assistant director, *California Split,* Columbia, 1974; assistant director, *The Long Goodbye,* 1974; director: *Welcome to L.A.,* Lion's Gate, 1977; *Remember My Name,* 1978; *Return Engagement,* The Production Company, 1978; *Roadie,* United Artists, 1980; *Endangered Species,* Metro-Goldwyn-Mayer/United Artists, 1982; *Songwriter,* Tri-Star, 1984; *Choose Me,* Glenwood, 1984; *Trouble in Mind,* 1985.

WRITINGS: SCREENPLAYS—*Buffalo Bill and the Indians, or Sitting Bull's History Lesson,* United Artists, 1976; *Welcome to L.A.,* Lion's Gate, 1977; *Remember My Name,* 1978; *Roadie,* United Artists, 1980; *Endangered Species,* Metro-Goldwyn-Mayer/ United Artists, 1982; *Songwriter,* Tri-Star, 1984; *Choose Me,* Glenwood, 1984; *Trouble in Mind,* 1985.

MEMBER: Directors Guild of America, Writers Guild of America.

ADDRESSES: AGENT—c/o Jim Wiatt, International Creative Management, 8899 Beverly Blvd., Los Angeles, CA 90048.*

*   *   *

RUSH, Barbara   1930-

PERSONAL: Born January 4, 1930, in Denver, CO; daughter of Roy L. and Marguerite Rush; married James Gruzalski, September 24, 1970; children: Christopher, Claudia. EDUCATION: Attended the University of California at Santa Barbara; trained for the stage at the Pasedena Playhouse Theatre Arts College.

VOCATION: Actress.

CAREER: FILM DEBUT—*Molly* (also known as *The Goldbergs*), 1950. PRINCIPAL FILM APPEARANCES—*The First Legion,* Paramount, 1951; *Quebec,* 1951; *When World's Collide,* Paramount, 1951; *It Came from Outer Space,* Paramount, 1953; *The Prince of Pirates,* 1953; *Taza, Son of Cochise,* 1954; *Magnificent Obsession,* Universal, 1954; *The Black Shield of Falworth,* 1954; *Captain Lightfoot,* Universal, 1955; *Kiss of Fire,* Universal, 1955; *The World in My Corner,* Universal, 1956; *Bigger Than Life,* Twentieth Century-Fox, 1956; *Oh, Men! Oh, Women!,* Twentieth Century-Fox, 1957; *No Down Payment,* Twentieth Century-Fox, 1957; *The Young Lions,* 1958; *Harry Black and the Tiger,* Twentieth Century-Fox, 1958; *The Young Philadelphians,* Warner Brothers, 1959; *Bramble Bush,* Warner Brothers, 1960; *Strangers When We Meet,* Columbia, 1960; *Come Blow Your Horn,* Paramount, 1963; *Robin and the Seven Hoods,* Warner Brothers, 1964; *Hombre,* Twentieth Century-Fox, 1967; *Airport,* Universal, 1970; *The Man,* Paramount, 1972; *Superdad,* Buena Vista, 1974; *Can't Stop the Music,* Associated, 1980; *Summer Lovers,* Filmways, 1982.

PRINCIPAL TELEVISION APPEARANCES—Series: Lizzie Hogan, *Saints and Sinners,* NBC, 1962-63; Marsha Russell, *Peyton Place,* ABC, 1968-69; Margot Brighton, *The New Dick Van Dyke Show,* CBS, 1973-74; Eudora Weldon, *Flamingo Road,* NBC, 1981-82. Episodic: *Ironside,* NBC. Movies: *Crime Club,* 1973; *The Last Day,* 1975.

STAGE DEBUT—*The Golden Ball,* Loberto Theatre, Santa Barbara, CA, 1940. PRINCIPAL STAGE APPEARANCES—*A Woman of Independent Means,* Back Alley Theatre, Los Angeles, then at the Biltmore Theatre, New York City, both 1983, and at the James A. Doolittle Theatre, Los Angeles, 1987; also appeared as Birdie, *The Little Foxes,* University of California at Santa Barbara; and in *Butterflies Are Free, Twigs, The Unsinkable Molly Brown, Hay Fever, Forty Carats, Father's Day,* and *Same Time, Next Year.*

MAJOR TOURS—*A Woman of Independent Means,* Dallas and Houston, TX, and Toronto, Canada.

AWARDS: Acting award in college, for *The Little Foxes;* Sarah Siddons Award, for *Forty Carats;* Los Angeles Drama Critics Circle Award, 1984, for *A Woman of Independent Means.*

MEMBER: Actors' Equity Association, Screen Actors Guild, American Federation of Television and Radio Artists.

ADDRESSES: AGENT—c/o Ro Diamond, Century Artists, Ltd., 9744 Wilshire Blvd., Suite 206, Beverly Hills, CA 90212. MANAGER—c/o Glenn Rose, The Bedford Company, 10000 Santa Monica Blvd., Suite 400, Los Angeles, CA 90067. PUBLICIST—c/o Warren Cowan, Rogers & Cowan, 10000 Santa Monica Blvd., Suite 400, Los Angeles, CA 90067.*

*   *   *

RUSH, Philip
See LARDNER, Ring, Jr.

*   *   *

RUSLER, Robert   1965-

PERSONAL: Born September 20, 1965, in Fort Wayne, IN; son of Richard C. and Maria Elena (Varela) Rusler. EDUCATION: Studied acting at the Loft Studio.

VOCATION: Actor.

CAREER: FILM DEBUT—Max, *Weird Science,* Universal, 1985. PRINCIPAL FILM APPEARANCES—*Nightmare on Elm Street, Part II,* New Line Cinema, 1986; *Vamp,* New World Pictures, 1987; also appeared in *Thrashin',* Fries Entertainment.

TELEVISION DEBUT—Kenny, *Tonight's the Night,* ABC, 1986. PRINCIPAL TELEVISION APPEARANCES—Episodic: *Facts of Life,* NBC.

MEMBER: Screen Actors Guild, American Federation of Television and Radio Artists.

ADDRESSES: AGENT—c/o Bob Gersh, Gersh Agency, 222 N. Canon, Beverly Hills, CA 90210.

*   *   *

RUSSELL, Ken   1927-

PERSONAL: Full name, Henry Kenneth Alfred Russell; born July 3, 1927, in Southampton, England; son of Henry (an owner of shoe stores) and Ethel (Smith) Russell; married Shirley Ann Kingdon (a costume designer), 1957 (divorced, 1979); married Vivian Jolly, June, 1984; children: (first marriage) Alex, James, Victoria, Xavier, Toby; (second marriage) Molly. EDUCATION: Attended Pangbourne Nautical College, 1941-44, Walthamstow Art School, 1949, and International Ballet School (London), 1950. RELIGION: Roman Catholic. MILITARY: Royal Air Force, 1946-49.

VOCATION: Director, producer and writer.

CAREER: PRINCIPAL FILM WORK—Also see *WRITINGS* below. Director: *Peepshow,* independent, 1956; *Amelia and the Angel,* independent, 1957; *Lourdes,* independent, 1958; *French Dressing,* Associated British, 1963; *Women in Love,* United Artists, 1969; *Billion Dollar Brain,* United Artists, 1970; also producer, *The Music Lovers,* United Artists, 1971; also co-producer, *The Devils,* Warner Brothers, 1971; also producer, *Savage Messiah,* Metro-Goldwyn-Mayer (MGM)/EMI, 1972; *The Boy Friend,* MGM/EMI, 1972; *Mahler,* Goodtimes Enterprises, 1974; also co-producer, *Tommy,* Columbia, 1975; *Liztomania,* Goodtimes Enterprises, 1975; *Valentino,* United Artists, 1977; *Altered States,* Warner Brothers, 1980; *Crimes of Passion,* New World Pictures, 1984; *Gothic,* Vestron, 1987.

PRINCIPAL TELEVISION WORK—Director of more than thirty-five productions for BBC, including: *Poet's London, Gordon Jacob, Guitar Craze, Variations on a Mechanical Theme, Portrait of a Goon,* and an untitled film on Robert McBryde and Robert Colquhoun, all 1959; *Marie Rambert Remembers, Architecture of Entertainment, Cranks at Work, The Miners' Picnic, Shelagh Delaney's Salford, A House in Bayswater,* and *The Light Fantastic,* all 1960; *Old Battersea House, Portrait of a Soviet Composer, London Moods,* and *Antonio Gaudi,* all 1961; *Pop Goes the Easel, Preservation Man, Mr. Chesher's Traction Engines, Elgar,* and (co-director) *Lotte Lenya Sings Kurt Weill,* all 1962; *Watch the Birdie,* 1963; *Lonely Shore, Bartok, The Dotty World of James Lloyd,* and *Diary of a Nobody,* all 1964; *Always on Sunday* and, also co-director, *The Debussy Film,* both 1965; *Don't Shoot the Composer* and *Isadora Duncan: The Biggest Dancer in the World,* both 1966; *Dante's Inferno,* 1967; *A Song of Summer,* 1968; *The*

Dance of the Seven Veils: A Comic Strip in Seven Episodes on the Life of Richard Strauss, 1970; *Clouds of Glory, Parts I and II,* 1978.

PRINCIPAL STAGE WORK—Director of operas: *A Rake's Progress,* 1982; *Die Soldaten,* 1983; also *Madame Butterfly* and *La Boheme.*

PRINCIPAL STAGE APPEARANCES—Dancer with the Norwegian Ballet Company, 1950; actor with the Garrick Players, U.K., 1951.

RELATED CAREER—Free-lance photographer, 1952-57.

NON-RELATED CAREER—Merchant marine, 1945.

WRITINGS: SCREENPLAYS—See production details above: *Peepshow,* 1956; *Amelia and the Angel,* 1957; *Lourdes,* 1958; (with Larry Kramer) *Women in Love,* based on the novel by the same title by D.H. Lawrence, 1969; *The Music Lovers,* 1971; *The Devils,* adapted from the play *The Devils of Loudon* by Aldous Huxley and the play by John Whiting, 1971; *The Boy Friend,* adapted from the musical by Sandy Wilson, 1972; *Mahler,* 1974; *Tommy,* adapted from the rock opera by Peter Townshend, 1975; *Lisztomania,* 1975; (with Mardick Martin) *Valentino,* 1977; *Gothic,* 1987.

TELEPLAYS—*Always on Sunday,* BBC, 1965; (with Melvyn Bragg) *The Debussy Film,* BBC, 1965.

BOOKS—(With John Baxter) *An Appalling Talent: Ken Russell* (autobiography), London, 1973.

PERIODICALS—Articles: "The Films I Do Best Are About People I Believe In," *Friends* (London), May, 1970; "Ken Russell Writes on Raising Kane," *Films and Filming* (London), May, 1972; "Ideas for Films," *Film,* January-February, 1973; "Personal Choice 1974," *Listener* (London), December, 1974; also contributor to *Books and Bookmen* and others.

AWARDS: Screen Writers' Guild awards, for *Elgar, The Debussy Film, Isadora Duncan: The Biggest Dancer in the World,* and *Dante's Inferno;* Delius Award; Guild of Television Producers and Directors Award, 1966; Desmond Davis Award, 1968; Best Director, Academy Award nomination, 1970, for *Women in Love.*

SIDELIGHTS: Known for his extravagant film biographies, particularly of famous composers, Ken Russell has been praised and damned for much the same reasons. Russell's films are characterized by wildly symbolic scenes, extreme violence, and a mixing of fantasy and reality. Joseph A. Gomez, a Russell admirer, pointed to the filmmaker's "shock editing, his obsessive camera movements, his penchant for theatricality and overblown performances, and his extraordinary, phantasmagoric images which overwhelm audiences." Russell, Gomez argued in his *Ken Russell: The Adaptor as Creator* (Frederick Muller, 1976), "goes to extremes to bring his audience to his position, which frequently rests somewhere between their conventional pieties or indifference and the presentation on the screen." Other critics have been less generous in their appraisals. Guy Flatley of the *New York Times* (October 15, 1972) claimed that the filmmaker's "disdain for cinematic decorum, coupled with an alleged distortion of fact in his film biographies, has won Russell the wrath of most American critics."

Russell began his career directing features for the British Broadcasting Corporation (BBC). With a series of biographies on such artists as dancer Isadora Duncan, composer Frederick Delius, and composer Richard Strauss, Russell won critical acclaim and was credited with having "raised the form to something like art," according to Fred Hauptfuhrer of *People* (March 30, 1981). Russell's innovations took the static documentary form favored by the BBC, a form which banned the use of actors or written dialogue, and transformed it into a dramatic and vital genre. *A Song of Summer,* Russell's biography of Delius, won particular recognition. In the October 19, 1975 *New York Times,* Peter G. Davis found that Russell's images in the film "are of such evocative power that ones feels instinctively how the profound mystery of natural forces came to pervade all of Delius's music."

When Russell graduated to making feature films, his early efforts were unsuccessful. His 1963 release, *French Dressing,* a farce about a small town's efforts to attract tourists, failed to draw attention at the box office. *Billion Dollar Brain,* an espionage thriller based on a Len Deighton novel, met a similar fate. But with his 1970 adaptation of the D.H. Lawrence novel *Women in Love,* Russell enjoyed critical success. Telling the story of two sisteers and their lovers, the film sensually explores the liberating and yet stifling nature of sexual relationships. Vincent Canby of the *New York Times* (March 29, 1970) called *Women in Love* "a loving, intelligent, faithful adaptation" of the novel. But Ian Leslie Christie of *Sight and Sound* (winter, 1969-70) believed that Russell's film "is not so much . . . an 'adaptation' . . . as a kind of critical recreation." He averred, "It stands or falls as a structure of sharply individualized sequences exploiting the range of Russell's ability to convey his meaning in purely cinematic terms."

After the success of *Women in Love,* Russell returned to the biographical film genre with *The Music Lovers,* a life of the Russian composer Peter Tchaikovsky. Russell's emphasis on the more sordid aspects of Tchaikovsky's life, including his homosexuality and his wife's nymphomania, help transform the film into what *Film Comment*'s Stephen Farber in the November-December, 1975 issue called "a pointed study of the decay of . . . nineteenth century romanticism." The critic also deemed it "precariously balanced between beauty and decay, romance and sexual nightmare." Although finding *The Music Lovers* flawed because of its uneven juxtaposition of "passages of great beauty" with "pronounced ugliness," Gordon Gow of *Films and Filming* (March, 1971) nonetheless called it "a work that affords us an impression of the artist's psyche, as distinct from a mere documentation of the known facts about his life and work."

The Music Lovers was a commercial failure, despite some positive reviews, as were Russell's next few films. *The Devils,* for example, was widely criticized for its offensive images: a corpse filled with squirming maggots; bald nuns at an orgy; graphic scenes of crucifixion. Of *Savage Messiah* Pauline Kael claimed in the November 18, 1972 *New Yorker,* "[The film] starts by lunging into the middle of a situation and then just keeps throwing things at you. You feel as if it were rushing through the projector at the wrong speed and with the sound turned up to panic level."

But with *Tommy,* the 1975 adaptation of the Who's rock opera, Russell regained critical and commercial acclaim. The story of a deaf, blind, and mute boy who wins international fame for his pinball-playing ability, the film, Hauptfuhrer reported, "made Russell a kind of cult hero and was his biggest commercial success." Critics who had dismissed previous Russell efforts as excessive and self-indulgent found the extravagant *Tommy* the ideal vehicle for the director's talents. "The opera and Russell were meant for each other,"Judith Crist commented in the April 7, 1975 *New York,* "or at very least serve each other well." "Like any pop artist," David Wilson observed in *Sight and Sound*(summer, 1975), "[Russell] needs a special relationship with his material. When he finds it, as he does in several of the units of *Tommy,* the effect can be dazzling." Gomez believed that "*Tommy,* perhaps, more than any other of his film adaptations, allowed Russell to be totally free in creating visuals from his own personal vision to match the songs and music."

A year after *Tommy* Russell released *Lisztomania,* a film biography of composer Franz Liszt with the Who's lead singer, Roger Daltry, as the star. As Farber remarked, "*Lisztomania* continues in the flamboyant circus style of *Tommy.. . . .* [But] the collage of wild comic images builds to a climax of unexpected intensity. This is a much more adventurous, imaginative film than *Tommy.*" Unfortunately for Russell, however, *Lisztomania* was "a commercial disaster," as Hauptfuhrer reported. Another ambitious film, 1977's *Valentino,* also lost money at the box office.

In 1980 Russell was called upon to direct the science fiction film *Altered States,* a film plagued by troubles. An earlier director had left the project in the planning stage, while Columbia Pictures had backed out of an agreement to distribute the movie. Most observers doubted that Russell was suited to do a science fiction film, but *Altered States,* the story of a research scientist whose experiments transform him into a primitive ape-man, proved to be a "*succes d'estime* and a solid hit at the box office," as Hauptfuhrer noted. Russell turned once again to a biographical inspiration for his 1987 release, *Gothic.* It offers a fictionalized account of the night in 1816 when the writers Lord Byron, Percy Shelley, and Mary Shelley smoked opium and spun out ghost stories to one another—the inspiration for Mary Shelley's writing of her classic tale *Frankenstein.* It opened in New York to "less-than-enthusiastic reviews," according to Richard Laermer in the April 12, 1987 *Daily News.*

Russell's work has long inspired heated reactions from his admirers and detractors alike. As Laermer explained, Russell "is the kind of film director people regard as a visionary—or a weirdo." Although Russell has maintained that he is "truly surprised that my films shock people," their shock effect does not bother him. "In some ways it's nice to be controversial," he told Laermer. "Then at least there are two sides to how people see you: Some like and some hate. I never want to be lukewarm."

ADDRESSES: AGENT—c/o Peter Rawley, International Creative Management, 8899 Beverly Boulevard, Los Angeles, CA 90048.*

RUTHERFORD, Mary   1945-

PERSONAL: Born May 19, 1945, in Toronto, ON, Canada; daughter of David Edward and Margaret Eleanor (McLaughlin) Rutherford. EDUCATION: Trained for the stage at the Drama Centre, London.

VOCATION: Actress.

CAREER: LONDON DEBUT—Fraulein Rabenjung, *The Tutor,* Royal Court Theatre, 1968. BROADWAY DEBUT—Hermia, *A Midsummer Night's Dream,* Royal Shakespeare Company, Billy Rose Theatre, 1971. PRINCIPAL STAGE APPEARANCES— Various roles, *The Hero Rises Up,* Round House Theatre, London, 1968; Glumdalclitch, *Gulliver's Travels,* Mermaid Theatre, London, 1969; Hazel Cook, *And These Is Not All,* Mercury Theatre, London, 1969; Alice, *Bartholomew Fair,* Royal Shakespeare Company (RSC), Aldwych Theatre, London, 1969; Princess Elizabeth, *Richard III,* Juliet, *Measure for Measure,* both RSC, Royal Shakespeare Theatre, Stratford-on-Avon, U.K., 1970; Hermia, *A Midsummer Night's Dream,* RSC, Royal Shakespeare Theatre, then Aldwych Theatre, both 1970; Nadya, *Enemies,* thief, *The Balcony,* both RSC, Aldwych Theatre, 1971; Lika, *The Promise,* Welsh Theatre Company, Cardiff, Wales, U.K., 1972; Ingrid, *The Green Woman,* Anitra, *Peer Gynt,* both University Theatre, Newcastle, U.K., 1973; Calpurnia, *Julius Caesar,* Octavia, *Antony and Cleopatra,* Alice Faulkner, *Sherlock Holmes,* all RSC, Aldwych Theatre, 1974; Olivia, *Twelfth Night,* RSC, Royal Shakespeare Theatre, then Aldwych Theatre, both 1975; Juliet, *Romeo and Juliet,* Haymarket Theatre, Leicester, U.K., 1975; Polly Eccles, *Caste,* Crewe Theatre, London, 1976; Dymphna Pugh-Gooch, *A Last Belch for the Great Auk,* Round House Theatre, then Young Vic Theatre, both London, 1977. Also appeared at the Stratford Shakespeare Festival, Stratford, ON, Canada, 1981.

MAJOR TOURS—Hermia, *A Midsummer Night's Dream,* RSC, U.K. and U.S. cities, 1971; Greta, *Metamorphosis,* London Theatre Group, U.K. cities, 1977.

PRINCIPAL TELEVISION APPEARANCES—Specials: *Antony and Cleopatra,* BBC.

MEMBER: British Actors' Equity Association.

SIDELIGHTS: RECREATIONS—Singing, bicycling, listening to Mozart.

ADDRESSES: AGENT—c/o Jean Diamond, London Management, 235 Regent Street, London W1, England.*

S

SAGAL, Katey

PERSONAL: Daughter of Boris Sagal (a director) and Sara Zwilling (a singer, writer, and director). EDUCATION: Attended California School of the Arts.

VOCATION: Actress and singer.

CAREER: PRINCIPAL TELEVISION APPEARANCES—Series: Jo Tucker, Mary, CBS, 1986; Peggy Bundy, Married. . . With Children, Fox Network, 1987. Movies: The Failing of Raymond, 1971.

PRINCIPAL STAGE APPEARANCES—Martha Rose and the Miners, Los Angeles Actors' Theatre, CA, 1982; My Beautiful Lady, Mark Taper Forum, Los Angeles, CA.

RELATED CAREER—Former backup singer for Bob Dylan, Etta James, and others; former member of the group, the Harlettes, with Bette Midler, for five years.

MEMBER: Actors' Equity Association, Association of Television and Radio Artists.

SIDELIGHTS: CTFT learned that Katey Sagal's mother was the first woman assistant director in live television in the 1950s and her father was the director of the television movie, The Failing of Raymond.

ADDRESSES: OFFICE—Fox Television Center, 5746 Sunset Blvd., Los Angeles, CA 90028.*

*   *   *

SAINT, Eva Marie   1924-

PERSONAL: Born July 4, 1924, in Newark, NJ; daughter of John Merle and Eva Marie (Rice) Saint; married Jeffery Hayden, October 27, 1951; children: Darrell, Laurette. EDUCATION: Bowling Green State University, B.A., 1946; trained for the stage at the Actors' Studio.

VOCATION: Actress.

CAREER: FILM DEBUT—On the Waterfront, Columbia, 1954. PRINCIPAL FILM APPEARANCES—That Certain Feeling, Paramount, 1956; Raintree County, Metro-Goldwyn-Mayer (MGM), 1957; A Hatful of Rain, MGM, 1957; Eve Kendall, North by Northwest, MGM, 1959; Exodus, United Artists, 1960; All Fall Down, MGM, 1962; The Sandpiper, MGM, 1965; 36 Hours,

MGM, 1965; Grand Prix, MGM, 1966; The Russians Are Coming! The Russians Are Coming!, United Artists, 1966; The Stalking Moon, National General, 1969; Loving, Columbia, 1970; Cancel My Reservation, Warner Brothers, 1972; Nothing in Common, Tri-Star, 1986.

PRINCIPAL TELEVISION APPEARANCES—Series: Claudia Barbour-Roberts, One Man's Family, NBC, 1950-52. Episodic: "Last Chance," The Web, CBS, 1953; "Our Town" (musical version), Producers' Showcase, NBC, 1955; Goodyear TV Playhouse, NBC; Taxi, ABC, 1978. Movies: The Macahans, 1976; A Christmas to Remember, 1978; When Hell Was in Session, 1980; The Best Little Girl in the World, 1981; Splendor in the Grass, 1981; Fatal Vision, 1984; A Year in the Life, NBC, 1986. Mini-Series: How the West Was Won.

BROADWAY DEBUT—A Trip to Bountiful, 1953. PRINCIPAL STAGE APPEARANCES—Judge Ruth Loomis, First Monday in October, Huntington Hartford Theatre, Los Angeles, then Blackstone Theatre, Chicago, 1979; Stephanie Abrahams, Duet for One, Northlight Repertory Theatre, Evanston, IL, and Roundabout Theatre, New York City, 1982-83; also appeared in Mr. Roberts and The Lincoln Mask.

PRINCIPAL RADIO WORK—Acted on radio in early career.

AWARDS: Outer Critics Circle Award, New York Drama Critics Award, and Theatre World Award, all 1953, for A Trip to Bountiful; Best Supporting Actress, Academy Award, 1955, for On the Waterfront.

MEMBER: Actors' Equity Association, Screen Actors Guild, American Federation of Television and Radio Artists.

ADDRESSES: AGENT—Paul Kohner, Inc., 9169 Sunset Blvd., Los Angeles, CA 90069.*

*   *   *

SALMI, Albert   1928-

PERSONAL: Born 1928, in Coney Island, NY; married Peggy Ann Garner (an actress), May 10, 1956; children: a daughter. EDUCATION: Trained for the stage at the Dramatic Workshop, The American Theatre Wing, and the Actors Studio, all in New York City.

VOCATION: Actor.

CAREER: OFF-BROADWAY DEBUT—*The Scarecrow,* Theatre de Lys, 1952. PRINCIPAL STAGE APPEARANCES—Roger Gatt, *End as a Man,* Theatre de Lys, and later at the Vanderbilt Theatre, both New York City, 1953; Jim Curry, *The Rainmaker,* Cort Theatre, New York City, 1954; Bo Decker, *Bus Stop,* Music Box Theatre, New York City, 1955; Yank Sun, *The Good Woman of Setzuan,* Phoenix Theatre, New York City, 1956; title role, *Howie,* 46th Street Theatre, New York City, 1958; He, *The Failures,* Fourth Street Theatre, New York City, 1959; John Paul Jones, *Once There Was a Russian,* Music Box Theatre, New York City, 1961; Matt Burke, *Anna Christie,* Huntington Hartford Theatre, Hollywood, CA, 1966; successor to the role of Victor Franz, *The Price,* Morosco Theatre, New York City, 1968, and later at the Duke of York's Theatre, London, 1969.

MAJOR TOURS—Bo Decker, *Bus Stop,* U.S. cities, 1955.

PRINCIPAL FILM APPEARANCES—*The Brothers Karamazov,* Metro-Goldwyn-Mayer, 1958; *The Bravados,* Twentieth Century-Fox, 1958; *The Unforgiven,* United Artists, 1960; *Wild River,* Twentieth Century-Fox, 1960; *The Outrage,* Metro-Goldwyn-Mayer, 1964; *The Flim-Flam Man,* Twentieth Century-Fox, 1967; *The Lawman,* United Artists, 1971; *Something Big,* National General, 1971; *The Deserter,* Paramount, 1971; *The Crazy World of Julius Vrooder,* Twentieth Century-Fox, 1974; *Empire of the Ants,* American International, 1977; Mr. Noonan, *Caddyshack,* Warner Brothers, 1980; *Steel,* 1980; Rory Poke, *Brubaker,* Twentieth Century-Fox, 1980; Inspector Sturgess, *The Witch,* 1981; Colonel Liakhov, *The Guns and the Fury,* 1981; *St. Helens, Killer Volcano,* 1981; Greil, *Dragonslayer,* United Artists, 1981; Captain Ellis, *Love Child,* Warner Brothers, 1982; Johnny Lawson, *Hard to Hold,* Universal, 1984; the U.S. Emissary, *Born American,* 1985.

PRINCIPAL TELEVISION APPEARANCES—Series: Yadkin, *Daniel Boone,* NBC, 1964-70; Peter Ritter, *Petrocelli,* NBC, 1974-76. Episodic: "Bang the Drum Slowly," *U.S. Steel Hour,* CBS, 1956; Holmes, "Survival," *U.S. Steel Hour,* CBS, 1956; Putnam Cox, "Most Blessed Woman," *Kraft Television Theatre,* NBC, 1957; *Man Under Glass,* CBS, 1958; Peter Sheeran, "The Old Foolishness," *Play of the Week,* WNTA, 1961; "Noon on Doomsday," *Theatre Guild,* CBS; "The Mary S. McDowall Story," *Profiles in Courage,* NBC, 1964; also *Destry,* ABC; *The Defenders,* CBS; *The Fugitive,* ABC; *Rawhide,* CBS; *The Eleventh Hour,* independent; *Trailmaster,* ABC; *Stoney Burke,* independent; *Twilight Zone,* CBS; *The Naked City,* independent; *The Virginian,* NBC; *I Spy,* NBC; *Laredo,* NBC; *The Untouchables,* ABC; *Shenandoah,* ABC; *Gunsmoke,* CBS; *The Big Valley,* ABC; *Voyage,* ABC; *Jesse James,* ABC; *Route 66,* independent; *The FBI,* ABC; *Twelve O'Clock High,* ABC; *Kung Fu,* ABC; *Barnaby Jones,* CBS. Movies: Hugh Glover, *Thou Shalt Not Kill,* 1982; Frank Taggert, *Female Artillary,* 1983; Ed Dietz, *Best Kept Secrets,* ABC, 1984; Judge Dupree, *Fatal Vision,* NBC, 1984; *Dress Gray,* NBC, 1986.

NON-RELATED CAREER—Formerly a Pinkerton detective.

AWARDS: Co-winner, Best Male Supporting Performance in a Play, *Variety* Poll of London Critics Award, 1969, for *The Price.*

MEMBER: Actors' Equity Association, Screen Actors Guild, American Federation of Television and Radio Artists.

SIDELIGHTS: RECREATIONS—Painting.

ADDRESSES: AGENT—Fred Amsel and Associates, 291 S. La Cienega Blvd., Suite 307, Beverly Hills, CA 90211.*

ENRIQUE SANDINO

SANDINO, Enrique 1951-

PERSONAL: Born December 3, 1951, in Jerusalem, Colombia; son of Oliverio (a veterinarian) and Diva Maria (a singer; maiden name, Velasquez); married Tilly Velasquez (a chef) January 25, 1951; children: Augusto Cesar. EDUCATION: Attended Escuela National de Pedagogia Artistica, London School of Contemporary Dance, and the Royal Academy of Dramatic Arts and Dance of Madrid; trained for the stage with Roberto McKay at the Experimental Theatre of Madrid. RELIGION: Roman Catholic.

VOCATION: Actor, dancer, choreographer, and writer.

CAREER: STAGE DEBUT—Alfredo, *La Venta de Las Votuntaded,* Atianza Colombo-Franesca, Bogota, Colombia, 1971, for ten performances. OFF-BROADWAY DEBUT— Astolfo, *Life Is a Dream,* Gramercy Arts Theatre, 1981. PRINCIPAL STAGE APPEARANCES—Valentin, *Kiss of the Spider Woman,* CAST Theatre, Hollywood, CA; Lazaro, *The Visionary,* Rich, *The Great Theatre of the World,* both Royal Theatre of Spain, New York City; Antonio, *And That's the Way It Is,* Writers Theatre, New York City; Astolfo, *Life Is a Dream,* Ismaelita, *The Pharaoh's Court,* Tenor, *Dona Francisquita,* King, *Secret Injury, Secret Revenge,* Mozo, *The Shoemaker's Prodigious Wife,* La Pera, *The Day That You'll Love Me;* all Spanish Repertory Theatre, New York City; son, *Walk around the Block,* L.A.T.E. INTAR Theatre, New York City.

MAJOR TOURS—Spanish Repertory Theatre, U.S. cities; Espacio Cero Ensemble, Madrid, Spain; Teatro Arte De Bogota and Ballet Cordillera, Bogata, Colombia.

PRINCIPAL TELEVISION APPEARANCES—Episodic: Gravas, "Definitely Miami,'' *Miami Vice*, NBC, 1985. Series: Clark, *Another World*, NBC. Also *Caso Juzgado, Dialogando, Teatro Popular Caracol, Un Angel Llamado Andrea, Memorias Fantasticas,* all on Latin American television, 1973-77.

PRINCIPAL FILM APPEARANCES—Chaco, *Game of Survival.*

WRITINGS: Three books of poetry, one of short stories, and a children's play.

MEMBER: Screen Actors Guild, Actors' Equity Association, American Federation of Television and Radio Artists.

ADDRESSES: HOME—839 N. Fuller Avenue, No. 8, Los Angeles, CA 90046. AGENT—Sanders Agency, 721 N. La Brea Avenue, Los Angeles, CA 90038; Cunningham Scott and Depene, 261 S. Robertson Boulevard, Beverly Hills, CA.

*   *   *

SARRAZIN, Michael   1940-

PERSONAL: Full name, Jacques Michel Andre Sarrazin; born May 22, 1940, in Quebec, Canada.

VOCATION: Actor.

CAREER: FILM DEBUT—*Gunfight in Abilene*, Universal, 1967. PRINCIPAL FILM APPEARANCES—*The Flim-Flam Man*, Twentieth Century-Fox, 1967; *The Sweet Ride*, Twentieth Century-Fox, 1968; *Journey to Shiloh*, Universal, 1968; *A Man Called Garrison*, Universal, 1969; *The Eye of the Cat*, Universal, 1969; *In Search of Gregory*, Universal, 1970; *They Shoot Horses, Don't They?*, Cinerama, 1969; *The Pursuit of Happiness*, Columbia, 1971; *Sometimes a Great Notion*, Universal, 1971; *Believe in Me*, Metro-Goldwyn-Mayer, 1971; *Harry in Your Pocket*, United Artists, 1973; *The Reincarnation of Peter Proud*, American International, 1975; *The Gumball Rally*, Warner Brothers, 1976; *Caravans*, Paramount, 1978; *The Seduction*, Embassy, 1982; *Fighting Back*, Paramount, 1982; *Joshua Then and Now*, 1985; also appeared in *Scaramouche.*

TELEVISION DEBUT—On CBC Television, Canada, at age seventeen. PRINCIPAL TELEVISION APPEARANCES—Episodic: *Bob Hope Presents the Chrysler Theatre*, NBC; *The Virginian*, NBC. Movies: The monster, *Frankenstein: The True Story*, 1973.

MEMBER: Screen Actors Guild, American Federation of Television and Radio Artists.

ADDRESSES: AGENT—c/o Mike Greenfield and Josh Basser, Charter Management, 9000 Sunset Boulevard, Suite 1112, Los Angeles, CA 90069.*

*   *   *

SAVAGE, John   1950-

PERSONAL: Born John Youngs, in 1950, in Old Bethpage, NY; wife's name Susan (an artist); children: Jennifer, Lachlan. EDUCATION: Trained for the stage at the American Academy of Dramatic Arts.

VOCATION: Actor.

CAREER: PRINCIPAL STAGE APPEARANCES—Bobby, *American Buffalo*, Ethel Barrymore Theatre, New York City, 1977; second waiter, *You Never Can Tell*, Roundabout Theatre, New York City, 1977; Lennie, *Of Mice and Men*, Roundabout Theatre, 1987; also appeared in *South Pacific*, City Center Theatre, New York City, 1967; Ari, Mark Hellinger Theatre, New York City, 1971; *Fiddler on the Roof*, Imperial Theatre, New York City; and *The Drunkard, Romeo and Juliet, Siamese Connections,* and *The Hostage.*

MAJOR TOURS—Billy Bibbit, *One Flew over the Cuckoo's Nest*, U.S. cities, 1973.

PRINCIPAL FILM APPEARANCES—*Bad Company*, Paramount, 1972; *Steelyard Blues*, Warner Brothers, 1973; *All the Kind Strangers*, 1974; *The Deer Hunter*, Universal, 1979; *Hair*, United Artists, 1979; *The Onion Field*, AVCO-Embassy, 1979; *Cattle Annie and Little Britches*, Universal, 1981; *Inside Moves*, Associated, 1980; *The Amateur*, Twentieth Century-Fox, 1982; *Brady's Escape*, Santori, 1984; *Maria's Lovers*, Cannon, 1985; Marco Venieri, *Hotel Colonial*, Orion and Yarno Cinematografica, 1987; Mr. Ellsworth, *The Beat*, Vestron, 1987; Beast/Prince, *Beauty and the Beast*, Cannon, 1987.

PRINCIPAL TELEVISION APPEARANCES—Episodic: *Cade's County*, CBS. Series: Jim Malloy, *Gibbsville*, NBC, 1976. Pilots: Jim Malloy, *The Turning Point of Jim Malloy*, NBC, 1975. Movies: Peter, *All the Kind Strangers*, ABC, 1974; Eric Swenson, *Eric*, NBC, 1975; Victor Herman, *Coming Out of the Ice*, CBS, 1982; Rick Cahill, *The Nairobi Affair*, CBS, 1984; Kevin Dunne, *Silent Witness*, NBC, 1985.

RELATED CAREER—Organizer of the Children's Theatre Group, which toured public housing projects in New York City.

AWARDS: Drama Critics Circle Award, for *One Flew over the Cuckoo's Nest.*

MEMBER: Actors' Equity Association, Screen Actors Guild, American Federation of Television and Radio Artists.

ADDRESSES: AGENT—c/o John Funicello, International Creative Management, 8899 Beverly Boulevard, Los Angeles, CA 90048.*

*   *   *

SCHEEDER, Louis W.   1946-

PERSONAL: Full name, Louis William Scheeder; born December 26, 1946, in New York, NY; son of Louis W. (an insurance agent) and Julia H. (a rental agent; maiden name, Callery) Scheeder; married Donna Wills, June 14, 1969. EDUCATION: Georgetown University, B.A., English literature, 1968; studied directing with Joseph Papp, acting with Jenny Egan, and theatre criticism with Albert Bermel at Columbia University, 1968-69.

VOCATION: Actor, director, producer, and stage manager.

CAREER: STAGE DEBUT—Boy, *The Rapists*, Gate Theatre, New York City, June, 1966.

PRINCIPAL STAGE WORK—Director, *Happy Days, The Promise,*

Twelfth Night, all Folger Theatre Group, Washington, DC, 1971; director, *Landscape and Silence, Total Eclipse, The Revenger's Tragedy,* all Folger Theatre Group, 1972; director, *1776,* Little Theatre on the Square, Sullivan, IL, 1972; director, *Winter's Tale,* Folger Theatre Group, 1973; director, *Creeps,* Folger Theatre Group, then Playhouse II Theatre, New York City, both 1973; director, *Applause,* Little Theatre on the Square, 1973; producer and director, *The Farm,* Folger Theatre Group, 1974; producer and director, *The Collected Works of Billy the Kid,* Folger Theatre Group, 1975; producer and director, *Henry V, The Fool,* both Folger Theatre Group, 1976; producer and director, *Mummer's End, Teeth 'n' Smiles, Two Gentlemen of Verona,* all Folger Theatre Group, 1977; producer and director, *Mackeral, Richard III, Whose Life Is It, Anyway?,* all Folger Theatre Group, 1978; producer and director, *As You Like It,* Folger Theatre Group, 1979; producer and director, *Custer,* Kennedy Center, Washington, DC, 1979; producer and director, *Charlie and Algernon,* Kennedy Center, 1980; producer and director, *Crossing Niagara, Love's Labour's Lost,* both Folger Theatre Group, 1981; producer, *How I Got That Story,* Westside Arts Theatre, New York City, 1982; director, *Julius Caesar,* Folger Theatre Group, 1982; director, *Hedda Gabler,* Center Stage, Toronto, ON, Canada, 1985; producer, *Diamonds,* Circle in the Square Downtown, New York City, 1985.

MAJOR TOURS—Director, *Black Elk Speaks,* Folger Theatre Group, U.S. cities, 1978.

RELATED CAREER—Assistant stage manager, Arena Stage, Washington, DC, 1969-70; resident director, Theatre Lobby, Washington, DC, 1969-70; director, Monday New Play Reading Series, Washington Theatre Club, Washington, DC, 1970; associate artistic director, then artistic director, later producer, Folger Theatre Group, Washington, DC, 1970-81; board of advisors, New Playwrights' Theatre of Washington, Washington, DC, 1975—; advisory council, Washington, DC, Commission on Arts and Humanities, 1976-80; advisory council, National Commission on Arts and Education, 1977—; artistic director, Centre Stage Productions, Toronto, ON, Canada, 1985; director, Manitoba Theatre Centre, Winnipeg, MB, Canada, 1982-84.

AWARDS: Dixon Award from Georgetown University, 1968; Alumni Achievement Award from the Georgetown University Alumni Club of Metropolitan Washington, DC, 1981; Mayor's Arts Award, Washington, DC, 1982.

MEMBER: Actors' Equity Association, Society of Stage Directors and Choreographers.

ADDRESSES: OFFICE—c/o Society of Stage Directors and Choreographers, 1501 Broadway, Suite 1614, New York, NY 10036.*

*   *   *

SCHEIDER, Roy   1935-

PERSONAL: Full name, Roy Richard Scheider; born November 10, 1935, in Orange, NJ; son of Roy Bernhard and Anna (Crosson) Scheider; married Cynthia Eddenfield Bebout (a film editor), November 8, 1962; children: Maximillia. EDUCATION: Franklin and Marshall College, B.A., 1955. RELIGION: Protestant. MILITARY: U.S. Air Force.

VOCATION: Actor.

CAREER: OFF-BROADWAY DEBUT—*Romeo and Juliet,* New York Shakespeare Festival, 1961. PRINCIPAL STAGE APPEARANCES—*The Chinese Prime Minister,* Broadway production, 1963; *Betrayal,* Trafalgar Theatre, New York City, 1980; Off-Broadway: *The Alchemist,* 1964; *Sergeant Musgrave's Dance,* 1967; *Stephen D.,* 1968; also appeared in *Richard III.*

PRINCIPAL FILM APPEARANCES—*Loving,* Paramount, 1972; *Paper Lion,* United Artists, 1968; *Star!,* Twentieth Century-Fox, 1968; *Puzzle of a Downfall Child,* Universal, 1970; *Klute,* Warner Brothers, 1971; *The French Connection,* Twentieth Century-Fox, 1971; *The Outside Man,* United Artists, 1973; *The Seven-Ups,* Twentieth Century-Fox, 1973; *Sheila Levine Is Dead And Living in New York,* Paramount, 1975; *Jaws,* Universal, 1975; *Marathon Man,* Paramount, 1976; *Sorcerer,* Paramount/Universal, 1977; *Jaws II,* Universal, 1978; *Last Embrace,* United Artists, 1979; *All That Jazz,* Twentieth Century-Fox, 1979; *Still of the Night,* Metro-Goldwyn-Mayer/United Artists, 1982; *In Our Hands,* Almi Classics, 1983; *Blue Thunder,* Columbia, 1983; *Tiger Town,* 1983; *2010,* Metro-Goldwyn-Mayer/United Artists, 1984; *Mishima: A Life in Four Chapters,* Warner Brothers, 1985; *The Men's Club,* 1986; *52 Pick-Up,* Cannon, 1986.

PRINCIPAL TELEVISION APPEARANCES—Episodic: *Hallmark Hall of Fame,* NBC; *Studio One,* CBS; *N.Y.P.D.,* ABC. Movies: Jacobo Timerman, *Prisoner without a Name, Cell without a Number,* 1983.

NON-RELATED CAREER—Co-owner, Joe Allen's Restaurant, in Paris and Los Angeles.

AWARDS: Obie Award, 1968, for *Stephen D.;* Best Supporting Actor, Academy Award nomination, 1972, for *The French Connection;* Best Actor, Academy Award nomination, 1980, for *All That Jazz;* Drama League of New York Award, 1980, for *Betrayal.*

MEMBER: Actors' Equity Association (councilor), Screen Actors Guild, American Federation of Television and Radio Artists.

SIDELIGHTS: Before entering the acting profession, Roy Scheider entered the New Jersey Diamond Gloves boxing competition as an amateur welterweight in 1951.

ADDRESSES: AGENT—c/o Sam Cohn, International Creative Management, 40 W. 57th Street, New York, NY 10019.*

*   *   *

SCHELL, Maxmilian   1930-

PERSONAL: Born December 8, 1930, in Vienna, Austria; son of Hermann Ferdinand (a playwright) and Margarethe (an actress; maiden name, Noe von Nordberg) Schell. EDUCATION: Attended the universities of Zurich, Basel, and Munich. MILITARY: Swiss Army, 1948-49.

VOCATION: Actor, director, producer, and writer.

CAREER: FILM DEBUT—*Kinder, Mutter, und ein General,* 1955. PRINCIPAL FILM APPEARANCES—*The Young Lions,* Twentieth

MAXIMILIAN SCHELL

Century-Fox, 1958; *Judgment at Nuremburg*, United Artists, 1961; *The Reluctant Saint*, Columbia, 1962; *The Condemned of Altona*, Twentieth Century-Fox, 1963; *Topkapi*, United Artists, 1964; *Return from the Ashes*, United Artists, 1965; *The Deadly Affair*, Columbia, 1967; *The Desperate Ones*, Commonwealth United, 1969; *The Castle*, Continental, 1969; *First Love*, UMC Pictures, 1970; *The Pedestrian*, Cinerama, 1973; *The Odessa File*, Columbia, 1975; *The Man in the Glass Booth*, American Film Theatre, 1975; *The End of the Game*, Twentieth Century-Fox, 1976; *St. Ives*, Warner Brothers, 1976; *A Bridge Too Far*, United Artists, 1977; *Cross of Iron*, AVCO-Embassy, 1977; *Julia*, Twentieth Century-Fox, 1977; *Players*, Paramount, 1979; *The Black Hole*, Buena Vista, 1979; *The Chosen*, Twentieth Century-Fox, 1982.

Also appeared in *Der 20. Juli, Reifende Jugend*, both 1955; *Ein Madchen aus Flandern, Die Ehe des Dr. Med. Danwitz, Ein Herz kehrt heim*, all 1956; *Die Letzten werden die Ersten sein, Taxichauffeur Banz, Der Meisterdieb*, all 1957; *Ein wunderbarer Sommer, Die Bernauerin, Die sechste Frau, Child of Our Time*, all 1958; *Perilous, Eine Dummheit macht auch der Gescheiteste*, both 1959; *The Observer, The Three Musketeers*, both 1960; *Five Finger Exercise*, 1961; *Letters of Mozart, John F. Kennedy*, both 1964; *Der seidene Schuh*, 1965; *A Time to Love*, 1966; *Beyond the Mountains, Counterpoint, Heide kehrt heim*, all 1967; *Krakatoa, East of Java* (also known as *Volcano*), 1968; *Simon Bolivar*, 1969; *Pope Joan*, 1971; *Paulina 1880, Trotta*, both 1972; *The Rehearsal*, 1974; *Assassination in Sarajevo*, 1975; *Amo non Amo, Avalanche Express, Gesprache mit Jedermann*, all 1978; *Geschichten aus dem Wiener Wald*, 1979; *Bernstein/Beethoven*, 1981; *Les Iles*, 1982;

The Great Hamlets, Tomorrow in Alabama, both 1983; *Man under Suspicion*, 1984; *The Assisi Underground*, 1985.

PRINCIPAL FILM WORK—Co-producer (with Rudolf Noelte), *The Castle*, Continental, 1969; co-producer, director, *First Love*, UMC Pictures, 1970; producer, director, *The Pedestrian*, Cinerama, 1973; director, *The End of the Game*, Twentieth Century-Fox, 1976; also producer, *The Clown*, 1975; producer, director, *Murder on the Bridge*, 1975; producer, *Der Richter und sein Henker*, 1976; producer, director, *Tales from the Vienna Woods*, 1978; producer, director, *Marlene*, 1983; producer, *Tomorrow in Alabama*, 1983.

STAGE DEBUT—At age three as a blade of grass in a pageant play written by his father. LONDON DEBUT—*Philotas, Leonce*, both with the Berlin Theatre am Kurfurstendamn, 1957. BROADWAY DEBUT—*Interlock*, American National Theatre Academy Playhouse, 1958. PRINCIPAL STAGE APPEARANCES—Title role, *Hamlet*, Munich, West Germany, 1968; also appeared in *Der Turn*, Salzburg Festival, Austria, 1959; *Sappho*, Hamburg, West Germany, 1959; *A Patriot for Me*, London, 1965, then Bremen, West Germany, 1966, later New York City, 1969; *The Venetian Twins*, Josefstadt, Vienna, 1966; *Herostrat*, Bochum, West Germany, 1966; *Old Times*, Vienna, Austria, 1973; *Poor Murderer*, Berlin, West Germany, 1982; appeared annually in *Everyman*, Salzburg Festival, 1978-82, and in *Der seidene Schuh*, 1982. Also appeared in *The Prince of Homburg, Mannerhouse*, and *Don Carlos*.

PRINCIPAL STAGE WORK—Director: *Tales from the Vienna Woods*, National Theatre, London, 1977; *The Undiscovered Country*, Salzburg Festival, 1979 and 1980; *Cornet*, Deutsche Opera, 1985; also *All the Best*, Bremen, then Vienna, both 1966; *Hamlet*, Munich, 1968; *Pygmalion*, Dusseldorf, West Germany, 1970; *La Traviata*, 1975.

PRINCIPAL TELEVISION APPEARANCES—Episodic: "Judgment at Nuremberg," *Playhouse 90*, CBS, 1959. Mini-Series: Title role, *Peter the Great*, NBC, 1986. Movies: *The Fifth Column*, 1959; *Turn the Key Deftly*, 1960; *The Diary of Ann Frank*, 1980; *The Phantom of the Opera*, 1982; also title role, *Hamlet*, for German television, 1960.

RELATED CAREER—Director, Volkstheater, Munich, West Germany, 1981—.

WRITINGS: SCREENPLAYS—*First Love*, UMC Pictures, 1970; (with Friedrich Durrenmatt) *The End of the Game*, Twentieth Century-Fox, 1976; also *Murder on the Bridge*, 1975; (with Christopher Hampton) *Tales from the Vienna Woods*, 1978; *Marlene*, 1983.

AWARDS: Best Actor, New York Critics Circle Award, 1961, Best Actor, Academy Award, 1961, Best Actor, Golden Globe, 1962, all for *Judgment at Nuremburg;* Best Picture, San Sebastian Film Festival Silver Medal, 1970, Best Picture, Filmband in Gold (Germany), 1971, Best Picture, Swiss Film Award, 1971, Best Foreign Film, Academy Award nomination, 1971, Best Director, Panama Film Festival, 1971, Special Award of the Jury, Cartagena Film Festival, 1971, all for *First Love;* Best Picture, Sorrento and Naples Film Festival Silver Sirene, 1973, Best Foreign Film, Chicago Film Critics Award, 1973, Best Picture, Golden Cup (Germany), 1974, Best Foreign Film, Academy Award nomination, 1974, Best Foreign Film, Golden Globe, 1974, all for *The Pedestrian.*

Best Actor, Academy Award nomination, 1975, for *The Man in the*

Glass Booth; Best Picture, San Sebastian Film Festival Silver Medal, 1975, Best Picture, Filmband in Silver (Germany), 1979, both for *Der Richter und sein Henker;* Best Supporting Actor, New York Film Critics Circle Award, 1978, Best Supporting Actor, Academy Award nomination, 1978, both for *Julia;* Best Foreign Film, Chicago Film Festival Golden Hugo Award, 1979, Best Picture, Filmband in Silver (Germany), 1980, Best Screenplay, Oxford Film Festival, 1980, all for *Tales from the Vienna Woods;* Best Picture, Berlin Festival Silver Bear Award, 1984, Best Actor, Golden Federation Award (Germany), 1984, both for *Tomorrow in Alabama.*

SIDELIGHTS: CTFT learned that Maximilian Schell is also a talented musician who has been described by Leonard Bernstein as "a remarkably good pianist."

ADDRESSES: OFFICE—2 Keplerstrasse, Munich 27, West Germany. AGENT—Nancy Seltzer and Associates, 8845 Ashcroft Avenue, Los Angeles, CA 90045.

*   *   *

SCHEPISI, Fred   1939-

PERSONAL: Full name, Frederic Alan Schepisi; born December 26, 1939, in Melbourne, Australia; son of Frederic Thomas and Loretto Ellen (Hare) Schepisi; married Joan Mary Ford, 1960 (marriage ended); married Rhonda Elizabeth Finlayson, 1973; children: two sons, four daughters. EDUCATION: Attended Assumption College, Marcillini College, and Marist Brothers' Juniorate, all in Australia.

VOCATION: Director, producer, and writer.

CAREER: PRINCIPAL FILM WORK—Director, *The Priest;* producer, director, and writer, *The Devil's Playground,* 1975; producer, director, and writer, *The Chant of Jimmy Blacksmith,* 1978; director, *Barbarosa,* Universal, 1982; director, *Iceman,* Universal, 1984; director, *Plenty,* RKO, 1984; director, *Roxanne,* Columbia Pictures, 1987.

RELATED CAREER—Television production manager, Daton Advisory Service, Melbourne, 1961-64; Victorian manager, Cinesound Productions, Melbourne, 1964-66; managing director, the Film House, Melbourne, 1964-66, chairman, 1979—.

ADDRESSES: HOME—159 Eastern Road, South Melbourne, Victoria, Australia. AGENT—c/o Sam Cohn, International Creative Management, 40 W. 57th Street, New York, NY 10019.*

*   *   *

SCHIFRIN, Lalo   1932-

PERSONAL: Born June 21, 1932, in Buenos Aires, Argentina; son of a conductor of the Teatro Colon in Buenos Aires. EDUCATION: Studied music in Argentina and at the Paris Conservatory.

VOCATION: Composer and conductor.

CAREER: PRINCIPAL FILM WORK—Composer of film scores: *Joy*

LALO SCHIFRIN

House (also known as *The Love Cage*), Metro-Goldwyn-Mayer (MGM), 1964; *The Cincinnati Kid,* MGM, 1965; *The Liquidator,* MGM, 1966; *Cool Hand Luke,* Warner Brothers/Seven Arts, 1967; *The President's Analyst,* Paramount, 1967; *The Fox,* Claridge, 1968; *Kelly's Heroes,* MGM, 1970; *The Hellstrom Chronicle,* Cinema V, 1971; *Dirty Harry,* Warner Brothers, 1972; *Magnum Force,* Warner Brothers, 1973; *Man on a Swing,* Warner Brothers, 1973; *The Master Gunfighter,* Taylor-Laughlin, 1975; *The Four Musketeers,* Twentieth Century-Fox, 1975; *Sky Riders,* Twentieth Century-Fox, 1976; *Day of the Animals,* Film Ventures, 1976; *Special Delivery,* American International, 1976; *St. Ives,* Warner Brothers, 1976; *Voyage of the Damned,* AVCO-Embassy, 1976; *The Eagle Has Landed,* Columbia, 1977; *Rollercoaster,* Universal, 1977; *Telefon,* United Artists, 1977; *The Manitou,* AVCO-Embassy, 1978; *Nunzio,* Universal, 1978; *The Cat from Outer Space,* Buena Vista, 1978; *Return from Witch Mountain,* Buena Vista, 1978; *Boulevard Nights,* Warner Brothers, 1979; *Escape to Athena,* Associated, 1979; *The Amityville Horror,* American International, 1979; *Concorde: Airport '79,* Universal, 1979.

The Nude Bomb, Universal, 1980; *The Competition,* Columbia, 1980; *The Big Brawl,* Warner Brothers, 1980; *Brubaker,* Twentieth Century-Fox, 1980; *Serial,* Paramount, 1980; *When Time Ran Out,* Warner Brothers, 1980; *Buddy Buddy,* United Artists, 1981; *Caveman,* United Artists, 1981; *Airplane II: The Sequel,* Paramount, 1982; *Amityville II: The Possession,* Orion, 1982; *The Seduction,* AVCO-Embassy, 1982; *A Stranger Is Watching,* Metro-Goldwyn-Mayer/United Artists, 1982; *The Class of 1984,* United Film, 1982; *Fast-Walking,* Lorimar, 1982; *Doctor Detroit,* Universal, 1983; *The Sting II,* Universal, 1983; *The Osterman Weekend,* Twentieth Century-Fox, 1983; *Sudden Impact,* Warner Brothers, 1983; *Tank,* Universal, 1983; *Bad Medicine,* Twentieth

Century-Fox, 1985; *The Mean Season,* Orion, 1985; *The New Kids,* Columbia, 1985; *Black Moon Rising,* New World, 1986; *The Ladies Club,* New Line Cinema, 1986; *The Fourth Protocol,* Rank, 1987; also *Love and Bullets,* 1979; *Loophole, Fridays of Eternity,* both 1981.

PRINCIPAL TELEVISION WORK—All as composer of theme music. Series: *Mission: Impossible,* CBS. Movies: *Foster and Laurie,* 1975; *Brenda Starr,* 1976; *Starsky and Hutch,* 1976; *Hollywood Wives,* 1986; *A.D.,* 1986; *Out on a Limb,* 1987.

PRINCIPAL STAGE WORK—Composer: (ballet) *Jazz Faust,* 1963; (orchestral) *Concerto for Guitar and Orchestra.*

RELATED CAREER—Formed own jazz group early in his career; Argentinian representative to the International Jazz Festival, Paris, 1955; arranger for Xavier Cugat's orchestra; pianist and composer with Dizzy Gillespie's band, 1962; teacher of music composition at University of California, Los Angeles, 1970-71; also guest conductor with philharmonic symphonies including those in Los Angeles, Israel, Buenos Aires, and Mexico, the Indianapolis and Atlanta symphonies, and the the Los Angeles Chamber Orchestra.

AWARDS: Winner of four Grammy Awards including two for his theme from *Mission: Impossible.*

MEMBER: Young Musicians Foundation (president and musical director, 1983).

ADDRESSES: AGENT—c/o Brian Loucks, Creative Artists Agency, 1888 Century Park E., Los Angeles, CA 90067.

*   *   *

SCHISGAL, Murray   1926-

PERSONAL: Born November 25, 1926, in Brooklyn, NY; son of Abraham (a tailor) and Irene (Sperling) Schisgal; married Reene Schapiro, June 29, 1958; children: Jane, Zachary. EDUCATION: Brooklyn Law School, LL.B., 1953; New School for Social Research, B.A., 1959; also attended the Brooklyn Conservatory of Music and Long Island University. MILITARY: U.S. Navy, 1944-46.

VOCATION: Playwright.

CAREER: Also see *WRITINGS* below.

NON-RELATED CAREER—Musician, 1947-50; attorney, 1953-55; teacher, 1955-59.

WRITINGS: PLAYS—*The Typists,* British Drama League Theatre, London, 1960, Orpheum Theatre, New York City, 1963, published by Coward McCann, 1963; *The Postman, A Simple Kind of Love Story,* both British Drama League Theatre, 1960; *Ducks and Lovers,* Arts Theatre, London, 1961, published by Dramatists Play Servuce, 1972; *The Tiger,* Orpheum Theatre, New York City, 1963, published by Coward McCann, 1963; *Knit One, Purl Two,* Poets Theatre, Boston, MA, 1963; *Luv,* Arts Theatre, 1963, then Booth Theatre, New York City, 1964, published by Coward McCann, 1965, in *The Best Plays of 1964-65,* Dodd, Mead & Company, 1965, in *Plays of Our Time,* Random House, 1967, and in *Luv and Other Plays,* Dodd, Mead & Company, 1983; *Windows,*

MURRAY SCHISGAL

produced in Los Angeles, CA, 1965, published in *Fragments, Windows, and Other Plays,* Coward McCann, 1965; *Fragments,* Cherry Lane Theatre, New York City, 1965, and at the Berkshire Playhouse, Stockbridge, MA, 1967, published in *Fragments, Windows, and Other Plays,* Coward McCann, 1965; *The Basement,* Cherry Lane Theatre, 1965; *Reverberations, The Old Jew,* both Berkshire Playhouse, Stockbridge, MA, 1967; *Memorial Day,* produced in Baltimore, MD, 1968; *Jimmy Shine,* Brooks Atkinson Theatre, New York City, 1968, published by Atheneum, 1969, and Dramatists Play Service, 1969; *The Chinese,* produced in Paris, France, 1968, then Ethel Barrymore Theatre, New York City, 1970, published by Dramatists Play Service, 1970, and in *Best Short Plays of the World Theatre, 1968-73,* Crown Publishers, 1974; *A Way of Life,* produced in 1969.

Doctor Fish, Ethel Barrymore Theatre, 1970, published by Dramatists Play Service, 1970; *An American Millionaire,* Circle in the Square, New York City, 1974, published by Dramatists Play Service, 1974; *All Over Town,* produced in New York City, 1974, published by Dramatists Play Service, 1975, and in *The Best Plays of 1974-75,* Dodd, Mead & Company, 1975; *Popkins,* Margo Jones Theatre, Dallas, TX, 1978, published by Dramatists Play Service, 1984; *The Pushcart Peddlers,* produced in New York City, 1979, published in *The Pushcart Peddlers, The Flatulist and Other Plays,* Dramatists Play Service, 1980, and in *Best Short Plays: 1981,* Chilton Book Company, 1981; *Walter and the Flatulist,* produced in New York City, 1980, produced in *The Pushcart Peddlars, The Flatulist and Other Plays,* Dramatists Play Service, 1980; *The Downstairs Boys* (previously *A Way of Life*), John Drew Theatre, East Hampton, NY, then Playhouse in the Park, Cincinnati, OH, both 1980; *An Original Jimmy Shine* (musical), University of California, Los Angeles, Los Angeles, CA, 1981; *A Need for*

Brussels Sprouts, Cort Theatre, New York City, then Mayfair Theatre, Los Angeles, CA, both 1982, published in *Twice Around the Park,* Samuel French, Inc., 1983, and in *Best Short Plays: 1983,* Chilton Book Company, 1983; *A Need for Less Expertise,* Cort Theatre, 1982, published in *Twice Around the Park,* Samuel French, Inc., 1983; *The New Yorkers,* Morse Center Trinity Theatre, New York City, 1984; *Jealousy,* produced in New York City, 1984, published by Dramatists Play Service, 1985; *Old Wine in a New Bottle,* Ranstadteater, Belgium, 1985, published by Dramatists Play Service, 1987; *Schneider,* reading at the Berkshire Theatre Festival, 1986; *The Rabbi and the Toyota Dealer,* Mayfair Theatre, 1987; *Road Show,* Circle Repertory Theatre, New York City, 1987; *What about Luv?* (musical), Lyric Hammersmith Theatre, London, 1987. Also published *Closet Madness and Other Plays,* Samuel French, Inc., 1984; and *There Are No Sacher Tortes in Our Society!,* Dramatists Play Service, 1985.

SCREENPLAYS—*Ducks and Lovers,* ABP, 1962; *The Tiger Makes Out,* Columbia, 1967; (with Don McGuire and Larry Gelbart) *Tootsie,* Columbia, 1982.

TELEPLAYS—*The Love Song of Barney Kempinski,* ABC, 1966; *Natasha Kovolina Pipishinsky,* ABC, 1976.

FICTION—*Days and Nights of a French Horn Player,* Little, Brown & Company, 1980.

AWARDS: Vernon Rice Award, Outer Circle Critics Award, *Saturday Review* Critics Poll Award, all 1963, for *The Typists* and *The Tiger;* Antoinette Perry Award nomination, Drama Critics Circle Award nomination, both 1964, for *Luv;* Outstanding Dramatic Program, Emmy Award nomination, 1966, for *The Love Song of Barney Kempinski;* Best Screenplay, Los Angeles Film Critics Award, New York Film Critics Award, National Society of Film Critics Award, Writers Guild of America Award, Academy Award nomination, British Academy Award nomination, all 1982, for *Tootsie.*

MEMBER: Screen Actors Guild.

ADDRESSES: AGENT—c/o Audrey Wood, International Creative Management, 40 W. 57th Street, New York, NY 10019.

*   *   *

SCHNEIDER, John

PERSONAL: Born April 8, in Mt. Kisco, NY.

VOCATION: Actor, singer, composer, and fashion model.

CAREER: PRINCIPAL STAGE APPEARANCES—*Night of 100 Stars,* Radio City Music Hall, New York City, 1982; also appeared in local and community theatres in Atlanta and in summer stock in New Hampshire.

PRINCIPAL FILM APPEARANCES—*Smokey and the Bandit,* Universal, 1977; *Eddie Macon's Run,* Universal, 1983; *Cocaine Wars,* Concorde/Cinema Group, 1985; also *Million Dollar Dixie Deliverance.*

PRINCIPAL TELEVISION APPEARANCES—Series: Bo Duke, *Dukes of Hazzard,* CBS, 1979-81. Movies: *Dream House,* 1981; *Happy*

Endings, 1983; *Stagecoach,* 1986. Specials: *John Schneider—Back Home.*

RELATED CAREER—Performed his own compositions and songs on guitar in cabarets in Atlanta; formerly a fashion model.

RECORDINGS: ALBUMS—*You Ain't Seen the Last of Me!,* MCA, 1987.

MEMBER: Screen Actors Guild, American Federation of Television and Radio Artists.

ADDRESSES: AGENT—Raymond Kate Enterprises, 9255 Sunset Blvd., Suite 1115, Los Angeles, CA 90069. PUBLICIST—c/o Lili Ungar, PMK Public Relations, Inc., 8436 W. Third Street, Suite 650, Los Angeles, CA 90048.*

*   *   *

SCHWAB, Sophie
See HAYDEN, Sophie

*   *   *

SCHWARTZ, Archibald
See McGOOHAN, Patrick

*   *   *

SCHWARTZ, Stephen   1948-

PERSONAL: Born March 6, 1948, in New York, NY; son of Stanley L. (in business) and Sheila L. (a teacher; maiden name, Siegal) Schwartz; married Carole Piasecki (an actress), June 6, 1969; children: Scott, Jessica. EDUCATION: Attended Juilliard School of Music, 1960-64; Carnegie Mellon University, B.F.A., 1964-68.

VOCATION: Composer, lyricist, and director.

CAREER: Also see *WRITINGS* below. FIRST STAGE WORK—Director, Playhouse Theatre, New London, NH, 1966. PRINCIPAL STAGE WORK—Director, *Working,* 46th Street Theatre, New York City, 1978. FIRST TELEVISION WORK— Director, *Working,* PBS American Playhouse, 1981.

RELATED CAREER—Artist and repertoire agent, RCA Records, 1969-71.

WRITINGS: MUSICALS—All as composer and lyricist unless indicated: *Godspell* Round House Theatre, London, then Cherry Lane Theatre, later Promenade Theatre, both New York City, 1971; (with Leonard Bernstein; lyricist only), *Mass* (English text), Kennedy Center, Washington, DC, 1971; *Pippin,* Imperial Theatre, New York City, 1972, then Her Majesty's Theatre, London, 1973; *The Magic Show,* Cort Theatre, New York City, 1974; (adaptor) *Working,* 46th Street Theatre, New York City, 1978; *The Baker's Wife,* 1976; *The Trip,* First All-Childrens' Theatre, New York City, 1983; (lyricist only) *Rags,* Mark Hellinger Theatre, New

STEPHEN SCHWARTZ

York City, 1986. SONGS—Composer, title song, *Butterflies Are Free,* Booth Theatre, New York City, 1969; four songs for *Working,* 46th Street Theatre, 1978; three songs for *Personals,* Minetta Lane Theatre, New York City, 1985.

FILM SCORES—Composer and lyricist, *Godspell,* Columbia, 1972.

TELEVISION SCORES—Composer, "The Flowering Oasis," *Nature,* PBS, 1987.

CHILDREN'S BOOKS—*The Perfect Peach,* Little, Brown & Company, 1977.

RECORDINGS: All original cast albums. Composer of music and lyrics: *Godspell,* Columbia, 1971; *Pippin,* Motown, 1973; *The Magic Show,* Bell, 1974. Producer: *The Last Sweet Days of Isaac; The Survival of Saint Joan.*

AWARDS: Best Score for Original Cast Album, Grammy Award, 1971, for *Godspell;* Most Promising Composer, Drama Desk Award, Best Composer, *Variety* Critics Poll Award, both 1971, for *Godspell;* Grand Prize from the International Film Office, Dineen Award from the National Theatre Arts Conference, both for the film version of *Godspell;* Best Director, Drama Desk Award, 1978, for *Working.*

MEMBER: Dramatists Guild, Directors Guild, American Society of Composers, Authors and Producers, Society of Stage Directors and Choreographers.

SIDELIGHTS: RECREATIONS—Tennis.

ADDRESSES: AGENT—c/o Shirley Bernstein, Paramuse Artists, 1414 Avenue of the Americas, New York, NY 10019.

*   *   *

SCORSESE, Martin   1942-

PERSONAL: Born November 17, 1942, in Flushing, NY; son of Charles and Catherine (Cappa) Scorsese (garment workers); married Laraine Marie Brennan, May 15, 1965 (divorced); married Julia Cameron (a writer; divorced); married Isabella Rosellini (a model and actress), September 29, 1979 (divorced, 1983); married Barbara DeFina (a film production worker), February, 1985; children: (first marriage) Catherine Terese Glinora Sophia; (second marriage) Dominica Elizabeth. EDUCATION: New York University, B.A., film communications, 1964, M.A., 1966.

VOCATION: Director, screenwriter, and actor.

CAREER: PRINCIPAL FILM WORK—Also see *WRITINGS* below. Director: *Who's That Knocking at My Door?* (also known as *J.R.*), Joseph Brenner Associates, 1968; (also associate producer and post production supervisor) *Boxcar Bertha,* American International, 1972; *Mean Streets,* Warner Brothers, 1973; *Alice Doesn't Live Here Anymore,* Warner Brothers, 1975; *Taxi Driver,* Columbia, 1976; *New York, New York,* United Artists, 1977; *The Last Waltz,* United Artists, 1978; *Raging Bull,* United Artists, 1980; *The King of Comedy,* Twentieth Century-Fox, 1983; *After Hours,* Geffen Films, 1985; *The Color of Money,* Buena Vista, 1986. Also directed *What's a Nice Girl Like You Doing in a Place Like This?,* 1963; *It's Not Just You, Murray,* 1964; *The Big Shave,* 1968; and worked on "The Last Temptation of Christ," cancelled by Paramount.

Supervising editor and assistant director, *Woodstock,* Warner Brothers, 1970; associate producer and post production supervisor, *Medicine Ball Caravan,* Warner Brothers, 1979. Also director and writer of documentaries, including *Street Scenes,* 1970; *Italian-American,* 1974, and *American Boy,* 1979.

PRINCIPAL FILM APPEARANCES—Gangster, *Who's That Knocking at My Door?,* Joseph Brenner Associates, 1968; client of bordello, *Boxcar Bertha,* American International, 1972; Shorty the hit man, *Mean Streets,* Warner Brothers, 1973; customer at Mel and Ruby's, *Alice Doesn't Live Here Anymore,* Warner Brothers, 1975; passenger, *Taxi Driver,* Columbia, 1976; as himself, *The Last Waltz,* United Artists, 1978; assistant, *The King of Comedy,* Twentieth Century-Fox, 1983; disco patron, *After Hours,* Geffen Films, 1985; also appeared in *Cannonball,* New World Pictures, 1976; *Hollywood's Wild Angel,* 1979; *Triple Play,* 1981.

PRINCIPAL STAGE WORK—Director, *The Act,* Majestic Theatre, New York City, 1977.

RELATED CAREER—Faculty assistant and instructor in the film department, New York University, 1963-66, instructor, 1968-70; director of television commercials in England, 1968; news editor, CBS-TV, 1968.

WRITINGS: SCREENPLAYS—*What's a Nice Girl Like You Doing in a Place Like This?,* 1963; *It's Not Just You, Murray,* 1964; *Bring on the Dancing Girls,* 1965; *I Call First,* 1967; *The Big Shave,* 1968; (with Betzi Manoogian) *Who's That Knocking at My Door?* (also known as *J.R.*), Joseph Brenner Associates, 1968; with

Mardik Martin) *Mean Streets,* Warner Brothers, 1973; (co-writer) *Italianamerican,* 1974.

AWARDS: Edward L. Kingsley Foundation Award, 1963, 1964; First Prize, Rosenthal Foundation Award, Society of Cinemetologists, 1964; Brown University Film Festival Award, 1965; First Prize, Screen Producer's Guild Award, 1965; Best Director, Academy Award nomination, 1976, for *Taxi Driver;* Best Director, Academy Award nomination, 1981, for *Raging Bull;* Best Director, Cannes Film Festival Award, 1986.

SIDELIGHTS: Director Martin Scorsese has created a body of work that includes the violent realism of *Mean Streets* and *Taxi Driver,* the poignant romance of *Alice Doesn't Live Here Any More,* the black comedy of *After Hours* and *The King of Comedy,* and the kinetic character study of *The Color of Money.* He has also made what some consider the best rock concert documentary, *The Last Waltz,* and what he himself terms a "musical noir," *New York, New York.* As early in Scorsese's career as February 8, 1976, film reporter Guy Flatley speculated in the *New York Times Magazine* that the variety represented "a shrewdly daring scheme to shift artistic gear from film to film, to alternate the grim and the glamorous, the harrowing and the happy, in an apparent effort to convince Hollywood that he is a jack-of-all-trades, a master of both the extravagant and the austere." Beneath the diversity, however, a number of critics have identified a consistent concern with individuals and with themes of alienation and redemption. The director told Flatley, "I look for a thematic idea running through my movies and I see that it's the outsider struggling for recognition," a role with which Scorsese strongly identifies.

Scorsese's chronic asthma isolated him as a child, preventing him from joining in sports at school and on the neighborhood streets of New York's Little Italy where he grew up. Instead, he joined his father on weekly outings to the movies, where he particularly enjoyed British films, westerns, and costume adventures, he recalled in *Anatomy of the Movies* (David Pirie, editor, Macmillan, 1981). While waiting after school for his parents to return from work, he would amuse himself by drawing out storyboards for his own epics at the kitchen table. Nevertheless, it was the priesthood, rather than filmmaking, that was Scorsese's original vocation. Expelled from a seminary, he did not distinguish himself at Cardinal Hayes High School and was not accepted at the Jesuit university to which he applied.

Instead he enrolled at New York University, located in Greenwich Village, just a few blocks, yet worlds away, from Little Italy. He recollected with Flatley: "When I went to the university, I met girls who were blond. As a kid, I had literally only known dark-haired girls." More significantly, Scorsese soon gave up his intention to major in English when he discovered the school's film study program. A renewed appreciation among critics for American film, the influx of French and Italian New Wave cinema represented by such directors as Francois Truffaut, Jean Luc Goddard, and Michelangelo Antonioni, and the rise of independent filmmakers like John Cassavetes were among the stimulating influences he encountered. "It was the best time to be a film student," he declared to Esther B. Fein (*New York Times,* September 29, 1985). Scorsese stayed on to earn a master's degree in film and returned later as an instructor, developing "the gritty sense of having made a movie by hand" he considered characteristic of NYU-trained directors, as opposed to those schooled in Hollywood, reported Fein.

Like a number of other directors of his generation, Scorsese got his start making commercial features with Roger Corman, whose

American International Pictures stocked drive-ins with a steady supply of violent B-movies done on a shoestring. After viewing Scorsese's early feature, *Who's That Knocking at My Door,* the producer offered him the job of directing *Boxcar Bertha,* a sequel to an earlier hit, *Bloody Mama.* Told that the project would involve costumes and guns, Scorsese agreed; working with Corman proved instructive. "You learn what's essential to a scene and how to get it quickly shot," he told Flatley. By this time, however, Scorsese had come to know John Cassavetes, whose free roaming camera technique had so impressed him in New York. Cassavetes reaction to *Boxcar Bertha,* according to *Anatomy of the Movies,* was: ". . . You've shown you can do that kind of action exploitation movie. But basically this isn't the kind of picture you should be doing." At his urging Scorsese returned to a semi-autobiographical project set in Little Italy.

Mean Streets centers on Charlie, a small-time hoodlum, and his conflicting desires to save his crazy, punk friend Johnny Boy (a widely hailed performance by Robert De Niro) from loan sharks, preserve his secretive romance with an epileptic neighbor, and still please his Mafioso uncle. Despite his criminal activities, Charlie likens himself to St. Francis of Assisi and carries on an internal dialogue with God. Harvey Keitel, who had the lead role, has appeared in a number of Scorsese's films; in the *New York Times Magazine* he applauded the director's handling of his cast: "Marty lets actors bring their own humanity—their eccentricities, their humor, their compassion—to a role." In addition to the characterizations, critics appreciated Scorsese's use of music and the way his jittery camera movement heightened the atmosphere of unpredictable violence in the episodic plot. Although it was not a popular success, when *Mean Streets* was screened at the prestigious New York Film Festival, it was "a shot heard all the way to Hollywood," reported the February, 1975 *Esquire.*

Warner Brothers tapped the young director to make *Alice Doesn't Live Here Any More* with Ellen Burstyn as a widow trying to make a career as a singer who has to settle for a waitress job to support her wise-cracking young son. Part of the project's appeal was its central female role, Pirie commented, since Scorsese wanted to disprove the notion *Mean Steets* inspired in some critics that he could not direct women. He also made a point of using women in the crew. In *Hollywood Renaissance* (A.S. Barnes, 1977), Dianne Jacobs described *Alice* as "a film about a conventional woman who, almost by chance, stumbles upon a relationship a little more fulfilling, a little more equitable than her first marriage." She found it to be "replete with fine moments," coming from both the characters and the filming techniques. The movie achieved major box office success.

Abruptly different in mood was Scorsese's next film, *Taxi Driver,* starring Robert De Niro as a psychopathic cab driver. Travis Bickle, the driver, cruises the streets of "a New York that steamed and simmered suspiciously like hell itself," *Newsweek* ventured in the May 16, 1977 issue. Spurned by a campaign worker, he tries to assassinate a presidential candidate; foiled, he attempts to restore a teenage prostitute to her parents through a shoot-out so violent that the motion picture ratings board threatened an "X" rating unless the color of the blood was toned down. Scorsese confessed to Flatley: "I *had* to make that movie. Not so much because of the social statement it makes, but because of its *feelings* about things, including things I don't like to admit about myself"—such as rage and rejection. Despite its subject matter, the film was a hit and Scorsese received an Academy Award nomination as best director. Jacobs asserted, "*Taxi Driver* establishes beyond question that Scorsese is one of the finest American directors working today."

His attempt at a full-scale musical in his next film, *New York, New York,* won support from neither audiences nor critics. Physically and emotionally the director was at a low ebb when he began to film *Raging Bull,* based on the rise and fall of the boxer Jake La Motta. Like *Taxi Driver,* the story was driven by violence, but the director told Pirie, "It's not only physical but psychological and it doesn't build to a climax the way *Taxi Driver* does." Again Scorsese saw something of himself in the main character. Furthermore, he believed it would be his last film, he confided to Mark Jacobson (*Rolling Stone,* April 14, 1983), so "he threw everything he knew into the wake of the beast. Visually the film is spectacular, the raucus jittery style of *Mean Streets* harnessed to create a great, silvery, remorseless machine." When it was finished, Scorsese felt the same satisfaction he had upon completing *Mean Streets;* he averred to Jacobson: ". . . They can leave it on the shelf and never show it because I got what I wanted out of it. I felt I had found my place, which was to make this kind of film and none other." *Raging Bull* achieved moderate success, nonetheless, and the director received another Academy Award nomination.

When he turned next to making *The King of Comedy,* he told Jacobson, he saw the aspiring comic Rupert Pupkin and his kidnap victim, established television host Jerry Langford, as "two pictures of me—the side that would do anything, *anything* to make a film, do anything to get somewhere, and the other side, the side that has gotten somewhere. And in both cases, I'm never satisfied." Rupert demands an appearance on Langford's show, including an introduction as "the king of comedy," as the ransom for his idol, whose kidnapping the director described as "polite." Critics found the style of the film controlled, a term not usually applied to Scorsese or to his stars, Robert De Niro and Jerry Lewis. "I wanted everything to be on an edge but not over it," Scorsese confirmed to Jacobson. He also termed the picture "transitional."

He intended to follow it with "The Last Temptation of Christ," a project he cultivated for a year and a half before it was cancelled by Paramount. The studio caved in to angry responses to its supposed depiction of Jesus as a homosexual. Scorsese denied the rumors to no avail, but was able to see a humorous parallel to his frustration over the experience in the misadventures of the protagonist of his next film, *After Hours.* In this comedy a young computer operator ventures from his middle class apartment to a Soho loft for an impromptu date with a girl he met in a coffee shop. Completely at odds with the bohemian downtown scene, he not only loses the girl and all his money, but is pursued by a pack of vigilantes who mistake him for a burglar. "I read the script and I said, 'I know just how this guy feels,'" Scorsese recalled to Fein. "This poor guy was being put through his paces by something other than his own actions." Yet he concluded: "I like seeing Paul going through all his troubles because then he resurrects, he has another chance. In a way, it's cathartic."

Scorsese's next chance came with *The Color of Money,* a sequel to the classic 1961 pool hall drama, *The Hustler.* After the middling success of his last few pictures, it marked a complete restoration of his acclaim among critics and audiences. Both the original and the sequel star Paul Newman as Fast Eddie Felsen, a pool prodigy who in the 1986 film has aged into a liquor salesman whose main source of pride is his luxury car and whose connection with pool is limited to staking younger players. But in attempting to groom the young enthusiast played by Tom Cruise in the art of big-time hustling—including deliberate strategic losses—Felsen regains his own determination to play, to prove himself again. Janet Maslin's October 26, 1986 *New York Times* review connected the film to the director's earlier explorations of manhood, guilt, and redemption

from *Mean Streets* and *Taxi Driver* through *Raging Bull* and praised its "visual brilliance." She concurred in the general acclaim for the casting and the way the actors were directed, saying that its players "join the ranks of players from Cybill Shepherd to Jodie Foster to Jerry Lewis, all of whom have been used with exceptional efficacy in Mr. Scorsese's work." Believing the film to demonstrate "both sides of [his] talent, the electrifying and the reflective," she hailed *The Color of Money* as a "return to the kind of pyrotechnics that put him on the map in the first place."

ADDRESSES: OFFICE—United Artists, 10202 W. Washington Boulevard, Culver City, CA 90230. AGENT—c/o Harry Ufland, Ufland-Roth Productions, Lions Gate Studio, 1861 S. Bundy Drive, Los Angeles, CA 90025.

*   *   *

SCOTT, Ridley   1939-

BRIEF ENTRY: Ridley Scott, the director responsible for terrifying countless movie-goers with the futuristic monster film *Alien,* was born in 1939 in South Shields, Tyne and Wear, England. After studying at the Royal College of Art in London and directing his first short film, *Boy on a Bicycle,* Scott became a set designer for BBC Television, where he also directed episodes of *Z Cars* in 1966. He worked on another British series, *The Informer* (1966-67), and then turned to directing commercials, completing more than two thousand over the next decade or so. His spot for Chanel No. 5 perfume won an award at the Venice Film Festival and his Orwellian 1984 commercial for Apple computers, costing some $580,000 to make, riveted viewers. The June, 1984 *Films and Filming* lauded Scott as the British director "who raised the level of the advertising film to an art form." His stunning visual style has impressed critics of his feature films as well, beginning with the 1977 release, *The Duellists,* a film about longstanding enmity between two French officers during the Napoleonic Wars, which critic Leonard Maltin described as "among [the] most staggeringly beautiful of its time." He followed the 1979 blockbuster *Alien* with another futuristic tale; set against the backdrop of the twenty-first century, *Blade Runner* concerns mutinous androids running amok on earth. Scott gave a fairy-tale setting to his 1985 feature, *Legend*—an allegorical tale about the nature of good and evil.

*   *   *

SCOTT, Tony   1944-

PERSONAL: Born June 21, 1944, in Newcastle, England; married Glynis Sanders (a producer of commercials). EDUCATION: Received degree in fine arts (first class), from Sunderland Art School; postgraduate work, Leeds College of Art, 1969; Royal College of Arts, M.F.A., 1972.

VOCATION: Director.

CAREER: FIRST FILM WORK—Director, *One of the Missing,* British Film Institute, 1969. PRINCIPAL FILM WORK— Director: *Loving Memory,* British Film Institute, 1972; *Author of Beltraffio,* 1983; *The Hunger,* Metro-Goldwyn-Mayer, 1983; *Top Gun,* Paramount, 1986; *Beverly Hills Cop II,* Paramount, 1987; *Presidio,* upcoming.

AWARDS: Clio awards and Cannes awards for television commercial work.

MEMBER: Directors Guild of America.

ADDRESSES: OFFICE—c/o Paramount Pictures, 5555 Melrose Boulevard, DeMille Room 194, Los Angeles, CA 90038. AGENT—c/o Bill Unger, 752 26th Street, Santa Monica, CA 90402.

*   *   *

SEAL, Elizabeth   1933-

PERSONAL: Born August 28, 1933, in Genoa, Italy; daughter of Frederick George (a ship broker) and Rill Alice (a model; maiden name, Read) Seal; married Peter Townsend (divorced); married Zack Matalon (divorced); married Michael Ward (a photographer); children: (second marriage) Sarah, Adam, Noah. EDUCATION: Studied dance with Karsavina, Margaret Clarke, and Molly Radcliff at the Royal Academy of Dancing.

VOCATION: Actress, dancer, and singer.

CAREER: LONDON DEBUT—*Gay's the Word*, Saville Theatre, 1951. BROADWAY DEBUT—Title role, *Irma La Douce*, Plymouth Theatre, 1960. PRINCIPAL STAGE APPEARANCES— Gladys, *The Pajama Game*, Coliseum Theatre, London, 1955; Esmeralda, *Camino Real*, Phoenix Theatre, London, 1957; Lola, *Damn Yankees*, Coliseum Theatre, 1957; title role, *Irma La Douce*, Lyric

ELIZABETH SEAL

Theatre, London, 1958, then National Theatre, Washington, DC, 1960; Lucette, *Cat amongst the Pidgeons*, Prince of Wales Theatre, London, 1969; Connie Kate Culpepper, *Liberty Ranch*, Greenwich Theatre, London, 1972; Sylvia, *The Recruiting Officer*, Sally Bowles, *Cabaret*, both Haymarket Theatre, Leicester, U.K., 1973; various roles, *In Order of Appearance*, Chichester Festival, Chichester, U.K., 1977; Roxie Hart, *Chicago*, Cambridge Theatre, London, 1980; Miss Ronberry, *The Corn Is Green*, Lunt-Fontanne Theatre, New York City, then Kennedy Center, both 1983; Desiree, *A Little Night Music*, Library Theatre, Manchester, U.K., 1987. Also appeared as Martha, *Who's Afraid of Virginia Woolf?*, Myra, *Hay Fever*, both Ipswich, U.K., 1974; Timothy's mother, various parts, *Salad Days*, Nottingham, U.K., then Bromley, U.K., later Duke of York's Theatre, London, 1976; Bertha, *Exiles*, Cleveland Playhouse, Cleveland, OH; and in *Farjeon Reviewed*, Mermaid Theatre, London, 1975; *ACT*, Shoreham Hotel, Washington, DC; *Cowdy Custard*, Farnham, U.K.; *Fifty Minute Act with Two Boys*, Country Cousins Theatre; *Wave Length*, Adeline Genee Theatre; *Mixed Doubles*, Winchester Theatre Royal, Winchester, U.K.

PRINCIPAL STAGE WORK—Choreographer, *An Evening of DeSilva Brown and Henderson*, Guildford School of Drama and Dance, Guildford, U.K., 1987; director, choreographer, *Gershwin Medley, Wild about Harry, Jule Styne Evening*, all Guildford School Drama and Dance; choreographer, *La Traviata* (opera), Welsh National Opera.

MAJOR TOURS—Josefa Lantenay, *A Shot in the Dark*, U.S. cities, 1962; Myra Arundel, *Hay Fever*, U.K. cities, 1975; Imogen Piper, *Murder by the Book*, U.K. cities, 1984.

PRINCIPAL TELEVISION APPEARANCES—Episodic: Avonia Bunn, *Trelawny of the Wells*, BBC; "Blues for a Left Foot," *Route 66*, CBS; two roles, *Supernatural*, BBC; *Jakanori Playhouse*, BBC; *My Son, My Son*, BBC; *Sunday Night at the Palladium; Mantovani Show; Ronnie Corbett Show; Z Cars*. Movies: *Softly Softly*, ITV; *Philby, Burgess and Maclean*, Granada; *Chelsea at 8.0*, Granada; *Chelsea at 9.0*, Granada. Guest: *Ed Sullivan Show*, CBS; *Perry Como Show*. Specials: *Music of Jerome Kern*, BBC; *Keith Michell Special*.

PRINCIPAL FILM APPEARANCES—*Town on Trial*, Columbia, 1956; appeared as Fiona, *Cone of Silence*, 1985; and in *Vampire Circus*, Hammer.

PRINCIPAL RADIO APPEARANCES—*House Husband: A Musical*.

RELATED CAREER—Teacher of musical theatre, Elmhurst Ballet School, Elmhurst, U.K.

AWARDS: Most Promising Newcomer, Variety Club of Great Britain Award, 1958, for *Irma La Douce;* Best Actress, Variety Club of Great Britain Award, 1958, for *The Pajama Game;* Best Actress in a Musical, Antoinette Perry Award, 1961, for *Irma La Douce.*

MEMBER: Actors' Equity Association, British Actors' Equity Association, Screen Actors Guild, American Federation of Television and Radio Artists.

ADDRESSES: AGENT—c/o Jan Kennedy, London Management, 235 Regent Street, London W1, England. MANAGER—c/o Dan Fuller Management Services, P.O. Box 1455, New York, NY 10185.

PETIE TRIGG SEALE

SEALE, Petie Trigg   1930-

PERSONAL: First name is pronounced "Peetee;" born Zenaide Alma Trigg, February 20, 1930, in Baltimore, MD; daughter of Frank Orren Saunders (an artist) and Loyse Gabrielle (a social worker; maiden name, Anderson) Trigg. Married Douglas R. Seale (an actor and director), November 9, 1964. EDUCATION: Boston University, B.S., 1951.

VOCATION: Actress, choreographer, and dancer.

CAREER: STAGE DEBUT—Monkee, *Noah,* Center Stage Theatre, Baltimore, MD, 1966, for thirty-two performances. PRINCIPAL STAGE APPEARANCES—Player queen, *Hamlet,* Miss Peake, *The Royal Family,* Sis Laura, *A Member of the Wedding,* all Center Stage Theatre, Baltimore, MD, 1966; Annie Dudgeon, *The Devil's Disciple,* Center Stage Theatre, 1968; Madrigal, *The Chalk Garden,* Old Town Players, Chicago, IL, 1970; Jenny, *The Threepenny Opera* Goodman Theatre, Chicago, IL, 1970; Lady Bracknell, *The Importance of Being Earnest,* Goodman Theatre, 1971; Golde, *Fiddler on the Roof,* Zela Bethbud, *Count Dracula,* both Red Barn Theatre, MI, 1971; Irma Kronkite, *Picnic,* Bucks County Playhouse, New Hope, PA, 1973; Mrs. Love, *Contributions,* Direct Theatre, New York City, 1974; Tillie Petunia, *Strivers' Row,* New Heritage Repertory Theatre, New York City, 1974; Louella, *Freed from the Met,* Mama Gail's Theatre, New York City, 1975; Clytemnestra/Christine, *Agamemnon/Homecoming,* Hopkins Center, Dartmouth College, Hanover, NH, 1975; Dr. Ludwig Schoen, *Earth Spirit,* Direct Theatre, 1975; Hecate, *Macbeth,* St. Clement's Church Theatre, New York City, 1976; Sylvia III, *Sylvia Plath,*

Nameless Theatre, New York City, 1976; chorus leader, *Medea,* Manhattan Plaza Theatre, New York City, 1978; nurse, *Romeo and Juliet,* Evelyn, *The Freeway,* Dilber, Fezziwig, *A Christmas Carol,* all Milwaukee Repertory Company, Milwaukee, WI, 1978; Clytemnestra, *Electra,* Equity Library Theatre, New York City, 1979.

Tillie Petunia, *Strivers' Row,* New Heritage Repertory Theatre, 1984; Irene, *Mojo,* New Day Repertory Theatre, New York City, 1985; Clytemnestra, *The Flies,* Amistad World Theatre, New York City, 1981; Fanny, *Clean Sheets Can't Soil,* Gertie, *Where Dewdrops of Mercy Shine Bright,* Annalois, *Mount Hope,* all Rights and Reason, Brown University, Providence, RI, 1983; Ash, *Zooman and the Sign,* Crossroads Theatre, New Brunswick, NJ, 1983; Blu, *Steal Away,* Crossroads Theatre, 1984; Carmela, *Sweet Daddy Love,* Crossroads Theatre, 1985; Mother Superior, *Agnes of God,* Crossroads Theatre, 1986. Also appeared as Sister Boxer, *The Amen Corner,* New York City, 1976; Eurydice, *Antigone,* New York City 1980; various roles, *The Actress,* New York City, 1985; Kat, *Tea at Kat's Place,* New York City, 1986; and in *Richard III,* American Folk Theatre, New York City, 1980; *Uncle Vanya,* American Academy of Dramatic Arts, New York City, 1982; *Home Again, Kathleen,* American Renaissance Theatre, New York City, 1983.

PRINCIPAL STAGE WORK—Director, *Journey of the Fifth Horse,* American Academy of Dramatic Arts, New York City, 1984; choreographer, *The Firebird,* Cricket Theatre, New York City; choreographer, *A Comedy of Errors, Hamlet,* both American Shakespeare Theatre Festival, Stratford, CT; choreographer, *Lady Audley's Secret, The Chinese Wall,* both Center Stage Theatre, Baltimore, MD.

PRINCIPAL CABARET APPEARANCES—All in New York City: Scene One, 1979; The Grand Finale, 1980; The Westbank Cafe, 1980; The Bushes, 1980 and 1981.

RELATED CAREER—Teacher and dancer, School for the Performing Arts, New York City, 1951-63; teacher, dancer, and choreographer, American Shakespeare Theatre, Stratford, CT, 1962-64.

MEMBER: Actors' Equity Association, Screen Actors Guild, American Federation of Television and Radio Artists, Audelco, Black Women in Theatre.

ADDRESSES: HOME—645 Hudson Street, New York, NY 10014.

*   *   *

SEARS, Austin   1947-

PERSONAL: Born November 2, 1947, in New York, NY; son of Bernard Horatio (an ivory and ostrich merchant) and Gustava N. (Pototska) Sears; married Margarita Malinova (a concert pianist); children: Judith, Sean, Jose, Prospero. EDUCATION: Columbia University, M.F.A., 1972; trained for the stage with Michael Shurtleff. MILITARY: French Foreign Legion, Lance Corporal, Cameroon, 1971-74.

VOCATION: Actor.

CAREER: PRINCIPAL STAGE APPEARANCES—Hillary McKenzie, *The Boiling Oil Machine,* Drury Lane Theatre, London, 1969; Dr.

Seward, *Dracula,* New Vic Theatre, London, 1973; John Dickinson, *1776,* Riverfront Stage, Philadelphia, PA, 1975; George, *Same Time, Next Year,* City Stage Theatre, Poughkeepsie, NY, 1979; Bluntschli, *Arms and the Man,* Cooperstown Theatre Festival, Cooperstown, NY, 1985; John Adams, *1776,* Cooperstown Theatre Festival, 1986. Also appeared as title role, *Hamlet,* National Shakespeare Company, International Repertory Theatre, 1974.

MAJOR TOURS—King Arthur, *Camelot,* U.S. cities, 1979 and 1983; John Adams, *1776,* U.S. cities, 1986.

FILM DEBUT—Homer, *Running,* Universal, 1979. PRINCIPAL FILM APPEARANCES—FBI Agent Jones, *Prince of the City,* Warner Brothers, 1981; *A Season in the Sun,* SAE Films, 1987.

TELEVISION DEBUT—Luke O'Hare, *Best of Families,* PBS, 1977.

AWARDS: Croix de Guerre.

MEMBER: Actors' Equity Association, American Federation of Television and Radio Artists, Screen Actors Guild; British-American Kangeroo Club.

SIDELIGHTS: FAVORITE ROLES—King Arthur in *Camelot;* John Adams in *1776.*

ADDRESSES: OFFICE—c/o Cooperstown Theatre, P.O. Box 851, Cooperstown, NY 13326.

*   *   *

SELBY, David

PERSONAL: Born in Morganstown, WV. EDUCATION: Attended the University of West Virginia.

VOCATION: Actor.

CAREER: PRINCIPAL STAGE APPEARANCES—John Buchanan, Jr., *The Eccentricities of a Nightingale,* Morosco Theatre, New York City, 1976; Dom, *I Won't Dance,* Studio Arena Theatre, Buffalo, NY, then at the Helen Hayes Theatre, New York City, 1981; *Hedda Gabler,* Hartman Theatre, Stamford, CT, 1981-82; also appeared with other regional theatres and in Off-Broadway productions.

PRINCIPAL FILM APPEARANCES—*Night of Dark Shadows,* Metro-Goldwyn-Mayer, 1971; *Up the Sandbox,* National General, 1972; Robert Hantz, *The Super Cops,* United Artists, 1974; *Lady in Blue,* 1975; *Rich Kids,* United Artists, 1979; *Rich and Famous,* 1981.

PRINCIPAL TELEVISION APPEARANCES—Series: *Dark Shadows,* ABC; Michael Tyrone, *Flamingo Road,* NBC, 1981-82; Richard Channing, *Falcon Crest,* CBS, 1982—. Episodic: *Family,* ABC. Mini-Series: *Washington Behind Closed Doors,* NBC. Movies: *Telethon,* 1977.

NON-RELATED CAREER—Former assistant instructor in literature, Southern Illinois University.

MEMBER: Actors' Equity Association, Screen Actors Guild, American Federation of Television and Radio Artists.

ADDRESSES: AGENT—c/o Ed Limato, William Morris Agency, 151 El Camino Drive, Beverly Hills, CA 90212.*

*   *   *

SELL, Janie   1941-

PERSONAL: Born October 1, 1941, in Detroit, MI. EDUCATION: Attended the University of Detroit.

VOCATION: Actress and choreographer.

CAREER: OFF-BROADWAY DEBUT—*Mixed Doubles,* Upstairs at the Downstairs, New York City, 1966. BROADWAY DEBUT—Madame Grimaldi, Mrs. Baker, *George M!,* Palace Theatre, 1968. PRINCIPAL STAGE APPEARANCES—Ruby, *Dames at Sea,* Bouwerie Lane Theatre, New York City, then as Mona Kent, Plaza 9 Music Hall, both New York City, 1970; Jane Burke, *Irene,* Minskoff Theatre, New York City, 1973; Mitzi, *Over Here!,* Shubert Theatre, New York City, 1974; Gladys, *Pal Joey,* Circle in the Square, New York City, 1976; Lieutenant Lillian Holliday, *Happy End,* Martin Beck Theatre, New York City, 1977; Monica, *I Love My Wife,* Ethel Barrymore Theatre, New York City, 1979; Sylvia Rosewater, *God Bless You, Mr. Rosewater,* Entermedia Theatre, New York City, 1979. Also appeared in *Dark Horses,* Upstairs at the Downstairs, New York City, 1966; *By Bernstein,* Chelsea Westside Theatre, New York City, 1975; *Real Life Funnies,* Manhattan Theatre Club, New York City, 1981; and with resident company, Old Globe Theatre, San Diego, CA, 1985.

PRINCIPAL STAGE WORK—Choreographer, *A Backers' Audition,* Manhattan Theatre Club, New York City, 1984.

AWARDS: Theatre World Award, 1974, for *Over Here!*

MEMBER: Actors' Equity Association.

ADDRESSES: OFFICE—c/o Actors' Equity Association, 165 W. 46th Street, New York, NY 10036.*

*   *   *

SEMPLE, Lorenzo, Jr.

VOCATION: Screenwriter.

WRITINGS: SCREENPLAYS—*Fathom,* Twentieth Century-Fox, 1967; *Pretty Poison,* Twentieth Century-Fox, 1968; (with Larry Cohen) *Daddy's Gone A-Hunting,* National General, 1969; *The Sporting Club,* AVCO-Embassy, 1970; *The Marriage of a Young Stockbroker,* Twentieth Century-Fox, 1971; (with Dalton Trumbo) *Papillon,* Allied Artists, 1973; *Super Cops,* United Artists, 1974; (with David Giler) *The Parallax View,* Paramount, 1974; (with Tracy Keenan Wynn and Walter Hill) *The Drowning Pool,* Warner Brothers, 1975; (with David Rayfiel) *Three Days of the Condor,* Paramount, 1975; *King Kong,* Paramount, 1976; *Hurricane,* Paramount, 1979; *Flash Gordon,* Universal, 1980; *Never Say Never Again,* Warner Brothers, 1983; *Sheena,* Columbia, 1984.

TELEPLAYS—Series: Batman, ABC, 1966. Movies: *Rearview Mirror,* NBC, 1984.

MEMBER: Writers Guild of America.

ADDRESSES: AGENT—Creative Artists Agency, 1888 Century Park E., Suite 1400, Los Angeles, CA 90067.

* * *

SERF, Joseph
  See McGOOHAN, Patrick

* * *

SHAGAN, Steve   1927-

PERSONAL: Surname rhymes with "pagan;" full name, Stephen H. Shagan; born October 25, 1927, in New York, NY; son of Barney (a pharmacy owner) and Rachel (Rosenzweig) Shagan; married Elizabeth Leslie Florance (a fashion model), November 18, 1956; children: Robert William. EDUCATION: Attended New York University. MILITARY: U.S. Coast Guard, 1944-46.

VOCATION: Writer and producer.

CAREER: Also see *WRITINGS* below. PRINCIPAL FILM WORK—Producer, *Save the Tiger,* Paramount, 1972; producer, *The Formula,* Metro-Goldwyn-Mayer/United Artists, 1980.

Photography by Jerry Bauer

STEVE SHAGAN

PRINCIPAL TELEVISION WORK—Episodic: *River of Mystery, Spanish Portrait, Sole Survivor, A Step Out of Line,* 1968-70. Series: Producer, *Tarzan,* 1966.

RELATED CAREER—Film technician, Consolidated Films Inc., New York City, 1952-56; assistant to the publicity director, Paramount Pictures, Hollywood, CA, 1962-63; guest lecturer in screenwriting, University of Southern California, Los Angeles, CA; assistant theatre director.

NON-RELATED CAREER—Technician with RCA, Cape Canaveral, FL, 1956-59; salesman; electrician; advertising copywriter.

WRITINGS: SCREENPLAYS—*Save the Tiger,* Paramount, 1972; *City of Angels* (also known as *Hustle*), Paramount, 1975; *Voyage of the Damned,* AVCO-Embassy, 1977; *The Formula,* Metro-Goldwyn-Mayer/United Artists, 1980. TELEPLAYS—*River of Mystery; Spanish Portrait; Sole Survivor; A Step Out of Line.*

FICTION—*Save the Tiger,* Dial Press, 1972; *City of Angels,* Putnam, 1975; *The Formula,* William Morrow, 1979; *The Circle,* William Morrow, 1982; *The Discovery,* William Morrow, 1984; *Vendetta,* William Morrow, 1986.

AWARDS: Best Drama Award from the Writers Guild of America, 1973; Best Screenplay, Academy Award nomination, 1973, for *Save the Tiger;* Best Screenplay, Academy Award nomination, 1976, for *Voyage of the Damned.*

MEMBER: Writers Guild of America-West (board of directors), Authors Guild of America, Mystery Writers Association.

SIDELIGHTS: Steve Shagan's novel *The Formula* has been translated into French, Italian, Portugese, Chinese, German, Japanese, and Serbo-Croatian.

ADDRESSES OFFICE—c/o Batjac Productions, 9570 Wilshire Boulevard, No. 400, Beverly Hills, CA 90212. AGENT— (Literary) c/o Morton Janklow, William Morris Agency, 151 El Camino Drive, Beverly Hills, CA 90212; (screenplays) c/o Ron Mardigian, William Morris Agency, 151 El Camino Drive, Beverly Hills, CA 90212.

* * *

SHANGE, Ntozake   1948-

PERSONAL: Name is pronounced "En-to-zaki Shong-gay;" born Paulette L. Williams, October 18, 1948, in Trenton, NJ; daughter of Paul T. (a surgeon) and Eloise (a psychiatric social worker and educator) Williams; married second husband, David Murray (a musician), July, 1977. EDUCATION: Barnard College, B.A. (magna cum laude), 1970; University of Southern California, Los Angeles, M.A., American studies, 1973.

VOCATION: Playwright, actress, director, and poet.

CAREER: Also see *WRITINGS* below. PRINCIPAL STAGE APPEARANCES—Lady in Yellow, *For Colored Girls Who Have Considered Suicide/When the Rainbow Is Enuf,* New York Shakespeare Festival (NYSF), Public Theatre, then Booth Theatre, both New York City, 1976; also appeared in *Where the Mississippi Meets the Amazon,* NYSF, Public Theatre, New York City, 1977.

PRINCIPAL STAGE WORK—Director: *The Mighty Gents,* New York Shakespeare Festival, Mobile Theatre, New York City, 1979; *A Photograph: A Study in Cruelty,* Equinox Theatre, New York City, 1979.

PRINCIPAL TELEVISION APPEARANCES—PBS documentary about her own work.

RELATED CAREER—Faculty member: Sonoma State University, 1973-75; Mills College, 1975; City College of New York, 1975; Douglass College, 1978. Guest artist, Alley Theatre, Houston, TX, 1986; performing member, Sounds in Motion dance company.

WRITINGS: PLAYS—*For Colored Girls Who Have Considered Suicide/When the Rainbow Is Enuf,* Studio Rivbea, New York City, 1975, then New York Shakespeare Festival (NYSF), Public Theatre later Booth Theatre, both New York City, 1976, then Syracuse Stage Theatre, Syracuse, NY, 1981, published by Shameless Hussy Press, 1976, and Macmillan, 1976; *A Photograph: A Study of Cruelty,* NYSF, Public Theatre, New York City, 1977; co-author, *Where the Mississippi Meets the Amazon,* NYSF, Public Theatre, New York City, 1977; *Spell #7,* NYSF, 1979; *Boogie-Woogie Landscapes,* NYSF, 1980; (translator) *Mother Courage,* 1980; (adaptor) *Educating Rita,* Alliance Theatre, Atlanta, GA, 1982.

BOOKS—*Sassafras* (novella), published by Shameless Hussy Press, 1976; *Natural Disasters and Other Festive Occasions,* published by Heirs, 1977; *Nappy Edges* (poetry), published by St. Martin's, 1978.

PERIODICALS—Contributor: *Black Scholar, Third World Women, Ms.,* and *Yardbird.*

TELEPLAYS—Specials: *Diana Ross Special,* NBC.

AWARDS: Outer Critics Circle Award, Obie Award from the *Village Voice,* Audelco Award, all 1977, for *For Colored Girls Who Have Considered Suicide/When the Rainbow Is Enuf;* Frank Silvera Writer's Workshop Award, 1978; *Los Angeles Times* Poetry Book Prize, 1981; Guggenheim Fellowship, 1981.

MEMBER: Actors' Equity Association, Dramatists Guild, National Academy of Television Arts and Sciences, Academy of American Poets, American Center for Poets and Writer's, Inc., PEN, New York Feminist Art Guild.

SIDELIGHTS: RECREATIONS—Playing violin; collecting Black memorabilia.

ADDRESSES: HOME—203 W. 23rd Street, No. 1016, New York, NY 10011. OFFICE—c/o Zaki Pony, 1270 Broadway, Suite 503, New York, NY 10001.*

*   *   *

SHANK, Theodore   1929-

PERSONAL: Born February 1, 1929, in Brawley, CA; son of Theodore Benjamin (a farmer) and Anna (Kretz) Shank; married Adele Edling (a playwright), 1967; children: Stan, Kendra. EDUCATION: University of California, Santa Barbara, B.A., 1950;

THEODORE SHANK

University of California, Los Angeles, M.A., 1952; Stanford University, Ph.D., 1956. MILITARY: U.S. Army.

VOCATION: Director and writer.

CAREER: FIRST STAGE WORK—Director, *Barbeque,* Magic Theatre, San Francisco, CA, 1979. PRINCIPAL STAGE WORK—Director: *Winterplay,* Magic Theatre, San Francisco, CA, 1980; *Stuck: A Freeway Comedy,* Magic Theatre, 1981; *Sin, Sex and Cinema, The Grass House,* both Magic Theatre, 1983; *War Horses,* Magic Theatre, 1985; *Sand Castles,* Actors Theatre, Louisville, KY, 1983; *Tumbleweed,* Los Angeles Theatre Center, Los Angeles, CA, 1986; *Electricity,* Minnesota Opera, MN, 1988.

RELATED CAREER—Founder, dramatic arts department, University of California, Davis.

WRITINGS: PLAYS—*Wild Indian,* Victory Gardens Theatre, Chicago, IL, 1985, then Magic Theatre, San Francisco, CA, 1986; *Electricity,* Minnesota Opera, MN, 1988. Also wrote *Codex* and *Dubliners* (opera), both 1987.

NON-FICTION—*The Art of Dramatic Art,* published in 1969; *Theatre in Real Time,* published in Torino, Italy, 1980; *Contemporary Experimental Theatre,* published in Frankfurt, West Germany, 1981; *American Alternative Theatre,* published in London and New York, both 1982.

AWARDS: Dramatists Guild/CBS New Play Award, 1985, Dramatists Guild/CBS Stage Two Award, 1986, both for *Wild Indian.*

MEMBER: Society of Stage Directors and Choreographers, Dramatists Guild, International Federation for Theatre Research.

ADDRESSES: HOME—1417 Shotwell Street, San Francisco, CA 94110; 42A Chalcot Road, London NW1 8LS, England. OFFICE—c/o Department of Dramatic Art, University of California, Davis, CA 95616.

*   *   *

SHAPIRO, Ken   1943-

PERSONAL: Born in 1943, in Brooklyn, NY. EDUCATION: Graduated from California State University, Northridge.

VOCATION: Producer and screenwriter.

CAREER: Also see *WRITINGS* below. PRINCIPAL TELEVISION WORK—All as producer. Series: *Cousteau's People of the Sea,* PBS. Specials: *Golden Globe Awards,* 1979, 1983-88; *Spectacular London,* Showtime; *Mumbo Jumbo, It's Magic,* HBO; *Sharks: The Death Machine,* NBC; *The Great Lounge Comedians,* cable; *An Evening with Alan King,* cable; *An Evening with Shecky Greene,* cable; *An Evening with Mort Sahl,* cable; *An Evening with Phyllis Diller,* cable; *An Evening with Henny Youngman,* cable. Videos: *Tommy Chong Roast; Playmate Playoffs; Cowboys of the Saturday Matinee.*

PRINCIPAL STAGE WORK—Producer of celebrity personal appearances Anthony Newley, Milton Berle, Wayne Newton, Barbara Mandrell, Tom Jones, Mel Tillis, Flip Wilson, and Lou Rawles.

WRITINGS: TELEPLAYS—Series: *Johnny Mann's Stand Up and Cheer,* syndicated, 1971-73; *TV's Bloopers and Practical Jokes,* NBC, 1985; also *Cousteau's People of the Sea,* PBS; *Love American Style,* ABC; *Playboy after Dark,* Playboy; *Hollywood Square,* syndicated; *The Newlywed Game,* syndicated; *Lorenzo and Henrietta Music Show,* CBS. Specials: *New Year's Rockin' Eve,* ABC, 1984-88; *Golden Globe Awards,* syndicated, 1979, 1983-88; also *America Versus the World Circus Challenge,* NBC; *Highlights of the Ringling Brothers and Barnum & Bailey Circus,* NBC; *The Sixth Annual International Circus Festival of Monte Carlo,* CBS; *TV's Censored Bloopers,* NBC; *More TV Censored Bloopers,* NBC; *TV Censored Bloopers,* numbers 3, 4, and 5, all NBC; *ABC Fall Saturday Morning Preview Party,* ABC; *ABC's Pac Preview Party,* ABC; *Best of Broadway,* Showtime; *Spectacular London,* Showtime; *Mumbo Jumbo It's Magic,* HBO; *The American Music Awards,* ABC; *An Evening with Alan King,* cable; *An Evening with Shecky Greene,* cable; *An Evening with Mort Sahl,* cable; *An Evening with Phyllis Diller,* cable; *An Evening with Henny Youngman,* cable; *The Great Lounge Comedians,* cable. Videos: *Tommy Chong Roast; Playmate Playoffs; Cowboys of the Saturday Matinee.*

MEMBER: Writers Guild of America-West.

ADDRESSES: OFFICE—c/o Writers Guild of America-West, 8955 Beverly Boulevard, Los Angeles, CA 90048.

*   *   *

SHARIF, Omar   1932-

PERSONAL: Born Michael Shalhoub, April 10, 1932, in Alexandria, Egypt; son of Joseph and Claire (Saada) Shalhoub; married Faten Hamama (an actress), February 5, 1955; children: son Tarek. EDUCATION: Attended Victoria College, Cairo, Egypt. RELIGION: Moslem.

VOCATION: Actor and writer.

CAREER: FILM DEBUT—*The Blazing Sun,* Talhamy, 1953. PRINCIPAL FILM APPEARANCES—Appeared in twenty-four Egyptian films and two French films, 1953-1962; *Lawrence of Arabia,* Columbia, 1962; *The Fall of the Roman Empire,* Paramount, 1964; *Behold a Pale Horse,* Columbia, 1964; *The Fabulous Adventures of Marco Polo,* 1964; *Doctor Zhivago,* Metro-Goldwyn-Mayer (MGM), 1965; *Genghis Khan,* 1965; *The Yellow Rolls Royce,* MGM, 1965; *The Night of the Generals,* Columbia, 1967; *More Than a Miracle,* Italian, 1967; *Cinderella—Italian Style,* MGM, 1967; *Funny Girl,* Columbia, 1968; *Mayerling,* MGM, 1969; *MacKenna's Gold,* Columbia, 1969; *The Appointment,* MGM, 1969; *Che!,* Twentieth Century-Fox, 1969; *The Last Valley,* Cinerama, 1971; *The Horsemen,* Columbia, 1971; *Le Casse,* 1971; *The Burglars,* Columbia, 1972; *The Mysterious Island of Captain Nemo,* Cinerama, 1974; *The Tamarind Seed,* AVCO-Embassy, 1974; *Juggernaut,* United Artists, 1974; *Funny Lady,* Columbia, 1975; *Crime and Passion,* 1976; *The Pink Panther Strikes Again,* United Artists, 1976; *Ashanti,* 1979; *S.H.E.,* 1979; *Bloodline,* 1979; *Oh, Heavenly Dog,* Twentieth Century-Fox, 1980; *Ace Up My Sleeve,* 1980; *The Baltimore Bullet,* AVCO-Embassy, 1980; *Green Ice,* 1981; *Return to Eden,* 1982; *Patience,* 1983; *Top Secret,* Paramount, 1984.

PRINCIPAL TELEVISION APPEARANCES—Mini-Series: *The Far Pavilions,* Home Box Office, 1984; *Peter the Great,* NBC, 1986; Czar Nicholas II, *Anastasia: The Story of Anna,* NBC, 1986. Movies: *Harem,* ABC, 1987.

PRINCIPAL STAGE APPEARANCES—*The Sleeping Prince,* England, 1983.

NON-RELATED CAREER—Formerly a salesman for a lumber importing firm.

WRITINGS: NON-FICTION—*The Eternal Male* (autobiography), 1977; *Omar Sharif's Life in Bridge,* Faber & Faber, 1983.

ARTICLES—Author of syndicated columns on bridge in newspapers and periodicals.

VIDEOS—*Play Bridge with Omar Sharif* (instructional), Best Film & Video Corporation, 1987.

AWARDS: Best Supporting Actor, Golden Globe Award, 1962, for *Lawrence of Arabia;* Best Newcomer, Golden Globe Award, 1963.

MEMBER: Screen Actors Guild, American Federation of Television and Radio Artists.

SIDELIGHTS: CTFT notes that Omar Shariff is an acknowleged international bridge expert. He also enjoys horse racing.

ADDRESSES: AGENT—William Morris Agency, 151 El Camino Drive, Beverly Hills, CA 90212.*

*   *   *

SHARKEY, Ray   1952-

PERSONAL: Born in 1952, in Brooklyn, NY.

VOCATION: Actor.

CAREER: FILM DEBUT—*Hot Tomorrows*, 1976. PRINCIPAL FILM APPEARANCES—*Stunts*, New Line Cinema, 1977; *Paradise Alley*, Universal, 1978; *Who'll Stop the Rain?*, United Artists, 1978; *Heart Beat*, Warner Brothers, 1979; *Willie and Phil*, Twentieth Century-Fox, 1980; *The Idolmaker*, United Artists, 1980; *Love and Money*, Paramount, 1982; *Some Kind of Hero*, Paramount, 1982; *Body Rock*, New World, 1984; *duBEAT-e-o*, 1984; *Hellhole*, Arkoff International, 1985; *Wise Guys*, Metro-Goldwyn-Mayer/United Artists, 1986; *No Mercy*, Tri-Star, 1986.

PRINCIPAL TELEVISION APPEARANCES—Episodic: *Kojak*, CBS; *Police Story*, CBS; *Barney Miller*, ABC; Sonny Steelgrave, *Wise Guy*, CBS, 1987. Movies: *Behind Enemy Lines*, 1985.

MEMBER: Screen Actors Guild, American Federation of Television and Radio Artists.

ADDRESSES: AGENT—McCartt, Oreck, Barrett, 10390 Santa Monica Blvd., Suite 310, Los Angeles, CA 90025.*

*   *   *

SHARPE, Cornelia   1943-

PERSONAL: Born October 18, 1943; daughter of Warner Jack, Jr. (a dental supplier) and Evelyn (a dental assistant and secretary; maiden name, Horne) Sharpe; married Martin Bregman (a produc-

CORNELIA SHARPE

er); children: Marissa Cornelia. EDUCATION: Trained for the stage with Peggy Feury and Lee Strasberg; studied voice with Colin Romoff and Maurice Jampol; studied dance with Thelma J. Baggs.

VOCATION: Actress, dancer, and singer.

CAREER: STAGE DEBUT—Adelia, *The House of Bernarda Alba*. PRINCIPAL STAGE APPEARANCES—*Play It Again, Sam*, Broadhurst Theatre, New York City, 1970.

FILM DEBUT—*Kansas City Bomber*, Metro-Goldwyn-Mayer, 1971. PRINCIPAL FILM APPEARANCES—*Serpico*, DeLaurentiis Films, 1974; *The Reincarnation of Peter Proud*, AVCO-Embassy, 1975; *The Next Man*, Allied Artists, 1976; also appeared in *Open Season*, 1974.

PRINCIPAL TELEVISION APPEARANCES—Series: Linda Allen, *Cover Girls*, NBC, 1977; Lavinia Keane, *S*H*E**, CBS, 1980.

AWARDS: Best Actress, Donatello Award, 1976, for *The Next Man*.

MEMBER: Screen Actors Guild.

ADDRESSES: OFFICE—641 Lexington Avenue, New York, NY 10022.

*   *   *

SHAWN, Dick   1929-1987

PERSONAL: Born Richard Schulefand, December 1, 1929 (some sources say 1923), in Buffalo, NY; died April 17, 1987, of a heart attack in San Diego, CA; children: one son, three daughters. EDUCATION: Attended the University of Miami, FL.

VOCATION: Actor and comedian.

CAREER: BROADWAY DEBUT—(As Richy Shawn) Milton Rubin, *For Heaven's Sake, Mother!*, Belasco Theatre, 1948. PRINCIPAL STAGE APPEARANCES—Member of company, *Betty Hutton and Her All-Star International Show*, Palace Theatre, New York City, 1953; Emile Magis, *The Egg*, Cort Theatre, New York City, 1962; Pseudolus, Prologus, *A Funny Thing Happened on the Way to the Forum*, Majestic Theatre, New York City, 1964; Peter, *Peterpat*, Longacre Theatre, New York City, 1965; Byron Prong, *Fade Out—Fade In*, Mark Hellinger Theatre, New York City, 1965; Yoni, Solomon, *I'm Solomon*, Mark Hellinger Theatre, 1968; Gordon Miller, *Room Service*, Edison Theatre, New York City, 1970; Tandy, *Steambath*, Truck and Warehouse Theatre, New York City, 1970; Major Upshaw, *Stag at Bay*, Hartman Theatre, Stamford, CT, 1976; Mendel, *The World of Sholem Aleichem*, Roundabout Theatre, New York City, 1976; *The Second Greatest Entertainer in the Whole Wide World* (one-man show) Promenade Theatre, New York City, 1977. Also appeared in *The Big House*, Yale Repertory Theatre, New Haven CT, 1971; *Halloween*, Bucks County Playhouse, New Hope, PA, 1972; *A Musical Jubilee*, St. James Theatre, New York City, 1975; *Bananas and Drums*, Westport Country Playhouse, Westport, CT, 1976; *Hey, Look Me Over!*, Avery Fisher Hall, New York City, 1981.

MAJOR TOURS—*The Second Greatest Entertainer in the Whole Wide World* (one-man show) U.S. cities, 1985.

PRINCIPAL FILM APPEARANCES—*The Opposite Sex*, Metro-Goldwyn-Mayer (MGM), 1956; *Wake Me When It's Over*, Twentieth-Century Fox, 1960; *Wizard of Baghdad*, Twentieth Century-Fox, 1961; *It's a Mad, Mad, Mad, Mad World*, United Artists, 1963; *A Very Special Favor*, Universal, 1965; *What Did You Do in the War, Daddy?*, United Artists, 1966; *Penelope*, MGM, 1966; *Way, Way Out*, Twentieth Century-Fox, 1966; *The Producers*, Embassy, 1968; *The Happy Ending*, Paramount, 1969; *Looking Up*, Levitt-Pickman, 1977; *Love at First Bite*, American International, 1979; *Young Warriors*, Cannon Films, 1983; *Angel*, New World, 1984; *Water*, Atlantic 1984. Appeared in *The Secret Diary of Sigmund Freud*, 1984; *Beer*, 1985; *The Check Is in the Mail*, 1985; *The Perils of P.K.*, 1986; *Maid to Order*, 1987; also *The Goony Birds; The Solid Gold Show; Goodbye Cruel World; Rented Lips.*

PRINCIPAL TELEVISION APPEARANCES—Episodic: *The Jimmy Dean Show*, ABC, 1963; *Love Boat*, ABC; *Legmen*, NBC, 1984; *The Fall Guy*, ABC; *Tales from the Darkside*, syndicated; *St. Elsewhere*, NBC; *Amazing Stories*, NBC; "The Emperor's New Clothes," *Faerie Tale Theatre*, 1984; *Hail to the Chief*. Series: *Mary*, CBS, 1978; *Mr. and Mrs. Dracula*. Pilot: Marshall Bing Bell, *Evil Roy Slade*, NBC, 1972; *You're Just Like Your Father*, 1976. Movies: Deke Edwards, *Fast Friends*, NBC, 1979. Specials: *Max Liebman Presents*, NBC, 1954-56; *Comic Relief*, HBO, 1986.

WRITINGS: SCREENPLAYS—Co-author, *Goodbye Cruel World.*

MEMBER: Actors' Equity Association, Screen Actors Guild, American Guild of Variety Artists, American Federation of Television and Radio Artists.

OBITUARIES AND OTHER SOURCES: *Variety*, 22, 1987.*

*   *   *

SHEA, John

PERSONAL: Full name, John Victor Shea III; born April 14, in North Conway, NH; son of John Victor, Jr. (an educator) and Elizabeth Mary (Fuller) Shea; married Laura Wilson Pettibone (a photographer), June 19, 1971; children: Jake Pettibone. EDUCATION: Bates College, B.F.A., drama, 1970; Yale School of Drama, M.F.A., directing, 1973.

VOCATION: Actor.

CAREER: STAGE DEBUT—Furniture removal man, *Juno and the Paycock*, Straight Wharf Theatre, Nantucket, MA, 1968, for thirty performances. BROADWAY DEBUT—Avigdor, *Yentl*, Eugene O'Neill Theatre, 1975, for two hundred thirty-four performances. LONDON DEBUT—Ned Weeks, *The Normal Heart*, Albery Theatre, 1986, for seventy performances. PRINCIPAL STAGE APPEARANCES—Paris, *Romeo and Juliet*, Circle in the Square, New York City, 1976; Stephen Hurt, *The Sorrows of Stephen*, New York Shakespeare Festival, Public Theatre, New York City, 1979; Don Sherman, *American Days*, Manhattan Theatre Club, New York City, 1981; *The Dining Room*, Playwrights Horizons, then Astor Place Theatre, both New York City, 1982; Michael Trent, *End of the World*, Music Box Theatre, New York City, 1984. Also appeared in *Long Day's Journey into Night*, Goodman Theatre,

Chicago, IL; *Battering Ram, Safe House, The Master and Margarita*, all New York City.

TELEVISION DEBUT—Joseph, *The Nativity*, ABC, 1978. PRINCIPAL TELEVISION APPEARANCES—Mini-Series: Terry Garrigan, *The Last Convertible*, NBC, 1981; Robert F. Kennedy, *Kennedy*, NBC, 1983. Movies: James Cookman, *Family Reunion*, NBC, 1981; Karl Hoffman, *Hitler's SS: Portrait of Evil*, NBC, 1985; Michael O'Donnell, *A Case of Deadly Force*, CBS, 1986. Also appeared in *Coast to Coast*, BBC, 1986; *Impossible Spy*, BBC, then HBO, both 1987.

FILM DEBUT—Emery Cole, *Hussy*, Kendon Films, 1980. PRINCIPAL FILM APPEARANCES—Charles Horman, *Missing . . .*, Universal, 1982; Hemdale, *Once We Were Dreamers*, Orion, 1987; also appeared in *Windy City*, Warner Brothers, 1984; *Lune De Miel* (*Honeymoon*), AAA Distributors, 1986; *A New Life*, Paramount, 1988; and *Stealing Home.*

AWARDS: Theatre World Award, 1975, for *Yentl;* Best Actor, Drama Desk Award nomination, 1981, for *American Days;* Best Actor, Montreal Film Festival, 1985, for *Windy City.*

MEMBER: Actors' Equity Association, Screen Actors Guild, American Federation of Television and Radio Artists.

ADDRESSES: AGENT—c/o International Creative Management, Inc., 40 W. 57th Street, New York, NY 10019.

JOHN SHEA

SHIRE, David   1937-

PERSONAL: Full name, David Lee Shire; born July 3, 1937, in Buffalo, NY; son of Irving Daniel and Esther Miriam (Sheinberg) Shire; married Talia Rose Coppola (an actress; professional name, Talia Shire), March 29, 1970, (divorced); married Didi Conn (an actress), February 11, 1984; children: (first marriage) Matthew Orlando. EDUCATION: Yale University, B.A., 1959. RELIGION: Jewish. MILITARY: U.S. Army National Guard, 1960-66.

VOCATION: Composer.

WRITINGS: MUSICAL SCORES—*The Sap of Life,* Sheridan Square Theatre, New York City, 1961; *Graham Crackers,* Upstairs at the Downstairs, New York City, 1962; *The Unknown Soldier and His Wife,* Vivian Beaumont Theatre, 1967; *Love Match,* Ahmanson Theatre, Los Angeles, CA, 1970; *Starting Here, Starting Now,* Barbarann Theatre, New York City, 1977; *Baby,* Ethel Barrymore Theatre, New York City, 1983. Also wrote the score for *How Do You Do, I Love You,* 1968; *Cyrano, The Grand Tour,* both produced by the Yale Dramatic Association.

FILM SCORES—*One More Train to Rob,* Universal, 1971; *Summertree,* Columbia, 1971; *Skin Game,* Warner Brothers, 1971; *Drive, He Said,* Columbia, 1972; *To Find a Man,* Columbia, 1972; (adaptor) *Steelyard Blues,* Warner Brothers, 1973; *Two People,* Universal, 1973; *Showdown,* Universal, 1973; *Class of '44,* Warner Brothers, 1973; *The Conversation,* Paramount, 1974; *The Taking of Pelham 1-2-3,* United Artists, 1974; (adaptor) *The Fortune,* Columbia, 1975; *Farewell, My Lovely,* AVCO-Embassy, 1975; *The Hindenburg,* Universal, 1975; *Harry and Walter Go to New*

DAVID SHIRE

York, Columbia, 1976; *All the President's Men,* Warner Brothers, 1976; *The Big Bus,* Paramount, 1976; (adaptor) *Saturday Night Fever,* Paramount, 1977; *Straight Time,* Warner Brothers, 1978; *The Promise,* Universal, 1979; *Old Boyfriends,* AVCO-Embassy, 1979; *Fast Break,* Columbia, 1979; *Norma Rae,* Twentieth Century-Fox, 1979; *The Night the Lights Went Out in Georgia,* AVCO-Embassy, 1981; *Only When I Laugh,* Columbia, 1981; *Paternity,* Paramount, 1981; *The Earthling,* Filmways, 1981; *Max Dugan Returns,* Twentieth Century-Fox, 1982; *The World According to Garp,* Warner Brothers, 1982; *2010,* Metro-Goldwyn-Mayer/United Artists, 1984; *Oh, God! You Devil,* Warner Brothers, 1984; *Return to Oz,* Buena Vista, 1985; *Short Circuit,* Tri-Star, 1986; *'night, Mother,* Universal, 1986; *Backfire,* ITC, 1988.

TELEVISION SCORES—Episodic: *CBS Playhouse,* CBS; *It Takes a Thief,* ABC; *The Virginian,* NBC; *Alias Smith and Jones,* ABC; *Getting Together,* ABC; *Love Story,* NBC; *Amazing Stories,* NBC; Series: *Tales of the Unexpected,* NBC; *Sirota's Court,* NBC; *Alice,* CBS; *The Practice,* NBC; *Joe and Sons,* CBS; *Three for the Road,* CBS; *Lucas Tanner,* NBC; *McCloud,* NBC; *Sarge,* NBC. Mini-Series: *Echos in the Darkness,* CBS, 1987. Pilots: *Lucas Tanner,* NBC, 1974; *The Healers,* NBC, 1974; also *Man about Town,* ABC. Movies: *McCloud: Who Killed Miss U.S.A.?,* NBC, 1970; *Marriage: Year One,* NBC, 1971; *Harpy,* CBS, 1971; *The Impatient Heart,* NBC, 1971; *The Priest Killer,* NBC, 1971; *Isn't It Shocking?,* ABC, 1973; *Killer Bees,* ABC, 1974; *Tell Me Where It Hurts,* CBS, 1974; *Sidekicks,* CBS, 1974; *The Tribe,* ABC, 1974; *The Godchild,* ABC, 1974; *Winner Take All,* NBC, 1975; *Oregon Trail,* NBC, 1976; *McNaughton's Daughter,* NBC, 1976; *Amelia Earhart,* NBC, 1976; *Raid on Entebbe,* NBC, 1977; *Something for Joey,* CBS, 1977; *The Greatest Thing That Almost Happened,* CBS, 1977; *The Storyteller,* NBC, 1977; *The Defection of Simas Kudirka,* CBS, 1978; *Daddy, I Don't Like This,* CBS, 1978; *Time Flyer* (also known as *The Blue Yonder*), ABC, 1986; *Do You Remember Love?,* CBS, 1985; *Promise,* CBS, 1986; *Convicted,* ABC, 1986; also *Chris,* PBS; *Three Faces of Love; Second Face; If I Had a Million; Three for the Road; The Clinic.*

SONGS—(Words and music with Richard Maltby, Jr.) "Autumn," recorded by Barbra Streisand and by Andy Williams; (words and music with Maltby) "Having Myself a Fine Time" (theme from *Summertree*), recorded by Hamilton Camp; (music only; words by Alan and Marilyn Bergman) "I'll Never Say Goodbye" (theme from *The Promise*), recorded by Melissa Manchester, by Judy Collins, and by Debby Boone; (music only; words by Norman Gimble) "It Goes Like It Goes" (theme from *Norma Rae*), recorded by Jennifer Warnes and by Glenn Campbell; (music only; words by Maltby) "No More Songs for Me," recorded by Barbra Streisand and by Lainie Kazan; (words and music with Bob Goldstein) "Washington Square," recorded by Marily May and by The Village Stompers; (music only; words by Carol Conners) "With You I'm Born Again" (theme from *Fast Break*), recorded by Billy Preston and Syreeta and by Johnny Mathis; "And So You Go," "Beautiful Changes," and "First Thing in the Morning," all recorded by Kathe Green; "Time Will Tell," recorded by Lani Hall; "Another Way," recorded by Dennis Weaver; "I'd Rather Be Rich," recorded by Robert Goulet and by Pearl Baily; "Take a Look Around," recorded by Tim Morgan and by Cliff Richard; "It's So Easy" and "Please Stay," both recorded by Billy Preston and Syreeta; "Halfway Home" (theme from *The Earthling*), recorded by Maureen McGovern; "Only When I Laugh," recorded by Brenda Lee; "Starting Here, Starting Now" and "The Morning After," both recorded by Barbra Streisand; "What about Today?," recorded by Barbra Streisand and by Shirley Bassey. Also wrote "Nobody's Perfect" (theme from *Harry and Walter Go to New*

York); "There's a New Girl in Town" (theme from *Alice*); "Baby Talk" (theme from *Paternity*); and "I Need You Strong for Me."

AWARDS: Best Original Score, Grammy Award nomination, 1977, for *Starting Here, Starting Now;* Emmy Award nomination, 1977, for *Raid on Entebbe;* Emmy Award nomination, 1978, for *The Defection of Simus Kudirka;* Best Original Song, Academy Award nomination, 1979, for "I'll Never Say Goodbye" (theme from *The Promise*); Best Original Song, Academy Award, 1979, for "It Goes Like It Goes" (theme from *Norma Rae*); Best Musical, Best Musical Score, both Antoinette Perry Award nominations, 1984, for *Baby;* Emmy Award nomination, 1985, for *Do You Remember Love?.*

MEMBER: Composers and Lyricists Guild of America, American Federation of Musicians, Broadcast Music, Inc. (BMI), Academy of Motion Picture Arts and Sciences, National Academy of Recording Arts and Sciences, Academy of Television Arts and Sciences.

ADDRESSES: AGENT—Gorfaine/Schwartz Agency, 3815 W. Olive Avenue, Suite 202, Burbank, CA 91505.

*   *   *

SHORT, Martin

PERSONAL: Born c. 1951; son of Charles Patrick (a steel company executive) and Olive (a violinist) Short; married Nancy Dolman (an actress); children: Katherine, Oliver. EDUCATION: Graduated from McMaster University, with social work major, 1972.

CAREER: STAGE DEBUT—*Godspell,* Toronto, ON, Canada, 1972. PRINCIPAL STAGE APPEARANCES—In revues and cabaret in Toronto, 1973-78, including as a member of Second City comedy troupe, 1977-78.

PRINCIPAL TELEVISION APPEARANCES—Series: Tucker Kerwin, *The Associates,* ABC, 1979, then 1980; Neal Stryker, *I'm a Big Girl Now,* ABC, 1980-81; *SCTV Network 90,* NBC, 1982-84; *Saturday Night Live,* NBC, 1985-86. Movies: Shucky Forme, "All's Well That Ends Strange," *Really Weird Tales,* 1987.

PRINCIPAL FILM APPEARANCES—Ned Nederlander, *Three Amigos,* Orion, 1986; hypochondriachal store clerk, *Innerspace,* Warner Brothers, 1987; also, as a salesman, *Cross My Heart,* 1987.

SIDELIGHTS: Comedian Martin Short has entertained audiences in the United States and his native Canada with his creation of such characters as the nerdy Ed Grimley and the lounge lizard Jackie Rogers, Jr., as well as hilarious impersonations of show business personalities ranging from Katharine Hepburn to Jerry Lewis. Having trained for a career in social work, Short hesitated before joining the Toronto unit of the famed Second City comedy troupe; he told Eric Pooley (*New York,* January 14, 1985), "Somehow, I felt a little funny about doing comedy for a living . . . ."

ADDRESSES: HOME—Pacific Palisades, CA.*

*   *   *

SHUKAT, Scott   1937-

PERSONAL: Born Sanford A. Shukat, March 9, 1937, in Brooklyn, NY; son of Harvy (in sales) and Florence (in sales; maiden

Photography by Susannah Gold

SCOTT SHUKAT

name, Halpern) Shukat; married Evelyn Monroe (a doctor), March 21, 1982; children: Jonathan Max. EDUCATION: School for the Performing Arts, 1950-54; Columbia College, B.A., music and history, 1958; trained for the stage at the Herbert Berghof Studios and with Sanford Meisner. MILITARY: U.S. Army, 1959-60.

VOCATION: Talent and literary agent, music publisher, and performer.

CAREER: Assistant agent, William Morris Agency, New York City, handling budgets for such New York City-based television shows as *Jimmy Dean Show,* ABC, *Sammy Davis, Jr. Show,* NBC, *Mitch Miller Show,* CBS, and *The Doctors,* ABC, all 1964-66; agent, William Morris Agency, handling recording contracts, artists, motion picture music, and music publishing, 1966-72; founder, Shukat Company, Ltd., a literary, personal management, and music publishing business which has developed such projects as: *Free to Be . . . You and Me* (written by clients Stephen Lawrence and Carol Hall) for ABC television, Bell Records (now Arista Records), and published as a book; co-publisher of score to *The Best Little Whorehouse in Texas* (written by client Carol Hall); produced (with clients Carol and Bruce Hart) *Sooner or Later* for ABC television, CBS records, and published by Avon who also published its sequel, *Waiting Games.* Listed among clients are composer and lyricist Alan Menken (*Little Shop of Horrors*), writer and producer Sherry Cober (creator of *Kate and Allie*), author Jane Waterhouse (*Playing for Keeps*), and record producer John Simon (*The Band* by the Band, *Jackrabbit Slim* by Steve Forbert), as well as the composers Lee Pockriss Skip Kenon, David Spencer, Isaiah Sheffer, and Anne Croswell, writer and lyricist David Axelrod, directors Robert Nigro and Bob Billig, and choreographers D.J. Giagni and Edie Cowan.

PRINCIPAL CABARET APPEARANCES—Playboy Club, Chicago; Jilly's, New York City.

MEMBER: Society of Authors Representatives.

ADDRESSES: OFFICE—Shukat Company Ltd., 340 W. 55th Street, New York, NY 10019.

*   *   *

SILLS, Paul

PERSONAL: Born in Chicago, IL; son of Viola Spolin (an improvisational theatre teacher and writer). EDUCATION: Attended the University of Chicago and Bristol University; studied improvisational theatre with his mother.

VOCATION: Director and writer.

CAREER: BROADWAY DEBUT—Director, *From the Second City,* Royale Theatre, 1961. PRINCIPAL STAGE WORK—Director unless indicated: *Seacoast of Bohemia, Alarums and Excursions,* both Square East Theatre, Chicago, IL, 1962; *To the Water Tower, When the Owl Screams,* both Square East Theatre, 1963; *Open Season at the Second City,* Chicago, IL, 1964; *Dynamite Tonite,* Second City Improvisational Company, Chicago, IL, 1964, then 1967; *Metamorphoses,* Yale Repertory Theatre, New Haven, CT, 1969, then Mark Taper Forum, Los Angeles, CA, 1971, later Ambassador Theatre, New York City, 1971; *Story Theatre,* Mark Taper Forum, Los Angeles, CA, then Ambassador Theatre, New York City, 1971; *Tales of the Hasidim,* New York Shakespeare Festival (NYSF), Public Theatre, New York City, 1977. Also directed *The American Revolution, Part 1,* Washington, DC, 1973; and *Sweet Bloody Liberty,* 1975.

RELATED CAREER—Co-founder, the Improvisational Playwright's Theatre Club, Chicago, IL, 1953, later known as Second City Improvisational Company, 1957.

WRITINGS: PLAYS—*Metamorphoses,* Yale Repertory Theatre, New Haven, CT, 1969; (with Arnold Weinstein) *The American Revolution, Part 1,* Washington, DC, 1973; (adaptor) *Tales of the Hasidim,* NYSF, Public Theatre, New York City, 1977.

AWARDS: Best Director, Antoinette Perry Award, 1971, for *Story Theatre.*

MEMBER: Actors' Equity Association, Society of Stage Directors and Choreographers.

ADDRESSES: OFFICE—c/o New York Shakespeare Festival, 425 Lafayette Street, New York, NY 10003.*

*   *   *

SIMMONS, J.K.   1955-

PERSONAL: Full name, Jonathan Kimble Simmons; born January 9, 1955, in Detroit, MI; son of Donald William (a college professor) and Patricia (an administrator; maiden name, Kimble) Simmons. EDUCATION: University of Montana, B.A., music, 1978; also

studied theatre and music at Ohio University and Ohio State University; trained for the stage with Hal Holden at the Herbert Berghof Studios and with Jacqueline Barton in New York City; studied voice with Mario Alch, Esther England, and John Mount.

VOCATION: Actor and singer.

CAREER: PRINCIPAL STAGE APPEARANCES—El Gallo, *The Fantasticks,* featured singer, *Five by Five,* both A Contemporary Theatre, Seattle, WA, 1981; Sailor Murphy, *Pal Joey,* Curtis, Vincentio, *The Taming of the Shrew,* Henrik, *An Enemy of the People,* Brannigan, *Guys and Dolls,* all Seattle Repertory Theatre, Seattle, WA, 1984-85. Also appeared as Huntington, *The Rise of David Levinsky,* George Street Playhouse, New Brunswick, NJ; Christian Brent, *Peg o' My Heart,* American Theatre Festival, VT; Miles Gloriosus, *A Funny Thing Happened on the Way to the Forum,* Alliance Theatre, Atlanta, GA; Carl-Magnus, *A Little Night Music,* Studio Arena Theatre, Buffalo, NY; Steve, *A Streetcar Named Desire,* Starkey, *Peter Pan,* both Pennsylvania Centre Stage; Osgood, *Sugar,* Shepard Henderson, *Bell, Book and Candle,* both Cirque Dinner Theatre; John the Baptist, *Godspell,* El Gallo, *The Fantasticks,* both Avenue Act One Theatre; Roy, *Lone Star,* Carl-Magnus, *A Little Night Music,* Johnny Brown, *The Unsinkable Molly Brown,* Fred, Petruchio, *Kiss Me, Kate,* all Bigfork Summer Playhouse; C.M. "Kid" Russell, *Cowboy,* Sun Valley Opera House.

MAJOR TOURS—Provost, B.D., Roland, *Doonesbury,* U.S. cities, 1984.

J.K. SIMMONS

PRINCIPAL TELEVISION APPEARANCES—Movies: Officer Miller, *Popeye Doyle,* NBC, 1986.

AWARDS: Best Actor award from the Bigfork Summer Theatre, 1978, 1979, and 1980.

MEMBER: Actors' Equity Association, Screen Actors Guild.

ADDRESSES: AGENT—c/o Sheldon Lubleiner, Professional Artists, 513 W. 54th Street, New York, NY 10019.

*　　*　　*

SIMPSON, Don　1945-

PERSONAL: Born October 29, 1945, in Anchorage, AK; father, a hunting guide. EDUCATION: Graduated from the University of Oregon, 1967. RELIGION: Fundamentalist Southern Baptist.

VOCATION: Producer, production executive, and writer.

CAREER: PRINCIPAL FILM WORK—Production supervisor in charge of marketing for Warner Brothers where he oversaw the marketing of such films as *Performance,* 1970; *A Clockwork Orange, Billy Jack,* both 1971; *Mean Streets,* 1973. Head of production at Paramount Pictures Corporation where he supervised production of such films as *American Gigolo, Little Darlings,* both 1980; *Urban Cowboy,* 1981; *An Officer and a Gentleman, 48 Hours,* both 1982. Producer (all with Jerry Bruckheimer): *Flashdance,* Paramount, 1983; *Thief of Hearts,* Paramount, 1984; *Beverly Hills Cop,* Paramount, 1984; *Top Gun,* Paramount, 1986; *Beverly Hills Cop II,* Paramount, 1987.

RELATED CAREER—Account executive, Jack Wodell Agency, San Francisco, CA, supervising the marketing of Warner Brothers films; marketing executive specializing in youth market, Warner Brothers, 1971; production executive, Paramount Pictures, 1975, then vice-president of production, 1977, senior vice-president of production, 1980; president, worldwide production for Paramount Pictures, 1981; formed partnership with Jerry Bruckheimer, Simpson-Bruckheimer Productions, 1982.

WRITINGS: SCREENPLAYS—*Aloha Bobby and Rose,* Columbia, 1975; *Cannonball,* New World Pictures, 1975.

AWARDS: Phi Beta Kappa, University of Oregon, 1967.

ADDRESSES: OFFICE—c/o Simpson-Bruckheimer Productions, Paramount Pictures, 5555 Melrose Avenue, Los Angeles, CA 90038.

*　　*　　*

SLOAN, Michael　1946-

PERSONAL: Born October 14, 1946, in New York, NY; son of Michael Nelson (a theatrical producer) and Paula (a theatrical producer; maiden name, Stone) Sloan. EDUCATION: Attended the Arts Educational Trust.

VOCATION: Writer and producer.

*CAREER:*PRINCIPAL TELEVISION WORK—Series: Supervising producer, *McCloud,* NBC, 1976; associate executive producer, *Quincy, M.E.,* NBC, 1977; supervising producer, *The Hardy Boys Mysteries,* ABC, 1977-79; supervising producer, *The Nancy Drew Mysteries,* ABC, 1977-79; supervising producer, *Sword of Justice,* NBC, 1979; supervising producer, *Battlestar Gallactica,* ABC, 1980; executive producer, *B.J. and the Bear,* NBC, 1979-81; creator and executive producer, *The Master,* NBC, 1984. Mini-Series: Supervising producer, *Evening in Byzantium,* syndicated, 1978. Pilots: Creator and executive producer, *The Equalizer,* CBS, 1985. Movies: Executive producer, *The Return of the Man from U.N.C.L.E.,* CBS, 1983; creator and executive producer, *Riviera,* ABC, 1985; executive producer, *The Return of the Six Million Dollar Man and the Bionic Woman,* ABC, 1987.

PRINCIPAL FILM WORK—Executive producer: *Hunted,* Columbia/Warner Brothers, 1971; *Assassin,* Columbia/Warner Brothers, 1972; *Moments,* Columbia/Warner Brothers, 1973; co-producer, *Caller,* Empire, 1987.

PRINCIPAL STAGE WORK—Director, *Wait until Dark,* Burbank Theatre Guild, 1986.

WRITINGS: PLAYS—*Underground,* produced in London, England, 1983. TELEPLAYS—Series: Eight episodes, *Harry O,* ABC, 1975; five episodes, *McCloud,* NBC, 1976; four episodes, *Quincy, M.E.,* NBC, 1977; eighteen episodes, *The Hardy Boys Mysteries,* ABC, 1977-79; four episodes, *The Nancy Drew Mysteries,* ABC, 1977-79; three episodes, *Sword of Justice,* NBC, 1979; six episodes, *Battlestar Gallactica,* ABC, 1980; twenty-five episodes, *B.J. and the Bear,* NBC, 1979-81; thirteen episodes, *The Master,* NBC, 1984. Mini-Series: *Evening in Byzantium,* syndicated, 1978. Pilots: (with Glen Larson) *Battles,* 1979. Movies: *The Return of the Man from U.N.C.L.E.,* CBS, 1983; *Riviera,* ABC, 1985-86; *The Return of the Six Million Dollar Man and the Bionic Woman,* ABC, 1987.

MEMBER: Writers Guild of America, Producers Guild of America.

ADDRESSES: OFFICE—c/o Universal Television, 100 Universal City Plaza, Universal City, CA 91608. AGENT—c/o Lou Pitt, International Creative Management, 8899 Beverly Boulevard, Beverly Hills, CA 90212.

*　　*　　*

SNODGRESS, Carrie　1946-

PERSONAL: Born October 27, 1946, in Barrington, IL. EDUCATION: Attended the University of Northern Illinois; trained for the stage at the Goodman Theatre, Chicago.

VOCATION: Actress.

CAREER: PRINCIPAL TELEVISION APPEARANCES—Episodic: *Marcus Welby, M.D.,* ABC; *Medical Center,* CBS; *Judd for the Defense,* ABC; *The Virginian,* NBC; *The Outsider,* NBC; *Murder, She Wrote,* CBS; *Highway to Heaven,* NBC. Movies: Megan Baker, *The Whole World Is Watching,* NBC, 1969; Janet, *Silent Night, Lonely Night,* NBC, 1969; Grace McCormack, *The Impatient Heart,* NBC, 1971; Nancy Warren, *Love's Dark Ride,* NBC, 1978; Sharon Keyes, *The Solitary Man,* CBS, 1979; Diana Hayward, *Fast Friends,* NBC, 1979; Stefanie Comeneci, *Nadia,* syndicated, 1984; Isobel Bennett, *A Reason to Live*, NBC, 1985; also appeared in *Andrea's Story* and *First Sign*.

FILM DEBUT—*Rabbit, Run*, Warner Brothers, 1970. PRINCIPAL FILM APPEARANCES—*Diary of a Mad Housewife*, Universal, 1970; *The Fury*, Twentieth Century-Fox, 1978; *A Night in Heaven*, 1983; *Pale Rider*, Warner Brothers, 1985; *Murphy's Law*, Cannon, 1986.

PRINCIPAL STAGE APPEARANCES—*All the Way Home, Oh! What a Lovely War, Caesar and Cleopatra, Tartuffe, The Balcony, The Boor*, all Goodman Theatre, Chicago, IL; *Curse of the Starving Class*, Tiffany Theatre, Los Angeles, CA.

AWARDS: Sarah Siddons Award, 1966, for *Tartuffe;* Best Actress, Academy Award nomination, two Golden Globe awards, all 1971, for *Diary of a Mad Housewife.*

MEMBER: Actors' Equity Association. Screen Actors Guild, American Federation of Television and Radio Artists.

ADDRESSES: AGENT—c/o David Shapira & Associates, 15301 Ventura Boulevard, Sherman Oaks, CA 91403.*

*   *   *

SPANO, Joe   1946-

PERSONAL: Born July 7, 1946, in San Francisco, CA; son of Vincent Dante (a physician) and Virginia Jean (Carpenter) Spano; married Joan Zerrien (a ceramic artist). EDUCATION: Received B.A., drama, from the University of California, Berkeley.

VOCATION: Actor, director, and producer.

CAREER: STAGE DEBUT—Paris, *Romeo and Juliet*, Alumni Repertory Theatre, University of California, Berkeley, 1967, for ten performances. PRINCIPAL STAGE APPEARANCES—Title role, *Hamlet*, Brick, *Cat on a Hot Tin Roof*, Duke Mantee, *The Petrified Forest*, Marchbanks, *Candida*, Theseus, Oberon, *A Midsummer Night's Dream*, Dick Dudgeon, *The Devil's Disciple*, Philip, *The Philanthropist*, Benedick, *Much Ado about Nothing*, Rocky, *The Iceman Cometh*, Antipholi, *Comedy of Errors*, all with the Berkeley Repertory Theatre, Berkeley, CA, 1968-78; also appeared in *We Won't Pay! We Can't Pay!*, Los Angeles Actors Theatre, Los Angeles, CA, 1981; *Three Guys Naked from the Waist Down, The Last Song of John Proffit, Loose Ends, Ring Around the Moon, Our Town, Cyrano de Bergerac, Measure for Measure, Cloud 9, Curse of the Starving Class*, all Playmakers Repertory Company, Chapel Hill, NC, 1984-85; Strangeweed's man, *Sheriff Bill*, Magic Theatre, San Francisco, CA; Nichols, *J.B.*, American Conservatory Theatre, San Francisco, CA; Luke Lovello, *Halloween*, One Act Theatre, San Francisco, CA; Maffuchi, *No Place to Be Somebody*, San Francisco, CA; Chauncey DeVille, Dracula, *Dracula: A Musical Nightmare*, title role, *Bullshot Crummond*, Vincent, *The Gingham Dog*, Zoot, *The Prisoner of Venice: A Hollywood Lullabye*, all Los Angeles, CA; and in *The Little Threepenny Cafe*, Los Angeles, CA, 1984; *Welcome to Transylvania*, San Francisco, CA, 1984.

PRINCIPAL STAGE WORK—Director, *Servant of Two Masters*, Berkeley Repertory Theatre, Berkeley, CA; producer, *Welcome to Transylvania*, San Francisco, CA, 1984; also director of improvisational comedy group, The Wing.

JOE SPANO

MAJOR TOURS—With The Wing (improvisational comedy group), U.K and U.S. cities, both 1974.

FILM DEBUT—Vic Lozier, *American Graffiti*, Universal, 1974. PRINCIPAL FILM APPEARANCES—*The Enforcer*, Warner Brothers, 1975; *The Incredible Shrinking Woman*, Universal, 1979; *Northern Lights*, Cine-Manifest, 1979; *Roadie*, United Artists, 1980; *Terminal Choice*, Magder Films, 1982; *Lovestruck*, Rainy Day Films, 1987; also appeared in *Over, Under, Sideways, Down; The Miller's Tale;* and with The Wing in *Storm Signals*, and *One Is a Lonely Number.*

TELEVISION DEBUT—*Streets of San Francisco*, ABC, 1974. PRINCIPAL TELEVISION APPEARANCES—Episodic: *Tenspeed and Brownshoe*, ABC, 1980; *Trapper John, M.D.*, CBS; *Lou Grant*, CBS; *A Child's Christmas in Wales*, KTVU-San Francisco. Series: Coroner Lavell, *Paris*, CBS, 1979; Henry Goldblume, *Hill Street Blues*, NBC, 1981-1987. Movies: Captain Murphy, *Fightin' Back: The Rocky Bleir Story*, ABC, 1980; Bob Grootemat, *Brotherhood of Justice*, ABC, 1986.

RELATED CAREER—Founding member, The Wing (improvisational comedy group), San Francisco, CA, 1968-78; trustee, Padua Hills Playwrights Festival.

AWARDS: Outstanding Achievement, Los Angeles Critics Award, 1978, for *Dracula: A Musical Nightmare;* Outstanding Supporting Actor in a Drama Series, Emmy Award nomination, 1983, for *Hill Street Blues;* Outstanding Undergraduate Actor, Sturgess Award, University of California, Berkeley.

MEMBER: Actors' Equity Association, American Federation of Television and Radio Artists, Screen Actors Guild.

ADDRESSES: OFFICE—c/o E.V. Associates, 9056 Santa Monica Boulevard, #307 Los Angeles, CA 90069. AGENT— c/o Susan Smith, 121 N. San Vicente Boulevard, Beverly Hills, CA 90211.

*   *   *

SPARER, Paul

PERSONAL: Born in Boston, MA; married Nancy Marchand (an actress).

VOCATION: Actor.

CAREER: PRINCIPAL STAGE APPEARANCES—Dumain, *Love's Labour's Lost*, City Center Theatre, New York City, 1953; Salanio, *The Merchant of Venice*, Cassio, *Othello*, Owen Glendower, Sir Walter Blunt, *Henry IV, Part I*, all City Center Theatre, 1955; Gilles de Rais, executioner, *Saint Joan*, Phoenix Theatre, New York City, 1956; Earl of Gloucester, *King Lear*, Players Theatre, New York City, 1959; Heracles, *Philoctetes*, Theatre de Lys, New York City, 1959; Borachio, *Much Ado about Nothing*, Lunt-Fontanne Theatre, New York City, 1959; John Brown, *Cut of the Axe*, Ambassador Theatre, New York City, 1960; Leone Gala, *The Rules of the Game*, Gramercy Arts Theatre, New York City, 1960; Lennox, *Macbeth*, Ulysses, *Troilus and Cressida*, Corin, *As You Like It*, all American Shakespeare Festival, Stratford, CT, 1961; prosecuting captain, *A Cook for Mr. General*, Playhouse Theatre, 1961; Auda Abu Tayi, *Ross*, Eugene O'Neill Theatre, New York City, 1961; Trigorin, *The Seagull*, Tom Allen, *The Tavern*, both Folksbiene Playhouse for APA, 1962, then Phoenix Theatre, 1964; Lamberto Laudisi, *Right You Are If You Think You Are*, Moliere, *Impromptu at Versailles*, Satin, *The Lower Depths*, all Phoenix Theatre, 1964; Mendoza, the Devil, *Man and Superman*, Dolokhov, *War and Peace*, Holofernes, *Judith*, all Phoenix Theatre, 1965; Mead, "The Pedestrian," David McLean, "The Veldt," stranger, "To the Chicago Abyss," all as *The World of Ray Bradbury*, Orpheum Theatre, New York City, 1965.

Robert Shallow, *Falstaff*, Sir Reginald Fitz Urse, *Murder in the Cathedral*, Cassius, *Julius Caesar*, all American Shakespeare Festival, 1966; lecturer, *After the Rain*, John Golden Theatre, New York City, 1967; Disley, *Teaparty*, Eastside Playhouse, New York City, 1968; title role, *In the Matter of J. Robert Oppenheimer*, Vivian Beaumont Theatre, New York City, 1969; General Browser, *Operation Sidewinder*, Vivian Beaumont Theatre, 1970; Richard Plantagenet, *Henry VI, Parts I and II*, New York Shakespeare Festival (NYSF), Delacorte Theatre, New York City, 1970; general, *The Happiness Cage*, Solness, *The Master Builder*, NYSF, Public Theatre, New York City, 1970; Albert Valpor, *The Water Hen*, Brooklyn Academy of Music, Brooklyn, NY, 1972; Leonato, *Much Ado about Nothing*, Winter Garden Theatre, New York City, 1973; Captain Melody, *A Touch of the Poet*, Hartford Stage Company, Hartford, CT, 1973; Giovanni, *The Burnt Flowerbed*, Roundabout Theatre, New York City, 1974; Emil Varec, *Duck Variations*, St. Clement's Church Theatre, New York City, 1975; chairman of council, *Zalmen*, Lyceum Theatre, New York City, 1976; *Heartbreak House*, Williamstown Theatre Festival, Williamstown, MA, 1976; various roles, *Poor Murderer*, Ethel Barrymore Theatre, New York City, 1976; Friedrich Reisen, *Cold Storage*, American Place Theatre, New York City, 1977; *The Sponsor*, St. Clem-

ent's Church Theatre, 1977; inquisitor, *Saint Joan*, Circle in the Square, New York City, 1977; *Awake and Sing*, Queen's Festival Playhouse, New York City, 1978; recorder, *Biography: A Game*, Chelsea Westside Theatre, New York City, 1979.

Title role, *Don Juan in Hell*, Roundabout Stage One Theatre, New York City, 1980; *The Millionairess*, Hartman Theatre, Stamford, CT, 1981; Creon, *Medea*, Clarence Brown Theatre Company, Knoxville, TN, then Cort Theatre, New York City, 1982; Tobias, *A Delicate Balance*, McCarter Theatre Company, Princeton, NJ, 1982; Jacob, *Awake and Sing*, Circle in the Square, 1984; Peter Stockman, *An Enemy of the People*, Roundabout Theatre, 1985. Also appeared in *Moby Dick*, City Center Theatre, 1955.

PRINCIPAL TELEVISION APPEARANCES—Movies: Sheriff, *Mayflower: The Pilgrims' Adventure*, CBS, 1979; Fritz Jack, *You Can't Go Home Again*, CBS, 1979.

MEMBER: Actors' Equity Association.

ADDRESSES: AGENT—c/o Arcasa, Bauman & Hiller, 850 Seventh Avenue, New York, NY 10019.*

*   *   *

SPIELBERG, David   1939-

PERSONAL: Born March 6, 1939, in Mercedes, TX; son of George (a merchant) and Manuela (an artist; maiden name, Benitez) Spielberg;

DAVID SPIELBERG

married Barbara Gladtone (a quilter) June 13, 1965; children: Daniel. EDUCATION: Attended the University of Texas; studied at the Ben Iden Payne School and with Alan Miller at the Herbert Berghof Studios. MILITARY: U.S. Naval Reserve, 1957-59.

VOCATION: Actor.

CAREER: STAGE DEBUT—King, *Ondine,* Hogg Auditorium, Austin TX, 1959. OFF-BROADWAY DEBUT—Polly, *A Man's a Man,* Maidman Theatre, 1963, for one hundred fifty performances. PRINCIPAL STAGE APPEARANCES—Mortimer, *Henry IV, Part I,* American Shakespeare Festival, Stratford, CT, 1962; Gordon, *Thieves,* Broadhurst Theatre, New York City, 1971; Larry Parks, *Are You Now or Have You Ever Been?,* CAST Theatre, Los Angeles, CA, 1974; Jack, *The Lady and the Clarinet,* Mark Taper Forum, Los Angeles, CA, 1981; Danforth, *I'm Not Rappaport,* Seattle Repertory Theatre, Seattle, WA, 1985; father, *Six Characters in Search of an Author,* Goodman Theatre, Chicago, IL, 1985; Kruk, *Ghetto,* Mark Taper Forum, 1986; Ben, *The Normal Heart,* Las Palmas Theatre, Los Angeles, CA, 1986. Also in *Funnyhouse of a Negro,* East End Theatre, New York City, 1964; *Macbird!,* Village Gate Theatre, New York City, 1969; *The Trial of the Catonsville Nine,* Lyceum Theatre, New York City, 1971; *Mary Barnes,* Long Wharf Theatre, New Haven, CT, 1979; *Sleep,* American Place Theatre, New York City; *Story Theatre,* Chicago, IL, then Yale Repertory Theatre, New Haven, CT; and appeared at the Williamstown Theatre Festival, Williamstown, MA, and the Stockbridge Festival Theatre, Stockbridge, MA.

MAJOR TOURS—Mickey, *After the Fall,* U.S. cities, 1964-65.

TELEVISION DEBUT—District Attorney Walberg, *The Bold Ones,* NBC, 1971. PRINCIPAL TELEVISION APPEARANCES— Episodic: *Two Brothers.* Series: Ted Henderson, *Bob and Carol and Ted and Alice,* ABC, 1973; Francis X. Casey, *The American Girls,* CBS, 1976; Dr. David Bedford, *The Practice,* NBC, 1976-77; Lieutenant/Captain Ross, *From Here to Eternity,* NBC, 1979-80; Max Kenyon, *Jessica Novack,* CBS, 1981; Peter Pan, *Mork and Mindy,* ABC. Pilots: Marlowe, *Toma,* ABC, 1973; Lieutenant Carey Roth, *Stone,* ABC, 1979. Mini-Series: Dr. Patterson, *Arthur Hailey's "Wheels,"* NBC, 1978; Lieutenant Ross, *From Here to Eternity,* NBC, 1979; Skip Morgan, *James A. Michener's "Space,"* CBS, 1985. Movies: Dr. Widdicomb, *Night of Terror,* ABC, 1972; Norman Ellsworth, *Force Five,* CBS, 1975; David Wilentz, *The Lindbergh Kidnapping Trial,* NBC, 1975; Dr. Mason, *In the Matter of Karen Ann Quinlan,* NBC, 1977; Louis Kellogg, *The Storyteller,* NBC, 1977; Frank Oberon, *The 3,000 Mile Chase,* NBC, 1977; David Beamer, *Kin,* NBC, 1978; David Addlestone, *Sergeant Matlovich vs. the U.S. Air Force,* NBC, 1978; Victor Burton, *Act of Love,* NBC, 1980; Mayor Frank Bellona, *The Henderson Monster,* CBS, 1980; Alan Porter, *Games Mother Never Taught You,* CBS, 1982; Harold Klumper, *Maid in America,* CBS, 1982; Steve Jones, *Police Woman Centerfold,* NBC, 1983; Sammler, *Obsessed with a Married Woman,* ABC, 1985.

FILM DEBUT—Mr. Goodman, *The Effect of Gamma Rays on Man-in-the-Moon Marigolds,* Twentieth Century-Fox, 1972. PRINCIPAL FILM APPEARANCES—*Law and Disorder,* Columbia, 1974; *Hustle,* Paramount, 1975; *Winterkills,* AVCO-Embassy, 1976; *The Choirboys,* Universal, 1977; *Real Life,* Paramount, 1979; *The Hunter,* Paramount, 1980; *The Children's War,* Paramount, 1983; *Christine,* Columbia, 1983; father, *Love and War,* Cannon, 1985; Dr. Hobby, *The Stranger,* Columbia, 1987.

RELATED CAREER—Associate instructor of acting, Yale School of

Drama, 1968-69; founding member, Open Theatre, 1962; company member, Long Wharf Theatre, 1965-80.

AWARDS: Distinguished Performance, Obie Award from the *Village Voice,* 1971, for *Sleep;* Best Performance Award, Los Angeles Drama Critics Circle Award, 1975, for *Are You Now or Have You Ever Been;* Emmy Award nomination, 1975, for *Lindbergh Kidnapping Trial.*

MEMBER: Actors' Equity Association, Screen Actors Guild, American Federation of Television and Radio Artists Academy of Television Arts and Sciences, Academy of Motion Picture Arts and Sciences.

ADDRESSES: AGENT—Artists Agency, 10000 Santa Monica Boulevard, Los Angeles, CA 90069.

*　　*　　*

STAGGE, Jonathan
　See WHEELER, Hugh

*　　*　　*

STANDER, Lionel   1908-

PERSONAL: Full name, Lionel Jay Stander; born January 11, 1908, in New York, NY; son of Louis E. (an accountant) and Bella Stander; married Lucy Dietz (an artist), 1928 (divorced, 1936); married Alice Twitchell (an artist), 1938 (divorced, 1942); married Vahanne Havens Monteagle, 1945 (divorced, 1950); married Diana Radbec (a singer), 1953 (divorced, 1963); married Maria Penn (an artist), 1964 (divorced, 1971); married Stephanie Van Hennik, 1971; children: (fist marriage) one daughter, (third marriage) two daughters, (fourth marriage) one daughter, (sixth marriage) one daughter. EDUCATION: Attended the University of North Carolina, 1927-28. MILITARY: U.S. Army Air Corps, 1942-45.

VOCATION: Actor and producer.

CAREER: PRINICIPAL FILM APPEARANCES—*Page Miss Glory,* Warner Brothers, 1935; *The Gay Deception,* Columbia, 1935; *The Scoundrel,* Paramount, 1935; *Mr. Deeds Goes to Town,* Columbia, 1936; *Meet Nero Wolfe,* Columbia, 1936; *Guadalcanal Diary,* Twentieth Century-Fox, 1943; *The Big Show-Off,* Republic, 1945; *In Old Sacramento,* Republic, 1946; *The Kid from Brooklyn,* RKO, 1946; *Gentelman Joe Palooka,* 1946; *Specter of the Rose,* Republic, 1946; *Mad Wednesday,* United Artists, 1947; *Call Northside 777,* Twentieth Century-Fox, 1948; *Unfaithfully Yours,* Twentieth Century-Fox, 1948; *Two Gals and a Guy,* United Artists, 1951; *St. Benny the Dip,* United Artists, 1951; *A Star is Born,* Warner Brothers, 1954; *Pal Joey,* Columbia, 1957; *The Loved One,* Metro-Goldwyn-Mayer, 1965; *Cul de Sac,* Sigma III, 1966; *Beyond the Law,* Grove, 1967; *A Dandy in Aspic,* Columbia, 1968; *Per Grazia Ricevuta,* Italy, 1970; *The Gang That Couldn't Shoot Straight,* Metro-Goldwyn-Mayer, 1971; *Pulp,* United Artists, 1972; *The Cassandra Crossing,* AVCO-Embassy, 1977; *New York, New York,* United Artists, 1977; *Matilda,* American International, 1978; *1941,* Universal, 1979. Also appeared in *Trouble Makers,* 1948; *The Black Bird,* 1975.

OFF-BROADWAY DEBUT—Cop and first fairy, *him*, Provincetown Playhouse, 1928. PRINCIPAL STAGE APPEARANCES—Yank, *S.S. Glencairn*, Provincetown Playhouse, New York City, 1929; Chock, *Little Ol' Boy*, Playhouse Theatre, New York City, 1933; Feodor Dobinsky, *The Drums Begin*, Shubert Theatre, New York City, 1933; Stephen, *The Bride of Torozko*, Henry Miller's Theatre, New York City, 1934; Lowell Ludlow, *Pal Joey*, Broadhurst Theatre, New York City, 1952; Sgt. Murdock, *The Conquering Hero*, American National Theatre Academy Playhouse, New York City, 1961; Commissioner of Police, *The Policeman*, Phoenix Theatre, New York City, 1961; Tetzel, *Luther*, St. James Theatre, New York City, 1963; J. Pierpont Mauler, *Saint Joan of the Stockyards*, Queen's Theatre, London, 1964.

PRINCIPAL STAGE WORK—Producer (with Bern Bernard), *Brooklyn, U.S.A.*, Forrest Theatre, New York City, 1941.

MAJOR TOURS—Lowell Ludlow, *Pal Joey*, U.S. cities, 1953.

PRINCIPAL TELEVISION APPEARANCES—Series: Max, *Hart to Hart*, ABC, 1979-84; also in *The Adventures of Pinocchio*, Italian Television, RAI-TV.

PRINCIPAL RADIO APPEARANCES—*The Fred Allen Show; The Eddie Cantor Show; The Rudy Vallee Show.*

NON-RELATED CAREER—Newspaper reporter.

MEMBER: Actors' Equity Association, Screen Actors Guild, American Federation of Television and Radio Artists, American Guild of Variety Artists.

ADDRESSES: AGENT—Paul Kohner, Inc., 9169 Sunset Boulevard, Los Angeles, CA 90069.*

*   *   *

STANTON, Harry Dean   1926-

PERSONAL: Born July 14, 1926, in Kentucky.

VOCATION: Actor.

CAREER: STAGE DEBUT—Pasadena Playhouse, CA.

FILM DEBUT—*Tomahawk Trail*, 1957. PRINCIPAL FILM APPEARANCES—*The Proud Rebel*, Buena Vista, 1958; *Pork Chop Hill*, 1959; *A Dog's Best Friend*, 1959; *Cool Hand Luke*, Warner Brothers, 1967; *Kelly's Heroes*, Metro-Goldwyn-Mayer, 1970; *Two-Lane Blacktop*, Universal, 1971; *Pat Garrett and Billy the Kid*, Metro-Goldwyn-Mayer, 1971; *Dillinger*, American International, 1973; *Zandy's Bride*, Warner Brothers, 1974; *The Godfather, Part II*, Paramount, 1974; *Rancho Deluxe*, United Artists, 1974; *Farewell, My Lovely*, AVCO-Embassy, 1975; *The Missouri Breaks*, United Artists, 1976; *92 in the Shade*, United Artists, 1976; *Renaldo & Clara*, 1977; *Straight Time*, Warner Brothers, 1977; *The Rose*, Twentieth Century-Fox, 1979; *Wise Blood*, 1979; *Deathwatch*, Quartet, 1979; *The Black Marble*, AVCO-Embassy, 1980; *UForia*, 1980; *Private Benjamin*, Warner Brothers, 1980; *Escape from New York*, AVCO-Embassy, 1981; *Young Doctors in Love*, Twentieth Century-Fox, 1982; *One from the Heart*, Columbia, 1982; *Tough Enough*, Twentieth Century-Fox, 1983; *Christine*, Columbia, 1983; *Repo*

Man, Universal, 1984; *The Bear*, Embassy, 1984; *Red Dawn*, Metro-Goldwyn-Mayer/United Artists, 1984; *Paris, Texas*, Twentieth Century-Fox, 1984; voice, *The Care Bears Movie*, Samuel Goldwyn, 1985; *One Magic Christmas*, Buena Vista, 1985; *Pretty in Pink*, Paramount, 1986; *Fool for Love*, Cannon, 1986.

PRINCIPAL TELEVISION APPEARANCES—Episodic: Title role, "Rip Van Winkle," *Faerie Tale Theatre*, Showtime, 1987.

MEMBER: Screen Actors Guild.

ADDRESSES: AGENT—c/o Toni Howard, William Morris Agency, Inc., 151 El Camino Drive, Beverly Hills, CA 90212. PUBLICIST—Guttman & Pam, Ltd., 8500 Wilshire Blvd., Suite 801, Beverly Hills, CA 90211.*

*   *   *

STEADMAN, Alison   1946-

PERSONAL: Born August 26, 1946, in Liverpool, England; daughter of George Percival and Marjorie (Evans) Steadman; married Mike Leigh. EDUCATION: Trained for the stage at the East 15 Acting School, 1966-69.

VOCATION: Actress.

CAREER: STAGE DEBUT—*The Prime of Miss Jean Brodie*, Theatre Royal, Lincoln, U.K., 1969. LONDON DEBUT— *Wholesome Glory*, Theatre Upstairs, 1973. PRINCIPAL STAGE APPEARANCES—Ophelia, *Hamlet*, Theatre Royal, Lincoln, U.K. 1969; *The Pope's Wedding*, Bush Theatre, London, 1973; Sylvia, *The Anchor*, Theatre Upstairs, London, 1974; Guinevere, *The King*, Shaw Theatre, London, 1974; Abigail, *Abigail's Party*, Hampstead Theatre Club, London, 1977; Anthea, *Joking Apart*, Globe Theatre, London, 1979; Sonya, *Uncle Vanya*, Hampstead Theatre Club, 1979. Also *The Plotters of Cabbage Patch Corner*, Bolton Theatre, Worcester, U.K.; *The Jaws of Death*, Traverse Theatre, Edinburgh, Scotland, U.K.; Desdemona, *Othello*, Nottingham Playhouse Theatre, Nottingham, U.K.

PRINCIPAL TELEVISION APPEARANCES—Episodic: *Hard Labour*, 1973; *Nuts in May*, 1976; *Through the Night*, 1979; *Pasmore*, 1980. Specials: *Abigail's Party*, 1977.

NON-RELATED CAREER—Secretary, Liverpool Probation Service.

AWARDS: Best Actress, *Evening Standard* Award, *Plays and Players* Award, both 1977, for *Abigail's Party*.

ADDRESSES: AGENT—c/o Bill Horne, 15 Little Newport Street, London WC2, England.*

*   *   *

STEEL, Dawn   1946-

PERSONAL: Born August 19, 1946, in New York, NY; married second husband, Charles Roven (a film producer); children: Rebecca. EDUCATION: Attended Boston University, 1964-65, and New York University, 1966-67.

VOCATION: Film studio executive.

CAREER: PRINCIPAL FILM WORK—Paramount Pictures Corporation, New York City and Los Angeles, CA: director of merchandising, 1978, vice-president of merchandising, 1979, senior vice-president of production, 1980-85, president of production, 1985-87, with major responsibility for such films as *Top Gun, Flashdance, Star Trek IV,* and *Fatal Attraction;* president of motion picture operations, Columbia Pictures Entertainment, Inc., Burbank, CA, 1987—.

RELATED CAREER—Director of merchandising, *Penthouse* magazine, 1969-75; founder and president, Oh, Dawn, Inc. (a merchandising company), New York City, 1975-78. Also acted as merchandising consultant to *Playboy.*

NON-RELATED CAREER—Receptionist, Stadia Publishing, New York City, then writer for Stadia publications *NFL Digest* and *Major League Digest,* 1968.

MEMBER: Academy of Motion Picture Arts and Sciences, Women in Film; California Abortion Rights Action League, AIDS Project Los Angeles, Neil Bogart Cancer Foundation.

SIDELIGHTS: Dawn Steel told Donna Rosenthal of the New York *Daily News* (November 1, 1987) that at the time she became vice-president of production at Paramount, "I'd never read a script—or even met a director." Nonetheless, the studio had some of their biggest-ever box office hits in the years she headed its production unit. Just before she moved to Columbia Pictures, Steel reportedly was considering becoming an independent producer but the October 28, 1987 *New York Times* quoted her reason for the change in plans: "I've never been asked to run a studio before. There are only six of these jobs in the business."

ADDRESSES: Columbia Pictures Entertainment, Inc., 4000 Warner Boulevard, Burbank, CA, 91522.*

*   *   *

STEIN, Ronald   1930-

PERSONAL: Born April 12, 1930, in St. Louis, MO. EDUCATION: Attended Washington University, St. Louis, 1947-51, Yale University, 1951-52, University of Southern California, Los Angeles, 1960-63. MILITARY: U.S. Army, 1952-54.

VOCATION: Composer, conductor, pianist, teacher, and filmmaker.

CAREER: PRINCIPAL FILM WORK—Documentary film director, writer, editor, and photographer.

PRINCIPAL TELEVISION WORK—Series: Editorial supervisior, *Dateline Yesterday.* Specials: Photographer and editor, *National Parks—A Road for the Future;* writer and director, *The Eye of the Mind.*

RELATED CAREER—Assistant music director, St. Louis Municipal Opera, 1950-51; assistant music director, Greek Theatre, Los Angeles, 1955; associate music director, Phoenix Star Theatre, 1964; professor of music, California State University at Northridge, 1960-61, University of Colorado, 1980-85; administrator, U.S. Educational Films; vice president of creative affairs, Techrev Communications.

RONALD STEIN

WRITINGS: FILM SCORES—*The Littlest Hobo,* Allied Artists, 1958; *Legend of Tom Dooley,* Columbia, 1959; *Raymie,* Allied Artists, 1960; *Premature Burial,* American International, 1962; *Of Love and Desire,* Twentieth Century-Fox, 1963; *Dime with a Halo,* Metro-Goldwyn-Mayer (MGM), 1963; *Dementia 13,* American International, 1964; *Psych-Out,* American International, 1968; *A Man Called Dagger,* MGM, 1968; *The Rain People,* Warner Brothers, 1969; *Getting Straight,* Columbia, 1970; *The Prisoners,* 1970; also *Frankenstein's Great Aunt Tillie, Stalemate,* others.

MEMBER: Academy of Motion Picture Arts and Sciences, American Society of Composers, Authors, and Publishers; American Federation of Musicians.

ADDRESSES: OFFICE—c/o American Society of Composers, Authors, and Publishers, 6430 Sunset Boulevard, Second Floor, Hollywood, CA 90028.

*   *   *

STEWART, Ellen

PERSONAL: Born in Alexandria, LA; daughter of a laborer and a school teacher; married five times. EDUCATION: Attended Arkansas State University and Illinois Institute of Technology.

VOCATION: Theatre producer, manager, and director.

CAREER: FIRST STAGE WORK—Producer and manager, *One*

Arm, Cafe La Mama, New York City, 1962. PRINCIPAL STAGE WORK—Producer, manager, and director, La Mama Experimental Theatre Club (La Mama ETC; originally known as Cafe La Mama), 1962—; has produced more than one thousand plays, including works by Harold Pinter, Fernando Arrabal, Leonard Melfi, Andre Gide, George Bernard Shaw, William Saroyan, Jean Anouilh, Gertrude Stein, Eugene Ionesco, Georg Buchner, Paul Foster, Lanford Wilson, Tom Eyen, Jean Genet, Sam Shepard, Jean-Claude van Itallie, Tom O'Horgan, H.M. Koutoukas, Megan Terry, Bertolt Brecht, Rochelle Owens, Ben Piazza, Ross Alexander, Israel Horowitz, Julie Bovasso, Maria Irene Fornes, Adrienne Kennedy, Alfred Jarry, Charles Ludlam, Slawomir Mrozek, Samuel Beckett, Wilford Leach, Ed Bullins, Peter Weiss, Edward Bond, Antonin Artaud, Robert Patrick, Eric Bentley, Andy Warhol, Jackie Curtis, William Shakespeare, Terrence McNally, August Strindberg, and Moliere.

As producer at La Mama ETC, has hosted productions by such visiting companies as: Open Theatre, American Indian Company, Los Grillos (from Peru), Tokyo Kid Brothers, Ridiculous Theatre, Le Grand Cirque de Magique de Paris, Esta Noche Teatro (from South America), Otrabunda Company (from the Virgin Islands), Asian American Repertory Company, and Andre Serban Troupe.

Founder of branches of La Mama in Boston, Amsterdam, Bogota, London, Melbourne, Munich, Paris, Tokyo, Toronto, Vienna, and in Israel and Morocco.

MAJOR TOURS—Producer and manager for La Mama ETC tours, European cities, 1965—, including presentation of *Tom Paine,* at Vaudeville Theatre, London, 1967, and the Edinburgh Festival, Edinburgh, Scotland, U.K.; *The Last Chance Saloon, Woyzeck,* both Arts Theatre, London, 1969; *Cinque, Rat's Mass, Ubu Roi, Arden of Faversham,* all Royal Court Theatre, London, 1970; *Emer, Renard,* Dubrovnik Festival, Yugoslavia, then West Berlin, Germany, and Copenhagen, Denmark, all 1971.

RELATED CAREER—Cultural ambassador to the Philippines for UNESCO, 1971.

NON-RELATED CAREER—Fashion designer, Saks Fifth Avenue, New York City, 1950-61; free-lance fashion designer in New York City, 1961-72.

AWARDS: Recipient of grants from Rockefeller Foundation, 1967, New York State Council on the Arts, 1973, and from Ford Foundation, National Arts Council, and Kaplan Fund; Margo Jones Award, 1969, for encouraging new playwrights; special Obie Award from the *Village Voice,* 1975, for Off-Off Broadway achievement; honorary doctorate from Bard College, 1975, and from Colby College.

SIDELIGHTS: Ellen Stewart's brainchild, La Mama Experimental Theatre Club (La Mama ETC), has been the birthplace of the avant-garde since its conception in 1962. "The oldest and perhaps most influential" of Off-Off Broadway theatres, according to the April 5, 1980 *New York Times,* La Mama numbers among its alumni such renowned playwrights, directors, and performers as Sam Shepard, Harvey Fierstein, Wilford Leach, Bette Midler, and Al Pacino. Joanne Mattera explained that the theatre got its name because it "was so much an extension of Stewart's warmly maternal personality that her friends simply called it what they called her" (*Women's Wear Daily,* August 5, 1985).

Stewart, nicknamed "Mama" by her friends, had no intention of

entering show business when she first came to New York City in 1950. Born in Louisiana and raised in Chicago, she wanted to become a fashion designer, but, being black, she was not allowed to enroll in design school in Illinois. To choose between the two cities where fashion schools did admit blacks—San Francisco and New York—Stewart "flipped a coin and came here," she told Mattera. Stewart calls what followed her "Cinderella story," according to Mattera. She went to work as a porter at Saks Fifth Avenue to earn tuition money, but the position "became her launching pad instead." Customers noticed the hand-made clothes Stewart wore under the blue smock she was required to wear while on the job; within three months she was promoted to executive designer. After a number of successful years with the department store, she left to work as a free-lance designer.

Yet, as late as 1961, "I was feeling sorry for myself because I didn't know what I wanted to do," Stewart told Lynn Gilbert in an interview published in the April, 1982 *Ms.* Her merchant friend Abraham Diamond often told Stewart she needed a symbolic "pushcart" in her life. "Even if all you have is in a pushcart," the producer quoted to Sidney Fields (*Daily News,* January 6, 1972), "push it, not only for yourself, but for the whole world." Stewart had been brooding about the problems her brother Fred Light and a friend, both playwrights, faced in finding a theatre to produce their plays, when she realized that she could help them and herself. "I saw a sign on Ninth Street: 'Basement for Rent': Ping! Pushcart!," she recalled to Josh Greenfeld in the July 9, 1967 *New York Times Magazine.* "I rushed in and asked for a lease," intending to set up a theatre there for her brother and other playwrights, which she would support with her income as a designer. "And my basement looked beautiful," she told Greenfeld. "No floor. No plumbing. No nothing. But to me it looked beautiful."

"Not knowing anything about theaters," she related to Gilbert, "I thought it was like playing house. . . . I would have this little theater and they would write plays and all their friends would be in them and live happily ever after." Difficulties soon arose, however, when the other tenants in her building, noticing the number of men entering the basement room to help fix it up, tried to get Stewart evicted for prostitution. "They didn't want to be living with a nigger," Stewart told Gilbert. Luckily, the officer called to inspect the case was a retired actor who became sympathetic when he learned of Stewart's plans for a performance space. Pointing out that theatre licenses were difficult to obtain, he offered to help get a restaurant permit so Stewart could open a coffeehouse where they could set up a stage for performances. When asked what the name of the place would be, one of the group suggested "Mama," Stewart recalled, and someone else said, "No, La Mama," and one of the first Greenwich Village coffeehouses was born.

Cafe La Mama, as it was called at that time, became an international theatre within a few years of its founding. "Publishers wouldn't publish our plays unless they had been reviewed," Stewart told Mattera, "and the critics wouldn't come to our little basement" with its twenty-five-seat theatre and stage "not much bigger than a bed." So in 1965 Stewart sent sixteen people with twenty plays to Europe, where she had heard that virtually every play produced was reviewed. "We would have gone to Timbuktu, anywhere to get critiques so that the plays could be published," she affirmed to Gilbert. Soon after the troupe returned, twelve of the plays were published; Stewart maintained the practice of sending her troupes abroad and, in addition, hosted New York productions by many groups they met on tours of France, Denmark, Sweden, Germany, and other countries. Moreover, branches of La Mama sprang up in Japan, Colombia, England, and elsewhere.

Despite the respect it earned worldwide, however, Stewart's coffeehouse still had to struggle locally to survive "against a background of Kafkaesque harassment which has resulted in two evictions, a union imbroglio and innumerable trips to the pawnshop," reported Greenfeld in 1967. To circumvent legal regulations governing the sale of theatre tickets, Stewart changed the coffeehouse/theatre into a theatre club in the mid-1960s, selling no tickets but collecting weekly "dues" from "members" who were allowed, after paying their fees, to attend an unlimited number of the week's performances. Helped by grant money, in 1969 La Mama moved to its present location, occupying six floors of rehearsal space and three stages, and for a time the theatre club thrived. La Mama's accomplishments have been numerous and varied, and include staging the first U.S. production of the British playwright Harold Pinter as well as premiering works by Americans who have subsequently achieved wide renown. La Mama presented a well-received version of William Shakespeare's *Hamlet* in Korean, five plays by the first American Indian theatre group, and an Eskimo *Antigone,* among many other unusual offerings in its over one thousand productions. "[Stewart's] success, in short, represents both a rare act of faith and an unflinching confrontation with the mechanics of moving mountains," Greenfeld declared.

During the 1980s, however, the National Endowment for the Arts and other supporting institutions began reducing their grants to La Mama considerably, which "has meant reducing the number of shows on [the theatre's] three stages, abandoning plans for a permanent repertory company and cutting the salaries of La Mama's staff," reported the *New York Times*'s Michiko Kakutani (April 5, 1980). Nevertheless, Stewart has remained optimistic about La Mama's future. After all, as she told Kakutani, "Maybe I'd still be in that little basement if I was never kicked out. . . . Each kick has become something new." She added, "I'm just an instrument through which La Mama functions. I never dictate. . . . Maybe it's fatalistic, but I know La Mama has its own spirit and if that spirit wishes to keep going, it will. All I can do is be a part of it."

Such mysticism, say those who have met Stewart, plays a significant role in her life. "I do not tell La Mama what to do," she explained to Mattera. "La Mama tells me, and I listen." Despite her twenty-five years experience in the industry, she claims to know little about theatre. "I don't know how to read a play, really, to tell the truth," she asserted to Gilbert. "I don't know because I don't have an academic education in theater. But I do know a little bit about how to read a person." Stewart chooses the plays La Mama will produce more on her assessment of the playwright than on her opinion of his or her play. "If the play is good, then it's good," she declared to Mel Gussow (*New York Times,* December 22, 1985). "If it's bad, that does not change my way of thinking about the person involved. . . . I've never been sorry about anything I put on." Director Alan Schneider lauded her ideal: "The important thing about La Mama," he asserted to Greenfeld, "is not whether the work is good or bad, but that Ellen Stewart helps keep theater alive by constantly giving new playwrights productions." "In some ways, she could be compared to a hostess who cannot help but ask guests to her house," Gussow observed. "Her art is in inspiring the art of others."

"I started La Mama so there would be a place where a playwright could write, see and learn," Stewart told Greenfeld. "My whole joy," she affirmed to Gussow, "is knowing the person is doing whatever he is doing." By keeping her theatre alive, Stewart believes she is helping to promote art, a calling she takes extremely seriously. "Art," she explained to Mattera, "is the only thing

that's free. . . . A mother singing to her child is art, even though she might have nothing to eat and a tent to live in. It's a God-given resource for all humankind to draw upon—many times there is nothing else." Stewart added, "A world without poverty or illiteracy would be wonderful, but without artistic expression it would be barren."

ADDRESSES: OFFICE—La Mama ETC, 74A E. 4th Street, New York, NY 10003.*

*   *   *

STEWART, Michael   1929-1987

OBITUARY NOTICE—See *CTFT* index for sketch: Born August 1, 1929 in New York City; died of pneumonia in New York City, September 20, 1987. Two-time Antoinette Perry Award winner Michael Stewart was the author of some of the most successful stage musicals in theatre history, having written the book, lyrics, or both for such shows as *Bye Bye Birdie, Hello Dolly!, George M.,* and *I Love My Wife.* Although his book for *Bye Bye Birdie* did not receive the best of critical notices, the show was the biggest hit of the 1960-61 season and was awarded most of the major Antoinette Perry awards in the musical categories, including best author for Stewart. A year later, Stewart's *Carnival* won the New York Drama Critics Circle Award and an Antoinette Perry Award nomination for best musical. In 1964 *Hello Dolly!* made its debut, again with enormous success, and Stewart once more received the Antoinette Perry and the New York Drama Critics Circle awards. *Hello Dolly!* was not only a box office smash which ran for 1,596 performances on Broadway, but has since been performed annually in summer stock and regional theatres throughout the world. Some of Michael Stewart's other notable works include the book and lyrics for *Mack and Mabel,* 1974, lyrics with Mark Bramble (his partner since 1974) for *42nd Street,* 1980, lyrics for *Barnum,* 1980, and for *Harrigan and Hart,* 1984. In 1986 Stewart collaborated with the composer Jule Styne to produce a musical version of Robert Louis Stevenson's *Treasure Island.*

OBITUARIES AND OTHER SOURCES: New York Times, September 21, 1987.

*   *   *

STIGWOOD, Robert   1934-

PERSONAL: Born April 16, 1934, in Adelaide, Australia; immigrated to London, England, 1956; son of Gordon and Gwendolyn (Burrows) Stigwood. EDUCATION: Attended Sacred Heart College in Adelaide, Australia.

VOCATION: Producer, executive, and talent agent.

CAREER: PRINCIPAL STAGE WORK—Producer: *Hair, Oh! Calcutta, Pippin, Jesus Christ Superstar,* and *Sweeney Todd,* all London productions; *The Dirtiest Show in Town,* London and New York City productions; *Evita,* London production and at the Broadway Theatre, New York City, 1979; *Joseph and the Amazing Technicolor Dreamcoat,* Royale Theatre, New York City, 1982.

MAJOR TOURS—Producer, *Evita,* U.S. cities, including Shubert

Theatre, Los Angeles, 1980, Masonic Temple, Detroit, MI, 1983, Minneapolis Orpheum Theatre, 1983.

PRINCIPAL FILM WORK—Producer: *Jesus Christ Superstar,* Universal, 1973; *Tommy,* Columbia, 1975; *Bugsy Malone,* Paramount, 1976; *Saturday Night Fever,* Paramount, 1977; *Grease,* Paramount, 1978; *Sergeant Pepper's Lonely Hearts Club Band,* Universal, 1978; *Moment by Moment,* Universal, 1978; *Times Square,* Associated Film Distributors, 1980; *Gallipoli,* Paramount, 1980; co-producer, *The Fan,* Paramount, 1981; *Grease 2,* Paramount, 1982; *Staying Alive,* Paramount, 1983.

PRINCIPAL TELEVISION WORK—Producer: Series—*Makin' It,* ABC, 1979. Movies—*The Entertainer,* 1975. Mini-Series—*The Prime of Miss Jean Brodie.*

PRINCIPAL RECORDING WORK—Producer for rock groups such as the Bee Gee's, Cream, others.

RELATED CAREER—Founder of his own talent agency, London, 1961-65; business manager, Graham Bond Organization; co-founder (with Brian Epstein) and co-manager, NEMS Enterprises, 1967; founder and chairman of the board, Robert Stigwood Organization (RSO), 1967, RSO Records, 1973; director, Polygram, 1976; co-founder (with Rupert Murdoch), R&R Films, 1979; founder, Music for UNICEF.

AWARDS: Named International Producer of the Year, ABC Interstate Theatres, 1976; awarded the Key to the City, Los Angeles, and Adelaide, Australia.

SIDELIGHTS: RECREATIONS—Tennis, swimming, sailing, and reading.

ADDRESSES: OFFICE—The Robert Stigwood Organization, Inc., 1775 Broadway, 21st Floor, New York, NY 10019.*

*　　　*　　　*

DON STITT

WRITINGS: PLAYS—*The Doonesbury Revue,* San Francisco State University Players Club, San Francisco, CA, 1975; *A Kid's Summer Night's Dream,* Artist Production Ensemble, New York City, 1979; *Potshots,* Network Theatre, New York City, 1980.

MEMBER: Actors' Equity Association.

ADDRESSES: HOME—11-34 44th Drive, No. 7, Long Island City, NY 11101. OFFICE—Box 1268, Long Island City, NY 11101. AGENT—Cunningham, Escot & Dipene, 118 E. 25th Street, New York, NY 10101.

*　　　*　　　*

STITT, Don　1956-

PERSONAL: Born January 25, 1956, in Stamford, CT; son of Donald William (a labor negotiator) and Margaret Rose (a medical secretary; maiden name, Porter) Stitt; married Elizabeth Popiel (a scenic designer), July 4, 1987. EDUCATION: San Francisco State University, B.A., theatre arts, 1977.

VOCATION: Actor and playwright.

CAREER: PRINCIPAL STAGE APPEARANCES—Ratzo Rizzo, *Beach Blanket Babylon Goes Bananas,* Fugazi Hall, San Francisco, CA, 1976; Felix Lindor, *Do Black Patent Leather Shoes Really Reflect Up?,* Alvin Theatre, New York City, 1982; Toulouse-Lautrec, *El Grande de Coca Cola,* Village Gate Downstairs, New York City, 1986; ensemble, *Waitin' in the Wings* (revue), Triplex Theatre, New York City, 1986; Vito, *Late Nite Comic,* Ritz Theatre, New York City, 1987.

MAJOR TOURS—*Do Black Patent Leather Shoes Really Reflect Up?,* various tours of U.S. cities, 1981-1987.

FILM DEBUT—Moonie, *Simon,* Warner Brothers, 1980.

STOCKWELL, Dean　1936-

PERSONAL: Born March 5, 1936, in Hollywood, CA; son of Harry (an actor) and Betty Veronica Stockwell.

VOCATION: Actor.

CAREER: PRINCIPAL STAGE APPEARANCES—*Innocent Voyage,* Theatre Guild, Belasco Theatre, New York City, 1943; *Compulsion,* Ambassador Theatre, New York City, 1958.

FILM DEBUT—*Anchors Aweigh,* Metro-Goldwyn-Mayer (MGM), 1945. PRINCIPAL FILM APPEARANCES—*The Valley of Decision,* MGM, 1945; *Abbott and Costello in Hollywood,* MGM, 1945; *The*

Green Years, 1946; *Home Sweet Homicide,* 1946; *The Mighty McGurk,* MGM, 1946; *The Arnelo Affair,* MGM, 1947; *The Romance of Rosy Ridge,* MGM, 1947; *Song of the Thin Man,* MGM, 1947; *Gentlemen's Agreement,* 1947; *Deep Waters,* 1948; *Down to the Sea in Ships,* 1949; *The Boy with Green Hair,* RKO, 1948; *The Secret Garden,* MGM, 1949; *The Happy Years,* MGM, 1950; *Kim,* MGM, 1950; *Stars in My Crown,* MGM, 1950; *Cattle Drive,* 1958; *Compulsion,* Twentieth Century-Fox, 1959; *Sons and Lovers,* 1960; *Long Day's Journey into Night,* Embassy, 1962; *Psych-Out,* American International, 1968; *The Dunwich Horror,* American International, 1970; *The Last Movie,* Universal, 1971; *The Loners,* 1972; *Tracks,* Rainbow Pictures, 1976; *Eadweard Muybridge, Zoopraxographer,* 1976; *Alsindo and the Condor,* 1981; *Wrong Is Right,* Columbia, 1982; *Human Highway,* 1982; *Sweet Scene of Death,* 1983; *Paris, Texas,* Twentieth Century-Fox, 1984; *Dune,* Universal, 1984; *The Legend of Billie Jean,* Tri-Star, 1985; *To Live and Die in L.A.,* MGM/United Artists, 1985; *Blue Velvet,* DEG, 1986; *Homer Thomas, Gardens of Stone,* Tri-Star, 1987; *Beverly Hills Cop, II,* Paramount, 1987; *Blue Iguana,* Propaganda, 1987; *Tucker,* Lucasfilm, 1988; *Palais Royale,* 1988; *Married to the Mob,* Orion, 1988.

PRINCIPAL RADIO WORK—*Death Valley Days* and *Dr. Christian.*

AWARDS: Named in the *Motion Picture Herald-Fame* "Stars of Tomorrow" poll, 1949; co-winner, Best Actor award, Cannes Film Festival, 1959, for *Compulsion;* Best Actor award, Cannes Film Festival, 1961, for *Long Day's Journey into Night;* also Golden Globe for *The Boy with Green Hair.*

MEMBER: Actors' Equity Association, Screen Actors Guild.

ADDRESSES: AGENT—c/o Chris Barrett, McCartt, Oreck, and Barrett, 10390 Santa Monica Boulevard, Suite 310, Los Angeles, CA 90025.

*   *   *

STRAUSS, Peter   1947-

PERSONAL: Born in 1947, in Croton-on-Hudson, NY. EDUCATION: Attended Northwestern University.

VOCATION: Actor.

CAREER: FILM DEBUT—*Hail Hero!,* National General, 1969. PRINCIPAL FILM APPEARANCES—*Soldier Blue,* AVCO-Embassy, 1970; *The Trial of the Cantonsville Nine,* Cinema 5, 1972; *The Last Tycoon,* Paramount, 1977; *The Secret of NIMH,* Metro-Goldwyn-Mayer, 1982; *Space Hunter: Adventures in the Forbidden Zone,* Columbia, 1983.

PRINCIPAL TELEVISION APPEARANCES—Mini-Series: Rudy Jordache, *Rich Man, Poor Man,* ABC, 1976-77; Senator Rudy Jordache, *Rich Man, Poor Man, Book II,* ABC, 1976-77; *Masada,* 1981; *Kane & Abel,* CBS, 1985. Movies: *Man without a Country,* 1973; *Attack on Terror: The FBI vs. the Klu Klux Klan,* 1975; *Heart of Steel,* 1983; *The Jericho Mile,* ABC, 1979; *Tender Is the Night,* Showtime, 1985; *Under Siege,* NBC, 1986; Kenneth Hoffman, *Penalty Phase,* CBS, 1986; also *The Forgotten Kennedy.*

PRINCIPAL STAGE APPEARANCES—Bill Allenson, *Einstein and the Polar Bear,* Cort Theatre, New York City, 1981; *Dance Next*

Door and *The Dirty Man,* both at the Mark Taper Forum, Los Angeles.

AWARDS: Outstanding Performance by a Leading Actor in a Special, Emmy Award, 1979, for *The Jericho Mile.*

ADDRESSES: AGENT—c/o Martha Lutrell, International Creative Management, 8899 Beverly Blvd., Los Angeles, CA 90068.*

*   *   *

SUSSKIND, David   1920-1987

PERSONAL: Full name, David Howard Susskind; born December 19, 1920, in New York, NY; died February 22, 1987, in New York, NY; son of Benjamin (an insurance executive) and Frances (Lear) Susskind; married Phyllis Briskin, August 23, 1939 (divorced); married Joyce Davidson, 1966 (divorced, 1986); children: (first marriage) Andrew, Diana, Pamela; (second marriage) Samantha. EDUCATION: Attended the University of Wisconsin, 1938-40; Harvard University, B.S., 1942. MILITARY: U.S. Navy, 1942-46.

VOCATION: Producer and talk show host.

CAREER: PRINCIPAL TELEVISION APPEARANCES—Series: Host, *Open End,* syndicated, 1958-67; host, *David Susskind Show,* syndicated, 1967-1986. Movies: Cameo, *Fear on Trial,* CBS, 1975.

PRINCIPAL TELEVISION WORK—All as producer or executive producer. Series: *Philco-Goodyear Playhouse,* NBC, 1948-52; *Mr. Peepers,* NBC, 1951-55; *Justice,* NBC, 1954-56; *Kaiser Aluminum Hour,* NBC, 1957; *Armstrong Circle Theatre,* NBC, 1955-57, then CBS, 1957-63; *Dupont Show of the Month,* CBS, 1957-61, then NBC, 1963-64; *Kraft Television Theatre,* NBC, 1959; *Play of the Week,* WNTA, New York City, 1959-61; *Way Out,* CBS, 1961; *East Side/West Side,* CBS, 1963-64; *Get Smart,* NBC, 1965-69, then CBS, 1969-70; *On Our Own,* CBS, 1977-78; *Good Company,* ABC, 1967; also *Esso Repertory Theatre,* 1964-65; *Festival of Performing Arts,* 1961-63; *The World Beyond.* Pilots: *Alice,* CBS, 1976. Movies: *The Glass Menagerie,* ABC, 1973; *All Creatures Great and Small,* NBC, 1975; *Eleanor and Franklin,* ABC, 1976; *The War between the Tates,* NBC, 1977; *Tell Me My Name,* CBS, 1977; *Johnny, We Hardly Knew Ye,* NBC, 1977; *Eleanor and Franklin: The White House Years,* ABC, 1977; *Goldenrod,* CBS, 1977; *Breaking Up,* ABC, 1978; *Home to Stay,* CBS, 1978; *Lovey: A Circle of Children, Part II,* CBS, 1978; *Who'll Save Our Children?,* CBS, 1978; *Walking through the Fire,* CBS, 1979; *Transplant,* CBS, 1979; *Sex and the Single Parent,* CBS, 1979; *The Family Man,* CBS, 1979; *Blind Ambition,* CBS, 1979; *Father Figure,* CBS, 1980; *Mom, the Wolfman, and Me,* syndicated, 1980; *The Plutonium Incident,* CBS, 1980; *The Bunker,* CBS, 1981; *Crisis at Central High,* CBS, 1981; *The Wall,* CBS, 1982; *Rita Hayworth: The Love Goddess,* CBS; 1983. Specials: *Rexall Specials,* NBC, 1956-60; *Death of a Salesman,* CBS, 1966; "The Price," *Hallmark Hall of Fame,* NBC, 1971; also *Look Homeward, Angel,* 1972; *If You Give a Dance, You Gotta Pay the Band,* 1972; *Harvey,* 1972; *The Shenyang Acrobatic Troupe Special,* 1973; *The Magic Show,* 1975; *Caesar and Cleopatra,* 1976; *Truman at Potsdam,* 1976; *Harry S. Truman: Plain Speaking,* 1976; *Richard Rodgers: The Sound of His Music,* 1976; *World of Darkness,* 1977; *Casey Stengle,* 1980; *Dear Liar,* 1980; *Ian McKellen: Acting Shakespeare,* 1981; *JFK: A One Man Show,*

1984; and *The Bridge of San Luis Rey; The Ages of Man; The Crucible; The Diary of Anne Frank; The Human Voice; Laura; Crown Matrimonial; Hedda Gabler; The Moon and Sixpence; A Moon for the Misbegotten; The Power and the Glory; The Picture of Dorian Gray; After He's Gone; Winston Churchill; Ike in Gettysburg.*

PRINCIPAL FILM APPEARANCES—Cameo, *Simon,* Warner Brothers, 1980. PRINCIPAL FILM WORK—All as producer or executive producer: *Edge of the City,* Metro-Goldwyn-Mayer, 1957; *A Raisin in the Sun,* Columbia, 1961; *Requiem for a Heavyweight,* Columbia, 1962; *All the Way Home,* Paramount, 1963; *The People Next Door,* AVCO-Embassy, 1970; *Lovers and Other Strangers,* Cinerama, 1970; *The Pursuit of Happiness,* Columbia, 1971; *Straw Dogs,* Cinerama, 1971; *Alice Doesn't Live Here Anymore,* Warner Brothers, 1975; *Buffalo Bill and the Indians, or Sitting Bull's History Lesson,* United Artists, 1976; *Loving Couples,* Twentieth Century-Fox, 1980; *Fort Apache, the Bronx,* Twentieth Century-Fox, 1981. Also *All Creatures Great and Small,* 1974; *All Things Bright and Beautiful* (also known as *It Shouldn't Happen to a Vet*), 1979.

PRINCIPAL STAGE WORK—Producer, all in New York City: *A Very Special Baby,* Playhouse Theatre, 1956; *A Handful of Fire,* Martin Beck Theatre, 1958; *Rashomon,* Music Box Theatre, 1959; *Kelly,* Broadhurst Theatre, 1965; *All in Good Time,* Royale Theatre, 1965; *Brief Lives,* 1967.

RELATED CAREER—Publicist, 1946-48; talent agent, 1948-52; co-owner and president, Talent Associates, Ltd., 1952-87 (merged with Time-Life Films, Inc., 1977).

AWARDS: Receipient of numerous awards including Emmy awards, George Foster Peabody awards, International Television Film Festival awards, Sylvania Television awards, *TV Film Daily* awards, Screen Producers Guild Award, Newspaper Guild awards, Robert Sherwood Award, Christopher awards, B'nai Brith awards, Protestant Council Award.

MEMBER: National Academy of Television Arts and Sciences (vice-president, board of governors), American Federation of Television and Radio Artists, Screen Producers Guild.

OBITUARIES AND OTHER SOURCES: New York Times, February 23, 1987; *Variety,* February 25, 1987.*

*　　　*　　　*

SUTHERLAND, Kiefer

BRIEF ENTRY: Being the son of actor Donald Sutherland proved a handicap to Kiefer Sutherland when, at age fifteen, he decided to pursue the same career. "I had the Catch-22 problem because of my father," he told Diana Maychick of the *New York Post* (August 18, 1986), referring to the way his name would open doors, yet make producers skeptical of his talent. After about a year of auditions, his persistence began to pay off. Born c. 1967 in London, England, but having moved to Toronto at age ten, Sutherland was cast in the title role of a boy coming of age in Canada during the 1930's in the 1984 film *The Bay Boy.* Later he appeared in the CBS TV movie *Trapped in Silence* as a traumatized child who refuses to speak, and he also performed in the theatrical releases *At Close Range* and *Crazy Moon.* It was two other film roles, however, that brought him wider attention; he was a menacing presence both as a

young thug in the 1986 hit film *Stand By Me* and as a teenaged vampire in *The Lost Boys,* 1987. Recently, Sutherland portrayed Tad Allagash in the film version of the best-selling novel, *Bright Lights, Big City,* 1988.

*　　　*　　　*

SYKES, Eric 1924-

PERSONAL: Born in 1924, in Oldham, England.

VOCATION: Actor, writer, director, and comedian.

CAREER: PRINCIPAL STAGE APPEARANCES—*Time and Time Again,* London, 1983; *Run for Your Wife,* London and Canadian productions.

MAJOR TOURS—*Big Bad House,* U.K. cities, 1977; *Summer Show Sykes,* Zimbabwe (formerly Rhodesia), Australian, and Canadian cities, 1978; one-man show, U.K. cities, 1982.

PRINCIPAL FILM APPEARANCES—*Watch Your Stern,* British, 1960; *Invasion Quartet,* Metro-Goldwyn-Mayer (MGM), 1962; *Kill or Cure,* MGM, 1962; *Heaven's Above,* British Lion, 1963; *One Way Pendulum,* Lopert, 1965; *Those Magnificent Men in Their Flying Machines,* Twentieth Century-Fox, 1965; *Rotten to the Core,* Universal, 1965; *The Liquidator,* MGM, 1966; *The Spy with the Cold Nose,* Embassy, 1966; also *Village of Daughters; The Bargee.*

PRINCIPAL FILM WORK—Director and writer: *The Plank.*

PRINCIPAL TELEVISION APPEARANCES—Series: *Sykes Versus TV,* BBC, 1958-65; also a member of a BBC panel show series. Episodic: *The Frankie Howerd Show,* BBC. Specials: *Sykes and a Big, Big, Show,* BBC, 1971 and 1978; also *The Plank, If You Go Down to the Woods Today, Cannon and Ball Show,* and *It's Your Move.*

WRITINGS: (In addition to the listing above) SCREENPLAYS—*Shalako,* Cinerama, 1968; *Theatre of Blood,* United Artists, 1973; also *The Monte Carlo Rally.*

TELEPLAYS—Series: *Educating Archie;* also wrote series for Frankie Howerd, Max Bygraves, and Harry Secombe, all BBC.

RADIO—Series: Writer for Frankie Howerd, Max Bygraves, and Harry Secombe.*

*　　　*　　　*

SYMONDS, Robert 1926-

PERSONAL: Born December 1, 1926, in Bristow, OK; son of Walter Stout and Nellie (Barry) Symonds; married Jan Kaderli. EDUCATION: Attended the University of Texas, 1943-44, 1948-54, and the University of Missouri, 1944-45; trained for the stage with Ben Iden Payne.

VOCATION: Actor, producer, and director.

CAREER: STAGE DEBUT—With the Actors Workshop, San Francisco, CA, 1954. OFF-BROADWAY DEBUT—Estragon, *Waiting for Godot*, York Theatre, 1958. PRINCIPAL STAGE APPEARANCES—Estragon, *Waiting for Godot*, Actors Workshop, Marines Memorial Theatre, San Francisco, CA, 1957, then World's Fair, Brussels, Belgium, 1962; Archie Rice, *The Entertainer*, Hamm, *Endgame*, Major Domo, *Ariadne auf Naxos*, all Actors Workshop, War Memorial Opera House, San Francisco, CA, 1959; title role, *Krapp's Last Tape*, Actors Workshop, 1961; title role, *Galileo*, Actors Workshop, 1962; title role, *Volpone*, Davies, *The Caretaker*, both Actors Workshop, 1963; Edgar, *Play Strindberg*, Studio Arena Theatre, Buffalo, NY, 1972; Fintan Kinmore, *Patrick Pearse Motel*, Olney Playhouse, MD, 1972; Edgar, *Comedy of Marriage*, Alley Theatre, Houston, TX, 1974; various roles, *The Death and Life of Jesse James*, Mark Taper Forum, Los Angeles, CA, 1974; Sergeant Coyne, *The Poison Tree*, Ambassador Theatre, New York City, 1976; Mr. Shaw, *In Celebration*, Manhattan Theatre Club, New York City, 1984. Also appeared in *The Show-Off*, Alley Theatre, 1976; *How the Other Half Loves*, Alley Theatre, 1977; *The Shadow Box*, Alley Theatre, 1978; *Artichoke, Don Juan in Hell, Side by Side by Sondheim*, all Alley Theatre, 1979; *A Month in the Country*, McCarter Theatre, Princeton, NJ, 1979; *Artaud at Rodez*, Los Angeles Actors Theatre, Los Angeles, CA, 1982; *An Enemy of the People*, Los Angeles Actors Theatre, 1983.

All with the Repertory Theatre of Lincoln Center, Vivian Beaumont Theatre, New York City, unless indicated: Robespierre, *Danton's Death*, Mr. Sparkish, *The Country Wife*, both 1965; judge, Azdak, *The Caucasian Chalk Circle*, Jeremy Butler, *The Alchemist*, both 1966; Federzoni, *Galileo*, 1967; Chaplain de Stogumer, *Saint Joan*, Demokos, *Tiger at the Gates*, title role, *Cyrano de Bergerac*, Kemp, *A Cry of Players*, all 1968; Dominic Christian, *The Inner Journey*, Harpagon, *The Miser*, Ward V. Evans, *In the Matter of J. Robert Oppenheimer*, Kit Carson, *The Time of Your Life*, all 1969; Mendacious Porpentine, *The Disintegration of James Cherry*, Forum Theatre, New York City, 1970; Duff, *Landscape*, Rumsey, *Silence*, both 1970; Lord Mulligan, *Camino Real*, 1971; Goldberg, *The Birthday Party*, Rumsey, *Silence*, Duff, *Landscape*, all Forum Theatre, 1971; *Scenes from American Life*, Edgar, *Play Strindberg*, both 1971; Sir Amias Paulet, *Mary Stuart*, Baso, *Narrow Road to the Deep North*, both 1971; Zekhar Bardin, *Enemies*, 1972; Duke of Venice, *The Merchant of Venice*, 1973.

PRINCIPAL STAGE WORK—Director: *The Maids*, Actors Workshop, San Francisco, CA, 1961; *Volpone, The Taming of the Shrew*, both Actors Workshop, 1963; *The Night of the Iguana*, Actors Workshop, 1964; *The Country Wife*, Repertory Theatre of Lincoln Center, Vivian Beaumont Theatre, New York City, 1966; *Bananas*, Repertory Theatre of Lincoln Center, 1968; *Amphitryon, The Good Woman of Setzuan*, both Repertory Theatre of Lincoln Center, 1970; *The Playboy of the Western World*, Repertory Theatre of Lincoln Center, 1971; *Endgame*, Alley Theatre, Houston, TX, 1977; *Root of the Mandrake*, Alley Theatre, 1978.

MAJOR TOURS—Prime Minister, *The Student Prince*, U.S. cities, 1973.

PRINCIPAL TELEVISION APPEARANCES—Pilots: Carruthers, *Shell Game*, CBS, 1975; *The Big Ripoff*, NBC, 1975. Mini-Series: Dave Goodwyn, *Loose Change* (also known as *Those Restless Years*), NBC, 1978; Cameron Fairchild, *Murder in Texas*, NBC, 1981; General Robert E. Lee, *The Blue and the Gray*, CBS, 1982; also appeared as Edward Gold, *Seventh Avenue*, 1974. Movies: Andrew Jennings, *The Legend of Lizzie Borden*, ABC, 1975; President Harry Truman, *Tail Gunner Joe*, NBC, 1977; Dr. Arnold, *Marian Rose White*, CBS, 1982; also appeared in *Wanted: The Sundance Woman* (also known as *Mrs. Sundance Rides Again*), ABC, 1976.

PRINCIPAL FILM APPEARANCES—*Gray Lady Down*, Universal, 1978; *And Justice for All*, Columbia, 1979; *The Ice Pirates*, Metro-Goldwyn-Mayer/United Artists, 1984; *Micki and Maude*, Columbia, 1984; also appeared in *The Witch*, 1981; *Crimewave*, 1985.

RELATED CAREER—Faculty member, University of California Extension, 1964-65; associate director, Repertory Theatre of Lincoln Center, New York City, 1966-1972.

ADDRESSES: AGENT—Hesseltine-Baker Associates, 119 W. 57th Street, New York, NY 10019.*

T

TABOR, Susan 1939-

PERSONAL: Born May 28, 1939, in Detroit, MI; daughter of Lawton Cline (a meat purveyor) and Sarah Alice (a teacher; maiden name, Kauffman) Tabor; married Thomas W. Wahman (a consultant), September 8, 1962; children: Jessica, Gwendolyn. EDUCATION: New York University, B.A., 1961; also attended Skidmore College, 1957-59; trained for the stage with Jane White and Bill Ball. POLITICS: Democrat.

VOCATION: Actress.

CAREER: OFF-BROADWAY DEBUT—Chorus, Electra, Players Theatre, 1962, for sixteen performances. PRINCIPAL STAGE APPEARANCES—Joy, Inadmissible Evidence, Belasco Theatre, then Shubert Theatre, both New York City, 1965; Lady Sybil, What Every Woman Knows, Roundabout Theatre, New York City, 1975;

SUSAN TABOR

Bunny, California Suite, Eugene O'Neill Theatre, New York City, 1976.

MAJOR TOURS—Tiffany, Mary, Mary, U.S. cities, 1963; Doreen, Seidman and Son, U.S. cities, 1963; Elsa, The Sound of Music, U.S. cities, 1978.

PRINCIPAL TELEVISION APPEARANCES—Series: Ruth, Ryan's Hope, ABC, 1977.

RELATED CAREER—Swimmer, Aqua Spectacular, U.S. cities, 1962; scuba diver, Lloyd Bridges's "Sea Hunt" at the World's Fair, New York City, 1964; actress, television commercials, 1963—.

NON-RELATED CAREER—Volunteer, American Field Service International Urban Scholarship Program, 1983—;

ADDRESSES: HOME—New York, NY. AGENT—c/o Cunningham, Escott, Dipene & Associates, 118 E. 25th Street, New York, NY 10010.

*   *   *

TAGG, Alan 1928-

PERSONAL: Born April 13, 1928, in Sutton-in-Ashfield, England; son of Thomas Bertram and Edith Annie (Hufton) Tagg. EDUCATION: Trained for the stage at the Old Vic Theatre School.

VOCATION: Set and costume designer.

CAREER: FIRST STAGE WORK—Set designer, The River Line, London, 1952. PRINCIPAL STAGE WORK—All as set designer unless indicated: Costume designer, Julius Caesar, Old Vic Theatre, London, 1955; Look Back in Anger, Lyceum Theatre, New York City, 1957; All in Good Time, Royale Theatre, New York City, 1965; Trelawny of the Wells, Chichester Festival Theatre, Chichester, U.K., 1965; The Fighting Cock, The Clandestine Marriage, The Cherry Orchard, Macbeth, all Chichester Festival Theatre, 1966; Black Comedy, National Theatre, London, 1966, then Ethel Barrymore Theatre, New York City, 1967; The Cherry Orchard, National Theatre, 1973; The Director of the Opera, Dandy Dick, both Chichester Festival Theatre, 1973; Confusions, Globe Theatre, London, 1976; Donkey's Years, Apollo Theatre, London, 1976; Same Time Next Year, Prince of Wales Theatre, London, 1976; Whose Life Is It, Anyway?, Mermaid Theatre, London, then Trafalgar Theatre, New York City, both 1978; The Millionairess, Haymarket Theatre, London, 1978; Alice's Boys,

357

Savoy Theatre, London, 1978; *Joking Apart,* Globe Theatre, 1979; *Bent,* Royal Court Theatre, then Criterion Theatre, both London, 1979; *Middle Age Spread,* Lyric Theatre, London, 1979; *Not Now Darling,* Savoy Theatre, London, 1979; *Whose Life Is It, Anyway?,* Wilshire Theatre, Los Angeles, CA, 1980, then Morris Mechanic Theatre, Baltimore, MD, 1981; *Corpse,* Helen Hayes Theatre, New York City, 1986.

Set designer, all in London unless indicated: *The Burning Glass, Waiting for Gillian, Both Ends Meet, Simon and Laura,* and *Bell, Book and Candle,* all 1954; *The Merchant of Venice,* Stratford-on-Avon, U.K., 1956; *Look Back in Anger, Cards of Identity,* both 1956; *The Member of the Wedding, The Entertainer,* both 1957; *Live Like Pigs,* New York City, 1958; *The Long and the Short and the Tall, One More River,* both 1959; *A Majority of One, Billy Liar, The Geese Are Getting Fat,* all 1960; *JB, Time and Yellow Roses, The American Dream, The Death of Bessie Smith, The Fire Raisers,* all 1961; *Play with a Tiger, Plays for England,* and *England, Our England,* all 1962; *Trap for a Lonely Man, Kelly's Eye, The Albatross,* all 1963; *A Cuckoo in the Nest,* 1964; *Meals on Wheels,* 1965; *Belcher's Luck,* 1966; *Halfway up the Tree,* 1967; *Spitting Image, Mr. and Mrs.,* both 1968; *Come as You Are, After Haggerty, London Assurance, How the Other Half Loves, Mrs. Warren's Profession,* all 1970; *Dear Antoine,* London, then Chichester Festival Theatre, both 1971; *Straight Up,* 1971; *Alpha Beta, Hedda Gabler, Time and Time Again,* all 1972; *Absurd Person Singular,* 1973; *The Constant Wife,* London, then New York City, 1973; *London Assurance,* New York City, 1974; *Alphabetical Order, The Gay Lord Quex, The Bed Before Yesterday, The Sea Gull, The Return of A.J. Raffles,* all 1975; *Candida, Waters of the Moon,* both 1977; *Sisterly Feelings, Taking Steps,* both 1980; *Moving, Arms and the Man,* both 1981; *Way Upstream,* 1982; *Corpse,* London, 1984; *A Chorus of Disapproval, The Corn Is Green, The Philanthropist,* all 1985; *Tons of Money,* 1986; *A View from the Bridge, A Small Family Business, Lettice and Lovage,* all 1987. Also designed shows for theatres in Europe and Australia.

ADDRESSES: OFFICE—19 Parsons Green, London SW6 4UL, England.

*   *   *

TAKEI, George

PERSONAL: Born April 20, in Los Angeles, CA. EDUCATION: Attended University of California at Los Angeles; trained at the Desilu Workshop, Hollywood.

VOCATION: Actor and writer.

CAREER: TELEVISION DEBUT—*Playhouse 90,* CBS. PRINCIPAL TELEVISION APPEARANCES—Series: Sulu, *Star Trek,* NBC, 1966-69. Episodic: *Perry Mason,* CBS; *Alcoa Premiere,* ABC; *Mr. Novak,* NBC; *The Wackiest Ship in the Army,* NBC; *I Spy,* NBC; *Magnum P.I.,* CBS; *Trapper John, M.D.,* CBS.

PRINCIPAL FILM APPEARANCES—*Ice Palace,* 1960; *A Majority of One,* Warner Brothers, 1962; *Hell to Eternity,* Allied Artists, 1962; *An American Dream,* Warner Brothers, 1962; *Walk, Don't Run,* Columbia, 1966; *The Green Berets,* Warner Brothers/Seven Arts, 1968; Sulu, *Star Trek: The Motion Picture,* Paramount, 1979; Sulu, *Star Trek II: Wrath of Khan,* Paramount, 1982; Sulu, *Star*

Trek III: Search for Spock, Paramount, 1984; Sulu, *Star Trek IV: The Voyage Home,* Paramount, 1986.

WRITINGS: BOOKS—*Mirror Friend, Mirror Foe.*

MEMBER: Screen Actors Guild, American Federation of Television and Radio Artists.

ADDRESSES: AGENT—c/o Steven R. Stevens, Twentieth Century Artists, Inc., 3800 Barham Boulevard, Suite 303, Los Angeles, CA 90068.

*   *   *

TARTIKOFF, Brandon

BRIEF ENTRY: As president of NBC Entertainment, Brandon Tartikoff is widely credited with devising the programming that raised the network to the top of the television ratings in 1985 after several years at the bottom. The victory culminated several years of trial-and-error adjustments to the schedule after Tartikoff, barely in his thirties, became director of programming in 1980. A 1970 graduate of Yale University, he had begun working in television as the director of advertising and promotion at station WLS-TV in Chicago and had a short stint at the ABC network before joining NBC in 1977 as the Burbank-based director of comedy programs. Tartikoff lured producers reluctant to air their shows on the low-rated NBC by pledging support to new programs. Such backing allowed quality shows like *St. Elsewhere* and *Cheers* to build viewers. "I like to challenge the audience," Tartikoff told *Time* (December 3, 1984); nevertheless, he enjoyed an immediate hit when he created *The Cosby Show* and also introduced such programs as *Knight Rider* and *Punky Brewster,* more popular with viewers than with critics. In 1986, under his leadership, NBC ventured into producing films for theatrical release, an area that piqued Tartikoff's interest when he became involved in financing *Terms of Endearment.* The first of the network-backed movies, each budgeted at a maximum of six million dollars according to the August 19, 1986 *New York Times,* was *Square Dance,* a story about a teenage girl's coming of age in Texas.

*   *   *

TAVEL, Ronald 1941-

PERSONAL: Surname is pronounced Tah-*vel;* born May 17, 1941, in Brooklyn, NY; son of George and Florence (Sterns) Tavel. EDUCATION: Received B.A. from Brooklyn College; University of Wyoming, M.A., 1961.

VOCATION: Playwright, screenwriter, and actor.

CAREER: PRINCIPAL FILM APPEARANCES—*Fifty Fantasticks,* 1964; *Bitch,* 1965; *Jail,* 1967; *Suicide Notions: Fire Escape,* 1972; *In Search of the Cobra Jewels,* 1972.

RELATED CAREER—Scenarist, Andy Warhol's Factory Film Studio, New York City, 1964-66; founder, Theatre of the Ridiculous, New York City, 1965; founding member, New York Theatre Strategy, 1971-79; literary advisor, *Scripts,* 1971-72; advisor, Subplot Theatre, American Place Theatre Complex, New York

City, 1972; also lecturer, New York State Council on the Arts. Playwright-in-residence: Play-House of the Ridiculous, 1965-67; Theatre of the Lost Continent, 1971-73; Actors Studio, 1972; Yale Divinity School, 1975, then 1977; Williamstown Theatre Festival, Williamstown, MA, 1977; O'Neill Playwrights Conference, 1977; New Playwrights Theatre, Washington, DC, 1978-79.

WRITINGS: PLAYS—*Christina's World*, 1958, published in *Chicago Review*, 1963; *Tarzan of the Flicks*, Goddard College, Plainfield, VT, 1965; *Screen Test*, 1965; *The Life of Juanita Castro, Shower*, both St. Mark's Playhouse, New York City, 1965, published in *Tri-Quarterly*, 1966, then *The Young American Writers*, Funk, 1967; *Vinyl*, Caffe Cino, New York City, 1967, published in *Clyde*, 1966; *The Life of Lady Godiva*, Play-House of the Ridiculous, New York City, 1966, published in *The New Underground Theatre*, Bantam, 1968; *Indira Gandhi's Daring Device, Screen Test*, both Play-House of *the Ridiculous*, 1966; *Kitchenette*, Play-House of the Ridiculous, 1967, published in *Partisan Review*, 1967; *Gorilla Queen*, Judson Poets Theatre, then Martinique Theatre, both New York City, 1967, published in *The Best of Off-Broadway Theatre*, Dutton, 1969, then in *The Off-Off-Broadway Book*, Bobbs-Merrill, 1972; *Canticle of the Nightingale*, produced in Stockholm, Sweden, 1968, then Manhattan Theatre Club, New York City, 1973; *Cleobis and Bito*, Extension Theatre, New York City, 1968; *Arenas of Lutetia*, Judson Poets Theatre, 1968, published in *Experiments in Prose*, Swallow Press, 1969; *Boy on the Straight-Back Chair*, American Place Theatre, New York City, 1969; *Vinyl Visits an FM Station*, Playwrights Unit, New York City, 1970, published in *Drama Review*, 1970; *Bigfoot*, Theatre Genesis, New York City, 1972; *Secrets of the Citizens Correction Committee*, St. Clements Church Theatre, New York City, 1973, published in *Scripts*, 1972; *How Jacqueline Kennedy Became Queen of Greece*, Theatre Genesis, 1973; *The Last Days of British Honduras*, New York Shakespeare Festival, Public Theatre, New York City, 1974; *Playbirth, The Clown's Tail*, both 1976; *Gazelle Boy, The Ovens of Anita Orangejuice*, both 1977; *The Ark of God, The Nutcracker in the Land of Nuts*, both 1979; *Success and Succession*, Theatre for the New City, New York City, 1983.

SCREENPLAYS—All produced by Andy Warhol Films, Inc.: *Harlot*, 1964, published in *Film Culture*, 1966; *The Life of Juanita Castro*, 1965; *Philip's Screen Test* (unreleased), 1965; *Kitchen*, 1965; *Horse*, 1965; *Space*, 1965; *Suicide*, 1965; *Withering Sights*, 1966; *The Chelsea Girls*, 1966; *Hedy, or the Fourteen Year Old Girl*, 1966; *Vinyl*, 1967; *Words for Bryan to Sing and Dance*, 1971.

NON-FICTION—*The Banana Diary* (book-length essay), published in *Film Culture*, 1966; *The New American Cinema*, Dutton, 1967. Also contributed poetry and criticism to *Inter/View, The Lyric, Poets at Le Metro, Writing at Wyoming, Chicago Review, Wormwood, Tri-Quarterly, Aspen, Film Culture, Graffiti*, and *Filmwise*.

FICTION—*Streets of Stairs*, selections published in *Chicago Review*, 1964, complete book published in 1968.

RECORDINGS: (Lyricist) *No More Masterpieces*, Mention Records, 1971.

AWARDS: Lyric poetry contest winner, 1955, for *Virginia Woolf;* Obie Award from the *Village Voice*, 1969, for *Boy on the Straight-Back Chair;* American Place Theatre Grant 1970; Rockefeller Foundation Fellowship, 1972; Creative Artists Public Service Program Fellowship, 1972; Guggenheim Foundation Grant, 1973; Obie Award, 1973, for *Bigfoot;* National Endowment for the Arts

Grant, 1974-75; New York State Council on the Arts Younger Audience Commission Grant, 1975-76.

SIDELIGHTS: RECREATIONS—Traveling, swimming.

ADDRESSES: HOME—438 West Broadway, New York, NY 10012. AGENT—c/o Helen Merrill, 337 W. 22nd Street, New York, NY 10011.*

*   *   *

TAYLOR, Don

PERSONAL: Born December 13, in Freeport, PA. EDUCATION: Attended Pennsylvania State University.

VOCATION: Actor, director, and writer.

CAREER: PRINCIPAL FILM APPEARANCES—*Girl Crazy*, Metro-Goldwyn-Mayer (MGM), 1943; *Winged Victory*, 1944; *For the Love of Money*, 1948; *Father of the Bride*, MGM, 1950; *Father's Little Dividend*, MGM, 1951; *Submarine Command*, 1951; *Flying Leathernecks*, RKO, 1951; *Blue Veil*, 1951; *Japanese War Bride*, 1952; *Stalag 17*, Paramount, 1953; *The Girls of Pleasure Island*, 1953; *Destination Gobi*, 1953; *Johnny Dark*, 1954; *I'll Cry Tomorrow*, Metro-Goldwyn-Mayer, 1955; *Bold and the Brave*, RKO, 1955; also *Battleground*.

PRINCIPAL FILM WORK—Director: *Jack of Diamonds*, MGM, 1967; *Five Man Army*, MGM, 1970; *Escape from the Planet of the Apes*, Twentieth Century-Fox, 1971; *Tom Sawyer*, United Artists, 1973; *Echoes of a Summer*, Cine Artists, 1976; *The Great Scout and Cathouse Thursday*, American International, 1976; *The Island of Dr. Moreau*, American International, 1977; *Damien: Omen II*, Twentieth Century-Fox, 1978; *The Final Countdown*, United Artists, 1980.

PRINCIPAL TELEVISION WORK—Movies: Director—*Red Flag: The Ultimate Game*, 1981; *Broken Promise*, 1981; *Drop-Out Father*, CBS, 1982; *September Gun*, CBS, 1983; *He's Not Your Son*, 1984; *Secret Weapons*, 1985; *My Wicked, Wicked Ways . . . The Legend of Errol Flynn*, CBS, 1985; *Going for the Gold: The Bill Johnson Story*, 1985; *Classified Cove*, 1986.

RELATED CAREER—Writer of short stories, radio dramas, one-act plays and television shows.

ADDRESSES: AGENT—The Gersh Agency, 222 N. Canon Drive, Beverly Hills, CA 90210.*

*   *   *

TAYLOR, John Russell   1935-

PERSONAL: Born June 19, 1935, in Dover, England; son of Arthur Russell and Kathleen Mary (Picker) Taylor. EDUCATION: Cambridge University, B.A., 1956; also attended the Courtauld Institute of Art.

VOCATION: Writer and critic.

CAREER: Editor, *Times Educational Supplement,* London, 1959-60; editorial assistant, *Times Literary Supplement,* London, 1960-62; film critic, *The Times,* London, 1962-73, then art critic, 1978—; editor, *Films and Filming,* 1983—; professor, Division of Cinema, University of Southern California, Los Angeles, 1972-78; also contributer of theatre criticism, *Plays and Players.*

WRITINGS: BOOKS—*Joseph L. Mankiewicz: An Index,* British Film Institute, 1960; *The Angry Theatre,* Hill and Wang, 1962, revised edition, Penguin, 1963, as *Anger and After: A Guide to the New British Drama,* Methuen, 1962; *Anatomy of a Television Play,* Weidenfeld and Nicholson, 1962; *Cinema Eye, Cinema Ear,* Methuen, 1964; (contributor) *Shakespeare: A Celebration,* Penguin, 1964; (editor and author of introductions) *John Arden: Three Plays,* Penguin, 1965; *New English Dramatists 8,* Penguin, 1965; *Penguin Dictionary of the Theatre,* Penguin, 1966; *The Art Nouveau Book in Britain,* Methuen, 1966, then M.I.T. Press, 1967; *The Rise and Fall of the Well-Made Play,* Hill and Wang, 1967; *Preston Sturges,* Secker and Warburg, 1967; (editor) *Look Back in Anger: A Casebook,* 1968; *Harold Pinter,* 1969; *The Art Dealers,* 1969; *The Hollywood Musical,* 1971; *The Second Wave: Hollywood Dramatists for the Seventies,* 1971; (editor) *The Pleasure Dome,* 1972; *Masterworks of the British Cinema,* 1974; *Directors and Directions: Peter Shaffer,* 1975; *Hitch,* 1978; *Cukor's Hollywood,* 1979; *Impressionism,* 1981; *Strangers in Paradise,* 1983; *Ingrid Bergman,* 1983; *Alec Guinness: A Celebration,* 1984; *Vivien Leigh,* 1984; *Hollywood 1940's,* 1985; (with John Kobal) *Portraits of the British Cinema,* 1986.

MEMBER: London Film and Television Press Guild, London Critics Circle, New York Society of Cinematologists.

SIDELIGHTS: RECREATIONS—Buying books, "talking to strange dogs."

ADDRESSES: HOME—11 Hollytree Close, Inner Park Road, London SW 19, England. OFFICE—c/o *The Times,* Gray's Inn Road, London W1X 8EZ, England. AGENT—c/o A.D. Peters, 10 Buckingham Street, London WC2, England.*

*   *   *

TERRY, Megan   1932-

PERSONAL: Born Megan Duffy, July 22, 1932, in Seattle, WA; daughter of Harold Joseph and Marguerite Cecilia (Henry) Duffy. EDUCATION: Received B.Ed. from the University of Washington; also attended the University of Alberta, Banff School of Fine Arts, and Yale Unversity; trained for the stage with Florence and Burton James at the Seattle Repertory Playhouse.

VOCATION: Playwright and teacher.

CAREER: Also see *WRITINGS* below.

RELATED CAREER—Founding member, Open Theatre, New York City, 1963; playwright in residence and literary manager, Omaha Magic Theatre, Omaha, NE, 1974—; Theatre Panel, National Endowment for the Arts, 1975-85, then Theatre Overview Panel, 1978, 81, 84-85, and Opera/Music Panel, 1985—; judge, American Theatre Association New Play Contest, 1977; member, Nebraska Committee for the Humanities, 1983; reorganized and toured with the Cornish Players, Seattle, WA; co-chair, Play-

MEGAN TERRY

Photography by Cynthia MacAdams

wrights Projects Committee, American Theatre Association; founding member, New York Theatre Strategy; founding member, Women's Theatre Council; Nebraska Dramatists Committee Selection Panel; Telecommunications Committee for the State of Nebraska; Theatre Grants Committee, Ford Foundation; Nebraska Arts Council; Bush Foundation; Ohio Arts Foundation; Wisconsin Arts Board; Rockefeller Foundation Theatre Panel.

Also Bingham Professor of Humanities, University of Louisville; Hill Professor of Fine Arts, University of Minnesota, Duluth. Lecturer: Rocky Mountain Theatre Conference, Colorado Women's College; Squaw Valley Community of Writers; Indiana University Writer's Conference; University of Southwestern Louisiana; University of North Dakota Writers' Conference; Cranbrook Writers' Conference; Notre Dame Literary Festival; National Playwrights Conference, Stanford University; Dancy Lectures, University of Montevallo; International Youth and Children's Theatre Festival; ASSITEJ World Theatre Symposium; Contemporary Arts Center, New Orleans, LA; University of Alabama; University of Minnesota; Miami-Dade Community College; playwriting seminars (with Caryl Churchill), Swarthmore College.

WRITINGS: PLAYS—*Beach Grass, Seascape, Go Out and Move the Car,* all Cornish Theatre, Seattle, WA, 1955; *New York Comedy: Two,* Saratoga Gallery Theatre, Saratoga, NY, 1961; *Ex-Miss Copper Queen on a Set of Pills,* Cherry Lane Theatre, New York City, 1963, then St. Joan Theatre, Chicago, IL, later Edinburgh Festival, Edinburgh, Scotland, U.K., both 1987, published in *Playwrights for Tomorrow, Vol. 1,* University of Minnesota Press, 1966, then by Samuel French, Inc., 1970, and in *A Century of Plays by American Women,* Rosen Press, 1979; *When My Girlhood Was Still All Flowers, Eat at Joe's,* both Open Theatre, New York City, 1963.

The Gloaming, Oh My Darling, Firehouse Theatre, Minneapolis, MN, 1965, published in *Viet Rock: Four Plays by Megan Terry,* Simon & Schuster, 1967, then in *Norton Introduction to Literature,* Norton, 1973, and by Samuel French, Inc., 1980; *Calm Down Mother,* Sheridan Square Playhouse, New York City, 1965, then Swarthmore College Theatre, Swarthmore, PA, 1987, published in *Eight Plays from Off-Off Broadway,* Bobbs-Merrill, 1966, then by Samuel French, Inc., 1970, and in *Plays by and about Women,* Random House, 1973; *Keep Tightly Closed in a Cool, Dry Place,* Sheridan Square Playhouse, 1965, then Edinburgh Festival, 1968, published in *Tulane Drama Review,* 1966, in *Viet Rock: Four Plays by Megan Terry,* Simon & Schuster, 1967, and by Samuel French, Inc., 1980; *The Magic Realists,* La Mama Experimental Theatre Club (ETC), New York City, 1966, published in *Best One-Act Plays of 1968,* Chilton Press, 1969, and by Samuel French, Inc., 1971; *Viet Rock,* La Mama ETC, 1966, then Yale University Theatre, New Haven, CT, 1966, later Martinique Theatre, New York City, 1967, and at Temple University Theatre, Philadelphia, PA, and Swarthmore College Theatre, and in New York City, all 1987, published in *Tulane Drama Review,* 1966, and in *Viet Rock: Four Plays by Megan Terry,* Simon & Schuster, 1967; *Comings and Goings,* La Mama ETC, 1966, then Edinburgh Festival, 1969, later Swarthmore College Theatre, 1987, published in *Viet Rock: Four Plays by Megan Terry,* 1967, and by Samuel French, Inc., 1980; *Jack-Jack,* Firehouse Theatre, then International Theatre Festival, Nancy, France, both 1968; *The Key Is at the Bottom,* Mark Taper Forum Theatre Lab, Los Angeles, CA, 1968; *Changes,* La Mama ETC, 1968; *Massachussetts Trust,* Brandeis University Theatre, Waltham, MA, 1968, published by Bobbs-Merrill, 1972; *The People vs. Ranchman,* Fortune Theatre, New York City, 1968, published by Samuel French, Inc., 1970; *The Tommy Allen Show,* College of the Immaculate Heart Theatre, Los Angeles, CA, 1969, then Omaha Magic Theatre, Omaha, NE, later Actors Studio, New York City, 1970, published in *Scripts 2,* 1971.

Approaching Simone, Boston University Theatre, Boston, MA, 1970, then University of Montreal Theatre, Montreal, PQ, Canada, and University of Western Maryland Theatre, both 1982, published by Feminist Press, 1973, in *Women in Drama,* Mentor Books (NAL), 1975, and by Samuel French, Inc., 1980; (with Jo Ann Schmidman) *Choose a Spot on the Floor,* Omaha Magic Theatre, 1972; *Grooving,* Brooklyn Academy of Music, Brooklyn, NY, 1972; (lyricist) *Thoughts,* Theatre de Lys, New York City, 1972; *Susan Peretz at the Manhattan Theatre Club,* New York Theatre Strategy Festival, New York City, 1973; *Saint Hydro-Clemency,* St. Clements Church Theatre, New York City, 1973; (with Sam Shepard and Jean Claude Van Itallie) *Nightwalk,* produced in New York City, 1973, published in *Three Works by the Open Theatre,* Bobbs-Merrill, 1975; *Couplings and Groupings,* published by Pantheon, 1973, then by Avon, 1974; *We Can Feed Everybody Here,* Westbeth Feminist's Collective Theatre, New York City, 1974; *The Narco Linguini Bust,* Omaha Magic Theatre, 1974; *Babes in the Bighouse,* Omaha Magic Theatre, 1974, then New York Theatre Strategy, Theatre 13, New York City, 1976, later Amherst College Theatre, MA, 1976, and Wilma Project Theatre, Philadelphia, PA, 1976, published in *High Energy Plays from the Omaha Magic Theatre,* Broadway Play Publishing, 1983; *The Pioneer,* Theatre Genesis, 1974, published by Ragnarok Press, 1975, and in *Two by Terry Plus One,* I.E. Clark, 1984; *Pro Game,* Theatre Genesis, 1974, then University of Notre Dame Theatre, 1983, published in *Two by Terry Plus One,* I.E. Clark, 1984; *Hospital Play,* Omaha Magic Theatre, 1974; *Hothouse,* Circle Repertory Theatre, then Chelsea Theatre Center, both New York City, 1974, later University of Nebraska Theatre, Lincoln, NE, 1980, Horizon Theatre, Atlanta, GA, 1984, and College of William

and Mary, Williamsburg, VA, 1987, published by Samuel French, Inc., 1975.

Mollie Bailey's Family Circus, Featuring Scenes from the Life of Mother Jones, Mark Taper Forum Theatre Lab, 1975, published by Broadway Play Publishing, 1983; *100,001 Horror Stories of the Plains,* Omaha Magic Theatre, 1976; *Brazil Fado,* Omaha Magic Theatre, 1977, then University of Notre Dame Theatre, 1983; *Willa-Willie-Bill's Dope Garden,* Ragnarok Press, 1977; *American King's English for Queens,* Omaha Magic Theatre, 1978, published in *High Energy Musicals from the Omaha Magic Theatre,* Broadway Play Publishing, 1983; (with Schmidman) *Running Gag,* Omaha Magic Theatre, 1979, then Winter Olympic Games Theatre, Lake Placid, NY, 1980, published by Broadway Play Publishing, 1983; *Fireworks,* Actors Theatre of Louisville, Louisville, KY, 1979, published by Earplay Publications, 1980; *Attempted Rescue on Avenue B.,* Chicago Theatre Strategy, Chicago, IL, 1979; *Goona Goona,* Omaha Magic Theatre, 1979, then Wichita State University, Wichita, KS, 1986.

Comings and Goings: The Musical, Advances, both Omaha Magic Theatre, 1980, then University of Kansas Theatre, Lawrence, KS, 1984; *Objective Love,* Omaha Magic Theatre, 1980; *Henna for Endurance, Scenes from Maps,* both University of Nebraska Theatre, Omaha, NE, 1980; *Winners,* Process Theatre, Santa Barbara, CA, 1981; *Katmandu,* Omaha Magic Theatre, 1981, published in *Humor in America,* Collins, 1985; *Kegger,* Omaha Magic Theatre, 1982, then Yuba College Theatre, Marysville, CA, 1984; *Fifteen Million Fifteen Year-Olds,* Omaha Magic Theatre, 1983; *X-Rayed-Iate,* Omaha Magic Theatre, 1984; *Family Talk,* Omaha Magic Theatre, 1986; *Sleazing toward Athens,* Omaha Magic Theatre, then University of Nebraska, Lincoln, both 1986; *Sea of Forms,* Omaha Magic Theatre, 1986, then Grinnell College, IA, 1987; *Dinner's in the Blender,* produced in Gordon, NE, 1987; *Pro-Jec-Tiles,* Omaha Magic Theatre, 1987; *Future Soap,* Omaha Magic Theatre, 1987, published as *Megan Terry's Home: Or Future Soap,* Samuel French, Inc., 1972; *Retro,* Omaha Magic Theatre, 1988.

TELEPLAYS—*The Dirt Boat,* KING-TV, Seattle, WA, 1955; *Home: Or Future Soap,* WNET, New York City, 1968, later in U.S. and Canada, 1969; *One More Little Drinkie,* PBS, 1970, published in *Three One-Act Plays by Megan Terry,* Samuel French, Inc., 1971; (with Anne Meara) *Special Material,* PBS, 1974; *Women and the Law,* PBS Nebraska, 1976.

RADIO PLAYS—*Sanibel and Captiva,* WGBH, Boston, then National Public Radio, both 1968, published in *Three One-Act Plays by Megan Terry,* Samuel French, Inc., 1971, and in *Spontaneous Combustion,* Winterhouse, 1972; ''American Wedding Ritual,'' *Earplay,* National Public Radio, then in Canada, both 1972, published in *Places: A Journal of the Theatre, Vol. 1,* 1973; ''Fireworks,'' *Earplay,* National Public Radio, then in Canada, both 1980.

PERIODICALS—''Cool Is Out! Uptight Is In,'' *New York Times,* January 14, 1968; ''Who Says Only Words Make Great Drama?,'' *New York Times,* November 10, 1968; ''American Experimental Theatre, Then and Now,'' *Performing Arts Journal,* Vol. 2, 1977; ''Two Pages a Day,'' *Drama Review,* 1977; ''Omaha Magic: Playwright's Theatre,'' *The Southwestern Review,* 1980. Also wrote the article ''Janis Joplin,'' for *Notable American Women,* Harvard University Press, 1980.

AWARDS: Best Play, Obie Award from the *Village Voice,* 1970, for *Approaching Simone;* Silver Medal, American Theatre Association, 1977, for "Distinguished Contribution to and Service in the American Theatre;" Dramatists Guild Award, 1983; Stanley Drama Award; American Theatre Association Award; Nebraska Poet Laureate nomination; Guggenheim Fellowship; two Office of Advanced Drama Research grants from the University of Minnesota; two Rockefeller grants; New York Stage CAPS Fellowship; ABC "Writing for the Camera" Fellowship from Yale University; Literature Fellowship, National Endowment for the Arts.

SIDELIGHTS: RECREATIONS—"Study of the living American language," fishing.

ADDRESSES: OFFICE—c/o The Magic Theatre, 1417 Farnam Street, Omaha, NE 68202. AGENT—c/o Elisabeth Marton, 96 Fifth Avenue, New York, NY 10011.

*   *   *

TESICH, Steve   1942-

PERSONAL: Born Stoyan Tesich, September 29, 1942, in Titovo Utice, Yugoslavia; immigrated to U.S., 1955, naturalized, 1961; son of Radisa (a steel mill worker) and Gospava (Bulaich) Tesich; married Rebecca Fletcher, May 24, 1971. EDUCATION: Indiana University, B.A., 1965; Columbia University, M.A., 1967. POLITICS: Democrat.

VOCATION: Writer.

CAREER: PRINCIPAL FILM WORK—Writer (see below).

NON-RELATED CAREER—Formerly a caseworker for the Department of Welfare, Brooklyn, NY, 1968.

WRITINGS: SCREENPLAYS—*Breaking Away,* Twentieth Century-Fox, 1979; *Eyewitness,* Twentieth Century-Fox, 1981; *Four Friends,* Filmways, 1981; *The World According to Garp,* Warner Brothers, 1982; *Eleni,* Warner Brothers, 1985; *American Flyers,* Warner Brothers, 1985.

PLAYS, PRODUCED AND PUBLISHED—*The Carpenters,* St. Clement's Church, 1970, New York City, published by Dramatists Play Service, 1971; *Nourish the Beast,* first produced as *Baba Goya,* American Place Theatre, New York City, 1973, published by Samuel French, 1974; *The Passing Game,* American Place Theatre, New York City, 1977, published by Samuel French, 1978; *Touching Bottom* (three one-acts, containing "The Road," "A Life," and "Baptismal") American Place Theatre, New York City, 1978, published by Samuel French; *Division Street,* Ahmanson Theatre, Los Angeles, 1980; published by Samuel French, also published in *Division Street & Other Plays,* PAJ Publications, 1981; also, *Gorky,* American Place Theatre, New York City, published by Samuel French. PLAYS, PRODUCED—*Lake of the Woods,* American Place Theatre, New York City.

FICTION—*Summer Crossing,* Random House, 1982.

AWARDS: Drama Desk Award, 1973, for *Baba Goya;* Best Screenplay, New York Film Critics Award and Academy Award, both 1979, for *Breaking Away;* Writers Guild of America Award, 1980; grants and fellowships: National Defense Education Act (NDEA) fellowship, 1965; Rockefeller Foundation grant, 1972.

MEMBER: Dramatists Guild, Writers Guild of America, Academy of Motion Picture Arts and Sciences; Phi Beta Kappa.

ADDRESSES: AGENT—c/o Sam Cohn, International Creative Management, 40 W. 57th Street, New York, NY 10019.*

*   *   *

TEWSON, Josephine

PERSONAL: Born in London, England; daughter of William (a musician) and Mary (a nurse; maiden name, Morley) Tewson; married Leonard Rossiter, September 27, 1958 (divorced, 1963); married Henry Newman (a dental surgeon), June 12, 1972. EDUCATION: Trained for the stage at the Royal Academy of Dramatic Art.

VOCATION: Actress.

CAREER: PRINCIPAL STAGE APPEARANCES—All in London: Dottie Otley, *Noises Off,* Savoy Theatre, 1985; *Woman in Mind,* Vaudeville Theatre, 1987; also appeared as Judith Bliss, *Hay Fever,* Mrs. Malaprop, *The Rivals,* and in *Free as Air; The Real Inspector Hound; Habeas Corpus; Rookery Nook.*

MAJOR TOURS—*Absurd Person Singular,* U.K. cities.

PRINCIPAL TELEVISION APPEARANCES—Episodic: All with BBC unless indicated: *The Two Ronnies; David Frost; Jimmy Tarbuck;*

JOSEPHINE TEWSON

Dick Emery; Harry Worth; Ken Dodd; Miss Bates; Hark at Barker; Wodehouse Playhouse; His Lordship Entertains; No Appointment Necessary; Odd Man Out; Terry and June; The Caucasian Chalk Circle, Thames TV. Series: *Rude Health.*

SIDELIGHTS: RECREATIONS—Going to concerts, watching cricket, reading.

ADDRESSES: AGENT—c/o International Artists Representation, Regent House, Regent Street, London W1, England.

* * *

THACKER, David   1950-

PERSONAL: Born December 21, 1950; married Margot Leicester (an actress); children: Thomas, William. EDUCATION: Received B.A., English and related literature, then M.A., Shakespeare studies, University of York.

VOCATION: Director.

CAREER: PRINCIPAL STAGE WORK—Director: *Othello, The Jail Diary of Albie Sachs, Stags and Hens, Macbeth, Hamlet, Measure for Measure, The Enemies Within, The Crucible, Romeo and Juliet, A Midsummer Night's Dream, Some Kind of Hero, Ghosts, Julius Caesar, Who's Afraid of Virginia Woolf?,* all Young Vic Theatre, London, 1984—; *Ghosts,* Wyndham's Theatre, London, 1986, then National Theatre of Norway, Oslo, Norway, 1987.

DAVID THACKER

RELATED CAREER—Founder, Rolling Stock Theatre Company; associate director, Arts Council of Great Britain Duke's Playhouse, Lancaster, U.K.; director, Duke's Playhouse, 1980.

ADDRESSES: HOME—22 Mount Grove, London N5, England. OFFICE—c/o The Young Vic, 66 The Cut, London SE1 8LZ, England. AGENT—Maggie Parker, c/o Al Parker, 55 Park Lane, London W1, England.

* * *

THOMAS, Gerald   1920-

PERSONAL: Born in 1920, in Hull, England.

VOCATION: Producer and director.

CAREER: PRINCIPAL FILM WORK—Producer and director of the British "Carry On . . ." comedy series for Governor Films, including: *Carry On Admiral* (also known as *The Ship Was Loaded*), 1957; *Carry On Sergeant, Carry On Nurse,* both 1959; *Carry On Regardless,* 1961; *Carry On Teacher,* 1962; *Carry On Spying, Carry On Cleo,* both 1965; *Carry On Doctor,* 1968; *Carry On Camping, Carry On Henry VIII,* both 1972; *Carry On Behind,* 1975; also *Carry On Cruising; Carry On Jack; Carry On Cowboy; Carry On Screaming; Carry On Up the Jungle; Carry On Up the Khyber; Carry On Loving; Carry On Again; Carry On at Your Convenience; Carry On Matron; Carry On Abroad; Carry On Girls; Carry On Dick; Carry On England; Carry On Emmanuelle.*

Producer: *The Sword and the Rose,* Buena Vista, 1953; *Doctor in the House,* Republic, 1954; *Above Us the Waves,* Republic, 1956; also *Tony Draws a Horse,* 1951; *Mad about Men,* 1954; *A Novel Affair,* 1958.

Producer and director: *A Day to Remember,* Republic, 1955; *Please Turn Over,* Governor, 1962; *Nurse on Wheels,* Janus, 1963; also *The Vicious Circle* (also known as *The Circle*), 1959; *Raising the Wind,* 1961; *Twice 'round the Daffodils,* 1962; *Follow That Camel,* 1967; *Appointment with Venus; Venetian Bird; After the Ball; Timelock; Chain of Events; Solitary Child; The Duke Wore Jeans; The Iron Maiden; Call Me a Cab; The Big Job; Don't Lose Your Head.*

PRINCIPAL TELEVISION WORK—Series: Producer and director, *Rob Roy,* BBC; producer, *Odd Man Out,* Thames. Specials: Producer, *Carry On Christmas,* Thames; producer, *Carry On Laughing,* ATV; director, *Best of Carry On,* Thames; director, *Just for Laughs,* Thames; director for Canadian television, *Comedy Tonight;* director, *What a Carry On,* Thames.*

* * *

THOMPSON, Evan   1931-

PERSONAL: Born Francis Marion Harlan Thompson, September 3, 1931, in New York, NY; son of Harlan (a producer, director, and writer) and Marian (a writer; maiden name, Spitzer) Thompson; married Joan Shepard (an actress and producer), December 13, 1959; children: Owen, Jennifer. EDUCATION: University of California, Berkeley, B.A., 1955; trained for the stage with William Hickey at the Herbert Berghof Studios, and with Jeff Corey in Hollywood. POLITICS: Democrat. MILITARY: U.S. Army, Korea, 1953-55.

VOCATION: Actor and director.

CAREER: STAGE DEBUT—Cassio, *Othello,* New Vic Theatre, Beverly Hills, CA, 1959, for ten performances. NEW YORK DEBUT—Sir Michael Audley, *Lady Audley's Secret,* Beechnut Theatre, New York World's Fair, Flushing, NY, 1964. BROADWAY DEBUT—Charles Hand, *Jimmy,* Winter Garden Theatre, 1969, for eighty performances. PRINCIPAL STAGE APPEARANCES—Demetrius, *A Midsummer Night's Dream,* American National Theatre Academy Playhouse, Hollywood, CA, 1961; Tom Wingfield, *The Glass Menagerie,* Citadel Theatre, Edmonton, AB, Canada, 1966; commentator, *Mahagonny,* Anderson Theatre, New York City, 1970; old actor, *The Fantasticks,* Sullivan Street Playhouse, New York City, 1975; Joseph Dobbs, *Child's Play,* Stage Company Theatre, Flushing, New York, 1976; Henry Drummond, *Inherit The Wind,* Heights Players Theatre, Brooklyn, NY, 1978; Andrew Crocker-Harris, *The Browning Version,* Wonderhorse Theatre, New York City, 1979.

Skipps, *The Lady's Not for Burning,* York Players, Church of the Heavenly Rest, New York City, 1980; Bayard Carsters, *Knitters in the Sun,* Theatre de Lys, New York City, 1980; Prospero, *The Tempest,* North Shore Music Theatre, Beverly, MA, 1980; Friar Laurence, *Romeo and Juliet,* North Shore Music Theatre, 1982; Sir Noel Cunliffe, *Half-Life,* Wonderhorse Theatre, 1981; father, *Fasnacht Day,* Vanya, *Uncle Vanya,* both Meat and Potatoes Company, Alvina Krause Theatre, New York City, 1981; Reverend Chasuble, *The Importance of Being Earnest,* Mercer Street Theatre, New York City, 1982; Byke, *Under the Gaslight,* Soho Repertory Theatre, New York City, 1983; James Gordon Bennett, *Miss Liberty,* Goodspeed Opera House, East Haddam, CT, 1983; Duke of Exeter, *Henry V,* Riverside Shakespeare Company, New York City, 1984; first actor, *The Dining Room,* Capital Repertory Theatre, Albany, NY, 1984; Reverend Duckworth, *Once on a Summer's Day,* Ensemble Studio Theatre, New York City, 1985; Browfield, *Walk the Dog, Willie,* Production Company Theatre, New York City, 1985; storyteller, *The Shawl, Prairie du Chien,* both Mitzi E. Newhouse Theatre, New York City, 1986; O'Brien, *1984,* Wilma Theatre, Philadelphia, PA, then Kennedy Center, Washington, DC, both 1986, later Joyce Theatre, New York City, 1987; Niles Harris, *Angels Fall,* Triangle Theatre, New York City, 1986; Sidney Bruhl, *Deathtrap,* River Repertory Theatre, Ivoryton, CT, 1987. Also appeared in *1776,* St. James Theatre, New York City, 1972; and as Butt, *Volunteers,* Westbeth, NY, 1982.

MAJOR TOURS—Knife grinder, *Oliver!,* U.S. cities, 1965; Billy Bones, Dr. Livesey, Israel Hands, *Treasure Island,* U.S. cities, 1975.

TELEVISION DEBUT—Doctor, *Climax,* CBS, 1955. PRINCIPAL TELEVISION APPEARANCES—Episodic: Intern, *The Untouchables,* ABC, 1960; reporter, *Donna Reed Show,* ABC, 1963; various roles, *Another World,* NBC, 1977-81; plainclothes cop, *Saturday Night Live,* NBC, 1983; various roles, *Loving,* ABC, 1983-85; various roles, *Ryan's Hope,* ABC, 1985-86; headwaiter, *Kate and Allie,* CBS, 1987.

PRINCIPAL FILM APPEARANCES—Cass Kelley, *The Chapman Report,* Warner Brothers, 1959; doctor, *The Electric Grandmother,* Highgate Pictures, 1981. PRINCIPAL FILM WORK—Assistant

director, *The Man Who Understood Women,* Twentieth Century-Fox, 1958.

RELATED CAREER—Artistic director, Fanfare Theatre, New York City, 1970—.

WRITINGS: MUSICALS—All for young audiences. (With Joan Shepard and Joe Bousard) *The Pied Piper of Hamelin,* WTIF-TV, Hershey, PA, 1966; (with Shepard and Phil Fleischman) *Rumplestiltskin;* (with Shepard and John Clifton): *Young Robinson Crusoe,* 1964; *Puss in Boots,* 1966; *Alice through the Looking Glass,* Felt Forum, Madison Square Garden, New York City, 1969; *Little Red Riding Hood,* 1969; *East of the Sun and West of the Moon,* 1971; *Annie Oakley and Buffalo Bill,* 1975; *Huckleberry Finn,* Detroit Institute of Art, then Morris Mechanic Theatre, Baltimore, MD, both 1977; *Goldilocks and the Three Bears,* 1981; *A Christmas Carol,* Westbury Music Fair, Long Island, New York, then Valley Forge Music Fair, both 1982; *Robin Hood,* 1987.

AWARDS: Villager Downtown Theatre Award, 1979, for *Knitters in the Sun;* Special Citation for Educational Excellence, Ohio State University, for *The Pied Piper of Hamelin.*

MEMBER: Actors' Equity Association, American Society of Composers, Authors and Publishers.

ADDRESSES: HOME—102 E. 4th Street, New York, NY 10003. OFFICE—100 E. 4th Street, New York, NY 10003. AGENT—c/o Kass & Woo, 156 Fifth Avenue, New York, NY 10010.

*   *   *

THORNE, Raymond   1933-

PERSONAL: Born Raymond Mihok, November 27, 1933, in Lackawanna, NY; married wife Andrea (an actress; maiden name, Cloak); children: Cecily, Gwendolyn, Dashiell. EDUCATION: University of Connecticut, B.A. MILITARY: U.S. Navy, Korean War.

VOCATION: Actor.

CAREER: STAGE DEBUT—Bo, *Bus Stop,* Port Players, Oconomowoc, WI, 1959, for eight performances. OFF-BROADWAY DEBUT— The lord, *Man with a Load of Mischief,* Jan Hus Theatre, 1966, for two hundred and thirty-two performances. PRINCIPAL STAGE APPEARANCES—Hennessey and the captain, *Dames at Sea,* Theatre de Lys and at the Plaza 9 Theatre, both New York City, 1969-70; F.D.R., *Annie,* Alvin Theatre, New York City, 1977; *Fallen Angels,* Barter Theatre, Abingdon, VA, 1983; Mac Moore, *Follow Thru,* Goodspeed Opera House, East Haddam, CT, 1984-85; Ben Miller, *Jack and Jill,* Riverwest Theatre, New York City, 1985; Dan King, *Plain & Fancy,* Equity Library Theatre, New York City; also appeared as Ben Marino, *Fiorello!;* Rutledge, *1776;* Mark Bruckner, *On a Clear Day;* Manningham, *Angel Street;* Brad, *Everybody Loves Opal;* Paul Verrall, *Born Yesterday;* Gil, *Janus;* Johnny, *Lullaby;* Jack Worthing, *The Importance of Being Earnest;* Murray, *A Thousand Clowns;* Mortimer, *Arsenic and Old Lace;* James, *That Championship Season;* Larry Kogin, *Seidman & Son;* Charlie, *Never Too Late;* appeared in *Knight of Olmedo* and *The Wedding,* both at the I.A.S.T.A. Theatre; *The Magistrate,* Equity Library Theatre; *Rose,* Provincetown Playhouse; other performances at the Theatre Under the Stars, Houston, TX, Playhouse on the Green, OH, Music Fair Enterprises, NY, Flint Musical Tent,

RAYMOND THORNE

MI, Houghton Lake Playhouse, MI, Cohoes Music Hall, NY, Washington Theatre Club, Washington, DC, and at the Cinncinnati Playhouse in the Park, OH.

MAJOR TOURS—Buzz Richards and Stan Harding, *Applause*, National, 1971-72.

FILM DEBUT—Dr. Jowdy, *Just Tell Me What You Want*, Warner Brothers, 1980.

PRINCIPAL TELEVISION APPEARANCES—Series: Dr. McKinley, *One Life to Live*, ABC; Pete Denton, *Love of Life*, CBS. Episodic: Assistant D.A., *The Defenders*, CBS. Movies: Florid man, *Found Money*, 1983.

MEMBER: Actors' Equity Association, Screen Actors Guild, American Federation of Television and Radio Artists.

ADDRESSES: HOME—463 West Street, New York, NY 10014. AGENT—Dulcina Eisen Associates, 154 E. 61st Street, New York, NY 10021.

*   *   *

TILLINGER, John   1939-

PERSONAL: Born Joachim Tillinger, June 28, 1939; son of Siegmund (an engineer) and Anna Marie (Gay) Tillinger; married Dorothy Cyman, December 1, 1971 (divorced, 1978); children: Emma,

Sebastian. EDUCATION: Trained for the stage with Duncan Ross at the Bristol Old Vic School.

VOCATION: Actor, director, and playwright.

CAREER: STAGE DEBUT—Innkeeper, *Rhinoceros*, Nottingham Playhouse Theatre, Nottingham, U.K., 1960. LONDON DEBUT—Caldaro, *Sport of My Mad Mother*, Royal Court Theatre, 1960. BROADWAY DEBUT—Man, *How's the World Treating You?*, Music Box Theatre, 1966. PRINCIPAL STAGE APPEARANCES—Man, *Ashes*, Public Theatre, New York City, 1977; Dick, *Chez Nous*, Manhattan Theatre Club, New York City, 1977; Freddie, *Joe Egg*, Haft Theatre, then Longacre Theatre, both New York City, 1985.

PRINCIPAL STAGE WORK—Director: *This Story of Yours*, Long Wharf Theatre, New Haven, CT, 1980; *Solomon's Child*, Long Wharf Theatre, 1980, then Little Theatre, New York City, 1982; *Entertaining Mr. Sloan*, Westside Mainstage, then Cherry Lane Theatre, both New York City, 1981; *A Call from the East*, Manhattan Theatre Club, New York City, 1981; *Another Country*, Long Wharf Theatre, 1982; *The Golden Age*, Jack Lawrence Theatre, New York City, 1983; *Serenading Louie*, Public Theatre, New York City, 1984; *Not Quite Jerusalem*, Long Wharf Theatre, 1984; *After the Fall*, Playhouse 91, New York City, 1984; *Total Eclipse*, Westside Arts Theatre, New York City, 1984; *The Lisbon Traviata*, Theatre-Off-Park, New York City, 1985; *Paris Bound*, Long Wharf Theatre, 1985; *Corpse!*, Helen Hayes Theatre, New York City, 1986; *Loot*, Manhattan Theatre Club, then Music Box Theatre, both New York City, 1986; *Sweet Sue*, Music Box Theatre, 1986, then Plymouth Theatre, 1987; *Another Antigone*, Old Globe Theatre, San Diego, CA, 1987, then Playwrights Horizons, New York City, 1988. Also directed *Progress*, Long Wharf Theatre.

FILM DEBUT—*Diary of a Mad Housewife*, Universal, 1970. PRINCIPAL FILM APPEARANCES—*Ressurection*, Universal, 1980; *A Little Sex*, Universal, 1982; also appeared in *Lovesick*.

PRINCIPAL TELEVISION APPEARANCES—Series: Brooks, *Another World*, NBC, 1978-81. Mini-Series: George III, *The Adams Chronicles*, PBS, 1975.

WRITINGS: (Adaptor) *House of Mirth*, Long Wharf Theatre, New Haven, CT; (adaptor) *Summerfolk*, Long Wharf Theatre; *A Christmas Garland*, Long Wharf Theatre.

AWARDS: Best Director, Antoinette Perry Award nomination, 1986, for *Loot;* also has received a Drama Desk Award, an Outer Critics Circle Award, and a Villager Award.

MEMBER: Society of Stage Directors and Choreographers, Actors' Equity Association, Screen Actors Guild, American Federation of Radio and Television Artists.

SIDELIGHTS: RECREATIONS—Travel.

ADDRESSES: AGENT—c/o G. Parker, William Morris Agency, 1350 Avenue of the Americas, New York, NY 10019.

*   *   *

TINKER, Grant   1926-

PERSONAL: Full name, Grant Almerin Tinker; born January 11, 1926, in Stamford, CT; son of a lumber supplier; married Ruth

Byerly (marriage ended, 1962); married Mary Tyler Moore (an actress, producer, and director), 1963 (divorced, 1981); children: (first marriage) three sons, one daughter. EDUCATION: Graduated from Dartmouth College, 1949.

VOCATION: Producer and television executive.

CAREER: PRINCIPAL TELEVISION WORK—Executive, NBC-TV, New York City, 1961-67, posts included vice-president of West Coast programming, 1961-66, and vice-president of New York programming, 1966-67; vice-president, Universal TV, Hollywood, CA, 1968-69; vice-president, Twentieth Century-Fox TV, Hollywood, 1969-70; president, MTM Enterprises, Studio City, CA, 1970-81, producing such series as *The Mary Tyler Moore Show,* CBS, 1970-77; *Lou Grant,* CBS, 1977-82; *The White Shadow,* CBS, 1978-81; *Mary,* CBS, 1978; *WKRP in Cincinnati,* CBS, 1978-82; *Mary Tyler Moore Hour,* CBS, 1979; *Hill Street Blues,* NBC, 1981-85; chairman and chief executive officer, NBC, New York City, 1981-87; president, GTG (Grant Tinker-Gannett) Entertainment, Culver City, CA, 1987—.

RELATED CAREER—Management trainee, National Broadcasting Co. (NBC), New York City, 1949; in television department, McCann-Erickson Advertising, New York City, 1954; in television department, Benton and Bowles Advertising, New York City, 1958. Also worked for NBC Radio and for Radio Free Europe.

AWARDS: Governor's Award, National Academy of Television Arts and Sciences, 1987.

SIDELIGHTS: Grant Tinker has come to represent "a kind of litmus test of commercial television's potential," according to Ben Brown (*American Film,* September, 1983). Tinker, a broadcasting executive who has founded and run two production companies, is widely credited with restoring the fortunes of the National Broadcasting Company (NBC), which he headed as chairman from 1981 until 1986. In an October 25, 1987 *New York Times Magazine* profile, Diane K. Shah observed that the self-effacing Tinker led NBC "away from the graveyard into gravy." She further reported: "During his chairmanship, NBC's profits soared—from $48 million in 1981 to more than $400 million in 1986. It owned America's living rooms during prime time, hooking the country on 'The Cosby Show,' 'Hill Street Blues' and 'Miami Vice'; keeping it hooked with Johnny Carson and David Letterman, hanging onto it through the early morning hours with the 'Today' show." Tinker effected the turnaround by going against the conventions of network programming—he kept faith in low-popularity but high-quality shows, renewing them even when their ratings suggested cancellation. "Audiences will appreciate good shows if we give them time," he affirmed in the March 9, 1986 *New York Times.* Validating this belief, reporter Sandra Salmans noted that in 1985, for instance, NBC not only "beat both CBS and ABC in total households and number of viewers," but it also garnered twenty-five Emmy Awards in the process—more than twice the total of either competing network. This accomplishment bore out Brown's conclusion that "if anyone can make television better,. . . Tinker's the man."

Tinker has made broadcasting his life's work. The son of a lumber supplier, he grew up in Stamford, Connecticut, determined not to follow in his father's business. Instead he attended Dartmouth College and at age twenty-three became a management trainee at NBC. As he rose in his profeesion through positions in studio production at Universal Studios, Twentieth Century-Fox, and two advertising agencies, he gained a reputation not as a creative

person, but as "an executive with a deep appreciation for creative people," Kay Gardella reported in a July 12, 1981 New York *Daily News* article. Tinker returned to NBC as a vice-president of television programming in 1961; throughout the 1960s, however, he was better known as the husband of actress Mary Tyler Moore than as a rising network executive. But in 1970, as founder with Moore and Arthur Price of MTM Enterprises, a television production company, Tinker began to gain recognition for his own achievements.

"What distinguished MTM from the big Hollywood studios where most television series are made was not only that it produced much of the best programming of the last 15 years—from 'The Mary Tyler Moore Show' to 'St. Elsewhere'—but the way it did so: by establishing an atmosphere in which writers and producers thrived," Salmans assessed. Steven Bochco, who created *Hill Street Blues* while at MTM, elaborated on that atmosphere in the *New York Times:* "Grant Tinker's real unique gift is in creating an environment where people feel safe, nurtured, protected to do what they do best." During Tinker's tenure at the helm of MTM and later at NBC, such shows as *Lou Grant, Hill Street Blues, Cheers,* and *Family Ties* were either created or produced or both. Tinker also became an outspoken critic of network programming that showed little imagination and less respect for the viewer. He told *People* (May 14, 1984): "If the networks have so little respect for the audience that we grind out pap and junk, we literally devalue our viewers, and we can't expect them to keep coming back to our programs."

Brown reported that Tinker was called "Mr. Quality Television" when he took over the lagging NBC network in 1981. As chairman he made stability his watchword and, although he stood behind shows that struggled at first to find their audiences—*Hill Street Blues* and *Cheers* among them, he also allowed the production of standard action-adventure series that were aimed at boosting ratings points. Ironically, *The A-Team,* one such action show, was NBC's first hit under Tinker. He told the January 7, 1983 *Christian Science Monitor:* "I can no longer live by the same rules that I did at MTM Enterprises, where we didn't offer to produce anything which we didn't feel had some real quality. And we concentrated on only a few shows. I dropped that way of living 20 minutes after I [came to NBC], because this has to be a more flexible schedule. I don't have any problems with programming for mass audiences, whatever the show is, even a lowest-common-denominator show. I just don't want to have 'em every night of the week." By 1985 NBC had moved from the least popular to the most popular commercial network on the strength of Tinker's support of *Cheers, The Cosby Show, Miami Vice,* and *The Golden Girls.* But Tinker also stood by shows like *Remington Steele, Knight Rider,* and *The A-Team,* which were also multi-season hits.

Tinker had signed on with NBC for five years and in the summer of 1986 he resigned. With numerous offers to consider, he decided to return to production; within a few months he formed a partnership with the Virginia-based Gannett Company. Under a multi-million dollar agreement for GTG (Grant Tinker-Gannett) Enterprises to create and produce shows for CBS, Tinker has his own studio in Los Angeles, the right to re-sell any programs rejected by CBS, and fifty per cent of the profits the new venture earns, in addition to his salary. The company plans to prepare between three and five shows—comedy and drama—for the fall, 1988 television season, and it has more than fifteen shows under preparation. Shah suggested, however, that Tinker might encounter more difficulties than he did when MTM Enterprises got under way in 1970. "Now, in a sense, Tinker's success has come back to haunt him," she wrote.

"The big names he helped create have risen beyond his budget and loom there as his competition. But Tinker has always managed to throw out the nets and haul in the next big-fish-to-be." Tinker told the *New York Times Magazine* that he feels additional pressure beyond the mere stresses of the budget because he has enjoyed such success in the preceding seventeen years. "I have a great sense of obligation and determination to succeed," he said of his new company. "Probably more than I've ever had. The others [MTM and NBC] would have been failures more easy to accept." Now in his early sixties and divorced from Moore, Tinker expresses no interest in retiring or even lessening his workload. "I don't mean I'd never like to sit in the backyard and watch the apples fall," he told the *New York Times.* "But I don't think I'll spend a lot of time doing that."

ADDRESSES: OFFICE—GTG Entertainment, 9336 Washington Boulevard, Culver City, CA 90232.*

*   *   *

TISCH, Laurence Alan   1923-

PERSONAL: Born March 15, 1923, in New York, NY; son of Al and Sadye (Brenner) Tisch; married Wilma Stein, October 31, 1948; children: Andrew, Daniel, James, Thomas. EDUCATION: New York University, B.S., 1942; University of Pennsylvania, M.A., industrial engineering, 1943; also attended Harvard Law School, 1946.

VOCATION: Executive.

CAREER: PRINCIPAL PROFESSIONAL AFFILIATIONS—Chairman of Executive Committee, Loews Theaters, Inc. (now Loews Corporation), New York City, 1959-65, chairman of the board of directors, 1960—; president, 1965-69, chief executive officer, 1969-86; chairman of the board, Columbia Broadcasting System (CBS), 1986—.

NON-RELATED CAREER—Chairman of the Board, CNA Financial Corporation, 1947—; president, Tisch Hotels, Inc., New York City, 1950-59; president, Americana Hotel, Inc., Miami Beach, 1956-59; director, Automatic Data Processing Corporation; chairman of the board and trustee, New York University; trustee: Legal Aid Society, Metropolitan Museum of Art, New York Public Library, Carnegie Corporation; trustee-at-large, Jewish Philanthropies of New York.

ADDRESSES: HOME—Island Drive, North Manursing Island, Rye, NY 10580. OFFICE—CBS, Inc., 51 W. 52nd Street, New York, NY 10019.*

*   *   *

TROOBNICK, Eugene   1926-

PERSONAL: Born August 23, 1926, in Boston, MA; son of Maurice and Lallie (Rothenberg) Troobnick. EDUCATION: Attended Ithaca College, Columbia University, and the University of Chicago.

VOCATION: Actor.

CAREER: STAGE DEBUT—Man, *Hello Out There,* Community

Players, Freeport, Long Island, NY, 1947. BROADWAY DEBUT—*From the Second City,* Royale Theatre, 1961. LONDON DEBUT—*Looking for Action,* Second City Troupe, Prince Charles Theatre, 1963. PRINCIPAL STAGE APPEARANCES—Mosca, *Volpone,* Playwrights Theatre Club, Chicago, IL, 1953; captain, *Dynamite Tonite,* Martinique Theatre, New York City, 1967; man, *Before You Go,* Henry Miller's Theatre, New York City, 1968; Androcles, *Androcles and the Lion,* American Shakespeare Festival, Stratford, CT, 1968; Sganarelle, *Don Juan,* Yale Repertory Theatre, New Haven, CT, 1968; Krupp, *The Time of Your Life,* Vivian Beaumont Theatre, New York City, 1969; Stan, *A Gun Play,* Cherry Lane Theatre, New York City, 1971; Hjalmar Ekdal, *The Wild Duck,* Yale Repertory Theatre, New Haven, CT, 1978; Sganarelle, *An Evening of Moliere,* Yale Repertory Theatre, then Public Theatre, New York City, 1978; Leon, *The Workroom,* South Street Theatre, New York City, 1982; Matt, *Talley's Folly,* Barter Theatre, Abingdon, VA, then Stagewest, West Springfield, MA, both 1982; Leo "the Lion Hearted" Loomis, *Requiem for a Heavyweight,* Martin Beck Theatre, New York City, 1985; Joseph Gribble, *Room Service,* Roundabout Theatre, New York City, 1986; Matt, *Talley's Folley,* York Theatre Company, New York City, 1986. Also appeared in *Tales of the Hasidim,* Public Theatre, 1977; *Biography,* Long Wharf Theatre, New Haven, CT, 1978; *A Lesson from Aloes,* Playhouse in the Park, Cincinnati, OH, 1982; *The Threepenny Opera,* Guthrie Theatre, Minneapolis, MN, 1983; *Seacoasts of Bohemia, Alarums and Excursions,* both Second City at the Square East Theatre, 1962; *To the Water Tower,* with the Second City, 1963; *Paul Sills' Story Theatre, Ovid's Metamorphoses,* both Ambassador Theatre, New York City, 1971; *In the Clap Shack,* Yale Repertory Theatre, 1972; appeared as Duncan, *Macbett,* 1973; Sganarelle, *Don Juan,* captain, *Dynamite Tonite!,* both 1975; Mr. Browfield, *Walk the Dog, Willie,* 1976; Howard Oates, *The Durango Flash,* judge, *Puntila,* father, *White Marriage,* all 1977; and in *Lear, The Mirror,* both 1973; General Gorgeous, *Ivanov,* both 1976; Off-Broadway in *Wings,* and *Damien;* and with the Guthrie Theatre, Minneapolis, MN, 1982-83.

PRINCIPAL TELEVISION APPEARANCES—Episodic: *That Was the Week That Was,* NBC; *Ed Sullivan Show,* CBS; *Hawaii Five-0,* CBS; also appeared in *The Second City,* and *Story Theatre.*

FILM DEBUT—*Harvey Middleman, Fireman,* Columbia, 1965. PRINCIPAL FILM APPEARANCES—*California Split,* Columbia, 1974; *Funny Lady,* Columbia, 1975.

PRINCIPAL RADIO APPEARANCES—Announcer, WNYC, New York City, and WFMT, Chicago, IL.

RELATED CAREER—Co-founder, Playwrights Theatre Club, Chicago, IL, 1953.

NON-RELATED CAREER—Associate editor, *Playboy.*

SIDELIGHTS: FAVORITE ROLES—Sganarelle; Androcles; Duncan; Mosca in *Volpone;* Macbeth; Iago in *Othello; Richard III; Cyrano.* RECREATIONS—Writing, cartooning.

ADDRESSES: HOME—2700 Neilson Way, Apartment 1632, Santa Monica, CA 90405.*

*   *   *

TRUSSLER, Simon   1942-

PERSONAL: Born June 11, 1942, in Tenterden, England; son of John (a farm worker) and Joan (Ovenden) Trussler; married Glenda

Leeming, 1966 (divorced); married Laverne Anderson, 1984; children: (first marriage) Nicholas, Anna; (second marriage) Jonathan. EDUCATION: University College, B.A., 1963, M.A., 1966.

VOCATION: Theatre writer and editor.

CAREER: Founding editor, *Prompt*, 1962-64; editorial assistant, *Plays and Players*, 1964-67; co-editor, *Encore*, 1965; London theatre critic, *Tulane Drama Review*, later called *The Drama Review*, New York, 1965-70; theatre critic, *Tribune*, London, 1966-72; radio critic, *The Listener*, London, 1969; founding editor, *Theatre Quarterly*, 1971-81; editor, *Theatre International*, International Theatre Institute, Paris, France, 1981-83; founding editor, *New Theatre Quarterly*, 1984—; general editor, *Writer-File* series, Methuen Publishers, London, 1985—; editor, *Swan Theatre Plays* series, Methuen Publishers, London, and Royal Shakespeare Company, Stratford-on-Avon, U.K., 1986—; lecturer: Tufts University London program, 1973-81; City University, 1980-82; University of California, Santa Barbara 1983; University of Kent, 1984-86; senior lecturer in drama, Goldsmiths' College, 1986—.

WRITINGS: BOOKS—(With Charles Marowitz) *Theatre at Work*, 1967; *John Osborne*, 1969; *The Plays of John Osborne*, 1969; *The Plays of Arnold Wesker*, 1971; *The Plays of John Whiting*, 1972; *The Plays of Harold Pinter*, 1973; *John Arden*, 1973; *A Classification for the Performing Arts*, 1974; *Edward Bond*, 1976; *Annual Bibliography of Theatre Studies, 1975-76*, 1977; *David Edgar: A Theatre Checklist*, 1979; *Royal Shakespeare Company: An Annual Record* (yearly), 1979-86; *New Theatre Voices of the Seventies*, 1981; *Twentieth-Century Drama*, 1982. Works also contained in *New English Dramatists 13*, 1968; *Burlesque Plays of the Eighteenth Century*, 1969; *Eighteenth Century Comedy*, 1969; four Elizabethan and Jacobean plays for the Methuen Student Edition Series, 1983-87; and in eight plays for the Swan Theatre Play Series, 1986-87.

ADDRESSES: OFFICE—c/o *New Theatre Quarterly*, Great Robhurst, Woodchurch, Ashford, Kent TN26 3TB, England; Drama Department, Goldsmiths' College, University of London, New Cross, London SE14 6NW, England.

*   *   *

TRYON, Thomas   1926-

PERSONAL: Born January 14, 1926, in Hartford, CT; son of Arthur Lane (a clothier) and Elizabeth (Lester) Tryon; married Anne Lilienthal, June, 1955 (divorced). EDUCATION: Yale University, B.A., 1949; also studied at the Art Students League. MILITARY: U.S. Naval Reserve, 1943-46.

VOCATION: Actor, writer, and producer.

CAREER: PRINCIPAL STAGE APPEARANCES—*Wish You Were Here*, *Cyrano de Bergerac*, and *Richard III*.

PRINCIPAL STAGE WORK—Set painter and assistant stage manager, Cape Playhouse, Dennis, MA.

FILM DEBUT—Marsh Marshall, *Scarlet Hour*, Paramount, 1956. PRINCIPAL FILM APPEARANCES—*Screaming Eagles*, Allied Artists, 1956; Cinch, *Three Violent People*, Paramount, 1957; Bill

Farrell, *I Married a Monster from Outer Space*, Paramount, 1958; *Moon Pilot*, Buena Vista, 1962; *The Longest Day*, Twentieth Century-Fox, 1962; *The Cardinal*, 1964; *Glory Guys*, United Artists, 1965; *In Harm's Way*, 1966; *Momento Mori*, 1968; *The Narco Men*, 1971.

PRINCIPAL FILM WORK—Executive producer, *The Other*, Twentieth Century Fox, 1971.

PRINCIPAL TELEVISION APPEARANCES—Episodic: Title role, "Texas John Slaughter," *Walt Disney*, ABC, 1958. Movies: Lin McAdam, *Winchester '73*, 1967.

RELATED CAREER—Former production assistant, CBS Television.

WRITINGS: FICTION—*The Other*, Knopf, 1971; *Harvest Home*, Knopf, 1973; *Lady*, Knopf, 1974; *Crowned Heads*, Knopf, 1976; *All That Glitters: Five Novellas*, Knopf, 1986. UNPUBLISHED WORKS—"What Is the Answer, What Was the Question?"

SCREENPLAYS—*The Other*, Twentieth Century-Fox, 1972.

TELEVISION—Movies: *Harvest Home*.

AWARDS: Prix Femina de Belgique, 1964; Laurel Award, Motion Picture Exhibitors, 1964.

ADDRESSES: HOME—145 Central Park West, New York, NY 10023. OFFICE—Alfred A. Knopf, Inc., 201 E. 50th Street, New York, NY 10021. AGENT—Arthur Riley, 32 Shadow Hill Road, Ridgefield, CT 06877.*

*   *   *

TUPOU, Manu

PERSONAL: Born January 5, on Lomaloma, Lau, Fiji Islands; son of Wilisoni Pau'u and Waimonana (Kalolaini) Fatafehi. EDUCATION: Received B.A. from the University of Hawaii,; also attended San Francisco State University and the University of London; trained for the stage with Uta Hagen, Herbert Berghof, Lee Strasberg, Elia Kazan, and Arthur Penn.

VOCATION: Actor.

CAREER: STAGE DEBUT—Recruiting officer, *Na'Au'Ao*, Honolulu Community Theatre, Honolulu, HI, 1961. BROADWAY DEBUT—Sitting Bull, *Indians*, Brooks Atkinson Theatre, 1969. PRINCIPAL STAGE APPEARANCES—Ragpicker, *The Madwoman of Chaillot*, Sokol Theatre, New York City, 1970; Sitting Bull, *Indians*, Seattle Repertory Theatre, Seattle, WA, 1970, then Bucks County Playhouse, New Hope, PA; title role, *Othello*, American Shakespeare Festival, Stratford, CT, 1971; *A Dramatized Anthology of Puerto Rican Short Stories*, Puerto Rican Traveling Theatre, New York City, 1971; Agamemnon, *The Wedding of Iphigenia*, Agamemnon, *Iphegenia in Concert*, both Public Theatre, New York City, 1971; Sidi el Assif, *Captain Brassbound's Conversion*, Ethel Barrymore Theatre, New York City, 1972; Creon Molina, *The Passion of Antigona Perez*, Cathedral Church, New York City, then Puerto Rican Traveling Theatre, both 1972; Assawamset, *Endecott and the Red Cross*, Reffyman, *My Kinsman, Major Molineaux*, both American Place Theatre, New York City, 1976;

title role, *Black Elk Lives,* Entermedia Theatre, New York City, 1981. Also appeared at Center Stage, Baltimore, MD, 1972-73.

FILM DEBUT—*Hawaii,* United Artists, 1966. PRINCIPAL FILM APPEARANCES—*A Man Called Horse,* National General, 1970; also appeared in *Castaway Cowboy,* 1974.

PRINCIPAL TELEVISION APPEARANCES—Episodic: *Hawaii Five-0,* CBS; *Quest in Paradise,* BBC.

RELATED CAREER—Writer and director of documentaries for Fiji Radio and BBC Overseas Service.

SIDELIGHTS: FAVORITE ROLES—Othello; Sitting Bull in *Indians.* RECREATIONS—Rugby, swimming, football, volleyball, reading.

ADDRESSES: HOME—11 W. 69th Street, New York, NY 10023.*

*   *   *

TURNER, Bridget   1939-

PERSONAL: Born February 22, 1939, in Cleethorpes, England; daughter of Eric and Phyllis Johanna (Blanchard) Turner; married Frank Cox. EDUCATION: Trained for the stage at the Royal Academy of Dramatic Art.

VOCATION: Actress.

BRIDGET TURNER

CAREER: STAGE DEBUT—Beatrice, *The Servant of Two Masters,* Welsh Children's Theatre, U.K. cities, 1959. BROADWAY DEBUT—Avril Hadfield, *Semi-Detached,* Music Box Theatre, 1963. PRINCIPAL STAGE APPEARANCES—Avril Hadfield, *Semi-Detached,* Belgrade Theatre, Coventry, U.K., 1962; Masha, *The Sea Gull,* Hampstead Theatre Club, London, 1962; Beatie, *Roots,* Royal Court Theatre, London, 1967; Pegeen Mike, *The Playboy of the Western World,* Juliet, *Romeo and Juliet,* both 69 Theatre Company, Manchester, U.K., 1967; Nina, *The Sea Gull,* Muriel Rye, *Brother and Sister,* both Bristol Old Vic Theatre, Bristol, U.K., 1968; Bess Hogg, *Sometime Never,* Fortune Theatre, London, 1969; Kate Hardcastle, *She Stoops to Conquer,* Garrick Theatre, London, 1969; Louisa, *Erb,* Strand Theatre, London, 1970; Jenny, *Me Times Me Times Me,* Phoenix Theatre, Leicester, U.K., 1971; Greenfly, *The Plotters of Cabbage Patch Corner,* Shaw Theatre, London, 1971; Anna, *Time and Time Again,* Comedy Theatre, London, 1972; Jane, *Absurd Person Singular,* Criterion Theatre, London, 1973; Ruth, *The Norman Conquests,* Globe Theatre, London, 1974; Patty, *The Fool,* Royal Court Theatre, 1975; Emilia, *Othello,* Maggie Hobson, *Hobson's Choice,* Madame Ranevsky, *The Cherry Orchard,* all Nottingham Playhouse Theatre, Nottinghan, U.K., 1976-77; Jeanette Fisher, *Last of the Red Hot Lovers,* Royal Exchange Theatre, Manchester, U.K., then Criterion Theatre, both 1979; Phyllis, *Season's Greetings,* Apollo Theatre, London, 1982; title role, *Stevie,* Barbican Theatre, Plymouth, U.K., 1983; Kate, *All My Sons,* Liverpool Playhouse, Liverpool, U.K., 1984; Clelia, *The Nerd,* Aldwych Theatre, London, 1984; Mrs. Watty, *The Corn Is Green,* Old Vic Theatre, London, 1985; Phyllis, *Leaving Home,* Soho Poly Theatre, London, 1986; Mrs. Munning, *Zack,* Royal Exchange Theatre, 1986; Lucy, *Laburnum Grove,* Watford Palace Theatre, Watford, U.K., 1987; Katherine, *Curtains,* Hampstead Theatre Club, 1987. Also appeared in *The Girl in the Square,* Hampstead Theatre Club, 1963.

MAJOR TOURS—Olga, *The Three Sisters,* Maria, *Twelfth Night,* both Royal Shakespeare Company, U.K. cities, 1978.

PRINCIPAL FILM APPEARANCES—*The Walking Stick,* Metro-Goldwyn-Mayer, 1970; also appeared in *Under Milk Wood,* 1973; and *Runners.*

PRINCIPAL TELEVISION APPEARANCES—Episodic: *Rusurrection; Slattery's Mounted Foot; Love Lies Bleeding; Two People; Jackanory; Home is the Sailor; Driving Ambition; The Brief; Season's Greetings.*

AWARDS: Clarence Derwent Award, 1972, for *Time and Time Again.*

SIDELIGHTS: RECREATIONS—Walking, listening to classical music.

ADDRESSES: AGENT—c/o Marmont Management, Langham House, 302-308 Regent Street, London W1R 5AL, England.

*   *   *

TURNER, Kathleen   1954-

PERSONAL: Born June 19, 1954, in Springfield, MO; married Jay Weiss (a realtor). EDUCATION: Attended Southwest Missouri State University; University of Maryland, M.F.A., 1977; trained for the stage at the Central School of Speech and Drama, London.

VOCATION: Actress.

CAREER: FILM DEBUT—Matty Walker, *Body Heat,* Warner Brothers, 1981. PRINCIPAL FILM APPEARANCES—*The Man with Two Brains,* Warner Brothers, 1983; *A Breed Apart,* 1984; *Romancing the Stone,* Twentieth Century-Fox, 1984; *Crimes of Passion,* New World, 1984; *Prizzi's Honor,* Twentieth Century-Fox, 1985; *The Jewel of the Nile,* Twentieth Century-Fox, 1985; title role, *Peggy Sue Got Married,* Tri-Star, 1986.

PRINCIPAL TELEVISION APPEARANCES—Series: *The Doctors,* NBC.

PRINCIPAL STAGE APPEARANCES—Judith Hastings, *Gemini,* Little Theatre, New York City, 1984; regional appearances include: Titania, *A Midsummer Night's Dream,* Arena Stage, Washington, DC; Nina, *The Seagull,* Manitoba Theatre Center, Winnipeg, Canada; others.

AWARDS: Best Actress, Los Angeles Film Critics Award and Best Actress in a Musical or Comedy, Golden Globe Award, both 1984, for *Romancing the Stone;* Best Actress, National Board of Review and Best Actress nomination, Academy Award, both 1987, for *Peggy Sue Got Married.*

ADDRESSES: AGENT—c/o Phil Gersh, The Gersh Agency, 222 N. Canon Drive, Suite 202, Beverly Hills, CA 90210.*

*   *   *

TURNER, Ted   1938-

PERSONAL: Full name, Robert Edward Turner III; born November 19, 1938, in Cincinnati, OH; son of a billboard advertising magnate; married second wife, Jane, c. 1964; children: Robert Edward IV, Beauregard, Laura Lee, Rhett, Sarah Jean (two from first marriage). EDUCATION: Attended Brown University.

VOCATION: Broadcasting and sports executive.

CAREER: Owner, WTBS (independent television station), Atlanta, GA, 1970—, broadcast nationally by satellite, 1976—; founder and owner, Turner Broadcasting System, Atlanta, 1979—, with services including Cable News Network, 1980—, Turner Network Television, 1988—, CNN2, CNN Radio, and Cable Music Channel; owner of some 3,600 films originally made for Metro-Goldwyn-Mayer, 1987—. Executive consultant for the film *Amazing Grace and Chuck,* Tri-Star, 1987.

NON-RELATED CAREER—Salesman, Turner Outdoor Advertising, Atlanta, GA, became president, 1963; owner and president, Atlanta Braves (baseball team), 1976—; part-owner and chairor of the board, Atlanta Hawks (basketball team), 1977—.

AWARDS: Named Yachtsman of the Year four times; winner of America's Cup as captain of the yacht *Courageous,* 1977.

SIDELIGHTS: Ted Turner, founder and president of the Turner Broadcasting System, is one of the most visible entrepreneurs in the cable television industry. In the August 14, 1983 *New York Times,* Sandra Salmans observed: "If cable has a single pioneer, it is arguably brash, outspoken Ted Turner. The so-called 'Mouth of the South,' Mr. Turner has shaken up the television industry repeatedly since he entered it in 1970." She went on to note: "While he is still a controversial and perhaps unpopular figure in broadcasting, there are few who would quibble with his claim—widely publicized in his trade promotions—that 'I was cable before cable was cool.'" Indeed, Turner has turned a failing Atlanta UHF television station into WTBS, a cable channel estimated to reach more than half of all viewers nationwide; the "Superstation" specializes in Atlanta Braves baseball, vintage movies, and reruns of family-oriented situation comedies. Since December, 1976, WTBS has been a regular feature of cable broadcasting, and since 1980 it has been joined by Turner's other successful venture, the Cable News Network, a twenty-four-hour news-only station. A past winner of the America's Cup for yacht racing who admittedly loves the limelight, Turner told *American Film* (July, 1982) that he intends to keep "going after the networks" on both the business and entertainment fronts. "All they're doing now is reacting to me," he asserted. "I give them hell because they don't serve the public interest. They look at the viewer the same way a slaughterhouse looks at its pigs and cattle. They sell them by the pound to the advertiser—the same way they sell ham hocks and spare ribs."

Such flamboyant statements are characteristic of Turner, according to a June 16, 1980 *Newsweek* feature by Harry F. Waters. He wrote: "Robert Edward Turner III has so incensed, perplexed and dazzled his many adversaries that he has become something of a Southern folk hero." Describing him as "ever the Confederate rebel," the reporter cited Turner's public carousing with his baseball players and yachting crew and his reputation as a ladies' man among the sources of criticism and continued: "His elephantine ego sometimes repels even his friends; his 10,000-watt exuberance charms even his enemies. If Ted Turner were a television show, he would be 'That's Incredible!'" Turner's rise to prominence demonstrates his creative use of his energies. At the age of twenty-four he inherited the family billboard business, then six million dollars in debt; business pressures had driven his father to suicide. Against the advice of financial consultants, Turner cancelled the sale of the business and then proceeded to restore it to success. Later he again ignored consultants' advice and bought a television station with annual losses of more than $500,000; within three years, Waters reported, it became one of the first independent stations in the country to show a substantial profit. As revenues increased, Turner purchased the Atlanta Braves baseball team and the Atlanta Hawks basketball team and began to show their games exclusively on his station. His other progamming included situation comedies and reruns aimed at family viewers who might find certain network television programming offensive.

In 1976 Turner paid to have his station transmitted into other states by means of an RCA Satcom satellite that serviced cable television. Thereby he quadrupled his audience overnight without altering his programming and was able to dub the Atlanta Braves "America's team" because of the span of households in the WTBS audience. As cable found its way into more and more homes, so did Turner's station; it quickly became the nation's most profitable single television station. The Turner Broadcasting System—officially so named in 1979—has had an uneven track record on profits, however, because the founder continually experiments with new broadcasting services, including a heavy investment in such exclusive programming as Jacques Cousteau oceanographic specials and MGM-United Artists movies, and because subscription prices were cut in order to compete with rival cable stations. Cable industry analyst Paul Kagan told the *New York Times* (April 14, 1983) that Turner's habit "has been to keep putting his reach beyond his grasp. It's his style to go for the next brass ring." Turner even attempted takeovers of two of the three major networks, CBS and ABC, between 1984 and 1987; he was unsuccessful in both cases. Early in 1987, reacting to a 1986 operating loss in excess of $100 million, Turner sold shares in his company retaining for himself just fifty-one percent of the stock and conceding a voice in management decisions to the new investors. In turn, the board of directors announced plans to create a new cable network, Turner Network Television, that will air original shows, exclusive specials, and vintage films. At a press conference in October, 1987, Turner told the *New York Times* that he plans to spearhead "cable's premier network" with major awards ceremonies, sporting events, and family specials as well as regular offerings.

Turner shared his vision of his role in the media in the June 16, 1980 *Newsweek:* "I can do more today in communications than any conqueror ever could have done. I want to be the hero of my country. I want to get it back to the principles that made us good. Television has led us . . . down the path of destruction. I intend to turn it around before it is too late. And the hour *is* late." Turner has affirmed his vigilance in the promotion of moral values on television, seeing this as a service to future generations. Twice married and the father of five children, Turner divides his time between business in Atlanta and a second home on a 5,200-acre South Carolina plantation "dominated by a white-pillared mansion that evokes Tara in 'Gone with the Wind,'" according to Waters, who concluded that whatever Turner's detractors may say, the Atlanta businessman "has enlivened and enriched all the games he has entered. Though he may occasionally mistake himself for one of his military heroes, his sheer exuberance is always infectious." The reporter added: "More important, in an age of play-it-safe corporate bureaucracy, bold spirits like Turner have become precious commodities. . . . He is pushing television . . . to its farthest frontiers."

ADDRESSES: HOME—Jacksonboro, SC and Atlanta, GA. OFFICE—c/o Turner Broadcasting System, 1050 Techwood Drive, N.W., Atlanta, GA, 30318; c/o Atlanta Braves, P.O. Box 4064, Atlanta, GA 30302.

*   *   *

TUTIN, Dorothy   1930-

PERSONAL: Born April 8, 1930; daughter of John and Adie Evelyn (Fryers) Tutin; married Derek Waring. EDUCATION: Trained for the stage at the Royal Academy of Dramatic Art.

VOCATION: Actress.

CAREER: STAGE DEBUT—Princess Margaret of England, *The Thistle and the Rose,* Boltons Theatre, 1949. BROADWAY DEBUT—*The Hollow Crown,* Henry Miller's Theatre, 1963. PRINCIPAL STAGE APPEARANCES—Phoebe, *As You Like It,* Anni, *Captain Carvallo,* Belinda, *The Provoked Wife,* all Bristol Old Vic Theatre, Bristol, U.K., 1950; Win-the-Fight Littlewit, *Bartholomew Fair,* Ann Page, *The Merry Wives of Windsor,* Princess Katharine, *Henry V,* all with the Old Vic Company, London, 1950-51; Martina, *Thor with Angels,* Lyric Hammersmith Theatre, London, 1951; Hero, *Much Ado about Nothing,* Phoenix Theatre, London, 1952; Rose Pemberton, *The Living Room,* Wyndham's Theatre, London, 1953; Sally Bowles, *I Am a Camera,* New Theatre, London, 1954; Joan, *The Lark,* Lyric Hammersmith Theatre, 1955; Hedvig, *The Wild Duck,* Saville Theatre, London, 1955; Jean Rice,

DOROTHY TUTIN

The Entertainer, Royal Court Theatre, London, 1957; Juliet, *Romeo and Juliet,* Viola, *Twelfth Night,* Ophelia, *Hamlet,* all Shakespeare Memorial Theatre Company, Stratford-on-Avon, U.K., 1958; Dolly, *Once More with Feeling,* New Theatre, 1959.

Portia, *The Merchant of Venice,* Viola, *Twelfth Night,* Cressida, *Troilus and Cressida,* all Shakespeare Memorial Theatre Company, Stratford-on-Avon, U.K., 1960; Viola, *Twelfth Night,* Sister Jeanne, *The Devils,* both Royal Shakespeare Company (RSC), Aldwych Theatre, London, 1961; Juliet, *Romeo and Juliet,* Desdemona, *Othello,* both RSC, Stratford-on-Avon, U.K., 1961; Varya, *The Cherry Orchard,* RSC, Aldwych Theatre, 1961; Sister Jeanne, *The Devils,* Cressida, *Troilus and Cressida,* both Edinburgh Festival, Edinburgh, Scotland, U.K., then Aldwych Theatre, 1962; Polly Peachum, *The Beggar's Opera,* Aldwych Theatre, 1963; Beatrice, *Beatrice et Benedict,* Festival Hall, London, 1976; Queen Victoria, *Portrait of a Queen,* Bristol Old Vic Theatre, then Vaudeville Theatre, London, both 1965, later Henry Miller's Theatre, New York City, 1968; title role, *Ann Veronica,* Belgrade Theatre, Coventry, U.K., 1969; *Rosalind, As You Like It,* RSC, Stratford-on-Avon, U.K., then Aldwych Theatre, later Ahmanson Theatre, Los Angeles, CA, all 1968.

Francine, *Play on Love,* St. Martin's Theatre, London, 1970; Alice, *Arden of Faversham,* RSC Theatre-Go-Round Festival, Round House Theatre, London, 1970; Kate, *Old Times,* Aldwych Theatre, 1971; title role, *Peter Pan,* Coliseum Theatre, London, 1971, then 1972; Natalya, *A Month in the Country,* Chichester Festival Theatre, Chichester, U.K., 1974, then Albery Theatre, London, 1975; Maggie Wylie, *What Every Woman Knows,* Albery

Theatre, 1974; Lady Macbeth, *Macbeth,* Arnaud Theatre, Guildford, U.K., 1976, then Olivier Theatre, London, 1978; Cleopatra, *Antony and Cleopatra,* Edinburgh Festival Theatre, then Old Vic Theatre, London, both 1977; Madame Ranevsky, *The Cherry Orchard,* Lady Plyant, *The Double Dealer,* both Olivier Theatre, 1978; Genia Hofreiter, *Undiscovered Country,* Olivier Theatre, 1979; Madame Dubarry, *Reflections,* Haymarket Theatre, London, 1980. Also appeared as Blanche, *Brighton Beach Memoirs,* Aldwych Theatre, London; Sarah Bernhardt, *After the Lions,* Manchester, U.K.; Madrigal, *The Chalk Garden;* and in *Ballerina, A Kind of Alaska,* and *Are You Sitting Comfortably?*

MAJOR TOURS—Caroline Traherne, *The Gates of Summer,* U.K. cities, 1956; Juliet, *Romeo and Juliet,* Viola, *Twelfth Night,* Ophelia, *Hamlet,* all RSC, Soviet cities, 1958; Maggie Wylie, *What Every Woman Knows,* U.K. cities, 1972.

PRINCIPAL TELEVISION APPEARANCES—Mini-Series: Anne Boleyn, *The Six Wives of Henry VIII.* Movies: Mildred Strete, *Agatha Christie's Murder with Mirrors,* CBS, 1985. Also appeared in *South Riding; Willow Cabins; Living Room; Victoria Regina; Invitation to a Voyage; Antigone; Colome; Carrington V.C.; The Hollow Crown; Scent of Fear; From Chekhov with Love; Flotsam and Jetsam; Mother And Son; Ghosts; Sister Dora; The Double Dealer; The Combination; La Ronde; Tales of the Unexpected; 10 Downing Street; Life after Death; King Lear; Landscape; The Father; The Demon Lover; Robin Hood.*

FILM DEBUT—Cecily Cardew, *The Importance of Being Earnest,* Rank, 1952. PRINCIPAL FILM APPEARANCES—Polly Peachum, *The Beggar's Opera,* 1953; also appeared in *A Tale of Two Cities,* Rank, 1958; *Cromwell,* Columbia, 1970; *Savage Messiah,* Metro-Goldwyn-Mayer, 1972; *The Shooting Party,* European Classics, 1984.

AWARDS: Best Actress, *Evening Standard* Award, 1960, for *Twelfth Night;* Best Actress, *Evening Standard* Award, 1975, for *A Month in the Country;* Dame Commander of the British Empire, 1967.

SIDELIGHTS: RECREATIONS—Music, mountain climbing.

ADDRESSES: AGENT—c/o Barry Burnett, Suite 42-43, Grafton House, Golden Square, London W1, England.

V

VADIM, Roger 1928-

PERSONAL: Born Roger Vadim Plemiannikov, January 26, 1928, in Paris, France; son of Igor Plemiannikov and Marie-Antoinette Ardilouze; married Brigitte Bardot, 1952 (divorced); married Annette Stroyberg, 1958 (divorced); married Jane Fonda, 1967 (divorced); married Catherine Schneider, 1975 (divorced); children: three.

VOCATION: Director, writer, producer, and actor.

CAREER: PRINCIPAL FILM WORK—Assistant to Marc Allegret, *Juliette*, 1953; dialogue writer, *Futures Vedettes*, 1954; co-adaptor, *En Effeuillant la Marguerite*, 1956; director and co-writer (unless otherwise stated): *Et. . . Dieu Crea la Femme (And. . . God Created Woman)*, 1956; *Sait-on Jamais?* (also known as *When the Devil Drives*), 1958; *Les Bijoutiers du Clair de Lune (Heaven Fell That Night)*, 1958; *Les Liaisons Dangereuses*, 1959; *Et Mourir de Plaisir (Blood and Roses)*, Paramount, 1961; *La Bride sur le Cou* (also known as *Please, Not Now*), 1961; "L'Orguiel (Pride)," from *Les Sept Pechees Capitaux (Seven Deadly Sins)*, 1962; *Le Repos du Guerrier (Warrior's Rest)*, 1962; also producer, *Le Vice et la Vertu (Vice and Virtue)*, Metro-Goldwyn-Mayer, 1965; *Chateau en Suede,* (also known as *Nutty Naughty Chateau*), 1963; also co-adaptor, *La Ronde (Circle of Love)*, Reade-Sterling, 1965; also producer, *La Curee (The Game Is Over)*, Royal International, 1967; "Metzengerstein," from *Histoires Extraordinaires (Spirits of the Dead)*, 1968; director only, *Barbarella*, Paramount, 1968; director only, *Pretty Maids All in a Row*, MGM, 1971; also story concept, *Helle*, 1972; also co-writer, *Don Juan 1973 ou Si Don Juan Etait une femme (Don Juan, or If Don Juan Were a Woman)*, 1973; also producer, *La Jeune Fille Assassinee* (also known as *Charlotte*), Gamma III, 1975; *Une Femme Fidele (A Faithful Woman)*, 1976; director only, *Night Games*, 1979; director only, *The Hot Touch*, 1980; also writer, *Surprise Party*, 1983.

PRINCIPAL FILM APPEARANCES—*La Jeunne Fille Assissinee (Charlotte)*, Gamma III, 1975.

PRINCIPAL TELEVISION WORK—Director, *Entree des Artistes*, 1956.

RELATED CAREER—Appeared as a stage actor, 1944-47; journalist, *Paris-Match*, 1952-54.

WRITINGS: BOOKS—*Memoirs of the Devil*, 1976; *The Hungry Angel* (English translation by William Attwood), Atheneum, 1984; *Bardot, Deneuve, Fonda: An Autobiography*, Simon & Shuster, 1986.

ADDRESSES: HOME—24-29 Beverly Avenue, Santa Monica, CA 90405. OFFICE—5 rue Turbigo, 75001 Paris, France. AGENT— c/o Robert Littman, Littman and Freifeld, Inc., 409 N. Camden Drive, Suite 105, Beverly Hills, CA 90210.*

* * *

VALDEZ, Luis 1940-

PERSONAL: Born June 26, 1940; son of Francisco (a farm worker) and Armeda Valdez; married wife, Guadalupe, August 23, 1969; children: Anahuac, Kinan, Lakin. EDUCATION: Graduated from San Jose State University, 1964.

VOCATION: Writer, director, and actor.

CAREER: STAGE DEBUT—*Huelga*, Committee Theatre, San Francisco, CA, 1966. PRINCIPAL STAGE APPEARANCES—With El Teatro Campesino, in U.S. and European cities, 1965—. FIRST NEW YORK STAGE WORK—Director, *La Carpa de los Rasquachis*, Chelsea Westside Theatre, 1973. PRINCIPAL STAGE WORK—Director: *Huelga*, Committe Theatre, San Francisco, CA, 1966; *La Virgen del Tepeyac*, Mission San Juan Bautista, CA, 1971; *Zoot Suit*, Mark Taper Forum, Los Angeles, CA, 1978, then Winter Garden Theatre, New York City, 1979; *Tibercio Vasquez*, 1980; also worked with Peter Brook on *Conference of the Birds*, Santa Cruz, CA, 1973.

MAJOR TOURS—Director and performer, *Actos*, U.S. and European cities, 1965-70; director, *I Don't Have to Show You No Stinking Badges*, U.S. cities, 1986.

PRINCIPAL FILM APPEARANCES—*Which Way Is Up?*, Universal, 1977. PRINCIPAL FILM WORK—Director: *Zoot Suit*, Universal, 1981; *La Bamba*, Columbia, 1987.

PRINCIPAL TELEVISION APPEARANCES—Episodic: *Visions*, PBS, 1976; *Corridos! Tales of Passion and Revolution*, PBS; also appeared in *Los Vendidos*, 1971, and *El Corrido*, 1976. PRINCIPAL TELEVISION WORK—Director, *Corridos! Tales of Passion and Revolution*, PBS.

RELATED CAREER—Founder, artistic director, El Teatro Campesino, 1965—; founding member, California Arts Council; writer, actor, director, United Farmworkers Organizing Committee, Delano, CA; board of directors, Theatre Communications Group; lecturer in Chicano History and Theatre, University of California, Santa Cruz, CA; lecturer in theatre arts, University of California, Berkeley, CA.

NON-RELATED CAREER—Union organizer, United Farm Workers.

WRITINGS: PLAYS—*The Shrunken Head of Pancho Villa,* produced at San Jose State College, San Jose, CA, 1964, published by El Centro Campesino Cultural, 1967; (adaptor) *La Virgen del Tepeyac,* produced at Mission San Juan Bautista, CA, 1971; *La Carpa de los Rasquachis,* Chelsea Westside Theatre, New York City, 1974; *El Fin del Mundo,* produced in 1976; *Zoot Suit,* Mark Taper Forum, Los Angeles, CA, 1978; *Tibercio Vasquez,* produced in 1980; *Corridos,* produced in San Francisco, CA, 1983; *I Don't Have to Show You No Stinking Badges,* Los Angeles Theatre Center, Los Angeles, CA, 1986; *Actos,* produced between 1965-70, published by Cucaracha Press, 1971.

SCREENPLAYS—*Which Way Is Up?,* Universal, 1977; *Zoot Suit,* Universal, 1981; *La Bamba,* Columbia, 1987; also *Gringo Viejo; La Carpa de los Rasquachis.*

TELEPLAYS—*Corridos! Tales of Passion and Revolution,* PBS.

BOOKS—(With Stan Steiner) *Aztlan: An Anthology of Mexican American Literature,* Knopf, 1972; *Pensamiento serpentino: A Chicano Approach to the Theater of Reality,* Cucaracha Publications, 1973.

AWARDS: Obie Award from the *Village Voice,* 1969, Los Angeles Drama Critics Circle Award, 1969 and 1972, all for his work with El Teatro Campesino; special Emmy Award, 1973, for directing; Rockefeller Foundation Grant, 1977; Distinguished Production, Los Angeles Drama Critics Circle Award, Outstanding Achievement in the Theatre, Drama-Logue Award, both 1978, for *Zoot Suit;* Best Musical Picture, Golden Globe nomination, 1981, for *Zoot Suit;* Best Musical, San Francisco Bay Critics Circle Award, 1983, for *Corridos.* Honorary degrees: Doctorate of Arts from Columbia College, Chicago.

MEMBER: Writers' Guild of America, Society of Stage Directors and Choreographers; California Arts Council.

ADDRESSES: HOME—53 Franklin Street, San Juan Bautista, CA 95045. OFFICE—705 Fourth Street, San Juan Bautista, CA 95045. AGENT—c/o Joan Scott, Writers and Artists Agency, 11726 San Vincente Boulevard, Suite 300 Los Angeles, CA 90049.

*   *   *

VALENTINE, Scott   1958-

PERSONAL: Born June 3, 1958, in Saratoga Springs, NY; son of Edward Eugene and Beverly Ann (Hanna) Valentine; married Kym Denyse Fisher (an actress), September 29, 1985; children: Trevin John. EDUCATION: Studied acting at the American Academy of Dramatic Arts, and with John Costopoulos at the Actors Studio West.

VOCATION: Actor.

CAREER: STAGE DEBUT—*No Place to Be Somebody,* Changing Place, New York City. PRINCIPAL STAGE APPEARANCES—Johnny, *Hatful of Rain,* American Academy of Dramatic Arts, New York City, 1980; *Festival Finale,* Union Square Theatre, New York City, 1980; Dan, *Home Remedies,* Actors Outlet, New York City, 1982.

FILM DEBUT—Peter, *Dead Time Stories,* 1982. PRINCIPAL FILM

APPEARANCES—*True Stories,* Island, 1986; Kaz, *My Demon Lover,* New Line Cinema, 1987.

PRINCIPAL TELEVISION APPEARANCES—Series: Nick, *Family Ties,* NBC, 1985-87; Nick, *The Art of Being Nick,* NBC, 1987. Pilots: Nick, *Taking It Home,* NBC, 1986.

MEMBER: Actors' Equity Association, Screen Actors Guild, American Federation of Television and Radio Artists.

ADDRESSES: AGENT—c/o Michael Slessinger, Actors Group, 8285 Sunset Boulevard, No. 12, Los Angeles, CA 90046. PUBLICIST—c/o Nancy Ryder, Nancy Ryder Public Relations, 8380 Melrose Avenue, No. 310A, Los Angeles, CA 90069.

*   *   *

VAN FLEET, Jo   1922-

PERSONAL: Born in 1922, in Oakland, CA; daughter of Roy H. and Elizabeth (Gardner) Van Fleet; married William Bales (a modern dance instructor); children: one son. EDUCATION: Received B.A. from College of the Pacific, Stockton, CA; trained for the stage with Sanford Meisner at the Neighborhood Playhouse and with Elia Kazan and Lee Strasberg at the Actors Studio.

VOCATION: Actress.

CAREER: STAGE DEBUT—Miss Phipps, *Uncle Harry,* National Theatre, Washington, DC, 1944. BROADWAY DEBUT—Dorcas, *The Winter's Tale,* Cort Theatre, 1946. PRINCIPAL STAGE APPEARANCES—Major Anna Orlov, *The Whole World Over,* Biltmore Theatre, New York City, 1947; Connie, *The Closing Door,* Empire Theatre, New York City, 1949; Regan, *King Lear,* National Theatre, New York City, 1950; Miss Foster, *Flight into Eqypt,* Music Box Theatre, New York City, 1952; Marguerite Gautier, *Camino Real,* National Theatre, 1953; Jessie Mae Watts, *The Trip to Bountiful,* Henry Miller's Theatre, New York City, 1953; Daisy, *My Aunt Daisy,* Westport Country Playhouse, Westport, CT, 1954; Eliza Gant, *Look Homeward, Angel,* Ethel Barrymore Theatre, New York City, 1957; Amanda Wingfield, *The Glass Menagerie,* Westport Country Playhouse, 1959; Frances Flint, *The Alligators,* Mrs. Kittel, *Rosemary,* both York Playhouse, New York City, 1960; Claire Zachanassian, *The Visit,* Playhouse-in-the-Park, Philadelphia, PA, 1961; Frieda Lawrence, *I Rise in Flame Cried the Phoenix,* title role, *The Lady of Larkspur Lotion,* both Festival of Two Worlds, Spoleto, Italy, 1961; Madame Rosepettle, *Oh Dad, Poor Dad, Mama's Hung You in the Closet and I'm Feelin' So Sad,* Phoenix Theatre, New York City, 1962; Amanda Wingfield, *The Glass Menagerie,* Brooks Atkinson Theatre, New York City, 1965; Beatrice, *The Effect of Gamma Rays on Man-in-the-Moon Marigolds,* Evy Meara, *The Gingerbread Lady,* both Studio Arena Theatre, Buffalo, NY, 1971; Linda Loman, *Death of a Salesman,* Arlington Park Theatre, Chicago, IL, 1972.

FILM DEBUT—*East of Eden,* Warner Brothers, 1955. PRINCIPAL FILM APPEARANCES—*I'll Cry Tomorrow,* Metro-Goldwyn-Mayer, 1955; *The Rose Tattoo,* Paramount, 1955; *The King and Four Queens,* United Artists, 1956; *Gunfight at the OK Corral,* Paramount, 1957; *This Angry Age,* Columbia, 1958; *Wild River,* Twentieth Century-Fox, 1960; *Cool Hand Luke,* Warner Brothers, 1967; *I Love You Alice B. Toklas,* Warner Brothers-Seven Arts, 1969; *Eighty Steps to Jonah,* Warner Brothers-Seven Arts, 1969;

The Gang That Couldn't Shoot Straight, Metro-Goldwyn-Mayer, 1971; *The Tenant,* Paramount, 1976.

PRINCIPAL TELEVISION APPEARANCES—Episodic: *Bonanza,* NBC; *Mod Squad,* ABC. Movies: Mama Rico, *The Family Rico,* CBS, 1972; Mrs. Jessica Williams, *Satan's School for Girls,* ABC, 1973; Mother Vanda, *Power,* NBC, 1980. Specials: Clara, *Paradise Lost,* 1971; *Cinderella.*

AWARDS: Antoinette Perry Award, Donaldson Award, Show Business Award, all 1954, for *The Trip to Bountiful;* Best Supporting Actress, Academy Award, 1956, for *East of Eden;* New York Drama Critics Award, 1958, for *Look Homeward, Angel.* Honorary degrees: D.F.A., College of the Pacific.

MEMBER: Actors' Equity Association, Screen Actors Guild, American Federation of Television and Radio Artists.

ADDRESSES: OFFICE—c/o Actors' Equity Association, 165 W. 46th Street, New York, NY 10036.

*   *   *

VAN GRIETHUYSEN, Ted   1934-

PERSONAL: Full name, Theodore Andre Van Griethuysen; born November 7, 1934, in Ponca City, OK; son of Theodore Andre (an oil company employee) and Treva Jan (Ogan) Van Griethuysen; married Rebecca Thompson (an actress), May 26, 1962. EDUCATION: University of Texas, B.F.A. (summa cum laude), 1956; Yale University School of Drama, graduate work, 1957-58; trained for the stage at the London Academy of Music and Dramatic Art, and with Ben Iden Payne, William Hickey, Michael Howard, and Eli Siegel.

VOCATION: Actor, director, and designer.

CAREER: STAGE DEBUT—Lion, *Androcles and the Lion,* Four Arts Theatre, Houston, TX, 1951. OFF-BROADWAY DEBUT—Rake, *The Failures,* Fourth Street Theatre, 1959. PRINCIPAL STAGE APPEARANCES—Sebastian, *Twelfth Night,* Four Arts Theatre, Houston, TX, 1952; Michael Brown, *O, Mistress Mine,* Little Theatre, Houston, TX, 1952; Ruddy Gibbons, *My Dear Delinquents,* Alley Theatre, Houston, TX, 1953; Orestes, *The Flies,* Alley Theatre, 1955; Claudio, *Measure for Measure,* Gremio, *The Taming of the Shrew,* Laertes, *Hamlet,* all Old Globe Theatre, San Diego Shakespeare Festival, San Diego, CA, 1955; Romeo, *Romeo and Juliet,* Clarence, *Richard III,* Guiderius, *Cymbeline,* King of Navarre, *Love's Labour's Lost,* all Oregon Shakespeare Festival, Ashland, OR, 1956; Pierre, *The Madwoman of Chaillot,* Prince, *Time Remembered,* both Williamstown Theatre Festival, Williamstown, MA, 1958; Li-Wang, *The Lute Song,* City Center Theatre, New York City, 1959; Octavius, *Man and Superman,* Judd Steiner, *Compulsion,* John Worthing, *The Importance of Being Earnest,* Thomas Mendip, *The Lady's Not for Burning,* Lord Brockhurst, *The Boy Friend,* all Stockbridge Theatre, Stockbridge, MA, 1959; Tom Lee, *Tea and Sympathy,* Equity Library Theatre, New York City, 1959; son, *The Purification,* Theatre de Lys, New York City, 1959; Florizel, *The Winter's Tale,* Adrian, *The Tempest,* Egyptian messenger, *Antony and Cleopatra,* all American Shakespeare Festival, Stratford, CT, 1960; Mr. Hastings, *She Stoops to Conquer,* Sergeant Tinley, *The Plough and the Stars,* both Phoenix Theatre, New York City, 1960.

Jules Thibodeaux, *The Octoroon,* Laertes, *Hamlet,* both Phoenix Theatre, 1961; Monsieur le Beau, *As You Like It,* Donalbain, *Macbeth,* Troilus, *Troilus and Cressida,* all American Shakespeare Festival, 1961; Young Marlow, *O, Marry Me!,* Gate Theatre, New York City, 1961; Ayamonn, *Red Roses for Me!,* Greenwich Mews Theatre, New York City, 1961; Aemilian, *Romulus,* Music Box Theatre, New York City, 1962; Oliver Brown, *The Moon Besieged,* Lyceum Theatre, New York City, 1962; title role, *Hamlet: Revisited,* Terrain Gallery Theatre, New York City, 1963; Richard III, *The White Rose and the Red,* Stage 73, New York City, 1963; Oberon, *A Midsummer Night's Dream,* New York Shakespeare Festival, New York City, 1964; Jones, *Inadmissible Evidence,* Belasco Theatre, New York City, 1965; Cardinal Bellarmine, *Galileo,* Vivian Beaumont Theatre, New York City, 1967; Tim Law, *The Basement,* Eastside Playhouse, New York City, 1968; Joseph Surface, *School for Scandal,* Mr. Horner, *The Country Wife,* Orestes, *Andromache,* all Terrain Gallery Theatre, New York City, 1969; Eilert Lovborg, *Hedda Gabler,* Terrain Gallery Theatre, then Actors Playhouse, New York City, 1970; title role, *Othello,* Rip Van Winkle/Richard III, *Goodbye Profit System,* both Terrain Gallery Theatre, 1972; P.T. Barnum, *First Time Anywhere,* Theatre-Off-Park, New York City, 1983; Big Daddy, *Cat on a Hot Tin Roof,* Long Wharf Theatre, New Haven, CT, 1985; Friar Laurence, *Romeo and Juliet,* Syracuse Stage, Syracuse, NY, 1986.

PRINCIPAL STAGE WORK—Production assistant, *The Tempest,* Drury Lane Theatre, London, 1958; costume designer, *The Crystal Heart,* East 74th Street Theatre, New York City, 1960; director, *Hamlet: Revisited,* Terrain Gallery Theatre, New York City, 1963; costume designer, *Javelin,* Actors Playhouse, New York City, 1966; director, *Hedda Gabler,* Terrain Gallery Theatre, 1969, then Actors Playhouse, 1970; director, *Othello,* Terrain Gallery Theatre, 1972.

PRINCIPAL TELEVISION APPEARANCES—Episodic: Mortimer, "Henry IV, Part I," *Play of the Week,* WNTA, 1960; son, "The Avenger," *The Defenders,* CBS, 1962; young sailor, "The Thunder of Ernie Bass," *The Nurses,* CBS, 1962; little fox, "The Pit," *Lamp unto My Feet,* CBS, 1965; Hansen, "Everybody Loved Him," *NYPD,* ABC, 1969; also appeared in title role, "Frankenstein," *The Human Stage,* WOR, New York. Specials: Mr. Fenno, "The Patriot," *Hallmark Hall of Fame,* NBC, 1963; Milton, "Lamp at Midnight," *Hallmark Hall of Fame,* NBC, 1966; Gilles de Rais, "Saint Joan," *Hallmark Hall of Fame,* NBC, 1967.

MEMBER: Actors' Equity Association, Screen Actors Guild, American Federation of Television and Radio Artists, United Scenic Artists.

ADDRESSES: OFFICE—259 W. 12th Street, New York, NY 10014.*

*   *   *

VANCE, Charles   1929-

PERSONAL: Born Charles Goldblatt, December 6, 1929, in Belfast, Northern Ireland; son of Eric (a leather merchant) and Sarah (Freeman) Goldblatt; married Imogen Anne Moynihan (an actress), April 23, 1966; children: Jacqueline. EDUCATION: Graduated from Queen's University, 1948; trained for the stage at the Ulster Group Theatre, Belfast and studied mime at the Marigny School, Paris.

VOCATION: Actor, director, and producing manager.

CAREER: STAGE DEBUT—With the Anew MacMaster Company, Gaiety Theatre, Dublin, Ireland, 1949. PRINCIPAL STAGE APPEARANCES—Sir Thomas More, *A Man for All Seasons,* Greenwood Theatre, 1975.

Also see *WRITINGS* below. FIRST STAGE WORK—Director, *The Glass Menagerie,* Arts Theatre, Cambridge, U.K., 1960. PRINCIPAL STAGE WORK—Producer and director of numerous theatrical presentations, including: Director, *Wuthering Heights,* 1972; director, *The Glass Menagerie, The Merchant of Venice,* both Gardner Centre Theatre, Brighton, U.K., 1973; director, *The Jolson Revue,* 1974; director, *Oh! What a Lovely War,* Greenwood Theatre, 1975; producer, *Stop the World, I Want to Get Off,* 1976; producer (with David Conville), *Salad Days,* 1977; director, *The Jolson Revue,* Australia, 1978; producer and director, *The Adventures of Paddington Bear,* 1978; director, *The Kingfisher,* 1981; director, *The Hollow,* 1982; director, *The Maing Game,* 1983; producer, *Mr. Cinders,* Blackpool, U.K., 1984; producer (with Bill Kenwright), *Joseph and the Amazing Technicolor Dreamcoat,* Scarborough, U.K., 1985; producer and director, *Jane Eyre,* 1985; producer, *For Love Nor Money,* Floral Hall Theatre, Scarborough, U.K., 1986. Also producer and director of pantomimes performed throughout the U.K.

MAJOR TOURS—Producer and director, *In Praise of Love,* U.K. cities, 1977; producer, *Witness for the Prosecution,* U.K. cities, 1979; director, *The Creeper,* U.K. cities, 1979; producer and director, *The Marriage Go-Round,* U.K. cities, 1979; producer and director, *Policy for Murder,* U.K. cities, 1984; producer, *Mr. Cinders,* U.K. cities, 1985; director, *Alice in Wonderland,* U.K. cities, 1986; director, *Wuthering Heights,* U.K. cities, 1988.

RELATED CAREER—Founder, Civic Theatre, Chelmsford, U.K., 1962; president, Theatrical Management Association, 1971-72, 1973-76, then executive vice-president, 1976-79; member, Theatres National Committee, 1971—; member, Provincial Theatre Council, 1971—; director, Theatres Investment Fund, 1974; member, Drama Advisory Panel, South East Arts Association, 1974-79; vice-chairor, Theatres Advisory Council, 1974—; chairor, Standing Advisory Committee on Local Authority and the Theatre, 1974—; manager, Floral Hall Theatre, Scarborough, U.K., 1985-86; chairor, Gala Committee, British Theatre Association, 1986—; manager, Beck Theatre, London, 1986—; manager, Manor Pavilion, Sidmouth, U.K., 1987—; editor-in-chief, Team Publishing, 1987—; editor, *Amateur Stage,* 1987—. Also director, Charles Vance Productions, later Charles Vance, Ltd.; founder, Vance-Offord Publications, Ltd.; executive producer, Entertainment Investments (theatre division); supervisor of repertory companies at Tunbridge Wells, Torquay, Whitby, Hastings, Eastbourne, and Folkestone; advisor to the government of Ghana for the building of a National Theatre; member, Fund Raising Committee, British Theatre Association.

NON-RELATED CAREER—Broadcaster.

WRITINGS: (Adpator) *Wuthering Heights,* 1972, revised 1988; *The Jolson Revue,* 1974; (adaptor) *Jane Eyre,* 1985; has also written numerous pantomimes which he has produced and directed in performances throughout the U.K.

MEMBER: British Actors' Equity Association, Theatrical Managers Association, Directors Guild, Royal Society of Arts, British Theatre Association; Hurlingham Club, Kennel Club, Wig and Pen Club.

SIDELIGHTS: RECREATIONS—Sailing, cooking, animals.

CTFT learned that Charles Vance sailed the Atlantic Ocean single-handedly in 1956.

ADDRESSES: OFFICE—Charles Vance, Ltd., 83 George Street, Marylebone, London W1H 5PL, England; Beck Theatre, Grange Road, Hayes, Middlesex UB3 2UE, England.

*   *   *

VAUGHAN, Stuart   1925-

PERSONAL: Born John Walker Vaughan, August 23, 1925, in Terre Haute, IN; son of John Harwood (in the U.S. Army Air Corps) and Pauletta Rosalie (Walker) Vaughan; married Gladys Regier (a director), 1948 (divorced, 1960); married Helen Quarrier (an actress), August 22, 1960, (died, December 25, 1963); married Anne Thompson (an actress), April 14, 1965. EDUCATION: Indiana State College, B.A., 1945; Indiana University, M.A., 1946; studied acting with Harold Clurman, 1954-56.

VOCATION: Director, actor, producer, and playwright.

CAREER: STAGE DEBUT—Fritz, *Claudia,* Belfry Theatre, Williams Bay, WI, 1945. BROADWAY DEBUT—Sergeant of the guard, *The Strong Are Lonely,* Broadhurst Theatre, 1953. PRINCIPAL STAGE APPEARANCES—(Understudy) *The Confidential Clerk,* Morosco Theatre, New York City, 1954; Mr. Lovewell, *The Clandestine Marriage,* Players Theatre, New York City, 1954; Hector, *Thieves' Carnival,* Cherry Lane Theatre, New York City, 1955; Algernon, *The Importance of Being Earnest,* Phoenix Theatre, New York City, 1961; Tanner, *Man and Superman,* Seattle Center Playhouse, Seattle, WA, 1964; Algernon, *The Importance of Being Earnest,* Seattle Center Playhouse, 1965; Duke, *Measure for Measure,* Chorus, *Antigone,* Colonel Triletski, *A Country Scandal,* CSC Repertory, Abbey Theatre, New York City, 1975. Also appeared in summer theatre productions at the Erie Playhouse, Erie, PA, 1950-52, and the Arena Theatre, Rochester, NY, 1952; appeared at the British Colonial Theatre, Nassau, Bahamas, and The Playhouse, Old Orchard Beach, ME, both 1953.

PRINCIPAL STAGE WORK—All as director, unless indicated: Assistant stage manager, *The Confidential Clerk,* Morosco Theatre, New York City, 1954; stage manager, *The Chalk Garden,* Ethel Barrymore Theatre, New York City, 1955; *I Knock at the Door, Pictures in the Hallway,* both Kaufmann Auditorium, New York City, 1956; *The Taming of the Shrew, Julius Caesar,* both New York Shakespeare Festival (NYSF), East Side Amphitheatre, New York City, 1956; *Pictures in the Hallway,* Playhouse Theatre, New York City, 1957; *The River Line,* Carnegie Hall Playhouse, New York City, 1957; *Romeo and Juliet, The Two Gentlemen of Verona, Macbeth,* all NYSF, Belvedere Lake Theatre, New York City, 1956; *I Knock at the Door,* Belasco Theatre, New York City, 1957; *Richard III,* NYSF, Heckscher Theatre, New York City, 1957; *As You Like It,* Heckscher Theatre, 1958; *Othello,* Belvedere Lake Theatre, 1958; *The Power and the Glory, The Family Reunion,* both Phoenix Theatre, New York City, 1958; *The Beaux' Stratagem,* Phoenix Theatre, 1959; *Julius Caesar,* NYSF, Belvedere Lake Theatre, 1959; *The Great God Brown,* Coronet Theatre, New York City, 1959; *Pictures in the Hallway,* Phoenix Theatre, 1959.

Continuing as director, unless indicated: *I Knock at the Door, Peer Gynt, She Stoops to Conquer, The Plough and the Stars,* and *Henry IV, Part I,* all Phoenix Theatre, 1960; *The Octoroon, Hamlet, The Importance of Being Earnest,* all Phoenix Theatre, 1961; *Medea,* Antioch Area Theatre, Yellow Springs, OH, 1962; *The Good Woman of Setzuan,* Studio Arena Theatre, Buffalo, NY, 1962; *Abe Lincoln in Illinois, The Taming of the Shrew,* both Anderson Theatre, New York City, 1963; *King Lear, The Firebugs,* both Seattle Center Playhouse, Seattle, WA, 1963; *The Lady's Not for Burning, Death of a Salesman, Shadows of Heros, Twelfth Night, Man and Superman,* all Seattle Center Playhouse, 1964; *Ah! Wilderness, The Cherry Orchard, Hamlet, The Importance of Being Earnest,* all Seattle Center Playhouse, 1965; *Heartbreak House,* Seattle Center Playhouse, 1966; producer, *Long Day's Journey into Night,* Seattle Center Playhouse, 1966; producer, *Charley's Aunt, Romeo and Juliet,* both Repertory Theatre of New Orleans, New Orleans, LA, 1966; producer, *Our Town, The Rivals, The Crucible, St. Joan,* all Repertory Theatre of New Orleans, 1967; producer, *A Midsummer Night's Dream, Tartuffe, Arms and the Man, Twelfth Night, An Enemy of the People,* all Repertory theatre of New Orleans, 1968; producer, *The Chairs, The Bald Soprano, Private Lives,* all Repertory Theatre of New Orleans, 1969; *The War of the Roses,* NYSF, Delacorte Theatre, New York City, 1969.

Continuing as director: *Assassination 1865,* Goodman Theatre, Chicago, IL, 1971; *Ghost Dance,* Trinity Square Repertory Theatre, Providence, RI, 1973; *A Country Scandal,* CSC Repertory, Abbey Theatre, New York City, 1975. Also directed, *The Taming of the Shrew,* Seattle and King County Parks, WA, 1965; directed at the Little Theatre, St. Augustine, FL, 1948-49; British Colonial Theatre, Nassau, Bahamas, and at The Playhouse, Old Orchard Beach, ME, both 1953; and the Belfry Theatre, Williams Bay, WI.

MAJOR TOURS—Stewart Kennedy, *Her Unborn Child,* U.S. cities, 1946; director, *Come and Be Killed,* U.S. cities, 1975.

PRINCIPAL TELEVISION WORK—Director, *The Lady's Not for Burning,* 1958.

RELATED CAREER—Drama instructor, Indiana State University, 1947-48; artistic director, New York Shakespeare Festival, New York City, 1956-58; artistic director, Phoenix Theatre, New York City, 1958-63; adjunct professor, Brooklyn College, 1960; artistic director, Seattle Repertory Theatre, Seattle, WA, 1963-66; founder and producer-director, Repertory Theatre of New Orleans, New Orleans, LA, 1966-69; visiting professor, Loyola University of the South, 1968; visiting director, Loeb Drama Center, Harvard University, 1970-71; adjunct professor, C.W. Post College, 1971; guest artist: University of Kansas, 1971-72, Ohio State University, 1974, University of Georgia, 1975, University of South Carolina, 1976; artistic adviser, Asolo State Theatre, Sarasota, FL, 1980-83.

WRITINGS: PLAYS—(Adaptor) "Henry VI, Parts I, II, and III" and "Richard III" as *The War of the Roses,* New York Shakespeare Festival, Delacorte Theatre, New York City, 1969; *Assassination 1865,* Goodman Theatre, Chicago, IL, 1971; *Ghost Dance,* Trinity Square Repertory Theatre, Providence, RI, 1973; (adaptor, with Anne Thompson) *The Servant of Two Masters,* Actors Theatre, Los Angeles, CA, 1975; (adaptor, with Thompson) *Amoreuse,* 1975. Also wrote *The Royal Game,* Dramatic Publishing Company, 1974; co-editor, *The Bantam Shakespeare,* Bantam, series of nineteen volumes published between 1960-64.

BOOKS—*A Possible Theatre,* 1969.

AWARDS: Best Director, Vernon Rice Award, Obie Award from the *Village Voice,* both 1958, for his work with the New York Shakespeare Festival; also received Rockefeller Grant, 1947; Fulbright Grant, 1949-50; Ford Foundation Grant, 1961-62.

MEMBER: Player's Club.

SIDELIGHTS: RECREATIONS—Fencing.

ADDRESSES: OFFICE—261 St. John's Avenue, Yonkers, NY 10704.*

*   *   *

VAUGHN, Robert   1932-

PERSONAL: Born November 22, 1932, in New York, NY.

VOCATION: Actor and writer.

CAREER: PRINCIPAL TELEVISION APPEARANCES—Series: Captain Ray Rambridge, *The Lieutenant,* NBC, 1963-64; Napoleon Solo, *The Man from U.N.C.L.E.,* NBC, 1964-68; Harry Rule, *The Protectors,* syndicated, 1972-73; Harlan Adams, *Emerald Point N.A.S.,* CBS, 1983-84. Episodic: *Telephone Time,* CBS; *General Electric True,* CBS. Mini-Series: Charles Desmond, *The Captains and the Kings,* NBC, 1976-77; *Washington: Behind Closed Doors,* ABC, 1977; Morgan Wendell, *Centennial,* NBC, 1978-79; President Woodrow Wilson, *Backstairs at the White House,* NBC, 1979; *The Blue and the Gray,* CBS, 1982; *Evergreen,* NBC, 1985. Movies: *International Airport,* 1985; also *The Spy in the Green Hat,* British.

PRINCIPAL FILM APPEARANCES—*Hell's Crossroads,* Republic, 1957; *No Time to Be Young,* Columbia, 1957; *Unwed Mother,* Allied Artists, 1958; *Good Day for a Hanging,* Columbia, 1959; *The Young Philadelphians,* Warner Brothers, 1959; *The Magnificent Seven,* United Artists, 1960; *The Big Show,* Twentieth Century-Fox, 1961; *The Caretakers,* 1963; *To Trap a Spy,* Metro-Goldwyn-Mayer (MGM), 1966; *The Spy with My Face,* MGM, 1966; *One Spy Too Many,* MGM, 1966; *One of Our Spies Is Missing,* MGM, 1966; *The Venetian Affair,* MGM, 1967; *How to Steal the World,* MGM, 1968; *Bullitt,* Warner Brothers-Seven Arts, 1968; *The Bridge at Remagen,* United Artists, 1969; *If It's Tuesday This Must Be Belgium,* United Artists, 1969; *Julius Caesar,* American International, 1970; *The Mind of Mr. Soames,* Columbia, 1970; *The Statue,* Cinerama, 1971; *The Clay Pigeon,* MGM, 1971; *The Towering Inferno,* Twentieth Century-Fox, 1974; *Wanted: Babysitter,* 1975; *Demon Seed,* United Artists, 1977; *Starship Invasions,* Warner Brothers, 1978; *Brass Target,* United Artists, 1979; *Cuba Crossing* (also known as *Assignment: Kill Castro* and *Kill Castro*), 1979; *Good Luck, Miss Wyckoff,* 1979; *Virus,* 1980; *Battle Beyond the Stars,* Orion, 1980; *Hanger 18,* Sunn Classic, 1980; *S.O.B.,* Paramount, 1981; *Superman III,* Warner Brothers, 1983; *Black Moon Rising,* 1985; *The Delta Force,* 1985; also *The City Jungle.*

PRINCIPAL STAGE APPEARANCES—Henry Drummond, *Inherit the Wind,* Paper Mill Playhouse, Millburn, NJ, 1984-85.

WRITINGS: BOOKS—*Only Victims,* 1972.

AWARDS: Best Supporting Actor, Academy Award nomination,

1959, for *The Young Philadelphians;* Outstanding Continuing Performance by a Supporting Actor in a Drama Series, Emmy Award, 1978, for *Washington: Behind Closed Doors.*

MEMBER: Screen Actors Guild, American Federation of Television and Radio Artists.

ADDRESSES: AGENT—c/o Joe Funicello, International Creative Management, 8899 Beverly Blvd., Los Angeles, CA 90068.*

*   *   *

VELEZ, Eddie   1958-

PERSONAL: Full name, Edwin Velez; born June 4, 1958, in New York, NY. EDUCATION: Attended the School of Visual Arts; studied acting with Jose Quintero, Estelle Harman, Sheila Weber, Dr. Doyne Mraz, and Sonia Weisman. MILITARY: U.S. Air Force.

VOCATION: Actor.

CAREER: TELEVISION DEBUT—*For Love and Honor,* NBC, 1983. PRINCIPAL TELEVISION APPEARANCES—Episodic: *Hill Street Blues,* NBC; *Houston Knights,* CBS; *Cagney and Lacey,* CBS; *Cápitol,* CBS; also *Double Dare.* Series: Pepe Garcia, *Bay City Blues,* NBC, 1983; Frankie Santana, *The A-Team,* NBC, 1987; *Trial and Error,* CBS, upcoming; also Migues, *Charlie and*

EDDIE VELEZ

Company, CBS; Julio Morales, *Berrenger's.* Movies: Stratis, *Summer Fantasy,* NBC, 1984; Tom, *Children of the Night,* CBS, 1985; Carlos, *C.A.T. Squad,* NBC, 1986.

PRINCIPAL STAGE APPEARANCES—*Balm in Gilead,* Pan Andreas Theatre, Hollywood, CA; *Delirious,* Pilot Theatre, Hollywood, CA; also appeared in *Steambath, The Petrified Forest, The Ritz, The Threepenny Opera, Mooney's Kids Don't Cry, The Valiant, Barefoot in the Park, Count Dracula, The Odd Couple,* and *Bell, Book and Candle,* at several theatres including the Palo Alto Playhouse, Theatre West, The Los Altos Conservatory, The One Act Theatre Company, and The Actors Ensemble.

PRINCIPAL FILM APPEARANCES—*Repo Man,* Universal, 1984; *Doin' Time,* 1985; *Extremities,* Atlantic, 1986; also *Kid Gloves; The Women's Club.*

RELATED CAREER—Stand-up comic; writer, producer, and director of productions at West Coast repertory theatre companies.

MEMBER: Actors' Equity Association, American Federation of Television and Radio Artists.

SIDELIGHTS: RECREATIONS—Writing, baseball, basketball, tennis.

ADDRESSES: MANAGER—J. Gerrard Management, 10661 Whipple, Tolica Lake, CA 91601.

*   *   *

VERNON, Richard   1925-

PERSONAL: Born March 7, 1925, in Reading, England; son of Evelyn and Violet Mary Stuart (Foley) Vernon; married Benedicta Leigh Hoskyns. EDUCATION: Trained for the stage at the Central School of Speech and Drama, London.

VOCATION: Actor.

CAREER: LONDON DEBUT—Hardwicke, *Stratton,* Mercury Theatre, 1950. PRINCIPAL STAGE APPEARANCES—Captain Hook/Mr. Darling, *Peter Pan,* Scala Theatre, London, 1953; Charles Parkin, M.P., *Any Other Business,* Westminster Theatre, London, 1958; Sir Harry Tremayne, *The Edwardians,* Saville Theatre, London, 1959; Mr. Bennett, *A Shred of Evidence,* Duchess Theatre, London, 1960; Mr. Brierly, *Kelly's Eye,* Royal Court Theatre, London, 1963; Sir John Holt, *A Friend in Need,* Royal Theatre, Windsor, U.K., 1965; Richard Greatham, *Hay Fever,* Duke of York's Theatre, London, 1968; Austin, *Highly Confidential,* Cambridge Theatre, London, 1969; Malcolm Garth-Bender, *George and Margaret,* Arnaud Theatre, Guildford, U.K., 1973; Antonio, *Saturday, Sunday, Monday,* Queen's Theatre, London, 1974; Lord Bogmore, *Dead Eyed Dicks,* Dublin Theatre Festival, Dublin, Ireland, 1976; Cedric Seward, *The Passion of Dracula,* Queen's Theatre, 1978. Also appeared in *Pack of Lies,* Lyric Theatre, London, 1983; *Look, No Hans,* Strand Theatre, London, 1985.

MAJOR TOURS—Jimmy Broadbent, *The Reluctant Debutante,* U.K. cities, 1975; Lord Bogmore, *Dead Eyed Dicks,* U.K. cities, 1976.

PRINCIPAL FILM APPEARANCES—*The Siege of Pinchgut* (also

known as *Four Desperate Men*), Continental, 1960; *The Village of the Damned*, Metro-Goldwyn-Mayer (MGM), 1961; *Cash on Demand*, Columbia, 1962; *Tomb of Ligeia*, American International, 1965; *Goldfinger*, United Artists, 1964; *A Hard Day's Night*, United Artists, 1964; *The Servant*, Landau, 1964; *The Secret of My Success*, MGM, 1965; *The Pink Panther Strikes Again*, United Artists, 1976; *The Human Factor*, Bryanston, 1975; *Oh, Heavenly Dog*, Twentieth Century-Fox, 1980; *Gandhi*, Columbia, 1982; *Evil under the Sun*, Universal, 1982. Also appeared in *Accidental Death*, 1963; *Alley France*, 1964; *Hot Enough for June*, 1964; *Early Bird*, 1965; *The Intelligence Men*, 1965; *She'll Follow You Anywhere*, 1971; *The Satanic Rites of Dracula*, 1973; *Lady Jane*, 1984; *A Month in the Country*, 1986; *The Storyteller*, 1987.

PRINCIPAL TELEVISION APPEARANCES—Episodic: *Ripping Yarns*. Series: *Upstairs, Downstairs; Edward VII; The Duchess of Duke Street; Hitchhiker's Guide to the Galaxy; Paradise Postponed*. Also appeared in *Man in Room 17; Lady Windemere's Fan; Happy; A Family and a Fortune; Persuasion; Sextet; Sarah; A Friend Indeed; Village Hall; Affairs of the Heart; Spawn; Aren't We All?; Sandbaggers; Suez; After Dinner Joke; Roger Doesn't Live Here Anymore; Adelaide Bartlett; Something in Disguise; Nanny; L for Lester; Witness for the Prosecution; Waters of the Moon; Roll over Beethoven; Learning; A Still Small Shout; Return of the Antelope; Hot Metal*.

SIDELIGHTS: RECREATIONS—Sailing.

ADDRESSES: AGENT—Julian Belfrage Associates, 60 St. James's Street, London W1, England.

*   *   *

VILLARD, Tom   1953-

PERSONAL: Full name, Thomas Louis Villard; born November 19, 1953, in Waipahu Ewa, HI; son of Ronald Louis (a photochemical engineer) and Diane Ruth (a teacher of the emotionally handicapped; maiden name, MacNaughton) Villard. EDUCATION: Attended Allegheny College; studied acting at the Lee Strasberg Institute, the American Academy of Dramatic Arts, and with Warren Robertson.

VOCATION: Actor.

CAREER: PRINCIPAL STAGE APPEARANCES—Prince Florizel, *The Winter's Tale*, Modern Artists Company, Los Angeles, CA; Jerry, *The Zoo Story*, Ogden Summer Theatre, NY; Bernard, *Feiffer's People*, Rochester Theatre, Rochester, NY; title role, *Butterfingers Angel*, Syracuse Stage, Syracuse, NY; ensemble, *Henry V*, Delacorte Theatre, New York Shakespeare Festival, New York City; Harlequin, *Inconstant Lovers*, Guthrie Theatre, Minneapolis, MN. Also appeared in *Vampire Tales*, with John Fleck & Company, Anti-Club, Los Angeles, CA; *Pagan Holiday*, with John Fleck & Company, Lhasha Club, Los Angeles, CA; *The Happiest Girl in the Whole Wide World*, Modern Artists Company, Los Angeles, CA.

PRINCIPAL FILM APPEARANCES—*Parasite*, Embassy, 1981; Johnny Ray, *Grease II*, Paramount, 1982; *Surf II*, Arista, 1983; *Weekend Warriors*, Convy-Frimberg Productions, 1985; *One Crazy Summer*, Warner Brothers, 1985; *Heartbreak Ridge*, Warner Brothers, 1986; also title role, *The Trouble with Dick*, 1986.

TOM VILLARD

PRINCIPAL TELEVISION APPEARANCES—Episodic: *Rags to Riches*, NBC; *The Golden Girls*, NBC; *Macgruder and Loud*, ABC; *Taxi*, ABC. Series: Jay Bostwick, *We Got It Made*, NBC, 1983-84, then syndicated, 1987. Movies: Eric, *Sidney Shorr: A Girl's Best Friend*, NBC, 1981; Crazy Leo Bandini, *High School, U.S.A.*, NBC, 1983; Keith, *Attack of Fear*, CBS, 1984.

NON-RELATED CAREER—Photographer.

WRITINGS: POETRY—*at the time*, 1977; *inside outside*, 1983.

MEMBER: Actors' Equity Association, Screen Actors Guild, American Federation of Television and Radio Artists.

SIDELIGHTS: Tom Villard told *CTFT* that a one-man exhibit of his color abstract photographs was held at the James Turcotte Gallery, Los Angeles, in 1983.

ADDRESSES: AGENT—Harris and Goldberg Talent Agency, 2121 Avenue of the Stars, Suite 950, Los Angeles, CA 90067.

*   *   *

VILLECHAIZE, Herve   1943-

PERSONAL: Full name, Herve Jean Pierre Villechaize; born April 23, 1943, in Paris, France; son of Andre and Eveline (Recchionni) Villechaize. EDUCATION: Studied art at the Beaux Art School, Paris; trained for the stage with Julie Bavasso, New York City.

VOCATION: Actor, painter, and singer.

CAREER: PRINCIPAL TELEVISION APPEARANCES—Series: Tatoo, *Fantasy Island,* ABC, 1978-83. Episodic: *Diff'rent Strokes,* NBC; *Taxi,* ABC; *The Fall Guy,* ABC; *Faery Tale Theatre,* Showtime. Guest: *Good Morning America, The Tonight Show with Johnny Carson, The Dinah Shore Show,* and *The Merv Griffin Show.*

FILM DEBUT—*The Guitar,* Spain. PRINCIPAL FILM APPEARANCES—*The Gang That Couldn't Shoot Straight,* Metro-Goldwyn-Mayer, 1971; *The Man with the Golden Gun,* United Artists, 1974; *Crazy Joe,* Columbia, 1974; *Seizure,* Canadian production, 1974; *The One and Only,* Paramount, 1978; *Forbidden Zone,* 1980; also *Hollywood Boulevard Number 2* and *Hot Tomorrow.*

PRINCIPAL STAGE APPEARANCES—*Elizabeth the First* and *Gloria and Esperanza,* both Broadway productions; *Ubu Roi,* with the Hartford Stage Company, CT; *Rosencrantz and Guildenstern Are Dead* and *Scuba Duba,* both at the Philadelphia Playhouse; *Jack Street,* Mark Taper Forum, Los Angeles; *Rigoletto, Pagliaci,* and *Carrie Nation,* both with the New York City Opera Company.

NON-RELATED CAREER—Painter, with exhibitions in galleries throughout the U.S.; partner: Art Students League, New York City, Mini Autos Corporation, Mexico City, and FW Spas, Inc.; founder, Venice Anti-Crime Hotline.

RECORDINGS: SONGS—"Why, When a Child Is Born," on the album *Children of the World.*

AWARDS: City of Paris Art Award.

MEMBER: American Federation of Television and Radio Artists; Suicide Hotline, Hogars Creative Center for Drug and Alcohol Abuse, Green Peace, The Flying Doctors of Mercy, Stop the Madness, Save the Seals, Save the Whales, Hathaway House for Children (board of directors), Sheenway School and Cultural Center, Wildlife Waystation, California Humane Society for Animals, LIGA International, International Association of Chiefs of Police, National Wildlife Association, St. Joseph's Lakota Council.

ADDRESSES: OFFICE—Midget Delight Productions, P.O. Box 1305, Burbank, CA 91507. AGENT—c/o John Kimble, Triad Artists, 10100 Santa Monica Blvd., Los Angeles, CA 90067.*

* * *

VILLIERS, James 1933-

PERSONAL: Born September 29, 1933, in London, England; son of Eric Hyde and Joan Ankaret (Talbot) Villiers; married Patricia Donovan. EDUCATION: Attended Wellington College; trained for the stage at the Royal Academy of Dramatic Art.

VOCATION: Actor.

CAREER: STAGE DEBUT—William Blore, *Ten Little Niggers,* Summer Theatre, Frinton, U.K., 1953. BROADWAY DEBUT—Bushy, *Richard II,* Winter Garden Theatre, 1956. PRINCIPAL STAGE APPEARANCES—Trebonius, *Julius Caeser,* Antenor, *Troilus and Cressida,* Bushy, *Richard II,* all with the Old Vic Company, London, 1955-56; Richard Kerstin, *Tomorrow with Pictures,* Lyric

Hammersmith Theatre, then Duke of York's Theatre, both London, 1960; Clive Rodingham, *Write Me a Murder,* Lyric Hammersmith Theatre, 1962; Vic, *Everybody Loves Opal,* Vaudeville Theatre, London, 1964; William, *The Burglar,* Vaudeville Theatre, 1967; Freddy Mayne, *The Happy Apple,* Apollo Theatre, London, 1970; Tito Belcredi, *Henry IV,* Her Majesty's Theatre, London, 1974; Earl of Warwick, *Saint Joan,* New Theatre, London, 1974; Philip, *The Little Hut,* New Theatre, then Duke of York's Theatre, both 1974; Sir Ralph Bonnington, *The Doctor's Dilemma,* Mermaid Theatre, London, 1975; Bracciano, *The White Devil,* Old Vic Theatre, London, 1976; *The Ghost Train,* Old Vic Theatre, 1976; Lord Godalming, *The Passion of Dracula,* Queen's Theatre, London, 1978; Mr. Darling/Captain Hook, *Peter Pan,* Shaftesbury Theatre, London, 1979.

MAJOR TOURS—Antenor, *Troilus and Cressida,* Bushy, *Richard II,* both with the Old Vic Theatre Company, U.S. and Canadian cities, 1956-57.

PRINCIPAL FILM APPEARANCES—*Half a Sixpence,* Paramount, 1968; *Otley,* Columbia, 1969; *The Ruling Class,* AVCO-Embassy, 1972; *King and Country,* Allied Artists, 1965.

SIDELIGHTS: RECREATIONS—Cricket, football.

ADDRESSES: OFFICE—29 Belsize Park, London NW3, England.*

* * *

VINCENT, Jan-Michael 1944-
(Michael Vincent)

PERSONAL: Born July 15, 1944, in Denver, CO. EDUCATION: Attended Ventura City College, art major. MILITARY: U.S. Army National Guard.

VOCATION: Actor.

CAREER: FILM DEBUT—(As Michael Vincent) *Los Bandidos,* Mexico. PRINCIPAL FILM APPEARANCES—*Journey to Shiloh,* Universal, 1968; *The Undefeated,* Twentieth Century-Fox, 1969; (as Jan-Michael Vincent:) *The Soldier Who Declared Peace* (originally made for television under the title, *Tribes,* released as a feature in Europe), 1970; *Going Home,* Metro-Goldwyn-Mayer, 1971; *The Mechanic,* United Artists, 1972; *The World's Greatest Athlete,* Buena Vista, 1973; *Buster and Billie,* Columbia, 1974; *Bite the Bullet,* Columbia, 1975; *White Line Fever,* Columbia, 1975; *Baby Blue Marine,* Columbia, 1976; *Vigilante Force,* United Artists, 1976; *Shadow of the Hawk,* Canadian production, 1976; *Damnation Alley,* Twentieth Century-Fox, 1977; *Big Wednesday,* Warner Brothers, 1978; *Hooper,* Warner Brothers, 1978; *Defiance,* American International, 1980; *Hard Country,* 1981; *The Last Plane Out,* 1983.

PRINCIPAL TELEVISION APPEARANCES—Series: Jeffrey Hastings, *The Survivors,* ABC, 1969-70; Stringfellow Hawke, *Airwolf,* CBS, 1984-86. Episodic: *Lassie,* CBS; *Bonanza,* NBC; *The Banana Splits Adventure Hour.* Movies: *Tribes,* 1970; *The Catcher,* 1971; *Sandcastles,* 1972.

MEMBER: Screen Actors Guild, American Federation of Television and Radio Artists.*

VINCENT, Michael
    See VINCENT, Jan-Michael

*   *   *

VON FURSTENBERG, Betsy   1931-

PERSONAL: Full name, Elizabeth Caroline Maria Agatha Felicitas Therese von Furstenberg-Hedringen; born August 16, 1931, in Neiheim Heusen, Germany; daughter of Count Franz-Egon and Elizabeth (Johnson) von Furstenberg; married Guy Vincent de la Maisoneuve (a mining engineer), June 16, 1954, (divorced); married John J. Reynolds, March 26, 1984; children: (first marriage) one son, one daughter. EDUCATION: Trained for the stage at the Neighborhood Playhouse with Sanford Meisner.

VOCATION: Actress.

CAREER: BROADWAY DEBUT—Thankful Mather, *Second Threshold*, Morosco Theatre, 1951. PRINCIPAL STAGE APPEARANCES—Lorraine, *Dear Barbarians*, Royale Theatre, New York City, 1952; Josephine Perry, *Josephine*, Playhouse Theatre, Wilmington, DE, 1953; Myra Hagerman, *Oh, Men! Oh, Women!*, Henry Miller's Theatre, New York City, 1953; Lady Sybil Tenterden, *What Every Woman Knows*, City Center Theatre, New York City, 1954; Laurel, *The Chalk Garden*, Ethel Barrymore Theatre, New York City, 1955; Kate, *Child of Fortune*, Royale Theatre, 1956; Maggie Turk, *Nature's Way*, Cornet Theatre, New York City, 1957; Elizabeth Compton, *The Making of Moo*, Rita Allen Theatre, New York City, 1958; Frankie Jordan, *Say, Darling*, Helen, *Wonderful Town*, both City Center Theatre, 1959; Cassandra Redwine, *Season of Choice*, Barbizon Plaza Theatre, New York City, 1959; Margaret, *Much Ado about Nothing*, Lunt-Fontanne Theatre, New York City, 1959.

Tiffany Richards, *Mary, Mary*, Helen Hayes Theatre, New York City, 1961; Sylvia Greer, *The Paisley Convertible*, Henry Miller's Theatre, 1967; Helen, *Wonderful Town*, City Center Theatre, 1967; Cecile Jeanrenaud, *Beyond Desire*, Theatre Four, New York City, 1967; Helen Claiborne, *Avanti!*, Booth Theatre, New York City, 1968; Sybil Chase, *Private Lives*, Theatre de Lys, New York City, 1968; Toby Landau, *The Gingerbread Lady*, Plymouth Theatre, New York City, 1970; Polly Raisen, *Does Anybody Here Do the Peabody?*, Wonderhorse Theatre, New York City, 1976. Also appeared in *For Love of Money*, Westport Country Playhouse, Westport, CT, 1951; *Second Man*, 1952; *Status Quo Vadis*, Ivanhoe Theatre, Chicago, IL, 1974.

MAJOR TOURS—Gabby, *The Petrified Forest*, Lisa, *Jason*, U.S. cities, both 1952; Josephine Perry, *Josephine*, U.S. cities, 1953; Toby Landau, *The Gingerbread Lady*, U.S. cities, 1971-72; Eva, *Absurd Person Singular*, U.S. cities, 1975-76.

PRINCIPAL TELEVISION APPEARANCES—Episodic: "Crimes of Passion," *Play of the Week*, WNTA, New York City, 1959; *The Fifth Column*, CBS, 1960; "Tonight in Samarkand," *Golden Show*, CBS; 1962; *Adventures in Paradise*, ABC; *Armstrong Circle Theatre*, NBC; *TV Sound Stage*, NBC; *Medallion Theatre*, CBS; *Omnibus*, CBS; *Appointment with Adventure*, CBS; *Robert Montgomery Presents*, NBC; *Kraft Television Theatre*, NBC; *Have Gun, Will Travel*, CBS; *Playhouse 90*, CBS; *Alfred Hitchcock Presents*, CBS; *The Defenders*, CBS. Series: *As the World Turns*, CBS. Movies: Jill Bennett, *Your Money or Your Wife*, CBS, 1972. Specials: Thankful Mather, "Second Threshold," *Pulitzer Prize Playhouse*, ABC, 1951.

PRINCIPAL FILM APPEARANCES—*Women without Names*, 1951.

NON-RELATED CAREER—Contributor of articles to newspapers and magazines.

MEMBER: Actors' Equity Association, Screen Actors Guild, American Federation of Television and Radio Artists.

SIDELIGHTS: FAVORITE ROLES—Maggie, *Cat on a Hot Tin Roof;* Laurel, *The Chalk Garden;* Toby Landau, *The Gingerbread Lady*. RECREATIONS—Tennis, painting, riding.

ADDRESSES: AGENT—Hartig-Josephson Agency, 527 Madison Avenue, New York, NY 10022; Beakel and Jennings Agency, 427 N. Canon Drive, Suite 205, Beverly Hills, CA 90210.*

*   *   *

VON SYDOW, Max   1929-

PERSONAL: Born Carl Adolf Von Sydow, April 10, 1929, in Lund, Sweden; son of Carl Wilhelm (a professor of Scandinavian and Irish folklore) and Greta (Rappe) Von Sydow; married Christina Olin (an actress), August 1, 1951; children: Clas Wilhelm, Per Henrik. EDUCATION: Trained for the stage at the Royal Dramatic Academy, Stockholm, 1948-51. MILITARY: Swedish Quartermaster Corps, 1947-48.

PERSONAL: Actor.

CAREER: PRINCIPAL FILM APPEARANCES—*Bara en Mor*, 1949; *Miss Julie*, 1951; *Ingen Mans Kvinna*, 1953; *Ratten att Alska*, 1956; *The Seventh Seal*, 1956; *Wild Strawberries*, Janus, 1957; *Prasten i Uddarbo*, 1958; Vogler, *The Face*, 1958; *Brink of Life*, 1958; *The Magician*, Janus, 1959; the father, *The Virgin Spring*, 1959; *Brollopsdagen* 1960; *Alskarinnan*, 1962; *Nils Holgerssons Underbara Resa*, 1962; *Through a Glass Darkly*, 1962; *Winter Light*, Janus, 1962; Jesus, *The Greatest Story Ever Told*, United Artists, 1965; *4 x 4*, 1965; *Hawaii*, United Artists, 1966; *The Reward*, Twentieth Century-Fox, 1965; *The Quiller Memorandum*, Twentieth Century-Fox, 1967; *Made in Sweden*, 1968; *Svarta Palmkronor*, 1968; Borg, *Hour of the Wolf*, Lopert, 1968; the musician, *Shame*, Lopert, 1969; *Utvandrarna*, 1970; *The Kremlin Letter*, Twentieth Century-Fox, 1970; *The Passion of Anna*, United Artists, 1970.

Night Visitor, UMC Pictures, 1971; *The Emigrants*, Warner Brothers, 1972; *The New Land*, Warner Brothers, 1973; Father Merin, *The Exorcist*, Warner Brothers, 1973; *Nybyggarna*, 1973; *Three Days of the Condor*, Paramount, 1975; *The Desert of the Tartars*, 1976; *Voyage of the Damned*, AVCO-Embassy, 1977; *Exorcist II: The Heretic*, Warner Brothers, 1977; *March or Die*, Columbia, 1977; *Death Watch*, Quartet Films, 1980; Ming, *Flash Gordon*, Universal, 1980; *Victory*, Paramount, 1981; *Conan the Barbarian*, Universal, 1982; *She Dances Alone*, 1982; *Never Say Never Again*, Warner Brothers, 1983; *Dreamscape*, Twentieth Century-Fox, 1984; *Dune*, Universal, 1984; *Code Name: Emerald*, Metro-Goldwyn-Mayer/United Artists, 1985; *Hannah and Her Sisters*, Orion, 1986; *Duet for One*, Cannon, 1986; Dr. Huber, *The Second Victory*, Films Around the World, 1987.

PRINCIPAL TELEVISION APPEARANCES—Mini-Series: *Christopher Columbus*, CBS, 1985. Movies: *Samson and Delilah*, ABC, 1984. Series: "Last Place on Earth," *Masterpiece Theatre*, 1985.

STAGE DEBUT—In high school productions of plays by Strindberg and Lagerkvist. BROADWAY DEBUT—August Stringberg, *The Night of the Tribades,* Helen Hayes Theatre, 1977. PRINCIPAL STAGE APPEARANCES—Appeared in *Peer Gynt, Henry IV* (Pirandello), *The Misanthrope, Faust,* and others, all in Sweden with the Municipal Theatre of Norrkoping-Linkoping, 1951-53, the Municipal Theatre of Halsingborg, 1953-55, the Municipal Theatre of of Malmo, 1955-60, and with the Royal Dramatic Theatre of Stockholm, 1960-74; Dr. Alfred Feldmann, *Duet for One,* Royale Theatre, New York City, 1981-82.

AWARDS: Royal Foundation of Culture Award, Sweden.

SIDELIGHTS: RECREATIONS—Gardening and studying nautical history.

ADDRESSES: AGENT—Paul Kohner Inc., 9169 Sunset Blvd., Los Angeles, CA 90069.*

W

WAGER, Michael 1925-

PERSONAL: Born Emanuel Weisgal, April 29, 1925, in New York, NY; son of Meyer W. and Shirley (Hirshfeld) Weisgal; married Mary Jo Van Ingen, December 21, 1948 (divorced, 1955); married Susan Blanchard Fonda, June 9, 1962 (divorced); children: (first marriage) one daughter; (second marriage) one son. EDUCATION: Harvard University, B.A., 1945, M.A., 1948; trained for the stage at the Actors Studio and with Herbert Berghof, Stella Adler, and Uta Hagen. MILITARY: U.S. Army, 1943-45.

VOCATION: Actor, director, producer, and playwright.

CAREER: STAGE DEBUT—Boy, *The Shoemaker's Prodigious Wife,* Harvard Dramatic Club, Brattle Theatre, Cambridge, MA, 1941. BROADWAY DEBUT—Young collector, *A Streetcar Named Desire,* Ethel Barrymore Theatre, 1949. PRINCIPAL STAGE APPEARANCES—Castro, *The Girl of the Golden West,* Westport Country Playhouse, Westport, CT, 1947; Henry, *The Skin of Our Teeth,* Westport Country Playhouse, 1948; Adolphus Cusins, *Major Barbara,* O'Connor, *Shadow and Substance,* both Brattle Theatre, Cambridge, MA, 1948; Julian, *Martine,* Lenox Hill Playhouse, New York City, 1949; Peter Mitchell, *The Small Hours,* National Theatre, New York City, 1951; Vernon Kinswood, *Bernardine,* Playhouse Theatre, New York City, 1952; Lorenzo, *The Merchant of Venice,* City Center Theatre, New York City, 1953; Bentley Summerhays, *Misalliance,* City Center Theatre, then Ethel Barrymore Theatre, New York City, both 1953; Wilbur Fifield, *The Remarkable Mr. Pennypacker,* Coronet Theatre, New York City, 1953; Roderigo, *Othello,* Prince Hal, *Henry IV, Part I,* both City Center Theatre, 1955; son, *Six Characters in Search of an Author,* Phoenix Theatre, New York City, 1955; Dauphin, *Saint Joan,* Phoenix Theatre, then Coronet Theatre, New York City, both 1956; Hermes, *Prometheus Bound,* Theatre of Herodus Atticus, Athens, Greece, 1957; Shendi, *The Firstborn,* Coronet Theatre, then Habimah Theatre, Tel Aviv, Israel, both 1958; Nick, *The Deserters,* Theatre Royal, Brighton, U.K., 1958; Sir Andrew Auguecheek, *Twelfth Night,* Malcolm, *Macbeth,* both Cambridge Drama Festival, Cambridge, MA, 1959.

Sasha, *The Cradle Will Rock,* New York City Opera Company, City Center Theatre, 1960; Mesa, *Noontide,* Marquee Theatre, New York City, 1961; Andrei, *The Three Sisters,* Morosco Theatre, New York City, 1964; Benya Crick, *Sunset,* 81st Street Theatre, New York City, 1966; Charles Bodie, *The Penny Friend,* Stage 73, New York City, 1966; Carlos, *The Cuban Thing,* Henry Miller's Theatre, New York City, 1968; Ferdinand Gadd, *Trelawny of The Wells,* Public Theatre, New York City, 1970; Petruchio, *The Taming of the Shrew,* Roundabout Theatre, New York City, 1972; John Dickinson, *1776,* Paper Mill Playhouse, Milburn, NJ, 1974; Thesee, *Syllabaire pour Phedre,* Metropolitan Opera House, New

York City, 1974; William Burroughs, *Visions of Kerouac,* Lions Theatre Club, New York City, 1977; Buckingham, *Richard III,* Actors Studio, New York City, 1978; Trigorin, *The Seagull,* Yale Repertory Theatre, New Haven, CT, 1979; Carl "Cubby" Steinbeck, *Rhinestone,* Richard Allen Center, New York City, 1982. Also appeared in *Brecht on Brecht,* Theatre de Lys, New York City, 1962; Marc Blitzstein Memorial Concert, Philharmonic Hall, New York City, 1964; *The Interview,* Pittsburgh Playhouse, Pittsburgh, PA, 1976; *Songs at Twilight,* La Mama Experimental Theatre Club, New York City, 1977; and as speaker, *Oedipus Rex* (opera), Boston Symphony Orchestra; narrator, *Historie du Soldat,* Chamber Music Society of Lincoln Center, New York City; and as narrator, *Lelio.*

PRINCIPAL STAGE WORK—Director, *Brecht on Brecht,* Washington Theatre Club, Washington, DC, 1963; producer, *Where's Daddy?,* Billy Rose Theatre, New York City, 1966; director, *Nag's Head,* New Theatre, New York City, 1969; also stage director, Westport Country Playhouse, Westport, CT, 1947-48.

MAJOR TOURS—Young collector, *A Streetcar Named Desire,* U.S. cities, 1950; James Browne, *The Dream,* U.S. cities, 1977; also toured with the Israel Philharmonic Orchestra, Israeli and German cities, 1978.

FILM DEBUT—Allen Goodman, *Hill 24 Does Not Answer,* 1954. PRINCIPAL FILM APPEARANCES—David Ben Ami, *Exodus,* United Artists, 1960; Thomas, *King of Kings,* Metro-Goldwyn-Mayer, 1961.

PRINCIPAL TELEVISION APPEARANCES—Episodic: Blind lover, *Mr. Om,* NBC, 1948.

RELATED CAREER—Founding member, director, Brattle Theatre, Cambridge, MA, 1947.

WRITINGS: PLAYS—(Co-adaptor with Sir Tyrone Guthrie) *Six Characters in Search of an Author,* Phoenix Theatre, New York City, 1955.

MEMBER: Actors' Equity Association, Screen Actors Guild, American Federation of Television and Radio Artists, Society of Stage Directors and Choreographers; Actors Studio Theatre, Signet Society.

SIDELIGHTS: FAVORITE ROLES—Dauphin in *Saint Joan;* Prince Hal in *Henry IV, Part I;* Andrei in *The Three Sisters;* Mesa in *Noontide.* RECREATIONS—Barn restoration, collecting operatic recordings and pirated Callas tapes.

ADDRESSES: OFFICE—126 Fifth Avenue, New York, NY 10011. HOME—Painter Hill Road, Roxbury, CT.*

© Susan Oristaglio, 1984

KENNETH WAISSMAN

WAISSMAN, Kenneth   1940-

PERSONAL: Born January 24, 1940, in Baltimore, MD; son of Charles William (a jewler) and Hilda (Shutz) Waissman; married Maxine Fox (a theatrical producer), June 17, 1973 (divorced, 1980). EDUCATION: Attended the University of Maryland and New York University.

VOCATION: Producer.

CAREER: PRINCIPAL STAGE WORK—Production assistant, *The Education of H*Y*M*A*N K*A*P*L*A*N,* Alvin Theatre, New York City, 1968; production assistant, *Fig Leaves Are Falling,* Broadhurst Theatre, New York City, 1969; producer, *Fortune and Men's Eyes,* Stage 73, New York City, 1969; producer (with Maxine Fox) *And Miss Reardon Drinks a Little,* Morosco Theatre, New York City, 1971; producer, *Grease,* Royale Theatre, New York City, 1972, then New Theatre, London, 1973; producer, *Over Here!,* Shubert Theatre, New York City, 1974; producer, *El Bravo!,* Entermedia Theatre, New York City, 1981; *Agnes of God,* Music Box Theatre, New York City, 1982; *Torch Song Trilogy,* Little Theatre, New York City, 1982; *The Octette Bridge Club,* Music Box Theatre, 1985. Also produced *VIP Night on Broadway,* New York City, 1979; *New York Salutes Congress,* New York City, 1979; *Today I Am a Fountain Pen,* New York City, 1986; *Asinamali,* New York City, 1987.

MAJOR TOURS—Producer: *Grease,* U.S. cities, 1973; *Agnes of God,* U.S. cities, 1982.

RELATED CAREER—Apprentice, Hilltop Playhouse, Owings Mills,

MD, 1959; producer and director of educational television programs while with the United States Peace Corps, Bogota, Colombia, 1964-66.

AWARDS: Best Musical, Antoinette Perry Award nomination, 1972, for *Grease;* Best Musical, Antoinette Perry Award nomination, 1974, for *Over Here!;* Best Play, Antoinette Perry Award, 1983, for *Torch Song Trilogy.*

MEMBER: League of New York Theatres and Producers; Players Club.

ADDRESSES: OFFICE—Waissman & Buckley Associates, 1501 Broadway, Suite 1518, New York, NY 10036.

*   *   *

WALES, William
See AMBROSE, David

*   *   *

WALKER, Zena   1934-

PERSONAL: Born March 7, 1934, in Birmingham, England; daughter of George (a trader) and Elizabeth Louise (Hammond) Walker; married Robert Urquhart, December, 1956 (divorced, 1961); married Julian Holloway (divorced); married John French (a theatrical agent), August 18, 1979; children: Mathew, Alison. EDUCATION: Trained for the stage at the Royal Academy of Dramatic Art.

VOCATION: Actress and writer.

CAREER: STAGE DEBUT—*Smooth-Faced Gentleman,* Alexandra Theatre, Birmingham, U.K., 1950. LONDON DEBUT— Angelina, *South,* Arts Theatre, 1955. BROADWAY DEBUT— Sheila, *A Day in the Death of Joe Egg,* Brooks Atkinson Theatre, 1968. PRINCIPAL STAGE APPEARANCES—Miranda, *The Tempest,* Royal Shakespeare Company (RSC), Memorial Theatre, Stratford-on-Avon, U.K., 1952; Juliet, *Romeo and Juliet,* RSC, Memorial Theatre, 1954; Katharine, *Henry V,* Perdita, *The Winter's Tale,* both Old Vic Theatre Company, London, 1955-56; Annabella, *'Tis Pity She's a Whore,* Mermaid Theatre, London, 1961; Violet, *Man and Superman,* Arts Theatre, London, 1965, then Vaudeville Theatre, London, 1966; Varya, *The Cherry Orchard,* Lady Macduff, *Macbeth,* both Chichester Festival Theatre, Chichester, U.K., 1966; Aglae, *The Fighting Cock,* Chichester Festival Theatre, then Duke of York's Theatre, London, both 1966; Sheila, *A Day in the Death of Joe Egg,* Comedy Theatre, London, 1967; June Elliot, *It's All in the Mind,* Hampstead Theatre Club, London, 1968; wife, *Marriages,* King's Head Theatre, London, 1973; Ghislaine de Ste. Euverte, *Waltz of the Toreadors,* Haymarket Theatre, London, 1974; Susan, *Away from It All,* ICA Theatre, London, 1974; Jenny Rastall, *The Case in Question,* Haymarket Theatre, 1975; Miss Cooper, *Separate Tables,* Apollo Theatre, London, 1977; Jenny, *Close of Play,* Lyttelton Theatre, London, 1979. Also appeared in *Passion Play,* London, 1984; and *The Women,* Old Vic Theatre Company, London, 1985.

PRINCIPAL FILM APPEARANCES—*The Reckoning,* Columbia,

1969; *Cromwell*, Columbia, 1970; *The Dresser*, Columbia, 1983; also appeared in *Sammy Going South*.

PRINCIPAL TELEVISION APPEARANCES—Movies: *Man at the Top; Abide with Me; Telford's Change; That Crazy Woman; Write Away.*

WRITINGS: RADIO PLAYS—*The Wake*, 1976.

AWARDS: Best Actress, Antoinette Perry Award, 1968, for *A Day in the Death of Joe Egg.*

MEMBER: British Actors' Equity Association.

SIDELIGHTS: RECREATIONS—Gardening, breeding ponies, home and family.

ADDRESSES: HOME—24 St Anselm's Place, London W1, England. AGENT—Joy Jameson, c/o French's, 26 Binney Street, London W1, England.

*   *   *

WALTHER, Gretchen   1938-

PERSONAL: Born March 8, 1938, in New York, NY; daughter of Francis Theodore (a musician and band leader) and Margot (a psychotherapist; maiden name, Wallace) Walther; married Egon Dumler (an entertainment attorney); children: Johnna Brooke,

GRETCHEN WALTHER

Matthew Benjamin. EDUCATION: Graduated from Northwestern University, 1960; studied acting with Charlotte Perry and Alvina Krause at Northwestern University; with Herbert Berghof, Sanford Meisner, and Bobby Lewis in New York City. RELIGION: Episcopalian.

VOCATION: Actress and dancer.

CAREER: BROADWAY DEBUT—*Something about a Soldier*, Ambassador Theatre, 1961. PRINCIPAL STAGE APPEARANCES— *Not a Way of Life*, Sheridan Square Playhouse, New York City, 1967; *How to Steal an Election*, Pocket Theatre, New York City, 1968; *The Gingham Dog*, John Golden Theatre, New York City, 1969; *Dear Oscar*, Playhouse Theatre, New York City, 1972; *Innocent Pleasures, Twice Removed, Salt Air*, all Ensemble Studio Theatre, New York City; *Barefoot in the Park, Diplomatic Relations, Thurber Carnival, Mr. Roberts, Old Acquaintance*, all Elitch's Garden Theatre, CO. Also appeared in *Villa Serena, The Everyday Business*, both Off-Broadway productions.

PRINCIPAL TELEVISION APPEARANCES—Episodic: *TV Workshop*, CBS; *Play of the Week*, WNET, New York; *As the World Turns*, CBS; *Love of Life*, NBC; *The Secret Storm*, CBS; *All My Children*, ABC; *Camera Three; The First Estate*. Series: Patti Tate, *Search for Tomorrow*, CBS; Dr. Kate Logan, *Hidden Faces*. Pilots: *The Cliffdwellers*.

PRINCIPAL FILM APPEARANCES—*The Young Doctors*, United Artists, 1961; *Act One*, Warner Brothers, 1963; *The Landlord*, United Artists, 1970.

RELATED CAREER—Dancer with the Sybil Shearer Company for two years.

MEMBER: Actors' Equity Association, Screen Actors Guild, American Federation of Television and Radio Artists; volunteer in programs for the homeless.

SIDELIGHTS: RECREATIONS—Gardening.

Gretchen Walther informs *CTFT* that she is a "committed environmentalist" and that she is a world traveler "with enough of six languages for travel purposes."

ADDRESSES: AGENT—Abrams Artists and Associates, Ltd. 420 Madison Avenue, New York, NY 10017.

*   *   *

WANG, Peter

BRIEF ENTRY: Former laser scientist Peter Wang directed the first movie co-produced by Chinese and American filmmakers, *A Great Wall*. This comedy of a Chinese-American family's visit to relatives in Beijing was also Wang's first outing as a director, though he had previously appeared in such ethnic-background films as *Chan Is Missing* and *Ah Ying*. Wang grew up in Taiwan, where his family had fled from Beijing after the revolution, but received his college and post-graduate education in the United States. In 1973 he left a comfortable job with IBM to move to San Francisco, where he joined the Asian Living Theatre. When he made *A Great Wall*, according to the June 3, 1986 *Village Voice*, he felt it "sees the Chinese in China." The director wanted the film to be accessible to audiences unfamiliar with the country, but also hoped to convey "the modernization of a beautiful old civilization." Living in New York City's Soho district by 1986, Wang planned for his next film to draw on his experience as a scientist.

*   *   *

WANG, Wayne   1949-

BRIEF ENTRY: "The Chinese have not really been given a chance to represent themselves in the media," asserted director Wayne Wang in the June 16-23, 1982 *Aquarian.* With two low-budget, independently made feature films that achieved a surprising success, he has begun to change that situation. Born in Hong Kong in 1949, Wang is the son of a Chinese engineer and businessman and his wife, both refugees from mainland China. He attended an English-language school run by Jesuits in Hong Kong and later came to the United States to study photography at the College of Arts and Crafts in Oakland, CA. Later, with a master's degree in film and television, Wang went back to Hong Kong, where he worked on a popular television comedy series and, in 1974, did his first film work as an assistant director for the Chinese sequences of *Golden Needles.* Returning to the United States, on the strength of an award-winning short film, *1944,* and the success in Europe of an earlier feature, *A Man, a Woman, and a Killer,* he won grants from the American Film Institute and the National Endowment for the Arts. He used them to finance the comedy *Chan Is Missing,* which he produced, directed, wrote, and edited at a cost of $22,000. In *American Film,* Wang explained, "*Chan Is Missing* was shot after I had been in Hong Kong and was feeling guilty about the fact that I could no longer fit in my own culture." He followed the success of his first film with *Dim Sum: A Little Bit of Heart,* another wry Chinese-American comedy which focused on a mother and daughter relationship.

*   *   *

WARD, Simon   1941-

PERSONAL: Born October 19, 1941, in London, England; son of Leonard Fox and Winifred Ward; married Alexandra Malcolm. EDUCATION: Trained for the stage at the Royal Academy of Dramatic Art.

VOCATION: Actor and director.

CAREER: LONDON DEBUT—Tom Phillips, *The Fourth of June,* St. Martin's Theatre, 1964. PRINCIPAL STAGE APPEARANCES—Fred Beenstock, *Hobson's Choice,* Northampton Repertory Theatre, Northampton, U.K., 1963; Alexander, *Alexander's Death,* Ashcroft Theatre, Croydon, U.K., 1964; Konstantin, *The Seagull,* Birmingham Repertory Theatre, Birmingham, U.K., 1964; Abel Drugger, *The Alchemist,* Oxford Playhouse, Oxford, U.K., 1965; Hippolytus, *Phedre,* Oxford Playhouse, 1966; Dennis, *Loot,* Jeannetta Cochrane Theatre, then Criterion Theatre, both London, 1966; Jerry, *Wise Child,* Wyndham's Theatre, London, 1967; Unknown Soldier, *The Unknown Soldier and His Wife,* Ferdinand, *The Tempest,* Henry, *The Skin of Our Teeth,* all Chichester Festival Theatre, Chichester, U.K., 1968; Donald, *Spoiled,* Haymarket Theatre, London, 1971; title role, *Romeo and Juliet,* Shaw Theatre, London, 1972; Teddy, *Clever Soldiers,* Hampstead Theatre Club, London, 1974; Troilus, *Troilus and Cressida,* Harry, *Four to One,*

both Young Vic Theatre, London, 1976; Ward, *Rear Column,* Globe Theatre, London, 1978. Also as Ken Harrison, *Whose Life Is It, Anyway?,* 1982; and in *House Guest,* 1982; *Heartbreak House,* 1983, *Dial M for Murder,* 1983, and *Ross,* Birmingham Repertory Theatre, Birmingham, U.K., 1986.

MAJOR TOURS—Valentine, *You Never Can Tell,* with the Cambridge Theatre Company, U.K. cities, 1973; Ken Harrison, *Whose Life Is It, Anyway?,* U.K. cities, 1980.

PRINCIPAL STAGE WORK—Co-director, *Henry IV, Part I,* National Youth Theatre, London, 1967.

FILM DEBUT—*Frankenstein Must Be Destroyed,* Warner Brothers, 1970. PRINCIPAL FILM APPEARANCES—*Young Winston,* Columbia, 1972; *Hitler: The Last Ten Days,* Paramount, 1972; *The Three Musketeers,* Twentieth Century-Fox, 1974; *The Four Musketeers,* Twentieth Century-Fox, 1975. Also *I Start Counting,* 1970; ; *Deadly Strangers,* 1975; *The Aces High,* 1976; *Battle Flag,* 1976; *Dominique,* 1977; *Holocaust 2000,* 1977; *The Chosen,* 1978; *Zulu Dawn,* 1979; *The Sabina,* 1979; *The Monster Club,* 1980; *Tug of Love,* 1983; *Supergirl,* 1984; *Leave All Fair,* 1985.

PRINCIPAL TELEVISION APPEARANCES—Series: *The Black Tulip,* BBC; *The Roads to Freedom,* BBC; *Holocaust,* BBC, then PBS; *The Rear Column,* BBC. Movies: Arthur Holmwood, *Dracula,* CBS, 1974; James Herriot, *All Creatures Great and Small,* NBC, 1975; William Trench, *The Four Feathers,* NBC, 1978; Jock Leslie-Melville, *The Last Giraffe,* CBS, 1979; Duc de Chateau Renaud, *The Corsican Brothers,* CBS, 1985; also *Chips with Everything,* BBC; *Bloomsday; Flowering Cherry.*

MEMBER: British Actors' Equity Association, Screen Actors Guild.

SIDELIGHTS: RECREATIONS—Gardening, music, reading, badminton.

ADDRESSES: AGENT—IFA Ltd., 11-12 Hanover Street, London W1, England.*

*   *   *

WARNER, David   1941-

PERSONAL: Born July 29, 1941, in Manchester, England; son of Herbert Simon Warner. EDUCATION: Trained for the stage at the Royal Academy of Dramatic Art.

VOCATION: Actor.

CAREER: LONDON DEBUT—Snout, *A Midsummer Night's Dream,* Royal Court Theatre, 1962. PRINCIPAL STAGE APPEARANCES—Conrade, *Much Ado about Nothing,* Belgrade Theatre, Coventry, U.K., 1962; Jim, *Afore Night Come,* New Arts Theatre, London, 1962; Trinculo, *The Tempest,* Cinna, *Julius Caesar,* title role, *Henry VI,* all Royal Shakespeare Company (RSC), Memorial Theatre, Stratford-on-Avon, U.K., 1963; Henry VI, *The Wars of the Roses,* RSC, Memorial Theatre, then Aldwych Theatre, London, 1964; title role, *Richard II,* Mouldy, *Henry IV, Part II,* both RSC, Memorial Theatre, 1964; Valentine Brose, *Eh?,* RSC, Aldwych Theatre, 1964; title role, *Hamlet,* RSC, Memorial Theatre, then Aldwych Theatre, both 1965; postmaster, *The Government Inspector,* RSC, Aldwych Theatre, 1966; title role, *Hamlet,* Sir Andrew Aguecheek, *Twelfth Night,* both RSC, Memorial Theatre, 1966; Julian, *Tiny Alice,* RSC, Aldwych Theatre, 1970; Hammett, *The*

Great Exhibition, Hampstead Theatre Club, London, 1972; *Claudius, I, Claudius,* Queen's Theatre, London, 1972. Also appeared in *The Rebel,* RSC, Aldwych Theatre, 1964.

FILM DEBUT—Blifil, *Tom Jones,* Lopert, 1963. PRINCIPAL FILM APPEARANCES—*The Bofors Gun,* Universal, 1968; *The Fixer,* Metro-Goldwyn-Mayer (MGM), 1968; *The Seagull,* Warner Brother/Seven-Arts, 1968; *Morgan—A Suitable Case for Treatment,* Cinema V, 1969; *The Ballad of Cable Hogue,* Warner Brothers, 1970; *Perfect Friday,* Chevron, 1970; *Straw Dogs,* Cinerama, 1971; *Tales from the Crypt,* Cinerama, 1972; *A Doll's House,* Paramount, 1973; *The Omen,* Twentieth Century-Fox, 1976; *Cross of Iron,* AVCO-Embassy, 1977; *Providence,* Cinema V, 1977; *Silver Bears,* Columbia, 1978; *The Disappearance,* Paramount, 1978; *Nightwing,* Columbia, 1979; *Time after Time,* Warner Brothers, 1979; *Airport '79—The Concorde,* Universal, 1979; *The Island,* Universal, 1980; *The French Lieutenant's Woman,* United Artists, 1981; *Time Bandits,* Embassy, 1981; *Tron,* Buena Vista, 1982; *The Man with Two Brains,* Warner Brothers, 1983; *The Company of Wolves,* Cannon, 1985. Also appeared in *Work Is a Four Letter Word,* 1967; *Little Malcolm,* 1975; *Mr. Quilp,* 1975; *Age of Innocence,* 1977; *The Thirty-Nine Steps,* 1978.

PRINCIPAL TELEVISION APPEARANCES—Series: *Clouds of Glory,* BBC, 1977; *Charlie,* BBC, 1984; also appeared in *The Pushover,* 1976. Mini-Series: Reinhard Heydrich, *Holocaust,* NBC, 1978; Pomponius Falco, *Masada,* ABC, 1981; Rustichello, *Marco Polo,* NBC, 1982. Movies: Laurence Beesley, *S.O.S. Titanic,* ABC, 1979; Bob Cratchit, *A Christmas Carol,* CBS, 1984; Reinhard Heydrich, *Hitler's SS: Portrait in Evil,* NBC, 1985.

MEMBER: British Actors' Equity Association, Screen Actors Guild.

ADDRESSES: AGENT—c/o Leading Artists, 60 St. James's Street, London SW1, England.*

*   *   *

WARNER, Malcolm-Jamal

BRIEF ENTRY: Malcolm-Jamal Warner was just thirteen years old when he signed on to play the only son in the television family on *The Cosby Show.* He won the role of Theo Huxtable even though the producers were seeking a taller, older youth to play the character modelled on the star's real-life son. The series meant returning to the East Coast (he was born in Jersey City, NJ) from Los Angeles. ''It wasn't a very happy time for my mom and me,'' the young actor told Gary Deeb of the *New York Post* (April 15, 1987). ''. . .We really loved California.'' His mother, Pamela Warner, gave up her job to manage his interests; but the move proved worthwhile for Warner, who soon found that being cast in a number-one rated network television show gave a boost to his acting career. In addition to his work on *Cosby,* he has hosted *Friday Night Videos* on NBC and, late in 1987, had a leading role in the NBC television movie *The Father Clements Story,* co-starring Louis Gosset, Jr.

*   *   *

WARREN, Jennifer

PERSONAL: Born August 12, in New York, NY; daughter of Barnet (a dentist) and Paula (an actress; maiden and professional name, Bauersmith) Warren; married Fritz DeBoer, September, 1964 (divorced, 1969); married Roger Gimbel (a producer), June 6, 1976; children: (second marriage) Barnett Warren. EDUCATION: Received B.A. from the University of Wisconsin, Madison; graduate work at Wesleyan University; studied acting with Uta Hagen at the Herbert Bergof Studios.

VOCATION: Actress.

CAREER: TELEVISION DEBUT—*Kojak,* CBS, 1975. PRINCIPAL TELEVISION APPEARANCES—Episodic: *The Bob Newhart Show,* CBS; *Fitzpatricks,* CBS. Series: Regular, *The Smothers Brothers Comedy Hour,* CBS, 1967-69; Dinah Caswell, *Paper Dolls,* ABC, 1984-85. Pilots: Molly Brannen, *Banjo Hackett: Roamin' Free,* NBC, 1976; Dinah Caswell, *Paper Dolls,* ABC, 1982. Movies: Carolyn, *Shark Kill,* NBC, 1976; Jesse Pfanner, *Steel Cowboy,* NBC, 1978; Erica Welles, *First, You Cry,* CBS, 1978; Camille Scoggin, *Champions: A Love Story,* CBS, 1979; Cloma Teeter, *Angel City,* CBS, 1980; Rachel Bellow, *Freedom,* ABC, 1981; Marsha Taylor, *The Choice,* CBS, 1981; Colette Beaudroux, *The Intruder Within,* ABC, 1981; Pat Price, *Confessions of a Married Man,* ABC, 1983; Martha Dalton, *Celebrity,* NBC, 1984; Dr. Diane Cosgrove, *Amazons,* ABC, 1984.

OFF-BROADWAY DEBUT—Jeannie Wonder, *Scuba Duba,* New Theatre, 1967. BROADWAY DEBUT—Wife, *6 RMS RIV VU,* Lunt-Fontaine Theatre, 1970. PRINCIPAL STAGE APPEARANCES—Nurse Kelly, *Harvey,* Phoenix Theatre, New York City, 1973; Stas, *Dusa, Fish, Stas, and Vi,* Mark Taper Forum, Los Angeles, CA, 1978; also appeared in *P.S. Your Cat Is Dead,* John Golden Theatre, New York City, 1975; *Saint Joan, Volpone, Henry V,* all

JENNIFER WARREN

Tyrone Guthrie Theatre, Minneapolis, MN; *Lemon Sky,* Washington Theatre Club, Washington, DC.

MAJOR TOURS—Nurse Kelly, *Harvey,* U.S. cities, 1973; appeared in *Scuba Duba,* U.S. cities, 1973.

FILM DEBUT—Paula, *Night Moves,* Warner Brothers, 1975. PRINCIPAL FILM APPEARANCES—Francine, *Slapshot,* Universal, 1977; *Another Man, Another Chance,* Metro-Goldwyn-Mayer, 1977; *Ice Castles,* Columbia, 1979; *Fatal Beauty,* Warner Brothers, 1987.

AWARDS: Theatre World Award, 1971, for *6 RMS RIV VU;* Screen World Award, 1975, for *Night Moves.*

MEMBER: Academy of Motion Picture Arts and Sciences.

ADDRESSES: AGENT—Leading Artists, 445 N. Bedford Drive, Beverly Hills, CA 90210.

*　　*　　*

WASSERMAN, Dale 1917-

PERSONAL: Born November 2, 1917, in Rhinelander, WI; son of Samuel (a motion picture theatre operator) and Hilda (Paykel) Wasserman; married Ramsay Ames (an actress), 1966.

VOCATION: Writer, producer, and artistic director.

CAREER: PRINCIPAL STAGE WORK—Writer (see below); founder and artistic director, Midwest Professional Playwrights Laboratory.

PRINCIPAL FILM WORK—Co-Producer: *Mr. Buddwing,* 1965; *A Walk with Love and Death,* 1969; *Man of La Mancha,* United Artists, 1972.

WRITINGS: PLAYS, PRODUCED AND PUBLISHED—(With Bruce Geller) *Living the Life,* Phoenix Theatre, New York City, 1955; *The Pencil of God,* Karamu Theatre, Cleveland, OH, 1961; *998,* Professional Workshop Theatre, Hollywood, CA, 1966; *One Flew Over the Cuckoo's Nest,* Cort Theatre, New York City, 1963, published by Samuel French, 1970; *Man of La Mancha* (book; music by Mitch Leigh, lyrics by Joe Darion), first produced at the Washington Square Theatre of the American National Theatre Academy, New York City, 1965 and later continued its run at the Martin Beck Theatre, New York City, until 1968, published by Random House, 1966; also *Play with Fire,* 1978; *Great Big River,* 1981; *Shakespeare and the Indians,* 1983.

SCREENPLAYS—*World of Strangers,* 1954; *The Vikings,* United Artists, 1955; *Two Faces to Go,* 1959; *Aboard the Flying Swan,* 1962; *Jangadeiro,* 1962; *Cleopatra,* Twentieth Century-Fox, 1963; *Quick, Before It Melts,* Metro-Goldwyn-Mayer, 1964; *Mister Buddwing,* Metro-Goldwyn-Mayer, 1965; *A Walk With Love and Death,* Twentieth Century-Fox, 1969; *Man of La Mancha,* United Artists, 1972.

TELEPLAYS—*Elisha and the Long Knives,* 1954; *Fiddlin' Man,* 1954; *Boys Will Be Boys,* 1955; *The Luck of Roaring Camp,* 1956; *The Fool Killer,* 1956; *Collision,* 1956; "The Fog," *Climax,* CBS, 1956; "The Time of the Draught," *Ponds' Theatre,* ABC, 1957; ; "Long After Summer," *Alcoa Hour,* NBC, 1957; "The Milwaukee Rocket," *Matinee Theatre,* NBC, 1957; "The Bequest," *Four*

Star Theatre, NBC, 1957; "The Forger," *Ponds' Theatre,* ABC; "The Man That Corrupted Hadleyburg," *Matinee Theatre,* NBC, 1958; *The Medallion,* 1958; *The Gentle Grafter,* 1958; *Eichmann,* 1958; *Look What's Going On,* 1959; *Engineer of Death,* 1959; "I, Don Quixote," *Dupont Show of the Month,* CBS, 1959; *The Citadel,* ABC, 1959; "American Primitive," *Studio One,* CBS, 1959; "Brotherhood of the Bell," *Studio One,* CBS, 1960; *The Power and the Glory,* 1960; "The Lincoln Murder Case," *Dupont Show of the Month,* NBC, 1962; "Circle of Death," *True,* CBS, 1962; "The Stranger," *Richard Boone Anthology,* NBC, 1963; also the author of nearly twenty-five additional teleplays from 1955-65. Pilots: *The Blue Angels,* 1960; *Grand Deception,* 1961.

PERIODICALS—Contributor: *Redbook, True, Argosy, Variety,* and *The New York Times.*

AWARDS: Top Television Play of the Year, 1954, for *Elisha and the Long Knives;* Writers Guild Award, 1957, for *The Fog;* Writers Guild Award and Emmy Award nomination, both 1960, for *I, Don Quixote;* Writers Guild Award and Emmy Award nomination, both 1961, for *The Lincoln Murder Case;* Antoinette Perry Award, New York Critics Circle, Outer Circle, *Saturday Review,* Spanish Pavilion, and *Variety* awards, and awards from France, Spain, and Czechoslovakia, all 1966, for *Man of La Mancha;* Joseph Jefferson Award, for *One Flew Over the Cuckoo's Nest;* honorary degree, University of Wisconsin, 1980.

MEMBER: Dramatists Guild, Authors League of America, Writers Guild of America East (national council, 1960-64), French Society of Authors and Composers, Spanish Society of Authors; Players Club.

SIDELIGHTS: *Man of La Mancha* is the third-longest running musical in the history of New York theatre.

ADDRESSES: HOME—Palm Springs, CA. OFFICE—3240 Moorpark Road, Moorpark, CA 93021.*

*　　*　　*

WATANABE, Gedde

PERSONAL: First name rhymes with "ready"; born Gary Watanabe, June 26, in Ogden, UT. EDUCATION: Trained for the stage at the American Conservatory Theatre, San Francisco.

VOCATION: Actor.

CAREER: BROADWAY DEBUT—Tree Boy, *Pacific Overtures,* Winter Garden Theatre, 1976. PRINCIPAL THEATRE APPEARANCES—Young man, *Oedipus the King,* Lepercq Space, Brooklyn Academy of Music, Brooklyn, NY, 1981; Paul, *Bullet Headed Birds,* Pan Asian Repertory Theatre, 28th Street Playhouse, New York City, 1981; Itsu Yoshiro, *Poor Little Lambs,* Theatre at St. Peter's Church, New York City, 1982; also appeared with the Shakespeare in the Park series, New York Shakespeare Festival, Delacorte Theatre, New York City.

MAJOR TOURS—Tree Boy, *Pacific Overtures,* U.S. cities.

FILM DEBUT—Long Duck Dong, *Sixteen Candles,* Paramount, 1984. PRINCIPAL FILM APPEARANCES—At-Toon, *Volunteers,*

© *Capital Cities/ABC, Inc.,* 1986

GEDDE WATANABE

Silver Screen-HBO, 1985; Kaz, *Gung Ho,* Paramount, 1986; Duncan, *Vamp,* New World, 1986.

TELEVISION DEBUT—Series: Kaz, *Gung Ho,* ABC, 1986.

MEMBER: Screen Actors Guild, American Federation of Television and Radio Artists, Association of Asian Pacific Artists.

SIDELIGHTS: FAVORITE ROLES—Kaz in *Gung Ho.* RECREATIONS—Tai-chi, folk guitar, ice and roller skating, learning Japanese.

Gedde Watanabe told *CTFT* that he has traveled extensively in the U.S., Europe, Mexico, and Japan.

ADDRESSES: PUBLICIST—c/o Brad Lemak, Lemak & Company, 7060 Hollywood Boulevard, Los Angeles, CA 90028.

*   *   *

WATERHOUSE, Keith Spencer   1929-
(Lee Gibb)

PERSONAL: Born February 6, 1929, in Leeds, England; son of Ernest and Elsie (Spencer) Waterhouse; married Joan Foster, October 21, 1950 (marriage ended); married Stella Bingham, 1984; children: (first marriage) Penelope, Sarah, Robert. MILITARY: Royal Air Force, 1947-49.

VOCATION: Playwright, novelist, and journalist.

CAREER: Also see *WRITINGS* below.

RELATED CAREER—Freelance journalist, Leeds, U.K., and London, 1950—; columnist, *The Daily Mirror,* 1970-86; columnist, *Daily Mail,* 1986—; contributor, *Punch,* member, *Punch* Table, 1966; also contributor, *New Statesman; Queen.*

WRITINGS: PLAYS—All with Willis Hall unless indicated: *Billy Liar,* Cambridge Theatre, London, 1960, then Gate Theatre, New York City, 1965, later Westside Theatre, New York City, 1982, published by Joseph, 1960, Norton, 1961; *Celebration: The Wedding and the Funeral,* produced in Nottingham, U.K., then in London, both 1961, published by Joseph, 1961, and with *All Things Bright and Beautiful,* Joseph, 1963; *England, Our England,* produced in London, 1962, published by Evans, 1964; *The Sponge Room, Squat Betty,* both produced in London, 1962, then East End Theatre, New York City, 1964, published by Evans, 1963; *All Things Bright and Beautiful,* produced in Bristol, U.K., then in London, both 1962, published by Joseph, 1963; *Come Laughing Home* (also known as *They Called the Bastard Steven*), produced in Bristol, U.K., 1964, and in Wimbledon, U.K., 1965, published by Evans, 1966; *Say Who You Are* (also known as *Help Stamp Out Marriage*), produced in Guildford, U.K., then London, both 1965, later Booth Theatre, New York City, 1966, published by Evans, 1965, and by Samuel French, Inc., 1966; *Joey, Joey,* produced in London, 1966; *Whoops-a-Daisy,* produced in Nottingham, U.K., 1968, published by Samuel French, Inc., 1968; *Children's Day,* produced in Edinburgh, Scotland, U.K., then in London, both 1969, published by Samuel French, Inc., 1975; *Who's Who,* produced in Coventry, U.K., 1971, then in London, 1973, published by Samuel French, Inc., 1974; (adaptors) *Saturday, Sunday, Monday,* produced in London, 1973, then in New York City, 1974, published by Heinemann, 1974; *The Card,* produced in Bristol, U.K., then in London, both 1973; (adaptor) *Filumena,* produced in London, 1977, then in New York, 1980, later Cleveland Playhouse, Cleveland, OH, 1981, published by Heinemann, 1978; *Worzel Gummidge,* produced in Birmingham, U.K., then in London, both 1981, published by Samuel French, Inc., 1984; (songs and sketches with Peter Tinniswood and Dick Vosburgh) *Steafel Variations,* produced in London, 1982; *Lost Empires,* produced in Darlington, U.K., then Cambridge Arts Festival, Cambridge, U.K., 1985; *Mr. and Mrs. Nobody,* produced in London, 1986.

TELEPLAYS—Series: (with Willis Hall) *Queenie's Castle,* 1970; (with Hall) *Budgie,* 1971-72; (with Hall) *The Upper Crusts,* 1973; (with Hall) *Billy Liar,* 1973-74; *The Upchat Line,* 1977; *The Upchat Connection,* 1978; (with Hall) *Worzel Gummidge,* 1979; *West End Tales,* 1981; *The Happy Apple,* 1983; *Charters and Caldicott,* 1984; (with Hall) *Worzel Gummidge Down Under,* 1987; *Andy Capp,* 1988; also wrote *Inside George Webley; There is a Happy Land.* Movies: (with Hall) *Happy Moorings,* 1963; (with Hall) *How Many Angels,* 1964; *The Warmonger,* 1970; (with Hall) *By Endeavor Alone,* 1973; *Charlie Muffin,* 1979; *This Office Life,* 1984; *Slip Up,* 1987.

SCREENPLAYS—All with Willis Hall: *Whistle down the Wind,* 1961; *A Kind of Loving,* Governor, 1962; *Billy Liar,* Continental, 1963; *Man in the Middle,* Twentieth Century-Fox, 1964; *Pretty Polly* (also known as *A Matter of Innocence*), Universal, 1968; *Lock Up Your Daughters,* Columbia, 1969; *The Valiant,* United Artists, 1969; *West Eleven,* 1970.

RADIO PLAYS—*The Town That Wouldn't Vote,* 1951; *There Is a*

Happy Land, 1962; *The Woolen Bank Forgeries,* 1964; *The Last Phone-In,* 1976; *The Big Broadcast of 1922,* 1979.

BOOKS—(With Guy Deghy) *Cafe Royal: Ninety Years of Bohemia,* Hutchinson, 1955; (with Paul Cave) *Britain's Voice Abroad,* Daily Mirror Newspapers, 1957; editor, *The Future of Television,* Daily Mirror Newspapers, 1958; (with Herald Froy, pseudonym for Deghy) *How to Survive Matrimony,* Muller, 1958; (with Froy) *How to Avoid Matrimony,* Muller, 1959; (with Deghy, under the joint pseudonym Lee Gibb) *The Joneses: How to Keep Up with Them,* Muller, 1959; (with Froy) *Can This Be Love?* Muller, 1960; (as Gibb) *The Higher Joneses,* Muller, 1961; (with Froy) *Maybe You're Just Inferior,* Muller, 1961; (with Froy) *O Mistress Mine,* Arthur Barker, 1962; co-editor (with Hall), *Writers' Theatre,* Heinemann, 1967; *The Passing of the Third Floor Buck,* Joseph, 1974; *Mondays, Thursdays,* Joseph, 1976; *Rhubarb, Rhubarb, and Other Noises,* Joseph, 1979; (with Hall) *Daily Mirror Style,* Mirror Books, 1981; *Fanny Peculiar,* Joseph, 1983; *Mrs. Pooter's Diary,* Joseph, 1983; *Waterhouse at Large,* Joseph, 1985; *The Collected Letters of a Nobody, The Theory and Practice of Lunch,* both Joseph, 1986.

FICTION—With Willis Hall: *The Television Adventures of Worzel Gummidge, More Television Adventures of Worzel Gummidge,* both Penguin, 1979, as one volume, Kestrel, 1981; *Worzel Gummidge at the Fair, The Trials of Worzel Gummidge,* both Penguin, 1980; *Worzel's Birthday,* Penguin, 1981; *New Television Adventures of Worzel Gummidge and Aunt Sally,* Sparrow, 1981; *Worzel Gummidge and Aunt Sally,* Severn House, 1982; *The Irish Adventures of Worzel Gummidge,* Severn House, 1984; *Worzel Gummidge Down Under,* Dragon, 1987. Also wrote *There Is a Happy Land,* Joseph, 1957; (with Guy Deghy, under the joint pseudonym Lee Gibb) *Billy Liar,* Joseph, 1960, Norton, 1960; (as Lee Gibb) *Jubb,* Joseph, 1963, Putnam, 1964; *The Bucket Shop,* Joseph, 1968, as *Everything Must Go,* Putnam, 1969; *Billy Liar on the Moon,* Joseph, 1975, Putnam, 1976; *Office Life,* Joseph, 1983; *Maggie Muggins, or Spring in Earl's Court,* Joseph, 1981; *In the Mood,* Joseph, 1983; *Thinks,* Joseph, 1984.

AWARDS: Granada Columnist of the Year Award, 1970; IPC Descriptive Writer of the Year Award, 1970; IPC Columnist of the Year Award, 1973; Columnist of the Year Award, British Press Awards 1978; Granada Special Quarter Century Award, 1982.

MEMBER: P.E.N.; Garrick Club, Chelsea Arts Club, Saville Club.

ADDRESSES: OFFICE—Jean Leyland, 29 Kenway Road, London SW5 ORP, England. AGENT—c/o London Management, 235/241 Regent Street, London W1, England; (literary) c/o David Higham Associates, 76 Dean Street, London W1, England.

*   *   *

WATERS, Jan   1937-

PERSONAL: Born January 28, 1937, in Bournemouth, England; daughter of Albert Edward and Florence May (Martin) Waters; married Peter Gilmore (divorced).

VOCATION: Actress and singer.

CAREER: STAGE DEBUT—Title role, *Cinderella* (pantomime), Adelphi Theatre, 1960. PRINCIPAL STAGE APPEARANCES—Tilda Mullen, *Do Re Mi,* Prince of Wales Theatre, London, 1961; Mary Grimaldi, *Joey,* Beatrice, *Much Ado about Nothing,* Liz Rivet, *Golden Rivet,* all Bristol Old Vic Theatre, Bristol, U.K., 1962-63; Ruth Condomine, *High Spirits,* Savoy Theatre, London, 1964; Polly Peachum, *The Beggar's Opera,* Apollo Theatre, London, 1968; Miss Ethel Monticue, *The Young Visitors,* Piccadilly Theatre, London, 1968; Vivien, *Don't Start without Me,* Garrick Theatre, London, 1971; Julie, *Showboat,* Adelphi Theatre, London, 1972; Eleanor, *Only a Game,* Shaw Theatre, London, 1973; Dionyza, *Pericles,* Her Majesty's Theatre, London, 1974; Carla, *Kennedy's Children,* King's Head Theatre, London, 1974; title role, *Susanna Andler,* Haymarket Theatre, London, 1975; *Buster,* Edinburgh Festival, Edinburgh, Scotland, U.K., then Old Vic Theatre, London, both 1977; Queenie, *Born in the Gardens,* Globe Theatre, London, 1980. Also appeared as Linda, *Pursuit of Love,* Bristol, U.K., 1967; Victoria, *Trumpets and Drums,* Edinburgh, Scotland, U.K., 1970; and in repertory at Coventry and Edinburgh, both 1969.

MAJOR TOURS—Doll Common, *The Alchemist,* Eileen Midway, *Semi-Detached,* both with the Cambridge Theatre Company, U.K. cities, 1970; Oello, *The Royal Hunt of the Sun,* Maria, *Twelfth Night,* Boult, Dionyza, *Pericles,* all with the Prospect Theatre Company, U.K. cities, 1973; Eliza Doolittle, *Pygmalion,* Portia, *Twelfth Night,* both with the Watford Palace Theatre Company, Far East cities, 1976.

FILM DEBUT—*Touch of Death,* 1962. PRINCIPAL FILM APPEARANCES—*Corruption,* Columbia, 1968.

MEMBER: British Actors' Equity Association, Screen Actors Guild.

SIDELIGHTS: FAVORITE ROLES—Polly Peachum in *The Beggars' Opera;* Victoria in *Trumpets and Drums.* RECREATIONS—Tapestry.

ADDRESSES: AGENT—c/o William Morris Agency, Ltd., 147-149 Wardour Street, London W1V 3TV, England.*

*   *   *

WATERS, John

BRIEF ENTRY: The current king of the midnight movie circuit, director and writer John Waters has gained a cult following with such films as *Pink Flamingos,* 1972, and *Polyester,* 1981. Waters's first films, shot with an eight-millimeter camera, included *Hag in a Black Leather Jacket* and an unfinished remake of *The Wizard of Oz* titled *Dorothy, the Kansas City Pothead.* But it was *Pink Flamingos,* about two families competing for the title ''The Filthiest People Alive,'' that established his reputation as a master of bad taste. *Polyester,* Waters's first commercial film, is his view of the ''typical'' American family. The ''heroine,'' played by Divine, a hefty female impersonator (who has appeared in virtually all of Waters's movies), is rescued from her middle-class existence by Todd Tomorrow, played by Tab Hunter. When charged that he had ''sold out'' by making a commercial movie, Waters told the *New York Post,* ''How could I have sold out? My movie stars a 300-pound transvestite and Tab Hunter.'' With his latest film *Hairspray,* 1988, described by Waters in the *New York Times* (January 1, 1988) as ''a satire of two dreaded genres: the teen flick and the message movie,'' the man who likes to purposely shock people may have been shocked himself when the film received a PG rating.

WEIDNER, Paul 1934-

PERSONAL: Full name, Paul Russell Weidner; born March 29, 1934, in Charleston, SC; son of Paul Russell (a teacher) and Joanna (Powers) Weidner. EDUCATION: College of Charleston, B.A., 1955; University of Besancon, France, graduate work, 1955-56; Yale School of Drama, M.F.A., directing, 1962; trained for the stage with Michael Howard, 1962-64. MILITARY: U.S. Army, 1956-58.

VOCATION: Actor, director, producer, and writer.

CAREER: STAGE DEBUT—*Six Characters in Search of an Author,* Martinique Theatre, New York City, 1963. PRINCIPAL STAGE APPEARANCES—Sir Andrew Aguecheek, *Twelfth Night,* Asolo Theatre, Sarasota, FL, 1964; Argan, *The Imaginary Invalid,* Asolo Theatre, then Hartford Stage Company, Hartford, CT, both 1964; Telyegin, *Uncle Vanya,* Hastings, *She Stoops to Conquer,* Vladimir, *Waiting for Godot,* Trinculo, *The Tempest,* all Hartford Stage Company, 1965; Polonius, *Hamlet,* Nano, *Volpone,* Demokos, *Tiger at the Gates,* all Asolo Theatre, 1965; Algernon, *The Importance of Being Earnest,* general, *The Balcony,* both Hartford Stage Company, 1966; Verges, *Much Ado about Nothing,* Harpagon, *The Miser,* Mr. Smith, *The Bald Soprano,* all Asolo Theatre, 1966; Chebutykin, *The Three Sisters,* Hartford Stage Company, 1966; mute, *Madwoman of Chaillot,* Asolo Theatre, 1967.

PRINCIPAL STAGE WORK—Director: *The Farce of Scapino,* Asolo Theatre, Sarasota, FL, 1967; *Look Back in Anger,* Asolo Theatre, 1968; *The Price,* Williamstown Theatre Festival, Williamstown, MA, 1970; *My Sister, My Sister,* Little Theatre, New York City, 1974; *A Delicate Balance,* McCarter Theatre, Princeton, NJ, 1982; *Come Back Little Sheba,* Roundabout Theatre, New York City, 1984; *Master Harold . . . and the Boys,* Seattle Repertory Theatre, Seattle, WA, 1984; also directed at the Milwaukee Repertory Theatre, Milwaukee, WI.

With the Hartford Stage Company, Hartford, CT, all as producer unless indicated: Director, *Tartuffe,* 1965; director, *Twelfth Night, Endgame, Act without Words,* all 1966; (also director) *The Servant of Two Masters,* 1967; *The Rose Tattoo,* 1968; *The Homecoming, Life with Father,* both 1969; (also director) *The Seagull, The Waltz Invention, A Delicate Balance, The Trial, The Farce of Scapino,* all 1969; *Joe Egg, Misalliance, Anything Goes, Ring Around the Moon,* all 1970; (also director) *The Trial of A. Lincoln, Rosencrantz and Guildenstern Are Dead,* both 1970; (also director) *A Gun Play, The Boys in the Band, Henry V,* all 1971; *Long Day's Journey into Night, Blithe Spirit, No Place to Be Somebody,* all 1971; (also director) *Rooted, Tiny Alice, The Misanthrope,* all 1972; *Charley's Aunt, Loot, A Streetcar Named Desire,* all 1972; *Juno and the Paycock, Getting Married,* both 1973; (also director) *My Sister, My Sister, Nightlight, Old Times, You Can't Take It with You,* all 1973; (also director) *Ubu Roi, A Touch of the Poet, School for Scandal, The Hot l Baltimore, The Cherry Orchard,* all 1974; *Arsenic and Old Lace,* 1974; (also director) *Afternoon Tea, Room Service, All Over,* all 1975; (also director) *The Estate, The Blood Knot, Waltz of the Toreadors,* all 1976; (also director) *A History of the American Film, All the Way Home, Past Tense,* all 1977; (also director) *Rain, Wedding Band,* both 1978; (also director) *Galileo, Bonjour la Bonjour,* both 1979; guest director, *The Lady from Dubuque,* 1981.

PRINCIPAL TELEVISION WORK—Director, *All Over,* WNET, 1975.

RELATED CAREER—Producing director, Hartford Stage Company, 1968-80.

WRITINGS: PLAYS—Translator, all produced by the Hartford Stage Company, Hartford, CT: *Servant of Two Masters,* 1967; *Scapino,* 1969; *Ubu Roi,* 1974.

MEMBER: Actors' Equity Association, Society of Stage Directors and Choreographers, League of Resident Theatres.

SIDELIGHTS: RECREATIONS—Reading history, skiing, travel.

ADDRESSES: OFFICE—c/o Society of Stage Directors and Choreographers, 1501 Broadway, New York, NY 10036.*

*   *   *

WELDON, Duncan Clark 1941-

PERSONAL: Born March 19, 1941, in Southport, England; son of Clarence and Margaret Mary (Andrew) Weldon; married Helen Shapiro (divorced); married Janet Mahoney.

VOCATION: Producer.

CAREER: FIRST STAGE WORK—Producer (with David Kossoff) *A Funny Kind of Evening,* Theatre Royal, Bath, U.K., 1965. PRINCIPAL STAGE WORK—Producer: *13 Rue de L'Amour,* Phoenix Theatre, London, 1976; *A Bedful of Foreigners,* Victoria Palace Theatre, London, 1976; *The Three Sisters,* Cambridge Theatre, London, 1976; *The Seagull,* Duke of York's Theatre, London, 1976; *Fringe Benefits,* Whitehall Theatre, London, 1976; *The Circle,* Haymarket Theatre, London, 1976; *Separate Tables,* Apollo Theatre, London, 1977; *Stevie, On Approval,* both Vaudeville Theatre, London, 1977; *Hedda Gabler, Laburnum Grove,* both Duke of York's Theatre, 1977; *The Good Woman of Setzuan,* Royal Court Theatre, London, 1977; *Romersholm,* Haymarket Theatre, 1977; *The Apple Cart,* Phoenix Theatre, 1977; *King and Clowns,* Phoenix Theatre, 1978; *The Travelling Music Show,* Her Majesty's Theatre, London, 1978; *Waters of the Moon, A Family, Look after Lulu, The Millionairess,* all Haymarket Theatre, 1978; *The Crucifer of Blood,* Haymarket Theatre, 1979; *Ben Kingsley as Edmund Kean,* Brooks Atkinson Theatre, New York City, 1983; *Beethoven's Tenth,* Center Theatre Group, Ahmanson Theatre, Los Angeles, CA, 1984; *Aren't We All?,* Brooks Atkinson Theatre, 1985; *Strange Interlude,* Nederlander Theatre, New York City, 1985. Also produced *When We Are Married,* London, 1970; *The Chalk Garden, Big Bad Mouse,* both London, 1971; *Bunny,* London, 1972; *Grease, The King and I,* London, 1973; *Dead Easy,* London, 1974; *Brief Lives,* New York City, 1974; *Hedda Gabler,* Royal Shakespeare Company, 1975; *The Case in Question, Dad's Army, Betzi, On Approval,* all London, 1975; *Reflections,* London, 1980.

MAJOR TOURS—Producer, *Aren't We All,?* U.S. cities, 1985.

PRINCIPAL TELEVISION WORK—Producer, *Big Bad Mouse,* 1971.

PRINCIPAL FILM WORK—Co-producer, *Hedda Gabler,* 1975.

RELATED CAREER—Founder (with Paul Elliott and Richard Todd), Triumph Theatre Productions, 1970.

NON-RELATED CAREER—Professional photographer.

MEMBER: Society of West End Producers; Green Room Club, MacReady's Club (London).

ADDRESSES: OFFICE—The Griffins, Abinger Hammer, Surrey, England.*

*   *   *

WENDERS, Wim   1945-

PERSONAL: Born Wilhelm Wenders, August 14, 1945, in Dusseldorf, Germany. EDUCATION: Studied film at Hochschule fur Fernsehen und Film, Munich, 1967-70.

VOCATION: Director, writer, and film critic.

CAREER: PRINCIPAL FILM WORK—Director: *Schauplatze (Locations)*, 1967; *Same Player Shoot Again*, 1967; *Silver City*, 1968; *Victor 1*, 1968; *Alabama*, 1969; *2,000 Light Years*, 1969; *Three Amerikanische LPs (Three American LPs)*, 1969; *Summer in the City* (also known as *Summer in the City: Dedicated to the Kinks*), Diploma Film, 1970; *Polizeifilm (Police Film)*, 1970; *Die Angst des Tormanns beim Elfmeter (The Goalie's Anxiety at the Penalty Kick)*, 1971; *Der Scharlachrote Buchstabe (The Scarlet Letter)*, 1972; *Alice in den Stadten (Alice in the Cities)*, 1973; *Falsche Bewegung (Wrong Movement)*, 1974; also writer, *Im Lauf der Zeit (Kings of the Road)*, 1976; also writer, *The Rule Without Exception*, 1976; also writer, *Der Amerikanische Freun (The American Friend)*, 1977; also writer, *Lightning Over Water*, 1981; *Hammett*, Zoetrope, 1982; *Chambre 666*, 1982; also writer, *Der Stand der Dinge (The State of Things)*, 1982; also writer, *Tokyo-Ga*, 1984; *Paris, Texas*, Twentieth Century-Fox, 1984; also writer and co-producer, *The Sky Over Berlin*, Road Movies, 1987.

PRINCIPAL FILM APPEARANCES—*I Played It for You*, Fox International, 1985.

PRINCIPAL TELEVISION WORK—Movies: Director, *Aus der Familie der Panzereschen (From the Family of the Crocodilia)* and *Die Insel (The Island)*, both 1974.

RELATED CAREER—Film critic, *Suddeutsche Zeitung* and *Filmkritik*, Munich, 1960s.

WRITINGS: SCREENPLAYS—See above. BOOKS—(With Fritz Muller-Scherz) *The Film by Wim Wenders: Kings of the Road*, Munich, 1976.

AWARDS: Best Feature Film Director, Cannes Film Festival Award, 1987, for *The Sky Over Berlin*.

SIDELIGHTS: Before taking an interest in filmmaking, Wim Wenders had studied medicine, philosophy, and painting.

ADDRESSES: AGENT—c/o Gary Salt, The Paul Kohner Agency, 9169 Sunset Blvd., Los Angeles, CA 90069.*

*   *   *

WESLEY, Richard   1945-

PERSONAL: Born July 11, 1945, in Newark, NJ; son of George Richard (a laborer) and Gertrude (Thomas) Wesley; married Valerie Wilson; children: Thembi. EDUCATION: Howard University, B.F.A., 1967; trained for the stage at the Black Theatre Workshop.

RICHARD WESLEY

VOCATION: Playwright and screenwriter.

CAREER: See *WRITINGS* below.

RELATED CAREER—Board of directors, Frank Silvera Writers' Workshop, 1974—.

WRITINGS: PLAYS—*The Black Terror*, Public Theatre, New York City, 1971, published in *New Lafayette Theatre Presents*, edited by Ed Bullins, Doubleday, 1973; *Gettin' It Together*, Public Theatre, 1972; *Strike Heaven on the Face*, Bijou Theatre, New York City, 1973; *Goin' thru Changes, The Past Is the Past*, both Eugene O'Neill Memorial Theatre Center, Waterford, CT, then Billie Holiday Theatre, New York City, 1974; *The Sirens*, Manhattan Theatre Club, New York City, 1974; *The Mighty Gents*, Eugene O'Neill Memorial Theatre, 1974, then Ambassador Theatre, New York City, 1978, later Repertory Theatre of St. Louis, St. Louis, MO, 1986; (book) *The Dream Team*, Goodspeed Opera House, East Haddam, CT, 1985. Also wrote the book for *On the Road to Babylon*, 1979.

SCREENPLAYS—*Uptown Saturday Night*, Warner Brothers, 1974; *Let's Do It Again*, Warner Brothers, 1975.

AWARDS: Outstanding Playwriting, Drama Desk Award, 1972, for *The Black Terror;* Image Award, NAACP, 1974, for *Uptown Saturday Night*.

MEMBER: Writer's Guild of America-East, Dramatists Guild.

SIDELIGHTS: Richard Wesley has stated that his plays are ''. . . inspired primarily by social and political conditions of Black people in the United States.''

ADDRESSES: HOME—57 Chestnut Street, East Orange, NJ, 07018. OFFICE—Nasaba Artists, Inc., 1860 Broadway, New York, NY 10025.

* * *

WEXLER, Peter 1936-

PERSONAL: Full name, Peter John Wexler; born October 31, 1936, in New York, NY; son of S. David and Berda (Sarnoff) Wexler; married Constance Ann Ross, November 30, 1962. EDUCATION: University of Michigan, B.S., design, 1958; also attended Yale School of Drama, 1958.

VOCATION: Set, lighting, and costume designer.

CAREER: FIRST NEW YORK STAGE WORK—Set, lighting, and costume designer, *Antony and Cleopatra,* New York Shakespeare Festival, Hecksher Theatre, 1959. PRINCIPAL STAGE WORK—Set, lighting, and costume designer, *The Big Knife,* Seven Arts Playhouse, New York City, 1959.

All as set and lighting designer, unless indicated: *Brecht on Brecht,* Theatre de Lys, New York City, 1962; *The Threepenny Opera,* Sacandaga Playhouse, Sacandaga, NY, 1962; *Portrait of the Artist as a Young Man,* (also costume designer) *The Barroom Monks,* both Martinique Theatre, New York City, 1962; (also costume designer) *The Taming of the Shrew, Abe Lincoln in Illinois,* both Phyllis Anderson Theatre, New York City, 1963; (also costume

PETER WEXLER

designer) *Capers* (ballet), Robert Joffrey Ballet at the Bolshoi, Moscow, U.S.S.R., 1964; *Watch the Birdie,* Coconut Grove Playhouse, Miami, FL, 1964; stage installation designer, *Laterna Magicka,* Carnegie Hall, New York City, 1964; set designer, *War and Peace* (opera), Phoenix Theatre, New York City, 1965; set and costume designer, *Venus and Adonis, Masque of Angels,* both Tyrone Guthrie Theatre, Minneapolis, MN, 1964; (also costume designer) *La Boheme* (opera), for the Corpus Christi Symphony Orchestra, New York City, 1965; *Lizzie Borden* (opera), New York City Opera, 1965; (also costume designer) *The White Devil* (opera), Circle in the Square, New York City, 1965; (also costume designer) *The Deputy,* The Theatre Group, Los Angeles, CA, 1965; *The Burnt Flower Bed,* Theatre Guild, New York City, 1965; (also costume designer) *A Joyful Noise,* Mark Hellinger Theatre, New York City, 1966; (also costume designer) *Candide,* Center Theatre Group, Los Angeles, CA, 1966; (also costume designer) *Cosi Fan Tutti* (opera), Corpus Christi Symphony Orchestra, Corpus Christi, TX, 1966; *The Magic Flute* (opera), Washington Opera Society, Washington, DC, 1966; *The Happy Time,* Broadway Theatre, New York City, 1968; set designer, *In the Matter of J. Robert Oppenheimer,* Vivian Beaumont Theatre, New York City, 1969.

Costume designer, *Camino Real,* Vivian Beaumont Theatre, 1970; set, lighting, and costume designer, *Minnie's Boys,* Imperial Theatre, New York City, 1970; set, lighting, and costume designer, *Murderous Angels,* Playhouse Theatre, New York City, 1971; set and lighting designer, *The Gershwin Years,* Philharmonic Hall, New York City, 1971; set designer, *The Trial of the Catonsville Nine,* Good Shepherd Faith Church, then Lyceum Theatre, both New York City, 1971; set, costume, and lighting designer, *The Web and the Rock,* Theatre de Lys, 1972; set and costume designer, *Curlew River* (opera), Central City Opera, Central City, CO, 1972; *Review of Reviews,* Philharmonic Hall, 1973; set, costume, and lighting designer, *Church Trilogy,* St. James Church, New York City, 1973; set, costume, and lighting designer, *Henry IV, Parts I and II,* Goodman Theatre, Chicago, IL, 1974; set, costume, and lighting designer, *Les Troyens* (opera), Metropolitan Opera House, New York City, 1973; set, costume, and lighting designer, *Le Prophete* (opera), Metropolitan Opera House, New York City, 1976; set designer, *Jockeys,* Promenade Theatre, New York City, 1977; (with Connie Wexler) set, costume, and lighting designer, *By Strouse,* Ballroom Theatre, New York City, 1978; set, costume, and lighting designer, *A Broadway Musical,* Lunt-Fontanne Theatre, New York City, 1978; director, *Cold Storage,* Arizona Theatre Company, Tucson, AZ, 1978; set, costume, and lighting designer, *Un Ballo in Maschera* (opera), Metropolitan Opera House, 1979; set, costume, and lighting designer, *Terra Nova,* Center Theatre Group, Los Angeles, CA, 1979, then (also director) Pittsburgh Public Theatre, Pittsburgh, PA, 1980-81; set, costume, and lighting designer, *Albert Herring* (opera), Savonlinna Opera Festival, Finland, 1981. Also set designer, *The Curate's Play, Tableaux,* both New York City, 1961; set, costume, and lighting designer, *The Mystery of Elche,* New York City, 1963; *Dreams* (ballet), New York City, 1964; set designer, *The Trial of A. Lincoln,* New York City, 1971; set, costume, and lighting designer, *The Philanthropist,* Chicago, IL, 1975; producer, *Star Festival 80,* Dallas Symphony Orchestra, Dallas, TX, 1980.

With the Center Theatre Group, Mark Taper Forum, Los Angeles, CA: Set, lighting, and costume designer, *The Devils, The Marriage of Mr. Mississippi,* set and costume designer, *Uncle Vanya,* all 1967; set designer, *Camino Real,* 1968; set designer, *Chemin de Fer, In the Matter of J. Robert Oppenheimer,* both 1969; set, lighting, and costume designer, *Murderous Angels,* costume designer, *Rosebloom,* both 1970; set designer, *The Trial of the*

Catonsville Nine, Godspell, both 1971; set designer, *Leonard Bernstein's Mass,* 1973; set and lighting designer, *Hamlet,* 1974.

MAJOR TOURS—Set, lighting, and costume designer, *The Deputy,* U.S. cities, 1965; set and lighting designer, *On a Clear Day You Can See Forever,* U.S. cities, 1966; also with the Mark Taper Forum Theatre Company, State Department tour of the Far East and Europe, 1969.

PRINCIPAL FILM WORK—Designer, *Andy,* Universal, 1965; set and lighting designer, editor, *Happy Talk,* New York Philharmonic Hall Films, 1973; set and lighting designer, editor, *Review of Reviews,* New York Philharmonic Hall Films, 1973; designer, *The Trial of the Catonsville Nine,* Universal, 1973; also designed *Watch the Birdie.*

PRINCIPAL TELEVISION WORK—Episodic: Set designer, *Say When,* 1962. Series: Designer, *The Merv Griffin Show,* CBS, 1965. Specials: Designer, *Cleo Awards Ceremony,* 1971.

RELATED CAREER—Designed the stage at the White House, Washington, DC, 1961; designed the interior for the New York Philharmonic Promenades, Philharmonic Hall, 1965; designed theatre complex, Upper West Theatre, New York City, 1970; designed Stage B, Twentieth Century-Fox complex, Los Angeles, CA, 1973; designed the Promenade Concerts and Rug Concerts at Avery Fisher Hall, 1973-77; co-designed the Hollywood Bowl, Los Angeles, CA, 1975; designed theatre space, Pittsburgh Public Theatre, Pittsburgh, PA, 1975; principal designer, Center Theatre Group, Mark Taper Forum, Los Angeles, CA, 1967-70; member of design team Frank O. Gehry & Associates; has exhibited design work in major galleries. Also teacher and lecturer: University of Michigan, State University of New York, and the University of Arizona at Tucson.

AWARDS: International Theatre Institute Award from the American National Theatre Academy, 1965; Most Imaginative Use of Scene Design Award from the *Saturday Review,* 1965; Best Designer, Drama Desk Award nomination, Joseph Maharam Award nomination, both 1966, for *The White Devils;* Best Designer, Drama Desk Award, Joseph Maharam Award, and Antoinette Perry Award nomination, all 1968, for *The Happy Time;* Best Designer, Drama Desk Award nomination, Joseph Maharam Award nomination, both 1969, for *In the Matter of J. Robert Oppenheimer;* Los Angeles Drama Critics Circle Award, 1971; Los Angeles Drama Critics Circle Award, 1979, for *Terra Nova.*

MEMBER: United Scenic Artists, Society of Stage Directors and Choreographers, International Alliance of Theatrical Stage Employees.

ADDRESSES: OFFICE—277 West End Avenue, New York, NY 10023.*

* * *

WHEATON, Wil

BRIEF ENTRY: A number of small roles on television and in films, beginning when he was just seven years old, preceded Wil Wheaton's casting in *Stand by Me,* the 1986 surprise hit movie in which he played the lead role of Gordie Lachance. The California-born actor's television credits include his debut performance in the 1981 NBC TV movie, *A Long Way Home,* a role as an unlucky private

detective's son in the ABC pilot *Long Time Gone,* appearances in two other pilots—*13 Thirteenth Avenue* and *The Man Who Fell to Earth,* in the TV movie *The Defiant Ones* and the special *The Shooting.* Wheaton made his film debut as a lonely teenaged matchmaker in the 1984 comedy *The Buddy System,* following it with *Hambone and Hillie, The Last Starfighter,* and the role of Zachary Hayes in *The Farm. Stand by Me*'s director Rob Reiner said of the young actor, "Wil Wheaton is an extraordinarily intelligent kid and his intelligence comes through" (*New York Times,* September 16, 1986). That quality is useful in Wheaton's role as the precocious Wesley Crusher on the 1987 syndicated science fiction series *Star Trek II: The Next Generation.*

* * *

WHEELER, Hugh   1912-1987
(Q. Patrick, Patrick Quentin, Jonathan Stagge)

PERSONAL: Full name, Hugh Callingham Wheeler; born March 19, 1912, in London; immigrated to the United States, 1934, became naturalized American citzen, 1942; died July 26, 1987, at the Berkshire Medical Center, Pittsfield, MA, after a long illness; son of Harold (a civil servant) and Florence (Scammell) Wheeler. EDUCATION: London University, B.A., 1932. MILITARY: U.S. Army.

VOCATION: Playwright and novelist.

WRITINGS: PLAYS—*Big Fish, Little Fish,* American National Theatre Academy Playhouse, New York City, 1961, then Duke of York's Theatre, London, 1962, published by Random House, 1961, and in *Broadway's Beautiful Losers,* edited by Marilyn Stasio, Delacorte, 1972; *Look: We've Come Through!,* Hudson Theatre, New York City, 1961, published by Dramatists Play Service, 1963; (adaptor) *Rich Little Rich Girl,* Walnut Street Theatre, Phildelphia, PA, 1964; *We Have Always Lived in the Castle,* Ethel Barrymore Theatre, New York City, 1966, published by Dramatists Play Service, 1967; (book) *A Little Night Music,* Shubert Theatre, New York City, 1973, published by Dodd, Mead, 1974; (adaptor, with Joseph Stein) *Irene,* Minskoff Theatre, New York City, 1973; (adaptor) *Candide,* Brooklyn Academy of Music, Brooklyn, NY, 1973, then Broadway Theatre, New York City, 1974; (book, with John Weidmann) *Pacific Overtures,* Winter Garden Theatre, New York City, 1976; (adaptor) *Sweeney Todd,* Uris Theatre, New York City, 1979; *The Little Prince and the Aviator,* Alvin Theatre, New York City, 1981. Also wrote the lyrics for *Love for Love,* New York City, 1974.

SCREENPLAYS—(With Peter Viertel) *Five Miles to Midnight,* United Artists, 1963; *Something for Everyone,* National General, 1970; (with Jay Presson Allen) *Cabaret,* Allied Artists, 1972; (with Allen) *Travels with My Aunt,* Metro-Goldwyn-Mayer, 1972; *A Little Night Music,* 1977; *Nijinski,* Paramount, 1980.

TELEPLAYS—Episodic: *The Snoop Sisters,* NBC, 1972-74.

NOVELS—*The Crippled Muse,* Hart Davis, 1951, Rinehart, 1952.

With Richard Wilson Webb, under the joint pseudonym Q. Patrick: *Death Goes to School,* Smith & Haas, 1936, Cassell, 1936; *The Grindle Nightmare,* Hartney Press, 1936, Gollancz (as *Darker Grows the Valley*), 1936; *Death for Dear Clara,* Simon & Schuster, 1937, Cassell, 1937; *File on Fenton and Farr,* Morrow, 1937,

Jarrolds, 1938; *File on Claudia Cragge,* Morrow, 1938, Jarrolds, 1938; *Death and the Maiden,* Simon & Schuster, 1939, Cassell, 1939; *Danger Next Door,* Cassell, 1951; *The Girl on the Gallows,* Fawcett, 1954. Also co-authors of *Famous Trials.*

With Richard Wilson Webb, under the joint psuedonym Jonathan Stagge: *Murder Gone to Earth,* Joseph, 1936, as *The Dogs Do Bark,* Doubleday, 1937; *Murder or Mercy,* Joseph, 1937, as *Murder by Prescription,* Doubleday, 1938; *The Stars Spell Death,* Doubleday, 1939, as *Murder in the Stars,* Joseph, 1940; *Turn of the Table,* Doubleday, 1940, as *Funeral for Five,* Joseph, 1940; *The Yellow Taxi,* Doubleday, 1942, as *Call a Hearse,* Joseph, 1942; *The Scarlet Circle,* Doubleday, 1943, as *Light from a Lantern,* Joseph, 1943; *Death My Darling Daughters,* Doubleday, 1945, as *Death and the Dear Girls,* Joseph, 1946; *Death's Old Sweet Song,* Doubleday, 1946, Joseph, 1947; *The Three Fears,* Doubleday, 1949, Joseph, 1949.

Under the pseudonym Patrick Quentin: (with Webb) *A Puzzle for Fools,* Simon & Schuster, 1936, Gollancz, 1936; (with Webb) *Puzzle for Players,* Simon & Schuster, 1938, Gollancz, 1939; (with Webb) *Puzzle for Puppets,* Simon & Schuster, 1944, Gollancz, 1944; (with Webb) *Puzzle for Wantons,* Simon & Schuster, 1945, Gollancz, 1946; (with Webb) *Puzzle for Fiends,* Simon & Schuster, 1946, Gollancz, 1947; (with Webb) *Puzzle for Pilgrims,* Simon & Schuster, 1947, Gollancz, 1948; (with Webb) *Run to Death,* Simon & Schuster, 1948, Gollancz, 1948; *The Follower,* Simon & Schuster, 1950, Gollancz, 1950; *Black Widow,* Simon & Schuster, 1952, as *Fatal Woman,* Gollancz, 1953; *My Son, the Murderer,* Simon & Schuster, 1954, as *The Wife of Ronald Sheldon,* Gollancz, 1954; *The Man with Two Wives,* Simon & Schuster, 1955, Gollancz, 1955; *The Man in the Net,* Simon & Schuster, 1956, Gollancz, 1956; *Suspicious Circumstances,* Simon & Schuster, 1957, Gollancz, 1957; *Shadow of Guilt,* Simon & Schuster, 1959, Gollancz, 1959; *The Green-Eyed Monster,* Simon & Schuster, 1960, Gollancz, 1960; *The Ordeal of Mrs. Snow and Other Stories,* Gollancz, 1961, Random House, 1962; *Family Skeletons,* Random House, 1965, Gollancz, 1965.

Also contributor of short stories and novelettes to numerous magazines under all three pseudonyms.

AWARDS: Edgar Allen Poe awards from the Mystery Writers of America, 1963, 1973; Best Musical, Antoinette Perry Award, Drama Critics Circle Award, Drama Desk Award, all 1973, for *A Little Night Music;* Best Musical, Antoinette Perry Award, Drama Critics Circle Award, Drama Desk Award, all 1974, for *Candide;* Drama Critics Circle Award, 1975, for *Pacific Overtures;* Best Musical, Antoinette Perry Award, Drama Critics Circle Award, Drama Desk Award, Outer Critics Circle Award, all 1979, for *Sweeney Todd.*

MEMBER: Dramatists Guild.

OBITUARIES AND OTHER SOURCES: Variety, July 29, 1987.*

*   *   *

WHITE, Michael   1936-

PERSONAL: Full name, Michael Simon White; born January 16, 1936, in Glasgow, Scotland; son of Victor (a theatrical director) and Doris (Cohen) White; married Sarah Hillsdon, January 15, 1965; children: two sons, one daughter. EDUCATION: Attended the Sorbonne.

VOCATION: Producer.

CAREER: PRINCIPAL STAGE WORK—Producer: (With Peter Daubeny) *The Connection,* Duke of York's Theatre, London, 1961; (with Oscar Lewenstein) *The Secret of the World, The Scatterin', Jungle of the Cities, The Voice of Shem,* all Theatre Royal, Stratford-on-Avon, U.K., 1962; *The Blood Knot,* Arts Theatre, London, 1963; *Cambridge Circus,* Arts Theatre, then Lyric Theatre, London, both 1963; *The *** Show,* Phoenix Theatre, London, 1963; (with William Donaldson) *Oscar Brown, Jr. Entertains,* Prince Charles' Theatre, London, 1963; *Merce Cunningham Dance Company,* Sadler's Wells Theatre, London, 1964; *Gracelia Martinez Dance Company,* Comedy Theatre, then Saville Theatre, both London, 1964; *Hamp,* Lyceum Theatre, Edinburgh, Scotland, U.K., 1964; *Son of Oblomov,* Comedy Theatre, 1964; *Any Wednesday,* Apollo Theatre, London, 1965; *Yvonne Rainer Dance Company,* Comedy Theatre, 1965; (with Ed Swann) *Saturday Night and Sunday Morning,* Prince of Wales Theatre, London, 1966; (with Philip Grout and Moray Watson) *How's the World Treating You?,* Comedy Theatre, 1966; *Merce Cunningham Dance Company,* Sadler's Wells Theatre, 1966; *The Trials of Brother Jero, The Blood Knot,* both Hampstead Theatre Club, London, 1966; (with Leonard Field) *Breakdown,* Gate Theatre, Dublin, Ireland, 1966; (with Field) *Hogan's Goat,* Olympia Theatre, Dublin, Ireland, 1966; *Yoko Ono—Music of the Mind,* Jeanette Cochrane Theatre, London, 1966; *The Burgler,* Vaudeville Theatre, London, 1967; *America Hurrah,* Royal Court Theatre, London, 1967; *Philadelphia Here I Come,* Apollo Theatre, 1967; *Tom Paine,* Vaudeville Theatre, 1967, then (with William Dorr) Stage 73, New York City, 1968; (with Michael Codron) *Fanghorn,* Fortune Theatre, London, 1967; *The Paper Bag Players,* Royal Court Theatre, 1967; (with Lewenstein) *Loot,* Criterion Theatre, London, 1967, then Biltmore Theatre, New York City, 1968; *Summer,* Fortune Theatre, 1968; (with Field) *The Au Pair Men,* Duchess Theatre, London, 1968; *Fortune and Men's Eyes,* Comedy Theatre, 1968; *The Beard,* Royal Court Theatre, 1968; (with Kenneth Tynan and Norman Granz) *Soldiers,* New Theatre, London, 1968; *The Resistable Rise of Arturo Ui,* Saville Theatre, London, 1969; *So What About Love?,* Criterion Theatre, 1969.

Sleuth, St. Martin's Theatre, London, then (with Helen Bonfils and Morton Gottlieb) Music Box Theatre, New York City, both 1970; *Widowers' Houses,* Royal Court Theatre, 1970; (with Robert Stigwood and Hillard Elkins) *Oh! Calcutta,* Royalty Theatre, London, then Duchess Theatre, both 1970; *Hamlet,* Fortune Theatre, 1971; (with Stigwood and Bob Swash) *The Dirtiest Show in Town,* Duchess Theatre, 1971; *As Time Goes By, Friday,* both Theatre Upstairs, London, 1971; *The Threepenny Opera,* Prince of Wales Theatre, 1972; *Julius Caesar,* New Theatre, 1972; *I, Claudius,* Piccadilly Theatre, London, 1972; (with Stigwood) *Joseph and the Amazing Technicolor Dreamcoat,* Round House Theatre, London, 1972, then Albery Theatre, London, 1973; *A Sense of Detachment,* Royal Court Theatre, 1972; (with Bernard Delfont) *A Doll's House,* Criterion Theatre, 1973; (with Stigwood) *Two Gentlemen of Verona,* Phoenix Theatre, 1973; *The Rocky Horror Show,* Classic Theatre, London, 1973; *The Ride across Lake Constance,* Hampstead Theatre Club, then May Fair Theatre, London, both 1973; *Judies,* Comedy Theatre, 1973; *Snap,* Vaudeville Theatre, 1974; *That Championship Season,* Garrick Theatre, London, 1974. Also produced *Saint's Day, The Star Spangled Jack Show,* both London, 1965; *I Wonder,* London, 1968; *The Island, Sizwe Banzi Is Dead,* both London, 1974, then New York City, 1975; *The Tooth of*

Crime, Play Mas, both London, 1974; *Murderer, Jeeves, Entertaining Mr. Sloane, Loot, What the Butler Saw, Too True to Be Good,* all London, 1975; *City Sugar, The Chairman, Housewife-Superstar, Baggage, A Chorus Line, Carte Blanche,* all London, 1976; *Censored Scenes from King Kong,* London, 1977; *Sleuth, Annie, I Was Sitting on My Patio This Guy Appeared I Thought I Was Hallucinating, Dracula, Deathtrap,* all London, 1978; *Ain't Misbehavin', Flowers for Algernon,* both London, 1979; *Pirates of Penzance, On Your Toes,* both London, 1980.

MAJOR TOURS—Producer (with Wolf Mankowitz), *Adam's Apple,* U.K. cities, 1966.

PRINCIPAL FILM WORK—Producer: *Moviemakers,* 1973; *Monty Python and the Holy Grail,* Cinema V, 1975; *Rocky Horror Picture Show,* 1975; *Jabberwocky,* 1977; *Rude Boy,* 1980; *My Dinner with Andre,* Pacific Arts, 1981; *Strangers Kiss,* 1984; also *Superglass; High Season; Eat the Rich; White Mischief.*

RELATED CAREER—Council member, Royal Court Theatre; council member, Institute of Contemporary Arts.

AWARDS: Best Play, Antoinette Perry Award, 1970, for *Sleuth.*

MEMBER: Society of West End Managers; Turf Club.

SIDELIGHTS: RECREATIONS—Skiing, painting, racing.

ADDRESSES: OFFICE—13 Duke Street, St. James's, London SW1, England.

*   *   *

WIDDOES, Kathleen   1939-

PERSONAL: Full name, Kathleen Effie Widdoes; born March 21, 1939, in Wilmington, DE; daughter of Eugene and Bernice (Delapo) Widdoes; married Richard Jordan (an actor), January 22, 1963. EDUCATION: Studied mime at the Universite au Theatre des Nations, Paris.

VOCATION: Actress.

CAREER: STAGE DEBUT—Alma, *Bus Stop,* Robin Hood Playhouse, Wilmington, DE, 1957. BROADWAY DEBUT— Teusret, *The Firstborn,* Coronet Theatre, 1958. PRINCIPAL STAGE APPEARANCES—Catherine, *A View from the Bridge,* Robin Hood Playhouse, Wilmington, DE, 1958; Teusret, *The Firstborn,* Habimah Theatre, Tel Aviv, Israel, 1958; tourist, *The World of Suzie Wong,* Broadhurst Theatre, New York City, 1958; Irina, *The Three Sisters,* Fourth Street Theatre, New York City, 1959; Sonja, *Notes from the Underground,* Theatre de Lys, New York City, 1959; Katherine, *Henry V,* Juliet, *Measure for Measure,* both New York Shakespeare Festival (NYSF), Belvedere Lake Theatre, New York City, 1960; Aglasia, *The Idiot,* Gate Theatre, New York City, 1960; Titania, *A Midsummer Night's Dream,* queen, *Richard II,* both NYSF, Central Park, New York City, 1961; Teresa del Castillo, *We Take the Town,* Shubert Theatre, New Haven, CT, 1962; Miranda, *The Tempest,* NYSF, Delacorte Theatre, New York City, 1962; Claire, *The Maids,* One Sheridan Square Theatre, New York City, 1963; Alice, *You Can't Take It with You,* Lyceum Theatre, New York City, 1966; Ersilia Drei, *To Clothe the Naked,* Sheridan Square Playhouse, New York City, 1967; *The Three*

Sisters, 'Tis Pity She's a Whore, both Yale Repertory Theatre, New Haven, CT, 1967; woman, *World War 2 1/2,* Martinique Theatre, New York City, 1969; Mildred, *Willie,* Other Stage Theatre, New York City, 1970; Polly Peachum, *The Beggar's Opera,* Brooklyn Academy of Music, Brooklyn, NY, then McAlpin Rooftop Theatre, New York City, both 1972; Beatrice, *Much Ado about Nothing,* NYSF, Delacorte Theatre, then Winter Garden Theatre, New York City, both 1972; Rosalind, *As You Like It,* NYSF, Delacorte Theatre, 1973; Desdemona, Juliet, Titania, *Shakespeare and the Performing Arts,* Kennedy Center, Washington, DC, 1973; Titania, *A Midsummer Night's Dream,* Mitzi E. Newhouse Theatre, New York City, 1975; Viola, *Twelfth Night,* Mariana, *Measure for Measure,* both Stratford Shakespeare Festival, Stratford, ON, Canada, 1975; *Castaways,* Promenade Theatre, New York City, 1977; Cecily Cardew, *The Importance of Being Earnest,* Circle in the Square, New York City, 1977; Donna, *Stops along the Way,* #2, *In Fireworks Lie Secret Codes,* both One Act Play Festival, Mitzi E. Newhouse Theatre, 1981; Gertrude, *Hamlet,* NYSF, Public Theatre, 1982; Blanche, *Brighton Beach Memoirs,* Neil Simon Theatre, New York City, 1983. Also appeared in *The Primrose Path,* Robin Hood Playhouse, 1958; and in *Ghosts,* American Repertory Theatre, Cambridge, MA, 1981.

MAJOR TOURS—Catherine, *A View from the Bridge,* Canadian cities, 1957, then U.S. cities, 1960.

TELEVISION DEBUT—*Lamp unto My Feet,* CBS, 1957. PRINCIPAL TELEVISION APPEARANCES—Episodic: *Dupont Show of the Month,* CBS, 1960; *Camera Three,* CBS, 1960; *The Defenders,* CBS, 1961, 1963, and 1965; *The Doctors,* NBC, 1963; *The Doctors/The Nurses,* CBS, 1965; *The Invaders,* ABC, 1965; *Memory Lane,* independent, 1965-66; *Twelve O'Clock High,* ABC, 1966; *Ford Star Time,* CBC. Movies: Margaret Howell Grant, *Punch and Jody,* NBC, 1974; Irene Hadrachi, *Happiness Is a Warm Clue,* NBC, 1979; Angela Giancana, *Mafia Princess,* NBC, 1986. Specials: Emily, *Our Town,* NBC, 1959; title role, *Colombe,* CBC, 1960; title role, *Ondine,* CBS, 1961; Joan, *The Lark,* CBC, 1962; Beatrice, *Much Ado about Nothing,* CBS, 1973.

PRINCIPAL FILM APPEARANCES—Helena Davis, *The Group,* United Artists, 1966; Masha, *The Sea Gull,* Warner Brothers/Seven Arts, 1968; also appeared in *Petulia,* Warner Brothers/Seven Arts, 1968; *Savages,* New World, 1973; *I'm Dancing As Fast As I Can,* Paramount, 1982; *Without a Trace,* Twentieth Century-Fox, 1983; and *The End of August,* 1981.

AWARDS: Fulbright Scholarship, 1962.

MEMBER: Actors' Equity Association, Screen Actors Guild, American Federation of Television and Radio Artists.

ADDRESSES: HOME—71 Horatio Street, New York, NY 10014.*

*   *   *

WIEST, Dianne   1948-

PERSONAL: Born March 28, 1948, in Kansas City, MO. EDUCATION: Attended the University of Maryland; trained as a ballet dancer.

VOCATION: Actress and director.

CAREER: FILM DEBUT—*I'm Dancing as Fast as I Can,* Paramount, 1982. PRINCIPAL FILM APPEARANCES—*Independence Day,* Warner Brothers, 1982; *Footloose,* Paramount, 1984; Isabella, *Falling in Love,* Paramount, 1984; *The Purple Rose of Cairo,* Orion, 1985; *Hannah and Her Sisters,* Orion, 1986; *Radio Days,* Orion, 1987; *September,* Orion, 1987; *Bright Lights, Big City,* United Artists, 1988.

PRINCIPAL STAGE APPEARANCES—Esther and Hadassah, *Esther,* Promenade Theatre, New York City, 1977; Elizabeth Sorrow, *Museum,* Public Theatre, New York Shakespeare Festival (NYSF), New York City, 1978; Lizzard, *Leave It to Beaver Is Dead,* Public Theatre, NYSF, 1978; Elizabeth Barrow Colt, *The Art of Dining,* Kennedy Center for the Performing Arts, then Public Theatre, 1979; Nicole, *Bonjour, LA, Bonjour,* with the Phoenix Repertory Company at the Marymount Manhattan Theatre, New York City, 1980; Elizabeth Lavenza, *Frankenstein,* Palace Theatre, New York City, 1981; title role, *Hedda Gabler,* Yale Repertory Theatre, New Haven, CT, 1981; Nora, *A Doll's House,* Yale Repertory Theatre, 1982; Masha, *The Three Sisters,* Manhattan Theatre Club, New York City, 1982; Desdemona, *Othello,* Circle in the Square Theatre, New York City, 1982; Prudence, *Beyond Therapy,* Brooks Atkinson Theatre, New York City, 1982; Deborah, *Other Places,* Manhattan Theatre Club, New York City, 1984; Maggie, *After the Fall,* Playhouse 91, New York City, 1984; *Hunting Cockroaches,* Manhattan Theatre Club at the City Center, New York City, 1987.

PRINCIPAL STAGE WORK—Director, *Not About Heroes,* Lucille Lortel Theatre, New York City, 1985.

AWARDS: Theatre World Award, 1979-80; Best Supporting Actress, Academy Award, National Society of Film Critics, National Critics Review Board, New York Film Critics, and Los Angeles Film Critics, all 1986, for *Hannah and Her Sisters.*

MEMBER: Actors' Equity Association, Screen Actors Guild.

ADDRESSES: AGENT—c/o Sam Cohn, International Creative Management, 40 W. 57th Street, New York, NY 10019.*

*　　*　　*

WILLIAMS, Clifford　1926-

PERSONAL: Born December 30, 1926, in Cardiff, Wales; son of George Frederick and Florence Maud (Gapper) Williams; married Josiane Peset; children: Anouk, Tara. EDUCATION: Attended Trinity College.

VOCATION: Director, writer, and actor.

CAREER: STAGE DEBUT—Larissa, *More Than Science,* both Chanticleer Theatre, London, 1945. PRINCIPAL STAGE APPEARANCES—Julius Caesar, *These Mortals,* People's Palace, London, 1948.

FIRST LONDON WORK—Director, *Yerma,* Arts Theatre, 1957. PRINCIPAL STAGE WORK—Director: *Radio Rescue,* Arts Theatre, London, 1958; *Dark Halo, Quartet for Five, The Marriage of Mr. Mississippi,* all Arts Theatre, 1959; *A Moon for the Misbegotten, The Shepherd's Chameleon, Victims of Duty,* all Arts Theatre, 1960; *The Flying Dutchman,* Covent Garden Theatre, London, 1966; *Volpone,* Yale School of Drama, New Haven, CT, 1967; *As*

CLIFFORD WILLIAMS

You Like It, National Theatre, London, 1967; *Back to Methuselah, Dido and Aeneas,* both Windsor Festival, Windsor, U.K., 1969; *Sleuth,* St. Martin's Theatre, London, then Music Box Theatre, New York City, both 1970; *Mardi Gras,* Prince of Wales Theatre, London, 1977; *Carte Blanche,* Phoenix Theatre, London, 1976; *Stevie,* Vaudeville Theatre, London, 1977; *The Old Country,* Queen's Theatre, London, 1977; *Rosmersholm,* Haymarket Theatre, London, 1977; *The Passion of Dracula,* Queen's Theatre, 1978; *To Grandmother's House We Go,* Biltmore Theatre, New York City, 1981; *Pack of Lies,* London 1983, then Royale Theatre, New York City, later Hamburg, West Germany, both 1985; *Aren't We All?,* London, 1984, then Brooks Atkinson Theatre, New York City, 1985, later Australia, 1986; *Breaking the Code,* London, 1986, then Neil Simon Theatre, New York City, 1987. Also directed twenty mime plays, Mime Theatre Company, 1950-53; *Race of Adam,* Llandaff Cathedral, U.K., 1961; *Our Man Crichton,* London, 1964; *The Gardener's Dog,* Finnish National Theatre, 1965; *The Meteor,* London, 1966; *The Merry Wives of Windsor,* Finnish National Theatre, 1967; *Othello,* Bulgarian National Theatre, 1968; *A Winter's Tale,* Yugoslav National Theatre, 1969; *Famine,* English Stage Society, 1969; *Henry IV,* New York City, then London, both 1974; *What Every Woman Knows,* 1974; *Murderer,* 1975; *The Threepenny Opera,* 1979; *Richard III,* Mexican National Theatre, 1979; *Born in the Gardens,* 1979; *The Love-Girl, The Innocent,* both 1980; *Scott,* 1981; *Overheard, The Carmelites, The Love-Girl,* all London, 1981; *Othello,* West Germany, 1982; *A Child's Christmas in Wales,* Cleveland, OH, 1982; *Richard III,* Madrid, Spain, 1983; *The Merry Wives of Windsor,* Cleveland, OH, 1983; *Mahoganny,* 1984; *The Cherry Orchard,* Tokyo, Japan, 1984; *Measure for Measure,* Sweden, 1985; *The Importance of Being Earnest,* Royal Danish Theatre, 1987; and with the Arena

Theatre, Birmingham, U.K.; Belgrade Theatre, Coventry, U.K.; Theatre Workshop; Theatre-in-the-Round; and National Theatre of the Deaf.

Director, all with the Royal Shakespeare Company, London and Stratford-on-Avon, U.K.: *Afore Night Come,* 1962; *The Comedy of Errors, The Tempest, The Representative,* all 1963; *Richard II, Henry IV, Parts I and II, Afore Night Come, The Jew of Malta,* all 1964; *The Merchant of Venice, The Jew of Malta, The Comedy of Errors,* all 1965; *Henry V, Twelfth Night,* both 1966; *Dr. Faustus,* 1968; *Major Barbara,* 1970; *The Duchess of Malfi,* 1971; *The Comedy of Errors,* 1972; *The Taming of the Shrew, A Lesson in Blood and Roses,* both 1973; *Cymbeline,* 1974; *The Mouth Organ, Too True to Be Good,* both 1975; *Wild Oats,* 1976; *Man and Superman,* 1977; *The Tempest,* 1978; *Wild Oats,* 1979; *The Innocent,* 1981; *The Happiest Days of Your Life,* 1984.

MAJOR TOURS—Director: *The Comedy of Errors,* for the Royal Shakespeare Company (RSC), U.S. cities, 1964; *Soldiers,* U.S. and Canadia cities, 1968; *Dr. Faustus,* U.S. cities, 1968; *Oh! Calcutta!,* European cities, 1970; *The Brass Hat,* RSC, 1972; *Lord Arthur Savile's Crime, Heartbreak House,* U.K. cities, both 1980; *Skin Game, The Cherry Orchard,* U.K. cities, both 1981; *Getting Married, Chapter 17, Do Not Disturb,* U.K. cities, all 1982; *Aren't We All?,* U.S. cities, 1985; *Saint Joan,* U.K. cities, 1985; *Legends,* U.S. cities, 1985.

RELATED CAREER—Founder, Mime Theatre Company, 1950-53; director of productions, Marlowe Theatre, Canterbury, U.K., 1956; director of productions, Queen's Theatre, Hornchurch, U.K., 1956; associate director, Royal Shakespeare Company, 1963.

WRITINGS: PLAYS—*The Sleeping Princess; The Goose Girl; The Secret Kingdom; Stephen Dedalus; The Disguises of Arlecchino.* Also wrote twenty mime plays for the Mime Theatre Company, 1950-53.

AWARDS: Best Director, Antoinette Perry Award nomination, 1971, for *Sleuth.*

MEMBER: British Theatre Association, (chairor, 1977—); fellow, Trinity College.

ADDRESSES: AGENT—c/o The Lantz Office, 888 Seventh Avenue, New York, NY 10106.

*   *   *

WILLIAMS, Dick Anthony   1938-

PERSONAL: Born August 9, 1938, in Chicago, IL.

VOCATION: Actor, director, and producer.

CAREER: PRINCIPAL STAGE APPEARANCES—Title role, *Big Time Buck White,* Village South Theatre, New York City, 1968; *Nigger Nightmare,* New York Shakespeare Festival, Public Theatre, New York City, 1971; *Ain't Supposed to Die a Natural Death,* Ethel Barrymore Theatre, New York City, 1971; Omar Butler I, *Jamimma,* Henry Street Playhouse, New York City, 1972; Rico, *What the Wine Sellers Buy,* New Federal Theatre, New York City, 1973, then Vivian Beaumont Theatre, New York City, and the New Theatre for Now, Los Angeles, CA, both 1974; Alexander, *Black*

Picture Show, Vivian Beaumont Theatre, 1975; Al Seaver, *We Interrupt This Program,* Ambassador Theatre, New York City, 1975; Bobby Foster, *The Poison Tree,* Ambassador Theatre, 1976.

PRINCIPAL STAGE WORK—Director, *The Pig Pen,* American Place Theatre, New York City, 1970; co-producer (with Woodie King), *Black Girl,* Theatre de Lys, New York City, 1971; director, *In New England Winter,* Henry Street Playhouse, New York City, 1971; producer, *A Recent Killing,* New Federal Theatre, New York City, 1973.

PRINCIPAL TELEVISION APPEARANCES—Mini-Series: Malcolm X, *King,* NBC, 1978; Gawain Butler, *James A. Michener's "Space,"* CBS, 1985. Movies: Anthony, *The Storyteller,* NBC, 1977; John Tubman, *A Woman Called Moses,* NBC, 1978; Danny York, *Hollow Image,* ABC, 1979; Dr. Hopstone, *Some Kind of Miracle,* CBS, 1979; Helmholtz Watson, *Brave New World,* NBC, 1980; Jim Downs, *The Night the City Screamed,* ABC, 1980; Ralph Joplin, *The Sophisticated Gents,* NBC, 1981; Detective Campbell, *A Gun in the House,* CBS, 1981; Reverend Richard Henderson, *Sister, Sister,* NBC, 1982; Morris Elliot, *Something So Right,* CBS, 1982; Leonard Hayes, *This Is Kate Bennett,* ABC, 1982; Detective Wylie, *Through Naked Eyes,* ABC, 1983; instructor, *Night Partners,* CBS, 1983; Dr. Hume, *Challenge of a Lifetime,* ABC, 1985.

PRINCIPAL FILM APPEARANCES—*Who Killed Mary What's 'ername?,* Cannon, 1971; *The Anderson Tapes,* Columbia, 1971; *Dog Day Afternoon,* Warner Brothers, 1975; *Deadly Hero,* AVCO-Embassy, 1976; *The Deep,* Columbia, 1977; *An Almost Perfect Affair,* Paramount, 1979; *The Jerk,* Universal, 1979; *The Star Chamber,* Twentieth Century-Fox, 1983.

MEMBER: Actors' Equity Association, Screen Actors Guild, American Federation of Television and Radio Artists.

ADDRESSES: HOME—4075 W. 29th Street, Los Angeles, CA, 90018.*

*   *   *

WILLIAMS, Emlyn   1905-1987

PERSONAL: Full name, George Emlyn Williams; born November 26, 1905, in Mostyn, Wales; died September 25, 1987, in London, following cancer surgery; son of Richard (a merchant seaman, greengrocer, village innkeeper, and foreman in an ironworks) and Mary (Williams) Williams; married Molly O'Shann, 1935 (died, 1970); children: two sons. EDUCATION: Christ Church, Oxford University, M.A., 1927.

VOCATION: Actor, director, and writer.

CAREER: LONDON DEBUT—Pelling's apprentice, *And So To Bed,* Savoy Theatre, 1927. BROADWAY DEBUT—Pepys' boy, *And So To Bed,* Shubert Theatre, 1927. PRINCIPAL STAGE APPEARANCES—Reverend Yorke, Billy Saunders, *The Pocket-Money Husband,* Arts Theatre, London, 1928; Jack, *Glamour,* Embassy Theatre, then Court Theatre, both London, 1928; Camille, *Therese Raquin,* Wyndham's Theatre, London, 1929; Beppo, *Mafro, Darling,* Berthold, *The Mock Emperor,* both Queen's Theatre, London, 1929; trumpeter, *The Silver Tassie,* Apollo Theatre, London, 1929; Captain Sandys, *Tunnel Trench,* Duchess Theatre, London, 1929;

Jules Marnier, *French Leave*, Vaudeville Theatre, London, 1930; Giovanni d'Amora, *La Piccola*, Arts Theatre, 1930; usher, *The Fire in the Opera House*, Everyman Theatre, London, 1930; Angelo, *On the Spot*, Commissar Neufeld, *The Mouthpiece*, both Wyndham's Theatre, 1930; Adolphe, *Devant la Porte*, Arts Theatre, 1930; title role, *Etienne*, St. James Theatre, London, 1931; Lord Lebanon, *The Case of the Frightened Lady*, Youssef el Tabah, *Port Said*, both Wyndham's Theatre, 1931; young Frenchman, *The Man I Killed*, Apollo Theatre, 1932; Jack, *Man Overboard*, Garrick Theatre, London, 1932; Lord Lebanon, *Criminal at Large* (American title for *The Case of the Frightened Lady*), Belasco Theatre, New York City, 1932; Patrick Branwell Bronte, *Wild Decembers*, Apollo Theatre, 1933; Piers Gaveston, *Rose and Glove*, Westminster Theatre, London, 1934; Eugene Beauharnais, *Josephine*, His Majesty's Theatre, London, 1934; Dan, *Night Must Fall*, Duchess Theatre, 1935, then Ethel Barrymore Theatre, New York City, 1936; Lambert, *He Was Born Gay*, Queen's Theatre, 937; Oswald, *Ghosts*, with the Old Vic Theatre Company, Buxton, U.K., 1937; Angelo, *Measure for Measure*, Duke of Gloucester, *Richard III*, both with the Old Vic Theatre Company, London, 1937; Morgan Evans, *The Corn Is Green*, Duchess Theatre, 1938.

Maddoc Thomas, *The Light of Heart*, Apollo Theatre, 1940; Cliff Parrilow, *The Morning Star*, Globe Theatre, London, 1941; Ambrose Ellis, *The Wind of Heaven*, St. James Theatre, 1945; Sir Robert Morton, *The Winslow Boy*, Lyric Theatre, London, 1946; Saivello, *Trespass*, Globe Theatre, 1947; Izquiredo, *Montserrat*, Fulton Theatre, New York City, 1949; Will Trenting, *Accolade*, Aldwych Theatre, London, 1950; *Charles Dickens* (one-man show), Lyric Hammersmith Theatre, London, 1951, then Criterion Theatre, London, and Duchess Theatre, all 1951, later John Golden Theatre, New York City, 1952; Charles Dickens, *Bleak House* (one-man show), Edinburgh Festival, Edinburgh, Scotland, U.K., 1952, then Ambassador's Theatre, London, later Bijou Theatre, New York City, 1952-53; *Charles Dickens* (Welsh translation of the one-man show) National Eisteddfod of Wales, Cardiff, Wales, U.K., 1953; Fenn, *Someone Waiting*, Globe Theatre, 1953; Dylan Thomas, *A Boy Growing Up* (one-man show), Globe Theatre, 1955, then Longacre Theatre, New York City, 1957, later Globe Theatre, 1958; Hjalmar Ekdal, *The Wild Duck*, Saville Theatre, London, 1955; Shylock, *The Merchant of Venice*, Iago, *Othello*, Angelo, *Measure for Measure*, all Royal Shakespeare Company, Memorial Theatre, Stratford-on-Avon, U.K., 1956; author, *Shadow of Heroes*, Piccadilly Theatre, London, 1958; man, "Lunch Hour," Mr. Chacterson, "The Form," Edward, "A Slight Ache," billed as *Three*, Arts Theatre, then Criterion Theatre, London, both 1961; Ascolini, *Daughter of Silence*, Music Box Theatre, New York City, 1961; Sir Thomas More, *A Man for All Seasons*, American National Theatre Academy (ANTA) Playhouse, New York City, 1962; Pope Pius XII, *The Deputy*, Brooks Atkinson Theatre, New York City, 1964; *Charles Dickens* (one-man show), Globe Theatre, 1965; Ignatyillyich, *A Month in the Country*, Cambridge Theatre, London, 1965; headmaster, *Forty Years On*, Apollo Theatre, 1969; *Charles Dickens* (one-man show), Haymarket Theatre, London, 1975; *Saki* (one-man show), Apollo Theatre, 1977; *Playboy of the Weekend World* (one-man show; American title for *Saki*), Playhouse Theatre, New York City, 1978; Dylan Thomas, *A Boy Growing Up*, Arnaud Theatre, Guildford, U.K., 1979, then Ambassador's Theatre, London, 1980.

MAJOR TOURS—Dan, *Night Must Fall*, Charles Condomine, *Blithe Spirit*, and in *Flare Path*, for Overseas Forces in the Middle East, all 1944; *Emlyn Williams as Charles Dickens*, U.S., Canadian, European, and South African cities, 1951, Australian and New Zealand cities, 1958, U.S., Canadian, and Far Eastern cities, 1965,

Australian , Soviet, and U.S. cities, 1970, U.S. and Canadian cities, 1980; Dylan Thomas, *A Boy Growing Up*, U.S. cities, 1959.

PRINCIPAL STAGE WORK—Director, all in London: *He Was Born Gay*, Queen's Theatre, 1937; *The Corn Is Green*, Duchess Theatre, 1938; *The Light of Heart*, Globe Theatre, 1940; *The Morning Star*, Globe Theatre, 1941; *Beth*, Apollo Theatre, 1958; also *A Murder Has Been Arranged*, 1930; *Watch on the Rhine*, *The Little Foxes*, both 1942; *The Druid's Rest*, 1944; *The Wind of Heaven*, 1945; *Trespass*, 1947.

FILM DEBUT—Lord Lebanon, *The Case of the Frightened Lady*, Beaconsfield, 1932. PRINCIPAL FILM APPEARANCES— *The Citadel*, Metro-Goldwyn-Mayer (MGM), 1938; *They Drive by Night* (English version), Warner Brothers, 1938; *Major Barbara*, United Artists, 1941; *The Stars Look Down*, MGM, 1941; *This England*, World Pictures, 1941; *The Last Days of Dolwyn*, London Films, 1948; *Three Husbands*, United Artists, 1951; *The Scarf*, United Artists, 1951; *Ivanhoe*, MGM, 1952; *The Deep Blue Sea*, Twentieth Century-Fox, 1955; *I Accuse*, MGM, 1958; *The Wreck of the Mary Deare*, MGM, 1959; *The L-Shaped Room*, Columbia, 1963; *The Eye of the Devil*, MGM, 1967; *The Walking Stick*, MGM, 1970. Also appeared in *Friday the Thirteenth*, *Evansong*, both 1934; *The Iron Duke*, *Men of Tomorrow*, *My Love for You*, *Loves of a Dictator*, all 1935; *Broken Blossoms*, 1937; *Dead Men Tell No Tales*, 1939; *Jamaica Inn*, 1939; *The Girl in the Mews*, 1941; *Hatter's Castle*, 1948; *Another Man's Poison*, 1952; *Beyond This Place*, 1958. PRINCIPAL FILM WORK— Director, *The Last Days of Dolwyn*, London Films, 1948.

PRINCIPAL TELEVISION APPEARANCES—Episodic: Gerald Lawen, "Mind over Murder," *The Defenders*, CBS, 1965; also *Rumpole of the Bailey*, BBC, then PBS; *Yob and Nabob*, BBC. Movies: Mr. Dick, *David Copperfield*, NBC, 1970; also appeared in *Every Picture Tells a Story*, *The Deadly Game*; *The Burning Bush*; *Past Caring*. Specials: *Emlyn Williams Special*, CBS, 1967; *Hall of Kings*, ABC, 1967; *Emlyn Williams as Charles Dickens*, 1981. Guest: *New York, New York*, ABC, 1964.

WRITINGS: PLAYS—*Vigil*, produced in Oxford, U.K., 1925, published in *The Second Book of One-Act-Plays*, Heinemann, 1954; *Full Moon*, produced in Oxford, U.K., 1927, then London, 1929; *Glamour*, Embassy Theatre, London, 1928; *A Murder Has Been Arranged: A Ghost Story*, produced in London, 1930, published by Collins, 1930, Samuel French, Inc., 1931; *Port Said*, Wyndham's Theatre, London, 1931, revised as *Vessels Departing*, produced in London, 1933; (adaptor) *The Late Christopher Bean*, produced in London, 1933, published by Gollancz, 1933; (adaptor) *Josephine*, His Majesty's Theatre, London, 1934; *Spring 1600*, produced in London, 1934, revised version produced in London, 1945, published by Heinemann, 1946; *Night Must Fall*, Duchess Theatre, London, 1935, then Ethel Barrymore Theatre, New York City, 1936, published by Gollancz, 1935, Random House, 1936, and in *Collected Plays I*, Random House, 1961; *He Was Born Gay*, Queen's Theatre, London, 1937, published by Heinemann, 1937, and in *Collected Plays I*; *The Corn Is Green*, Duchess Theatre, 1938, then National Theatre, New York City, 1940, published by Heinemann, 1937, by Random House, 1941, in *The Corn Is Green, with Two Other Plays*, Pan, 1950, and in *Collected Plays I*.

The *Light of Heart*, Globe Theatre, London, 1941, published by Heinemann, 1940, and in *Collected Plays*, 1961; *The Morning Star*, Globe Theatre, 1941, published by Heinemann, 1942; *Yesterday's Magic*, Guild Theatre, New York City, 1942; *Pen Don*, Blackpool, U.K., 1943; (adaptor) *A Month in the Country*, Globe

Theatre, 1943, published by Heinemann, 1943, revised version produced in Chicago, IL, 1956, published by Samuel French, Inc., 1957; *The Druid's Rest*, produced in London, 1944, published by Heinemann, 1944, and in *The Corn Is Green, with Two Other Plays; The Wind of Heaven*, St. James Theatre, London, 1945, then Westport Country Playhouse, Westport, CT, 1963, published by Heinemann, 1945, and in *The Corn Is Green, with Two Other Plays; Thinking Aloud*, produced in London, 1945, then in New York City, 1975, published as *Thinking Aloud: A Dramatic Sketch*, Samuel French, Inc., 1946; *Trespass*, Globe Theatre, 1947, published by Heinemann, 1947; *Dear Evelyn*, produced in Rutherglen, Lanarkshire, U.K., 1948, published by Samuel French, Inc.

Accolade, Aldwych Theatre, London, 1950, published by Heinemann, 1951; *Emlyn Williams as Charles Dickens*, Lyric Hammersmith Theatre, then Criterion Theatre, London, 1951, (see above for tours, 1951 through 1981), published as *Readings from Dickens* Folio Society, 1953; *Bleak House* (dramatic reading based on the novel by Dickens), Edinburgh, Scotland, U.K., and London, 1952, then in New York City, 1953; *Someone Waiting*, produced in Liverpool, U.K., then Globe Theatre, 1953, later in New York City, 1956, published by Heinemann, 1954, and Dramatists Play Service, 1956; *A Boy Growing Up* (dramatic reading based on the works of Dylan Thomas), Globe Theatre, 1955, then Longacre Theatre, New York City, 1957; *Beth*, produced in Brighton, U.K., then Apollo Theatre, London, 1958, published by Heinemann, 1959; (adaptor) *The Master Builder*, produced in London, 1964, published by Theatre Arts Books, 1967.

SCREENPLAYS—*Friday the Thirteenth*, 1933; *Evergreen*, 1934; (contributor) *The Man Who Knew Too Much*, 1934; dialogue (with Ian Dalrymple, Frank Wead, and Elizabeth Hill) *The Citadel*, MGM, 1938; (with A.R. Rawlinson and Bridget Boland) *This England*, World Pictures, 1941; *The Last Days of Dolwyn*, London Films, 1948; *Time without Pity*, 1957.

TELEPLAYS—*A Month in the Country*, 1947; *Every Picture Tells a Story*, 1949; *In Tonight*, 1954; *A Blue Movie of My Own True Love*, 1968; *The Power of Dawn*, 1975. RADIO PLAYS—*Pepper and Sand: A Duologue*, BBC, 1948, published by Deane, 1948; *Emlyn* (adapted from his own book), 1974.

BOOKS—*George: An Early Autobiography*, Hamish Hamilton, 1961, Random House, 1962; *Beyond Belief: A Study in Murder*, Hamish Hamilton, 1967, Random House, 1968; *Emlyn: An Early Autobiography, 1927-1935*, Bodley Head, 1973, Viking Press, 1974; *Doctor Crippen's Diary, Headlong*, both 1981.

AWARDS: Order of Commander of the British Empire, 1962; New York Drama Critics Circle Award, 1941, for *The Corn Is Green*. Honorary degrees: LL.D., University College of North Wales, 1949.

OBITUARIES AND OTHER SOURCES: *Variety*, September 30, 1987.*

*   *   *

WILLIAMS, Michael   1935-

PERSONAL: Born July 9, 1935, in Manchester, England; son of Michael Leonard and Elizabeth (Mulligan) Williams; married Judi Dench (an actress). EDUCATION: Attended St. Edward's College; trained for the stage at the Royal Academy of Dramatic Art.

VOCATION: Actor.

CAREER: STAGE DEBUT—Auguste, *Take the Fool Away*, Nottingham Playhouse Theatre, Nottingham, U.K., 1959. LONDON DEBUT—Bernard Fuller, *Celebration*, Duchess Theatre, 1961. BROADWAY DEBUT—Herald, *Marat/Sade*, Martin Beck Theatre, 1965. PRINCIPAL STAGE APPEARANCES—All with the Royal Shakespeare Company: Puck, *A Midsummer Night's Dream*, Filch, *The Beggar's Opera*, Adolf Eichmann, *The Representative*, all Aldwych Theatre, London, 1963; Oswald, *King Lear*, Aldwych Theatre, then State Theatre, New York City, 1964; Pinch, *The Comedy of Errors*, Kokol, *Marat/Sade*, Lodowick, *The Jew of Malta*, all Aldwych Theatre, 1964; sergeant, *Don't Make Me Laugh*, Aldwych Theatre, 1965; Dromio of Syracuse, *The Comedy of Errors*, painter, *Timon of Athens*, Guildenstern, *Hamlet*, all Memorial Theatre, Stratford-on-Avon, U.K., 1965; Arthur, *Tango*, Aldwych Theatre, 1966; Petruchio, *The Taming of the Shrew*, Orlando, *As You Like It*, all Aldwych Theatre, 1967; Fool, *King Lear*, Orlando, *As You Like It*, Troilus, *Troilus and Cressida*, all Memorial Theatre, 1968; Troilus, *Troilus and Cressida*, Aldwych Theatre, 1969.

Charles Courtly, *London Assurance*, Aldwych Theatre, 1970; Bassanio, *The Merchant of Venice*, Ferdinand, *The Duchess of Malfi*, title role, *Henry V*, all Memorial Theatre, 1971; Mole, *Toad of Toad Hall*, Memorial Theatre, 1972; Charles Courtly, *London Assurance*, New Theatre, London, 1972; Stellio, *Content to Whisper*, Theatre Royal, York, U.K., 1973; Ian, *Jingo*, Aldwych Theatre, 1975; Scribes, University Theatre, Newcastle, U.K., 1975; Private Meek, *Too True to Be Good*, Globe Theatre, London, 1975; Autolycus, *The Winter's Tale*, Memorial Theatre, 1976; title role, *Schweik in the Second World War*, Other Place Theatre,

MICHAEL WILLIAMS

Stratford-on-Avon, U.K., 1976, then Warehouse Theatre, London, 1977; Dromio, *The Comedy of Errors,* Fool, *King Lear,* both Memorial Theatre, 1976, then Aldwych Theatre, 1977. Also appeared in the Royal Shakespeare Company's *Theatre-Go-Round Festival,* Round House Theatre, London, 1970.

FILM DEBUT—*Marat/Sade,* United Artists, 1966. PRINCIPAL FILM APPEARANCES—*Eagle in a Cage,* National General, 1971; *Dead Certain,* 1974; *Educating Rita,* Columbia, 1983.

PRINCIPAL TELEVISION APPEARANCES—Mini-Series: *Elizabeth R.; Love in a Cold Climate* Movies: *A Raging Calm; The Hanged Man.* Specials: *The Comedy of Errors,* BBC; *My Son, My Son; A Fine Romance; Blunt.*

MEMBER: British Actors' Equity Association, Screen Actors Guild; The Garrick Club.

SIDELIGHTS: FAVORITE ROLES—Petruchio in *The Taming of the Shrew;* the Fool in *King Lear.*

ADDRESSES: AGENT—Michael Whitehall, Ltd., 125 Gloucester Road, London SW7 4TL, England.

*　　*　　*

WILSON, August   1945-

BRIEF ENTRY: Dramatist and poet August Wilson has announced his goal of writing a play for each decade of the twentieth century, delineating the Black experience in America. The first two plays in the cycle to reach Broadway have earned the author two Pulitzer Prizes, among other honors. Wilson never completed high school in his native Pittsburgh, PA; he recalled for Brent Staples of *Essence* that when his history teacher accused him of plagiarism on a paper, "I tore it up, threw it in the trash basket, walked out, and never looked back." His literary career began with poems most often published in Afro-American small magazines, but he also founded Minnesota's Black Horizons Theatre Company. His play cycle on Black American despair and alienation includes *Joe Turner's Come and Gone* (set in 1911), *The Piano Lesson* (1936), *Fullerton Street* (1941), and *Jitney* (1971); the dramas of the twenties and fifties are the award-winning *Ma Rainey's Black Bottom* (1927) and *Fences* (1957). The former, which was also selected Best New Play of 1984-85 by the New York Drama Critics Circle, centers on the blues singer Ma Rainey and her pain at being held at the mercy of white record producers. *Fences,* which earned Wilson the 1987 Antoinette Perry Award for Best Drama, concerns a family that is being torn apart by the appearance of a child from the father's extramarital affair and by a son who is growing up in the early stages of America's Civil Rights Movement. In the December 10, 1987 *New York Times,* Frank Rich observed, "Mr. Wilson has this gift for making an audience feel that it . . . has pulled a chair up to the table of history, to partake intimately of an epic feast."

*　　*　　*

WILSON, Robert   1941-

PERSONAL: Born October 4, 1941, in Waco, TX; son of D.M. (a lawyer) and Loree Velma (Hamilton) Wilson. EDUCATION: At-

ROBERT WILSON

tended the University of Texas, 1959-62; Pratt Institute, B.F.A., 1965.

VOCATION: Director, playwright, set designer, and performer.

CAREER: Also see *WRITINGS* below. PRINCIPAL STAGE WORK— All as director, unless indicated: Set designer, *America Hurrah,* Pocket Theatre, New York City, 1965; "Dance Event," New York World's Fair, Queen's, NY, 1965; "Solo Performance," Byrd Hoffman Studio, New York City, 1966; "Theatre Activity," Bleecker Street Theatre, then American Theatre Laboratory, both New York City, 1967; *ByrdwoMAN,* Byrd Hoffman Studio, 1968; *The King of Spain,* Anderson Theatre, New York City, 1969; *The Life and Times of Sigmund Freud,* Brooklyn Academy of Music, Brooklyn, NY, 1969.

Deafman Glance, University Theatre, Iowa City, IA, 1970, then Brooklyn Academy of Music, 1971; *Program Prologue Now, Overture for a Deafman,* Espace Pierre Cardin, Paris, France, 1971; *Overture,* Byrd Hoffman Studio, then Khaneh-e Zinatolmolle, Shiraz, Iran, later Musee Galliera and Opera Comique, Paris, all 1972; *KA MOUNTAIN AND GUARDenia TERRACE,* Haft Tan Mountain, Shiraz, Iran, 1972; *The Life and Times of Joseph Stalin,* Det Ny Theatre, Copenhagen, Denmark, the Brooklyn Academy of Music, both 1973, later produced as *The Life and Times of Dave Clark,* Teatro Municipal, Sao Paulo, Brazil, 1974; *King Lyre and Lady in the Wasteland,* Byrd Hoffman Studio, 1973; *Prologue to "A Letter for Queen Victoria,"* Teatro Six O'Clock, Spoleto, Italy, 1974; *A Mad Man a Mad Giant a Mad Dog a Mad Urge a Mad Face,* Teatro di Roma, Rome, Italy, then Kennedy Center, Washington, DC, later Shirza Festival, Shirza, Iran, all 1974; *A Letter for Queen Victoria,* American National Theatre Academy Playhouse, New York City, 1975; *To Street,* Kultur Forum, Bonn, West Germany, 1975; *The $ Value of Man,* Brooklyn Academy of Music, 1975; *Dia Log,* Public Theatre, New York City, 1975; *Einstein on the Beach* (opera), Metropolitan Opera House, New York City, 1976; *I Was Sitting on My Patio This Guy Appeared I Thought I Was Hallucinating,* Cherry Lane Theatre, New York City, 1977; *Overture to the Fourth Act of "Deafman Glance,"* Manhattanville College, Purchase, NY, then John Drew Theatre, East Hampton, NY, both 1978, then Barcelona Theatre Festival, Barcelona, Spain, 1986, later International Theatre Conference, Delphi, Greece, 1987; *Edison,* Lion Theatre, New York City (as a work-in-progress), then Theatre Nationale Populaire, Lyons, France, both 1979; *Death, Destruction, and Detroit,* Schaubuhne Theatre, Berlin, West Germany, 1979.

Dia Log/Curious George, Mitzie E. Newhouse Theatre, New York City, 1980; *Medea,* Kennedy Center, 1981, then Aaron Davis Hall, City College of New York, New York City, 1982, later Opera de Lyons, Lyons, France, and Theatre des Champs Elysees, Paris, France, both 1984; *The Man in the Raincoat,* Theatre de Wilte, Cologne, West Germany, 1981; *Great Day in the Morning,* Theatre des Champs Elysees, 1982; *The Golden Windows,* Kammerspiele, Munich, West Germany, 1982, then Brooklyn Academy of Music, 1985; *the CIVIL warS/The Knee Plays,* Walker Art Center, Guthrie Theatre, Minneapolis, MN, 1984; (also set designer) *Medee* (opera), Opera de Lyons, 1984; *King Lear,* University of California, Los Angeles, Los Angeles, CA (as a work-in-progress), 1985; "Readings," Dublin Theatre Festival, Dublin, Ireland, then Museum van Hedendaagse Kunst, Ghent, Belgium, both 1985; (also set designer) *Alcestis,* American Repertory Theatre, Cambridge, MA, then Festival d'Automne, Paris, France, both 1986, later Staatstheatre, Stuttgart, West Germany, 1987; (also set designer) *Hamletmachine,* New York University, New York City, then Thalia Theatre, Hamburg, West Germany, both 1986, later Berlin Festspiele Theatretreffen, West Germany, 1987; (also set designer) *Alceste* (opera), Staatsoper, Stuttgart, West Germany, 1986, then 1987; (also set designer) *Salome* (opera), Teatro alla Scala, Milan, Italy, 1987; *Death, Destruction, and Detroit II,* Schaubuhne Theatre, Berlin, West Germany, 1987; (also set designer) *Quartett,* Schauspielhaus Ludwigsburg, West Germany, 1987.

MAJOR TOURS—Director: *Deafman Glance,* European cities, 1971; *A Letter for Queen Victoria,* European cities, 1974; *Einstein on the Beach,* European cities, 1976; *I Was Sitting on My Patio This Guy Appeared I Thought I Was Hallucinating,* U.S. cities, 1977, then European cities, 1978; *Dia Log,* U.S. cities, 1978; *Dia Log/Curious George,* European cities, 1980; *Overture to the Fourth Act of Deafman "Glance,"* Japanese and West German cities, 1982; *the CIVIL warS,* European cities, 1983, then U.S. cities, 1984 and 1986.

PRINCIPAL TELEVISION WORK—All as director. Specials: *Slant,* WNET, New York City, 1967; also *The House,* 1963; *Overture for a Deafman,* 1971. Videos: *Spaceman,* 1976; *Video 50,* 1978; *Deafman Glance,* 1981; *Stations,* 1982.

RELATED CAREER—Lecturer: International Theatre Institute, Durden France; BITEF, Belgrade, Yugoslavia; International School, Paris, France; University of Torino; Harvard University; New York University; Miami-Dade County Community College; Congres Internacional de Theatre a Catalunya, Barcelona, Spain; Delphi International Theatre Festival, Delphi, Greece; Arts Club of Chicago; Carnegie Mellon University; University of Texas, Austin.

Artistic director, Byrd Hoffman Foundation, Inc.; trustee, National Institute of Music Theatre; honorary board member, American Repertory Theatre.

NON-RELATED CAREER—Painter and artist whose works have appeared in numerous one-man and group exhibitions around the world; among the museums containing Robert Wilson's works in their private collections are: Australian National Gallery, Canberra; Kunstmuseum, Berne;, Museum of Fine Arts, Houston, TX; Museum of Fine Arts, Boston, MA; Museum of Modern Art, New York City; Museum of Modern Art, Paris; Centre Georges Pomipdou, Paris; Museum of Contemporary Art, Los Angeles; Metropolitan Museum of Art, New York City; and the Rhode Island School of Design Museum of Art, Providence.

WRITINGS: PLAYS—See productions details above, unless indicated: "Dance Event," 1965; "Solo Performance," 1966; "Theatre Activity," 1967; *ByrdwoMAN,* 1968; *The King of Spain,* 1969; *The Life and Times of Sigmund Freud,* 1969; *Deafman Glance,* 1970; *Program Prologue Now, Overture for a Deafman,* 1971; *Deafman Glance,* 1971; *Overture,* 1972; *KA MOUNTAIN AND GUARDenia TERRACE,* 1972; *The Life and Times of Joseph Stalin,* 1973; *King Lyre and Lady in the Wasteland,* 1973; *Prologue to "A Letter for Queen Victoria,"* 1974; (with Christopher Knowles) *A Mad Man a Mad Giant a Mad Dog a Mad Urge a Mad Face,* 1974; *A Letter for Queen Victoria,* 1974, published by Byrd Hoffman Foundation, 1974; *To Street,* 1975; *The $ Value of Man,* 1975; (with Christopher Knowles) *Dia Log,* 1975; (with Philip Glass) *Einstein on the Beach* (opera), 1976, published by EOS Enterprises, 1976; *I Was Sitting on My Patio This Guy Appeared I Thought I Was Hallucinating,* 1977, published by Byrd Hoffman Foundation, 1978; *Overture to the Fourth Act of "Deafman Glance,"* 1978; *Edison,* 1979; with Christoper Knowles) *Dia Log/Curious George,* 1979; *Death, Destruction, and Detroit,* 1979, published by Schaubuhne am Halleschen Ufer, 1979; (with Gavin Bryars) *Medea,* 1981; *The Man in the Raincoat,* 1981; (with Jessye Norman) *Great Day in the Morning,* 1982; *The Golden Windows,* 1982, published by Carl Hanser Verlag, 1982; *the CIVIL warS/Knee Plays,* 1983; *King Lear,* 1985; (adaptor; additional text by Heiner Muller) *Alcestis,* 1986; *Death, Destruction, and Detroit II,* 1987.

RECORDINGS: ALBUMS—*The Life and Times of Joseph Stalin,* Byrd Hoffman Foundation, 1973; (with Philip Glass) *Einstein on the Beach,* CBS Masterworks, 1979; *the CIVIL warS/The Knee Plays,* Warner Brothers, 1985.

AWARDS: Best Foreign Play, Critics Award from Le Syndicat de la Critique Musicale (Paris), and Best Director, Drama Desk Award, both 1971, for *Deafman Glance;* Guggenheim Foundation Fellowship, 1971; Directors's Citation, Obie Award from the *Village Voice,* 1974, for *The Life and Times of Joseph Stalin;* Best Set Design, Maharam Award, Best Score and Lyrics, Antoinette Perry Award nomination, both 1975, for *A Letter for Queen Victoria;* Playwriting Fellowship from the Rockefeller Foundation, 1975; Best Musical Theatre, Critics Award from Syndicat de la Critique Musicale, Grand Prize, BITEF (Belgrade, Yugoslavia), and Lumen Award for Design, all 1977, for *Einstein on the Beach;* First Prize, German Press Award for Playwrights and German Critics Award, both 1979, for *Death, Destruction, and Detroit;* Guggenheim Foundation Fellowship, 1980; Rockefeller Foundation Award, 1981; citation from Harvard University, 1982, for *The Golden Windows;* San Sebastian Film and Video Festival award, 1984, for *Stations;* Directors' Citation, Obie Award, 1986, for *Hamletmachine;* Picasso Award from the Malaga Theatre Festival, 1986, for *Overture to the Fourth Act of "Deafman Glance;"* sole nominee,

Pulitzer Prize for Drama (prize not awarded), 1986, for *the CIVIL warS/The Knee Plays;* Skowhegan Medal from the Skowhegan School of Painting, 1987.

MEMBER: Society of Stage Directors and Choreographers, Dramatists Guild, P.E.N. American Center, Societe des Auteurs et Compositeurs Dramatiques.

ADDRESSES: OFFICE—Byrd Hoffman Foundation, Inc., 325 Spring Street, Room 328, New York, NY 10013.

*　　*　　*

WINTERS, Jonathan 1925-

PERSONAL: Full name, Jonathan Harshman Winters III; born November 11, 1925, in Dayton, OH; son of Jonathan H. (an investment broker) and Alice Kilgore (a radio personality; maiden name, Rodgers) Winters; married Eileen Ann Schauder, September 11, 1948; children: Jonathan IV, Lucinda Kelley. EDUCATION: Attended Kenyon College, 1946; Dayton Art Institute, 1946-49, awarded B.F.A. for life experience, 1976. MILITARY: U.S. Marine Corps, 1943-46.

VOCATION: Comedian, actor, and writer.

CAREER: PRINCIPAL TELEVISION APPEARANCES—Episodic: *Omnibus,* CBS, 1954; *The Steve Allen Show,* NBC, 1954-61; *Shirley Temple's Storybook,* ABC, 1959; *NBC Monitor Show,* NBC, 1963; also, *Good Morning, America,* ABC; voice, *Wait Till Your Father Gets Home* (cartoon), syndicated; *The Mouse Factory,* syndicated; *The Dean Martin Show,* NBC.

Series: *The Garry Moore Show,* CBS, 1954-63; *And Here's the Show,* NBC, 1955; *NBC Comedy Hour,* NBC, 1956; *The Jonathan Winters Show,* NBC, 1956-57; panelist, *Masquerade Party,* CBS, 1958; *The Jack Paar Program,* NBC, 1962-63; *The Andy Williams Show,* NBC, 1965-67, 1970-71; *The Wacky World of Jonathan Winters,* syndicated, 1972-74; Mearth, *Mork and Mindy,* ABC, 1981-82; *Hee Haw,* CBS, 1983-84. Pilots: *Take One,* NBC, 1981. Movies: Jeremiah Klay, *Now You See It, Now You Don't,* NBC, 1986; Professor Albert Paradine II, *More Wild, Wild West,* CBS, 1980; Humpty Dumpty, *Alice in Wonderland,* CBS, 1985. Guest: *Hollywood Squares,* NBC.

Specials: *Jonathan Winters Presents a Wild Winters Night,* NBC, 1964; *Jonathan Winters Presents Two Hundred Years of American Humor,* NBC, 1976; *From Tahiti, Bob Hope's Comedy Special,* NBC, 1987.

PRINCIPAL FILM APPEARANCES—Van driver, *It's a Mad, Mad, Mad, Mad World,* United Artists, 1963; Hollywood promoter, cemetery director (dual role), *The Loved One,* Metro-Goldwyn-Mayer (MGM), 1965; deputy sheriff, *The Russians Are Coming! The Russians Are Coming!,* United Artists, 1966; National Guard commander, *Viva Max,* Commonwealth United, 1969; also *Penelope,* MGM, 1966; *Eight on the Lam,* United Artists, 1967; *Oh Dad, Poor Dad, Mama's Hung You in the Closet and I'm Feeling So Sad,* Paramount, 1967; *The Fish That Saved Pittsburgh,* United Artists, 1979; and *The Midnight Oil,* 1967; *Long Shot,* 1981.

PRINCIPAL STAGE APPEARANCES—*John Murray Anderson's Almanac* (revue), Imperial Theatre, New York City, 1954; ap-

peared in nightclubs and cabarets, 1953-59, and in concert halls, 1961—.

RELATED CAREER—Radio disc jockey, WING, Dayton, OH, 1949; television announcer and comedian, WBNS-TV, Columbus, OH, 1950-53.

WRITINGS: BOOKS—*Mouse Breath, Conformity, and Other Social Ills,* Bobbs Merrill, 1965; *Winters' Tales: Stories and Observations for the Unusual,* Random House, 1987.

RECORDINGS: COMEDY ALBUMS—All for Verve-MGM, 1960-64: *The Wonderful World of Jonathan Winters; Down to Earth with Jonathan Winters; Here's Jonathan; Humor Seen through the Eyes of Jonathan Winters; Whistle-Stopping with Jonathan Winters.* Also recorded an album with Columbia Records.

SIDELIGHTS: Comedian Jonathan Winters "has been called a genius by enough peers to convince you that there is truth in that description," declared Robert Hilburn in the August 29, 1971 *Chicago Sun-Times.* Winters is perhaps best known to the public for his repertoire of comic characters, including midwestern hick Elwood P. Suggins, sports announcer Boom Boom Bailey, stuffy Englishman Sir Trafalgar Whittley, blowhard financier B.B. Bindlestiff, and the redoubtable grandmother Maude Frickert. His improvisational skill awes his fellow professionals; Hilburn deemed him "the master of the free-form situation" and Charles Champlin noted his "fantastic energy and a fertile imagination which seem to blur the line between reality and fantasy" in the September 13, 1966 *New York World-Journal-Tribune.* In the December 20, 1987 *Parade,* Winters's wife gave her opinion of the source of his genius: "The thing is, Jon *thinks* funny."

Winters has cited his paternal grandfather as one of the influences on his comedy. Despite his position as a bank president, the elder Winters was known to walk the streets of his hometown of Dayton, Ohio, "flapping his arms at his pal Orville Wright and screeching, 'How's the airplane, Orville?'" according to *Time* (October 13, 1958). The comic's own parents were divorced when he was seven, and his mother, a radio actress, left Dayton for nearby Springfield, taking her son along. His childhood was a painful one; he explained to *People*'s Lois Armstrong in the January 26, 1976 issue, "I was expecting love, and it wasn't there, and that threw me." When he became a parent himself, Winters was determined to preserve his relationship with his children. In *Parade* he recalled to Cleveland Amory that he once suggested to his son that the boy go fishing alone because he had a club date: "'Dad,' he said, 'it's not much fun alone.' . . . From then on, I gave up all my club dates and a lot of other stuff and spent every bit of time I could with my family."

It was Winters's wife, Eileen, who first urged him to try making a living with his comedy. She suggested he enter a talent contest to win a wristwatch they could not otherwise afford; he did and was offered a job as a disk jockey for a Dayton radio station. As well as playing music for station WING, Winters did interviews; when he ran out of guests, he began to create character voices and interview himself. "I'd make up people like Dr. Hardbody of the Atomic Energy Commission or an Englishman whose blimp had crash-landed in Dayton," he told Hilburn. He left this job to try television on a local Columbus station.

In 1953 Winters left Ohio for New York City. There he attracted the attention of television personalities Garry Moore and Jack Paar while he was working in such fashionable nightclubs as the Blue Angel and Ruban Bleu. His appearances on their shows were an immediate hit. In the January 12, 1969 *New York Sunday News,* Bob Lardine recollected how ''people went wild over Winters' impersonations and amazingly accurate re-creation of everyday sounds.'' During the early 1960s Winters was regularly featured on the *Jack Paar Show;* in Chris Bachman's opinion (*Films in Review,* November, 1986), this was his heyday. Perhaps it was the comfortable atmosphere and leisurely pace which induced his creative energies to flow so freely,'' speculated Bachman. ''Whatever the reason, a cast of zany characters was unleashed, searing the telewaves with high speed double-edged humor. This was the era of choice Winters.''

His television work of this period was a happy contrast with his earlier experience working lounges. ''Most club audiences ignore you,'' he told Lardine. ''They're either part of the Virgina Woolf crowd that's always playing games, or they're sauced out of their heads.'' To Hammond the comedian remarked: ''All the clowns in the world go into the gin mills. They're all bombed and they feel like they own you.'' In 1959, in fact, the pressures of performing under these conditions drove Winters to what Hammond termed ''a dramatic nervous collapse.'' Winters had already begun to confront his own drinking problem and during his recuperation, ''he decided the money he was making was less important then being happy and seeing more of his family,'' according to Hammond.

Working in television and films allowed him to do that. Over the years he made a few hour-long specials, had two series of his own, and made a pilot for a third. None of these, however, matched the success of his earlier appearances on other people's shows. In Bachman's opinion, the networks did not understand the demands of Winters's particular brand of comedy: ''He needed time to develop character and material, and time to play it out to some logical or absurd conclusion—whichever came first.'' The critic felt that the earlier days of television had given Winters an appropriate setting, but in his own programs, he was presented ''*without time,* but expected to deliver *instant comedy* all the same.'' Similar problems crippled the pilot *Take One,* where ''the sketches [were] obviously edited, creating a certain choppiness and reducing much of the material to snippets,'' assessed the *New York Times*'s John J. O'Connor (May 1, 1981). ''With nothing but improvisation,''he observed, ''even a half hour tends to become tedious.''

Winters won better reviews when he joined Robin Williams and Pam Dawber in the fourth season of their show *Mork and Mindy.* Comedian Williams ''often acknowledges Winter as his idol,'' noted Bachman. Terry Kelleher reported in the *New York Sunday News* of December 6, 1981 that it was Williams's ''often-repeated praise of Winters [that] lured the older comedian to accept a recurring role [on] 'Mork and Mindy.''' Typical of critics' response was Bachman's comment: ''The chemistry between Winters, as son Mearth, and Williams' Mork was marvelous! They were as two giant Cabbage Patch dolls set loose to scatter mayhem in the playpen.'' On at least one occasion—when Mork was attempting to photograph the infant Mearth—the two discarded the script for the show and improvised. Kelleher described the results: ''''This one's for Playboy!' Williams called. A shocked Winters clutched his ridiculously undersized baby blanket over his bosom. 'This one's for After Dark!' A split-second's consideration, and Winters dangled it hanky-like from his pocket.'' As Bachman noted, ''The scenes they shared were so short that neither got to carry lunacy to extremes.'' Althouth the response to Winters's characterization of Mearth was generally enthusiastic, *Mork and Mindy* was cancelled not long after the older comedian joined the cast.

Despite the acclaim he has won from critics, Winters has received

little formal recognition for his work, but this apparent lack of acknowledgment does not bother him. ''Is that what life has to offer?'' he asked Alan Gill of *TV Guide* in the February 8, 1964 issue. ''An Oscar? An Emmy? A medal? I was a medals guy. I went after them by [performing continually]. But the only real awards that have come to me are my wife and two kids Lucinda and Jay, my friends, and my work; and they don't hang on walls.'' For many years Winters has been working on an autobiography. It reportedly bears a dedication that reflects his own philosophy: ''To all people who are overly sensitive. Don't be ashamed of it. It beats being overly bitter.''

ADDRESSES: AGENT—Triad Artists, Inc., 10100 Santa Monica Boulevard, Los Angeles, CA 90067.*

* * *

WINTERS, Time   1956-

PERSONAL: Born Timothy G. Winters, February 3, 1956, in Lebanon, OR; son of Lyle R. (an elementary school principal) and Adalee C. (an elementary school teacher; maiden name, McKinney) Winters. EDUCATION: Lane Community College, A.A., 1976; Stephen's College, B.F.A., 1978; studied acting with Michael Howard, Michael Kahn, Henry Banister, and Jean Muir; studied singing with William Reed, Dennis English, and Earl Coleman; studied dance and movement with Flip Reade and Richard Morse; studied combat and fencing with B.H. Barry and John Elliott.

TIME WINTERS

VOCATION: Actor.

CAREER: STAGE DEBUT—Iago, *Othello,* Champlain Shakespeare Festival, Burlington, VT, 1978, for thirty performances. BROADWAY DEBUT—Salieri's valet, *Amadeus,* Broadhurst Theatre, New York City, 1983. PRINCIPAL STAGE APPEARANCES—Tom, *Round and Round the Garden,* St. Malachy's Theatre, New York City, 1981; Nym and Orleans, *Henry V,* with the Riverside Shakespeare Company at the Shakespeare Center, New York City, 1984; Flute and Thisbe, *A Midsummer Night's Dream,* Walnut Street Theatre, Philadelphia, PA, 1985; *The Taming of the Shrew,* Colonades Theatre, New York City, 1985; Friar Bonafides, *Nathan the Wise,* Soho Repertory Theatre, New York City, 1987; also appeared as a priest, *Rashomon,* Asolo State Theatre, NY; Orsino, *Twelfth Night,* Champlain Shakespeare Festival; Ligurio, *The Mandrake* and Jack Worthing, *The Importance of Being Earnest,* both at the Portland Stage Company, OR; Slim, *Cowboy Mouth* and Corin, *As You Like It,* both at the Oregon Shakespeare Festival; Peter Kershaw, *Whose Life Is It, Anyway?,* Mike Endicott, *The Front Page,* and Bellerose and Raganeau (standby), *Cyrano De Bergerac,* all at the Williamstown Theatre Festival; Clive and Edward, *Cloud 9* and Cletis Fullernoy, *Lone Star,* both at the Philadelphia Stage Company; John, *A Life in the Theatre,* Wilma Theatre, Philadelphia, PA; Bob Cratchit, *A Christmas Carol,* GeVa Theatre, NY; Willy Banbury, *Fallen Angels,* Missouri Repertory Company; Truffaldino, *The Servant of Two Masters,* IRT Theatre, New York City; Cheng K'uan, *Fanshen* and Philpot, *Ragged Trousered Philanthropists,* both at the Soho Repertory Theatre, New York City; Charlie Baker, *The Foreigner,* Dorset Theatre, VT; Mr. Mell, *The Play's the Thing,* Pittsburgh Public Theatre, PA.

FILM DEBUT—Trapper Bauman, *Sasquatch: The Legend of Bigfoot,* North American Wildlife Films, 1975. PRINCIPAL FILM APPEARANCES—Radio technician, *The Purple Rose of Cairo,* Orion, 1985.

TELEVISION DEBUT—Charles Nicholson, *Jay Leno Special,* NBC, 1986. PRINCIPAL TELEVISION APPEARANCES—Episodic: Heckler, *One Life to Live,* ABC.

MEMBER: Actor's Equity Association, Screen Actors Guild, American Federation of Television and Radio Artists, National Academy of Television Arts and Sciences.

ADDRESSES: AGENT—Ann Wright Representatives, 136 E. 57th Street, New York, NY 10022.

*　　　*　　　*

WOOD, John 1931-

PERSONAL: Born in 1931, in Derbyshire, England. EDUCATION: Attended Oxford University. MILITARY: Lieutenant, Royal Horse Artillery.

VOCATION: Actor.

CAREER: PRINCIPAL STAGE APPEARANCES—Lennox, *Macbeth,* with the Old Vic Company, London, 1954; Bushy, Exton, *Richard II,* Sir Oliver Martext, *As You Like It,* Pistol, *The Merry Wives of Windsor,* all with the Old Vic Company, 1955; Helenus, *Troilus and Cressida,* with the Old Vic Company, 1956; Don Quixote, *Camino Real,* Phoenix Theatre, London, 1957; Wali,

Brouhaha, Aldwych Theatre, London, 1958; Henry Albertson, *The Fantasticks,* Apollo Theatre, London, 1961; Guildenstern, *Rosencrantz and Guildenstern Are Dead,* Alvin Theatre, New York City, 1967; Frederick II, *The Sorrows of Frederick,* Birmingham Repertory Theatre, Birmingham, U.K., 1970; Richard Rowan, *Exiles,* Mermaid Theatre, London, 1970; Yakov Bardin, *Enemies,* Sir Fopling Flutter, *The Man of Mode,* Richard Rowan, *Exiles,* Mark, *The Balcony,* all Royal Shakespeare Company (RSC), Aldwych Theatre, 1971; Brutus, *Julius Caesar,* Saturninus, *Titus Andronicus,* all RSC, Stratford-on-Avon, U.K., 1972, then Aldwych Theatre, 1973; Antipholus of Syracuse, *The Comedy of Errors,* RSC, Stratford-on-Avon, U.K., 1972; Harry Winter, *Collaborators,* Duchess Theatre, 1973; title role, *Sherlock Holmes,* Aldwych Theatre, then Broadhurst Theatre, New York City, both 1974; Henry Carr, *Travesties,* Aldwych Theatre, 1974, then Ethel Barrymore Theatre, New York City, 1975; General Burgoyne, *The Devil's Disciple,* title role, *Ivanov,* both Aldwych Theatre, 1976; Sidney Bruhl, *Deathtrap,* Music Box Theatre, New York City, 1978, then Biltmore Theatre, New York City, 1982; Friedrich Hofreiter, *Undiscovered Country,* Richard of Gloucester, *Richard III,* both Olivier Theatre, London, 1979; Antonio Salieri, *Amadeus,* Broadhurst Theatre, 1980. Also appeared in *The Making of Moo,* Royal Court Theatre, London, 1957; and as Monsieur Luc, *A Lesson in Blood,* Place Theatre, 1973; Alceste, *The Misanthrope,* with the Melbourne Theatre Company, 1974; Ivanov, *Every Good Boy Deserves Favour,* Royal Festival Hall, 1977.

MAJOR TOURS—Ivanov, *Every Good Boy Deserves Favour,* U.S. cities, 1978.

PRINCIPAL FILM APPEARANCES—*Nicholas and Alexandra,* Columbia, 1971; *Slaughterhouse Five,* Universal, 1972; *Somebody Killed Her Husband,* Columbia, 1978; *War Games,* Metro-Goldwyn-Mayer/United Artists, 1982; *Ladyhawke,* Warner Brothers, 1984; *The Purple Rose of Cairo,* Orion, 1984; *Lady Jane,* Paramount, 1986; *Heartburn,* Paramount, 1986. Also appeared in *Blue Fire Lady,* 1978; *Ginger Meggs,* 1982; *The Empty Beach,* 1985; *Twelfth Night,* 1985; *Jumpin' Jack Flash,* 1986.

PRINCIPAL TELEVISION APPEARANCES—Specials: *A Tale of Two Cities; Barnaby Rudge.*

AWARDS: Best Actor, Antoinette Perry Award, 1976, for *Travesties.*

ADDRESSES: OFFICE—c/o National Theatre, South Bank, London SE1, England.*

*　　　*　　　*

WOODARD, Alfre

BRIEF ENTRY: Actress Alfre Woodard has earned accolades for her work on television, stage, and in films. With her parents' support, she left her native Tulsa, OK, to study acting at Boston University. Not long after her graduation she began winning roles in such plays as *Horatio* and *Saved* in theatres in Washington, DC. Moving to Los Angeles to pursue opportunities in television and film, she again found quick recognition of her talent. Her performance as Geechee, Marjorie Kinnan Rawling's illiterate housekeeper in *Cross Creek,* earned her an Academy Award nomination as best supporting actress, while the role of an embittered mother of a child killed by a police officer on *Hill Street Blues* won her an Emmy Award. Other television work has included a continuing role as the head of obstetrics on *St. Elsewhere;* the part of Marcia Fulbright on *Tucker's Witch;* Mattie Custer in "The Killing Floor" on the PBS series *American Playhouse;* the NBC movie *Unnatural Causes,* in which she played a Veterans Administration counselor fighting for the rights of victims of the herbicide Agent Orange; and the role of Winnie Mandela in the HBO movie *Mandela.* She also has continued to work on the stage, as in the Mark Taper Forum production of *For Colored Girls Who Have Considered Suicide/When the Rainbow Is Enuf* and in the 1985 Off-Broadway production of *A Map of the World.*

* * *

WOODS, James 1947-

PERSONAL: Born April 18, 1947, in Vernal, UT. EDUCATION: Attended Massachusetts Institute of Technology.

VOCATION: Actor.

CAREER: FILM DEBUT—*The Visitors,* United Artists, 1972. PRINCIPAL FILM APPEARANCES—*The Way We Were,* Columbia, 1973; *The Gambler,* Paramount, 1974; *Night Moves,* Warner Brothers, 1975; *Alex and the Gypsy,* Twentieth Century-Fox, 1976; *The Choir Boys,* Universal, 1977; *The Onion Field,* AVCO-Embassy, 1979; *The Black Marble,* AVCO-Embassy, 1980; *Eyewitness,* Twentieth Century-Fox, 1981; *Split Image,* Orion, 1982; *Fast-Walking,* Lorimar, 1982; *Videodrome,* Universal, 1983; *Against All Odds,* Columbia, 1984; *Once Upon a Time in America,*

JAMES WOODS

Warner Brothers, 1984; *Cat's Eye,* Metro-Goldwyn-Mayer/United Artists, 1985; *Joshua, Then and Now,* Twentieth Century-Fox, 1985; *Salvador,* Hemdale, 1986; *Best Seller,* Orion, 1987.

PRINCIPAL TELEVISION APPEARANCES—Mini-series: *Holocaust,* 1978. Movies: *Footsteps,* 1972; *A Great American Tragedy,* 1972; *The Disappearance of Aimee,* 1976; *Raid on Entebbe,* 1977; *The Gift of Love,* 1978; *And Your Name Is Jonah,* 1979; *Badge of the Assassin,* 1985; *Promise,* 1986; *In Love and War,* 1987; also *All the Way Home; Billion Dollar Bubble.*

PRINCIPAL STAGE APPEARANCES—*Borstal Boy,* Lyceum Theatre, New York City, 1970; *Conduct Unbecoming,* Ethel Barrymore Theatre, New York City, 1970; *Saved,* Chelsea Theatre Center, Brooklyn Academy of Music, Brooklyn, NY, 1970; *The Trial of the Catonsville Nine,* Good Shepherd-Faith Church, New York City, then Lyceum Theatre, both 1971; *Green Julia,* Sheridan Square Playhouse, New York City, 1972; *Finishing Touches,* Plymouth Theatre, New York City, 1973. Also appeared in *Moonchildren,* New York City.

AWARDS: Best Actor, Academy Award nomination, 1987, for *Salvador;* Outstanding Lead Actor in a Miniseries or Special, Emmy Award, and Best Actor in a Telefilm, Golden Globe, both 1987, for *Promise;* also an Obie Award from the *Village Voice* and Clarence Derwent Award, both for *Saved;* Theatre World Award for *Moonchildren.*

ADDRESSES: AGENT—c/o Todd Smith, Creative Artists Agency, 1888 Century Park E., Suite 1400, Los Angeles, CA 90067.

* * *

WOODWARD, Charles, Jr.

VOCATION: Producer.

CAREER: FIRST NEW YORK STAGE WORK—Producer (with Richard Barr and Clinton Wilder), *Johnny No-Trump,* Cort Theatre, 1967. PRINCIPAL STAGE WORK—Producer: *The Boys in the Band,* Theatre Four, New York City, 1968; *The Front Page,* Ethel Barrymore Theatre, New York City, 1969; *Watercolor, Criss-Crossing,* both American National Theatre Academy (ANTA) Playhouse, New York City, 1970; *What the Butler Saw,* McAlpin Rooftop Theatre, New York City, 1970; *All Over,* Martin Beck Theatre, New York City, 1971; *Drat!,* McAlpin Rooftop Theatre, 1971; *The Grass Harp,* Martin Beck Theatre, 1971; *The Last of Mrs. Lincoln,* ANTA Playhouse, 1972; *Noel Coward in Two Keys,* Ethel Barrymore Theatre, 1974; *P.S. Your Cat is Dead!,* John Golden Theatre, New York City, 1975; *Seascape,* Shubert Theatre, New York City, 1975; *Sweeney Todd,* Uris Theatre, New York City, 1979; *Home Front,* Theatre Three, Dallas, TX, 1985. Also produced *Detective Store,* Philadelphia, PA, 1973.

ADDRESSES: OFFICE—P.O. Box 8868, St. Thomas, Virgin Islands, 00801.

* * *

WURTZEL, Stuart 1940-

PERSONAL: Born August 2, 1940, in Newark, NJ; son of Nathan and Pearl Sylvia (Spirn) Wurtzel; married Patrizia von Brandenstein (a designer), October 19, 1969; children: Kimberly. EDUCATION: Carnegie Mellon University, B.F.A., 1962, M.F.A., 1964.

VOCATION: Production designer.

CAREER: FIRST FILM WORK—Production designer, *Hester Street,* Midwest Films, 1975. PRINCIPAL FILM WORK— Production designer: *The Next Man,* Allied Artists, 1976; *Between the Lines,* Midwest Films, 1977; *Hair,* United Artists, 1979; *Simon,* Warner Brothers, 1980; *Times Square,* Associated Films, 1980; *Tattoo,* Twentieth Century-Fox, 1981; *The Chosen,* Twentieth Century-Fox, 1982; *The Ballad of Gregorio Cortez,* Embassy, 1983; *The Purple Rose of Cairo,* Orion, 1985; *Hannah and Her Sisters,* Orion, 1986; *Brighton Beach Memoirs,* Universal, 1987; also production designer for *Night of the Juggler,* 1980.

PRINCIPAL TELEVISION WORK—Series: Art director, *The Today Show,* NBC. Movies (all as production designer): *Bernice Bobs Her Hair,* PBS, 1973; *Little Gloria . . . Happy at Last,* NBC, 1982; *Pope John Paul II,* CBS, 1984.

AWARDS: Emmy Award nomination, *Little Gloria . . . Happy at Last;* Academy Award nomination, *Hannah and Her Sisters,* 1986.

ADDRESSES: HOME—460 Greenwich Street, New York, NY 10013. AGENT—c/o Clifford Stevens, STE Representation, 888 Seventh Avenue, New York, NY 10019.

Y-Z

YORK, Susannah   1941-

PERSONAL: Born Susannah Johnson, January 9, 1941, in London, England; daughter of Joseph Gwynne and Florence Edith (Chown) Johnson; married Michael Wells, 1960; children: Sasha, Orlando. EDUCATION: Attended the Royal Academy of Dramatic Art.

VOCATION: Actress, writer, and producer.

CAREER: OFF-BROADWAY DEBUT—Title role, *Hedda Gabler*, Roundabout Theatre, April 14, 1981, for fifty-one performances. PRINCIPAL STAGE APPEARANCES—*Appearances*, 1980; *Agnes of God*, 1983; *Cinderella*, 1983; *The Human Voice*, 1984; *Penthisilea*, 1984; *The Apple Cart*, 1986; also appeared in *The Women, A Cheap Bunch of Nice Flowers, Wings of a Dove, A Singular Man, The Singular Life of Albert Nobbs, Man and Superman, Mrs. Warren's*

SUSANNAH YORK

Profession, Peter Pan, The Maids, The Great Ban, Private Lives, and *The Importance of Being Earnest.*

FILM DEBUT—*There Was a Crooked Man*, 1960. PRINCIPAL FILM APPEARANCES—*Tunes of Glory*, United Artists, 1960; *The Greengage Summer* (also known as *Loss of Innocence*), Columbia, 1961; *Freud*, Universal, 1962; *The Secret Passion*, 1962; *Tom Jones*, Lopert, 1963; *The Seventh Dawn*, United Artists, 1964; *Scene Nun—Take One*, 1964; *Sands of the Kalahari*, Paramount, 1965; *A Man For All Seasons*, Columbia, 1966; *Scruggs*, 1966; *Kaleidoscope*, Warner Brothers, 1966; *Sebastian*, Paramount, 1968; *The Killing of Sister George*, Cinerama, 1968; *Duffy*, Columbia, 1968; *Oh! What A Lovely War*, Paramount, 1969; *The Battle of Britain*, United Artists, 1969; *Lock Up Your Daughters*, Columbia, 1969; *They Shoot Horses, Don't They?*, Cinerama, 1969; *Brotherly Love* (also known as *Country Dance,*), Metro-Goldwyn-Mayer, 1969; *Zee* (also known as *Zee & Co.*), Columbia, 1972; *Happy Birthday, Wanda June*, Columbia, 1971; *Images*, Columbia 1972; *The Maids*, American Film Theatre, 1975; *Gold*, Allied Artists, 1974; *Conduct Unbecoming*, Allied Artists, 1975; *That Lucky Touch*, 1975; *Sky Riders*, Twentieth Century-Fox, 1976; *Eliza Fraser*, 1976; *Silent Partner*, Canadian, 1978; *Memories*, 1977; *Superman*, Warner Brothers, 1978; *The Shout*, Columbia, 1979; *Alice*, 1979; *The Awakening*, Warner Brothers, 1980; *Superman II*, Warner Brothers, 1980; *Falling in Love Again*, 1980; *Head On*, Greentree Productions, 1980 (Canadian, released in the U.S. as *Fatal Attraction*, 1985); *Yellowbeard*, Orion, 1983; *Loophole*, 1983; *Mio, My Mio*, 1985; also *Spectre on the Bridge, While the Tiger Sleeps,* and *Heaven Save Us from Our Friends.*

TELEVISION DEBUT—1959. PRINCIPAL TELEVISION APPEARANCES—Teleplays: *The Crucible*, 1960; *The Rebel and the Soldier*, 1960; *The Richest Man in the World*, 1960; *Fallen Angels*, 1974; *Second Chance*, 1981; *We'll Meet Again*, 1982; *The Other Side of Me*, 1982; *Prince Regent*, 1983; *Macho*, 1984; *A Christmas Carol*, 1984; *Star Quality*, 1985; *Two Ronnies*, 1985; also *The Creditors, La Grande Breteche, Slaughter of St. Teresa's Day, Kiss on a Grass Green Pillow,* and *Benjamin's Britain.* Movies: *Jane Eyre*, 1970; *Star Quality.*

PRINCIPAL TELEVISION WORK—Producer, *The Big One: A Variety Show for Peace,* 1984.

WRITINGS: FICTION—Juvenile: *In Search of Unicorns*, Hodder & Stoughton, 1973, reprinted in 1986; also *Lark's Castle*, Hodder & Stoughton.

AWARDS: Academy Award nomination, 1969, for *They Shoot Horses, Don't They?*

ADDRESSES: AGENT—Jeremy Conway, 109 Jermyn Street, London SW1Y 6HB, England.

YOUNG, Burt   1940-

PERSONAL: Born April 30, 1940, in New York City; son of Michael and Josephine Young; married May 20, 1961 (wife died); children: Richard, Anne Susan. EDUCATION: Trained for the stage at the Actors Studio. RELIGION: Roman Catholic. MILITARY: U.S. Marine Corps, 1957-59.

VOCATION: Actor and screenwriter.

CAREER: PRINCIPAL FILM APPEARANCES—*Cinderella Liberty*, Twentieth Century-Fox, 1974; *The Gambler*, Paramount, 1971; *Chinatown*, Paramount, 1974; *The Killer Elite*, United Artists, 1975; *Harry and Walter Go to New York*, Columbia, 1976; *Rocky*, United Artists, 1977; *The Choirboys*, Universal, 1977; *Twilight's Last Gleaming*, Allied Artists, 1977; *Convoy*, United Artists, 1978; *Uncle Joe Shannon*, United Artists, 1979; *Rocky II*, United Artists, 1979; *Blood Beach*, 1980; *All the Marbles*, United Artists, 1981; *Rocky III*, Metro-Goldwyn-Mayer/United Artists (MGM/UA), 1972; *Lookin' to Get Out*, Paramount, 1982; *Amityville II: The Possession*, Orion, 1982; *Over the Brooklyn Bridge*, MGM/UA, 1984; *Once Upon a Time in America*, Warner Brothers, 1984; *The Pope of Greenwich Village*, MGM/UA, 1984; *Rocky IV*, MGM/UA, 1985.

PRINCIPAL TELEVISION APPEARANCES—Episodic: *M.A.S.H.*, CBS; *Baretta*, ABC; *Miami Vice*, NBC. Series: Nick Chase, *Roomies*, NBC, 1987. Pilots: Alec Rosen, *Serpico: The Deadly Game*, NBC, 1976. Movies: Ernie, *The Connection*, ABC, 1973; Ace Tully, *The Great Niagra*, ABC, 1974; Gustavino, *Hustling*, ABC, 1975; Ralph Rodino, *Woman of the Year*, CBS, 1976; Rocco Agnelli, *Daddy, I Don't Like It Like This*, CBS, 1977; Palumbo, *Murder Can Hurt You!*, ABC, 1980; Fidel Fargo, *A Summer to Remember*, CBS, 1985.

PRINCIPAL STAGE APPEARANCES—Smitty, "Escape from Deep Hammock during the Hurricane of '52," Dr. Pinkney, "The Organ Recital at the New Grand," Bobby Terry, "The Men's Room," all as *The Men's Room*, Actors Repertory Theatre, New York City, 1982; Jackie, *Cuba and His Teddy Bear*, Public Theatre, New York City, 1986; *S.O.S.* (one-man show), Actors Playhouse, New York City, 1988.

RELATED CAREER—Director, Sunshine Film Company.

NON-RELATED CAREER—President, White Crown Carpet Cleaners, 1964-67; Aurura Carpet Installation Company, 1966-69; owner, operator, Burt's Blues Tapes/Records, 1978; also was a boxer and a truck driver.

WRITINGS: TELEPLAYS—Movies: *Daddy, I Don't Like It Like This*, CBS, 1977. SCREENPLAYS—*Uncle Joe Shannon*, United Artists, 1979.

AWARDS: Best Supporting Actor, Academy Award nomination, 1976, for *Rocky*.

MEMBER: Academy of Motion Picture Arts and Sciences, Writers Guild of America; Hole in the Wall Gang of Corona.

ADDRESSES: AGENT—Triad Artists, 10100 Santa Monica Boulevard, Los Angeles, CA 90067.*

JACKLYN ZEMAN

ZEMAN, Jacklyn

PERSONAL: Born March 6, in Englewood, NJ; daughter of Richard S. Zeman (a systems engineer) and Rita Zeman-Rohlman (a magazine supervisor). EDUCATION: Attended New York University; trained for the stage with Wynn Handman and Sonia Moore.

VOCATION: Actress and writer.

CAREER: TELEVISION DEBUT—Lana McLain, *One Life to Live*, ABC, 1976. PRINCIPAL TELEVISION APPEARANCES— Episodic: *Mickey Spillane's Mike Hammer*, CBS; *The Edge of Night*, ABC; *Sledgehammer*, ABC. Series: Bobbie Spencer Brock, *General Hospital*, ABC, 1977—; co-host, *Travel Shoppin'*, syndicated; co-host, *Epcot Magazine;* co-host, *AM San Francisco;* co-host, *330.*

FILM DEBUT—Jane Washburn, *National Lampoon's Class Reunion*, Twentieth Century-Fox, 1982. PRINCIPAL FILM APPEARANCES—*Young Doctors in Love*, Twentieth Century-Fox, 1982.

PRINCIPAL STAGE APPEARANCES—*Barefoot in the Park, The Boyfriend, Gypsy, Luv in a Pub*, all in New York City.

PRINCIPAL RADIO APPEARANCES—*Soap Talk*, ABC; also celebrity talk shows.

RELATED CAREER—Featured performer, New Jersey Dance Theatre, 1969, then 1978.

NON-RELATED CAREER—Style editor, *Soap Opera People Magazine;* writer of a question and answer column for *Rona Barrett's Daytimers Magazine.*

WRITINGS: BOOKS—*Beauty on the Go,* Simon & Schuster, 1986.

AWARDS: Soapy Award, 1979; Emmy Award nomination, 1981; Hollywood International Daytime Performer of the Year Award, 1984.

MEMBER: American Federation of Television and Radio Artists; Women in Film; national ambassador, Where Are the Children?.

SIDELIGHTS: RECREATIONS—Water sports, motorcycling, aerobics, travel.

ADDRESSES: OFFICE—c/o General Hospital, ABC Television, 1415 Gordon Street, Hollywood, CA 90028. AGENT—c/o CNA, 8721 Sunset Boulevard, Los Angeles, CA 90069.

Cumulative Index

To provide continuity with *Who's Who in the Theatre,* this index interfiles references to *Who's Who in the Theatre,* 1st-17th Editions, and *Who Was Who in the Theatre* (Gale Research Co., 1978) with references to *Contemporary Theatre, Film, and Television,* Volumes 1-5.

References in the index are identified as follows:

CTFT and volume number—*Contemporary Theatre, Film, and Television,* Volumes 1-5
WWT and edition number—*Who's Who in the Theatre,* 1st-17th Editions
WWasWT—*Who Was Who in the Theatre*

Bannen, Ian 1928– CTFT-5
Earlier sketch in WWT-17
Banner, Bob 1921– CTFT-3
Bannerman, Celia 1946– CTFT-5
Earlier sketch in WWT-17
Bannerman, Kay 1919– CTFT-4
Earlier sketch in WWT-17
Bannerman, Margaret 1896– . . . . . . WWasWT
Bannister, Harry 1893–1961 . . . . . . WWasWT
Bantry, Bryan 1956– CTFT-1
Baraka, Imamu Amiri 1934– WWT-17
Baranski, Christine 1952– CTFT-4
Earlier sketch in WWT-17
Barbeau, Adrienne CTFT-4
Barbee, Richard 1887– . . . . WWasWT
Barber, John CTFT-1
Barbera, Joseph R. CTFT-1
Barbor, H. R. 1893–1933 . . . . WWasWT
Barbour, Elly 1945– CTFT-2
Barbour, Joyce 1901– . . . . WWasWT
Barbour, Thomas 1921– CTFT-2
Barcelo, Randy 1946– CTFT-4
Bard, Wilkie 1874–? . . . . WWasWT
Bardon, Henry 1923– WWT-17
Bardot, Brigitte 1934– CTFT-3
Barge, Gillian 1940– WWT-17
Baring, Maurice 1874–1945 . . . . . . WWasWT
Barker, Bob 1923– CTFT-2
Barker, Clive 1931– WWT-17
Barker, Felix WWT-17
Barker, H. Granville-
See Granville-Barker, Harley– . . . WWasWT
Barker, Helen Granville-
See Granville-Barker, Helen . . . . WWasWT
Barker, Howard 1946– WWT-17
Barker, Ronnie 1929– WWT-17
Barkworth, Peter 1929– WWT-17
Barlog, Boleslaw 1906– . . . . WWasWT
Barlow, Billie 1862–1937 . . . . WWasWT
Barlow, H. J. 1892–1970 . . . . WWasWT
Barnabe, Bruno 1905– WWT-17
Barnard, Ivor 1887–1953 . . . . WWasWT
Barner, Barry K. 1906–1965 . . . . . . WWasWT
Barnes, Binnie 1905– . . . . WWasWT
Barnes, Clive Alexander 1927– CTFT-3
Earlier sketch in WWT-17
Barnes, Fran 1931– CTFT-1
Barnes, Fred 1884–? . . . . WWasWT
Barnes, Howard 1904–1968 . . . . . . WWasWT
Barnes, J. H. 1850–1925 . . . . WWasWT
Barnes, Kenneth (Ralph)
1878–1957 . . . . WWasWT
Barnes, Peter 1931– CTFT-5
Earlier sketch in WWT-17
Barnes, Wade 1917– CTFT-4
Barnes, Winifred 1894–1935 . . . . . . WWasWT
Barney, Jay 1913–1985 . . . . CTFT-1
Baron, Alec CTFT-5
Baron, Evelyn 1948– CTFT-2
Baronova, Irina 1919– . . . . WWasWT
Barr, Patrick 1908– WWT-17
Barr, Richard 1917– WWT-17
Barranger, Millie S. 1937– WWT-17
Barratt, Augustus . . . . WWasWT
Barratt, Watson 1884–1962 . . . . . . WWasWT
Barrault, Jean-Louis 1910– . . . . . . WWasWT
Barre, Gabriel 1957– CTFT-4
Barrett, Edith 1906– . . . . WWasWT
Barrett, George 1869–1935 . . . . WWasWT
Barrett, Leslie 1919– CTFT-4
Earlier sketch in WWT-17
Barrett, Lester . . . . WWasWT
Barrett, Oscar 1875–1941 . . . . WWasWT

Barrett, Rona 1936– CTFT-4
Barrett, Wilson 1900– . . . . WWasWT
Barrie, Amanda 1939– WWT-17
Barrie, Barbara 1931– CTFT-3
Earlier sketch in WWT-17
Barrie, Frank 1939– WWT-17
Barrie, James Matthew 1860–1937 . . WWasWT
Barrington, Rutland 1853–1922 . . . WWasWT
Barron, Marcus 1925–1944 . . . . WWasWT
Barron, Muriel 1906– . . . . WWasWT
Barrs, Norman 1917– CTFT-1
Barry, B. Constance 1913– CTFT-1
Barry, B. H. 1940– CTFT-5
Earlier sketch in CTFT-1
Barry, Christine 1911– . . . . WWasWT
Barry, Gene 1922– CTFT-5
Earlier sketch in CTFT-2
Barry, Jack 1918–1984 . . . . CTFT-2
Barry, Joan 1901– . . . . WWasWT
Barry, John 1933– CTFT-4
Barry, Michael 1910– WWT-17
Barry, Paul 1931– CTFT-5
Earlier sketch in CTFT-1
Barry, Philip 1896–1949 . . . . WWasWT
Barry, Raymond J. 1939– CTFT-1
Barry, Shiel 1882–1937 . . . . WWasWT
Barrymore, Diana 1921–1960 . . . . . WWasWT
Barrymore, Drew 1975– CTFT-5
Brief Entry in CTFT-2
Barrymore, Ethel 1879–1959 . . . . . WWasWT
Barrymore, John 1882–1942 . . . . . . WWasWT
Barrymore, Lionel 1878–1954 . . . . WWasWT
Bart, Lionel 1930– CTFT-3
Earlier sketch in WWT-17
Bart, Peter 1932– CTFT-2
Bartenieff, George 1935– CTFT-1
Bartet, Jeanne Julia 1854– . . . . WWasWT
Barth, Cecil ?–1949 . . . . WWasWT
Bartholomae, Phillip H. ?–1947 . . . WWasWT
Bartlett, Basil 1905– . . . . WWasWT
Bartlett, Clifford 1903–1936 . . . . . . WWasWT
Bartlett, D'Jamin 1948– CTFT-5
Earlier sketch in WWT-17
Bartlett, Elise . . . . WWasWT
Bartlett, Hall 1925– CTFT-1
Bartlett, Michael 1901– . . . . WWasWT
Barton, Dora ?–1966 . . . . WWasWT
Barton, James 1890–1962 . . . . WWasWT
Barton, John 1928– WWT-17
Barton, Margaret 1926– . . . . WWasWT
Barton, Mary ?–1970 . . . . WWasWT
Barty, Jack 1888–1942 . . . . WWasWT
Baryshnikov, Mikhail 1948– CTFT-3
Basehart, Richard 1914–1984 . . . . . . CTFT-2
Earlier sketch in WWasWT
Basinger, Kim CTFT-2
Baskcomb, A. W. 1880–1939 . . . . . WWasWT
Baskcomb, Lawrence 1883–1962 . . . WWasWT
Bass, Alfred 1921–1987 . . . . CTFT-5
Earlier sketch in WWasWT
Bass, George Houston 1938– CTFT-1
Bassett, Alfred Leon 1870–? . . . . . WWasWT
Bataille, Henry 1872–1940 . . . . WWasWT
Bate, Anthony WWT-17
Bateman, Jason CTFT-5
Brief Entry in CTFT-2
Bateman, Justine CTFT-5
Earlier sketch in CTFT-2
Bateman, Leah 1892– . . . . WWasWT
Bateman, Miss 1842–1917 . . . . WWasWT
Bateman, Virginia Frances
See Compton, Mrs. Edward . . . . WWasWT
Bateman, Zitlah 1900–1970 . . . . . . WWasWT

Bates, Alan 1934– CTFT-2
Earlier sketch in WWT-17
Bates, Bianche 1873–1941 . . . . WWasWT
Bates, Kathy 1948– CTFT-1
Bates, Michael 1920– WWT-16
Bates, Sally 1907– . . . . WWasWT
Bates, Thorpe 1883–1958 . . . . WWasWT
Bateson, Timothy 1926– WWT-17
Bath, Hubert 1883– . . . . WWasWT
Batley, Dorothy 1902– . . . . WWasWT
Battles, John 1921– . . . . WWasWT
Batty, Archibald 1884–1961 . . . . . . WWasWT
Baty, Gaston 1885–1952 . . . . WWasWT
Bauersmith, Paula 1909–1987 . . . . . . CTFT-5
Earlier sketch in WWT-17
Baughan, Edward Algernon
1865–1938 . . . . WWasWT
Baughman, Renee CTFT-2
Baumann, K. T. CTFT-1
Baumgarten, Craig 1949– CTFT-1
Bawn, Harry 1872–? . . . . WWasWT
Bax, Clifford 1886–1962 . . . . WWasWT
Baxley, Barbara 1927– CTFT-2
Earlier sketch in WWT-17
Baxter, Alan 1908– . . . . WWasWT
Baxter, Anne 1923–1985 . . . . CTFT-3
Earlier sketch in WWT-17
Baxter, Barry 1894–1922 . . . . WWasWT
Baxter, Beryl 1926– . . . . WWasWT
Baxter, Beverly 1891– . . . . WWasWT
Baxter, Cash 1937– CTFT-5
Baxter, Jane 1909– WWT-17
Baxter, Keith 1935– CTFT-4
Earlier sketch in WWT-17
Baxter, Stanley 1926– WWT-17
Baxter, Trevor 1932– WWT-17
Bay, Howard 1912–1986 . . . . CTFT-4
Earlier sketch in WWT-17
Bayes, Nora 1880–1928 . . . . WWasWT
Bayler, Terence 1930– CTFT-3
Bayley, Caroline 1890– . . . . WWasWT
Bayley, Hilda ?–1971 . . . . WWasWT
Baylis, Lilian 1874–1937 . . . . WWasWT
Bayliss, Peter WWT-17
Bayly, Caroline . . . . WWasWT
Baynton, Henry 1892–1951 . . . . WWasWT
Beach, Ann 1938– WWT-17
Beach, Gary 1947– CTFT-1
Beacham, Stephanie 1947– CTFT-4
Earlier sketch in WWT-17
Beal, John 1909– WWT-17
Bealby, George 1877–1931 . . . . WWasWT
Beals, Jennifer 1963– CTFT-5
Brief Entry in CTFT-2
Bean, Orson 1928– CTFT-3
Earlier sketch in WWT-17
Beardsley, Alice 1925– CTFT-1
Beaton, Cecil 1904–1980 . . . . WWT-16
Beatty, Harcourt . . . . WWasWT
Beatty, John Lee 1948– CTFT-2
Earlier sketch in WWT-17
Beatty, May ?–1945 . . . . WWasWT
Beatty, Robert 1909– WWT-17
Beatty, Roberta 1891– . . . . WWasWT
Beatty, Warren 1938– CTFT-3
Beauchamp, John ?–1921 . . . . WWasWT
Beaufort, John 1912– WWT-17
Beaumont, Cyril William 1891– . . . WWasWT
Beaumont, Diana 1909–1964 . . . . . WWasWT
Beaumont, Gabrielle 1942– CTFT-1
Beaumont, Hugh 1908– . . . . WWasWT
Beaumont, John 1902– . . . . WWasWT
Beaumont, Muriel 1881–1957 . . . . . WWasWT

C

E

F

I

N